FOOTBALL REGISTER

1988 EDITION

S0-BYE-542

Editors/Football Register
HOWARD BALZER
BARRY SIEGEL

Contributing Editor/Football Register
DAVE SLOAN

President-Chief Executive Officer
RICHARD WATERS

Editor
TOM BARNIDGE

Director of Books and Periodicals
RON SMITH

Published by

The Sporting News

1212 North Lindbergh Boulevard
P.O. Box 56 — St. Louis, MO 63166

Copyright © 1988
The Sporting News Publishing Company

A Times Mirror
Company

ISBN 0-89204-286-9   ISSN 0071-7258

TABLE
of
CONTENTS

ON THE COVER: San Francisco wide receiver Jerry Rice led the NFL with 22 touchdown catches last season while leading the 49ers to the NFC West Division title and earning Player of the Year honors from The Sporting News.

Photo by Richard Pilling

EXPLANATION OF ABBREVIATIONS

AAFC—All America Football Conference. AFL—American Football League. CFL—Canadian Football League. CoFL—Continental Football League. EFL—Eastern Football League. NFL—National Football League. PFLA—Professional Football League of America. USFL—United States Football League. WFL—World Football League.

Att.—Attempts. Avg.—Average. Blk.—Blocked punts. Cmp.—Pass completions. F—Fumbles. FG—Field goals made. FGA—Field goal attempts. G—Games. Gain—Yards gained passing. No.—Number. P.C.—Passes caught. Pct.—Percentage completed. P.I.—Passes intercepted. Pts.—Total points scored. TD—Touchdowns. T.P.—Touchdown passes thrown. XP—Extra points made. XPM—Extra points missed. Yds.—Net yards gained.

Veteran Players

Please note for statistical comparisons: In 1982, only nine of 16 games were played due to the cancellation of games because of players' strike. In 1987, only 15 of 16 games were played due to the cancellation of games during week three because of players' strike. Most NFL players also missed games scheduled during weeks four through six.

*Indicates led league or tied for leadership.

VINCENT STEVEN ABBOTT
(Vince)
Placekicker—San Diego Chargers

Born May 31, 1958, at London, England.
Height, 5.11. Weight, 206.
High School—Tsawwassen, Vancouver, Canada, South Delta.
Attended University of Washington and received bachelor of arts degree in accounting
from California State University at Fullerton in 1981.

Signed as free agent by Los Angeles Rams, June 15, 1981.
Released by Los Angeles Rams, August 7, 1981; signed as free agent by San Francisco 49ers, April 20, 1982.
Released by San Francisco 49ers, August 24, 1982; awarded on waivers to Miami Dolphins, August 25, 1982.
Released by Miami Dolphins, August 31, 1982; signed as free agent by Los Angeles Express, November 1, 1982.
Released by Los Angeles Express, February 21, 1984; signed as free agent by Chicago Bears, April 13, 1984.
Released by Chicago Bears, August 21, 1984; signed as free agent by Tampa Bay Buccaneers for 1985, November 9, 1984.
Released by Tampa Bay Buccaneers, August 19, 1985; signed as free agent by Los Angeles Raiders, June 21, 1986.
Released by Los Angeles Raiders, August 19, 1986; signed as free agent by San Diego Chargers, April 13, 1987.

		——PLACE KICKING——				
Year	Club	G.	XP.	XPM.	FG.	FGA.	Pts.
1983—Los Angeles USFL...		18	31	3	17	30	82
1987—San Diego NFL.........		12	22	1	13	22	61
Pro Totals—2 Years.......		30	53	4	30	52	143

WALTER AUGUSTUS ABERCROMBIE
Running Back—Pittsburgh Steelers

Born September 26, 1959, at Waco, Tex.
Height, 6.00. Weight, 210.
High School—Waco, Tex., University.
Attended Baylor University.

Selected by Pittsburgh in 1st round (12th player selected) of 1982 NFL draft.
On injured reserve with knee injury, September 7 through November 26, 1982; activated, November 27, 1982.

		——RUSHING——				PASS RECEIVING				—TOTAL—		
Year	Club	G.	Att.	Yds.	Avg.	TD.	P.C.	Yds.	Avg.	TD.	TD.	Pts.	F.
1982—Pittsburgh NFL..........................		6	21	100	4.8	2	1	14	14.0	0	2	12	0
1983—Pittsburgh NFL..........................		15	112	446	4.0	4	26	391	15.0	3	7	42	2
1984—Pittsburgh NFL..........................		14	145	610	4.2	1	16	135	8.4	0	1	6	0
1985—Pittsburgh NFL..........................		16	227	851	3.7	7	24	209	8.7	2	9	54	5
1986—Pittsburgh NFL..........................		16	214	877	4.1	6	47	395	8.4	2	8	48	4
1987—Pittsburgh NFL..........................		12	123	459	3.7	2	24	209	8.7	0	2	12	4
Pro Totals—6 Years....................		79	842	3343	4.0	22	138	1353	9.8	7	29	174	15

Additional pro statistics: Returned seven kickoffs for 139 yards (19.9 avg.) and recovered two fumbles, 1982; recovered one fumble, 1985; recovered three fumbles for two yards, 1987.
Played in AFC Championship Game following 1984 season.

ROBERT ABRAHAM
Linebacker—New York Giants

Born July 13, 1960, at Myrtle Beach, S. C.
Height, 6.01. Weight, 236.
High School—Myrtle Beach, S. C.
Attended North Carolina State University.

Selected by Houston in 3rd round (77th player selected) of 1982 NFL draft.
On injured reserve with broken leg, December 7 through remainder of 1983 season.
On injured reserve with groin injury, September 8 through November 27, 1987; activated, November 28, 1987.
On injured reserve with hamstring injury, December 12 through remainder of 1987 season.
Released by Houston Oilers, February 22, 1988; awarded on waivers to New York Giants, March 4, 1988.
Houston NFL, 1982 through 1987.
Games: 1982 (9), 1983 (14), 1984 (16), 1985 (16), 1986 (16), 1987 (2). Total—73.
Pro statistics: Recovered one fumble, 1982 and 1986; intercepted one pass for no yards, 1983; intercepted one pass for one yard, 1984; recovered four fumbles, 1985.

CURTIS LADONN ADAMS
Running Back—San Diego Chargers

Born April 30, 1962, at Muskegon, Mich.
Height, 5.11. Weight, 194.
High School—Muskegon, Mich., Orchard View.
Attended Central Michigan University.

Selected by Orlando in 9th round (117th player selected) of 1985 USFL draft.

Selected by San Diego in 8th round (207th player selected) of 1985 NFL draft.
Signed by San Diego Chargers, June 19, 1985.
On injured reserve with knee injury, September 12 through remainder of 1985 season.
On injured reserve with shoulder injury, September 2 through November 7, 1986; activated, November 8, 1986.

Year Club	G.	—RUSHING—				PASS RECEIVING				—TOTAL—		
		Att.	Yds.	Avg.	TD.	P.C.	Yds.	Avg.	TD.	TD.	Pts.	F.
1985—San Diego NFL	1	16	49	3.1	1	1	12	12.0	0	1	6	0
1986—San Diego NFL	7	118	366	3.1	4	4	26	6.5	0	4	24	3
1987—San Diego NFL	12	90	343	3.8	1	4	38	9.5	0	1	6	1
Pro Totals—3 Years	20	224	758	3.4	6	9	76	8.4	0	6	36	4

Additional pro statistics: Returned two kickoffs for 50 yards, 1985; returned five kickoffs for 100 yards and recovered one fumble, 1986; returned four kickoffs for 32 yards, 1987.

GEORGE WALLACE ADAMS
Running Back—New York Giants
Born December 22, 1962, at Lexington, Ky.
Height, 6.01. Weight, 225.
High School—Lexington, Ky., Lafayette.
Attended University of Kentucky.

Selected by Orlando in 3rd round (33rd player selected) of 1985 USFL draft.
Selected by New York Giants in 1st round (19th player selected) of 1985 NFL draft.
Signed by New York Giants, July 22, 1985.
On injured reserve with hip injury, September 1 through entire 1986 season.

Year Club	G.	—RUSHING—				PASS RECEIVING				—TOTAL—		
		Att.	Yds.	Avg.	TD.	P.C.	Yds.	Avg.	TD.	TD.	Pts.	F.
1985—New York Giants NFL	16	128	498	3.9	2	31	389	12.5	2	4	24	7
1987—New York Giants NFL	12	61	169	2.8	1	35	298	8.5	1	2	12	3
Pro Totals—2 Years	28	189	667	3.5	3	66	687	10.4	3	6	36	10

	KICKOFF RETURNS				
Year Club	G.	No.	Yds.	Avg.	TD.
1985—N.Y. Giants NFL	16	14	241	17.2	0
1987—N.Y. Giants NFL	12	9	166	18.4	0
Pro Totals—2 Years	28	23	407	17.7	0

Additional pro statistics: Attempted one pass with no completions and recovered two fumbles, 1985; recovered one fumble, 1987.

MICHAEL ADAMS
Cornerback—New Orleans Saints
Born April 5, 1964, at Shelby, Miss.
Height, 5.10. Weight, 195.
High School—Shelby, Miss., Broad Street.
Attended Mississippi Delta Junior College and Arkansas State University.

Selected by New Orleans in 3rd round (67th player selected) of 1987 NFL draft.
Signed by New Orleans Saints, August 3, 1987.
On injured reserve with hamstring injury, September 11 through September 29, 1987; activated, September 30, 1987.
Crossed picket line during player's strike, September 30, 1987.
New Orleans NFL, 1987.
Games: 1987 (7).
Pro statistics: Returned four kickoffs for 52 yards, recovered two fumbles and fumbled once, 1987.

STEFON LEE ADAMS
Safety—Los Angeles Raiders
Born August 11, 1963, at High Point, N. C.
Height, 5.10. Weight, 190.
High School—High Point, N. C., Southwest Guilford.
Attended East Carolina University.

Selected by Baltimore in 4th round (58th player selected) of 1985 USFL draft.
Selected by Los Angeles Raiders in 3rd round (80th player selected) of 1985 NFL draft.
Signed by Los Angeles Raiders, July 17, 1985.
On injured reserve with hamstring injury, September 2 through entire 1985 season.

	KICKOFF RETURNS				
Year Club	G.	No.	Yds.	Avg.	TD.
1986—L.A. Raiders NFL	16	27	573	21.2	0
1987—L.A. Raiders NFL	9	3	61	20.3	0
Pro Totals—2 Years	25	30	634	21.1	0

Additional pro statistics: Intercepted one pass for 32 yards and recovered two fumbles, 1986; intercepted one pass for eight yards and returned five punts for 39 yards, 1987.

JOHN M. ADICKES
Name pronounced ADD-dix.
Center—Chicago Bears
Born June 29, 1964, at St. Albans, N. Y.
Height, 6.03. Weight, 264.
High School—Killeen, Tex.
Received degree in finance and real estate from Baylor University in 1987.
Brother of Mark Adickes, guard with Kansas City Chiefs.

Selected by Chicago in 6th round (154th player selected) of 1987 NFL draft.
Signed by Chicago Bears, July 30, 1987.
Chicago NFL, 1987.
Games: 1987 (6).

MARK ADICKES
Name pronounced ADD-dix.
Guard—Kansas City Chiefs
Born April 22, 1961, at Badconstadt, West Germany.
Height, 6.04. Weight, 270.
High School—Killeen, Tex.
Attended Baylor University.
Brother of John Adickes, center with Chicago Bears.
Named as offensive tackle on THE SPORTING NEWS College All-America Team, 1983.
Selected by Houston in 1984 USFL territorial draft.
USFL rights traded with rights to center Mike Ruether by Houston Gamblers to Los Angeles Express for 2nd round pick in 1985 and 1986 draft, February 13, 1984.
Signed by Los Angeles Express, February 13, 1984.
Granted roster exemption, February 13, 1984; activated, February 24, 1984.
On injured reserve with knee injury, March 6 through remainder of 1984 season.
Selected by Kansas City in 1st round (5th player selected) of 1984 NFL supplemental draft.
Released by Los Angeles Express, August 1, 1985; re-signed by Express, August 2, 1985.
Released by Los Angeles Express, April 3, 1986; signed by Kansas City Chiefs, June 5, 1986.
Los Angeles USFL, 1984 and 1985; Kansas City NFL, 1986 and 1987.
Games: 1984 (2), 1985 (11), 1986 (15), 1987 (12). Total USFL—13. Total NFL—27. Total Pro—40.
Pro statistics: Caught one pass for three yards and a touchdown and recovered one fumble, 1987.

DAVID IVER AHRENS
Name pronounced AIR-ens.
(Dave)
Linebacker—Indianapolis Colts
Born December 5, 1958, at Cedar Falls, Ia.
Height, 6.04. Weight, 247.
High School—Oregon, Wis.
Attended University of Wisconsin.
Selected by St. Louis in 6th round (143rd player selected) of 1981 NFL draft.
Traded by St. Louis Cardinals to Indianapolis Colts for 10th round pick in 1986 draft, August 27, 1985.
St. Louis NFL, 1981 through 1984; Indianapolis NFL, 1985 through 1987.
Games: 1981 (16), 1982 (9), 1983 (16), 1984 (16), 1985 (16), 1986 (16), 1987 (12). Total—101.
Pro statistics: Intercepted one pass for 14 yards, 1981; returned one kickoff for five yards, 1982; recovered one fumble, 1982 and 1985; caught one pass for four yards, 1983; returned one punt for no yards and recovered two fumbles, 1987.

VINCE DENADER ALBRITTON
Safety—Dallas Cowboys
Born July 23, 1962, at Oakland, Calif.
Height, 6.02. Weight, 217.
High School—Oakland, Calif., McClymond.
Attended University of Washington.
Selected by Philadelphia in 16th round (326th player selected) of 1984 USFL draft.
Signed as free agent by Dallas Cowboys, May 3, 1984.
On injured reserve with hamstring injury, August 20 through November 7, 1985; activated after clearing procedural waivers, November 9, 1985.
Dallas NFL, 1984 through 1987.
Games: 1984 (16), 1985 (7), 1986 (16), 1987 (11). Total—50.
Pro statistics: Recovered two fumbles, 1984 and 1986.

DAN LAMARR ALEXANDER
Guard-Offensive Tackle—New York Jets
Born June 17, 1955, at Houston, Tex.
Height, 6.04. Weight, 274.
High School—Houston, Tex., Lamar.
Received degree in law enforcement from Louisiana State University.
Selected by New York Jets in 8th round (200th player selected) of 1977 NFL draft.
New York Jets NFL, 1977 through 1987.
Games: 1977 (14), 1978 (16), 1979 (16), 1980 (16), 1981 (16), 1982 (9), 1983 (16), 1984 (16), 1985 (16), 1986 (16), 1987 (12). Total—163.
Pro statistics: Recovered one fumble, 1978 and 1982; recovered two fumbles, 1987.
Played in AFC Championship Game following 1982 season.

—DID YOU KNOW—
That The New Orleans Saints ended the 1987 regular season with a nine-game winning streak, breaking their old mark of three?

DAVID ALEXANDER
Offensive Tackle—Philadelphia Eagles
Born July 28, 1964, at Silver Spring, Md.
Height, 6.03. Weight, 275.
High School—Broken Arrow, Okla.
Attended The University of Tulsa.

Selected by Philadelphia in 5th round (121st player selected) of 1987 NFL draft.
Signed by Philadelphia Eagles, August 5, 1987.
Philadelphia NFL, 1987.
Games: 1987 (12).

ROGERS ALEXANDER
Linebacker—Indianapolis Colts
Born August 11, 1964, at Washington, D.C.
Height, 6.03. Weight, 219.
High School—Hyattsville, Md., DeMatha Catholic.
Received degree in administrator of justice from Penn State University in 1986.

Selected by Baltimore in 1986 USFL territorial draft.
Selected by New York Jets in 4th round (105th player selected) of 1986 NFL draft.
Signed by New York Jets, July 16, 1986.
Released by New York Jets, August 30, 1986; re-signed by Jets, October 29, 1986.
Released by New York Jets, November 5, 1986; re-signed by Jets, February 19, 1987.
Released by New York Jets, August 27, 1987; signed as free agent replacement player by New England Patriots, September 24, 1987.
Released by New England Patriots, October 23, 1987; signed as free agent by Indianapolis Colts, April 22, 1988.
New York Jets NFL, 1986; New England NFL, 1987.
Games: 1986 (1), 1987 (3). Total—4.
Pro statistics: Returned one kickoff for four yards, 1987.

VERNEST RAYNARD ALEXANDER
(Ray)
Wide Receiver—Dallas Cowboys
Born January 8, 1962, at Miami, Fla.
Height, 6.04. Weight, 196.
High School—Mobile, Ala., John S. Shaw.
Attended Florida A&M University.

Selected by Tampa Bay in 1984 USFL territorial draft.
Signed as free agent by Denver Broncos, May 2, 1984.
Released by Denver Broncos, August 27, 1984; re-signed by Broncos, September 27, 1984.
Released by Denver Broncos, August 26, 1985; signed as free agent by Calgary Stampeders, September 8, 1985.
Granted free agency, March 1, 1987; signed as free agent by Dallas Cowboys, March 23, 1987.
On injured reserve with broken wrist, September 1 through entire 1987 season.
Crossed picket line during player's strike, October 14, 1987.

		—PASS RECEIVING—			
Year Club	G.	P.C.	Yds.	Avg.	TD.
1984—Denver NFL	8	8	132	16.5	1
1985—Calgary CFL	8	22	361	16.4	1
1986—Calgary CFL	18	88	1590	18.1	10
NFL Total—1 Year	8	8	132	16.5	1
CFL Totals—2 Years	26	110	1951	17.7	11
Pro Totals—3 Years	34	118	2083	17.7	12

Additional pro statistics: Fumbled once, 1985; scored one 2-point conversion, 1986.

RAUL ENRIQUE ALLEGRE
Placekicker—New York Giants
Born June 15, 1959, at Torreon, Coahuila, Mex.
Height, 5.10. Weight, 167.
High School—Shelton, Wash.
Attended University of Montana and received degree in civil engineering from University of Texas.

Signed as free agent by Dallas Cowboys, April 28, 1983.
Traded by Dallas Cowboys to Baltimore Colts for 9th round pick in 1984 draft, August 29, 1983.
Franchise transferred to Indianapolis, March 31, 1984.
Released by Indianapolis Colts, September 1, 1986; signed as free agent by New York Giants, September 25, 1986.

		—PLACE KICKING—				
Year Club	G.	XP.	XPM.	FG.	FGA.	Pts.
1983—Baltimore NFL	16	22	2	30	35	112
1984—Indianapolis NFL	12	14	0	11	18	47
1985—Indianapolis NFL	16	36	3	16	26	84
1986—N.Y. Giants NFL	13	33	0	24	32	105
1987—N.Y. Giants NFL	12	25	1	17	27	76
Pro Totals—5 Years	69	130	6	98	138	424

Played in NFC Championship Game following 1986 season.
Played in NFL Championship Game following 1986 season.

ANTHONY DERRICK ALLEN
Running Back—Washington Redskins
Born June 29, 1959, at McComb, Miss.
Height, 5.11. Weight, 182.
High School—Seattle, Wash., Garfield.
Attended University of Washington.
Brother of Patrick Allen, cornerback with Houston Oilers.

Selected by Tampa Bay in 3rd round (36th player selected) of 1983 USFL draft.
Selected by Atlanta in 6th round (156th player selected) of 1983 NFL draft.
USFL rights traded by Tampa Bay Bandits to Los Angeles Express for 4th round pick in 1984 draft, May 9, 1983.
Signed by Los Angeles Express, May 9, 1983.
Granted roster exemption, May 9, 1983; activated, May 14, 1983.
Traded by Los Angeles Express to Michigan Panthers for draft pick, April 18, 1984.
Not protected in merger of Michigan Panthers and Oakland Invaders; selected by Baltimore Stars in USFL dispersal draft, December 6, 1984.
Released by Baltimore Stars, February 18, 1985; signed as free agent by Portland Breakers, April 4, 1985.
Released by Portland Breakers, May 14, 1985; signed by Atlanta Falcons, July 18, 1985.
On injured reserve with knee injury, October 8 through remainder of 1986 season.
Released by Atlanta Falcons, September 7, 1987; signed as free agent replacement player by Washington Redskins, October 1, 1987.
Released by Washington Redskins, November 28, 1987; re-signed by Redskins, December 9, 1987.

Year Club	G.	—RUSHING—				PASS RECEIVING				—TOTAL—		
		Att.	Yds.	Avg.	TD.	P.C.	Yds.	Avg.	TD.	TD.	Pts.	F.
1983—Los Angeles USFL	8	1	—6	—6.0	0	37	613	16.6	3	3	18	1
1984—Los Angeles (8)-Mich. (10) USFL	18	2	0	0.0	0	34	535	15.7	3	3	18	4
1985—Portland USFL	6		None			9	125	13.9	2	2	12	0
1985—Atlanta NFL	16		None			14	207	14.8	2	2	12	0
1986—Atlanta NFL	5		None			10	156	15.6	2	2	12	1
1987—Washington NFL	3		None			13	337	25.9	3	3	18	0
USFL Totals—3 Years	32	3	—6	—2.0	0	80	1273	15.9	8	8	48	5
NFL Totals—3 Years	24	0	0	0.0	0	37	700	18.9	7	7	42	1
Pro Totals—6 Years	56	3	—6	—2.0	0	117	1973	16.9	15	15	90	6

Year Club	G.	—PUNT RETURNS—				—KICKOFF RET.—			
		No.	Yds.	Avg.	TD.	No.	Yds.	Avg.	TD.
1983—Los Angeles USFL	8	15	105	7.0	0	11	211	19.2	0
1984—Los Angeles (8)-Michigan (10) USFL	18	36	233	6.5	0	2	31	15.5	0
1985—Portland USFL	6		None				None		
1985—Atlanta NFL	16	21	141	6.7	0	8	140	17.5	0
1986—Atlanta NFL	5	2	10	5.0	0		None		
1987—Washington NFL	3		None				None		
USFL Totals—3 Years	32	51	338	6.6	0	13	242	18.6	0
NFL Totals—3 Years	24	23	151	6.6	0	8	140	17.5	0
Pro Totals—6 Years	56	74	489	6.6	0	21	382	18.2	0

Additional USFL statistics: Attempted one pass with no completions and recovered one fumble, 1983.
Additional NFL statistics: Recovered one fumble, 1985 and 1986.
Played in NFC Championship Game following 1987 season.
Member of Washington Redskins for NFL Championship Game following 1987 season; inactive.

DOUG ALLEN
Wide Receiver—Indianapolis Colts ✳
Born April 22, 1963, at Columbus, O.
Height, 5.10. Weight, 175.
High School—Baldwin Park, Calif.
Attended Arizona State University.
Brother of Gary Allen, running back with Houston Oilers and Dallas Cowboys, 1982 through 1984.

Selected by Arizona in 1985 USFL territorial draft.
Selected by New York Jets in 4th round (94th player selected) of 1985 NFL draft.
Signed by New York Jets, July 22, 1985.
Released by New York Jets, August 27, 1985; signed as free agent by San Francisco 49ers for 1986, December 20, 1985.
Released by San Francisco 49ers, August 16, 1986; signed as free agent by Edmonton Eskimos, September 9, 1986.
Released by Edmonton Eskimos, June 19, 1987; signed as free agent by Indianapolis Colts, February 12, 1988.
Played in CFL Championship Game following 1986 season.

EGYPT TYRONE ALLEN
Defensive Back—Chicago Bears
Born July 28, 1964, at Dallas, Tex.
Height, 6.00. Weight, 203.
High School—Dallas, Tex., South Oak Cliff.
Attended Texas Christian University.

Signed as free agent by Chicago Bears, May 10, 1986.
Released by Chicago Bears, August 18, 1986; signed as replacement player by Bears, September 24, 1987.
Chicago NFL, 1987.
Games: 1987 (6).
Pro statistics: Recovered two fumbles, 1987.

LLOYD PATRICK ALLEN
(Known by middle name.)
Cornerback—Houston Oilers
Born August 26, 1961, at Seattle, Wash.
Height, 5.10. Weight, 179.
High School—Seattle, Wash., Garfield.
Attended Utah State University.
Brother of Anthony Allen, running back with Washington Redskins.

Selected by Washington in 2nd round (27th player selected) of 1984 USFL draft.
Selected by Houston in 4th round (100th player selected) of 1984 NFL draft.
Signed by Houston Oilers, July 18, 1984.

			—INTERCEPTIONS—		
Year Club	G.	No.	Yds.	Avg.	TD.
1984—Houston NFL	16	1	2	2.0	0
1985—Houston NFL	16		None		
1986—Houston NFL	16	3	20	6.7	0
1987—Houston NFL	11	1	37	37.0	0
Pro Totals—4 Years	59	5	59	11.8	0

Additional pro statistics: Returned 11 kickoffs for 210 yards (19.1 avg.), 1984; recovered two fumbles, 1985; recovered one fumble, 1987.

MARCUS ALLEN
Running Back—Los Angeles Raiders
Born March 26, 1960, at San Diego, Calif.
Height, 6.02. Weight, 205.
High School—San Diego, Calif., Lincoln.
Attended University of Southern California.
Brother of Damon Allen, quarterback with Edmonton Eskimos.

Named THE SPORTING NEWS NFL Player of the Year, 1985.
Named to THE SPORTING NEWS NFL All-Star Team, 1985.
Named THE SPORTING NEWS NFL Rookie of the Year, 1982.
Heisman Trophy winner, 1981.
Named THE SPORTING NEWS College Player of the Year, 1981.
Named as running back on THE SPORTING NEWS College All-America Team, 1981.
Established NFL record for most combined yards, season (2,314), 1985.
Tied NFL record for most consecutive games, 100 yards rushing (9), 1985.
Selected by Los Angeles Raiders in 1st round (10th player selected) of 1982 NFL draft.

		—RUSHING—				PASS RECEIVING				—TOTAL—		
Year Club	G.	Att.	Yds.	Avg.	TD.	P.C.	Yds.	Avg.	TD.	TD.	Pts.	F.
1982—Los Angeles Raiders NFL	9	160	697	4.4	*11	38	401	10.6	3	*14	*84	5
1983—Los Angeles Raiders NFL	15	266	1014	3.8	9	68	590	8.7	2	12	72	*14
1984—Los Angeles Raiders NFL	16	275	1168	4.2	13	64	758	11.8	5	*18	108	8
1985—Los Angeles Raiders NFL	16	380	*1759	4.6	11	67	555	8.3	3	14	84	3
1986—Los Angeles Raiders NFL	13	208	759	3.6	5	46	453	9.8	2	7	42	7
1987—Los Angeles Raiders NFL	12	200	754	3.8	5	51	410	8.0	0	5	30	3
Pro Totals—6 Years	81	1489	6151	4.1	54	334	3167	9.5	15	70	420	40

Additional pro statistics: Completed one of four pass attempts for 47 yards, 1982; recovered two fumbles, 1982 and 1985; attempted seven passes with four completions for 111 yards and three touchdowns and recovered two fumbles (including one in end zone for a touchdown), 1983; attempted four passes with one completion for 38 yards and recovered three fumbles, 1984; attempted two passes with one completion for 16 yards, 1985; recovered one fumble, 1986; attempted two passes with one completion for 23 yards, 1987.
Played in AFC Championship Game following 1983 season.
Played in NFL Championship Game following 1983 season.
Played in Pro Bowl (NFL All-Star Game) following 1982, 1984, 1985 and 1987 seasons.
Named to play in Pro Bowl following 1986 season; replaced due to injury by Sammy Winder.

TY HUNTER ALLERT
Linebacker—Philadelphia Eagles
Born July 23, 1963, at Rosenberg, Tex.
Height, 6.02. Weight, 233.
High School—Houston, Tex., Northbrook.
Attended University of Texas.

Selected by San Diego in 4th round (95th player selected) of 1986 NFL draft.
Signed by San Diego Chargers, July 25, 1986.
Released by San Diego Chargers, November 3, 1987; awarded on waivers to Philadelphia Eagles, November 4, 1987.
San Diego NFL, 1986; San Diego (3)-Philadelphia (7) NFL, 1987.
Games: 1986 (16), 1987 (10). Total—26.

JOHN MICHAEL ALT
Offensive Tackle—Kansas City Chiefs
Born May 30, 1962, at Stuttgart, West Germany.
Height, 6.07. Weight, 278.
High School—Columbia Heights, Minn.
Attended University of Iowa.

Selected by Oklahoma in 3rd round (46th player selected) of 1984 USFL draft.
Selected by Kansas City in 1st round (21st player selected) of 1984 NFL draft.
Signed by Kansas City Chiefs, July 18, 1984.
On injured reserve with back injury, December 6 through remainder of 1985 season.
On physically unable to perform/reserve with back injury, August 18 through November 7, 1986; activated, November 8, 1986.
On injured reserve with knee injury, December 9 through remainder of 1987 season.
Kansas City NFL, 1984 through 1987.
Games: 1984 (15), 1985 (13), 1986 (7), 1987 (9). Total—44.

JIM ALTHOFF
Defensive Lineman—Chicago Bears
Born September 27, 1961, at McHenry, Ill.
Height, 6.03. Weight, 278.
High School—McHenry, Ill., Community.
Attended Winona State University.

Signed as free agent by Buffalo Bills, July 16, 1987.
Released by Buffalo Bills, August 10, 1987; signed as free agent replacement player by Chicago Bears, September 24, 1987.
On injured reserve with back injury, December 14, 1987 through remainder of season.
Chicago NFL, 1987.
Games: 1987 (4).
Pro statistics: Recovered one fumble, 1987.

STEVEN LEE ALVORD
(Steve)
Defensive Tackle—Phoenix Cardinals
Born October 2, 1964, at Bellingham, Wash.
Height, 6.04. Weight, 272.
High School—Bellingham, Wash.
Attended University of Washington.

Selected by St. Louis in 8th round (201st player selected) of 1987 NFL draft.
Signed by St. Louis Cardinals, July 18, 1987.
Franchise transferred to Phoenix, March 15, 1988.
St. Louis NFL, 1987.
Games: 1987 (12).

MORTEN ANDERSEN
Placekicker—New Orleans Saints
Born August 19, 1960, at Struer, Denmark.
Height, 6.02. Weight, 221.
High School—Indianapolis, Ind., Davis.
Attended Michigan State University.

Named to THE SPORTING NEWS NFL All-Star Team, 1985 through 1987.
Named as placekicker on THE SPORTING NEWS College All-America Team, 1981.
Established NFL record for highest field goal percentage, career (79.6).
Selected by New Orleans in 4th round (86th player selected) of 1982 NFL draft.
On injured reserve with sprained ankle, September 15 through November 19, 1982; activated, November 20, 1982.

	—PLACE KICKING—					
Year Club	G.	XP.	XPM.	FG.	FGA.	Pts.
1982—New Orleans NFL...	8	6	0	2	5	12
1983—New Orleans NFL...	16	37	1	18	24	91
1984—New Orleans NFL...	16	34	0	20	27	94
1985—New Orleans NFL...	16	27	2	31	35	120
1986—New Orleans NFL...	16	30	0	26	30	108
1987—New Orleans NFL...	12	37	0	★28	★36	121
Pro Totals—6 Years.......	84	171	3	125	157	546

Played in Pro Bowl (NFL All-Star Game) following 1985 through 1987 seasons.

ALFRED ANTHONY ANDERSON
Running Back—Minnesota Vikings
Born August 4, 1961, at Waco, Tex.
Height, 6.01. Weight, 220.
High School—Waco, Tex., Richfield.
Attended Baylor University.

Selected by San Antonio in 1984 USFL territorial draft.
Selected by Minnesota in 3rd round (67th player selected) of 1984 NFL draft.
Signed by Minnesota Vikings, May 18, 1984.

		—RUSHING—				PASS RECEIVING				—TOTAL—		
Year Club	G.	Att.	Yds.	Avg.	TD.	P.C.	Yds.	Avg.	TD.	TD.	Pts.	F.
1984—Minnesota NFL.........................	16	201	773	3.8	2	17	102	6.0	1	3	18	8
1985—Minnesota NFL.........................	12	50	121	2.4	4	16	175	10.9	1	5	30	0
1986—Minnesota NFL.........................	16	83	347	4.2	2	17	179	10.5	2	4	24	3
1987—Minnesota NFL.........................	10	68	319	4.7	2	7	69	9.9	0	2	12	1
Pro Totals—4 Years.................	54	402	1560	3.9	10	57	525	9.2	4	14	84	12

Year Club	G.	No.	Yds.	Avg.	TD.
		KICKOFF RETURNS			
1984—Minnesota NFL	16	30	639	21.3	0
1985—Minnesota NFL	12		None		
1986—Minnesota NFL	16	3	38	12.7	0
1987—Minnesota NFL	10		None		
Pro Totals—4 Years	54	33	677	20.5	0

Additional pro statistics: Attempted seven passes with three completions for 95 yards with two touchdowns and one interception, 1984; recovered two fumbles, 1984 and 1986; attempted two passes with one completion for 17 yards, 1986.

Played in NFC Championship Game following 1987 season.

CHARLES NEAL ANDERSON

(Known by middle name.)

Running Back—Chicago Bears

Born August 14, 1964, at Graceville, Fla.
Height, 5.11. Weight, 210.
High School—Graceville, Fla.
Received degree in public relations from University of Florida in 1986.

Selected by Tampa Bay in 1986 USFL territorial draft.
Selected by Chicago in 1st round (27th player selected) of 1986 NFL draft.
Signed by Chicago Bears, August 15, 1986.

Year Club	G.	Att.	Yds.	Avg.	TD.	P.C.	Yds.	Avg.	TD.	TD.	Pts.	F.
		RUSHING				PASS RECEIVING				—TOTAL—		
1986—Chicago NFL	14	35	146	4.2	0	4	80	20.0	1	1	6	1
1987—Chicago NFL	11	129	586	4.5	3	47	467	9.9	3	6	36	2
Pro Totals—2 Years	25	164	732	4.5	3	51	547	10.7	4	7	42	3

Additional pro statistics: Returned four kickoffs for 26 yards, 1986.

EDDIE LEE ANDERSON JR.

Safety—Los Angeles Raiders

Born July 22, 1963, at Warner Robins, Ga.
Height, 6.01. Weight, 199.
High School—Warner Robins, Ga.
Attended Fort Valley State College.

Selected by Seattle in 6th round (153rd player selected) of 1986 NFL draft.
Signed by Seattle Seahawks, July 16, 1986.
On injured reserve with back injury, September 11 through November 20, 1986; activated, November 21, 1986.
Released by Seattle Seahawks, September 1, 1987; signed as free agent replacement player by Los Angeles Raiders, September 24, 1987.
Seattle NFL, 1986; Los Angeles Raiders NFL, 1987.
Games: 1986 (5), 1987 (13). Total—18.
Pro statistics: Intercepted one pass for 58 yards and recovered one fumble, 1987.

GARY ALLAN ANDERSON

Placekicker—Pittsburgh Steelers

Born July 16, 1959, at Parys, Orange Free State, South Africa.
Height, 5.11. Weight, 170.
High School—Durban, South Africa, Brettonwood.
Received bachelor of science degree in management and accounting
from Syracuse University in 1982.
Son of Rev. Douglas Anderson, former pro soccer player in England.

Selected by Buffalo in 7th round (171st player selected) of 1982 NFL draft.
Released by Buffalo Bills, September 6, 1982; claimed on waivers by Pittsburgh Steelers, September 7, 1982.

Year Club	G.	XP.	XPM.	FG.	FGA.	Pts.
		PLACE KICKING				
1982—Pittsburgh NFL	9	22	0	10	12	52
1983—Pittsburgh NFL	16	38	1	27	31	119
1984—Pittsburgh NFL	16	45	0	24	32	117
1985—Pittsburgh NFL	16	40	0	*33	*42	139
1986—Pittsburgh NFL	16	32	0	21	32	95
1987—Pittsburgh NFL	12	21	0	22	27	87
Pro Totals—6 Years	85	198	1	137	176	609

Played in AFC Championship Game following 1984 season.
Played in Pro Bowl (NFL All-Star Game) following 1983 and 1985 seasons.

GARY WAYNE ANDERSON

Running Back—San Diego Chargers

Born April 18, 1961, at Columbia, Mo.
Height, 6.00. Weight, 180.
High School—Columbia, Mo., Hickman.
Attended University of Arkansas

Named as running back on THE SPORTING NEWS USFL All-Star Team, 1985.
Selected by New Jersey in 1st round (5th player selected) of 1983 USFL draft.

Selected by San Diego in 1st round (20th player selected) of 1983 NFL draft.
USFL rights traded by New Jersey Generals to Tampa Bay Bandits for 1st round pick in 1984 draft, May 9, 1983.
Signed by Tampa Bay Bandits, May 9, 1983.
Granted roster exemption, May 9 through May 13, 1983; activated, May 14, 1983.
Released by Tampa Bay Bandits, September 27, 1985; signed by San Diego Chargers, September 30, 1985.
Granted roster exemption, September 30 through October 4, 1985; activated, October 5, 1985.

Year Club	G.	—RUSHING— Att.	Yds.	Avg.	TD.	PASS RECEIVING P.C.	Yds.	Avg.	TD.	—TOTAL— TD.	Pts.	F.
1983—Tampa Bay USFL	8	97	516	5.3	4	29	347	12.0	0	4	24	7
1984—Tampa Bay USFL	18	268	1008	3.8	*19	66	682	10.3	2	*21	126	8
1985—Tampa Bay USFL	18	276	1207	4.4	16	72	678	9.4	4	20	120	11
1985—San Diego NFL	12	116	429	3.7	4	35	422	12.1	2	7	42	5
1986—San Diego NFL	16	127	442	3.5	1	80	871	10.9	8	9	54	5
1987—San Diego NFL	12	80	260	3.3	3	47	503	10.7	2	5	30	4
USFL Totals—3 Years	44	641	2731	4.3	39	167	1707	10.2	6	45	270	26
NFL Totals—3 Years	40	323	1131	3.5	8	162	1796	11.1	12	21	126	14
Pro Totals—6 Years	84	964	3862	4.0	47	329	3503	10.6	18	66	396	40

Year Club	G.	—PUNT RETURNS— No.	Yds.	Avg.	TD.	—KICKOFF RET.— No.	Yds.	Avg.	TD.
1983—Tampa Bay USFL	8	2	—1	—0.5	0	3	47	15.7	0
1984—Tampa Bay USFL	18	4	22	5.5	0		None		
1985—Tampa Bay USFL	18		None			0	2	0.0	0
1985—San Diego NFL	12		None			13	302	23.2	1
1986—San Diego NFL	16	25	227	9.1	0	24	482	20.1	0
1987—San Diego NFL	12		None			22	433	19.7	0
USFL Totals—3 Years	44	6	21	3.5	0	3	49	16.3	0
NFL Totals—3 Years	40	25	227	9.1	0	59	1217	20.6	1
Pro Totals—6 Years	84	31	248	8.0	0	62	1266	20.4	1

Additional USFL statistics: Attempted one pass with no completions and recovered one fumble, 1983; attempted three passes with two completions for 44 yards, one touchdown and one interception and recovered two fumbles, 1984; attempted three passes with two completions for three yards and a touchdown and recovered five fumbles, 1985.
Additional NFL statistics: Recovered three fumbles, 1985; attempted one pass with one completion for four yards and a touchdown and recovered two fumbles, 1986; recovered one fumble, 1987.
Played in Pro Bowl (NFL All-Star Game) following 1986 season.

OTTIS JEROME ANDERSON
(O. J.)
Running Back—New York Giants
Born November 19, 1957, at West Palm Beach, Fla.
Height, 6.02. Weight, 225.
High School—West Palm Beach, Fla., Forest Hill.
Received degree in physical education from University of Miami (Fla.).
Step-brother of Mike Taliferro, defensive lineman with Denver Gold, 1985.

Tied NFL record for most 100-yard games by rookie, season (9), 1979.
Named THE SPORTING NEWS NFL Rookie of the Year, 1979.
Named THE SPORTING NEWS NFC Player of the Year, 1979.
Named to THE SPORTING NEWS NFC All-Star Team, 1979.
Selected by St. Louis in 1st round (8th player selected) of 1979 NFL draft.
Traded by St. Louis Cardinals to New York Giants for 2nd and 7th round picks in 1987 draft, October 8, 1986.

Year Club	G.	—RUSHING— Att.	Yds.	Avg.	TD.	PASS RECEIVING P.C.	Yds.	Avg.	TD.	—TOTAL— TD.	Pts.	F.
1979—St. Louis NFL	16	331	1605	4.8	8	41	308	7.5	2	10	60	10
1980—St. Louis NFL	16	301	1352	4.5	9	36	308	8.6	0	9	54	5
1981—St. Louis NFL	16	328	1376	4.2	9	51	387	7.6	0	9	54	13
1982—St. Louis NFL	8	145	587	4.0	3	14	106	7.6	0	3	18	2
1983—St. Louis NFL	15	296	1270	4.3	5	54	459	8.5	1	6	36	10
1984—St. Louis NFL	15	289	1174	4.1	6	70	611	8.7	2	8	48	8
1985—St. Louis NFL	9	117	479	4.1	4	23	225	9.8	0	4	24	3
1986—St. Louis (4)-N.Y. Giants (8) NFL	12	75	237	3.2	3	19	137	7.2	0	3	18	2
1987—New York Giants NFL	4	2	6	3.0	0	2	16	8.0	0	0	0	0
Pro Totals—9 Years	111	1884	8086	4.3	47	310	2557	8.2	5	52	312	53

Additional pro statistics: Recovered one fumble, 1979, 1982, 1984 and 1985; attempted one pass with no completions, 1979; recovered four fumbles, 1980; recovered three fumbles, 1981 and 1983.
Played in NFC Championship Game following 1986 season.
Played in NFL Championship Game following 1986 season.
Played in Pro Bowl (NFL All-Star Game) following 1979 and 1980 seasons.

ROGER JOHN ANDERSON
(Known by middle name.)
Linebacker—Green Bay Packers
Born February 14, 1956, at Waukesha, Wis.
Height, 6.03. Weight, 229.
High School—Waukesha, Wis., South.
Received bachelor of arts degree in environmental studies from University
of Michigan in 1978.

Selected by Green Bay in 1st round (26th player selected) of 1978 NFL draft.
On injured reserve with broken arm, December 6 through remainder of 1978 season.
On injured reserve with broken arm, August 28 through October 29, 1979; activated, October 30, 1979.
On injured reserve with broken arm, November 5 through remainder of 1980 season.
On injured reserve with torn ligaments in ankle and fractured fibula, October 1 through remainder of 1986 season.

Year Club	G.	No.	Yds.	Avg.	TD.
1978—Green Bay NFL	13	5	27	5.4	0
1979—Green Bay NFL	7		None		
1980—Green Bay NFL	9		None		
1981—Green Bay NFL	16	3	12	4.0	0
1982—Green Bay NFL	9	3	22	7.3	0
1983—Green Bay NFL	16	5	54	10.8	1
1984—Green Bay NFL	16	3	24	8.0	0
1985—Green Bay NFL	16	2	2	1.0	0
1986—Green Bay NFL	4	1	3	3.0	0
1987—Green Bay NFL	12	2	22	11.0	0
Pro Totals—10 Years	118	24	166	6.9	1

Additional pro statistics: Recovered one fumble, 1978 through 1980 and 1983 through 1985; scored four points, kicking one field goal on one attempt and one extra point on two attempts, 1979; recovered four fumbles for 22 yards, 1981; recovered two fumbles, 1982; returned one kickoff for 14 yards, 1985; recovered three fumbles, 1987.

MITCHELL DEAN ANDREWS
(Mitch)
Tight End—Denver Broncos
Born March 4, 1964, at Houma, La.
Height, 6.02. Weight, 239.
High School—Houma, La., H.L. Bourgeois.
Attended Louisiana State University.

Signed as free agent by Denver Broncos, May 1, 1986.
Released by Denver Broncos, July 31, 1986; re-signed by Broncos, May 1, 1987.
Released by Denver Broncos, August 17, 1987; re-signed as replacement player by Broncos, September 25, 1987.
Released by Denver Broncos, November 3, 1987; re-signed by Broncos, November 11, 1987.

Year Club	G.	P.C.	Yds.	Avg.	TD.
1987—Denver NFL	8	4	53	13.3	0

Played in AFC Championship Game following 1987 season.
Member of Denver Broncos for NFL Championship Game following 1987 season; inactive.

SAM ANNO
(Last name originally was Aono.)
Linebacker—Minnesota Vikings
Born January 26, 1965, at Silver Springs, Md.
Height, 6.02. Weight, 230.
High School—Santa Monica, Calif.
Attended University of Southern California.

Signed as free agent by Los Angeles Rams, May 14, 1987.
Released by Los Angeles Rams, September 7, 1987; re-signed by Rams, September 8, 1987.
Crossed picket line during players' strike, October 14, 1987.
Released by Los Angeles Rams, November 3, 1987; signed as free agent by Minnesota Vikings, November 18, 1987.
Los Angeles Rams (3)-Minnesota (6) NFL, 1987.
Games: 1987 (9).
Played in NFC Championship Game following 1987 season.

EVAN ANTHONY ARAPOSTATHIS
Placekicker—Denver Broncos
Born October 30, 1963, at San Diego, Calif.
Height, 5.10. Weight, 165.
High School—La Mesa, Calif., Helix.
Attended Grossmount College and received bachelor of arts degree in psychology and sociology from Eastern Illinois University in 1986.

Signed as free agent by St. Louis Cardinals, July 6, 1986.
Released by St. Louis Cardinals, August 20, 1986; re-signed by Cardinals, September 1, 1986.
Released by St. Louis Cardinals, October 7, 1986; signed as free agent by Cincinnati Bengals, February 4, 1987.
Released by Cincinnati Bengals, May 8, 1987; signed as free agent by Dallas Cowboys, June 26, 1987.
Released by Dallas Cowboys, August 14, 1987; signed as free agent replacement player by Denver Broncos, September 25, 1987.
Released by Denver Broncos, October 19, 1987; re-signed by Broncos for 1988, December 29, 1987.

Year Club	G.	No.	Avg.	Blk.
1986—St. Louis NFL	5	30	38.0	0

Additional pro statistics: Attempted one pass with no completions, 1986.

DAVID ARCHER
(Dave)
Quarterback—Miami Dolphins

Born February 15, 1962, at Fayetteville, N.C.
Height, 6.02. Weight, 208.
High School—Soda Springs, Ida.
Attended Snow College and Iowa State University.

Selected by Denver in 9th round (171st player selected) of 1984 USFL draft.
Signed as free agent by Atlanta Falcons, May 2, 1984.
On injured reserve with separated shoulder, November 17 through remainder of 1986 season.
Granted free agency, February 1, 1988; withdrew qualify offer, April 27, 1988.
Signed by Miami Dolphins, May 27, 1988.

		—————PASSING—————						—RUSHING—			—TOTAL—		
Year Club	G.	Att.	Cmp.	Pct.	Gain	T.P.	P.I.	Avg.	Att.	Yds.	Avg.	TD.	TD.	Pts.	F.
1984—Atlanta NFL	2	18	11	61.1	181	1	1	10.06	6	38	6.3	0	0	0	1
1985—Atlanta NFL	16	312	161	51.6	1992	7	17	6.38	70	347	5.0	2	2	12	9
1986—Atlanta NFL	11	294	150	51.0	2007	10	9	6.83	52	298	5.7	0	0	0	8
1987—Atlanta NFL	9	23	9	39.1	95	0	2	4.13	2	8	4.0	0	0	0	0
Pro Totals—4 Years	38	647	331	51.2	4275	18	29	6.61	130	691	5.3	2	2	12	18

Quarterback Rating Points: 1984 (90.3), 1985 (56.5), 1986 (71.6), 1987 (15.7). Total—62.9.
Additional pro statistics: Recovered two fumbles, 1985; recovered one fumble and fumbled eight times for minus three yards, 1986.

WILLIAM DONOVAN ARD
(Billy)
Guard—New York Giants

Born March 12, 1959, at East Orange, N.J.
Height, 6.03. Weight, 270.
High School—Watchung, N.J.
Attended Wake Forest University.

Named as guard on THE SPORTING NEWS College All-America Team, 1980.
Selected by New York Giants in 8th round (221st player selected) of 1981 NFL draft.
On injured reserve with knee injury, December 11 through remainder of 1984 season.
New York Giants NFL, 1981 through 1987.
Games: 1981 (13), 1982 (9), 1983 (16), 1984 (15), 1985 (16), 1986 (16), 1987 (12). Total—97.
Pro statistics: Recovered one fumble, 1981; recovered one fumble for one yard, 1986.
Played in NFC Championship Game following 1986 season.
Played in NFL Championship Game following 1986 season.

BRUCE ARMSTRONG
Guard-Offensive Tackle—New England Patriots

Born September 7, 1965, at Miami, Fla.
Height, 6.04. Weight, 284.
High School—Miami, Fla., Central.
Attended University of Louisville.

Selected by New England in 1st round (23rd player selected) of 1987 NFL draft.
Signed by New England Patriots, July 23, 1987.
New England NFL, 1987.
Games: 1987 (12).

HARVEY LEE ARMSTRONG
Nose Tackle—Indianapolis Colts

Born December 29, 1959, at Houston, Tex.
Height, 6.03. Weight, 265.
High School—Houston, Tex., Kashmere.
Received degree in business management from Southern Methodist University.

Selected by Philadelphia in 7th round (190th player selected) of 1982 NFL draft.
Released by Philadelphia Eagles, August 20, 1985; signed as free agent by Indianapolis Colts, May 21, 1986.
Philadelphia NFL, 1982 through 1984; Indianapolis NFL, 1986 and 1987.
Games: 1982 (8), 1983 (16), 1984 (16), 1986 (16), 1987 (11). Total—67.
Pro statistics: Recovered two fumbles, 1983 and 1987; intercepted one pass for four yards and recovered three fumbles, 1986.

JAMES EDWARD ARNOLD
(Jim)
Punter—Detroit Lions

Born January 31, 1961, at Dalton, Ga.
Height, 6.03. Weight, 211.
High School—Dalton, Ga.
Attended Vanderbilt University.

Named to THE SPORTING NEWS NFL All-Star Team, 1987.
Named as punter on THE SPORTING NEWS College All-America Team, 1982.

Led NFL in net punting average with 39.6 in 1987.
Led NFL in punting yards with 4,397 in 1984.
Selected by Kansas City in 5th round (119th player selected) of 1983 NFL draft.
Released by Kansas City Chiefs, August 26, 1986; signed as free agent by Detroit Lions, November 5, 1986.
Released by Detroit Lions, September 7, 1987; re-signed by Lions, September 14, 1987.

Year Club	G.	No.	Avg.	Blk.
1983—Kansas City NFL	16	93	39.9	0
1984—Kansas City NFL	16	*98	*44.9	0
1985—Kansas City NFL	16	*93	41.2	*2
1986—Detroit NFL	7	36	42.6	1
1987—Detroit NFL	11	46	43.6	0
Pro Totals—5 Years	66	366	42.3	3

Additional pro statistics: Rushed once for no yards, recovered two fumbles and fumbled once for minus nine yards, 1984.
Played in Pro Bowl (NFL All-Star Game) following 1987 season.

DOUGLAS ARONSON
(Doug)
Guard—Cincinnati Bengals
Born August 14, 1964, at San Francisco, Calif.
Height, 6.03. Weight, 290.
High School—South San Francisco, Calif.
Attended San Diego State University.

Signed as free agent by Cincinnati Bengals, May 1, 1987.
On injured reserve with Achilles heel injury, August 26 through November 13, 1987; activated, November 14, 1987.
Cincinnati NFL, 1987.
Games: 1987 (2).

WALKER LEE ASHLEY
(Walker Lee)
Linebacker—Minnesota Vikings
Born July 28, 1960, at Bayonne, N.J.
Height, 6.00. Weight, 232.
High School—Jersey City, N.J., Snyder.
Received degree in community development from Penn State University.

Selected by Philadelphia in 1983 USFL territorial draft.
Selected by Minnesota in 3rd round (73rd player selected) of 1983 NFL draft.
Signed by Minnesota Vikings, June 10, 1983.
On injured reserve with ruptured Achilles tendon, August 20 through entire 1985 season.
Minnesota NFL, 1983, 1984, 1986 and 1987.
Games: 1983 (15), 1984 (15), 1986 (16), 1987 (12). Total—58.
Pro statistics: Recovered one fumble, 1986.
Played in NFC Championship Game following 1987 season.

GENE REYNARD ATKINS
Defensive Back—New Orleans Saints
Born August 31, 1964, at Tallahassee, Fla.
Height, 6.01. Weight, 200.
High School—Tallahassee, Fla., James S. Rickards.
Attended Florida A&M University.

Selected by New Orleans in 7th round (179th player selected) of 1987 NFL draft.
Signed by New Orleans Saints, July 25, 1987.
On injured reserve with eye injury, September 7 through September 30, 1987; activated, October 1, 1987.
Crossed picket line during players' strike, October 1, 1987.
New Orleans NFL, 1987.
Games: 1987 (13).
Pro statistics: Intercepted three passes for 12 yards and recovered one fumble, 1987.

JESS GERALD ATKINSON
Placekicker—Washington Redskins
Born December 11, 1961, at Ann Arbor, Mich.
Height, 5.09. Weight, 168.
High School—Camy Springs, Md., Crossland.
Received bachelor of science degree in business from University of Maryland.

Selected by Baltimore in 6th round (87th player selected) of 1985 USFL draft.
Signed as free agent by New England Patriots, May 21, 1985.
Released by New England Patriots, August 19, 1985; signed as free agent by New York Giants, September 17, 1985.
Released by Ney York Giants, October 28, 1985; awarded on waivers to St. Louis Cardinals, October 29, 1985.
Released by St. Louis Cardinals, November 13, 1985; signed as free agent by Washington Redskins, May 8, 1986.
Released by Washington Redskins, August 6, 1986; re-signed by Redskins, December 16, 1986.
On injured reserve with dislocated ankle, September 16 through remainder of 1987 season.

Year Club	—PLACE KICKING—					
	G.	XP.	XPM.	FG.	FGA.	Pts.
1985—NYG(6)-StL(2) NFL	8	17	1	10	18	†53
1986—Washington NFL.....	1	3	0	0	0	3
1987—Washington NFL......	1	1	0	1	1	4
Pro Totals—3 Years.......	10	21	1	11	19	60

†Includes six points scored on a 14-yard run for a touchdown.
Played in NFC Championship Game following 1986 season.

CLIFF AUSTIN
Running Back—Tampa Bay Buccaneers
Born March 2, 1960, at Atlanta, Ga.
Height, 6.01. Weight, 213.
High School—Avondale Estates, Ga.
Attended Clemson University.

Selected by Washington in 1983 USFL territorial draft.
Selected by New Orleans in 3rd round (66th player selected) of 1983 NFL draft.
Signed by New Orleans Saints, June 21, 1983.
On injured reserve with separated shoulder and hamstring injuries, August 30 through October 7, 1983; activated, October 8, 1983.
Released by New Orleans Saints, August 27, 1984; signed as free agent by Atlanta Falcons, September 4, 1984.
On injured reserve with sprained ankle, December 10 through remainder of 1985 season.
Traded by Atlanta Falcons to Tampa Bay Buccaneers for 6th round pick in 1988 draft, September 7, 1987.
On injured reserve with knee injury, November 14 through remainder of 1987 season.

Year Club		—RUSHING—				PASS RECEIVING				—TOTAL—		
	G.	Att.	Yds.	Avg.	TD.	P.C.	Yds.	Avg.	TD.	TD.	Pts.	F.
1983—New Orleans NFL....................	11	4	16	4.0	0	2	25	12.5	0	0	0	0
1984—Atlanta NFL	15	4	7	1.8	0		None			0	0	0
1985—Atlanta NFL	14	20	110	5.5	0	1	21	21.0	0	1	6	0
1986—Atlanta NFL	15	62	280	4.5	1	3	21	7.0	0	1	6	0
1987—Tampa Bay NFL	3	19	32	1.7	1	5	51	10.2	0	1	6	0
Pro Totals—5 Years.......................	58	109	445	4.1	2	11	118	10.7	0	3	18	1

Year Club	KICKOFF RETURNS				
	G.	No.	Yds.	Avg.	TD.
1983—New Orleans NFL........	11	7	112	16.0	0
1984—Atlanta NFL	15	4	77	19.3	0
1985—Atlanta NFL	14	39	838	21.5	1
1986—Atlanta NFL	15	7	120	17.1	0
1987—Tampa Bay NFL	3		None		
Pro Totals—5 Years............	58	57	1147	20.1	1

Additional pro statistics: Recovered one fumble, 1986.

ROBERT MITCHELL AWALT
(Name pronounced A-walt.)
Tight End—Phoenix Cardinals
Born April 9, 1964, at Landsthul, West Germany.
Height, 6.05. Weight, 248.
High School—Sacramento, Calif., Valley.
Attended University of Nevada at Reno (did not play football), Sacramento City College and San Diego State University.

Named THE SPORTING NEWS Rookie of the Year, 1987.
Selected by St. Louis in 3rd round (62nd player selected) of 1987 NFL draft.
Signed by St. Louis Cardinals, July 31, 1987.
Franchise transferred to Phoenix, March 15, 1988.

Year Club	—PASS RECEIVING—				
	G.	P.C.	Yds.	Avg.	TD.
1987—St. Louis NFL.................	12	42	526	12.5	6

Additional pro statistics: Rushed twice for minus nine yards and recovered one fumble, 1987.

WILLIAM LESLIE AYDELETTE
(Buddy)
Offensive Tackle-Center—Pittsburgh Steelers
Born August 19, 1956, at Mobile, Ala.
Height, 6.04. Weight, 262.
High School—Mobile, Ala., Murphy.
Attended University of Alabama.

Named as guard on THE SPORTING NEWS USFL All-Star Team, 1983 through 1985.
Selected by Green Bay in 7th round (169th player selected) of 1980 NFL draft.
On injured reserve with knee injury, November 15 through remainder of 1980 season.
On injured reserve with knee injury, August 31 through entire 1981 season.
Retired and released by Green Bay Packers, August 11, 1982; signed as free agent by Birmingham Stallions, December 23, 1982.
On developmental squad, June 14 through remainder of 1985 season.
Granted free agency when USFL suspended operations, August 7, 1986; signed as free agent by Minnesota Vikings, March 3, 1987.

Released by Minnesota Vikings, September 2, 1987; awarded on waivers to Pittsburgh Steelers, September 3, 1987.
On developmental squad for 2 games with Birmingham Stallions in 1985.
Green Bay NFL, 1980; Birmingham USFL, 1983 through 1985; Pittsburgh NFL, 1987.
Games: 1980 (9), 1983 (18), 1984 (17), 1985 (16), 1987 (12). Total USFL—51. Total NFL—21. Total Pro—72.
USFL statistics: Recovered one fumble, 1983; recovered two fumbles, 1984.
Additional NFL statistics: Recovered one fumble for five yards, 1987.

MICHEAL JAMES BAAB
(Mike)
Center—Cleveland Browns
Born December 6, 1959, at Fort Worth, Tex.
Height, 6.04. Weight, 270.
High School—Euless, Tex., Trinity.
Attended Tarrant County Junior College, Austin Community College
and University of Texas.

Selected by Cleveland in 5th round (115th player selected) of 1982 NFL draft.
Cleveland NFL, 1982 through 1987.
Games: 1982 (7), 1983 (15), 1984 (16), 1985 (16), 1986 (16), 1987 (12). Total—82.
Pro statistics: Fumbled once for minus 11 yards, 1984; rushed once for no yards and fumbled once for minus two yards, 1985.
Played in AFC Championship Game following 1986 and 1987 seasons.

STEVEN WILLIAM BAACK
Name pronounced Bock.
(Steve)
Guard—Detroit Lions
Born November 16, 1960, at Ames, Ia.
Height, 6.04. Weight, 265.
High School—John Day, Ore., Grant Union.
Received bachelor of science degree in psychology from University of Oregon in 1984.

Selected by Philadelphia in 9th round (184th player selected) of 1984 USFL draft.
Selected by Detroit in 3rd round (75th player selected) of 1984 NFL draft.
Signed by Detroit Lions, June 20, 1984.
On injured reserve with knee injury, September 11 through October 30, 1987; activated, October 31, 1987.
Detroit NFL, 1984 through 1987.
Games: 1984 (16), 1985 (16), 1986 (16), 1987 (7). Total—55.
Pro statistics: Recovered one fumble, 1985.

RICHARD ALAN BADANJEK
(Rick)
Running Back—Atlanta Falcons
Born April 25, 1962, at Warren, O.
Height, 5.08. Weight, 217.
High School—Southington, O., Chalker.
Attended University of Maryland.

Selected by Baltimore in 1986 USFL territorial draft.
Selected by Washington in 7th round (186th player selected) of 1986 NFL draft.
Signed by Washington Redskins, July 18, 1986.
On injured reserve with hamstring injury, October 18 through remainder of 1986 season.
Released by Washington Redskins, August 31, 1987; signed as free agent replacement player by Atlanta Falcons, October 7, 1987.
Released by Atlanta Falcons, October 19, 1987; re-signed by Falcons, February 22, 1988.

		——RUSHING——				PASS RECEIVING				—TOTAL—		
Year Club	G.	Att.	Yds.	Avg.	TD.	P.C.	Yds.	Avg.	TD.	TD.	Pts.	F.
1986—Washington NFL	6			None				None		0	0	0
1987—Atlanta NFL	2	29	87	3.0	1	6	35	5.8	0	1	6	1
Pro Totals—2 Years	8	29	87	3.0	1	6	35	5.8	0	1	6	1

Additional pro statistics: Returned two kickoffs for 27 yards, 1987.

CHRIS BAHR
Placekicker—Los Angeles Raiders
Born February 3, 1953, at State College, Pa.
Height, 5.10. Weight, 170.
High School—Langhorne, Pa., Neshaminy Langhorne.
Received bachelor of science degree in biology from Penn State University in 1976, attended Chase
Law School at Northern Kentucky University and graduated from Southwestern Law School in 1986.
Brother of Matt Bahr, placekicker with Cleveland Browns.

Named to THE SPORTING NEWS AFC All-Star Team, 1977.
Named as placekicker on THE SPORTING NEWS College All-America Team, 1975.
Selected by Cincinnati in 2nd round (51st player selected) of 1976 NFL draft.
Released by Cincinnati Bengals, August 26, 1980; signed as free agent by Oakland Raiders, September 1, 1980.
Franchise transferred to Los Angeles, May 7, 1982.
Crossed picket line during players' strike, October 14, 1987.
Played with Philadelphia Atoms of North American Soccer League, 1975 (22 games, 11 goals, 2 assists).

Year Club		——PLACE KICKING——				
	G.	XP.	XPM.	FG.	FGA.	Pts.
1976—Cincinnati NFL........	14	39	3	14	27	81
1977—Cincinnati NFL........	14	25	1	19	27	82
1978—Cincinnati NFL	16	26	3	16	30	74
1979—Cincinnati NFL........	16	40	2	13	23	79
1980—Oakland NFL............	16	41	3	19	37	98
1981—Oakland NFL............	16	27	6	14	24	69
1982—L.A. Raiders NFL....	9	★32	1	10	16	62
1983—L.A. Raiders NFL....	16	51	2	21	27	114
1984—L.A. Raiders NFL....	16	40	2	20	27	100
1985—L.A. Raiders NFL....	16	40	2	20	32	100
1986—L.A. Raiders NFL....	16	36	0	21	28	99
1987—L.A. Raiders NFL....	13	27	1	19	29	84
Pro Totals—12 Years.....	178	424	26	206	327	1042

Additional pro statistics: Punted twice for 44.0 average, 1977; punted four times for 27.0 average, 1978; punted twice for 21.5 average, 1981.
Played in AFC Championship Game following 1980 and 1983 seasons.
Played in NFL Championship Game following 1980 and 1983 seasons.

MATTHEW DAVID BAHR
(Matt)
Placekicker—Cleveland Browns
Born July 6, 1956, at Philadelphia, Pa.
Height, 5.10. Weight, 175.
High School—Langhorne, Pa., Neshaminy Langhorne.
Received bachelor of science degree in electrical engineering from Penn State University in 1979; attending Carnegie-Mellon University for master's degree in industrial administration.
Brother of Chris Bahr, placekicker with Los Angeles Raiders.
Selected by Pittsburgh in 6th round (165th player selected) of 1979 NFL draft.
Released by Pittsburgh Steelers, August 31, 1981; signed as free agent by San Francisco 49ers, September 8, 1981.
Traded by San Francisco 49ers to Cleveland Browns for 9th round pick in 1983 draft, October 6, 1981.
On injured reserve with knee injury, November 26 through remainder of 1986 season.
On physically unable to perform/reserve with knee injury, September 1 through December 11, 1987; activated, December 12, 1987.
Played with Colorado Caribous and Tulsa Roughnecks of North American Soccer League, 1978 (26 games, 3 assists).

Year Club		——PLACE KICKING——				
	G.	XP.	XPM.	FG.	FGA.	Pts.
1979—Pittsburgh NFL........	16	★50	2	18	30	104
1980—Pittsburgh NFL........	16	39	3	19	28	96
1981—SF (4)-Cle (11) NFL	15	34	0	15	26	79
1982—Cleveland NFL.........	9	17	0	7	15	38
1983—Cleveland NFL.........	16	38	2	21	24	101
1984—Cleveland NFL.........	16	25	0	24	32	97
1985—Cleveland NFL.........	16	35	0	14	18	77
1986—Cleveland NFL.........	12	30	0	20	26	90
1987—Cleveland NFL.........	3	9	1	4	5	21
Pro Totals—9 Years.......	119	277	8	142	204	703

Played in AFC Championship Game following 1979 and 1987 seasons.
Played in NFL Championship Game following 1979 season.

EDWIN RAYMOND BAILEY
Guard—Seattle Seahawks
Born May 15, 1959, at Savannah, Ga.
Height, 6.04. Weight, 276.
High School—Savannah, Ga., Tompkins.
Attended South Carolina State College.
Selected by Seattle in 5th round (114th player selected) of 1981 NFL draft.
On injured reserve with knee injury, November 10 through December 7, 1984; activated, December 8, 1984.
On injured reserve with knee injury, September 11 through October 10, 1986; activated, October 11, 1986.
Seattle NFL, 1981 through 1987.
Games: 1981 (16), 1982 (9), 1983 (16), 1984 (12), 1985 (16), 1986 (12), 1987 (12). Total—93.
Pro statistics: Recovered one fumble, 1982; caught one pass for three yards, 1986.
Played in AFC Championship Game following 1983 season.

STACEY DWAYNE BAILEY
Wide Receiver—Atlanta Falcons
Born February 10, 1960, at San Rafael, Calif.
Height, 6.01. Weight, 160.
High School—San Rafael, Calif., Terra Linda.
Attended San Jose State University.
Selected by Atlanta in 3rd round (63rd player selected) of 1982 NFL draft.
On inactive list, September 12 and September 19, 1982.
On injured reserve with hamstring injury, September 2 through October 31, 1986; activated, November 1, 1986.

Year Club	—PASS RECEIVING—				
	G.	P.C.	Yds.	Avg.	TD.
1982—Atlanta NFL	5	2	24	12.0	1
1983—Atlanta NFL	15	55	881	16.0	6
1984—Atlanta NFL	16	67	1138	17.0	6
1985—Atlanta NFL	15	30	364	12.1	0
1986—Atlanta NFL	6	3	39	13.0	0
1987—Atlanta NFL	7	20	325	16.3	3
Pro Totals—6 Years	64	177	2771	15.7	16

Additional pro statistics: Fumbled once, 1982 through 1985 and 1987; rushed twice for minus five yards and recovered one fumble, 1983; rushed once for minus three yards, 1985; rushed once for six yards, 1986.

CHARLES EDWARD BAKER
(Charlie)
Linebacker—Phoenix Cardinals
Born September 26, 1957, at Mt. Pleasant, Tex.
Height, 6.02. Weight, 234.
High School—Odessa, Tex., Ector.
Attended University of New Mexico.

Selected by St. Louis in 3rd round (81st player selected) of 1980 NFL draft.
On injured reserve with abdominal strain, October 5 through November 8, 1984; activated, November 9, 1984.
Granted free agency, February 1, 1987; re-signed by Cardinals, August 31, 1987.
Granted roster exemption, August 31 through September 3, 1987; activated, September 4, 1987.
Crossed picket line during players' strike, October 7, 1987.
Franchise transferred to Phoenix, March 15, 1988.
St. Louis NFL, 1980 through 1987.
Games: 1980 (16), 1981 (14), 1982 (9), 1983 (16), 1984 (9), 1985 (15), 1986 (16), 1987 (14). Total—109.
Pro statistics: Ran 27 yards with lateral on kickoff return, 1980; recovered one fumble, 1981 and 1986; recovered two fumbles, 1982.

JAMES ALBERT LONDON BAKER
(Al or Bubba)
Defensive End—Cleveland Browns
Born December 9, 1956, at Jacksonville, Fla.
Height, 6.06. Weight, 270.
High School—Newark, N. J., Weequahic.
Attended Colorado State University.

Named THE SPORTING NEWS NFC Rookie of the Year, 1978.
Selected by Detroit in 2nd round (40th player selected) of 1978 NFL draft.
On reserve-retired list, August 19 through September 10, 1980; activated, September 11, 1980.
On physically unable to perform/active list with groin injury, July 29 through August 30, 1982; activated, August 31, 1982.
Traded by Detroit Lions to St. Louis Cardinals for defensive tackle Mike Dawson and 3rd round pick in 1984 draft, July 18, 1983.
Granted free agency, February 1, 1986; re-signed by Cardinals, August 26, 1986.
Granted roster exemption, August 26 and 27, 1986; activated, August 28, 1986.
Traded by St. Louis Cardinals to Cleveland Browns for 5th round pick in 1988 draft, September 3, 1987.
Detroit NFL, 1978 through 1982; St. Louis NFL, 1983 through 1986; Cleveland NFL, 1987.
Games: 1978 (16), 1979 (16), 1980 (15), 1981 (11), 1982 (9), 1983 (16), 1984 (15), 1985 (16), 1986 (16), 1987 (12). Total—142.
Pro statistics: Recovered one fumble, 1978 through 1980, 1982, 1985 and 1987; intercepted one pass for no yards, 1980; intercepted one pass for nine yards, 1981; intercepted two passes for 24 yards and recovered two fumbles, 1983.
Played in AFC Championship Game following 1987 season.
Played in Pro Bowl (NFL All-Star Game) following 1978 through 1980 seasons.

RONALD BAKER
(Ron)
Guard—Philadelphia Eagles
Born November 19, 1954, at Gary, Ind.
Height, 6.04. Weight, 274.
High School—Gary, Ind., Emerson.
Attended Indian Hills Junior College and Oklahoma State University.

Selected by Baltimore in 10th round (277th player selected) of 1977 NFL draft.
On injured reserve with ankle injury entire 1977 season.
Traded by Baltimore Colts to Philadelphia Eagles for 8th round pick in 1981 draft, August 26, 1980.
On injured reserve with knee injury, December 17 through remainder of 1987 season.
Baltimore NFL, 1978 and 1979; Philadelphia NFL, 1980 through 1987.
Games: 1978 (16), 1979 (16), 1980 (16), 1981 (16), 1982 (9), 1983 (16), 1984 (16), 1985 (15), 1986 (16), 1987 (10). Total—146.
Pro statistics: Returned one kickoff for six yards, 1980; recovered one fumble, 1982 through 1984 and 1987.
Played in NFC Championship Game following 1980 season.
Played in NFL Championship Game following 1980 season.

STEPHEN BAKER
Wide Receiver—New York Giants
Born August 30, 1964, at San Antonio, Tex.
Height, 5.08. Weight, 160.
High School—Los Angeles, Calif., Hamilton.
Attended West Los Angeles College and Fresno State University.
Selected by New York Giants in 3rd round (83rd player selected) of 1987 NFL draft.
Signed by New York Giants, July 27, 1987.

		—PASS RECEIVING—			
Year Club	G.	P.C.	Yds.	Avg.	TD.
1987—New York Giants NFL	12	15	277	18.5	2

Additional pro statistics: Rushed once for 18 yards, returned three punts for 16 yards and fumbled once, 1987.

TONY FERRINO BAKER
Running Back—Cleveland Browns
Born June 11, 1964, at High Point, N.C.
Height, 5.10. Weight, 176.
High School—High Point, N.C., T. Wingate Andrews.
Attended East Carolina University.
Selected by Atlanta in 10th round (252nd player selected) of 1986 NFL draft.
Selected by Memphis in 2nd round (14th player selected) of 1986 USFL draft.
Signed by Atlanta Falcons, July 15, 1986.
Released by Atlanta Falcons, September 9, 1986; re-signed by Falcons, October 9, 1986.
Released by Atlanta Falcons, October 18, 1986; awarded on waivers to Cleveland Browns, October 20, 1986.
Released by Cleveland Browns, November 22, 1986; re-signed by Browns, March 17, 1987.
On injured reserve with wrist injury, September 7 through entire 1987 season.
Atlanta (2)-Cleveland (2) NFL, 1986.
Games: 1986 (4).
Pro statistics: Rushed once for three yards, 1986.

GARY THOMAS BALDINGER
Defensive Tackle-Defensive End—Kansas City Chiefs
Born October 4, 1963, at Philadelphia, Pa.
Height, 6.03. Weight, 265.
High School—Massapequa, N.Y.
Received degree in history from Wake Forest University in 1986.
Brother of Brian Baldinger, guard with Dallas Cowboys, 1982 through 1984, 1986 and 1987; and
Rich Baldinger, guard-offensive tackle with Kansas City Chiefs.
Selected by Kansas City in 9th round (229th player selected) of 1986 NFL draft.
Signed by Kansas City Chiefs, July 17, 1986.
Released by Kansas City Chiefs, September 1, 1986; re-signed by Chiefs, September 2, 1986.
Released by Kansas City Chiefs, October 10, 1986; re-signed by Chiefs, February 12, 1987.
On injured reserve with back injury, October 30 through December 4, 1987; activated, December 5, 1987.
Kansas City NFL, 1986 and 1987.
Games: 1986 (5), 1987 (7). Total—12.

RICHARD L. BALDINGER
(Rich)
Guard-Offensive Tackle—Kansas City Chiefs
Born December 31, 1959, at Camp Le Jeune, N.C.
Height, 6.04. Weight, 285.
High School—Massapequa, N.Y.
Attended Wake Forest University.
Brother of Brian Baldinger, guard with Dallas Cowboys, 1982 through 1984, 1986 and 1987; and
Gary Baldinger, defensive tackle-defensive end with Kansas City Chiefs.
Selected by New York Giants in 10th round (270th player selected) of 1982 NFL draft.
On inactive list, September 12, 1982.
Released by New York Giants, August 29, 1983; re-signed by Giants, September 8, 1983.
Released by New York Giants, October 7, 1983; signed as free agent by Kansas City Chiefs, October 26, 1983.
New York Giants NFL, 1982; New York Giants (2)-Kansas City (6) NFL, 1983; Kansas City NFL, 1984 through 1987.
Games: 1982 (1), 1983 (8), 1984 (14), 1985 (16), 1986 (16), 1987 (12). Total—67.
Pro statistics: Recovered one fumble, 1987.

DONALD WAYNE BALDWIN
(Don)
Defensive End—New York Jets
Born July 9, 1964, at St. Charles, Mo.
Height, 6.03. Weight, 263.
High School—St. Charles, Mo., West.
Attended Purdue University.
Signed as free agent by New York Jets, June 26, 1986.
Released by New York Jets, August 25, 1986; re-signed by Jets, March 26, 1987.
Crossed picket line during players' strike, October 14, 1987.
New York Jets NFL, 1987.
Games: 1987 (8).

KEITH MANNING BALDWIN
Defensive End—San Diego Chargers
Born October 13, 1960, at Houston, Tex.
Height, 6.04. Weight, 270.
High School—Houston, Tex., M.B. Smiley.
Attended Texas A&M University.
Selected by Cleveland in 2nd round (31st player selected) of 1982 NFL draft.
On injured reserve with knee injury, August 18 through entire 1986 season.
Granted free agency, February 1, 1987; withdrew qualifying offer, June 25, 1987.
Signed by San Diego Chargers, July 20, 1987.
On injured reserve with knee injury, September 7 through November 20, 1987; activated, November 21, 1987.
Cleveland NFL, 1982 through 1985; San Diego NFL, 1987.
Games: 1982 (9), 1983 (16), 1984 (16), 1985 (10), 1987 (6). Total—57.

THOMAS BURKE BALDWIN
(Tom)
Defensive Tackle—New York Jets
Born May 13, 1961, at Evergreen Park, Ill.
Height, 6.04. Weight, 270.
High School—Lansing, Ill., Thornton Fractional South.
Attended University of Wisconsin, Thornton Community College and
and received degree in education from The University of Tulsa.
Brother of Brian Baldwin, pitcher in Los Angeles Dodgers' organization, 1977 through 1979.
Selected by Oklahoma in 1984 USFL territorial draft.
Selected by New York Jets in 9th round (234th player selected) of 1984 NFL draft.
Signed by New York Jets, May 29, 1984.
On injured reserve with stress fracture in foot, September 1 through entire 1987 season.
New York Jets NFL, 1984 through 1986.
Games: 1984 (16), 1985 (16), 1986 (16). Total—48.
Pro statistics: Recovered one fumble for nine yards and a touchdown, 1985; returned two kickoffs for three yards, recovered one fumble and fumbled once, 1986.

JERRY LEE BALL
Nose Tackle—Detroit Lions
Born December 15, 1964, at Beaumont, Tex.
Height, 6.01. Weight, 283.
High School—Westbrook, Tex.
Attended Southern Methodist University.
Selected by Detroit in 3rd round (63rd player selected) of 1987 NFL draft.
Signed by Detroit Lions, July 6, 1987.
Detroit NFL, 1987.
Games: 1987 (12).
Pro statistics: Returned two kickoffs for 23 yards, 1987.

TED BANKER
Guard-Center—New York Jets
Born February 17, 1961, at Belleville, Ill.
Height, 6.02. Weight, 275.
High School—Belleville, Ill., Althoff.
Attended Southeast Missouri State University.
Signed as free agent by New York Jets, June 20, 1983.
On injured reserve with knee injury, August 12 through entire 1983 season.
On injured reserve with broken leg, December 24 through remainder of 1985 season playoffs.
Crossed picket line during players' strike, October 14, 1987.
New York Jets NFL, 1984 through 1987.
Games: 1984 (14), 1985 (16), 1986 (15), 1987 (13). Total—58.
Pro statistics: Returned one kickoff for five yards, 1984; recovered one fumble, 1987.

CARL BANKS
Linebacker—New York Giants
Born August 29, 1962, at Flint, Mich.
Height, 6.04. Weight, 235.
High School—Flint, Mich., Beecher.
Attended Michigan State University.
Named to THE SPORTING NEWS NFL All-Star Team, 1987.
Named as linebacker on THE SPORTING NEWS College All-America Team, 1983.
Selected by Michigan in 1984 USFL territorial draft.
Selected by New York Giants in 1st round (3rd player selected) of 1984 NFL draft.
Signed by New York Giants, July 12, 1984.
On injured reserve with knee injury, October 12 through November 8, 1985; activated, November 9, 1985.
New York Giants NFL, 1984 through 1987.
Games: 1984 (16), 1985 (12), 1986 (16), 1987 (12). Total—56.
Pro statistics: Recovered one fumble, 1984 and 1985; recovered two fumbles for five yards, 1986; intercepted one pass for no yards, 1987.
Played in NFC Championship Game following 1986 season.

Played in NFL Championship Game following 1986 season.
Played in Pro Bowl (NFL All-Star Game) following 1987 season.

CHUCK EDWARD BANKS
Running Back—Indianapolis Colts
Born January 4, 1964, at Baltimore, Md.
Height, 6.01. Weight, 225.
High School—Hyattsville, Md., Northwestern.
Attended Ferrum College and West Virginia Institute of Technology.

Selected by Houston in 12th round (310th player selected) of 1986 NFL draft.
Selected by Arizona in 9th round (62nd player selected) of 1986 USFL draft.
Signed by Houston Oilers, July 21, 1986.
Released by Houston Oilers, October 31, 1986; re-signed by Oilers, November 12, 1986.
Released by Houston Oilers, September 6, 1987; signed as free agent replacement player by Indianapolis Colts, September 23, 1987.
On injured reserve with knee and ankle injuries, November 6 through remainder of 1987 season.

		——RUSHING——				PASS RECEIVING				—TOTAL—		
Year Club	G.	Att.	Yds.	Avg.	TD.	P.C.	Yds.	Avg.	TD.	TD.	Pts.	F.
1986—Houston NFL	13	29	80	2.8	0	7	71	10.1	0	0	0	1
1987—Indianapolis NFL	3	50	245	4.9	0	9	50	5.6	0	0	0	1
Pro Totals—2 Years	16	79	325	4.1	0	16	121	7.6	0	0	0	2

FREDERICK RAY BANKS
(Fred)
Wide Receiver—Miami Dolphins
Born May 26, 1962, at Columbus, Ga.
Height, 5.10. Weight, 177.
High School—Columbus, Ga., Baker.
Attended Chowan College and Liberty Baptist College.

Selected by Denver in 8th round (107th player selected) of 1985 USFL draft.
Selected by Cleveland in 8th round (203rd player selected) of 1985 NFL draft.
Signed by Cleveland Browns, July 11, 1985.
On injured reserve with pulled hamstring, October 9 through November 15, 1985; activated, November 16, 1985.
On physically unable to perform/reserve with ankle injury, August 19 through September 15, 1986.
Released by Cleveland Browns, September 16, 1986; signed as free agent by Miami Dolphins for 1987, November 24, 1986.
Released by Miami Dolphins, December 12, 1987; re-signed by Dolphins, December 15, 1987.

	——PASS RECEIVING——				
Year Club	G.	P.C.	Yds.	Avg.	TD.
1985—Cleveland NFL	10	5	62	12.4	2
1987—Miami NFL	3	1	10	10.0	1
Pro Totals—2 Years	13	6	72	12.0	3

GORDON GERARD BANKS
Wide Receiver—Dallas Cowboys
Born March 12, 1958, at Los Angeles, Calif.
Height, 5.10. Weight, 173.
High School—Los Angeles, Calif., Loyola.
Received degree in political science from Stanford University.

Signed as free agent by New Orleans Saints, May 19, 1980.
Released by New Orleans Saints, August 26, 1980; re-signed by Saints after clearing procedural waivers, November 4, 1980.
Released by New Orleans Saints, Octoer 13, 1981; signed as free agent by San Diego Chargers, July 7, 1982.
Released by San Diego Chargers, August 31, 1982; signed as free agent by Oakland Invaders, January 26, 1983.
Placed on reserve/did not report list, January 30 through February 2, 1984; activated, February 3, 1984.
Protected in merger of Michigan Panthers and Oakland Invaders, December 6, 1984.
Released by Oakland Invaders, August 8, 1985; signed as free agent by Dallas Cowboys and placed on reserve/future list, November 6, 1985.
Activated from reserve/future list, December 5, 1985.
On injured reserve with foot injury, December 5 through remainder of 1987 season.

		——RUSHING——				PASS RECEIVING				—TOTAL—		
Year Club	G.	Att.	Yds.	Avg.	TD.	P.C.	Yds.	Avg.	TD.	TD.	Pts.	F.
1980—New Orleans NFL	7	1	—5	—5.0	0	1	7	7.0	0	0	0	0
1981—New Orleans NFL	6		None			2	18	9.0	0	0	0	2
1983—Oakland USFL	18	5	20	4.0	0	61	855	14.0	2	2	12	5
1984—Oakland USFL	18	1	8	8.0	0	64	937	14.6	5	5	30	6
1985—Oakland USFL	18		None			62	1115	18.0	5	5	†32	1
1985—Dallas NFL	2	1	—1	—1.0	0		None			0	0	0
1986—Dallas NFL	16		None			17	202	11.9	0	0	0	4
1987—Dallas NFL	5		None			15	231	15.4	1	1	6	1
NFL Totals—5 Years	36	2	—6	—3.0	0	35	458	13.1	1	1	6	7
USFL Totals—3 Years	54	6	28	4.7	0	187	2907	15.5	12	12	74	12
Pro Totals—8 Years	90	8	22	2.8	0	222	3365	15.2	13	13	80	19

Year Club			——PUNT RETURNS——		
	G.	No.	Yds.	Avg.	TD.
1980—New Orleans NFL........	7			None	
1981—New Orleans NFL........	6	2	0	0.0	0
1983—Oakland USFL.............	18	30	292	9.7	0
1984—Oakland USFL.............	18	25	147	5.9	0
1985—Oakland USFL.............	18	13	82	6.3	0
1985—Dallas NFL	2	3	27	9.0	0
1986—Dallas NFL	16	27	160	5.9	0
1987—Dallas NFL	5	5	33	6.6	0
NFL Totals—5 Years..........	36	37	220	5.9	0
USFL Totals—3 Years........	54	68	521	7.7	0
Pro Totals—8 Years............	90	105	741	7.1	0

†Includes one 2-point conversion.

Additional NFL statistics: Returned one kickoff for nine yards, 1981; recovered one fumble, 1981 and 1987; returned one kickoff for 56 yards and recovered three fumbles, 1986.

Additional USFL statistics: Returned three kickoffs for 27 yards and recovered one fumble, 1983; recovered two fumbles, 1984; recovered one fumble for minus eight yards, 1985.

Played in USFL Championship Game following 1985 season.

ROY F. BANKS
Wide Receiver—Indianapolis Colts
Born November 29, 1965, at Detroit, Mich.
Height, 5.10. Weight, 190.
High School—Detroit, Mich., Martin Luther King.
Attended Eastern Illinois University.

Selected by Indianapolis in 5th round (114th player selected) of NFL draft.
Signed by Indianapolis Colts, July 24, 1987.
On injured reserve with ankle injury, September 7 through December 10, 1987; activated, December 11, 1987.
Indianapolis NFL, 1987.
Games: 1987 (1).

WILLIAM CHIP BANKS
(Known by middle name.)
Linebacker—San Diego Chargers
Born September 18, 1959, at Fort Lawton, Okla.
Height, 6.04. Weight, 233.
High School—Augusta, Ga., Lucy Laney.
Attended University of Southern California.

Named as linebacker on THE SPORTING NEWS College All-America Team, 1981.
Selected by Cleveland in 1st round (3rd player selected) of 1982 NFL draft.
Traded with 3rd round pick in 1985 draft and 1st and 6th round picks in 1986 draft by Cleveland Browns to Buffalo Bills for 1st round pick in 1985 supplemental draft, April 9, 1985 (Bills received 1st round pick in 1985 draft from Browns when Banks did not report).
Placed on did not report list, August 18 through August 31, 1986; activated, September 1, 1986.
Granted roster exemption, September 1 through September 5, 1986; activated, September 6, 1986.
Traded with 1st and 2nd round picks in 1987 draft by Cleveland Browns to San Diego Chargers for 1st and 2nd round picks in 1987 draft, April 28, 1987.

Year Club			——INTERCEPTIONS——		
	G.	No.	Yds.	Avg.	TD.
1982—Cleveland NFL.............	9	1	14	14.0	0
1983—Cleveland NFL.............	16	3	95	31.7	1
1984—Cleveland NFL.............	16	1	8	8.0	0
1985—Cleveland NFL.............	16			None	
1986—Cleveland NFL.............	16			None	
1987—San Diego NFL	12	1	20	20.0	0
Pro Totals—6 Years............	85	6	137	22.8	1

Additional pro statistics: Recovered one fumble, 1983; recovered three fumbles for 17 yards, 1984; recovered two fumbles, 1986 and 1987.

Played in AFC Championship Game following 1986 season.
Played in Pro Bowl (NFL All-Star Game) following 1982, 1983 and 1986 seasons.
Named to play in Pro Bowl following 1985 season; replaced due to injury by Clay Matthews.

ROLAND ANTHONY BARBAY JR.
Nose Tackle—Seattle Seahawks
Born October 1, 1964, at New Orleans, La.
Height, 6.04. Weight, 260.
High School—New Orleans, La., Holy Cross.
Attended Louisiana State University.

Selected by Seattle in 7th round (184th player selected) of 1987 NFL draft.
Signed by Seattle Seahawks, July 21, 1987.
On injured reserve with back injury, September 7 through November 29, 1987; activated, November 30, 1987.
Seattle NFL, 1987.
Games: 1987 (5).

MARION BARBER
Fullback—New York Jets
Born December 6, 1959, at Fort Lauderdale, Fla.
Height, 6.03. Weight, 228.
High School—Detroit, Mich., Chadsey.
Received degree in juvenile behavior from University of Minnesota.
Selected by New York Jets in 2nd round (30th player selected) of 1981 NFL draft.
On injured reserve with concussion, August 17 through entire 1981 season.
On inactive list, September 12 and September 19, 1982.
On injured reserve with cracked rib, November 5 through remainder of 1985 season.

| Year   Club | G. | RUSHING | | | PASS RECEIVING | | | | —TOTAL— | | |
		Att.	Yds.	Avg.	TD.	P.C.	Yds.	Avg.	TD.	TD.	Pts.	F.
1982—New York Jets NFL	6	8	24	3.0	0	None				0	0	0
1983—New York Jets NFL	14	15	77	5.1	1	7	48	6.9	1	2	12	0
1984—New York Jets NFL	14	31	148	4.8	2	10	79	7.9	0	2	12	3
1985—New York Jets NFL	8	9	41	4.6	0	3	46	15.3	0	0	0	0
1986—New York Jets NFL	15	11	27	2.5	0	5	36	7.2	0	0	0	1
1987—New York Jets NFL	12		None			None				0	0	0
Pro Totals—6 Years	69	74	317	4.3	3	25	209	8.4	1	4	24	4

Additional pro statistics: Returned one kickoff for nine yards and recovered two fumbles, 1983; recovered one fumble, 1984; returned two kickoffs for five yards, 1987.
Played in AFC Championship Game following 1982 season.

LEO BARKER
Linebacker—Cincinnati Bengals
Born November 7, 1959, at Cristobal, Panama.
Height, 6.02. Weight, 227.
High School—Cristobal, Panama.
Attended New Mexico State University.
Selected by Arizona in 1984 USFL territorial draft.
Selected by Cincinnati in 7th round (177th player selected) of 1984 NFL draft.
Signed by Cincinnati Bengals, June 26, 1984.
Cincinnati NFL, 1984 through 1987.
Games: 1984 (16), 1985 (16), 1986 (16), 1987 (12). Total—60.
Pro statistics: Intercepted two passes for seven yards, 1986.

ROD DEAN BARKSDALE
Wide Receiver—Dallas Cowboys
Born September 8, 1962, at Los Angeles, Calif.
Height, 6.01. Weight, 193.
High School—Compton, Calif.
Received bachelor of science degree in political science
from University of Arizona in 1985.
Cousin of Jeremiah Castille, defensive back with Denver Broncos.
Signed as free agent by Los Angeles Raiders, May 11, 1985.
On injured reserve with ankle injury, August 20 through entire 1985 season.
Traded by Los Angeles Raiders to Dallas Cowboys for cornerback Ron Fellows, August 2, 1987.

| Year   Club | PASS RECEIVING | | | | |
	G.	P.C.	Yds.	Avg.	TD.
1986—L.A. Raiders NFL	16	18	434	24.1	2
1987—Dallas NFL	12	12	165	13.8	1
Pro Totals—2 Years	28	30	599	20.0	3

Additional pro statistics: Recovered one fumble and fumbled once, 1986.

JEFF BARNES
Linebacker—Los Angeles Raiders
Born March 1, 1955, at Philadelphia, Pa.
Height, 6.02. Weight, 230.
High School—Hayward, Calif.
Attended Chabot College and University of California at Berkeley.
Selected by Oakland in 5th round (139th player selected) of 1977 NFL draft.
Franchise transferred to Los Angeles, May 7, 1982.
On injured reserve with foot injury, December 3 through remainder of 1987 season.
Oakland NFL, 1977 through 1981; Los Angeles Raiders NFL, 1982 through 1987.
Games: 1977 (14), 1978 (16), 1979 (16), 1980 (16), 1981 (15), 1982 (9), 1983 (16), 1984 (16), 1985 (16), 1986 (16), 1987 (7). Total—157.
Pro statistics: Recovered two fumbles, 1977; intercepted one pass for eight yards, 1979; recovered one fumble, 1980 and 1984; intercepted one pass for 15 yards, 1984; intercepted one pass for no yards and recovered four fumbles for 14 yards, 1985; intercepted two passes for seven yards and fumbled once, 1986.
Played in AFC Championship Game following 1977, 1980 and 1983 seasons.
Played in NFL Championship Game following 1980 and 1983 seasons.

LEW ERIC BARNES
Wide Receiver—Chicago Bears

Born December 27, 1962, at Long Beach, Calif.
Height, 5.08. Weight, 163.
High School—San Diego, Calif., Abraham Lincoln.
Attended San Diego Mesa College and University of Oregon.

Selected by Chicago in 5th round (138th player selected) of 1986 NFL draft.
Signed by Chicago Bears, July 16, 1986.
On injured reserve with broken leg, August 27 through entire 1987 season.

		PASS RECEIVING				–PUNT RETURNS–				—KICKOFF RET.—				—TOTAL—		
Year	Club	G.	P.C.	Yds.	Avg.	TD.	No.	Yds.	Avg.	TD.	No.	Yds.	Avg.	TD.	TD.	Pts.	F.
1986—Chicago NFL		16	4	54	13.5	0	*57	482	8.5	0	3	94	31.3	*1	1	6	5

Additional pro statistics: Recovered three fumbles, 1986.

TOMMY RAY BARNHARDT
Punter—Chicago Bears

Born June 11, 1963, at Salisbury, N.C.
Height, 6.03. Weight, 205.
High School—China Grove, N.C., South Rowan.
Attended East Carolina University and received degree in industrial relations
from University of North Carolina in 1986.

Selected by Baltimore in 1986 USFL territorial draft.
Selected by Tampa Bay in 9th round (223rd player selected) of 1986 NFL draft.
Signed by Tampa Bay Buccaneers, July 16, 1986.
Released by Tampa Bay Buccaneers, August 25, 1986; re-signed by Buccaneers, February 6, 1987.
Released by Tampa Bay Buccaneers, August 5, 1987; signed as free agent replacement player by New Orleans Saints, September 23, 1987.
Released by New Orleans Saints, November 3, 1987; signed as free agent by Chicago Bears, December 16, 1987.

		——PUNTING——			
Year	Club	G.	No.	Avg.	Blk.
1987—N.O. (3)-Chi. (2) NFL		5	17	42.3	0

Additional pro statistics: Rushed once for minus 13 yards, 1987.

SCOTT MARTIN BARROWS
Guard-Center—Detroit Lions

Born March 31, 1963, at Marietta, O.
Height, 6.02. Weight, 278.
High School—Marietta, O.
Attended West Virginia University.

Selected by Tampa Bay in 11th round (150th player selected) of 1985 USFL draft.
Signed as free agent by Detroit Lions, May 9, 1986.
Released by Detroit Lions, August 27, 1986; re-signed by Lions, April 21, 1986.
Detroit NFL, 1986 and 1987.
Games: 1986 (16), 1987 (12). Total—28.
Pro statistics: Recovered one fumble, 1986 and 1987.

STEPHEN JAMES BARTALO
(Steve)
Running Back—San Francisco 49ers

Born July 15, 1964, at Limestone, Me.
Height, 5.09. Weight, 200.
High School—Colorado Springs, Colo., Thomas B. Doherty.
Received degree in physical education from Colorado State University.

Selected by Tampa Bay in 6th round (143rd player selected) of 1987 NFL draft.
Signed by Tampa Bay Buccaneers, July 18, 1987.
Released by Tampa Bay Buccaneers, May 4, 1988; awarded on waivers to San Francisco 49ers, May 17, 1988.

		——RUSHING——					PASS RECEIVING				—TOTAL—		
Year	Club	G.	Att.	Yds.	Avg.	TD.	P.C.	Yds.	Avg.	TD.	TD.	Pts.	F.
1987—Tampa Bay NFL		9	9	30	3.3	1	1	5	5.0	0	1	6	0

Additional pro statistics: Returned one kickoff for 15 yards and had only pass attempt intercepted, 1987.

HARRIS SCOTT BARTON
Offensive Tackle—San Francisco 49ers

Born April 19, 1964, at Atlanta, Ga.
Height, 6.04. Weight, 280.
High School—Dunwoody, Ga.
Received bachelor of science degree from University of North Carolina in 1987.

Selected by San Francisco in 1st round (22nd player selected) of 1987 NFL draft.
Signed by San Francisco 49ers, July 22, 1987.
San Francisco NFL, 1987.
Games: 1987 (12).
Pro statistics: Recovered one fumble, 1987.

WILLIAM FREDERICK BATES
(Bill)
Safety—Dallas Cowboys

Born June 6, 1961, at Knoxville, Tenn.
Height, 6.01. Weight, 201.
High School—Knoxville, Tenn., Farragut.
Attended University of Tennessee.

Selected by New Jersey in 1983 USFL territorial draft.
Signed as free agent by Dallas Cowboys, April 28, 1983.
On injured reserve with hip injury, September 3 through September 27, 1984; activated, September 28, 1984.

		-INTERCEPTIONS-				-PUNT RETURNS-				—TOTAL—		
Year Club	G.	No.	Yds.	Avg.	TD.	No.	Yds.	Avg.	TD.	TD.	Pts.	F.
1983—Dallas NFL	16	1	29	29.0	0		None			0	0	1
1984—Dallas NFL	12	1	3	3.0	0		None			0	0	0
1985—Dallas NFL	16	4	15	3.8	0	22	152	6.9	0	0	0	0
1986—Dallas NFL	15		None				None			0	0	0
1987—Dallas NFL	12	3	28	9.3	0		None			0	0	0
Pro Totals—5 Years	71	9	75	8.3	0	22	152	6.9	0	0	0	1

Additional pro statistics: Recovered two fumbles, 1983; recovered one fumble, 1984.
Played in Pro Bowl (NFL All-Star Game) following 1984 season.

GREGORY JAMES BATY
(Greg)
Tight End—Los Angeles Rams

Born August 28, 1964, at Haistings, Mich.
Height, 6.05. Weight, 241.
High School—Sparta, N.J.
Received bachelor of arts degree in human biology from Stanford University in 1986.

Selected by New England in 8th round (220th player selected) of 1986 NFL draft.
Signed by New England Patriots, July 18, 1986.
Released by New England Patriots, November 12, 1987; awarded on waivers to Los Angeles Rams, November 13, 1987.

	——PASS RECEIVING——				
Year Club	G.	P.C.	Yds.	Avg.	TD.
1986—New England NFL	16	37	331	8.9	2
1987—N.E.(5)-Rams(4) NFL .	9	18	175	9.7	2
Pro Totals—2 Years	25	55	506	9.2	4

THOMAS A. BAUGH
(Tom)
Center—Kansas City Chiefs

Born December 1, 1963, at Chicago, Ill.
Height, 6.03. Weight, 274.
High School—Riverside, Ill., Brookfield.
Received degree in construction management from University of Southern Illinois in 1986.

Selected by Kansas City in 4th round (87th player selected) of 1986 NFL draft.
Signed by Kansas City Chiefs, June 10, 1986.
On injured reserve with broken finger, September 9 through November 27, 1986; activated, November 28, 1986.
Kansas City NFL, 1986 and 1987.
Games: 1986 (5), 1987 (12). Total—17.
Pro statistics: Recovered two fumbles and fumbled once, 1987.

MARK BAVARO
Tight End—New York Giants

Born April 28, 1963, at Winthrop, Mass.
Height, 6.04. Weight, 245.
High School—Danvers, Mass.
Received bachelor of arts degree in history from University of Notre Dame in 1985.

Named to THE SPORTING NEWS NFL All-Star Team, 1986 and 1987.
Selected by Orlando in 15th round (212th player selected) of 1985 USFL draft.
Selected by New York Giants in 4th round (100th player selected) of 1985 NFL draft.
Signed by New York Giants, July 7, 1985.

	——PASS RECEIVING——				
Year Club	G.	P.C.	Yds.	Avg.	TD.
1985—N.Y. Giants NFL	16	37	511	13.8	4
1986—N.Y. Giants NFL	16	66	1001	15.2	4
1987—N.Y. Giants NFL	12	55	867	15.8	8
Pro Totals—3 Years	44	158	2379	15.1	16

Additional pro statistics: Recovered two fumbles and fumbled three times, 1986; returned one kickoff for 16 yards and fumbled twice, 1987.
Played in NFC Championship Game following 1986 season.
Played in NFL Championship Game following 1986 season.
Played in Pro Bowl (NFL All-Star Game) following 1986 season.
Named to play in Pro Bowl following 1987 season; replaced due to injury by Hoby Brenner.

MARTIN BAYLESS
Safety—San Diego Chargers
Born October 11, 1962, at Dayton, O.
Height, 6.02. Weight, 200.
High School—Dayton, O., Belmont.
Attended Bowling Green State University.

Selected by Memphis in 1st round (20th player selected) of 1984 USFL draft.
Selected by St. Louis in 4th round (101st player selected) of 1984 NFL draft.
Signed by St. Louis Cardinals, July 20, 1984.
Released by St. Louis Cardinals, September 19, 1984; awarded on waivers to Buffalo Bills, September 20, 1984.
On injured reserve with pinched nerve in neck, December 6 through remainder of 1985 season.
Traded by Buffalo Bills to San Diego Chargers for cornerback Wayne Davis, August 26, 1987.
St. Louis (3)-Buffalo (13) NFL, 1984; Buffalo NFL, 1985 and 1986; San Diego NFL, 1987.
Games: 1984 (16), 1985 (12), 1986 (16), 1987 (12). Total—56.
Pro statistics: Intercepted two passes for 10 yards and recovered one fumble, 1985; intercepted one pass for no yards, 1986.

PATRICK JESSE BEACH
(Pat)
Tight End—Indianapolis Colts
Born December 28, 1959, at Grant's Pass, Ore.
Height, 6.04. Weight, 252.
High School—Pullman, Wash.
Attended Washington State University.

Named as tight end on THE SPORTING NEWS College All-America team, 1981.
Selected by Baltimore in 6th round (140th player selected) of 1982 NFL draft.
Franchise transferred to Indianapolis, March 31, 1984.
On non-football injury list with ankle injury, August 10 through August 21, 1984.
On injured reserve with ankle injury, August 22 through entire 1984 season.

Year Club	G.	P.C.	Yds.	Avg.	TD.
1982—Baltimore NFL	9	4	45	11.3	1
1983—Baltimore NFL	16	5	56	11.2	1
1985—Indianapolis NFL	16	36	376	10.4	6
1986—Indianapolis NFL	16	25	265	10.6	1
1987—Indianapolis NFL	12	28	239	8.5	0
Pro Totals—5 Years	69	98	981	10.0	9

Additional pro statistics: Returned one kickoff for no yards, 1983; recovered one fumble for five yards and fumbled three times, 1985; recovered one fumble and fumbled twice, 1986.

KURT FRANK BECKER
Guard—Chicago Bears
Born December 22, 1958, at Aurora, Ill.
Height, 6.05. Weight, 280.
High School—Aurora, Ill., East.
Received bachelor of arts degree in business administration from University of Michigan.

Selected by Chicago in 6th round (146th player selected) of 1982 NFL draft.
On inactive list, September 12 and September 19, 1982.
On injured reserve with knee injury, October 4 through remainder of 1985 season.
Chicago NFL, 1982 through 1987.
Games: 1982 (5), 1983 (16), 1984 (16), 1985 (3), 1986 (14), 1987 (12). Total—66.
Played in NFC Championship Game following 1984 season.

MARK GERALD BEHNING
Name pronounced BEN-ing.
Offensive Tackle—Pittsburgh Steelers
Born September 26, 1961, at Alpena, Mich.
Height, 6.06. Weight, 277.
High School—Denton, Tex.
Attended University of Nebraska.

Selected by Pittsburgh in 2nd round (47th player selected) of 1985 NFL draft.
Signed by Pittsburgh Steelers, July 19, 1985.
On injured reserve with broken arm, August 20 through entire 1985 season.
On injured reserve with torn Achilles tendon, August 31 through entire 1987 season.
Pittsburgh NFL, 1986.
Games: 1986 (16).

ANTHONY DEWITT BELL
Linebacker—St. Louis Cardinals
Born July 2, 1964, at Miami, Fla.
Height, 6.03. Weight, 231.
High School—Fort Lauderdale, Fla., Boyd H. Anderson.
Attended Michigan State University.

Selected by St. Louis in 1st round (5th player selected) of 1986 NFL draft.
Signed by St. Louis Cardinals, August 11, 1986.
Franchise transferred to Phoenix, March 15, 1988.
St. Louis NFL, 1986 and 1987.
Games: 1986 (16), 1987 (12). Total—28.
Pro statistics: Intercepted one pass for 13 yards and fumbled once, 1987.

GREG LEON BELL
Running Back—Los Angeles Rams
Born August 1, 1962, at Columbus, O.
Height, 5.10. Weight, 210.
High School—Columbus, O., South.
Received bachelor of arts degree in economics from University of Notre Dame in 1984.

Selected by Chicago in 1984 USFL territorial draft.
Selected by Buffalo in 1st round (26th player selected) of 1984 NFL draft.
Signed by Buffalo Bills, July 23, 1984.
On injured reserve with groin injury, October 18 through December 12, 1986; activated, December 13, 1986.
On injured reserve with groin injury, December 20 through remainder of 1986 season.
Traded with 1st round pick in 1988 draft and 1st and 2nd round picks in 1989 draft by Buffalo Bills to Los Angeles Rams in exchange for Indianapolis Colts trading rights to linebacker Cornelius Bennett, October 31, 1987; Rams also acquired 1st and 2nd round picks in 1988 draft, 2nd round pick in 1989 draft and running back Owen Gill from Colts for running back Eric Dickerson.
On injured reserve with shoulder injury, December 4 through remainder of 1987 season.

		—RUSHING—				PASS RECEIVING				—TOTAL—		
Year Club	G.	Att.	Yds.	Avg.	TD.	P.C.	Yds.	Avg.	TD.	TD.	Pts.	F.
1984—Buffalo NFL	16	262	1100	4.2	7	34	277	8.1	1	8	48	5
1985—Buffalo NFL	16	223	883	4.0	8	58	576	9.9	1	9	54	8
1986—Buffalo NFL	6	90	377	4.2	4	12	142	11.8	2	6	36	2
1987—Buffalo (2)-L.A. Rams (2) NFL	4	22	86	3.9	0	9	96	10.7	1	1	6	1
Pro Totals—4 Years	42	597	2446	4.1	19	113	1091	9.7	5	24	144	16

Additional pro statistics: Returned one kickoff for 15 yards and recovered three fumbles, 1984; attempted one pass with no completions, 1985; recovered two fumbles, 1985 and 1986.
Played in Pro Bowl (NFL All-Star Game) following 1984 season.

KENNETH SHAWN BELL
(Ken)
Running Back—Denver Broncos
Born November 16, 1964, at Greenwich, Conn.
Height, 5.10. Weight, 190.
High School—Greenwich, Conn.
Received bachelor of arts degree from Boston College in 1986.

Signed as free agent by Denver Broncos, May 1, 1986.
Selected by Baltimore in 8th round (57th player selected) of 1986 USFL draft.
Released by Denver Broncos, September 7, 1987; re-signed by Broncos, September 8, 1987.

		—RUSHING—				PASS RECEIVING				—TOTAL—		
Year Club	G.	Att.	Yds.	Avg.	TD.	P.C.	Yds.	Avg.	TD.	TD.	Pts.	F.
1986—Denver NFL	16	9	17	1.9	0	2	10	5.0	0	0	0	1
1987—Denver NFL	12	13	43	3.3	0	1	8	8.0	0	0	0	2
Pro Totals—2 Years	28	22	60	2.7	0	3	18	6.0	0	0	0	3

		KICKOFF RETURNS			
Year Club	G.	No.	Yds.	Avg.	TD.
1986—Denver NFL	16	23	531	23.1	0
1987—Denver NFL	12	15	323	21.5	0
Pro Totals—2 Years	28	38	854	22.5	0

Pro statistics: Recovered one fumble, 1987.
Played in AFC Championship Game following 1986 and 1987 seasons.
Played in NFL Championship Game following 1986 and 1987 seasons.

LEONARD CHARLES BELL
Safety—Cincinnati Bengals
Born March 14, 1964, at Rockford, Ill.
Height, 5.11. Weight, 201.
High School—Rockford, Ill., Thomas Jefferson.
Attended Indiana University.

Selected by Cincinnati in 3rd round (76th player selected) of 1987 NFL draft.
Signed by Cincinnati Bengals, July 26, 1987.
On injured reserve with strained Achilles heal injury, September 1 through December 25, 1987; activated, December 26, 1987.
Cincinnati NFL, 1987.
Games: 1987 (1).

—DID YOU KNOW—
That last year was the first time since 1966 that the Buffalo Bills defeated the Miami Dolphins twice in the same season?

MIKE J. BELL
Defensive End—Kansas City Chiefs
Born August 30, 1957, at Wichita, Kan.
Height, 6.04. Weight, 260.
High School—Wichita, Kan., Bishop Carroll.
Attended Colorado State University.
Twin brother of Mark E. Bell, tight end with Seattle Seahawks and Baltimore-Indianapolis
Colts, 1979, 1980 and 1982 through 1984.

Named as defensive lineman on THE SPORTING NEWS College All-America Team, 1978.
Selected by Kansas City in 1st round (2nd player selected) of 1979 NFL draft.
On injured reserve with knee injury, October 9 through November 16, 1979; activated, November 17, 1979.
On injured reserve with torn bicep, September 20 through remainder of 1980 season.
On injured reserve with groin injury, December 14 through remainder of 1982 season.
On injured reserve with knee injury, December 13 through remainder of 1984 season.
Granted roster exemption/leave of absence with drug problem, November 20 through remainder of 1985 season.
Placed on reserve/did not report, August 11 through entire 1986 season (included prison term on drug charges, August 11 through December 10, 1986); reinstated, March 25, 1987.
Kansas City NFL, 1979 through 1985 and 1987.
Games: 1979 (11), 1980 (2), 1981 (16), 1982 (6), 1983 (16), 1984 (15), 1985 (11), 1987 (12). Total—89.
Pro statistics: Recovered one fumble, 1979, 1981, 1983 and 1985; recovered two fumbles, 1984 and 1987; fumbled once, 1984.

TODD ANTHONY BELL
Safety
Born November 28, 1958, at Middletown, O.
Height, 6.01. Weight, 212.
High School—Middletown, O.
Attended Ohio State University.

Named to THE SPORTING NEWS NFL All-Star Team, 1984.
Selected by Chicago in 4th round (95th player selected) of 1981 NFL draft.
Granted free agency, February 1, 1985.
On reserve/unsigned free agency list, August 20 through remainder of 1985 season.
Re-signed by Chicago Bears, August 16, 1986.
Released by Chicago Bears, May 10, 1988.

| | | —INTERCEPTIONS— | | | |
Year Club	G.	No.	Yds.	Avg.	TD.
1981—Chicago NFL	16	1	92	92.0	1
1982—Chicago NFL	9		None		
1983—Chicago NFL	15		None		
1984—Chicago NFL	16	4	46	11.5	1
1986—Chicago NFL	15	1	—1	—1.0	0
1987—Chicago NFL	12		None		
Pro Totals—6 Years	83	6	137	22.8	2

Additional pro statistics: Recovered one fumble, 1981 and 1987; returned one kickoff for 14 yards, 1982; returned two kickoffs for 18 yards and recovered one fumble for 10 yards, 1983; returned two kickoffs for 33 yards and recovered two fumbles for four yards, 1984; returned one kickoff for 18 yards and fumbled once, 1987.
Played in NFC Championship Game following 1984 season.
Played in Pro Bowl (NFL All-Star Game) following 1984 season.

RODNEY CARWELL BELLINGER
Cornerback—Tampa Bay Buccaneers
Born June 4, 1962, at Miami, Fla.
Height, 5.08. Weight, 189.
High School—Coral Gables, Fla.
Attended University of Miami (Fla.).

Selected by Houston in 2nd round (40th player selected) of 1984 USFL draft.
Selected by Buffalo in 3rd round (77th player selected) of 1984 NFL draft.
Signed by Buffalo Bills, July 12, 1984.
On injured reserve with fractured cervical disc, September 13 through October 25, 1984; activated, October 26, 1984.
Released by Buffalo Bills, September 1, 1987; signed as free agent by Cleveland Browns, March 4, 1988.
Released by Cleveland Browns, April 11, 1988; signed as free agent by Tampa Bay Buccaneers, May 17, 1988.

| | | —INTERCEPTIONS— | | | |
Year Club	G.	No.	Yds.	Avg.	TD.
1984—Buffalo NFL	10	1	0	0.0	0
1985—Buffalo NFL	16	2	64	32.0	0
1986—Buffalo NFL	16	1	14	14.0	0
Pro Totals—3 Years	42	4	78	19.5	0

Additional pro statistics: Recovered one fumble, 1985; recovered four fumbles for 15 yards and a touchdown and returned two kickoffs for 32 yards, 1986.

MARK JOSEPH BELLINI
Wide Receiver—Indianapolis Colts
Born January 19, 1964, at San Leandro, Calif.
Height, 5.11. Weight, 185.
High School—San Leandro, Calif.
Attended Brigham Young University.

Selected by Indianapolis in 7th round (170th player selected) of 1987 NFL draft.
Signed by Indianapolis Colts, July 26, 1987.
Crossed picket line during players' strike, October 14, 1987.

	——PASS RECEIVING——			
Year Club	G.	P.C.	Yds.	Avg. TD.
1987—Indianapolis NFL.........	10	5	69	13.8 0

DAN BENISH
Defensive Tackle—Washington Redskins
Born November 21, 1961, at Youngstown, O.
Height, 6.05. Weight, 280.
High School—Hubbard, O.
Attended Clemson University.

Selected by Washington in 1983 USFL territorial draft.
Signed as free agent by Atlanta Falcons, May 3, 1983.
Released by Atlanta Falcons, October 9, 1986; signed as free agent by Miami Dolphins, March 9, 1987.
Released by Miami Dolphins after failing physical, May 4, 1987; signed as free agent by Tampa Bay Buccaneers, July 18, 1987.
Released by Tampa Bay Buccaneers, September 7, 1987; signed as free agent replacement player by Washington Redskins, September 23, 1987.
On injured reserve with elbow injury, October 27 through remainder of 1987 season.
Atlanta NFL, 1983 through 1986; Washington NFL, 1987.
Games: 1983 (16), 1984 (15), 1985 (16), 1986 (5), 1987 (3). Total—55.
Pro statistics: Recovered one fumble, 1985 and 1987.

BARRY MARTIN BENNETT
Defensive End-Defensive Tackle—Los Angeles Raiders
Born December 10, 1955, at St. Paul, Minn.
Height, 6.04. Weight, 257.
High School—St. Paul, Minn., North.
Received bachelor of science degree in physical education from Concordia College in 1977.

Selected by New Orleans in 3rd round (60th player selected) of 1978 NFL draft.
On injured reserve with neck injury, October 2 through remainder of 1981 season.
Released by New Orleans Saints, June 24, 1982; signed as free agent by Minnesota Vikings, July 20, 1982.
Released by Minnesota Vikings, September 6, 1982; signed as free agent by New York Jets, September 8, 1982.
On inactive list, September 19, 1982.
Crossed picket line during players' strike, October 14, 1987.
Waived by New York Jets, February 26, 1988; recalled by Jets, March 8, 1988.
Traded by New York Jets to Los Angeles Raiders for 1989 draft pick, March 9, 1988.
New Orleans NFL, 1978 through 1981; New York Jets NFL, 1982 through 1987.
Games: 1978 (16), 1979 (16), 1980 (15), 1981 (3), 1982 (7), 1983 (13), 1984 (15), 1985 (16), 1986 (16), 1987 (13). Total—130.
Pro statistics: Recovered four fumbles for six yards, 1984.
Member of New York Jets for AFC Championship Game following 1982 season; did not play.

CHARLES A. BENNETT
Defensive Tackle—Miami Dolphins
Born February 9, 1963, at Alligator, Miss.
Height, 6.05. Weight, 250.
High School—Clarksdale, Miss., Coahoma County.
Attended Mississippi Delta Junior College and University of Southwestern Louisiana.

Selected by Portland in 5th round (65th player selected) of 1985 USFL draft.
Selected by Chicago in 7th round (190th player selected) of 1985 NFL draft.
Signed by Chicago Bears, July 19, 1985.
Released by Chicago Bears, August 27, 1985; signed as free agent by Saskatchewan Roughriders, November 2, 1985.
Released by Saskatchewan Roughriders, June 12, 1986; signed as free agent by Dallas Cowboys, June 27, 1986.
Released by Dallas Cowboys, August 19, 1986; signed as free agent by Miami Dolphins for 1987, November 30, 1986.
Released by Miami Dolphins, August 31, 1987; re-signed as replacement player by Dolphins, September 24, 1987.
Released by Miami Dolphins, November 3, 1987; re-signed by Dolphins for 1988, December 12, 1987.
Saskatchewan CFL, 1985; Miami NFL, 1987.
Games: 1985 (1), 1987 (3). Total—4.

CORNELIUS O'LANDA BENNETT
Linebacker—Buffalo Bills
Born August 25, 1965, at Birmingham, Ala.
Height, 6.02. Weight, 235.
High School—Birmingham, Ala., Ensley.
Attended University of Alabama.

Named as linebacker on THE SPORTING NEWS College All-America Team, 1986.
Selected by Indianapolis in 1st round (2nd player selected) of 1987 NFL draft.
Placed on reserve/unsigned list, August 31 through October 30, 1987.
Rights traded by Indianapolis Colts to Buffalo Bills in exchange for Bills trading 1st round pick in 1988 draft, 1st and 2nd round picks in 1989 draft and running back Greg Bell to Los Angeles Rams, October 31, 1987; Rams also traded running back Eric Dickerson to Colts for 1st and 2nd round picks in 1988 draft, 2nd round pick in 1989 draft and running back Owen Gill.

Signed by Buffalo Bills, October 31, 1987.
Granted roster exemption, October 31 through November 6, 1987; activated, November 7, 1987.
Buffalo NFL, 1987.
Games: 1987 (8).

ROY BENNETT
Defensive Back—San Diego Chargers
Born July 5, 1961, at Birmingham, Ala.
Height, 6.02. Weight, 200.
High School—Birmingham, Ala., West End.
Attended Jackson State University.

Selected by Jacksonville in 15th round (315th player selected) of 1984 USFL draft.
Signed by Jacksonville Bulls, January 6, 1984.
Released by Jacksonville Bulls, January 30, 1984; signed as free agent by Dallas Cowboys, May 15, 1984.
Released by Dallas Cowboys, July 25, 1984; signed as free agent by Winnipeg Blue Bombers, March, 1985.
Granted free agency, March 1, 1988; signed by San Diego Chargers, April 13, 1988.

Year Club	G.	No.	Yds.	Avg.	TD.
1985—Winnipeg CFL	16	5	105	21.0	0
1986—Winnipeg CFL	17	8	204	25.5	2
1987—Winnipeg CFL	18	*13	146	11.2	0
CFL Totals—3 Years	51	26	455	17.5	2

Additional CFL statistics: Returned one punt for 10 yards, 1985; recovered one fumble, 1985 and 1987; returned two punts for minus four yards and fumbled once, 1986.

WOODROW BENNETT JR.
(Woody)
Fullback—Miami Dolphins
Born March 24, 1955, at York, Pa.
Height, 6.02. Weight, 244.
High School—York, Pa., William Penn.
Attended Arizona Western Junior College and University of Miami.

Signed as free agent by Montreal Alouettes, April, 1979.
Released by Montreal Alouettes, June 22, 1979; signed as free agent by New York Jets, July 9, 1979.
Released by New York Jets, November 17, 1980; claimed on waivers by Miami Dolphins, November 18, 1980.
On injured reserve with knee injury, September 22 through remainder of 1981 season.
On physically unable to perform/active list with knee injury, July 22 through August 23, 1982; activated, August 24, 1982.
On injured reserve with knee injury, September 7 through December 30, 1982; activated, December 31, 1982.

Year Club	G.	Att.	Yds.	Avg.	TD.	P.C.	Yds.	Avg.	TD.	TD.	Pts.	F.
1979—New York Jets NFL	15	2	4	2.0	1	1	9	9.0	0	1	6	1
1980—New York Jets (8)-Miami (4) NFL	12	46	200	4.3	0	3	26	8.7	1	1	6	2
1981—Miami NFL	3	28	104	3.7	0	4	22	5.5	0	0	0	1
1982—Miami NFL	1	9	15	1.7	0			None		0	0	0
1983—Miami NFL	16	49	197	4.0	2	6	35	5.8	0	2	12	1
1984—Miami NFL	16	144	606	4.2	7	6	44	7.3	1	8	48	4
1985—Miami NFL	16	54	256	4.7	0	10	101	10.1	1	1	6	0
1986—Miami NFL	16	36	162	4.5	0	4	33	8.3	0	0	0	1
1987—Miami NFL	12	25	102	4.1	0	4	18	4.5	0	0	0	0
Pro Totals—9 Years	107	393	1646	4.2	10	38	288	7.6	3	13	78	10

Additional pro statistics: Returned one kickoff for seven yards, 1979; recovered two fumbles, 1980 and 1984; returned six kickoffs for 88 yards, 1980; recovered one fumble, 1981 and 1983; returned one kickoff for six yards, 1983.
Played in AFC Championship Game following 1982, 1984 and 1985 seasons.
Played in NFL Championship Game following 1982 and 1984 seasons.

CHARLES HENRY BENSON
Defensive End—Detroit Lions
Born November 21, 1960, at Houston, Tex.
Height, 6.03. Weight, 267.
High School—Houston, Tex., Aldine.
Attended Baylor University.

Selected by New Jersey in 10th round (118th player selected) of 1983 USFL draft.
Selected by Miami in 3rd round (76th player selected) of 1983 NFL draft.
Signed by Miami Dolphins, July 9, 1983.
On injured reserve with groin injury, August 30 through October 27, 1983; activated, October 28, 1983.
Released by Miami Dolphins, August 27, 1985; signed as free agent by Indianapolis Colts, December 19, 1985.
Released by Indianapolis Colts, August 26, 1986; signed as free agent by Detroit Lions, July 30, 1987.
Released by Detroit Lions, September 1, 1987; re-signed as replacement player by Lions, September 24, 1987.
Released by Detroit Lions, October 22, 1987; re-signed by Lions, February 12, 1988.
Miami NFL, 1983 and 1984; Indianapolis NFL, 1985; Detroit NFL, 1987.
Games: 1983 (8), 1984 (16), 1985 (1), 1987 (3). Total—28.
Pro statistics: Recovered one fumble, 1987.
Played in AFC Championship Game following 1984 season.
Played in NFL Championship Game following 1984 season.

CLIFFORD ANTHONY BENSON
(Cliff)
Tight End—New Orleans Saints
Born August 28, 1961, at Chicago, Ill.
Height, 6.0¼. Weight, 238.
High School—Palos Heights, Ill., Alan B. Shepard.
Received bachelor of arts degree in social work from Purdue University in 1984.

Selected by Oakland in 1st round (11th player selected) of 1984 USFL draft.
Selected by Atlanta Falcons in 5th round (132nd player selected) of 1984 NFL draft.
Signed by Atlanta Falcons, July 12, 1984.
Released by Atlanta Falcons, August 26, 1986; signed as free agent by San Francisco 49ers, March 10, 1987.
Released by San Francisco 49ers, August 24, 1987; awarded on waivers to Washington Redskins, August 25, 1987.
Released by Washington Redskins, September 7, 1987; re-signed by Redskins, September 8, 1987.
Released by Washington Redskins, November 3, 1987; awarded on waivers to New Orleans Saints, November 4, 1987.

		——PASS RECEIVING——			
Year Club	G.	P.C.	Yds.	Avg.	TD.
1984—Atlanta NFL	16	26	244	9.4	0
1985—Atlanta NFL	16	10	37	3.7	0
1987—Wash.(2)-N.O.(8) NFL .	10	2	11	5.5	0
Pro Totals—3 Years	42	38	292	7.7	0

Additional pro statistics: Rushed three times for eight yards, 1984.

THOMAS CARL BENSON
Linebacker—San Diego Chargers
Born September 6, 1961, at Ardmore, Okla.
Height, 6.02. Weight, 235.
High School—Ardmore, Okla.
Attended University of Oklahoma.
Cousin of Rich Turner, defensive tackle with Green Bay Packers, 1981 through 1983.

Selected by Oklahoma in 1984 USFL territorial draft.
Selected by Atlanta in 2nd round (36th player selected) of 1984 NFL draft.
Signed by Atlanta Falcons, July 22, 1984.
Traded by Atlanta Falcons to San Diego Chargers for 6th round pick in 1987 draft, July 25, 1986.
Granted free agency, February 1, 1987; re-signed by San Diego Chargers, September 8, 1987.
Granted roster exemption, September 8 through September 18, 1987; activated, September 19, 1987.
Atlanta NFL, 1984 and 1985; San Diego NFL, 1986 and 1987.
Games: 1984 (16), 1985 (16), 1986 (16), 1987 (11). Total—59.
Pro statistics: Recovered two fumbles, 1985 and 1986; recovered one fumble, 1987.

TROY B. BENSON
Linebacker—New York Jets
Born July 30, 1963, at Altoona, Pa.
Height, 6.02. Weight, 235.
High School—Altoona, Pa.
Attended University of Pittsburgh.
Brother of Brad Benson, offensive tackle with New York Giants, 1977 through 1987.

Selected by Baltimore in 1985 USFL territorial draft.
Selected by New York Jets in 5th round (120th player selected) of 1985 NFL draft.
Signed by New York Jets, July 22, 1985.
On injured reserve with ankle injury, August 22 through entire 1985 season.
New York Jets NFL, 1986 and 1987.
Games: 1986 (15), 1987 (11). Total—26.

ALBERT TIMOTHY BENTLEY
Running Back—Indianapolis Colts
Born August 15, 1960, at Naples, Fla.
Height, 5.11. Weight, 214.
High School—Immokalee, Fla.
Attended University of Miami (Fla.).

Selected by Chicago in 1st round (7th player selected) of 1984 USFL draft.
USFL rights traded by Chicago Blitz to Michigan Panthers for safety John Arnaud, April 17, 1984.
Signed by Michigan Panthers, April 17, 1984.
Granted roster exemption, April 17 through May 4, 1984; activated, May 5, 1984.
Selected by Indianapolis in 2nd round (36th player selected) of 1984 NFL supplemental draft.
Not protected in merger of Michigan Panthers and Oakland Invaders; selected by Oakland Invaders in USFL dispersal draft, December 6, 1984.
Released by Oakland Invaders, August 1, 1985; signed by Indianapolis Colts, September 3, 1985.
Granted roster exemption, September 3 through September 11, 1985; activated, September 12, 1985.
On injured reserve with ankle injury, October 20 through November 20, 1986; activated, November 21, 1986.

		——RUSHING——				PASS RECEIVING			—TOTAL—		
Year Club	G.	Att.	Yds.	Avg.	TD.	P.C.	Yds.	Avg.	TD.	Pts.	F.
1984—Michigan USFL	8	18	60	3.3	0	2	7	3.5	0	0	0	1
1985—Oakland USFL	18	191	1020	5.3	4	42	441	10.5	3	7	42	6
1985—Indianapolis NFL	15	54	288	5.3	2	11	85	7.7	0	2	12	1

Year Club	G.	Att.	RUSHING Yds.	Avg.	TD.	PASS RECEIVING P.C. Yds.		Avg.	TD.	—TOTAL— TD. Pts.		F.
1986—Indianapolis NFL	12	73	351	4.8	3	25	230	9.2	0	3	18	2
1987—Indianapolis NFL	12	142	631	4.4	7	34	447	13.1	2	9	54	3
USFL Totals—2 Years	26	209	1080	5.2	4	44	448	10.2	3	7	42	7
NFL Totals—3 Years	39	269	1270	4.7	12	70	762	10.9	2	14	84	6
Pro Totals—5 Years	65	478	2350	4.9	16	114	1210	10.6	5	21	126	13

Year Club	G.	No.	KICKOFF RETURNS Yds.	Avg.	TD.
1984—Michigan USFL	8	19	425	22.4	0
1985—Oakland USFL	18	7	177	25.3	0
1985—Indianapolis NFL	15	27	674	25.0	0
1986—Indianapolis NFL	12	32	687	21.5	0
1987—Indianapolis NFL	12	22	500	22.7	0
USFL Totals—2 Years	26	26	602	23.2	0
NFL Totals—3 Years	39	81	1861	23.0	0
Pro Totals—5 Years	65	107	2463	23.0	0

Additional USFL statistics: Recovered two fumbles, 1984 and 1985; attempted one pass with no completions, 1985.
Additional NFL statistics: Attempted one pass with one completion for six yards and recovered one fumble, 1985; recovered one fumble for nine yards, 1986; recovered three fumbles, 1987.
Played in USFL Championship Game following 1985 season.

RAY RUSSELL BENTLEY
Linebacker—Buffalo Bills
Born November 25, 1960, at Grand Rapids, Mich.
Height, 6.02. Weight, 245.
High School—Hudsonville, Mich.
Attended Central Michigan University.

Named as inside linebacker on THE SPORTING NEWS USFL All-Star Team, 1983.
Selected by Michigan in 1983 USFL territorial draft.
Signed by Michigan Panthers, January 24, 1983.
On developmental squad, May 4 through June 4, 1983; activated, June 5, 1983.
Protected in merger of Michigan Panthers and Oakland Invaders, December 6, 1984.
Sold by Oakland Invaders to Arizona Outlaws, August 14, 1985.
Traded by Arizona Outlaws to Memphis Showboats for rights to linebacker Steve Hathaway, September 17, 1985.
Granted free agency when USFL suspended operations, August 7, 1986; signed as free agent by Tampa Bay Buccaneers, August 12, 1986.
Granted roster exemption, August 12 through August 21, 1986; activated, August 22, 1986.
Released by Tampa Bay Buccaneers, August 30, 1986; signed as free agent by Buffalo Bills, September 17, 1986.
Released by Buffalo Bills, October 18, 1986; re-signed by Bills, October 21, 1986.
On developmental squad for 5 games with Michigan Panthers in 1983.
Michigan USFL, 1983 and 1984; Oakland USFL, 1985; Buffalo NFL, 1986 and 1987.
Games: 1983 (14), 1984 (18), 1985 (18), 1986 (13), 1987 (9). Total USFL—50. Total NFL—22. Total Pro—72.
Pro statistics: Intercepted two passes for 11 yards and credited with one sack for nine yards, 1983; recovered one fumble, 1983 through 1985; intercepted two passes for 10 yards and credited with 1½ sacks for 12½ yards, 1984; credited with two sacks for 20 yards and intercepted two passes for nine yards, 1985.
Played in USFL Championship Game following 1983 and 1985 seasons.

GREGORY KARL BERNARD
(Known by middle name.)
Running Back—Detroit Lions
Born October 12, 1964, at New Orleans, La.
Height, 5.11. Weight, 205.
High School—Baton Rouge, La., Catholic.
Attended Louisiana State University and University of Southwestern Louisiana.

Signed as free agent by Detroit Lions, May 27, 1987.

Year Club	G.	Att.	RUSHING Yds.	Avg.	TD.	PASS RECEIVING P.C. Yds.		Avg.	TD.	—TOTAL— TD. Pts.		F.
1987—Detroit NFL	8	45	187	4.2	2	13	91	7.0	0	2	12	3

Additional pro statistics: Returned four kickoffs for 54 yards and recovered one fumble, 1987.

ROD EARL BERNSTINE
Tight End—San Diego Chargers
Born February 8, 1965, at Fairfield, Calif.
Height, 6.03. Weight, 235.
High School—Bryan, Tex.
Attended Texas A&M University.

Selected by San Diego in 1st round (24th player selected) of 1987 NFL draft.
Signed by San Diego Chargers, August 11, 1987.
On injured reserve with hamstring injury, September 8 through October 23, 1987; activated, October 24, 1987.

Year Club	G.	P.C.	PASS RECEIVING Yds.	Avg.	TD.
1987—San Diego NFL	10	10	76	7.6	1

Additional pro statistics: Rushed once for nine yards, returned one kickoff for 13 yards, and recovered one fumble, 1987.

EDWARD BERRY JR.
(Ed)
Defensive Back—San Francisco 49ers
Born September 28, 1963, at San Francisco, Calif.
Height, 5.10. Weight, 183.
High School—Belmont, Calif., Carlmont.
Attended Utah State University.
Selected by Green Bay in 7th round (183rd player selected) of 1986 NFL draft.
Selected by Jacksonville in 12th round (86th player selected) of 1986 USFL draft.
Signed by Green Bay Packers, July 19, 1986.
Released by Green Bay Packers, September 7, 1987; signed as free agent replacement player by San Diego Chargers, September 23, 1987.
Released by San Diego Chargers, October 22, 1987; signed as free agent by San Francisco 49ers, January 4, 1988.
Green Bay NFL, 1986; San Diego NFL, 1987.
Games: 1986 (16), 1987 (2). Total—18.
Pro statistics: Returned one kickoff for 16 yards and recovered one fumble, 1986.

RAYMOND LENN BERRY
(Ray)
Linebacker—Minnesota Vikings
Born October 28, 1963, at Lovington, N. M.
Height, 6.02. Weight, 230.
High School—Abilene, Tex., Cooper.
Received degree in business management and real estate from Baylor University in 1987.
Selected by Minnesota in 2nd round (44th player selected) of 1987 NFL draft.
Signed by Minnesota Vikings, August 10, 1987.
Minnesota NFL, 1987.
Games: 1987 (11).
Pro statistics: Recovered one fumble, 1987.
Played in NFC Championship Game following 1987 season.

BILL BERTHUSEN
Defensive Tackle—New York Giants
Born June 26, 1964, at Grinnell, Ia.
Height, 6.05. Weight, 285.
High School—Marshalltown, Ia.
Attended Iowa State University.
Selected by New York Giants in 12th round (321st player selected) of 1987 NFL draft.
Signed by New York Giants, July 27, 1987.
Released by New York Giants, August 31, 1987; signed as free agent replacement player by Cincinnati Bengals, September 25, 1987.
Released by Cincinnati Bengals, October 19, 1987; signed as free agent by New York Giants, December 1, 1987.
Cincinnati (3)-New York Giants (1) NFL, 1987.
Games: 1987 (4).
Pro statistics: Recovered one fumble for one yard, 1987.

DOUGLAS LLOYD BETTERS
(Doug)
Defensive End—Miami Dolphins
Born June 11, 1956, at Lincoln, Neb.
Height, 6.07. Weight, 265.
High School—Arlington Heights, Ill., Arlington.
Attended University of Montana and University of Nevada at Reno.
Named to THE SPORTING NEWS NFL All-Star Team, 1983.
Selected by Miami in 6th round (163rd player selected) of 1978 NFL draft.
Granted free agency, February 1, 1986; re-signed by Dolphins, September 2, 1986.
Granted roster exemption, September 2 through September 5, 1986; activated, September 6, 1986.
Miami NFL, 1978 through 1987.
Games: 1978 (16), 1979 (16), 1980 (16), 1981 (15), 1982 (9), 1983 (16), 1984 (16), 1985 (14), 1986 (16), 1987 (12). Total—146.
Pro statistics: Recovered one fumble, 1980 and 1984; recovered four fumbles, 1983.
Played in AFC Championship Game following 1982, 1984 and 1985 seasons.
Played in NFL Championship Game following 1982 and 1984 seasons.
Played in Pro Bowl (NFL All-Star Game) following 1983 season.

DEAN BIASUCCI
Placekicker—Indianapolis Colts
Born July 25, 1962, at Niagara Falls, N.Y.
Height, 6.00. Weight, 191.
High School—Miramar, Fla.
Attended Western Carolina University.
Signed as free agent by Atlanta Falcons, May 16, 1984.
Released by Atlanta Falcons, August 14, 1984; signed as free agent by Indianapolis Colts, September 8, 1984.
Released by Indianapolis Colts, August 27, 1985; re-signed by Colts, April 22, 1986.

| | | —PLACE KICKING— | | | | |
Year Club	G.	XP.	XPM.	FG.	FGA.	Pts.
1984—Indianapolis NFL....	15	13	1	3	5	22
1986—Indianapolis NFL....	16	26	1	13	25	65
1987—Indianapolis NFL....	12	24	0	24	27	96
Pro Totals—3 Years.......	43	63	2	40	57	183

Played in Pro Bowl (NFL All-Star Game) following 1987 season.

DUANE CLAIR BICKETT

Name pronounced BIK-ett.

Linebacker—Indianapolis Colts

Born December 1, 1962, at Los Angeles, Calif.
Height, 6.05. Weight, 241.
High School—Glendale, Calif.
Received degree in accounting from University of Southern California in 1986.

Named as linebacker on THE SPORTING NEWS College All-America Team, 1984.
Selected by Los Angeles in 1985 USFL territorial draft.
Selected by Indianapolis in 1st round (5th player selected) of 1985 NFL draft.
Signed by Indianapolis Colts, August 7, 1985.
Indianapolis NFL, 1985 through 1987.
Games: 1985 (16), 1986 (16), 1987 (12). Total—44.
Pro statistics: Intercepted one pass for no yards and recovered two fumbles, 1985; intercepted two passes for 10 yards and recovered one fumble, 1986; recovered two fumbles for 32 yards and fumbled once, 1987.
Played in Pro Bowl (NFL All-Star Game) following 1987 season.

LEWIS KENNETH BILLUPS

Cornerback—Cincinnati Bengals

Born October 10, 1963, at Tampa, Fla.
Height, 5.11. Weight, 190.
High School—Niceville, Fla.
Attended University of North Alabama.

Selected by Birmingham in 1986 USFL territorial draft.
Selected by Cincinnati in 2nd round (38th player selected) of 1986 NFL draft.
Signed by Cincinnati Bengals, August 13, 1986.
On injured reserve with knee injury, October 17 through November 9, 1986; activated, November 10, 1986.
Cincinnati NFL, 1986 and 1987.
Games: 1986 (12), 1987 (11). Total—23.
Pro statistics: Recovered one fumble for two yards, 1986; recovered one fumble, 1987.

GUY RICHARD BINGHAM

Center-Guard—New York Jets

Born February 25, 1958, at Koiaumi Gumma Ken, Japan.
Height, 6.03. Weight, 260.
High School—Aberdeen, Wash., Weatherwax.
Received degree in physical education from University of Montana.

Selected by New York Jets in 10th round of 1980 NFL draft.
On injured reserve with knee injury, September 7 through November 18, 1982; activated, November 19, 1982.
New York Jets NFL, 1980 through 1987.
Games: 1980 (16), 1981 (16), 1982 (7), 1983 (16), 1984 (16), 1985 (16), 1986 (16), 1987 (12). Total—115.
Pro statistics: Returned one kickoff for 19 yards, 1980; recovered one fumble, 1984 and 1986.
Played in AFC Championship Game following 1982 season.

CRAIG BIRDSONG

(Known by middle name.)

Safety—Houston Oilers

Born August 16, 1964, at Kaufman, Tex.
Height, 6.02. Weight, 217.
High School—Kaufman, Tex.
Attended North Texas State University.

Signed as free agent replacement player by Houston Oilers, September 23, 1987.
On injured reserve with ruptured hernia, October 24, 1987 through January 8, 1988; activated, January 9, 1988.
Houston NFL, 1987.
Games: 1987 (3).

KEITH BRYAN BISHOP

Center-Guard—Denver Broncos

Born March 10, 1957, at San Diego, Calif.
Height, 6.03. Weight, 265.
High School—Midland, Tex., Robert E. Lee.
Attended University of Nebraska and Baylor University.

Selected by Denver in 6th round (157th player selected) of 1980 NFL draft.
On injured reserve with ankle injury, August 18 through entire 1981 season.
Denver NFL, 1980 and 1982 through 1987.

Games: 1980 (16), 1982 (9), 1983 (16), 1984 (16), 1985 (14), 1986 (16), 1987 (12). Total—99.
Pro statistics: Recovered one fumble, 1982, 1983 and 1986.
Played in AFC Championship Game following 1986 and 1987 seasons.
Played in NFL Championship Game following 1986 and 1987 seasons.
Played in Pro Bowl (NFL All-Star Game) following 1986 and 1987 seasons.

MEL BLACK
Linebacker—Los Angeles Raiders
Born February 7, 1962, at New Haven, Conn.
Height, 6.02. Weight, 228.
High School—West Haven, Conn.
Attended Santa Ana College and Eastern Illinois University.
Signed as free agent by New England Patriots, May 10, 1986.
Released by New England Patriots, August 12, 1986; re-signed by Patriots, November 28, 1986.
On injured reserve with hamstring injury, January 2 through remainder of 1986 season playoffs.
Released by New England Patriots, August 25, 1987; re-signed as replacement player by Patriots, September 24, 1987.
Released by New England Patriots, October 23, 1987; signed as free agent by Los Angeles Raiders, April 27, 1988.
New England NFL, 1986 and 1987.
Games: 1986 (3), 1987 (3). Total—6.

MICHAEL DAVID BLACK
(Mike)
Offensive Tackle—New York Giants
Born August 24, 1964, at Auburn, Calif.
Height, 6.04. Weight, 280.
High School—Loomis, Calif., Del Oro.
Attended California State University at Sacramento.
Selected by Seattle in 9th round (237th player selected) of 1986 NFL draft.
Signed by Seattle Seahawks, July 16, 1986.
Released by Seattle Seahawks, August 19, 1986; signed as free agent by Philadelphia Eagles, November 6, 1986.
Released by Philadelphia Eagles, August 31, 1987; re-signed as replacement player by Eagles, September 23, 1987.
Left Philadelphia Eagles camp voluntarily and released, September 25, 1987; signed as free agent replacement player by New York Giants, October 6, 1987.
On injured reserve with foot injury, November 7 through December 16, 1987.
Released by New York Giants, December 17, 1987; re-signed by Giants for 1988, December 23, 1987.
Philadelphia NFL, 1986; New York Giants NFL, 1987.
Games: 1986 (1), 1987 (2). Total—3.
Pro statistics: Recovered one fumble and fumbled once, 1986.

TODD ALAN BLACKLEDGE
Quarterback—Pittsburgh Steelers
Born February 25, 1961, at Canton, O.
Height, 6.03. Weight, 219.
High School—North Canton, O., Hoover.
Received degree in speech communications from Penn State University in 1983.
Son of Ron Blackledge, offensive line coach with Pittsburgh Steelers.
Selected by Kansas City in 1st round (7th player selected) of 1983 NFL draft.
Selected by Philadelphia in 1984 USFL territorial draft.
Granted free agency, February 1, 1988; re-signed by Chiefs and traded to Pittsburgh Steelers for 4th round pick in 1988 draft, March 29, 1988.

Year Club	G.	Att.	Cmp.	Pct.	Gain	T.P.	P.I.	Avg.	Att.	Yds.	Avg.	TD.	TD.	Pts.	F.
				PASSING						RUSHING			TOTAL		
1983—Kansas City NFL............	4	34	20	58.8	259	3	0	7.62	1	0	0.0	0	0	0	1
1984—Kansas City NFL............	11	294	147	50.0	1707	6	11	5.81	18	102	5.7	1	1	6	8
1985—Kansas City NFL............	12	172	86	50.0	1190	6	14	6.92	17	97	5.7	0	0	0	3
1986—Kansas City NFL............	10	211	96	45.5	1200	10	6	5.69	23	60	2.6	0	0	0	5
1987—Kansas City NFL............	3	31	15	48.4	154	1	1	4.97	5	21	4.2	0	0	0	2
Pro Totals—5 Years..........	40	742	364	49.1	4510	26	32	6.08	64	280	4.4	1	1	6	19

Quarterback Rating Points: 1983 (112.3), 1984 (59.2), 1985 (50.3), 1986 (67.6), 1987 (60.4). Total—62.1.
Additional pro statistics: Recovered four fumbles and fumbled eight times for minus three yards, 1984; recovered one fumble, 1985; recovered two fumbles and fumbled five times for minus six yards, 1986; fumbled twice for minus six yards, 1987.

GLENN ALLEN BLACKWOOD
Safety—Miami Dolphins
Born February 23, 1957, at San Antonio, Tex.
Height, 6.00. Weight, 188.
High School—San Antonio, Tex., Churchill
Received bachelor of science degree in pre-dental studies from University of Texas in 1979.
Brother of Lyle Blackwood, safety with Cincinnati Bengals,
Seattle Seahawks, Baltimore Colts and Miami Dolphins, 1973 through 1986.
Selected by Miami in 8th round (215th player selected) of 1979 NFL draft.
On injured reserve with knee injury, November 19 through remainder of 1979 season.
Granted free agency, February 1, 1985; re-signed by Dolphins, September 12, 1985.
Granted roster exemption, September 12 through September 20, 1985; activated, September 21, 1985.

On injured reserve with thigh injury, September 2 through October 17, 1986; activated, October 18, 1986.
On injured reserve with knee injury, December 15 through remainder of 1987 season.

Year Club	G.	No.	Yds.	Avg.TD.	
			—INTERCEPTIONS—		
1979—Miami NFL	11		None		
1980—Miami NFL	16	3	0	0.0	0
1981—Miami NFL	16	4	124	31.0	0
1982—Miami NFL	9	2	42	21.0	*1
1983—Miami NFL	16	3	0	0.0	0
1984—Miami NFL	16	6	169	28.2	0
1985—Miami NFL	14	6	36	6.0	0
1986—Miami NFL	10	2	10	5.0	0
1987—Miami NFL	10	3	17	5.7	0
Pro Totals—9 Years	118	29	398	13.7	1

Additional pro statistics: Returned one punt for no yards, 1980 and 1986; recovered four fumbles, 1980 and 1983; returned two punts for eight yards and recovered one fumble for five yards, 1981; returned two punts for two yards, 1982; recovered one fumble, 1982, 1984 and 1985; fumbled once, 1982; returned one punt for 10 yards, 1983; returned three punts for 20 yards, 1985; recovered two fumbles and fumbled twice, 1986; returned one punt for one yard, 1987.
Played in AFC Championship Game following 1982, 1984 and 1985 seasons.
Played in NFL Championship Game following 1982 and 1984 seasons.

BRIAN TIMOTHY BLADOS
Guard—Cincinnati Bengals
Born January 11, 1962, at Arlington, Va.
Height, 6.05. Weight, 295.
High School—Arlington, Va., Washington Lee.
Attended University of North Carolina.
Selected by Pittsburgh in 1984 USFL territorial draft.
Selected by Cincinnati in 1st round (28th player selected) of 1984 NFL draft.
Signed by Cincinnati Bengals, June 28, 1984.
Cincinnati NFL, 1984 through 1987.
Games: 1984 (16), 1985 (16), 1986 (16), 1987 (11). Total—59.
Pro statistics: Caught one pass for four yards, 1985.

PAUL KEVIN BLAIR
Offensive Tackle—Chicago Bears
Born March 8, 1963, at Edmond, Okla.
Height, 6.04. Weight, 295.
High School—Edmond, Okla., Memorial.
Received degree in finance from Oklahoma State University in 1987.
Selected by New Jersey in 1986 USFL territorial draft.
Selected by Chicago in 4th round (110th player selected) of 1986 NFL draft.
Signed by Chicago Bears, July 17, 1986.
Chicago NFL, 1986 and 1987.
Games: 1986 (14), 1987 (10). Total—24.

CARL NATHANIEL BLAND
Wide Receiver—Detroit Lions
Born August 17, 1961, at Fluvanna County, Va.
Height, 5.11. Weight, 182.
High School—Richmond, Va., Thomas Jefferson.
Attended Virginia Union University.
Signed as free agent by Detroit Lions, May 3, 1984.
On injured reserve with hamstring injury, August 20 through November 7, 1984; activated after clearing procedural waivers, November 9, 1984.
Released by Detroit Lions, September 3, 1985; re-signed by Lions, October 17, 1985.
Released by Detroit Lions, October 31, 1985; re-signed by Lions, November 4, 1985.
On injured reserve with knee injury, September 7 through October 23, 1987; activated, October 24, 1987.

Year Club	G.	P.C.	Yds.	Avg.TD.	
			—PASS RECEIVING—		
1984—Detroit NFL	3		None		
1985—Detroit NFL	8	12	157	13.1	0
1986—Detroit NFL	16	44	511	11.6	2
1987—Detroit NFL	10	2	14	7.0	1
Pro Totals—4 Years	37	58	682	11.8	3

Additional pro statistics: Returned six kickoffs for 114 yards, recovered two fumbles for eight yards and fumbled once, 1986; returned two kickoffs for 44 yards, 1987.

BRIAN PATRICK BLANKENSHIP
Guard-Center—Pittsburgh Steelers
Born April 7, 1963, at Omaha, Neb.
Height, 6.01. Weight, 281.
High School—Omaha, Neb., Daniel J. Gross.
Attended University of Nebraska at Omaha and University of Nebraska at Lincoln.
Selected by Memphis in 1986 USFL territorial draft.

Signed as free agent by Pittsburgh Steelers, May 13, 1986.
Released by Pittsburgh Steelers, September 1, 1986; signed as free agent by Indianapolis Colts, May 11, 1987.
Released by Indianapolis Colts, August 7, 1987; signed as free agent replacement player by Pittsburgh Steelers, September 24, 1987.
Pittsburgh NFL, 1987.
Games: 1987 (13).

DENNIS BLIGEN
Running Back—New York Jets
Born March 3, 1962, at New York, N.Y.
Height, 5.11. Weight, 215.
High School—New York, N.Y., Murray Bergtraum.
Attended St. John's University.

Signed as free agent by New York Jets, May 16, 1984.
On injured reserve with fractured thumb, July 31 through October 24, 1984; activated after clearing procedural waivers, October 26, 1984.
Released by New York Jets, November 24, 1984; re-signed by Jets, December 6, 1984.
On injured reserved with rib injury, August 27 through October 23, 1985; activated after clearing procedural waivers, October 25, 1985.
On injured reserve with knee injury, October 20 through December 10, 1986; awarded on procedural waivers to Tampa Bay Buccaneers, December 12, 1986.
Released by Tampa Bay Buccaneers, August 5, 1987; signed as free agent by New York Jets, August 7, 1987.
Released by New York Jets, September 6, 1987; re-signed as replacement player by Jets, October 7, 1987.

			RUSHING			PASS RECEIVING				—TOTAL—		
Year Club	G.	Att.	Yds.	Avg.	TD.	P.C.	Yds.	Avg.	TD.	TD.	Pts.	F.
1984—New York Jets NFL	1		None				None			0	0	0
1985—New York Jets NFL	9	22	107	4.9	1	5	43	8.6	0	1	6	1
1986—N.Y. Jets (4)-Tampa Bay (1) NFL	5	20	65	3.3	1	2	6	3.0	0	1	6	2
1987—New York Jets NFL	6	31	128	4.1	1	11	81	7.4	0	1	6	1
Pro Totals—4 Years	21	73	300	4.1	3	18	130	7.2	0	3	18	4

Additional pro statistics: Recovered one fumble, 1987.

DWAINE P. BOARD
Defensive End—San Francisco 49ers
Born November 29, 1956, at Union Hall, Va.
Height, 6.05. Weight, 248.
High School—Rocky Mount, Va., Franklin County.
Received bachelor of science degree in industrial technology from
North Carolina A&T State University in 1979.

Selected by Pittsburgh in 5th round (137th player selected) of 1979 NFL draft.
Released by Pittsburgh Steelers, August 27, 1979; claimed on waivers by San Francisco 49ers, August 28, 1979.
On injured reserve with knee injury, September 23 through remainder of 1980 season.
On injured reserve with knee injury, September 16 through remainder of 1982 season.
Crossed picket line during players' strike, October 7, 1987.
San Francisco NFL, 1979 through 1987.
Games: 1979 (16), 1980 (3), 1981 (16), 1982 (1), 1983 (16), 1984 (16), 1985 (16), 1986 (16), 1987 (14). Total—114.
Pro statistics: Recovered five fumbles (including one in end zone for a touchdown), 1983; recovered one fumble, 1984, 1985 and 1987; recovered two fumbles for 16 yards, 1986.
Played in NFC Championship Game following 1981, 1983 and 1984 seasons.
Played in NFL Championship Game following 1981 and 1984 seasons.

TONY L. BODDIE
Running Back—Denver Broncos
Born November 11, 1960, at Portsmouth, Va.
Height, 5.11. Weight, 195.
High School—Bremerton, Wash.
Attended Montana State University.

Selected by Los Angeles in 12th round (144th player selected) of 1983 USFL draft.
On developmental squad, March 23 through March 28, 1985; activated, March 29, 1985.
On developmental squad, April 26 through May 23, 1985; activated, May 24, 1985.
Released by Los Angeles Eppress, July 9, 1985; signed as free agent by Los Angeles Raiders, July 19, 1985.
Released by Los Angeles Raiders, July 25, 1985; signed as free agent by Denver Broncos, March 24, 1986.
Released by Denver Broncos, August 26, 1986; re-signed by Broncos, September 9, 1986.
Released by Denver Broncos, September 17, 1986; re-signed by Broncos for 1987, November 28, 1986.
On injured reserve with knee injury, September 1 through October 30, 1987; activated, October 31, 1987.
Released by Denver Broncos, November 3, 1987; re-signed by Broncos, November 25, 1987.
On developmental squad for 5 games with Los Angeles Express in 1985.

			RUSHING			PASS RECEIVING				—TOTAL—		
Year Club	G.	Att.	Yds.	Avg.	TD.	P.C.	Yds.	Avg.	TD.	TD.	Pts.	F.
1983—Los Angeles USFL	18	109	403	3.7	3	46	434	9.4	2	5	30	7
1984—Los Angeles USFL	18	16	31	1.9	0	20	170	8.5	1	1	6	1
1985—Los Angeles USFL	13	49	208	4.2	1	17	124	7.3	1	2	12	3
1986—Denver NFL	1	1	2	2.0	0		None			0	0	0
1987—Denver NFL	5	3	7	2.3	1	9	85	9.4	0	1	6	0
USFL Totals—3 Years	49	174	642	3.7	4	83	728	8.8	4	8	48	11
NFL Totals—2 Years	6	4	9	2.3	1	9	85	9.4	0	1	6	0
Pro Totals—5 Years	55	178	651	3.7	5	92	813	8.8	4	9	54	11

		KICKOFF RETURNS			
Year Club	G.	No.	Yds.	Avg.	TD.
1983—Los Angeles USFL........	18	7	132	18.9	0
1984—Los Angeles USFL........	18	33	782	23.7	0
1985—Los Angeles USFL........	13	29	517	17.8	0
1986—Denver NFL	1		None		
1987—Denver NFL	5		None		
USFL Totals—3 Years........	49	69	1431	20.7	0
NFL Totals—2 Years..........	6	0	0	0.0	0
Pro Totals—5 Years............	55	69	1431	20.7	0

Additional pro statistics: Recovered two fumbles, 1983; attempted one pass with no completions, 1985; recovered one fumble, 1987.
Played in AFC Championship Game following 1987 season.
Played in NFL Championship Game following 1987 season.

RICKEY ALLEN BOLDEN
Offensive Tackle—Cleveland Browns
Born September 8, 1961, at Dallas, Tex.
Height, 6.06. Weight, 280.
High School—Dallas, Tex., Hillcrest.
Attended Southern Methodist University.

Selected by Oakland in 4th round (72nd player selected) of 1984 USFL draft.
Selected by Cleveland in 4th round (96th player selected) of 1984 NFL draft.
Signed by Cleveland Browns, May 17, 1984.
On injured reserve with dislocated shoulder, November 21 through remainder of 1984 season.
On injured reserve with broken arm, October 8 through December 12, 1986; activated, December 13, 1986.
Crossed picket line during players' strike, October 14, 1987.
On injured reserve with fractured ankle, November 3 through remainder of 1987 season.
Cleveland NFL, 1984 through 1987.
Games: 1984 (12), 1985 (16), 1986 (7), 1987 (5). Total—40.
Pro statistics: Caught one pass for 19 yards and fumbled once, 1984.
Played in AFC Championship Game following 1986 season.

STEVEN CHRISTOPHER BONO
(Steve)
Quarterback—Pittsburgh Steelers
Born May 11, 1962, at Norristown, Pa.
Height, 6.04. Weight, 215.
High School—Norristown, Pa.
Attended University of California at Los Angeles.

Selected by Memphis in 1985 USFL territorial draft.
Selected by Minnesota in 6th round (142nd player selected) of 1985 NFL draft.
Signed by Minnesota Vikings, July 10, 1985.
Released by Minnesota Vikings, October 4, 1986; re-signed by Vikings, November 19, 1986.
Released by Minnesota Vikings, December 9, 1986; signed as free agent by Pittsburgh Steelers, March 25, 1987.
Released by Pittsburgh Steelers, September 7, 1987; re-signed as replacement player by Steelers, September 24, 1987.

		—————PASSING—————							——RUSHING——				—TOTAL—		
Year Club	G.	Att.	Cmp.	Pct.	Gain	T.P.	P.I.	Avg.	Att.	Yds.	Avg.	TD.	TD.	Pts.	F.
1985—Minnesota NFL................	1	10	1	10.0	5	0	0	0.50		None			0	0	0
1986—Minnesota NFL................	1	1	1	100.0	3	0	0	3.00		None			0	0	0
1987—Pittsburgh NFL................	3	74	34	45.9	438	5	2	5.92	8	27	3.4	1	1	6	5
Pro Totals—3 Years..........	5	85	36	42.4	446*	5	2	5.25	8	27	3.4	1	1	6	5

Quarterback Rating Points: 1985 (39.6), 1986 (79.2), 1987 (76.3). Total—69.0.
Additional pro statistics: Caught one pass for two yards and recovered three fumbles, 1987.

JON L. BORCHARDT
Offensive Tackle—Seattle Seahawks
Born August 13, 1957, at Minneapolis, Minn.
Height, 6.05. Weight, 272.
High School—Brooklyn Park, Minn., Park Center.
Received bachelor of science degree in microbiology from Montana State University in 1979.

Selected by Buffalo in 3rd round (62nd player selected) of 1979 NFL draft.
Traded by Buffalo Bills to Seattle Seahawks for 7th round pick in 1986 draft, April 26, 1985.
Released by Seattle Seahawks, September 1, 1986; re-signed by Seahawks, September 3, 1986.
Buffalo NFL, 1979 through 1984; Seattle NFL, 1985 through 1987.
Games: 1979 (16), 1980 (16), 1981 (16), 1982 (9), 1983 (16), 1984 (16), 1985 (13), 1986 (16), 1987 (12). Total—130.
Pro statistics: Recovered one fumble, 1981.

KYLE CRAIG BORLAND
Linebacker—San Diego Chargers
Born July 5, 1961, at Denison, Ia.
Height, 6.03. Weight, 228.
High School—Fort Atkinson, Wis.
Attended University of Wisconsin.

— 38 —

Signed by Michigan Panthers, February 5, 1983.
On developmental squad, March 4 through April 3, 1983; activated, April 4, 1983.
Not protected in merger of Michigan Panthers and Oakland Invaders, selected by New Jersey Generals in USFL dispersal draft, December 6, 1984.
On developmental squad, May 18 through May 24, 1985; activated, May 25, 1985.
On developmental squad, June 1 through June 9, 1985; activated, June 10, 1985.
Released by New Jersey Generals, July 31, 1985; awarded on waivers to Orlando Renegades, August 1, 1985.
Released by Orlando Renegades, February 20, 1986; signed as free agent by Los Angeles Raiders, June 27, 1986.
Released by Los Angeles Raiders, August 12, 1986; signed as free agent by Los Angeles Rams, May 1, 1987.
Released by Los Angeles Rams, September 7, 1987; re-signed as replacement player by Rams, October 5, 1987.
On injured reserve with elbow injury, October 21 through remainder of 1987 season.
Granted free agency with option not exercised, February 1, 1988; signed by San Diego Chargers, April 18, 1988.
On developmental squad for 4 games with Michigan Panthers in 1983.
On developmental squad for 2 games with New Jersey Generals in 1985.
Michigan USFL, 1983 and 1984; New Jersey USFL, 1985; Los Angeles Rams NFL, 1987.
Games: 1983 (14), 1984 (18), 1985 (16), 1987 (2). Total USFL—48. Total Pro—50.
Pro statistics: Credited with two sacks for 22 yards and recovered three fumbles, 1983; intercepted one pass for no yards, 1983 and 1984; credited with 7½ sacks for 58½ yards and recovered two fumbles for 38 yards and a touchdown, 1984; recovered one fumble, 1985.
Played in USFL Championship Game following 1983 season.

MARK STEVEN BORTZ
Guard—Chicago Bears
Born February 12, 1961, at Pardeeville, Wis.
Height, 6.06. Weight, 275.
High School—Pardeeville, Wis.
Attended University of Iowa.

Selected by Los Angeles in 4th round (48th player selected) of 1983 USFL draft.
Selected by Chicago in 8th round (219th player selected) of 1983 NFL draft.
Signed by Chicago Bears, June 2, 1983.
Chicago NFL, 1983 through 1987.
Games: 1983 (16), 1984 (15), 1985 (16), 1986 (15), 1987 (12). Total—74.
Pro statistics: Caught one pass for eight yards, 1986.
Played in NFC Championship Game following 1984 and 1985 seasons.
Played in NFL Championship Game following 1985 season.

JOHN WILFRED BOSA
Defensive End—Miami Dolphins
Born January 10, 1964, at Keene, N. H.
Height, 6.04. Weight, 263.
High School—Keene, N. H.
Received bachelor of science degree in marketing from Boston College in 1987.

Selected by Miami in 1st round (16th player selected) of 1987 NFL draft.
Signed by Miami Dolphins, September 1, 1987.
Granted roster exemption, September 1 and September 2, 1987; activated, September 3, 1987.
Miami NFL, 1987.
Games: 1987 (12).
Pro statistics: Recovered two fumbles, 1987.

CASPER N. BOSO
(Name pronounced BO-sew.)
(Cap)
Tight End—Chicago Bears
Born September 10, 1962, at Kansas City, Mo.
Height, 6.03. Weight, 224.
High School—Indianapolis, Ind., Bishop Chatard.
Attended Joliet Junior College and received liberal arts and sciences degree
in sociology from University of Illinois in 1986.

Selected by Orlando in 1986 USFL territorial draft.
Selected by Pittsburgh in 8th round (207th player selected) of 1986 NFL draft.
Signed by Pittsburgh Steelers, July 18, 1986.
Released by Pittsburgh Steelers, September 1, 1986; signed as free agent by St. Louis Cardinals, December 10, 1986.
Released by St. Louis Cardinals, September 7, 1987; awarded on waivers to Chicago Bears, September 8, 1987.

| | | —PASS RECEIVING— | | | |
Year Club	G.	P.C.	Yds.	Avg.	TD.
1986—St. Louis NFL	2		None		
1987—Chicago NFL	12	17	188	11.1	2
Pro Totals—2 Years	14	17	188	11.1	2

—DID YOU KNOW—
That Miami's Dan Marino in 1986 became the first quarterback in NFL history to throw 30 or more touchdown passes in three different seasons? Marino did it in consecutive seasons, throwing a record 48 scoring passes in 1984, 30 in '85 and 44 in '86.

JEFF BOSTIC
Center—Washington Redskins
Born September 18, 1958, at Greensboro, N. C.
Height, 6.02. Weight, 260.
High School—Greensboro, N. C., Benjamin L. Smith.
Attended Clemson University.
Brother of Joe Bostic, guard with Phoenix Cardinals.

Signed as free agent by Philadelphia Eagles, May 20, 1980.
Released by Philadelphia Eagles, August 26, 1980; signed as free agent by Washington Redskins, September 1, 1984.
On injured reserve with knee injury, October 23 through remainder of 1984 season.
On injured reserve with knee injury, August 24 through October 18, 1985; activated, October 19, 1985.
Washington NFL, 1980 through 1987.
Games: 1980 (16), 1981 (16), 1982 (9), 1983 (16), 1984 (8), 1985 (10), 1986 (16), 1987 (12). Total—103.
Pro statistics: Recovered one fumble, 1981 and 1985; caught one pass for minus four yards, 1981; recovered three fumbles, 1983; recovered two fumbles, 1984; recovered one fumble for one yard, 1986.
Played in NFC Championship Game following 1982, 1983, 1986 and 1987 seasons.
Played in NFL Championship Game following 1982, 1983 and 1987 seasons.
Played in Pro Bowl (NFL All-Star Game) following 1983 season.

JOE EARL BOSTIC JR.
Guard—Phoenix Cardinals
Born April 20, 1957, at Greensboro, N.C.
Height, 6.03. Weight, 265.
High School—Greensboro, N.C., Benjamin L. Smith.
Attended Clemson University.
Brother of Jeff Bostic, center with Washington Redskins.

Selected by St. Louis in 3rd round (64th player selected) of 1979 NFL draft.
On injured reserve with knee injury, December 3 through remainer of 1986 season.
On injured reserve with knee injury, December 12 through remainder of 1987 season.
Franchise transferred to Phoenix, March 15, 1988.
St. Louis NFL, 1979 through 1987.
Games: 1979 (16), 1980 (16), 1981 (14), 1982 (8), 1983 (14), 1984 (16), 1985 (16), 1986 (13), 1987 (9). Total—122.
Pro statistics: Recovered one fumble, 1983.

KEITH BOSTIC
Safety—Houston Oilers
Born January 17, 1961, at Ann Arbor, Mich.
Height, 6.01. Weight, 223.
High School—Ann Arbor, Mich., Pioneer.
Attended University of Michigan.

Selected by Michigan in 1983 USFL territorial draft.
Selected by Houston in 2nd round (42nd player selected) of 1983 NFL draft.
Signed by Houston Oilers, June 27, 1983.

| | | —INTERCEPTIONS— | | | |
Year Club	G.	No.	Yds.	Avg.	TD.
1983—Houston NFL	16	2	0	0.0	0
1984—Houston NFL	16	None			
1985—Houston NFL	16	3	28	9.3	0
1986—Houston NFL	16	1	0	0.0	0
1987—Houston NFL	12	6	—14	—2.3	0
Pro Totals—5 Years	76	12	14	1.2	0

Additional pro statistics: Recovered two fumbles for 25 yards and a touchdown, 1984; recovered one fumble, 1985 and 1986; recovered one fumble for two yards and fumbled once, 1987.
Played in Pro Bowl (NFL All-Star Game) following 1987 season.

BRIAN KEITH BOSWORTH
Linebacker—Seattle Seahawks
Born March 9, 1965, at Oklahoma City, Okla.
Height, 6.02. Weight, 248.
High School—Irving, Tex., MacArthur.
Received degree in business from University of Oklahoma in 1987.

Named as linebacker on THE SPORTING NEWS College All-America Team, 1986.
Selected by Seattle in 1st round of 1987 NFL supplemental draft, June 12, 1987.
Signed by Seattle Seahawks, August 14, 1987.
Seattle NFL, 1987.
Games: 1987 (12).
Pro statistics: Recovered two fumbles for 38 yards, 1987.

MATTHEW KYLE BOUZA
(Matt)
Wide Receiver—Indianapolis Colts
Born April 8, 1958, at San Jose, Calif.
Height, 6.03. Weight, 211.
High School—Sacramento, Calif., Jesuit.
Received degree in political science from University of California at Berkeley.

Signed as free agent by San Francisco 49ers, May 8, 1981.
Released by San Francisco 49ers, August 31, 1981; re-signed by 49ers, September 1, 1981.
Released by San Francisco 49ers, September 9, 1981; signed as free agent by Baltimore Colts, May 15, 1982.
On injured reserve with separated shoulder, November 18 through remainder of 1983 season.
Franchise transferred to Indianapolis, March 31, 1984.
On injured reserve with knee injury, November 1 through November 28, 1985; activated, November 29, 1985.

		—PASS RECEIVING—			
Year Club	G.	P.C.	Yds.	Avg.	TD.
1981—San Francisco NFL	1		None		
1982—Baltimore NFL	9	22	287	13.0	2
1983—Baltimore NFL	11	25	385	15.4	0
1984—Indianapolis NFL	16	22	270	12.3	0
1985—Indianapolis NFL	12	27	381	14.1	2
1986—Indianapolis NFL	16	71	830	11.7	5
1987—Indianapolis NFL	12	42	569	13.5	4
Pro Totals—7 Years............	77	209	2722	13.0	13

Additional pro statistics: Returned three kickoffs for 31 yards, returned two punts for no yards and recovered one fumble, 1982; fumbled once, 1982 through 1984; returned one kickoff for minus four yards, 1983; returned three punts for 17 yards, 1984; rushed once for 12 yards, 1986; fumbled twice, 1987.

TODD ROBERT BOWLES
Safety—Washington Redskins
Born November 18, 1963, at Elizabeth, N.J.
Height, 6.02. Weight, 203.
High School—Elizabeth, N.J.
Attended Temple University.

Selected by Baltimore in 1986 USFL territorial draft.
Signed as free agent by Washington Redskins, May 6, 1986.

		—INTERCEPTIONS—			
Year Club	G.	No.	Yds.	Avg.	TD.
1986—Washington NFL	15	2	0	0.0	0
1987—Washington NFL	12	4	24	6.0	0
Pro Totals—2 Years............	27	6	24	4.0	0

Additional pro statistics: Recovered one fumble, 1987.
Played in NFC Championship Game following 1986 and 1987 seasons.
Played in NFL Championship Game following 1987 season.

JAMES EDWIN BOWMAN
(Jim)
Safety—New England Patriots
Born October 26, 1963, at Cadillac, Mich.
Height, 6.02. Weight, 210.
High School—Cadillac, Mich.
Attended Central Michigan University.

Selected by Oakland in 11th round (153rd player selected) of 1985 USFL draft.
Selected by New England in 2nd round (52nd player selected) of 1985 NFL draft.
Signed by New England Patriots, July 23, 1985.
New England NFL, 1985 through 1987.
Games: 1985 (16), 1986 (16), 1987 (12). Total—44.
Pro statistics: Returned one punt for minus three yards, 1985; intercepted two passes for three yards and recovered one fumble for six yards, 1987.
Played in AFC Championship Game following 1985 season.
Played in NFL Championship Game following 1985 season.

KEVIN GERARD BOWMAN
Wide Receiver—Tampa Bay Buccaneers
Born February 23, 1962, at Sacramento, Calif.
Height, 6.03. Weight, 205.
High School—Sacramento, Calif., Luther Burbank.
Attended San Jose State University.

Selected by Oakland in 1985 USFL territorial draft.
Signed as free agent by Dallas Cowboys, May 3, 1985.
Released by Dallas Cowboys, July 26, 1985; signed as free agent by San Francisco 49ers, March 2, 1986.
Released by San Francisco 49ers, August 13, 1986; signed as free agent by British Columbia Lions, April 7, 1987.
Released by British Columbia Lions, August 11, 1987; signed as free agent replacement player by Philadelphia Eagles, September 24, 1987.
Released by Philadelphia Eagles, October 19, 1987; signed as free agent by Tampa Bay Buccaneers, December 30, 1987.

		—PASS RECEIVING—			
Year Club	G.	P.C.	Yds.	Avg.	TD.
1987—British Columbia CFL.	2	4	43	10.8	0
1987—Philadelphia NFL	3	6	127	31.2	1
Pro Totals—2 Years............	5	10	170	17.0	1

Additional NFL statistics: Returned seven kickoffs for 153 yards (21.9 avg.) and returned four punts for 43 yards (10.8 avg.), 1987.

WALTER NATHANIEL BOWYER JR.

Name pronounced BOY-er.

(Walt)
Defensive End—Denver Broncos

Born September 8, 1960, at Pittsburgh, Pa.
Height, 6.04. Weight, 260.
High School—Winkinsburg, Pa.
Attended Arizona State University.

Selected by Denver in 10th round (254th player selected) of 1983 NFL draft.
Released by Denver Broncos, August 27, 1985; re-signed by Broncos for 1986, December 14, 1985.
Released by Denver Broncos, September 1, 1986; re-signed by Broncos, August 19, 1987.
Released by Denver Broncos, September 7, 1987; re-signed by Broncos, September 8, 1987.
Crossed picket line during players' strike, October 2, 1987.
Denver NFL, 1983, 1984 and 1987.
Games: 1983 (14), 1984 (16), 1987 (15). Total—45.
Pro statistics: Recovered one fumble, 1983 and 1984.
Played in AFC Championship Game following 1987 season.
Played in NFL Championship Game following 1987 season.

GERARD MARK JOSEPH BOYARSKY

Name pronounced Boy-ARE-ski.

(Jerry)
Nose Tackle—Green Bay Packers

Born May 15, 1959, at Scranton, Pa.
Height, 6.03. Weight, 290.
High School—Jermyn, Pa., Lakeland.
Received bachelor of arts degree in political science from University of Pittsburgh in 1981.

Selected by New Orleans in 5th round (128th player selected) of 1981 NFL draft.
On injured reserve with knee injury, September 1 through October 1, 1981; activated, October 2, 1981.
Released by New Orleans Saints, September 6, 1982; signed as free agent by Cincinnati Bengals, December 1, 1982 and 1983.
Released by Cincinnati Bengals, September 3, 1986; signed as free agent by Buffalo Bills, September 10, 1986.
Released by Buffalo Bills, November 21, 1986; signed as free agent by Green Bay Packers, December 2, 1986.
Released by Green Bay Packers, December 15, 1986; re-signed by Packers, February 24, 1987.
New Orleans NFL, 1981; Cincinnati NFL, 1982 through 1985; Buffalo (10)-Green Bay (2) NFL, 1986; Green Bay NFL, 1987.
Games: 1981 (11), 1982 (2), 1983 (15), 1984 (15), 1985 (16), 1986 (12), 1987 (12). Total—83.

MARK HEARN BOYER
Tight End—Indianapolis Colts

Born September 16, 1962, at Huntington Beach, Calif.
Height, 6.04. Weight, 239.
High School—Huntington Beach, Calif., Edison.
Attended University of Southern California.

Selected by Los Angeles in 1985 USFL territorial draft.
Selected by Indianapolis in 9th round (229th player selected) of 1985 NFL draft.
Signed by Indianapolis Colts, July 18, 1985.
On injured reserve with broken arm, October 26 through December 3, 1987; activated, December 4, 1987.

| | | | —PASS RECEIVING— | | |
Year	Club	G.	P.C.	Yds.	Avg.	TD.
1985—Indianapolis NFL		16	25	274	11.0	0
1986—Indianapolis NFL		16	22	237	10.8	1
1987—Indianapolis NFL		7	10	73	7.3	0
Pro Totals—3 Years		39	57	584	10.2	1

Additional pro statistics: Recovered one fumble, 1985; fumbled once, 1986.

DONALD CRAIG BRACKEN
(Don)
Punter—Green Bay Packers

Born February 16, 1962, at Coalinga, Calif.
Height, 6.00. Weight, 211.
High School—Thermopolis, Wyo., Hot Springs County.
Received bachelor of science degree in physical education from University of Michigan.

Selected by Michigan in 1984 USFL territorial draft.
Signed by Michigan Panthers, January 8, 1984.
Released by Michigan Panthers, February 16, 1984; signed as free agent by Kansas City Chiefs, May 4, 1984.
Released by Kansas City Chiefs, June 1, 1984; signed as free agent by Indianapolis Colts, June 14, 1984.
Released by Indianapolis Colts, August 6, 1984; signed as free agent by Denver Broncos, January 30, 1985.
Released by Denver Broncos, August 26, 1985; signed as free agent by Green Bay Packers, November 6, 1985.
On injured reserve with dislocated elbow, December 5 through remainder of 1986 season.
Released by Green Bay Packers, September 7, 1987; re-signed by Packers, September 8, 1987.

Year Club		PUNTING		
	G.	No.	Avg.	Blk.
1985—Green Bay NFL	7	26	40.5	0
1986—Green Bay NFL	13	55	40.1	2
1987—Green Bay NFL	12	72	40.9	1
Pro Totals—3 Years	32	153	40.5	3

ED JOHN BRADY
Linebacker—Cincinnnati Bengals
Born June 17, 1960, at Morris, Ill.
Height, 6.02. Weight, 235.
High School—Morris, Ill.
Attended University of Illinois.

Selected by Chicago in 1984 USFL territorial draft.
Selected by Los Angeles Rams in 8th round (215th player selected) of 1984 NFL draft.
Signed by Los Angeles Rams, July 14, 1984.
Released by Los Angeles Rams, August 27, 1984; re-signed by Rams, August 28, 1984.
Released by Los Angeles Rams, September 1, 1986; awarded on waivers to Cincinnati Bengals, September 2, 1986.
Los Angeles Rams NFL, 1984 and 1985; Cincinnati NFL, 1986 and 1987.
Games: 1984 (16), 1985 (16), 1986 (16), 1987 (12). Total—60.
Pro statistics: Recovered one fumble, 1985 and 1987; fumbled once for minus seven yards, 1986.
Played in NFC Championship Game following 1985 season.

STEPHEN BRAGGS
Defensive Back—Cleveland Browns
Born August 29, 1965, at Houston, Tex.
Height, 5.09. Weight, 173.
High School—Smiley, Tex.
Attended University of Texas.

Selected by Cleveland in 6th round (165th player selected) of 1987 NFL draft.
Signed by Cleveland Browns, July 26, 1987.
Cleveland NFL, 1987.
Games: 1987 (12).
Played in AFC Championship Game following 1987 season.

REGINALD ETOY BRANCH
(Reggie)
Running Back—Washington Redskins
Born October 22, 1962, at Sanford, Fla.
Height, 5.11. Weight, 235.
High School—Sanford, Fla., Seminole.
Attended West Virginia State College and East Carolina University.
Nephew of Tony Collins, running back with New England Patriots, 1981 through 1987.

Signed as free agent by Washington Redskins, May 2, 1985.
Released by Washington Redskins, August 27, 1985; re-signed by Redskins, October 1, 1985.
Released by Washington Redskins, November 12, 1985; re-signed by Redskins, December 11, 1985.
Released by Washington Redskins, August 26, 1986; re-signed by Redskins, December 17, 1986.
Washington NFL, 1985 through 1987.
Games: 1985 (8), 1986 (1), 1987 (12). Total—21.
Pro statistics: Rushed four times for nine yards and a touchdown and returned four kickoffs for 61 yards, 1987.
Played in NFC Championship Game following 1986 and 1987 seasons.
Played in NFL Championship Game following 1987 season.

JOHN WESLEY BRANDES
Tight End—Indianapolis Colts
Born April 2, 1964, at Fort Riley, Kan.
Height, 6.02. Weight, 237.
High School—Arlington, Tex., Lamar.
Attended Cameron University.

Signed as free agent by Indianapolis Colts, May 11, 1987.
Crossed picket line during players' strike, October 7, 1987.

Year Club		PASS RECEIVING			
	G.	P.C.	Yds.	Avg.	TD.
1987—Indianapolis NFL	12	5	35	7.0	0

DAVID SHERROD BRANDON
Linebacker—San Diego Chargers
Born February 9, 1965, at Memphis, Tenn.
Height, 6.04. Weight, 225.
High School—Memphis, Tenn., Mitchell.
Attended Memphis State University.

Selected by Buffalo in 3rd round (60th player selected) of 1987 NFL draft.
Signed by Buffalo Bills, July 25, 1987.

— 43 —

Traded with 4th round pick in 1988 draft by Buffalo Bills to San Diego Chargers for Wide Receiver Trumaine Johnson and 7th round pick in 1988 draft, August 31, 1987.
San Diego NFL, 1987.
Games: 1987 (8).
Pro statistics: Recovered blocked punt in end zone for a touchdown, 1987.

ROBERT LEE BRANNON
Defensive End—New Orleans Saints
Born March 26, 1961, at Charleston, S.C.
Height, 6.07. Weight, 260.
High School—Columbia, S.C., A.C. Flora.
Attended University of Arkansas.

Selected by Portland in 3rd round (37th player selected) of 1985 USFL draft.
Signed by Portland Breakers, January 20, 1985.
On developmental squad, February 21 through March 15, 1985; activated, March 16, 1985.
On developmental squad, April 1 through April 5, 1985; activated, April 6, 1985.
On developmental squad, May 21 through May 29, 1985; activated, May 30, 1985.
Released by Portland Breakers, July 31, 1985; signed as free agent by Tampa Bay Buccaneers, August 5, 1985.
Released by Tampa Bay Buccaneers, August 19, 1985; signed as free agent replacement player by Cleveland Browns, September 23, 1987.
Traded with running back Kirk Jones by Cleveland Browns to New Orleans Saints for draft pick, October 15, 1987.
Released by New Orleans Saints, October 21, 1987; re-signed by Saints, February 22, 1988.
On developmental squad for 5 games with Portland Breakers in 1985.
Portland USFL, 1985; Cleveland (1)-New Orleans (1) NFL, 1987.
Games: 1985 (13), 1987 (2). Total—15.
Pro statistics: Credited with two sacks for 14 yards, 1985.

RHEUGENE JAMES BRANTON
First name pronounced ROO-jean.
(Gene)
Wide Receiver—Los Angeles Raiders
Born November 23, 1960, at Tampa, Fla.
Height, 6.04. Weight, 210.
High School—Tampa, Fla., King.
Attended Texas Southern University.

Selected by Tampa Bay in 6th round (148th player selected) of 1983 NFL draft.
On injured reserve with knee injury, September 9 through remainder of 1983 season.
On injured reserve with pulled hamstring, August 27 through entire 1984 season.
Released by Tampa Bay Buccaneers, September 25, 1985; signed as free agent by Los Angeles Raiders, June 27, 1986.
On injured reserve with ankle injury, August 18 through entire 1986 season.
On injured reserve with knee injury, September 7 through December 25, 1987; activated, December 26, 1987.
Crossed picket line during players' strike, October 14, 1987.
Active for 1 game with Los Angeles Raiders in 1987; did not play.
Tampa Bay NFL, 1983 and 1985; Los Angeles Raiders NFL, 1987.
Games: 1983 (1), 1985 (3). Total—4.

TYRONE SCOTT BRAXTON
Safety—Denver Broncos
Born December 17, 1964, at Madison, Wis.
Height, 5.11. Weight, 174.
High School—Madison, Wis., James Madison Memorial.
Attended North Dakota State University.
Related to Jim Braxton, fullback with Buffalo Bills and Miami Dolphins, 1971 through 1978.

Selected by Denver in 12th round (334th player selected) of 1987 NFL draft.
Signed by Denver Broncos, July 18, 1987.
On injured reserve with shoulder injury, September 1 through December 17, 1987; activated, December 18, 1987.
Denver NFL, 1987.
Games: 1987 (2).
Played in AFC Championship Game following 1987 season.
Played in NFL Championship Game following 1987 season.

JAMES THOMAS BREECH
(Jim)
Placekicker—Cincinnati Bengals
Born April 11, 1956, at Sacramento, Calif.
Height, 5.06. Weight, 161.
High School—Sacramento, Calif.
Attended University of California.

Selected by Detroit in 8th round (206th player selected) of 1978 NFL draft.
Released by Detroit Lions, August 23, 1978; signed as free agent by Oakland Raiders, December 12, 1978.
Released by Oakland Raiders, September 1, 1980; signed as free agent by Cincinnati Bengals, November 25, 1980.
Active for 1 game with Oakland Raiders in 1978; did not play.

Year Club	G.	XP.	XPM.	FG.	FGA.	Pts.
1979—Oakland NFL............	16	41	4	18	27	95
1980—Cincinnati NFL........	4	11	1	4	7	23
1981—Cincinnati NFL........	16	49	2	22	32	115
1982—Cincinnati NFL........	9	25	1	14	18	67
1983—Cincinnati NFL........	16	39	2	16	23	87
1984—Cincinnati NFL........	16	37	0	22	31	103
1985—Cincinnati NFL........	16	48	2	24	33	120
1986—Cincinnati NFL........	16	50	1	17	32	101
1987—Cincinnati NFL........	12	25	2	24	30	97
Pro Totals—10 Years.....	121	325	15	161	233	808

Additional pro statistics: Punted twice for 33.5 yard average, 1980; fumbled once, 1983; punted five times for 30.6 average, 1985.

Played in AFC Championship Game following 1981 season.

Played in NFL Championship Game following 1981 season.

LOUIS EVERETT BREEDEN
Cornerback—Indianapolis Colts
Born October 26, 1953, at Hamlet, N. C.
Height, 5.11. Weight, 185.
High School—Hamlet., N. C.
Attended Richmond Technical Institute and received bachelor of science degree
from North Carolina Central University in 1977.

Tied NFL record for most yards, interception return (102), vs. San Diego Chargers, November 8, 1981.

Selected by Cincinnati in 7th round (187th player selected) of 1977 NFL draft.

On injured reserve, September 8 through entire 1977 season.

On injured reserve with shoulder injury, November 13 through remainder of 1979 season.

On injured reserve with back injury, September 8 through October 29, 1987; activated, October 30, 1987.

Granted free agency with no qualifying offer, February 1, 1988.

Signed by Indianapolis Colts, May 16, 1988.

		—INTERCEPTIONS—			
Year Club	G.	No.	Yds.	Avg.	TD.
1978—Cincinnati NFL............	16	3	25	8.3	0
1979—Cincinnati NFL............	10		None		
1980—Cincinnati NFL............	16	7	91	13.0	0
1981—Cincinnati NFL............	16	4	145	*36.3	1
1982—Cincinnati NFL............	6	2	9	4.5	0
1983—Cincinnati NFL............	14	2	47	23.5	0
1984—Cincinnati NFL............	16	4	96	24.0	0
1985—Cincinnati NFL............	16	2	24	12.0	0
1986—Cincinnati NFL............	16	7	72	10.3	1
1987—Cincinnati NFL............	8	2	49	24.5	0
Pro Totals—10 Years..........	134	33	558	16.9	2

Additional pro statistics: Recovered one fumble, 1978 and 1983; returned six punts for minus 12 yards, returned one kickoff for 12 yards and fumbled twice, 1978; recovered one fumble for 10 yards, 1981; fumbled once, 1982 and 1984.

Played in AFC Championship Game following 1981 season.

Played in NFL Championship Game following 1981 season.

JEFFERY BRYAN BREGEL
(Jeff)
Guard—San Francisco 49ers
Born May 1, 1964, at Redondo Beach, Calif.
Height, 6.04. Weight, 280.
High School—Los Angeles, Calif., John F. Kennedy.
Attended University of Southern California.

Named as guard on THE SPORTING NEWS College All-America Team, 1986.

Selected by San Francisco in 2nd round (37th player selected) of 1987 NFL draft.

Signed by San Francisco 49ers, July 20, 1987.

On injured reserve with knee injury, September 7 through October 30, 1987; activated, October 31, 1987.

On injured reserve with back injury, December 18 through remainder of 1987 season.

San Francisco NFL, 1987.

Games: 1987 (5).

BRIAN MICHAEL BRENNAN
Wide Receiver—Cleveland Browns
Born February 15, 1962, at Bloomfield, Mich.
Height, 5.09. Weight, 178.
High School—Birmingham, Mich., Brother Rice.
Received bachelor of science degree in finance from Boston College in 1984.

Selected by Denver in 16th round (324th player selected) in 1984 USFL draft.

Selected by Cleveland in 4th round (104th player selected) of 1984 NFL draft.

Signed by Cleveland Browns, May 18, 1984.

On injured reserve with separated shoulder, September 4 through October 1, 1985; activated, October 2, 1985.

Crossed picket line during players' strike, October 14, 1987.

Year Club	G.	P.C.	-PASS RECEIVING- Yds.	Avg.	TD.	No.	-PUNT RETURNS- Yds.	Avg.	TD.	-TOTAL- TD.	Pts.	F.
1984—Cleveland NFL	15	35	455	13.0	3	25	199	8.0	0	3	18	1
1985—Cleveland NFL	12	32	487	15.2	0	19	153	8.1	1	1	6	3
1986—Cleveland NFL	16	55	838	15.2	6		None			7	42	0
1987—Cleveland NFL	13	43	607	14.1	6		None			6	36	1
Pro Totals—4 Years	56	165	2387	14.5	15	44	352	8.0	1	17	102	5

Additional pro statistics: Attempted one pass with one completion for 33 yards and a touchdown, 1985; recovered fumble in end zone for a touchdown, attempted one pass with one completion for 35 yards and fumbled once, 1986; recovered one fumble, 1987.

Played in AFC Championship Game following 1986 and 1987 seasons.

HOBY F. J. BRENNER
Tight End—New Orleans Saints

Born June 2, 1959, at Linwood, Calif.
Height, 6.04. Weight, 240.
High School—Fullerton, Calif.
Attended University of Southern California.

Selected by New Orleans in 3rd round (71st player selected) of 1981 NFL draft.
On injured reserve with turf toe, September 1 through October 22, 1981; activated, October 23, 1981.
On injured reserve with knee injury, December 31 through remainder of 1982 season.
On injured reserve with separated shoulder, September 27 through October 23, 1987; activated, October 24, 1987.

Year Club	G.	P.C.	——PASS RECEIVING—— Yds.	Avg.	TD.
1981—New Orleans NFL	9	7	143	20.4	0
1982—New Orleans NFL	8	16	171	10.7	0
1983—New Orleans NFL	16	41	574	14.0	3
1984—New Orleans NFL	16	28	554	19.8	6
1985—New Orleans NFL	16	42	652	15.5	3
1986—New Orleans NFL	15	18	286	15.9	0
1987—New Orleans NFL	12	20	280	14.0	2
Pro Totals—7 Years	92	172	2660	15.5	14

Additional pro statistics: Fumbled once, 1981, 1982 and 1985; recovered one fumble, 1982.
Played in Pro Bowl (NFL All-Star Game) following 1987 season.

TOM BRIEHL
Name pronounced Breel.
Linebacker—San Diego Chargers

Born September 8, 1962, at Phoenix, Ariz.
Height, 6.03. Weight, 247.
High School—Phoenix, Ariz., Gerard Catholic.
Attended Stanford University.

Selected by Oakland in 1985 USFL territorial draft.
Selected by Houston in 4th round (87th player selected) of 1985 NFL draft.
Signed by Houston Oilers, July 19, 1985.
On injured reserve with fractured ankle, August 12 through entire 1986 season.
Released by Houston Oilers, September 6, 1987; re-signed as replacement player by Oilers, September 24, 1987.
Released by Houston Oilers, October 27, 1987; signed as free agent by San Diego Chargers, May 10, 1988.
Houston NFL, 1985 and 1987.
Games: 1985 (16), 1987 (3). Total—19.
Pro statistics: Returned one kickoff for five yards, 1985.

DARRICK JOSEPH BRILZ
Guard—Washington Redskins

Born February 14, 1964, at Richmond, Calif.
Height, 6.03. Weight, 264.
High School—Pinole, Calif., Pinole Valley.
Attended Oregon State University.

Signed as free agent by Washington Redskins, May 1, 1987.
Released by Washington Redskins, August 31, 1987; re-signed as replacement player by Redskins, September 23, 1987.
On injured reserve with pinched nerve in neck, December 12 through remainder of 1987 season.
Washington NFL, 1987.
Games: 1987 (7).

WALTER ANDREW BRISTER III
(Bubby)
Quarterback—Pittsburgh Steelers

Born August 15, 1962, at Alexandria, La.
Height, 6.03. Weight, 195.
High School—Monroe, La., Neville.
Attended Tulane University and Northeast Louisiana University.

Selected by Pittsburgh in 3rd round (67th player selected) of 1986 NFL draft.
Selected by New Jersey in 11th round (80th player selected) of 1986 USFL draft.
Signed by Pittsburgh Steelers, July 25, 1986.

Year Club	G.	Att.	Cmp.	Pct.	Gain	T.P.	P.I.	Avg.	Att.	Yds.	Avg.	TD.	TD.	Pts.	F.
				PASSING						RUSHING				TOTAL	
1986—Piitsburgh NFL	2	60	21	35.0	291	0	2	4.85	6	10	1.7	1	1	6	1
1987—Pittsburgh NFL	2	12	4	33.3	20	0	3	1.67			None		0	0	0
Pro Totals—2 Years	4	72	25	34.7	311	0	5	4.32	6	10	1.7	1	1	6	1

Quarterback Rating Points: 1986 (37.6), 1987 (2.8). Total—20.3.

RECORD AS BASEBALL PLAYER

Year Club	League	Pos.	G.	AB.	R.	H.	2B.	3B.	HR.	RBI.	B.A.	PO.	A.	E.	F.A.
1981—Bristol	Appal.	OF-SS	39	111	12	20	7	0	0	10	.180	46	11	9	.864
1982—Bristol†‡	Appal.					(Did not play)									

Selected by Detroit Tigers' organization in 4th round of free-agent draft, June 8, 1981.
†On suspended list, June 22, 1982 through entire season.
‡Placed on restricted list, October 7, 1982.

LOUIS CLARK BROCK JR.
(Lou)
Cornerback—San Diego Chargers
Born May 8, 1964, at Chicago, Ill.
Height, 5.10. Weight, 175.
High School—St. Louis, Mo., Horton Watkins.
Attended University of Southern California.
Son of Lou Brock Sr., Hall of Fame outfielder with Chicago Cubs
and St. Louis Cardinals, 1961 through 1979.

Selected by San Diego in 2nd round (53rd player selected) of 1987 NFL draft.
Signed by San Diego Chargers, July 25, 1987.
On injured reserve with lymph infection in groin, November 3 through remainder of 1987 season.
Selected by Montreal Expos' organization in 17th round of free-agent draft, June 7, 1982.
San Diego NFL, 1987.
Games: 1987 (1).

PETER ANTHONY BROCK
(Pete)
Center—New England Patriots
Born July 14, 1954, at Portland, Ore.
Height, 6.05. Weight, 275.
High School—Beaverton, Ore., Jesuit.
Received bachelor of science degree in biology from University of Colorado in 1976.
Brother of Stan Brock, offensive tackle with New Orleans Saints; Willie Brock, center with
Detroit Lions, 1978; and Ray Brock, rookie center with Kansas City Chiefs.

Named as center on THE SPORTING NEWS College All-America Team, 1975.
Selected by New England in 1st round (12th player selected) of 1976 NFL draft.
On injured reserve with knee injury, October 26 through November 29, 1985; activated, November 30, 1985.
Granted free agency, February 1, 1986; re-signed by Patriots, August 18, 1986.
Granted roster exemption, August 18 through August 20, 1986; activated, August 21, 1986.
Granted free agency, February 1, 1987; option not exercised, June 1, 1987.
Re-signed by New England Patriots, July 31, 1987.
On injured reserve with knee injury, November 3 through December 17, 1987; activated, December 18, 1987.
New England NFL, 1976 through 1987.
Games: 1976 (14), 1977 (14), 1978 (15), 1979 (16), 1980 (16), 1981 (16), 1982 (9), 1983 (13), 1984 (12), 1985 (9), 1986 (16), 1987 (4). Total—154.
Pro statistics: Recovered one fumble, 1976, 1980 through 1982 and 1986; caught one pass for six yards and a touchdown, 1976; fumbled twice, 1979; fumbled once, 1986.
Played in AFC Championship Game following 1985 season.
Played in NFL Championship Game following 1985 season.

STANLEY JAMES BROCK
(Stan)
Offensive Tackle—New Orleans Saints
Born June 8, 1958, at Portland, Ore.
Height, 6.06. Weight, 292.
High School—Beaverton, Ore., Jesuit.
Attended University of Colorado.
Brother of Pete Brock, center with New England Patriots; Willie Brock, center with
Detroit Lions, 1978; and Ray Brock, rookie center with Kansas City Chiefs.

Named as offensive tackle on THE SPORTING NEWS College All-America Team, 1979.
Selected by New Orleans in 1st round (12th player selected) of 1980 NFL draft.
On injured reserve with knee injury, December 5 through remainder of 1984 season.
New Orleans NFL, 1980 through 1987.
Games: 1980 (16), 1981 (16), 1982 (9), 1983 (16), 1984 (14), 1985 (16), 1986 (16), 1987 (12). Total—115.
Pro statistics: Recovered one fumble, 1980, 1983 and 1985; returned two kickoffs for 18 yards and recovered two fumbles, 1981; returned one kickoff for 15 yards, 1983; returned one kickoff for 11 yards, 1987.

MITCHELL EUGENE BROOKINS
Wide Receiver—San Diego Chargers
Born December 10, 1960, at Chicago, Ill.
Height, 5.11. Weight, 196.
High School—Chicago, Ill., Wendell Phillips.
Received bachelor of science degree in political science from University of Illinois in 1984.
Selected by Chicago in 1984 USFL territorial draft.
Selected by Buffalo in 4th round (95th player selected) of 1984 NFL draft.
Signed by Buffalo Bills, June 1, 1984.
On injured reserve with knee injury, October 12 through remainder of 1985 season.
On injured reserve with knee injury, August 22 through entire 1986 season.
Released by Buffalo Bills, September 1, 1987; signed as free agent replacement player by Los Angeles Raiders, October 9, 1987.
Released by Los Angeles Raiders, October 15, 1987; signed as free agent by San Diego Chargers, April 18, 1988.

		—PASS RECEIVING—				
Year Club		G.	P.C.	Yds.	Avg.	TD.
1984—Buffalo NFL		16	18	318	17.7	1
1985—Buffalo NFL		5	3	71	23.7	0
Pro Totals—2 Years		21	21	389	18.5	1

Additional pro statistics: Rushed twice for 27 yards, 1984; returned six kickoffs for 152 yards, 1985.

JAMES ROBERT BROOKS
Running Back—Cincinnati Bengals
Born December 28, 1958, at Warner Robins, Ga.
Height, 5.10. Weight, 182.
High School—Warner Robins, Ga.
Attended Auburn University.
Selected by San Diego in 1st round (24th player selected) of 1981 NFL draft.
Traded by San Diego Chargers to Cincinnati Bengals for running back Pete Johnson, May 29, 1984.

		—RUSHING—				PASS RECEIVING				—TOTAL—		
Year Club	G.	Att.	Yds.	Avg.	TD.	P.C.	Yds.	Avg.	TD.	TD.	Pts.	F.
1981—San Diego NFL	14	109	525	4.8	3	46	329	7.2	3	6	36	7
1982—San Diego NFL	9	87	430	4.9	6	13	66	5.1	0	6	36	4
1983—San Diego NFL	15	127	516	4.1	3	25	215	8.6	0	3	18	8
1984—Cincinnati NFL	15	103	396	3.8	2	34	268	7.9	2	4	24	4
1985—Cincinnati NFL	16	192	929	4.8	7	55	576	10.5	5	12	72	7
1986—Cincinnati NFL	16	205	1087	*5.3	5	54	686	12.7	4	9	54	2
1987—Cincinnati NFL	9	94	290	3.1	1	22	272	12.4	2	3	18	0
Pro Totals—7 Years	94	917	4173	4.6	27	249	2412	9.7	16	43	258	32

		—PUNT RETURNS—				—KICKOFF RET.—			
Year Club		G.	No.	Yds.	Avg.	TD.	No.	Yds.	Avg. TD.
1981—San Diego NFL		14	22	290	13.2	0	40	949	23.7 0
1982—San Diego NFL		9	12	138	11.5	0	*33	*749	22.7 0
1983—San Diego NFL		15	18	137	7.6	0	32	607	19.0 0
1984—Cincinnati NFL		15	None				7	144	20.6 0
1985—Cincinnati NFL		16	None				3	38	12.7 0
1986—Cincinnati NFL		16	None				None		
1987—Cincinnati NFL		9	None				2	42	21.0 0
Pro Totals—7 Years		94	52	565	10.9	0	117	2529	21.6 0

Additional pro statistics: Recovered two fumbles, 1981; recovered one fumble, 1982 and 1985; recovered three fumbles, 1983; attempted one pass with one completion for eight yards and a touchdown, 1985; attempted one pass with no completions, 1986.
Played in AFC Championship Game following 1981 season.
Played in Pro Bowl (NFL All-Star Game) following 1986 season.

KEVIN CRAIG BROOKS
Defensive Tackle—Dallas Cowboys
Born February 9, 1963, at Detroit, Mich.
Height, 6.06. Weight, 278.
High School—Detroit, Mich., MacKenzie.
Received bachelor of general studies degree from University of Michigan in 1985.
Selected by Tampa Bay in 10th round (141st player selected) of 1985 USFL draft.
Selected by Dallas in 1st round (17th player selected) of 1985 NFL draft.
Signed by Dallas Cowboys, July 17, 1985.
On injured reserve with knee injury, August 21 through October 24, 1986; activated, October 25, 1986.
Crossed picket line during players' strike, October 7, 1987.
Dallas NFL, 1985 through 1987.
Games: 1985 (11), 1986 (9), 1987 (13). Total—33.
Pro statistics: Recovered one fumble, 1987.

—DID YOU KNOW—
That the Kansas City Chiefs have won their first and last games in each of the last five seasons? Their winning streak in finales goes back to 1980.

MICHAEL BROOKS
Linebacker—Denver Broncos
Born October 2, 1964, at Ruston, La.
Height, 6.01. Weight, 235.
High School—Ruston, La.
Attended Louisiana State University.

Selected by Denver in 3rd round (86th player selected) of 1987 NFL draft.
Signed by Denver Broncos, July 24, 1987.
Denver NFL, 1987.
Games: 1987 (12).
Pro statistics: Recovered one fumble, 1987.
Played in AFC Championship Game following 1987 season.
Played in NFL Championship Game following 1987 season.

WILLIAM BROOKS JR.
(Bill)
Wide Receiver—Indianapolis Colts
Born April 6, 1964, at Boston, Mass.
Height, 6.00. Weight, 190.
High School—Framingham, Mass., North.
Received bachelor of science degree in business administration
from Boston University in 1986.

Selected by Indianapolis in 4th round (86th player selected) of 1986 NFL draft.
Signed by Indianapolis Colts, June 23, 1986.

		PASS RECEIVING			-PUNT RETURNS-				—KICKOFF RET.—				—TOTAL—		
Year	Club	G.	P.C.	Yds.	Avg.	TD.	No.	Yds.	Avg.	TD.	No.	Yds.	Avg.	TD.	TD.	Pts.	F.
1986—Indianapolis NFL	....	16	65	1131	17.4	8	18	141	7.8	0	8	143	17.9	0	8	48	2
1987—Indianapolis NFL	....	12	51	722	14.2	3	22	136	6.2	0		None			3	18	3
Pro Totals—2 Years	....	28	116	1853	16.0	11	40	277	6.9	0	8	143	17.9	0	11	66	5

Additional pro statistics: Rushed four times for five yards and recovered one fumble, 1986; rushed twice for minus two yards, 1987.

JAMES JAY BROPHY
(Known by middle name.)
Linebacker—Tampa Bay Buccaneers
Born July 27, 1960, at Akron, O.
Height, 6.03. Weight, 233.
High School—Akron, O., John R. Buchtel.
Attended University of Miami (Fla.).

Selected by Tampa Bay in 4th round (73rd player selected) of 1984 USFL draft.
Selected by Miami in 2nd round (53rd player selected) of 1984 NFL draft.
Signed by Miami Dolphins, May 24, 1984.
Released by Miami Dolphins, September 1, 1986; re-signed by Dolphins, September 17, 1986.
Released by Miami Dolphins, October 18, 1986; signed as free agent by New York Jets, February 25, 1987.
Released by New York Jets, August 31, 1987; re-signed as replacement player by Jets, September 24, 1987.
Released by New York Jets, October 26, 1987; signed as free agent by Tampa Bay Buccaneers, February 18, 1988.
Miami NFL, 1984 through 1986; New York Jets NFL, 1987.
Games: 1984 (11), 1985 (16), 1986 (4), 1987 (3). Total—34.
Pro statistics: Intercepted one pass for 41 yards and recovered one fumble, 1985.
Played in AFC Championship Game following 1984 and 1985 seasons.
Played in NFL Championship Game following 1984 season.

ROBERT JOHN BROTZKI
(Bob)
Offensive Tackle—Indianapolis Colts
Born December 24, 1962, at Sandusky, O.
Height, 6.05. Weight, 293.
High School—Sandusky, O., Saint Mary's Central Catholic.
Received bachelor of science degree in marketing from Syracuse University in 1986.

Selected by New Jersey in 1986 USFL territorial draft.
Selected by Indianapolis in 9th round (228th player selected) of 1986 NFL draft.
Signed by Indianapolis Colts, July 17, 1986.
On injured reserve with back injury, August 30 through November 6, 1986; activated, November 7, 1986.
Indianapolis NFL, 1986 and 1987.
Games: 1986 (2), 1987 (11). Total—13.

WALTER CRAIG BROUGHTON
Wide Receiver—Buffalo Bills
Born October 20, 1962, at Brewton, Ala.
Height, 5.10. Weight, 180.
High School—Brewton, Ala., T.R. Miller.
Attended Jacksonville State University.

Selected by Michigan in 2nd round (35th player selected) of 1984 USFL draft.
Signed by Michigan Panthers, February 6, 1984.

Not protected in merger of Michigan Panthers and Oakland Invaders; selected by Houston Gamblers in USFL dispersal draft, December 6, 1984.

Released by Houston Gamblers, February 18, 1985; awarded on waivers to New Jersey Generals, February 19, 1985.

On developmental squad, February 21 through March 18, 1985; activated, March 19, 1985.

Released by New Jersey Generals, July 31, 1985; awarded on waivers to Baltimore Stars, August 1, 1985.

Released by Baltimore Stars, August 2, 1985; signed as free agent by Buffalo Bills, May 10, 1986.

On injured reserve with thigh injury, November 7 through remainder of 1986 season.

On developmental squad for 2 games with New Jersey Generals in 1985.

		PASS RECEIVING				—PUNT RETURNS—				—KICKOFF RET.—				—TOTAL—		
Year Club	G.	P.C.	Yds.	Avg.	TD.	No.	Yds.	Avg.	TD.	No.	Yds.	Avg.	TD.	TD.	Pts.	F.
1984—Michigan USFL............	18	35	593	16.9	5	16	110	6.9	0	11	220	20.0	0	5	30	2
1985—New Jersey USFL.......	15	21	359	17.1	3		None			1	0	0.0	0	3	18	1
1986—Buffalo NFL.................	8	3	71	23.7	0	12	53	4.4	0	11	243	22.1	0	0	0	5
1987—Buffalo NFL.................	9	5	90	18.0	1		None				None			1	6	0
USFL Totals—2 Years....	33	56	952	17.0	8	16	110	6.9	0	12	220	18.3	0	8	48	3
NFL Totals—2 Years.....	17	8	161	20.1	1	12	53	4.4	0	11	243	22.1	0	1	6	5
Pro Totals—4 Years.......	50	64	1113	17.4	9	28	163	5.8	0	23	463	20.1	0	9	54	8

Additional USFL statistics: Recovered one fumble, 1984; recovered one fumble for five yards, 1985.
Additional NFL statistics: Rushed once for minus six yards and recovered one fumble, 1986.

WILLIE LEE BROUGHTON
Nose Tackle—Indianapolis Colts
Born September 9, 1964, at Fort Pierce, Fla.
Height, 6.05. Weight, 281.
High School—Fort Pierce, Fla., Central.
Attended University of Miami (Fla.).
Brother of Dock Luckie, nose tackle with Winnipeg Blue Bombers, 1981.

Selected by Orlando in 1985 USFL territorial draft.
Selected by Indianapolis in 4th round (88th player selected) of 1985 NFL draft.
Signed by Indianapolis Colts, August 9, 1985.
On injured reserve with knee injury, August 5 through entire 1987 season.
Crossed picket line during players' strike, September 29, 1987.
Indianapolis NFL, 1985 and 1986.
Games: 1985 (15), 1986 (15). Total—30.
Pro statistics: Recovered one fumble, 1986.

ARNOLD LEE BROWN
Cornerback—Denver Broncos
Born August 27, 1962, at Wilmington, N.C.
Height, 5.11. Weight, 185.
High School—Wilmington, N.C., E.A. Laney.
Attended North Carolina Central University.

Selected by Oakland in 8th round (108th player selected) of 1985 USFL draft.
Selected by Seattle in 5th round (128th player selected) of 1985 NFL draft.
Signed by Seattle Seahawks, July 21, 1985.
Released by Seattle Seahawks, August 27, 1985; signed as free agent by Detroit Lions, September 10, 1985.
On injured reserve with fractured elbow, November 2 through remainder of 1985 season.
On injured reserve with groin injury, August 22 through entire 1986 season.
Released by Detroit Lions, August 26, 1987; signed as free agent replacement player by Seattle Seahawks, October 9, 1987.
Released by Seattle Seahawks, October 20, 1987; signed as free agent by Denver Broncos, March 28, 1988.
Detroit NFL, 1985; Seattle NFL, 1987.
Games: 1985 (7), 1987 (2). Total—9.
Pro statistics: Recovered one fumble, 1987.

CEDRICK BROWN
Cornerback—Philadelphia Eagles
Born September 6, 1964, at Compton, Calif.
Height, 5.10. Weight, 182.
High School—Compton, Calif.
Attended Washington State University.

Signed as free agent by Philadelphia Eagles, May 7, 1986.
On injured reserve with hamstring injury, August 19 through entire 1986 season.
Philadelphia NFL, 1987.
Games: 1987 (12).
Pro statistics: Intercepted one pass for nine yards, returned one kickoff for 13 yards and returned one punt for minus one yard, 1987.

CHARLES LEE BROWN
(Bud)
Safety—Miami Dolphins
Born April 19, 1961, at DeKalb, Miss.
Height, 6.00. Weight, 194.
High School—DeKalb, Miss., West Kemper.
Attended University of Southern Mississippi.

Selected by New Orleans in 1984 USFL territorial draft.
Selected by Miami in 11th round (305th player selected) of 1984 NFL draft.
Signed by Miami Dolphins, June 26, 1984.
Released by Miami Dolphins, August 27, 1984; re-signed by Dolphins, August 28, 1984.

		—INTERCEPTIONS—			
Year Club	G.	No.	Yds.	Avg.	TD.
1984—Miami NFL	16	1	53	53.0	0
1985—Miami NFL	16	2	40	20.0	0
1986—Miami NFL	16	1	3	3.0	0
1987—Miami NFL	9	1	0	0.0	0
Pro Totals—4 Years	57	5	96	19.2	0

Additional pro statistics: Recovered five fumbles for six yards, 1985; recovered two fumbles for six yards, 1986; fumbled once, 1986 and 1987; returned two punts for eight yards and recovered one fumble, 1987.
Played in AFC Championship Game following 1984 and 1985 seasons.
Played in NFL Championship Game following 1984 season.

CHARLIE BROWN
Wide Receiver—Indianapolis Colts
Born October 29, 1958, at Charleston, S.C.
Height, 5.10. Weight, 184.
High School—St. John's Island, S.C.
Received bachelor's degree in physical education from South Carolina State College.
Related to Marion Brown, wide receiver with New Orleans-Portland Breakers, 1984 and 1985.

Selected by Washington in 8th round (201st player selected) of 1981 NFL draft.
On injured reserve with knee injury, September 1 through entire 1981 season.
On injured reserve with stress fracture in leg, October 23 through November 23, 1984; activated, November 24, 1984.
Traded by Washington Redskins to Atlanta Falcons for guard R.C. Thielemann, August 26, 1985.
Granted free agency, February 1, 1987; re-signed by Falcons, September 21, 1987.
Granted free agency, February 1, 1988; re-signed by Falcons and traded to Indianapolis Colts for conditional 12th round pick in 1989 draft, April 27, 1988.

		—PASS RECEIVING—			
Year Club	G.	P.C.	Yds.	Avg.	TD.
1982—Washington NFL	9	32	690	*21.6	8
1983—Washington NFL	15	78	1225	15.7	8
1984—Washington NFL	9	18	200	11.1	3
1985—Atlanta NFL	13	24	412	17.2	2
1986—Atlanta NFL	16	63	918	14.6	4
1987—Atlanta NFL	6	5	103	20.6	0
Pro Totals—6 Years	68	220	3548	16.1	25

Additional pro statistics: Recovered one fumble, 1982 and 1983; fumbled once, 1982 and 1986; rushed four times for 53 yards, 1983.
Played in NFC Championship Game following 1982 and 1983 seasons.
Played in NFL Championship Game following 1982 and 1983 seasons.
Played in Pro Bowl (NFL All-Star Game) following 1982 and 1983 seasons.

CLIFTON D. BROWN
(Sonny)
Safety—Houston Oilers
Born November 12, 1963, at Tinker AFB, Okla.
Height, 6.02. Weight, 200.
High School—Alice, Tex.
Attended University of Oklahoma.

Signed as free agent by Houston Oilers, May 21, 1987.
Released by Houston Oilers, November 7, 1987; re-signed by Oilers, May 18, 1988.
Houston NFL, 1987.
Games: 1987 (2).

DAVID STEVEN BROWN
(Dave)
Defensive Back—Green Bay Packers
Born January 16, 1953, at Akron, O.
Height, 6.01. Weight, 195.
High School—Akron, O., Garfield.
Received bachelor of arts degree in speech from University of Michigan.

Tied NFL record for most touchdowns scored by interception, game (2), vs. Kansas City Chiefs, November 4, 1984.
Named as safety on THE SPORTING NEWS College All-America Team, 1974.
Selected by Pittsburgh in 1st round (26th player selected) of 1975 NFL draft.
Selected from Pittsburgh Steelers by Seattle Seahawks in NFL expansion draft, March 30, 1976.
Granted free agency, February 1, 1985; re-signed by Seahawks, August 19, 1985.
Granted roster exemption, August 19 through August 29, 1985; activated, August 30, 1985.
Traded by Seattle Seahawks to Green Bay Packers for 11th round pick in 1988 draft, August 26, 1987.

		—INTERCEPTIONS—				—PUNT RETURNS—				—TOTAL—		
Year Club	G.	No.	Yds.	Avg.	TD.	No.	Yds.	Avg.	TD.	TD.	Pts.	F.
1975—Pittsburgh NFL	13	None				22	217	9.9	0	0	0	1

Year Club	G.	INTERCEPTIONS				PUNT RETURNS				TOTAL		
		No.	Yds.	Avg.	TD.	No.	Yds.	Avg.	TD.	TD.	Pts.	F.
1976—Seattle NFL	14	4	70	17.5	0	13	74	5.6	0	0	2	0
1977—Seattle NFL	14	4	68	17.0	1		None			1	6	0
1978—Seattle NFL	16	3	44	14.7	0		None			0	0	0
1979—Seattle NFL	16	5	46	9.2	0		None			0	0	0
1980—Seattle NFL	16	6	32	5.3	0		None			0	0	0
1981—Seattle NFL	10	2	2	1.0	0		None			0	0	0
1982—Seattle NFL	9	1	3	3.0	0		None			0	0	0
1983—Seattle NFL	16	6	83	13.8	0		None			0	0	1
1984—Seattle NFL	16	8	179	22.4	*2		None			2	12	0
1985—Seattle NFL	16	6	58	9.7	*1		None			1	6	0
1986—Seattle NFL	16	5	58	11.6	1		None			1	6	0
1987—Green Bay NFL	12	3	16	5.3	0		None			0	0	0
Pro Totals—13 Years	184	53	659	12.4	5	35	291	8.3	0	4	26	2

Additional pro statistics: Returned six kickoffs for 126 yards, 1975; scored one safety, 1976; recovered one fumble for eight yards, 1981; recovered two fumbles for 15 yards, 1982; recovered three fumbles, 1983; recovered one fumble, 1984 through 1986.

Played in AFC Championship Game following 1975 and 1983 seasons.

Played in NFL Championship Game following 1975 season.

Played in Pro Bowl (NFL All-Star Game) following 1984 season.

DONALD BROWN
Cornerback—New York Giants
Born November 28, 1963, at Annapolis, Md.
Height, 5.11. Weight, 189.
High School—Annapolis, Md.
Attended University of Oklahoma and University of Maryland.

Selected by Baltimore in 1986 USFL territorial draft.
Selected by San Diego in 5th round (129th player selected) of 1986 NFL draft.
Signed by San Diego Chargers, July 21, 1986.
Released by San Diego Chargers, December 2, 1986; signed as free agent by Miami Dolphins, December 9, 1986.
Released by Miami Dolphins, August 18, 1987; signed as free agent by Los Angeles Raiders, August 20, 1987.
Released by Los Angeles Raiders, August 27, 1987; signed as free agent replacement player by New York Giants, October 2, 1987.
Released by New York Giants, October 19, 1987; re-signed by Giants, December 23, 1987.
San Diego (13)-Miami (2) NFL, 1986; New York Giants NFL, 1987.
Games: 1986 (15), 1987 (3). Total—18.
Pro statistics: Intercepted one pass for 23 yards and recovered two fumbles, 1986; intercepted one pass for four yards and recovered one fumble, 1987.

EDDIE LEE BROWN
Wide Receiver—Cincinnati Bengals
Born December 17, 1962, at Miami, Fla.
Height, 6.00. Weight, 185.
High School—Miami, Fla., Senior.
Attended Navarro College and University of Miami (Fla.).

Named THE SPORTING NEWS NFL Rookie of the Year, 1985.
Selected by Orlando in 1985 USFL territorial draft.
Selected by Cincinnati in 1st round (13th player selected) of 1985 NFL draft.
Signed by Cincinnati Bengals, August 7, 1985.

Year Club	G.	RUSHING				PASS RECEIVING				TOTAL		
		Att.	Yds.	Avg.	TD.	P.C.	Yds.	Avg.	TD.	TD.	Pts.	F.
1985—Cincinnati NFL	16	14	129	9.2	0	53	942	17.8	8	8	48	2
1986—Cincinnati NFL	16	8	32	4.0	0	58	964	16.6	4	4	24	0
1987—Cincinnati NFL	12	1	0	0.0	0	44	608	13.8	3	3	18	3
Pro Totals—3 Years	44	23	161	7.0	0	155	2514	16.2	15	15	90	5

Additional pro statistics: Returned one kickoff for six yards, 1985; recovered one fumble, 1985 and 1987; recovered two fumbles, 1986.

GREGORY LEE BROWN
(Greg)
Defensive End—Atlanta Falcons
Born January 5, 1957, at Washington, D.C.
Height, 6.05. Weight, 265.
High School—Washington, D.C., Woodson.
Attended Kansas State University and Eastern Illinois University.

Signed as free agent by Philadelphia Eagles, May 16, 1981.
Traded by Philadelphia Eagles to Atlanta Falcons for defensive end Mike Pitts, September 7, 1987.
Philadelphia NFL, 1981 through 1986; Atlanta NFL, 1987.
Games: 1981 (16), 1982 (9), 1983 (16), 1984 (16), 1985 (16), 1986 (16), 1987 (12). Total—101.
Pro statistics: Recovered two fumbles for seven yards and one touchdown, 1981; recovered two fumbles, one for a touchdown, 1982; recovered one fumble, 1984, recovered two fumbles, 1985; credited with a safety, 1986.

JEROME BROWN
Defensive Tackle—Philadelphia Eagles
Born February 4, 1965, at Brooksville, Fla.
Height, 6.02. Weight, 288.
High School—Brooksville, Fla., Hernando.
Attended University of Miami (Fla.).
Cousin of Maulty Moore, offensive tackle with Miami Dolphins,
Cincinnati Bengals and Tampa Bay Buccaneers, 1972 through 1976.

Named as defensive lineman on THE SPORTING NEWS College All-America Team, 1986.
Selected by Philadelphia in 1st round (9th player selected) of 1987 NFL draft.
Signed by Philadelphia Eagles, August 21, 1987.
Philadelphia NFL, 1987.
Games: 1987 (12).
Pro statistics: Intercepted two passes for seven yards and recovered one fumble for 37 yards, 1987.

LEONARD RAY BROWN JR.
(Known by middle name.)
Guard-Offensive Tackle—Phoenix Cardinals
Born December 12, 1962, at West Memphis, Ark.
Height, 6.05. Weight, 280.
High School—Marion, Ark.
Attended Memphis State University, Arizona State University
and Arkansas State University.

Selected by St. Louis in 8th round (201st player selected) of 1986 NFL draft.
Signed by St. Louis Cardinals, July 14, 1986.
On injured reserve with knee injury, October 17 through November 20, 1986; activated, November 21, 1986.
Released by St. Louis Cardinals, September 7, 1987; re-signed as free agent replacement player by Cardinals, September 25, 1987.
On injured reserve with disclosed finger, November 12 through December 11, 1987; activated, December 12, 1987.
Franchise transferred to Phoenix, March 15, 1988.
St. Louis NFL, 1986 and 1987.
Games: 1986 (11), 1987 (7). Total—18.

LOMAS BROWN JR.
Offensive Tackle—Detroit Lions
Born March 30, 1963, at Miami, Fla.
Height, 6.04. Weight, 282.
High School—Miami Springs, Fla.
Attended University of Florida.
Cousin of Joe Taylor, defensive back with Chicago Bears, 1967 through 1974;
and Guy McIntyre, guard with San Francisco 49ers.

Named as tackle on THE SPORTING NEWS College All-America Team, 1984.
Selected by Orlando in 2nd round (18th player selected) of 1985 USFL draft.
Selected by Detroit in 1st round (6th player selected) of 1985 NFL draft.
Signed by Detroit Lions, August 9, 1985.
Detroit NFL, 1985 through 1987.
Games: 1985 (16), 1986 (16), 1987 (11). Total—43.

MARK ANTHONY BROWN
Linebacker—Miami Dolphins
Born July 18, 1961, at New Brunswick, N.J.
Height, 6.02. Weight, 235.
High School—Inglewood, Calif.
Attended Los Angeles Southwest Community College and Purdue University.

Selected by Boston in 10th round (115th player selected) of 1983 USFL draft.
Selected by Miami in 9th round (250th player selected) of 1983 NFL draft.
Signed by Miami Dolphins, June 15, 1983.
Miami NFL, 1983 through 1987.
Games: 1983 (14), 1984 (16), 1985 (15), 1986 (14), 1987 (12). Total—71.
Pro statistics: Intercepted one pass for no yards, returned one kickoff for no yards and recovered one fumble, 1983; intercepted one pass for five yards and recovered two fumbles, 1985; recovered four fumbles for 11 yards, 1986; recovered one fumble for one yard, 1987.
Played in AFC Championship Game following 1984 and 1985 seasons.
Played in NFL Championship Game following 1984 season.

RICHARD SOLOMON BROWN
Linebacker—Los Angeles Rams
Born September 21, 1965, at Western Samoa.
Height, 6.03. Weight, 240.
High School—Westminster, Calif.
Attended San Diego State University.

Signed as free agent by Los Angeles Rams, May 14, 1987.
On injured reserve with hamstring injury, August 31 through November 2, 1987; activated, November 3, 1987.
Los Angeles Rams NFL, 1987.
Games: 1987 (8).

ROBERT LEE BROWN
Defensive End—Green Bay Packers
Born May 21, 1960, at Edenton, N.C.
Height, 6.02. Weight, 267.
High School—Edenton, N.C., John A. Holmes.
Attended Chowan Junior College and Virginia Polytechnic Institute and State University.
Selected by Green Bay in 4th round (98th player selected) of 1982 NFL draft.
On inactive list, September 20, 1982.
Green Bay NFL, 1982 through 1987.
Games: 1982 (8), 1983 (16), 1984 (16), 1985 (16), 1986 (16), 1987 (12). Total—84.
Pro statistics: Recovered one fumble, 1982 and 1986; intercepted one pass for five yards and a touchdown, 1984; credited with one safety, 1985; recovered four fumbles, 1985 and 1987.

RONALD WILLIAM BROWN
(Ron)
Wide Receiver—Phoenix Cardinals
Born January 11, 1963, at Long Island, N. Y.
Height, 5.10. Weight, 186.
High School—Pasadena, Calif., John Muir.
Attended Colorado University and Pasadena City College.
Selected by New York Giants in 6th round (139th player selected) of 1986 NFL draft.
Selected by New Jersey in 6th round (40th player selected) of 1986 USFL draft.
Signed by New York Giants, July 16, 1986.
Released by New York Giants, August 21, 1986; signed as free agent by Saskatchewan Roughriders, September 16, 1986.
Released by Saskatchewan Roughriders, June 19, 1987; signed as free agent by St. Louis Cardinals, July 16, 1987.
Released by St. Louis Cardinals, August 17, 1987; awarded on waivers to New Orleans Saints, August 18, 1987.
Released by New Orleans Saints, September 7, 1987; signed as free agent replacement player by St. Louis Cardinals, September 25, 1987.
Franchise transferred to Phoenix, March 15, 1988.

		—PASS RECEIVING—			
Year Club	G.	P.C.	Yds.	Avg.	TD.
1986—Saskatchewan CFL......	4	7	121	17.3	1
1987—St. Louis NFL.................	7	2	16	8.0	0
Pro Totals—2 Years............	11	9	137	15.2	1

Additional CFL statistics: Returned one kickoff for 25 yards, 1986.
Additional NFL statistics: Returned one kickoff for 40 yards and rushed once for nine yards, 1987.

STEVE BROWN
Cornerback—Houston Oilers
Born March 20, 1960, at Sacramento, Calif.
Height, 5.11. Weight, 188.
High School—Sacramento, Calif., C.K. McClatchy.
Attended University of Oregon.
Selected by Arizona in 7th round (74th player selected) of 1983 USFL draft.
Selected by Houston in 3rd round (83rd player selected) of 1983 NFL draft.
Signed by Houston Oilers, June 28, 1983.

		-INTERCEPTIONS-				—KICKOFF RET.—				—TOTAL—		
Year Club	G.	No.	Yds.	Avg.	TD.	No.	Yds.	Avg.	TD.	TD.	Pts.	F.
1983—Houston NFL..	16	1	16	16.0	0	31	795	25.6	★1	1	6	2
1984—Houston NFL..	16	1	26	26.0	0	3	17	5.7	0	0	0	1
1985—Houston NFL..	15	5	41	8.2	0	2	45	22.5	0	0	0	1
1986—Houston NFL..	16	2	34	17.0	0		None			0	0	0
1987—Houston NFL..	10	2	45	22.5	0		None			0	0	1
Pro Totals—5 Years.................	73	11	162	14.7	0	36	857	23.8	1	1	6	5

Additional pro statistics: Recovered one fumble, 1984, 1985 and 1987.

THOMAS MARTIN BROWN
(Tom)
Fullback—Miami Dolphins
Born November 20, 1964, at Ridgway, Pa.
Height, 6.01. Weight, 218.
High School—Lower Burrell, Pa., Burrell.
Attended University of Pittsburgh.
Selected by Miami in 7th round (182nd player selected) of 1987 NFL draft.
Signed by Miami Dolphins, July 22, 1987.
On injured reserve with ankle injury, September 8 through October 30, 1987; activated, October 31, 1987.
On injured reserve with knee injury, November 3 through remainder of 1987 season.
Miami NFL, 1987.
Games: 1987 (1).
Pro statistics: Rushed three times for three yards and caught one pass for six yards, 1987.

JOEY MATTHEW BROWNER
Safety—Minnesota Vikings

Born May 15, 1960, at Warren, O.
Height, 6.02. Weight, 212.
High Schools—Warren, O., Western Reserve; and Atlanta, Ga., Southwest.
Attended University of Southern California.
Brother of Ross Browner, defensive end with Green Bay Packers;
brother of Jim Browner, defensive back with Cincinnati Bengals,
1979 and 1980; and Keith Browner, linebacker with San Diego Chargers.

Named to THE SPORTING NEWS NFL All-Star Team, 1987.
Selected by Los Angeles in 1983 USFL territorial draft.
Selected by Minnesota in 1st round (19th player selected) of 1983 NFL draft.
Signed by Minnesota Vikings, April 30, 1983.

| | | —INTERCEPTIONS— | | | |
Year Club	G.	No.	Yds.	Avg.	TD.
1983—Minnesota NFL............	16	2	0	0.0	0
1984—Minnesota NFL............	16	1	20	20.0	0
1985—Minnesota NFL............	16	2	17	8.5	*1
1986—Minnesota NFL............	16	4	62	15.5	1
1987—Minnesota NFL............	12	6	67	11.2	0
Pro Totals—5 Years............	76	15	166	11.1	2

Additional pro statistics: Recovered four fumbles for four yards, 1983; fumbled once, 1983 and 1985; recovered three fumbles for 63 yards and a touchdown, 1984; returned one kickoff for no yards and recovered three fumbles for five yards, 1985; recovered four fumbles, 1986; recovered one fumble, 1987.
Played in NFC Championship Game following 1987 season.
Played in Pro Bowl (NFL All-Star Game) following 1985 through 1987 seasons.

KEITH TELLUS BROWNER
Linebacker—San Diego Chargers

Born January 24, 1962, at Warren, O.
Height, 6.06. Weight, 245.
High School—Atlanta, Ga., Southwest.
Attended University of Southern California.
Brother of Ross Browner, defensive end with Cincinnati Bengals; Jim Browner, defensive back
with Cincinnati Bengals, 1979 and 1980; and Joey Browner, safety with Minnesota Vikings.

Selected by Los Angeles in 1984 USFL territorial draft.
Selected by Tampa Bay in 2nd round (30th player selected) of 1984 NFL draft.
Signed by Tampa Bay Buccaneers, May 30, 1984.
Placed on suspended list, December 13 through December 16, 1986; reinstated, December 17, 1986.
Traded by Tampa Bay Buccaneers to San Francisco 49ers for 6th round pick in 1988 draft, February 27, 1987.
Released by San Francisco 49ers, September 7, 1987; re-signed as replacement player by 49ers, September 24, 1987.
Traded by San Francisco 49ers to Los Angeles Raiders for cash, October 7, 1987.
On injured reserve with ankle injury, October 19 through November 2, 1987.
Released by Los Angeles Raiders, November 3, 1987; release voided due to injured status and placed on injured reserve with ankle injury, November 9 through November 23, 1987.
Released by Los Angeles Raiders, November 24, 1987; signed as free agent by San Diego Chargers, April 13, 1988.
Tampa Bay NFL, 1984 through 1986; San Francisco (1)-Los Angeles Raiders (1) NFL, 1987.
Games: 1984 (16), 1985 (16), 1986 (15), 1987 (2). Total—49.
Pro statistics: Recovered one fumble, 1984 and 1985; intercepted one pass for 25 yards and fumbled once, 1985; intercepted one pass for 16 yards and recovered two fumbles, 1986.

ROSS BROWNER
Defensive End—Green Bay Packers

Born March 22, 1954, at Warren, O.
Height, 6.03. Weight, 265.
High School—Warren, O., Western Reserve.
Received bachelor of arts degree in economics from University of Notre Dame in 1978.
Brother of Jim Browner, defensive back with Cincinnati Bengals, 1979 and 1980; Keith Browner,
linebacker with San Diego Chargers; and Joey Browner, safety with Minnesota Vikings.

Outland Trophy winner, 1976.
Named defensive end on THE SPORTING NEWS College All-America Team, 1976 and 1977.
Selected by Cincinnati in 1st round (8th player selected) of 1978 NFL draft.
On suspended list for violating league drug policy, July 25 through September 25, 1983; reinstated, September 26, 1983.
Granted roster exemption, September 26, 1983; activated September 27, 1983.
Granted free agency, February 1, 1985; signed by Houston Gamblers, May 24, 1985.
Released by Houston Gamblers, July 23, 1985; re-signed by Bengals, August 27, 1985.
Granted roster exemption, August 27 through August 29, 1985; activated, August 30, 1985.
Released by Cincinnati Bengals, September 9, 1987; signed as free agent by Green Bay Packers, September 11, 1987.
Cincinnati NFL, 1978 through 1986; Houston USFL, 1985; Green Bay NFL, 1987.
Games: 1978 (11), 1979 (16), 1980 (15), 1981 (16), 1982 (9), 1983 (12), 1984 (16), 1985 USFL (5), 1985 NFL (16), 1986 (16), 1987 (11). Total NFL—138. Total Pro—143.
NFL statistics: Recovered three fumbles for 21 yards, 1978; returned two kickoff for 29 yards, 1979; recovered one fumble, 1979 through 1984 and 1986; intercepted one pass for 29 yards, 1982; credited with one extra point, 1983; recovered two fumbles and credited with one safety, 1985.
USFL statistics: Credited with ½ sack for 5½ yards, 1985.
Played in AFC Championship Game following 1981 season.
Played in NFL Championship Game following 1981 season.

ROBERT LOUIS BRUDZINSKI
(Bob)
Linebacker—Miami Dolphins
Born January 1, 1955, at Fremont, O.
Height, 6.04. Weight, 223.
High School—Fremont, O., Ross.
Received bachelor of science degree in business (marketing) from Ohio State University in 1977.

Named as linebacker on THE SPORTING NEWS College All-America Team, 1976.
Selected by Los Angeles in 1st round (23rd player selected) of 1977 NFL draft.
Granted roster exemption when left camp, September 2, 1980; reinstated, September 6, 1980.
Left camp, November 5, 1980; granted roster exemption, November 6, 1980.
On retired-reserve list, November 12 through remainder of 1980 season.
Traded with 2nd round pick in 1981 draft by Los Angeles Rams to Miami Dolphins for 2nd and 3rd round picks in 1981 draft and 2nd round pick in 1982 draft, April 28, 1981.
Granted free agency, February 1, 1985; re-signed by Dolphins, September 21, 1985.

		—INTERCEPTIONS—					—INTERCEPTIONS—			
Year Club	G.	No.	Yds.	Avg.TD.	Year Club	G.	No.	Yds.	Avg.TD.
1977—Los Angeles NFL........	14	2	24	12.0	0	1983—Miami NFL...................	16	None			
1978—Los Angeles NFL.........	16	1	31	31.0	1	1984—Miami NFL...................	16	1	0	0.0	0
1979—Los Angeles NFL.........	16	1	26	26.0	0	1985—Miami NFL...................	14	1	6	6.0	0
1980—Los Angeles NFL.........	9	None			1986—Miami NFL...................	16	None			
1981—Miami NFL...................	16	2	35	17.5	0	1987—Miami NFL...................	12	None			
1982—Miami NFL...................	9	1	5	5.0	0	Pro Totals—11 Years.......... 154	9	127	14.1	1	

Additional pro statistics: Recovered one fumble for three yards, 1979; recovered one fumble, 1982, 1983 and 1986; recovered two fumbles for seven yards and a touchdown, 1985.
Played in NFC Championship Game following 1978 and 1979 seasons.
Played in AFC Championship Game following 1982, 1984 and 1985 seasons.
Played in NFL Championship Game following 1979, 1982 and 1984 seasons.

RICK DON BRYAN
Defensive End—Atlanta Falcons
Born March 20, 1962, at Tulsa, Okla.
Height, 6.04. Weight, 265.
High School—Coweta, Okla.
Attended University of Oklahoma.
Brother of Steve Bryan, defensive lineman with Denver Broncos.

Named as defensive lineman on THE SPORTING NEWS College All-America Team, 1983.
Selected by Oklahoma in 1984 USFL territorial draft.
Selected by Atlanta in 1st round (9th player selected) of 1984 NFL draft.
Signed by Atlanta Falcons, July 20, 1984.
Atlanta NFL, 1984 through 1987.
Games: 1984 (16), 1985 (16), 1986 (16), 1987 (9). Total—57.
Pro statistics: Credited with one safety, 1984; caught extra point and ran four yards with lateral on fumble recovery, 1985; recovered one fumble, 1987.

STEVE RAY BRYAN
Defensive Lineman—Denver Broncos
Born May 6, 1964, at Wagoner, Okla.
Height, 6.02. Weight, 256.
High School—Coweta, Okla.
Received bachelor of arts degree in communications from
University of Oklahoma in 1987.
Brother of Rick Bryan, defensive end with Atlanta Falcons.

Selected by Chicago in 5th round (120th player selected) of 1987 NFL draft.
Signed by Chicago Bears, July 31, 1987.
Released by Chicago Bears, September 7, 1987; signed as free agent replacement player by Denver Broncos, September 25, 1987.
Denver NFL, 1987.
Games: 1987 (4).
Played in AFC Championship Game following 1987 season.
Member of Denver Broncos for NFL Championship Game following 1987 season; inactive.

WILLIAM KIRBY BRYAN
(Bill)
Center—Denver Broncos
Born June 21, 1955, at Burlington, N. C.
Height, 6.02. Weight, 258.
High School—Burlington, N. C., Walter Williams.
Received bachelor of arts degree in economics from Duke University in 1977.

Selected by Denver in 4th round (101st player selected) of 1977 NFL draft.
On injured reserve, October 3 through remainder of 1977 season.
Crossed picket line during players' strike, October 1, 1987.
On injured reserve with knee injury, October 20 through remainder of 1987 season.
Denver NFL, 1978 through 1987.
Games: 1978 (13), 1979 (16), 1980 (16), 1981 (14), 1982 (9), 1983 (16), 1984 (16), 1985 (16), 1986 (16), 1987 (4).
Total—136.

Pro statistics: Recovered two fumbles, 1979; recovered one fumble, 1980, 1985 and 1987; fumbled twice for minus 20 yards, 1980; fumbled once, 1981 and 1984.
Played in AFC Championship Game following 1986 season.
Played in NFL Championship Game following 1986 season.

DOMINGO GARCIA BRYANT
Safety—Houston Oilers
Born December 8, 1963, at Nacagdoches, Tex.
Height, 6.04. Weight, 175.
High School—Garrison, Tex.
Attended Texas A&M University.

Selected by Jacksonville in 1986 USFL territorial draft.
Selected by Pittsburgh in 6th round (148th player selected) of 1986 NFL draft.
Signed by Pittsburgh Steelers, July 10, 1986.
On injured reserve with broken finger, August 19 through September 3, 1986.
Released by Pittsburgh Steelers, September 4, 1986; signed as free agent by Houston Oilers for 1987, November 13, 1986.
Released by Houston Oilers, September 1, 1987; re-signed as replacement player by Oilers, September 23, 1987.

		——INTERCEPTIONS——			
Year Club	G.	No.	Yds.	Avg.	TD.
1987—Houston NFL	13	4	75	18.8	0

Additional pro statistics: Recovered one fumble, 1987.

JEFF DWIGHT BRYANT
Defensive End—Seattle Seahawks
Born May 22, 1960, at Atlanta, Ga.
Height, 6.05. Weight, 270.
High School—Decatur, Ga., Gordon.
Attended Clemson University.

Selected by Seattle in 1st round (6th player selected) of 1982 NFL draft.
On injured reserve with ankle injury, November 14 through December 12, 1986; activated, December 13, 1986.
Seattle NFL, 1982 through 1987.
Games: 1982 (9), 1983 (16), 1984 (16), 1985 (16), 1986 (12), 1987 (12). Total—81.
Pro statistics: Recovered one fumble, 1983 and 1987; intercepted one pass for one yard, credited with one safety and recovered two fumbles, 1984; recovered four fumbles, 1985.
Played in AFC Championship Game following 1983 season.

KELVIN LeROY BRYANT
Running Back—Washington Redskins
Born September 26, 1960, at Tarboro, N.C.
Height, 6.02. Weight, 195.
High School—Tarboro, N.C.
Attended University of North Carolina.

Named as running back on THE SPORTING NEWS USFL All-Star Team, 1983 and 1984.
Selected by Philadelphia in 1983 USFL territorial draft.
Signed by Philadelphia Stars, February 8, 1983.
Selected by Washington in 7th round (196th player selected) of 1983 NFL draft.
On developmental squad, July 1 through July 4, 1983; activated, July 5, 1983.
On developmental squad, April 8 through April 25, 1984; activated, April 26, 1984.
Franchise transferred to Baltimore, November 1, 1984.
On developmental squad, March 31 through April 12, 1985; activated, April 13, 1985.
Granted free agency when USFL suspended operations, August 7, 1986; signed by Washington Redskins, August 13, 1986.
Granted roster exemption, August 13 through August 22, 1986; activated, August 23, 1986.
On injured reserve with knee and ankle injuries, September 16 through October 31, 1986; activated, November 1, 1986.
On developmental squad for 1 game with Philadelphia Stars in 1983.
On developmental squad for 3 games with Philadelphia Stars in 1984.
On developmental squad for 2 games with Baltimore Stars in 1985.

		——RUSHING——				PASS RECEIVING				—TOTAL—		
Year Club	G.	Att.	Yds.	Avg.	TD.	P.C.	Yds.	Avg.	TD.	TD.	Pts.	F.
1983—Philadelphia USFL	17	318	1442	4.5	16	53	410	7.7	1	17	102	4
1984—Philadelphia USFL	15	*297	1406	4.7	13	48	453	9.4	1	15	90	8
1985—Baltimore USFL	15	238	1207	5.1	12	40	407	10.2	4	16	96	3
1986—Washington NFL	10	69	258	3.7	4	43	449	10.4	3	7	42	2
1987—Washington NFL	11	77	406	5.3	1	43	490	11.4	5	6	36	4
USFL Totals—3 Years	47	853	4055	4.8	41	141	1270	9.0	6	48	288	15
NFL Totals—2 Years	21	146	664	4.5	5	86	939	10.9	8	13	78	6
Pro Totals—5 Years	68	999	4719	4.7	46	227	2209	9.7	14	61	366	21

Additional USFL statistics: Recovered two fumbles, 1983; recovered three fumbles for 38 yards and a touchdown, 1984; recovered one fumble and attempted one pass with no completions, 1985.
Additional NFL statistics: Recovered one fumble, 1986 and 1987; attempted one pass with no completions, 1987.
Played in USFL Championship Game following 1983 through 1985 seasons.
Played in NFC Championship Game following 1986 and 1987 seasons.
Played in NFL Championship Game following 1987 season.

JASON OGDEN BUCK
Defensive End—Cincinnati Bengals
Born July 27, 1963, at Moses Lake, Wash.
Height, 6.05. Weight, 264.
High School—St. Anthony, Ida., South Fremont.
Attended Ricks College (Ida.) and Brigham Young University.
Named as defensive lineman on THE SPORTING NEWS College All-America Team, 1986.
Selected by Cincinnati in 1st round (17th player selected) of 1987 NFL draft.
Signed by Cincinnati Bengals, September 8, 1987.
Granted roster exemption, September 8, 1987.
Cincinnati NFL, 1987.
Games: 1987 (12).

JOHN ROBERT BUCZKOWSKI
(Bob)
Defensive End—Los Angeles Raiders
Born May 5, 1964, at Pittsburgh, Pa.
Height, 6.05. Weight, 260.
High School—Monroeville, Pa., Gateway.
Attended University of Pittsburgh.
Selected by Los Angeles Raiders in 1st round (24th player selected) of 1986 NFL draft.
Signed by Los Angeles Raiders, July 17, 1986.
On injured reserve with back injury, August 26 through entire 1986 season.
On non-football injury list with hepatitis, September 9 through October 13, 1987; activated, October 14, 1987.
Crossed picket line during player's strike, October 14, 1987.
On injured reserve with ankle injury, November 11 through December 11, 1987; activated, December 12, 1987.
Los Angeles Raiders NFL, 1987.
Games: 1987 (2).

BRAD EDWARD BUDDE
Name pronounced Buddy.
Guard—Los Angeles Raiders
Born May 9, 1958, at Detroit, Mich.
Height, 6.04. Weight, 271.
High School—Kansas City, Mo., Rockhurst.
Received bachelor of science degree in public administration from
University of Southern California.
Son of Ed Budde, guard with Kansas City Chiefs, 1963 through 1976;
and brother of John Budde, defensive end at Michigan State University.
Named as guard on THE SPORTING NEWS College All-America Team, 1979.
Selected by Kansas City in 1st round (11th player selected) of 1980 NFL draft.
On injured reserve with knee injury, November 23 through remainder of 1983 season.
On injured reserve with shoulder injury, November 8 through remainder of 1985 season.
On injured reserve with abdomen strain, September 7 through entire 1987 season.
Granted free agency with no qualifying offer, February 1, 1988; signed by Los Angeles Raiders, March 31, 1988.
Kansas City NFL, 1980 through 1986.
Games: 1980 (16), 1981 (16), 1982 (9), 1983 (12), 1984 (16), 1985 (7), 1986 (16). Total—92.
Pro statistics: Returned three kickoffs for 28 yards, 1980.

MAURY ANTHONY BUFORD
Punter—Denver Broncos
Born February 18, 1960, at Mount Pleasant, Tex.
Height, 6.01. Weight, 191.
High School—Mount Pleasant, Tex.
Received business degree from Texas Tech University in 1982.
Selected by San Diego in 8th round (215th player selected) of 1982 NFL draft.
Traded by San Diego Chargers to Chicago Bears for 12th round pick in 1986 draft, August 20, 1985.
Released by Chicago Bears, September 7, 1987; signed as free agent by Denver Broncos, April 28, 1988.

| | | —————PUNTING——— | | |
Year Club	G.	No.	Avg.	Blk.
1982—San Diego NFL	9	21	41.3	*2
1983—San Diego NFL	16	63	43.9	0
1984—San Diego NFL	16	66	42.0	0
1985—Chicago NFL	16	68	42.2	1
1986—Chicago NFL	16	69	41.3	1
Pro Totals—5 Years	73	287	42.2	4

Additional pro statistics: Attempted one pass with no completions, 1983; attempted one pass with one completion for five yards, 1985; rushed once for minus 13 yards and fumbled once, 1986.
Played in NFC Championship Game following 1985 season.
Played in NFL Championship Game following 1985 season.

CHRIS BURKETT
Wide Receiver—Buffalo Bills

Born August 21, 1962, at Laurel, Miss.
Height, 6.04. Weight, 210.
High School—Collins, Miss.
Attended Jackson State University.

Selected by Baltimore in 1st round (14th player selected) of 1985 USFL draft.
Selected by Buffalo in 2nd round (42nd player selected) of 1985 NFL draft.
Signed by Buffalo Bills, July 23, 1985.

			—PASS RECEIVING—		
Year Club	G.	P.C.	Yds.	Avg.	TD.
1985—Buffalo NFL..............	16	21	371	17.7	0
1986—Buffalo NFL..............	14	34	778	★22.9	4
1987—Buffalo NFL..............	12	56	765	13.7	4
Pro Totals—3 Years...........	42	111	1914	17.2	8

Additional pro statistics: Fumbled once, 1986 and 1987.

SHAWN SPENCER BURKS
Linebacker—New Orleans Saints

Born February 10, 1963, at Baton Rouge, La.
Height, 6.01. Weight, 230.
High School—Baton Rouge, La., Central.
Attended Louisiana State University.

Signed as free agent by Washington Redskins, May 6, 1986.
Released by Washington Redskins, November 8, 1986; re-signed by Redskins, November 12, 1986.
Released by Washington Redskins, August 31, 1987; signed as free agent by New Orleans Saints, March 8, 1988.
Washington NFL, 1986.
Games: 1986 (15).
Played in NFC Championship Game following 1986 season.

DERRICK D. BURROUGHS
Cornerback—Buffalo Bills

Born May 18, 1962, at Mobile, Ala.
Height, 6.01. Weight, 180.
High School—Prichard, Ala., M. T. Blount.
Attended Memphis State University.

Selected by Memphis in 1985 USFL territorial draft.
Selected by Buffalo in 1st round (14th player selected) of 1985 NFL draft.
Signed by Buffalo Bills, May 17, 1985.
On injured reserve with knee injury, December 17 through remainder of 1986 season.

			—INTERCEPTIONS—		
Year Club	G.	No.	Yds.	Avg.	TD.
1985—Buffalo NFL..............	14	2	7	3.5	0
1986—Buffalo NFL..............	15	2	49	24.5	0
1987—Buffalo NFL..............	12	2	11	5.5	0
Pro Totals—3 Years...........	41	6	67	11.2	0

Additional pro statistics: Recovered one fumble, 1987.

LLOYD EARL BURRUSS JR.
Safety—Kansas City Chiefs

Born October 31, 1957, at Charlottesville, Va.
Height, 6.00. Weight, 209.
High School—Charlottesville, Va.
Received bachelor of arts degree in general studies from University of Maryland in 1981.

Selected by Kansas City in 3rd round (78th player selected) of 1981 NFL draft.
On injured reserve with knee injury, December 23 through remainder of 1987 season.

			—INTERCEPTIONS—		
Year Club	G.	No.	Yds.	Avg.	TD.
1981—Kansas City NFL..........	14	4	75	18.8	1
1982—Kansas City NFL..........	9	1	25	25.0	0
1983—Kansas City NFL..........	12	4	46	11.5	0
1984—Kansas City NFL..........	16	2	16	8.0	0
1985—Kansas City NFL..........	15	1	0	0.0	0
1986—Kansas City NFL..........	15	5	★193	38.6	★3
1987—Kansas City NFL..........	11			None	
Pro Totals—7 Years...........	92	17	355	20.9	4

Additional pro statistics: Returned five kickoffs for 91 yards, recovered one fumble for four yards and fumbled once, 1981; recovered two fumbles for 26 yards, 1983; recovered one fumble, 1984 and 1986; returned blocked field goal 78 yards for a touchdown, 1986.
Played in Pro Bowl (NFL All-Star Game) following 1986 season.

TONY LEE BURSE
Fullback—Seattle Seahawks
Born April 4, 1965, at Lafayette, Ga.
Height, 6.00. Weight, 220.
High School—Lafayette, Ga.
Attended Middle Tennessee State University.

Selected by Seattle in 12th round (324th player selected) of 1987 NFL draft.
Signed by Seattle Seahawks, July 22, 1987.

Year Club	G.	RUSHING				PASS RECEIVING				—TOTAL—		
		Att.	Yds.	Avg.	TD.	P.C.	Yds.	Avg.	TD.	TD.	Pts.	F.
1987—Seattle NFL	12	7	36	5.1	0	None				0	0	1

Additional pro statistics: Returned one kickoff for one yard, 1987.

JAMES P. BURT
(Jim)
Nose Tackle—New York Giants
Born June 7, 1959, at Buffalo, N. Y.
Height, 6.01. Weight, 260.
High School—Orchard Park, N. Y.
Attended University of Miami (Fla.).

Signed as free agent by New York Giants, May 4, 1981.
On injured reserve with back injury, December 24 through remainder of 1982 season.
On injured reserve with back injury, November 2 through remainder of 1983 season.
On injured reserve with back injury, December 7 through remainder of 1987 season.
New York Giants NFL, 1981 through 1987.
Games: 1981 (13), 1982 (4), 1983 (7), 1984 (16), 1985 (16), 1986 (13), 1987 (8). Total—77.
Pro statistics: Recovered one fumble, 1983; recovered two fumbles, 1984 and 1985; recovered three fumbles for one yard, 1986.
Played in NFC Championship Game following 1986 season.
Played in NFL Championship Game following 1986 season.
Played in Pro Bowl (NFL All-Star Game) following 1986 season.

LEONARD BERNARD BURTON
Offensive Tackle—Buffalo Bills
Born June 18, 1964, at Memphis, Tenn.
Height, 6.03. Weight, 265.
High School—Memphis, Tenn., Oakhaven.
Attended Northwest Mississippi Junior College and University of South Carolina.

Selected by Jacksonville in 1986 USFL territorial draft.
Selected by Buffalo in 3rd round (77th player selected) of 1986 NFL draft.
USFL rights traded with rights to offensive tackle Doug Williams by Jacksonville Bulls to Memphis Showboats for rights to wide receiver Tim McGee, May 6, 1986.
Signed by Buffalo Bills, July 24, 1986.
On injured reserve with knee injury, December 17 through remainder of 1986 season.
Buffalo NFL, 1986 and 1987.
Games: 1986 (14), 1987 (12). Total—26.

RONALD LEON BURTON
(Ron)
Linebacker—Dallas Cowboys
Born May 2, 1964, at Richmond, Va.
Height, 6.01. Weight, 245.
High School—Highland Springs, Va.
Received bachelor of industrial relations degree from
University of North Carolina in 1987.

Signed as free agent by Dallas Cowboys, April 30, 1987.
Dallas NFL, 1987.
Games: 1987 (12).

BLAIR WALTER BUSH
Center—Seattle Seahawks
Born November 25, 1956, at Fort Hood, Tex.
Height, 6.03. Weight, 272.
High School—Palos Verdes, Calif.
Received degree in education from University of Washington.

Selected by Cincinnati in 1st round (16th player selected) of 1978 NFL draft.
Traded by Cincinnati Bengals to Seattle Seahawks for 1st round pick in 1985 draft, June 29, 1983.
On injured reserve with knee injury, October 22 through remainder of 1986 season.
Crossed picket line during players' strike, October 14, 1987.
On injured reserve with broken hand, December 18 through remainder of 1987 season.
Cincinnati NFL, 1978 through 1982; Seattle, NFL, 1983 through 1987.
Games: 1978 (16), 1979 (12), 1980 (16), 1981 (16), 1982 (8), 1983 (16), 1984 (16), 1985 (16), 1986 (7), 1987 (11). Total—134.
Pro statistics: Recovered one fumble for 12 yards, 1981; recovered one fumble, 1985.

Played in AFC Championship Game following 1981 and 1983 seasons.
Played in NFL Championship Game following 1981 season.

STEVE RAY BUSICK
Linebacker—San Diego Chargers
Born December 10, 1958, at Los Angeles, Calif.
Height, 6.04. Weight, 227.
High School—Temple City, Calif.
Attended University of Southern California.

Selected by Denver in 7th round (181st player selected) of 1981 NFL draft.
Traded by Denver Broncos to Los Angeles Rams for 11th round pick in 1987 draft and 7th round pick in 1988 draft, September 2, 1986.
On injured reserve with knee injury, September 30 through remainder of 1986 season.
Released by Los Angeles Rams after failing physical, September 1, 1987; signed as free agent replacement player by San Diego Chargers, October 13, 1987.
On injured reserve with knee injury, October 16 through December 11, 1987; activated, December 12, 1987.
Denver NFL, 1981 through 1985; Los Angeles Rams NFL, 1986; San Diego NFL, 1987.
Games: 1981 (16), 1982 (9), 1983 (16), 1984 (16), 1985 (16), 1986 (4), 1987 (1). Total—78.
Pro statistics: Recovered two fumbles for three yards, 1981; intercepted two passes for 21 yards, 1984; recovered one fumble, 1984 and 1985.

BARNEY A. BUSSEY
Safety—Cincinnati Bengals
Born May 20, 1962, at Lincolnton, Ga.
Height, 6.00. Weight, 195.
High School—Lincolnton, Ga., Lincoln County.
Attended South Carolina State College.

Named as strong safety on THE SPORTING NEWS USFL All-Star Team, 1985.
Selected by Memphis in 1st round (4th player selected) of 1984 USFL draft.
Selected by Cincinnati in 5th round (119th player selected) of 1984 NFL draft.
Signed by Memphis Showboats, May 8, 1984.
Granted roster exemption, May 8 through May 14, 1984; activated, May 15, 1984.
On developmental squad, March 16 through March 23, 1985; activated, March 24, 1985.
Granted free agency when USFL suspended operations, August 7, 1986; signed by Cincinnati Bengals, August 12, 1986.
On developmental squad for 1 game with Memphis Showboats in 1985.
Memphis USFL, 1984 and 1985; Cincinnati NFL, 1986 and 1987.
Games: 1984 (6), 1985 (17), 1986 (16), 1987 (12). Total USFL—23. Total NFL—28. Total Pro—51.
USFL statistics: Recovered on fumble, 1984; intercepted three passes for 11 yards, credited with one sack for four yards and recovered one fumble for 12 yards, 1985.
NFL statistics: Intercepted one pass for 19 yards, 1986; intercepted one pass for no yards, returned 21 kickoffs for 406 yards (19.3 avg.) and fumbled once, 1987.

PAUL MARTIN BUTCHER
Linebacker—Detroit Lions
Born November 8, 1963, at Detroit, Mich.
Height, 6.00. Weight, 219.
High School—Dearborn, Mich., St. Alphonsus.
Received degree in mechanical engineering from Wayne State University in 1986.

Signed as free agent by Detroit Lions, July 23, 1986.
Released by Detroit Lions, August 18, 1986; re-signed by Lions, October 3, 1986.
Detroit NFL, 1986 and 1987.
Games: 1986 (12), 1987 (12). Total—24.

JERRY O'DELL BUTLER
Wide Receiver—Buffalo Bills
Born October 2, 1957, at Ware Shoals, S.C.
Height, 6.00. Weight, 178.
High School—Ware Shoals, S.C.
Received bachelor of arts degree in recreation and parks administration
from Clemson University in 1980.

Named as wide receiver on THE SPORTING NEWS College All-America Team, 1978.
Named THE SPORTING NEWS AFC Rookie of the Year, 1979.
Selected by Buffalo in 1st round (5th player selected) of 1979 NFL draft.
On did not report list, August 24 through September 2, 1982.
Granted two-game roster exemption, September 3, 1982; activated, September 11, 1982.
On injured reserve with knee injury, November 4 through remainder of 1983 season.
On physically unable to perform/reserve with knee injury, August 14 through entire 1984 season.
On injured reserve with fractured fibula, November 17 through remainder of 1986 season.
On injured reserve with leg injury, September 7 through entire 1987 season.

Year Club	G.	P.C.	Yds.	Avg.	TD.	Year Club	G.	P.C.	Yds.	Avg.	TD.
1979—Buffalo NFL	13	48	834	17.4	4	1983—Buffalo NFL	9	36	385	10.7	3
1980—Buffalo NFL	16	57	832	14.6	6	1985—Buffalo NFL	16	41	770	18.8	2
1981—Buffalo NFL	16	55	842	15.3	8	1986—Buffalo NFL	11	15	302	20.1	2
1982—Buffalo NFL	7	26	336	12.9	4	Pro Totals—7 Years	88	278	4301	15.5	29

Additional pro statistics: Rushed twice for 13 yards, 1979; fumbled once, 1979 and 1983; rushed once for 18 yards, 1980; rushed once for one yard and fumbled twice, 1981.

JOHN KEITH BUTLER
(Known by middle name.)
Linebacker—Seattle Seahawks
Born May 16, 1956, at Anniston, Ala.
Height, 6.04. Weight, 238.
High School—Huntsville, Ala., Lee.
Attending Memphis State University.

Selected by Seattle in 2nd round (36th player selected) of 1978 NFL draft.
Seattle NFL, 1978 through 1987.
Games: 1978 (16), 1979 (14), 1980 (16), 1981 (16), 1982 (8), 1983 (16), 1984 (16), 1985 (16), 1986 (16), 1987 (12). Total—146.
Pro statistics: Recovered two fumbles, 1978; intercepted one pass for four yards, 1979; intercepted two passes for 11 yards, 1980; intercepted two passes for no yards and fumbled once, 1981; intercepted one pass for no yards, 1983; intercepted two passes for 31 yards and recovered three fumbles, 1985; recovered one fumble, 1987.
Played in AFC Championship Game following 1983 season.

KEVIN GREGORY BUTLER
Placekicker—Chicago Bears
Born July 24, 1962, at Savannah, Ga.
Height, 6.01. Weight, 204.
High School—Redan, Ga.
Attended University of Georgia.

Selected by Jacksonville in 1985 USFL territorial draft.
Selected by Chicago in 4th round (105th player selected) of 1985 NFL draft.
Signed by Chicago Bears, July 23, 1985.

Year Club	G.	XP.	XPM.	FG.	FGA.	Pts.
1985—Chicago NFL	16	51	0	31	37	*144
1986—Chicago NFL	16	36	1	28	*41	120
1987—Chicago NFL	12	28	2	19	28	85
Pro Totals—3 Years	44	115	3	78	106	349

Played in NFC Championship Game following 1985 season.
Played in NFL Championship Game following 1985 season.

RAYMOND LEONARD BUTLER
(Ray)
Wide Receiver—Seattle Seahawks
Born June 28, 1956, at Port Lavaca, Tex.
Height, 6.03. Weight, 206.
High School—Sweeny, Tex.
Attended Wharton County Junior College and received
degree in speech from University of Southern California in 1980.

Selected by Baltimore in 4th round (88th player selected) of 1980 NFL draft.
On injured reserve with broken arm, November 28 through remainder of 1983 season.
Franchise transferred to Indianapolis, March 31, 1984.
Released by Indianapolis Colts, November 18, 1985; signed as free agent by Seattle Seahawks, December 4, 1985.

Year Club	G.	P.C.	Yds.	Avg.	TD.
1980—Baltimore NFL	16	34	574	16.9	2
1981—Baltimore NFL	16	46	832	18.1	9
1982—Baltimore NFL	9	17	268	15.8	2
1983—Baltimore NFL	11	10	207	20.7	3
1984—Indianapolis NFL	16	43	664	15.4	6
1985—Ind.(11)-Sea.(2) NFL	13	19	345	18.2	2
1986—Seattle NFL	16	19	351	18.5	4
1987—Seattle NFL	12	33	465	14.1	5
Pro Totals—8 Years	109	221	3706	16.8	33

Additional pro statistics: Rushed three times for 10 yards and recovered one fumble, 1982; rushed once for minus one yard, 1985; fumbled once, 1987.

ROBERT CALVIN BUTLER
(Bobby)
Cornerback—Atlanta Falcons
Born May 28, 1959, at Boynton Beach, Fla.
Height, 5.11. Weight, 175.
High School—Delray Beach, Fla., Atlantic.
Attended Florida State University.
Cousin of James (Cannonball) Butler, running back with Pittsburgh Steelers,
Atlanta Falcons and St. Louis Cardinals, 1965 through 1972.

Selected by Atlanta in 1st round (25th player selected) of 1981 NFL draft.
On injured reserve with broken leg, October 20 through remainder of 1986 season.

Year Club	G.	No.	Yds.	Avg.	TD.
			—INTERCEPTIONS—		
1981—Atlanta NFL	16	5	86	17.2	0
1982—Atlanta NFL	9	2	0	0.0	0
1983—Atlanta NFL	16	4	12	3.0	0
1984—Atlanta NFL	15	2	25	12.5	0

Year Club	G.	No.	Yds.	Avg.	TD.
			—INTERCEPTIONS—		
1985—Atlanta NFL	16	5	−4	−0.8	0
1986—Atlanta NFL	7	1	33	22.0	1
1987—Atlanta NFL	12	4	48	12.0	0
Pro Totals—7 Years	91	23	200	8.7	1

Additional pro statistics: Returned one kickoff for 17 yards and recovered one fumble, 1983; recovered one fumble for 10 yards, 1984.

DAVID ROY BUTZ
(Dave)
Defensive Tackle—Washington Redskins
Born June 23, 1950, at Lafayette, Ala.
Height, 6.07. Weight, 295.
High School—Park Ridge, Ill., Maine South.
Received bachelor of science degree in physical education,
health and safety from Purdue University in 1973.
Nephew of Earl Butz, former secretary of agriculture.

Named as defensive tackle on THE SPORTING NEWS College All-America Team, 1972.
Named to THE SPORTING NEWS NFL All-Star Team, 1983.
Selected by St. Louis in 1st round (5th player selected) of 1973 NFL draft.
Played out option with St. Louis Cardinals and signed by Washington Redskins, August 5, 1975; Cardinals received three draft choices (1st round picks in 1977 and 1978 and 2nd round pick in 1979) in exchange for three draft choices (5th and 15th round picks in 1976 and 6th round pick in 1977) as compensation, September 4, 1975.
St. Louis NFL, 1973 and 1974; Washington NFL, 1975 through 1986.
Games: 1973 (12), 1974 (1), 1975 (14), 1976 (14), 1977 (12), 1978 (16), 1979 (15), 1980 (16), 1981 (16), 1982 (9), 1983 (16), 1984 (15), 1985 (16), 1986 (16), 1987 (12). Total—200.
Pro statistics: Returned one kickoff for 23 yards, 1973; recovered one fumble, 1973, 1976 and 1982 through 1985; intercepted one pass for three yards, 1978; intercepted one pass for 26 yards, 1981.
Played in NFC Championship Game following 1982, 1983, 1986 and 1987 seasons.
Played in NFL Championship Game following 1982, 1983 and 1987 seasons.
Played in Pro Bowl (NFL All-Star Game) following 1983 season.

KEITH BYARS
Running Back—Philadelphia Eagles
Born October 14, 1963, at Dayton, O.
Height, 6.01. Weight, 238.
High School—Dayton, O., Nettie Lee Roth.
Attended Ohio State University.

Named as running back on THE SPORTING NEWS College All-America Team, 1984.
Selected by New Jersey in 1986 USFL territorial draft.
Selected by Philadelphia in 1st round (10th player selected) of 1986 NFL draft.
Signed by Philadelphia Eagles, July 25, 1986.

Year Club	G.	—RUSHING—				PASS RECEIVING				—TOTAL—		
		Att.	Yds.	Avg.	TD.	P.C.	Yds.	Avg.	TD.	TD.	Pts.	F.
1986—Philadelphia NFL	16	177	577	3.3	1	11	44	4.0	0	1	6	3
1987—Philadelphia NFL	10	116	426	3.7	3	21	177	8.4	1	4	24	3
Pro Totals—2 Years	26	293	1003	3.4	4	32	221	6.9	1	5	30	6

Additional pro statistics: Returned two kickoffs for 47 yards, attempted two passes with one completion for 55 yards and one touchdown, 1986; recovered two fumbles, 1986 and 1987.

EARNEST ALEXANDER BYNER
Running Back—Cleveland Browns
Born September 15, 1962, at Milledgeville, Ga.
Height, 5.10. Weight, 215.
High School—Milledgeville, Ga., Baldwin.
Attended East Carolina University.

Selected by Cleveland in 10th round (280th player selected) of 1984 NFL draft.
On injured reserve with ankle injury, October 21, 1986 through January 9, 1987; activated, January 10, 1987.

Year Club	G.	—RUSHING—				PASS RECEIVING				—TOTAL—		
		Att.	Yds.	Avg.	TD.	P.C.	Yds.	Avg.	TD.	TD.	Pts.	F.
1984—Cleveland NFL	16	72	426	5.9	2	11	118	10.7	0	3	18	3
1985—Cleveland NFL	16	244	1002	4.1	8	45	460	10.2	2	10	60	5
1986—Cleveland NFL	7	94	277	2.9	2	37	328	8.9	2	4	24	1
1987—Cleveland NFL	12	105	432	4.1	8	52	552	10.6	2	10	60	5
Pro Totals—4 Years	51	515	2137	4.1	20	145	1458	10.1	6	27	162	14

Year Club	G.	No.	Yds.	Avg.	TD.
		KICKOFF RETURNS			
1984—Cleveland NFL	16	22	415	18.9	0
1985—Cleveland NFL	16		None		
1986—Cleveland NFL	7		None		
1987—Cleveland NFL	12	1	2	2.0	0
Pro Totals—4 Years	51	23	417	18.1	0

Additional pro statistics: Recovered two fumbles for 55 yards and a touchdown, 1984; recovered four fumbles, 1985; recovered one fumble, 1987.
Played in AFC Championship Game following 1986 and 1987 seasons.

GILL ARNETTE BYRD
Defensive Back—San Diego Chargers
Born February 20, 1961, at San Francisco, Calif.
Height, 5.11. Weight, 194.
High School—San Francisco, Calif., Lowell.
Received degree in business administration and finance
from San Jose State University in 1982.
Nephew of MacArthur Byrd, linebacker with Los Angeles Rams, 1965.
Selected by Oakland in 1983 USFL territorial draft.
Selected by San Diego in 1st round (22nd player selected) of 1983 NFL draft.
Signed by San Diego Chargers, May 20, 1983.
On injured reserve with pulled hamstring, December 12 through remainder of 1984 season.

Year Club	G.	No.	Yds.	Avg.	TD.
1983—San Diego NFL	14	1	0	0.0	0
1984—San Diego NFL	13	4	157	39.3	*2
1985—San Diego NFL	16	1	25	25.0	0
1986—San Diego NFL	15	5	45	9.0	0
1987—San Diego NFL	12		None		
Pro Totals—5 Years	70	11	227	20.6	2

Additional pro statistics: Recovered one fumble, 1985 and 1987.

RICHARD BYRD
Defensive End—Houston Oilers
Born March 20, 1962, at Natchez, Miss.
Height, 6.04. Weight, 264.
High School—Jackson, Miss., Jim Hill.
Attended University of Southern Mississippi.
Selected by Portland in 1985 USFL territorial draft.
Selected by Houston in 2nd round (36th player selected) of 1985 NFL draft.
Signed by Houston Oilers, July 19, 1985.
Houston NFL, 1985 through 1987.
Games: 1985 (15), 1986 (16), 1987 (12). Total—43.
Pro statistics: Recovered one fumble, 1985 and 1986.

CARL EDWARD BYRUM
Fullback—Buffalo Bills
Born June 29, 1963, at Olive Branch, Miss.
Height, 6.00. Weight, 232.
High School—Southaven, Miss.
Attended Mississippi Valley State University.
Selected by Buffalo in 5th round (111th player selected) of 1986 NFL draft.
Signed by Buffalo Bills, July 19, 1986.
On injured reserve with knee injury, December 13 through remainder of 1986 season.
Crossed picket line during players' strike, October 7, 1987.

Year Club	G.	Att.	Yds.	Avg.	TD.	P.C.	Yds.	Avg.	TD.	TD.	Pts.	F.
			RUSHING			PASS RECEIVING				—TOTAL—		
1986—Buffalo NFL	13	38	156	4.1	0	13	104	8.0	1	1	6	0
1987—Buffalo NFL	13	66	280	4.2	0	3	23	7.7	0	0	0	4
Pro Totals—2 Years	26	104	436	4.2	0	16	127	7.9	1	1	6	4

Additional pro statistics: Recovered one fumble, 1987.

TOMMORIES CADE
(Mossy)
Cornerback—Green Bay Packers
Born December 26, 1961, at Eloy, Ariz.
Height, 6.01. Weight, 195.
High School—Eloy, Ariz., Santa Cruz Valley Union.
Attended University of Texas.
Named as defensive back on THE SPORTING NEWS College All-America Team, 1983.
Selected by San Antonio in 1984 USFL territorial draft.
Selected by San Diego in 1st round (6th player selected) of 1984 NFL draft.
USFL rights traded by San Antonio Gunslingers to Memphis Showboats for defensive back Vic Minor and draft choice, October 3, 1984.
Signed by Memphis Showboats, October 3, 1984.
On developmental squad, June 1 through June 14, 1984; activated, June 15, 1984.
On developmental squad, June 22 through June 29, 1984; activated, June 30, 1984.
Released by Memphis Showboats, September 5, 1984.
NFL rights traded by San Diego Chargers to Green Bay Packers for 1st round pick in 1986 draft and 5th round pick in 1987 draft, September 6, 1985.
Signed by Green Bay Packers, September 5, 1985.
Granted roster exemption, September 5 through September 15, 1985; activated, September 16, 1985.
On reserve/did not report list, August 15 through entire 1987 season.
On developmental squad for 3 games with Memphis Showboats in 1984.

Year Club		G.	No.	Yds.	Avg.	TD.
			—INTERCEPTIONS—			
1985—Memphis USFL		15	2	0	0.0	0
1985—Green Bay NFL		14	1	0	0.0	0
1986—Green Bay NFL		16	4	26	6.5	0
USFL Totals—1 Year		15	2	0	0.0	0
NFL Totals—2 Years		30	5	26	5.2	0
Pro Totals—3 Years		45	7	26	3.7	0

Additional USFL statistics: Recovered two fumbles for 39 yards, 1985.
Additional NFL statistics: Recovered one fumble, 1985.

DARRYL CALDWELL
Guard—New York Jets
Born February 2, 1960, at Birmingham, Ala.
Height, 6.05. Weight, 245.
High School—Birmingham, Ala., C.W. Hayes.
Attended Tennessee State University.

Signed as free agent by Buffalo Bills, May 25, 1983.
Released by Buffalo Bills, August 27, 1984; signed as free agent by Memphis Showboats, September 18, 1984.
Released by Memphis Showboats, January 28, 1985; re-signed by Bills, May 6, 1986.
Released by Buffalo Bills, August 18, 1986; signed as free agent by New York Jets, April 7, 1987.
On injured reserve with rotator cuff injury, August 31 through entire 1987 season.
Buffalo NFL, 1983.
Games: 1983 (14).
Pro statistics: Recovered one fumble, 1983.

RAVIN CALDWELL JR.
Linebacker—Washington Redskins
Born August 4, 1963, at Port Arthur, Tex.
Height, 6.03. Weight, 229.
High School—Fort Smith, Ark., Northside.
Attended University of Arkansas.

Selected by Memphis in 1986 USFL territorial draft.
Selected by Washington in 5th round (113th player selected) of 1986 NFL draft.
Signed by Washington Redskins, July 18, 1986.
On injured reserve with knee injury, August 23 through entire 1986 season.
Washington NFL, 1987.
Games: 1987 (12).
Played in NFC Championship Game following 1987 season.
Played in NFL Championship Game following 1987 season.

KEVIN BRADLEY CALL
Offensive Tackle—Indianapolis Colts
Born November 13, 1961, at Boulder, Colo.
Height, 6.07. Weight, 302.
High School—Boulder, Colo., Fairview.
Attended Colorado State University.

Selected by Denver in 1984 USFL territorial draft.
Selected by Indianapolis in 5th round (130th player selected) of 1984 NFL draft.
Signed by Indianapolis Colts, July 24, 1984.
Indianapolis NFL, 1984 through 1987.
Games: 1984 (15), 1985 (14), 1986 (16), 1987 (12). Total—57.

RICHARD JON CAMARILLO
(Rich)
Punter—New England Patriots
Born November 29, 1959, at Whittier, Calif.
Height, 5.11. Weight, 185.
High School—Pico Rivera, Calif., El Rancho.
Attended Cerritos Junior College and University of Washington.
Nephew of Leo Camarillo, professional on rodeo circuit.

Named to THE SPORTING NEWS NFL All-Star Team, 1983.
Led NFL in punting yards with 3,953 in 1985.
Led NFL in net punting average with 37.1 in 1983.
Signed as free agent by New England Patriots, May 11, 1981.
Released by New England Patriots, August 24, 1981; re-signed by Patriots after clearing procedural waivers, October 20, 1981.
On injured reserve with knee injury, August 28 through November 2, 1984; activated, November 3, 1984.

Year Club	G.	No.	Avg.	Blk.	Year Club	G.	No.	Avg.	Blk.
		—PUNTING—					—PUNTING—		
1981—New England NFL	9	47	41.7	0	1985—New England NFL	16	92	43.0	0
1982—New England NFL	9	49	43.7	0	1986—New England NFL	16	89	42.1	★3
1983—New England NFL	16	81	44.6	0	1987—New England NFL	12	62	40.1	1
1984—New England NFL	7	48	42.1	0	Pro Totals—7 Years	85	468	42.6	4

Additional pro statistics: Recovered one fumble and fumbled once, 1981; rushed once for no yards, 1987.
Played in AFC Championship Game following 1985 season.
Played in NFL Championship Game following 1985 season.
Played in Pro Bowl (NFL All-Star Game) following 1983 season.

REGGIE LOUIS CAMP
Defensive End—Cleveland Browns
Born February 28, 1961, at San Francisco, Calif.
Height, 6.04. Weight, 280.
High School—Daly City, Calif., Jefferson.
Attended University of California at Berkley.

Selected by Oakland in 1983 USFL territorial draft.
Selected by Cleveland in 3rd round (68th player selected) of 1983 NFL draft.
Signed by Cleveland Browns, May 31, 1983.
On injured reserve with knee injury, November 19, 1987 through January 7, 1988; activated, January 8, 1988.
Cleveland NFL, 1983 through 1987.
Games: 1983 (16), 1984 (16), 1985 (16), 1986 (16), 1987 (6). Total—70.
Pro statistics: Recovered one fumble, 1984 and 1985.
Played in AFC Championship Game following 1986 and 1987 seasons.

ROBERT SCOTT CAMPBELL
(Known by middle name.)
Quarterback—Atlanta Falcons
Born April 15, 1962, at Hershey, Pa.
Height, 6.00. Weight, 195.
High School—Hershey, Pa.
Attended Purdue University.
Son of Ken Campbell, wide receiver with New York Titans of AFL, 1960.

Selected by Philadelphia in 4th round (76th player selected) of 1984 USFL draft.
Selected by Pittsburgh in 7th round (191st player selected) of 1984 NFL draft.
Signed by Pittsburgh Steelers, May 19, 1984.
Released by Pittsburgh Steelers, September 24, 1986; signed as free agent by Atlanta Falcons for 1987, November 7, 1986.
Signed for 1986 season, November 17, 1986.

Year Club	G.	Att.	Cmp.	Pct.	Gain	T.P.	P.I.	Avg.	Att.	Yds.	Avg.	TD.	TD.	Pts.	F.
1984—Pittsburgh NFL	5	15	8	53.3	109	1	1	7.27	3	—5	—1.7	0	0	0	1
1985—Pittsburgh NFL	16	96	43	44.8	612	4	6	6.38	9	28	3.1	0	0	0	3
1986—Pitt.(3)-Atl.(1)NFL	4	7	1	14.3	7	0	0	1.00	1	7	7.0	0	0	0	0
1987—Atlanta NFL	12	260	136	52.3	1728	11	14	6.65	21	102	4.9	2	2	12	4
Pro Totals—4 Years	37	378	188	49.7	2456	16	21	6.50	34	132	3.9	2	2	12	8

Quarterback Rating Points: 1984 (71.3), 1985 (53.8), 1986 (39.6), 1987 (65.0). Total—61.3.
Additional pro statistics: Recovered one fumble, 1984; recovered three fumbles, 1985; recovered two fumbles, 1987.
Member of Pittsburgh Steelers for AFC Championship Game following 1984 season; did not play.

JAMES F. CAMPEN
Center—New Orleans Saints
Born June 11, 1964, at Sacramento, Calif.
Height, 6.03. Weight, 260.
High School—Shingle Springs, Calif., Ponderosa.
Attended Sacramento City College and Tulane University.

Signed as free agent by New Orleans Saints, May 13, 1986.
Released by New Orleans Saints, August 25, 1986; re-signed by Saints for 1987, October 23, 1986.
On injured reserve with rotator cuff injury, September 7 through September 27, 1987; activated, September 28, 1987.
Crossed picket line during players' strike, September 28, 1987.
New Orleans NFL, 1987.
Games: 1987 (3).
Pro statistics: Recovered one fumble, 1987.

JOHN RAYMOND CANNON
Defensive End—Tampa Bay Buccaneers
Born July 30, 1960, at Long Branch, N.J.
Height, 6.05. Weight, 260.
High School—Holmdel, N.J.
Received bachelor of business administration degree from
College of William & Mary in 1982.

Selected by Tampa Bay in 3rd round (83rd player selected) of 1982 NFL draft.
USFL rights traded by Memphis Showboats to Houston Gamblers for rights to defensive end Ray Yakavonis, February 13, 1985.
On injured reserve with leg injury, October 23 through December 11, 1986; activated, December 12, 1986.
Tampa Bay NFL, 1982 through 1987.
Games: 1982 (9), 1983 (14), 1984 (16), 1985 (16), 1986 (9), 1987 (11). Total—75.
Pro statistics: Recovered one fumble, 1983, 1984 and 1987; intercepted one pass for no yards, 1984; recovered three fumbles, 1985; recovered two fumbles, 1986.

MARK MAIDA CANNON
Center—Green Bay Packers
Born June 14, 1962, at Whittier, Calif.
Height, 6.03. Weight, 258.
High School—Austin, Tex., S.F. Austin.
Attended University of Texas at Arlington.

Selected by Tampa Bay in 3rd round (62nd player selected) of 1984 USFL draft.
Selected by Green Bay in 11th round (294th player selected) of 1984 NFL draft.
Signed by Green Bay Packers, July 12, 1984.
Granted free agency, February 1, 1986; re-signed by Packers, August 20, 1986.
Granted roster exemption, August 20 through August 28, 1986; activated, August 29, 1986.
On injured reserve with knee injury, October 11 through November 14, 1986; activated, November 15, 1986.
On injured reserve with knee injury, November 26 through remainder of 1986 season.
Green Bay NFL, 1984 through 1987.
Games: 1984 (16), 1985 (16), 1986 (7), 1987 (12). Total—51.
Pro statistics: Recovered two fumbles, 1985; fumbled once for minus eight yards, 1987.

JOSEPH J. CARAVELLO
(Joe)
Tight End—Washington Redskins
Born June 6, 1963, at Santa Monica, Calif.
Height, 6.03. Weight, 270.
High School—El Segundo, Calif.
Attended Tulane University.

Signed as free agent by Atlanta Falcons, May 2, 1986.
Released by Atlanta Falcons, September 1, 1986; re-signed by Falcons, March 13, 1987.
Released by Atlanta Falcons, September 7, 1987; signed as free agent replacement player by Washington Redskins, September 24, 1987.
Washington NFL, 1987.
Games: 1987 (11).
Pro statistics: Caught two passes for 29 yards and recovered one fumble, 1987.
Member of Washington Redskins for NFL Championship Game following 1987 season; inactive.

MATTHEW CODY CARLSON
(Known by middle name.)
Quarterback—Houston Oilers
Born November 5, 1963, at Dallas, Tex.
Height, 6.03. Weight, 203.
High School—San Antonio, Tex., Winston Churchill.
Received bachelor of science degree in marketing management
from Baylor University in 1987.

Selected by Houston in 3rd round (64th player selected) of 1987 NFL draft.
Signed by Houston Oilers, June 3, 1987.
Active for 4 games with Houston Oilers in 1987; did not play.
Houston NFL, 1987.

ROGER EUGENE CARON
Offensive Tackle—New Orleans Saints
Born June 3, 1962, at Boston, Mass.
Height, 6.05. Weight, 275.
High School—Norwell, Mass.
Received bachelor of arts degree from Harvard University in 1985.

Selected by Baltimore in 2nd round (30th player selected) of 1985 USFL draft.
Selected by Indianapolis in 5th round (117th player selected) of 1985 NFL draft.
Signed by Indianapolis Colts, July 18, 1985.
Traded by Indianapolis Colts to Buffalo Bills for 8th round pick in 1987 draft, April 13, 1987.
Placed on did not report/reserve, July 19, 1987.
Released by Buffalo Bills, March 4, 1988; signed as free agent by New Orleans Saints, May 3, 1988.
Indianapolis NFL, 1985 and 1986.
Games: 1985 (7), 1986 (3). Total—10.

GREGG KEVIN CARR
Linebacker—Pittsburgh Steelers
Born March 31, 1962, at Birmingham, Ala.
Height, 6.02. Weight, 224.
High School—Birmingham, Ala., Woodlawn.
Attended Auburn University.

Selected by Birmingham in 1985 USFL territorial draft.
Selected by Pittsburgh in 6th round (160th player selected) of 1985 NFL draft.
Signed by Pittsburgh Steelers, July 19, 1985.
Pittsburgh NFL, 1985 through 1987.
Games: 1985 (16), 1986 (16), 1987 (12). Total—44.
Pro statistics: Recovered two fumbles, 1985; credited with a safety, 1987.

JOHN MARK CARRIER
(Known by middle name.)
Wide Receiver—Tampa Bay Buccaneers
Born October 28, 1965, at Lafayette, La.
Height, 6.00. Weight, 182.
High School—Church Point, La.
Attended Nicholls State University.

Selected by Tampa Bay in 3rd round (57th player selected) of 1987 NFL draft.
Signed by Tampa Bay Buccaneers, July 18, 1987.

		——PASS RECEIVING——				
Year	Club		G.	P.C.	Yds.	Avg. TD.
1987—Tampa Bay NFL			10	26	423	16.3 3

Additional pro statistics: Returned one kickoff for no yards, 1987.

ALPHONSO CARREKER
Name pronounced CARE-uh-ker.
Defensive End—Green Bay Packers
Born May 25, 1962, at Columbus, O.
Height, 6.06. Weight, 271.
High School—Columbus, O., Marion Franklin.
Attended Florida State University.

Selected by Tampa Bay in 1984 USFL territorial draft.
Selected by Green Bay in 1st round (12th player selected) of 1984 NFL draft.
Signed by Green Bay Packers, June 20, 1984.
Green Bay NFL, 1984 through 1987.
Games: 1984 (14), 1985 (16), 1986 (16), 1987 (12). Total—58.
Pro statistics: Recovered two fumbles, 1986; intercepted one pass for six yards, 1987.

PAUL OTT CARRUTH
(Paul Ott)
Running Back—Green Bay Packers
Born July 12, 1961, at Hattiesburg, Miss.
Height, 6.01. Weight, 220.
High School—McComb, Miss., Parklane.
Received bachelor of science degree in communications from University of Alabama.

Selected by Birmingham in 1985 USFL territorial draft.
Signed by Birmingham Stallions, January 28, 1985.
Granted free agency when USFL suspended operations, August 7, 1986; signed as free agent by Green Bay Packers, August 14, 1986.
Granted roster exemption, August 14 through August 21, 1986; activated, August 22, 1986.

			——RUSHING——				PASS RECEIVING				—TOTAL—		
Year	Club	G.	Att.	Yds.	Avg.	TD.	P.C.	Yds.	Avg.	TD.	TD.	Pts.	F.
1985—Birmingham USFL		18	57	265	4.7	2	2	11	5.5	0	2	12	2
1986—Green Bay NFL......................		16	81	308	3.8	2	24	134	5.6	2	4	24	1
1987—Green Bay NFL......................		12	64	192	3.0	3	10	78	7.8	1	4	24	0
Pro Totals—3 Years....................		46	202	765	3.8	7	36	223	6.2	3	10	60	3

		KICKOFF RETURNS				
Year	Club	G.	No.	Yds.	Avg.	TD.
1985—Birmingham USFL		18	26	477	18.4	0
1986—Green Bay NFL............		16	4	40	10.0	0
1987—Green Bay NFL............		12	1	8	8.0	0
Pro Totals—3 Years............		46	31	525	16.9	0

Additional pro statistics: Attempted one pass with one completion for three yards and a touchdown, 1987.

CARLOS A. CARSON
Wide Receiver—Kansas City Chiefs
Born December 28, 1958, at Lake Worth, Fla.
Height, 5.11. Weight, 180.
High School—Lake Worth, Fla., John I. Leonard.
Attended Louisana State University.
Cousin of Darrin Nelson, running back with Minnesota Vikings; and Kevin Nelson,
running back with Los Angeles Express, 1984 and 1985.

Selected by Kansas City in 5th round (114th player selected) of 1980 NFL draft.
On injured reserve with broken foot, September 23 through December 11, 1981; activated, December 12, 1981.
On injured reserve with foot injury, November 28 through December 26, 1986; activated, December 27, 1986.

			——RUSHING——				PASS RECEIVING				—TOTAL—		
Year	Club	G.	Att.	Yds.	Avg.	TD.	P.C.	Yds.	Avg.	TD.	TD.	Pts.	F.
1980—Kansas City NFL...................		16	2	41	20.5	0	5	68	13.6	0	0	0	1
1981—Kansas City NFL...................		5	1	−1	−1.0	0	7	179	25.6	1	1	6	1
1982—Kansas City NFL...................		9		None			27	494	18.3	2	2	12	1
1983—Kansas City NFL...................		16	2	20	10.0	0	80	1351	16.9	7	7	42	2
1984—Kansas City NFL...................		16	1	−8	−8.0	0	57	1078	18.9	4	4	24	0
1985—Kansas City NFL...................		15	3	25	8.3	0	47	843	17.9	4	4	24	0
1986—Kansas City NFL...................		10		None			21	497	23.7	4	4	24	1
1987—Kansas City NFL...................		12	1	−7	−7.0	0	55	1044	19.0	7	7	42	1
Pro Totals—8 Years....................		99	10	70	7.0	0	299	5554	18.6	29	29	174	7

Year Club	G.	No.	KICKOFF RETURNS Yds.	Avg.TD.	
1980—Kansas City NFL.........	16	40	917	22.9	0
1981—Kansas City NFL.........	5	10	227	22.7	0
1982—Kansas City NFL.........	9			None	
1983—Kansas City NFL.........	16	1	12	12.0	0
1984—Kansas City NFL.........	16	1	2	2.0	0
1985—Kansas City NFL.........	15			None	
1986—Kansas City NFL.........	10	5	88	17.6	0
1987—Kansas City NFL.........	12			None	
Pro Totals—8 Years............	99	57	1246	21.9	0

Additional pro statistics: Recovered one fumble, 1980 and 1981; attempted one pass with one completion for 48 yards and one touchdown, 1983; recovered two fumbles, 1984.

Played in Pro Bowl (NFL All-Star Game) following 1983 and 1987 seasons.

HAROLD DONALD CARSON
(Harry)
Linebacker—New York Giants

Born November 26, 1953, at Florence, S. C.
Height, 6.02. Weight, 240.
High School—Florence, S. C., McClenaghan.
Received bachelor of science degree in physical education
from South Carolina State College.

Named to THE SPORTING NEWS NFL All-Star Team, 1984.
Named to THE SPORTING NEWS NFC All-Star Team, 1979.
Selected by New York Giants in 4th round (105th player selected) of 1976 NFL draft.
On injured reserve with knee injury, October 16 through November 13, 1980; activated, November 14, 1980.
On injured reserve, November 24 through remainder of 1980 season.
On injured reserve with knee injury, September 19 through October 28, 1983; activated, October 29, 1983.

Year Club	G.	——INTERCEPTIONS—— No.	Yds.	Avg.TD.		Year Club	G.	——INTERCEPTIONS—— No.	Yds.	Avg.TD.
1976—N.Y. Giants NFL	12			None		1983—N.Y. Giants NFL	10			None
1977—N.Y. Giants NFL	14			None		1984—N.Y. Giants NFL	16	1	6	6.0 0
1978—N.Y. Giants NFL	16	3	86	28.7 0		1985—N.Y. Giants NFL	16			None
1979—N.Y. Giants NFL	16	3	28	9.3 0		1986—N.Y. Giants NFL	16	1	20	20.0 0
1980—N.Y. Giants NFL	8			None		1987—N.Y. Giants NFL	12			None
1981—N.Y. Giants NFL	16			None		Pro Totals—12 Years.........	161	9	146	16.2 0
1982—N.Y. Giants NFL	9	1	6	6.0 0						

Additional pro statistics: Recovered one fumble, 1976 through 1978, 1980, 1984 and 1987; returned one kickoff for five yards, 1976; recovered three fumbles for 22 yards and one touchdown, 1979; recovered one fumble for two yards, 1981; caught one pass for 13 yards and a touchdown and recovered two fumbles, 1986.

Played in NFC Championship Game following 1986 season.
Played in NFL Championship Game following 1986 season.
Played in Pro Bowl (NFL All-Star Game) following 1978, 1979 and 1981 through 1987 seasons.

ANTHONY CARTER
Wide Receiver—Minnesota Vikings

Born September 17, 1960, at Riviera Beach, Fla.
Height, 5.11. Weight, 175.
High School—Riviera Beach, Fla., Sun Coast.
Attended University of Michigan.
Cousin of Leonard Coleman, cornerback with Indianapolis Colts.

Named as wide receiver on THE SPORTING NEWS USFL All-Star Team, 1985.
Named as punt returner on THE SPORTING NEWS USFL All-Star Team, 1983.
Named as wide receiver on THE SPORTING NEWS College All-America Team, 1981 and 1982.
Selected by Michigan in 1983 USFL territorial draft.
Signed by Michigan Panthers, February 26, 1983.
Selected by Miami in 12th round (334th player selected) of 1983 NFL draft.
On injured reserve with broken arm, April 5 through remainder of 1984 season.
Protected in merger of Michigan Panthers and Oakland Invaders, December 6, 1984.
On developmental squad, June 24 through June 29, 1985; activated, June 30, 1985.
NFL rights traded by Miami Dolphins to Minnesota Vikings for linebacker Robin Sendlein and 2nd round pick in 1986 NFL draft, August 15, 1985.
Released by Oakland Invaders, August 23, 1985; signed by Minnesota Vikings, August 25, 1985.
Granted roster exemption, August 25 through August 28, 1985; activated, August 29, 1985.
On injured reserve with knee injury, September 5 through October 3, 1986; activated, October 4, 1986.
On developmental squad for 1 game with Oakland Invaders in 1985.

Year Club	G.	-PASS RECEIVING- P.C. Yds. Avg. TD.				-PUNT RETURNS- No. Yds. Avg. TD.				—TOTAL— TD. Pts. F.		
1983—Michigan USFL..............	18	60	1181	19.7	9	40	387	9.7	★1	10	60	6
1984—Michigan USFL..............	6	30	538	17.9	4	5	21	4.2	0	4	24	2
1985—Oakland USFL...............	17	70	1323	18.9	14			None		15	90	0
1985—Minnesota NFL.............	16	43	821	19.1	8	9	117	13.0	0	8	48	1
1986—Minnesota NFL.............	12	38	686	18.1	7			None		7	42	1
1987—Minnesota NFL.............	12	38	922	★24.3	7	3	40	13.3	0	7	42	0
USFL Totals—3 Years.................	41	160	3042	19.0	27	45	408	9.1	1	29	174	8
NFL Totals—3 Years..................	40	119	2429	20.4	22	12	157	13.1	0	22	132	2
Pro Totals—6 Years....................	81	279	5471	19.6	49	57	565	9.9	1	51	306	10

Additional USFL statistics: Rushed three times for one yard and recovered three fumbles, 1983; recovered one fumble, 1984; recovered one fumble in end zone for a touchdown and attempted one pass with no completions, 1985.

Additional NFL statistics: Recovered one fumble, 1985; rushed once for 12 yards, 1986.

Played in NFC Championship Game following 1987 season.

Played in USFL Championship Game following 1983 and 1985 seasons.

Played in Pro Bowl (NFL All-Star Game) following 1987 season.

CARL ANTHONY CARTER
Cornerback—Phoenix Cardinals
Born March 7, 1964, at Fort Worth, Tex.
Height, 5.11. Weight, 180.
High School—Fort Worth, Tex., O. D. Wyatt.
Attended Texas Tech University.

Selected by St. Louis in 4th round (89th player selected) of 1986 NFL draft.

Signed by St. Louis Cardinals, July 12, 1986.

Franchise transferred to Phoenix, March 15, 1988.

			—INTERCEPTIONS—		
Year Club	G.	No.	Yds.	Avg.	TD.
1986—St. Louis NFL	14	2	12	6.0	0
1987—St. Louis NFL	12	1	0	0.0	0
Pro Totals—2 Years	26	3	12	4.0	0

Additional pro statistics: Returned two kickoffs for 21 yards, returned one punt for no yards and fumbled once, 1986; recovered one fumble, 1986 and 1987.

CRIS CARTER
Wide Receiver—Philadelphia Eagles
Born November 25, 1965, at Middletown, O.
Height, 6.03. Weight, 194.
High School—Middletown, O.
Attended Ohio State University.

Selected by Philadelphia in 4th round of 1987 NFL supplemental draft, September 4, 1987.

Signed by Philadelphia Eagles, September 17, 1987.

Granted roster exemption, September 17 through October 25, 1987; activated, October 26, 1987.

		PASS RECEIVING				—KICKOFF RET.—				—TOTAL—		
Year Club	G.	P.C.	Yds.	Avg.	TD.	No.	Yds.	Avg.	TD.	TD.	Pts.	F.
1987—Philadelphia NFL	9	5	84	16.8	2	12	271	20.1	0	2	12	0

Additional pro statistics: Attempted one pass with no completions, 1987.

GERALD LOUIS CARTER
Wide Receiver—Tampa Bay Buccaneers
Born June 19, 1957, at Bryan, Tex.
Height, 6.01. Weight, 190.
High School—Bryan, Tex.
Attended Tyler Junior College and Texas A&M University.

Selected by Tampa Bay in 9th round (240th player selected) of 1980 NFL draft

Released by Tampa Bay Buccaneers, August 25, 1980; claimed on procedural waivers by New York Jets, October 23, 1980.

Released by New York Jets, November 17, 1980; signed as free agent by Tampa Bay Buccaneers, December 12, 1980.

Active for 2 games with Tampa Bay Buccaneers in 1980; did not play.

		—PASS RECEIVING—			
Year Club	G.	P.C.	Yds.	Avg.	TD.
1980—N.Y.J. (3)-T.B. (0) NFL	3		None		
1981—Tampa Bay NFL	16	1	10	10.0	0
1982—Tampa Bay NFL	9	10	140	14.0	0
1983—Tampa Bay NFL	16	48	694	14.5	2
1984—Tampa Bay NFL	16	60	816	13.6	5
1985—Tampa Bay NFL	16	40	557	13.9	3
1986—Tampa Bay NFL	15	42	640	15.2	2
1987—Tampa Bay NFL	12	38	586	15.4	5
Pro Totals—8 Years	103	239	3443	14.4	17

Additional pro statistics: Returned one kickoff for 12 yards, 1980; fumbled once, 1980, 1984 and 1985; fumbled three times and rushed once for no yards, 1983; recovered one fumble and rushed once for 16 yards, 1984; rushed once for 13 yards, 1985; rushed once for minus five yards and fumbled twice, 1986.

MICHAEL D'ANDREA CARTER
Nose Tackle—San Francisco 49ers
Born October 29, 1960, at Dallas, Tex.
Height, 6.02. Weight, 285.
High School—Dallas, Tex., Thomas Jefferson.
Received bachelor of science degree in sociology from Southern Methodist University in 1984.
Won silver medal in shot put during 1984 Olympics.

Named to THE SPORTING NEWS NFL All-Star Team, 1987.

Selected by Los Angeles in 10th round (194th player selected) of 1984 USFL draft.

Selected by San Francisco in 5th round (121st player selected) of 1984 NFL draft.
USFL rights traded by Los Angeles Express to New Orleans Breakers for past considerations, June 19, 1984.
Signed by San Francisco 49ers, August 14, 1984.
On injured reserve with torn hamstring, September 28 through October 25, 1985; activated, October 26, 1985.
San Francisco NFL, 1984 through 1987.
Games: 1984 (16), 1985 (12), 1986 (15), 1987 (12). Total—55.
Played in NFC Championship Game following 1984 season.
Played in NFL Championship Game following 1984 season.
Played in Pro Bowl (NFL All-Star Game) following 1985 and 1987 seasons.

RODNEY CARL CARTER
Running Back—Pittsburgh Steelers
Born October 30, 1964, at Elizabeth, N.J.
Height, 6.00. Weight, 212.
High School—Elizabeth, N.J.
Received bachelor of social sciences degree in criminology
and criminal justice from Purdue University in 1986.

Selected by Pittsburgh in 7th round (175th player selected) of 1986 NFL draft.
Signed by Pittsburgh Steelers, July 10, 1986.
On injured reserve with knee injury, August 26 through entire 1986 season.
Released by Pittsburgh Steelers, September 7, 1987; re-signed as replacement player by Steelers, September 24, 1987.

Year Club	G.	Att.	Yds.	Avg.	TD.	P.C.	Yds.	Avg.	TD.	TD.	Pts.	F.
		—RUSHING—				PASS RECEIVING				—TOTAL—		
1987—Pittsburgh NFL	11	5	12	2.4	0	16	180	11.3	3	3	18	0

RUSSELL EDMONDS CARTER JR.
Defensive Back—Los Angeles Raiders
Born February 10, 1962, at Philadelphia, Pa.
Height, 6.02. Weight, 195.
High School—Ardmore, Pa., Lower Merion.
Attended Southern Methodist University.

Named as defensive back on THE SPORTING NEWS College All-America Team, 1983.
Selected by Denver in 1st round (9th player selected) of 1984 USFL draft.
Selected by New York Jets in 1st round (10th player selected) of 1984 NFL draft.
Signed by New York Jets, May 25, 1984.
On injured reserve with back injury, November 16 through December 26, 1985; activated, December 27, 1985.
On injured reserve with separated shoulder, December 9 through remainder of 1987 season.
Granted free agency, February 1, 1988; re-signed by Jets and traded to Los Angeles Raiders for 6th round pick in 1989 draft, May 21, 1988.
New York Jets NFL, 1984 through 1987.
Games: 1984 (11), 1985 (8), 1986 (13), 1987 (8). Total—40.
Pro statistics: Intercepted four passes for 26 yards, 1984; recovered one fumble, 1986 and 1987.

MAURICE CARTHON
Running Back—New York Giants
Born April 24, 1961, at Chicago, Ill.
Height, 6.01. Weight, 225.
High School—Osceola, Ark.
Attended Arkansas State University.

Selected by New Jersey in 8th round (94th player selected) of 1983 USFL draft.
Signed by New Jersey Generals, January 19, 1983.
On developmental squad, June 17 through remainder of 1983 season.
Signed by New York Giants, March 7, 1985, for contract to take effect after being granted free agency after 1985 USFL season.
Placed on did not report list, January 21 through January 27, 1985; activated, January 28, 1985.
Granted roster exemption, January 28 through February 3, 1985; activated, February 4, 1985.
On developmental squad for 3 games with New Jersey Generals in 1983.

Year Club	G.	Att.	Yds.	Avg.	TD.	P.C.	Yds.	Avg.	TD.	TD.	Pts.	F.
		—RUSHING—				PASS RECEIVING				—TOTAL—		
1983—New Jersey USFL	11	90	334	3.7	3	20	170	8.5	0	3	†24	4
1984—New Jersey USFL	18	238	1042	4.4	11	26	194	7.5	1	12	72	4
1985—New Jersey USFL	18	175	726	4.2	6	18	154	8.6	0	6	36	3
1985—New York Giants NFL	16	27	70	2.6	0	8	81	10.1	0	0	0	1
1986—New York Giants NFL	16	72	260	3.6	0	16	67	4.2	0	0	0	1
1987—New York Giants NFL	11	26	60	2.3	0	8	71	8.9	0	0	0	0
USFL Totals—3 Years	47	503	2102	4.2	20	64	518	8.1	1	21	132	11
NFL Totals—3 Years	43	125	390	3.1	0	32	219	6.8	0	0	0	2
Pro Totals—6 Years	90	628	2492	4.0	20	96	737	7.7	1	21	132	13

†Includes three 2-point conversions.
Additional pro statistics: Recovered one fumble, 1984.
Played in NFC Championship Game following 1986 season.
Played in NFL Championship Game following 1986 season.

MELVIN CARVER
(Mel)
Running Back—Indianapolis Colts

Born July 14, 1959, at Pensacola, Fla.
Height, 5.11. Weight, 215.
High School—Alameda, Calif., Encinal.
Attended Laney Junior College and University of Nevada at Las Vegas.
Signed as free agent by Tampa Bay Buccaneers, May 3, 1982.
On injured reserve with stress fracture of shin, October 3 through remainder of 1984 season.
Released by Tampa Bay Buccaneers, September 16, 1985; signed as free agent by Indianapolis Colts, June 27, 1986.
Released by Indianapolis Colts, August 11, 1986; re-signed as replacement player by Colts, October 13, 1987.
Released by Indianapolis Colts, November 2, 1987; re-signed by Colts for 1988, December 3, 1987.

Year Club	G.	Att.	Yds.	Avg.	TD.	P.C.	Yds.	Avg.	TD.	TD.	Pts.	F.
1982—Tampa Bay NFL	9	70	229	3.3	1	4	46	11.5	1	2	12	2
1983—Tampa Bay NFL	16	114	348	3.1	0	32	262	8.2	1	1	6	6
1984—Tampa Bay NFL	5	11	44	4.0	0	3	27	9.0	0	0	0	1
1985—Tampa Bay NFL	2			None				None		0	0	0
1987—Indianapolis NFL	1	2	3	1.5	0			None		0	0	0
Pro Totals—5 Years	33	197	624	3.2	1	39	335	8.6	2	3	18	9

Column groups: RUSHING (Att. Yds. Avg. TD.), PASS RECEIVING (P.C. Yds. Avg. TD.), TOTAL (TD. Pts. F.)

Additional pro statistics: Returned three kickoffs for 62 yards and recovered three fumbles, 1982; returned two kickoffs for 24 yards and recovered two fumbles, 1983.

JEFFREY SCOTT CASE
(Known by middle name.)
Cornerback—Atlanta Falcons

Born May 17, 1962, at Waynoka, Okla.
Height, 6.00. Weight, 178.
High Schools—Alva, Okla.; and Edmond, Okla., Memorial.
Attended Northeastern Oklahoma A&M and University of Oklahoma.
Selected by Oklahoma in 1984 USFL territorial draft.
Selected by Atlanta in 2nd round (32nd player selected) of 1984 NFL draft.
Signed by Atlanta Falcons, July 20, 1984.

Year Club	G.	No.	Yds.	Avg.	TD.
1984—Atlanta NFL	16		None		
1985—Atlanta NFL	14	4	78	19.5	0
1986—Atlanta NFL	16	4	41	10.3	0
1987—Atlanta NFL	11	1	12	12.0	0
Pro Totals—4 Years	57	9	131	14.6	0

Column group: INTERCEPTIONS

Additional pro statistics: Credited with one safety and recovered one fumble for 13 yards, 1985.

TONY STEVEN CASILLAS
Nose Tackle—Atlanta Falcons

Born October 26, 1963, at Tulsa, Okla.
Height, 6.03. Weight, 280.
High School—Tulsa, Okla., East Central.
Received degree from University of Oklahoma in 1986.
Named as defensive lineman on THE SPORTING NEWS College All-America Team, 1984 and 1985.
Selected by Atlanta in 1st round (2nd player selected) of 1986 NFL draft.
Selected by Arizona in 1st round (2nd player selected) of 1986 USFL draft.
Signed by Atlanta Falcons, July 20, 1986.
Atlanta NFL, 1986 and 1987.
Games: 1986 (16), 1987 (9). Total—25.
Pro statistics: Recovered one fumble, 1986 and 1987.

JEREMIAH CASTILLE
Name pronounced Cass-TEEL.
Defensive Back—Denver Broncos

Born January 15, 1961, at Columbus, Ga.
Height, 5.10. Weight, 175.
High School—Phenix City, Ala., Central.
Received degree in broadcasting from University of Alabama.
Cousin of Rod Barksdale, wide receiver with Dallas Cowboys.
Selected by Birmingham in 1983 USFL territorial draft.
Selected by Tampa Bay in 3rd round (72nd player selected) of 1983 NFL draft.
Signed by Tampa Bay Buccaneers, May 18, 1983.
Released by Tampa Bay Buccaneers, August 24, 1987; awarded on waivers to Denver Broncos, August 25, 1987.

Year Club	G.	No.	Yds.	Avg.TD.		Year Club	G.	No.	Yds.	Avg.TD.
1983—Tampa Bay NFL	15	1	69	69.0	1	1986—Tampa Bay NFL	13		None	
1984—Tampa Bay NFL	16	3	38	12.7	0	1987—Denver NFL	11		None	
1985—Tampa Bay NFL	16	7	49	7.0	0	Pro Totals—5 Years	71	11	156	14.2 1

Column groups: INTERCEPTIONS

Additional pro statistics: Recovered two fumbles for 16 yards, 1984; recovered two fumbles and fumbled once, 1985.
Played in AFC Championship Game following 1987 season.
Played in NFL Championship Game following 1987 season.

SEBASTIAN TOBIAS CASTON
(Toby)
Linebacker—Houston Oilers
Born July 17, 1965, at Monroe, La.
Height, 6.01. Weight, 235.
High School—Monroe, La., Neville.
Attended Louisiana State University.

Selected by Houston in 6th round (159th player selected) of 1987 NFL draft.
Signed by Houston Oilers, July 27, 1987.
On injured reserve with foot and arch injuries, November 24 through remainder of 1987 season.
Houston NFL, 1987.
Games: 1987 (6).

MATTHEW ANDREW CAVANAUGH
(Matt)
Quarterback—Philadelphia Eagles
Born October 27, 1956, at Youngstown, O.
Height, 6.02. Weight, 212.
High School—Youngstown, O., Chaney.
Received bachelor of science degree in administration of justice from University of Pittsburgh.

Selected by New England in 2nd round (50th player selected) of 1978 NFL draft.
Traded by New England Patriots to San Francisco 49ers for 7th round pick in 1984 draft, 8th round pick in 1985 draft and 7th round pick in 1986 draft, August 10, 1983.
Traded by San Francisco 49ers to Philadelphia Eagles for 3rd round pick in 1986 draft and 2nd round pick in 1987 draft, April 29, 1986.
Active for 16 games with New England Patriots in 1978; did not play.

					—PASSING—						—RUSHING—			—TOTAL—		
Year Club	G.	Att.	Cmp.	Pct.	Gain	T.P.	P.I.	Avg.	Att.	Yds.	Avg.	TD.	TD.	Pts.	F.
1979—New England NFL...........	13	1	1	100.0	10	0	0	10.00	1	—2	—2.0	0	0	0	0
1980—New England NFL...........	16	105	63	60.0	885	9	5	8.43	19	97	5.1	0	0	0	1
1981—New England NFL...........	16	219	115	52.5	1633	5	13	7.46	17	92	5.4	3	3	18	2
1982—New England NFL...........	7	60	27	45.0	490	5	5	8.17	2	3	1.5	0	0	0	1
1983—San Francisco NFL	5				None				1	8	8.0	0	0	0	0
1984—San Francisco NFL	8	61	33	54.1	449	4	0	7.36	4	—11	—2.8	0	0	0	0
1985—San Francisco NFL	16	54	28	51.9	334	1	1	6.19	4	5	1.3	0	0	0	0
1986—Philadelphia NFL	10	58	28	48.3	397	2	4	6.84	9	26	2.9	0	0	0	2
1987—Philadelphia NFL	3				None				1	—2	—2.0	0	0	0	0
Pro Totals—10 Years........	94	558	295	52.9	4198	26	28	7.52	58	216	3.7	3	3	18	6

Quarterback Rating Points: 1979 (108.3), 1980 (95.9), 1981 (60.0), 1982 (66.7), 1984 (99.7), 1985 (69.5), 1986 (53.6). Total—72.3.
Additional pro statistics: Recovered one fumble and fumbled once for minus four yards, 1980; caught one pass for nine yards, 1981.
Played in NFC Championship Game following 1984 season.
Member of San Francisco 49ers for NFC Championship Game following 1983 season; did not play.
Member of San Francisco 49ers for NFL Championship Game following 1984 season; did not play.

JEFFREY ALLAN CHADWICK
(Jeff)
Wide Receiver—Detroit Lions
Born December 16, 1960, at Detroit, Mich.
Height, 6.03. Weight, 190.
High School—Dearborn, Mich., Divine Child.
Attended Grand Valley State College.

Signed as free agent by Detroit Lions, May 15, 1983.
On injured reserve with broken collarbone, November 4 through remainder of 1985 season.
On injured reserve with Achilles heal injury, December 17 through remainder of 1986 season.
On injured reserve with broken hand, December 1 through remainder of 1987 season.

		—PASS RECEIVING—			
Year Club	G.	P.C.	Yds.	Avg.	TD.
1983—Detroit NFL..................	16	40	617	15.4	4
1984—Detroit NFL..................	16	37	540	14.6	2
1985—Detroit NFL..................	7	25	478	19.1	3
1986—Detroit NFL..................	15	53	995	18.8	5
1987—Detroit NFL..................	8	30	416	13.9	0
Pro Totals—5 Years............	62	185	3046	16.5	14

Additional pro statistics: Rushed once for 12 yards and a touchdown, 1984; fumbled once, 1986; rushed once for minus six yards, 1987.

THORNTON GREENE CHANDLER
Tight End—Dallas Cowboys
Born November 27, 1963, at Jacksonville, Fla.
Height, 6.05. Weight, 245.
High School—Jacksonville, Fla., William M. Raines.
Attended Florida A&M University and University of Alabama.

Selected by Dallas in 6th round (140th player selected) of 1986 NFL draft.
Signed by Dallas Cowboys, July 6, 1986.

			—PASS RECEIVING—			
Year	Club	G.	P.C.	Yds.	Avg.	TD.
1986—Dallas NFL		15	6	57	9.5	2
1987—Dallas NFL		12	5	25	5.0	1
Pro Totals—2 Years		27	11	82	7.5	3

Additional pro statistics: Fumbled once, 1986; returned one kickoff for seven yards, 1987.

WESLEY SANDY CHANDLER
(Wes)
Wide Receiver—San Francisco 49ers
Born August 22, 1956, at New Smyrna Beach, Fla.
Height, 6.00. Weight, 188.
High School—New Smyrna Beach, Fla.
Received degree in speech pathology from University of Florida.

Named as wide receiver on THE SPORTING NEWS College All-America Team, 1977.
Selected by New Orleans in 1st round (3rd player selected) of 1978 NFL draft.
Traded by New Orleans Saints to San Diego Chargers for wide receiver Aundra Thompson and 1st and 3rd round picks in 1982 draft, September 29, 1981.
Traded with conditional 1989 draft pick by San Diego Chargers to San Francisco 49ers for center Fred Quillan and conditional 1989 draft pick, June 3, 1988.

			PASS RECEIVING				—PUNT RETURNS—				—KICKOFF RET.—				—TOTAL—		
Year	Club	G.	P.C.	Yds.	Avg.	TD.	No.	Yds.	Avg.	TD.	No.	Yds.	Avg.	TD.	TD.	Pts.	F.
1978—New Orleans NFL		16	35	472	13.5	2	34	233	6.9	0	32	760	23.8	0	2	12	1
1979—New Orleans NFL		16	65	1069	16.4	6	3	13	4.3	0	7	136	19.4	0	6	36	0
1980—New Orleans NFL		16	65	975	15.0	6	8	36	4.5	0		None			6	36	2
1981—N.O. (4)-S.D. (12) NFL.		16	69	1142	16.6	6	5	79	15.8	0	8	125	15.6	0	6	36	1
1982—San Diego NFL		8	49	*1032	21.1	*9		None				None			9	54	0
1983—San Diego NFL		16	58	845	14.6	5	8	26	3.3	0		None			5	30	3
1984—San Diego NFL		15	52	708	13.6	6		None				None			6	36	0
1985—San Diego NFL		15	67	1199	17.9	10		None				None			10	60	1
1986—San Diego NFL		16	56	874	15.6	4	3	13	4.3	0	1	11	11.0	0	4	24	2
1987—San Diego NFL		12	39	617	15.8	2		None				None			2	12	1
Pro Totals—10 Years		146	555	8933	16.1	56	61	400	6.6	0	48	1032	21.5	0	56	336	11

Additional pro statistics: Rushed twice for 10 yards, 1978; punted eight times for 31.0 average, 1979; attempted one pass with one completion for 43 yards and recovered two fumbles, 1980; rushed once for nine yards, 1980 and 1985; recovered one fumble for 51 yards, rushed five times for minus one yard and attempted two passes with no completions, 1981; rushed five times for 32 yards, 1982; rushed twice for 25 yards and recovered one fumble, 1983; punted five times for a 33.4 average, 1986; recovered one fumble, 1987.
Played in AFC Championship Game following 1981 season.
Played in Pro Bowl (NFL All-Star Game) following 1979, 1982, 1983 and 1985 seasons.

RICHARD HARRY CHAPURA JR.
Name pronounced Sha-POOR-a.
(Dick)
Defensive Tackle—Chicago Bears
Born June 15, 1964, at Sarasota, Fla.
Height, 6.03. Weight, 280.
High School—Sarasota, Fla., Riverview.
Attended University of Missouri.

Selected by Chicago in 10th round (277th player selected) of 1987 NFL draft.
Signed by Chicago Bears, July 27, 1987.
On injured reserve with knee injury, August 27 through November 15, 1987; activated, November 16, 1987.
Chicago NFL, 1987.
Games: 1987 (2).

MICHAEL WILLIAM CHARLES
(Mike)
Nose Tackle—San Diego Chargers
Born September 23, 1962, at Newark, N.J.
Height, 6.04. Weight, 287.
High School—Newark, N.J., Central.
Received bachelor of science degree in speech communications from Syracuse University.

Selected by New Jersey in 1983 USFL territorial draft.
Selected by Miami in 2nd round (55th player selected) of 1983 NFL draft.
Signed by Miami Dolphins, July 12, 1983.
On injured reserve with knee injury, November 17 through December 27, 1984; activated, December 28, 1984.
On suspended list, September 6 through September 25, 1986; activated, September 26, 1986.

On injured reserve with knee injury, October 1 through October 31, 1986; activated, November 1, 1986.
Released by Miami Dolphins, July 31, 1987; awarded on waivers to Tampa Bay Buccaneers, August 3, 1987.
Released by Tampa Bay Buccaneers, August 17, 1987; awarded on waivers to San Diego Chargers, August 18, 1987.
Miami NFL, 1983 through 1986; San Diego NFL, 1987.
Games: 1983 (16), 1984 (10), 1985 (16), 1986 (9), 1987 (11). Total—62.
Pro statistics: Recovered one fumble and credited with one safety, 1983; intercepted one pass for two yards, 1986.
Played in AFC Championship Game following 1984 and 1985 seasons.
Played in NFL Championship Game following 1984 season.

DERON LEIGH CHERRY

First name pronounced Da-RON.

Safety—Kansas City Chiefs

Born September 12, 1959, at Riverside, N.J.
Height, 5.11. Weight, 196.
High School—Palmyra, N.J.
Attended Rutgers University.
Related to Raphel Cherry, safety with Detroit Lions.

Named to THE SPORTING NEWS NFL All-Star Team, 1986.
Tied NFL record for most interceptions, game (4), against Seattle Seahawks, September 29, 1985.
Signed as free agent by Kansas City Chiefs, May 4, 1981.
Released by Kansas City Chiefs, August 31, 1981; re-signed by Chiefs, September 23, 1981.
On inactive list, September 19, 1982.
On injured reserve with shoulder separation, December 30 through remainder of 1982 season.

		—INTERCEPTIONS—			
Year Club	G.	No.	Yds.	Avg.	TD.
1981—Kansas City NFL..........	13	1	4	4.0	0
1982—Kansas City NFL..........	7		None		
1983—Kansas City NFL..........	16	7	100	14.3	0
1984—Kansas City NFL..........	16	7	140	20.0	0
1985—Kansas City NFL..........	16	7	87	12.4	*1
1986—Kansas City NFL..........	16	9	150	16.7	0
1987—Kansas City NFL..........	8	3	58	19.3	0
Pro Totals—7 Years..........	92	34	539	15.9	1

Additional pro statistics: Returned three kickoffs for 52 yards, 1981; returned one kickoff for 39 yards, 1982; returned two kickoffs for 54 yards, recovered two fumbles for four yards and fumbled twice, 1983; returned one kickoff for no yards, 1984; recovered blocked punt in end zone twice for two touchdowns and recovered two fumbles for seven yards, 1986; recovered one fumble, 1987.
Played in Pro Bowl (NFL All-Star Game) following 1983 through 1987 seasons.

RAPHEL JEROME CHERRY

First name pronounced RA-fehl.

Safety—Detroit Lions

Born December 19, 1961, at Little Rock, Ark.
Height, 6.00. Weight, 194.
High School—Los Angeles, Calif., Washington.
Attended University of Hawaii.
Related to Deron Cherry, safety with Kansas City Chiefs.

Selected by Houston in 1st round (6th player selected) of 1985 USFL draft.
Selected by Washington in 5th round (122nd player selected) of 1985 NFL draft.
Signed by Washington Redskins, July 18, 1985.
Released by Washington Redskins, September 1, 1986; signed as free agent by San Francisco 49ers, December 23, 1986.
Released by San Francisco 49ers, September 7, 1987; signed as free agent by Detroit Lions to begin play after strike is settled, October 5, 1987.

		—INTERCEPTIONS—			
Year Club	G.	No.	Yds.	Avg.	TD.
1985—Washington NFL..........	16	2	29	14.5	0
1987—Detroit NFL.................	10	1	2	2.0	0
Pro Totals—2 Years..........	26	3	31	10.3	0

Additional pro statistics: Returned four punts for 22 yards, returned one kickoff for nine yards and caught one pass for 11 yards, 1985.

WILLIAM KIMBLE CHERRY

(Bill)

Center-Guard—Green Bay Packers

Born January 5, 1961, at Deland, Fla.
Height, 6.04. Weight, 277.
High School—Dover, Tenn., Stewart County.
Attended Middle Tennessee State University.

Signed as free agent by Memphis Showboats, January 16, 1984.
Released by Memphis Showboats, February 12, 1984; signed as free agent by Tampa Bay Bandits, October 31, 1984.
Released by Tampa Bay Bandits, December 19, 1984; signed as free agent by Green Bay Packers, March 28, 1986.
Green Bay NFL, 1986 and 1987.
Games: 1986 (16), 1987 (12). Total—28.
Pro statistics: Fumbled once for minus 23 yards, 1986.

ANTHONY PAUL CHICKILLO

Name pronounced CHI-kill-o.

(Tony)

Nose Tackle—New York Jets

Born July 8, 1960, at Miami, Fla.
Height, 6.03. Weight, 257.
High School—Miami, Fla., Southwest.
Received degree in recreational therapy from University of Miami (Fla.) in 1983.
Son of Nick Chickillo, guard with Chicago Cardinals, 1953.

Selected by New Jersey in 16th round (191st player selected) of 1983 USFL draft.
Selected by Tampa Bay in 5th round (131st player selected) of 1983 NFL draft.
Signed by Tampa Bay Buccaneers, June 6, 1983.
On injured reserve with ankle injury, August 22 through entire 1983 season.
Released by Tampa Bay Buccaneers, August 20, 1984; awarded on waivers to Indianapolis Colts, August 21, 1984.
Released by Indianapolis Colts, August 27, 1984.
USFL rights traded by New Jersey Generals to Orlando Renegades for rights to defensive tackle Charles Cook, October 31, 1984.
Signed as free agent by San Diego Chargers, December 13, 1984.
Released by San Diego Chargers, October 5, 1985; signed as free agent by Miami Dolphins, April 30, 1986.
Released by Miami Dolphins, August 21, 1986; signed as free agent by New York Jets, March 27, 1987.
Released by New York Jets after failing physical, May 20, 1987; re-signed as replacement player by Jets, September 24, 1987.
Released by New York Jets, October 19, 1987; re-signed by Jets, April 15, 1988.
San Diego NFL, 1984 and 1985; New York Jets NFL, 1987.
Games: 1984 (1), 1985 (4), 1987 (2). Total—7.

RAY CHILDRESS

Defensive End—Houston Oilers

Born October 20, 1962, at Memphis, Tenn.
Height, 6.06. Weight, 276.
High School—Richardson, Tex., J.J. Pearce.
Attended Texas A&M University.

Named as defensive lineman on THE SPORTING NEWS College All-America Team, 1984.
Selected by Houston in 1985 USFL territorial draft.
Selected by Houston in 1st round (3rd player selected) of 1985 NFL draft.
Signed by Houston Oilers, August 24, 1985.
Granted roster exemption, August 24 through August 29, 1985; activated, August 30, 1985.
Crossed picket line during players' strike, October 14, 1987.
Houston NFL, 1985 through 1987.
Games: 1985 (16), 1986 (16), 1987 (13). Total—45.
Pro statistics: Recovered one fumble, 1985 and 1986; recovered one fumble for one yard, 1987.

GENE ALAN CHILTON

Offensive Tackle—Phoenix Cardinals

Born March 27, 1964, at Houston, Tex.
Height, 6.03. Weight, 271.
High School—Houston, Tex., Memorial.
Attended University of Texas.

Selected by St. Louis in 3rd round (59th player selected) of 1986 NFL draft.
Signed by St. Louis Cardinals, July 25, 1986.
Franchise transferred to Phoenix, March 15, 1988.
St. Louis NFL, 1986 and 1987.
Games: 1986 (16), 1987 (11). Total—27.
Pro statistics: Recovered one fumble, 1986.

TODD JAY CHRISTENSEN

Tight End—Los Angeles Raiders

Born August 3, 1956, at Bellefonte, Pa.
Height, 6.03. Weight, 230.
High School—Eugene, Ore., Sheldon.
Attended Brigham Young University.

Named to THE SPORTING NEWS NFL All-Star Team, 1983 and 1985.
Selected by Dallas in 2nd round (56th player selected) of 1978 NFL draft.
On injured reserve with broken foot, August 28 through entire 1978 season.
Released by Dallas Cowboys, August 27, 1979; claimed on waivers by New York Giants, August 28, 1979.
Released by New York Giants, September 4, 1979; signed as free agent by Oakland Raiders, September 26, 1979.
Franchise transferred to Los Angeles, May 7, 1982.
On did not report list, August 14 through August 22, 1984.
Reported and granted roster exemption, August 23 through August 31, 1984; activated, September 1, 1984.

			—PASS RECEIVING—			
Year Club	G.	P.C.	Yds.	Avg.	TD.	
1979—NYG (1)-Oak (12) NFL	13		None			
1980—Oakland NFL	16		None			
1981—Oakland NFL	16	8	115	14.4	2	
1982—L.A. Raiders NFL	9	42	510	12.1	4	
1983—L.A. Raiders NFL	16	*92	1247	13.6	12	
1984—L.A. Raiders NFL	16	80	1007	12.6	7	
1985—L.A. Raiders NFL	16	82	987	12.0	6	
1986—L.A. Raiders NFL	16	*95	1153	12.1	8	
1987—L.A. Raiders NFL	12	47	663	14.1	2	
Pro Totals—9 Years	130	446	5682	12.7	41	

Additional pro statistics: Recovered two fumbles for one yard, 1979; recovered one fumble in end zone for a touchdown and returned one kickoff for 10 yards, 1980; returned four kickoffs for 54 yards and credited with one safety, 1981; recovered one fumble, 1981 and 1983 through 1985; rushed once for minus six yards and fumbled three times, 1982; fumbled once, 1983, 1984 and 1986.

Played in AFC Championship Game following 1980 and 1983 seasons.

Played in NFL Championship Game following 1980 and 1983 seasons.

Played in Pro Bowl (NFL All-Star Game) following 1983 through 1987 seasons.

DARRYL E. CLACK
Running Back—Dallas Cowboys
Born October 29, 1963, at San Antonio, Tex.
Height, 5.10. Weight, 218.
High School—Security, Colo., Widefield.
Attended Arizona State University.

Selected by Arizona in 1986 USFL territorial draft.
Selected by Dallas in 2nd round (33rd player selected) of 1986 NFL draft.
Signed by Dallas Cowboys, July 21, 1986.

		—RUSHING—				PASS RECEIVING				—TOTAL—		
Year Club	G.	Att.	Yds.	Avg.	TD.	P.C.	Yds.	Avg.	TD.	TD.	Pts.	F.
1986—Dallas NFL	16	4	19	4.8	0	1	18	18.0	0	0	0	3
1987—Dallas NFL	12		None				None			0	0	1
Pro Totals—2 Years	28	4	19	4.8	0	1	18	18.0	0	0	0	4

		KICKOFF RETURNS			
Year Club	G.	No.	Yds.	Avg.	TD.
1986—Dallas NFL	16	19	421	22.2	0
1987—Dallas NFL	12	29	635	21.9	0
Pro Totals—2 Years	28	48	1056	22.0	0

SAM CLANCY
Defensive End—Cleveland Browns
Born May 29, 1958, at Pittsburgh, Pa.
Height, 6.07. Weight, 260.
High School—Pittsburgh, Pa., Brashear.
Attended University of Pittsburgh.

Selected by Phoenix in 3rd round (62nd player selected) of 1981 NBA draft.
Released by Phoenix Suns, October 19, 1981; signed by Billings Volcanos (CBA), November 12, 1981.
Selected by Seattle in 11th round (284th player selected) of 1982 NFL draft.
On injured reserve with knee injury, August 16 through entire 1982 season.
Granted free agency, February 1, 1984; signed by Pittsburgh Maulers, February 10, 1984.
Franchise disbanded, October 25, 1984.
Selected by Memphis Showboats in USFL dispersal draft, December 6, 1984.
Granted free agency, August 1, 1985; re-signed by Seahawks and traded to Cleveland Browns for 7th round pick in 1986 draft, August 27, 1985.
Granted roster exemption, August 27 through September 5, 1985; activated, September 6, 1985.
Crossed picket line during players' strike, October 14, 1987.
Seattle NFL, 1983; Pittsburgh USFL, 1984; Memphis USFL, 1985; Cleveland NFL, 1985 through 1987.
Games: 1983 (13), 1984 (18), 1985 USFL (18), 1985 NFL (14), 1986 (16), 1987 (13). Total NFL—56. Total USFL—36. Total Pro—92.
USFL statistics: Credited with 15 sacks for 136 yards and recovered two fumbles, 1984; credited with four sacks for 28 yards, 1985.
NFL statistics: Recovered one fumble, 1986; recovered two fumbles, 1987.
Played in AFC Championship Game following 1986 and 1987 seasons.

BASKETBALL RECORD AS PLAYER

								3-pt.	3-pt.							Blk.	
Year—Team	G	Min.	FGM	FGA	Pct.	FTM	FTA	Pct.	Made	Att.	Pts.	Avg.	Reb.	Avg.	Ast.	PF	Shots	Steals
81-82 Billings CBA	41	1170	190	355	53.5	89	128	69.5	1	5	472	11.5	342	8.3	50	144	41	67

PLAYOFF RECORD

								3-pt.	3-pt.							Blk.	
Year—Team	G	Min.	FGM	FGA	Pct.	FTM	FTA	Pct.	Made	Att.	Pts.	Avg.	Reb.	Avg.	Ast.	PF	Shots	Steals
81-82 Billings CBA	5	167	24	46	52.1	12	19	63.1	1	1	63	12.6	54	10.8	8	23	5	8

SAM JACK CLAPHAN

Name pronounced Clap-in.

Guard-Offensive Tackle—San Diego Chargers

Born October 10, 1956, at Tahlequah, Okla.
Height, 6.06. Weight, 288.
High School—Stillwell, Okla.
Received bachelor of science degree in special education from University of Oklahoma in 1979.

Selected by Cleveland in 2nd round (47th player selected) of 1979 NFL draft.
On injured reserve with back injury, August 27 through entire 1979 season.
Released by Cleveland Browns, August 26, 1980; signed as free agent by San Diego Chargers, May 1, 1981.
On inactive list, September 12 and September 19, 1982.
On injured reserve with knee injury, December 4 through remainder of 1985 season.
San Diego NFL, 1981 through 1987.
Games: 1981 (16), 1982 (2), 1983 (16), 1984 (16), 1985 (12), 1986 (16), 1987 (9). Total—87.
Pro statistics: Recovered one fumble, 1985.
Played in AFC Championship Game following 1981 season.

BRET CLARK

Safety—Atlanta Falcons

Born February 24, 1961, at Nebraska City, Neb.
Height, 6.03. Weight, 200.
High School—Nebraska City, Neb.
Attended University of Nebraska.

Selected by Denver in 1985 USFL territorial draft.
USFL rights traded by Denver Gold to Tampa Bay Bandits for pick in 1986 draft and $5,000, May 10, 1985.
Signed by Tampa Bay Bandits, May 10, 1985.
Selected by Los Angeles Raiders in 7th round (191st player selected) of 1985 NFL draft.
Released by Tampa Bay Bandits, March 7, 1986.
NFL rights traded by Los Angeles Raiders to Atlanta Falcons for 4th round pick in 1986 draft, April 29, 1986.
Signed by Atlanta Falcons, July 14, 1986.
On injured reserve with fractured fibula, September 14 through remainder of 1987 season.

Year Club	G.	No.	Yds.	Avg.	TD.
1985—Tampa Bay USFL	7	1	0	0.0	0
1986—Atlanta NFL	16	5	94	18.8	0
1987—Atlanta NFL	1			None	
USFL Totals—1 Year	7	1	0	0.0	0
NFL Totals—2 Years	17	5	94	18.8	0
Pro Totals—3 Years	24	6	94	15.7	0

Additional USFL statistics: Credited with one sack for nine yards and returned two kickoffs for 19 yards, 1985.
Additional NFL statistics: Rushed twice for eight yards and recovered two fumbles, 1986.

BRUCE CLARK

Defensive End—New Orleans Saints

Born March 31, 1958, at New Castle, Pa.
Height, 6.03. Weight, 274.
High School—New Castle, Pa.
Attended Penn State University.

Selected by Green Bay in 1st round (4th player selected) of 1980 NFL draft.
Signed by Toronto Argonauts, May 26, 1980.
Granted free agency, March 1, 1982; traded by Green Bay Packers to New Orleans Saints for 1st round pick in 1983 draft, June 10, 1982.
Crossed picket line during players' strike, September 30, 1987.
Toronto CFL, 1980 and 1981; New Orleans NFL, 1982 through 1987.
Games: 1980 (16), 1981 (16), 1982 (9), 1983 (15), 1984 (15), 1985 (16), 1986 (16), 1987 (15). Total CFL—32. Total NFL—86. Total Pro—118.
CFL statistics: Intercepted one pass for no yards and recovered four fumbles for six yards, 1980; recovered one fumble, 1981.
NFL statistics: Recovered one fumble, 1983; intercepted one pass for nine yards and recovered two fumbles for five yards, 1984; recovered one fumble for four yards, 1985; recovered three fumbles for 28 yards, 1986; recovered two fumbles and credited with a safety, 1987.
Played in Pro Bowl (NFL All-Star Game) following 1984 season.

GARY C. CLARK

Wide Receiver—Washington Redskins

Born May 1, 1962, at Radford, Va.
Height, 5.09. Weight, 175.
High School—Dublin, Va., Pulaski County.
Attended James Madison University.

Selected by Jacksonville in 1st round (6th player selected) of 1984 USFL draft.
Signed by Jacksonville Bulls, January 16, 1984.
On developmental squad, May 9 through May 15, 1984; activated, May 16, 1984.
On developmental squad, June 4 through June 11, 1984; activated, June 12, 1984.
Selected by Washington in 2nd round (55th player selected) of 1984 NFL supplemental draft.
On developmental squad, March 17 through March 19, 1985; activated, March 20, 1985.

Released by Jacksonville Bulls, May 1, 1985; signed by Washington Redskins, May 13, 1985.
On developmental squad for 2 games with Jacksonville Bulls in 1984.
On developmental squad for 1 game with Jacksonville Bulls in 1985.

			PASS RECEIVING			-PUNT RETURNS-				—KICKOFF RET.—				—TOTAL—		
Year	Club	G.	P.C.	Yds.	Avg.	TD.	No.	Yds.	Avg.	TD.	No.	Yds.	Avg.	TD.	TD.	Pts.	F.
1984—Jacksonville USFL		16	56	760	13.6	2	20	84	4.2	0	19	341	18.0	0	2	12	5
1985—Jacksonville USFL		9	10	61	6.1	1	7	44	6.3	0	3	56	18.7	0	1	6	1
1985—Washington NFL		16	72	926	12.9	5		None				None			5	30	0
1986—Washington NFL		15	74	1265	17.1	7	1	14	14.0	0		None			7	42	1
1987—Washington NFL		12	56	1066	19.0	7		None				None			7	42	3
USFL Totals—2 Years		25	66	821	12.4	3	27	128	4.7	0	22	397	18.0	0	3	18	6
NFL Totals—3 Years		43	202	3257	16.1	19	1	14	14.0	0	0	0	0.0	0	19	114	4
Pro Totals—5 Years		68	268	4078	15.2	22	28	142	5.1	0	22	397	18.0	0	22	132	10

Additional USFL statistics: Rushed twice for nine yards and recovered four fumbles, 1984; recovered one fumble, 1985.
Additional NFL statistics: Rushed twice for 10 yards and recovered one fumble, 1986; rushed once for no yards, 1987.
Played in NFC Championship Game following 1986 and 1987 seasons.
Played in NFL Championship Game following 1987 season.
Played in Pro Bowl (NFL All-Star Game) following 1986 and 1987 seasons.

JESSIE L. CLARK
Fullback—Green Bay Packers
Born January 3, 1960, at Thebes, Ark.
Height, 6.00. Weight, 228.
High School—Crossett, Ark.
Attended Louisiana Tech University and received bachelor of arts
degree in criminal justice from University of Arkansas in 1983.
Cousin of Dennis Woodberry, cornerback with Washington Redskins.

Selected by Green Bay in 7th round (188th player selected) of 1983 NFL draft.
On injured reserve with muscle tear in elbow, November 16 through remainder of 1984 season.
On injured reserve with elbow injury, November 19 through remainder of 1986 season.

			——RUSHING——				PASS RECEIVING				—TOTAL—		
Year	Club	G.	Att.	Yds.	Avg.	TD.	P.C.	Yds.	Avg.	TD.	TD.	Pts.	F.
1983—Green Bay NFL		16	71	328	4.6	0	18	279	15.5	1	1	6	2
1984—Green Bay NFL		11	87	375	4.3	4	29	234	8.1	2	6	36	2
1985—Green Bay NFL		16	147	633	4.3	5	24	252	10.5	2	7	42	4
1986—Green Bay NFL		5	18	41	2.3	0	6	41	6.8	0	0	0	1
1987—Green Bay NFL		12	56	211	3.8	0	22	119	5.4	1	1	6	0
Pro Totals—5 Years		60	379	1588	4.2	9	99	925	9.3	6	15	90	9

Additional pro statistics: Recovered one fumble, 1983; recovered two fumbles, 1985.

KEVIN RANDALL CLARK
(K. C.)
Defensive Back—Denver Broncos
Born June 8, 1964, at Sacramento, Calif.
Height, 5.10. Weight, 185.
High School—Sacramento, Calif., K. C. McClatchy.
Attended San Jose State University.

Signed as free agent by Denver Broncos, May 1, 1987.
Released by Denver Broncos, September 7, 1987; re-signed as replacement player by Broncos, September 25, 1987.

			INTERCEPTIONS			-PUNT RETURNS-				—KICKOFF RET.—				—TOTAL—		
Year	Club	G.	No.	Yds.	Avg.	TD.	No.	Yds.	Avg.	TD.	No.	Yds.	Avg.	TD.	TD.	Pts.	F.
1987—Denver NFL		11	3	105	35.0	0	18	233	12.9	1	2	33	16.5	0	1	6	1

Additional pro statistics: Recovered one fumble, 1987.
Played in AFC Championship Game following 1987 season.
Played in NFL Championship Game following 1987 season.

LOUIS STEVEN CLARK
Wide Receiver—Seattle Seahawks
Born July 3, 1964, at Shannon, Miss.
Height, 6.02. Weight, 225.
High School—Shannon, Miss.
Attended Mississippi State University.
Brother of Dave Clark, outfielder in Cleveland Indians' organization.

Selected by Seattle in 10th round (270th player selected) of 1987 NFL draft.
Signed by Seattle Seahawks, July 21, 1987.
On injured reserve with pulled hamstring, November 16 through remainder of 1987 season.
Seattle NFL, 1987.
Games: 1987 (2).

—DID YOU KNOW—
That Charles White of the Los Angeles Rams led the NFL in rushing with 1,324 yards in
1987? His career rushing total entering the '87 season was 1,378.

ROBERT CLARK
Wide Receiver—New Orleans Saints
Born August 6, 1965, at Brooklyn, N.Y.
Height, 5.11. Weight, 175.
High School—Richmond, Va., Maggie L. Walker.
Attended North Carolina Central University.

Selected by New Orleans in 10th round (263rd player selected) of 1987 NFL draft.
Signed by New Orleans Saints, July 24, 1987.
On injured reserve with stress fracture of leg, October 30 through remainder of 1987 season.
New Orleans NFL, 1987.
Games: 1987 (2).
Pro statistics: Caught three passes for 38 yards, 1987.

ROBERT JAMES CLASBY
(Bob)
Defensive Tackle—Phoenix Cardinals
Born September 28, 1960, at Detroit, Mich.
Height, 6.05. Weight, 258.
High School—Dorchester, Mass., Boston College.
Received bachelor of business administration degree in finance from Notre Dame University.
Cousin of former President John F. Kennedy, former Senator Robert F. Kennedy
and Senator Edward Kennedy (D-Mass.).

Selected by Chicago in 1983 USFL territorial draft.
Selected by Seattle in 9th round (236th player selected) of 1983 NFL draft.
Signed by Seattle Seahawks, May 8, 1983.
Released by Seattle Seahawks, August 23, 1983; signed by Chicago Blitz, September 24, 1983.
Traded by Chicago Blitz to Arizona Wranglers for rights to offensive tackle Russ Washington, January 24, 1984.
Released by Arizona Wranglers, February 24, 1984; signed as free agent by Chicago Blitz, March 6, 1984.
On developmental squad, March 24 through March 28, 1984; activated, March 29, 1984.
Traded by Chicago Blitz to Jacksonville Bulls for defensive back Kerry Baird, April 17, 1984.
Granted free agency when USFL suspended operations, August 7, 1986; signed as free agent by St. Louis Cardinals, August 15, 1986.
Granted roster exemption, August 15 through August 20, 1986; activated, August 21, 1986.
Franchise transferred to Phoenix, March 15, 1988.
On developmental squad for 1 game with Chicago Blitz in 1984.
Chicago (3)-Jacksonville (10) USFL, 1984; Jacksonville, 1985; St. Louis NFL, 1986 and 1987.
Games: 1984 (13), 1985 (18), 1986 (16), 1987 (12). Total USFL—31. Total NFL—28. Total Pro—59.
USFL statistics: Credited with five sacks for 43 yards and recovered two fumbles, 1984; credited with 3½ sacks for 38½ yards and recovered one fumble, 1985.
NFL statistics: Recovered one fumble, 1986 and 1987.

JOHN GREGORY CLAY
Offensive Tackle—Los Angeles Raiders
Born May 1, 1964, at St. Louis, Mo.
Height, 6.05. Weight, 295.
High School—St. Louis, Mo., Northwest.
Attended University of Missouri.

Selected by Los Angeles Raiders in 1st round (15th player selected) of 1987 NFL draft.
Signed by Los Angeles Raiders, July 29, 1987.
Los Angeles Raiders NFL, 1987.
Games: 1987 (10).
Pro statistics: Recovered one fumble, 1987.

RAYMOND DE WAYNE CLAYBORN
(Ray)
Cornerback—New England Patriots
Born January 2, 1955, at Fort Worth, Tex.
Height, 6.00. Weight, 186.
High School—Fort Worth, Tex., Trimble.
Received degree in communications from University of Texas.

Named as cornerback on THE SPORTING NEWS College All-America Team, 1976.
Named to THE SPORTING NEWS NFL All-Star Team, 1983.
Selected by New England in 1st round (16th player selected) of 1977 NFL draft.
Crossed picket line during players' strike, October 2, 1987.
On injured reserve with knee injury, November 23 through remainder of 1987 season.

| | | -INTERCEPTIONS- | | | —KICKOFF RET.— | | | | —TOTAL— | | |
Year Club	G.	No.	Yds.	Avg.	TD.	No.	Yds.	Avg.	TD.	TD.	Pts.	F.
1977—New England NFL	14		None			28	869	★31.0	★3	3	†20	1
1978—New England NFL	16	4	72	18.0	0	27	636	23.6	0	0	0	0
1979—New England NFL	16	5	56	11.2	0	2	33	16.5	0	0	0	0
1980—New England NFL	16	5	87	17.4	0		None			0	0	0
1981—New England NFL	16	2	39	19.5	0		None			0	0	0
1982—New England NFL	9	1	26	26.0	0		None			0	0	0
1983—New England NFL	16		None				None			0	0	0
1984—New England NFL	16	3	102	34.0	0		None			0	0	0

Year Club	G.	-INTERCEPTIONS- No. Yds. Avg. TD.	—KICKOFF RET.— No. Yds. Avg. TD.	—TOTAL— TD. Pts. F.
1985—New England NFL	16	6 80 13.3 *1	None	1 6 0
1986—New England NFL	16	3 4 1.3 0	None	0 0 0
1987—New England NFL	10	2 24 12.0 0	None	1 6 0
Pro Totals—11 Years	161	31 490 15.8 1	57 1538 27.0 3	5 32 1

†Includes one safety.
Additional pro statistics: Recovered one fumble, 1978, 1980, 1982 and 1987; recovered two fumbles for four yards, 1981; recovered two fumbles, 1986; returned blocked field goal attempt 71 yards for a touchdown, 1987.
Played in AFC Championship Game following 1985 season.
Played in NFL Championship Game following 1985 season.
Played in Pro Bowl (NFL All-Star Game) following 1983, 1985 and 1986 seasons.

HARVEY JEROME CLAYTON
Cornerback—New York Giants

Born April 4, 1961, at Kendall, Fla.
Height, 5.09. Weight, 186.
High School—Miami, Fla., South Dade.
Attended Florida State University.

Selected by Tampa Bay in 1983 USFL territorial draft.
Signed as free agent by Pittsburgh Steelers, May 19, 1983.
Traded by Pittsburgh Steelers to Detroit Lions for draft pick, September 7, 1987.
Released by Detroit Lions, September 11, 1987; signed as free agent by New York Giants, September 16, 1987.
On injured reserve with injured ribs, November 14 through remainder of 1987 season.

Year Club	G.	——INTERCEPTIONS—— No. Yds. Avg.TD.
1983—Pittsburgh NFL	14	1 70 70.0 1
1984—Pittsburgh NFL	14	1 0 0.0 0
1985—Pittsburgh NFL	14	None
1986—Pittsburgh NFL	15	3 18 6.0 0
1987—N.Y. Giants NFL	2	None
Pro Totals—5 Years	59	5 88 17.6 1

Additional pro statistics: Returned one punt for no yards and recovered one fumble, 1984.
Played in AFC Championship Game following 1984 season.

MARK GREGORY CLAYTON
Wide Receiver—Miami Dolphins

Born April 8, 1961, at Indianapolis, Ind.
Height, 5.09. Weight, 172.
High School—Indianapolis, Ind., Cathedral.
Attended University of Louisville.

Established NFL record for most touchdown receptions, season (18), 1984.
Selected by Miami in 8th round (223rd player selected) of 1983 NFL draft.

Year Club	G.	-PASS RECEIVING- P.C. Yds. Avg. TD.	-PUNT RETURNS- No. Yds. Avg. TD.	—TOTAL— TD. Pts. F.
1983—Miami NFL	14	6 114 19.0 1	41 392 9.6 *1	2 12 3
1984—Miami NFL	15	73 1389 19.0 *18	8 79 9.9 0	*18 108 2
1985—Miami NFL	16	70 996 14.2 4	2 14 7.0 0	4 24 2
1986—Miami NFL	15	60 1150 19.2 10	1 0 0.0 0	10 60 1
1987—Miami NFL	12	46 776 16.9 7	None	7 42 0
Pro Totals—5 Years	72	255 4425 17.4 40	52 485 9.3 1	41 246 8

Additional pro statistics: Rushed twice for nine yards, returned one kickoff for 25 yards, attempted one pass with one completion for 48 yards and a touchdown, 1983; recovered one fumble, 1983 through 1985; rushed three times for 35 yards, returned two kickoffs for 15 yards and attempted one pass with one interception, 1984; rushed once for 10 yards, 1985; rushed twice for 33 yards, 1986; rushed twice for eight yards, 1987.
Played in AFC Championship Game following 1984 and 1985 seasons.
Played in NFL Championship Game following 1984 season.
Played in Pro Bowl (NFL All-Star Game) following 1984 through 1986 seasons.

MICHAEL LUTRELL CLEMONS
Running Back-Punt Returner—Kansas City Chiefs

Born January 15, 1965, at Clearwater, Fla.
Height, 5.05. Weight, 166.
High School—Dunedin, Fla.
Attended College of William and Mary.

Selected by Kansas City in 8th round (218th player selected) of 1987 NFL draft.
Signed by Kansas City Chiefs, July 16, 1987.

Year Club	G.	——PUNT RETURNS—— No. Yds. Avg.TD.
1987—Kansas City NFL	8	19 162 8.5 0

Additional pro statistics: Rushed twice for seven yards, returned one kickoff for three yards, recovered one fumble and fumbled three times, 1987.

KYLE CLIFTON
Linebacker—New York Jets

Born August 23, 1962, at Onley, Tex.
Height, 6.04. Weight, 233.
High School—Bridgeport, Tex.
Received degree in business management from Texas Christian University.
Selected by Birmingham in 1st round (12th player selected) of 1984 USFL draft.
Selected by New York Jets in 3rd round (64th player selected) of 1984 NFL draft.
Signed by New York Jets, July 12, 1984.

| | | | —INTERCEPTIONS— | | |
Year Club	G.	No.	Yds.	Avg.	TD.
1984—N.Y. Jets NFL	16	1	0	0.0	0
1985—N.Y. Jets NFL	16	3	10	3.3	0
1986—N.Y. Jets NFL	16	2	8	4.0	0
1987—N.Y. Jets NFL	12			None	
Pro Totals—4 Years	60	6	18	3.0	0

Additional pro statistics: Intercepted one pass for no yards, 1984; recovered one fumble, 1984 and 1986; recovered two fumbles, 1985.

JACKIE WAYNE CLINE
Nose Tackle—Miami Dolphins

Born March 13, 1960, at Kansas City, Kan.
Height, 6.05. Weight, 274.
High School—McCalla, Ala., McAdory.
Received bachelor of science degree in advertising from University of Alabama.
Selected by Birmingham in 1983 USFL territorial draft.
Signed by Birmingham Stallions, January 26, 1983.
On developmental squad, April 16 through April 22, 1983; activated, April 23, 1983.
On developmental squad, May 5 through May 25, 1984; activated, May 26, 1984.
Released by Birmingham Stallions, August 7, 1986; signed as free agent by Green Bay Packers, August 14, 1986.
Granted roster exemption, August 14 through August 24, 1986.
Released by Green Bay Packers, August 25, 1986; signed as free agent by Cleveland Browns, July 17, 1987.
Released by Cleveland Browns, September 7, 1987; signed as free agent replacement player by Pittsburgh Steelers, October 8, 1987.
Released by Pittsburgh Steelers, November 7, 1987; awarded on waivers to Miami Dolphins, November 9, 1987.
On developmental squad for 1 game with Birmingham Stallions in 1983.
On developmental squad for 3 games with Birmingham Stallions in 1984.
Birmingham USFL, 1983 through 1985; Pittsburgh (1)-Miami (7) NFL, 1987.
Games: 1983 (17), 1984 (15), 1985 (18), 1987 (8). Total USFL—50. Total Pro—58.
Pro statistics: Credited with 5½ sacks for 45 yards and recovered one fumble for two yards, 1983; credited with one safety and four sacks for 37 yards and recovered one fumble, 1984; credited with five sacks for 47 yards, 1985.

WILLIAM JOSEPH CLINKSCALES
(Joey)
Wide Receiver—Pittsburgh Steelers

Born May 21, 1964, at Asheville, N. C.
Height, 6.00. Weight, 204.
High School—Knoxville, Tenn., Austin-East.
Received bachelor of arts degree in liberal arts from University of Tennessee in 1987.
Selected by Pittsburgh in 9th round (233rd player selected) of 1987 NFL draft.
Signed by Pittsburgh Steelers, July 26, 1987.
Released by Pittsburgh Steelers, August 31, 1987; re-signed as replacement player by Steelers, September 24, 1987.

| | | —PASS RECEIVING— | | | |
Year Club	G.	P.C.	Yds.	Avg.	TD.
1987—Pittsburgh NFL	7	13	240	18.5	1

GARRY WILBERT COBB
Linebacker—Philadelphia Eagles

Born March 16, 1957, at Carthage, N. C.
Height, 6.02. Weight, 227.
High School—Stamford, Conn.
Attended University of Southern California.
Selected by Dallas in 9th round (247th player selected) of 1979 NFL draft.
Released by Dallas Cowboys, August 21, 1979; signed as free agent by Detroit Lions, October 24, 1979.
Granted free agency, February 1, 1985; re-signed by Lions and traded to Philadelphia Eagles for running back Wilbert Montgomery, August 21, 1985.

| | —INTERCEPTIONS— | | | | | | —INTERCEPTIONS— | | | |
Year Club	G.	No.	Yds.	Avg.	TD.	Year Club	G.	No.	Yds.	Avg.	TD.
1979—Detroit NFL	8			None		1984—Detroit NFL	16			None	
1980—Detroit NFL	16			None		1985—Philadelphia NFL	16			None	
1981—Detroit NFL	16	3	32	10.7	0	1986—Philadelphia NFL	16	1	3	3.0	0
1982—Detroit NFL	6	2	12	6.0	0	1987—Philadelphia NFL	12			None	
1983—Detroit NFL	15	4	19	4.8	0	Pro Totals—9 Years	121	10	66	6.6	0

Additional pro statistics: Caught one pass for 19 yards, 1981; recovered three fumbles, 1981 and 1987; caught one pass for 25 yards, 1982; recovered two fumbles, 1983; recovered one fumble, 1986.

SHERMAN COCROFT
Defensive Back—Kansas City Chiefs
Born August 29, 1961, at Watsonville, Calif.
Height, 6.01. Weight, 195.
High School—Watsonville, Calif.
Attended Cabrillo College and San Jose State University.

Selected by Oakland in 1984 USFL territorial draft.
Signed as free agent by Seattle Seahawks, May 3, 1984.
Released by Seattle Seahawks, August 21, 1984; signed as free agent by Kansas City Chiefs for 1985, October 15, 1984.

| | | —INTERCEPTIONS— | | | |
Year Club	G.	No.	Yds.	Avg.	TD.
1985—Kansas City NFL	16	3	27	9.0	0
1986—Kansas City NFL	16	3	32	10.7	0
1987—Kansas City NFL	12		None		
Pro Totals—3 Years	44	6	59	9.8	0

Additional pro statistics: Recovered two fumbles, 1985; returned one kickoff for 23 yards and recovered one fumble, 1986; returned one punt for no yards, 1987.

MICHAEL LYNN COFER
(Mike)
Linebacker—Detroit Lions
Born April 7, 1960, at Knoxville, Tenn.
Height, 6.05. Weight, 245.
High School—Knoxville, Tenn., Rule.
Attended University of Tennessee.
Brother of James Cofer, linebacker with Baltimore Stars, 1985.

Selected by New Jersey in 1983 USFL territorial draft.
Selected by Detroit in 3rd round (67th player selected) of 1983 NFL draft.
Signed by Detroit Lions, July 1, 1983.
On injured reserve with hip injury, October 25 through remainder of 1985 season.
Detroit NFL, 1983 through 1987.
Games: 1983 (16), 1984 (16), 1985 (7), 1986 (16), 1987 (11). Total—66.
Pro statistics: Recovered one fumble, 1983, 1984 and 1987; recovered three fumbles, 1986.

PAUL RANDOLPH COFFMAN
Tight End—New Orleans Saints
Born March 29, 1956, at St. Louis, Mo.
Height, 6.03. Weight, 225.
High School—Chase, Kan.
Received degree in grain milling science from Kansas State University in 1982.

Signed as free agent by Green Bay Packers, May 18, 1978.
Released by Green Bay Packers, September 1, 1986; signed as free agent by Kansas City Chiefs, September 9, 1986.
Granted free agency with no qualifying offer, February 1, 1988; signed by New Orleans Saints, May 10, 1988.

| | | —PASS RECEIVING— | | | |
Year Club	G.	P.C.	Yds.	Avg.	TD.
1978—Green Bay NFL	16		None		
1979—Green Bay NFL	16	56	711	12.7	4
1980—Green Bay NFL	16	42	496	11.8	3
1981—Green Bay NFL	16	55	687	12.5	4
1982—Green Bay NFL	9	23	287	12.5	2
1983—Green Bay NFL	16	54	814	15.1	11
1984—Green Bay NFL	14	43	562	13.1	9
1985—Green Bay NFL	16	49	666	13.6	6
1986—Kansas City NFL	15	12	75	6.3	2
1987—Kansas City NFL	12	5	42	8.4	1
Pro Totals—10 Years	146	339	4340	12.8	42

Additional pro statistics: Fumbled four times, 1979; rushed once for three yards, 1980; returned three kickoffs for 77 yards, 1981; recovered one fumble, 1981, 1984 and 1986; fumbled once, 1981 and 1983 through 1986; recovered two fumbles, 1987.
Played in Pro Bowl (NFL All-Star Game) following 1982 through 1984 seasons.

TIMMY LEE COFIELD
(Tim)
Linebacker—Kansas City Chiefs
Born May 18, 1963, at Murfreesboro, N.C.
Height, 6.02. Weight, 245.
High School—Murfreesboro, N.C.
Attended Elizabeth City State University.

Selected by Baltimore in 6th round (45th player selected) of 1986 USFL draft.
Signed as free agent by Kansas City Chiefs, May 8, 1986.
Kansas City NFL, 1986 and 1987.
Games: 1986 (15), 1987 (12). Total—27.
Pro statistics: Recovered one fumble, 1986 and 1987.

DARRELL RAY COLBERT
Wide Receiver—Kansas City Chiefs
Born November 16, 1964, at Beaumont, Tex.
Height, 5.10. Weight, 174.
High School—Beaumont, Tex., Westbrook.
Attended Texas Southern University.

Signed as free agent by Kansas City Chiefs, May 13, 1987.
Kansas City NFL, 1987.
Games: 1987 (12).

Pro statistics: Caught three passes for 21 yards, returned one punt for 11 yards and returned one kickoff for 18 yards, 1987.

LEWIS WELTON COLBERT
Punter—Kansas City Chiefs
Born August 23, 1963, at Phenix City, Ala.
Height, 5.11. Weight, 180.
High School—Phenix City, Ala., Glenwood Academy.
Attended Auburn University.

Named as punter on THE SPORTING NEWS College All-America Team, 1985.
Selected by Birmingham in 1986 USFL territorial draft.
Selected by Kansas City in 8th round (196th player selected) of 1986 NFL draft.
Signed by Kansas City Chiefs, July 18, 1986.
On injured reserve with back injury, November 3 through remainder of 1987 season.

Year Club	G.	No.	——PUNTING—— Avg.	Blk.
1986—Kansas City NFL	16	99	40.7	0
1987—Kansas City NFL	2	10	37.7	0
Pro Totals—2 Years	18	109	40.4	0

ROBIN COLE
Linebacker—Pittsburgh Steelers
Born September 11, 1955, at Los Angeles, Calif.
Height, 6.02. Weight, 225.
High School—Compton, Calif.
Attended University of New Mexico.
Cousin of Willie Davis, Hall of Fame defensive end with Cleveland Browns and Green Bay Packers, 1958 through 1969.

Selected by Pittsburgh in 1st round (21st player selected) of 1977 NFL draft.
Pittsburgh NFL, 1977 through 1987.
Games: 1977 (8), 1978 (16), 1979 (13), 1980 (14), 1981 (14), 1982 (9), 1983 (16), 1984 (16), 1985 (16), 1986 (16), 1987 (12). Total—150.

Pro statistics: Recovered two fumbles, 1977 and 1986; recovered one fumble, 1979, 1981 and 1987; returned one kickoff for three yards, 1979; intercepted one pass for 34 yards and recovered one fumble for 14 yards, 1980; intercepted one pass for 29 yards, 1981; recovered two fumbles for 20 yards, 1983; intercepted one pass for 12 yards and recovered one fumble for eight yards, 1984; intercepted one pass for four yards and recovered three fumbles, 1985; intercepted one pass for no yards, 1987.
Played in AFC Championship Game following 1978, 1979 and 1984 seasons.
Played in NFL Championship Game following 1978 and 1979 seasons.
Played in Pro Bowl (NFL All-Star Game) following 1984 season.

GREG JEROME COLEMAN
Punter—Minnesota Vikings
Born September 9, 1954, at Jacksonville, Fla.
Height, 6.00. Weight, 185.
High School—Jacksonville, Fla., William M. Raines.
Received degree in criminology from Florida A&M University.
Cousin of Vince Coleman, outfielder with St. Louis Cardinals.

Selected by Cincinnati in 14th round (398th player selected) of 1976 NFL draft.
Released by Cincinnati Bengals, August, 1976; signed as free agent by Cleveland Browns, March, 1977.
Released by Cleveland Browns, August 30, 1978; signed as free agent by Minnesota Vikings, October 20, 1978.

Year Club	G.	No.	——PUNTING—— Avg.	Blk.
1977—Cleveland NFL	14	61	39.2	0
1978—Minnesota NFL	9	51	39.0	1
1979—Minnesota NFL	16	90	39.5	1
1980—Minnesota NFL	16	81	38.8	0
1981—Minnesota NFL	15	88	41.4	0
1982—Minnesota NFL	9	*58	41.1	0
1983—Minnesota NFL	16	91	41.5	0
1984—Minnesota NFL	16	82	42.4	0
1985—Minnesota NFL	16	67	42.8	0
1986—Minnesota NFL	16	67	41.4	0
1987—Minnesota NFL	9	45	39.7	1
Pro Totals—11 Years	152	781	40.7	3

Additional pro statistics: Rushed once for minus three yards, 1977; rushed twice for 22 yards, 1978; recovered one fumble, 1981 and 1985; rushed once for 15 yards, 1982; rushed once for minus nine yards, 1983; rushed twice for 11 yards and attempted one pass with no completions, 1984; rushed twice for no yards and fumbled once, 1985; rushed twice for 46 yards, 1986.

LEONARD DAVID COLEMAN
Safety—Indianapolis Colts
Born January 30, 1962, at Boynton Beach, Fla.
Height, 6.02. Weight, 202.
High School—Lake Worth, Fla.
Attended Vanderbilt University.
Cousin of Anthony Carter, wide receiver with Minnesota Vikings.
Selected by Memphis in 1984 USFL territorial draft.
Selected by Indianapolis in 1st round (8th player selected) of 1984 NFL draft.
Signed by Memphis Showboats, September 13, 1984.
Released by Memphis Showboats, September 18, 1985; signed by Indianapolis Colts, September 18, 1985.
Granted roster exemption, September 18 through September 29, 1985; activated, September 30, 1985.
On injured reserve with broken thumb, December 8 through remainder of 1987 season.

		—INTERCEPTIONS—			
Year Club	G.	No.	Yds.	Avg.	TD.
1985—Memphis USFL............	18	2	6	3.0	0
1985—Indianapolis NFL.........	12		None		
1986—Indianapolis NFL........	16	4	36	9.0	0
1987—Indianapolis NFL........	4		None		
USFL Totals—1 Year.........	18	2	6	3.0	0
NFL Totals—3 Years..........	32	4	36	9.0	0
Pro Totals—4 Years............	50	6	42	7.0	0

Additional USFL statistics: Credited with one sack for nine yards and recovered four fumbles for 31 yards and a touchdown, 1985.
Additional NFL statistics: Recovered one fumble, 1986.

MONTE COLEMAN
Linebacker—Washington Redskins
Born November 4, 1957, at Pine Bluff, Ark.
Height, 6.02. Weight, 230.
High School—Pine Bluff, Ark.
Attended Central Arkansas University.
Selected by Washington in 11th round (289th player selected) of 1979 NFL draft.
On injured reserve with thigh injury, September 16 through October 16, 1983; activated, October 17, 1983.
On injured reserve with strained hamstring, September 25 through November 8, 1985; activated, November 9, 1985.
On injured reserve with pulled hamstring, October 8 through November 7, 1986; activated, November 8, 1986.

		—INTERCEPTIONS—			
Year Club	G.	No.	Yds.	Avg.	TD.
1979—Washington NFL..........	16	1	13	13.0	0
1980—Washington NFL..........	16	3	92	30.7	0
1981—Washington NFL..........	12	3	52	17.3	1
1982—Washington NFL..........	8		None		
1983—Washington NFL..........	10		None		
1984—Washington NFL..........	16	1	49	49.0	1
1985—Washington NFL..........	10		None		
1986—Washington NFL..........	11		None		
1987—Washington NFL..........	12	2	53	26.5	0
Pro Totals—9 Years............	111	10	259	25.9	2

Additional pro statistics: Recovered three fumbles, 1979; caught one pass for 12 yards, 1980; recovered two fumbles, 1980 and 1983; recovered one fumble for two yards, 1981; ran 27 yards with lateral on punt return and recovered one fumble, 1984.
Played in NFC Championship Game following 1982, 1983, 1986 and 1987 seasons.
Played in NFL Championship Game following 1982, 1983 and 1987 seasons.

BRUCE STOKES COLLIE
Offensive Tackle-Guard—San Francisco 49ers
Born June 27, 1962, at Nuremburg, Germany.
Height, 6.06. Weight, 275.
High School—San Antonio, Tex., Robert E. Lee.
Attended University of Texas at Arlington.
Selected by Baltimore in 6th round (78th player selected) of 1985 USFL draft.
Selected by San Francisco in 5th round (140th player selected) of 1985 NFL draft.
Signed by San Francisco 49ers, June 25, 1985.
San Francisco NFL, 1985 through 1987.
Games: 1985 (16), 1986 (16), 1987 (11). Total—43.

—DID YOU KNOW—

That Reggie White of the Philadelphia Eagles led the NFL in sacks with 21 in 1987? White played in only 12 games while the record-holder, Mark Gastineau of the Jets, had 22 sacks in 16 games in 1984.

STEVEN ANDRE COLLIER
(Steve)
Offensive Tackle—Green Bay Packers
Born April 19, 1963, at Chicago, Ill.
Height, 6.07. Weight, 342.
High School—Chicago, Ill., Whitney-Young.
Attended Garden City Community College, University of Illinois and Bethune-Cookman College.
Signed as free agent by Cleveland Browns, May 6, 1985.
Released by Cleveland Browns, August 21, 1985; signed as free agent by San Diego Chargers, April 15, 1986.
Released by San Diego Chargers, July 19, 1986; signed as free agent replacement player by Green Bay Packers, September 25, 1987.
Green Bay NFL, 1987.
Games: 1987 (10).

GLEN LEON COLLINS
Defensive End—Indianapolis Colts
Born July 10, 1959, at Jackson, Miss.
Height, 6.06. Weight, 265.
High School—Jackson, Miss., Jim Hill.
Attended Mississippi State University.
Named as defensive tackle on THE SPORTING NEWS College All-America Team, 1981.
Selected by Cincinnati in 1st round (26th player selected) of 1982 NFL draft.
On inactive list, September 19, 1982.
Traded by Cincinnati Bengals to Green Bay Packers for draft choice, May 12, 1986.
Released by Green Bay Packers, August 25, 1986; signed as free agent replacement player by San Francisco 49ers, September 24, 1987.
Released by San Francisco 49ers, October 27, 1987; signed as free agent by Indianapolis Colts, February 11, 1988.
Cincinnati NFL, 1982 through 1985; San Francisco NFL, 1987.
Games: 1982 (7), 1983 (16), 1984 (16), 1985 (16), 1987 (3). Total—58.
Pro statistics: Recovered one fumble, 1983 and 1984.

JAMES BRIAN COLLINS
(Jim)
Linebacker—Los Angeles Rams
Born June 11, 1958, at Orange, N.J.
Height, 6.02. Weight, 230.
High School—Mendham, N.J.
Received bachelor of science degree in psychology from Syracuse University in 1981.
Named to THE SPORTING NEWS NFL All-Star Team, 1985.
Selected by Los Angeles in 2nd round (43rd player selected) of 1981 NFL draft.
On injured reserve with pulled stomach muscle, September 1 through October 2, 1981; activated October 3, 1981.
On injured reserve with knee injury, December 4 through remainder of 1981 season.
On injured reserve with shoulder injury, August 25 through entire 1986 season.
Crossed picket line during players' strike, October 2, 1987.

| | | | —INTERCEPTIONS— | | |
Year Club	G.	No.	Yds.	Avg.	TD.
1981—L.A. Rams NFL............	7		None		
1982—L.A. Rams NFL............	6		None		
1983—L.A. Rams NFL............	16	2	46	23.0	0
1984—L.A. Rams NFL............	16	2	43	21.5	0
1985—L.A. Rams NFL............	16	2	8	4.0	0
1987—L.A. Rams NFL............	15		None		
Pro Totals—6 Years............	76	6	97	16.2	0

Additional pro statistics: Recovered one fumble, 1983 and 1985; recovered two fumbles for 17 yards and fumbled once, 1984; recovered two fumbles, 1987.
Played in NFC Championship Game following 1985 season.
Played in Pro Bowl (NFL All-Star Game) following 1985 season.

MARK COLLINS
Cornerback—New York Giants
Born January 16, 1964, at San Bernardino, Calif.
Height, 5.10. Weight, 190.
High School—San Bernardino, Calif., Pacific.
Attended California State University at Fullerton.
Named as defensive back on THE SPORTING NEWS College All-America Team, 1985.
Selected by New York Giants in 2nd round (44th player selected) of 1986 NFL draft.
Signed by New York Giants, July 30, 1986.
On injured reserve with back injury, December 23 through remainder of 1987 season.

| | | -INTERCEPTIONS- | | | | —KICKOFF RET.— | | | | —TOTAL— | | |
Year Club	G.	No.	Yds.	Avg.	TD.	No.	Yds.	Avg.	TD.	TD.	Pts.	F.
1986—New York Giants NFL	15	1	0	0.0	0	11	204	18.5	0	0	0	2
1987—New York Giants NFL	11	2	28	14.0	0		None			0	0	0
Pro Totals—2 Years....................	26	3	28	9.3	0	11	204	18.5	0	0	0	2

Additional pro statistics: Returned three punts for 11 yards and recovered three fumbles for five yards, 1986.

Played in NFC Championship Game following 1986 season.
Played in NFL Championship Game following 1986 season.

ANTHONY CRIS COLLINSWORTH
(Known by middle name.)
Wide Receiver—Cincinnati Bengals
Born January 27, 1959, at Dayton, O.
Height, 6.06. Weight, 192.
High School—Titusville, Fla., Astronaut.
Received degree in accounting from University of Florida in 1981.

Selected by Cincinnati in 2nd round (37th player selected) of 1981 NFL draft.
Signed by Tampa Bay Bandits, June 27, 1983, for contract to take effect after being granted free agency, February 1, 1985.
Released by Tampa Bay Bandits, February 18, 1984; re-signed by Bengals, February 21, 1984.

		—PASS RECEIVING—				
Year Club	G.	P.C.	Yds.	Avg.	TD.
1981—Cincinnati NFL	16	67	1009	15.1	8
1982—Cincinnati NFL	9	49	700	14.3	1
1983—Cincinnati NFL	14	66	1130	17.1	5
1984—Cincinnati NFL	15	64	989	15.5	6
1985—Cincinnati NFL	16	65	1125	17.3	5
1986—Cincinnati NFL	16	62	1024	16.5	10
1987—Cincinnati NFL	8	31	494	15.9	0
Pro Totals—7 Years	94	404	6471	16.0	35

Additional pro statistics: Recovered one fumble, 1981, 1983 and 1984; fumbled three times, 1981; rushed once for minus 11 yards, 1982; fumbled once, 1982, 1985 and 1986; rushed twice for two yards and fumbled twice, 1983; rushed once for seven yards, 1984; rushed once for three yards and attempted one pass with one interception, 1985; rushed twice for minus 16 yards, 1986.
Played in AFC Championship Game following 1981 season.
Played in NFL Championship Game following 1981 season.
Played in Pro Bowl (NFL All-Star Game) following 1981 through 1983 seasons.

ANTHONY IVAR COLORITO
(Tony)
Defensive End—Denver Broncos
Born September 8, 1964, at Brooklyn, N.Y.
Height, 6.05. Weight, 260.
High School—Brooklyn, N.Y., Midwood.
Received degree in biology from University of Southern California in 1986.

Selected by Denver in 5th round (134th player selected) of 1986 NFL draft.
Signed by Denver Broncos, July 16, 1986.
On injured reserve with knee injury, August 20 through entire 1987 season.
Crossed picket line during players' strike, October 14, 1987.
Denver NFL, 1986.
Games: 1986 (15).
Pro statistics: Recovered two fumbles, 1986.
Played in AFC Championship Game following 1986 season.
Played in NFL Championship Game following 1986 season.

GEORGE CURTIS COLTON
Guard—Atlanta Falcons
Born July 28, 1963, at Lindenhurst, N.Y.
Height, 6.03. Weight, 279.
High School—Lindenhurst, N.Y.
Received degree in general studies from University of Maryland in 1986.

Selected by New England in 9th round (248th player selected) of 1986 NFL draft.
Signed by New England Patriots, July 18, 1986.
Released by New England Patriots, August 21, 1986; re-signed by Patriots, March 18, 1987.
Released by New England Patriots, August 31, 1987; re-signed as replacement player by Patriots, September 24, 1987.
Released by New England Patriots, March 2, 1988; awarded on waivers to Atlanta Falcons, March 15, 1988.
New England NFL, 1987.
Games: 1987 (3).
Pro statistics: Recovered one fumble, 1987.

DARREN COMEAUX
Linebacker—San Francisco 49ers
Born April 15, 1960, at San Diego, Calif.
Height, 6.01. Weight, 227.
High School—San Diego, Calif.
Attended San Diego Mesa College and Arizona State University.

Signed as free agent by Denver Broncos, April 30, 1982.
On injured reserve with broken foot, September 7 through December 15, 1982; activated, December 16, 1982.
Released by Denver Broncos, August 29, 1983; re-signed by Broncos, September 13, 1983.

Released by Denver Broncos, September 2, 1985; re-signed by Broncos, September 3, 1985.
On injured reserve with broken thumb, October 16 through November 21, 1985; activated, November 22, 1985.
Released by Denver Broncos, September 7, 1987; signed as free agent replacement player by San Francisco 49ers, October 8, 1987.
Released by San Francisco 49ers, November 3, 1987; re-signed by 49ers, November 6, 1987.
Denver NFL, 1982 through 1986; San Francisco NFL, 1987.
Games: 1982 (3), 1983 (14), 1984 (16), 1985 (11), 1986 (16), 1987 (8). Total—68.
Pro statistics: Intercepted one pass for five yards, 1984; recovered one fumble, 1984 and 1986.
Played in AFC Championship Game following 1986 season.
Played in NFL Championship Game following 1986 season.

CHARLES EDWARD COMMISKEY
(Chuck)
Guard—New Orleans Saints
Born March 2, 1958, at Killeen, Tex.
Height, 6.04. Weight, 290.
High School—Pascagoula, Miss.
Attended University of Mississippi.

Selected by Philadelphia in 9th round (247th player selected) of 1981 NFL draft.
On injured reserve with dislocated shoulder, August 25 through entire 1981 season.
Released by Philadelphia Eagles, September 6, 1982.
USFL rights traded by Birmingham Stallions to Philadelphia Stars for rights to defensive back Charles Grandjean, October 12, 1982.
Signed by Philadelphia Stars, January 16, 1983.
Franchise transferred to Baltimore, November 1, 1984.
Granted free agency when USFL suspended operations, August 7, 1986; signed as free agent by New Orleans Saints, August 13, 1986.
Granted roster exemption, August 13 through August 21, 1986; activated, August 22, 1986.
Released by New Orleans Saints, August 26, 1986; re-signed by Saints, September 2, 1986.
Philadelphia USFL, 1983 and 1984; Baltimore USFL, 1985; New Orleans NFL, 1986 and 1987.
Games: 1983 (18), 1984 (18), 1985 (18), 1986 (16), 1987 (12). Total USFL—54. Total NFL—28. Total Pro—82.
Pro statistics: Rushed once for minus three yards and recovered one fumble, 1983.
Played in USFL Championship Game following 1983 through 1985 seasons.

SHANE PATRICK CONLAN
Linebacker—Buffalo Bills
Born April 3, 1964, at Frewsburg, N.Y.
Height, 6.03. Weight, 230.
High School—Frewsburg, N.Y., Central.
Received degree in administration of justice from Penn State University in 1987.
Brother of Michael Conlan, linebacker at Rutgers University.

Selected by Buffalo in 1st round (8th player selected) of 1987 draft.
Signed by Buffalo Bills, August 9, 1987.
Buffalo NFL, 1987.
Games: 1987 (12).

CHRISTOPHER HOWARD CONLIN
(Chris)
Guard—Miami Dolphins
Born June 7, 1965, at Philadelphia, Pa.
Height, 6.04. Weight, 290.
High School—Wyncote, Pa., Bishop McDevitt.
Attended Penn State University.
Brother of Craig Conlin, basketball center at LaSalle University.

Selected by Miami in 5th round (132nd player selected) of 1987 NFL draft.
Signed by Miami Dolphins, July 23, 1987.
On injured reserve with knee injury, December 4 through remainder of 1987 season.
Miami NFL, 1987.
Games: 1987 (3).

WILLIAM CONTZ
(Bill)
Offensive Tackle—New Orleans Saints
Born May 12, 1961, at Belle Vernon, Pa.
Height, 6.05. Weight, 270.
High School—Belle Vernon, Pa.
Received bachelor of science degree in business logistics
from Penn State University in 1983.

Selected by Philadelphia in 1983 USFL territorial draft.
Selected by Cleveland in 5th round (122nd player selected) of 1983 NFL draft.
Signed by Cleveland Browns, May 31, 1983.
On injured reserve with knee injury, December 12 through remainder of 1984 season.
On physically unable to perform/active with knee injury, August 20 through October 18, 1985; activated, October 19, 1985.
Released by Cleveland Browns, September 10, 1986; signed as free agent by New Orleans Saints, September 23, 1986.

Cleveland NFL, 1983 through 1985; Cleveland (1)-New Orleans (13) NFL, 1986; New Orleans NFL, 1987.
Games: 1983 (16), 1984 (15), 1985 (4), 1986 (14), 1987 (3). Total—52.
Pro statistics: Returned one kickoff for three yards, 1983; returned one kickoff for 10 yards, 1984; recovered two fumbles, 1986.

JOSEPH STANISLAUS CONWELL
(Joe)
Offensive Tackle—Philadelphia Eagles
Born February 24, 1961, at Philadelphia, Pa.
Height, 6.05. Weight, 286.
High School—Ardmore, Pa., Lower Merion.
Received bachelor of arts degree in industrial relations from University of North Carolina.

Selected by Philadelphia in 1984 USFL territorial draft.
Signed by Philadelphia Stars, January 20, 1984.
On reserve/physically unable to perform, February 20 through April 18, 1984; activated, April 19, 1984.
On developmental squad, April 19 through April 26, 1984; activated, April 27, 1984.
On developmental squad, May 3 through June 20, 1984; activated, June 21, 1984.
Selected by San Francisco in 2nd round (51st player selected) of 1984 NFL supplemental draft.
Franchise transferred to Baltimore, November 1, 1984.
Granted free agency when USFL suspended operations, August 7, 1986.
NFL rights traded by San Francisco 49ers to Philadelphia Eagles for 11th round pick in 1987 draft, August 20, 1986.
Signed by Philadelphia Eagles, August 20, 1986.
Granted roster exemption, August 20 through August 28, 1986; activated, August 29, 1986.
On developmental squad for 8 games with Philadelphia Stars in 1984.
Philadelphia USFL, 1984; Baltimore USFL, 1985; Philadelphia NFL, 1986 and 1987.
Games: 1984 (10), 1985 (18), 1986 (16), 1987 (12). Total USFL—28. Total NFL—28. Total Pro—56.
USFL statistics: Recovered two fumbles, 1985.
NFL statistics: Recovered one fumble, 1986.
On developmental squad for USFL Championship Game following 1984 season.
Played in USFL Championship Game following 1985 season.

KELLY EDWARD COOK
Running Back—Green Bay Packers
Born August 20, 1962, at Cushing, Okla.
Height, 5.10. Weight, 225.
High School—Midwest City, Okla.
Received bachelor of science in agricultural economics from Oklahoma State in 1986.

Signed as free agent by Buffalo Bills, May 6, 1986.
Released by Buffalo Bills, August 11, 1986; signed as free agent by Green Bay Packers, May 26, 1987.

| | | KICKOFF RETURNS | | | |
Year Club	G.	No.	Yds.	Avg.TD.	
1987—Green Bay NFL............	11	10	147	14.7	0

Additional pro statistics: Rushed twice for three yards, 1987.

TOI FITZGERALD COOK
(First name pronounced Toy.)
Safety—New Orleans Saints
Born December 3, 1964, at Chicago, Ill.
Height, 5.11. Weight, 188.
High School—Montclair, Calif.
Attended Stanford University.

Selected by New Orleans in 8th round (207th player selected) of 1987 NFL draft.
Signed by New Orleans Saints, July 24, 1987.
Selected by Minnesota Twins' organization in 38th round of free-agent draft, June 2, 1987.
New Orleans NFL, 1987.
Games: 1987 (7).
Pro statistics: Returned one punt for three yards, 1987.

JOHNIE EARL COOKS
Linebacker—Indianapolis Colts
Born November 23, 1958, at Leland, Miss.
Height, 6.04. Weight, 251.
High School—Leland, Miss.
Received degree in physical education from Mississippi State University.

Named as linebacker on THE SPORTING NEWS College All-America Team, 1981.
Selected by Baltimore in 1st round (2nd player selected) of 1982 NFL draft.
Franchise transferred to Indianapolis, March 31, 1984.
Baltimore NFL, 1982 and 1983; Indianapolis NFL, 1984 through 1987.
Games: 1982 (9), 1983 (16), 1984 (16), 1985 (16), 1986 (15), 1987 (10). Total—82.
Pro statistics: Recovered one fumble, 1982 and 1987; intercepted one pass for 15 yards and recovered two fumbles for 52 yards and a touchdown, 1983; fumbled once, 1983 and 1987; intercepted one pass for seven yards, 1985; intercepted one pass for one yard, 1986; intercepted one pass for two yards, 1987.

RAYFORD E. COOKS
Defensive End—Houston Oilers
Born August 25, 1962, at Dallas, Tex.
Height, 6.03. Weight, 245.
High School—Dallas, Tex., L.G. Pinkston.
Attended North Texas State University.

Selected by Houston in 15th round (314th player selected) of 1984 USFL draft.
Signed by Houston Gamblers, October 1, 1984.
On developmental squad, February 21 through March 23, 1985; activated, March 24, 1985.
Released by Houston Gamblers, July 31, 1985; awarded on waivers to Jacksonville Bulls, August 1, 1985.
Granted free agency when USFL suspended operations, August 7, 1986; signed by Montreal Alouettes, August 27, 1986.
Granted free agency when Montreal Alouettes suspended operations, June 24, 1987; signed as replacement player by Houston Oilers, September 23, 1987.
On developmental squad for 4 games with Houston Gamblers in 1985.
Houston USFL, 1985; Montreal CFL, 1986; Houston NFL, 1987.
Games: 1985 (14), 1986 (6), 1987 (10). Total—30.
USFL statistics: Credited with 3½ sacks for 27½ yards and recovered three fumbles, 1985.
CFL statistics: Recovered one fumble, 1986.

EVAN COOPER
Safety—Philadelphia Eagles
Born June 28, 1962, at Miami, Fla.
Height, 5.11. Weight, 194.
High School—Miami, Fla., Killian.
Received bachelor of science degree in communications
from University of Michigan in 1984.

Selected by Michigan in 1984 USFL territorial draft.
Selected by Philadelphia in 4th round (88th player selected) of 1984 NFL draft.
Signed by Philadelphia Eagles, June 11, 1984.

Year Club	G.	INTERCEPTIONS				–PUNT RETURNS–				—KICKOFF RET.—				—TOTAL—		
		No.	Yds.	Avg.	TD.	No.	Yds.	Avg.	TD.	No.	Yds.	Avg.	TD.	TD.	Pts.	F.
1984—Philadelphia NFL	16	None				40	250	6.3	0	17	299	17.6	0	0	0	0
1985—Philadelphia NFL	16	2	13	6.5	0	43	364	8.5	0	3	32	10.7	0	0	0	1
1986—Philadelphia NFL	16	3	20	6.7	0	16	139	8.7	0	2	42	21.0	0	0	0	2
1987—Philadelphia NFL	12	2	0	0.0	0	None				5	86	17.2	0	0	0	1
Pro Totals—4 Years.......	60	7	33	4.7	0	99	753	7.6	0	27	459	17.0	0	0	0	4

Additional pro statistics: Recovered one fumble, 1985 and 1986.

GEORGE JUNIOUS COOPER
Linebacker—San Francisco 49ers
Born December 24, 1958, at Detroit, Mich.
Height, 6.02. Weight, 225.
High School—Detroit, Mich., Northern.
Received bachelor of arts degree in art and industrial design from Michigan State University in 1982.

Signed as free agent by Pittsburgh Steelers, May 22, 1982.
Released by Pittsburgh Steelers, August 30, 1982.
USFL rights traded with rights to offensive tackles Bob Gruber and Brad Oates, quarterback Dan Kendra and tight end Al Kimichik by Michigan Panthers to Philadelphia Stars for rights to quarterback Dan Feraday, running back Jim Jodat and linebacker Ed O'Neil, September 27, 1982.
Signed by Philadelphia Stars, September 27, 1982.
On developmental squad, April 2 through May 5, 1983; activated, May 6, 1983.
Franchise transferred to Baltimore, November 1, 1984.
Granted free agency when USFL suspended operations, August 7, 1986; signed as free agent by San Francisco 49ers, May 20, 1987.
Crossed picket line during players' strike, October 7, 1987.
On injured reserve with ankle injury, November 21 through December 14, 1987.
Released by San Francisco 49ers, December 15, 1987; re-signed by 49ers after clearing procedural waivers, December 18, 1987.
On developmental squad for 5 games with Philadelphia Stars in 1983.
Philadelphia USFL, 1983 and 1984; Baltimore USFL, 1985; San Francisco NFL, 1987.
Games: 1983 (13), 1984 (18), 1985 (18), 1987 (10). USFL—49. Total Pro—59.
Pro statistics: Intercepted one pass for 16 yards, credited with ½ sack for 5½ yards and recovered one fumble, 1983; credited with six sacks for 52 yards, intercepted two passes for 10 yards and recovered one fumble for four yards, 1984; intercepted two passes for six yards, credited with four sacks for 30 yards and recovered two fumbles, 1985.
Played in USFL Championship Game following 1983 through 1985 seasons.

LOUIS COOPER
Linebacker—Kansas City Chiefs
Born August 5, 1963, at Marion, S.C.
Height, 6.02. Weight, 240.
High School—Marion, S.C.
Attended West Carolina University.

Selected by Orlando in 6th round (76th player selected) of 1985 USFL draft.
Selected by Seattle in 11th round (305th player selected) of 1985 NFL draft.
Signed by Seattle Seahawks, July 17, 1985.

Released by Seattle Seahawks, August 27, 1985; signed as free agent by Kansas City Chiefs, September 17, 1985.
On injured reserve with ankle injury, October 14 through November 20, 1985; activated after clearing procedural waivers, November 22, 1985.
Released by Kansas City Chiefs, August 26, 1986; re-signed by Chiefs, September 2, 1986.
Kansas City NFL, 1985 through 1987.
Games: 1985 (8), 1986 (16), 1987 (12). Total—36.
Pro statistics: Recovered one fumble, 1986; intercepted one pass for no yards, 1987.

MARK SAMUEL COOPER
Offensive Tackle—Tampa Bay Buccaneers
Born February 14, 1960, at Camden, N.J.
Height, 6.05. Weight, 267.
High School—Miami, Fla., Killian.
Received bachelor of arts degree in communications
from University of Miami (Fla.) in 1983.
Selected by New Jersey in 5th round (60th player selected) of 1983 USFL draft.
Selected by Denver in 2nd round (31st player selected) of 1983 NFL draft.
Signed by Denver Broncos, June 26, 1983.
On injured reserve with sprained ankle, December 13 through remainder of 1984 season.
On injured reserve with foot injury, October 22 through December 4, 1986; activated, December 5, 1986.
Released by Denver Broncos, November 10, 1987; signed as free agent by Tampa Bay Buccaneers, November 17, 1987.
Denver NFL, 1983 through 1986; Denver (5)-Tampa Bay (4) NFL, 1987.
Games: 1983 (10), 1984 (15), 1985 (15), 1986 (8), 1987 (9). Total—57.
Pro statistics: Caught one pass for 13 yards, 1985.
Played in AFC Championship Game following 1986 season.
Played in NFL Championship Game following 1986 season.

DOUGLAS DURANT COSBIE
(Doug)
Tight End—Dallas Cowboys
Born March 27, 1956, at Palo Alto, Calif.
Height, 6.06. Weight, 238.
High School—Mt. View, Calif., St. Francis.
Attended College of the Holy Cross, DeAnza College and received bachelor of science degree
in marketing from University of Santa Clara in 1979.
Selected by Dallas in 3rd round (76th player selected) of 1979 NFL draft.
USFL rights traded by Michigan Panthers to Oakland Invaders for rights to placekicker Wilson Alvarez, September 2, 1982.

| | | —PASS RECEIVING— | | | |
Year Club	G.	P.C.	Yds.	Avg.	TD.
1979—Dallas NFL	16	5	36	7.2	0
1980—Dallas NFL	16	2	11	5.5	1
1981—Dallas NFL	16	17	225	13.2	5
1982—Dallas NFL	9	30	441	14.7	4
1983—Dallas NFL	16	46	588	12.8	6
1984—Dallas NFL	16	60	789	13.2	4
1985—Dallas NFL	16	64	793	12.4	6
1986—Dallas NFL	16	28	312	11.1	1
1987—Dallas NFL	12	36	421	11.7	3
Pro Totals—9 Years............	133	288	3616	12.6	30

Additional pro statistics: Fumbled once, 1979, 1981 and 1984; returned one kickoff for 13 yards and recovered two fumbles, 1980; rushed four times for 33 yards and returned one kickoff for no yards, 1981; rushed once for minus two yards and returned one kickoff for four yards, 1982; returned two kickoffs for 17 yards, 1983; fumbled twice, 1985; rushed once for nine yards, 1986; rushed once for minus five yards, 1987.
Played in NFC Championship Game following 1980 through 1982 seasons.
Played in Pro Bowl (NFL All-Star Game) following 1983 through 1985 seasons.

JOSEPH PATRICK COSTELLO JR.
(Joe)
Linebacker—Atlanta Falcons
Born June 1, 1960, at New York, N.Y.
Height, 6.03. Weight, 244.
High School—Stratford, Conn.
Received bachelor of science degree in accounting from Central Connecticut State University in 1982.
Signed as free agent by Montreal Concordes, March, 1982.
Released by Montreal Concordes, June 30, 1983; signed by Jacksonville Bulls, October 20, 1983.
Released by Jacksonville Bulls, February 28, 1986; signed as free agent by Cleveland Browns, April 21, 1986.
Released by Cleveland Browns, September 3, 1986; signed as free agent by Atlanta Falcons, September 17, 1986.
On injured reserve with broken arm, August 31 through October 30, 1987; activated, October 31, 1987.
Crossed picket line during player's strike, October 2, 1987.
Montreal CFL, 1982; Jacksonville USFL, 1984 and 1985; Atlanta NFL, 1986 and 1987.
Games: 1982 (2), 1984 (18), 1985 (18), 1986 (14), 1987 (9). Total USFL—36. Total NFL—23. Total Pro—61.
Pro statistics: Credited with 4½ sacks for 40½ yards, 1984; credited with 4½ sacks for 36 yards, 1985.

JAMES PAUL COVERT
(Jim)
Offensive Tackle—Chicago Bears
Born March 22, 1960, at Conway, Pa.
Height, 6.04. Weight, 275.
High School—Freedom, Pa., Area.
Attended University of Pittsburgh.

Named to THE SPORTING NEWS NFL All-Star Team, 1985 and 1986.
Selected by Tampa Bay in 1st round (12th player selected) of 1983 USFL draft.
Selected by Chicago in 1st round (6th player selected) of 1983 NFL draft.
Signed by Chicago Bears, July 20, 1983.
Chicago NFL, 1983 through 1987.
Games: 1983 (16), 1984 (16), 1985 (15), 1986 (16), 1987 (9). Total—72.
Pro statistics: Recovered one fumble, 1983, 1986 and 1987; recovered two fumbles, 1984.
Played in NFC Championship Game following 1984 and 1985 seasons.
Played in NFL Championship Game following 1985 season.
Played in Pro Bowl (NFL All-Star Game) following 1985 and 1986 seasons.

ARTHUR COX
Tight End—San Diego Chargers
Born February 5, 1961, at Plant City, Fla.
Height, 6.02. Weight, 262.
High School—Plant City, Fla.
Attended Texas Southern University.

Signed as free agent by Atlanta Falcons, May 4, 1983.
Granted free agency, February 1, 1988; withdrew qualifying offer, May 2, 1988.
Signed by San Diego Chargers, May 10, 1988.

Year Club	G.	P.C.	Yds.	Avg.	TD.
1983—Atlanta NFL	15	9	83	9.2	1
1984—Atlanta NFL	16	34	329	9.7	3
1985—Atlanta NFL	16	33	454	13.8	2
1986—Atlanta NFL	16	24	301	12.5	1
1987—Atlanta NFL	12	11	101	9.2	0
Pro Totals—5 Years	75	111	1268	11.4	7

Additional pro statistics: Fumbled once, 1983, 1984 and 1986; recovered two fumbles, 1986; fumbled twice and returned one kickoff for 11 yards, 1987.

ROBERT LLOYD COX
Offensive Tackle—Los Angeles Rams
Born December 30, 1963, at San Francisco, Calif.
Height, 6.05. Weight, 258.
High School—Dublin, Calif.
Attended Chabot College and University of California at Los Angeles.

Selected by Arizona in 1986 USFL territorial draft.
Selected by Los Angeles Rams in 6th round (144th player selected) of 1986 NFL draft.
Signed by Los Angeles Rams, July 22, 1986.
On injured reserve with ankle injury, August 27 through entire 1986 season.
Los Angeles Rams NFL, 1987.
Games: 1987 (10).
Pro statistics: Returned one kickoff for 12 yards, 1987.

STEVE COX
Punter-Placekicker—Washington Redskins
Born May 11, 1958, at Shreveport, La.
Height, 6.04. Weight, 195.
High School—Charleston, Ark.
Received bachelor of science degree in banking and finance from University of Arkansas in 1982.

Selected by Cleveland in 5th round (134th player selected) of 1981 NFL draft.
On injured reserve with head injury, August 30 through November 1, 1983; activated, November 2, 1983.
Released by Cleveland Browns, August 27, 1985; signed as free agent by Washington Redskins, October 1, 1985.

Year Club	G.	No.	Avg.	Blk.	XP.	XPM.	FG.	FGA.	Pts.
1981—Cleveland NFL	16	68	42.4	*2	0	0	0	1	0
1982—Cleveland NFL	9	48	39.1	1	0	0	0	1	0
1983—Cleveland NFL	7		None		0	0	1	1	3
1984—Cleveland NFL	16	74	43.4	2	0	0	1	3	3
1985—Washington NFL	12	52	41.8	0	0	0	0	1	0
1986—Washington NFL	16	75	43.6	0	0	0	3	5	9
1987—Washington NFL	12	63	40.8	1	3	0	1	2	6
Pro Totals—7 Years	88	380	42.1	6	3	0	6	14	21

Additional pro statistics: Rushed twice for minus 11 yards and recovered one fumble, 1982; attempted one pass with one completion for 16 yards, 1984; attempted one pass with one completion for 11 yards, 1985.
Played in NFC Championship Game following 1986 and 1987 seasons.
Played in NFL Championship Game following 1987 season.

ROBERT EDWARD CRABLE
(Bob)
Linebacker—New York Jets

Born September 22, 1959, at Cincinnati, O.
Height, 6.03. Weight, 228.
High School—Cincinnati, O., Moeller.
Received bachelor of science degree in business administration from
University of Notre Dame in 1982.

Named as linebacker on THE SPORTING NEWS College All-America Team, 1980 and 1981.
Selected by New York Jets in 1st round (23rd player selected) of 1982 NFL draft.
On physically unable to perform/active with knee injury, July 14 through August 20, 1984; activated, August 21, 1984.
On injured reserve with knee injury, August 28 through September 27, 1984; activated, September 28, 1984.
On injured reserve with knee injury, November 5 through remainder of 1984 season.
On physically unable to perform/active with knee injury, July 25 through October 13, 1985; activated, October 14, 1985.
New York Jets NFL, 1982 through 1987.
Games: 1982 (9), 1983 (14), 1984 (5), 1985 (10), 1986 (16), 1987 (12). Total—66.
Pro statistics: Intercepted one pass for no yards, 1983; recovered one fumble, 1985; intercepted one pass for 26 yards and recovered three fumbles for 42 yards, 1986; intercepted one pass for eight yards, 1987.

ROGER TIMOTHY CRAIG
Fullback—San Francisco 49ers

Born July 10, 1960, at Davenport, Ia.
Height, 6.00. Weight, 222.
High School—Davenport, Ia., Central.
Attended University of Nebraska.

Established NFL record for most pass receptions by running back, season (92), 1985.
Selected by Boston in 1983 USFL territorial draft.
Selected by San Francisco in 2nd round (49th player selected) of 1983 NFL draft.
Signed by San Francisco 49ers, June 13, 1983.
Crossed picket line during players' strike, October 7, 1987.

		—RUSHING—			PASS RECEIVING				—TOTAL—		
Year Club	G.	Att.	Yds.	Avg. TD.	P.C.	Yds.	Avg.	TD.	TD.	Pts.	F.
1983—San Francisco NFL	16	176	725	4.1 8	48	427	8.9	4	12	72	6
1984—San Francisco NFL	16	155	649	4.2 7	71	675	9.5	3	10	60	3
1985—San Francisco NFL	16	214	1050	4.9 9	*92	1016	11.0	6	15	90	5
1986—San Francisco NFL	16	204	830	4.1 7	81	624	7.7	0	7	42	4
1987—San Francisco NFL	14	215	815	3.8 3	66	492	7.5	1	4	24	5
Pro Totals—5 Years	78	964	4069	4.2 34	358	3234	9.0	14	48	288	23

Additional pro statistics: Recovered one fumble, 1983, 1984 and 1986; recovered two fumbles, 1987.
Played in NFC Championship Game following 1983 and 1984 seasons.
Played in NFL Championship Game following 1984 season.
Played in Pro Bowl (NFL All-Star Game) following 1985 and 1987 seasons.

CHARLES CRAWFORD
Running Back—Philadelphia Eagles

Born March 8, 1964, at Bristow, Okla.
Height, 6.02. Weight, 243.
High School—Bristow, Okla.
Attended Oklahoma State University.

Selected by Philadelphia in 7th round of 1986 NFL supplemental draft.
Signed by Philadelphia Eagles, August 2, 1986.
Released by Philadelphia Eagles, November 5, 1987; release voided due to injured status and placed on injured reserve with broken hand, November 11 through remainder of 1987 season.

		—RUSHING—			PASS RECEIVING				—TOTAL—		
Year Club	G.	Att.	Yds.	Avg. TD.	P.C.	Yds.	Avg.	TD.	TD.	Pts.	F.
1986—Philadelphia NFL	16	28	88	3.1 1		None			1	6	1
1987—Philadelphia NFL	2		None			None			0	0	0
Pro Totals—2 Years	18	28	88	3.1 1	0	0	0.0	0	1	6	1

		KICKOFF RETURNS		
Year Club	G.	No.	Yds.	Avg.TD.
1986—Philadelphia NFL	16	27	497	18.4 0
1987—Philadelphia NFL	2		None	
Pro Totals—2 Years	18	27	497	18.4 0

Additional pro statistics: Recovered one fumble, 1986 and 1987.

DERRICK LORWENZO CRAWFORD
Wide Receiver-Kick Returner—San Francisco 49ers

Born September 3, 1960, at Memphis, Tenn.
Height, 5.10. Weight, 185.
High School—Memphis, Tenn., East.
Attended Memphis State University.

Named as kickoff returner on THE SPORTING NEWS USFL All-Star Team, 1984.

Selected by Memphis in 1984 USFL territorial draft.
Signed by Memphis Showboats, January 21, 1984.
Selected by San Francisco in 1st round (24th player selected) of 1984 NFL supplemental draft.
Granted free agency when USFL suspended operations, August 7, 1986; signed by San Francisco 49ers, August 12, 1986.
On injured reserve with shoulder injury, August 26 through October 17, 1986; activated, October 18, 1986.
On injured reserve with foot injury, August 28 through entire 1987 season.

| | | | —RUSHING— | | | PASS RECEIVING | | | | —TOTAL— | | |
Year Club	G.	Att.	Yds.	Avg.	TD.	P.C.	Yds.	Avg.	TD.	TD.	Pts.	F.
1984—Memphis USFL	18	13	27	2.1	0	61	703	11.5	12	13	78	7
1985—Memphis USFL	18	1	6	6.0	0	70	1057	15.1	9	10	60	1
1986—San Francisco NFL	10		None			5	70	14.0	0	0	0	1
USFL Totals—2 Years	36	14	33	2.4	0	131	1760	13.4	21	23	138	8
NFL Totals—1 Year	10	0	0	0.0	0	5	70	14.0	0	0	0	1
Pro Totals—3 Years	46	14	33	2.4	0	136	1830	13.5	21	23	138	9

| | | —PUNT RETURNS— | | | | —KICKOFF RET.— | | | |
Year Club	G.	No.	Yds.	Avg.	TD.	No.	Yds.	Avg.	TD.
1984—Memphis USFL	18	3	—1	—0.3	0	*47	*1237	*26.3	*1
1985—Memphis USFL	18	8	184	23.0	1	11	263	23.9	0
1986—San Francisco NFL	10	4	15	3.8	0	15	280	18.7	0
USFL Totals—2 Years	36	11	183	16.6	1	58	1500	25.9	1
NFL Totals—1 Year	10	4	15	3.8	0	15	280	18.7	0
Pro Totals—3 Years	46	15	198	13.2	1	73	1780	24.4	1

Additional USFL statistics: Recovered five fumbles, 1984; recovered three fumbles, 1985.
Additional NFL statistics: Recovered one fumble, 1986.

JOE STANIER CRIBBS
Running Back—San Francisco 49ers
Born January 5, 1958, at Sulligent, Ala.
Height, 5.11. Weight, 190.
High School—Sulligent, Ala.
Attended Auburn University.

Named as running back on THE SPORTING NEWS USFL All-Star Team, 1984.
Selected by Buffalo in 2nd round (29th player selected) of 1980 NFL draft.
On did not report list, August 24 through November 19, 1982; activated, November 20, 1982.
Signed by Birmingham Stallions, July 2, 1983, for contract to take affect after being granted free agency, February 1, 1984.
Granted roster exemption, February 15, 1984; activated, February 25, 1984.
On suspended list, May 9 through May 22, 1984; activated, May 23, 1984.
On developmental squad, June 3 through June 7, 1985; activated, June 8, 1985.
Released by Birmingham Stallions, October 14, 1985; re-signed by Buffalo Bills, October 11, 1985.
Granted roster exemption, October 11 through October 18, 1985; activated, October 19, 1985.
Traded by Buffalo Bills to San Francisco 49ers for 3rd round pick in 1987 draft and 5th round pick in 1988 draft, August 19, 1986.
Crossed picket line during players' strike, October 7, 1987.
On developmental squad for 1 game with Birmingham Stallions in 1985.

| | | | —RUSHING— | | | PASS RECEIVING | | | | —TOTAL— | | |
Year Club	G.	Att.	Yds.	Avg.	TD.	P.C.	Yds.	Avg.	TD.	TD.	Pts.	F.
1980—Buffalo NFL	16	306	1185	3.9	11	52	415	8.0	1	12	72	*16
1981—Buffalo NFL	15	257	1097	4.3	3	40	603	15.1	7	10	60	12
1982—Buffalo NFL	7	134	633	4.7	3	13	99	7.6	0	3	18	5
1983—Buffalo NFL	16	263	1131	4.3	3	57	524	9.2	7	10	60	6
1984—Birmingham USFL	16	*297	*1467	4.9	8	39	500	12.8	5	13	78	7
1985—Birmingham USFL	17	267	1047	3.9	7	41	287	7.0	1	8	48	3
1985—Buffalo NFL	10	122	399	3.3	1	18	142	7.9	0	1	6	5
1986—San Francisco NFL	14	152	590	3.9	5	35	346	9.9	0	5	30	5
1987—San Francisco NFL	11	70	300	4.3	1	9	70	7.8	0	2	12	1
NFL Totals—7 Years	89	1294	5335	4.1	27	224	2199	9.8	15	43	258	50
USFL Totals—2 Years	33	564	2514	4.5	15	80	787	9.8	6	21	126	10
Pro Totals—9 Years	122	1858	7849	4.2	42	304	2986	9.8	21	64	384	60

| | | —PUNT RETURNS— | | | |
Year Club	G.	No.	Yds.	Avg.	TD.
1980—Buffalo NFL	16	29	154	5.3	0
1981—Buffalo NFL	15		None		
1982—Buffalo NFL	7		None		
1983—Buffalo NFL	16		None		
1984—Birmingham USFL	16		None		
1985—Birmingham USFL	17		None		
1985—Buffalo NFL	10		None		
1986—San Francisco NFL	14		None		
1987—San Francisco NFL	11		None		
NFL Totals—7 Years	89	29	154	5.3	0
USFL Totals—2 Years	33	0	0	0.0	0
Pro Totals—9 Years	122	29	154	5.3	0

Additional NFL statistics: Attempted one pass with one completion for 13 yards; returned two kickoffs for 39 yards

(19.5 average), and recovered one fumble for minus seven yards, 1980; attempted one pass with one completion for nine yards, 1981; attempted one pass with one interception and recovered two fumbles, 1982; recovered one fumble, 1981, 1983, 1985 and 1986; attempted two passes with one completion for three yards, 1983; returned 13 kickoffs for 327 yards (25.2 avg.) and a touchdown, 1987.

Additional USFL statistics: Recovered one fumble, 1984 and 1985.

Played in Pro Bowl (NFL All-Star Game) following 1980 and 1983 seasons.

Named to Pro Bowl following 1981 season (replaced due to injury by Pete Johnson).

NOLAN NEIL CROMWELL
Safety—Los Angeles Rams
Born January 30, 1955, at Smith Center, Kan.
Height, 6.01. Weight, 200.
High School—Ransom, Kan.
Attended University of Kansas.

Named to THE SPORTING NEWS NFL All-Star Team, 1980.

Selected by Los Angeles in 2nd round (31st player selected) of 1977 NFL draft.

On injured reserve with knee injury, November 13 through remainder of 1984 season.

Crossed picket line during players' strike, October 2, 1987.

| | | ——INTERCEPTIONS—— | | | |
Year Club	G.	No.	Yds.	Avg.	TD.
1977—L.A. Rams NFL............	14		None		
1978—L.A. Rams NFL............	16	1	31	31.0	0
1979—L.A. Rams NFL............	16	5	109	21.8	0
1980—L.A. Rams NFL............	16	8	140	17.5	1
1981—L.A. Rams NFL............	16	5	94	18.8	0
1982—L.A. Rams NFL............	9	3	33	11.0	0
1983—L.A. Rams NFL............	16	3	76	25.3	1
1984—L.A. Rams NFL............	11	3	54	18.0	1
1985—L.A. Rams NFL............	16	2	5	2.5	0
1986—L.A. Rams NFL............	16	5	101	20.2	1
1987—L.A. Rams NFL............	15	2	28	14.0	0
Pro Totals—11 Years..........	161	37	671	18.1	4

Additional pro statistics: Recovered two fumbles for three yards, 1977; returned one punt for eight yards, recovered one fumble in end zone for a touchdown and rushed once for 16 yards, 1978; rushed once for five yards and a touchdown and recovered three fumbles, 1979; scored one point on run for extra point, rushed twice for no yards, attempted one pass with no completions, fumbled twice and recovered one fumble for minus one yard, 1980; rushed once for 17 yards and recovered three fumbles for four yards, 1981; rushed once for 17 yards and a touchdown and recovered one fumble for six yards, 1982; rushed once for no yards and recovered two fumbles, 1983; recovered one fumble, 1984 and 1986; returned one kickoff for three yards and recovered four fumbles for 12 yards, 1985. Total—Rushed seven times for 55 yards and three touchdowns, scored one point on run for extra point, returned one punt for eight yards, returned one kickoff for three yards, recovered 18 fumbles for 24 yards and one touchdown, attempted one pass with no completions and fumbled twice.

Played in NFC Championship Game following 1978, 1979 and 1985 seasons.

Played in NFL Championship Game following 1979 season.

Played in Pro Bowl (NFL All-Star Game) following 1980 through 1983 seasons.

RANDALL LAUREAT CROSS
(Randy)
Guard-Center—San Francisco 49ers
Born April 25, 1954, at Brooklyn, N.Y.
Height, 6.03. Weight, 265.
High School—Encino, Calif., Crespi.
Received degree in political science from University of California at Los Angeles in 1976.
Son of Dennis Cross, former television actor.

Selected by San Francisco in 2nd round (42nd player selected) of 1976 NFL draft.

On injured reserve with ankle injury, November 3 through remainder of 1978 season.

On injured reserve with knee injury, December 18 through remainder of 1985 season.

San Francisco NFL, 1976 through 1987.

Games: 1976 (14), 1977 (14), 1978 (9), 1979 (16), 1980 (16), 1981 (16), 1982 (9), 1983 (16), 1984 (16), 1985, (15), 1986 (16), 1987 (12). Total—169.

Pro statistics: Recovered one fumble, 1976, 1982 and 1986; fumbled once for minus 37 yards; 1977; fumbled once, 1978; recovered two fumbles, 1979.

Played in NFC Championship Game following 1981, 1983 and 1984 seasons.

Played in NFL Championship Game following 1981 and 1984 seasons.

Played in Pro Bowl (NFL All-Star Game) following 1981, 1982 and 1984 seasons.

DAVID RODNEY CROUDIP
Cornerback—Atlanta Falcons
Born January 25, 1959, at Indianapolis, Ind.
Height, 5.08. Weight, 183.
High School—Compton, Calif.
Attended Ventura College and San Diego State University.

Selected by Los Angeles in 7th round (78th player selected) of 1983 USFL draft.

Selected by Houston in 18th round (107th player selected) of USFL expansion draft, September 6, 1983.

Released by Houston Gamblers, February 29, 1984; signed as free agent by Los Angeles Rams, April 2, 1984.

Released by Los Angeles Rams, August 27, 1984; re-signed by Rams, August 28, 1984.

Released by Los Angeles Rams, September 19, 1984; re-signed by Rams, September 21, 1984.
Released by Los Angeles Rams, September 2, 1985; re-signed by Rams, September 3, 1985.
Released by Los Angeles Rams, September 5, 1985; signed as free agent by San Diego Chargers, September 10, 1985.
Released by San Diego Chargers, October 5, 1985; signed as free agent by Atlanta Falcons, October 8, 1985.
Los Angeles USFL, 1983; Houston USFL, 1984; Los Angeles Rams NFL, 1984; San Diego (2)-Atlanta (11) NFL, 1985; Atlanta NFL, 1986 and 1987.
Games: 1983 (18), 1984 USFL (1), 1984 NFL (16), 1985 (13), 1986 (15), 1987 (12). Total USFL—19. Total NFL—56. Total Pro—75.
USFL statistics: Recovered one fumble, 1983.
NFL statistics: Recovered two fumbles, 1984; recovered one fumble, 1985; intercepted two passes for 35 yards and returned one kickoff for 20 yards, 1986; intercepted two passes for 40 yards and returned one kickoff for 18 yards, 1987.

RANDALL CUNNINGHAM
Quarterback—Philadelphia Eagles
Born March 27, 1963, at Santa Barbara, Calif.
Height, 6.04. Weight, 201.
High School—Santa Barbara, Calif.
Attended University of Nevada at Las Vegas.
Brother of Sam Cunningham, running back with New England Patriots,
1973 through 1979, 1981 and 1982.

Named as punter on THE SPORTING NEWS College All-America Team, 1984.
Selected by Arizona in 1985 USFL territorial draft.
Selected by Philadelphia in 2nd round (37th player selected) of 1985 NFL draft.
Signed by Philadelphia Eagles, July 22, 1985.

Year Club	G.	Att.	Cmp.	Pct.	Gain	T.P.	P.I.	Avg.	Att.	Yds.	Avg.	TD.	TD.	Pts.	F.
				PASSING							RUSHING			TOTAL	
1985—Philadelphia NFL	6	81	34	42.0	548	1	8	6.77	29	205	7.1	0	0	0	3
1986—Philadelphia NFL	15	209	111	53.1	1391	8	7	6.66	66	540	8.2	5	5	30	7
1987—Philadelphia NFL	12	406	223	54.9	2786	23	12	6.86	76	505	6.6	3	3	18	*12
Pro Totals—3 Years	33	696	368	52.9	4725	32	27	6.79	171	1250	7.3	8	8	48	22

Quarterback Rating Points: 1985 (29.8), 1986 (72.9), 1987 (83.0). Total—73.6.
Additional pro statistics: Punted twice for 27.0 avg. and recovered four fumbles, 1986; caught one pass for minus three yards, recovered six fumbles and fumbled 12 times for minus seven yards, 1987.

TRAVIS CURTIS
Safety—Phoenix Cardinals
Born September 27, 1965, at Potomac, Md.
Height, 5.10. Weight, 180.
High School—Potomac, Md., Winston Churchill.
Attended West Virginia University.

Signed as free agent by St. Louis Cardinals, May 20, 1987.
Released by St. Louis Cardinals, September 7, 1987; re-signed by Cardinals, September 9, 1987.
Crossed picket line during player's strike, October 14, 1987.
Franchise transferred to Phoenix, March 15, 1988.

Year Club	G.	No.	Yds.	Avg.	TD.
		INTERCEPTIONS			
1987—St. Louis NFL	13	5	65	13.0	0

JEFFERY DWAYNE DALE
Safety—San Diego Chargers
Born October 6, 1962, at Pineville, La.
Height, 6.03. Weight, 214.
High School—Winnfield, La.
Attended Louisiana State University.

Selected by Portland in 1985 USFL territorial draft.
Selected by San Diego in 2nd round (55th player selected) of 1985 NFL draft.
Signed by San Diego Chargers, July 26, 1985.
On injured reserve with back injury, September 1 through entire 1987 season.
Crossed picket line during players' strike, October 13, 1987.

Year Club	G.	No.	Yds.	Avg.	TD.
		INTERCEPTIONS			
1985—San Diego NFL	16	2	83	41.5	*1
1986—San Diego NFL	16	4	153	38.3	0
Pro Totals—2 Years	32	6	236	39.3	1

KENNETH RAY DALLAFIOR
Name pronounced DAL-uh-for.
(Ken)
Guard—San Diego Chargers
Born August 26, 1959, at Royal Oak, Mich.
Height, 6.04. Weight, 277.
High School—Madison Heights, Mich., Madison.
Received bachelor of arts and science degree in business studies
from University of Minnesota in 1982.

Selected by Pittsburgh in 5th round (124th player selected) of 1982 NFL draft.
On injured reserve with sprained neck, September 6 through entire 1982 season.
Released by Pittsburgh Steelers, August 29, 1983; signed as free agent by Michigan Panthers, October 26, 1983.
Not protected in merger of Michigan Panthers and Oakland Invaders; selected by New Jersey Generals, December 6, 1984.
Released by New Jersey Generals, January 28, 1985; signed as free agent by San Diego Chargers, June 21, 1985.
Released by San Diego Chargers, September 2, 1985; re-signed by Chargers, December 4, 1985.
On injured reserve with knee injury, August 26 through October 4, 1986; activated after clearing procedural waivers, October 6, 1986.
Michigan USFL, 1984: San Diego NFL, 1985 through 1987.
Games: 1984 (18), 1985 (3), 1986 (12), 1987 (8). Total NFL—23. Total Pro—41.

COACHING RECORD

Assistant coach at Madison High School, Madison Heights, Mich., 1985.

EUGENE DANIEL JR.
Cornerback—Indianapolis Colts
Born May 4, 1961, at Baton Rouge, La.
Height, 5.11. Weight, 179.
High School—Baton Rouge, La., Robert E. Lee.
Received degree in marketing from Louisiana State University.

Selected by New Orleans in 1984 USFL territorial draft.
Selected by Indianapolis in 8th round (205th player selected) of 1984 NFL draft.
Signed by Indianapolis Colts, June 21, 1984.

Year Club	G.	No.	Yds.	Avg.	TD.
1984—Indianapolis NFL	15	6	25	4.2	0
1985—Indianapolis NFL	16	8	53	6.6	0
1986—Indianapolis NFL	15	3	11	3.7	0
1987—Indianapolis NFL	12	2	34	17.0	0
Pro Totals—4 Years	58	19	123	6.5	0

Additional pro statistics: Returned one punt for six yards, recovered three fumbles for 25 yards and fumbled once, 1985; returned blocked punt 13 yards for a touchdown and recovered one fumble, 1986.

GARY DENNIS DANIELSON
Quarterback—Cleveland Browns
Born September 10, 1951, at Detroit, Mich.
Height, 6.02. Weight, 196.
High School—Dearborn, Mich., Divine Child.
Received bachelor of arts degree in business management and master's degree
in sports administration, both from Purdue University.

Signed as free agent by New York Stars (WFL), 1974.
Traded by Charlotte Hornets (WFL) to Chicago Winds (WFL) for future considerations, 1975.
Signed as free agent by Detroit Lions after World Football League folded, 1976.
On injured reserve with knee injury, August 28 through entire 1979 season.
On injured reserve with broken wrist, October 8 through November 24, 1981; activated, November 25, 1981.
USFL rights traded by Michigan Panthers to Arizona Wranglers for 4th round pick in 1984 draft, April 4, 1983.
Traded by Detroit Lions to Cleveland Browns for 3rd round pick in 1986 draft, May 1, 1985.
On injured reserve with broken ankle, September 1 through entire 1986 season.
Crossed picket line during players' strike, October 14, 1987.

Year Club	G.	Att.	Cmp.	Pct.	Gain	T.P.	P.I.	Avg.	Att.	Yds.	Avg.	TD.	TD.	Pts.	F.
1974—N.Y.-Char. WFL	....	60	28	46.7	305	1	0	5.08	10	51	5.1	3	3	21	....
1975—Chicago WFL	....	15	9	60.0	107	0	2	7.13	None				0	0	....
1976—Detroit NFL	1	None							None				0	0	0
1977—Detroit NFL	13	100	42	42.0	445	1	5	4.45	7	62	8.9	0	0	0	0
1978—Detroit NFL	16	351	199	56.7	2294	18	17	6.54	22	93	4.2	0	0	0	5
1980—Detroit NFL	16	417	244	58.5	3223	13	11	7.73	48	232	4.8	2	2	12	11
1981—Detroit NFL	6	96	56	58.3	784	3	5	8.17	9	23	2.6	2	2	12	2
1982—Detroit NFL	8	197	100	50.8	1343	10	14	6.82	23	92	4.0	0	0	0	6
1983—Detroit NFL	10	113	59	52.2	720	7	4	6.37	6	8	1.3	0	0	0	2
1984—Detroit NFL	15	410	252	61.5	3076	17	15	7.50	41	218	5.3	3	4	24	7
1985—Cleveland NFL	8	163	97	59.5	1274	8	6	7.82	25	126	5.0	0	0	0	5
1987—Cleveland NFL	6	33	25	75.8	281	4	0	8.52	1	0	0.0	0	0	0	2
WFL Totals—2 Years	....	75	37	49.3	412	1	2	5.49	10	51	5.1	3	3	21	....
NFL Totals—10 Years	99	1880	1074	57.1	13440	81	77	7.15	182	854	4.7	7	8	48	40
Pro Totals—12 Years	....	1955	1111	56.8	13852	82	79	7.09	192	905	4.7	10	11	69	....

NFL Quarterback Rating Points: 1977 (38.1), 1978 (73.6), 1980 (82.6), 1981 (73.4), 1982 (60.3), 1983 (78.0), 1984 (83.1), 1985 (85.3), 1987 (140.3). Total—76.7.
Additional pro statistics: Recovered one fumble, 1977, 1982 and 1983; recovered two fumbles and fumbled five times for minus 12 yards, 1978; recovered four fumbles and fumbled 11 times for minus two yards, 1980; fumbled six times for minus 11 yards, 1982; caught one pass for 22 yards and a touchdown, recovered two fumbles and fumbled seven times for minus five yards, 1984; recovered one fumble and fumbled five times for minus 17 yards, 1985; recovered two fumbles and fumbled twice for minus two yards, 1987.
Member of Cleveland Browns for AFC Championship Game following 1987 season; did not play.

BYRON DARBY
Defensive End—Indianapolis Colts
Born June 4, 1960, at Los Angeles, Calif.
Height, 6.04. Weight, 260.
High School—Inglewood, Calif.
Attended University of Southern California.

Selected by Los Angeles in 1983 USFL territorial draft.
Selected by Philadelphia in 5th round (120th player selected) of 1983 NFL draft.
Signed by Philadelphia Eagles, May 25, 1983.
On injured reserve with knee injury, September 25 through November 4, 1985; activated, November 5, 1985.
Granted free agency, February 1, 1987; withdrew qualifying offer, August 1, 1987.
Signed by Indianapolis Colts, August 3, 1987.
Philadelphia NFL, 1983 through 1986; Indianapolis NFL, 1987.
Games: 1983 (16), 1984 (16), 1985 (10), 1986 (16), 1987 (12). Total—70.
Pro statistics: Returned two kickoffs for three yards and fumbled once, 1983; caught two passes for 16 yards, 1986.

MATTHEW WAYNE DARWIN
(Matt)
Offensive Tackle—Philadelphia Eagles
Born March 11, 1963, at Houston, Tex.
Height, 6.04. Weight, 275.
High Schools—Colorado Springs, Colo., Cheyenne Mountain;
and Houston, Tex., Klein.
Attended Texas A&M University.

Selected by Houston in 1985 USFL territorial draft.
Selected by Dallas in 5th round (119th player selected) of 1985 NFL draft.
On reserve/did not sign entire 1985 season through April 28, 1986.
Selected by Philadelphia in 4th round (106th player selected) of 1986 NFL draft.
Signed by Philadelphia Eagles, July 31, 1986.
Philadelphia NFL, 1986 and 1987.
Games: 1986 (16), 1987 (12). Total—28.
Pro statistics: Recovered one fumble, 1987.

RONALD DONOVAN DAVENPORT
(Ron)
Fullback—Miami Dolphins
Born December 22, 1962, at Summerset, Bermuda.
Height, 6.02. Weight, 230.
High School—Atlanta, Ga., Walter F. George.
Attended University of Louisville.

Selected by Memphis in 9th round (120th player selected) of 1985 USFL draft.
Selected by Miami in 6th round (167th player selected) of 1985 NFL draft.
Signed by Miami Dolphins, July 15, 1985.

		——RUSHING——				PASS RECEIVING				—TOTAL—		
Year Club	G.	Att.	Yds.	Avg.	TD.	P.C.	Yds.	Avg.	TD.	TD.	Pts.	F.
1985—Miami NFL	16	98	370	3.8	11	13	74	5.7	2	13	78	2
1986—Miami NFL	16	75	314	4.2	0	20	177	8.9	1	1	6	4
1987—Miami NFL	10	32	114	3.6	1	27	249	9.2	1	2	12	0
Pro Totals—3 Years	42	205	798	3.9	12	60	500	8.3	4	16	96	6

		KICKOFF RETURNS		
Year Club	G.	No.	Yds.	Avg.TD.
1985—Miami NFL	16		None	
1986—Miami NFL	16	16	285	17.8 0
1987—Miami NFL	10		None	
Pro Totals—3 Years	42	16	285	17.8 0

Additional pro statistics: Recovered one fumble, 1986.
Played in AFC Championship Game following 1985 season.

BRIAN DAVIS
Cornerback—Washington Redskins
Born August 31, 1963, at Phoenix, Ariz.
Height, 6.02. Weight, 190.
High School—Phoenix, Ariz., Cortez.
Attended Glendale Community College and University of Nebraska.

Selected by Washington in 2nd round (30th player selected) of 1987 NFL draft.
Signed by Washington Redskins, July 26, 1987.
On injured reserve with hamstring injury, November 3 through December 4, 1987; activated, December 5, 1987.
Washington NFL, 1987.
Games: 1987 (7).
Pro statistics: Recovered one fumble for 11 yards, 1987.
Played in NFC Championship Game following 1987 season.
Played in NFL Championship Game following 1987 season.

BRUCE E. DAVIS
Wide Receiver—Indianapolis Colts

Born February 25, 1963, at Dallas, Tex.
Height, 5.08. Weight, 170.
High School—Dallas, Tex., Franklin D. Roosevelt.
Received bachelor of arts degree in radio and television communications from Baylor University.

Selected by San Antonio in 1984 USFL territorial draft.
Selected by Cleveland in 2nd round (50th player selected) of 1984 NFL draft.
Signed by Cleveland Browns, June 6, 1984.
Released by Cleveland Browns, August 30, 1985; signed as free agent by Los Angeles Raiders for 1986, November 29, 1985.
Released by Los Angeles Raiders, August 8, 1986; signed as free agent by Calgary Stampeders, March 7, 1987.
Released by Calgary Stampeders, June 3, 1987; signed as free agent by San Diego Chargers, July 20, 1987.
Released by San Diego Chargers, August 27, 1987; re-signed as replacement player by Chargers, September 24, 1987.
Released by San Diego Chargers, October 20, 1987; signed as free agent by Indianapolis Colts, February 11, 1988.
Active for 1 game with San Diego Chargers in 1987; did not play.

		PASS RECEIVING			—KICKOFF RET.—			—TOTAL—		
Year Club	G.	P.C.	Yds.	Avg.	TD.	No.	Yds.	Avg.	TD.	TD. Pts. F.
1984—Cleveland NFL	14	7	119	17.0	2	18	369	20.5	0	2 12 2

Additional pro statistics: Rushed once for six yards, 1984.

BRUCE EDWARD DAVIS
Offensive Tackle—Houston Oilers

Born June 21, 1956, at Rutherfordton, N.C.
Height, 6.06, Weight, 280.
High School—Marbury, Md., Lackey.
Attended University of California at Los Angeles.

Selected by Oakland in 11th round (294th player selected) of 1979 NFL draft.
Franchise transferred to Los Angeles, May 7, 1982.
Traded by Los Angeles Raiders to Houston Oilers for 2nd round pick in 1988 draft, November 3, 1987.
Oakland NFL, 1979 through 1981; Los Angeles Raiders NFL, 1982 through 1986; Los Angeles Raiders (4)-Houston (7) NFL, 1987.
Games: 1979 (12), 1980 (16), 1981 (16), 1982 (9), 1983 (16), 1984 (16), 1985 (16), 1986 (16), 1987 (11). Total—128.
Pro statistics: Recovered one fumble, 1982 and 1983.
Played in AFC Championship Game following 1980 and 1983 seasons.
Played in NFL Championship Game following 1980 and 1983 seasons.

C. WAYNE DAVIS
(Known by middle name.)
Linebacker—Phoenix Cardinals

Born March 10, 1964, at Tuscaloosa, Ala.
Height, 6.01. Weight, 213.
High School—Gordo, Ala.
Attended University of Alabama.

Selected by St. Louis in 9th round (229th player selected) of 1987 NFL draft.
Signed by St. Louis Cardinals, July 2, 1987.
Franchise transferred to Phoenix, March 15, 1988.
St. Louis NFL, 1987.
Games: 1987 (12).

ELGIN DAVIS
Running Back—New England Patriots

Born October 23, 1965, at Jacksonville, Fla.
Height, 5.10. Weight, 192.
High School—Jacksonville, Fla., Ribault.
Attended University of Central Florida.

Selected by New England in 12th round (330th player selected) of 1987 NFL draft.
Signed by New England Patriots, July 17, 1987.
On injured reserve with quadricep injury, September 7 through October 6, 1987; activated, October 7, 1987.
Crossed picket line during players' strike, October 7, 1987.

		—RUSHING—				PASS RECEIVING				—TOTAL—	
Year Club	G.	Att.	Yds.	Avg.	TD.	P.C.	Yds.	Avg.	TD.	TD. Pts. F.	
1987—New England NFL	4	9	43	4.8	0	None				0 0 0	

Additional pro statistics: Returned five kickoffs for 134 yards (26.8 avg.), 1987.

JAMES STEVEN DAVIS
Safety—Los Angeles Raiders

Born June 12, 1957, at Los Angeles, Calif.
Height, 6.00. Weight, 200.
High School—Los Angeles, Calif., Crenshaw.
Attended Los Angeles Southwest Junior College and Southern University.

Selected by Oakland in 5th round (118th player selected) of 1981 NFL draft.
On injured reserve, August 25 through entire 1981 season.

Franchise transferred to Los Angeles, May 7, 1982.
Released by Los Angeles Raiders, September 7, 1987; re-signed by Raiders, September 8, 1987.
Crossed picket line during players' strike, October 14, 1987.

Year Club	G.	No.	Yds.	Avg.	TD.
			—INTERCEPTIONS—		
1982—L.A. Raiders NFL.........	9	2	*107	53.5	*1
1983—L.A. Raiders NFL.........	16	1	10	10.0	0
1984—L.A. Raiders NFL.........	15	1	8	8.0	0
1985—L.A. Raiders NFL.........	15		None		
1986—L.A. Raiders NFL.........	16		None		
1987—L.A. Raiders NFL.........	12		None		
Pro Totals—6 Years.............	83	4	125	31.3	1

Additional pro statistics: Recovered one fumble, 1982, 1983 and 1987; recovered two fumbles, 1984; returned one punt for no yards and fumbled once, 1987.
Played in AFC Championship Game following 1983 season.
Played in NFL Championship Game following 1983 season.

JEFFERY EUGENE DAVIS
(Jeff)
Linebacker—Tampa Bay Buccaneers
Born January 26, 1960, at Greensboro, N.C.
Height, 6.00. Weight, 230.
High School—Greensboro, N.C., Dudley.
Received degree in industrial management from Clemson University in 1984.

Selected by Tampa Bay in 5th round (128th player selected) of 1982 NFL draft.
Tampa Bay NFL, 1982 through 1987.
Games: 1982 (9), 1983 (15), 1984 (16), 1985 (16), 1986 (16), 1987 (11). Total—83.
Pro statistics: Returned one kickoff for no yards and fumbled once, 1982; recovered one fumble, 1982, 1984 and 1986; intercepted one pass for no yards, 1984 and 1986; intercepted one pass for 22 yards and recovered two fumbles, 1985; recovered two fumbles for three yards, 1987.

JOHN HENRY DAVIS
Guard—Houston Oilers
Born August 22, 1965, at Ellijay, Ga.
Height, 6.04. Weight, 304.
High School—Ellijay, Ga., Gilmer.
Attended Georgia Tech.

Selected by Houston in 11th round (287th player selected) of 1987 NFL draft.
Signed by Houston Oilers, July 24, 1987.
On injured reserve with ankle injury, December 19 through remainder of 1987 season.
Houston NFL, 1987.
Games: 1987 (6).

KENNETH EARL DAVIS
Running Back—Green Bay Packers
Born April 16, 1962, at Williamson County, Tex.
Height, 5.10. Weight, 209.
High School—Temple, Tex.
Attended Texas Christian University.

Named as running back on THE SPORTING NEWS College All-America Team, 1984.
Selected by Green Bay in 2nd round (41st player selected) of 1986 NFL draft.
Signed by Green Bay Packers, May 17, 1986.

Year Club	G.	Att.	Yds.	Avg.	TD.	P.C.	Yds.	Avg.	TD.	TD.	Pts.	F.
		—RUSHING—				PASS RECEIVING				—TOTAL—		
1986—Green Bay NFL............................	16	114	519	4.6	0	21	142	6.8	1	1	6	2
1987—Green Bay NFL............................	10	109	413	3.8	3	14	110	7.9	0	3	18	2
Pro Totals—2 Years................................	26	223	932	4.2	3	35	252	7.2	1	4	24	4

Year Club	G.	No.	Yds.	Avg.	TD.
		KICKOFF RETURNS			
1986—Green Bay NFL...........	16	12	231	19.3	0
1987—Green Bay NFL...........	10		None		
Pro Totals—2 Years...........	26	12	231	19.3	0

LEE ANDREW DAVIS
Cornerback—New York Jets
Born December 18, 1962, at Okolona, Miss.
Height, 5.11. Weight, 198.
High School—Amory, Miss.
Attended University of Mississippi.

Selected by Cincinnati in 5th round (129th player selected) of 1985 NFL draft.
Signed by Cincinnati Bengals, June 25, 1985.
Released by Cincinnati Bengals, September 2, 1985; re-signed by Bengals, September 3, 1985.
Released by Cincinnati Bengals, October 24, 1985; signed as free agent by Seattle Seahawks, April 15, 1986.
Released by Seattle Seahawks, August 18, 1986; signed as free agent by Los Angeles Raiders, May 2, 1987.

Released by Los Angeles Raiders, August 27, 1987; signed as free agent replacement player by Indianapolis Colts, September 23, 1987.
Released by Indianapolis Colts, October 19, 1987; signed as free agent by New York Jets, May 3, 1988.
Cincinnati NFL, 1985; Indianapolis NFL, 1987.
Games: 1985 (7), 1987 (3). Total—10.
Pro statistics: Intercepted one pass for seven yards and recovered one fumble, 1987.

MICHAEL LEONAR DAVIS
(Mike)
Safety—San Diego Chargers
Born April 15, 1956, at Los Angeles, Calif.
Height, 6.03. Weight, 205.
High School—Los Angeles, Calif., Alain Leroy Locke.
Attended East Los Angeles Junior College and received bachelor of science degree
in communications from University of Colorado in 1977.

Selected by Oakland in 2nd round (35th player selected) of 1977 NFL draft.
On injured reserve entire 1977 season.
On injured reserve with knee and ankle injuries, September 23 through November 20, 1981; activated, November 21, 1981.
Franchise transferred to Los Angeles, May 7, 1982.
On injured reserve with knee injury, November 13 through December 22, 1985; activated, December 23, 1985.
On injured reserve with knee injury, August 26 through entire 1986 season.
Released by Los Angeles Raiders, September 1, 1987; signed as free agent by San Diego Chargers, October 24, 1987.

| | | | —INTERCEPTIONS— | | | |
Year	Club	G.	No.	Yds.	Avg.	TD.
1978—Oakland NFL		16	1	0	0.0	0
1979—Oakland NFL		16	2	22	11.0	0
1980—Oakland NFL		16	3	88	29.3	0
1981—Oakland NFL		7	1	0	0.0	0
1982—L.A. Raiders NFL		9	1	56	56.0	*1
1983—L.A. Raiders NFL		16	1	3	3.0	0
1984—L.A. Raiders NFL		16	2	11	5.5	0
1985—L.A. Raiders NFL		11		None		
1987—San Diego NFL		8		None		
Pro Totals—9 Years		115	11	180	16.4	1

Additional pro statistics: Recovered one fumble, 1978, 1982, 1984 and 1985; returned one punt for six yards and recovered three fumbles for 14 yards, 1979; recovered three fumbles for 35 yards, 1980; recovered two fumbles, 1983.
Played in AFC Championship Game following 1980 and 1983 seasons.
Played in NFL Championship Game following 1980 and 1983 seasons.

TYRONE DAVIS
(Ty)
Cornerback—Denver Broncos
Born November 17, 1961, at Athens, Ga.
Height, 6.01. Weight, 190.
High School—Athens, Ga., Cedar Shoals.
Attended Clemson University.

Selected by Orlando in 1985 USFL territorial draft.
Selected by New York Giants in 3rd round (58th player selected) of 1985 NFL draft.
Signed by New York Giants, June 4, 1985.
On injured reserve with back injury, November 1 through remainder of 1985 season.
On injured reserve with knee injury, August 25 through entire 1986 season.
Released by New York Giants, August 31, 1987; awarded on waivers to Detroit Lions, September 1, 1987.
Released by Detroit Lions, September 7, 1987; signed as free agent by Denver Broncos, April 7, 1988.
New York Giants NFL, 1985.
Games: 1985 (7).

WAYNE ELLIOT DAVIS
Cornerback—Buffalo Bills
Born July 17, 1963, at Cincinnati, O.
Height, 5.11. Weight, 175.
High School—Cincinnati, O., Mount Healthy.
Attended Indiana State University.

Selected by Baltimore in 2nd round (21st player selected) of 1985 USFL draft.
Selected by San Diego in 2nd round (39th player selected) of 1985 NFL draft.
Signed by San Diego Chargers, June 14, 1985.
Traded by San Diego Chargers to Buffalo Bills for safety Martin Bayless, August 26, 1987.
On injured reserve with hamstring injury, September 8 through October 22, 1987; activated, October 23, 1987.

| | | | —INTERCEPTIONS— | | | |
Year	Club	G.	No.	Yds.	Avg.	TD.
1985—San Diego NFL		16	2	29	14.5	0
1986—San Diego NFL		16		None		
1987—Buffalo NFL		10	1	0	0.0	0
Pro Totals—3 Years		42	3	29	9.7	0

Additional pro statistics: Recovered one fumble, 1985.

JAMES LINWOOD DAWSON
(Lin)
Tight End—New England Patriots
Born June 24, 1959, at Norfolk, Va.
Height, 6.03. Weight, 240.
High School—Kinston, N.C.
Attended North Carolina State University.
Selected by New England in 8th round (212th player selected) of 1981 NFL draft.
On inactive list, September 19, 1982.
On injured reserve with knee injury, August 19 through entire 1986 season.

			—PASS RECEIVING—			
Year	Club	G.	P.C.	Yds.	Avg.	TD.
1981—New England NFL		15	7	126	18.0	0
1982—New England NFL		8	13	160	12.3	1
1983—New England NFL		13	9	84	9.3	1
1984—New England NFL		16	39	427	10.9	4
1985—New England NFL		16	17	148	8.7	0
1987—New England NFL		12	12	81	6.8	0
Pro Totals—6 Years		80	97	1026	10.6	6

Additional pro statistics: Recovered one fumble, 1984 and 1985; fumbled once, 1985.
Played in AFC Championship Game following 1985 season.
Played in NFL Championship Game following 1985 season.

KEVIN JAMES DEAN
Linebacker—San Francisco 49ers
Born February 5, 1965, at Newton, Tex.
Height, 6.01. Weight, 235.
High School—Newton, Tex.
Attended Texas Christian University.
Related to Ernie Holmes, defensive tackle with Pittsburgh Steelers, 1972 through 1977;
and Fred Dean, defensive end with San Diego Chargers and San Francisco 49ers, 1975 through 1985.
Signed as free agent by San Francisco 49ers, May 12, 1987.
Crossed picket line during players' strike, October 9, 1987.
On injured reserve with ankle injury, November 2 through remainder of 1987 season.
San Francisco NFL, 1987.
Games: 1987 (4).

VERNON DEAN
Cornerback
Born May 5, 1959, at Los Angeles, Calif.
Height, 5.11. Weight, 178.
High School—Los Angeles, Calif.
Attended Los Angeles Valley Junior College, U.S. International University
and San Diego State University.
Selected by Washington in 2nd round (49th player selected) of 1982 NFL draft.
Released by Washington Redskins, May 17, 1988.

			—INTERCEPTIONS—			
Year	Club	G.	No.	Yds.	Avg.	TD.
1982—Washington NFL		9	3	62	20.7	0
1983—Washington NFL		16	5	54	10.8	0
1984—Washington NFL		16	7	114	16.3	*2
1985—Washington NFL		16	5	8	1.6	0
1986—Washington NFL		16	1	5	5.0	0
1987—Washington NFL		12			None	
Pro Totals—6 Years		85	21	243	11.6	2

Additional pro statistics: Recovered three fumbles (including one in end zone for a touchdown), 1983; recovered one fumble for six yards, 1984; returned one punt for no yards, 1985; recovered one fumble, 1985 and 1987.
Played in NFC Championship Game following 1982, 1983, 1986 and 1987 seasons.
Played in NFL Championship Game following 1982, 1983 and 1987 seasons.

JULIAN LUIS DeAYALA
(Kiki)
Linebacker—Cincinnati Bengals
Born October 23, 1961, at Miami, Fla.
Height, 6.01. Weight, 226.
High School—Houston, Tex., Memorial.
Received bachelor of arts degree in advertising from University of Texas.
Selected by Washington in 11th round (124th player selected) of 1983 USFL draft.
Selected by Cincinnati in 6th round (152nd player selected) of 1983 NFL draft.
USFL rights traded by Washington Federals to Houston Gamblers for 5th round pick in 1984 draft, June 7, 1983.
Signed by Houston Gamblers, June 7, 1983.
Released by Houston Gamblers, May 28, 1986; awarded on waivers to Arizona Outlaws, May 29, 1986.
Granted free agency when USFL suspended operations, August 7, 1986; signed by Cincinnati Bengals, August 19, 1986.

Granted roster exemption, August 19 through August 21, 1986; activated, August 22, 1986.
Houston USFL, 1984 and 1985; Cincinnati NFL, 1986 and 1987.
Games: 1984 (18), 1985 (18), 1986 (16), 1987 (12). Total USFL—36. Total NFL—28. Total Pro—64.
USFL statistics: Intercepted one pass for seven yards, credited with 1½ sacks for 10½ yards, returned one kickoff for two yards and fumbled once, 1984; recovered one fumble, 1984 and 1985; intercepted four passes for 37 yards and credited with five sacks for 37 yards, 1985.
NFL statistics: Recovered two fumbles, 1987.

STEVEN L. DeBERG
(Steve)
Quarterback—Kansas City Chiefs
Born January 19, 1954, at Oakland, Calif.
Height, 6.03. Weight, 210.
High School—Anaheim, Calif., Savanna.
Attended Fullerton Junior College and received bachelor of science degree
from San Jose State University in 1980.

Selected by Dallas in 10th round (275th player selected) of 1977 NFL draft.
Claimed on waivers from Dallas Cowboys by San Francisco 49ers, September 12, 1977.
Traded by San Francisco 49ers to Denver Broncos for 4th round pick in 1983 draft, August 31, 1981.
USFL rights traded by Oakland Invaders to Denver Gold for rights to tight end John Thompson and offensive tackle Randy Van Divier, October 7, 1983.
On injured reserve with separated shoulder, November 16 through December 21, 1983; activated, December 22, 1983.
Granted free agency, February 1, 1984; re-signed by Broncos and traded to Tampa Bay Buccaneers for 4th round pick in 1984 draft and 2nd round pick in 1985 draft, April 24, 1984.
Granted free agency, February 1, 1988; re-signed by Buccaneers and traded to Kansas City Chiefs for safety Mark Robinson and 4th and 8th round picks in 1988 draft, March 31, 1988.
Active for 5 games with San Francisco 49ers in 1977; did not play.

Year Club	G.	Att.	Cmp.	Pct.	Gain	T.P.	P.I.	Avg.	Att.	Yds.	Avg.	TD.	TD.	Pts.	F.
				—PASSING—						—RUSHING—			—TOTAL—		
1978—San Francisco NFL	12	302	137	45.4	1570	8	22	5.20	15	20	1.3	1	1	6	9
1979—San Francisco NFL	16	*578	*347	60.0	3652	17	21	6.32	17	10	0.6	0	0	0	6
1980—San Francisco NFL	11	321	186	57.9	1998	12	17	6.22	6	4	0.7	0	0	0	4
1981—Denver NFL	14	108	64	59.3	797	6	6	7.38	9	40	4.4	0	0	0	2
1982—Denver NFL	9	223	131	58.7	1405	7	11	6.30	8	27	3.4	1	1	6	4
1983—Denver NFL	10	215	119	55.3	1617	9	7	7.52	13	28	2.2	1	1	6	5
1984—Tampa Bay NFL	16	509	308	60.5	3554	19	18	6.98	28	59	2.1	2	2	12	15
1985—Tampa Bay NFL	11	370	197	53.2	2488	19	18	6.72	9	28	3.1	0	0	0	3
1986—Tampa Bay NFL	16	96	50	52.1	610	5	12	6.35	2	1	0.5	1	1	6	2
1987—Tampa Bay NFL	12	275	159	57.8	1891	14	7	6.88	8	—8	—1.0	0	0	0	7
Pro Totals—11 Years	127	2997	1698	56.7	19582	116	139	6.53	115	209	1.8	6	6	36	57

Quarterback Rating Points: 1978 (39.8), 1979 (73.1), 1980 (66.5), 1981 (77.6), 1982 (67.2), 1983 (79.9), 1984 (79.3), 1985 (71.3), 1986 (49.7), 1987 (85.3). Total—70.4.
Additional pro statistics: Recovered two fumbles and fumbled nine times for minus five yards, 1978; recovered two fumbles and fumbled six times for minus 17 yards, 1979; fumbled four times for minus six yards, 1980; recovered two fumbles and fumbled 15 times for minus eight yards, 1984; recovered one fumble and fumbled twice for minus five yards, 1986; recovered two fumbles and fumbled seven times for minus two yards, 1987.

ALBERT LOUIS DEL GRECO JR.
(Al)
Placekicker—Phoenix Cardinals
Born March 2, 1962, at Providence, R. I.
Height, 5.10. Weight, 191.
High School—Coral Gables, Fla.
Attended Auburn University.

Signed as free agent by Miami Dolphins, May 17, 1984.
Released by Miami Dolphins, August 27, 1984; signed as free agent by Green Bay Packers, October 17, 1984.
Released by Green Bay Packers, November 25, 1987; signed as free agent by St. Louis Cardinals, December 8, 1987.
Franchise transferred to Phoenix, March 15, 1988.

Year Club	G.	XP.	XPM.	FG.	FGA.	Pts.
		—PLACE KICKING—				
1984—Green Bay NFL	9	34	0	9	12	61
1985—Green Bay NFL	16	38	2	19	26	95
1986—Green Bay NFL	16	29	0	17	27	80
1987—G.B.(5)-St.L.(3) NFL	8	19	1	9	15	46
Pro Totals—4 Years	49	120	3	54	80	282

JEFFREY ALAN DELLENBACH
(Jeff)
Offensive Tackle—Miami Dolphins
Born February 14, 1963, at Wausau, Wis.
Height, 6.06. Weight, 280.
High School—Wausau, Wis., East.
Attended University of Wisconsin.

Selected by Jacksonville in 1985 USFL territorial draft.

Selected by Miami in 4th round (111th player selected) of 1985 NFL draft.
Signed by Miami Dolphins, July 15, 1985.
Miami NFL, 1985 through 1987.
Games: 1985 (11), 1986 (13), 1987 (11). Total—35.
Pro statistics: Fumbled once for minus 13 yards, 1987.
Played in AFC Championship Game following 1985 season.

JACK DEL RIO
Linebacker—Kansas City Chiefs
Born April 4, 1963, at Castro Valley, Calif.
Height, 6.04. Weight, 235.
High School—Hayward, Calif.
Attended University of Southern California.
Selected by Los Angeles in 1985 USFL territorial draft.
Selected by New Orleans in 3rd round (68th player selected) of 1985 NFL draft.
Signed by New Orleans Saints, July 31, 1985.
Traded by New Orleans Saints to Kansas City Chiefs for 5th round pick in 1988 draft, August 17, 1987.
Selected by Toronto Blue Jays' organization in 22nd round of free-agent draft, June 8, 1981.
New Orleans NFL, 1985 and 1986; Kansas City NFL, 1987.
Games: 1985 (16), 1986 (16), 1987 (10). Total—42.
Pro statistics: Recovered five fumbles for 22 yards and a touchdown and intercepted two passes for 13 yards, 1985; rushed once for 16 yards, 1986.

MARK FRANCIS DENNIS
Offensive Tackle—Miami Dolphins
Born April 15, 1965, at Junction City, Kan.
Height, 6.06. Weight, 291.
High School—Washington, Ill.
Attended University of Illinois.
Selected by Miami in 8th round (212th player selected) of 1987 NFL draft.
Signed by Miami Dolphins, July 23, 1987.
Miami NFL, 1987.
Games: 1987 (5).

GLENN DENNISON
Tight End—New York Jets
Born November 17, 1961, at Beaver Falls, Pa.
Height, 6.03. Weight, 225.
High School—Beaver Falls, Pa.
Attended University of Miami (Fla.).
Selected by Houston in 3rd round (64th player selected) of 1984 USFL draft.
Selected by New York Jets in 2nd round (39th player selected) of 1984 NFL draft.
Signed by New York Jets, May 29, 1984.
On physically unable to perform/reserve with back injury, July 27 through August 18, 1985.
On injured reserve with back injury, August 19 through entire 1985 season.
Released by New York Jets, August 25, 1986; signed as free agent by New England Patriots for 1987, November 17, 1986.
Traded by New England Patriots to Washington Redskins for draft choice, August 20, 1987.
Released by Washington Redskins, October 27, 1987; signed as free agent by New York Jets, November 4, 1987.
Released by New York Jets, December 1, 1987; re-signed by Jets, April 8, 1988.

| Year   Club | —PASS RECEIVING— | | | | |
	G.	P.C.	Yds.	Avg.	TD.
1984—N.Y. Jets NFL	16	16	141	8.8	1
1987—Washington NFL	2	2	8	4.0	0
Pro Totals—2 Years	18	18	149	8.3	1

Additional pro statistics: Rushed once for four yards, 1984.

RICK STEVEN DENNISON
Linebacker—Denver Broncos
Born June 22, 1958, at Kalispell, Mont.
Height, 6.03. Weight, 220.
High School—Fort Collins, Colo., Rocky Mountain.
Received bachelor of science degree in civil engineering from Colorado State University in 1980.
Signed as free agent by Buffalo Bills, May 9, 1980.
Released by Buffalo Bills, August 20, 1980; signed as free agent by Denver Broncos, December 29, 1980.
Released by Denver Broncos, August 31, 1981; signed as free agent by Buffalo Bills, February 26, 1982.
Released by Buffalo Bills, August 31, 1982; signed as free agent by Denver Broncos, September 7, 1982.
Denver NFL, 1982 through 1987.
Games: 1982 (9), 1983 (16), 1984 (16), 1985 (15), 1986 (16), 1987 (12). Total—84.
Pro statistics: Returned two kickoffs for 27 yards and recovered one fumble, 1984; intercepted one pass for five yards, 1986; intercepted one pass for 10 yards, 1987.
Played in AFC Championship Game following 1986 and 1987 seasons.
Played in NFL Championship Game following 1986 and 1987 seasons.

BURNELL JOSEPH DENT
Linebacker—Green Bay Packers
Born March 16, 1963, at New Orleans, La.
Height, 6.01. Weight, 236.
High School—Destrehan, La.
Received bachelor of science degree in physical education from Tulane University in 1986.

Selected by Green Bay in 6th round (143rd player selected) of 1986 NFL draft.
Signed by Green Bay Packers, July 18, 1986.
On injured reserve with knee injury, September 1 through October 23, 1987; activated, October 24, 1987.
Green Bay NFL, 1986 and 1987.
Games: 1986 (16), 1987 (9). Total—25.

RICHARD LAMAR DENT
Defensive End—Chicago Bears
Born December 13, 1960, at Atlanta, Ga.
Height, 6.05. Weight, 263.
High School—Atlanta, Ga., Murphy.
Attended Tennessee State University.

Selected by Philadelphia in 8th round (89th player selected) of 1983 USFL draft.
Selected by Chicago in 8th round (203rd player selected) of 1983 NFL draft.
Signed by Chicago Bears, May 12, 1983.
Chicago NFL, 1983 through 1987.
Games: 1983 (16), 1984 (16), 1985 (16), 1986 (15), 1987 (12). Total—75.
Pro statistics: Recovered one fumble, 1984; intercepted two passes for 10 yards and a touchdown and recovered two fumbles, 1985; recovered two fumbles for 11 yards, 1987.
Played in NFC Championship Game following 1984 and 1985 seasons.
Played in NFL Championship Game following 1985 season.
Played in Pro Bowl (NFL All-Star Game) following 1984 and 1985 seasons.

STEVEN LEONARD DeOSSIE
(Steve)
Linebacker—Dallas Cowboys
Born November 22, 1962, at Tacoma, Wash.
Height, 6.02. Weight, 248.
High School—Boston, Mass., Don Bosco Technical.
Received bachelor of science degree in communications from Boston College in 1984.

Selected by New Jersey in 1st round (14th player selected) of 1984 USFL draft.
Selected by Dallas in 4th round (110th player selected) of 1984 NFL draft.
Signed by Dallas Cowboys, May 3, 1984.
Dallas NFL, 1984 through 1987.
Games: 1984 (16), 1985 (16), 1986 (16), 1987 (11). Total—59.

JOSEPH DEVLIN
(Joe)
Offensive Tackle—Buffalo Bills
Born February 23, 1954 at Phoenixville, Pa.
Height, 6.05. Weight, 280.
High School—Frazer, Pa., Great Valley.
Attended University of Iowa.

Named as guard on THE SPORTING NEWS College All-America Team, 1975.
Selected by Buffalo in 2nd round (52nd player selected) of 1976 NFL draft.
On injured reserve with knee injury, December 13 through remainder of 1978 season.
On injured reserve with broken ankle, August 22 through entire 1983 season.
Buffalo NFL, 1976 through 1982 and 1984 through 1987.
Games: 1976 (14), 1977 (14), 1978 (14), 1979 (16), 1980 (16), 1981 (16), 1982 (9), 1984 (16), 1985 (16), 1986 (16), 1987 (12). Total—159.
Pro statistics: Recovered one fumble, 1978 and 1982; recovered two fumbles, 1979.

ERIC DEMETRIC DICKERSON
Running Back—Indianapolis Colts
Born September 2, 1960, at Sealy, Tex.
Height, 6.03. Weight, 218.
High School—Sealy, Tex.
Attended Southern Methodist University.
Cousin of Dexter Manley, defensive end with Washington Redskins.

Named as running back on THE SPORTING NEWS College All-America Team, 1982.
Named THE SPORTING NEWS NFL Player of the Year, 1983.
Named to THE SPORTING NEWS NFL All-Star Team, 1983, 1984, 1986 and 1987.
Established NFL records for most yards rushing by rookie (1,808), 1983; most touchdowns rushing by rookie (18), 1983; most yards rushing, season (2,105), 1984; most games, 100 yards rushing, season (12), 1984; most seasons, 2,000 yards rushing and receiving combined (3).
Selected by Arizona in 1st round (6th player selected) of 1983 USFL draft.
Selected by Los Angeles Rams in 1st round (2nd player selected) of 1983 NFL draft.

Signed by Los Angeles Rams, July 12, 1983.
On did not report list, August 20 through September 12, 1985.
Reported and granted roster exemption, September 13 through September 19, 1985; activated, September 20, 1985.
Crossed picket line during players' strike, October 14, 1987.
Traded by Los Angeles Rams to Indianapolis Colts for 1st and 2nd round picks in 1988 draft, 2nd round pick in 1989 draft and running back Owen Gill, October 31, 1987; Rams also acquired 1st round pick in 1988 draft, 1st and 2nd round picks in 1989 draft and running back Greg Bell from Buffalo Bills in exchange for Colts trading rights to linebacker Cornelius Bennett to Bills.

			RUSHING			PASS RECEIVING				TOTAL		
Year Club	G.	Att.	Yds.	Avg.	TD.	P.C.	Yds.	Avg.	TD.	TD.	Pts.	F.
1983—Los Angeles Rams NFL	16	*390	*1808	4.6	18	51	404	7.9	2	20	120	13
1984—Los Angeles Rams NFL	16	379	*2105	5.6	*14	21	139	6.6	0	14	84	14
1985—Los Angeles Rams NFL	14	292	1234	4.2	12	20	126	6.3	0	12	72	10
1986—Los Angeles Rams NFL	16	*404	*1821	4.5	11	26	205	7.9	0	11	66	12
1987—L.A. Rams (3)-Ind. (9) NFL	12	283	1288	4.6	6	18	171	9.5	0	6	36	7
Pro Totals—5 Years	74	1748	8256	4.7	61	136	1045	7.7	2	63	378	56

Additional pro statistics: Recovered one fumble, 1983; attempted one pass with one interception and recovered four fumbles, 1984; recovered three fumbles, 1985 and 1987; attempted one pass with one completion for 15 yards and a touchdown and recovered two fumbles, 1986.
Played in NFC Championship Game following 1985 season.
Played in Pro Bowl (NFL All-Star Game) following 1983, 1984, 1986 and 1987 seasons.

CLINT DIDIER
Tight End—Washington Redskins
Born April 4, 1959, at Connell, Wash.
Height, 6.05. Weight, 240.
High School—Connell, Wash.
Attended Columbia Basin Junior College and Portland State University.

Selected by Washington in 12th round (314th player selected) of 1981 NFL draft.
On injured reserve with pulled hamstring, August 18 through entire 1981 season.
On injured reserve with fractured leg, August 28 through September 28, 1984; activated, September 29, 1984.
On injured reserve with hamstring injury, September 8 through October 23, 1987; activated, October 24, 1987.

		PASS RECEIVING			
Year Club	G.	P.C.	Yds.	Avg.	TD.
1982—Washington NFL	8	2	10	5.0	1
1983—Washington NFL	16	9	153	17.0	4
1984—Washington NFL	11	30	350	11.7	5
1985—Washington NFL	16	41	433	10.6	4
1986—Washington NFL	14	34	691	20.3	4
1987—Washington NFL	9	13	178	13.7	1
Pro Totals—6 Years	74	129	1815	14.1	19

Additional pro statistics: Recovered one fumble in end zone for a touchdown and fumbled once, 1983.
Played in NFC Championship Game following 1982, 1983, 1986 and 1987 seasons.
Played in NFL Championship Game following 1982, 1983 and 1987 seasons.

CURT JOSEPH DiGIACOMO
Guard—Kansas City Chiefs
Born October 24, 1963, at San Diego, Calif.
Height, 6.04. Weight, 275.
High School—Sacramento, Calif., Foothill.
Attended American River College and University of Arizona.

Signed as free agent by San Diego Chargers, May 22, 1986.
On injured reserve with Achilles tendon injury, September 1 through December 2, 1986; activated after clearing procedural waivers, December 4, 1986.
On injured reserve with ankle injury, September 7 through October 26, 1987.
Released by San Diego Chargers, October 27, 1987; signed as free agent by Kansas City Chiefs, May 2, 1988.
San Diego NFL, 1986.
Games: 1986 (3).

STEPHEN WHITFIELD DILS
(Steve)
Quarterback—Los Angeles Rams
Born December 8, 1955, at Seattle, Wash.
Height, 6.01. Weight, 191.
High School—Vancouver, Wash., Fort Vancouver.
Received bachelor of arts degree in economics from Stanford University in 1979.

Selected by Minnesota in 4th round (97th player selected) of 1979 NFL draft.
Traded by Minnesota Vikings to Los Angeles Rams for 4th round pick in 1985 draft, September 18, 1984.
Crossed picket line during players' strike, October 1, 1987.

		PASSING							RUSHING				TOTAL		
Year Club	G.	Att.	Cmp.	Pct.	Gain	T.P.	P.I.	Avg.	Att.	Yds.	Avg.	TD.	TD.	Pts.	F.
1979—Minnesota NFL	1				None						None		0	0	0
1980—Minnesota NFL	16	51	32	62.7	352	3	0	6.90	3	26	8.7	0	0	0	0
1981—Minnesota NFL	2	102	54	52.9	607	1	2	5.95	4	14	3.5	0	0	0	3
1982—Minnesota NFL	9	26	11	42.3	68	0	0	2.62	1	5	5.0	0	0	0	0
1983—Minnesota NFL	16	444	239	53.8	2840	11	16	6.40	16	28	1.8	0	0	0	13

Year Club	G.	Att.	Cmp.	Pct.	Gain	T.P.	P.I.	Avg.	Att.	Yds.	Avg.	TD.	TD.	Pts.	F.
				PASSING						RUSHING			TOTAL		
1984—Min. (3)-Rams (7) NFL....	10	7	4	57.1	44	1	1	6.29			None		0	0	0
1985—Los Angeles Rams NFL..	15				None				2	—4	—2.0	0	0	0	0
1986—Los Angeles Rams NFL..	15	129	59	45.7	693	4	4	5.37	10	5	0.5	0	0	0	4
1987—Los Angeles Rams NFL..	15	114	56	49.1	646	5	4	5.67	7	—4	—0.6	0	0	0	2
Pro Totals—9 Years..........	99	873	455	52.1	5250	25	27	6.01	43	70	1.6	0	0	0	22

Quarterback Rating Points: 1980 (102.8), 1981 (66.0), 1982 (49.8), 1983 (66.8), 1984 (75.9), 1986 (60.0), 1987 (66.6). Total—67.3.

Additional pro statistics: Recovered two fumbles, 1981; recovered six fumbles, 1983; recovered one fumble and fumbled four times for minus six yards, 1986; recovered one fumble and fumbled twice for minus one yard, 1987.

Member of Los Angeles Rams for NFC Championship Game following 1985 season; did not play.

FLOYD EUGENE DIXON
Wide Receiver—Atlanta Falcons
Born April 9, 1964, at Beaumont, Tex.
Height, 5.09. Weight, 170.
High School—Beaumont, Tex., Hebert.
Received degree from Stephen F. Austin State University in 1987.

Selected by Atlanta in 6th round (154th player selected) of 1986 NFL draft.
Signed by Atlanta Falcons, July 17, 1986.

Year Club	G.	Att.	Yds.	Avg.	TD.	P.C.	Yds.	Avg.	TD.	TD.	Pts.	F.
			RUSHING				PASS RECEIVING			TOTAL		
1986—Atlanta NFL	16	11	67	6.1	0	42	617	14.7	2	2	12	3
1987—Atlanta NFL	12	3	—3	—1.0	0	36	600	16.7	5	5	30	0
Pro Totals—2 Years..................	28	14	64	4.6	0	78	1217	15.6	7	7	42	3

Year Club	G.	No.	Yds.	Avg.	TD.
			PUNT RETURNS		
1986—Atlanta NFL	16	26	151	5.8	0
1987—Atlanta NFL	12			None	
Pro Totals—2 Years............	28	26	151	5.8	0

Additional pro statistics: Returned one kickoff for 13 yards and recovered two fumbles, 1986.

HANFORD DIXON
Cornerback—Cleveland Browns
Born December 25, 1958, at Mobile, Ala.
Height, 5.11. Weight, 186.
High School—Theodore, Ala.
Attended University of Southern Mississippi.
Cousin of Lyneal Alston, wide receiver with Pittsburgh Steelers.

Named to THE SPORTING NEWS NFL All-Star Team, 1986 and 1987.
Named as defensive back on THE SPORTING NEWS College All-America Team, 1980.
Selected by Cleveland in 1st round (22nd player selected) of 1981 NFL draft.

Year Club	G.	No.	Yds.	Avg.	TD.
			INTERCEPTIONS		
1981—Cleveland NFL.............	16			None	
1982—Cleveland NFL.............	9	4	22	5.5	0
1983—Cleveland NFL.............	16	3	41	13.7	0
1984—Cleveland NFL.............	16	5	31	6.2	0
1985—Cleveland NFL.............	16	3	65	21.7	0
1986—Cleveland NFL.............	16	5	35	7.0	0
1987—Cleveland NFL.............	12	3	5	1.7	0
Pro Totals—7 Years............	101	23	199	8.7	0

Additional pro statistics: Fumbled once, 1982 and 1986; recovered one fumble, 1984; recovered two fumbles, 1986.
Played in AFC Championship Game following 1986 and 1987 seasons.
Played in Pro Bowl (NFL All-Star Game) following 1986 and 1987 seasons.

RANDY C. DIXON
Offensive Tackle—Indianapolis Colts
Born March 12, 1965, at Clewiston, Fla.
Height, 6.03. Weight, 293.
High School—Clewiston, Fla.
Attended University of Pittsburgh.

Named as offensive tackle on THE SPORTING NEWS College All-America Team, 1986.
Selected by Indianapolis in 4th round (85th player selected) of 1987 NFL draft.
Signed by Indianapolis Colts, July 24, 1987.
Indianapolis NFL, 1987.
Games: 1987 (3).

—DID YOU KNOW—

That the New York Jets' Joe Walton, with a 41-38 record after five seasons, is the only head coach in Jets history to have a career record over .500?

WILLIE JOE DIXON JR.

(Known by middle name.)

Defensive Tackle—Atlanta Falcons

Born January 8, 1964, at Fort Smith, Ark.
Height, 6.02. Weight, 276.
High School—Pocola, Okla.
Attended University of Tulsa.
Cousin of Rod Shoate, linebacker with New England Patriots, New Jersey Generals
and Memphis Showboats, 1975, 1977 through 1981, 1983 and 1984.

Signed as free agent by Los Angeles Raiders, May 2, 1986.
Released by Los Angeles Raiders, August 6, 1986; awarded on waivers to Houston Oilers, August 7, 1986.
Released by Houston Oilers, August 25, 1986; re-signed by Oilers, March 25, 1987.
Released by Houston Oilers, October 27, 1987; signed as free agent by Atlanta Falcons for 1988, December 24, 1987.
Houston NFL, 1987.
Games: 1987 (2).

KIRK JAMES DODGE

Linebacker—Denver Broncos

Born June 4, 1962, at Whittier, Calif.
Height, 6.01. Weight, 231.
High School—San Francisco, Calif., Lowell.
Attended Fullerton College and University of Nevada at Las Vegas.

Selected by Los Angeles in 6th round (112th player selected) of 1984 USFL draft.
Selected by Atlanta in 7th round (175th player selected) of 1984 NFL draft.
Signed by Atlanta Falcons, June 10, 1984.
Released by Atlanta Falcons, August 26, 1984; signed as free agent by Detroit Lions, October 2, 1984
On injured reserve with shoulder injury, August 20 through entire 1985 season.
Released by Detroit Lions, August 18, 1986; signed as free agent by Houston Oilers, October 24, 1986.
Released by Houston Oilers, September 3, 1987; signed as free agent replacement player by Denver Broncos,
September 25, 1987.
Released by Denver Broncos, October 19, 1987; re-signed by Broncos, April 5, 1988.
Detroit NFL, 1984; Houston NFL, 1986; Denver NFL, 1987.
Games: 1984 (11), 1986 (9), 1987 (3). Total—23.
Pro statistics: Recovered one fumble, 1984.

STEPHEN GUGEL DOIG

(Steve)

Linebacker—Los Angeles Raiders

Born March 28, 1960, at Melrose, Mass.
Height, 6.02. Weight, 242.
High School—North Reading, Mass.
Attended University of New Hampshire.

Selected by Detroit in 3rd round (69th player selected) of 1982 NFL draft.
On injured reserve with ankle injury, October 8 through November 11, 1983; activated, November 12, 1983.
Released by Detroit Lions, August 27, 1985; signed as free agent by New England Patriots, February 24, 1986.
On injured reserve with foot injury, August 26 through Septmeber 29, 1986.
Released by New England Patriots, September 30, 1986; re-signed by Patriots after clearing procedural waivers,
November 19, 1986.
Released by New England Patriots, September 7, 1987; re-signed by Patriots, September 16, 1987.
Crossed picket line during players' strike, October 14, 1987.
On injured reserve with strained stomach muscle, November 3 through November 30, 1987.
Released by New England Patriots, December 1, 1987; signed as free agent by Los Angeles Raiders, April 15, 1988.
Detroit NFL, 1982 through 1984; New England NFL, 1986 and 1987.
Games: 1982 (9), 1983 (9), 1984 (16), 1986 (5), 1987 (1). Total—40.
Pro statistics: Recovered one fumble, 1986.

CHRISTOPHER JOHN DOLEMAN

(Chris)

Defensive End—Minnesota Vikings

Born October 16, 1961, at Indianapolis, Ind.
Height, 6.05. Weight, 262.
High Schools—Wayne, Pa., Valley Forge Military Academy;
and York, Pa., William Penn.
Attended University of Pittsburgh.
Brother of Ty Doleman, basketball player at University of Pittsburgh at Johnstown.

Selected by Baltimore in 1985 USFL territorial draft.
Selected by Minnesota in 1st round (4th player selected) of 1985 NFL draft.
Signed by Minnesota Vikings, August 8, 1985.
Minnesota NFL, 1985 through 1987.
Games: 1985 (16), 1986 (16), 1987 (12). Total—44.
Pro statistics: Intercepted one pass for five yards and recovered three fumbles, 1985; intercepted one pass for 59
yards and a touchdown, 1986.
Played in NFC Championship Game following 1987 season.
Played in Pro Bowl (NFL All-Star Game) following 1987 season.

JAMES MATTHEW DOMBROWSKI
(Jim)
Offensive Tackle—New Orleans Saints
Born October 19, 1963, at Williamsville, N.Y.
Height, 6.05. Weight, 298.
High School—Williamsville, N.Y., South.
Received bachelor's degree in biology from University of Virginia in 1986.

Named as offensive tackle on THE SPORTING NEWS College All-America Team, 1985.
Selected by Orlando in 1986 USFL territorial draft.
Selected by New Orleans in 1st round (6th player selected) of 1986 NFL draft.
Signed by New Orleans Saints, August 1, 1986.
On injured reserve with broken foot, September 22 through remainder of 1986 season.
New Orleans NFL, 1986 and 1987.
Games: 1986 (3), 1987 (10). Total—13.

JEFF DONALDSON
Safety—Houston Oilers
Born April 19, 1962, at Fort Collins, Colo.
Height, 6.00. Weight, 193.
High School—Fort Collins, Colo.
Attended University of Colorado.

Selected by Denver in 1984 USFL territorial draft.
Selected by Houston in 9th round (228th player selected) of 1984 NFL draft.
Signed by Houston Oilers, July 17, 1984.

| | | —INTERCEPTIONS— | | | |
Year Club	G.	No.	Yds.	Avg.	TD.
1984—Houston NFL	16		None		
1985—Houston NFL	16		None		
1986—Houston NFL	16	1	0	0.0	0
1987—Houston NFL	12	4	16	4.0	0
Pro Totals—4 Years	60	5	16	3.2	0

Additional pro statistics: Returned six punts for 35 yards, returned five kickoffs for 93 yards and fumbled once, 1985; recovered two fumbles, 1985 and 1987; recovered two fumbles for one yard and a touchdown, 1986.

RAYMOND CANUTE DONALDSON
(Ray)
Center—Indianapolis Colts
Born May 18, 1958, at Rome, Ga.
Height, 6.03. Weight, 288.
High School—Rome, Ga., East.
Attended University of Georgia.
Step-brother of John Tutt, outfielder in Baltimore Orioles' and San Diego Padres'
organizations, 1981 through 1986; and Aguas of Mexican League, 1983;
and cousin of Robert Lavette, running back with Atlanta Falcons.

Selected by Baltimore in 2nd round (32nd player selected) of 1980 NFL draft.
Franchise transferred to Indianapolis, March 31, 1984.
Baltimore NFL, 1980 through 1983; Indianapolis NFL, 1984 through 1987.
Games: 1980 (16), 1981 (16), 1982 (9), 1983 (16), 1984 (16), 1985 (16), 1986 (16), 1987 (12). Total—117.
Pro statistics: Recovered one fumble, 1981, 1982 and 1985; fumbled once, 1983; fumbled twice for minus four yards, 1986.
Played in Pro Bowl (NFL All-Star Game) following 1986 and 1987 seasons.

RICK DONNELLY
Punter—Atlanta Falcons
Born May 17, 1962, at Miller Place, N.Y.
Height, 6.00. Weight, 190.
High School—Miller Place, N.Y.
Attended University of Wyoming.

Selected by San Antonio in 14th round (192nd player selected) of 1985 USFL draft.
Signed as free agent by New England Patriots, May 8, 1985.
Released by New England Patriots, August 19, 1985; signed as free agent by Atlanta Falcons, August 23, 1985.
On injured reserve with knee injury, November 18 through remainder of 1985 season.

| | | —PUNTING— | | |
Year Club	G.	No.	Avg.	Blk.
1985—Atlanta NFL	11	59	43.6	0
1986—Atlanta NFL	16	78	43.9	1
1987—Atlanta NFL	12	61	*44.0	*2
Pro Totals—3 Years	39	198	43.8	3

Additional pro statistics: Rushed twice for minus five yards, 1985; recovered one fumble, 1985 and 1987; successful on only extra point attempt, 1986; rushed three times for minus six yards and fumbled twice for minus four yards, 1987.

KEITH ROBERT DORNEY
Guard-Offensive Tackle—Detroit Lions
Born December 3, 1957, at Allentown, Pa.
Height, 6.05. Weight, 285.
High School—Emmaus, Pa.
Received bachelor of science degree in business from Penn State University in 1979.

Named as offensive tackle on THE SPORTING NEWS College All-America Team, 1978.
Selected by Detroit in 1st round (10th player selected) of 1979 NFL draft.
On injured reserve with knee injury, October 15 through December 5, 1980; activated, December 6, 1980.
On injured reserve with knee injury, September 12 through October 10, 1986; activated, October 11, 1986.
On injured reserve with elbow injury, October 31 through November 24, 1987; activated, November 25, 1987.
On injured reserve with knee injury, December 17 through remainder of 1987 season.
Detroit NFL, 1979 through 1987.
Games: 1979 (16), 1980 (9), 1981 (16), 1982 (9), 1983 (13), 1984 (16), 1985 (16), 1986 (12), 1987 (5). Total—112.
Pro statistics: Recovered one fumble, 1981.
Played in Pro Bowl (NFL All-Star Game) following 1982 season.

ANTHONY DREW DORSETT
Name pronounced Dor-SETT.
(Tony)
Running Back—Denver Broncos
Born April 7, 1954, at Rochester, Pa.
Height, 5.11. Weight, 185.
High School—Aliquippa, Pa., Hopewell.
Attended University of Pittsburgh.

Established NFL record for longest run from scrimmage (99 yards), January 3, 1983, against Minnesota Vikings.
Named THE SPORTING NEWS NFC Rookie of the Year, 1977.
Named to THE SPORTING NEWS NFL All-Star Team, 1981.
Named as running back on THE SPORTING NEWS College All-America Team, 1976.
Named THE SPORTING NEWS College Player of the Year, 1976.
Heisman Trophy winner, 1976.
Selected by Dallas in 1st round (2nd player selected) of 1977 NFL draft.
Crossed picket line during players' strike, October 1, 1987.
Traded by Dallas Cowboys to Denver Broncos for conditional pick in 1989 draft, June 3, 1988.

| | | ——RUSHING—— | | | | PASS RECEIVING | | | | —TOTAL— | | |
Year	Club	G.	Att.	Yds.	Avg.	TD.	P.C.	Yds.	Avg.	TD.	TD.	Pts.	F.
1977—Dallas NFL		14	208	1007	4.8	12	29	273	9.4	1	13	78	7
1978—Dallas NFL		16	290	1325	4.6	7	37	378	10.2	2	10	60	12
1979—Dallas NFL		14	250	1107	4.4	6	45	375	8.3	1	7	42	9
1980—Dallas NFL		15	278	1185	4.3	11	34	263	7.7	0	11	66	8
1981—Dallas NFL		16	342	1646	4.8	4	32	325	10.2	2	6	36	10
1982—Dallas NFL		9	★177	745	4.2	5	24	179	7.5	0	5	30	6
1983—Dallas NFL		16	289	1321	4.6	8	40	287	7.2	1	9	54	5
1984—Dallas NFL		16	302	1189	3.9	6	51	459	9.0	1	7	42	12
1985—Dallas NFL		16	305	1307	4.3	7	46	449	9.8	3	10	60	7
1986—Dallas NFL		13	184	748	4.1	5	25	267	10.7	1	6	36	5
1987—Dallas NFL		12	130	456	3.5	1	19	177	9.3	1	2	12	3
Pro Totals—11 Years		157	2755	12036	4.4	72	382	3432	9.0	13	86	516	84

Additional pro statistics: Attempted one pass with one completion for 34 yards, 1977; recovered four fumbles for 54 yards and one touchdown, 1978; attempted one pass with no completions, 1978, 1980, 1982 and 1983; recovered one fumble, 1979, 1980, 1982 and 1983; recovered one fumble for minus 21 yards, 1984; recovered two fumbles, 1981 and 1986; attempted one pass with one interception, 1984; recovered three fumbles, 1985.
Played in NFC Championship Game following 1977, 1978 and 1980 through 1982 seasons.
Played in NFL Championship Game following 1977 and 1978 seasons.
Played in Pro Bowl (NFL All-Star Game) following 1978 and 1981 through 1983 seasons.

DEAN DORSEY
Placekicker—Philadelphia Eagles
Born March 13, 1957, at Toronto, Ontario, Can.
Height, 5.11. Weight, 190.
Attended University of Toronto.

Signed as free agent by Cincinnati Bengals, July 10, 1982.
Released by Cincinnati Bengals, August 23, 1982; signed as free agent by Toronto Argonauts, September 1982.
Released by Toronto Argonauts, June 17, 1983; signed as free agent by New England Patriots, July 15, 1983.
Released by New England Patriots, August 10, 1983.
USFL rights traded by Memphis Showboats to Washington Federals for past considerations, September 12, 1983.
Signed by Washington Federals, October 13, 1983.
Released by Washington Federals, February 13, 1984; signed as free agent by Ottawa Rough Riders, March 2, 1984.
Granted free agency, March 1, 1988; signed by Philadelphia Eagles, March 23, 1988.

| | | ——PLACE KICKING—— | | | | | |
Year	Club	G.	XP.	XPM.	FG.	FGA.	Pts.
1982—Toronto CFL		7	15	0	12	17	55
1984—Ottawa CFL		16	37	0	26	31	122
1985—Ottawa CFL		16	24	0	28	38	120
1986—Ottawa CFL		18	28	0	33	42	134
1987—Ottawa CFL		16	28	0	36	44	141
CFL Totals—5 Years		73	132	0	135	172	†572

†Includes 35 singles.
Additional CFL statistics: Scored four singles and punted 57 times for a 40.5 average, 1982; scored seven singles, 1984; scored 12 singles, 1985; scored seven singles and fumbled once, 1986; scored five singles, 1987.

ERIC HALL DORSEY
Defensive End—New York Giants
Born August 5, 1964, at Washington, D.C.
Height, 6.05. Weight, 280.
High School—McLean, Vir.
Received bachelor of business administration degree in marketing from University of Notre Dame in 1988.
Cousin of Allen Pinkett, running back with Houston Oilers.
Selected by Orlando in 1986 USFL territorial draft.
Selected by New York Giants in 1st round (19th player selected) of 1986 NFL draft.
Signed by New York Giants, August 8, 1986.
New York Giants NFL, 1986 and 1987.
Games: 1986 (16), 1987 (12). Total—28.
Pro statistics: Returned one kickoff for 13 yards, 1987.
Played in NFC Championship Game following 1986 season.
Played in NFL Championship Game following 1986 season.

JOHN MICHAEL DORSEY
Linebacker—Green Bay Packers
Born August 31, 1960, at Leonardtown, Md.
Height, 6.02. Weight, 243.
High School—Leonardtown, Md., Fort Union.
Attended University of Connecticut.
Selected by Philadelphia in 7th round (142nd player selected) of 1984 USFL draft.
Selected by Green Bay in 4th round (99th player selected) of 1984 NFL draft.
Signed by Green Bay Packers, July 12, 1984.
Green Bay NFL, 1984 through 1987.
Games: 1984 (16), 1985 (16), 1986 (16), 1987 (12). Total—60.
Pro statistics: Recovered two fumbles, 1985 and 1986.

DAVID GLENN DOUGLAS
Offensive Tackle—Cincinnati Bengals
Born March 20, 1963, at Spring City, Tenn.
Height, 6.04. Weight, 280.
High School—Evansville, Tenn., Rhea County.
Attended University of Tennessee.
Selected by Memphis in 1986 USFL territorial draft.
Selected by Cincinnati in 8th round (204th player selected) of 1986 NFL draft.
Signed by Cincinnati Bengals, July 10, 1986.
Cincinnati NFL, 1986 and 1987.
Games: 1986 (14), 1987 (12). Total—26.

MAURICE GERRARD DOUGLASS
Defensive Back—Chicago Bears
Born February 12, 1964, at Muncie, Ind.
Height, 5.11. Weight, 200.
High School—Trotwood, O., Madison.
Attended Coffeyville Community College and University of Kentucky.
Selected by Chicago in 8th round (221st player selected) of 1986 NFL draft.
Signed by Chicago Bears, June 22, 1986.
Released by Chicago Bears, September 1, 1986; re-signed by Bears, November 28, 1986.
Chicago NFL, 1986 and 1987.
Games: 1986 (4), 1987 (12). Total—16.
Pro statistics: Intercepted two passes for no yards and recovered one fumble, 1987.

WESLEY WALTER DOVE
(Wes)
Defensive End—Seattle Seahawks
Born February 9, 1964, at Buffalo, N.Y.
Height, 6.07. Weight, 270.
High School—Tonawanda, N.Y., Kenmore East.
Received degree in economics from Syracuse University in 1987.
Selected by Seattle in 12th round (312th player selected) of 1987 NFL draft.
Signed by Seattle Seahawks, July 14, 1987.
Seattle NFL, 1987.
Games: 1987 (2).

MICHAEL LYNN DOWNS
Safety—Dallas Cowboys
Born June 9, 1959, at Dallas, Tex.
Height, 6.03. Weight, 212.
High School—Dallas, Tex., South Oak Cliff.
Received degree in business, political science and physical education from Rice University in 1981.
Signed as free agent by Dallas Cowboys, May, 1981.

		—INTERCEPTIONS—			
Year Club	G.	No.	Yds.	Avg.	TD.
1981—Dallas NFL	15	7	81	11.6	0
1982—Dallas NFL	9	1	22	22.0	0
1983—Dallas NFL	16	4	80	20.0	0
1984—Dallas NFL	16	7	126	18.0	1
1985—Dallas NFL	16	3	11	3.7	0
1986—Dallas NFL	16	6	54	9.0	0
1987—Dallas NFL	12	4	56	14.0	0
Pro Totals—7 Years	100	32	430	13.4	1

Additional pro statistics: Recovered one fumble, 1981 and 1987; recovered three fumbles for 87 yards and one touchdown, 1982; recovered two fumbles for 10 yards and a touchdown, 1983; recovered two fumbles for 28 yards, 1984; recovered three fumbles, 1985; recovered one fumble for 17 yards, 1986.
Played in NFC Championship Game following 1981 and 1982 seasons.

WILLIAM HENRY DOZIER JR.
(D. J.)
Running Back—Minnesota Vikings
Born September 21, 1965, at Norfolk, Va.
Height, 6.00. Weight, 198.
High School—Virginia Beach, Va., Kempsville.
Attended Penn State University.
Selected by Minnesota in 1st round (14th player selected) of 1987 NFL draft.
Signed by Minnesota Vikings, July 6, 1987.
Selected by Detroit Tigers' organization in 18th round of free-agent draft, June 6, 1983.

		—RUSHING—				PASS RECEIVING				—TOTAL—		
Year Club	G.	Att.	Yds.	Avg.	TD.	P.C.	Yds.	Avg.	TD.	TD.	Pts.	F.
1987—Minnesota NFL	9	69	257	3.7	5	12	89	7.4	2	7	42	2

Additional pro statistics: Returned two kickoffs for 23 yards, 1987.
Played in NFC Championship Game following 1987 season.

DWIGHT DRANE
Safety—Buffalo Bills
Born May 6, 1962, at Miami, Fla.
Height, 6.02. Weight, 205.
High School—Miami, Fla., Central.
Attended University of Oklahoma.
Selected by Oklahoma in 1984 USFL territorial draft.
Rights traded by Oklahoma Outlaws to Los Angeles Express for rights to running back Andrew Lazarus, February 29, 1984.
Signed by Los Angeles Express, March 2, 1984.
Granted roster exemption, March 2 through March 8, 1984; activated, March 9, 1984.
Selected by Buffalo in 1st round (14th player selected) of 1984 NFL supplemental draft.
On developmental squad, June 9 through remainder of 1985 season.
Traded with running back Mel Gray, guard Wayne Jones, tight end Ken O'Neal, defensive backs John Warren and Troy West and linebacker Howard Carson by Los Angeles Express to Arizona Outlaws for past considerations, August 1, 1985.
Granted free agency when USFL suspended operations, August 7, 1986; signed by Buffalo Bills, September 10, 1986.
Granted roster exemption, September 10 through September 21, 1986; activated, September 22, 1986.
On developmental squad for 3 games with Los Angeles Express in 1985.
Los Angeles USFL, 1984 and 1985; Buffalo NFL, 1986 and 1987.
Games: 1984 (16), 1985 (15), 1986 (13), 1987 (11). Total USFL—31. Total NFL—24. Total Pro—55.
USFL statistics: Intercepted three passes for 43 yards and a touchdown and recovered one fumble for 50 yards, 1984.
NFL statistics: Recovered one fumble, 1987.

CHRIS DRESSEL
Tight End—Cleveland Browns
Born February 7, 1961, at Placentia, Calif.
Height, 6.04. Weight, 238.
High School—Placentia, Calif., El Dorado.
Attended Stanford University.
Selected by Oakland in 1983 USFL territorial draft.
Selected by Houston in 3rd round (69th player selected) of 1983 NFL draft.
Signed by Houston Oilers, June 22, 1983.
Traded by Houston Oilers to Washington Redskins for conditional 1988 draft choice, June 22, 1987.
Released by Washington Redskins, September 1, 1987; signed as free agent replacement player by San Francisco 49ers, September 24, 1987.

Released by San Francisco 49ers, October 14, 1987; signed as free agent by Cleveland Browns, November 19, 1987. Released by Cleveland Browns, December 10, 1987; re-signed by Browns, April 30, 1988.

		—PASS RECEIVING—			
Year Club	G.	P.C.	Yds.	Avg.	TD.
1983—Houston NFL	16	32	316	9.9	4
1984—Houston NFL	16	40	378	9.5	2
1985—Houston NFL	16	3	17	5.7	1
1986—Houston NFL	16		None		
1987—San Francisco NFL	1	1	8	8.0	0
Pro Totals—5 Years	65	76	719	9.5	7

Additional pro statistics: Returned four kickoffs for 40 yards and rushed once for three yards, 1983; fumbled once, 1984; recovered one fumble, 1985.

WILLIE DREWREY
Wide Receiver-Kick Returner—Houston Oilers
Born April 28, 1963, at Columbus, N.J.
Height, 5.07. Weight, 164.
High School—Columbus, N.J., Northern Burlington.
Attended West Virginia University.

Named as kick returner on THE SPORTING NEWS College All-America Team, 1984.
Selected by Birmingham in 1985 USFL territorial draft.
Selected by Houston in 11th round (281st player selected) of 1985 NFL draft.
Signed by Houston Oilers, July 18, 1985.

		PASS RECEIVING				–PUNT RETURNS–				—KICKOFF RET.—				—TOTAL—		
Year Club	G.	P.C.	Yds.	Avg.	TD.	No.	Yds.	Avg.	TD.	No.	Yds.	Avg.	TD.	TD.	Pts.	F.
1985—Houston NFL	14	2	28	14.0	0	24	215	9.0	0	26	642	24.7	0	0	0	2
1986—Houston NFL	15	18	299	16.6	0	34	262	7.7	0	25	500	20.0	0	0	0	3
1987—Houston NFL	12	11	148	13.5	0	3	11	3.7	0	8	136	17.0	0	0	0	0
Pro Totals—3 Years	41	31	475	15.3	0	61	488	8.0	0	59	1278	21.7	0	0	0	5

Additional pro statistics: Rushed twice for minus four yards, 1985; recovered one fumble, 1986.

DOUG DuBOSE
Running Back—San Francisco 49ers
Born March 14, 1964, at New London, Conn.
Height, 5.11. Weight, 190.
High School—Oakdale, Conn., Montville.
Attended University of Nebraska.

Signed as free agent by San Francisco 49ers, June 30, 1987.
On injured reserve with shoulder injury, September 8 through October 11, 1987; activated, October 12, 1987.
Crossed picket line during players' strike, October 12, 1987.
On injured reserve with knee injury, December 17 through remainder of 1987 season.

		——RUSHING——				PASS RECEIVING				—TOTAL—		
Year Club	G.	Att.	Yds.	Avg.	TD.	P.C.	Yds.	Avg.	TD.	TD.	Pts.	F.
1987—San Francisco NFL	2	10	33	3.3	0	4	37	9.3	0	0	0	0

MARK DAVID DUDA
Nose Tackle—Phoenix Cardinals
Born February 4, 1961, at Wilkes Barre, Pa.
Height, 6.03. Weight, 279.
High School—Plymouth, Pa., Wyoming Valley West.
Attended University of Maryland.

Selected by Washington in 1983 USFL territorial draft.
Selected by St. Louis in 4th round (96th player selected) of 1983 NFL draft.
Signed by St. Louis Cardinals, May 9, 1983.
On injured reserve with dislocated kneecap, November 6 through remainder of 1984 season.
On injured reserve with knee injury, October 27 through remainder of 1987 season.
Franchise transferred to Phoenix, March 15, 1988.
St. Louis NFL, 1983 through 1987.
Games: 1983 (14), 1984 (8), 1985 (16), 1986 (14), 1987 (3). Total—55.
Pro statistics: Returned one kickoff for 12 yards and recovered two fumbles, 1983; recovered one fumble, 1984 and 1985.

BRIAN CHRISTOPHER DUDLEY
Safety—Cleveland Browns
Born August 30, 1960, at Los Angeles, Calif.
Height, 6.00. Weight, 180.
High School—Los Angeles, Calif., Fairfax.
Attended Bethune-Cookman College.

Signed as free agent by Montreal Alouettes, March, 1984.
Released by Montreal Alouettes, June, 1984; re-signed by Alouettes, May, 1985.
Released by Montreal Alouettes, June, 1985; re-signed by Alouettes, April 12, 1986.
Released by Montreal Alouettes, June 12, 1987; signed as free agent replacement player by Cleveland Browns, September 23, 1987.
Released by Cleveland Browns, October 19, 1987; re-signed by Browns, March 4, 1988.
Montreal CFL, 1986; Cleveland NFL, 1987.

Games: 1986 (16), 1987 (3). Total—19.

CFL statistics: Intercepted two passes for 32 yards, returned three punts for 17 yards, recovered four fumbles and credited with two sacks, 1986.

DAVID RUSSELL DUERSON
(Dave)
Safety—Chicago Bears
Born November 28, 1960, at Muncie, Ind.
Height, 6.01. Weight, 210.
High School—Muncie, Ind., Northside.
Received bachelor of arts degree in economics and communications from
University of Notre Dame in 1983.
Cousin of Allen Leavell, guard with Houston Rockets.

Named to THE SPORTING NEWS NFL All-Star Team, 1986.
Selected by Chicago in 1983 USFL territorial draft.
Selected by Chicago in 3rd round (64th player selected) of 1983 NFL draft.
Signed by Chicago Bears, June 25, 1983.

| | | | —INTERCEPTIONS— | | | | –PUNT RETURNS– | | | | —TOTAL— | | |
Year	Club	G.	No.	Yds.	Avg.	TD.	No.	Yds.	Avg.	TD.	TD.	Pts.	F.
1983—Chicago NFL		16		None				None			0	0	0
1984—Chicago NFL		16	1	9	9.0	0	1	4	4.0	0	0	0	0
1985—Chicago NFL		15	5	53	10.6	0	6	47	7.8	0	0	0	1
1986—Chicago NFL		16	6	139	23.2	0		None			0	0	0
1987—Chicago NFL		12	3	0	0.0	0	1	10	10.0	0	0	0	0
Pro Totals—5 Years		75	15	201	13.4	0	8	61	7.6	0	0	0	1

Additional pro statistics: Returned three kickoffs for 66 yards, 1983; returned four kickoffs for 95 yards, 1984; recovered one fumble, 1985; recovered two fumbles for six yards, 1986; recovered one fumble for 10 yards, 1987.
Played in NFC Championship Game following 1984 and 1985 seasons.
Played in NFL Championship Game following 1985 season.
Played in Pro Bowl (NFL All-Star Game) following 1985 through 1987 seasons.

JAMIE DONNELL DUKES
Guard—Atlanta Falcons
Born June 14, 1964, at Schnectady, N.Y.
Height, 6.01. Weight, 278.
High School—Orlando, Fla., Evans.
Attended Florida State University.

Selected by Tampa Bay in 1986 USFL territorial draft.
Signed as free agent by Atlanta Falcons, May 4, 1986.
Atlanta NFL, 1986 and 1987.
Games: 1986 (14), 1987 (4). Total—18.
Pro statistics: Recovered one fumble, 1986.

JONATHAN DUMBAULD
(Jon)
Defensive End—Philadelphia Eagles
Born February 14, 1963, at Anaheim, Calif.
Height, 6.04. Weight, 259.
High School—Troy, O.
Attended University of Kentucky.

Selected by New Orleans in 10th round (253rd player selected) of 1986 NFL draft.
Selected by Memphis in 6th round (41st player selected) of 1986 USFL draft.
Signed by New Orleans Saints, July 19, 1986.
Released by New Orleans Saints, August 27, 1986; re-signed by Saints, October 14, 1986.
Released by New Orleans Saints, September 7, 1987; awarded on waivers to Philadelphia Eagles, September 8, 1987.
On injured reserve with foot fracture, November 27 through remainder of 1987 season.
New Orleans NFL, 1986; Philadelphia NFL, 1987.
Games: 1986 (9), 1987 (6). Total—15.

CURTIS EVERETT DUNCAN
Wide Receiver-Kick Returner—Houston Oilers
Born January 26, 1965, at Detroit, Mich.
Height, 5.11. Weight, 184.
High School—Detroit, Mich., Redford.
Received bachelor of science degree in business/pre-law from Northwestern University in 1987.

Selected by Houston in 10th round (258th player selected) of 1987 NFL draft.
Signed by Houston Oilers, July 30, 1987.

| | | | PASS RECEIVING | | | | –PUNT RETURNS– | | | | —KICKOFF RET.— | | | | —TOTAL— | | |
Year	Club	G.	P.C.	Yds.	Avg.	TD.	No.	Yds.	Avg.	TD.	No.	Yds.	Avg.	TD.	TD.	Pts.	F.
1987—Houston NFL		10	13	237	18.2	5	8	23	2.9	0	28	546	19.5	0	5	30	0

GARY EDWARD DUNN
Nose Tackle—Pittsburgh Steelers
Born August 24, 1953, at Coral Gables, Fla.
Height, 6.03. Weight, 275.
High School—Coral Gables, Fla.
Received bachelor of business administration degree from University of Miami (Fla.) in 1976.
Son of Eddie Dunn, head coach at University of Miami (Fla.), 1943 and 1944.

Selected by Pittsburgh in 6th round (159th player selected) of 1976 NFL draft.
On injured reserve entire 1977 season.
Crossed picket line during players' strike, October 14, 1987.
Pittsburgh NFL, 1976 and 1978 through 1987.
Games: 1976 (5), 1978 (16), 1979 (16), 1980 (16), 1981 (16), 1982 (9), 1983 (13), 1984 (16), 1985 (10), 1986 (16), 1987 (13). Total—146.
Pro statistics: Recovered one fumble, 1978, 1986 and 1987; recovered two fumbles, 1979; recovered one fumble for one yard, 1981; recovered three fumbles, 1985.
Played in AFC Championship Game following 1978, 1979 and 1984 seasons.
Played in NFL Championship Game following 1978 and 1979 seasons.

KELDRICK A. DUNN
(K. D.)
Tight End—New York Jets
Born April 28, 1963, at Fort Hood, Tex.
Height, 6.03. Weight, 235.
High School—Decatur, Ga., Gordon.
Attended Clemson University.

Selected by Orlando in 1985 USFL territorial draft.
Selected by St. Louis in 5th round (116th player selected) of 1985 NFL draft.
Signed by St. Louis Cardinals, July 3, 1985.
Released by St. Louis Cardinals, August 26, 1985; signed as free agent by Tampa Bay Buccaneers, November 5, 1985.
Released by Tampa Bay Buccaneers, August 22, 1986; re-signed by Buccaneers, November 4, 1986.
Released by Tampa Bay Buccaneers, August 24, 1987; signed as free agent replacement player by Washington Redskins, September 23, 1987.
Released by Washington Redskins, October 20, 1987; signed as free agent by New York Jets, May 3, 1988.
Tampa Bay NFL, 1985 and 1986; Washington NFL, 1987.
Games: 1985 (7), 1986 (7), 1987 (3). Total—17.
Pro statistics: Caught three passes for 83 yards and returned one kickoff for no yards, 1986.

JON REGINALD DUPARD
(Reggie)
Running Back—New England Patriots
Born October 30, 1963, at New Orleans, La.
Height, 5.11. Weight, 205.
High School—River Ridge, La., John Curtis Christian.
Attended Southern Methodist University.

Selected by New England in 1st round (26th player selected) of 1986 NFL draft.
Selected by Birmingham in 1st round (6th player selected) of 1986 USFL draft.
Signed by New England Patriots, August 5, 1986.
On injured reserve with sprained toe, September 1 through November 12, 1986; activated, November 13, 1986.
On injured reserve with hip injury, September 8 through October 30, 1987; activated, October 31, 1987.

Year Club	G.	—RUSHING— Att. Yds. Avg. TD.				PASS RECEIVING P.C. Yds. Avg. TD.				—TOTAL— TD. Pts. F.		
1986—New England NFL	6	15	39	2.6	0	None				0	0	1
1987—New England NFL	8	94	318	3.4	3	3	1	0.3	0	3	18	2
Pro Totals—2 Years	14	109	357	3.3	3	3	1	0.3	0	3	18	3

Additional pro statistics: Returned three kickoffs for 50 yards, 1986; returned four kickoffs for 61 yards and recovered one fumble, 1987.

MARK SUPER DUPER
(Given name at birth was Mark Kirby Dupas.)
Wide Receiver—Miami Dolphins
Born January 25, 1959, at Pineville, La.
Height, 5.09. Weight, 187.
High School—Moreauville, La.
Attended Northwestern (La.) State University.

Selected by Miami in 2nd round (52nd player selected) of 1982 NFL draft.
On inactive list, September 12 and September 19, 1982.
On injured reserve with broken leg, September 16 through November 8, 1985; activated, November 9, 1985.

Year Club	—PASS RECEIVING— G. P.C. Yds. Avg. TD.					Year Club	—PASS RECEIVING— G. P.C. Yds. Avg. TD.				
1982—Miami NFL	2		None			1986—Miami NFL	16	67	1313	19.6	11
1983—Miami NFL	16	51	1003	19.7	10	1987—Miami NFL	11	33	597	18.1	8
1984—Miami NFL	16	71	1306	18.4	8	Pro Totals—6 Years	70	257	4869	18.9	40
1985—Miami NFL	9	35	650	18.6	3						

Additional pro statistics: Recovered one fumble, 1984; recovered one fumble for three yards and fumbled once, 1985; rushed once for minus 10 yards, 1986.
Played in AFC Championship Game following 1984 and 1985 seasons.
Played in NFL Championship Game following 1984 season.
Member of Miami Dolphins for AFC and NFL Championship Game following 1982 season; did not play.
Played in Pro Bowl (NFL All-Star Game) following 1983 and 1984 seasons.
Named to play in Pro Bowl following 1986 season; replaced due to injury by Mark Clayton.

MICHAEL RAY DURRETTE
Guard—Minnesota Vikings
Born August 11, 1957, at Charlottesville, Va.
Height, 6.04. Weight, 280.
High School—Charlottesville, Va., Miller Military of Albemarle.
Attended Ferrum Junior College and West Virginia University.
Related to Walter White, tight end with Kansas City Chiefs, 1975 through 1979.

Signed by Los Angeles Express, January 10, 1983.
On developmental squad, May 18 through June 8, 1985; activated, June 9, 1985.
Released by Los Angeles Express, August 1, 1985; signed as free agent by San Francisco 49ers, February 7, 1986.
On injured reserve with wrist injury, August 25 through October 8, 1986; activated after clearing procedural waivers, October 10, 1986.
On injured reserve with back injury, January 2, 1987 through 1986 season playoffs.
Released by San Francisco 49ers, September 7, 1987; re-signed as replacement player by 49ers, September 24, 1987.
Released by San Francisco 49ers, November 3, 1987; signed as free agent by Minnesota Vikings, November 18, 1987.
Released by Minnesota Vikings, December 1, 1987; re-signed by Vikings for 1988, December 3, 1987.
On developmental squad for 3 games with Los Angeles Express in 1985.
Los Angeles USFL, 1983 through 1985; San Francisco NFL, 1986 and 1987.
Games: 1983 (17), 1984 (18), 1985 (16), 1986 (9), 1987 (3). Total USFL—51. Total NFL—12. Total Pro—63.
Pro statistics: Rushed twice for no yards, caught one pass for four yards and recovered two fumbles, 1983; returned one kickoff for five yards and fumbled once, 1984.

SEAN RENE DYKES
Cornerback—New York Jets
Born August 8, 1964, at New Orleans, La.
Height, 5.10. Weight, 170.
High School—New Orleans, La., Joseph S. Clark.
Attended Eastern Arizona Junior College and Bowling Green State University.

Signed as free agent by San Diego Chargers, May 15, 1986.
Released by San Diego Chargers, August 11, 1986; signed as free agent by New York Jets, March 26, 1987.
Released by New York Jets, August 20, 1987; re-signed as replacement player by Jets, September 24, 1987.
Released by New York Jets, October 26, 1987; re-signed by Jets, December 2, 1987.
New York Jets NFL, 1987.
Games: 1987 (6).

KENNY EASLEY
Safety—Seattle Seahawks
Born January 15, 1959, at Chesapeake, Va.
Height, 6.03. Weight, 198.
High School—Chesapeake, Va., Oscar Smith.
Received degree in political science from University of California at Los Angeles.
Cousin of Walt Easley, running back with San Francisco 49ers, Chicago Blitz and Pittsburgh Maulers, 1981 through 1984.

Named to THE SPORTING NEWS NFL All-Star Team, 1984 and 1985.
Named as defensive back on THE SPORTING NEWS College All-America Team, 1978 through 1980.
Selected by Chicago Bulls in 10th round of 1981 NBA draft.
Selected by Seattle in 1st round (4th player selected) of 1981 NFL draft.
On injured reserve with ankle injury, November 21 through remainder of 1986 season.

Year	Club	G.	No.	Yds.	Avg.	TD.	No.	Yds.	Avg.	TD.	TD.	Pts.	F.
			-INTERCEPTIONS-				-PUNT RETURNS-				—TOTAL—		
1981—Seattle NFL		14	3	155	51.7	1	None				1	6	0
1982—Seattle NFL		8	4	48	12.0	0	1	15	15.0	0	0	0	0
1983—Seattle NFL		16	7	106	15.1	0	1	6	6.0	0	0	0	0
1984—Seattle NFL		16	*10	126	12.6	*2	16	194	12.1	0	2	12	0
1985—Seattle NFL		13	2	22	11.0	0	8	87	10.9	0	0	0	2
1986—Seattle NFL		10	2	34	17.0	0	None				0	0	0
1987—Seattle NFL		12	4	47	11.8	0	None				0	0	0
Pro Totals—7 Years		89	32	538	16.8	3	26	302	11.6	0	3	18	2

Additional pro statistics: Recovered four fumbles for 25 yards, 1981; recovered one fumble, 1982, 1984, 1985 and 1987; recovered three fumbles for 29 yards, 1983.
Played in AFC Championship Game following 1983 season.
Played in Pro Bowl (NFL All-Star Game) following 1982 through 1985 and 1987 seasons.

—DID YOU KNOW—
That the Detroit Lions have lost to the Washington Redskins 12 consecutive times (including one playoff game)? The Lions' last win over Washington was on October 3, 1965.

BO EASON
Safety—San Francisco 49ers

Born March 10, 1961, at Walnut Grove, Calif.
Height, 6.02. Weight, 205.
High School—Walnut Grove, Calif., Delta.
Attended University of California at Davis.
Brother of Tony Eason, quarterback with New England Patriots.

Selected by Oakland in 1st round (18th player selected) of 1984 USFL draft.
Selected by Houston in 2nd round (54th player selected) of 1984 NFL draft.
Signed by Houston Oilers, July 22, 1984.
On injured reserve with knee injury, October 25 through November 23, 1984; activated, November 24, 1984.
On injured reserve with ankle injury, November 3 through remainder of 1986 season.
On injured reserve with knee injury, August 31 through December 11, 1987; activated, December 12, 1987.
Granted free agency, February 1, 1988; re-signed by Oilers and traded to San Francisco 49ers for conditional 5th round pick in 1989 draft and conditional 4th round pick in 1990 draft, June 6, 1988.

			—INTERCEPTIONS—		
Year	Club	G.	No.	Yds.	Avg.TD.
1984—Houston NFL		10	1	20	20.0	0
1985—Houston NFL		16	3	55	18.3	0
1986—Houston NFL		9	2	16	8.0	0
1987—Houston NFL		3		None	
Pro Totals—4 Years		38	6	91	15.2	0

Additional pro statistics: Recovered one fumble, 1984 and 1986; fumbled once, 1985 and 1986.

CHARLES CARROLL EASON IV
(Tony)
Quarterback—New England Patriots

Born October 8, 1959, at Blythe, Calif.
Height, 6.04. Weight, 212.
High School—Clarksburg, Calif., Delta.
Attended American River College and received bachelor of science degree
in physical education from University of Illinois in 1983.
Brother of Bo Eason, safety with San Francisco 49ers.

Selected by Chicago in 1983 USFL territorial draft.
USFL rights traded with running back Calvin Murray and 1st round pick in 1983 draft by Chicago Blitz to Arizona Wranglers for rights to placekicker Frank Corral and 1st round pick in 1983 draft, January 4, 1983.
Selected by New England in 1st round (15th player selected) of 1983 NFL draft.
Signed by New England Patriots, June 2, 1983.
On injured reserve with separated shoulder, November 3 through remainder of 1987 season.

			—PASSING—						—RUSHING—				—TOTAL—		
Year	Club	G.	Att.	Cmp.	Pct.	Gain	T.P.	P.I.	Avg.	Att.	Yds.	Avg.	TD.	TD.	Pts.	F.
1983—New England NFL		16	95	46	48.4	557	1	5	5.86	19	39	2.1	0	0	0	5
1984—New England NFL		16	431	259	60.1	3228	23	8	7.49	40	154	3.9	5	5	30	7
1985—New England NFL		16	299	168	56.2	2156	11	17	7.21	22	70	3.2	1	1	6	4
1986—New England NFL		15	448	276	61.6	3328	19	10	7.43	35	170	4.9	0	0	0	4
1987—New England NFL		4	79	42	53.2	453	3	2	5.73	3	25	8.3	0	0	0	1
Pro Totals—5 Years		67	1352	791	58.5	9722	57	42	7.19	119	458	3.8	6	6	36	21

Quarterback Rating Points: 1983 (48.4), 1984 (93.4), 1985 (67.5), 1986 (89.2), 1987 (72.4). Total—81.9.
Additional pro statistics: Recovered one fumble, 1983; recovered two fumbles and fumbled seven times for minus five yards, 1984; recovered one fumble and fumbled four times for minus 19 yards, 1985; recovered three fumbles, 1986.
Played in AFC Championship Game following 1985 season.
Played in NFL Championship Game following 1985 season.

IRVIN H. EATMAN
(Irv)
Offensive Tackle—Kansas City Chiefs

Born January 1, 1961, at Birmingham, Ala.
Height, 6.07. Weight, 293.
High School—Dayton, O., Meadowdale.
Attended University of California at Los Angeles.

Named as offensive tackle on THE SPORTING NEWS USFL All-Star Team, 1983 and 1984.
Selected by Philadelphia in 1st round (8th player selected) of 1983 USFL draft.
Signed by Philadelphia Stars, February 8, 1983.
Selected by Kansas City in 8th round (204th player selected) of 1983 NFL draft.
Franchise transferred to Baltimore, November 1, 1984.
Granted free agency when USFL suspended operations, August 7, 1986; signed by Kansas City Chiefs, August 10, 1986.
Philadelphia USFL, 1983 and 1984; Baltimore USFL, 1985; Kansas City NFL, 1986 and 1987.
Games: 1983 (18), 1984 (18), 1985 (18), 1986 (16), 1987 (12). Total USFL—54. Total NFL—28. Total Pro—82.
Played in USFL Championship Game following 1983 through 1985 seasons.

BRAD M. EDELMAN
Guard—New Orleans Saints

Born September 3, 1960, at Jacksonville, Fla.
Height, 6.06. Weight, 270.
High School—Creve Coeur, Mo., Parkway North.
Attended University of Missouri.

Named as center on THE SPORTING NEWS College All-America Team, 1981.
Selected by New Orleans on 2nd round (30th player selected) of 1982 NFL draft.
On injured reserve with knee injury, October 9 through November 18, 1984; activated, November 19, 1984.
On injured reserve with knee injury, September 24 through November 15, 1985; activated, November 16, 1985.
New Orleans NFL, 1982 through 1987.
Games: 1982 (9), 1983 (16), 1984 (11), 1985 (8), 1986 (13), 1987 (11). Total—68.
Pro statistics: Recovered one fumble, 1986.
Played in Pro Bowl (NFL All-Star Game) following 1987 season.

BOBBY JOE EDMONDS JR.
(Bobby Joe)
Running Back—Seattle Seahawks
Born September 26, 1964, at Nashville, Tenn.
Height, 5.11. Weight, 186.
High School—St. Louis, Mo., Lutheran North.
Attended University of Arkansas.
Son of Bobby Joe Edmonds Sr., player with Indiana Pacers of ABA, 1967-68 and 1969-70.
Named as punt returner to THE SPORTING NEWS NFL All-Star Team, 1986.
Selected by Memphis in 1986 USFL territorial draft.
Selected by Seattle in 5th round (126th player selected) of 1986 NFL draft.
Signed by Seattle Seahawks, July 17, 1986.
Selected by St. Louis Cardinals' organization in 12th round of free-agent draft, June 7, 1982.
Selected by St. Louis Cardinals' organization in secondary phase of free-agent draft, June 6, 1983.

		–PUNT RETURNS–				—KICKOFF RET.—				—TOTAL—		
Year Club	G.	No.	Yds.	Avg.	TD.	No.	Yds.	Avg.	TD.	TD.	Pts.	F.
1986—Seattle NFL	15	34	419	*12.3	1	34	764	22.5	0	1	6	4
1987—Seattle NFL	11	20	251	12.6	0	27	564	20.9	0	0	0	1
Pro Totals—2 Years	26	54	670	12.4	1	61	1328	21.8	0	1	6	5

Additional pro statistics: Rushed once for minus 11 yards, 1986; recovered one fumble, 1986 and 1987.
Played in Pro Bowl (NFL All-Star Game) following 1986 season.

DAVID LEE EDWARDS
(Dave)
Safety—Tampa Bay Buccaneers
Born March 31, 1962, at Senoia, Ga.
Height, 6.00. Weight, 196.
High School—Decatur, Ga., Columbia.
Received bachelor of arts degree in history from University of Illinois in 1985.
Selected by Baltimore in 13th round (188th player selected) of 1985 USFL draft.
Signed as free agent by Pittsburgh Steelers, May 3, 1985.
On injured reserve with foot injury, December 10 through remainder of 1985 season.
Released by Pittsburgh Steelers, August 31, 1987; re-signed as replacement player by Steelers, September 24, 1987.
Released by Pittsburgh Steelers, October 20, 1987; signed as free agent by Tampa Bay Buccaneers, February 18, 1988.
Pittsburgh NFL, 1985 through 1987.
Games: 1985 (14), 1986 (16), 1987 (3). Total—33.
Pro statistics: Credited with one safety, 1986.

EDDIE EDWARDS
Defensive End—Cincinnati Bengals
Born April 25, 1954, at Sumter, S. C.
Height, 6.05. Weight, 256.
High School—Fort Pierce, Fla., Central.
Attended Arizona Western College and University of Miami (Fla.).
Selected by Cincinnati in 1st round (3rd player selected) of 1977 NFL draft.
Crossed picket line during players' strike, October 7, 1987.
Cincinnati NFL, 1977 through 1987.
Games: 1977 (12), 1978, (16), 1979 (14), 1980 (16), 1981 (14), 1982 (9), 1983 (16), 1984 (16), 1985 (16), 1986 (16), 1987 (14). Total—159.
Pro statistics: Recovered one fumble for three yards, 1977; recovered two fumbles, 1978, 1979 and 1985; intercepted one pass for two yards, 1978; recovered one fumble, 1980 through 1983 and 1987; recovered three fumbles for minus two yards, 1984; recovered two fumbles (including one in end zone for a touchdown), 1986.
Played in AFC Championship Game following 1981 season.
Played in NFL Championship Game following 1981 season.

KELVIN EDWARDS
Wide Receiver—Dallas Cowboys
Born July 19, 1964, at Birmingham, Ala.
Height, 6.02. Weight, 205.
High School—Eastpoint, Ga., Russell.
Attended Liberty Baptist College.
Selected by New Orleans in 4th round (88th player selected) of 1986 NFL draft.
Signed by New Orleans Saints, July 16, 1986.
Released by New Orleans Saints, September 7, 1987; signed as free agent replacement player by Dallas Cowboys, September 23, 1987.

Year Club	G.	PASS RECEIVING				-PUNT RETURNS-				—KICKOFF RET.—				—TOTAL—		
		P.C.	Yds.	Avg.	TD.	No.	Yds.	Avg.	TD.	No.	Yds.	Avg.	TD.	TD.	Pts.	F.
1986—New Orleans NFL	14	10	132	13.2	0	3	2	0.7	0	None				0	0	2
1987—Dallas NFL	13	34	521	15.3	3	8	75	9.4	0	7	155	22.1	0	4	24	1
Pro Totals—2 Years	27	44	653	14.8	3	11	77	7.0	0	7	155	22.1	0	4	24	3

Additional pro statistics: Rushed once for six yards and recovered two fumbles, 1986; rushed twice for 61 yards and a touchdown, 1987.

RICHARD RANDOLPH EDWARDS
(Randy)
Nose Tackle—Tampa Bay Buccaneers

Born March 9, 1961, at Marietta, Ga.
Height, 6.04. Weight, 267.
High School—Marietta, Ga., Wheeler.
Received degree in corporate finance from University of Alabama.

Selected by Birmingham in 1984 USFL territorial draft.
Signed as free agent by Seattle Seahawks, May 2, 1984.
On injured reserve with back injury, November 30 through remainder of season.
Traded with 1989 draft pick by Seattle Seahawks to Tampa Bay Buccaneers for offensive tackle Ron Heller, May 4, 1988.
Seattle NFL, 1984 through 1987.
Games: 1984 (13), 1985 (16), 1986 (16), 1987 (7). Total—52.
Pro statistics: Recovered one fumble, 1985; returned one kickoff for 13 yards, 1986.

CHARLES KALEV EHIN

(Middle name is an Estonian name meaning Atlas, or great person.)

(Chuck)
Nose Tackle—San Diego Chargers

Born July 1, 1961, at Marysville, Calif.
Height, 6.04. Weight, 266.
High School—Layton, Utah.
Attended Brigham Young University.

Selected by Chicago in 17th round (198th player selected) of 1983 USFL draft.
Selected by San Diego in 12th round (329th player selected) of 1983 NFL draft.
Signed by San Diego Chargers, June 6, 1983.
On injured reserve with knee injury, November 24 through remainder of 1986 season.
San Diego NFL, 1983 through 1987.
Games: 1983 (9), 1984 (16), 1985 (16), 1986 (12), 1987 (12). Total—65.
Pro statistics: Recovered one fumble, 1984 through 1986; recovered one fumble for 27 yards and fumbled once, 1987.

STANLEY EMERSON EISENHOOTH
(Stan)
Center—Seattle Seahawks

Born July 8, 1963, at Harrisburg, Pa.
Height, 6.06. Weight, 300.
High School—Wingate, Pa., Bald Eagle Area.
Attended Arizona Western College and Towson State University.
Brother of John Eisenhooth, defensive tackle with Seattle Seahawks, 1987.

Signed as free agent by Seattle Seahawks, May 8, 1986.
On injured reserve with shoulder injury, September 3 through entire 1986 season.
On injured reserve with broken hand, September 1 through December 17, 1987; activated, December 18, 1987.
Crossed picket line during players' strike, September 28, 1987; returned to picket line, October 1, 1987.
Active for 2 games with Seattle Seahawks in 1987; did not play.
Seattle NFL, 1987.

CARL FREDERICK EKERN

Name pronounced EH-kern.

Linebacker—Los Angeles Rams

Born May 27, 1954, at Richland, Wash.
Height, 6.03. Weight, 222.
High School—Sunnyvale, Calif., Fremont.
Received bachelor of business administration degree from San Jose State University and attending California State University at Long Beach for master's degree in business administration.
Cousin of Andy Ekern, offensive tackle with Indianapolis Colts, 1984.

Selected by Los Angeles in 5th round (128th player selected) of 1976 NFL draft.
On injured reserve with knee injury, August 20 through entire 1979 season.
On injured reserve with knee injury, November 23 through remainder of 1982 season.
Los Angeles Rams NFL, 1976 through 1978 and 1980 through 1987.
Games: 1976 (14), 1977 (14), 1978 (16), 1980 (15), 1981 (16), 1982 (3), 1983 (16), 1984 (16), 1985 (16), 1986 (13), 1987 (11). Total—150.
Pro statistics: Returned one kickoff for eight yards, 1977; intercepted one pass for nine yards, 1982; intercepted one pass for one yard and recovered two fumbles, 1983; recovered one fumble, 1984; intercepted two passes for 55 yards and a touchdown, 1985; intercepted one pass for seven yards, 1987.
Played in NFC Championship Game following 1976, 1978 and 1985 seasons.
Played in Pro Bowl (NFL All-Star Game) following 1986 season.

ONZY WARREN ELAM

(Name pronounced ON-zee EE-lam.)
Linebacker—New York Jets

Born December 1, 1964, at Miami, Fla.
Height, 6.02. Weight, 225.
High School—Miami, Fla., Northwestern.
Received degree in criminal justice from Tennessee State University in 1987.

Selected by New York Jets in 3rd round (75th player selected) of 1987 NFL draft.
Signed by New York Jets, July 23, 1987.
New York Jets NFL, 1987.
Games: 1987 (5).

DONALD EUGENE ELDER

(Donnie)
Cornerback—Tampa Bay Buccaneers

Born December 13, 1962, at Chattanooga, Tenn.
Height, 5.09. Weight, 175.
High School—Chattanooga, Tenn., Brainerd.
Attended Memphis State University.

Selected by Memphis in 1985 USFL territorial draft.
Selected by New York Jets in 3rd round (67th player selected) of 1985 NFL draft.
Signed by New York Jets, July 17, 1985.
On injured reserve with hip injury, November 16 through remainder of 1985 season.
Released by New York Jets, August 25, 1986; awarded on waivers to Pittsburgh Steelers, August 26, 1986.
Released by Pittsburgh Steelers, November 28, 1986; signed as free agent by Detroit Lions, December 3, 1986.
On injured reserve with knee injury, September 7 through November 16, 1987.
Released by Detroit Lions, November 17, 1987; signed as free agent by Tampa Bay Buccaneers, February 18, 1988.

		KICKOFF RETURNS			
Year	Club	G.	No.	Yds.	Avg.TD.
1985—N.Y. Jets NFL		10	3	42	14.0 0
1986—Pitt.(9)-Det.(3) NFL		12	22	435	19.8 0
Pro Totals—2 Years		22	25	477	19.1 0

Additional pro statistics: Fumbled once, 1985 and 1986; recovered one fumble, 1986.

HENRY ELLARD
Wide Receiver—Los Angeles Rams

Born July 21, 1961, at Fresno, Calif.
Height, 5.11. Weight, 175.
High School—Fresno, Calif., Hoover.
Attended Fresno State University.

Named as punt returner to THE SPORTING NEWS NFL All-Star Team, 1984 and 1985.
Selected by Oakland in 1983 USFL territorial draft.
Selected by Los Angeles Rams in 2nd round (32nd player selected) of 1983 NFL draft.
Signed by Los Angeles Rams, July 22, 1983.
Granted free agency, February 1, 1986; re-signed by Rams, October 22, 1986.
Granted roster exemption, October 22 through October 24, 1986; activated, October 25, 1986.

		PASS RECEIVING				–PUNT RETURNS–				—KICKOFF RET.—				—TOTAL—		
Year	Club	G.	P.C.	Yds.	Avg. TD.	No.	Yds.	Avg. TD.		No.	Yds.	Avg. TD.		TD.	Pts.	F.
1983—L.A. Rams NFL		12	16	268	16.8 0	16	217	*13.6	*1	15	314	20.9 0		1	6	2
1984—L.A. Rams NFL		16	34	622	18.3 6	30	403	13.4	*2	2	24	12.0 0		8	48	4
1985—L.A. Rams NFL		16	54	811	15.0 5	37	501	13.5	1		None			6	36	5
1986—L.A. Rams NFL		9	34	447	13.1 4	14	127	9.1	0	1	18	18.0 0		4	24	3
1987—L.A. Rams NFL		12	51	799	15.7 3	15	107	7.1	0	1	8	8.0 0		3	18	3
Pro Totals—5 Years		65	189	2947	15.6 18	112	1355	12.1	4	19	364	19.2 0		22	132	17

Additional pro statistics: Rushed three times for seven yards, 1983; recovered two fumbles, 1983 and 1984; rushed three times for minus five yards, 1984; rushed three times for eight yards and recovered five fumbles, 1985; rushed once for minus 15 yards, 1986; recovered one fumble, 1986 and 1987; rushed once for four yards, 1987.
Played in NFC Championship Game following 1985 season.
Played in Pro Bowl (NFL All-Star Game) following 1984 season.

GARY ELLERSON
Running Back-Kick Returner—Detroit Lions

Born July 17, 1963, at Albany, Ga.
Height, 5.11. Weight, 220.
High School—Albany, Ga., Monroe.
Attended University of Wisconsin.

Selected by Green Bay in 7th round (182nd player selected) of 1985 NFL draft.
Signed by Green Bay Packers, July 19, 1985.
On injured reserve with knee injury, September 7 through September 21, 1987.
Released by Green Bay Packers, September 22, 1987; signed as free agent replacement player by Detroit Lions, October 15, 1987.

Year Club	G.	RUSHING Att.	Yds.	Avg.	TD.	PASS RECEIVING P.C.	Yds.	Avg.	TD.	TOTAL TD.	Pts.	F.
1985—Green Bay NFL	15	32	205	6.4	2	2	15	7.5	0	2	12	3
1986—Green Bay NFL	16	90	287	3.2	3	12	130	10.8	0	3	18	3
1987—Detroit NFL	8	47	196	4.2	3	5	48	9.6	1	4	24	0
Pro Totals—3 Years	39	169	688	4.1	8	19	193	10.2	1	9	54	6

Year Club	G.	KICKOFF RETURNS No.	Yds.	Avg.	TD.
1985—Green Bay NFL	15	29	521	18.0	0
1986—Green Bay NFL	16	7	154	22.0	0
1987—Detroit NFL	8		None		
Pro Totals—3 Years	39	36	675	18.8	0

Additional pro statistics: Recovered three fumbles, 1985.

ANTHONY ROBERT ELLIOTT
(Tony)
Nose Tackle—New Orleans Saints
Born April 28, 1959, at New York, N.Y.
Height, 6.02. Weight, 295.
High School—Bridgeport, Conn., Harding.
Attended University of Wisconsin and North Texas State University.

Selected by New Orleans in 5th round (114th player selected) of 1982 NFL draft.
On reserve/non-football injury, November 11 through December 8, 1983; activated, December 9, 1983.
Released by New Orleans Saints, July 12, 1984; re-signed by Saints, October 26, 1984.
Granted roster exemption, October 26 through November 23, 1984; activated, November 24, 1984.
On injured reserve with knee injury, December 20 through remainder of 1986 season.
Crossed picket line during players' strike, September 30, 1987.
New Orleans NFL, 1982 through 1987.
Games: 1982 (9), 1983 (12), 1984 (4), 1985 (16), 1986 (15), 1987 (14). Total—70.
Pro statistics: Recovered one fumble, 1982; recovered two fumbles, 1985.

KERWIN RAY ELLIS
(Known by middle name.)
Safety—Indianapolis Colts
Born April 27, 1959, at Canton, O.
Height, 6.01. Weight, 196.
High School—Canton, O., McKinley.
Attended Ohio State University.

Selected by Philadelphia in 12th round (331st player selected) of 1981 NFL draft.
Released by Philadelphia Eagles, September 3, 1986; signed as free agent by Cleveland Browns, September 9, 1986.
Granted free agency, February 1, 1988; withdrew qualifying offer, April 22, 1988.
Signed by Indianapolis Colts, April 25, 1988.

Year Club	G.	INTERCEPTIONS No.	Yds.	Avg.	TD.
1981—Philadelphia NFL	16		None		
1982—Philadelphia NFL	9		None		
1983—Philadelphia NFL	16	1	18	18.0	0
1984—Philadelphia NFL	16	7	119	17.0	0
1985—Philadelphia NFL	16	4	32	8.0	0
1986—Cleveland NFL	15	2	12	6.0	0
1987—Cleveland NFL	12		None		
Pro Totals—7 Years	100	14	181	12.9	0

Additional pro statistics: Recovered one fumble, 1981, 1983 and 1984; returned seven kickoffs for 119 yards, 1983; returned two kickoffs for 25 yards and fumbled once, 1984; recovered three fumbles for eight yards, 1985; recovered two fumbles for 27 yards and a touchdown, 1987.
Played in AFC Championship Game following 1986 and 1987 seasons.

RIKI MORGAN ELLISON
(Formerly known as Riki Gray.)
Linebacker—San Francisco 49ers
Born August 15, 1960, at Christchurch, New Zealand.
Height, 6.02. Weight, 225.
High School—Tucson, Ariz., Amphitheater.
Received bachelor of arts degree in international relations, certificate of defense and strategic studies
and physical education from University of Southern California in 1983; and attending
University of Southern California for master's degree in international relations and foreign policy.

Selected by Los Angeles in 1983 USFL territorial draft.
Selected by San Francisco in 5th round (117th player selected) of 1983 NFL draft.
Signed by San Francisco 49ers, June 1, 1983.
On injured reserve with broken arm, September 14 through December 16, 1987; activated, December 17, 1987.
San Francisco NFL, 1983 through 1987.
Games: 1983 (16), 1984 (16), 1985 (16), 1986 (16), 1987 (3). Total—67.
Pro statistics: Recovered two fumbles for seven yards, 1985; recovered one fumble, 1986.
Played in NFC Championship Game following 1983 and 1984 seasons.
Played in NFL Championship Game following 1984 season.

JOHN ALBERT ELWAY
Quarterback—Denver Broncos
Born June 28, 1960, at Port Angeles, Wash.
Height, 6.03. Weight, 210.
High School—Granada Hills, Calif.
Received bachelor of arts degree in economics from Stanford University in 1983.
Son of Jack Elway, head football coach at Stanford University.

Named to THE SPORTING NEWS NFL All-Star Team, 1987.
Named as quarterback on THE SPORTING NEWS College All-America Team, 1980 and 1982.
Selected by Oakland in 1983 USFL territorial draft.
Selected by Baltimore in 1st round (1st player selected) of 1983 NFL draft.
Rights traded by Baltimore Colts to Denver Broncos for quarterback Mark Herrmann, rights to offensive lineman Chris Hinton and 1st round pick in 1984 draft, May 2, 1983.
Signed by Denver Broncos, May 2, 1983.

					PASSING					RUSHING				TOTAL	
Year	Club	G.	Att.	Cmp.	Pct.	Gain	T.P.	P.I.	Avg.	Att.	Yds.	Avg.	TD.	TD.	Pts.	F.
1983—Denver NFL		11	259	123	47.5	1663	7	14	6.42	28	146	5.2	1	1	6	6
1984—Denver NFL		15	380	214	56.3	2598	18	15	6.84	56	237	4.2	1	1	6	14
1985—Denver NFL		16	*605	327	54.0	3891	22	23	6.43	51	253	5.0	0	0	0	7
1986—Denver NFL		16	504	280	55.6	3485	19	13	6.91	52	257	4.9	1	2	12	8
1987—Denver NFL		12	410	224	54.6	3198	19	12	7.80	66	304	4.6	4	4	24	2
Pro Totals—5 Years		70	2158	1168	54.1	14835	85	77	6.87	253	1197	4.7	7	8	48	37

Quarterback Rating Points: 1983 (54.9), 1984 (76.8), 1985 (70.2), 1986 (79.0), 1987 (83.4). Total—73.8.
Additional pro statistics: Recovered three fumbles, 1983; recovered five fumbles and fumbled 14 times for minus 10 yards, 1984; recovered two fumbles and fumbled seven times for minus 35 yards, 1985; caught one pass for 23 yards and a touchdown, recovered one fumble and fumbled eight times for minus 13 yards, 1986; fumbled twice for minus one yard and punted once for 31 yards, 1987.
Played in AFC Championship Game following 1986 and 1987 seasons.
Played in NFL Championship Game following 1986 and 1987 seasons.
Played in Pro Bowl (NFL All-Star Game) following 1986 and 1987 seasons.

RECORD AS BASEBALL PLAYER

Year	Club	League	Pos.	G.	AB.	R.	H.	2B.	3B.	HR.	RBI.	B.A.	PO.	A.	E.	F.A.
1982—Oneonta	NYP		OF	42	151	26	48	6	2	4	25	.318	69	8	0	1.000

Selected by Kansas City Royals' organization in 18th round of free-agent draft, June 5, 1979.
Selected by New York Yankees' organization in 2nd round of free-agent draft, June 8, 1981.

JON W. EMBREE
Tight End—Los Angeles Rams
Born October 15, 1965, at Los Angeles, Calif.
Height, 6.02. Weight, 225.
High School—Englewood, Colo., Cherry Creek.
Attended University of Colorado.
Son of John Embree, wide receiver with Denver Broncos, 1969 and 1970.

Selected by Los Angeles Rams in 6th round (166th player selected) of 1987 NFL draft.
Signed by Los Angeles Rams, July 24, 1987.
On injured reserve with elbow injury, November 13 through remainder of 1987 season.
Los Angeles Rams NFL, 1987.
Games: 1987 (1).

LARRY G. EMERY JR.
Running Back—Atlanta Falcons
Born July 13, 1964, at Macon, Ga.
Height, 5.09. Weight, 195.
High School—Macon, Ga., Northeast.
Attended University of Wisconsin.

Selected by Atlanta in 12th round (320th player selected) of 1987 NFL draft.
Signed by Atlanta Falcons, July 26, 1987.
On injured reserve with blood clot in arm, September 11 through November 2, 1987; activated, November 3, 1987.
On injured reserve with back injury, December 18 through remainder of 1987 season.

			RUSHING				PASS RECEIVING				TOTAL	
Year	Club	G.	Att.	Yds.	Avg.	TD.	P.C.	Yds.	Avg.	TD.	TD.	Pts.	F.
1987—Atlanta NFL		5	1	5	5.0	0	5	31	6.2	0	0	0	0

			KICKOFF RETURNS		
Year	Club	G.	No.	Yds.	Avg.TD.
1987—Atlanta NFL		5	21	440	21.0	0

PHILLIP EARL EPPS
(Phil)
Wide Receiver—Green Bay Packers
Born November 11, 1959, at Atlanta, Tex.
Height, 5.10. Weight, 165.
High School—Atlanta, Tex.
Received bachelor of science degree in criminal justice from Texas Christian University.
Cousin of Cedric Mack, cornerback with Phoenix Cardinals.

Selected by Green Bay in 12th round (321st player selected) of 1982 NFL draft.
USFL rights traded with future draft picks by San Antonio Gunslingers to Philadelphia Stars for rights to running back Billy Campfield, March 5, 1984.
Granted free agency, February 1, 1986; re-signed by Packers, August 18, 1986.
Granted roster exemption, August 18 through August 21, 1986; activated, August 22, 1986.
On injured reserve with knee injury, November 26 through remainder of 1986 season.

		PASS RECEIVING				-PUNT RETURNS-				—KICKOFF RET.—				—TOTAL—		
Year Club	G.	P.C.	Yds.	Avg.	TD.	No.	Yds.	Avg.	TD.	No.	Yds.	Avg.	TD.	TD.	Pts.	F.
1982—Green Bay NFL..........	9	10	226	22.6	2	20	150	7.5	0		None			2	12	1
1983—Green Bay NFL..........	16	18	313	17.4	0	36	324	9.0	*1		None			1	6	2
1984—Green Bay NFL..........	16	26	435	16.7	3	29	199	6.9	0	12	232	19.3	0	3	18	1
1985—Green Bay NFL..........	16	44	683	15.5	3	15	146	9.7	0	12	279	23.3	0	4	24	1
1986—Green Bay NFL..........	12	49	612	12.5	4		None			1	21	21.0	0	4	24	0
1987—Green Bay NFL..........	10	34	516	15.2	2		None				None			2	12	1
Pro Totals—6 Years.......	79	181	2785	15.4	14	100	819	8.2	1	25	532	21.3	0	16	96	6

Additional pro statistics: Recovered one fumble, 1984; rushed five times for 103 yards and a touchdown, 1985; rushed four times for 18 yards, 1986; rushed once for no yards, 1987.

NORMAN JULIUS ESIASON
(Boomer)
Quarterback—Cincinnati Bengals
Born April 17, 1961, at West Islip, N.Y.
Height, 6.04. Weight, 220.
High School—Islip Terrace, N.Y., East Islip.
Attended University of Maryland.
Selected by Washington in 1984 USFL territorial draft.
Selected by Cincinnati in 2nd round (38th player selected) of 1984 NFL draft.
Signed by Cincinnati Bengals, June 19, 1984.

		PASSING							RUSHING				—TOTAL—		
Year Club	G.	Att.	Cmp.	Pct.	Gain	T.P.	P.I.	Avg.	Att.	Yds.	Avg.	TD.	TD.	Pts.	F.
1984—Cincinnati NFL.................	10	102	51	50.0	530	3	3	5.20	19	63	3.3	2	2	12	4
1985—Cincinnati NFL.................	15	431	251	58.2	3443	27	12	7.99	33	79	2.4	1	1	6	9
1986—Cincinnati NFL.................	16	469	273	58.2	3959	24	17	*8.44	44	146	3.3	1	1	6	12
1987—Cincinnati NFL.................	12	440	240	54.5	3321	16	19	7.55	52	241	4.6	0	0	0	10
Pro Totals—4 Years..........	53	1442	815	56.5	11253	70	51	7.80	148	529	3.6	4	4	24	35

Quarterback Rating Points: 1984 (62.9), 1985 (93.2), 1986 (87.7), 1987 (73.1). Total—83.4.
Additional pro statistics: Recovered two fumbles and fumbled four times for minus two yards, 1984; recovered four fumbles and fumbled nine times for minus five yards, 1985; punted once for 31 yards, recovered five fumbles and fumbled 12 times for minus 10 yards, 1986; punted twice for a 34.0 average, recovered four fumbles and fumbled 10 times for minus eight yards, 1987.
Played in Pro Bowl (NFL All-Star Game) following 1986 season.

BYRON NELSON EVANS
Linebacker—Philadelphia Eagles
Born February 23, 1964, at Phoenix, Ariz.
Height, 6.02. Weight, 225.
High School—Phoenix, Ariz., South Mountain.
Attended University of Arizona.
Selected by Philadelphia in 4th round (93rd player selected) of 1987 NFL draft.
Signed by Philadelphia Eagles, August 6, 1987.
Philadelphia NFL, 1987.
Games: 1987 (12).
Pro statistics: Intercepted one pass for 12 yards and recovered one fumble, 1987.

DAVID W. EVANS
Cornerback—Tampa Bay Buccaneers
Born May 1, 1959, at Naples, Tex.
Height, 6.00. Weight, 178.
High School—Naples, Tex., Paul H. Pewitt.
Received bachelor of science degree in physical education from University of Central Arkansas.
Signed as free agent by Birmingham Stallions, May 21, 1983.
On developmental squad, May 21 through June 10, 1983; activated, June 11, 1983.
Granted free agency when USFL suspended operations, August 7, 1986; signed as free agent by Minnesota Vikings, August 11, 1986.
Granted roster exemption, August 11 through August 20, 1986; activated, August 21, 1986.
Released by Minnesota Vikings, September 7, 1987; re-signed as replacement player by Vikings, September 24, 1987.
Released by Minnesota Vikings, October 19, 1987; signed as free agent by Tampa Bay Buccaneers, April 5, 1988.
On developmental squad for 3 games with Birmingham Stallions in 1983.

		INTERCEPTIONS						INTERCEPTIONS		
Year Club	G.	No.	Yds.	Avg.TD.		Year Club	G.	No.	Yds.	Avg.TD.
1983—Birmingham USFL......	5		None			1987—Minnesota NFL.............	3		None	
1984—Birmingham USFL......	18	3	60	20.0 1		USFL Totals—3 Years........	41	4	64	16.0 1
1985—Birmingham USFL......	18	1	4	4.0 0		NFL Totals—2 Years..........	19	0	0	0.0 0
1986—Minnesota NFL.............	16		None			Pro Totals—5 Years............	60	4	64	16.0 1

Additional USFL statistics: Recovered one fumble for five yards and a touchdown, 1984; recovered one fumble, 1985.

Additional NFL statistics: Recovered one fumble, 1987.

DONALD LEE EVANS
Fullback—Los Angeles Rams
Born March 14, 1964, at Raleigh, N.C.
Height, 6.02. Weight, 256.
High School—Raleigh, N.C., Athens Drive.
Attended Winston-Salem State University.

Selected by Los Angeles Rams in 2nd round (47th player selected) of 1987 NFL draft.
Signed by Los Angeles Rams, August 1, 1987.
On injured reserve with strained abdomen, September 7 through December 7, 1987; activated, December 8, 1987.
Los Angeles Rams NFL, 1987.
Games: 1987 (1).
Pro statistics: Rushed three times for 10 yards, 1987.

JAMES MARCUS EVANS
Fullback—Tampa Bay Buccaneers
Born August 17, 1963, at Prichard, Ala.
Height, 6.00. Weight, 220.
High School—Prichard, Ala., M.T. Blount.
Attended Southern University & A&M.

Selected by Kansas City in 10th round (271st player selected) of 1987 NFL draft.
Signed by Kansas City Chiefs, July 16, 1987.
Released by Kansas City Chiefs, December 2, 1987; awarded on waivers to Tampa Bay Buccaneers, December 3, 1987.
Active for 1 game with Tampa Bay Buccaneers in 1987; did not play.
Kansas City (2)-Tampa Bay (0) NFL, 1987.
Games: 1987 (2).

VINCENT TOBIAS EVANS
(Vince)
Quarterback—Los Angeles Raiders
Born June 14, 1955, at Greensboro, N.C.
Height, 6.02. Weight, 205.
High School—Greensboro, N.C., Benjamin L. Smith.
Attended Los Angeles City College and University of Southern California.

Selected by Chicago in 6th round (140th player selected) of 1977 NFL draft.
On injured reserve with staph infection, October 12 through remainder of 1979 season.
USFL rights traded by Los Angeles Express to Washington Federals for rights to cornerback Johnny Lynn, November 11, 1983.
Signed by Chicago Blitz, November 14, 1983, for contract to take effect after being granted free agency, February 1, 1984.
USFL rights traded by Washington Federals to Chicago Blitz for linebacker Ben Apuna and rights to wide receiver Waddell Smith, December 27, 1983.
Franchise disbanded, November 20, 1984.
Traded with linebackers Kelvin Atkins, Jay Wilson and Ed Thomas by Chicago Blitz to Denver Gold for past consideration, December 6, 1984.
Contract rights returned to Chicago Blitz, August 2, 1985.
Granted free agency when USFL suspended operations, August 7, 1986; signed as replacement player by Los Angeles Raiders, September 24, 1987.

Year Club	G.	Att.	Cmp.	Pct.	Gain	T.P.	P.I.	Avg.	Att.	Yds.	Avg.	TD.	TD.	Pts.	F.
		PASSING							RUSHING				TOTAL		
1977—Chicago NFL	13	None							1	0	0.0	0	0	0	3
1978—Chicago NFL	3	3	1	33.3	38	0	1	12.67	6	23	3.8	0	0	0	0
1979—Chicago NFL	4	63	32	50.8	508	4	5	8.06	12	72	6.0	1	1	6	1
1980—Chicago NFL	13	278	148	53.2	2039	11	16	7.33	60	306	5.1	8	8	48	4
1981—Chicago NFL	16	436	195	44.7	2354	11	20	5.40	43	218	5.1	3	3	18	13
1982—Chicago NFL	4	28	12	42.9	125	0	4	4.46	2	0	0.0	0	0	0	1
1983—Chicago USFL	9	145	76	52.4	1108	5	7	7.64	22	142	6.5	1	1	6	4
1984—Chicago USFL	15	411	200	48.7	2624	14	22	6.38	30	144	4.8	6	6	36	6
1985—Denver USFL	14	325	157	48.3	2259	12	16	6.95	43	283	6.6	7	7	42	3
1987—L.A. Raiders NFL	3	83	39	47.0	630	5	4	7.59	11	144	13.1	1	1	6	1
NFL Totals—8 Years	65	1036	503	48.6	6802	36	57	6.57	157	905	5.8	14	14	84	26
USFL Totals—2 Years	29	736	357	48.5	4883	26	38	6.63	73	427	5.8	13	13	78	9
Pro Totals—10 Years	94	1772	860	48.5	11685	62	95	6.59	230	1332	5.8	27	27	1620	35

NFL Quarterback Rating Points: 1978 (42.3), 1979 (66.1), 1980 (66.1), 1981 (51.0), 1982 (16.8), 1983 (69.0), 1987 (72.9). Total—58.7.
USFL Quarterback Rating Points: 1984 (58.3), 1985 (63.1). Total—60.1.
Additional NFL statistics: Returned 13 kickoffs for 253 yards (19.5 average) and recovered two fumbles, 1977; fumbled once for minus two yards, 1979; fumbled four times for minus three yards, 1980; recovered two fumbles and fumbled 13 times for minus 10 yards, 1981; fumbled once for minus 24 yards, 1982.
Additional USFL statistics: Recovered two fumbles, 1984.

JAMES SAMUEL EVERETT III
(Jim)
Quarterback—Los Angeles Rams

Born January 3, 1963, at Emporia, Kan.
Height, 6.05. Weight, 212.
High School—Albuquerque, N.M., Eldorado.
Received degree in finance from Purdue University in 1986.

Selected by Houston in 1st round (3rd player selected) of 1986 NFL draft.
Selected by Memphis in 1st round (4th player selected) of 1986 USFL draft.
NFL rights traded by Houston Oilers to Los Angeles Rams for guard Kent Hill, defensive end William Fuller, 1st and 5th round picks in 1987 draft and 1st round pick in 1988 draft, September 18, 1986.
Signed by Los Angeles Rams, September 25, 1986.
Granted roster exemption, September 25 through September 29, 1986; activated, September 30, 1986.
Crossed picket line during players' strike, October 14, 1987.

			PASSING						RUSHING				TOTAL		
Year	Club	G.	Att.	Cmp.	Pct.	Gain	T.P.	P.I.	Avg.	Att.	Yds.	Avg.	TD.	TD.	Pts.	F.
1986—L.A. Rams NFL		6	147	73	49.7	1018	8	8	6.93	16	46	2.9	1	1	6	2
1987—L.A. Rams NFL		11	302	162	53.6	2064	10	13	6.83	18	83	4.6	1	1	6	2
Pro Totals—2 Years		17	449	235	52.3	3082	18	21	6.86	34	129	3.8	2	2	12	4

Quarterback Rating Points: 1986 (67.8), 1987 (68.4). Total—68.0.
Additional pro statistics: Fumbled twice for minus two yards, 1986; recovered one fumble, 1987.

MAJOR DONEL EVERETT
Running Back—Atlanta Falcons

Born January 4, 1960, at New Hebron, Miss.
Height, 5.10. Weight, 215.
High School—New Hebron, Miss.
Received degree in mathematics from Mississippi College.

Selected by Birmingham in 13th round (149th player selected) of 1983 NFL draft.
Signed by Birmingham Stallions, January 21, 1983.
Released by Birmingham Stallions, February 7, 1983; signed as free agent by Philadelphia Eagles, May 12, 1983.
Released by Philadelphia Eagles, August 19, 1986; signed as free agent by Cleveland Browns, October 21, 1986.
Released by Cleveland Browns, September 1, 1987; re-signed as replacement player by Browns, September 30, 1987.
Released by Cleveland Browns, November 3, 1987; signed as free agent by Atlanta Falcons, November 10, 1987.

			RUSHING				PASS RECEIVING				TOTAL		
Year	Club	G.	Att.	Yds.	Avg.	TD.	P.C.	Yds.	Avg.	TD.	TD.	Pts.	F.
1983—Philadelphia NFL		16	5	7	1.4	0	2	18	9.0	0	0	0	0
1984—Philadelphia NFL		16		None				None			0	0	0
1985—Philadelphia NFL		15	4	13	3.3	0	4	25	6.3	0	0	0	2
1986—Cleveland NFL		9	12	43	3.6	0		None			0	0	0
1987—Cleveland (4)-Atlanta (7) NFL		11	34	95	2.8	0	8	41	5.1	0	0	0	0
Pro Totals—5 Years		67	55	158	2.9	0	14	84	6.0	0	0	0	2

			KICKOFF RETURNS			
Year	Club	G.	No.	Yds.	Avg.	TD.
1983—Philadelphia NFL		16	14	275	19.6	0
1984—Philadelphia NFL		16	3	40	13.3	0
1985—Philadelphia NFL		15		None		
1986—Cleveland NFL		9		None		
1987—Cle. (4)-Atl. (7) NFL		11	2	23	16.5	0
Pro Totals—5 Years		67	19	348	18.3	0

Additional pro statistics: Recovered one fumble, 1983; recovered two fumbles, 1985 and 1986.
Played in AFC Championship Game following 1986 season.

THOMAS GREGORY EVERETT
Safety-Punt Returner—Pittsburgh Steelers

Born November 21, 1964, at Daingerfield, Tex.
Height, 5.09. Weight, 179.
High School—Daingerfield, Tex.
Attended Baylor University.

Named as defensive back on THE SPORTING NEWS College All-America Team, 1986.
Selected by Pittsburgh in 4th round (94th player selected) of 1987 NFL draft.
Signed by Pittsburgh Steelers, July 26, 1987.

			INTERCEPTIONS			
Year	Club	G.	No.	Yds.	Avg.	TD.
1987—Pittsburgh NFL		12	3	22	7.3	0

Additional pro statistics: Returned four punts for 22 yards, recovered two fumbles for seven yards and fumbled once, 1987.

—DID YOU KNOW—

That Raiders running back Marcus Allen's 759 yards rushing in 1986 was exactly 1,000 yards less than his league-leading total of 1,759 in 1985?

SINATAUSILINUU FAAOLA

(Name pronounced SEENA-tau-sili-E-NEW-oo Fa-O-la.)

(Nuu)
Running Back—New York Jets

Born January 15, 1964, at Honolulu, Haw.
Height, 5.11. Weight, 210.
High School—Kalihi, Haw., Farrington.
Attended University of Hawaii.

Selected by New York Jets in 9th round (245th player selected) of 1986 NFL draft.
Signed by New York Jets, May 28, 1986.
Released by New York Jets, August 30, 1986; re-signed by Jets, September 30, 1986.

Year Club	G.	—RUSHING— Att.	Yds.	Avg.	TD.	PASS RECEIVING P.C.	Yds.	Avg.	TD.	—TOTAL— TD.	Pts.	F.
1986—New York Jets NFL	12	3	5	1.7	0	None				0	0	0
1987—New York Jets NFL	12	14	43	3.1	2	1	16	16.0	0	2	12	0
Pro Totals—2 Years	24	17	48	2.8	2	1	16	16.0	0	2	12	0

Additional pro statistics: Returned one kickoff for four yards and recovered one fumble for three yards, 1987.

KEVIN FAGAN

Defensive End—San Francisco 49ers

Born April 25, 1963, at Lake Worth, Fla.
Height, 6.03. Weight, 260.
High School—Lake Worth, Fla., John I. Leonard.
Attended University of Miami (Fla.).

Selected by Orlando in 1986 USFL territorial draft.
Selected by San Francisco in 4th round (102nd player selected) of 1986 NFL draft.
Signed by San Francisco 49ers, July 20, 1986.
On non-football injury list with knee injury, July 22 through entire 1986 season.
San Francisco NFL, 1987.
Games: 1987 (7).
Pro statistics: Recovered one fumble for six yards, 1987.

JAMES JOHN FAHNHORST

(Jim)
Linebacker—San Francisco 49ers

Born November 8, 1958, at St. Cloud, Minn.
Height, 6.04. Weight, 230.
High School—St. Cloud, Minn., Technical.
Attended University of Minnesota.
Brother of Keith Fahnhorst, offensive tackle with San Francisco 49ers, 1974 through 1987.

Selected by Minnesota in 4th round (92nd player selected) of 1982 NFL draft.
Signed by Chicago Blitz, August 16, 1982.
USFL rights subsequently traded by Los Angeles Express to Chicago Blitz for rights to tight end Mike Sherrod and wide receiver Kris Haines and 6th, 7th and 8th round picks in 1983 draft, November 2, 1982.
Franchise transferred to Arizona, September 30, 1983.
Signed by San Francisco 49ers, June 13, 1984; Minnesota Vikings did not exercise right of first refusal, June 28, 1984.
On injured reserve with knee injury, December 5 through remainder of 1984 season.
Released by San Francisco 49ers, September 7, 1987; re-signed by 49ers, September 14, 1987.
Chicago USFL, 1983; Arizona USFL, 1984; San Francisco NFL, 1984 through 1987.
Games: 1983 (18), 1984 USFL (18), 1984 NFL (14), 1985 (15), 1986 (16), 1987 (11). Total USFL—36. Total NFL—56. Total Pro—92.
USFL statistics: Intercepted one pass for 19 yards, recovered three fumbles for six yards and credited with one sack for nine yards, 1983; intercepted one pass for no yards, credited with one sack for seven yards and recovered one fumble, 1984.
NFL statistics: Intercepted two passes for nine yards, 1984; intercepted four passes for 52 yards, 1986; intercepted one pass for no yards, 1987.
Played in USFL Championship Game following 1984 season.

PAUL JAY FAIRCHILD

Center-Guard—New England Patriots

Born September 14, 1961, at Carroll, Ia.
Height, 6.04. Weight, 270.
High School—Glidden, Ia., Ralston.
Attended Ellsworth Junior College and received bachelor of general science degree in liberal arts from University of Kansas in 1984.

Selected by Houston in 6th round (124th player selected) of 1984 USFL draft.
Selected by New England in 5th round (124th player selected) of 1984 NFL draft.
Signed by New England Patriots, June 18, 1984.
New England NFL, 1984 through 1987.
Games: 1984 (7), 1985 (16), 1986 (15), 1987 (11). Total—49.
Played in AFC Championship Game following 1985 season.
Played in NFL Championship Game following 1985 season.

ERIC JEROME FAIRS
Linebacker—Houston Oilers
Born February 17, 1964, at Memphis, Tenn.
Height, 6.03. Weight, 235.
High School—Memphis, Tenn., Northside.
Attended Memphis State University.

Selected by Memphis in 1986 USFL territorial draft.
Signed as free agent by Houston Oilers, May 21, 1986.
Released by Houston Oilers, August 26, 1986; re-signed by Oilers, October 2, 1986.
Houston NFL, 1986 and 1987.
Games: 1986 (12), 1987 (12). Total—24.

SEAN WARD FARRELL
Guard-Offensive Tackle—New England Patriots
Born May 25, 1960, at Southampton, N.Y.
Height, 6.03. Weight, 260.
High School—Westhampton Beach, N.Y.
Received bachelor of arts degree in general arts and sciences from Penn State University in 1982.

Named to THE SPORTING NEWS NFL All-Star Team, 1984.
Named as guard on THE SPORTING NEWS College All-America Team, 1981.
Selected by Tampa Bay in 1st round (17th player selected) of 1982 NFL draft.
Granted free agency, February 1, 1987; re-signed by Buccaneers and traded to New England Patriots for 2nd, 7th and 9th round picks in 1987 draft, February 19, 1987.
Crossed picket line during players' strike, October 2, 1987.
Tampa Bay NFL, 1982 through 1986; New England NFL, 1987.
Games: 1982 (9), 1983 (10), 1984 (15), 1985 (14), 1986 (16), 1987 (14). Total—78.
Pro statistics: Recovered one fumble, 1983; recovered two fumbles, 1984.

PAUL V. FARREN
Offensive Tackle-Guard—Cleveland Browns
Born December 24, 1960, at Weymouth, Mass.
Height, 6.05. Weight, 280.
High School—Cohasset, Mass.
Received bachelor of arts degree in marketing finance from Boston University in 1983.

Selected by Boston in 1983 USFL territorial draft.
Selected by Cleveland in 12th round (316th player selected) of 1983 NFL draft.
Signed by Cleveland Browns, May 31, 1983.
On injured reserve with knee injury, December 30 through remainder of 1985 season playoffs.
Cleveland NFL, 1983 through 1987.
Games: 1983 (16), 1984 (15), 1985 (13), 1986 (16), 1987 (12). Total—72.
Pro statistics: Recovered one fumble, 1984 and 1987.
Played in AFC Championship Game following 1986 and 1987 seasons.

GRANT EARL FEASEL
Center—Seattle Seahawks
Born June 28, 1960, at Barstow, Calif.
Height, 6.07. Weight, 278.
High School—Barstow, Calif.
Received bachelor of science degree in biology from Abilene Christian University in 1983.
Brother of Greg Feasel, offensive tackle with San Diego Chargers.

Selected by Baltimore in 6th round (161st player selected) of 1983 NFL draft.
Franchise transferred to Indianapolis, March 31, 1984.
Released by Indianapolis Colts, October 10, 1984; signed as free agent by Minnesota Vikings, October 17, 1984.
On injured reserve with knee injury, August 29 through entire 1985 season.
Granted free agency with option not exercised, February 1, 1986; re-signed by Vikings, June 21, 1986.
On injured reserve with knee injury, August 19 through October 27, 1986.
Released by Minnesota Vikings, October 28, 1986; re-signed by Vikings after clearing procedural waivers, November 20, 1986.
Released by Minnesota Vikings, November 28, 1986; signed as free agent by Seattle Seahawks, February 25, 1987.
Active for 1 game with Minnesota Vikings in 1986; did not play.
Baltimore NFL, 1983; Indianapolis (6)-Minnesota (9) NFL, 1984; Minnesota NFL, 1986; Seattle NFL, 1987.
Games: 1983 (11), 1984 (15), 1987 (12). Total—38.
Additional pro statistics: Recovered one fumble and fumbled once for minus 19 yards, 1987.

GREGORY DUANE FEASEL
(Greg)
Offensive Tackle—San Diego Chargers
Born November 7, 1957, at Barstow, Calif.
Height, 6.07. Weight, 301.
High School—Barstow, Calif.
Attended Barstow Junior College and received bachelor of science degree in health and physical education from Abilene Christian University in 1981.
Brother of Grant Feasel, center with Seattle Seahawks.

Signed as free agent by Seattle Seahawks, May 2, 1980.

Released by Seattle Seahawks, July 20, 1980; signed as free agent by Philadelphia Eagles, May 15, 1981.
Released by Philadelphia Eagles, July 31, 1981; signed as free agent by Houston Oilers, May 4, 1982.
Released by Houston Oilers, August 23, 1982; signed by Denver Gold, October 29, 1982.
Released by Denver Gold, February 27, 1983; resigned by Gold, March 11, 1983.
On developmental squad, May 19 through June 1, 1984; activated, June 2, 1984.
On developmental squad, April 18 through remainder of 1985 season.
Franchise merged with Jacksonville, February 19, 1986.
Granted free agency when USFL suspended operations, August 7, 1986; signed as free agent by Green Bay Packers, August 11, 1986.
Granted roster exemption, August 11 through August 21, 1986; activated, August 22, 1986.
Traded by Green Bay Packers to Houston Oilers for conditional draft pick, August 31, 1987.
Released by Houston Oilers, September 6, 1987; signed as free agent replacement player by San Diego Chargers, September 27, 1987.
Released by San Diego Chargers, October 27, 1987; re-signed by Chargers, April 17, 1988.
On developmental squad for 2 games with Denver Gold in 1984.
On developmental squad for 10 games with Denver Gold in 1985.
Denver USFL 1983 through 1985; Green Bay NFL, 1986; San Diego NFL, 1987.
Games 1983 (15), 1984 (16), 1985 (8), 1986 (15), 1987 (3). Total USFL—39. Total NFL—18. Total Pro—57.

GERRY FEEHERY
Name pronounced FEER-ee.
Center—Philadelphia Eagles
Born March 9, 1960, at Philadelphia, Pa.
Height, 6.02. Weight, 268.
High School—Springfield, Pa., Cardinal O'Hara.
Received bachelor of science degree in marketing from Syracuse University.

Selected by New Jersey in 1983 USFL territorial draft.
Signed as free agent by Philadelphia Eagles, May 4, 1983.
On injured reserve with knee injury, November 4 through remainder of 1983 season.
On injured reserve with knee injury, October 14 through remainder of 1986 season.
Philadelphia NFL, 1983 through 1987.
Games: 1983 (2), 1984 (6), 1985 (15), 1986 (6), 1987 (12). Total—41.

RONALD LEE FELLOWS
(Ron)
Cornerback—Los Angeles Raiders
Born November 7, 1958, at South Bend, Ind.
Height, 6.00. Weight, 173.
High School—South Bend, Ind., Washington.
Attended Butler (Kan.) County Community College and University of Missouri.

Selected by Dallas in 7th round (173rd player selected) of 1981 NFL draft.
Granted free agency, February 1, 1987; re-signed by Cowboys and traded to Los Angeles Raiders for wide receiver Ron Barksdale, August 2, 1987.

		INTERCEPTIONS			–PUNT RETURNS–				—KICKOFF RET.—				—TOTAL—		
Year Club	G.	No.	Yds.	Avg. TD.	No.	Yds.	Avg.	TD.	No.	Yds.	Avg.	TD.	TD.	Pts.	F.
1981—Dallas NFL	16		None		11	44	4.0	0	8	170	21.3	0	0	0	0
1982—Dallas NFL	9		None		25	189	7.6	0	16	359	22.4	0	0	0	3
1983—Dallas NFL	16	5	139	27.8	1	10	75	7.5	0	43	855	19.9	0	2	12	4
1984—Dallas NFL	16	3	3	1.0	0		None		6	94	15.7	0	0	0	3
1985—Dallas NFL	13	4	52	13.0	0		None			None			0	0	0
1986—Dallas NFL	16	5	46	9.2	1		None			None			1	6	0
1987—L.A. Raiders NFL	12		None		2	19	9.5	0		None			0	0	0
Pro Totals—7 Years	98	17	240	14.1	2	48	327	6.8	0	73	1478	20.2	0	3	18	10

Additional pro statistics: Recovered one fumble, 1982; returned blocked field goal attempt 62 yards for a touchdown and recovered three fumbles, 1983; recovered one fumble for 12 yards, 1984; recovered two fumbles for two yards, 1986.
Played in NFC Championship Game following 1981 and 1982 seasons.

RICKY DALE FENNEY
(Rick)
Running Back—Minnesota Vikings
Born December 7, 1964, at Everett, Wash.
Height, 6.01. Weight, 240.
High School—Snohomish, Wash.
Attended University of Washington.

Selected by Minnesota in 8th round (211th player selected) of 1987 NFL draft.
Signed by Minnesota Vikings, July 30, 1987.

		——RUSHING——				PASS RECEIVING				—TOTAL—		
Year Club	G.	Att.	Yds.	Avg.	TD.	P.C.	Yds.	Avg.	TD.	TD.	Pts.	F.
1987—Minnesota NFL	11	42	174	4.1	2	7	27	3.9	0	2	12	0

Played in NFC Championship Game following 1987 season.

JOE CARLTON FERGUSON JR.
Quarterback—Tampa Bay Buccaneers

Born April 23, 1950, at Alvin, Tex.
Height, 6.01. Weight, 195.
High School—Shreveport, La., Woodlawn.
Received bachelor of science degree in physical education from
University of Arkansas in 1973.

Established NFL record for fewest passes intercepted among qualifiers, season (1), 1976.
Tied NFL records for most fumbles and most own fumbles recovered, game (4), September 18, 1977, against Miami Dolphins.
Selected by Buffalo in 3rd round (57th player selected) of 1973 NFL draft.
Traded by Buffalo Bills to Detroit Lions for 7th round pick in 1986 draft, April 30, 1985.
Granted free agency with no qualifying offer, February 1, 1988; signed by Indianapolis Colts, April 22, 1988.
Traded by Indianapolis Colts to Tampa Bay Buccaneers for 12th round pick in 1989 draft, April 29, 1988.
Active for 12 games with Detroit Lions in 1987; did not play.

Year Club	G.	Att.	Cmp.	Pct.	Gain	T.P.	P.I.	Avg.	Att.	Yds.	Avg.	TD.	TD.	Pts.	F.
		PASSING							RUSHING				TOTAL		
1973—Buffalo NFL	14	164	73	44.5	939	4	10	5.73	48	147	3.1	2	2	12	7
1974—Buffalo NFL	14	232	119	51.3	1588	12	12	6.84	54	111	2.1	2	2	12	*14
1975—Buffalo NFL	14	321	169	52.6	2426	*25	17	7.56	23	82	3.6	1	1	6	4
1976—Buffalo NFL	7	151	74	49.0	1086	9	1	7.19	18	81	4.5	0	0	0	2
1977—Buffalo NFL	14	*457	221	48.4	*2803	12	*24	6.13	41	279	6.8	2	2	12	12
1978—Buffalo NFL	16	330	175	53.0	2136	16	15	6.47	27	76	2.8	0	0	0	5
1979—Buffalo NFL	16	458	238	52.0	3572	14	15	7.80	22	68	3.1	1	1	6	5
1980—Buffalo NFL	16	439	251	57.2	2805	20	18	6.39	31	65	2.1	0	0	0	9
1981—Buffalo NFL	16	498	252	50.6	3652	24	20	7.33	20	29	1.5	1	1	6	2
1982—Buffalo NFL	9	264	144	54.5	1597	7	*16	6.05	16	46	2.9	1	2	12	5
1983—Buffalo NFL	16	508	281	55.3	2995	26	25	5.90	20	88	4.4	0	0	0	3
1984—Buffalo NFL	12	344	191	55.5	1991	12	17	5.79	19	102	5.4	0	0	0	8
1985—Detroit NFL	8	54	31	57.4	364	2	3	6.74	4	12	3.0	1	1	6	1
1986—Detroit NFL	6	155	73	47.1	941	7	7	6.07	5	25	5.0	0	0	0	3
Pro Totals—15 Years	178	4375	2292	52.4	28895	190	200	6.60	348	1211	3.5	11	12	72	80

Quarterback Rating Points: 1973 (45.6), 1974 (69.0), 1975 (81.3), 1976 (90.0), 1977 (54.6), 1978 (70.5), 1979 (74.5), 1980 (74.6), 1981 (74.1), 1982 (56.3), 1983 (69.3), 1984 (63.5), 1985 (67.2), 1986 (62.9). Total—68.4.
Additional pro statistics: Recovered four fumbles, fumbled seven times for minus three yards and caught one pass for minus three yards, 1973; recovered five fumbles and fumbled 14 times for minus 13 yards, 1974; recovered three fumbles, 1975, 1978, 1979 and 1983; fumbled four times for minus one yard, 1975; recovered seven fumbles and fumbled 12 times for minus seven yards, 1977; fumbled five times for minus three yards and caught one pass for minus six yards, 1978; recovered one fumble and fumbled nine times for minus 12 yards, 1980; recovered two fumbles, one for a touchdown and fumbled five times for minus 10 yards, 1982; recovered two fumbles and fumbled eight times for minus 26 yards, 1984; recovered two fumbles, 1986.

KEITH TYRONE FERGUSON
Defensive End—Detroit Lions

Born April 3, 1959, at Miami, Fla.
Height, 6.05. Weight, 260.
High School—Miami, Fla., Edison.
Attended Ohio State University.

Selected by San Diego in 5th round (131st player selected) of 1981 NFL draft.
Released by San Diego Chargers, November 20, 1985; awarded on waivers to Detroit Lions, November 21, 1985.
San Diego NFL, 1981 through 1984; San Diego (10)-Detroit (5) NFL, 1985; Detroit NFL, 1986 and 1987.
Games: 1981 (16), 1982 (9), 1983 (16), 1984 (16), 1985 (15), 1986 (16), 1987 (12). Total—100.
Pro statistics: Recovered one fumble, 1982 and 1984 through 1987; recovered two fumbles, 1983; intercepted one pass for seven yards and fumbled once, 1986.
Played in AFC Championship Game following 1981 season.

MERVYN FERNANDEZ
Wide Receiver—Los Angeles Raiders

Born December 29, 1959, at Merced, Calif.
Height, 6.03. Weight, 205.
High School—San Jose, Calif., Andrew Hill.
Attended De Anza College and San Jose State University.

Signed as free agent by British Columbia Lions, March 11, 1982.
Selected by Los Angeles Raiders in 10th round (277th player selected) of 1983 NFL draft.
On injured list, July 1 through September 2, 1986.
Granted free agency, March 1, 1987; signed by Los Angeles Raiders, March 4, 1987.
Crossed picket line during players' strike, October 14, 1987.
On injured reserve with shoulder injury, November 21 through remainder of 1987 season.

Year Club	G.	P.C.	Yds.	Avg.	TD.	Year Club	G.	P.C.	Yds.	Avg.	TD.
	PASS RECEIVING						PASS RECEIVING				
1982—British Columbia CFL.	16	64	1046	16.3	8	1987—L.A. Raiders NFL	7	14	236	16.9	0
1983—British Columbia CFL.	16	78	1284	16.5	10	CFL Totals—5 Years	74	374	6408	17.1	55
1984—British Columbia CFL.	15	89	*1486	16.7	17	NFL Totals—1 Year	7	14	236	16.9	0
1985—British Columbia CFL.	16	95	*1727	18.2	*15	Pro Totals—6 Years	81	388	6644	17.1	55
1986—British Columbia CFL.	11	48	865	18.0	5						

Additional CFL statistics: Scored one two-point conversion, 1982 and 1983; returned 20 punts for 179 yards and one touchdown, returned one kickoff for 32 yards, rushed twice for one yard and fumbled twice, 1982; returned two punts

for 19 yards and fumbled twice, 1983; rushed three times for 33 yards, returned one kickoff for three yards, attempted one pass with one completion for 55 yards and fumbled once, 1985; punted 14 times for 34.0 yard average and attempted one pass with one completion for 86 yards, 1986.
Additional NFL statistics: Fumbled once, 1987.

EARL THOMAS FERRELL
Fullback—Phoenix Cardinals
Born March 27, 1958, at Halifax, Va.
Height, 6.00. Weight, 240.
High School—South Boston, Va., Halifax County.
Received degree in physical education from East Tennessee State University.

Selected by St. Louis in 5th round (125th player selected) of 1982 NFL draft.
On non-football injury list with drug problems, November 21 through remainder of 1985 season.
Crossed picket line during players' strike, October 2, 1987.
On injured reserve with knee injury, December 5 through remainder of 1987 season.
Franchise transferred to Phoenix, March 15, 1988.

| | | ——RUSHING—— | | | | PASS RECEIVING | | | | —TOTAL— | | |
Year	Club	G.	Att.	Yds.	Avg.	TD.	P.C.	Yds.	Avg.	TD.	TD.	Pts.	F.
1982—St. Louis NFL		9			None				None		0	0	0
1983—St. Louis NFL		16	7	53	7.6	1			None		1	6	2
1984—St. Louis NFL		16	41	190	4.6	1	26	218	8.4	1	2	12	3
1985—St. Louis NFL		11	46	208	4.5	2	25	277	11.1	2	4	24	2
1986—St. Louis NFL		16	124	548	4.4	0	56	434	7.8	3	3	18	6
1987—St. Louis NFL		11	113	512	4.5	7	23	262	11.4	0	7	42	0
Pro Totals—6 Years		79	331	1511	4.6	11	130	1191	9.2	6	17	102	13

| | | KICKOFF RETURNS | | | | |
Year	Club	G.	No.	Yds.	Avg.	TD.
1982—St. Louis NFL		9	4	88	22.0	0
1983—St. Louis NFL		16	13	257	19.8	0
1984—St. Louis NFL		16	1	0	0.0	0
1985—St. Louis NFL		11			None	
1986—St. Louis NFL		16	3	41	13.7	0
1987—St. Louis NFL		11	1	10	10.0	0
Pro Totals—6 Years		79	22	396	18.0	0

Additional pro statistics: Returned one punt for six yards, 1982; returned one punt for 17 yards, 1983; recovered one fumble, 1985 and 1987.

ALFRED FIELDS
(Jitter)
Defensive Back-Kick Returner—Kansas City Chiefs
Born August 16, 1962, at Dallas, Tex.
Height, 5.09. Weight, 180.
High School—Dallas, Tex., H. Grady Spruce.
Attended University of Texas.

Selected by San Antonio in 1984 USFL territorial draft.
Selected by New Orleans in 5th round (123rd player selected) of 1984 NFL draft.
Signed by New Orleans Saints, June 23, 1984.
Released by New Orleans Saints, August 20, 1985; signed as free agent replacement player by Indianapolis Colts, September 23, 1987.
Released by Indianapolis Colts, October 9, 1987; awarded on waivers to Kansas City Chiefs, October 12, 1987.
Released by Kansas City Chiefs, November 3, 1987; re-signed by Chiefs, December 12, 1987.

| | | -PUNT RETURNS- | | | | —KICKOFF RET.— | | | | —TOTAL— | | |
Year	Club	G.	No.	Yds.	Avg.	TD.	No.	Yds.	Avg.	TD.	TD.	Pts.	F.
1984—New Orleans NFL		13	27	236	8.7	0	19	356	18.7	0	0	0	2
1987—Ind. (1)-Kan. City (5) NFL		6	8	161	20.1	1	1	13	13.0	0	1	6	0
Pro Totals—2 Years		19	35	397	11.3	1	20	369	18.4	0	1	6	2

Additional pro statistics: Recovered one fumble, 1984.

DAN CLEMENT FIKE JR.
Guard—Cleveland Browns
Born June 16, 1961, at Mobile, Ala.
Height, 6.07. Weight, 280.
High School—Pensacola, Fla., Pine Forest.
Attended University of Florida.

Selected by Tampa Bay in 1984 USFL territorial draft.
Selected by New York Jets in 10th round (274th player selected) of 1983 NFL draft.
Signed by New York Jets, June 10, 1983.
Released by New York Jets, August 29, 1983; signed by Tampa Bay Bandits, November 13, 1983.
Signed by Cleveland Browns, January 20, 1985, to take affect after being granted free agency following 1985 USFL season.
Tampa Bay USFL, 1984 and 1985; Cleveland NFL, 1985 through 1987.
Games: 1984 (18), 1985 USFL (18), 1985 NFL (13), 1986 (16), 1987 (12). Total USFL—36. Total NFL—41. Total Pro—77.
Pro statistics: Recovered one fumble, 1986.
USFL statistics: Recovered one fumble, 1985.
Played in AFC Championship Game following 1986 and 1987 seasons.

JAMES JOSEPH FitzPATRICK III
Guard-Offensive Tackle—San Diego Chargers
Born February 1, 1964, at Heidelberg, Germany.
Height, 6.07. Weight, 286.
High School—Beaverton, Ore.
Attended University of Southern California.

Selected by New Jersey in 1986 USFL territorial draft.
Selected by San Diego in 1st round (13th player selected) of 1986 NFL draft.
Signed by San Diego Chargers, July 25, 1986.
On injured reserve with back injury, October 6 through remainder of 1986 season.
San Diego NFL, 1986 and 1987.
Games: 1986 (4), 1987 (10). Total—14.

R. TERRENCE FLAGLER
(Known by middle name.)
Running Back—San Francisco 49ers
Born September 24, 1964, at New York, N.Y.
Height, 6.00. Weight, 200.
High School—Fernandina Beach, Fla.
Attended Clemson University.

Selected by San Francisco in 1st round (25th player selected) of 1987 NFL draft.
Signed by San Francisco 49ers, July 24, 1987.

Year Club	G.	Att.	Yds.	Avg.	TD.	P.C.	Yds.	Avg.	TD.	TD.	Pts.	F.
		——RUSHING——				PASS RECEIVING				—TOTAL—		
1987—San Francisco NFL	3	6	11	1.8	0	2	28	14.0	0	0	0	2

Additional pro statistics: Returned three kickoffs for 31 yards and recovered one fumble, 1987.

SIMON RAYNARD FLETCHER
Defensive End—Denver Broncos
Born February 18, 1962, at Bay City, Tex.
Height, 6.05. Weight, 240.
High School—Bay City, Tex.
Attended University of Houston.
Related to Pat Franklin, running back with San Diego Chargers.

Selected by Houston in 1985 USFL territorial draft.
Selected by Denver in 2nd round (54th player selected) of 1985 NFL draft.
Signed by Denver Broncos, July 16, 1985.
Denver NFL, 1985 through 1987.
Games: 1985 (16), 1986 (16), 1987 (12). Total—44.
Pro statistics: Recovered two fumbles, 1986; recovered one fumble, 1987.
Played in AFC Championship Game following 1986 and 1987 seasons.
Played in NFL Championship Game following 1986 and 1987 seasons.

TOM FLICK
Quarterback—New York Jets
Born August 30, 1958, at Patuxent River, Md.
Height, 6.02. Weight, 190.
High School—Belleville, Wash.
Received bachelor of arts degree in communications from University of Washington in 1981.

Selected by Washington in 4th round (90th player selected) of 1981 NFL draft.
Traded by Washington Redskins to New England Patriots for quarterback Tom Owen, August 25, 1982.
On inactive list, September 12 and September 19, 1982.
On injured reserve with elbow injury, August 16 through September 28, 1983.
Released by New England Patriots, September 29, 1983; signed as free agent by Cleveland Browns, January 3, 1984.
Released by Cleveland Browns, July 28, 1985; signed as free agent by San Diego Chargers, May 15, 1986.
Released by San Diego Chargers, August 29, 1987; signed as free agent replacement player by New York Jets, October 14, 1987.
Active for 1 game with New York Jets in 1987; did not play.

Year Club	G.	Att.	Cmp.	Pct.	Gain	T.P.	P.I.	Avg.	Att.	Yds.	Avg.	TD.	TD.	Pts.	F.
		——————PASSING——————							——RUSHING——				—TOTAL—		
1981—Washington NFL	6	27	13	48.1	143	0	2	5.30	None				0	0	2
1982—New England NFL	3	5	0	0.0	0	0	0	0.00	None				0	0	0
1984—Cleveland NFL	1	1	1	100.0	2	0	0	2.00	None				0	0	1
1986—San Diego NFL	11	73	33	45.2	361	2	8	4.95	6	5	0.8	1	1	6	1
Pro Totals—5 Years	21	106	47	44.3	506	2	10	4.77	6	5	0.8	1	1	6	4

Quarterback Rating Points: 1981 (33.4), 1982 (39.6), 1984 (79.2), 1986 (29.9). Total—26.1.
Additional pro statistics: Recovered one fumble, 1981 and 1986.

KENNETH C. FLOWERS
(Kenny)
Running Back—Atlanta Falcons
Born March 14, 1964, at Daytona Beach, Fla.
Height, 6.00. Weight, 210.
High School—Daytona Beach, Fla., Spruce Creek.
Attended Clemson University.

Selected by Atlanta in 2nd round (31st player selected) in 1987 NFL draft.
Signed by Atlanta Falcons, July 31, 1987.
On injured reserve with hamstring injury, November 10 through December 11, 1987; activated, December 12, 1987.

Year Club			——RUSHING——				PASS RECEIVING				—TOTAL—		
	G.	Att.	Yds.	Avg.	TD.		P.C.	Yds.	Avg.	TD.	TD.	Pts.	F.
1987—Atlanta NFL	8	14	61	4.4	0		7	50	7.1	0		0	0	1

Year Club	KICKOFF RETURNS				
	G.	No.	Yds.	Avg.	TD.
1987—Atlanta NFL	8	4	72	18.0	0

Additional pro statistics: Recovered one fumble, 1987.

DOUG FLUTIE
Quarterback—New England Patriots
Born October 23, 1962, at Manchester, Md.
Height, 5.09. Weight, 176.
High School—Natick, Mass.
Attended Boston College.

Heisman Trophy winner, 1984.
Named THE SPORTING NEWS College Football Player of the Year, 1984.
Named as quarterback on THE SPORTING NEWS College All-America Team, 1984.
Selected by New Jersey in 1985 USFL territorial draft.
Signed by New Jersey Generals, February 4, 1985.
Granted roster exemption, February 4 through February 14, 1985; activated, February 15, 1985.
Selected by Los Angeles Rams in 11th round (285th player selected) of 1985 NFL draft.
On developmental squad, June 10 through remainder of 1985 season.
NFL rights traded with 4th round pick in 1987 draft by Los Angeles Rams to Chicago Bears for 3rd and 6th round picks in 1987 draft, October 14, 1986.
Signed by Chicago Bears, October 21, 1986.
Granted roster exemption, October 21 through November 3, 1986; activated, November 4, 1986.
Crossed picket line during players' strike, October 13, 1987.
Traded by Chicago Bears to New England Patriots for 8th round pick in 1988 draft, October 13, 1987.
On developmental squad for 3 games with New Jersey Generals in 1985.

Year Club		——————PASSING——————							——RUSHING——				—TOTAL—		
	G.	Att.	Cmp.	Pct.	Gain	T.P.	P.I.	Avg.	Att.	Yds.	Avg.	TD.	TD.	Pts.	F.
1985—New Jersey USFL	15	281	134	47.7	2109	13	14	7.51	65	465	7.2	6	6	36	3
1986—Chicago NFL	4	46	23	50.0	361	3	2	7.85	9	36	4.0	1	1	6	3
1987—Chi. (1)-N.E. (1) NFL.......	2	25	15	60.0	199	1	0	7.96	6	43	7.2	0	0	0	1
USFL Totals—1 Year........	15	281	134	47.7	2109	13	14	7.51	65	465	7.2	6	6	36	3
NFL Totals—2 Years.........	6	71	38	53.5	560	4	2	7.89	15	79	5.3	1	1	6	4
Pro Totals—3 Years...........	21	352	172	48.9	2669	17	16	7.58	80	544	6.8	7	7	42	7

USFL Quarterback Rating Points: 1985 (67.8).
NFL Quarterback Rating Points: 1986 (80.1), 1987 (98.6). Total—86.6.
Additional USFL statistics: Recovered two fumbles, 1985.
Additional NFL statistics: Recovered two fumbles and fumbled three times for minus four yards, 1986; recovered one fumble, 1987.

THOMAS JEFFERY FLYNN
(Tom)
Safety—New York Giants
Born March 24, 1962, at Verona, Pa.
Height, 6.00. Weight, 195.
High School—Pittsburgh, Pa., Penn Hills.
Attended University of Pittsburgh.

Selected by Pittsburgh in 1984 USFL territorial draft.
Selected by Green Bay in 5th round (126th player selected) of 1984 NFL draft.
Signed by Green Bay Packers, July 1, 1984.
Released by Green Bay Packers, October 21, 1986; signed as free agent by New York Giants, December 9, 1986.

Year Club		-INTERCEPTIONS-				-PUNT RETURNS-				—TOTAL—		
	G.	No.	Yds.	Avg.	TD.	No.	Yds.	Avg.	TD.	TD.	Pts.	F.
1984—Green Bay NFL............................	16	9	106	11.8	0	15	128	8.5	0	0	0	1
1985—Green Bay NFL............................	16	1	7	7.0	0	7	41	5.9	0	0	0	0
1986—G.B.(7)-NYG(2) NFL..................	9	1	0	0.0	0		None			1	6	0
1987—New York Giants NFL	12		None				None			1	6	0
Pro Totals—4 Years................................	53	11	113	10.3	0	22	169	7.7	0	2	12	0

Additional pro statistics: Recovered three fumbles for three yards, 1984; returned one kickoff for 20 yards and recovered one fumble, 1985; returned blocked punt 36 yards for a touchdown, 1986; recovered blocked punt in end zone for a touchdown, 1987.
Played in NFC Championship Game following 1986 season.
Played in NFL Championship Game following 1986 season.

—DID YOU KNOW—

That when Marv Levy won his first game as Buffalo coach on November 9, 1986 (a 16-12 defeat of Pittsburgh), he became the first of 10 head coaches in Bills history to win his debut game?

STEVE MARK FOLSOM
Tight End—Dallas Cowboys
Born March 21, 1958, at Los Angeles, Calif.
Height, 6.05. Weight, 236.
High School—Santa Fe Springs, Calif.
Attended California State University at Long Beach and received bachelor of science
degree in commercial recreation from University of Utah in 1981.

Selected by Miami in 10th round (261st player selected) of 1981 NFL draft.
Released by Miami Dolphins, August 17, 1981; signed as free agent by Philadelphia Eagles, November 25, 1981.
On injured reserve with pulled hamstring, December 26 through remainder of 1981 season playoffs.
On injured reserve with neck injury, September 6, 1982.
Released by Philadelphia Eagles, September 7, 1982; signed as free agent by New York Giants, September 13, 1982.
On inactive list, September 20, 1982.
Released by New York Giants, November 30, 1982.
USFL rights traded by Los Angeles Express to Philadelphia Stars for rights to defensive back Chuck Scicli,
September 9, 1982.
Signed by Philadelphia Stars, January 27, 1983.
On developmental squad, June 21 through remainder of 1984 season.
Franchise transferred to Baltimore, November 1, 1984.
On physically unable to perform, February 18 through April 5, 1985; activated, April 6, 1985.
On developmental squad, May 15 through June 13, 1985; activated, June 14, 1985.
Granted free agency when USFL suspended operations, August 7, 1986; signed as free agent by Dallas Cowboys,
April 30, 1987.
Released by Dallas Cowboys, September 7, 1987; re-signed by Cowboys, October 20, 1987.
On developmental squad for 1 game with Philadelphia Stars in 1984.
On developmental squad for 4 games with Baltimore Stars in 1985.

				—PASS RECEIVING—			
Year	Club		G.	P.C.	Yds.	Avg.	TD.
1981—Philadelphia NFL		....	3		None		
1983—Philadelphia USFL		......	18	26	286	11.0	1
1984—Philadelphia USFL		......	17	46	485	10.5	6
1985—Baltimore USFL		....	8	1	4	4.0	0
1987—Dallas NFL		....	9		None		
USFL Totals—3 Years		....	43	73	775	10.6	7
NFL Totals—2 Years		....	12	0	0.0	0.0	0
Pro Totals—5 Years		....	55	73	775	10.6	7

Additional pro statistics: Fumbled once, 1983; returned one kickoff for three yards, 1984.
Played in USFL Championship Game following 1983 and 1985 seasons.
On developmental squad for USFL Championship Game following 1984 season.

HERMAN FONTENOT
Running Back—Cleveland Browns
Born September 12, 1963, at St. Elizabeth, Tex.
Height, 6.00. Weight, 206.
High School—Beaumont, Tex., Charlton-Pollard.
Attended Louisiana State University.

Selected by New Jersey in 9th round (127th player selected) of 1985 USFL draft.
Signed as free agent by Cleveland Browns, May 6, 1985.
On injured reserve with broken bone in back, August 27 through October 24, 1985; activated, October 25, 1985.

			—RUSHING—				PASS RECEIVING				—TOTAL—		
Year	Club		G.	Att.	Yds.	Avg.	TD.	P.C.	Yds.	Avg.	TD.	TD.	Pts.	F.
1985—Cleveland NFL		......	9		None			2	19	9.5	0	0	0	1
1986—Cleveland NFL		......	16	25	105	4.2	1	47	559	11.9	1	2	12	2
1987—Cleveland NFL		......	12	15	33	2.2	0	4	40	10.0	0	0	0	0
Pro Totals—3 Years		......	37	40	138	3.5	1	53	618	11.7	1	2	12	3

			KICKOFF RETURNS			
Year	Club		G.	No.	Yds.	Avg.TD.
1985—Cleveland NFL		....	9	8	215	26.9	0
1986—Cleveland NFL		....	16	7	99	14.1	0
1987—Cleveland NFL		....	12	9	130	14.4	0
Pro Totals—3 Years		....	37	24	444	18.5	0

Additional pro statistics: Attempted one pass with no completions, 1985; attempted one pass with one completion
for 46 yards and a touchdown and recovered one fumble, 1986; attempted one pass with one completion for 14 yards,
1987.
Played in AFC Championship Game following 1986 and 1987 seasons.

CHRIS D. FOOTE
Center—Minnesota Vikings
Born December 2, 1956, at Louisville, Ky.
Height, 6.04. Weight, 265.
High School—Boulder, Colo., Fairview.
Received bachelor of arts degree in communications from
University of Southern California in 1980.

Selected by Baltimore in 6th round (144th player selected) of 1980 NFL draft.
Released by Baltimore Colts, September 6, 1982; signed as free agent by New York Giants, September 17, 1982.

Traded by New York Giants to New York Jets for future draft pick, August 23, 1983.
Released by New York Jets, August 29, 1983; signed as free agent by New York Giants, September 12, 1983.
Signed by Los Angeles Express, November 13, 1983, for contract to take effect after being granted free agency, February 1, 1984.
Traded by Los Angeles Express to Tampa Bay Bandits for past considerations, March 12, 1984.
On developmental squad, April 5 through April 18, 1985; activated, April 19, 1985.
Granted free agency when USFL suspended operations, August 7, 1986; re-signed by New York Giants and traded to Minnesota Vikings for conditional pick in 1988 draft, May 7, 1987.
On injured reserve with broken hand, September 1 through November 9, 1987.
Released by Minnesota Vikings, November 10, 1987; re-signed by Vikings after clearing procedural waivers, November 17, 1987.
On developmental squad for 2 games with Tampa Bay Bandits in 1985.
Baltimore NFL, 1980 and 1981; New York Giants NFL, 1982 and 1983; Los Angeles (3)-Tampa Bay (15) USFL, 1984; Tampa Bay USFL, 1985; Minnesota NFL, 1987.
Games: 1980 (16), 1981 (16), 1982 (7), 1983 (11), 1984 (18), 1985 (16), 1987 (6). Total NFL—56. Total USFL—34. Total Pro—90.
NFL statistics: Returned one kickoff for nine yards and recovered one fumble, 1980; returned one kickoff for no yards, 1981.
USFL statistics: Recovered one fumble, 1985.
Played in NFC Championship Game following 1987 season.

PHIL L. FORNEY
Linebacker—New York Jets
Born September 18, 1963, at Rutherfordton, N.C.
Height, 6.02. Weight, 220.
High Scool—Rutherfordton, N.C., Central.
Attended East Tennessee State University.

Selected by Jacksonville in 11th round (148th player selected) of 1985 USFL draft.
Signed by Jacksonville Bulls, January 19, 1985.
Released by Jacksonville Bulls, February 12, 1985; re-signed by Bulls, April 29, 1985.
Granted free agency when USFL suspended operations, August 7, 1986; signed as replacement player by St. Louis Cardinals, September 25, 1987.
Released by St. Louis Cardinals, October 20, 1987; signed as free agent by New York Jets, April 15, 1988.
Jacksonville USFL, 1985; St. Louis NFL, 1987.
Games: 1985 (8), 1987 (3). Total—11.

JEROME FOSTER
Defensive End-Defensive Tackle—New York Jets
Born July 25, 1960, at Detroit, Mich.
Height, 6.02. Weight, 275.
High School—Detroit, Mich., Kettering.
Attended Ohio State University.

Selected by Oakland in 5th round (55th player selected) of 1983 USFL draft.
Selected by Houston in 5th round (139th player selected) of 1983 NFL draft.
Signed by Houston Oilers, June 22, 1983.
On injured reserve with knee injury, September 20 through November 9, 1984; activated, November 10, 1984.
Released by Houston Oilers, September 2, 1985; signed as free agent by Miami Dolphins, March 6, 1986.
Released by Miami Dolphins, December 13, 1986; signed as free agent by New York Jets, December 17, 1986.
On injured reserve with injured calf muscle, September 7 through December 6, 1987; activated, December 7, 1987.
Houston NFL, 1983 and 1984; Miami (14)-New York Jets (1) NFL, 1986; New York Jets NFL, 1987.
Games: 1983 (16), 1984 (9), 1986 (15), 1987 (4). Total—44.
Pro statistics: Recovered one fumble, 1986.

ROY ALLEN FOSTER
Guard—Miami Dolphins
Born May 24, 1960, at Los Angeles, Calif.
Height, 6.04. Weight, 272.
High Schools—Woodland Hills, Calif., Taft; and Shawnee Mission, Kan., West.
Attended University of Southern California.

Named as guard on THE SPORTING NEWS College All-America Team, 1981.
Selected by Miami in 1st round (24th player selected) of 1982 NFL draft.
Miami NFL, 1982 through 1987.
Games: 1982 (9), 1983 (16), 1984 (16), 1985 (16), 1986 (16), 1987 (12). Total—85.
Pro statistics: Recovered one fumble, 1984 and 1987; recovered two fumbles, 1986.
Played in AFC Championship Game following 1982, 1984 and 1985 seasons.
Played in NFL Championship Game following 1982 and 1984 seasons.
Played in Pro Bowl (NFL All-Star Game) following 1985 and 1986 seasons.

ELBERT FOULES
Cornerback—Philadelphia Eagles
Born July 4, 1961, at Greenville, Miss.
Height, 5.11. Weight, 193.
High School—Greenville, Miss.
Attended Alcorn State University.

Cousin of Wilbert Montgomery, running back with Philadelphia Eagles and Detroit Lions, 1977 through 1985; and Cle Montgomery, wide receiver with Cincinnati Bengals, Cleveland Browns and Oakland-Los Angeles Raiders, 1980 through 1985.

Signed as free agent by Philadelphia Eagles, May 12, 1983.

Year Club	G.	No.	Yds.	Avg.TD.	
1983—Philadelphia NFL	16	1	0	0.0	0
1984—Philadelphia NFL	16	4	27	6.8	0
1985—Philadelphia NFL	16		None		
1986—Philadelphia NFL	16	1	14	14.0	0
1987—Philadelphia NFL	9	4	6	1.5	0
Pro Totals—5 Years............	73	10	47	4.7	0

Additional pro statistics: Returned one punt for seven yards, 1983; returned one kickoff for seven yards and recovered one fumble, 1985; recovered two fumbles, 1986.

JOHN CHARLES FOURCADE
Quarterback—New Orleans Saints
Born October 11, 1960, at Gretna, La.
Height, 6.01. Weight, 208.
High School—Marrero, La., Archbishop Shaw.
Received bachelor of science degree in education
and sports marketing from University of Mississippi.

Signed as free agent by Toronto Argonauts, May 5, 1982.
Traded by Toronto Argonauts to British Columbia Lions, May 20, 1982.
Released by British Columbia Lions, July 4, 1982; re-signed by Lions, July 8, 1982.
Released by British Columbia Lions, June 30, 1983; signed by Birmingham Stallions, October 10, 1983.
Released by Birmingham Stallions, February 13, 1984; signed as free agent by Memphis Showboats, May 31, 1984.
On developmental squad, May 31 through remainder of 1984 season.
Released by Memphis Showboats, January 23, 1985; signed as free agent by New York Giants, May 3, 1985.
Released by New York Giants, July 22, 1985; signed as free agent by New Orleans Saints, May 13, 1986.
Released by New Orleans Saints, August 19, 1986; signed as free agent by Denver Dynamite of Arena Football League, July 15, 1987.
Granted free agency, August 15, 1987; re-signed as replacement player by New Orleans Saints, September 24, 1987.
On developmental squad for 4 games with Memphis Showboats in 1984.

		PASSING						RUSHING				TOTAL		
Year Club	G.	Att.	Cmp.	Pct.	Gain	T.P.	P.I.	Avg.	Att.	Yds.	Avg.	TD.	TD. Pts. F.	
1982—British Columbia CFL.....	4	14	5	35.7	55	0	3	3.93	2	37	18.5	0	0 0 0	
1987—New Orleans NFL.............	3	89	48	53.9	597	4	3	6.71	19	134	7.1	0	0 0 1	
Pro Totals—2 Years...........	7	103	53	51.5	652	4	6	6.33	21	171	8.1	0	0 0 1	

NFL Quarterback Rating Points: 1987 (75.9).

STEVEN TODD FOWLER
(Known by middle name.)
Fullback—Dallas Cowboys
Born June 9, 1962, at Van, Tex.
Height, 6.03. Weight, 222.
High School—Van, Tex.
Attended Henderson County Junior College and Stephen F. Austin State University.

Selected by Houston in 16th round (329th player selected) of 1984 USFL draft.
Signed by Houston Gamblers, January 20, 1984.
Selected by Dallas in 1st round (25th player selected) of 1984 NFL supplemental draft.
Signed by Dallas Cowboys, September 24, 1984, for contract to take effect after being granted free agency after 1985 USFL season.
On developmental squad, February 21 through March 30, 1985; activated, March 31, 1985.
On injured reserve with knee injury, August 27 through October 28, 1985; activated, October 29, 1985.
On developmental squad for 5 games with Houston Gamblers in 1985.

		RUSHING				PASS RECEIVING				TOTAL		
Year Club	G.	Att.	Yds.	Avg.	TD.	P.C.	Yds.	Avg.	TD.	TD.	Pts.	F.
1984—Houston USFL...........................	18	170	1003	5.9	11	24	301	12.5	2	13	78	4
1985—Houston USFL...........................	13	92	402	4.4	3	27	239	8.9	1	4	†26	5
1985—Dallas NFL.................................	8	7	25	3.6	0	5	24	4.8	0	0	0	0
1986—Dallas NFL.................................	16	6	5	0.8	0	1	19	19.0	0	0	0	1
1987—Dallas NFL.................................	12		None			1	6	6.0	0	0	0	0
USFL Totals—2 Years....................	31	262	1405	5.4	14	51	540	10.6	3	17	104	9
NFL Totals—3 Years......................	36	13	30	2.3	0	7	49	7.0	0	0	0	1
Pro Totals—5 Years......................	67	275	1435	5.2	14	58	589	10.2	3	17	104	10

†Includes one 2-point conversion.
Additional USFL statistics: Recovered four fumbles, 1984; recovered two fumbles, 1985.
Additional NFL statistics: Returned three kickoffs for 48 yards, 1985; recovered one fumble, 1986.

CHAS FOX
Wide Receiver—Buffalo Bills
Born October 3, 1963, at Lafayette, Ind.
Height, 5.11. Weight, 190.
High School—Rapid City, S.D., Stevens.
Attended Furman University.

Selected by New Jersey in 6th round (85th player selected) of 1985 USFL draft.

Selected by Kansas City in 4th round (90th player selected) of 1986 NFL draft.
Signed by Kansas City Chiefs, June 3, 1986.
Released by Kansas City Chiefs, August 26, 1986; signed as free agent by St. Louis Cardinals, September 23, 1986.
Released by St. Louis Cardinals, October 20, 1986; signed as free agent by Kansas City Chiefs, February 7, 1987.
Released by Kansas City Chiefs, September 7, 1987; signed as free agent replacement player by Buffalo Bills, October 8, 1987.
On injured reserve with knee injury, October 16 through remainder of 1987 season.

Year Club			—PASS RECEIVING—		
	G.	P.C.	Yds.	Avg.	TD.
1986—St. Louis NFL	4	5	59	11.8	1

Additional pro statistics: Returned six kickoffs for 161 yards (26.8 avg.), 1986.

TODD L. FRAIN
Tight End—New York Jets
Born January 31, 1962, at Council Bluffs, Ia.
Height, 6.02. Weight, 235.
High School—Treynor, Ia.
Received bachelor of science in education from University of Nebraska in 1986.

Signed as free agent by Washington Redskins, May 8, 1986.
On injured reserve with foot injury, August 19 through December 14, 1986; activated after clearing procedural waivers, December 16, 1986.
On injured reserve with concussion, January 9 through 1986 season playoffs.
Released by Washington Redskins, August 31, 1987; signed as free agent replacement player by New England Patriots, September 24, 1987.
Released by New England Patriots, October 21, 1987; signed as free agent by New York Jets, March 30, 1988.
Washington NFL, 1986; New England NFL, 1987.
Games: 1986 (1), 1987 (3). Total—4.

WILLIAM P. FRALIC JR.
(Bill)
Guard—Atlanta Falcons
Born October 31, 1962, at Penn Hills, Pa.
Height, 6.05. Weight, 280.
High School—Pittsburgh, Pa., Penn Hills.
Attended University of Pittsburgh.

Named to THE SPORTING NEWS NFL All-Star Team, 1986 and 1987.
Named as offensive tackle on THE SPORTING NEWS College Football All-America Team, 1983 and 1984.
Selected by Baltimore in 1985 USFL territorial draft.
Selected by Atlanta in 1st round (2nd player selected) of 1985 NFL draft.
Signed by Atlanta Falcons, July 22, 1985.
Atlanta NFL, 1985 through 1987.
Games: 1985 (15), 1986 (16), 1987 (12). Total—43.
Played in Pro Bowl (NFL All-Star Team) following 1986 and 1987 seasons.

JON CHARLES NAEKAUNA FRANCIS
Running Back—Los Angeles Rams
Born June 21, 1964, at Corvallis, Ore.
Height, 5.11. Weight, 207.
High School—Corvallis, Ore.
Attended Taft College, Colorado State University and Boise State University.

Selected by New York Giants in 7th round (184th player selected) of 1986 NFL draft.
Signed by New York Giants, July 17, 1986.
On injured reserve with leg injury, August 19 through September 1, 1986.
Released by New York Giants, September 2, 1986; signed as free agent by New England Patriots, May 28, 1987.
Released by New England Patriots, August 25, 1987; signed as free agent replacement player by Los Angeles Rams, September 23, 1987.
Released by Los Angeles Rams, November 3, 1987; re-signed by Rams, November 5, 1987.
Released by Los Angeles Rams, November 10, 1987; re-signed by Rams, November 19, 1987.

Year Club		—RUSHING—				PASS RECEIVING			—TOTAL—		
	G.	Att.	Yds.	Avg.	TD.	P.C.	Yds.	Avg.	TD.	TD.	Pts.	F.
1987—Los Angeles Rams NFL	9	35	138	3.9	0	8	38	4.8	2	2	12	0

RONALD BERNARD FRANCIS
(Ron)
Cornerback—Dallas Cowboys
Born April 7, 1964, at LaMarque, Tex.
Height, 5.09. Weight, 199.
High School—LaMarque, Tex.
Attended Baylor University.
Brother of James Francis, linebacker (football) and forward (basketball) at Baylor University.

Selected by Dallas in 2nd round (39th player selected) of 1987 NFL draft.
Signed by Dallas Cowboys, July 24, 1987.
Dallas NFL, 1987.
Games: 1987 (11).
Pro statistics: Intercepted two passes for 18 yards and a touchdown and recovered one fumble for two yards, 1987.

RUSSELL ROSS FRANCIS
(Russ)
Tight End—New England Patriots

Born April 3, 1953, at Seattle, Wash.
Height, 6.06. Weight, 242.
High Schools—Kailua, Oahu, Hawaii; and Pleasant Hill, Ore.
Attended University of Oregon.
Son of Ed Francis, former part-time scout with New England Patriots.

Selected by New England in 1st round (16th player selected) of 1975 NFL draft.
On did not report list, August 18 through entire 1981 season.
Traded with 2nd round pick in 1982 draft by New England Patriots to San Francisco 49ers for 1st, 4th and two 2nd round picks in 1982 draft, April 27, 1982.
On injured reserve with neck injury, October 23 through December 6, 1984; activated, December 7, 1984.
On injured reserve with Achilles heel injury, September 7 through October 5, 1987; activated, October 6, 1987.
Crossed picket line during players' strike, October 6, 1987.
On injured reserve with back injury, December 4 through December 14, 1987.
Released by San Francisco 49ers, December 15, 1987; signed as free agent by New England Patriots, December 23, 1987.
Selected by Kansas City Royals' organization in 9th round of free-agent draft, June 5, 1974.

| | | | —PASS RECEIVING— | | |
Year Club	G.	P.C.	Yds.	Avg.	TD.
1975—New England NFL	14	35	636	18.2	4
1976—New England NFL	13	26	367	14.1	3
1977—New England NFL	10	16	229	14.3	4
1978—New England NFL	15	39	543	13.9	4
1979—New England NFL	12	39	557	14.3	5
1980—New England NFL	15	41	664	16.2	8
1982—San Francisco NFL	9	23	278	12.1	4
1983—San Francisco NFL	16	33	357	10.8	4
1984—San Francisco NFL	10	23	285	12.4	2
1985—San Francisco NFL	16	44	478	10.9	3
1986—San Francisco NFL	16	41	505	12.3	1
1987—S.F. (8)-N.E. (1) NFL	9	22	202	9.2	0
Pro Totals—12 Years	155	382	5042	13.2	40

Additional pro statistics: Fumbled once, 1975, 1976, 1978 and 1984; rushed twice for 12 yards and recovered one fumble, 1976 and 1978; recovered one fumble for three yards, 1977; attempted one pass with one completion for 45 yards, 1982; fumbled twice, 1982, 1983 and 1985; recovered two fumbles, 1984.
Played in NFC Championship Game following 1983 and 1984 seasons.
Played in NFL Championship Game following 1984 season.
Played in Pro Bowl (NFL All-Star Game) following 1976 and 1977 seasons.
Named to play in Pro Bowl following 1978 season; replaced due to injury by Riley Odoms.

JOHN E. FRANK
Tight End—San Francisco 49ers

Born April 17, 1962, at Pittsburgh, Pa.
Height, 6.03. Weight, 225.
High School—Pittsburgh, Pa., Mount Lebanon.
Received bachelor of arts degree in pre-med from Ohio State University in 1984.

Selected by New Jersey in 1984 USFL territorial draft.
USFL rights traded with rights to guard Joe Lukens by New Jersey Generals to Pittsburgh Maulers for cornerback Kerry Justin, November 15, 1983.
Selected by San Francisco in 2nd round (56th player selected) of 1984 NFL draft.
Signed by San Francisco 49ers, July 16, 1984.

| | | | —PASS RECEIVING— | | |
Year Club	G.	P.C.	Yds.	Avg.	TD.
1984—San Francisco NFL	15	7	60	8.6	1
1985—San Francisco NFL	16	7	50	7.1	1
1986—San Francisco NFL	16	9	61	6.8	2
1987—San Francisco NFL	12	26	296	11.4	3
Pro Totals—4 Years	59	49	467	9.5	7

Additional pro statistics: Returned one kickoff for one yard, 1985; rushed once for minus three yards and returned two kickoffs for 24 yards, 1986; rushed once for two yards and fumbled twice, 1987.
Played in NFC Championship Game following 1984 season.
Member of San Francisco 49ers for NFL Championship Game following 1984 season; did not play.

ANTHONY RAY FRANKLIN
(Tony)
Placekicker—New England Patriots

Born November 18, 1956, at Big Spring, Tex.
Height, 5.08. Weight, 182.
High School—Fort Worth, Tex., Arlington Heights.
Attended Texas A&M University.

Selected by Philadelphia in 3rd round (74th player selected) of 1979 NFL draft.
Traded by Philadelphia Eagles to New England Patriots for 6th round pick in 1985 draft, February 21, 1984.
Crossed picket line during players' strike, October 7, 1987.

Year Club		——PLACE KICKING——				
	G.	XP.	XPM.	FG.	FGA.	Pts.
1979—Philadelphia NFL ...	16	36	3	23	31	105
1980—Philadelphia NFL ...	16	48	0	16	31	96
1981—Philadelphia NFL ...	16	41	2	20	31	101
1982—Philadelphia NFL ...	9	23	2	6	9	41
1983—Philadelphia NFL ...	16	24	3	15	26	69
1984—New England NFL..	16	42	0	22	28	108
1985—New England NFL..	16	40	1	24	30	112
1986—New England NFL..	16	44	1	*32	*41	*140
1987—New England NFL..	14	37	1	15	26	82
Pro Totals—9 Years.......	135	335	13	173	253	854

Additional pro statistics: Punted once for 32 yards, 1979; punted once for 13 yards, 1981, rushed once for minus five yards, 1985.

Played in NFC Championship Game following 1980 season.
Played in AFC Championship Game following 1985 season.
Played in NFL Championship Game following 1980 and 1985 seasons.
Played in Pro Bowl (NFL All-Star Game) following 1986 season.

BYRON PAUL FRANKLIN
Wide Receiver—Seattle Seahawks
Born September 3, 1958, at Florence, Ala.
Height, 6.01. Weight, 183.
High School—Sheffield, Ala.
Attended Auburn University.

Selected by Buffalo in 2nd round (50th player selected) of 1981 NFL draft.
On injured reserve with sciatic nerve injury, September 6 through entire 1982 season.
Traded by Buffalo Bills to Seattle Seahawks for tight end Pete Metzelaars, August 20, 1985.
On injured reserve with knee injury, December 4 through remainder of 1985 season.
On injured reserve with knee injury, December 10 through remainder of 1986 season.
On physically unable to perform/reserve with knee injury, September 1 through November 15, 1987; activated, November 16, 1987.

Year Club		PASS RECEIVING				—KICKOFF RET.—				—TOTAL—		
	G.	P.C.	Yds.	Avg.	TD.	No.	Yds.	Avg.	TD.	TD.	Pts.	F.
1981—Buffalo NFL............................	13	2	29	14.5	0	21	436	20.8	0	0	0	2
1983—Buffalo NFL............................	15	30	452	15.1	4		None			4	24	0
1984—Buffalo NFL............................	16	69	862	12.5	4		None			4	24	4
1985—Seattle NFL............................	13	10	119	11.9	0		None			0	0	0
1986—Seattle NFL............................	14	33	547	16.6	2		None			2	12	0
1987—Seattle NFL............................	6	1	7	7.0	0		None			0	0	0
Pro Totals—6 Years................	77	145	2016	13.9	10	21	436	20.8	0	10	60	6

Additional pro statistics: Rushed once for minus 11 yards and returned five punts for 45 yards, 1981; rushed once for three yards, 1983; rushed once for minus seven yards, 1984; rushed once for five yards, 1985; rushed once for two yards, 1986.

PATRICK DIJON FRANKLIN
(Pat)
Running Back—San Diego Chargers
Born August 16, 1963, at Bay City, Tex.
Height, 6.01. Weight, 230.
High School—Bay City, Tex.
Attended University of Houston and Southwest Texas State University.
Related to Simon Fletcher, defensive end with Denver Broncos; and Harold Smith, quarterback with Saskatchewan Roughriders of CFL.

Selected by Cincinnati in 7th round (177th player selected) of 1986 NFL draft.
Selected by Orlando in 2nd round (9th player selected) of 1986 USFL draft.
Signed by Cincinnati Bengals, July 24, 1986.
Released by Cincinnati Bengals, September 1, 1986; signed as free agent by Tampa Bay Buccaneers, October 21, 1986.
Released by Tampa Bay Buccaneers, August 31, 1987; awarded on waivers to Indianapolis Colts, September 1, 1987.
Released by Indianapolis Colts, September 7, 1987; signed as free agent replacement player by Cincinnati Bengals, September 25, 1987.
Released by Cincinnati Bengals, October 19, 1987; signed as free agent by San Diego Chargers, May 23, 1988.

Year Club		——RUSHING——				PASS RECEIVING				—TOTAL—		
	G.	Att.	Yds.	Avg.	TD.	P.C.	Yds.	Avg.	TD.	TD.	Pts.	F.
1986—Tampa Bay NFL	8	7	7	1.0	0	7	29	4.1	1	2	12	1
1987—Cincinnati NFL	2		None				None			0	0	0
Pro Totals—2 Years....................	10	7	7	1.0	0	7	29	4.1	1	2	12	1

Additional pro statistics: Recovered one fumble in end zone for a touchdown and returned three kickoffs for 23 yards, 1986.

LORENZO Z. FREEMAN
Nose Tackle-Defensive Tackle—Pittsburgh Steelers
Born May 23, 1964, at East Camden, N.J.
Height, 6.05. Weight, 270.
High School—Camden, N.J., Woodrow Wilson.
Attended University of Pittsburgh.

Selected by Green Bay in 4th round (89th player selected) of 1987 NFL draft.
Signed by Green Bay Packers, July 25, 1987.
On injured reserve with ankle injury, September 7 through September 21, 1987; activated, September 22, 1987.
Released by Green Bay Packers, November 3, 1987; signed as free agent by Pittsburgh Steelers, November 18, 1987.
Pittsburgh NFL, 1987.
Games: 1987 (6).

MICHAEL JOSEPH FREEMAN
(Mike)
Guard—Denver Broncos
Born October 13, 1961, at Mt. Holly, N.J.
Height, 6.03. Weight, 256.
High Schools—Tucson, Ariz., Sahuaro; and Fountain Valley, Calif.
Attended University of Arizona.
Nephew of Bob Freeman, defensive back with Cleveland Browns, Green Bay Packers,
Philadelphia Eagles and Washington Redskins, 1957 through 1962.

Signed as free agent by Denver Broncos, May 2, 1984.
On injured reserve with sprained knee, August 20 through entire 1985 season.
On injured reserve with knee injury, August 25 through November 13, 1986; activated, November 14, 1986.
Released by Denver Broncos, September 7, 1987; re-signed as replacement player by Broncos, September 30, 1987.
Denver NFL, 1984, 1986 and 1987.
Games: 1984 (9), 1986 (4), 1987 (13). Total—26.
Played in AFC Championship Game following 1986 and 1987 seasons.
Played in NFL Championship Game following 1986 and 1987 seasons.

PHILLIP EMERY FREEMAN
(Phil)
Wide Receiver—Tampa Bay Buccaneers
Born December 9, 1962, at St. Paul, Minn.
Height, 5.11. Weight, 185.
High School—Santa Monica, Calif., St. Monica.
Attended University of Arizona.

Selected by Arizona in 1985 USFL territorial draft.
Selected by Tampa Bay in 8th round (204th player selected) of 1985 NFL draft.
Signed by Tampa Bay Buccaneers, June 24, 1985.
On injured reserve with broken wrist, December 10 through remainder of 1985 season.
On injured reserve with knee injury, December 14 through remainder of 1987 season.

		PASS RECEIVING				—KICKOFF RET.—				—TOTAL—		
Year	Club	G.	P.C.	Yds.	Avg.	TD.	No.	Yds.	Avg.	TD.	TD.	Pts.	F.
1985—Tampa Bay NFL	14		None				48	1085	22.6	0	0	0	1
1986—Tampa Bay NFL	15	14	229	16.4	2	31	582	18.8	0	2	12	1
1987—Tampa Bay NFL	8	8	141	17.6	2		None			2	12	1
Pro Totals—3 Years	37	22	370	16.8	4	79	1667	21.1	0	4	24	3

Additional pro statistics: Recovered one fumble, 1986; rushed once for one yard, 1987.

STEVEN JAY FREEMAN
(Steve)
Safety—Minnesota Vikings
Born May 8, 1953, at Lamesa, Tex.
Height, 5.11. Weight, 185.
High School—Memphis, Tenn., Whitehaven.
Received degree in agricultural economics from Mississippi State University.

Named to THE SPORTING NEWS NFL All-Star Team, 1983.
Selected by New England in 5th round (117th player selected) of 1975 NFL draft.
Claimed on waivers from New England Patriots by Buffalo Bills, August 21, 1975.
Traded by Buffalo Bills to Minnesota Vikings for past considerations, March 11, 1987.
Released by Minnesota Vikings, September 7, 1987; re-signed by Vikings, September 8, 1987.

		—INTERCEPTIONS—						—INTERCEPTIONS—			
Year	Club	G.	No.	Yds.	Avg.	TD.	Year	Club	G.	No.	Yds.	Avg.	TD.
1975—Buffalo NFL	14	2	44	22.0	1	1982—Buffalo NFL	9	3	27	9.0	0
1976—Buffalo NFL	14		None			1983—Buffalo NFL	16	3	40	13.3	0
1977—Buffalo NFL	14	1	4	4.0	0	1984—Buffalo NFL	15	3	45	15.0	0
1978—Buffalo NFL	16		None			1985—Buffalo NFL	16		None		
1979—Buffalo NFL	16	3	62	20.7	1	1986—Buffalo NFL	16	1	0	0.0	0
1980—Buffalo NFL	16	7	107	15.3	1	1987—Minnesota NFL	12		None		
1981—Buffalo NFL	16		None			Pro Totals—13 Years	190	23	329	14.3	3

Additional pro statistics: Recovered one fumble, 1975, 1976, 1982 and 1984; recovered two fumbles, 1979; returned one kickoff for no yards, 1981; recovered two fumbles for 31 yards, 1983.
Played in NFC Championship Game following 1987 season.

PAUL MITCHAEL FREROTTE
(Name pronounced Fur-ROT.)
Guard—Buffalo Bills
Born March 30, 1965, at Kittanning, Pa.
Height, 6.03. Weight, 280.
High School—Kittanning, Pa.
Attended Penn State University.

Signed as free agent by Buffalo Bills, July 22, 1987.
Buffalo NFL, 1987.
Games: 1987 (12).

WILLIAM JASPER FRIZZELL
Safety—Philadelphia Eagles
Born September 8, 1962, at Greenville, N.C.
Height, 6.03. Weight, 205.
High School—Greenville, N.C., J.H. Rose.
Attended North Carolina Central University.

Selected by Detroit in 10th round (259th player selected) of 1984 NFL draft.
On injured reserve with ankle injury, September 2 through November 1, 1985; activated, November 2, 1985.
Released by Detroit Lions, August 26, 1986; signed as free agent by Philadelphia Eagles, October 8, 1986.
Released by Philadelphia Eagles, November 6, 1986; re-signed by Eagles, November 26, 1986.
Detroit NFL, 1984 and 1985; Philadelphia NFL, 1986 and 1987.
Games: 1984 (16), 1985 (8), 1986 (8), 1987 (12). Total—44.
Pro statistics: Intercepted one pass for three yards, 1985; recovered one fumble, 1987.

IRVING DALE FRYAR
Wide Receiver-Kick Returner—New England Patriots
Born September 28, 1962, at Mount Holly, N.J.
Height, 6.00. Weight, 200.
High School—Mount Holly, N.J., Rancocas Valley Regional.
Attended University of Nebraska.
Cousin of Charles Fryar, cornerback at University of Nebraska.

Named as wide receiver on THE SPORTING NEWS College All-America Team, 1983.
Selected by Chicago in 1st round (3rd player selected) of 1984 USFL draft.
Signed by New England Patriots, April 11, 1984.
Selected officially by New England in 1st round (1st player selected) of 1984 NFL draft.

| | | —RUSHING— | | | | PASS RECEIVING | | | | —TOTAL— | | |
Year Club	G.	Att.	Yds.	Avg.	TD.	P.C.	Yds.	Avg.	TD.	TD.	Pts.	F.
1984—New England NFL	14	2	—11	—5.5	0	11	164	14.9	1	1	6	4
1985—New England NFL	16	7	27	3.9	1	39	670	17.2	7	10	60	4
1986—New England NFL	14	4	80	20.0	0	43	737	17.1	6	7	42	4
1987—New England NFL	12	9	52	5.8	0	31	467	15.1	5	5	30	2
Pro Totals—4 Years	56	22	148	6.7	1	124	2038	16.4	19	23	138	14

| | | —PUNT RETURNS— | | | | —KICKOFF RET.— | | |
Year Club	G.	No.	Yds.	Avg.	TD.	No.	Yds.	Avg.TD.
1984—New England NFL	14	36	347	9.6	0	5	95	19.0 0
1985—New England NFL	16	37	520	★14.1	★2	3	39	13.0 0
1986—New England NFL	14	35	366	10.5	1	10	192	19.2 0
1987—New England NFL	12	18	174	9.7	0	6	119	19.8 0
Pro Totals—4 Years	56	126	1407	11.2	3	24	445	18.5 0

Additional pro statistics: Recovered one fumble, 1984 and 1986.
Played in NFL Championship Game following 1985 season.
Played in Pro Bowl (NFL All-Star Game) following 1985 season.

DAVID FRYE
(Dave)
Linebacker—Miami Dolphins
Born June 21, 1961, at Cincinnati, O.
Height, 6.02. Weight, 227.
High School—Cincinnati, O., Woodward.
Attended Santa Ana College and Purdue University.

Signed as free agent by Atlanta Falcons, May 9, 1983.
On non-football injury list with drug problem, September 27 through October 8, 1985; activated, October 9, 1985.
Released by Atlanta Falcons, August 26, 1986; signed as free agent by Miami Dolphins, October 24, 1986.
Atlanta NFL, 1983 through 1985; Miami NFL, 1986 and 1987.
Games: 1983 (16), 1984 (16), 1985 (14), 1986 (9), 1987 (12). Total—67.
Pro statistics: Recovered two fumbles, 1983 and 1984; intercepted one pass for 20 yards and recovered one fumble for 13 yards, 1985; recovered one fumble, 1986.

DAVID DWAYNE FULCHER
Safety—Cincinnati Bengals
Born September 28, 1964, at Los Angeles, Calif.
Height, 6.03. Weight, 228.
High School—Los Angeles, Calif., John C. Fremont.
Attended Arizona State University.

Named as defensive back on THE SPORTING NEWS College All-America Team, 1984 and 1985.
Selected by Cincinnati in 3rd round (78th player selected) of 1986 NFL draft.
Selected by Arizona in 1986 USFL supplemental territorial draft.
Signed by Cincinnati Bengals, July 19, 1986.
On injured reserve with back injury, December 26 through remainder of 1987 season.

			—INTERCEPTIONS—		
Year	Club	G.	No.	Yds.	Avg. TD.
1986—Cincinnati NFL		16	4	20	5.0 0
1987—Cincinnati NFL		11	3	30	10.0 0
Pro Totals—2 Years		27	7	50	7.1 0

Additional pro statistics: Recovered one fumble, 1986 and 1987; returned one kickoff for no yards, 1987.

SCOTT ALAN FULHAGE
Punter—Cincinnati Bengals
Born November 17, 1961, at Beloit, Kan.
Height, 5.11. Weight, 191.
High School—Beloit, Kan.
Received bachelor of science degree in agricultural economics
from Kansas State University in 1985.

Signed as free agent by Buffalo Bills, June 20, 1985.
Released by Buffalo Bills, August 5, 1985; signed as free agent by Washington Redskins, June 29, 1986.
Released by Washington Redskins, August 18, 1986; signed as free agent by Cincinnati Bengals, February 4, 1987.
Released by Cincinnati Bengals, September 7, 1987; re-signed as replacement player by Bengals, September 25, 1987.
Released by Cincinnati Bengals, October 19, 1987; awarded on waivers to Green Bay Packers, October 20, 1987.
Released by Green Bay Packers, November 3, 1987; signed as free agent by Cincinnati Bengals, November 5, 1987.

			—PUNTING—		
Year	Club	G.	No.	Avg.	Blk.
1987—Cincinnati NFL		11	52	41.7	0

JEFFERY AVERY FULLER
(Jeff)
Safety-Linebacker—San Francisco 49ers
Born August 8, 1962, at Dallas, Tex.
Height, 6.02. Weight, 216.
High School—Dallas, Tex., Franklin D. Roosevelt.
Attended Texas A&M University.

Selected by Houston in 1984 USFL territorial draft.
Selected by San Francisco in 5th round (139th player selected) of 1984 NFL draft.
Signed by San Francisco 49ers, May 29, 1984.
On injured reserve with knee injury, September 10 through November 21, 1986; activated, November 22, 1986.
Crossed picket line during players' strike, October 7, 1987.

			—INTERCEPTIONS—		
Year	Club	G.	No.	Yds.	Avg. TD.
1984—San Francisco NFL		13	1	38	38.0 0
1985—San Francisco NFL		16	1	4	4.0 0
1986—San Francisco NFL		6	4	44	11.0 0
1987—San Francisco NFL		14		None	
Pro Totals—4 Years		49	6	86	14.3 0

Additional pro statistics: Recovered one fumble and fumbled twice, 1986; credited with a safety and recovered three fumbles, 1987.
Played in NFC Championship Game following 1984 season.
Played in NFL Championship Game following 1984 season.

STEPHEN RAY FULLER
(Steve)
Quarterback—San Diego Chargers
Born January 5, 1957, at Enid, Okla.
Height, 6.04. Weight, 198.
High School—Spartanburg, S.C.
Received degree from Clemson University.

Selected by Kansas City in 1st round (23rd player selected) of 1979 NFL draft.
On injured reserve with knee injury, December 18 through remainder of 1980 season.
Traded by Kansas City Chiefs to Los Angeles Rams for cornerback Lucious Smith and 5th round pick in 1985 draft, August 19, 1983.
Traded by Los Angeles Rams to Chicago Bears for 11th round pick in 1984 draft and 6th round pick in 1985 draft, April 30, 1984.
On injured reserve with separated shoulder, August 28 through October 5, 1984; activated, October 6, 1984.
On physically unable to perform/reserve with shoulder injury, August 27 through entire 1987 season.
Released by Chicago Bears, February 23, 1988; signed as free agent by San Diego Chargers, May 10, 1988.
Active for 16 games with Los Angeles Rams in 1983; did not play.

			—PASSING—						—RUSHING—				—TOTAL—		
Year	Club	G.	Att.	Cmp.	Pct.	Gain	T.P.	P.I.	Avg.	Att.	Yds.	Avg.	TD.	TD.	Pts.	F.
1979—Kansas City NFL		16	270	146	54.1	1484	6	14	5.50	50	264	5.3	1	1	6	6
1980—Kansas City NFL		14	320	193	60.3	2250	10	12	7.03	60	274	4.6	4	4	24	*16

Year Club	G.	Att.	Cmp.	Pct.	Gain	T.P.	P.I.	Avg.	Att.	Yds.	Avg.	TD.	TD.	Pts.	F.
				PASSING						RUSHING			TOTAL		
1981—Kansas City NFL	13	134	77	57.5	934	3	4	6.97	19	118	6.2	0	0	0	4
1982—Kansas City NFL	9	93	49	52.7	665	3	2	7.15	10	56	5.6	0	0	0	3
1984—Chicago NFL	6	78	53	67.9	595	3	0	7.63	15	89	5.9	1	1	6	0
1985—Chicago NFL	16	107	53	49.5	777	1	5	7.26	24	77	3.2	5	5	30	3
1986—Chicago NFL	16	64	34	53.1	451	2	4	7.05	8	30	3.8	0	0	0	2
Pro Totals—8 Years	90	1066	605	56.8	7156	28	41	6.71	186	908	4.9	11	11	66	34

Quarterback Rating Points: 1979 (55.8), 1980 (76.1), 1981 (73.9), 1982 (77.3), 1984 (103.3), 1985 (57.3), 1986 (60.1). Total—70.2.

Additional pro statistics: Recovered three fumbles and fumbled six times for minus four yards, 1979; recovered seven fumbles and fumbled 16 times for minus 43 yards, 1980; recovered one fumble and fumbled four times for minus six yards, 1981; recovered two fumbles, 1982; recovered one fumble and fumbled three times for minus 15 yards, 1985; recovered one fumble and fumbled twice for minus three yards, 1986.

Played in NFL Championship Game following 1984 and 1985 seasons.
Played in NFL Championship Game following 1985 season.

WILLIAM HENRY FULLER JR.
Defensive End—Houston Oilers
Born March 8, 1962, at Norfolk, Va.
Height, 6.03. Weight, 258.
High School—Chesapeake, Va., Indian River.
Attended University of North Carolina.

Named as defensive tackle on THE SPORTING NEWS College All-America Team, 1983.
Named as defensive end on THE SPORTING NEWS USFL All-Star Team, 1985.
Selected by Philadelphia in 1984 USFL territorial draft.
Signed by Philadelphia Stars, February 6, 1984.
On injured reserve with fractured ankle, May 18 through June 22, 1984; activated, June 23, 1984.
Selected by Los Angeles Rams in 1st round (21st player selected) of 1984 NFL supplemental draft.
Franchise transferred to Baltimore, November 1, 1984.
Granted free agency when USFL suspended operations, August 7, 1986; signed by Los Angeles Rams, September 10, 1986.
Traded with guard Kent Hill, 1st and 5th round picks in 1987 draft and 1st round pick in 1988 draft by Los Angeles Rams to Houston Oilers for rights to quarterback Jim Everett, September 8, 1986.
Granted roster exemption, September 18 through September 21, 1986; activated, September 22, 1986.
Philadelphia USFL, 1984; Baltimore USFL, 1985; Houston NFL, 1986 and 1987.
Games: 1984 (13), 1985 (18), 1986 (13), 1987 (12). Total USFL—31. Total NFL—25. Total Pro—56.
USFL statistics: Credited with two sacks for 18 yards and recovered one fumble, 1984; credited with 8½ sacks for 102 yards, intercepted one pass for 35 yards and recovered four fumbles for 17 yards, 1985.
NFL statistics: Recovered one fumble and returned one kickoff for no yards, 1987.
Played in USFL Championship Game following 1984 and 1985 seasons.

BRENT LANARD FULLWOOD
Running Back—Green Bay Packers
Born October 10, 1963, at Kissimmee, Fla.
Height, 5.11. Weight, 209.
High School—St. Cloud, Fla.
Attended Auburn University.

Named as running back on THE SPORTING NEWS College All-America Team, 1986.
Selected by Green Bay Packers in 1st round (4th player selected) of 1987 NFL draft.
Signed by Green Bay Packers, August 4, 1987.

Year Club	G.	Att.	Yds.	Avg.	TD.	P.C.	Yds.	Avg.	TD.	TD.	Pts.	F.
			RUSHING			PASS RECEIVING				TOTAL		
1987—Green Bay NFL	11	84	274	3.3	5	2	11	5.5	0	5	30	2

Year Club	G.	No.	Yds.	Avg.TD.
		KICKOFF RETURNS		
1987—Green Bay NFL	11	24	510	21.3 0

Additional pro statistics: Recovered one fumble, 1987.

ANTHONY JOSEPH FURJANIC
(Tony)
Linebacker—Buffalo Bills
Born February 26, 1964, at Chicago, Ill.
Height, 6.01. Weight, 228.
High School—Chicago, Ill., Mt. Carmel.
Received bachelor of business administration degree in marketing from
University of Notre Dame in 1986.

Selected by Orlando in 1986 USFL territorial draft.
Selected by Buffalo in 8th round (202nd player selected) of 1986 NFL draft.
Signed by Buffalo Bills, July 23, 1986.
Released by Buffalo Bills, September 7, 1987; re-signed by Bills, October 20, 1987.
Buffalo NFL, 1986 and 1987.
Games: 1986 (14), 1987 (8). Total—22.

BOBBY LEE FUTRELL

Name pronounced Few-TRELL.

Defensive Back—Tampa Bay Buccaneers

Born August 4, 1962, at Ahoskie, N.C.
Height, 5.11. Weight, 190.
High School—Ahoskie, N.C.
Attended Elizabeth City State University.

Selected by Michigan in 5th round (93rd player selected) of 1984 USFL draft.
Signed by Michigan Panthers, January 23, 1984.
Not protected in merger of Michigan Panthers and Oakland Invaders; selected by Tampa Bay Bandits in USFL dispersal draft, December 6, 1984.
Released by Tampa Bay Bandits, February 18, 1985; re-signed by Bandits, February 19, 1985.
Released by Tampa Bay Bandits, April 19, 1985; awarded on waivers to Oakland Invaders, April 23, 1985.
On developmental squad, May 23 through June 14, 1985; activated, June 15, 1985.
Released by Oakland Invaders, August 2, 1985; signed as free agent by Tampa Bay Buccaneers, April 2, 1986.
On developmental squad for 3 games with Oakland Invaders in 1985.

Year Club	G.	INTERCEPTIONS				-PUNT RETURNS-				—KICKOFF RET.—				—TOTAL—		
		No.	Yds.	Avg.	TD.	No.	Yds.	Avg.	TD.	No.	Yds.	Avg.	TD.	TD.	Pts.	F.
1984—Michigan USFL............	18	1	29	29.0	0	3	17	5.7	0	27	576	21.3	0	0	0	4
1985—TB (8)-Oak. (6) USFL..	14			None				None		10	199	19.9	0	0	0	0
1986—Tampa Bay NFL.........	16			None		14	67	4.8	0	5	115	23.0	0	0	0	1
1987—Tampa Bay NFL.........	12	2	46	23.0	0	24	213	8.9	0	31	609	19.6	0	0	0	2
USFL Totals—2 Years....	32	1	29	29.0	0	3	17	5.7	0	37	775	20.9	0	0	0	4
NFL Totals—2 Years.....	28	2	46	23.0	0	38	280	7.4	0	36	724	20.1	0	0	0	3
Pro Totals—4 Years.......	60	3	75	25.0	0	41	297	7.2	0	73	1499	20.5	0	0	0	7

Additional USFL statistics: Recovered two fumbles, 1984.
Additional NFL statistics: Recovered one fumble, 1986; recovered two fumbles, 1987.
On developmental squad for USFL Championship Game following 1985 season.

DENNIS RICHARD GADBOIS

Wide Receiver—New England Patriots

Born September 18, 1963, at Biddleford, Me.
Height, 6.01. Weight, 185.
High School—Biddleford, Me.
Attended Boston University.

Signed as free agent by New England Patriots, May 5, 1987.
Released by New England Patriots, August 25, 1987; re-signed as replacement player by Patriots, September 24, 1987.
Released by New England Patriots, October 23, 1987; re-signed by Patriots, December 2, 1987.
New England NFL, 1987.
Games: 1987 (3).
Pro statistics: Caught three passes for 51 yards, 1987.

STEVE GAGE

Safety—Washington Redskins

Born May 10, 1964, at Claremore, Okla.
Height, 6.03. Weight, 210.
High School—Claremore, Okla.
Attended The University of Tulsa.

Selected by Washington in 6th round (144th player selected) of 1987 NFL draft.
Signed by Washington Redskins, July 26, 1987.
Released by Washington Redskins, September 7, 1987; re-signed as replacement player by Redskins, October 8, 1987.
On injured reserve, January 9, 1988 through remainder of 1987 season playoffs.
Washington NFL, 1987.
Games: 1987 (4).
Pro statistics: Intercepted one pass for seven yards, 1987.

ROBERT FRANK GAGLIANO

(Bob)

Quarterback—San Francisco 49ers

Born September 5, 1958, at Los Angeles, Calif.
Height, 6.03. Weight, 195.
High School—Glendale, Calif., Hoover.
Attended Glendale Junior College, U.S. International
University and Utah State University.

Selected by Kansas City in 12th round (319th player selected) of 1981 NFL draft.
Released by Kansas City Chiefs, August 25, 1981; re-signed by Chiefs, August 27, 1981.
On inactive list, September 12 and September 19, 1982.
USFL rights traded with rights to wide receiver Dave Dorn by New Jersey Generals to Chicago Blitz for rights to offensive tackle Jeff Weston and linebacker Bobby Leopold, November 23, 1983.
USFL rights traded by Chicago Blitz to San Antonio Gunslingers for defensive tackle Broderick Thompson and 1st round pick in 1984 draft, January 3, 1984.
Signed by San Antonio Gunslingers, January 6, 1984, for contract to take effect after being granted free agency, February 1, 1984.

Traded by San Antonio Gunslingers to Denver Gold or linebacker Putt Choate and 9th round pick in 1985 draft, February 13, 1984.
On developmental squad, February 24 through March 16, 1984; activated, March 17, 1984.
On developmental squad, April 28 through May 24, 1984; activated, May 25, 1984.
On developmental squad, June 2 through June 7, 1984; activated June 8, 1984.
On developmental squad, June 15 through remainder of 1984 season.
Franchise merged with Jacksonville Bulls, February 19, 1986.
Released by Jacksonville Bulls, March 18, 1986; signed as free agent by San Francisco 49ers, October 29, 1986.
Released by San Francisco 49ers, November 7, 1986; re-signed by 49ers for 1987, November 13, 1986.
Released by San Francisco 49ers, September 7, 1987; re-signed as replacement player by 49ers, September 24, 1987.
On developmental squad for 10 games with Denver Gold in 1984.
Active for 16 games with Kansas City Chiefs in 1981; did not play.
Active for 1 game with San Francisco 49ers in 1986; did not play.

Year Club	G.	Att.	Cmp.	Pct.	Gain	T.P.	P.I.	Avg.	Att.	Yds.	Avg.	TD.	TD.	Pts.	F.
					PASSING					RUSHING			TOTAL		
1982—Kansas City NFL..............	1	1	1	100.0	7	0	0	7.00		None			0	0	0
1983—Kansas City NFL..............	1				None					None			0	0	0
1984—Denver USFL	8	31	20	64.5	236	2	1	7.61	1	7	7.0	0	0	†2	2
1985—Denver USFL	18	358	205	57.3	2695	13	17	7.53	34	111	3.3	2	2	12	5
1987—San Francisco NFL	3	29	16	55.2	229	1	1	7.90		None			0	0	0
NFL Totals—5 Years........	5	30	17	56.7	236	1	1	7.87	0	0	0.0	0	0	0	0
USFL Totals—2 Years.......	26	389	225	57.8	2931	15	18	7.53	35	118	3.4	2	2	14	7
Pro Totals—7 Years...........	31	419	242	57.8	3167	16	19	7.56	35	118	3.4	2	2	14	7

†Includes one 2-point conversion.
Additional pro statistics: Recovered two fumbles, 1984, recovered three fumbles, 1985.
USFL Quarterback Rating Points: 1984 (95.6), 1985 (73.5). Total—75.5.
NFL Quarterback Rating Points: 1987 (78.1).

GREGORY SCOTT GAINES
(Greg)
Linebacker—Seattle Seahawks
Born October 16, 1958, at Martinsville, Va.
Height, 6.03. Weight, 220.
High School—Hermitage, Tenn., DuPont.
Attended University of Tennessee.
Nephew of Ray Oldham, safety with Baltimore Colts, Pittsburgh Steelers,
New York Giants and Detroit Lions, 1973 through 1982; and brother of Chris Gaines,
rookie linebacker with Phoenix Cardinals.
Signed as free agent by Seattle Seahawks, May 6, 1981.
On injured reserve with knee injury, October 28 through remainder of 1981 season.
On injured reserve with knee injury, August 31 through entire 1982 season.
Seattle NFL, 1981 and 1983 through 1987.
Games: 1981 (8), 1983 (16), 1984 (16), 1985 (16), 1986 (16), 1987 (11). Total—83.
Pro statistics: Recovered one fumble, 1981, 1986 and 1987; recovered four fumbles, 1983; intercepted one pass for 18 yards, 1984; recovered two fumbles for seven yards, 1985; intercepted one pass for eight yards, 1986.
Played in AFC Championship Game following 1983 season.

JIM PATRICK GALLERY
Placekicker—Phoenix Cardinals
Born September 15, 1961, at Morton, Minn.
Height, 6.01. Weight, 190.
High School—Morton, Minn.
Attended University of Minnesota.
Selected by Tampa Bay in 10th round (254th player selected) of 1984 NFL draft.
NFL rights released by Tampa Bay Buccaneers, July 5, 1984; signed as free agent by Buffalo Bills, July 9, 1984.
Released by Buffalo Bills, August 14, 1984; re-signed by Bills, May 10, 1985.
Released by Buffalo Bills, August 5, 1985.
USFL rights traded by Birmingham Stallions to Arizona Outlaws for past considerations, June 23, 1986.
Signed as free agent by New England Patriots, May 9, 1987.
Released by New England Patriots, September 7, 1987; awarded on waivers to St. Louis Cardinals, September 8, 1987.
Crossed picket line during players' strike, October 14, 1987.
Franchise transferred to Phoenix, March 15, 1988.

Year Club	G.	XP.	XPM.	FG.	FGA.	Pts.
			PLACE KICKING			
1987—St. Louis NFL............	13	30	1	9	19	57

DAVID LAWRENCE GALLOWAY
Defensive End—Phoenix Cardinals
Born February 16, 1959, at Tampa, Fla.
Height, 6.03. Weight, 277.
High School—Brandon, Fla.
Attended University of Florida.
Selected by St. Louis in 2nd round (38th player selected) of 1982 NFL draft.
On injured reserve with dislocated elbow, September 8 through November 30, 1982; activated, December 1, 1982.
On injured reserve with broken arm, September 1 through December 4, 1987; activated, December 5, 1987.

Franchise transferred to Phoenix, March 15, 1988.
St. Louis NFL, 1982 through 1987.
Games: 1982 (5), 1983 (16), 1984 (14), 1985 (16), 1986 (14), 1987 (4). Total—69.
Pro statistics: Intercepted one pass for 17 yards and credited with one safety, 1983; recovered one fumble, 1983 and 1985; recovered two fumbles, 1986.

DUANE KEITH GALLOWAY
Defensive Back—Detroit Lions

Born November 7, 1961, at Los Angeles, Calif.
Height, 5.08. Weight 181.
High School—Los Angeles, Calif., Crenshaw.
Attended Santa Monica City College and Arizona State University.

Selected by Los Angeles in 19th round (217th player selected) of 1983 USFL draft.
Signed by Los Angeles Express, January 26, 1983.
Released by Los Angeles Express, February 20, 1983; signed as free agent by Saskatchewan Roughriders, March 15, 1983.
Released by Saskatchewan Roughriders, June 28, 1983; re-signed by Roughriders, July 27, 1983.
Released by Saskatchewan Roughriders, September 11, 1983; signed as free agent by Indianapolis Colts, May 15, 1984.
On injured reserve with thigh injury, August 13 through September 17, 1984.
Released by Indianapolis Colts, September 18, 1984; signed as free agent by Detroit Lions, May 9, 1985.
On injured reserve with broken arm, September 10 through December 20, 1985; activated, December 21, 1985.

			—INTERCEPTIONS—			
Year	Club	G.	No.	Yds.	Avg.	TD.
1983—Saskatchewan CFL		6		None		
1985—Detroit NFL		2		None		
1986—Detroit NFL		16	4	58	14.5	0
1987—Detroit NFL		10	3	46	15.3	0
CFL Totals—1 Year		6	0	0	0.0	0
NFL Totals—3 Years		28	7	104	14.9	0
Pro Totals—4 Years		34	7	104	14.9	0

Additional pro statistics: Recovered one fumble, 1986.

VINCENT LUCKY GAMACHE
(Vince)
Punter—San Francisco 49ers

Born November 18, 1961, at Los Angeles, Calif.
Height, 5.11. Weight, 176.
High School—Los Angeles, Calif., Venice.
Attended California State University at Fullerton.

Signed as free agent by Los Angeles Raiders, July 10, 1985.
Released by Los Angeles Raiders, July 24, 1985; signed as free agent by Seattle Seahawks, April 15, 1986.
Released by Seattle Seahawks, September 1, 1987; signed as free agent replacement player by Los Angeles Raiders, September 24, 1987.
Released by Los Angeles Raiders, October 21, 1987; signed as free agent by San Francisco 49ers for 1988, December 8, 1987.

			—PUNTING—		
Year	Club	G.	No.	Avg.	Blk.
1986—Seattle NFL		16	79	38.6	0
1987—L.A. Raiders NFL		3	13	39.9	1
Pro Totals—2 Years		19	92	38.8	1

MIKE ALAN GANN
Defensive End—Atlanta Falcons

Born October 19, 1963, at Stillwater, Okla.
Height, 6.05. Weight, 275.
High School—Lakewood, Colo.
Received bachelor of business administration degree
from University of Notre Dame in 1985.

Selected by Tampa Bay in 1st round (12th player selected) of 1985 USFL draft.
Selected by Atlanta in 2nd round (45th player selected) of 1985 NFL draft.
Signed by Atlanta Falcons, July 23, 1985.
Atlanta NFL, 1985 through 1987.
Games: 1985 (16), 1986 (16), 1987 (12). Total—44.
Pro statistics: Recovered one fumble for 42 yards and a touchdown, 1985; credited with a safety and recovered three fumbles for 12 yards, 1986.

RICHARD JOSEPH GANNON
(Rich)
Quarterback—Minnesota Vikings

Born December 20, 1965, at Philadelphia, Pa.
Height, 6.03. Weight, 197.
High School—Philadelphia, Pa., St. Joseph's Prep.
Received degree in criminal justice from University of Delaware in 1987.

Selected by New England in 4th round (98th player selected) of 1987 NFL draft.
Rights traded by New England Patriots to Minnesota Vikings for 4th and 11th round picks in 1988 draft, May 6, 1987.
Signed by Minnesota Vikings, July 30, 1987.
Minnesota NFL, 1987.
Games: 1987 (4).
Pro statistics: Attempted six passes with two completions for 18 yards and one interception, 1987.
Member of Minnesota Vikings for NFC Championship Game following 1987 season; did not play.

BRIAN KEITH GANT
Linebacker—Tampa Bay Buccaneers
Born September 6, 1965, at Gary, Ind.
Height, 6.00. Weight, 235.
High School—Gary, Ind., Roosevelt.
Attended Illinois State University.

Signed as free agent by Tampa Bay Buccaneers, May 4, 1987.
Released by Tampa Bay Buccaneers, August 31, 1987; re-signed as replacement player by Buccaneers, September 24, 1987.
Tampa Bay NFL, 1987.
Games: 1987 (11).
Pro statistics: Intercepted one pass for five yards, 1987.

MARK PATRICK GARALCZYK
(Name pronounced Guh-RAL-chik.)
Defensive Tackle—Phoenix Cardinals
Born August 12, 1965, at Roseville, Mich.
Height, 6.05. Weight, 272.
High School—Fraser, Mich.
Received bachelor of science degree in communications
from Western Michigan University in 1987.

Selected by St. Louis in 6th round (146th player selected) of 1987 NFL draft.
Signed by St. Louis Cardinals, June 9, 1987.
On injured reserve with pulled thigh muscle, September 7 through September 28, 1987; activated, September 29, 1987.
Crossed picket line during players' strike, September 29, 1987.
Franchise transferred to Phoenix, March 15, 1988.
St. Louis NFL, 1987.
Games: 1987 (11).
Pro statistics: Recovered one fumble, 1987.

HAL E. GARNER JR.
Linebacker—Buffalo Bills
Born January 18, 1962, at New Iberia, La.
Height, 6.04. Weight, 235.
High School—Logan, Utah.
Attended Utah State University.

Selected by Baltimore in 3rd round (44th player selected) of 1985 USFL draft.
Selected by Buffalo in 3rd round (63rd player selected) of 1985 NFL draft.
Signed by Buffalo Bills, July 19, 1985.
On injured reserve with toe injury, December 6 through remainder of 1985 season.
On injured reserve with knee injury, September 1 through entire 1987 season.
Buffalo NFL, 1985 and 1986.
Games: 1985 (13), 1986 (16). Total—29.

GREGG DAVID GARRITY
Wide Receiver—Philadelphia Eagles
Born November 24, 1961, at Pittsburgh, Pa.
Height, 5.10. Weight, 171.
High School—Wexford, Pa., North Allegheny.
Received bachelor of science degree in industrial arts education
from Penn State University in 1983.

Selected by Philadelphia in 1983 USFL territorial draft.
Selected by Pittsburgh in 5th round (140th player selected) of 1983 NFL draft.
Signed by Pittsburgh Steelers, May 20, 1983.
Released by Pittsburgh Steelers, October 23, 1984; awarded on waivers to Philadelphia Eagles, October 24, 1984.
On injured reserve with broken finger, August 19 through September 24, 1986; activated after clearing procedural waivers, September 26, 1986.

| Year Club | G. | —PASS RECEIVING— | | | | —PUNT RETURNS— | | | | —TOTAL— | | |
		P.C.	Yds.	Avg.	TD.	No.	Yds.	Avg.	TD.	TD.	Pts.	F.
1983—Pittsburgh NFL	15	19	279	14.7	1	None				0	0	1
1984—Pitt. (6)-Phi. (4) NFL	10	2	22	11.0	0	None				0	0	0
1985—Philadelphia NFL	12	7	142	20.3	0	None				0	0	0
1986—Philadelphia NFL	12	12	227	18.9	0	17	187	11.0	1	1	6	0
1987—Philadelphia NFL	12	12	242	20.2	2	4	16	4.0	0	2	12	2
Pro Totals—5 Years	61	52	912	17.5	3	21	203	9.7	1	4	24	3

Additional pro statistics: Recovered one fumble, 1983.

KEITH JERROLD GARY
Defensive End—Pittsburgh Steelers
Born September 14, 1959, at Bethesda, Md.
Height, 6.03. Weight, 260.
High School—Fairfax, Va., Chantilly.
Attended Ferrum Junior College and University of Oklahoma.
Selected by Pittsburgh in 1st round (17th player selected) of 1981 NFL draft.
Signed by Montreal Alouettes, July 7, 1981.
On reserve, August 30 through September 4, 1982.
On injured list, September 5 through remainder of 1982 season.
Granted free agency, March 11, 1983; signed by Pittsburgh Steelers, April 15, 1983.
On injured reserve with hamstring and knee injuries, October 22 through November 22, 1985; activated, November 23, 1985.
Montreal CFL, 1981 and 1982; Pittsburgh NFL, 1983 through 1987.
Games: 1981 (13), 1982 (7), 1983 (16), 1984 (16), 1985 (12), 1986 (16), 1987 (11). Total CFL—20. Total NFL—71. Total Pro—91.
CFL statistics: Recovered one fumble for 20 yards, 1982.
NFL statistics: Recovered two fumbles for 17 yards, 1983; recovered one fumble for six yards, 1984; recovered one fumble, 1985.
Played in AFC Championship Game following 1984 season.

RUSSELL CRAIG GARY
Safety—Philadelphia Eagles
Born July 31, 1959, at Minneapolis, Minn.
Height, 5.11. Weight, 200.
High School—Minneapolis, Minn., Central.
Attended University of Nebraska.
Selected by New Orleans in 2nd round (29th player selected) of 1981 NFL draft.
On injured reserve with knee injury, September 25 through remainder of 1985 season.
Released by New Orleans Saints, October 28, 1986; awarded on waivers to Philadelphia Eagles, October 29, 1986.
Released by Philadelphia Eagles, December 8, 1986; re-signed by Eagles, July 28, 1987.

| | | | —INTERCEPTIONS— | | |
Year Club	G.	No.	Yds.	Avg.	TD.
1981—New Orleans NFL	14	1	0	0.0	0
1982—New Orleans NFL	9	2	25	12.5	0
1983—New Orleans NFL	14	3	70	23.3	0
1984—New Orleans NFL	16		None		
1985—New Orleans NFL	2		None		
1986—N.O. (7)-Phi. (6) NFL...	13	1	14	14.0	0
1987—Philadelphia NFL	12		None		
Pro Totals—7 Years	80	7	109	15.6	0

Additional pro statistics: Recovered two fumbles, 1982; fumbled once, 1983; recovered one fumble for five yards, 1984; recovered one fumble for 19 yards, 1987.

MARCUS D. GASTINEAU
Name pronounced GAS-tin-oh.
(Mark)
Defensive End—New York Jets
Born November 20, 1956, at Ardmore, Okla.
Height, 6.05. Weight, 255.
High School—Springerville, Ariz., Round Valley.
Attended Eastern Arizona Junior College, Arizona State University and
East Central (Okla.) University
Son of Ernie Gastineau, former professional boxer.
Named to THE SPORTING NEWS NFL All-Star Team, 1984 and 1985.
Selected by New York Jets in 2nd round (41st player selected) of 1979 NFL draft.
On injured reserve with knee injury, November 20 through December 25, 1986; activated, December 26, 1986.
Crossed picket line during players' strike, September 23, 1987.
New York Jets NFL, 1979 through 1987.
Games: 1979 (16), 1980 (16), 1981 (16), 1982 (9), 1983 (16), 1984 (16), 1985 (16), 1986 (10), 1987 (15). Total—130.
Pro statistics: Recovered two fumbles, 1981; recovered two fumbles (including one in end zone for a touchdown), 1983; recovered one fumble in end zone for a touchdown, 1984; recovered three fumbles, 1985.
Played in AFC Championship Game following 1982 season.
Played in Pro Bowl (NFL All-Star Game) following 1981 through 1985 seasons.

WILLIE JAMES GAULT
Wide Receiver—Chicago Bears
Born September 5, 1960, at Griffin, Ga.
Height, 6.01. Weight, 183.
High School—Griffin, Ga.
Attended University of Tennessee.
Selected by New Jersey in 1983 USFL territorial draft.
Selected by Chicago in 1st round (18th player selected) of 1983 NFL draft.
Signed by Chicago Bears, August 16, 1983.

Year Club	G.	RUSHING				PASS RECEIVING				TOTAL		
		Att.	Yds.	Avg.	TD.	P.C.	Yds.	Avg.	TD.	TD.	Pts.	F.
1983—Chicago NFL	16	4	31	7.8	0	40	836	20.9	8	8	48	1
1984—Chicago NFL	16		None			34	587	17.3	6	6	36	1
1985—Chicago NFL	16	5	18	3.6	0	33	704	21.3	1	2	12	0
1986--Chicago NFL	16	8	79	9.9	0	42	818	19.5	5	5	30	1
1987—Chicago NFL	12	2	16	8.0	0	35	705	20.1	7	7	42	0
Pro Totals—5 Years	76	19	144	7.6	0	184	3650	19.8	27	28	168	3

Year Club	G.	KICKOFF RETURNS			
		No.	Yds.	Avg.	TD.
1983—Chicago NFL	16	13	276	21.2	0
1984—Chicago NFL	16	1	12	12.0	0
1985—Chicago NFL	16	22	577	26.2	1
1986—Chicago NFL	16	1	20	20.0	0
1987—Chicago NFL	12		None		
Pro Totals—5 Years	76	37	885	23.9	1

Additional pro statistics: Returned nine punts for 60 yards, 1983; recovered one fumble, 1983 and 1987.
Played in NFC Championship Game following 1984 and 1985 seasons.
Played in NFL Championship Game following 1985 season.

WILLIAM H. GAY
(Bill)
Defensive End—Minnesota Vikings
Born May 28, 1955, at San Francisco, Calif.
Height, 6.05. Weight, 260.
High School—San Diego, Calif., Herbert Hoover.
Attended San Diego City College and University of Southern California.
Related to Dwight McDonald, wide receiver with San Diego Chargers, 1975 through 1978.

Selected by Denver in 2nd round (55th player selected) of 1978 NFL draft.
Traded by Denver Broncos to Detroit Lions for defensive back Charlie West and 6th round pick in 1979 draft, August 14, 1978.
Crossed picket line during players' strike, October 14, 1987.
Granted free agency with no qualifying offer, February 1, 1988; signed by Minnesota Vikings, April 8, 1988.
Detroit NFL, 1978 through 1987.
Games: 1978 (16), 1979 (15), 1980 (16), 1981 (16), 1982 (9), 1983 (15), 1984 (16), 1985 (16), 1986 (16), 1987 (11). Total—146.
Pro statistics: Recovered one fumble, 1978, 1981, 1982 and 1986; returned one kickoff for no yards, recovered one fumble in end zone for a touchdown and fumbled once, 1979; intercepted one pass for seven yards, 1982 and 1985; recovered one fumble for 11 yards, 1983; recovered two fumbles for 30 yards, 1984; recovered six fumbles for three yards, 1985.
Played in Pro Bowl (NFL All-Star Game) following 1983 season.

SHAUN LaNARD GAYLE
Safety—Chicago Bears
Born March 8, 1962, at Newport News, Va.
Height, 5.11. Weight, 195.
High School—Hampton, Va., Bethel.
Received bachelor of science degree in education from Ohio State University in 1984.

Selected by Michigan in 14th round (288th player selected) of 1984 USFL draft.
Selected by Chicago in 10th round (271st player selected) of 1984 NFL draft.
Signed by Chicago Bears, June 21, 1984.
On injured reserve with broken ankle, December 12 through remainder of 1984 season.
On injured reserve with ankle injury, September 8 through November 5, 1987; activated, November 6, 1987.
Chicago NFL, 1984 through 1987.
Games: 1984 (15), 1985 (16), 1986 (16), 1987 (8). Total—55.
Pro statistics: Intercepted one pass for minus one yard, 1984; recovered one fumble, 1985 and 1986; intercepted one pass for 13 yards, 1986; intercepted one pass for 20 yards and a touchdown, 1987.
Played in NFC Championship Game following 1985 season.
Played in NFL Championship Game following 1985 season.

DOUG GAYNOR
Quarterback—Los Angeles Rams
Born July 5, 1963, at Fresno, Calif.
Height, 6.02. Weight, 205.
High School—Fresno, Calif., Roosevelt.
Attended Fresno City College and California State University at Long Beach.

Selected by Cincinnati in 4th round (99th player selected) of 1986 NFL draft.
Signed by Cincinnati Bengals, July 28, 1986.
On injured reserve with finger injury, December 19 through remainder of 1986 season.
Released by Cincinnati Bengals, September 9, 1987; signed as free agent by Los Angeles Rams, March 8, 1988.
Cincinnati NFL, 1986.
Games; 1986 (1).
Pro statistics: Attempted three passes with three completions for 30 yards and rushed once for four yards, 1986.

JAMES GEATHERS
Defensive End—New Orleans Saints
Born June 26, 1960, at Georgetown, S.C.
Height, 6.07. Weight, 290.
High School—Georgetown, S.C., Choppee.
Attended Paducah Community College and Wichita State University.
Brother of Robert Geathers, defensive end with Boston Breakers, 1983.
Selected by Oklahoma in 1984 USFL territorial draft.
Selected by New Orleans in 2nd round (42nd player selected) of 1984 NFL draft.
Signed by New Orleans Saints, May 30, 1984.
On injured reserve with knee injury, September 1 through December 25, 1987; activated, December 26, 1987.
New Orleans NFL, 1984 through 1987.
Games: 1984 (16), 1985 (16), 1986 (16), 1987 (1). Total—49.
Pro statistics: Recovered one fumble, 1986.

MARK GEHRING
Tight End—Washington Redskins
Born April 16, 1964, at Burien, Wash.
Height, 6.04. Weight, 235.
High School—Des Moines, Wash., Mount Rainier.
Attended Olympic College and Eastern Washington University.
Signed as free agent by Minnesota Vikings, May 3, 1986.
Released by Minnesota Vikings, June 10, 1986; signed as free agent by Houston Oilers, July 8, 1986.
Released by Houston Oilers, August 7, 1986; signed as free agent by Calgary Stampeders, April 22, 1987.
Released by Calgary Stampeders, July 1, 1987; re-signed as replacement player by Houston Oilers, September 23, 1987.
Released by Houston Oilers, November 10, 1987; signed as free agent by Washington Redskins, April 8, 1988.
Calgary CFL, 1987; Houston NFL, 1987.
Games: 1987 CFL (2), 1987 NFL (6). Total —8.
CFL statistics: Caught one pass for 12 yards, 1987.
NFL statistics: Caught five passes for 64 yards and a touchdown, 1987.

STANLEY MORRIS GELBAUGH
(Stan)
Quarterback—Buffalo Bills
Born December 4, 1962, at Carlisle, Pa.
Height, 6.03. Weight, 207.
High School—Mechanicsburg, Pa., Cumberland Valley.
Received bachelor of science degree in marketing from University of Maryland in 1986.
Selected by Baltimore in 1986 USFL territorial draft.
Selected by Dallas in 6th round (150th player selected) of 1986 NFL draft.
Signed by Dallas Cowboys, July 5, 1986.
Released by Dallas Cowboys, August 18, 1986; signed as free agent by Saskatchewan Roughriders, August 27, 1986.
Released by Saskatchewan Roughriders, October 7, 1986; signed as free agent by Buffalo Bills, November 18, 1986.
On injured reserve with elbow injury, September 8 through entire 1987 season.
Active for 5 games with Buffalo Bills in 1986; did not play.
Saskatchewan CFL, 1986; Buffalo NFL, 1986.
Games: 1986 CFL (5).

DENNIS LOUIS GENTRY
Wide Receiver—Chicago Bears
Born February 10, 1959, at Lubbock, Tex.
Height, 5.08. Weight, 180.
High School—Lubbock, Tex., Dunbar.
Attended Baylor University.
Selected by Chicago in 4th round (89th player selected) of 1982 NFL draft.

Year Club		G.	Att.	Yds.	Avg.	TD.	P.C.	Yds.	Avg.	TD.	TD.	Pts.	F.
			—RUSHING—				PASS RECEIVING				—TOTAL—		
1982—Chicago NFL		9	4	21	5.3	0	1	9	9.0	0	0	0	4
1983—Chicago NFL		15	16	65	4.1	0	2	8	4.0	0	0	0	1
1984—Chicago NFL		16	21	79	3.8	1	4	29	7.3	0	1	6	0
1985—Chicago NFL		16	30	160	5.3	2	5	77	15.4	0	3	18	0
1986—Chicago NFL		15	11	103	9.4	1	19	238	12.5	0	3	18	0
1987—Chicago NFL		12	6	41	6.8	0	17	183	10.8	1	2	12	2
Pro Totals—6 Years		83	88	469	5.3	4	48	544	11.3	1	9	54	7

Year Club		G.	No.	Yds.	Avg.	TD.	No.	Yds.	Avg.	TD.
			—PUNT RETURNS—				—KICKOFF RET.—			
1982—Chicago NFL		9	17	89	5.2	0	9	161	17.9	0
1983—Chicago NFL		15		None			7	130	18.6	0
1984—Chicago NFL		16		None			11	209	19.0	0
1985—Chicago NFL		16	0	47	....	0	18	466	25.9	1
1986—Chicago NFL		15		None			20	576	*28.8	*1
1987—Chicago NFL		12		None			25	621	24.8	1
Pro Totals—6 Years		83	17	136	8.0	0	90	2163	24.0	3

Additional pro statistics: Recovered one fumble, 1982; recovered blocked punt in end zone for a touchdown, 1986.

Played in NFC Championship Game following 1984 and 1985 seasons
Played in NFL Championship Game following 1985 season.

JOHN CHRISTIAN GESEK JR.
Guard—Los Angeles Raiders
Born February 18, 1963, at San Francisco, Calif.
Height, 6.05. Weight, 275.
High Schools—Danville, Calif., San Ramon Valley; and Bellflower, Calif.
Attended Diablo Valley College (did not play football) and
California State University at Sacramento.

Selected by Los Angeles Raiders in 10th round (265th player selected) of 1987 NFL draft.
Signed by Los Angeles Raiders, July 11, 1987.
On injured reserve with back injury, September 7 through October 13, 1987; activated, October 14, 1987.
Crossed picket line during players' strike, October 13, 1987.
On injured reserve with knee injury, October 19 through December 4, 1987; activated, December 5, 1987.
Los Angeles Raiders NFL, 1987.
Games: 1987 (3).

RALPH GIACOMARRO
Punter—Los Angeles Raiders
Born January 17, 1961, at Passaic, N.J.
Height, 6.01. Weight, 194.
High School—Saddle Brook, N.J.
Attended Penn State University.

Selected by Philadelphia in 1983 USFL territorial draft.
Selected by Atlanta in 10th round (268th player selected) of 1983 NFL draft.
Signed by Atlanta Falcons, July 15, 1983.
Released by Atlanta Falcons, August 26, 1985; re-signed by Falcons, November 26, 1985.
Granted free agency, February 1, 1986; withdrew qualifying offer, June 6, 1986.
Signed as free agent replacement player by Denver Broncos, September 25, 1987.
Released by Denver Broncos, October 19, 1987; signed as free agent by Los Angeles Raiders, April 22, 1988.

Year Club	G.	No.	Avg.	Blk.
1983—Atlanta NFL	16	70	40.3	1
1984—Atlanta NFL	16	68	42.0	2
1985—Atlanta NFL	5	29	39.9	2
1987—Denver NFL	3	18	42.1	0
Pro Totals—4 Years	40	185	41.0	5

Additional pro statistics: Rushed twice for 13 yards and attempted one passe with one completion for 23 yards, 1983; recovered one fumble and fumbled once, 1983 and 1984; rushed once for no yards, 1984.

ANTONIO MARICE GIBSON
Safety—New Orleans Saints
Born July 5, 1962, at Jackson, Miss.
Height, 6.03. Weight, 206.
High School—Jackson, Miss., Murrah.
Attended Hinds Junior College and University of Cincinnati.

Selected by Philadelphia in 4th round (41st player selected) of 1983 USFL draft.
Signed by Philadelphia Stars, January 7, 1983.
Franchise transferred to Baltimore, November 1, 1984.
On developmental squad, February 24 through February 27, 1985; activated, February 28, 1985.
Granted free agency when USFL suspended operations, August 7, 1986; signed as free agent by New Orleans Saints, August 11, 1986.
Crossed picket line during players' strike, October 1, 1987.
On injured reserve with broken arm, November 25, 1987 through January 1, 1988; activated, January 2, 1988.
On developmental squad for 1 game with Baltimore Stars in 1985.
Philadelphia USFL, 1983 and 1984; Baltimore USFL, 1985; New Orleans NFL, 1986 and 1987.
Games: 1983 (18), 1984 (18), 1985 (17), 1986 (16), 1987 (10). Total USFL—53. Total NFL—26. Total Pro—79.
USFL statistics: Recovered one fumble, 1983 and 1985; credited with one sack for one yard and intercepted three passes for no yards, 1983; credited with two sacks for 13 yards, ran four yards with lateral on kickoff return and fumbled once, 1984; credited with two sacks for 12 yards and intercepted one pass for 50 yards and a touchdown, 1985.
NFL statistics: Intercepted two passes for 43 yards and recovered one fumble, 1986; intercepted one pass for 17 yards, 1987.
Played in USFL Championship Game following 1983 through 1985 seasons.

DENNIS MICHAEL GIBSON
Linebacker—Detroit Lions
Born February 8, 1964, at Des Moines, Ia.
Height, 6.02. Weight, 240.
High School—Ankeny, Ia.
Attended Iowa State University.

Selected by Detroit in 8th round (203rd player selected) of 1987 NFL draft.
Signed by Detroit Lions, July 25, 1987.
Detroit NFL, 1987.
Games: 1987 (12).
Pro statistics: Intercepted one pass for five yards, 1987.

ERNEST GERARD GIBSON
Cornerback—New England Patriots
Born October 3, 1961, at Jacksonville, Fla.
Height, 5.10. Weight, 185.
High School—Jacksonville, Fla., Bishop Kenny.
Received bachelor of arts degree in political science from Furman University in 1984.

Selected by Memphis in 3rd round (44th player selected) of 1984 USFL draft.
USFL rights traded by Memphis Showboats to Birmingham Stallions for rights to quarterback Walter Lewis, January 16, 1984.
Selected by New England in 6th round (151st player selected) of 1984 NFL draft.
Signed by New England Patriots, June 6, 1984.
On injured reserve with chest injury, September 2 through October 3, 1985; activated, October 4, 1985.
New England NFL, 1984 through 1987.
Games: 1984 (15), 1985 (9), 1986 (15), 1987 (12). Total—51.
Pro statistics: Intercepted two passes for four yards, returned one punt for three yards and recovered one fumble, 1984; intercepted two passes for 17 yards, 1987.
Played in AFC Championship Game following 1985 season.
Played in NFL Championship Game following 1985 season.

JON WILLIAM GIESLER
Name pronounced Geese-ler.
Offensive Tackle—Miami Dolphins
Born December 23, 1956, at Toledo, O.
Height, 6.05. Weight, 265.
High School—Elmore, O., Woodmore.
Received bachelor of science degree in education from University of Michigan in 1979.

Selected by Miami in 1st round (24th player selected) of 1979 NFL draft.
On injured reserve with shoulder injury, September 2 through October 9, 1980; activated, October 10, 1980.
On physically unable to perform/reserve with knee injury, August 18 through October 17, 1986; activated, October 18, 1986.
On injured reserve with knee injury, December 12 through remainder of 1986 season.
On physically unable to perform/reserve with knee injury, August 31 through October 23, 1987; activated, October 24, 1987.
Miami NFL, 1979 through 1987.
Games: 1979 (16), 1980 (10), 1981 (16), 1982 (9), 1983 (16), 1984 (16), 1985 (13), 1986 (7), 1987 (10). Total—113.
Pro statistics: Recovered one fumble, 1981 and 1985.
Played in AFC Championship Game following 1982, 1984 and 1985 seasons.
Played in NFL Championship Game following 1982 and 1984 seasons.

DAREN GILBERT
Offensive Tackle—New Orleans Saints
Born October 3, 1963, at San Diego, Calif.
Height, 6.06. Weight, 295.
High School—Compton, Calif., Dominguez.
Attended California State University at Fullerton.

Selected by Los Angeles in 1985 USFL territorial draft.
Selected by New Orleans in 2nd round (38th player selected) of 1985 NFL draft.
Signed by New Orleans Saints, August 5, 1985.
Crossed picket line during players' strike, October 2, 1987.
New Orleans NFL, 1985 through 1987.
Games: 1985 (16), 1986 (9), 1987 (6). Total—31.

FREDDIE GENE GILBERT
Defensive End—Denver Broncos
Born April 8, 1962, at Griffin, Ga.
Height, 6.04. Weight, 275.
High School—Griffin, Ga.
Attended University of Georgia.

Selected by Jacksonville in 1984 USFL territorial draft.
USFL rights traded by Jacksonville Bulls to New Jersey Generals for rights to running back Archie Griffin and draft choice, January 16, 1984.
Signed by New Jersey Generals, January 24, 1984.
On injured reserve with knee injury, March 27 through June 14, 1984; activated, June 15, 1984.
Selected by Denver Broncos in 1st round (19th player selected) of 1984 NFL supplemental draft.
On developmental squad, March 23 through March 29, 1985; activated, March 30, 1985.
On developmental squad, May 5 through June 9, 1985; activated, June 10, 1985.
On developmental squad, June 22 through June 30, 1985; activated , July 1, 1985.
Released by New Jersey Generals, July 31, 1985; re-signed by Generals, August 1, 1985.
Granted free agency when USFL suspended operations, August 7, 1986; signed by Denver Broncos, August 24, 1986.
Granted roster exemption, August 24 through September 7, 1986; activated, September 8, 1986.
On developmental squad for 7 games with New Jersey Generals in 1985.
New Jersey USFL, 1984 and 1985; Denver NFL, 1986 and 1987.
Games: 1984 (7), 1985 (11), 1986 (15), 1987 (7). Total USFL—18. Total NFL—22. Total Pro—40.
USFL statistics: Credited with three fumbles for 14 yards, 1984; credited with 3½ sacks for 41 yards and recovered one fumble for 31 yards and a touchdown, 1985.
NFL statistics: Recovered one fumble, 1987.
Played in AFC Championship Game following 1986 and 1987 seasons.
Played in NFL Championship Game following 1986 and 1987 seasons.

GALE GILBERT
Quarterback—Seattle Seahawks
Born December 20, 1961, at Red Bluff, Calif.
Height, 6.03. Weight, 206.
High School—Red Bluff, Calif.
Attended University of California at Berkeley.

Selected by Oakland in 1985 USFL territorial draft.
Signed as free agent by Seattle Seahawks, May 2, 1985.
On injured reserve with knee injury, September 8 through entire 1987 season.

Year Club	G.	Att.	Cmp.	Pct.	Gain	T.P.	P.I.	Avg.	Att.	Yds.	Avg.	TD.	TD.	Pts.	F.
				PASSING						RUSHING				TOTAL	
1985—Seattle NFL	9	40	19	47.5	218	1	2	5.45	7	4	0.6	0	0	0	1
1986—Seattle NFL	16	76	42	55.3	485	3	3	6.38	3	8	2.7	0	0	0	1
Pro Totals—2 Years	25	116	61	52.6	703	4	5	6.06	10	12	1.2	0	0	0	2

Quarterback Rating Points: 1985 (51.9), 1986 (71.4). Total—64.6.
Additional pro statistics: Recovered one fumble and fumbled once for minus five yards, 1985.

JIMMIE GILES JR.
Name pronounced Jiles.
Tight End—Philadelphia Eagles
Born November 8, 1954, at Natchez, Miss.
Height, 6.03. Weight, 240.
High School—Greenville, Miss.
Received bachelor of science degree in business administration from Alcorn State University in 1977.
Related to Sammy White, wide receiver with Minnesota Vikings, 1976 through 1985.

Selected by Houston in 3rd round (70th player selected) of 1977 NFL draft.
Traded with four draft choices (1st and 2nd round in 1978 and 3rd and 5th round in 1979) by Houston Oilers to Tampa Bay Buccaneers for 1st round pick in 1978 draft, April 24, 1978.
On reserve/did not report, August 16 through August 26, 1983.
Reinstated and granted roster exemption, August 27 through September 1, 1983; activated, September 2, 1983.
Released by Tampa Bay Buccaneers, October 20, 1986; signed as free agent by Detroit Lions, October 24, 1986.
Granted free agency, February 1, 1987; re-signed by Lions, September 8, 1987.
Granted roster exemption, September 8 through September 10, 1987; activated, September 11, 1987.
Traded by Detroit Lions to Philadelphia Eagles for 9th round pick in 1988 draft, November 3, 1987.

Year Club	G.	P.C.	Yds.	Avg.	TD.
		PASS RECEIVING			
1977—Houston NFL	14	17	147	8.6	0
1978—Tampa Bay NFL	16	23	324	14.1	2
1979—Tampa Bay NFL	16	40	579	14.5	7
1980—Tampa Bay NFL	16	33	602	18.2	4
1981—Tampa Bay NFL	16	45	786	17.5	6
1982—Tampa Bay NFL	9	28	499	17.8	3
1983—Tampa Bay NFL	11	25	349	14.0	1
1984—Tampa Bay NFL	14	24	310	12.9	2
1985—Tampa Bay NFL	16	43	673	15.7	8
1986—T.B. (7)-Det. (9) NFL	16	37	376	10.2	4
1987—Det. (4)-Phi. (8) NFL	12	13	157	12.1	1
Pro Totals—11 Years	156	328	4802	14.6	38

Additional pro statistics: Rushed once for minus 10 yards, 1977; returned five kickoffs for 60 yards, rushed once for minus one yard, 1978; fumbled once, 1978 and 1983; rushed twice for seven yards, 1979; recovered one fumble, 1979, 1980 and 1982; fumbled twice, 1980 and 1982; rushed once for one yard, 1982; fumbled three times, 1985.
Played in NFC Championship Game following 1979 season.
Played in Pro Bowl (NFL All-Star Game) following 1980 through 1982 and 1985 seasons.

RECORD AS BASEBALL PLAYER
Selected by Los Angeles Dodgers' organization in 12th round of free-agent draft, June 8, 1976.
Placed on restricted list, July 14, 1977.

Year Club	League	Pos.	G.	AB.	R.	H.	2B.	3B.	HR.	RBI.	B.A.	PO.	A.	E.	F.A.
1976—Bellingham	Northw.	O-1-3	29	51	4	4	0	0	0	0	.078	16	5	2	.913

OWEN GILL
Fullback—Tampa Bay Buccaneers
Born February 19, 1962, at London, England.
Height, 6.01. Weight, 230.
High School—Brooklyn, N.Y., Samuel J. Tilden.
Attended University of Iowa.

Selected by Oakland in 1985 USFL territorial draft.
Selected by Seattle in 2nd round (53rd player selected) of 1985 NFL draft.
Signed by Seattle Seahawks, June 3, 1985.
Released by Seattle Seahawks, September 4, 1985; awarded on waivers to Indianapolis Colts, September 5, 1985.
On injured reserve with broken leg, September 8 through October 29, 1987; activated, October 30, 1987.
Traded with 1st and 2nd round picks in 1988 draft and 2nd round pick in 1989 draft by Indianapolis Colts to Los Angeles Rams for running back Eric Dickerson, October 31, 1987; Rams also acquired 1st round pick in 1988 draft, 1st and 2nd round picks in 1989 draft and running back Greg Bell from Buffalo Bills in exchange for Colts trading rights to linebacker Cornelius Bennett to Bills.
Released by Los Angeles Rams, December 1, 1987; signed as free agent by Tampa Bay Buccaneers for 1988, December 18, 1987.

Year	Club	G.	Att.	RUSHING Yds.	Avg.	TD.	PASS RECEIVING P.C.	Yds.	Avg.	TD.	TOTAL TD.	Pts.	F.
1985—Indianapolis NFL		15	45	262	5.8	2	5	52	10.4	0	2	12	1
1986—Indianapolis NFL		16	53	228	4.3	1	16	137	8.6	0	1	6	4
1987—Los Angeles Rams NFL		1		None				None			0	0	0
Pro Totals—3 Years		32	98	490	5.0	3	21	189	9.0	0	3	18	5

Additional pro statistics: Returned one kickoff for six yards, 1985; returned five kickoffs for 73 yards, 1986.

WILLIE E. GILLESPIE
Wide Receiver—Indianapolis Colts
Born October 24, 1961, at Starkville, Miss.
Height, 5.09. Weight, 170.
High School—Starkville, Miss.
Attended East Mississippi Junior College and University of Tennessee-Chattanooga.
Selected by Tampa Bay in 6th round (181st player selected) of 1983 USFL draft.
Signed by Tampa Bay Bandits, January 21, 1983.
On developmental squad, March 9 through April 14, 1985; activated, April 15, 1985.
Granted free agency when USFL suspended operations, August 7, 1986; signed as free agent by Tampa Bay Buccaneers, August 12, 1986.
Granted roster exemption, August 12 through August 25, 1986.
On injured reserve with hamstring injury, August 26 through October 23, 1986; activated, October 24, 1986.
Released by Tampa Bay Buccaneers, August 31, 1987; signed as free agent replacement player by Minnesota Vikings, October 14, 1987.
Released by Minnesota Vikings, October 19, 1987; signed as free agent by Indianapolis Colts, February 10, 1988.
On developmental squad for 5 games with Tampa Bay Bandits in 1985.

Year	Club	G.	PASS RECEIVING P.C.	Yds.	Avg.	TD.	KICKOFF RET. No.	Yds.	Avg.	TD.	TOTAL TD.	Pts.	F.
1983—Tampa Bay USFL		18	38	639	16.8	4	10	166	16.0	0	0	0	2
1984—Tampa Bay USFL		18	50	803	16.1	5		None			5	†32	0
1985—Tampa Bay USFL		13	33	487	14.8	1		None			1	6	1
1986—Tampa Bay NFL		2	1	18	18.0	0		None			0	0	0
1987—Minnesota NFL		1	2	28	14.0	0		None			0	0	0
USFL Totals—3 Years		49	121	1929	15.9	10	10	166	16.0	0	6	38	3
NFL Totals—2 Years		3	3	46	15.3	0	0	0	0.0	0	0	0	0
Pro Totals—5 Years		52	124	1975	15.9	10	10	166	16.0	0	6	38	3

†Includes one 2-point conversion.
Additional pro statistics: Rushed twice for three yards and returned one punt for one yard, 1983; recovered one fumble, 1983 through 1985; rushed four times for 19 yards, 1984; rushed twice for 35 yards and returned three punts for 16 yards, 1985.

JAMES THOMAS GILMORE
(Jim)
Guard—Miami Dolphins
Born December 19, 1962, at Philadelphia, Pa.
Height, 6.05. Weight, 275.
High School—Philadelphia, Pa., North Catholic.
Attended Villanova University and Ohio State University.
Signed as free agent by Philadelphia Eagles, May 7, 1986.
Released by Philadelphia Eagles, September 1, 1986; re-signed by Eagles, September 2, 1986.
Released by Philadelphia Eagles, October 16, 1986; signed as free agent by Los Angeles Raiders, June 22, 1987.
Released by Los Angeles Raiders, September 1, 1987; signed as free agent replacement player by Miami Dolphins, September 23, 1987.
On injured reserve with leg injury, October 20 through remainder of 1987 season.
Philadelphia NFL, 1986; Miami NFL, 1987.
Games: 1986 (2), 1987 (3). Total—5.

ERNEST P. GIVINS
Wide Receiver—Houston Oilers
Born September 3, 1964, at St. Petersburg, Fla.
Height, 5.09. Weight, 175.
High School—St. Petersburg, Fla., Lakewood.
Attended Northeastern Oklahoma A&M and University of Louisville.
Selected by Houston in 2nd round (34th player selected) of 1986 NFL draft.
Selected by Tampa Bay in 1st round (8th player selected) of 1986 USFL draft.
Signed by Houston Oilers, August 1, 1986.

Year	Club	G.	Att.	RUSHING Yds.	Avg.	TD.	PASS RECEIVING P.C.	Yds.	Avg.	TD.	TOTAL TD.	Pts.	F.
1986—Houston NFL		15	9	148	16.4	1	61	1062	17.4	3	4	24	0
1987—Houston NFL		12	1	−13	−13.0	0	53	933	17.6	6	6	36	2
Pro Totals—2 Years		27	10	135	13.5	1	114	1995	17.5	9	10	60	2

Additional pro statistics: Attempted two passes with no completions and returned eight punts for 80 yards, 1986.

NESBY LEE GLASGOW
Safety—Indianapolis Colts
Born April 15, 1957, at Los Angeles, Calif.
Height, 5.10. Weight, 188.
High School—Gardena, Calif.
Attended University of Washington.
Tied NFL record for most combined kick returns, game (12), September 2, 1979, vs. Denver Broncos.
Selected by Baltimore in 8th round (207th player selected) of 1979 NFL draft.
Franchise transferred to Indianapolis, March 31, 1984.

		INTERCEPTIONS				-PUNT RETURNS-				—KICKOFF RET.—				—TOTAL—		
Year Club	G.	No.	Yds.	Avg.	TD.	No.	Yds.	Avg.	TD.	No.	Yds.	Avg.	TD.	TD.	Pts.	F.
1979—Baltimore NFL	16	1	−1	−1.0	0	44	352	8.0	1	50	1126	22.5	0	1	6	8
1980—Baltimore NFL	16	4	65	16.3	0	23	187	8.1	0	33	743	22.5	0	0	0	5
1981—Baltimore NFL	14	2	35	17.5	0		None			1	35	35.0	0	0	0	0
1982—Baltimore NFL	9		None			4	24	6.0	0		None			0	0	0
1983—Baltimore NFL	16	3	35	11.7	0	1	9	9.0	0		None			0	0	0
1984—Indianapolis NFL	16	1	8	8.0	0	7	79	11.3	0		None			0	0	1
1985—Indianapolis NFL	16		None				None				None			0	0	0
1986—Indianapolis NFL	14		None				None				None			0	0	0
1987—Indianapolis NFL	11	1	0	0.0	0		None				None			0	0	0
Pro Totals—9 Years	128	12	142	11.8	0	79	651	8.2	1	84	1904	22.7	0	1	6	14

Additional pro statistics: Recovered two fumbles, 1979 through 1981 and 1986; recovered one fumble, 1984 and 1987.

KERRY R. GLENN
Cornerback—New York Jets
Born March 31, 1962, at St. Louis, Mo.
Height, 5.09. Weight, 175.
High School—East St. Louis, Ill.
Attended University of Minnesota.
Selected by Orlando in 4th round (46th player selected) of 1985 USFL draft.
Selected by New York Jets in 10th round (262nd player selected) of 1985 NFL draft.
Signed by New York Jets, July 26, 1985.
On injured reserve with sprained foot, September 10 through remainder of 1986 season.
On injured reserve with knee injury, December 4 through remainder of 1987 season.
New York Jets NFL, 1985 through 1987.
Games: 1985 (16), 1986 (1), 1987 (8). Total—25.
Pro statistics: Intercepted four passes for 15 yards and a touchdown, returned five kickoffs for 71 yards and recovered two fumbles for 31 yards, 1985; recovered one fumble, 1986.

VENCIE LEONARD GLENN
Safety—San Diego Chargers
Born October 26, 1964, at Grambling, La.
Height, 6.00. Weight, 187.
High School—Silver Springs, Md., John F. Kennedy.
Attended Indiana State University.
Selected by New England in 2nd round (54th player selected) of 1986 NFL draft.
Signed by New England Patriots, July 29, 1986.
Traded by New England Patriots to San Diego Chargers for 5th round pick in 1987 draft and cash, September 29, 1986.

		——INTERCEPTIONS——			
Year Club	G.	No.	Yds.	Avg.	TD.
1986—San Diego NFL	12	2	31	15.5	0
1987—San Deigo NFL	12	4	*166	41.5	1
Pro Totals—2 Years	24	6	197	32.8	1

Additional pro statistics: Recovered two fumbles for 32 yards, 1986; recovered one fumble, 1987.

CLYDE M. GLOVER
Defensive End—San Francisco 49ers
Born July 16, 1960, at New Orleans, La.
Height, 6.06. Weight, 280.
High School—Las Vegas, Nev., Sunset.
Attended Walla Walla Community College and Fresno State University.
Selected by Oakland in 1984 USFL territorial draft.
Signed as free agent by New England Patriots, May 14, 1984.
Released by New England Patriots, August 21, 1984; signed as free agent by Kansas City Chiefs for 1985, October 15, 1984.
Released by Kansas City Chiefs, June 7, 1985; signed as free agent by Toronto Argonauts, June 10, 1985.
Released by Toronto Argonauts, August 4, 1985; signed as free agent by San Francisco 49ers, March 10, 1986.
Released by San Francisco 49ers, August 19, 1986; re-signed by 49ers for 1987, October 29, 1986.
Released by San Francisco 49ers, September 7, 1987; re-signed as replacement player by 49ers, September 24, 1987.
Toronto CFL, 1985; San Francisco NFL, 1987.
Games: 1985 (5), 1987 (13). Total—18.

KEVIN BERNARD GLOVER
Center-Guard—Detroit Lions
Born June 17, 1963, at Washington, D.C.
Height, 6.02. Weight, 267.
High School—Largo, Md.
Attended University of Maryland.

Named as center on THE SPORTING NEWS College All-America Team, 1984.
Selected by Tampa Bay in 1985 USFL territorial draft.
Selected by Detroit in 2nd round (34th player selected) of 1985 NFL draft.
Signed by Detroit Lions, July 23, 1985.
On injured reserve with knee injury, December 7 through remainder of 1985 season.
On injured reserve with knee injury, September 29 through December 19, 1986; activated, December 20, 1986.
Detroit NFL, 1985 through 1987.
Games: 1985 (10), 1986 (4), 1987 (12). Total—26.
Additional pro statistics: Returned one kickoff for 19 yards, 1987.

CHRISTOPHER JAMES GODFREY
(Chris)
Guard—New York Giants
Born May 17, 1958, at Detroit, Mich.
Height, 6.03. Weight, 265.
High Schools—Detroit, Mich., De LaSalle; and Miami, Fla., Lake.
Received bachelor of science degree in business from University of Michigan in 1980.

Signed as free agent by Washington Redskins, May 20, 1980.
Released by Washington Redskins, August 26, 1980; signed as free agent by New York Jets, September 23, 1980.
On physically unable to perform/active list with knee injury, July 17 through August 10, 1981.
Released by New York Jets, August 11, 1981; claimed on waivers by Green Bay Packers, August 13, 1981.
On injured reserve with knee injury, August 31 through entire 1981 season.
Released by Green Bay Packers, August 30, 1982; signed by Michigan Panthers, January 24, 1983.
Signed by New York Giants, April 28, 1984, to contract to take effect after being granted free agency, November 30, 1984.
On developmental squad, May 13 through May 19, 1984; activated, May 20, 1984.
On developmental squad, June 2 through remainder of 1984 season.
On injured reserve with knee injury, September 28 through November 13, 1987; activated, November 14, 1987.
On developmental squad for 5 games with Michigan Panthers in 1984.
New York Jets NFL, 1980; Michigan USFL, 1983 and 1984; New York Giants NFL, 1984 through 1987.
Games: 1980 (6), 1983 (18), 1984 USFL (13), 1984 NFL (10), 1985 (16), 1986 (16), 1987 (8). Total NFL—56. Total USFL—31. Total Pro—87.
Pro statistics: Recovered two fumbles, 1983.
Played in USFL Championship Game following 1983 season.
Played in NFC Championship Game following 1986 season.
Played in NFL Championship Game following 1986 season.

KEVIN PATRICK GOGAN
Offensive Tackle—Dallas Cowboys
Born November 2, 1964, at San Francisco, Calif.
Height, 6.07. Weight, 310.
High School—San Francisco, Calif., Sacred Heart.
Received degree in sociology from University of Washington in 1987.

Selected by Dallas in 8th round (206th player selected) of 1987 NFL draft.
Signed by Dallas Cowboys, July 18, 1987.
Dallas NFL, 1987.
Games: 1987 (11).
Pro Statistics: Recovered one fumble, 1987.

MIKE GOLIC
Name pronounced Go-lick.
Defensive Lineman—Philadelphia Eagles
Born December 12, 1962, at Willowick, O.
Height, 6.05. Weight, 272.
High School—Cleveland, O., St. Joseph.
Received bachelor of business administration degree in management from University of Notre Dame in 1985.
Son of Louis Golic, former player with Montreal Alouettes, Hamilton Tiger-Cats and Saskatchewan Roughriders; and brother of Bob Golic, nose tackle with Cleveland Browns.

Selected by Orlando in 15th round (204th player selected) of 1985 USFL draft.
Selected by Houston in 10th round (255th player selected) of 1985 NFL draft.
Signed by Houston Oilers, July 18, 1985.
On injured reserve with ankle injury, August 27 through entire 1985 season.
Released by Houston Oilers, November 3, 1987; signed as free agent by Philadelphia Eagles, November 11, 1987.
Houston NFL, 1986; Houston (2)-Philadelphia (6) NFL, 1987.
Games: 1986 (16), 1987 (8). Total—24.
Pro statistics: Recovered two fumbles for four yards, 1986.

ROBERT PERRY GOLIC

Name pronounced Go-lick.

(Bob)

Nose Tackle—Cleveland Browns

Born October 26, 1957, at Cleveland, O.
Height, 6.02. Weight, 270.
High School—Cleveland, O., St. Joseph.
Received bachelor of business administration degree in management from
University of Notre Dame in 1979.
Son of Louis Golic, former player with Montreal Alouettes, Hamilton Tiger-Cats and Saskatchewan
Roughriders; and brother of Mike Golic, defensive lineman with Philadelphia Eagles.

Named to THE SPORTING NEWS NFL All-Star Team, 1985.
Selected by New England in 2nd round (52nd player selected) of 1979 NFL draft.
On injured reserve with shoulder injury, August 28 through December 14, 1979; activated, December 15, 1979.
Released by New England Patriots, August 31, 1982; signed as free agent by Cleveland Browns, September 2, 1982.
On inactive list, September 12, 1982.
On injured reserve with broken arm, December 30 through remainder of 1987 season playoffs.
New England NFL, 1979 through 1982; Cleveland NFL, 1983 through 1987.
Games: 1979 (1), 1980 (16), 1981 (16), 1982 (6), 1983 (16), 1984 (15), 1985 (16), 1986 (16), 1987 (12). Total—114.
Pro statistics: Recovered one fumble, 1981; intercepted one pass for seven yards and a touchdown, 1983; recovered
one fumble for 18 yards, 1984.
Played in AFC Championship Game following 1986 season.
Played in Pro Bowl (NFL All-Star Game) following 1985 and 1986 seasons.
Named to play in Pro Bowl following 1987 season; replaced due to injury by Tim Krumrie.

KELLY JOE GOODBURN

Punter—Kansas City Chiefs

Born April 14, 1962, at Cherokee, Ia.
Height, 6.02. Weight, 195.
High School—Correctionville,Ia., Eastwood Community.
Attended Iowa State University and received degree in physical education
from Emporia State University in 1987.

Signed as free agent by Kansas City Chiefs, May 3, 1986.
Released by Kansas City Chiefs, August 19, 1986; re-signed by Chiefs, April 7, 1987.
Released by Kansas City Chiefs, August 31, 1987; re-signed as replacement player by Chiefs, September 25, 1987.

| | | ———PUNTING——— | | |
Year Club	G.	No.	Avg.	Blk.
1987—Kansas City NFL	13	59	40.9	0

Additional pro statistics: Rushed once for 16 yards, 1987.

CHRIS GOODE

(Name pronounced Good.)

Defensive Back—Indianapolis Colts

Born September 17, 1963, at Town Creek, Ala.
Height, 6.00. Weight, 193.
High School—Town Creek, Ala., Hazelwood.
Attended University of North Alabama and University of Alabama.

Selected by Indianapolis in 10th round (253rd player selected) of 1987 NFL draft.
Signed by Indianapolis Colts, July 23, 1987.
On injured reserve with strained abdomen, September 7 through November 5, 1987; activated, November 6, 1987.
Indianapolis NFL, 1987.
Games: 1987 (8).

CONRAD LAWRENCE GOODE

Name pronounced Goodie.

Offensive Lineman—Chicago Bears

Born January 19, 1962, at St. Louis, Mo.
Height, 6.06. Weight, 285.
High School—Creve Coeur, Mo., Parkway Central.
Attended University of Missouri.
Stepson of Irv Goode, guard-center with St. Louis Cardinals, Buffalo Bills and
Miami Dolphins, 1962 thrugh 1974.

Selected by Oklahoma in 1st round (22nd player selected) of 1984 USFL draft.
Selected by New York Giants in 4th round (87th player selected) of 1984 NFL draft.
Signed by New York Giants, June 8, 1984.
Released by New York Giants, September 1, 1986; signed as free agent by Tampa Bay Buccanners, March 21, 1987.
Granted free agency, February 1, 1988; withdrew qualifying offer, May 16, 1988.
Signed by Chicago Bears, May 18, 1988.
New York Giants NFL, 1984 and 1985; Tampa Bay NFL, 1987.
Games: 1984 (8), 1985 (16), 1987 (11). Total—35.
Pro statistics: Recovered one fumble, 1987.

JOHN TIMOTHY GOODE
Tight End—Cincinnati Bengals
Born November 5, 1962, at Cleveland Heights, O.
Height, 6.02. Weight, 243.
High School—Cleveland, O. Benedictine.
Attended Youngstown State University.
Selected by Oklahoma in 5th round (85th player selected) of 1984 USFL draft.
Selected by St. Louis in 5th round (136th player selected) of 1984 NFL draft.
Signed by St. Louis Cardinals, July 19, 1984.
Released by St. Louis Cardinals, September 2, 1985; signed as free agent by Philadelphia Eagles, September 13, 1985.
Released by Philadelphia Eagles, July 29, 1986; signed as free agent by Detroit Lions, August 1, 1986.
Released by Detroit Lions, August 18, 1986; signed as free agent by New York Jets, May 15, 1987.
Released by New York Jets, August 18, 1987; signed as free agent by Cincinnati Bengals, April 8, 1988.

		—PASS RECEIVING—			
Year Club	G.	P.C.	Yds.	Avg.	TD.
1984—St. Louis NFL	16	3	23	7.7	0
1985—Philadelphia NFL	14		None		
Pro Totals—2 Years	30	3	23	7.7	0

EUGENE GOODLOW
Wide Receiver—San Diego Chargers
Born December 19, 1958, at St. Louis, Mo.
Height, 6.02. Weight, 186.
High School—Rochester, N.Y., McQuaid Jesuit.
Attended Kansas State University.
Signed by Winnipeg Blue Bombers, September 22, 1980.
Selected by New Orleans in 3rd round (66th player selected) of 1982 NFL draft.
On injured list with neck injury, August 20 through remainder of 1982 season.
Granted free agency, March 1, 1983; signed by New Orleans Saints, March 2, 1983.
On injured reserve with pulled hamstring, October 5 through November 18, 1984; activated, November 19, 1984.
On injured reserve with knee injury, October 11 through November 7, 1985; activated, November 8, 1985.
On injured reserve with leg injury, September 1 through September 6, 1987.
Released by New Orleans Saints, September 7, 1987; signed as free agent by San Diego Chargers, May 23, 1988.

		—PASS RECEIVING—			
Year Club	G.	P.C.	Yds.	Avg.	TD.
1980—Winnipeg CFL	5	17	206	12.1	1
1981—Winnipeg CFL	16	*100	1494	14.9	4
1982—Winnipeg CFL	6	30	515	17.2	8
1983—New Orleans NFL	16	41	487	11.9	2
1984—New Orleans NFL	10	22	281	12.8	3
1985—New Orleans NFL	12	32	603	18.8	3
1986—New Orleans NFL	16	20	306	15.3	2
CFL Totals—3 Years	27	147	2215	15.1	13
NFL Totals—4 Years	54	115	1677	14.6	10
Pro Totals—7 Years	81	262	3892	14.9	23

Additional CFL statistics: Returned three punts for 22 yards, two kickoffs for 38 yards and fumbled once, 1980; returned four kickoffs for 72 yards and recovered two fumbles, 1981.
Additional NFL statistics: Rushed once for three yards, 1983 and 1985; rushed once for five yards, 1984; recovered one fumble and fumbled once, 1986.

ALEX GRONCIER GORDON
Linebacker—New York Jets
Born September 14, 1964, at Jacksonville, Fla.
Height, 6.05. Weight, 246.
High School—Jacksonville, Fla., Englewood.
Attended University of Cincinnati.
Selected by New York Jets in 2nd round (42nd player selected) of 1987 NFL draft.
Signed by New York Jets, July 22, 1987.
New York Jets NFL, 1987.
Games: 1987 (12).

DENMAN PRESTON GORDON
(Sonny)
Defensive Back—Tampa Bay Buccaneers
Born July 30, 1965, at Lynn, Mass.
Height, 5.11. Weight, 192.
High School—Middletown, O.
Attended Ohio State University.
Selected by Cincinnati in 6th round (157th player selected) of 1987 NFL draft.
Signed by Cincinnati Bengals, July 22, 1987.
Released by Cincinnati Bengals, September 7, 1987; signed as free agent by Tampa Bay Buccaneers, September 19, 1987.
Tampa Bay NFL, 1987.
Games: 1987 (7).

TIM CARVELLE GORDON
Safety—Atlanta Falcons
Born May 7, 1965, at Ardmore, Okla.
Height, 6.00. Weight, 188.
High School—Ardmore, Okla.
Attended University of Tulsa.

Signed as free agent by Atlanta Falcons, May 6, 1987.
Released by Atlanta Falcons, September 1, 1987; re-signed by Falcons, September 16, 1987.
Atlanta NFL, 1987.
Games: 1987 (11).
Pro statistics: Intercepted two passes for 28 yards and recovered one fumble, 1987.

JEFFERY ALAN GOSSETT
(Jeff)
Punter—Houston Oilers
Born January 25, 1957, at Charleston, Ill.
Height, 6.02. Weight, 197.
High School—Charleston, Ill.
Received bachelor of science degree in physical education from Eastern Illinois University in 1982.

Signed as free agent by Dallas Cowboys, May, 1980.
Released by Dallas Cowboys, August 25, 1980; signed as free agent by San Diego Chargers, April 6, 1981.
Released by San Diego Chargers, August 31, 1981; signed as free agent by Kansas City Chiefs, November 5, 1981.
Released by Kansas City Chiefs, December 14, 1982; re-signed by Chiefs, December 21, 1982.
Released by Kansas City Chiefs, August 29, 1983; awarded on waivers to Cleveland Browns, August 30, 1983.
Signed by Chicago Blitz, December 20, 1983, for contract to take effect after being granted free agency, February 1, 1984.
USFL rights traded with placekicker Efren Herrera by Pittsburgh Maulers to Chicago Blitz for rights to linebacker Bruce Huther, December 30, 1983.
Franchise disbanded, November 20, 1984; signed as free agent by Portland Breakers, February 4, 1985.
Signed by Cleveland Browns for 1985 season, May 20, 1985.
Released by Portland Breakers, June 26, 1985.
Crossed picket line during players' strike, October 14, 1987.
Released by Cleveland Browns, November 17, 1987; signed as free agent by Houston Oilers, December 3, 1987.

		—PUNTING—		
Year Club	G.	No.	Avg.	Blk.
1981—Kansas City NFL	7	29	39.3	0
1982—Kansas City NFL	8	33	41.4	0
1983—Cleveland NFL	16	70	40.8	0
1984—Chicago USFL	18	85	*42.5	....
1985—Portland USFL	18	74	42.2	....
1985—Cleveland NFL	16	81	40.3	0
1986—Cleveland NFL	16	83	41.2	0
1987—Cle. (5)-Hou. (4) NFL	9	44	40.4	1
NFL Totals—6 Years	72	340	40.7	1
USFL Totals—2 Years	36	159	42.3	
Pro Totals—8 Years	108	499	41.2	....

Additional NFL statistics. Recovered one fumble, 1982; attempted one pass with no completions, 1985; attempted two passes with one completion for 30 yards and one interception, 1986.
Additional USFL statistics: Rushed once for no yards, 1984; attempted one pass with one interception, rushed once for minus four yards, recovered one fumble and fumbled once, 1985.
Played in AFC Championship Game following 1986 season.

RECORD AS BASEBALL PLAYER
Selected by New York Mets' organization in 5th round of free-agent draft, June 6, 1978.
Placed on restricted list, April 30, 1980.

Year Club League	Pos.	G.	AB.	R.	H.	2B.	3B.	HR.	RBI.	B.A.	PO.	A.	E.	F.A.
1978—Lynchburg Carol.	3B-OF	10	21	1	5	1	0	0	4	.238	6	8	6	.700
1978—Little Falls NYP	3B-OF	61	233	30	59	12	4	4	36	.253	54	102	19	.891
1979—Lynchburg Carol.	3B	112	386	56	98	25	2	13	53	.254	71	200	*32	.894

PRESTON GOTHARD
Tight End—Pittsburgh Steelers
Born February 23, 1962, at Montgomery, Ala.
Height, 6.04. Weight, 240.
High School—Montgomery, Ala., Lowndes Academy.
Attended University of Alabama.

Signed as free agent by Pittsburgh Steelers, May 3, 1985.
On injured reserve with knee injury, November 18 through remainder of 1987 season.

		—PASS RECEIVING—		
Year Club	G.	P.C.	Yds.	Avg.	TD.
1985—Pittsburgh NFL	16	6	83	13.8	0
1986—Pittsburgh NFL	16	21	246	11.7	1
1987—Pittsburgh NFL	2	2	9	4.5	1
Pro Totals—3 Years	34	29	338	11.7	2

Additional pro statistics: Recovered one fumble, 1985.

KURT KEOLA GOUVEIA
Linebacker—Washington Redskins
Born September 14, 1964, at Honolulu, Haw.
Height, 6.01. Weight, 227.
High School—Waianae, Haw.
Attended Brigham Young University.
Selected by Washington in 8th round (213th player selected) of 1986 NFL draft.
Signed by Washington Redskins, July 18, 1986.
On injured reserve with knee injury, August 25 through entire 1986 season.
Washington NFL, 1987.
Games: 1987 (11).
Played in NFC Championship Game following 1987 season.
Played in NFL Championship Game following 1987 season.

CORNELL ANTHONY GOWDY
Defensive Back—Pittsburgh Steelers
Born October 2, 1963, at Washington, D. C.
Height, 6.01. Weight, 197.
High School—Seat Pleasant, Md., Central.
Received bachelor of science degree in business administration
from Morgan State University in 1985.
Signed as free agent by Pittsburgh Steelers, July 15, 1985.
Released by Pittsburgh Steelers, July 30, 1985; signed as free agent by Dallas Cowboys, May 2, 1986.
Released by Dallas Cowboys, September 23, 1986; signed as free agent by New York Giants for 1987, October 27, 1986.
Released by New York Giants, August 31, 1987; signed as free agent replacement player by Pittsburgh Steelers, September 24, 1987.
Dallas NFL, 1986; Pittsburgh NFL, 1987.
Games: 1986 (3), 1987 (13). Total—16.
Pro statistics: Intercepted two passes for 50 yards and a touchdown, recovered two fumbles for one yard and returned one kickoff for no yards, 1987.

SAMUEL LOUIS GRADDY
(Sam)
Wide Receiver—Denver Broncos
Born February 10, 1964, At Gaffney, S. C.
Height, 5.10. Weight, 165.
High School—Atlanta, Ga., Northside.
Received bachelor of arts degree in economics from University of Tennessee in 1987.
Signed as free agent by Denver Broncos, May 1, 1987.
On injured reserve with hamstring injury, September 1 through December 11, 1987; activated, December 12, 1987.
Denver NFL, 1987.
Games: 1987 (1).
Member of Denver Broncos for NFL Championship Game following 1987 season; inactive.

RICHARD GLENN GRAF
(Rick)
Linebacker—Miami Dolphins
Born August 29, 1963, at Iowa City, Ia.
Height, 6.05. Weight, 239.
High School—Madison, Wis., James Madison Memorial.
Received bachelor of arts degree in communication arts from University of Wisconsin in 1987.
Selected by Miami in 2nd round (43rd player selected) of 1987 NFL draft.
Signed by Miami Dolphins, August 1, 1987.
Miami NFL, 1987.
Games: 1987 (12).
Pro statistics: Recovered one fumble, 1987.

DONALD JOHN GRAHAM
(Don)
Linebacker—Tampa Bay Buccaneers
Born January 31, 1964, at Pittsburgh, Pa.
Height, 6.02. Weight, 244.
High School—Pittsburgh, Pa., Brentwood.
Received degree in hotel, restaurant and institutional management
from Penn State University in 1987.
Selected by Tampa Bay in 4th round (84th player selected) of 1987 NFL draft.
Signed by Tampa Bay Buccaneers, July 18, 1987.
On injured reserve with stomach injury, November 7 through remainder of 1987 season.
Tampa Bay NFL, 1987.
Games: 1987 (2).

DARRYL GRANT
Defensive Tackle—Washington Redskins
Born November 22, 1959, at San Antonio, Tex.
Height, 6.01. Weight, 275.
High School—San Antonio, Tex., Highlands.
Attended Rice University.

Selected by Washington in 9th round (231st player selected) of 1981 NFL draft.
On injured reserve with knee injury, November 2 through remainder of 1985 season.
Washington NFL, 1981 through 1987.
Games: 1981 (15), 1982 (9), 1983 (16), 1984 (15), 1985 (8), 1986 (16), 1987 (12). Total—91.
Pro statistics: Returned one kickoff for 20 yards, 1981; recovered two fumbles, 1983; recovered four fumbles for 22 yards and a touchdown, 1984; recovered one fumble, 1987.
Played in NFC Championship Game following 1982, 1983, 1986 and 1987 seasons.
Played in NFL Championship Game following 1982, 1983 and 1987 seasons.

JERRY GRAY
Cornerback—Los Angeles Rams
Born December 2, 1962, at Lubbock, Tex.
Height, 6.00. Weight, 185.
High School—Lubbock, Tex., Estacado.
Attended University of Texas.

Named as defensive back on THE SPORTING NEWS College All-America Team, 1984.
Selected by San Antonio in 1985 USFL territorial draft.
Selected by Los Angeles Rams in 1st round (21st player selected) of 1985 NFL draft.
Signed by Los Angeles Rams, August 1, 1985.
Crossed picket line during players' strike, October 14, 1987.

Year Club	G.	No.	Yds.	Avg.	TD.
1985—L.A. Rams NFL.............	16		None		
1986—L.A. Rams NFL.............	16	8	101	12.6	0
1987—L.A. Rams NFL.............	12	2	35	17.5	0
Pro Totals—3 Years.............	44	10	136	13.6	0

Additional pro statistics: Recovered one fumble, 1986 and 1987; recovered blocked punt in end zone for a touchdown, 1987.
Played in NFC Championship Game following 1985 season.
Played in Pro Bowl (NFL All-Star Game) following 1986 and 1987 seasons.

MEL GRAY
Running Back—New Orleans Saints
Born March 16, 1961, at Williamsburg, Va.
Height, 5.09. Weight, 166.
High School—Williamsburg, Va., Lafayette.
Attended Coffeyville Junior College and Purdue University.

Named as punt returner to THE SPORTING NEWS All-Star Team, 1987.
Named as kickoff returner to THE SPORTING NEWS NFL All-Star Team, 1986.
Selected by Chicago in 7th round (132nd player selected) of 1984 USFL draft.
USFL rights traded by Chicago Blitz to Los Angeles Express for wide receiver Kris Haines, February 11, 1984.
Signed by Los Angeles Express, February 16, 1984.
On developmental squad, February 24 through March 8, 1984; activated, March 9, 1984.
On developmental squad, May 26 through June 8, 1984; activated, June 9, 1984.
Selected by New Orleans in 2nd round (42nd player selected) of 1984 NFL supplemental draft.
Traded with defensive backs Dwight Drane, John Warren and Troy West, guard Wayne Jones, linebacker Howard Carson and tight end Ken O'Neal by Los Angeles Express to Arizona Outlaws for past considerations, August 1, 1985.
Granted free agency when USFL suspended operations, August 7, 1986; signed by New Orleans Saints, August 18, 1986.
Granted roster exemption, August 18 through August 28, 1986; activated, August 29, 1986.
On developmental squad for 4 games with Los Angeles Express in 1984

Year Club	G.	—RUSHING—				PASS RECEIVING				—TOTAL—		
		Att.	Yds.	Avg.	TD.	P.C.	Yds.	Avg.	TD.	TD.	Pts.	F.
1984—Los Angeles USFL..................................	15	133	625	4.7	3	27	288	10.7	1	4	24	10
1985—Los Angeles USFL..................................	16	125	526	4.2	1	20	101	5.1	0	1	6	7
1986—New Orleans NFL...................................	16	6	29	4.8	0	2	45	22.5	0	1	6	0
1987—New Orleans NFL...................................	12	8	37	4.6	1	6	30	5.0	0	1	6	3
USFL Totals—2 Years..............................	31	258	1151	4.5	4	47	389	8.3	1	5	30	17
NFL Totals—2 Years...............................	28	14	66	4.7	1	8	75	9.4	0	2	12	3
Pro Totals—4 Years................................	59	272	1217	4.5	5	55	464	8.4	1	7	42	20

Year Club	G.	—PUNT RETURNS—				—KICKOFF RET.—			
		No.	Yds.	Avg.	TD.	No.	Yds.	Avg.	TD.
1984—Los Angeles USFL..................................	15		None			20	332	16.6	0
1985—Los Angeles USFL..................................	16		None			11	203	18.5	0
1986—New Orleans NFL...................................	16		None			31	866	27.9	*1
1987—New Orleans NFL...................................	12	24	352	*14.7	0	30	636	21.2	0
USFL Totals—2 Years..............................	31		None			31	535	17.3	0
NFL Totals—2 Years...............................	28	24	352	14.7	0	61	1502	24.6	1
Pro Totals—4 Years................................	59	24	352	14.7	0	92	2037	22.1	1

Additional USFL statistics: Attempted one pass with one completion for 29 yards and recovered two fumbles, 1984; recovered one fumble, 1985.
Additional NFL statistics: Recovered one fumble, 1987.

DAVID LEE GRAYSON
(Dave)
Linebacker—Cleveland Browns
Born February 27, 1964, at San Diego, Calif.
Height, 6.02. Weight, 229.
High School—San Diego, Calif., Abraham Lincoln.
Attended California State Poly University and Fresno State University.
Son of Dave Grayson, defensive back with Dallas Texans-Kansas City Chiefs
and Oakland Raiders, 1961 through 1970.

Selected by San Francisco in 8th round (217th player selected) of 1987 NFL draft.
Signed by San Francisco 49ers, July 15, 1987.
Released by San Francisco 49ers, August 28, 1987; signed as free agent replacement player by Cleveland Browns, September 23, 1987.
Cleveland NFL, 1987.
Games: 1987 (11).
Pro statistics: Recovered one fumble for 17 yards and a touchdown and returned one kickoff for six yards, 1987.
Played in AFC Championship Game following 1987 season.

CURTIS GREEN
Defensive End-Nose Tackle—Detroit Lions
Born June 3, 1957, at Quincy, Fla.
Height, 6.03. Weight, 265.
High School—Quincy, Fla., James A. Shanks.
Attended Alabama State University.

Selected by Detroit in 2nd round (46th player selected) of 1981 NFL draft.
On inactive list, September 19, 1982.
Detroit NFL, 1981 through 1987.
Games: 1981 (14), 1982 (7), 1983 (16), 1984 (16), 1985 (15), 1986 (16), 1987 (12). Total—96.
Pro statistics: Recovered one fumble, 1981 and 1985; returned one kickoff for no yards and fumbled once, 1987.

DARRELL GREEN
Cornerback—Washington Redskins
Born February 15, 1960, at Houston, Tex.
Height, 5.08. Weight, 170.
High School—Houston, Tex., Jesse Jones.
Attended Texas A&I University.

Selected by Denver in 10th round (112th player selected) of 1983 USFL draft.
Selected by Washington in 1st round (28th player selected) of 1983 NFL draft.
Signed by Washington Redskins, June 10, 1983.

| | | -INTERCEPTIONS- | | | -PUNT RETURNS- | | | | —TOTAL— | | |
Year Club	G.	No.	Yds.	Avg.	TD.	No.	Yds.	Avg.	TD.	TD.	Pts.	F.
1983—Washington NFL	16	2	7	3.5	0	4	29	7.3	0	0	0	1
1984—Washington NFL	16	5	91	18.2	1	2	13	6.5	0	1	6	0
1985—WashingtonNFL	16	2	0	0.0	0	16	214	13.4	0	0	0	2
1986—Washington NFL	16	5	9	1.8	0	12	120	10.0	0	0	0	0
1987—Washington NFL	12	3	65	21.7	0	5	53	10.6	0	1	6	0
Pro Totals—5 Years	76	17	172	10.1	1	39	429	11.0	0	2	12	3

Additional pro statistics: Recovered one fumble, 1983, 1985 and 1986; rushed once for six yards, 1985; fumbled once, 1986; recovered one fumble for 26 yards and a touchdown, 1987.
Played in NFC Championship Game following 1983, 1986 and 1987 seasons.
Played in NFL Championship Game following 1983 and 1987 seasons.
Played in Pro Bowl (NFL All-Star Game) following 1984, 1986 and 1987 seasons.

HUGH DONELL GREEN
Linebacker—Miami Dolphins
Born July 27, 1959, at Natchez, Miss.
Height, 6.02. Weight, 225.
High School—Natchez, Miss., North.
Attended University of Pittsburgh.

Named THE SPORTING NEWS College Player of the Year, 1980.
Named as defensive end on THE SPORTING NEWS College All-America Team, 1979 and 1980.
Named to THE SPORTING NEWS NFL All-Star Team, 1980.
Selected by Tampa Bay in 1st round (7th player selected) of 1981 NFL draft.
On non-football injury list with eye and wrist injury, November 1 through November 29, 1984; activated, November 30, 1984.
Traded by Tampa Bay Buccaneers to Miami Dolphins for 1st and 2nd round picks in 1986 draft, October 9, 1985.
On injured reserve with knee injury, September 23 through remainder of 1986 season.
On injured reserve with knee injury, September 7 through October 23, 1987; activated, October 24, 1987.

Year Club	G.	No.	Yds.	Avg.	TD.
		—INTERCEPTIONS—			
1981—Tampa Bay NFL	16	2	56	28.0	0
1982—Tampa Bay NFL	9	1	31	31.0	0
1983—Tampa Bay NFL	16	2	54	27.0	*2
1984—Tampa Bay NFL	8		None		
1985—T.B.(5)-Mia.(11) NFL...	16	1	28	28.0	0
1986—Miami NFL	3		None		
1987—Miami NFL	9		None		
Pro Totals—7 Years............	77	6	169	28.2	2

Additional pro statistics: Recovered one fumble, 1981 and 1985; recovered two fumbles for 11 yards and fumbled once, 1983.
Played in AFC Championship Game following 1985 season.
Played in Pro Bowl (NFL All-Star Game) following 1982 and 1983 seasons.

JACOB CARL GREEN
Defensive End—Seattle Seahawks
Born January 21, 1957, at Pasadena, Tex.
Height, 6.03. Weight, 255.
High School—Houston, Tex., Kashmere.
Attended Texas A&M University.
Cousin of George Small, defensive tackle with New York Giants and
Calgary Stampeders, 1980 through 1983.

Named to THE SPORTING NEWS NFL All-Star Team, 1984.
Selected by Seattle in 1st round (10th player selected) of 1980 NFL draft.
Seattle NFL, 1980 through 1987.
Games: 1980 (14), 1981 (16), 1982 (9), 1983 (16), 1984 (16), 1985 (16), 1986 (16), 1987 (12). Total—115.
Pro statistics: Recovered one fumble, 1981, 1986 and 1987; intercepted one pass for 73 yards and a touchdown and recovered two fumbles, 1983; recovered four fumbles, 1984; recovered two fumbles for 79 yards and a touchdown and intercepted one pass for 19 yards and a touchdown, 1985.
Played in AFC Championship Game following 1983 season.
Played in Pro Bowl (NFL All-Star Game) following 1986 and 1987 seasons.

ROY GREEN
Wide Receiver—Phoenix Cardinals
Born June 30, 1957, at Magnolia, Ark.
Height, 6.00. Weight, 195.
High School—Magnolia, Ark.
Attended Henderson State University.

Tied NFL record for longest kickoff return, game (106 yards), against Dallas Cowboys, October 21, 1979.
Named as kick returner to THE SPORTING NEWS NFC All-Star Team, 1979.
Named to THE SPORTING NEWS NFL All-Star Team, 1983 and 1984.
Selected by St. Louis in 4th round (89th player selected) of 1979 NFL draft.
On injured reserve with knee injury, December 15 through remainder of 1980 season.
On injured reserve with ankle injury, September 23 through October 23, 1986; activated, October 24, 1986.
Crossed picket line during players' strike, September 30, 1987.
Franchise transferred to Phoenix, March 15, 1988.

Year Club	G.	—RUSHING—				PASS RECEIVING				—TOTAL—		
		Att.	Yds.	Avg.	TD.	P.C.	Yds.	Avg.	TD.	TD.	Pts.	F.
1979—St. Louis NFL................................	16	None				1	15	15.0	0	1	6	4
1980—St. Louis NFL................................	15	None				None				1	6	2
1981—St. Louis NFL................................	16	3	60	20.0	1	33	708	21.5	4	5	30	2
1982—St. Louis NFL................................	9	6	8	1.3	0	32	453	14.2	3	3	18	1
1983—St. Louis NFL................................	16	4	49	12.3	0	78	1227	15.7	*14	14	84	3
1984—St. Louis NFL................................	16	1	−10	−10.0	0	78	*1555	19.9	12	12	72	1
1985—St. Louis NFL................................	13	1	2	2.0	0	50	693	13.9	5	5	30	2
1986—St. Louis NFL................................	11	2	−4	−2.0	0	42	517	12.3	6	6	36	1
1987—St. Louis NFL................................	12	2	34	17.0	0	43	731	17.0	4	4	24	1
Pro Totals—9 Years................................	124	19	139	7.3	1	357	5899	16.5	48	51	306	17

Year Club	G.	—PUNT RETURNS—				—KICKOFF RET.—			
		No.	Yds.	Avg.	TD.	No.	Yds.	Avg.	TD.
1979—St. Louis NFL................................	16	8	42	5.3	0	41	1005	24.5	*1
1980—St. Louis NFL................................	15	16	168	10.5	1	32	745	23.3	0
1981—St. Louis NFL................................	16	None				8	135	16.9	0
1982—St. Louis NFL................................	9	3	20	6.7	0	None			
1983—St. Louis NFL................................	16	None				1	14	14.0	0
1984—St. Louis NFL................................	16	None				1	18	18.0	0
1985—St. Louis NFL................................	13	None				None			
1986—St. Louis NFL................................	11	None				None			
1987—St. Louis NFL................................	12	None				None			
Pro Totals—9 Years................................	124	27	230	8.5		83	1917	23.1	1

Additional pro statistics: Recovered two fumbles, 1979; intercepted one pass for 10 yards, 1980; intercepted two passes for 44 yards, 1981; attempted one pass with no completions and recovered one fumble for two yards, 1982; recovered one fumble, 1983.
Played in Pro Bowl (NFL All-Star Game) following 1983 and 1984 seasons.

TIMOTHY JOHN GREEN
(Tim)
Linebacker—Atlanta Falcons
Born December 16, 1963, at Liverpool, N.Y.
Height, 6.02. Weight, 245.
High School—Liverpool, N.Y.
Received degree in English literature from Syracuse University in 1986.
Named as defensive lineman on THE SPORTING NEWS College All-America Team, 1984 and 1985.
Selected by New Jersey in 1986 USFL territorial draft.
Selected by Atlanta in 1st round (17th player selected) of 1986 NFL draft.
Signed by Atlanta Falcons, August 14, 1986.
Granted roster exemption, August 14 through August 21, 1986; activated, August 22, 1986.
On injured reserve with pulled calf, September 6 through October 10, 1986; activated, October 11, 1986.
Crossed picket line during players' strike, October 2, 1987.
On injured reserve with knee injury, November 17 through remainder of 1987 season.
Atlanta NFL, 1986 and 1987.
Games: 1986 (11), 1987 (9). Total—20.
Pro statistics: Recovered two fumbles for 35 yards, 1987.

GEORGE GREENE
(Tiger)
Defensive Back—Green Bay Packers
Born February 15, 1962, at Hendersonville, N.C.
Height, 6.00. Weight, 194.
High School—Flat Rock, N.C., East Henderson.
Attended Western Carolina University.
Selected by Memphis in 14th round (191st player selected) of 1985 USFL draft.
Signed as free agent by Atlanta Falcons, May 3, 1985.
On injured reserve with knee injury, September 16 through October 18, 1985; activated, October 19, 1985.
On injured reserve with ankle injury, December 10 through remainder of 1985 season.
Released by Atlanta Falcons, August 22, 1986; signed as free agent by Green Bay Packers, September 25, 1986.

| | | —INTERCEPTIONS— | | | |
Year Club	G.	No.	Yds.	Avg.TD.	
1985—Atlanta NFL	10	2	27	13.5	0
1986—Green Bay NFL............	13	2	0	0.0	0
1987—Green Bay NFL............	11	1	11	11.0	0
Pro Totals—3 Years............	34	5	38	7.6	0

Additional pro statistics: Recovered two fumbles, 1987.

KEVIN DARWIN GREENE
Linebacker—Los Angeles Rams
Born July 31, 1962, at New York, N.Y.
Height, 6.03. Weight, 238.
High School—Granite City, Ill., South.
Attended Auburn University.
Selected by Birmingham in 1985 USFL territorial draft.
Selected by Los Angeles Rams in 5th round (113th player selected) of 1985 NFL draft.
Signed by Los Angeles Rams, July 12, 1985.
Crossed picket line during players' strike, October 14, 1987.
Los Angeles Rams NFL, 1985 through 1987.
Games: 1985 (15), 1986 (16), 1987 (9). Total—40.
Pro statistics: Recovered one fumble for 13 yards, 1986; intercepted one pass for 25 yards and a touchdown, 1987.
Played in NFC Championship Game following 1985 season.

THEODORE DANIEL GREENE II
(Danny)
Wide Receiver—San Diego Chargers
Born December 26, 1961, at Compton, Calif.
Height, 5.11. Weight, 190.
High School—Compton, Calif.
Attended University of Washington.
Selected by Portland in 1985 USFL territorial draft.
Selected by Seattle in 3rd round (81st player selected) of 1985 NFL draft.
Signed by Seattle Seahawks, July 21, 1985.
On injured reserve with hamstring injury, October 2 through remainder of season.
On injured reserve with broken finger, August 26 through entire 1986 season.
Released by Seattle Seahawks, September 1, 1987; signed as free agent replacement player by San Diego Chargers, October 16, 1987.
Released by San Diego Chargers, November 3, 1987; re-signed by Chargers, May 3, 1988.

| | | PASS RECEIVING | | | | -PUNT RETURNS- | | | | —KICKOFF RET.— | | | | —TOTAL— | | |
Year Club	G.	P.C.	Yds.	Avg.	TD.	No.	Yds.	Avg.	TD.	No.	Yds.	Avg.	TD.	TD.	Pts.	F.
1985—Seattle NFL..................	4	2	10	5.0	1	11	60	5.5	0	5	144	28.8	0	1	6	1

CURTIS WILLIAM GREER
Defensive End—Phoenix Cardinals
Born November 10, 1957, at Detroit, Mich.
Height, 6.04. Weight, 258.
High School—Detroit, Mich., Cass Tech.
Received bachelor of science degree in speech communication
from University of Michigan in 1979.

Selected by St. Louis in 1st round (6th player selected) of 1980 NFL draft.
On injured reserve with concussion, September 9 through October 9, 1980; activated, October 10, 1980.
On injured reserve with broken thumb, December 15 through remainder of 1980 season.
On injured reserve with knee injury, September 2 through entire 1986 season.
Crossed picket line during players' strike, September 23, 1987.
On injured reserve with back injury, December 5 through remainder of 1987 season.
Franchise transferred to Phoenix, March 15, 1987.
St. Louis NFL, 1980 through 1985 and 1987.
Games: 1980 (11), 1981 (16), 1982 (9), 1983 (16), 1984 (16), 1985 (16), 1987 (10). Total—94.
Pro statistics: Recovered four fumbles for two yards, 1981; recovered three fumbles, 1982; recovered one fumble for five yards, 1983; recovered one fumble, 1985.

TERRY LEE GREER
Wide Receiver—San Francisco 49ers
Born September 27, 1957, at Memphis, Tenn.
Height, 6.01. Weight, 192.
High School—Memphis, Tenn., Messick.
Received bachelor of science degree in business administration from Alabama State University in 1980.

Signed as free agent by Toronto Argonauts, March 21, 1980.
Selected by Los Angeles Rams in 11th round (304th player selected) of 1980 NFL draft.
On injured reserve, August 10 through remainder of 1981 season.
Granted free agency, March 1, 1986.
Los Angeles Rams matched Cleveland Browns offer sheet and traded him to Cleveland Browns for 4th round pick in 1986 draft, April 18, 1986.
On injured reserve with knee injury, October 10 through November 9, 1986; activated, November 10, 1986.
On injured reserve with bruised thumb, December 23 through remainder of 1986 season playoffs.
Released by Cleveland Browns, September 7, 1987; signed as free agent replacement player by San Francisco 49ers, September 30, 1987.
Released by San Francisco 49ers, November 3, 1987; re-signed by 49ers, April 5, 1988.

		——RUSHING——				PASS RECEIVING				—TOTAL—		
Year Club	G.	Att.	Yds.	Avg.	TD.	P.C.	Yds.	Avg.	TD.	TD.	Pts.	F.
1980—Toronto CFL	14	2	38	19.0	1	37	552	14.9	2	3	18	0
1981—Toronto CFL	6	1	22	22.0	0	21	284	13.5	3	4	24	1
1982—Toronto CFL	15	7	52	7.4	1	85	1466	17.2	11	12	†74	1
1983—Toronto CFL	16	2	15	7.5	0	★113	★2003	17.7	8	8	48	1
1984—Toronto CFL	15	2	13	6.5	0	70	1189	17.0	14	14	84	1
1985—Toronto CFL	16	3	45	15.0	0	78	1323	17.0	9	9	54	0
1986—Cleveland NFL	11	3	51	17.0	0	3	51	17.0	0	0	0	0
1987—San Francisco NFL	3		None			6	111	18.5	1	1	6	0
CFL Totals—6 Years	82	17	185	10.9	2	404	6817	16.9	47	50	302	4
NFL Totals—2 Years	14	3	51	17.0	0	9	162	18.0	1	1	6	0
Pro Totals—8 Years	96	20	236	11.8	2	413	6979	16.9	48	51	308	4

		KICKOFF RETURNS		
Year Club	G.	No.	Yds.	Avg.TD.
1980—Toronto CFL	14	23	533	23.2 0
1981—Toronto CFL	6	11	418	38.0 1
1982—Toronto CFL	15	12	285	23.8 0
1983—Toronto CFL	16	1	0	0.0 0
1984—Toronto CFL	15	3	31	10.3 0
1985—Toronto CFL	16		None	
1986—Cleveland NFL	11		None	
1987—San Francisco NFL	3		None	
CFL Totals—6 Years	82	50	1267	25.3 1
NFL Totals—2 Years	14	0	0	0.0 0
Pro Totals—8 Years	96	50	1267	25.3 1

†Scored one 2-point conversion.
Additional pro statistics: Attempted one pass with one completion for 39 yards and a touchdown, 1982; attempted two passes with one completion for 39 yards with one touchdown and one interception, 1983; attempted three passes with one completion for 42 yards and a touchdown, 1984; attempted two passes with one completion for minus one yard and recovered one fumble for two yards, 1985.
Played in CFL Championship Game following 1982 and 1983 seasons.

DONALD FREDERICK GRIFFIN
(Don)
Cornerback—San Francisco 49ers
Born March 17, 1964, at Pelham, Ga.
Height, 6.00. Weight, 176.
High School—Pelham, Ga., Mitchell-Baker.
Attended Middle Tennessee State University.

Selected by Memphis in 1986 USFL territorial draft.
Selected by San Francisco in 6th round (162nd player selected) of 1986 NFL draft.
Signed by San Francisco 49ers, July 21, 1986.

Year Club	G.	No.	Yds.	Avg.	TD.	No.	Yds.	Avg.	TD.	TD.	Pts.	F.
		\-INTERCEPTIONS-				\-PUNT RETURNS-				—TOTAL—		
1986—San Francisco NFL	16	3	0	0.0	0	38	377	9.9	1	1	6	3
1987—San Francisco NFL	12	5	1	0.2	0	9	79	8.8	0	0	0	0
Pro Totals—2 Years	28	8	1	0.1	0	47	456	9.7	1	1	6	3

Additional pro statistics: Returned five kickoffs for 97 yards and recovered two fumbles, 1986; recovered one fumble for seven yards, 1987.

JAMES VICTOR GRIFFIN
Safety—Detroit Lions
Born September 7, 1961, at Camilla, Ga.
Height, 6.02. Weight, 197.
High School—Camilla, Ga., Mitchell.
Attended Middle Tennessee State University.

Selected by Cincinnati in 7th round (193rd player selected) of 1983 NFL draft.
Released by Cincinnati Bengals, September 1, 1986; signed as free agent by Detroit Lions, September 4, 1986.

		—INTERCEPTIONS—			
Year Club	G.	No.	Yds.	Avg.	TD.
1983—Cincinnati NFL	16	1	41	41.0	1
1984—Cincinnati NFL	16	1	57	57.0	1
1985—Cincinnati NFL	16	7	116	16.6	*1
1986—Detroit NFL	16	2	34	17.0	0
1987—Detroit NFL	12	6	130	21.7	0
Pro Totals—5 Years	76	17	378	22.2	3

Additional pro statistics: Recovered two fumbles, 1984; returned one kickoff for no yards and recovered one fumble for 29 yards, 1985.

KEITH GRIFFIN
Running Back—Washington Redskins
Born October 26, 1961, at Columbus, O.
Height, 5.08. Weight, 185.
High School—Columbus, O., Eastmoor.
Attended University of Miami (Fla.).
Brother of Archie Griffin, running back with Cincinnati Bengals and Jacksonville Bulls, 1976 through 1982 and 1984; and Ray Griffin, defensive back with Cincinnati Bengals, 1978 through 1984.

Selected by Oklahoma in 11th round (212th player selected) of 1984 USFL draft.
Selected by Washington in 10th round (279th player selected) of 1984 NFL draft.
Signed by Washington Redskins, July 13, 1984.

		—RUSHING—				PASS RECEIVING				—TOTAL—		
Year Club	G.	Att.	Yds.	Avg.	TD.	P.C.	Yds.	Avg.	TD.	TD.	Pts.	F.
1984—Washington NFL	16	97	408	4.2	0	8	43	5.4	0	0	0	7
1985—Washington NFL	16	102	473	4.6	3	37	285	7.7	0	3	18	1
1986—Washington NFL	16	62	197	3.2	0	11	110	10.0	0	0	0	0
1987—Washington NFL	9	62	242	3.9	0	3	13	4.3	1	1	6	3
Pro Totals—4 Years	57	323	1320	4.1	3	59	451	7.6	1	4	24	11

		KICKOFF RETURNS			
Year Club	G.	No.	Yds.	Avg.	TD.
1984—Washington NFL	16	9	164	18.2	0
1985—Washington NFL	16	7	142	20.3	0
1986—Washington NFL	16	8	156	19.5	0
1987—Washington NFL	9	25	478	19.1	0
Pro Totals—4 Years	57	49	940	19.2	0

Played in NFC Championship Game following 1986 season.
Played in NFL Championship Game following 1987 season.

LARRY ANTHONY GRIFFIN
Defensive Back—Pittsburgh Steelers
Born January 11, 1963, at Chesapeake, Vir.
Height, 6.00. Weight, 197.
High School—Chesapeake, Vir., Great Bridge.
Attended University of North Carolina.

Selected by Baltimore in 1986 USFL territorial draft.
Selected by Houston in 8th round (199th player selected) of 1986 NFL draft.
Signed by Houston Oilers, July 21, 1986.
Released by Houston Oilers, August 25, 1986; re-signed by Oilers, October 1, 1986.
Released by Houston Oilers, October 22, 1986; signed as free agent by Miami Dolphins, February 23, 1987.
Released by Miami Dolphins, September 7, 1987; signed as free agent replacement player by Pittsburgh Steelers, September 28, 1987.
Houston NFL, 1986; Pittsburgh NFL, 1987.
Games: 1986 (3), 1987 (7). Total—10.
Pro statistics: Intercepted two passes for two yards, 1987.

LEONARD JAMES GRIFFIN
Defensive End—Kansas City Chiefs
Born September 22, 1962, at Lake Providence, La.
Height, 6.04. Weight, 258.
High School—Lake Providence, La.
Attended Grambling State University.
Brother of Elinor Griffin, member of 1980 U.S. Women's Olympic Basketball team.
Selected by Kansas City in 3rd round (63rd player selected) of 1986 NFL draft.
Signed by Kansas City Chiefs, July 26, 1986.
On injured reserve with ankle injury, September 2 through October 24, 1986; activated, October 25, 1986.
Kansas City NFL, 1986 and 1987.
Games: 1986 (9), 1987 (12). Total—21.

STEVE BROADUS GRIFFIN
Running Back—Atlanta Falcons
Born December 17, 1963, at Charlotte, N. C.
Height, 5.10. Weight, 185.
High School—Charlotte, N. C., South Mecklenburg.
Attended Clemson University.
Signed as free agent by Atlanta Falcons, June 30, 1987.
Released by Atlanta Falcons, September 7, 1987; re-signed by Falcons, September 11, 1987.
Released by Atlanta Falcons, November 3, 1987; re-signed by Falcons, February 16, 1988.
Atlanta NFL, 1987.
Games: 1987 (4).
Pro statistics: Rushed once for minus two yards and returned one kickoff for 21 yards, 1987.

ANTHONY GRIGGS
Linebacker—Cleveland Browns
Born February 12, 1960, at Lawton, Okla.
Height, 6.03. Weight, 230.
High School—Willingboro, N.J., John F. Kennedy.
Attended Ohio State University and received degree in communications from Villanova University.
Cousin of Billy Griggs, tight end with New York Jets.
Selected by Philadelphia in 4th round (104th player selected) of 1982 NFL draft.
Traded by Philadelphia Eagles to Cleveland Browns for 8th round pick in 1986 draft, April 29, 1986.
Philadelphia NFL, 1982 through 1985; Cleveland NFL, 1986 and 1987.
Games: 1982 (9), 1983 (16), 1984 (16), 1985 (16), 1986 (16), 1987 (12). Total—85.
Pro statistics: Recovered one fumble, 1982; intercepted three passes for 61 yards, 1983; recovered one fumble for three yards, 1986.
Played in AFC Championship Game following 1986 and 1987 seasons.

WILLIAM EDWARD GRIGGS
(Billy)
Tight End—New York Jets
Born August 4, 1962, at Camden, N.J.
Height, 6.03. Weight, 230.
High School—Pennsauken, N.J.
Received bachelor of arts degree in sociology from University of Virginia in 1984.
Cousin of Anthony Griggs, linebacker with Cleveland Browns.
Selected by New York Jets in 8th round (203rd player selected) of 1984 NFL draft.
On injured reserve with ankle injury, August 14 through entire 1984 season.
New York Jets NFL, 1985 through 1987.
Games: 1985 (16), 1986 (16), 1987 (12). Total—44.
Pro statistics: Caught two passes for 17 yards and a touchdown and returned one kickoff for 13 yards, 1987.

RANDALL COLLINS GRIMES
(Randy)
Center—Tampa Bay Buccaneers
Born July 20, 1960, at Tyler, Tex.
Height, 6.04. Weight, 270.
High School—Tyler, Tex., Robert E. Lee.
Attended Baylor University.
Selected by New Jersey in 6th round (70th player selected) of 1983 USFL draft.
Selected by Tampa Bay in 2nd round (45th player selected) of 1983 NFL draft.
Signed by Tampa Bay Buccaneers, June 6, 1983.
Tampa Bay NFL, 1983 through 1987.
Games: 1983 (15), 1984 (10), 1985 (16), 1986 (16), 1987 (12). Total—69.
Pro statistics: Recovered one fumble, 1983.

—DID YOU KNOW—
That the Atlanta Falcons (205 points) and San Diego Chargers (253) combined scored fewer points in 1987 than the San Francisco 49ers (459)?

RUSS GRIMM
Center-Guard—Washington Redskins
Born May 2, 1959, at Scottsdale, Pa.
Height, 6.03. Weight, 275.
High School—Southmoreland, Pa.
Attended University of Pittsburgh.

Named to THE SPORTING NEWS NFL All-Star Team, 1985.
Selected by Washington in 3rd round (69th player selected) of 1981 NFL draft.
On injured reserve with knee injury, November 14 through December 24, 1987; activated, December 25, 1987.
Washington NFL, 1981 through 1987.
Games: 1981 (14), 1982 (9), 1983 (16), 1984 (16), 1985 (16), 1986 (15), 1987 (6). Total—92.
Pro statistics: Recovered one fumble, 1981 and 1982; recovered two fumbles, 1984 and 1986.
Played in NFC Championship Game following 1982, 1983, 1986 and 1987 seasons.
Played in NFL Championship Game following 1982, 1983 and 1987 seasons.
Played in Pro Bowl (NFL All-Star Game) following 1983 through 1986 seasons.

EDWARD PAUL GRIMSLEY
(Ed)
Linebacker—Indianapolis Colts
Born March 22, 1963, at Canton, O.
Height, 6.00. Weight, 235.
High School—Canton, O., McKinley.
Attended University of Akron.

Signed as free agent by Indianapolis Colts, May 11, 1987.
Released by Indianapolis Colts, August 31, 1987; re-signed as replacement player by Colts, September 23, 1987.
On injured reserve with knee injury, November 2 through remainder of 1987 season.
Indianapolis NFL, 1987.
Games: 1987 (5).
Pro statistics: Recovered one fumble, 1987.

JOHN GLENN GRIMSLEY
Linebacker—Houston Oilers
Born February 25, 1962, at Canton, O.
Height, 6.02. Weight, 232.
High School—Canton, O., McKinley.
Attended University of Kentucky.

Selected by Denver in 3rd round (59th player selected) of 1984 USFL draft.
Selected by Houston in 6th round (141st player selected) of 1984 NFL draft.
Signed by Houston Oilers, July 7, 1984.
Houston NFL, 1984 through 1987.
Games: 1984 (16), 1985 (15), 1986 (16), 1987 (12). Total—59.
Pro statistics: Recovered one fumble for five yards, 1985; recovered two fumbles, 1986; recovered one fumble, 1987.

STEVEN JAMES GROGAN
(Steve)
Quarterback—New England Patriots
Born July 24, 1953, at San Antonio, Tex.
Height, 6.04. Weight, 210.
High School—Ottawa, Kan.
Received bachelor of science degree in physical education from Kansas State University in 1975.
Son of Jim Grogan, assistant football coach at Ottawa University (Kan.); and brother of Scott Grogan, assistant football coach at University of Nebraska at Omaha.

Selected by New England in 5th round (116th player selected) of 1975 NFL draft.
On injured reserve with broken leg, November 30, 1985 through January 3, 1986; activated, January 4, 1986.

Year Club	G.	Att.	Cmp.	Pct.	Gain	T.P.	P.I.	Avg.	Att.	Yds.	Avg.	TD.	TD.	Pts.	F.
				PASSING						RUSHING			TOTAL		
1975—New England NFL	13	274	139	50.7	1976	11	18	7.21	30	110	3.7	3	3	18	6
1976—New England NFL	14	302	145	48.0	1903	18	20	6.30	60	397	6.6	12	13	78	6
1977—New England NFL	14	305	160	52.5	2162	17	21	7.09	61	324	5.3	1	1	6	7
1978—New England NFL	16	362	181	50.0	2824	15	23	7.80	81	539	*6.7	5	5	30	9
1979—New England NFL	16	423	206	48.7	3286	*28	20	7.77	64	368	5.8	2	2	12	12
1980—New England NFL	12	306	175	57.2	2475	18	22	*8.09	30	112	3.7	1	1	6	4
1981—New England NFL	8	216	117	54.2	1859	7	16	*8.61	12	49	4.1	2	2	12	5
1982—New England NFL	6	122	66	54.1	930	7	4	7.62	9	42	4.7	1	1	6	2
1983—New England NFL	12	303	168	55.4	2411	15	12	7.96	23	108	4.7	2	2	12	4
1984—New England NFL	3	68	32	47.1	444	3	6	6.53	7	12	1.7	0	0	0	4
1985—New England NFL	7	156	85	54.5	1311	7	5	8.40	20	29	1.5	2	2	12	6
1986—New England NFL	4	102	62	60.8	976	9	2	9.57	9	23	2.6	1	1	6	2
1987—New England NFL	7	161	93	57.8	1183	10	9	7.35	20	37	1.9	2	2	12	8
Pro Totals—13 Years	132	3100	1629	52.5	23740	165	178	7.66	426	2150	5.0	34	35	210	75

Quarterback Rating Points: 1975 (60.2), 1976 (60.8), 1977 (65.3), 1978 (63.3), 1979 (77.5), 1980 (73.1), 1981 (63.0), 1982 (84.2), 1983 (81.4), 1984 (46.4), 1985 (84.1), 1986 (113.8), 1987 (78.2). Total—71.7.
Additional pro statistics: Recovered four fumbles and fumbled six times for minus 12 yards, 1975; recovered four fumbles and one touchdown and fumbled six times for minus 18 yards, 1976; recovered two fumbles and fumbled seven times for minus 41 yards, 1977; recovered two fumbles and fumbled nine times for minus 24 yards, 1978; recovered four fumbles and fumbled 12 times for minus 12 yards, 1979; recovered one fumble and fumbled four times for minus 10

yards, 1980; recovered two fumbles, caught two passes for 27 yards and fumbled five times for minus eight yards, 1981; recovered one fumble 1982, 1983 and 1986; caught one pass for minus eight yards, 1983; recovered two fumbles and fumbled four times for minus three yards, 1984; recovered one fumble and fumbled six times for minus 10 yards, 1985; recovered six fumbles and fumbled eight times for minus six yards, 1987.

Member of New England Patriots for AFC Championship Game following 1985 season; did not play.

Played in NFL Championship Game following 1985 season.

ALFRED E. GROSS
(Al)
Safety—Cleveland Browns
Born January 4, 1961, at Stockton, Calif.
Height, 6.03. Weight, 195.
High School—Stockton, Calif., Franklin.
Attended University of Arizona.

Selected by Arizona in 1983 USFL territorial draft.
Selected by Dallas in 9th round (246th player selected) of 1983 NFL draft.
Signed by Dallas Cowboys, June 20, 1983.
Released by Dallas Cowboys, August 2, 1983; awarded on waivers to Cleveland Browns, August 4, 1983.
On injured reserve with knee injury, September 9 through November 21, 1986; activated, November 22, 1986.

| | | —INTERCEPTIONS— | | | |
Year Club	G.	No.	Yds.	Avg.	TD.
1983—Cleveland NFL..............	16	1	18	18.0	0
1984—Cleveland NFL..............	16	5	103	20.6	0
1985—Cleveland NFL..............	16	5	109	21.8	*1
1986—Cleveland NFL..............	4		None		
1987—Cleveland NFL..............	6		None		
Pro Totals—5 Years............	58	11	230	20.9	1

Additional pro statistics: Recovered one fumble for four yards, 1983; recovered two fumbles for 28 yards, 1984; recovered two fumbles for two yards, 1985; recovered one fumble in end zone for a touchdown, 1986.

Played in AFC Championship Game following 1986 season.

ROBERT LEON GRUBER JR.
(Bob)
Offensive Tackle—Miami Dolphins
Born June 7, 1958, at Del Rio, Tex.
Height, 6.05. Weight, 280.
High School—Greenville, Pa.
Received degree in criminal justice from University of Pittsburgh.

Selected by Los Angeles in 10th round (276th player selected) of 1980 NFL draft.
On injured reserve, August 18 through entire 1980 season.
Released by Los Angeles Rams, August 24, 1981; signed as free agent by Miami Dolphins, February 15, 1982.
Released by Miami Dolphins, September 6, 1982.
USFL rights traded with linebacker George Cooper, offensive tackle Brad Oates, quarterback Dan Kendra and tight end Al Kimichik by Michigan Panthers to Philadelphia Stars for rights to quarterback Dan Feraday, running back Jim Jodat and linebacker Ed O'Neil, September 27, 1982.
Signed by Philadelphia Stars, November 20, 1982.
Released by Philadelphia Stars, February 27, 1983; awarded on waivers to Birmingham Stallions, February 28, 1983.
On reserve/did not report, March 2 through entire 1983 season.
Selected by Jacksonville Bulls in 18th round (104th player selected) of USFL expansion draft, September 6, 1983.
Traded by Jacksonville Bulls to Memphis Showboats for draft choice, February 28, 1986.
Granted free agency when USFL suspended operations, August 7, 1986; signed as free agent by Cleveland Browns, August 12, 1986.
Released by Cleveland Browns, August 26, 1986; re-signed by Browns, August 28, 1986.
On injured reserve with knee injury, September 1 through October 8, 1986; activated after clearing procedural waivers, October 10, 1986.
Released by Cleveland Browns, December 13, 1986; re-signed by Browns, April 22, 1987.
Released by Cleveland Browns, September 7, 1987; signed as free agent replacement player by Green Bay Packers, October 15, 1987.
Released by Green Bay Packers, October 22, 1987; signed as free agent by Miami Dolphins, December 15, 1987.
Active for 9 games with Cleveland Browns in 1986; did not play.
Active for 2 games with Miami Dolphins in 1987; did not play.
Jacksonville USFL, 1984 and 1985; Cleveland NFL, 1986; Green Bay (1)-Miami (0) NFL, 1987.
Games: 1984 (18), 1985 (18), 1987 (1). Total USFL—36. Total Pro—37.
Pro statistics: Recovered one fumble, 1984.

NEAL E. GUGGEMOS
Safety—Minnesota Vikings
Born June 14, 1964, at Winsted, Minn.
Height, 6.00. Weight, 187.
High School—Winsted, Minn., Holy Trinity.
Attended College of St. Thomas.

Signed as free agent by Minnesota Vikings, May 2, 1986.
On injured reserve with broken thumb, August 18 through November 24, 1986; activated after clearing procedural waivers, November 26, 1986.

Year Club	G.	No.	Yds.	Avg.TD.	
1986—Minnesota NFL.............	4			None	
1987—Minnesota NFL.............	12	36	808	22.4	0
Pro Totals—2 Years...........	16	36	808	22.4	0

Additional pro statistics: Intercepted one pass for 26 yards, recovered three fumbles and fumbled four times, 1987.
Played in NFC Championship Game following 1987 season.

MICHAEL DONALD GUMAN
(Mike)
Fullback—Los Angeles Rams

Born April 21, 1958, at Allentown, Pa.
Height, 6.02. Weight, 218.
High School—Bethlehem, Pa., Catholic.
Received bachelor of science degree in marketing from Penn State University in 1980.

Selected by Los Angeles in 6th round (154th player selected) of 1980 NFL draft.
On injured reserve with knee injury, September 19 through November 14, 1985; activated, November 15, 1985.
On injured reserve with knee injury, November 25 through remainder of 1986 season.
Released by Los Angeles Rams, September 7, 1987; re-signed by Rams, September 8, 1987.
Crossed picket line during players' strike, October 1, 1987.

		——RUSHING——				PASS RECEIVING				—TOTAL—		
Year Club	G.	Att.	Yds.	Avg.	TD.	P.C.	Yds.	Avg.	TD.	TD.	Pts.	F.
1980—Los Angeles Rams NFL	16	100	410	4.1	4	14	131	9.4	0	4	24	4
1981—Los Angeles Rams NFL	16	115	433	3.8	4	18	130	7.2	0	4	24	2
1982—Los Angeles Rams NFL	9	69	266	3.9	2	31	310	10.0	0	2	12	3
1983—Los Angeles Rams NFL	16	7	42	6.0	0	34	347	10.2	4	4	24	0
1984—Los Angeles Rams NFL	16	1	2	2.0	0	19	161	8.5	0	1	6	0
1985—Los Angeles Rams NFL	8	11	32	2.9	0	3	23	7.7	0	0	0	1
1986—Los Angeles Rams NFL	12	2	2	1.0	0	9	68	7.6	0	0	0	0
1987—Los Angeles Rams NFL	12	36	98	2.7	1	22	263	12.0	0	1	6	0
Pro Totals—8 Years....................	105	341	1285	3.8	11	150	1433	9.6	4	16	96	10

Additional pro statistics: Attempted one pass with one completion for 31 yards and a touchdown, returned two punts for six yards and returned two kickoffs for 25 yards, 1980; attempted one pass with one completion for seven yards and a touchdown and returned one kickoff for 10 yards, 1981; attempted one pass with one interception and returned eight kickoffs for 102 yards, 1982; returned two kickoffs for 30 yards, 1983 and 1985; returned one kickoff for 43 yards and a touchdown and recovered one fumble, 1984; returned two kickoffs for 28 yards, 1986; returned two kickoffs for 18 yards, 1987.
Played in NFC Championship Game following 1985 season.

JAMES JOEL GUSTAFSON
(Jim)
Wide Receiver—Minnesota Vikings

Born March 16, 1961, at Minneapolis, Minn.
Height, 6.01. Weight, 178.
High School—Bloomington, Minn., Lincoln.
Received degree in finance from St. Thomas College in 1983.

Signed as free agent by Cincinnati Bengals, April 28, 1983.
Released by Cincinnati Bengals, August 29, 1983; signed as free agent by Minnesota Vikings, March 3, 1984.
Released by Minnesota Vikings, August 13, 1984; re-signed by Vikings, April 21, 1985.
On injured reserve with separated shoulder, August 20 through entire 1985 season.

		——PASS RECEIVING——			
Year Club	G.	P.C.	Yds.	Avg.	TD.
1986—Minnesota NFL.............	14	5	61	12.2	2
1987—Minnesota NFL.............	12	4	55	13.8	0
Pro Totals—2 Years............	26	9	116	12.9	2

Additional pro statistics: Rushed once for minus two yards, 1987.
Played in NFC Championship Game following 1987 season.

KEITH EDWIN GUTHRIE
Nose Tackle—Kansas City Chiefs

Born August 17, 1962, at Tyler, Tex.
Height, 6.04. Weight, 275.
High School—Tyler, Tex., John Tyler.
Attended Texas A&M University.

Selected by Houston in 1984 USFL territorial draft.
Selected by San Diego in 6th round (144th player selected) of 1984 NFL draft.
Signed by San Diego Chargers, June 10, 1984.
On injured reserve with chipped tailbone, August 28 through September 27, 1984; activated, September 28, 1984.
Released by San Diego Chargers, August 26, 1985; signed as free agent by Houston Oilers, June 4, 1987.
Released by Houston Oilers, September 1, 1987; signed as free agent replacement player by Kansas City Chiefs, September 24, 1987.
On injured reserve with knee injury, October 3 through remainder of 1987 season.
San Diego NFL, 1984.
Games: 1984 (11).

BARRY DEAN HACKETT
(Dino)
Linebacker—Kansas City Chiefs
Born June 28, 1964, at Greensboro, N.C.
Height, 6.03. Weight, 225.
High School—Greensboro, N.C., Southern Guilford.
Received degree in criminal justice from Appalachian State University in 1986.
Brother of Joey Hackett, tight end with Green Bay Packers.

Selected by Kansas City in 2nd round (35th player selected) of 1986 NFL draft.
Signed by Kansas City Chiefs, July 23, 1986.
Kansas City NFL, 1986 and 1987.
Games: 1986 (16), 1987 (11). Total—27.
Pro statistics: Intercepted one pass for no yards and recovered two fumbles, 1986.

JOSEPH GLENN HACKETT
(Joey)
Tight End—Green Bay Packers
Born September 29, 1958, at Greensboro, N.C.
Height, 6.05. Weight, 267.
High School—Greensboro, N.C., Southern Guilford.
Received degree from Elon College in 1980.
Brother of Dino Hackett, linebacker with Kansas City Chiefs.

Signed as free agent by Dallas Cowboys, May, 1981.
Released by Dallas Cowboys, August 24, 1981; signed as free agent by Washington Redskins, April 2, 1982.
Released by Washington Redskins, June 21, 1982; signed by New Jersey Generals, November 11, 1982.
Released by New Jersey Generals, February 20, 1983; re-signed by Generals, March 2, 1983.
On developmental squad, March 4 through March 18, 1983; activated, March 19, 1983.
On developmental squad, March 26 through May 17, 1983.
On injured reserve with broken hand, May 18 through June 26, 1983; activated from injured reserve after clearing procedural waivers, June 28, 1983.
On developmental squad, June 28 through remainder of 1983 season.
Selected by San Antonio Gunslingers in 14th round (81st player selected) of USFL expansion draft, September 6, 1983.
Released by San Antonio Gunslingers, July 23, 1985; signed as free agent by Denver Broncos, May 17, 1986.
Released by Denver Broncos, September 7, 1987; signed as free agent by Green Bay Packers, September 16, 1987.
On developmental squad for 11 games with New Jersey Generals in 1983.

		——PASS RECEIVING——			
Year Club	G.	P.C.	Yds.	Avg.	TD.
1984—San Antonio USFL........	18	29	431	14.9	5
1985—San Antonio USFL........	18	34	515	15.2	3
1986—Denver NFL.................	16	3	48	16.0	0
1987—Green Bay NFL............	11		None		
USFL Totals—2 Years........	36	63	946	15.0	8
NFL Totals—2 Years..........	27	3	48	16.0	0
Pro Totals—4 Years............	63	66	994	15.1	8

Additional USFL statistics: Recovered one fumble, 1984; fumbled twice, 1985.
Additional NFL statistics: Recovered one fumble, 1986.
Played in AFC Championship Game following 1986 season.
Played in NFL Championship Game following 1986 season.

MICHAEL HADDIX
Fullback—Philadelphia Eagles
Born December 27, 1961, at Tippah County, Miss.
Height, 6.02. Weight, 225.
High School—Walnut, Miss.
Attended Mississippi State University.
Cousin of Wayne Haddix, cornerback with New York Giants.

Selected by Denver in 2nd round (16th player selected) of 1983 USFL draft.
Selected by Philadelphia in 1st round (8th player selected) of 1983 NFL draft.
Signed by Philadelphia Eagles, May 13, 1983.

		——RUSHING——				PASS RECEIVING				—TOTAL—		
Year Club	G.	Att.	Yds.	Avg.	TD.	P.C.	Yds.	Avg.	TD.	TD.	Pts.	F.
1983—Philadelphia NFL	14	91	220	2.4	2	23	254	11.0	0	2	12	4
1984—Philadelphia NFL	14	48	130	2.7	1	33	231	7.0	0	1	6	2
1985—Philadelphia NFL	16	67	213	3.2	0	43	330	7.7	0	0	0	2
1986—Philadelphia NFL	16	79	276	3.5	0	26	150	5.8	0	0	0	1
1987—Philadelphia NFL	12	59	165	2.8	0	7	58	8.3	0	0	0	1
Pro Totals—5 Years.....................	72	344	1004	2.9	3	132	1023	7.8	0	3	18	10

Additional pro statistics: Returned three kickoffs for 51 yards, 1983; recovered one fumble, 1986; returned two kickoffs for 16 yards, 1987.

—DID YOU KNOW—
That the Chicago Bears went 7-0 in divisional play in 1987 while the Cincinnati Bengals were 0-6 within their division?

WAYNE HADDIX
Cornerback—New York Giants

Born July 23, 1965, at Bolivar, Tenn.
Height, 6.01. Weight, 203.
High School—Middleton, Tenn.
Attended Liberty Baptist.
Cousin of Michael Haddix, fullback with Philadelphia Eagles.

Signed as free agent by New York Giants, May 11, 1987.
On injured reserve with knee injury, September 7 through November 6, 1987; activated, November 7, 1987.
New York Giants NFL, 1987.
Games: 1987 (5).

MICHAEL HAIGHT
(Mike)

Name pronounced Hate.

Guard-Offensive Tackle—New York Jets

Born October 6, 1962, at Manchester, Ia.
Height, 6.04. Weight, 270.
High School—Dyersville, Ia., Beckman.
Attended University of Iowa.
Brother of Dave Haight, nose tackle at University of Iowa.

Selected by New York Jets in 1st round (22nd player selected) of 1986 NFL draft.
Selected by Orlando in 1st round (1st player selected) of 1986 USFL draft.
Signed by New York Jets, July 23, 1986.
On injured reserve with knee injury, September 2 through October 3, 1986; activated, October 4, 1986.
New York Jets NFL, 1986 and 1987.
Games: 1986 (2), 1987 (6). Total—8.

CARL BLAKE HAIRSTON
Defensive End—Cleveland Browns

Born December 15, 1952, at Martinsville, Va.
Height, 6.04. Weight, 260.
High School—Martinsville, Va.
Received bachelor of arts degree in education from University of Maryland (Eastern Shore) in 1985.

Selected by Philadelphia in 7th round (191st player selected) of 1976 NFL draft.
Traded by Philadelphia Eagles to Cleveland Browns for 9th round pick in 1985 draft, February 9, 1984.
Crossed picket line during players' strike, October 7, 1987.
Philadelphia NFL, 1976 through 1983; Cleveland NFL, 1984 through 1987.
Games: 1976 (14), 1977 (14), 1978 (16), 1979 (15), 1980 (16), 1981 (16), 1982 (9), 1983 (16), 1984 (16), 1985 (16), 1986 (16), 1987 (14). Total—178.
Pro statistics: Recovered one fumble, 1977, 1980, 1981 and 1985 through 1987; intercepted one pass for no yards, 1980; recovered two fumbles for 24 yards, 1982; recovered two fumbles, 1983; ran 40 yards with lateral from interception, 1987.
Played in NFC Championship Game following 1980 season.
Played in AFC Championship Game following 1986 and 1987 seasons.
Played in NFL Championship Game following 1980 season.

ALI HAJI-SHEIKH

Name pronounced Hodgie-Sheek.

Placekicker—Washington Redskins

Born January 11, 1961, at Ann Arbor, Mich.
Height, 6.00. Weight, 172.
High School—Arlington, Tex.
Attended University of Michigan.

Established NFL record for most field goals, season (35), 1983.
Named to THE SPORTING NEWS NFL All-Star Team, 1983.
Selected by Michigan in 1983 USFL territorial draft.
Selected by New York Giants in 9th round (237th player selected) of 1983 NFL draft.
Signed by New York Giants, June 13, 1983.
On injured reserve with hamstring injury, September 17 through remainder of 1985 season.
On injured reserve with groin injury, September 1 through September 16, 1986.
Released by New York Giants, September 17, 1986; signed as free agent by Atlanta Falcons, November 12, 1986.
Released by Atlanta Falcons, August 25, 1987; signed as free agent by Washington Redskins, September 16, 1987.

		—————PLACE KICKING—————					
Year	Club	G.	XP.	XPM.	FG.	FGA.	Pts.
1983—N.Y. Giants NFL		16	22	1	*35	42	127
1984—N.Y. Giants NFL		16	32	3	17	33	83
1985—N.Y. Giants NFL		2	5	0	2	5	11
1986—Atlanta NFL		6	7	1	9	12	34
1987—Washington NFL		11	29	*3	13	19	68
Pro Totals—5 Years		51	95	8	76	111	323

Additional pro statistics: Had only attempted punt blocked, 1984.
Played in NFC Championship Game following 1987 season.
Played in NFL Championship Game following 1987 season.
Played in Pro Bowl (NFL All-Star Game) following 1983 season.

CHARLES LEWIS HALEY
Defensive End—San Francisco 49ers
Born January 6, 1964, at Gladys, Va.
Height, 6.05. Weight, 230.
High School—Naruna, Va., William Campbell.
Attended James Madison University.

Selected by San Francisco in 4th round (96th player selected) of 1986 NFL draft.
Signed by San Francisco 49ers, May 27, 1986.
San Francisco NFL, 1986 and 1987.
Games: 1986 (16), 1987 (12). Total—28.
Pro statistics: Intercepted one pass for eight yards; recovered two fumbles for three yards and fumbled once, 1986.

DARRYL HALEY
Offensive Tackle-Guard—Cleveland Browns
Born February 16, 1961, at Los Angeles, Calif.
Height, 6.04. Weight, 265.
High School—Los Angeles, Calif., Alin Leroy Locke.
Attended University of Utah.
Cousin of Darrell Jackson, pitcher with Minnesota Twins, 1978 through 1982.

Selected by New England in 2nd round (55th player selected) of 1982 NFL draft.
On non-football injury list with colitis, August 28 through entire 1985 season.
Traded by New England Patriots to Tampa Bay Buccaneers for conditional draft pick, July 27, 1987.
Released by Tampa Bay Buccaneers, August 5, 1987; signed as free agent by San Diego Chargers, August 11, 1987.
Released by San Diego Chargers, August 27, 1987; signed as free agent replacement player by Cleveland Browns, October 10, 1987.
New England NFL, 1982 through 1984 and 1986; Cleveland NFL, 1987.
Games: 1982 (9), 1983 (16), 1984 (16), 1986 (16), 1987 (9). Total—66.
Played in AFC Championship Game following 1987 season.

DELTON DWAYNE HALL
Cornerback—Pittsburgh Steelers
Born January 16, 1965, at Greensboro, N.C.
Height, 6.01. Weight, 205.
High School—Greensboro, N.C., Grimsley.
Attended Clemson University.

Selected by Pittsburgh in 2nd round (38th player selected) of 1987 NFL draft.
Signed by Pittsburgh Steelers, August 6, 1987.

		——INTERCEPTIONS——			
Year	Club	G.	No.	Yds.	Avg.TD.
1987—Pittsburgh NFL............		12	3	29	9.7 1

Additional pro statistics: Recovered two fumbles for 50 yards and a touchdown and fumbled once, 1987.

RONALD A. HALL
(Ron)
Tight End—Tampa Bay Buccaneers
Born March 15, 1964, at Fort Huachuca, Ariz.
Height, 6.04. Weight, 238.
High School—Escondido, Calif., San Pasqual.
Attended California State Poly University and University of Hawaii.

Selected by Tampa Bay in 4th round (87th player selected) of 1987 NFL draft.
Signed by Tampa Bay Buccaneers, July 18, 1987.

		——PASS RECEIVING——			
Year	Club	G.	P.C.	Yds.	Avg. TD.
1987—Tampa Bay NFL..........		11	16	169	10.6 1

RONALD DAVID HALLSTROM
(Ron)
Guard—Green Bay Packers
Born June 11, 1959, at Holden, Mass.
Height, 6.06. Weight, 290.
High School—Moline, Ill.
Attended Iowa Central Junior College and University of Iowa.

Selected by Green Bay in 1st round (22nd player selected) of 1982 NFL draft.
On inactive list, September 12 and September 20, 1982.
Green Bay NFL, 1982 through 1987.
Games: 1982 (6), 1983 (16), 1984 (16), 1985 (16), 1986 (16), 1987 (12). Total—82.
Pro statistics: Recovered two fumbles for one yard, 1984; recovered one fumble, 1985 and 1987.

MIKE HAMBY
Defensive End—Buffalo Bills
Born November 2, 1962, at Salt Lake City, Utah.
Height, 6.04. Weight, 270.
High School—Lehi, Utah.
Attended Utah State University.

Selected by Jacksonville in 2nd round (27th player selected) of 1985 USFL draft.
Selected by Buffalo in 6th round (141st player selected) of 1985 NFL draft.
Signed by Buffalo Bills, July 19, 1985.
On injured reserve with knee injury, August 19 through entire 1985 season.
On injured reserve with groin injury, September 1 through entire 1987 season.
Crossed picket line during players' strike, October 14, 1987.
Buffalo NFL, 1986.
Games: 1986 (16).
Pro statistics: Recovered one fumble, 1986.

DEAN HAMEL
Defensive Tackle—Washington Redskins
Born July 7, 1961, at Detroit, Mich.
Height, 6.03. Weight, 290.
High School—Warren, Mich., Mott.
Attended Coffeyville Community College and University of Tulsa.

Selected by Washington in 12th round (309th player selected) in 1985 NFL draft.
Signed by Washington Redskins, June 14, 1985.
Washington NFL, 1985 through 1987.
Games: 1985 (16), 1986 (16), 1987 (12). Total—44.
Pro statistics: Returned one kickoff for 14 yards, 1985.
Played in NFC Championship Game following 1986 and 1987 seasons.
Played in NFL Championship Game following 1987 season.

HARRY E. HAMILTON
Safety—New York Jets
Born November 29, 1962, at Jamaica, N.Y.
Height, 6.00. Weight, 193.
High School—Nanticoke, Pa., John S. Fine.
Received bachelor of arts degree in pre-law and liberal arts from Penn State University in 1984.

Selected by Philadelphia in 1984 USFL territorial draft.
Selected by New York Jets in 7th round (176th player selected) of 1984 NFL draft.
Signed by New York Jets, May 29, 1984.
On injured reserve with knee injury, October 22 through remainder of 1984 season.
On injured reserve with shoulder injury, October 14 through November 15, 1985; activated, November 16, 1985.

		——INTERCEPTIONS——			
Year Club	G.	No.	Yds.	Avg.	TD.
1984—N.Y. Jets NFL	8	None			
1985—N.Y. Jets NFL	11	2	14	7.0	0
1986—N.Y. Jets NFL	15	1	29	29.0	0
1987—N.Y. Jets NFL	12	3	25	8.3	0
Pro Totals—4 Years............	46	6	68	11.3	0

Additional pro statistics: Recovered one fumble, 1985 and 1987; recovered two fumbles for 28 yards, 1986.

STEVEN HAMILTON
(Steve)
Defensive End-Defensive Tackle—Washington Redskins
Born September 28, 1961, at Niagara Falls, N.Y.
Height, 6.04. Weight, 270.
High School—Williamsville, N.Y., East
Attended Fork Union Military Academy and East Carolina University.

Selected by Michigan in 4th round (79th player selected) of 1984 USFL draft.
Selected by Washington in 2nd round (55th player selected) of 1984 NFL draft.
Signed by Washington Redskins, June 5, 1984.
On injured reserve with fractured ankle, August 20 through entire 1984 season.
On injured reserve with shoulder injury, September 3, through November 1, 1985; activated, November 2, 1985.
On injured reserve with knee injury, December 6, 1986 through January 8, 1987; activated, January 9, 1987.
Washington NFL, 1985 through 1987.
Games: 1985 (7), 1986 (12), 1987 (12). Total—31.
Pro statistics: Recovered one fumble, 1987.
Played in NFC Championship Game following 1986 and 1987 seasons.
Played in NFL Championship Game following 1987 season.

BOB HAMM
Defensive End—Indianapolis Colts
Born April 24, 1959, at Kansas City, Mo.
Height, 6.04. Weight, 263.
High School—Mountain View, Calif., St. Francis.
Attended University of Nevada at Reno.

Signed as free agent by Kansas City Chiefs, May 9, 1983.
On injured reserve with knee injury, August 28 through September 27, 1984; activated, September 28, 1984.
Released by Kansas City Chiefs, August 29, 1983; awarded on waivers to Houston Oilers, August 30, 1983.
Traded with 4th round pick in 1986 draft by Houston Oilers to Kansas City Chiefs for 5th and 6th round picks in 1985 draft, April 30, 1985.

On injured reserve with knee injury, December 11 through remainder of 1985 season.
On injured reserve with knee injury, August 25 through November 3, 1986.
Released by Kansas City Chiefs, November 4, 1986; signed as free agent by New York Jets, March 26, 1987.
Released by New York Jets, June 10, 1987; signed as free agent replacement player by Indianapolis Colts, September 23, 1987.
Released by Indianapolis Colts, October 20, 1987; re-signed by Colts for 1988, December 10, 1987.
Houston NFL, 1983 through 1985; Indianapolis NFL, 1987.
Games: 1983 (16), 1984 (12), 1985 (14), 1987 (3). Total—45.
Pro statistics: Recovered one fumble, 1984.

MICHAEL SCOTT HAMMERSTEIN
(Mike)
Defensive End—Cincinnati Bengals
Born March 29, 1963, at Kokomo, Ind.
Height, 6.04. Weight, 270.
High School—Wapakoneta, O.
Received degree from University of Michigan in 1987.

Selected by Baltimore in 1986 USFL territorial draft.
Selected by Cincinnati in 3rd round (65th player selected) of 1986 NFL draft.
Signed by Cincinnati Bengals, July 26, 1986.
Cincinnati NFL, 1986 and 1987.
Games: 1986 (15), 1987 (11). Total—26.

STEVEN REED HAMMOND
(Steve)
Linebacker—Buffalo Bills
Born February 5, 1960, at Hartford, Conn.
Height, 6.04. Weight, 225.
High School—Merrick, N.Y., Sanford H. Calhoun.
Attended Wake Forest University.

Selected by New Jersey in 23rd round (267th player selected) of 1983 USFL draft.
Signed by New Jersey Generals, January 19, 1983.
On developmental squad, April 2 through April 22, 1983; activated, April 23, 1983.
Traded with running back Dwight Sullivan by New Jersey Generals to Los Angeles Express for rights to quarterback Brian Sipe, December 27, 1983.
Traded by Los Angeles Express to Memphis Showboats for rights to linebacker Doug West, January 21, 1984.
Granted free agency when USFL suspended operations, August 7, 1986; signed as free agent by Buffalo Bills, May 11, 1987.
On injured reserve with ankle injury, September 8 through entire 1987 season.
On developmental squad for 3 games with New Jersey Generals in 1983.
New Jersey USFL, 1983; Memphis USFL, 1984 and 1985.
Games: 1983 (15), 1984 (18), 1985 (17). Total—50.
Pro statistics: Credited with $\frac{1}{2}$ sack for three yards and recovered one fumble for three yards, 1983; credited with one sack for 14 yards and recovered four fumbles, 1984; credited with $2\frac{1}{2}$ sacks for $20\frac{1}{2}$ yards and recovered two fumbles, 1985.

DANIEL OLIVER HAMPTON
(Dan)
Defensive End—Chicago Bears
Born September 19, 1957, at Oklahoma City, Okla.
Height, 6.05. Weight, 270.
High School—Jacksonville, Ark.
Attended University of Arkansas.

Named to THE SPORTING NEWS NFL All-Star Team, 1984.
Selected by Chicago in 1st round (4th player selected) of 1979 NFL draft.
On injured reserve with knee injury, November 16 through December 13, 1987; activated, December 14, 1987.
Chicago NFL, 1979 through 1987.
Games: 1979 (16), 1980 (16), 1981 (16), 1982 (9), 1983 (11), 1984 (15), 1985 (16), 1986 (16), 1987 (8). Total—123.
Pro statistics: Recovered two fumbles, 1979 and 1986; recovered three fumbles, 1984 and 1985; credited with a safety, 1982.
Played in NFC Championship Game following 1984 and 1985 seasons.
Played in NFL Championship Game following 1985 season.
Played in Pro Bowl (NFL All-Star Game) following 1980, 1982, 1984 and 1985 seasons.

LORENZO TIMOTHY HAMPTON
Running Back—Miami Dolphins
Born March 12, 1962, at Lake Wales, Fla.
Height, 6.00. Weight, 203.
High School—Lake Wales, Fla.
Attended University of Florida.

Selected by Tampa Bay in 1985 USFL territorial draft.
USFL rights traded with rights to running back Greg Allen by Tampa Bay Bandits to Orlando Renegades for rights to running back Jeff McCall, December 21, 1984.
Selected by Miami in 1st round (27th player selected) of 1985 NFL draft.
Signed by Miami Dolphins, July 19, 1985.

Year Club	G.	Att.	Yds.	Avg.	TD.	P.C.	Yds.	Avg.	TD.	TD.	Pts.	F.
			RUSHING			PASS RECEIVING				—TOTAL—		
1985—Miami NFL	16	105	369	3.5	3	8	56	7.0	0	3	18	3
1986—Miami NFL	16	186	830	4.5	9	61	446	7.3	3	12	72	4
1987—Miami NFL	12	75	289	3.9	1	23	223	9.7	0	1	6	4
Pro Totals—3 Years	44	366	1488	4.1	13	92	725	7.9	3	16	96	11

Year Club	G.	No.	Yds.	Avg.	TD.
		KICKOFF RETURNS			
1985—Miami NFL	16	45	1020	22.7	0
1986—Miami NFL	16	9	182	20.2	0
1987—Miami NFL	12	16	304	19.0	0
Pro Totals—3 Years	44	70	1506	21.5	0

Additional pro statistics: Recovered one fumble, 1985 through 1987.
Played in AFC Championship Game following 1985 season.

KEVIN DREW HANCOCK
Linebacker—Indianapolis Colts
Born January 6, 1962, at Longview, Tex.
Height, 6.02. Weight, 224.
High School—Texas City, Tex.
Attended Baylor University.

Selected by San Antonio in 1985 USFL territorial draft.
Selected by Detroit in 4th round (90th player selected) of 1985 NFL draft.
Signed by Detroit Lions, July 21, 1985.
On injury reserve with knee injury, August 13 through entire 1985 season.
Released by Detroit Lions, September 5, 1986; signed as free agent by New York Jets, May 10, 1987.
Released by New York Jets, August 20, 1987; signed as free agent by Indianapolis Colts, December 23, 1987.
Indianapolis NFL, 1987.
Games: 1987 (1).

JON THOMAS HAND
Defensive End—Indianapolis Colts
Born November 13, 1963, at Sylacauga, Ala.
Height, 6.07. Weight, 298.
High School—Sylacauga, Ala.
Attended University of Alabama.

Named as defensive lineman of THE SPORTING NEWS College All-America Team, 1985.
Selected by Birmingham in 1986 USFL territorial draft.
Selected by Indianapolis in 1st round (4th player selected) of 1986 NFL draft.
Signed by Indianapolis Colts, August 7, 1986.
Indianapolis NFL, 1986 and 1987.
Games: 1986 (15), 1987 (12). Total—27.
Pro statistics: Intercepted one pass for eight yards and recovered two fumbles, 1986.

CHARLES ALVIN HANNAH
(Charley)
Guard—Los Angeles Raiders
Born July 26, 1955, at Albertville, Ala.
Height, 6.05. Weight, 265.
High School—Chattanooga, Tenn., Baylor.
Attended University of Alabama.
Son of Herb Hannah, tackle with New York Giants, 1951; and brother
of John Hannah, guard with New England Patriots, 1973 through 1985.

Selected by Tampa Bay in 3rd round (56th player selected) of 1977 NFL draft.
On injured reserve, November 14 through remainder of 1977 season.
On injured reserve with knee injury, December 7 through December 26, 1979; activated, December 27, 1979.
Traded by Tampa Bay Buccaneers to Los Angeles Raiders for defensive end Dave Browning and 4th round pick in 1984 draft, July 18, 1983.
Granted free agency, February 1, 1986; re-signed by Raiders, September 1, 1986.
Granted roster exemption, September 1 through September 14, 1986; activated, September 15, 1986.
On injured reserve with calf injury, December 19 through remainder of 1987 season.
Tampa Bay NFL, 1977 through 1982; Los Angeles Raiders NFL, 1983 through 1987.
Games: 1977 (9), 1978 (16), 1979 (14), 1980 (16), 1981 (15), 1982 (7), 1983 (16), 1984 (15), 1985 (15), 1986 (12), 1987 (5).
Total—140.
Pro statistics: Recovered one fumble for eight yards and fumbled once for minus 32 yards, 1978; attempted one pass with no completions, 1980; recovered one fumble, 1985; recovered one fumble for two yards, 1987.
Played in NFC Championship Game following 1979 season.
Played in AFC Championship Game following 1983 season.
Played in NFL Championship Game following 1983 season.

BRIAN HANSEN
Punter—New Orleans Saints
Born October 18, 1960, at Hawarden, Ia.
Height, 6.03. Weight, 209.
High School—Hawarden, Ia., West Sioux Community.
Attended Sioux Falls College.

Selected by New Orleans in 9th round (237th player selected) of 1984 NFL draft.

			——PUNTING——		
Year	Club	G.	No.	Avg.	Blk.
1984—New Orleans NFL		16	69	43.8	1
1985—New Orleans NFL		16	89	42.3	0
1986—New Orleans NFL		16	81	42.7	1
1987—New Orleans NFL		12	52	40.5	0
Pro Totals—4 Years		60	291	42.4	2

Additional pro statistics: Rushed twice for minus 27 yards, 1984; attempted one pass with one completion for eight yards, 1985; rushed once for no yards, recovered one fumble and fumbled once, 1986; rushed twice for minus six yards, 1987.
Played in Pro Bowl (NFL All-Star Game) following 1984 season.

BRUCE B. HANSEN
Running Back—New England Patriots
Born September 18, 1961, at American Fork, Utah.
Height, 6.01. Weight, 225.
High School—American Fork, Utah.
Attended Brigham Young University.
Brother of Regan Hansen, linebacker at Brigham Young University.

Signed as free agent replacement player by New England Patriots, September 24, 1987.
Released by New England Patriots, October 27, 1987; re-signed by Patriots, November 24, 1987.
On injured reserve with ankle injury, December 19 through remainder of 1987 season.

			——RUSHING——				PASS RECEIVING				—TOTAL—		
Year	Club	G.	Att.	Yds.	Avg.	TD.	P.C.	Yds.	Avg.	TD.	TD.	Pts.	F.
1987—New England NFL		6	16	44	2.8	0	1	22	22.0	0	0	0	0

Additional pro statistics: Returned one kickoff for 14 yards and recovered one fumble, 1987.

JAMES JOSEPH HARBAUGH
(Jim)
Quarterback—Chicago Bears
Born December 23, 1963, at Toledo, O.
Height, 6.03. Weight, 202.
High Schools—Ann Arbor, Mich., Pioneer; and Palo Alto, Calif.
Received bachelor's degree in communications
from University of Michigan in 1987.
Son of Jack Harbaugh, assistant coach, and cousin of Mike Gottfried,
head coach, both at University of Pittsburgh.

Selected by Chicago in 1st round (26th player selected) of 1987 NFL draft.
Signed by Chicago Bears, August 3, 1987.

			————————PASSING————————							——RUSHING——				—TOTAL—		
Year	Club	G.	Att.	Cmp.	Pct.	Gain	T.P.	P.I.	Avg.	Att.	Yds.	Avg.	TD.	TD.	Pts.	F.
1987—Chicago NFL		6	11	8	72.7	62	0	0	5.64	4	15	3.8	0	0	0	0

Additional pro statistics: 1987 (86.2).

MICHAEL HARDEN
(Mike)
Cornerback—Denver Broncos
Born February 16, 1959, at Memphis, Tenn.
Height, 6.01. Weight, 190.
High School—Detroit, Mich., Central.
Received bachelor of arts degree in political science from University of Michigan in 1980.

Selected by Denver in 5th round (131st player selected) of 1980 NFL draft.
On injured reserve with knee injury, December 16 through remainder of 1982 season.
On injured reserve with broken arm, January 16, 1988 through remainder of 1987 season playoffs.

			-INTERCEPTIONS-				—KICKOFF RET.—				—TOTAL—		
Year	Club	G.	No.	Yds.	Avg.	TD.	No.	Yds.	Avg.	TD.	TD.	Pts.	F.
1980—Denver NFL		16		None			12	214	17.8	0	0	0	1
1981—Denver NFL		16	2	34	17.0	0	11	178	16.2	0	0	0	0
1982—Denver NFL		5	2	3	1.5	0		None			0	0	0
1983—Denver NFL		15	4	127	31.8	0	1	9	9.0	0	0	0	0
1984—Denver NFL		16	6	79	13.2	1	1	4	4.0	0	1	6	1
1985—Denver NFL		16	5	100	20.0	*1		None			1	6	0
1986—Denver NFL		16	6	179	29.8	2		None			3	18	0
1987—Denver NFL		12	4	85	21.3	0	2	11	5.5	0	0	0	0
Pro Totals—8 Years		112	29	607	20.9	4	27	416	15.4	0	5	30	2

Additional pro statistics: Returned two punts for 36 yards and recovered one fumble, 1981; recovered one fumble for 13 yards, 1982; recovered three fumbles, 1983; recovered two fumbles, 1984; recovered two fumbles for five yards, 1985; returned one punt for 41 yards and a touchdown, 1986; recovered one fumble for 14 yards, 1987.
Played in AFC Championship Game following 1986 season.
Played in NFL Championship Game following 1986 season.

WILLIAM DAVID HARDISON
(Dee)
Defensive End—San Diego Chargers
Born May 2, 1956, at Jacksonville, N. C.
Height, 6.04. Weight, 291.
High School—Newton Grove, N. C., Hobbton.
Attended University of North Carolina.

Selected by Buffalo in 2nd round (32nd player selected) of 1978 NFL draft.
Released by Buffalo Bills, August 25, 1981; signed as free agent by New York Giants, December 8, 1981.
On injured reserve with hip injury, November 30 through December 30, 1982; activated, December 31, 1982.
Released by New York Giants, September 1, 1986; awarded on waivers to San Diego Chargers, September 2, 1986.
Active for 2 games with New York Giants in 1981; did not play.
Buffalo NFL, 1978 through 1980; New York Giants NFL, 1981 through 1985; San Diego NFL, 1986 and 1987.
Games: 1978 (16), 1979 (16), 1980 (16), 1982 (5), 1983 (16), 1984 (15), 1985 (13), 1986 (15), 1987 (3). Total—115.
Pro statistics: Recovered one fumble, 1983 and 1986.

ANDRE HARDY
Running Back-Kick Returner—Seattle Seahawks
Born November 28, 1961, at San Diego, Calif.
Height, 6.01. Weight, 233.
High School—San Diego, Calif., Herbert Hoover.
Attended San Diego City College, Weber State College and received
bachelor of science degree in communications from St. Mary's College (Cal.) in 1984.

Selected by San Antonio in 5th round (86th player selected) of 1984 USFL draft.
Selected by Philadelphia in 5th round (116th player selected) of 1984 NFL draft.
Signed by Philadelphia Eagles, May 31, 1984.
Released by Philadelphia Eagles, September 4, 1985; signed as free agent by Seattle Seahawks, October 9, 1985.
Released by Seattle Seahawks, November 6, 1985; re-signed by Seahawks, November 11, 1985.
Released by Seattle Seahawks, November 21, 1985; signed as free agent by San Francisco 49ers, March 7, 1986.
Released by San Francisco 49ers, August 19, 1986; re-signed as replacement player by 49ers, September 24, 1987.
Traded by San Francisco 49ers to Seattle Seahawks for draft choice, October 7, 1987.
On injured reserve with hand injury, October 9 through remainder of 1987 season.

Year Club	G.	Att.	Yds.	Avg.	TD.	P.C.	Yds.	Avg.	TD.	TD.	Pts.	F.
			RUSHING				PASS RECEIVING				—TOTAL—	
1984—Philadelphia NFL	6	14	41	2.9	0	2	22	11.0	0	0	0	0
1985—Seattle NFL	3	5	5	1.0	0	3	7	2.3	0	0	0	1
1987—San Francisco NFL	1			None				None		0	0	0
Pro Totals—3 Years	10	19	46	2.4	0	5	29	5.8	0	0	0	1

Additional pro statistics: Returned one kickoff for 20 yards, 1984; recovered one fumble, 1985.

BRUCE ALAN HARDY
Tight End—Miami Dolphins
Born June 1, 1956, at Murray, Utah.
Height, 6.05. Weight, 232.
High School—Copperton, Utah, Bingham.
Received bachelor of science degree in business administration
from Arizona State University.
Brother of Bryan Hardy, pitcher in Chicago Cubs' organization, 1979, 1980 and 1982.

Selected by Miami in 9th round (247th player selected) of 1978 NFL draft.

Year Club	G.	P.C.	Yds.	Avg.	TD.
		PASS RECEIVING			
1978—Miami NFL	16	4	32	8.0	2
1979—Miami NFL	16	30	386	12.9	3
1980—Miami NFL	16	19	159	8.4	2
1981—Miami NFL	16	15	174	11.6	0
1982—Miami NFL	9	12	66	5.5	2
1983—Miami NFL	15	22	202	9.2	0
1984—Miami NFL	16	28	257	9.2	5
1985—Miami NFL	16	39	409	10.5	4
1986—Miami NFL	16	54	430	8.0	5
1987—Miami NFL	12	28	292	10.4	2
Pro Totals—10 Years	148	251	2407	9.6	25

Additional pro statistics: Returned two kickoffs for 27 yards, 1978; attempted one pass with no completions, 1979; fumbled once, 1980, 1981 and 1985; rushed once for two yards, 1983; returned one kickoff for 11 yards, 1985; returned three kickoffs for 39 yards and fumbled twice, 1986; returned five kickoffs for 62 yards and fumbled once for minus seven yards, 1987.
Played in AFC Championship Game following 1982, 1984 and 1985 seasons.
Played in NFL Championship Game following 1982 and 1984 seasons.

—DID YOU KNOW—

Trailing 28-3 after three quarters against Tampa Bay on November 8, 1987, the St. Louis Cardinals scored four touchdowns for the biggest fourth-quarter comeback in NFL history? The Cardinals won, 31-28.

RONNIE KEITH HARMON
Running Back—Buffalo Bills
Born May 7, 1964, at Queens, N. Y.
Height, 5.11. Weight, 192.
High School—Queens, N. Y., Bayside.
Attended University of Iowa.
Brother of Derrick Harmon, running back with San Francisco 49ers, 1984 through 1986;
and Kevin Harmon, rookie running back with Seattle Seahawks.
Selected by Buffalo in 1st round (16th player selected) of 1986 NFL draft.
Signed by Buffalo Bills, August 13, 1986.
Granted roster exemption, August 13 through August 24, 1986; activated, August 25, 1986.

			RUSHING			PASS RECEIVING				—TOTAL—		
Year Club	G.	Att.	Yds.	Avg.	TD.	P.C.	Yds.	Avg.	TD.	TD.	Pts.	F.
1986—Buffalo NFL	14	54	172	3.2	0	22	185	8.4	1	1	6	2
1987—Buffalo NFL	12	116	485	4.2	2	56	477	8.5	2	4	24	2
Pro Totals—2 Years	26	170	657	3.9	2	78	662	8.5	3	5	30	4

		KICKOFF RETURNS			
Year Club	G.	No.	Yds.	Avg.	TD.
1986—Buffalo NFL	14	18	321	17.8	0
1987—Buffalo NFL	12	1	30	30.0	0
Pro Totals—2 Years	26	19	351	18.5	0

MARK HARPER
Cornerback—Cleveland Browns
Born November 5, 1961, at Memphis, Tenn.
Height, 5.09. Weight, 174.
High School—Memphis, Tenn., Northside.
Received degree from Alcorn State University in 1982.
Signed by Chicago Blitz, July 31, 1983.
Franchise transferred to Arizona, September 30, 1983.
Traded by Arizona Wranglers to Pittsburgh Maulers for draft choice, February 13, 1984.
On developmental squad, February 24 through March 28, 1984; activated, March 29, 1984.
Franchise disbanded, October 25, 1984.
Selected by Jacksonville Bulls in USFL dispersal draft, December 6, 1984.
On developmental squad, April 25 through June 13, 1985; activated, June 14, 1985.
Released by Jacksonville Bulls, February 28, 1986; signed as free agent by Cleveland Browns, April 7, 1986.
On developmental squad for 5 games with Pittsburgh Maulers in 1984.
On developmental squad for 7 games with Jacksonville Bulls in 1985.

		INTERCEPTIONS			-PUNT RETURNS-				—KICKOFF RET.—				—TOTAL—		
Year Club	G.	No.	Yds.	Avg.	TD.	No.	Yds.	Avg.	TD.	No.	Yds.	Avg.	TD.	TD.	Pts.	F.
1984—Pittsburgh USFL	12		None			22	157	7.1	0	7	130	18.6	0	0	0	1
1985—Jacksonville USFL	11	1	10	10.0	0		None				None			0	0	0
1986—Cleveland NFL	16	1	31	31.0	0		None				None			0	0	0
1987—Cleveland NFL	12	2	16	8.0	0		None				None			0	0	0
USFL Totals—2 Years	23	1	10	10.0	0	22	157	7.1	0	7	130	18.6	0	0	0	1
NFL Totals—2 Years	28	3	47	15.7	0	0	0	0.0	0	0	0	0.0	0	0	0	0
Pro Totals—4 Years	51	4	57	14.3	0	22	157	7.1	0	7	130	18.6	0	0	0	1

Additional USFL statistics: Recovered three fumbles, 1984.
Additional NFL statistics: Recovered two fumbles, 1986.
Played in AFC Championship Game following 1986 and 1987 seasons.

MICHAEL HARPER
Wide Receiver—New York Jets
Born May 11, 1961, at Kansas City, Mo.
Height, 5.10. Weight, 180.
High School—Kansas City, Mo., Hickman Mills.
Received bachelor of arts degree in business from University of Southern California.
Selected by Los Angeles in 1984 USFL territorial draft.
Selected by Los Angeles Rams in 11th round (293rd player selected) of 1984 NFL draft.
Signed by Los Angeles Rams, July 9, 1984.
Released by Los Angeles Rams, August 27, 1984; re-signed by Rams, July 24, 1985.
Released by Los Angeles Rams, September 2, 1985; signed as free agent by New York Jets, April 23, 1986.
Released by New York Jets, September 6, 1987; re-signed as replacement player by Jets, September 24, 1987.
On injured reserve with knee injury, October 20 through remainder of 1987 season.

		PASS RECEIVING			
Year Club	G.	P.C.	Yds.	Avg.	TD.
1986—N. Y. Jets NFL	16		None		
1987—N. Y. Jets NFL	3	18	225	12.5	1
Pro Totals—2 Years	19	18	225	12.5	1

Additional pro statistics: Returned seven kickoffs for 71 yards and recovered three fumbles, 1986; returned four punts for 93 yards (23.3 avg.) and a touchdown and returned four kickoffs for 75 yards, 1987.

JAMES CLEARANCE HARRELL JR.
Linebacker—Kansas City Chiefs
Born July 19, 1957, at Tampa, Fla.
Height, 6.02. Weight, 240.
High School—Tampa, Fla., Chamberlain.
Received bachelor of science degree in public relations from University of Florida.

Named as outside linebacker on THE SPORTING NEWS USFL All-Star Team, 1984.
Signed as free agent by Denver Broncos, May 12, 1979.
Released by Denver Broncos, August 27, 1979; claimed on waivers by Detroit Lions, August 28, 1979.
On injured reserve with shoulder injury, August 29 through October 19, 1979; activated, October 20, 1979.
On injured reserve with knee injury, October 15 through remainder of 1980 season.
Granted free agency, February 1, 1984; signed by Tampa Bay Bandits, March 23, 1984.
On developmental squad, June 7 through June 27, 1985; activated, June 28, 1985.
Granted free agency, August 1, 1985; signed by Detroit Lions, August 13, 1985.
On injured reserve with back injury, October 24 through remainder of 1985 season.
Released by Detroit Lions, September 7, 1987; signed as free agent replacement player by Kansas City Chiefs, October 1, 1987.
On developmental squad for 3 games with Tampa Bay Bandits in 1985.
Detroit NFL, 1979 through 1983, 1985 and 1986; Tampa Bay USFL, 1984 and 1985; Kansas City NFL, 1987.
Games: 1979 (9), 1980 (5), 1981 (16), 1982 (9), 1983 (16), 1984 (14), 1985 USFL (15), 1985 NFL (7), 1986 (16), 1987 (11). Total NFL—89. Total USFL—29. Total Pro—118.
NFL statistics: Returned one kickoff for no yards, 1981; intercepted one pass for 20 yards, 1985; recovered two fumbles, 1986 and 1987.
USFL statistics: Intercepted one pass for eight yards, credited with 1½ sacks for 14 yards and recovered one fumble for 18 yards, 1984; intercepted two passes for 19 yards and credited with four sacks for 33 yards, 1985.

ALFRED CARL HARRIS
(Al)
Linebacker-Defensive End—Chicago Bears
Born December 31, 1956, at Bangor, Me.
Height, 6.05. Weight, 270.
High School—Wahiawa, Hawaii, Leilehua.
Received bachelor of science degree in communications from Arizona State University.
Cousin of Ricky Bell, running back with Tampa Bay Buccaneers and San Diego Chargers,
1977 through 1982; and Archie Bell, lead singer of Archie Bell and the Drells.

Named as defensive lineman on THE SPORTING NEWS College All-America Team, 1978.
Selected by Chicago in 1st round (9th player selected) of 1979 NFL draft.
On injured reserve with knee injury, August 28 through October 25, 1979; activated, October 26, 1979.
On inactive list, September 19, 1982.
Granted free agency, February 1, 1985.
On reserve/unsigned free agency list, August 20 through entire 1985 season.
Re-signed by Bears, July 16, 1986.
Chicago NFL, 1979 through 1984, 1986 and 1987.
Games: 1979 (4), 1980 (16), 1981 (16), 1982 (8), 1983 (13), 1984 (16), 1986 (16), 1987 (12). Total—101.
Pro statistics: Caught one pass for 18 yards, intercepted one pass for 44 yards and a touchdown and recovered three fumbles for five yards, 1981; recovered two fumbles, 1983; intercepted one pass for 34 yards, 1984.
Played in NFC Championship Game following 1984 season.

HERBERT H. HARRIS
Wide Receiver—New Orleans Saints
Born May 4, 1961, at Houston, Tex.
Height, 6.01. Weight, 206.
High School—Houston, Tex., Kashmere.
Received bachelor of science degree in secondary education from Lamar University.

Signed as free agent by Tampa Bay Buccaneers, May 3, 1983.
Released by Tampa Bay Buccaneers, August 23, 1983; signed by Houston Gamblers, October 28, 1983.
Released by Houston Gamblers, November 15, 1983; awarded on waivers to Philadelphia Stars, November 22, 1983.
Franchise transferred to Baltimore, November 1, 1984.
On developmental squad, April 13 through April 25, 1985; activated, April 26, 1985.
On developmental squad, May 31 through June 13, 1985; activated, June 14, 1985.
On developmental squad, June 21 through remainder of 1985 season.
Granted free agency, August 1, 1985; signed as free agent by Philadelphia Eagles, August 5, 1985.
Released by Philadelphia Eagles, September 2, 1985; signed as free agent by New Orleans Saints, May 15, 1986.
On injured reserve with hamstring injury, September 2 through October 28, 1986; activated after clearing procedural waivers, October 30, 1986.
On injured reserve with hamstring injury, September 7 through October 23, 1987; activated, October 24, 1987.
On injured reserve with hamstring injury, November 3 through November 30, 1987.
Released by New Orleans Saints, December 1, 1987; re-signed by Saints after clearing procedural waivers, December 3, 1987.
Released by New Orleans Saints, December 24, 1987; re-signed by Saints, March 8, 1988.
On developmental squad for 5 games with Baltimore Stars in 1985.

Year Club	G.	P.C.	Yds.	Avg.	TD.	Year Club	G.	P.C.	Yds.	Avg.	TD.
1984—Philadelphia USFL	17	18	309	17.2	2	1987—New Orleans NFL	2		None		
1985—Baltimore USFL	12	16	210	13.1	3	USFL Totals—2 Years	29	34	519	15.3	5
1986—New Orleans NFL	7	11	148	13.5	0	NFL Totals—2 Years	9	11	148	13.5	0
						Pro Totals—4 Years	38	45	667	14.8	5

Additional USFL statistics: Ran 33 yards with lateral on punt return, returned four kickoffs for 73 yards and recovered three fumbles for seven yards, 1984; fumbled once, 1984 and 1985; returned nine kickoffs for 199 yards, 1985.
Additional NFL statistics: Returned seven kickoffs for 122 yards and fumbled once, 1986.
Played in USFL Championship Game following 1984 season.
On developmental squad for USFL Championship Game following 1985 season.

JAMIE A. HARRIS
Wide Receiver—New York Jets
Born March 23, 1962, at McKinney, Tex.
Height, 5.08. Weight, 170.
High School—McKinney, Tex.
Attended Texas Tech University and Oklahoma State University.
Brother of Leonard Harris, wide receiver with Denver Gold, 1984.

Selected by Denver in 1985 USFL territorial draft.
Selected by Washington in 7th round (177th player selected) of 1985 NFL draft.
Signed by Washington Redskins, July 23, 1985.
Released by Washington Redskins, August 20, 1985; signed as free agent by British Columbia Lions, November 15, 1985.
Traded with linebacker Mike Emery by British Columbia Lions to Calgary Stampeders for 3rd round pick in 1987 CFL draft, June 10, 1986.
Released by Calgary Stampeders, June 15, 1987; signed as free agent by New York Jets, May 17, 1988.

		PASS RECEIVING				-PUNT RETURNS-				—KICKOFF RET.—				—TOTAL—		
Year	Club	G.	P.C.	Yds.	Avg.	TD.	No.	Yds.	Avg.	TD.	No.	Yds.	Avg.	TD.	TD.	Pts.	F.
1986—Calgary CFL		8	14	223	15.9	7	19	114	6.0	0	8	216	27.0	0	7	42	2

Additional CFL statistics: Rushed once for nine yards, 1986.

JOHN EDWARD HARRIS
Safety—Minnesota Vikings
Born June 13, 1956, at Fort Benning, Ga.
Height, 6.02. Weight, 200.
High School—Miami, Fla., Jackson.
Received bachelor of science degree in political science from Arizona State University in 1978.

Selected by Seattle in 7th round (173rd player selected) of 1978 NFL draft.
On did not report list, August 31 through September 1, 1982; activated and granted two-game roster exemption, September 2, 1982.
Activated, September 10, 1982.
Granted free agency, February 1, 1986; re-signed by Seahawks, August 31, 1986.
Granted roster exemption, August 31 and September 1, 1986.
Traded by Seattle Seahawks to Minnesota Vikings for 7th round pick in 1987 draft, September 2, 1986.
Granted roster exemption, September 2 through September 4, 1986; activated, September 5, 1986.

		——INTERCEPTIONS——				
Year	Club	G.	No.	Yds.	Avg.	TD.
1978—Seattle NFL		16	4	65	16.3	0
1979—Seattle NFL		14	2	30	15.0	0
1980—Seattle NFL		16	6	28	4.7	0
1981—Seattle NFL		16	10	155	15.5	2
1982—Seattle NFL		9	4	33	8.3	0
1983—Seattle NFL		16	2	15	7.5	0
1984—Seattle NFL		16	6	79	13.2	0
1985—Seattle NFL		16	7	20	2.9	0
1986—Minnesota NFL		16	3	69	23.0	0
1987—Minnesota NFL		12	3	20	6.7	0
Pro Totals—10 Years		147	47	514	10.9	2

Additional pro statistics: Returned five punts for 58 yards, 1978; fumbled once, 1978, 1979 and 1981; returned eight punts for 70 yards and returned one kickoff for 21 yards, 1979; recovered one fumble, 1979, 1980, 1984 and 1987; recovered three fumbles, 1981; returned two punts for 27 yards and recovered three fumbles for 62 yards, 1983; returned one kickoff for seven yards, 1984; returned three punts for 24 yards and recovered two fumbles, 1985.
Played in AFC Championship Game following 1983 season.
Played in NFC Championship Game following 1987 season.

LEONARD MILTON HARRIS
Wide Receiver—Houston Oilers
Born November 27, 1960, at McKinney, Tex.
Height, 5.08. Weight, 185.
High School—McKinney, Tex.
Attended Austin College and Texas Tech University.
Cousin of Judson Flint, defensive back with Cleveland Browns and Buffalo Bills, 1980 through 1983.

Selected by Denver in 1984 USFL territorial draft.
Signed by Denver Gold, January 24, 1984.
Franchise merged with Jacksonville, February 19, 1986.
Granted free agency when USFL suspended operations, August 7, 1986; signed as free agent by Tampa Bay Buccaneers, August 12, 1986.
Granted roster exemption, August 12 through August 21, 1986; activated, August 22, 1986.
On injured reserve with hamstring injury, November 10 through remainder of 1986 season.
Released by Tampa Bay Buccaneers, June 11, 1987; signed as free agent by Washington Redskins, June 26, 1987.
Released by Washington Redskins, August 31, 1987; signed as free agent replacement player by Houston Oilers, September 23, 1987.

On injured reserve with knee injury, October 24 through remainder of 1987 season.

Year	Club	G.	PASS RECEIVING				—KICKOFF RET.—				—TOTAL—		
			P.C.	Yds.	Avg.	TD.	No.	Yds.	Avg.	TD.	TD.	Pts.	F.
1984—Denver USFL		18	35	657	18.8	4	43	1086	25.3	0	4	24	2
1985—Denver USFL		18	101	*1432	14.2	8	4	86	21.5	0	8	48	8
1986—Tampa Bay NFL		6	3	52	17.3	0	4	63	15.8	0	0	0	1
1987—Houston NFL		3	10	164	16.4	0	3	87	29.0	0	0	0	0
USFL Totals—2 Years		36	136	2089	15.4	12	47	1172	24.9	0	12	72	10
NFL Totals—2 Years		9	13	216	16.6	0	7	150	21.4	0	0	0	1
Pro Totals—4 Years		45	149	2305	15.5	12	54	1322	24.5	0	12	72	11

Additional USFL statistics: Returned one punt for four yards, 1984; recovered two fumbles, 1984 and 1985; returned seven punts for 35 yards and rushed six times for one yard, 1985.
Additional NFL statistics: Returned three punts for 16 yards, 1986; rushed once for 17 yards, 1987.

TIMOTHY DAVID HARRIS
(Tim)
Linebacker—Green Bay Packers

Born September 10, 1964, at Birmingham, Ala.
Height, 6.05. Weight, 235.
High Schools—Birmingham, Ala., Woodlawn; and Memphis, Tenn., Catholic.
Attended Memphis State University.

Selected by Memphis in 1986 USFL territorial draft.
Selected by Green Bay in 4th round (84th player selected) of 1986 NFL draft.
Signed by Green Bay Packers, May 17, 1986.
Green Bay NFL, 1986 and 1987.
Games: 1986 (16), 1987 (12). Total—28.
Pro statistics: Recovered one fumble, 1986.

WILLIAM MILTON HARRIS
Tight End—Phoenix Cardinals

Born February 10, 1965, at Houston, Tex.
Height, 6.04. Weight, 243.
High School—Houston, Tex., M. B. Smiley.
Attended University of Texas and Bishop College.

Selected by St. Louis in 7th round (195th player selected) of 1987 NFL draft.
Signed by St. Louis Cardinals, July 18, 1987.
Released by St. Louis Cardinals, September 1, 1987; re-signed as replacement player by Cardinals, September 25, 1987.
Franchise transferred to Phoenix, March 15, 1988.
St. Louis NFL, 1987.
Games: 1987 (10).
Pro statistics: Caught one pass for eight yards, 1987.

EMILE MICHAEL HARRY
Wide Receiver—Kansas City Chiefs

Born April 5, 1963, at Los Angeles, Calif.
Height, 5.11. Weight, 175.
High School—Fountain Valley, Calif.
Received bachelor of arts degree in political science
from Stanford University in 1985.

Selected by Oakland in 1985 USFL territorial draft.
Selected by Atlanta in 4th round (89th player selected) of 1985 NFL draft.
Signed by Atlanta Falcons, July 19, 1985.
Released by Atlanta Falcons, September 2, 1985; signed as free agent by Kansas City Chiefs, January 18, 1986.
Released by Kansas City Chiefs, September 1, 1986; re-signed by Chiefs, September 30, 1986.
On injured reserve with shoulder injury, August 14 through entire 1987 season.

			——PASS RECEIVING——			
Year	Club	G.	P.C.	Yds.	Avg.	TD.
1986—Kansas City NFL		12	9	211	23.4	1

Additional pro statistics: Returned six kickoff for 115 yards, returned six punts for 20 yards and fumbled once, 1986.

JAMES DONALD HASLETT
(Jim)
Linebacker—New York Jets

Born December 9, 1957, at Pittsburgh, Pa.
Height, 6.03. Weight, 236.
High School—Pittsburgh, Pa., Avalon.
Attended Indiana (Pa.) University.
Cousin of Hal Stringert, defensive back with The Hawaiians
(WFL) and San Diego Chargers, 1974 through 1980.

Selected by Buffalo in 2nd round (51st player selected) of 1979 NFL draft.
On injured reserve with back injury, September 13 through November 17, 1983; activated, November 18, 1983.
On injured reserve with broken leg, September 1 through entire 1986 season.

Released by Buffalo Bills, September 7, 1987; signed as free agent replacement player by New York Jets, September 30, 1987.

On injured reserve with back injury, October 20 through remainder of 1987 season.

| | | —INTERCEPTIONS— | | | |
Year Club	G.	No.	Yds.	Avg.	TD.
1979—Buffalo NFL	16	2	15	7.5	0
1980—Buffalo NFL	16	2	30	15.0	0
1981—Buffalo NFL	16		None		
1982—Buffalo NFL	6		None		
1983—Buffalo NFL	5		None		
1984—Buffalo NFL	15		None		
1985—Buffalo NFL	16	1	40	40.0	0
1987—N. Y. Jets NFL	3	1	9	9.0	0
Pro Totals—8 Years	93	6	94	15.7	0

Additional pro statistics: Recovered two fumbles, 1979; recovered one fumble, 1980 through 1982 and 1987; caught one pass for four yards, 1982; recovered three fumbles for 10 yards, 1984; recovered three fumbles and fumbled once, 1985.

ROGER DALE HATCHER
(Known by middle name.)
Punter—Los Angeles Rams
Born April 5, 1963, at Cheraw, S.C.
Height, 6.02. Weight, 200.
High School—Cheraw, S.C.
Attended Clemson University.

Named to The Sporting News NFL All-Star Team, 1985.
Led NFL in punting yards with 3,140 in 1987.
Led NFL in net punting average with 38.0 in 1985.
Selected by Orlando in 8th round (114th player selected) of 1985 USFL draft.
Selected by Los Angeles Rams in 3rd round (77th player selected) of 1985 NFL draft.
Signed by Los Angeles Rams, July 12, 1985.
Crossed picket line during players' strike, October 2, 1987.

| | | —PUNTING— | | |
Year Club	G.	No.	Avg.	Blk.
1985—L.A. Rams NFL	16	87	43.2	1
1986—L.A. Rams NFL	16	97	38.6	1
1987—L. A. Rams NFL	15	76	41.3	1
Pro Totals—3 Years	47	260	41.0	3

Played in NFC Championship Game following 1985 season.
Played in Pro Bowl (NFL All-Star Game) following 1985 season.

ANTHONY JAMES HAWKINS
(Andy)
Linebacker—Kansas City Chiefs
Born March 31, 1958, at Bay City, Tex.
Height, 6.02. Weight, 230.
High School—Van Vleck, Tex.
Attended Texas A&I University.
Brother of Mike Hawkins, linebacker with New England Patriots,
Los Angeles Raiders and Houston Gamblers, 1978 through 1982, 1984 and 1985.

Named as outside linebacker on The Sporting News USFL All-Star Team, 1985.
Selected by Tampa Bay in 10th round (267th player selected) of 1980 NFL draft.
On injured reserve with sprained knee, October 12 through remainder of 1983 season.
Signed by Houston Gamblers, September 13, 1983, for contract to take effect after being granted free agency, February 1, 1984.
On developmental squad, May 4 through June 7, 1984; activated, June 8, 1984.
Traded with defensive backs Luther Bradley, Will Lewis, Mike Mitchell and Durwood Roquemore, defensive end Pete Catan, quarterbacks Jim Kelly and Todd Dillon, defensive tackles Tony Fitzpatrick, Van Hughes and Hosea Taylor, running back Sam Harrell, linebacker Ladell Wills, wide receivers Richard Johnson, Scott McGhee, Gerald McNeil, Ricky Sanders and Clarence Verdin, guard Rich Kehr, center Billy Kidd and offensive tackles Chris Riehm and Tommy Robison by Houston Gamblers to New Jersey Generals for past considerations, March 7, 1986.
Granted free agency when USFL suspended operations, August 7, 1986; re-signed by Tampa Bay Buccaneers and traded to San Diego Chargers for 6th round pick in 1987 draft, August 20, 1986.
Granted roster exemption August 20 and August 21, 1986; activated, August 22, 1986.
On injured reserve with groin injury, September 2 through October 5, 1986; activated, October 6, 1986.
Released by San Diego Chargers, October 27, 1987; signed as free agent by Kansas City Chiefs, February 26, 1988.
On developmental squad for 5 games with Houston Gamblers in 1984.
Tampa Bay NFL, 1980 through 1983; Houston USFL, 1984 and 1985; San Diego NFL, 1986 and 1987.
Games: 1980 (16), 1981 (16), 1982 (9), 1983 (6), 1984 (14), 1985 (18), 1986 (10), 1987 (2). Total NFL—59. Total USFL—32. Total Pro—91.
Additional NFL statistics: Recovered one fumble, 1980; intercepted one pass for 16 yards and recovered one fumble for three yards, 1981.
Additional USFL statistics: Credited with one sack for nine yards, 1984; intercepted two passes for 13 yards and a touchdown, credited with 1½ sacks for 20 yards and recovered one fumble, 1985.

JONATHAN MICHAEL HAYES
Tight End—Kansas City Chiefs
Born August 11, 1962, at South Fayette, Pa.
Height, 6.05. Weight, 240.
High School—McDonald, Pa., South Fayette.
Received degree in criminology from University of Iowa in 1986.
Brother of Jay Hayes, defensive end with Michigan Panthers,
San Antonio Gunslingers and Memphis Showboats, 1984 and 1985.

Selected by Kansas City in 2nd round (41st player selected) of 1985 NFL draft.
Signed by Kansas City Chiefs, June 19, 1985.

		—PASS RECEIVING—			
Year	Club	G.	P.C.	Yds.	Avg.	TD.
1985—Kansas City NFL		16	5	39	7.8	1
1986—Kansas City NFL		16	8	69	8.6	0
1987—Kansas City NFL		12	21	272	13.0	2
Pro Totals—3 Years		44	34	380	11.2	3

Additional pro statistics: Returned one kickoff for no yards, 1985; recovered one fumble, 1987.

LESTER HAYES
Cornerback—Los Angeles Raiders
Born January 22, 1955, at Houston, Tex.
Height, 6.00. Weight, 200.
High School—Houston, Tex., Wheatley.
Attended Texas A&M University.

Named to THE SPORTING NEWS NFL All-Star Team, 1980 and 1981.
Named as safety on THE SPORTING NEWS College All-America Team, 1976.
Selected by Oakland in 5th round (126th player selected) of 1977 NFL draft.
Franchise transferred to Los Angeles, May 7, 1982.
On injured reserve with broken foot, December 10 through remainder of 1986 season.
On injured reserve with toe injury, September 7 through entire 1987 season.
Crossed picket line during players' strike, October 7, 1987.

		—INTERCEPTIONS—			
Year	Club	G.	No.	Yds.	Avg.	TD.
1977—Oakland NFL		14	1	27	27.0	0
1978—Oakland NFL		16	4	86	21.5	0
1979—Oakland NFL		16	7	100	14.3	*2
1980—Oakland NFL		16	*13	*273	21.0	1
1981—Oakland NFL		16	3	0	0.0	0
1982—L.A. Raiders NFL		9	2	0	0.0	0
1983—L.A. Raiders NFL		16	2	49	24.5	0
1984—L.A. Raiders NFL		16	1	3	3.0	0
1985—L.A. Raiders NFL		16	4	27	6.8	*1
1986—L.A. Raiders NFL		14	2	7	3.5	0
Pro Totals—10 Years		149	39	572	14.7	4

Additional pro statistics: Recovered two fumbles for minus three yards, returned three kickoffs for 57 yards and fumbled once, 1977; returned one kickoff for no yards, 1980 and 1985; recovered two fumbles, 1980; recovered one fumble, 1985; recovered two fumbles for 42 yards and a touchdown, 1986.
Played in AFC Championship Game following 1977, 1980 and 1983 seasons.
Played in NFL Championship Game following 1980 and 1983 seasons.
Played in Pro Bowl (NFL All-Star Game) following 1980 through 1984 seasons.

JAMES HAYNES
Linebacker—New Orleans Saints
Born August 9, 1960, at Tallulah, La.
Height, 6.02. Weight, 233.
High School—Tallulah, La.
Attended Coahoma Junior College and Mississippi Valley State University.

Signed as free agent by New Orleans Saints, June 20, 1984.
On injured reserve with rotator cuff injury, August 27 through October 4, 1984; activated after clearing procedural waivers, October 5, 1984.
New Orleans NFL, 1984 through 1987.
Games: 1984 (10), 1985 (16), 1986 (16), 1987 (12). Total—54.
Pro statistics: Caught one pass for eight yards and recovered two fumbles, 1985; intercepted one pass for 17 yards and a touchdown and recovered two fumbles for seven yards, 1986.

MARK HAYNES
Cornerback—Denver Broncos
Born November 6, 1958, at Kansas City, Kan.
Height, 5.11. Weight, 198.
High School—Kansas City, Kan., Harmon.
Attended University of Colorado.

Selected by New York Giants in 1st round (8th player selected) of 1980 NFL draft.
Left camp voluntarily and granted roster exemption, August 21 through August 27, 1984; returned and activated, August 28, 1984.
On injured reserve with knee injury, December 14 through remainder of 1984 season.

Granted free agency, February 1, 1985; re-signed by Giants, October 16, 1985.
Granted roster exemption, October 16 through October 27, 1985; activated, October 28, 1985.
On injured reserve with groin injury, December 14 through remainder of 1985 season.
Traded by New York Giants to Denver Broncos for 2nd and 6th round picks in 1986 draft and 2nd round pick in 1987 draft, April 29, 1986.
On injured reserve with thigh injury, September 2 through October 9, 1986; activated, October 10, 1986.

			——INTERCEPTIONS——		
Year Club	G.	No.	Yds.	Avg.	TD.
1980—N.Y. Giants NFL	15	1	6	6.0	0
1981—N.Y. Giants NFL	16	1	9	9.0	0
1982—N.Y. Giants NFL	9	1	0	0.0	0
1983—N.Y. Giants NFL	15	3	18	6.0	0
1984—N.Y. Giants NFL	15	7	90	12.9	0
1985—N.Y. Giants NFL	5		None		
1986—Denver NFL	11		None		
1987—Denver NFL	12	3	39	13.0	1
Pro Totals—8 Years............	98	16	162	10.1	1

Additional pro statistics: Returned two kickoffs for 40 yards, 1980; recovered one fumble, 1981; recovered two fumbles for four yards, 1983; recovered two fumbles for 12 yards, 1984; recovered one fumble for 24 yards, 1987.
Played in AFC Championship Game following 1987 season.
Member of Denver Broncos for AFC Championship Game following 1986 season; did not play.
Played in NFL Championship Game following 1986 and 1987 seasons.
Played in Pro Bowl (NFL All-Star Game) following 1982 and 1983 seasons.
Named to play in Pro Bowl following 1984 season; replaced due to injury by Eric Wright.

MICHAEL JAMES HAYNES
(Mike)
Cornerback—Los Angeles Raiders
Born July 1, 1953, at Denison, Tex.
Height, 6.02. Weight, 190.
High School—Los Angeles, Calif., John Marshall.
Attending Arizona State University.
Brother of Reggie Haynes, tight end with Washington Redskins, 1978.

Named to THE SPORTING NEWS NFL All-Star Team, 1984 and 1985.
Named to THE SPORTING NEWS AFC All-Star Team, 1976, 1978 and 1979.
Named by THE SPORTING NEWS as AFC Rookie of the Year, 1976.
Named as defensive back on THE SPORTING NEWS College All-America Team, 1975.
Selected by New England in 1st round (5th player selected) of 1976 NFL draft.
On did not report list, September 1 through September 22, 1980.
Granted roster exemption, September 23 through September 28, 1980; activated, September 29, 1980.
On injured reserve with collapsed lung, November 6 through December 10, 1981; activated, December 11, 1981.
Granted free agency, February 1, 1983; signed by Los Angeles Raiders, November 2, 1983 (Haynes had sued NFL when trade to Raiders was voided because it was after trading deadline).
Contract awarded to Raiders in settlement, November 10, 1983, with Patriots receiving 1st round pick in 1984 draft and 2nd round pick in 1985 draft and Raiders receiving 7th round pick in 1985 draft.
Granted roster exemption, November 10, 1983; activated, November 18, 1983.

		INTERCEPTIONS				PUNT RETURNS				—TOTAL—		
Year Club	G.	No.	Yds.	Avg.	TD.	No.	Yds.	Avg.	TD.	TD.	Pts.	F.
1976—New England NFL...............	14	8	90	11.3	0	45	608	13.5	2	2	12	3
1977—New England NFL...............	14	5	54	10.8	0	24	200	8.3	0	0	0	4
1978—New England NFL...............	16	6	123	20.5	1	14	183	13.1	0	1	6	1
1979—New England NFL...............	16	3	66	22.0	0	5	16	3.2	0	0	0	1
1980—New England NFL...............	13	1	31	31.0	0	17	140	8.2	0	1	6	2
1981—New England NFL...............	8	1	3	3.0	0	6	12	2.0	0	0	0	0
1982—New England NFL...............	9	4	26	6.5	0		None			0	0	0
1983—Los Angeles Raiders NFL	5	1	0	0.0	0		None			0	0	0
1984—Los Angeles Raiders NFL	16	6	*220	36.7	1		None			1	6	0
1985—Los Angeles Raiders NFL	16	4	8	2.0	0	1	9	9.0	0	0	0	0
1986—Los Angeles Raiders NFL	13	2	28	14.0	0		None			0	0	0
1987—Los Angeles Raiders NFL	8	2	9	4.5	0		None			0	0	0
Pro Totals—12 Years..............	148	43	658	15.3	2	112	1168	10.4	2	5	30	11

Additional pro statistics: Recovered three fumbles, 1976 and 1979; recovered two fumbles, 1977; returned blocked field goal 65 yards for a touchdown and recovered three fumbles for six yards, 1980.
Played in AFC Championship Game following 1983 season.
Played in NFL Championship Game following 1983 season.
Played in Pro Bowl (NFL All-Star Game) following 1976 through 1980, 1982, 1985 and 1986 seasons.
Member of Pro Bowl following 1984 season; did not play.

THOMAS W. HAYNES JR.
(Tommy)
Defensive Back—Dallas Cowboys
Born February 6, 1963, at Chicago, Ill.
Height, 6.02. Weight, 190.
High School—Covina, Calif.
Attended Mt. San Antonio College and University of Southern California.

Selected by Los Angeles in 1985 USFL territorial draft.
USFL rights traded by Los Angeles Express to Portland Breakers for draft choice, February 19, 1985.

Signed by Portland Breakers, February 20, 1985.
Granted roster exemption, February 20 through February 22, 1985; activated, February 23, 1985.
Released by Portland Breakers, July 31, 1985; signed as free agent by Dallas Cowboys, August 2, 1985.
Released by Dallas Cowboys, August 20, 1985; re-signed by Cowboys, March 7, 1986.
On injured reserve with thumb injury, August 26 through November 4, 1986.
Released by Dallas Cowboys, November 5, 1986; signed as free agent by Los Angeles Rams, May 1, 1987.
Released by Los Angeles Rams, September 1, 1987; signed as free agent replacement player by Dallas Cowboys, September 23, 1987.
Released by Dallas Cowboys, October 26, 1987; re-signed by Cowboys for 1988, October 28, 1987.
Portland USFL, 1985; Dallas NFL, 1987.
Games: 1985 (16), 1987 (3). Total—19.
USFL statistics: Intercepted one pass for 29 yards, 1985.
NFL statistics: Intercepted three passes for seven yards, 1987.

ANDREW ROOSEVELT HEADEN
(Andy)
Linebacker—New York Giants
Born July 8, 1960, at Asheboro, N.C.
Height, 6.05. Weight, 242.
High School—Asheboro, N.C., Eastern Randolph.
Attended Clemson University.

Selected by Washington in 1983 USFL territorial draft.
Selected by New York Giants in 8th round (205th player selected) of 1983 NFL draft.
Signed by New York Giants, June 13, 1983.
On injured reserve with sprained foot, October 10 through November 16, 1984; activated, November 17, 1984.
New York Giants NFL, 1983 through 1987.
Games: 1983 (16), 1984 (11), 1985 (16), 1986 (15), 1987 (12). Total—70.
Pro statistics: Intercepted one pass for four yards and recovered one fumble for 81 yards and a touchdown, 1984; intercepted two passes for seven yards, 1985; intercepted one pass for one yard, 1986; intercepted two passes for 25 yards and recovered one fumble, 1987.
Played in NFC Championship Game following 1986 season.
Played in NFL Championship Game following 1986 season.

HERMAN WILLIE HEARD JR.
Running Back—Kansas City Chiefs
Born November 24, 1961, at Denver, Colo.
Height, 5.10. Weight, 182.
High School—Denver, Colo., South.
Attended Fort Lewis College and University of Southern Colorado.

Selected by Kansas City in 3rd round (61st player selected) of 1984 NFL draft.

		—————RUSHING—————				PASS RECEIVING				—TOTAL—		
Year Club	G.	Att.	Yds.	Avg.	TD.	P.C.	Yds.	Avg.	TD.	TD.	Pts.	F.
1984—Kansas City NFL	16	165	684	4.1	4	25	223	8.9	0	4	24	5
1985—Kansas City NFL	16	164	595	3.6	4	31	257	8.3	2	6	36	4
1986—Kansas City NFL	15	71	295	4.2	2	17	83	4.9	0	2	12	4
1987—Kansas City NFL	12	82	466	5.7	3	14	118	8.4	0	3	18	5
Pro Totals—4 Years	59	482	2040	4.2	13	87	681	7.8	2	15	90	18

Additional pro statistics: Recovered three fumbles, 1984; recovered one fumble, 1985; recovered two fumbles, 1987.

BOBBY JOSEPH HEBERT JR.
Name pronounced A-bear.
Quarterback—New Orleans Saints
Born August 19, 1960, at Baton Rouge, La.
Height, 6.04. Weight, 215.
High School—Galliano, La., South Lafourche.
Received degree in business administration from Northwestern Louisiana State University in 1983.
Brother of Billy Bob Herbert, quarterback at Nicholls State University.

Named THE SPORTING NEWS USFL Player of the Year, 1983.
Named as quarterback on THE SPORTING NEWS USFL All-Star Team, 1983.
Selected by Michigan in 3rd round (34th player selected) of 1983 USFL draft.
Signed by Michigan Panthers, January 22, 1983.
On reserve/did not report, January 23 through February 15, 1984; activated, February 16, 1984.
Protected in merger of Michigan Panthers and Oakland Invaders, December 6, 1984.
Granted free agency, July 15, 1985; signed by New Orleans Saints, August 7, 1985.
On injured reserve with broken foot, September 22 through November 7, 1986; activated, November 8, 1986.

		————————PASSING————————							——RUSHING——				—TOTAL—		
Year Club	G.	Att.	Cmp.	Pct.	Gain	T.P.	P.I.	Avg.	Att.	Yds.	Avg.	TD.	TD.	Pts.	F.
1983—Michigan USFL	18	451	257	57.0	3568	*27	17	*7.91	28	35	1.3	3	3	†20	8
1984—Michigan USFL	17	500	272	54.4	3758	24	22	7.52	18	76	4.2	1	1	6	8
1985—Oakland USFL	18	456	244	53.5	3811	30	19	8.36	12	31	2.6	1	1	6	5
1985—New Orleans NFL	6	181	97	53.6	1208	5	4	6.67	12	26	2.2	0	1	6	1
1986—New Orleans NFL	5	79	41	51.9	498	2	8	6.30	5	14	2.8	0	0	0	3
1987—New Orleans NFL	12	294	164	55.8	2119	15	9	7.21	13	95	7.3	0	0	0	4
USFL Totals—3 Years	53	1407	773	54.9	11137	81	58	7.92	58	142	2.4	5	5	32	21
NFL Totals—3 Years	23	554	302	54.5	3825	22	21	6.90	30	135	4.5	0	1	6	8
Pro Totals—6 Years	76	1961	1075	54.8	14962	103	79	7.63	88	277	3.1	5	6	38	29

†Includes one 2-point conversion.
USFL Quarterback Rating Points: 1983 (86.7), 1984 (76.4), 1985 (86.1). Total—83.1.
NFL Quarterback Rating Points: 1985 (74.6), 1986 (40.5), 1987 (82.9). Total—73.8.
Additional USFL statistics: Recovered two fumbles, 1983; recovered three fumbles, 1984; recovered three fumbles and fumbled five times for minus two yards, 1985.
Additional NFL statistics: Caught one pass for seven yards and a touchdown and recovered one fumble, 1985; caught one pass for one yard, 1986; recovered two fumbles, 1987.
Played in USFL Championship Game following 1983 and 1985 seasons.

JOHNNY LYNDELL HECTOR
Running Back—New York Jets
Born November 26, 1960, at Lafayette, La.
Height, 5.11. Weight, 197.
High School—New Iberia, La.
Attended Texas A&M University.
Selected by Chicago in 2nd round (19th player selected) of 1983 USFL draft.
Selected by New York Jets in 2nd round (51st player selected) of 1983 NFL draft.
Signed by New York Jets, June 9, 1983.

Year Club	G.	Att.	Yds.	Avg.	TD.	P.C.	Yds.	Avg.	TD.	TD.	Pts.	F.
		——RUSHING——				PASS RECEIVING				—TOTAL—		
1983—New York Jets NFL	10	16	85	5.3	0	5	61	12.2	1	1	6	2
1984—New York Jets NFL	13	124	531	4.3	1	20	182	9.1	0	1	6	2
1985—New York Jets NFL	14	145	572	3.9	6	17	164	9.6	0	6	36	2
1986—New York Jets NFL	13	164	605	3.7	8	33	302	9.2	0	8	48	2
1987—New York Jets NFL	11	111	435	3.9	*11	32	249	7.8	0	11	66	2
Pro Totals—5 Years	61	560	2228	4.0	26	107	958	9.0	1	27	162	10

Year Club	G.	No.	Yds.	Avg.	TD.
	KICKOFF RETURNS				
1983—New York Jets NFL	10	14	274	19.6	0
1984—New York Jets NFL	13		None		
1985—New York Jets NFL	14	11	274	24.9	0
1986—New York Jets NFL	13		None		
1987—New York Jets NFL	11		None		
Pro Totals—5 Years	61	25	548	21.9	0

Additional pro statistics: Recovered one fumble, 1985 and 1987.

MICHAEL WILLIAM HEGMAN
(Mike)
Linebacker—Dallas Cowboys
Born January 17, 1953, at Memphis, Tenn.
Height, 6.01. Weight, 225.
High School—Memphis, Tenn., Northside.
Attended Alabama A&M University and received degree in physical education
from Tennessee State University.
Selected by Dallas in 7th round (173rd player selected) of 1975 NFL draft.
On injured reserve with broken arm, September 8 through October 14, 1981; activated, October 15, 1981.
Did not play in 1975.
On injured reserve with broken leg, December 18 through remainder of 1987 season.
Dallas NFL, 1976 through 1986.
Games: 1976 (14), 1977 (14), 1978 (16), 1979 (16), 1980 (16), 1981 (11), 1982 (9), 1983 (16), 1984 (16), 1985 (16), 1986 (16), 1987 (10). Total—170.
Pro statistics: Recovered one fumble, 1976, 1977, 1984, 1985 and 1987; intercepted one pass for no yards, 1977; recovered two fumbles, 1978; intercepted two passes for two yards and recovered one fumble in end zone for a touchdown, 1980; recovered one fumble for nine yards and a touchdown, 1983; intercepted three passes for three yards, 1984; intercepted one pass for seven yards, 1985.
Played in NFC Championship Game following 1977, 1978, 1981 and 1982 seasons.
Member of Dallas Cowboys for NFC Championship Game following 1980 season; did not play.
Played in NFL Championship Game following 1977 and 1978 seasons.

RONALD JEFFERY HELLER
(Ron)
Tight End—San Francisco 49ers
Born September 18, 1963, at Gross Valley, Calif.
Height, 6.03. Weight, 235.
High School—Clark Fork, Ida.
Attended Oregon State University.
Signed as free agent by Dallas Cowboys, May 1, 1986.
Released by Dallas Cowboys, July 24, 1986; signed as free agent by San Francisco 49ers, July 29, 1986.
On injured reserve with neck and head injuries, September 1 through entire 1986 season.
Crossed picket line during players' strike, October 7, 1987.

Year Club	G.	P.C.	Yds.	Avg.	TD.
	——PASS RECEIVING——				
1987—San Francisco NFL	13	12	165	13.8	3

Additional pro statistics: Fumbled once, 1987.

RONALD RAMON HELLER
(Ron)
Offensive Tackle—Seattle Seahawks
Born August 25, 1962, at East Meadow, N.Y.
Height, 6.06. Weight, 280.
High School—Farming Dale, N.Y.
Received bachelor of science degree in administration of justice
from Penn State University in 1984.

Selected by Philadelphia in 1984 USFL territorial draft.
Selected by Tampa Bay in 4th round (112th player selected) of 1984 NFL draft.
Signed by Tampa Bay Buccaneers, June 6, 1984.
Granted free agency, February 1, 1988; re-signed by Buccaneers and traded to Seattle Seahawks for defensive end Randy Edwards and 1989 draft pick, May 4, 1988.
Tampa Bay NFL, 1984 through 1987.
Games: 1984 (14), 1985 (16), 1986 (16), 1987 (12). Total—58.
Pro statistics: Caught one pass for one yard and a touchdown and recovered one fumble, 1986.

DALE ROBERT HELLESTRAE
Name pronounced Hellus-TRAY.
Offensive Tackle—Buffalo Bills
Born July 11, 1962, at Phoenix, Ariz.
Height, 6.05. Weight, 275.
High School—Scottsdale, Ariz., Saguaro.
Attended Southern Methodist University.

Selected by Houston in 1985 USFL territorial draft.
Selected by Buffalo in 4th round (112th player selected) of 1985 NFL draft.
Signed by Buffalo Bills, July 19, 1985.
On injured reserve with broken thumb, October 4 through remainder of 1985 season.
On injured reserve with broken wrist, September 17 through November 14, 1986; activated, November 15, 1986.
On injured reserve with hip injury, September 1 through entire 1987 season.
Buffalo NFL, 1985 and 1986.
Games: 1985 (4), 1986 (8). Total—12.
Pro statistics: Fumbled once for minus 14 yards, 1986.

ANDREW CAREY HENDEL
(Andy)
Linebacker—Buffalo Bills
Born March 4, 1961, at Rochester, N.Y.
Height 6.01. Weight, 230.
High School—Irondequoit, N.Y.
Attended North Carolina State University.

Selected by Jacksonville in 1984 USFL territorial draft.
Signed by Jacksonville Bulls, January 16, 1984.
On developmental squad, May 16 through May 30, 1984; activated, May 31, 1984.
On developmental squad, June 20 through remainder of 1984 season.
Released injured by Jacksonville Bulls, February 23, 1985; signed as free agent by Miami Dolphins, March 6, 1986.
On injured reserve with leg injury, September 7 through entire 1987 season.
Granted free agency with option not exercised, February 1, 1988; signed by Buffalo Bills, March 8, 1988.
On developmental squad for 3 games with Jacksonville Bulls in 1984.
Jacksonville USFL, 1984; Miami NFL, 1986.
Games: 1984 (15), 1986 (16). Total—31.
Pro statistics: Intercepted three passes for 84 yards and credited with one sack for three yards, 1984.

WYMON HENDERSON
Defensive Back—Minnesota Vikings
Born December 15, 1961, at North Miami Beach, Fla.
Height, 5.10. Weight, 186.
High School—Miami Beach, Fla., North.
Attended Hancock Junior College and University of Nevada at Las Vegas.

Selected by Los Angeles in 8th round (96th player selected) of 1983 USFL draft.
Signed by Los Angeles Express, January 20, 1983.
Granted free agency, August 1, 1985; signed by San Francisco 49ers, August 7, 1985.
Released by San Francisco 49ers, August 20, 1985; re-signed by 49ers, February 3, 1986.
On injured reserve with foot injury, August 19 through entire 1986 season.
Granted free agency with option not exercised, February 1, 1987; signed by Minnesota Vikings, April 20, 1987.

Year Club	G.	No.	Yds.	Avg.	TD.
1983—Los Angeles USFL	16		None		
1984—Los Angeles USFL	18	3	23	7.7	0
1985—Los Angeles USFL	18	4	44	11.0	0
1987—Minnesota NFL	12	4	33	8.3	0
USFL Totals—3 Years	52	7	67	9.6	0
NFL Totals—1 Year	12	4	33	8.3	0
Pro Totals—4 Years	64	11	100	9.1	0

Additional pro statistics: Recovered one fumble for 30 yards and one touchdown, 1983; returned one punt for three yards and recovered two fumbles, 1984; recovered one fumble and fumbled three times, 1985.
Played in NFC Championship Game following 1987 season.

MANUEL HENDRIX
(Manny)
Cornerback—Dallas Cowboys
Born October 20, 1964, at Phoenix, Ariz.
Height, 5.10. Weight, 178.
High School—Phoenix, Ariz., South Mountain.
Attended University of Utah.

Signed as free agent by Dallas Cowboys, May 1, 1986.
Released by Dallas Cowboys, August 26, 1986; re-signed by Cowboys, September 23, 1986.
Dallas NFL, 1986 and 1987.
Games: 1986 (13), 1987 (12). Total—25.
Pro statistics: Recovered one fumble, 1986 and 1987.

OSCAR ANTHONY HENTON
(Known by middle name.)
Linebacker—Pittsburgh Steelers
Born July 27, 1963, at Bessemer, Ala.
Height, 6.01. Weight, 234.
High School—Bessemer, Ala., Jess Lanier.
Attended Troy State University.

Selected by Birmingham in 1986 USFL territorial draft.
Selected by Pittsburgh in 9th round (234th player selected) of 1986 NFL draft.
Signed by Pittsburgh Steelers, July 14, 1986.
On physically unable to perform/reserve with knee injury, September 1 through entire 1987 season.
Pittsburgh NFL, 1986.
Games: 1986 (16).
Pro statistics: Recovered one fumble, 1986.

MARK DONALD HERRMANN
Quarterback—Indianapolis Colts
Born January 8, 1959, at Cincinnati, O.
Height, 6.04. Weight, 207.
High School—Carmel, Ind.
Received bachelor of science degree in business
management from Purdue University in 1981.

Selected by Denver in 4th round (98th player selected) of 1981 NFL draft.
On inactive list, September 19, 1982.
Traded with rights to offensive tackle Chris Hinton and 1st round pick in 1984 draft by Denver Broncos to Baltimore Colts for rights to quarterback John Elway, May 2, 1983.
On injured reserve with broken collarbone, August 30 through October 27, 1983; activated, October 28, 1983.
Franchise transferred to Indianapolis, March 31, 1984.
On injured reserve with broken thumb, August 28 through October 19, 1984; activated, October 20, 1984.
Granted free agency, February 1, 1985; re-signed by Colts and traded to San Diego Chargers for 10th round pick in 1986 draft, March 27, 1985.
Traded by San Diego Chargers to Indianapolis Colts for future considerations, April 27, 1988.
Active for 16 games with Denver Broncos in 1981; did not play.

		PASSING							RUSHING				TOTAL		
Year Club	G.	Att.	Cmp.	Pct.	Gain	T.P.	P.I.	Avg.	Att.	Yds.	Avg.	TD.	TD.	Pts.	F.
1982—Denver NFL	2	60	32	53.3	421	1	4	7.02	3	7	2.3	1	1	6	1
1983—Baltimore NFL	2	36	18	50.0	256	0	3	7.11	1	0	0.0	0	0	0	2
1984—Indianapolis NFL	3	56	29	51.8	352	1	6	6.29		None			0	0	0
1985—San Diego NFL	9	201	132	65.7	1537	10	10	7.65	18	—8	—0.4	0	0	0	8
1986—San Diego NFL	6	97	51	52.6	627	2	3	6.46	2	6	3.0	0	0	0	2
1987—San Diego NFL	3	57	37	64.9	405	1	5	7.11	4	—1	—0.3	0	0	0	1
Pro Totals—7 Years	25	507	299	59.0	3598	15	31	7.10	28	4	0.1	1	1	6	14

Quarterback Rating Points: 1982 (53.5), 1983 (38.7), 1984 (37.8), 1985 (84.5), 1986 (66.8), 1987 (55.1). Total—65.4.
Additional pro statistics: Recovered one fumble, 1983; recovered two fumbles and fumbled eight times for minus 26 yards, 1985; recovered one fumble and fumbled once for minus five yards, 1987.

JESSIE LEE HESTER
Wide Receiver—Los Angeles Raiders
Born January 21, 1963, at Belle Glade, Fla.
Height, 5.11. Weight, 170.
High School—Belle Glade, Fla., Central.
Received degree in social science from Florida State University.

Selected by Tampa Bay in 1985 USFL territorial draft.
Selected by Los Angeles Raiders in 1st round (23rd player selected) of 1985 NFL draft.
Signed by Los Angeles Raiders, July 23, 1985.

		——PASS RECEIVING——			
Year Club	G.	P.C.	Yds.	Avg.	TD.
1985—L.A. Raiders NFL........	16	32	665	20.8	4
1986—L.A. Raiders NFL........	13	23	632	27.5	6
1987—L.A. Raiders NFL........	10	1	30	30.0	0
Pro Totals—3 Years............	39	56	1327	23.7	10

Additional pro statistics: Rushed once for 13 yards and a touchdown, and recovered one fumble, 1985.

CLIFFORD WENDELL HICKS JR.
(Cliff)
Cornerback—Los Angeles Rams

Born August 18, 1964, at San Diego, Calif.
Height, 5.10. Weight, 188.
High School—San Diego, Calif., Kearny.
Attended San Diego Mesa College and University of Oregon.

Selected by Los Angeles Rams in 3rd round (74th player selected) of 1987 NFL draft.
Signed by Los Angeles Rams, July 23, 1987.

		——PUNT RETURNS——			
Year Club	G.	No.	Yds.	Avg.	TD.
1987—L.A. Rams NFL.............	11	13	110	8.5	0

Additional pro statistics: Intercepted one pass for nine yards, returned four kickoffs for 119 yards (29.8 avg.) and fumbled once, 1987.

ALONZO WALTER HIGHSMITH
Fullback—Houston Oilers

Born February 26, 1965, at Bartow, Fla.
Height 6.01. Weight, 235.
High School—Miami, Fla., Christopher Columbus.
Received bachelor of science degree in business management from University of Miami in 1987.
Son of Walter Highsmith, offensive lineman with Charleston of Continental Football League,
1965 through 1967; Denver Broncos and Houston Oilers, 1968, 1969 and 1972; with
Montreal Alouettes; and currently assistant coach at Florida A&M University.

Selected by Houston in 1st round (3rd player selected) of 1987 NFL draft.
Placed on reserve/unsigned list, August 31 through October 27, 1987.
Signed by Houston Oilers, October 28, 1987.
Granted roster exemption, October 28 through November 6, 1987; activated, November 7, 1987.

		——RUSHING——				PASS RECEIVING				—TOTAL—		
Year Club	G.	Att.	Yds.	Avg.	TD.	P.C.	Yds.	Avg.	TD.	TD.	Pts.	F.
1987—Houston NFL...	8	29	106	3.7	1	4	55	13.8	1	2	12	2

JAY WALTER HILGENBERG
Center—Chicago Bears

Born March 21, 1960, at Iowa City, Ia.
Height, 6.03. Weight, 260.
High School—Iowa City, Ia., City.
Attended University of Iowa.
Brother of Joel Hilgenberg, center-guard with New Orleans Saints; and nephew of Wally Hilgenberg,
linebacker with Detroit Lions and Minnesota Vikings, 1964 through 1979.

Named to THE SPORTING NEWS NFL All-Star Team, 1987.
Signed as free agent by Chicago Bears, May 8, 1981.
Chicago NFL, 1981 through 1987.
Games: 1981 (16), 1982 (9), 1983 (16), 1984 (16), 1985 (16), 1986 (16), 1987 (12). Total—101.
Pro statistics: Recovered one fumble for five yards, 1982; recovered one fumble, 1983 and 1985; fumbled once for minus 28 yards, 1986.
Played in NFC Championship Game following 1984 and 1985 seasons.
Played in NFL Championship Game following 1985 season.
Played in Pro Bowl (NFL All-Star Game) following 1985 through 1987 seasons.

JOEL HILGENBERG
Center-Guard—New Orleans Saints

Born July 10, 1962, at Iowa City, Ia.
Height, 6.02. Weight, 253.
High School—Iowa City, Ia., City.
Attended University of Iowa.
Brother of Jay Hilgenberg, center with Chicago Bears; and nephew of Wally Hilgenberg,
linebacker with Detroit Lions and Minnesota Vikings, 1964 through 1979.

Selected by Washington in 6th round (109th player selected) of 1984 USFL draft.
USFL rights traded with 1st round pick in 1985 draft by Washington Federals to Birmingham Stallions for quarterback Reggie Collier, January 12, 1984.
Selected by New Orleans in 4th round (97th player selected) of 1984 NFL draft.
Signed by New Orleans Saints, July 24, 1984.
On injured reserve with dislocated elbow, October 30 through December 6, 1984; activated, December 7, 1984.
New Orleans NFL, 1984 through 1987.
Games: 1984 (10), 1985 (15), 1986 (16), 1987 (12). Total—53.
Pro statistics: Recovered one fumble, 1985 and 1987.

RUSSELL TODD HILGER
(Rusty)
Quarterback—Los Angeles Raiders
Born May 9, 1962, at Oklahoma City, Okla.

Height, 6.04. Weight, 205.

High School—Oklahoma City, Okla., Southeast.

Attended Oklahoma State University.

Selected by Denver in 1985 USFL territorial draft.

Selected by Los Angeles Raiders in 6th round (143rd player selected) of 1985 NFL draft.

Signed by Los Angeles Raiders, July 21, 1985.

Crossed picket line during players' strike, October 14, 1987.

					PASSING						RUSHING			TOTAL		
Year	Club	G.	Att.	Cmp.	Pct.	Gain	T.P.	P.I.	Avg.	Att.	Yds.	Avg.	TD.	TD.	Pts.	F.
1985—L.A. Raiders NFL		4	13	4	30.8	54	1	0	4.15	3	8	2.7	0	0	0	1
1986—L.A. Raiders NFL		2	38	19	50.0	266	1	1	7.00	6	48	8.0	0	0	0	3
1987—L.A. Raiders NFL		5	106	55	51.9	706	2	6	6.66	8	8	1.0	0	0	0	3
Pro Totals—3 Years		11	157	78	49.7	1026	4	7	6.54	17	64	3.8	0	0	0	7

Quarterback Rating Points: 1985 (70.7), 1986 (70.7), 1987 (55.8). Total—60.3.

Additional pro statistics: Recovered one fumble, 1985 and 1987; recovered one fumble and fumbled three times for minus seven yards, 1986.

ANDREW HILL
(Drew)
Wide Receiver—Houston Oilers
Born February 5, 1956, at Newman, Ga.

Height, 5.09. Weight, 170.

High School—Newman, Ga.

Received bachelor of arts degree in industrial management from Georgia Tech in 1981.

Established NFL record for most kickoff returns, season (60), 1981.

Selected by Los Angeles in 12th round (328th player selected) of 1979 NFL draft.

On injured reserve with back injury, August 24 through entire 1983 season.

Traded by Los Angeles Rams to Houston Oilers for 7th round pick in 1986 draft and 4th round pick in 1987 draft, July 3, 1985.

			PASS RECEIVING				KICKOFF RET.				TOTAL		
Year	Club	G.	P.C.	Yds.	Avg.	TD.	No.	Yds.	Avg.	TD.	TD.	Pts.	F.
1979—Los Angeles Rams NFL		16	4	94	23.5	1	40	803	20.1	0	1	6	2
1980—Los Angeles Rams NFL		16	19	416	21.9	2	43	880	20.5	*1	3	18	2
1981—Los Angeles Rams NFL		16	16	355	22.2	3	*60	1170	19.5	0	3	18	1
1982—Los Angeles Rams NFL		9	7	92	13.1	0	2	42	21.0	0	0	0	0
1984—Los Angeles Rams NFL		16	14	390	27.9	4	26	543	20.9	0	4	24	0
1985—Houston NFL		16	64	1169	18.3	9	1	22	22.0	0	9	54	0
1986—Houston NFL		16	65	1112	17.1	5		None			5	30	0
1987—Houston NFL		12	49	989	20.2	6		None			6	36	1
Pro Totals—8 Years		117	238	4617	19.4	30	172	3460	20.1	1	31	186	6

Additional pro statistics: Returned one punt for no yards, 1979; recovered one fumble and rushed once for four yards, 1980; rushed once for 14 yards, returned two punts for 22 yards and recovered one fumble, 1981; attempted one pass with no completions, 1987.

Played in NFC Championship Game following 1979 season.

Played in NFL Championship Game following 1979 season.

BRUCE EDWARD HILL
Wide Receiver—Tampa Bay Buccaneers
Born February 29, 1964, at Fort Dix, N. J.

Height, 6.00. Weight, 175.

High School—Lancaster, Calif., Antelope Valley.

Attended Arizona State University.

Selected by Tampa Bay in 4th round (106th player selected) of 1987 NFL draft.

Signed by Tampa Bay Buccaneers, July 20, 1987.

On injured reserve with knee injury, September 7 through November 6, 1987; activated, November 7, 1987.

		PASS RECEIVING				
Year	Club	G.	P.C.	Yds.	Avg.	TD.
1987—Tampa Bay NFL		8	23	402	17.5	2

Additional pro statistics: Rushed three times for three yards, returned one kickoff for eight yards, recovered one fumble and fumbled once, 1987.

DAVID HILL
Tight End—Detroit Lions
Born January 1, 1954, at San Antonio, Tex.

Height, 6.02. Weight, 235.

High School—San Antonio, Tex., Highlands.

Attended Texas A&I University.

Brother of Jim Hill, defensive back with San Diego Chargers, Green Bay Packers and Cleveland Browns, 1969 through 1975; and cousin of Gary Green, cornerback with Kansas City Chiefs and Los Angeles Rams, 1977 through 1985.

Selected by Detroit in 2nd round (46th player selected) of 1976 NFL draft.

Traded by Detroit Lions to Los Angeles Rams for cornerback Rod Perry and 3rd round pick in 1984 draft, August 19, 1983.

Placed on waivers by Los Angeles Rams, February 10, 1987; awarded on waivers to Detroit Lions, February 23, 1987.

Granted free agency with option not exercised, February 1, 1988; re-signed by Lions, April 19, 1988.

Year Club	G.	Att.	Yds.	Avg.	TD.	P.C.	Yds.	Avg.	TD.	TD.	Pts.	F.
1976—Detroit NFL	14		None			19	249	13.1	5	5	30	2
1977—Detroit NFL	14	4	10	2.5	0	32	465	14.5	2	2	12	1
1978—Detroit NFL	16	3	12	4.0	0	53	633	11.9	4	4	24	1
1979—Detroit NFL	16	1	15	15.0	0	47	569	12.1	3	3	18	1
1980—Detroit NFL	16		None			39	424	10.9	1	1	6	1
1981—Detroit NFL	15		None			33	462	14.0	4	4	24	1
1982—Detroit NFL	9		None			22	252	11.5	4	4	24	0
1983—Los Angeles Rams NFL	16		None			28	280	10.0	2	2	12	1
1984—Los Angeles Rams NFL	16		None			31	300	9.7	1	1	6	2
1985—Los Angeles Rams NFL	16		None			29	271	9.3	1	1	6	2
1986—Los Angeles Rams NFL	16		None			14	202	14.4	1	1	6	1
1987—Los Angeles Rams NFL	12		None			11	105	9.5	0	0	0	0
Pro Totals—12 Years	176	8	37	4.6	0	358	4212	11.8	28	28	168	13

Additional pro statistics: Attempted one pass with one interception, 1976; recovered one fumble, 1976 through 1979, 1983, 1984 and 1987; attempted one pass with no completions, 1977; recovered two fumbles, 1986.

Played in NFC Championship Game following 1985 season.

Played in Pro Bowl (NFL All-Star Game) following 1979 season.

GREG HILL
Cornerback—Kansas City Chiefs
Born February 12, 1961, at Orange, Tex.
Height, 6.01. Weight, 199.
High School—West Orange, Tex., Stark.
Attended Oklahoma State University.

Selected by Philadelphia in 3rd round (32nd player selected) of 1983 USFL draft.

Selected by Houston in 4th round (86th player selected) of 1983 NFL draft.

Signed by Houston Oilers, June 25, 1983.

Released by Houston Oilers, August 27, 1984; awarded on waivers to Kansas City Chiefs, August 28, 1984.

On injured reserve with sprained wrist, December 5 through remainder of 1986 season.

Released by Kansas City Chiefs, August 31, 1987; awarded on waivers to St. Louis Cardinals, September 1, 1987.

Released by St. Louis Cardinals, September 7, 1987; signed as free agent replacement player by Los Angeles Raiders, October 9, 1987.

Released by Los Angeles Raiders, November 3, 1987; signed as free agent by Houston Oilers, November 19, 1987.

Released by Houston Oilers, November 27, 1987; awarded on waivers to Kansas City Chiefs, November 30, 1987.

Year Club	G.	No.	Yds.	Avg.	TD.
1983—Houston NFL	14		None		
1984—Kansas City NFL	15	2	−1	−0.5	0
1985—Kansas City NFL	16	3	37	12.3	0
1986—Kansas City NFL	13	3	64	21.3	1
1987—Raid. (2)-K.C. (4) NFL	6		None		
Pro Totals—5 Years	64	8	100	12.5	1

Additional pro statistics: Fumbled once, 1984.

KENNETH HILL
(Kenny)
Safety—New York Giants
Born July 25, 1958, at Oak Grove, La.
Height, 6.00. Weight, 195.
High School—Oak Grove, La.
Received bachelor of science degree in molecular biophysics from Yale University in 1980.

Selected by Oakland in 8th round (194th player selected) of 1980 NFL draft.

On injured reserve with hip pointer, August 26 through entire 1980 season.

On injured reserve with pulled hamstring, August 31 through October 18, 1981; activated after clearing procedural waivers, October 20, 1981.

Franchise transferred to Los Angeles, May 7, 1982.

Traded by Los Angeles Raiders to New York Giants for 7th round pick in 1985 draft, August 27, 1984.

On injured reserve with hamstring injury, September 3 through October 3, 1985; activated, October 4, 1985.

Year Club	G.	No.	Yds.	Avg.	TD.	No.	Yds.	Avg.	TD.	TD.	Pts.	F.
1981—Oakland NFL	9		None			1	21	21.0	0	0	0	0
1982—Los Angeles Raiders NFL	9		None			2	20	10.0	0	0	0	1
1983—Los Angeles Raiders NFL	16		None				None			0	0	0
1984—New York Giants NFL	12		None			1	27	27.0	0	0	0	0
1985—New York Giants NFL	12	2	30	15.0	0	11	186	16.9	0	0	0	1
1986—New York Giants NFL	16	3	25	8.3	0	5	61	12.2	0	0	0	1
1987—New York Giants NFL	12	1	1	1.0	0		None			0	0	0
Pro Totals—7 Years	86	6	56	9.3	0	20	315	15.8	0	0	0	3

Additional pro statistics: Recovered two fumbles, 1985; recovered three fumbles, 1986; recovered one fumble for six yards, 1987.

Played in AFC Championship Game following 1983 season.
Played in NFC Championship Game following 1986 season.
Played in NFL Championship Game following 1983 and 1986 seasons.

LONZELL RAMON HILL
Wide Receiver—New Orleans Saints
Born September 25, 1965, at Stockton, Calif.
Height, 5.11. Weight, 189.
High School—Stockton, Calif., Amos Alonzo Stagg.
Attended University of Washington.
Son of J. D. Hill, Sr., wide receiver with Buffalo Bills and Detroit Lions,
1971 through 1977; brother of J. D. Hill, Jr., wide receiver at University of Washington;
and cousin of Paul Dunn, former wide receiver with Cincinnati Bengals, Washington Redskins
and Philadelphia Bell (WFL).

Selected by New Orleans in 2nd round (40th player selected) of 1987 NFL draft.
Signed by New Orleans Saints, August 8, 1987.

			—PASS RECEIVING—			
Year	Club	G.	P.C.	Yds.	Avg.	TD.
1987—New Orleans NFL		10	19	322	16.9	2

Additional pro statistics: Rushed once for minus nine yards and recovered one fumble, 1987.

IRA McDONALD HILLARY
Wide Receiver—Cincinnati Bengals
Born November 13, 1962, at Edgefield, S. C.
Height, 5.11. Weight, 190.
High School—Johnston, S. C., Strom Thurmond.
Received bachelor of arts degree in interdisciplinary studies (management)
from University of South Carolina in 1985.

Selected by Los Angeles in 1985 USFL territorial draft.
Selected by Kansas City in 8th round (210th player selected) of 1985 NFL draft.
Signed by Kansas City Chiefs, July 15, 1985.
Released by Kansas City Chiefs, August 26, 1985; signed as free agent by Cincinnati Bengals, February 18, 1986.
On injured reserve with Achilles heel injury, August 26 through entire 1986 season.

			—PASS RECEIVING—			
Year	Club	G.	P.C.	Yds.	Avg.	TD.
1987—Cincinnati NFL		11	5	65	13.0	0

Additional pro statistics: Returned one kickoff for 15 yards, 1987.

DALTON HILLIARD
Running Back—New Orleans Saints
Born January 21, 1964, at Patterson, La.
Height, 5.08. Weight, 204.
High School—Patterson, La.
Attended Louisiana State University.

Selected by Tampa Bay in 1986 USFL territorial draft.
Signed by New Orleans in 2nd round (31st player selected) of 1986 NFL draft.
Signed by New Orleans Saints, July 21, 1986.

			——RUSHING——				PASS RECEIVING				—TOTAL—		
Year	Club	G.	Att.	Yds.	Avg.	TD.	P.C.	Yds.	Avg.	TD.	TD.	Pts.	F.
1986—New Orleans NFL		16	121	425	3.5	5	17	107	6.3	0	5	30	3
1987—New Orleans NFL		12	123	508	4.1	7	23	264	11.5	1	8	48	4
Pro Totals—2 Years		28	244	933	3.8	12	40	371	9.3	1	13	78	7

			KICKOFF RETURNS			
Year	Club	G.	No.	Yds.	Avg.	TD.
1986—New Orleans NFL		16		None		
1987—New Orleans NFL		12	10	248	24.8	0
Pro Totals—2 Years		26	10	248	24.8	0

Additional pro statistics: Attempted three passes with one completion for 29 yards and a touchdown, 1986; attempted one pass with one completion for 23 yards and a touchdown, 1987.

CARL PATRICK HILTON
Tight End—Minnesota Vikings
Born February 28, 1964, at Galveston, Tex.
Height, 6.03. Weight, 236.
High School—Galveston, Tex., Ball.
Attended University of Houston.

Named as tight end on The Sporting News College All-America Team, 1984.
Selected by Minnesota in 7th round (179th player selected) of 1986 NFL draft.
Signed by Minnesota Vikings, July 27, 1986.
Minnesota NFL, 1986 and 1987.
Games: 1986 (16), 1987 (11). Total—27.
Pro statistics: Caught two passes for 16 yards and two touchdowns and returned one kickoff for 13 yards, 1987.
Played in NFC Championship Game following 1987 season.

BRYAN ERIC HINKLE
Linebacker—Pittsburgh Steelers
Born June 4, 1959, at Long Beach, Calif.
Height, 6.02. Weight, 215.
High School—Silverdale, Wash., Central Kitsap.
Received degree in business from University of Oregon.

Selected by Pittsburgh in 6th round (156th player selected) of 1981 NFL draft.
On injured reserve with ankle injury and concussion, August 31 through entire 1981 season.
On injured reserve with torn quadricep, January 7 through remainder of 1982 season playoffs.

			—INTERCEPTIONS—		
Year Club	G.	No.	Yds.	Avg.	TD.
1982—Pittsburgh NFL.............	9		None		
1983—Pittsburgh NFL.............	16	1	14	14.0	1
1984—Pittsburgh NFL.............	15	3	77	25.7	0
1985—Pittsburgh NFL.............	14		None		
1986—Pittsburgh NFL.............	16	3	7	2.3	0
1987—Pittsburgh NFL.............	12	3	15	5.0	0
Pro Totals—6 Years............	82	10	113	11.3	1

Additional pro statistics: Recovered two fumbles for four yards, 1983; recovered two fumbles for 21 yards and a touchdown, 1984; recovered one fumble, 1986 and 1987; fumbled once, 1987.
Played in AFC Championship Game following 1984 season.

WILLIAM DEWAYNE HINSON
(Billy)
Guard—Atlanta Falcons
Born January 8, 1963, at Folkston, Ga.
Height, 6.01. Weight, 278.
High School—Hilliard, Fla.
Attended University of Florida.

Selected by Tampa Bay in 1985 USFL territorial draft.
Selected by Denver in 5th round (139th player selected) of 1985 NFL draft.
Signed by Denver Broncos, July 11, 1985.
On injured reserve with hand injury, August 26 through entire 1985 season.
Released by Denver Broncos, September 1, 1986; signed as free agent by Atlanta Falcons, December 13, 1986.
On injured reserve with calf injury, August 31 through entire 1987 season.
Active for 2 games with Atlanta Falcons in 1986; did not play.
Atlanta NFL, 1986.

CHRISTOPHER JERROD HINTON
(Chris)
Offensive Tackle—Indianapolis Colts
Born July 31, 1961, at Chicago, Ill.
Height, 6.04. Weight, 295.
High School—Chicago, Ill., Wendell Phillips.
Received degree in sociology from Northwestern University.

Named to THE SPORTING NEWS NFL All-Star Team, 1987.
Named as offensive tackle on THE SPORTING NEWS All-America Team, 1982.
Selected by Chicago in 1983 USFL territorial draft.
Selected by Denver in 1st round (4th player selected) of 1983 NFL draft.
Rights traded with quarterback Mark Herrmann, and 1st round pick in 1984 draft by Denver Broncos to Baltimore Colts for rights to quarterback John Elway, May 2, 1983.
Signed by Baltimore Colts, May 12, 1983.
Franchise transferred to Indianapolis, March 31, 1984.
On injured reserve with fractured fibula, October 8 through remainder of 1984 season.
Baltimore NFL, 1983; Indianapolis NFL, 1984 through 1987.
Games: 1983 (16), 1984 (6), 1985 (16), 1986 (16), 1987 (12). Total—66.
Pro statistics: Recovered one fumble, 1983 and 1987; recovered two fumbles, 1986.
Played in Pro Bowl (NFL All-Star Game) following 1983 and 1985 through 1987 seasons.

ERIC ELLSWORTH HIPPLE
Quarterback—Detroit Lions
Born September 16, 1957, at Lubbock, Tex.
Height, 6.02. Weight, 196.
High School—Downey, Calif., Warren.
Received bachelor of science degree in business administration from
Utah State University in 1980.

Selected by Detroit in 4th round (85th player selected) of 1980 NFL draft.
On injured reserve with knee injury, October 18 through December 13, 1984; activated, December 14, 1984.
On injured reserve with broken thumb, September 8 through entire 1987 season.

		—PASSING—							—RUSHING—				—TOTAL—		
Year Club	G.	Att.	Cmp.	Pct.	Gain	T.P.	P.I.	Avg.	Att.	Yds.	Avg.	TD.	TD.	Pts.	F.
1980—Detroit NFL......................	15		None							None			0	0	0
1981—Detroit NFL......................	16	279	140	50.2	2358	14	15	8.45	41	168	4.1	7	7	42	*14
1982—Detroit NFL......................	9	86	36	41.9	411	2	4	4.78	10	57	5.7	0	0	0	1
1983—Detroit NFL......................	16	387	204	52.7	2577	12	18	6.66	41	171	4.2	3	3	18	12
1984—Detroit NFL......................	8	38	16	42.1	246	1	1	6.47	2	3	1.5	0	0	0	0

Year	Club	G.	Att.	PASSING Cmp.	Pct.	Gain	T.P.	P.I.	Avg.	RUSHING Att.	Yds.	Avg.	TD.	TOTAL TD.	Pts.	F.
1985—Detroit NFL		16	406	223	54.9	2952	17	18	7.27	32	89	2.8	2	2	12	13
1986—Detroit NFL		16	305	192	*63.0	1919	9	11	6.29	16	46	2.9	0	0	0	7
Pro Totals—7 Years		96	1501	811	54.0	10463	55	67	6.97	142	534	3.8	12	12	72	47

Quarterback Rating Points: 1981 (73.3), 1982 (66.9), 1983 (64.7), 1984 (62.0), 1985 (73.6), 1986 (75.6). Total—69.7.

Additional pro statistics: Recovered four fumbles and fumbled 14 times for minus 10 yards; recovered six fumbles, 1983; recovered three fumbles and fumbled 13 times for minus three yards, 1985; recovered two fumbles and fumbled seven times for minus two yards, 1986.

RAY HITCHCOCK
Center-Guard—Washington Redskins
Born June 20, 1965, at St. Paul, Minn.
Height, 6.02. Weight, 289.
High School—St. Paul, Minn., Johnson.
Attended University of Minnesota.

Selected by Washington in 12th round (331st player selected) of 1987 NFL draft.
Signed by Washington Redskins, July 26, 1987.
On injured reserve with hamstring injury, September 1 through November 22, 1987; activated, November 23, 1987.
On injured reserve with hamstring injury, December 25 through remainder of 1987 season.
Washington NFL, 1987.
Games: 1987 (5).

TERRELL LEE HOAGE
(Terry)
Safety—Philadelphia Eagles
Born April 11, 1962, at Ames, Ia.
Height, 6.03. Weight, 199.
High School—Huntsville, Tex.
Received degree in genetics from University of Georgia.

Named as defensive back on THE SPORTING NEWS College All-America Team, 1983.
Selected by Jacksonville in 1984 USFL territorial draft.
Selected by New Orleans in 3rd round (68th player selected) of 1984 NFL draft.
Signed by New Orleans Saints, July 25, 1984.
Released by New Orleans Saints, August 26, 1986; signed as free agent by Philadelphia Eagles, September 3, 1986.

Year	Club	G.	INTERCEPTIONS No.	Yds.	Avg.	TD.
1984—New Orleans NFL		14		None		
1985—New Orleans NFL		16	4	79	19.8	*1
1986—Philadelphia NFL		16	1	18	18.0	0
1987—Philadelphia NFL		11	2	3	1.5	0
Pro Totals—4 Years		57	7	100	14.3	1

Additional pro statistics: Recovered one fumble, 1984; recovered two fumbles, 1985 through 1987.

LIFFORT HOBLEY
Safety—Miami Dolphins
Born May 12, 1962, at Shreveport, La.
Height, 6.00. Weight, 199.
High School—Shreveport, La., C.E. Byrd.
Attended Louisiana State University.

Selected by Portland in 1985 USFL territorial draft.
Selected by Pittsburgh in 3rd round (74th player selected) of 1985 NFL draft.
Signed by Pittsburgh Steelers, June 5, 1985.
Released by Pittsburgh Steelers, August 25, 1985; signed as free agent by San Diego Chargers, August 28, 1985.
Released by San Diego Chargers after failing physical, August 29, 1985; signed as free agent by St. Louis Cardinals, September 11, 1985.
Released by St. Louis Cardinals, October 15, 1985; signed as free agent by Miami Dolphins, March 6, 1986.
Released by Miami Dolphins, August 19, 1986; re-signed by Dolphins, April 21, 1987.
Released by Miami Dolphins, September 7, 1987; re-signed by Dolphins, September 8, 1987.
Crossed picket line during players' strike, October 7, 1987.
St. Louis NFL, 1985; Miami NFL, 1987.
Games: 1985 (5), 1987 (14). Total—19.
Pro statistics: Intercepted two passes for seven yards and recovered four fumbles for 55 yards and a touchdown, 1987.

MILFORD HODGE
Defensive Lineman—New England Patriots
Born March 11, 1961, at Los Angeles, Calif.
Height, 6.03. Weight, 278.
High School—San Francisco, Calif., South.
Attended Washington State University.

Selected by New England in 8th round (224th player selected) of 1985 NFL draft.
Signed by New England Patriots, July 19, 1985.
Released by New England Patriots, August 28, 1985; re-signed by Patriots, February 24, 1986.

On injured reserve with thumb injury, August 18 through September 29, 1986.
Released by New England Patriots, September 30, 1986; signed as free agent by New Orleans Saints, October 10, 1986.
Released by New Orleans Saints, October 14, 1986; signed as free agent by New England Patriots, November 14, 1986.
Released by New England Patriots, September 7, 1987; re-signed by Patriots, September 8, 1987.
Granted free agency with no qualifying offer, February 1, 1988; re-signed by Patriots, April 26, 1988.
New Orleans (1)-New England (6) NFL, 1986; New England NFL, 1987.
Games: 1986 (7), 1987 (12). Total—19.

MERRIL D. HOGE
(Name pronounced Hodge.)
Running Back—Pittsburgh Steelers
Born January 26, 1965, at Pocatello, Ida.
Height, 6.02. Weight, 212.
High School—Pocatello, Ida., Highland.
Attended Idaho State University.

Selected by Pittsburgh in 10th round (261st player selected) of 1987 NFL draft.
Signed by Pittsburgh Steelers, July 26, 1987.
Crossed picket line during players' strike, October 13, 1987.

		——RUSHING——				PASS RECEIVING				—TOTAL—		
Year	Club	G.	Att.	Yds.	Avg.	TD.	P.C.	Yds.	Avg.	TD.	TD.	Pts.	F.
1987—Pittsburgh NFL		13	3	8	2.7	0	7	97	13.9	1	1	6	0

Additional pro statistics: Returned one kickoff for 13 yards, 1987.

GARY KEITH HOGEBOOM
Name pronounced HOAG-ih-boom.
Quarterback—Indianapolis Colts
Born August 21, 1958, at Grand Rapids, Mich.
Height, 6.04. Weight, 207.
High School—Grand Rapids, Mich., Northview.
Attended Central Michigan University.

Selected by Dallas in 5th round (133rd player selected) of 1980 NFL draft.
Traded with 2nd round pick in 1986 draft by Dallas Cowboys to Indianapolis Colts for 2nd round pick in 1986 draft and conditional 1987 pick, April 28, 1986.
On injured reserve with separated shoulder, September 16 through December 4, 1986; activated, December 5, 1986.
Crossed picket line during players' strike, September 23, 1987.

		——————PASSING——————							——RUSHING——				—TOTAL—		
Year	Club	G.	Att.	Cmp.	Pct.	Gain	T.P.	P.I.	Avg.	Att.	Yds.	Avg.	TD.	TD.	Pts.	F.
1980—Dallas NFL		2		None							None			0	0	0
1981—Dallas NFL		1		None							None			0	0	0
1982—Dallas NFL		4	8	3	37.5	45	0	1	5.63	3	0	0.0	0	0	0	2
1983—Dallas NFL		6	17	11	64.7	161	1	1	9.47	6	—10	—1.7	0	0	0	0
1984—Dallas NFL		16	367	195	53.1	2366	7	14	6.45	15	19	1.3	0	0	0	8
1985—Dallas NFL		16	126	70	55.6	978	5	7	7.76	8	48	6.0	1	1	6	0
1986—Indianapolis NFL		5	144	85	59.0	1154	6	6	8.01	10	20	2.0	1	1	6	3
1987—Indianapolis NFL		6	168	99	58.9	1145	9	5	6.82	3	3	1.0	0	0	0	1
Pro Totals—8 Years		56	830	463	55.8	5849	28	34	7.05	45	80	1.8	2	2	12	14

Quarterback Rating Points: 1982 (17.2), 1983 (90.6), 1984 (63.7), 1985 (70.8), 1986 (81.2), 1987 (85.0). Total—72.2.
Additional pro statistics: Recovered four fumbles and fumbled eight times for minus three yards, 1984; recovered two fumbles and fumbled three times for 50 yards, 1986; recovered one fumble and fumbled once for minus one yard, 1987.
Member of Dallas Cowboys for NFC Championship Game following 1980 and 1981 seasons; did not play.
Played in NFC Championship Game following 1982 season.

WILLIAM BENJAMIN HOGGARD
(D. D.)
Cornerback—Philadelphia Eagles
Born May 7, 1961, at Windsor, N.C.
Height, 6.00. Weight, 188.
High School—Windsor, N.C., Bertie.
Attended North Carolina State University.

Selected by Washington in 12th round (141st player selected) of 1983 USFL draft.
Signed as free agent by Washington Redskins, April 28, 1983.
Released by Washington Redskins, July 30, 1983; signed by Washington Federals, October 21, 1983.
On developmental squad, March 2 through March 6, 1984.
Released by Washington Federals, March 7, 1984; signed by Cleveland Browns, May 6, 1985.
Released by Cleveland Browns, September 2, 1985; re-signed by Browns, October 9, 1985.
Released by Cleveland Browns, October 23, 1985; re-signed by Browns for 1986 season, November 1, 1985.
On injured reserve with ankle injury, September 7 through December 24, 1987; activated, December 25, 1987.
Traded with 6th round pick in 1988 draft and conditional 1989 draft pick by Cleveland Browns to Philadelphia Eagles for defensive tackle Chris Pike, March 25, 1988.
On developmental squad for 1 game with Washington Federals in 1984.
Washington USFL, 1984; Cleveland NFL, 1985 through 1987.
Games: 1984 (1), 1985 (2), 1986 (16), 1987 (1). Total NFL—19. Total Pro—20.
Played in AFC Championship Game following 1986 and 1987 seasons.

JAMIE LORENZA HOLLAND
Wide Receiver—San Diego Chargers
Born February 1, 1964, at Raleigh, N. C.
Height, 6.01. Weight, 186.
High School—Wake Forest, N. C., Rolesville.
Attended Butler County (Kan.) Community College and received
bachelor's degree in education from Ohio State University in 1986.

Selected by San Diego in 7th round (173rd player selected) of 1987 NFL draft.
Signed by San Diego Chargers, July 25, 1987.

			PASS RECEIVING			—KICKOFF RET.—				—TOTAL—		
Year	Club	G.	P.C.	Yds.	Avg.	TD.	No.	Yds.	Avg.	TD.	TD.	Pts.	F.
1987—San Diego NFL		12	6	138	23.0	0	19	410	21.6	0	0	0	0

Additional pro statistics: Rushed once for 17 yards, 1987.

JOHNNY RAY HOLLAND
Linebacker—Green Bay Packers
Born March 11, 1965, at Bellville, Tex.
Height, 6.02. Weight, 221.
High School—Hempstead, Tex.
Attended Texas A&M University.

Selected by Green Bay in 2nd round (41st player selected) of 1987 NFL draft.
Signed by Green Bay Packers, July 25, 1987.
Green Bay NFL, 1987.
Games: 1987 (12).
Pro statistics: Intercepted two passes for four yards and recovered one fumble, 1987.

ERIC W. HOLLE
Defensive Tackle—Kansas City Chiefs
Born September 5, 1960, at Houston, Tex.
Height, 6.05. Weight, 265.
High School—Austin, Tex., LBJ.
Attended University of Texas.

Selected by San Antonio in 1984 USFL territorial draft.
Selected by Kansas City in 5th round (117th player selected) of 1984 NFL draft.
Signed by Kansas City Chiefs, July 12, 1984.
On injured reserve with hip injury, December 5 through remainder of 1987 season.
Kansas City NFL, 1984 through 1987.
Games: 1984 (16), 1985 (16), 1986 (16), 1987 (8). Total—56.
Pro statistics: Recovered one fumble for two yards, 1984.

DOUGLAS HOLLIE
(Doug)
Defensive End—Seattle Seahawks
Born December 15, 1960, at Detroit, Mich.
Height, 6.04. Weight, 250.
High School—Highland Park, Mich.
Attended City College of San Francisco and Southern Methodist University.
Son of Alvin (Blue) Lewis, former heavyweight boxer.

Selected by Pittsburgh in 2nd round (30th player selected) of 1984 USFL draft.
Signed by Pittsburgh Maulers, January 11, 1984.
Selected by Detroit in 3rd round (74th player selected) of 1984 NFL supplemental draft.
Franchise disbanded, October 25, 1984.
Selected by Oakland Invaders in USFL dispersal draft, December 6, 1984.
Released by Oakland Invaders, May 28, 1986; signed by Detroit Lions, July 16, 1986.
Released by Detroit Lions, August 6, 1986; signed as free agent by Los Angeles Raiders, June 22, 1987.
Released by Los Angeles Raiders, August 12, 1987; signed as free agent replacement player by Seattle Seahawks, October 9, 1987.
Released by Seattle Seahawks, October 20, 1987; re-signed by Seahawks for 1988, October 22, 1987.
Pittsburgh USFL, 1984; Oakland USFL, 1985; Seattle NFL, 1987.
Games: 1984 (18), 1985 (18), 1987 (2). Total USFL—36. Total Pro—38.
Pro statistics: Credited with eight sacks for 48 yards, 1984; credited with three sacks for nine yards, 1987.
Played in USFL Championship Game following 1985 season.

DAVID LANIER HOLLIS
Cornerback—Seattle Seahawks
Born April 4, 1965, at Harbor City, Calif.
Height, 5.11. Weight, 175.
High School—Gardena, Calif.
Attended University of Nevada at Las Vegas.

Signed as free agent by Seattle Seahawks, May 12, 1987.

			-PUNT RETURNS-			—KICKOFF RET.—				—TOTAL—		
Year	Club	G.	No.	Yds.	Avg.	TD.	No.	Yds.	Avg.	TD.	TD.	Pts.	F.
1987—Seattle NFL		11	6	33	5.5	0	10	263	26.3	0	0	0	0

BRIAN DOUGLASS HOLLOWAY
Offensive Tackle—Los Angeles Raiders
Born July 25, 1959, at Omaha, Neb.
Height, 6.07. Weight, 275.
High School—Potomac, Md., Winston Churchill.
Received bachelor of arts degree in economics from Stanford University in 1981.
Son-in-law of John McKenzie, forward with Chicago Black Hawks, Detroit Red Wings, New York Rangers, Boston Bruins, Philadelphia-Vancouver Blazers, Minnesota Fighting Saints, Cincinnati Stingers and New England Whalers, 1958 through 1961 and 1963 through 1979;
and brother of Jonathan Holloway, linebacker at Stanford University.
Selected by New England in 1st round (19th player selected) of 1981 NFL draft.
Traded by New England Patriots to Los Angeles Raiders for 5th round pick in 1988 draft, September 1, 1987.
New England NFL, 1981 through 1986; Los Angeles Raiders NFL, 1987.
Games: 1981 (16), 1982 (9), 1983 (16), 1984 (16), 1985 (16), 1986 (15), 1987 (12). Total—100.
Pro statistics: Recovered one fumble, 1981 and 1986; recovered two fumbles, 1985; caught one pass for five yards, 1986.
Played in AFC Championship Game following 1985 season.
Played in NFL Championship Game following 1985 season.
Played in Pro Bowl (NFL All-Star Game) following 1983 through 1985 seasons.

JOHNNY OWEN HOLLOWAY
Cornerback—Seattle Seahawks
Born November 8, 1963, at Galveston, Tex.
Height, 5.11. Weight, 182.
High School—Houston, Tex., Mirabeau B. Lamar.
Attended Northwestern University, Butler County Community College (Kan.) and University of Kansas.
Selected by Dallas in 7th round (185th player selected) of 1986 NFL draft.
Signed by Dallas Cowboys, July 5, 1986.
Released by Dallas Cowboys, September 7, 1987; awarded on waivers to St. Louis Cardinals, September 8, 1987.
Released by St. Louis Cardinals after failing physical, September 9, 1987; re-signed by Cardinals, November 12, 1987.
Released by St. Louis Cardinals, December 8, 1987; signed as free agent by Seattle Seahawks, May 11, 1988.
Dallas NFL, 1986; St. Louis NFL, 1987.
Games: 1986 (16), 1987 (3). Total—19.
Pro statistics: Intercepted one pass for one yard, returned one punt for no yards and fumbled once, 1986.

STEVE HOLLOWAY
Tight End—Miami Dolphins
Born August 23, 1964, at Montgomery, Ala.
Height, 6.03. Weight, 235.
High School—Montgomery, Ala., Jeff Davis.
Attended Tennessee State University.
Signed as free agent by Tampa Bay Buccaneers, May 11, 1987.
Released by Tampa Bay Buccaneers, September 7, 1987; re-signed as replacement player by Buccaneers, September 24, 1987.
Released by Tampa Bay Buccaneers, November 17, 1987; signed as free agent by Miami Dolphins for 1988, December 17, 1987.

		——PASS RECEIVING——				
Year	Club	G.	P.C.	Yds.	Avg.	TD.
1987—Tampa Bay NFL		6	10	127	12.7	0

Additional pro statistics: Recovered one fumble, 1987.

RODNEY A. HOLMAN
Tight End—Cincinnati Bengals
Born April 20, 1960, at Ypsilanti, Mich.
Height, 6.03. Weight, 238.
High School—Ypsilanti, Mich.
Received degree from Tulane University in 1981.
Cousin of Preston Pearson, running back with Baltimore Colts, Pittsburgh Steelers and Dallas Cowboys, 1967 through 1980.
Selected by Cincinnati in 3rd round (82nd player selected) of 1982 NFL draft.

		——PASS RECEIVING——				
Year	Club	G.	P.C.	Yds.	Avg.	TD.
1982—Cincinnati NFL		9	3	18	6.0	1
1983—Cincinnati NFL		16	2	15	7.5	0
1984—Cincinnati NFL		16	21	239	11.4	1
1985—Cincinnati NFL		16	38	479	12.6	7
1986—Cincinnati NFL		16	40	570	14.3	2
1987—Cincinnati NFL		12	28	438	15.6	2
Pro Totals—6 Years		85	132	1759	13.3	13

Additional pro statistics: Recovered one fumble, 1984, 1985 and 1987; fumbled once, 1984 through 1986; returned one kickoff for 18 yards, 1986.

DARRYL DeWAYNE HOLMES
Defensive Back—New England Patriots
Born September 6, 1964, at Birmingham, Ala.
Height, 6.02. Weight, 190.
High School—Warner Robins, Ga., Northside.
Attended Fort Valley State College.

Signed as free agent by New England Patriots, May 12, 1987.
Released by New England Patriots, September 7, 1987; re-signed by Patriots, September 8, 1987.
Crossed picket line during players' strike, October 2, 1987.
New England NFL, 1987.
Games: 1987 (15).
Pro statistics: Intercepted one pass for four yards and recovered one fumble, 1987.

DON IRA HOLMES
Wide Receiver—Phoenix Cardinals
Born April 1, 1961, at Miami, Fla.
Height, 5.10. Weight, 180.
High School—Miami, Fla., Northwestern.
Attended University of Colorado, Gavilan College and Mesa College (Colo.).

Selected by Oakland in supplemental round (404th player selected) of 1984 USFL draft.
Selected by Atlanta in 12th round (318th player selected) of 1986 NFL draft.
Signed by Atlanta Falcons, April 29, 1985.
Released by Atlanta Falcons, August 23, 1985; signed as free agent by Indianapolis Colts for 1986, December 6, 1985.
On injured reserve with toe injury, August 18 through September 28, 1986.
Released after clearing procedural waivers, September 29, 1986; awarded to St. Louis Cardinals, September 30, 1986.
Franchise transferred to Phoenix, March 15, 1988.

		—PASS RECEIVING—			
Year Club	G.	P.C.	Yds.	Avg.	TD.
1986—St. Louis NFL	12		None		
1987—St. Louis NFL	11	11	132	12.0	0
Pro Totals—2 Years	23	11	132	12.0	0

Additional pro statistics: Returned one kickoff for two yards, 1986; returned one kickoff for 25 yards, 1987.

JERRY HOLMES
Cornerback—New York Jets
Born December 22, 1957, at Newport News, Va.
Height, 6.02. Weight, 175.
High School—Hampton, Va., Bethel.
Attended Chowan Junior College and received degree in
personnel management from University of West Virginia.

Named as cornerback on THE SPORTING NEWS USFL All-Star Team, 1984 and 1985.
Signed as free agent by New York Jets, June 4, 1980.
On injured reserve with knee injury, October 21 through November 21, 1980; activated, November 22, 1980.
Signed by Pittsburgh Maulers, September 2, 1983, for contract to take effect after being granted free agency, February 1, 1984.
Franchise disbanded, October 25, 1984.
Assigned to Baltimore Stars, November 1, 1984.
Assigned by USFL to New Jersey Generals, January 18, 1985.
On developmental squad, February 23 through March 22, 1985; activated, March 23, 1985.
Granted free agency when USFL suspended operations, August 7, 1986; re-signed by New York Jets, August 30, 1986.
Granted roster exemption, August 30 through September 9, 1986; activated, September 10, 1986.
On injured reserve with broken rib, November 16 through December 18, 1987; activated, December 19, 1987.
On developmental squad for 4 games when New Jersey Generals in 1985.

	—INTERCEPTIONS—						—INTERCEPTIONS—				
Year Club	G.	No.	Yds.	Avg.	TD.	Year Club	G.	No.	Yds.	Avg.	TD.
1980—New York Jets NFL	12		None			1986—New York Jets NFL	15	6	29	4.8	0
1981—New York Jets NFL	16	1	0	0.0	0	1987—New York Jets NFL	8	1	20	20.0	0
1982—New York Jets NFL	9	3	2	0.7	0	NFL Totals—6 Years	76	14	158	11.3	1
1983—New York Jets NFL	16	3	107	35.7	1	USFL Totals—2 Years	32	5	27	5.4	0
1984—Pittsburgh USFL	18	2	0	0.0	0	Pro Totals—8 Years	108	19	185	9.7	1
1985—New Jersey USFL	14	3	27	9.0	0						

Additional pro statistics: Recovered one fumble, 1981; ran back blocked field goal attempt 57 yards for a touchdown and recovered one fumble for three yards, 1983; recovered three fumbles and fumbled once, 1985.
Played in AFC Championship Game following 1982 season.

—DID YOU KNOW—
That three of the top nine players selected in the 1987 draft were from Miami (Fla.), the best by one school since Southern California had three of the top five in 1977? Vinny Testaverde, Alonzo Highsmith and Jerome Brown were top Hurricanes in 1987; Ricky Bell, Marvin Powell and Gary Jeter were the Trojans chosen in 1977.

RONALD HOLMES
(Ron)
Defensive End—Tampa Bay Buccaneers

Born August 26, 1963, at Fort Benning, Ga.
Height, 6.04. Weight, 255.
High School—Lacey, Wash., Timberline.
Attended University of Washington.

Selected by Portland in 1985 USFL territorial draft.
USFL rights traded with rights to linebacker Tim Meamber by Portland Breakers to Baltimore Stars for rights to defensive end Kenny Neil, February 13, 1985.
Selected by Tampa Bay in 1st round (8th player selected) of 1985 NFL draft.
Signed by Tampa Bay Buccaneers, August 4, 1985.
Tampa Bay NFL, 1985 through 1987.
Games: 1985 (16), 1986 (14), 1987 (10). Total—40.
Pro statistics: Recovered two fumbles, 1985; recovered fumble, 1986 and 1987.

TOM HOLMOE
Safety—San Francisco 49ers

Born March 7, 1960, at Los Angeles, Calif.
Height, 6.02. Weight, 195.
High School—La Crescenta, Calif., Valley.
Attended Brigham Young University.

Selected by Boston in 9th round (102nd player selected) of 1983 USFL draft.
Selected by San Francisco in 4th round (90th player selected) of 1983 NFL draft.
Signed by San Francisco 49ers, July 16, 1983.
On injured reserve with separated shoulder, September 1 through entire 1985 season.
Released by San Francisco 49ers, August 19, 1986; re-signed by 49ers, August 25, 1986.
San Francisco NFL, 1983, 1984, 1986 and 1987.
Games: 1983 (16), 1984 (16), 1986 (16), 1987 (11). Total—59.
Pro statistics: Recovered one fumble, 1983; intercepted three passes for 149 yards and two touchdowns and recovered three fumbles, 1986; intercepted one pass for no yards, 1987.
Played in NFC Championship Game following 1983 and 1984 seasons.
Played in NFL Championship Game following 1984 season.

PETER JOSEPH HOLOHAN
(Pete)
Tight End—Los Angeles Rams

Born July 25, 1959, at Albany, N.Y.
Height, 6.04. Weight, 232.
High School—Liverpool, N.Y.
Attended University of Notre Dame.

Selected by San Diego in 7th round (189th player selected) of 1981 NFL draft.
Left San Diego Chargers voluntarily and placed on left-camp retired list; October 28, 1981; reinstated, April 30, 1982.
USFL rights traded with wide receiver Neil Balholm, defensive end Bill Purifoy, tight end Mike Hirn and linebacker Orlando Flanagan by Chicago Blitz to Denver Gold for center Glenn Hyde and defensive end Larry White, December 28, 1983.
Traded by San Diego Chargers to Los Angeles Rams for 4th round pick in 1988 draft, April 24, 1988.

| | | —PASS RECEIVING— | | | |
Year Club	G.	P.C.	Yds.	Avg.	TD.
1981—San Diego NFL	7	1	14	14.0	0
1982—San Diego NFL	9		None		
1983—San Diego NFL	16	23	272	11.8	2
1984—San Diego NFL	15	56	734	13.1	1
1985—San Diego NFL	15	42	458	10.9	3
1986—San Diego NFL	16	29	356	12.3	1
1987—San Diego NFL	12	20	239	12.0	0
Pro Totals—7 Years	90	171	2073	12.1	7

Additional pro statistics: Recovered one fumble, 1982 and 1987; attempted one pass with no completions, 1983 and 1985; attempted two passes with one completion for 25 yards and a touchdown and recovered two fumbles for 19 yards, 1984; returned one kickoff for no yards and fumbled once, 1985; attempted two passes with one completion for 21 yards, 1986.

ISSIAC HOLT III
Cornerback—Minnesota Vikings

Born October 4, 1962, at Birmingham, Ala.
Height, 6.02. Weight, 197.
High School—Birmingham, Ala., Carver.
Attended Alcorn State University.

Selected by San Antonio in 1st round (3rd player selected) of 1985 USFL draft.
Selected by Minnesota in 2nd round (30th player selected) of 1985 NFL draft.
Signed by Minnesota Vikings, May 24, 1985.

Year Club		—INTERCEPTIONS—			
	G.	No.	Yds.	Avg.	TD.
1985—Minnesota NFL............	15	1	0	0.0	0
1986—Minnesota NFL............	16	8	54	6.8	0
1987—Minnesota NFL............	9	2	7	3.5	0
Pro Totals—3 Years............	40	11	61	5.5	0

Additional pro statistics: Recovered blocked punt in end zone for a touchdown and fumbled once, 1986. Played in NFC Championship Game following 1987 season.

JOHN STEPHANIE HOLT
Cornerback—Indianapolis Colts

Born May 14, 1959, at Lawton, Okla.
Height, 5.10. Weight, 180.
High School—Enid, Okla.
Attended West Texas State University.

Selected by Tampa Bay in 4th round (89th player selected) of 1981 NFL draft.
USFL rights traded with rights to defensive end Clenzie Pierson by Denver Gold to Houston Gamblers for rights to center George Yarno, September 23, 1983.
Traded by Tampa Bay Buccaneers to Indianapolis Colts for 8th round pick in 1987 draft, August 13, 1986.

Year Club		-INTERCEPTIONS-				-PUNT RETURNS-				—TOTAL—		
	G.	No.	Yds.	Avg.	TD.	No.	Yds.	Avg.	TD.	TD.	Pts.	F.
1981—Tampa Bay NFL...................	16	1	13	13.0	0	9	100	11.1	0	0	0	1
1982—Tampa Bay NFL	9		None			16	81	5.1	0	0	0	2
1983—Tampa Bay NFL...................	16	3	43	14.3	0	5	43	8.6	0	0	0	1
1984—Tampa Bay NFL	15	1	25	25.0	0	6	17	2.8	0	0	0	0
1985—Tampa Bay NFL...................	16	1	3	3.0	0		None			0	0	0
1986—Indianapolis NFL..................	16	1	80	80.0	0		None			0	0	0
1987—Indianapolis NFL..................	12		None				None			0	0	0
Pro Totals—7 Years...................	100	7	164	23.4	0	36	241	6.7	0	0	0	4

Additional pro statistics: Returned 11 kickoffs for 274 yards (24.9 avg.), 1981; recovered one fumble, 1982 through 1984; recovered two fumbles, 1985; recovered four fumbles, 1986.

JAMES HOOD
Wide Receiver—Seattle Seahawks

Born September 9, 1961, at Los Angeles, Calif.
Height, 6.01. Weight, 175.
High School—Los Angeles, Calif., Westchester.
Attended Arizona State University.

Signed as free agent by Oakland Invaders, January 12, 1984.
Released by Oakland Invaders, February 9, 1984; signed as free agent by Winnipeg Blue Bombers, April 21, 1984.
Released by Winnipeg Blue Bombers, June 16, 1984; re-signed by Blue Bombers, May 7, 1985.
Released by Winnipeg Blue Bombers, June 18, 1986; signed as free agent by Montreal Alouettes, June 24, 1986.
Selected by Ottawa Rough Riders in dispersal draft after Montreal Alouettes suspended operations, June 24, 1987.
Released by Ottawa Rough Riders, September 13, 1987; signed as free agent by Seattle Seahawks, October 21, 1987.
On injured reserve with pulled groin, November 6 through remainder of 1987 season.

Year Club		——PASS RECEIVING——			
	G.	P.C.	Yds.	Avg.	TD.
1985—Winnipeg CFL...............	5	23	281	12.2	0
1986—Montreal CFL...............	18	95	1411	14.9	2
1987—Ottawa CFL	9	39	446	11.4	3
CFL Totals—3 Years	32	157	2138	13.6	5

Additional CFL statistics: Rushed once for two yards, recovered one fumble and fumbled once, 1987.

WINFORD DeWAYNE HOOD
Guard—Denver Broncos

Born March 29, 1962, at Atlanta, Ga.
Height, 6.03. Weight, 262.
High School—Atlanta, Ga., Therrell.
Attended University of Georgia.

Selected by Jacksonville in 1984 USFL territorial draft.
Selected by Denver in 8th round (207th player selected) of 1984 NFL draft.
Signed by Denver Broncos, May 21, 1984.
Released by Denver Broncos, August 25, 1986; re-signed by Broncos, September 17, 1986.
Released by Denver Broncos, October 10, 1986; re-signed by Broncos, October 22, 1986.
Released by Denver Broncos, December 5, 1986; re-signed by Broncos, May 1, 1987.
On injured reserve with wrist injury, September 1 through September 30, 1987; activated, October 1, 1987.
Crossed picket line during players' strike, October 1, 1987.
On injured reserve with knee injury, October 21 through remainder of 1987 season.
Denver NFL, 1984 through 1987.
Games: 1984 (16), 1985 (16), 1986 (9), 1987 (3). Total—44.

—DID YOU KNOW—

That the 49ers won their final three regular season games in '87 by a combined score of 124-7? The touchdown against was scored on a kickoff return.

WES HOPKINS
Safety—Philadelphia Eagles

Born September 26, 1961, at Birmingham, Ala.
Height, 6.01. Weight, 210.
High School—Birmingham, Ala., John Carroll.
Attended Southern Methodist University.

Named to THE SPORTING NEWS NFL All-Star Team, 1985.
Selected by New Jersey in 4th round (46th player selected) of 1983 USFL draft.
Selected by Philadelphia in 2nd round (35th player selected) of 1983 NFL draft.
Signed by Philadelphia Eagles, May 26, 1983.
On injured reserve with knee injury, October 1 through remainder of 1986 season.
On physically unable to perform/reserve with knee injury, September 6 through entire 1987 season.
Crossed picket line during players' strike, October 14, 1987.

| | | —INTERCEPTIONS— | | | |
Year Club	G.	No.	Yds.	Avg.	TD.
1983—Philadelphia NFL	14		None		
1984—Philadelphia NFL	16	5	107	21.4	0
1985—Philadelphia NFL	15	6	36	6.0	*1
1986—Philadelphia NFL	4		None		
Pro Totals—4 Years	49	11	143	13.0	1

Additional pro statistics: Recovered three fumbles, 1984; recovered two fumbles for 42 yards and fumbled once, 1985; recovered one fumble for minus four yards, 1986.
Played in Pro Bowl (NFL All-Star Game) following 1985 season.

MICHAEL WILLIAM HORAN
Name pronounced Hor-RAN.
(Mike)
Punter—Denver Broncos

Born February 1, 1959, at Orange, Calif.
Height, 5.11. Weight, 190.
High School—Fullerton, Calif., Sunny Hills.
Attended Fullerton College and received degree in mechanical engineering
from California State University at Long Beach.

Selected by Atlanta in 9th round (235th player selected) of 1982 NFL draft.
Released by Atlanta Falcons, September 4, 1982; signed as free agent by Green Bay Packers, March 15, 1983.
Released by Green Bay Packers after failing physical, May 6, 1983; signed as free agent by Buffalo Bills, May 25, 1983.
Released by Buffalo Bills, August 22, 1983; signed as free agent by Philadelphia Eagles, May 7, 1984.
Released by Philadelphia Eagles, August 28, 1986; signed as free agent by Minnesota Vikings, October 31, 1986.
Released by Minnesota Vikings, November 3, 1986; signed as free agent by Denver Broncos, November 25, 1986.
Active for 1 game with Minnesota Vikings in 1986; did not play.

| | | —PUNTING— | | |
Year Club	G.	No.	Avg.	Blk.
1984—Philadelphia NFL	16	92	42.2	0
1985—Philadelphia NFL	16	91	41.5	0
1986—Minn. (0)-Den. (4) NFL	4	21	41.1	0
1987—Denver NFL	12	44	41.1	*2
Pro Totals—4 Years	48	248	41.7	2

Additional pro statistics: Rushed once for 12 yards, 1985; rushed once for no yards, recovered one fumble and fumbled once for minus 12 yards, 1986.
Played in AFC Championship Game following 1986 and 1987 seasons.
Played in NFL Championship Game following 1986 and 1987 seasons.

GREG HORNE
Punter—Phoenix Cardinals

Born November 22, 1964, at Russellville, Ark.
Height, 6.00. Weight, 188.
High School—Russellville, Ark.
Attended University of Arkansas.

Selected by Cincinnati in 5th round (139th player selected) of 1987 NFL draft.
Signed by Cincinnati Bengals, July 23, 1987.
Released by Cincinnati Bengals, November 5, 1987; signed as free agent by St. Louis Cardinals, November 25, 1987.
Franchise transferred to Phoenix, March 15, 1988.

| | | —PUNTING— | | |
Year Club	G.	No.	Avg.	Blk.
1987—Cinc. (4)-St.L. (5) NFL	9	43	40.2	0

ETHAN SHANE HORTON
Running Back—Los Angeles Raiders

Born December 19, 1962, at Kannapolis, N.C.
Height, 6.03. Weight, 228.
High School—Kannapolis, N.C., A.L. Brown.
Attended University of North Carolina.

Selected by Baltimore in 1985 USFL territorial draft.

Selected by Kansas City in 1st round (15th player selected) of 1985 NFL draft.
Signed by Kansas City Chiefs, July 26, 1985.
Released by Kansas City Chiefs, September 1, 1986; signed as free agent by Los Angeles Raiders, May 6, 1987.
Released by Los Angeles Raiders, September 7, 1987; re-signed by Raiders, September 16, 1987.
Crossed picket line during players' strike, October 2, 1987.
Released by Los Angeles Raiders, November 3, 1987; re-signed by Raiders, April 27, 1988.

Year Club	G.	—RUSHING—				PASS RECEIVING				—TOTAL—		
		Att.	Yds.	Avg.	TD.	P.C.	Yds.	Avg.	TD.	TD.	Pts.	F.
1985—Kansas City NFL	16	48	146	3.0	3	28	185	6.6	1	4	24	2
1987—Los Angeles Raiders NFL	4	31	95	3.1	0	3	44	14.7	1	1	6	2
Pro Totals—2 Years	20	79	241	3.1	3	31	229	7.4	2	5	30	4

Additional pro statistics: Attempted one pass with no completions, 1985.

RAYMOND ANTHONY HORTON
(Ray)
Cornerback—Cincinnati Bengals
Born April 12, 1960, at Tacoma, Wash.
Height, 5.11. Weight, 190.
High School—Tacoma, Wash., Mt. Tahoma.
Received bachelor of arts degree in sociology from University of Washington in 1983.
Selected by Los Angeles in 3rd round (25th player selected) of 1983 USFL draft.
Selected by Cincinnati in 2nd round (53rd player selected) of 1983 NFL draft.
Signed by Cincinnati Bengals, May 21, 1983.

Year Club	G.	-INTERCEPTIONS-				-PUNT RETURNS-				—TOTAL—		
		No.	Yds.	Avg.	TD.	No.	Yds.	Avg.	TD.	TD.	Pts.	F.
1983—Cincinnati NFL	16	5	121	24.2	1	1	10	10.0	0	1	6	1
1984—Cincinnati NFL	15	3	48	16.0	1	2	—1	—0.5	0	1	6	0
1985—Cincinnati NFL	16	2	3	1.5	0		None			0	0	1
1986—Cincinnati NFL	16	1	4	4.0	0	11	111	10.1	0	0	0	0
1987—Cincinnati NFL	12		None			1	0	0.0	0	0	0	0
Pro Totals—5 Years	75	11	176	16.0	2	15	120	8.0	0	2	12	2

Additional pro statistics: Returned five kickoffs for 128 yards (25.6 avg.), 1983; recovered one fumble, 1983 and 1984; recovered two fumbles, 1985; fumbled twice, 1986.

JEFF W. HOSTETLER
Quarterback—New York Giants
Born April 22, 1961, at Hollsopple, Pa.
Height, 6.03. Weight, 212.
High School—Johnstown, Pa., Conemaugh Valley.
Attended West Virginia University.
Son-in-law of Don Nehlen, head coach at West Virginia University.
Selected by Pittsburgh in 1984 USFL territorial draft.
Selected by New York Giants in 3rd round (59th player selected) of 1984 NFL draft.
USFL rights traded with rights to cornerback Dwayne Woodruff by Pittsburgh Maulers to Arizona Wranglers for draft choice, May 2, 1984.
Signed by New York Giants, June 12, 1984.
On injured reserve with pulled hamstring, December 14 through remainder of 1985 season.
On injured reserve with leg injury, December 6 through remainder of 1986 season.
On injured reserve with kidney injury, September 7 through November 6, 1987; activated, November 7, 1987.
Crossed picket line during players' strike, October 14, 1987.
Active for 16 games with New York Giants in 1984; did not play.
Active for 2 games with New York Giants in 1987; did not play.
New York Giants NFL, 1984 through 1987.
Games: 1985 (5), 1986 (13). Total—18.
Pro statistics: Rushed once for one yard, 1986.

KEVIN NATHANIEL HOUSE
Wide Receiver—Los Angeles Rams
Born December 20, 1957, at St. Louis, Mo.
Height, 6.01. Weight, 185.
High School—University City, Mo.
Attended Southern Illinois University.
Selected by Tampa Bay in 2nd round (49th player selected) of 1980 NFL draft.
Released by Tampa Bay Buccaneers, October 20, 1986; awarded on waivers to Los Angeles Rams, October 21, 1986.
Selected by St. Louis (baseball) Cardinals' organization in 27th round of free-agent draft, June 5, 1979.
Selected by Chicago White Sox' organization in 20th round of free-agent draft, June 3, 1980.

Year Club		——PASS RECEIVING——			
	G.	P.C.	Yds.	Avg.	TD.
1980—Tampa Bay NFL	14	24	531	22.1	5
1981—Tampa Bay NFL	16	56	1176	21.0	9
1982—Tampa Bay NFL	9	28	438	15.6	2
1983—Tampa Bay NFL	16	47	769	16.4	5
1984—Tampa Bay NFL	16	76	1005	13.2	5
1985—Tampa Bay NFL	16	44	803	18.3	5
1986—T.B. (7)-Rams (8) NFL	15	18	384	21.3	2
1987—L.A. Rams NFL	12	6	63	10.5	1
Pro Totals—8 Years	114	299	5169	17.3	34

Additional pro statistics: Rushed once for 32 yards, 1980; fumbled once, 1980 and 1982; rushed twice for nine yards, attempted one pass with no completions and fumbled twice, 1981; rushed once for minus one yard, 1982; rushed once for minus four yards, 1983; recovered one fumble, 1984 and 1985; rushed twice for five yards, 1986.

BOBBY HOWARD
Running Back—Tampa Bay Buccaneers
Born June 1, 1964, at Pittsburgh, Pa.
Height, 6.00. Weight, 210.
High School—Pittsburgh, Pa., Langley.
Attended Indiana University.
Selected by Philadelphia in 12th round (325th player selected) of 1986 NFL draft.
Selected by Orlando in 6th round (44th player selected) of 1986 USFL draft.
Signed by Philadelphia Eagles, July 16, 1986.
Released by Philadelphia Eagles, August 26, 1986; signed as free agent by Tampa Bay Buccaneers, October 28, 1986.

		—RUSHING—			PASS RECEIVING				—TOTAL—		
Year Club	G.	Att.	Yds.	Avg. TD.	P.C.	Yds.	Avg.	TD.	TD.	Pts.	F.
1986—Tampa Bay NFL	7	30	110	3.7 1	5	60	12.0	0	1	6	1
1987—Tampa Bay NFL	12	30	100	3.3 1	10	123	12.3	0	1	6	1
Pro Totals—2 Years	19	60	210	3.5 2	15	183	12.2	0	2	12	2

Additional pro statistics: Returned four kickoffs for 71 yards, 1986; returned one kickoff for five yards, 1987.

CARL DELANO HOWARD JR.
Defensive Back—New York Jets
Born September 20, 1961, at Newark, N.J.
Height, 6.02. Weight, 190.
High School—Irvington, N.J., Technical.
Received degree in economics from Rutgers University.
Selected by New Jersey in 1984 USFL territorial draft.
Signed as free agent by Dallas Cowboys, May 3, 1984.
On injured reserve with knee injury, November 20 through remainder of 1984 season.
Released by Dallas Cowboys, September 2, 1985; awarded on waivers to Houston Oilers, September 3, 1985.
Released by Houston Oilers, September 7, 1985; signed as free agent by Tampa Bay Buccaneers, October 15, 1985.
Released by Tampa Bay Buccaneers, November 12, 1985; signed as free agent by New York Jets, December 5, 1985.
Released by New York Jets, August 30, 1986; re-signed by Jets, September 14, 1986.
Dallas NFL, 1984; Tampa Bay (4)-New York Jets (3) NFL, 1985; New York Jets NFL, 1986 and 1987.
Games: 1984 (10), 1985 (7), 1986 (14), 1987 (12). Total—43.
Pro statistics: Recovered one fumble for four yards, 1986; intercepted three passes for 29 yards, 1987.

DAVID HOWARD
Linebacker—Minnesota Vikings
Born December 8, 1961, at Enterprise, Ala.
Height, 6.02. Weight, 232.
High School—Long Beach, Calif., Poly.
Attended Oregon State University and California State University at Long Beach.
Selected by Los Angeles in 1984 USFL territorial draft.
Signed by Los Angeles Express, February 10, 1984.
On developmental squad, April 28 through May 10, 1984; activated, May 11, 1984.
Selected by Minnesota in 3rd round (67th player selected) of 1984 NFL supplemental draft.
Released by Los Angeles Express, August 22, 1985; signed by Minnesota Vikings, August 25, 1985.
Granted roster exemption, August 25 through September 6, 1985; activated, September 7, 1985.
On developmental squad for 2 games with Los Angeles Express in 1984.
Los Angeles USFL, 1984 and 1985; Minnesota NFL, 1985 through 1987.
Games: 1984 (15), 1985 USFL (18), 1985 NFL (16), 1986 (14), 1987 (10). Total USFL—33. Total NFL—40. Total Pro—73.
USFL statistics: Intercepted two passes for 14 yards, credited with 4½ sacks for 39 yards, recovered three fumbles and fumbled once, 1984; intercepted one pass for six yards, recovered four fumbles for 12 yards, credited with three sacks for 30 yards and returned two kickoffs for 10 yards, 1985.
NFL statistics: Intercepted one pass for one yard, 1987.
Played in NFC Championship Game following 1987 season.

ERIK HOWARD
Nose Tackle—New York Giants
Born November 12, 1964, at Pittsfield, Mass.
Height, 6.04. Weight, 268.
High School—San Jose, Calif., Bellarmine College Prep.
Attended Washington State University.
Selected by New York Giants in 2nd round (46th player selected) of 1986 NFL draft.
Selected by Baltimore in 1st round (7th player selected) of 1986 USFL draft.
Signed by New York Giants, July 30, 1986.
On injured reserve with hand injury, October 9 through December 5, 1986; activated, December 6, 1986.
New York Giants NFL, 1986 and 1987.
Games: 1986 (8), 1987 (12). Total—20.
Pro statistics: Recovered one fumble, 1987.

Played in NFC Championship Game following 1986 season.
Played in NFL Championship Game following 1986 season.

WALTER LEE HOWARD
(Todd)
Linebacker—Kansas City Chiefs
Born February 18, 1965, at Bryan, Tex.
Height, 6.02. Weight, 235.
High School—Bryan, Tex.
Attended Texas A&M University.

Selected by Kansas City in 3rd round (73rd player selected) of 1987 NFL draft.
Signed by Kansas City Chiefs, July 22, 1987.
Kansas City NFL, 1987.
Games: 1987 (12).

BOBBY GLEN HOWE
(Known by middle name.)
Offensive Tackle—New York Jets
Born October 18, 1961, at New Albany, Miss.
Height, 6.07. Weight, 298.
High School—New Albany, Miss., W.P. Daniel.
Attended University of Southern Mississippi.

Selected by New Orleans in 1984 USFL territorial draft.
Selected by Atlanta in 9th round (233rd player selected) of 1984 NFL draft.
Signed by Atlanta Falcons, June 4, 1984.
Released by Atlanta Falcons, August 26, 1984; signed as free agent by Pittsburgh Steelers, May 9, 1985.
Released by Pittsburgh Steelers, September 2, 1985; re-signed by Steelers, September 3, 1985.
Released by Pittsburgh Steelers, October 4, 1985; signed as free agent by Atlanta Falcons, November 19, 1985.
On injured reserve with back injury, August 26 through October 15, 1986; activated after clearing procedural waivers, October 17, 1986.
Released by Atlanta Falcons, September 7, 1987; signed as free agent by Dallas Cowboys, September 15, 1987.
Released by Dallas Cowboys, November 2, 1987; signed as free agent by New York Jets, April 29, 1988.
Active for 1 game with Dallas Cowboys in 1987; did not play.
Pittsburgh (2)-Atlanta (5) NFL, 1985; Atlanta NFL, 1986; Dallas NFL, 1987.
Games: 1985 (7), 1986 (7). Total—14.

GORDON HUDSON
Tight End—Denver Broncos
Born June 22, 1962, at Kennewick, Wash.
Height, 6.04. Weight, 241.
High School—Kennewick, Wash.
Attended Brigham Young University.

Named as tight end on THE SPORTING NEWS USFL All-Star Team, 1985.
Selected by Los Angeles in 8th round (154th player selected) of 1984 USFL draft.
Signed by Los Angeles Express, January 16, 1984.
On reserve/did not report, February 14 through entire 1984 season.
Selected by Seattle in 1st round (22nd player selected) of 1984 NFL supplemental draft.
Activated from reserve/did not report, January 26, 1985.
On developmental squad, May 19 through remainder of 1985 season.
Released by Los Angeles Express, November 13, 1985; signed by Seattle Seahawks for 1986, November 14, 1985.
Released by Seattle Seahawks, September 7, 1987; signed as free agent by Denver Broncos for 1988, December 29, 1987.
On developmental squad for 6 games with Los Angeles Express in 1985.

| | | —PASS RECEIVING— | | | |
Year Club	G.	P.C.	Yds.	Avg.	TD.
1985—Los Angeles USFL	11	34	476	14.0	0
1986—Seattle NFL	16	13	131	10.1	1
Pro Totals—2 Years	27	47	607	12.9	1

Additional USFL statistics: Recovered one fumble and fumbled once, 1985.
Additional NFL statistics: Fumbled once, 1986.

DAVID LAMBERT HUFFMAN
(Dave)
Offensive Tackle—Minnesota Vikings
Born April 4, 1957, at Canton, O.
Height, 6.06. Weight, 284.
High School—Dallas, Tex., Thomas Jefferson.
Recieved bachelor of arts degree in anthropology from
University of Notre Dame in 1979.
Brother of Tim Huffman, guard with Green Bay Packers, 1981 through 1985.

Named as center on THE SPORTING NEWS College All-America Team, 1978.
Selected by Minnesota in 2nd round (43rd player selected) of 1979 NFL draft.
Signed by Arizona Wranglers, January 6, 1984, for contract to take effect after being granted free agency, February 1, 1984.

Traded by Arizona Wranglers to Memphis Showboats for past consideration, December 6, 1984.
Released by Memphis Showboats, August 20, 1985; re-signed by Minnesota Vikings, September 5, 1985.
Granted roster exemption, September 5 through September 13, 1985; activated, September 14, 1985.
Minnesota NFL, 1979 through 1983 and 1985 through 1987; Arizona USFL, 1984; Memphis USFL, 1985.
Games: 1979 (13), 1980 (16), 1981 (13), 1982 (9), 1983 (15), 1984 (18), 1985 USFL (18), 1985 NFL (15), 1986 (16), 1987 (12). Total NFL—109. Total USFL—36. Total Pro—145.
NFL statistics: Recovered blocked fumble in end zone for a touchdown, returned three kickoffs for 42 yards and recovered two fumbles, 1983; fumbled once for minus 26 yards, 1985.
USFL statistics: Returned one kickoff for eight yards, 1984; caught one pass for two yards and a touchdown and recovered two fumbles, 1985.
Played in NFC Championship Game following 1987 season.
Played in USFL Championship Game following 1984 season.

JAMES KENT HULL
(Known by middle name.)
Center—Buffalo Bills
Born January 13, 1961, at Ponotoc, Miss.
Height, 6.04. Weight, 275.
High School—Greenwood, Miss.
Received bachelor of arts degree from Mississippi State University.

Named as center on THE SPORTING NEWS USFL All-Star Team, 1985.
Selected by New Jersey in 7th round (75th player selected) of 1983 USFL draft.
Signed by New Jersey Generals, January 19, 1983.
Granted free agency when USFL suspended operations, August 7, 1986; signed as free agent by Buffalo Bills, August 18, 1986.
Granted roster exemption, August 18 through August 21, 1986; activated, August 22, 1986.
New Jersey USFL, 1983 through 1985; Buffalo NFL, 1986 and 1987.
Games: 1983 (18), 1984 (18), 1985 (18), 1986 (16), 1987 (12). Total USFL—54. Total NFL—28. Total Pro—82.

ROBERT CHARLES HUMPHERY
(Bobby)
Cornerback-Kick Returner—New York Jets
Born August 23, 1961, at Lubbock, Tex.
Height 5.10. Weight, 180.
High School—Lubbock, Tex., Estacado.
Received degree in social work from New Mexico State University.

Named as kick returner to THE SPORTING NEWS NFL All-Star Team, 1984.
Selected by New York Jets in 9th round (247th player selected) of 1983 NFL draft.
On injured reserve with broken finger, August 1 through entire 1983 season.
On injured reserve with fractured wrist, September 3 through October 4, 1985; activated, October 5, 1985.

| | | PASS RECEIVING | | | | —KICKOFF RET.— | | | | —TOTAL— | | |
Year Club	G.	P.C.	Yds.	Avg.	TD.	No.	Yds.	Avg.	TD.	TD.	Pts.	F.
1984—New York Jets NFL	16	14	206	14.7	1	22	675	★30.7	★1	2	12	1
1985—New York Jets NFL	12		None			17	363	21.4	0	0	0	2
1986—New York Jets NFL	16		None			28	655	23.4	★1	1	6	1
1987—New York Jets NFL	12		None			18	357	19.8	0	1	6	1
Pro Totals—4 Years	56	14	206	14.7	1	85	2050	24.1	2	4	24	6

Additional pro statistics: Recovered two fumbles, 1984; returned one punt for no yards, ran once for 10 yards and recovered one fumble, 1985; credited with a safety, 1986; recovered two fumbles for 46 yards and a touchdown, 1987.

STEFAN GOVAN HUMPHRIES
Guard—Denver Broncos
Born January 20, 1962, at Fort Lauderdale, Fla.
Height, 6.03. Weight, 265.
High School—Fort Lauderdale, Fla., St. Thomas Aquinas.
Received bachelor of science degree in engineering science
from University of Michigan in 1984.

Named as guard on THE SPORTING NEWS College All-America Team, 1983.
Selected by Michigan in 1984 USFL territorial draft.
Selected by Chicago in 3rd round (71st player selected) of 1984 NFL draft.
Signed by Chicago Bears, July 2, 1984.
On injured reserve with knee injury, December 5 through remainder of 1984 season.
On injured reserve with knee injury, September 3 through October 3, 1985; activated, October 4, 1985.
On injured reserve with broken foot, August 26 through November 26, 1986; activated after clearing procedural waivers, November 28, 1986.
Traded by Chicago Bears to Denver Broncos for punter Bryan Wagner and draft pick, August 25, 1987.
On injured reserve with pulled thigh muscle, Sepmber 8 through November 9, 1987; activated, November 10, 1987.
Chicago NFL, 1984 through 1986; Denver NFL, 1987.
Games: 1984 (9), 1985 (11), 1986 (4), 1987 (7). Total—31.
Played in NFC Championship Game following 1985 season.
Played in AFC Championship Game following 1987 season.
Played in NFL Championship Game following 1985 and 1987 seasons.

KENNETH LaMONTE HUNLEY

(Known by middle name.)

Linebacker—Miami Dolphins

Born January 31, 1963, at Richmond, Va.
Height, 6.02. Weight, 241.
High School—Petersburg, Pa.
Attended University of Arizona.
Brother of Ricky Hunley, linebacker with Denver Broncos.

Selected by Arizona in 1985 USFL territorial draft.
Signed as free agent by Indianapolis Colts, May 14, 1985.
On injured reserve with foot injury, October 20 through remainder of 1986 season.
Released by Indianapolis Colts, September 7, 1987; signed as free agent by Miami Dolphins, March 22, 1988.
Indianapolis NFL, 1985 and 1986.
Games: 1985 (16), 1986 (6). Total—22.
Pro statistics: Recovered one fumble, 1986.

RICKY CARDELL HUNLEY

Linebacker—Denver Broncos

Born November 11, 1961, at Petersburg, Va.
Height, 6.02. Weight, 238.
High School—Petersburg, Va.
Received degree in business from University of Arizona in 1984.
Brother of LaMonte Hunley, linebacker with Miami Dolphins.

Selected by Arizona in 1984 USFL territorial draft.
Selected by Cincinnati in 1st round (7th player selected) in 1984 NFL draft.
NFL rights traded by Cincinnati Bengals to Denver Broncos for 1st and 3rd round picks in 1986 draft and 5th round pick in 1987 draft, October 9, 1984.
Signed by Denver Broncos, October 16, 1984.
Granted roster exemption, October 16 though October 25, 1984; activated, October 26, 1984.
Selected by Pittsburgh Pirates' organization in 26th round of free-agent draft, June 3, 1980.
Denver NFL, 1984 through 1987.
Games: 1984 (8), 1985 (16), 1986 (16), 1987 (12). Total—52.
Pro statistics: Intercepted one pass for 22 yards, returned two kickoffs for 11 yards and recovered one fumble, 1986; intercepted two passes for 64 yards and a touchdown, 1987.
Played in AFC Championship Game following 1986 and 1987 seasons.
Played in NFL Championship Game following 1986 and 1987 seasons.

BYRON RAY HUNT

Linebacker—New York Giants

Born December 17, 1958, at Longview, Tex.
Height, 6.05. Weight, 242.
High School—Longview, Tex., White Oak.
Received degree in political science from Southern Methodist University.
Brother of Sam Hunt, defensive end with New England Patriots
and Green Bay Packers, 1974 through 1980.

Selected by New York Giants in 9th round (224th player selected) of 1981 NFL draft.
New York Giants NFL, 1981 through 1987.
Games: 1981 (16), 1982 (9), 1983 (16), 1984 (13), 1985 (16), 1986 (16), 1987 (12). Total—98.
Pro statistics: Intercepted one pass for seven yards, 1981; intercepted one pass for 14 yards and recovered two fumbles, 1984; recovered one fumble, 1985.
Played in NFC Championship Game following 1986 season.
Played in NFL Championship Game following 1986 season.

DANIEL LEWIS HUNTER

Cornerback—San Diego Chargers

Born September 1, 1962, at Arkadelphia, Ark.
Height, 5.11. Weight, 180.
High School—Arkadelphia, Ark.
Attended Henderson State University.

Signed as free agent by Los Angeles Express, January 13, 1984.
Released by Los Angeles Express, February 22, 1984; signed as free agent by Dallas Cowboys, May 10, 1984.
Released by Dallas Cowboys, August 13, 1984; signed as free agent by Denver Broncos, February 27, 1985.
Released by Denver Broncos, November 14, 1986; signed as free agent by San Diego Chargers, November 20, 1986.
Denver NFL, 1985; Denver (10)-San Diego (5) NFL, 1986; San Diego NFL, 1987.
Games: 1985 (16), 1986 (15), 1987 (12). Total—43.
Pro statistics: Intercepted one pass for 20 yards and returned two kickoffs for 32 yards, 1985; returned one kickoff for no yards, 1987.

EDWARD LEE HUNTER

(Eddie)

Running Back—Tampa Bay Buccaneers

Born January 20, 1965, at Reno, Nev.
Height, 5.10. Weight, 195.
High School—Forestville, Md., Bishop McNamara.
Attended Virginia Tech.

Selected by New York Jets in 8th round (196th player selected) of 1987 NFL draft.
Signed by New York Jets, June 29, 1987.
Released by New York Jets, September 6, 1987; re-signed as replacement player by Jets, September 24, 1987.
Released by New York Jets, November 9, 1987; signed as free agent by Tampa Bay Buccaneers, November 19, 1987.

Year Club		—RUSHING—				PASS RECEIVING				—TOTAL—		
	G.	Att.	Yds.	Avg.	TD.	P.C.	Yds.	Avg.	TD.	TD.	Pts.	F.
1987—N.Y. Jets (3)-Tampa Bay (3) NFL	6	56	210	3.8	0	7	28	4.0	2	2	12	3

Year Club	KICKOFF RETURNS			
	G.	No.	Yds.	Avg. TD.
1987—N.Y.J. (3)-T.B. (3) NFL	6	8	123	15.4 0

PATRICK EDWARD HUNTER
Cornerback—Seattle Seahawks
Born October 24, 1964, at San Francisco, Calif.
Height, 5.11. Weight, 185.
High School—South San Francisco, Calif.
Attended University of Nevada at Reno.
Cousin of Louis Wright, cornerback with Denver Broncos, 1975 through 1986;
and brother of Ezra Hunter, basketball swingman at St. Mary's College.
Selected by Seattle in 3rd round (68th player selected) of 1986 NFL draft.
Signed by Seattle Seahawks, July 16, 1986.
Seattle NFL, 1986 and 1987.
Games: 1986 (16), 1987 (11). Total—27.
Pro statistics: Intercepted one pass for three yards, 1987.

JEFFERY TONJA HURD
(Jeff)
Linebacker—Dallas Cowboys
Born May 25, 1964, at Monroe, La.
Height, 6.02. Weight, 245.
High School—Kansas City, Mo., Lincoln Academy.
Attended Kansas State University.
Signed as free agent by Dallas Cowboys, April 30, 1987.
Released by Dallas Cowboys, August 17, 1987; re-signed as replacement player by Cowboys, September 23, 1987.
Released by Dallas Cowboys, October 26, 1987; re-signed by Cowboys for 1988, October 27, 1987.
Signed for 1987 season, December 16, 1987.
Dallas NFL, 1987.
Games: 1987 (5).

DONALD AMECHI IGWEBUIKE
Name pronounced Ig-way-BWEE-kay.

(Middle name means "You can't predict tomorrow.")
Placekicker—Tampa Bay Buccaneers
Born December 27, 1960, at Anambra, Nigeria.
Height, 5.09. Weight, 185.
High School—Anambra, Nigeria, Immaculate Conception.
Attended Clemson University.
Selected by Tampa Bay in 10th round (260th player selected) of 1985 NFL draft.
Signed by Tampa Bay Buccaneers, June 6, 1985.

Year Club	—PLACE KICKING—					
	G.	XP.	XPM.	FG.	FGA.	Pts.
1985—Tampa Bay NFL	16	30	2	22	32	96
1986—Tampa Bay NFL	16	26	1	17	24	77
1987—Tampa Bay NFL	12	24	2	14	18	66
Pro Totals—3 Years	44	80	5	53	74	239

TUNCH ALI ILKIN
Name pronounced TOON-ch ILL-kin.
Offensive Tackle—Pittsburgh Steelers
Born September 23, 1957, at Istanbul, Turkey.
Height, 6.03. Weight, 265.
High School—Highland Park, Ill.
Received bachelor of science degree in broadcasting from Indiana State University in 1980.
Selected by Pittsburgh in 6th round (165th player selected) of 1980 NFL draft.
Released by Pittsburgh Steelers, August 25, 1980; re-signed by Steelers, October 15, 1983.
On injured reserve with shoulder injury, August 30 through September 29, 1983; activated, September 30, 1983.
Pittsburgh NFL, 1980 through 1987.
Games: 1980 (10), 1981 (16), 1982 (8), 1983 (11), 1984 (16), 1985 (16), 1986 (15), 1987 (11). Total—103.
Pro statistics: Recovered one fumble, 1981, 1983 and 1985.
Played in AFC Championship Game following 1984 season.

TIMOTHY JAMES INGLIS
(Tim)
Linebacker—Cincinnati Bengals

Born March 10, 1964, at Toledo, O.
Height, 6.03. Weight, 232.
High School—Toledo, O., St. John's.
Received bachelor of business administration degree from University of Toledo in 1987.

Signed as free agent by Cincinnati Bengals, May 1, 1987.
Released by Cincinnati Bengals, August 24, 1987; re-signed as replacement player by Bengals, September 25, 1987.
Released by Cincinnati Bengals, October 19, 1987; re-signed by Bengals, October 29, 1987.
Cincinnati NFL, 1987.
Games: 1987 (8).

BYRON KYMBLE INGRAM
Guard—Kansas City Chiefs

Born November 17, 1964, at Lexington, Ky.
Height, 6.02. Weight, 295.
High School—Lexington, Ky., Henry Clay.
Attended Eastern Kentucky University.

Signed as free agent by Kansas City Chiefs, June 26, 1987.
On injured reserve with neck injury, September 7 through October 29, 1987; activated, October 30, 1987.
Kansas City NFL, 1987.
Games: 1987 (1).

MARK INGRAM
Wide Receiver—New York Giants

Born August 23, 1965, at Rockford, Ill.
Height, 5.10. Weight, 188.
High School—Flint, Mich., Northwestern.
Attended Michigan State University.

Selected by New York Giants in 1st round (28th player selected) of 1987 NFL draft.
Signed by New York Giants, July 31, 1987.
New York Giants NFL, 1987.
Games: 1987 (9).
Pro statistics: Caught two passes for 32 yards and returned six kickoffs for 114 yards, 1987.

LeROY IRVIN JR.
Cornerback—Los Angeles Rams

Born September 15, 1957, at Fort Dix, N.J.
Height, 5.11. Weight, 184.
High School—Augusta, Ga., Glenn Hills.
Attended University of Kansas.

Established NFL record for most punt return yards, game (207), against Atlanta Falcons, October 11, 1981.
Tied NFL record for most touchdowns, punt returns, game (2), against Atlanta Falcons, October 11, 1981.
Named to THE SPORTING NEWS NFL All-Star Team, 1986.
Named as punt returner to THE SPORTING NEWS NFL All-Star Team, 1981.
Selected by Los Angeles in 3rd round (70th player selected) of 1980 NFL draft.
Placed on suspended list, November 4 through November 9, 1987; activated, November 10, 1987.

| | | -INTERCEPTIONS- | | | | -PUNT RETURNS- | | | | —TOTAL— | | |
Year Club	G.	No.	Yds.	Avg.	TD.	No.	Yds.	Avg.	TD.	TD.	Pts.	F.
1980—Los Angeles Rams NFL	16	2	80	40.0	0	42	296	7.0	0	0	0	5
1981—Los Angeles Rams NFL	16	3	18	6.0	0	46	*615	*13.4	*3	3	18	3
1982—Los Angeles Rams NFL	9		None			22	242	11.0	1	1	6	4
1983—Los Angeles Rams NFL	15	4	42	10.5	0	25	212	8.5	0	0	0	4
1984—Los Angeles Rams NFL	16	5	166	33.2	*2	9	83	9.2	0	2	12	0
1985—Los Angeles Rams NFL	16	6	83	13.8	*1		None			1	6	0
1986—Los Angeles Rams NFL	16	6	150	25.0	1		None			3	18	1
1987—Los Angeles Rams NFL	10	2	47	23.5	1	1	0	0.0	0	1	6	0
Pro Totals—8 Years	114	28	586	20.9	5	145	1448	10.0	4	11	66	17

Additional pro statistics: Returned one kickoff for five yards and recovered three fumbles, 1980; recovered three fumbles for 14 yards, 1981; recovered two fumbles, 1982 and 1983; returned one kickoff for 22 yards, 1983; returned two kickoffs for 33 yards, 1984; returned blocked field goal 65 yards for a touchdown and recovered three fumbles for 55 yards and a touchdown, 1986.
Played in NFC Championship Game following 1985 season.
Played in Pro Bowl (NFL All-Star Game) following 1985 and 1986 seasons.

TIMOTHY EDWARD IRWIN
(Tim)
Offensive Tackle—Minnesota Vikings

Born December 13, 1958, at Knoxville, Tenn.
Height, 6.07. Weight, 290.
High School—Knoxville, Tenn., Central.
Received degree in political science from University of Tennessee in 1981.

Selected by Minnesota in 3rd round (74th player selected) of 1981 NFL draft.

Minnesota NFL, 1981 through 1987.
Games: 1981 (7), 1982 (9), 1983 (16), 1984 (16), 1985 (16), 1986 (16), 1987 (12). Total—92.
Pro statistics: Recovered one fumble, 1983; recovered one fumble for two yards, 1984; returned one kickoff for no yards and recovered two fumbles, 1986.
Played in NFC Championship Game following 1987 season.

RAYMOND CLINTON ISOM
(Ray)
(Name pronounced Eye-SUM.)
Defensive Back—Tampa Bay Buccaneers
Born December 27, 1965, at Harrisburg, Pa.
Height, 5.09. Weight, 190.
High School—Harrisburg, Pa.
Attended Penn State University.

Signed as free agent by Tampa Bay Buccaneers, May 4, 1987.
On injured reserve with ankle injury, September 7 through November 13, 1987; activated, November 14, 1987.
Tampa Bay NFL, 1987.
Games: 1987 (6).
Pro statistics: Intercepted two passes for 67 yards, 1987.

ANDREW LEON JACKSON
Running Back—Tampa Bay Buccaneers
Born May 6, 1964, at Los Angeles, Calif.
Height, 5.10. Weight, 195.
High School—Los Angeles, Calif., Manual Arts.
Attended El Camino College, University of Southern California
and Iowa State University.

Signed as free agent replacement player by Houston Oilers, September 23, 1987.
Released by Houston Oilers, November 24, 1987; signed as free agent by Tampa Bay Buccaneers for 1988, December 9, 1987.

		—RUSHING—				PASS RECEIVING				—TOTAL—		
Year	Club	G.	Att.	Yds.	Avg.	TD.	P.C.	Yds.	Avg.	TD.	TD.	Pts.	F.
1987—Houston NFL		7	60	232	3.9	1	10	44	4.4	0	1	6	0

EARNEST JACKSON
Running Back—Pittsburgh Steelers
Born December 18, 1959, at Needville, Tex.
Height, 5.09. Weight, 219.
High School—Rosenburg, Tex., Lamar.
Attended Texas A&M University.

Selected by Oakland in 9th round (103rd player selected) of 1983 USFL draft.
USFL rights traded by Oakland Invaders to Michigan Panthers for 8th round pick in 1984 draft, March 24, 1983.
Selected by San Diego in 8th round (202nd player selected) of 1983 NFL draft.
Signed by San Diego Chargers, July 11, 1983.
Traded by San Diego Chargers to Philadelphia Eagles for 4th round pick in 1986 draft and 8th round pick in 1987 draft, September 2, 1985.
Released by Philadelphia Eagles, September 16, 1986; signed as free agent by Pittsburgh Steelers, September 23, 1986.
Crossed picket line during players' strike, September 30, 1987.
Active for 2 games with Philadelphia Eagles in 1986; did not play.

		—RUSHING—				PASS RECEIVING				—TOTAL—		
Year	Club	G.	Att.	Yds.	Avg.	TD.	P.C.	Yds.	Avg.	TD.	TD.	Pts.	F.
1983—San Diego NFL		12	11	39	3.5	0	5	42	8.4	0	0	0	1
1984—San Diego NFL		16	296	1179	4.0	8	39	222	5.7	1	9	54	3
1985—Philadelphia NFL		16	282	1028	3.6	5	10	126	12.6	1	6	36	3
1986—Phi. (0)-Pitt. (13) NFL		13	216	910	4.2	5	17	169	9.9	0	5	30	3
1987—Pittsburgh NFL		12	180	696	3.9	1	7	52	7.4	0	1	6	2
Pro Totals—5 Years		69	985	3852	3.9	19	78	611	7.8	2	21	126	12

		KICKOFF RETURNS			
Year	Club	G.	No.	Yds.	Avg.	TD.
1983—San Diego NFL	12	11	201	18.3	0
1984—San Diego NFL	16	1	10	10.0	0
1985—Philadelphia NFL	16		None		
1986—Phi. (0)-Pitt. (13) NFL.	13		None		
1987—Pittsburgh NFL	12		None		
Pro Totals—5 Years	69	12	211	17.6	0

Additional pro statistics: Recovered one fumble, 1983 and 1986; recovered two fumbles, 1984; recovered three fumbles, 1987.
Played in Pro Bowl (NFL All-Star Game) following 1984 and 1986 seasons.

—DID YOU KNOW—
That Philadelphia's John Teltschik set a National Football League record when he punted 15 times in a December 6 overtime game against the Giants?

JEFFERY PAUL JACKSON
(Jeff)
Linebacker—San Diego Chargers
Born October 9, 1961, at Shreveport, Ga.
Height, 6.01. Weight, 228.
High School—Griffin, Ga.
Attended Auburn University.

Selected by Birmingham in 1984 USFL territorial draft.
Selected by Atlanta in 8th round (206th player selected) of 1984 NFL draft.
Signed by Atlanta Falcons, June 10, 1984.
Released by Atlanta Falcons, November 21, 1985; re-signed by Falcons, January 21, 1986.
Released by Atlanta Falcons, August 18, 1986; signed as free agent by San Diego Chargers, April 22, 1987.
Released by San Diego Chargers, September 7, 1987; re-signed as replacement player by Chargers, September 24, 1987.
Atlanta NFL, 1984 and 1985; San Diego NFL, 1987.
Games: 1984 (16), 1985 (11), 1987 (11). Total—38.
Pro statistics: Intercepted one pass for 35 yards and a touchdown, 1984; recovered one fumble, 1984 and 1987.

KIRBY JACKSON
Cornerback—Buffalo Bills
Born February 2, 1965, at Sturgis, Miss.
Height, 5.10. Weight, 180.
High School—Sturgis, Miss.
Attended Mississippi State University.

Selected by New York Jets in 5th round (129th player selected) of 1987 NFL draft.
Signed by New York Jets, July 24, 1987.
Released by New York Jets, September 6, 1987; signed as free agent replacement player by Los Angeles Rams, September 23, 1987.
Released by Los Angeles Rams, November 16, 1987; signed as free agent by Buffalo Bills, November 27, 1987.
Los Angeles Rams NFL, 1987.
Games: 1987 (5).
Pro statistics: Intercepted one pass for 36 yards and recovered blocked punt in end zone for a touchdown, 1987.

MARK ANTHONY JACKSON
Wide Receiver—Denver Broncos
Born July 23, 1963, at Chicago, Ill.
Height, 5.09. Weight, 174.
High School—Terre Haute, Ind., South Vigo.
Received bachelor's degree in public relations from Purdue University in 1986.

Selected by Denver in 6th round (161st player selected) of 1986 NFL draft.
Selected by New Jersey in 2nd round (11th player selected) of 1986 USFL draft.
Signed by Denver Broncos, July 16, 1986.

		—PASS RECEIVING—			
Year Club	G.	P.C.	Yds.	Avg.	TD.
1986—Denver NFL	16	38	738	19.4	1
1987—Denver NFL	12	26	436	16.8	2
Pro Totals—2 Years	28	64	1174	18.3	3

Additional pro statistics: Rushed twice for six yards, returned two punts for seven yards, returned one kickoff for 16 yards and fumbled three times, 1986.
Played in AFC Championship Game following 1986 and 1987 seasons.
Played in NFL Championship Game following 1986 and 1987 seasons.

MARK DEVALON JACKSON
Cornerback—Phoenix Cardinals
Born March 16, 1962, at Amarillo, Tex.
Height, 5.09. Weight, 180.
High School—Amarillo, Tex., Tascosa.
Attended Abilene Christian University.

Signed as free agent by Buffalo Bills, May 16, 1984.
Released by Buffalo Bills, August 27, 1984; signed as free agent by St. Louis Cardinals, July 10, 1987.
Released by St. Louis Cardinals, September 7, 1987; re-signed as replacement player by Cardinals, September 25, 1987.
Franchise transferred to Phoenix, March 15, 1988.
St. Louis NFL, 1987.
Games: 1987 (11).
Pro statistics: Recovered one fumble for 77 yards and a touchdown, 1987.

RICKEY ANDERSON JACKSON
Linebacker—New Orleans Saints
Born March 20, 1958, at Pahokee, Fla.
Height, 6.02. Weight, 243.
High School—Pahokee, Fla.
Attended University of Pittsburgh.

Named to THE SPORTING NEWS NFL All-Star Team, 1987.
Selected by New Orleans in 2nd round (51st player selected) of 1981 NFL draft.
New Orleans NFL, 1981 through 1987.
Games: 1981 (16), 1982 (9), 1983 (16), 1984 (16), 1985 (16), 1986 (16), 1987 (12). Total—101.
Pro statistics: Recovered one fumble, 1981 and 1986; intercepted one pass for 32 yards and recovered two fumbles, 1982; intercepted one pass for no yards and recovered two fumbles for minus two yards, 1983; fumbled once, 1983 and 1984; recovered four fumbles for four yards and intercepted one pass for 14 yards, 1984; intercepted one pass for one yard, 1986; intercepted two passes for four yards, 1987.
Played in Pro Bowl (NFL All-Star Game) following 1983 through 1986 seasons.

ROBERT MICHAEL JACKSON
Safety—Cincinnati Bengals
Born October 10, 1958, at Grand Rapids, Mich.
Height, 5.10. Weight, 186.
High School—Allendale, Mich.
Attended Central Michigan University.

Selected by Cincinnati in 11th round (285th player selected) of 1981 NFL draft.
On injured reserve with knee injury, August 10 through entire 1981 season.
On injured reserve with elbow injury, September 16 through November 9, 1986; activated, November 10, 1986.

| | | —INTERCEPTIONS— | | | |
Year Club	G.	No.	Yds.	Avg.	TD.
1982—Cincinnati NFL............	9		None		
1983—Cincinnati NFL............	16	2	21	10.5	0
1984—Cincinnati NFL............	16	4	32	8.0	1
1985—Cincinnati NFL............	16	6	100	16.7	*1
1986—Cincinnati NFL............	7		None		
1987—Cincinnati NFL............	12	3	49	16.3	0
Pro Totals—6 Years...........	76	15	202	13.5	2

Additional pro statistics: Recovered one fumble, 1982, 1985 and 1987; recovered three fumbles, 1984.

VESTEE JACKSON II
Cornerback—Chicago Bears
Born August 14, 1963, at Fresno, Calif.
Height, 6.00. Weight, 186.
High School—Fresno, Calif., McLane.
Attended University of Washington.

Selected by Chicago in 2nd round (55th player selected) of 1986 NFL draft.
Signed by Chicago Bears, July 24, 1986.

| | | —INTERCEPTIONS— | | | |
Year Club	G.	No.	Yds.	Avg.	TD.
1986—Chicago NFL.................	16	3	0	0.0	0
1987—Chicago NFL.................	12	1	0	0.0	0
Pro Totals—2 Years...........	28	4	0	0.0	0

Additional pro statistics: Recovered two fumbles for minus seven yards, 1986.

VINCENT EDWARD JACKSON
(Bo)
Running Back—Los Angeles Raiders
Born November 30, 1962, at Bessemer, Ala.
Height, 6.01. Weight, 230.
High School—McCalla, Ala., McAdory.
Attended Auburn University, Auburn, Ala.

Heisman Trophy winner, 1985.
Named college football Player of the Year by THE SPORTING NEWS, 1985.
Named as running back on THE SPORTING NEWS College All-America Team, 1985.
Selected by Tampa Bay in 1st round (1st player selected) of 1986 NFL draft.
Selected by Birmingham in 1986 USFL territorial draft.
On reserve/did not sign entire 1986 football season through April 27, 1987.
Selected by Los Angeles Raiders in 7th round (183rd player selected) of 1987 NFL draft.
Signed by Los Angeles Raiders, July 17, 1987.
On did not report/reserve, August 27 through October 23, 1987; activated, October 24, 1987.

| | | —RUSHING— | | | | PASS RECEIVING | | | | —TOTAL— | | |
Year Club	G.	Att.	Yds.	Avg.	TD.	P.C.	Yds.	Avg.	TD.	TD.	Pts.	F.
1987—Los Angeles Raiders NFL	7	81	554	6.8	4	16	136	8.5	2	6	36	2

Additional pro statistics: Recovered one fumble, 1987.

RECORD AS BASEBALL PLAYER
Tied major league records for most strikeouts, nine-inning game (5), April 18, 1987; most strikeouts, inning (2), April 8, 1987, fourth inning.
Major League stolen bases: 1986 (3), 1987 (10). Total—13.

Year Club	League	Pos.	G.	AB.	R.	H.	2B.	3B.	HR.	RBI.	B.A.	PO.	A.	E.	F.A.
1986—Memphis†............ South.		OF	53	184	30	51	9	3	7	25	.277	116	8	7	.947
1986—Kansas City.......... Amer.		OF	25	82	9	17	2	1	2	9	.207	29	2	4	.886
1987—Kansas City.......... Amer.		OF	116	396	46	93	17	2	22	53	.235	180	9	9	.955
Major League Totals—2 Years................			141	478	55	110	19	3	24	62	.230	209	11	13	.944

Selected by New York Yankees' organization in 2nd round of free-agent draft, June 7, 1982.
Selected by California Angels' organization in 20th round of free-agent draft, June 3, 1985.
Selected by Kansas City Royals' organization in 4th round of free-agent draft, June 2, 1986.
†On temporary inactive list, June 20 to June 30, 1986.

JOE JACOBY
Offensive Tackle—Washington Redskins
Born July 6, 1959, at Louisville, Ky.
Height, 6.07. Weight, 305.
High School—Louisville, Ky., Western.
Attended University of Louisville.

Named to THE SPORTING NEWS NFL All-Star Team, 1983 and 1984.
Signed as free agent by Washington Redskins, May 1, 1981.
Washington NFL, 1981 through 1987.
Games: 1981 (14), 1982 (9), 1983 (16), 1984 (16), 1985 (11), 1986 (16), 1987 (12). Total—94.
Pro statistics: Recovered one fumble, 1981 and 1982; recovered fumble in end zone for a touchdown, 1984.
Played in NFC Championship Game following 1982, 1983, 1986 and 1987 seasons.
Played in NFL Championship Game following 1982, 1983 and 1987 seasons.
Played in Pro Bowl (NFL All-Star Game) following 1983 through 1986 seasons.

JEFF TODD JAEGER
(Name pronounced JAY-ger.)
Placekicker—Cleveland Browns
Born November 26, 1964, at Tacoma, Wash.
Height, 5.11. Weight, 189.
High School—Kent, Wash., Kent-Meridian.
Attended University of Washington.

Selected by Cleveland in 3rd round (82nd player selected) of 1987 NFL draft.
Signed by Cleveland Browns, July 26, 1987.
Crossed picket line during players' strike, October 14, 1987.

		——PLACE KICKING——				
Year	Club	G.	XP.	XPM.	FG.	FGA.	Pts.
1987—Cleveland NFL.........		10	33	0	14	22	75

Additional pro statistics: Attempted one pass with no completions and recovered one fumble, 1987.

VAN JAKES
Cornerback—New Orleans Saints
Born May 10, 1961, at Phenix City, Ala.
Height, 6.00. Weight, 190.
High School—Buffalo, N.Y., Seneca Vocational.
Attended Kent State University.

Signed as free agent by Kansas City Chiefs, May 5, 1983.
On injured reserve with ankle injury, October 16 through November 27, 1984.
Released by Kansas City Chiefs, November 28, 1984; re-signed by Chiefs, December 11, 1984.
Signed by Jacksonville Bulls, December 31, 1984, to contract to take effect after being granted free agency, February 1, 1985.
Released by Jacksonville Bulls, August 28, 1985; signed as free agent by New Orleans Saints, July 11, 1986.
On injured reserve with knee injury, December 3 through remainder of 1986 season.

		——INTERCEPTIONS——			
Year	Club	G.	No.	Yds.	Avg.TD.
1983—Kansas City NFL..........		14		None	
1984—Kansas City NFL..........		7		None	
1985—Jacksonville USFL.......		18	3	13	4.3	0
1986—New Orleans NFL.......		12	2	6	3.0	0
1987—New Orleans NFL.......		12	3	32	10.7	0
NFL Totals—4 Years..........		45	5	38	7.6	0
USFL Totals—1 Year..........		18	3	13	4.3	0
Pro Totals—5 Years............		63	8	51	6.4	0

Additional USFL statistics: Credited with one sack for 18 yards and recovered one fumble, 1985.
Additional NFL statistics: Recovered one fumble for 30 yards, 1987.

GARRY MALCOM JAMES
Running Back—Detroit Lions
Born September 4, 1963, at Marrero, La.
Height, 5.10. Weight, 214.
High School—Harvey, La., West Jefferson.
Attended Louisiana State University.

Cousin of Louis Lipps, wide receiver with Pittsburgh Steelers.
Selected by Tampa Bay in 1986 USFL territorial draft.
Selected by Detroit in 2nd round (29th player selected) of 1986 NFL draft.
Signed by Detroit Lions, July 23, 1986.

Year Club	G.	Att.	RUSHING Yds.	Avg.	TD.	PASS RECEIVING P.C.	Yds.	Avg.	TD.	—TOTAL— TD.	Pts.	F.
1986—Detroit NFL	16	159	688	4.3	3	34	219	6.4	0	3	18	3
1987—Detroit NFL	8	82	270	3.3	4	16	215	13.4	0	4	24	3
Pro Totals—2 Years	24	241	958	4.0	7	50	434	8.7	0	7	42	6

Additional pro statistics: Recovered one fumble, 1986 and 1987.

JESSE CRAIG JAMES

(Known by middle name.)

Fullback—New England Patriots

Born January 2, 1961, at Jacksonville, Tex.
Height, 6.00. Weight, 215.
High School—Houston, Tex., Stratford.
Received degree in history from Southern Methodist University.
Brother of Chris James, outfielder with Philadelphia Phillies.
Selected by Washington in 1st round (4th player selected) of 1983 USFL draft.
Signed by Washington Federals, January 12, 1983.
Selected by New England in 7th round (187th player selected) of 1983 NFL draft.
On developmental squad, March 19 through April 14, 1983; activated, April 15, 1983.
On developmental squad, March 9 through April 11, 1984.
Released with knee injury by Washington Federals, April 12, 1984; signed by New England Patriots, April 20, 1984.
On injured reserve with knee injury, October 26 through remainder of 1987 season.
On developmental squad for 4 games with Washington Federals in 1983.
On developmental squad for 5 games with Washington Federals in 1984.

Year Club	G.	Att.	RUSHING Yds.	Avg.	TD.	PASS RECEIVING P.C.	Yds.	Avg.	TD.	—TOTAL— TD.	Pts.	F.
1983—Washington USFL	14	202	823	4.1	4	40	342	8.6	2	6	36	6
1984—Washington USFL	2	16	61	3.8	0	1	13	13.0	0	0	0	0
1984—New England NFL	15	160	790	4.9	1	22	159	7.2	0	1	6	4
1985—New England NFL	16	263	1227	4.7	5	27	360	13.3	2	7	42	8
1986—New England NFL	13	154	427	2.8	4	18	129	7.2	0	4	24	5
1987—New England NFL	2	4	10	2.5	0		None			0	0	0
USFL Totals—2 Years	16	218	884	4.1	4	41	355	8.7	2	6	36	6
NFL Totals—4 Years	46	581	2454	4.2	10	67	648	9.7	2	12	72	17
Pro Totals—6 Years	62	799	3338	4.2	14	108	1003	9.3	4	18	108	23

Additional pro statistics: Returned one kickoff for no yards, attempted two passes with two completions for 16 yards and two touchdowns and recovered four fumbles, 1985; attempted four passes with one completion for 10 yards with one touchdown and one interception and recovered one fumble, 1986.
Played in AFC Championship Game following 1985 season.
Played in NFL Championship Game following 1985 season.
Played in Pro Bowl (NFL All-Star Game) following 1985 season.

JUNE JAMES IV

Linebacker—Indianapolis Colts

Born December 2, 1962, at Jennings, La.
Height, 6.01. Weight, 236.
High School—Kansas City, Mo., Southeast.
Attended University of Texas.
Selected by San Antonio in 1985 USFL territorial draft.
Selected by Detroit in 9th round (230th player selected) of 1985 NFL draft.
Signed by Detroit Lions, July 21, 1985.
Released by Detroit Lions, August 18, 1986; signed as free agent by Indianapolis Colts, May 11, 1987.
Detroit NFL, 1985; Indianapolis NFL, 1987.
Games: 1985 (16), 1987 (11). Total—27.
Pro statistics: Recovered one fumble, 1985.

LIONEL JAMES

Wide Receiver—San Diego Chargers

Born May 25, 1962, at Albany, Ga.
Height, 5.06. Weight, 172.
High School—Albany, Ga., Dougherty.
Attended Auburn University.
Established NFL records for most combined yards gained, season (2,535), 1985; most 300-yard combined yardage games, season (2), 1985; most pass reception yards by running back, season (1,027), 1985.
Selected by Birmingham in 1984 USFL territorial draft.
Selected by San Diego in 5th round (118th player selected) of 1984 NFL draft.
Signed by San Diego Chargers, June 8, 1984.
On injured reserve with foot injury, October 24 through remainder of 1986 season.

Year Club	G.	Att.	RUSHING Yds.	Avg.	TD.	PASS RECEIVING P.C.	Yds.	Avg.	TD.	—TOTAL— TD.	Pts.	F.
1984—San Diego NFL	16	25	115	4.6	0	23	206	9.0	0	1	6	9
1985—San Diego NFL	16	105	516	4.9	0	86	1027	11.9	6	8	48	9
1986—San Diego NFL	7	51	224	4.4	0	23	173	7.5	0	0	0	5
1987—San Diego NFL	12	27	102	3.8	2	41	593	14.5	3	6	36	6
Pro Totals—4 Years	51	208	957	4.6	4	173	1999	11.6	9	15	90	29

Year Club	G.	—PUNT RETURNS—				—KICKOFF RET.—			
		No.	Yds.	Avg.	TD.	No.	Yds.	Avg.	TD.
1984—San Diego NFL	16	30	208	6.9	1	*43	*959	22.3	0
1985—San Diego NFL	16	25	213	8.5	0	36	779	21.6	0
1986—San Diego NFL	7	9	94	10.4	0	18	315	17.5	0
1987—San Diego NFL	12	32	400	12.5	1	2	41	20.5	0
Pro Totals—4 Years	51	96	915	9.5	2	99	2094	21.2	0

Additional pro statistics: Attempted two passes with no completions and one interception and recovered four fumbles, 1984; recovered one fumble, 1985 and 1986; fumbled six times for minus eight yards, 1987.

ROLAND ORLANDO JAMES
Safety—New England Patriots
Born February 18, 1958, at Xenia, O.
Height, 6.02. Weight, 191.
High School—Jamestown, O., Greenview.
Attended University of Tennessee.

Named as cornerback on THE SPORTING NEWS College All-America Team, 1979.
Selected by New England in 1st round (14th player selected) of 1980 NFL draft.
On injured reserve with knee injury, January 6, 1983 through remainder of 1982 season playoffs.
On injured reserve with knee injury, September 8 through October 22, 1987; activated, October 23, 1987.

Year Club	G.	-INTERCEPTIONS-				-PUNT RETURNS-				—TOTAL—		
		No.	Yds.	Avg.	TD.	No.	Yds.	Avg.	TD.	TD.	Pts.	F.
1980—New England NFL	16	4	32	8.0	0	33	331	10.0	1	1	6	2
1981—New England NFL	16	2	29	14.5	0	7	56	8.0	0	0	0	1
1982—New England NFL	7	3	12	4.0	0	None				0	0	1
1983—New England NFL	16	5	99	19.8	0	None				0	0	0
1984—New England NFL	15	2	14	7.0	0	None				0	0	0
1985—New England NFL	16	4	51	12.8	0	2	13	6.5	0	0	0	1
1986—New England NFL	15	2	39	19.5	0	None				0	0	0
1987—New England NFL	9	1	27	27.0	0	None				0	0	0
Pro Totals—8 Years	110	23	303	13.2	0	42	400	9.5	1	1	6	5

Additional pro statistics: Recovered one fumble, 1980, 1981 and 1984; recovered four fumbles, 1983; credited with one safety, 1984.
Played in AFC Championship Game following 1985 season.
Played in NFL Championship Game following 1985 season.

GEORGE R. JAMISON
Linebacker—Detroit Lions
Born September 30, 1962, at Bridgeton, N.J.
Height, 6.01. Weight, 228.
High School—Bridgeton, N.J.
Attended University of Cincinnati.
Cousin of Anthony (Bubba) Green, defensive tackle with Baltimore Colts, 1981;
and Larry Milbourne, infielder with Houston Astros, Seattle Mariners, New York Yankees,
Minnesota Twins, Cleveland Indians and Philadelphia Phillies, 1975 through 1984.

Selected by Philadelphia in 2nd round (34th player selected) of 1984 USFL draft.
Signed by Philadelphia Stars, January 17, 1984.
On developmental squad, February 24 through March 1, 1984; activated, March 2, 1984.
On developmental squad, June 21 through remainder of 1984 season.
Selected by Detroit in 2nd round (47th player selected) of 1984 NFL supplemental draft.
Franchise transferred to Baltimore, November 1, 1984.
On developmental squad, May 3 through May 9, 1985; activated, May 10, 1985.
Granted free agency when USFL suspended operations, August 7, 1986; signed by Detroit Lions, August 17, 1986.
On injured reserve with Achilles tendon injury, August 30 through entire 1986 season.
On developmental squad for 2 games with Philadelphia Stars in 1984.
On developmental squad for 1 game with Baltimore Stars in 1985.
Philadelphia USFL, 1984; Baltimore USFL, 1985; Detroit NFL, 1987.
Games: 1984 (15), 1985 (17), 1987 (12). Total USFL—32. Total Pro—44.
USFL statistics: Credited with four sacks for 37 yards, 1984; intercepted one pass for 16 yards and credited with five sacks for 40½ yards, 1985.
NFL statistics: Credited with a safety, 1987.
Played in USFL Championship Game following 1984 and 1985 seasons.

ILIA JAROSTCHUK
(Name pronounced ILL-ee-uh Jur-ROST-chuk.)
Linebacker—Phoenix Cardinals
Born August 1, 1964, at Utica, N. Y.
Height, 6.03. Weight, 231.
High School—Whitesboro, N. Y., Central.
Received bachelor of science degree in civil engineering
from University of New Hampshire in 1987.

Selected by St. Louis in 5th round (127th player selected) of 1987 NFL draft.
Signed by St. Louis Cardinals, July 20, 1987.
Franchise transferred to Phoenix, March 15, 1988.
St. Louis NFL, 1987.
Games: 1987 (12).

CURTIS JARVIS JR.
(Curt)
Defensive Lineman—Tampa Bay Buccaneers
Born January 28, 1965, at Birmingham, Ala.
Height, 6.02. Weight, 266.
High School—Gardendale, Ala.
Attended University of Alabama.

Selected by Tampa Bay in 7th round (169th player selected) of 1987 NFL draft.
Signed by Tampa Bay Buccaneers, July 16, 1987.
On injured reserve with knee injury, August 31 through November 27, 1987; activated, November 28, 1987.
Tampa Bay NFL, 1987.
Games: 1987 (2).

RONALD VINCENT JAWORSKI
(Ron)
Quarterback—Miami Dolphins
Born March 23, 1951, at Lackawanna, N. Y.
Height, 6.01. Weight, 196.
High School—Lackawanna, N. Y.
Attended Youngstown State University.

Tied NFL record for longest completed passing play from scrimmage when he threw a 99-yard touchdown pass to wide receiver Mike Quick against Atlanta Falcons, November 10, 1985.
Selected by Los Angeles in 2nd round (37th player selected) of 1973 NFL draft.
Member of Los Angeles Rams' taxi squad, 1973.
Traded by Los Angeles Rams to Philadelphia Eagles for tight end Charle Young, March 10, 1977.
On injured reserve with broken fibula, November 27 through remainder of 1984 season.
On injured reserve with torn tendon in finger, November 13 through remainder of 1986 season.
Granted free agency, March 1, 1987; signed by Miami Dolphins, August 18, 1987.
Active for 2 games with Miami Dolphins in 1987; did not play.

				—PASSING—					—RUSHING—				—TOTAL—		
Year Club	G.	Att.	Cmp.	Pct.	Gain	T.P.	P.I.	Avg.	Att.	Yds.	Avg.	TD.	TD.	Pts.	F.
1974—Los Angeles NFL	5	24	10	41.7	144	0	1	6.00	7	34	4.9	1	1	6	1
1975—Los Angeles NFL	14	48	24	50.0	302	0	2	6.29	12	33	2.8	2	2	12	1
1976—Los Angeles NFL	5	52	20	38.5	273	1	5	5.25	2	15	7.5	1	1	6	0
1977—Philadelphia NFL	14	346	166	48.0	2183	18	21	6.31	40	124	3.1	5	5	30	6
1978—Philadelphia NFL	16	398	206	51.8	2487	16	16	6.25	30	79	2.6	0	0	0	7
1979—Philadelphia NFL	16	374	190	50.8	2669	18	12	7.14	43	119	2.8	2	2	12	12
1980—Philadelphia NFL	16	451	257	57.0	3529	27	12	7.82	27	95	3.5	1	1	6	6
1981—Philadelphia NFL	16	461	250	54.2	3095	23	20	6.71	22	128	5.8	0	0	0	3
1982—Philadelphia NFL	9	286	167	58.4	2076	12	12	7.26	10	9	0.9	0	0	0	9
1983—Philadelphia NFL	16	446	235	52.7	3315	20	18	7.43	25	129	5.2	1	1	6	11
1984—Philadelphia NFL	13	427	234	54.8	2754	16	14	6.45	5	18	3.6	1	1	6	5
1985—Philadelphia NFL	16	484	255	52.7	3450	17	20	7.13	17	35	2.1	2	2	12	5
1986—Philadelphia NFL	10	245	128	52.2	1405	8	6	5.73	13	33	2.5	0	0	0	4
Pro Totals—14 Years	166	4042	2142	53.0	27682	176	159	6.85	253	851	3.4	16	16	96	70

Quarterback Rating Points: 1974 (44.3), 1975 (52.5), 1976 (22.8), 1977 (60.3), 1978 (68.0), 1979 (76.8), 1980 (90.9), 1981 (74.0), 1982 (77.5), 1983 (75.1), 1984 (73.5), 1985 (70.2), 1986 (70.2). Total—73.2.
Additional pro statistics: Recovered two fumbles and fumbled once for minus three yards, 1975; recovered three fumbles and fumbled six times for minus four yards, 1977; recovered three fumbles and fumbled seven times for minus one yard, 1978; recovered five fumbles and fumbled 12 times for minus 23 yards, 1979; recovered four fumbles, 1980 and 1983; recovered three fumbles and fumbled three times for minus two yards, 1981; recovered four fumbles and fumbled nine times for minus 11 yards, 1982; recovered two fumbles, 1984 and 1985; recovered one fumble, 1986.
Played in NFC Championship Game following 1975 and 1980 seasons.
Member of Los Angeles Rams for NFC Championship Game following 1974 and 1976 seasons; did not play.
Played in NFL Championship Game following 1980 season.
Played in Pro Bowl (NFL All-Star Game) following 1980 season.

JAMES GARTH JAX
(Known by middle name.)
Linebacker—Dallas Cowboys
Born September 16, 1963, at Houston, Tex.
Height, 6.02. Weight, 225.
High School—Houston, Tex., Strake Jesuit Preparatory.
Received bachelor of science degree in criminology from
Florida State University in 1986.

Selected by Tampa Bay in 1986 USFL territorial draft.
Selected by Dallas in 11th round (296th player selected) of 1986 NFL draft.
Signed by Dallas Cowboys, July 1, 1986.
Released by Dallas Cowboys, September 1, 1986; re-signed by Cowboys, September 8, 1986.
On injured reserve with fractured wrist, November 2 through remainder of 1987 season.
Dallas NFL, 1986 and 1987.
Games: 1986 (16), 1987 (3). Total—19.

JAMES WILSON JEFFCOAT JR.
(Jim)
Defensive End—Dallas Cowboys
Born April 1, 1961, at Long Branch, N.J.
Height, 6.05. Weight, 263.
High School—Matawan, N.J., Regional.
Received bachelor of arts degree in communications
from Arizona State University in 1983.

Selected by Arizona in 1983 USFL territorial draft.
Selected by Dallas in 1st round (23rd player selected) of 1983 NFL draft.
Signed by Dallas Cowboys, May 24, 1983.
Dallas NFL, 1983 through 1987.
Games: 1983 (16), 1984 (16), 1985 (16), 1986 (16), 1987 (12). Total—76.
Pro statistics: Recovered fumble in end zone for a touchdown, 1984; intercepted one pass for 65 yards and a touchdown and recovered two fumbles, 1985; recovered two fumbles for eight yards, 1986 and 1987; intercepted one pass for 26 yards and a touchdown, 1987.

NORMAN JEFFERSON JR.
Defensive Back—Green Bay Packers
Born August 7, 1964, at Marrero, La.
Height, 5.10. Weight, 183.
High School—Marrero, La., John Ehret.
Attended Louisiana State University.

Selected by Green Bay in 12th round (335th player selected) of 1987 NFL draft.
Signed by Green Bay Packers, July 23, 1987.
Green Bay NFL, 1987.
Games: 1987 (12).
Pro statistics: Returned two kickoffs for 30 yards, 1987.

HAYWOOD FRANKLIN JEFFIRES
Wide Receiver—Houston Oilers
Born December 12, 1964, at Greensboro, N. C.
Height, 6.02. Weight, 198.
High School—Greensboro, N. C., Page.
Received bachelor of arts degree in recreation administration
from North Carolina State University in 1987.

Selected by Houston in 1st round (20th player selected) of 1987 NFL draft.
Signed by Houston Oilers, July 22, 1987.
Crossed picket line during players' strike, October 14, 1987.

		——PASS RECEIVING——			
Year Club	G.	P.C.	Yds.	Avg.	TD.
1987—Houston NFL	9	7	89	12.7	0

KEYVAN JENKINS
Running Back—Kansas City Chiefs
Born January 6, 1961, at Stockton, Calif.
Height, 5.10. Weight, 190.
Attended University of Nevada at Las Vegas.

Signed as free agent by British Columbia Lions, April 12, 1984.
Granted free agency, March 1, 1987; signed as free agent by San Diego Chargers, April 11, 1987.
Released by San Diego Chargers, August 27, 1987; re-signed as replacement player by Chargers, September 24, 1987.
Released by San Diego Chargers, October 27, 1987; signed as free agent by Kansas City Chiefs, March 28, 1988.

		——RUSHING——				PASS RECEIVING			—TOTAL—		
Year Club	G.	Att.	Yds.	Avg.	TD.	P.C.	Yds.	Avg.	TD.	TD.	Pts.	F.
1984—British Columbia CFL	3	30	170	5.7	2	7	56	8.0	0	2	12	3
1985—British Columbia CFL	14	193	964	5.0	8	51	437	8.6	3	11	66	5
1986—British Columbia CFL	11	131	496	3.8	7	34	329	9.7	0	7	42	6
1987—San Diego NFL	3	22	88	4.0	0	8	40	5.0	0	0	0	0
CFL Totals—3 Years	28	354	1630	4.6	17	92	822	8.9	3	20	120	14
NFL Totals—1 Year	3	22	88	4.0	0	8	40	5.0	0	0	0	0
Pro Totals—4 Years	31	376	1718	4.6	17	100	862	8.6	3	20	120	14

		KICKOFF RETURNS			
Year Club	G.	No.	Yds.	Avg.	TD.
1984—British Columbia CFL	3	6	173	28.8	0
1985—British Columbia CFL	14	35	720	20.6	0
1986—British Columbia CFL	11	23	502	21.8	0
1987—San Diego NFL	3	2	46	23.0	0
CFL Totals—3 Years	28	64	1395	21.8	0
NFL Totals—1 Year	3	2	46	23.0	0
Pro Totals—4 Years	31	66	1441	21.8	0

Additional CFL statistics: Recovered two fumbles, 1985.

MELVIN JENKINS
Cornerback—Seattle Seahawks
Born March 16, 1962, at Jackson, Miss.
Height, 5.10. Weight, 170.
High School—Jackson, Miss., Wingfield.
Attended University of Cincinnati.

Signed as free agent by Calgary Stampeders, April 17, 1984.
Granted free agency, March 1, 1987; signed as free agent by Seattle Seahawks, April 22, 1987.

Year Club	G.	INTERCEPTIONS No.	Yds.	Avg.	TD.	-PUNT RETURNS- No.	Yds.	Avg.	TD.	—KICKOFF RET.— No.	Yds.	Avg.	TD.	—TOTAL— TD.	Pts.	F.
1984—Calgary CFL	13	3	50	16.7	1	41	349	8.5	0	15	312	20.8	0	1	6	4
1985—Calgary CFL	9	1	—5	—5.0	0	7	74	10.6	0	6	110	18.3	0	0	0	1
1986—Calgary CFL	18	7	139	19.9	1	1	10	10.0	0			None		1	6	0
1987—Seattle NFL	12	3	46	15.3	0			None				None		0	0	1
CFL Totals—3 Years	40	11	184	16.7	2	49	433	8.8	0	21	422	20.1	0	2	12	5
NFL Totals—1 Year	12	3	46	15.3	0	0	0	0.0	0	0	0	0.0	0	0	0	1
Pro Totals—4 Years	52	14	230	16.4	2	49	433	8.8	0	21	422	20.1	0	2	12	6

Additional CFL statistics: Recovered three fumbles, 1984; recovered one fumble, 1985 and 1986.

STANFORD JAMISON JENNINGS
Running Back—Cincinnati Bengals
Born March 12, 1962, at Summerville, S.C.
Height, 6.01. Weight, 205.
High School—Summerville, S.C.
Attended Furman University.

Selected by Michigan in 1st round (17th player selected) of 1984 USFL draft.
Selected by Cincinnati in 3rd round (65th player selected) of 1984 NFL draft.
Signed by Cincinnati Bengals, July 2, 1984.

Year Club	G.	——RUSHING—— Att.	Yds.	Avg.	TD.	PASS RECEIVING P.C.	Yds.	Avg.	TD.	—TOTAL— TD.	Pts.	F.
1984—Cincinnati NFL	15	79	379	4.8	2	35	346	9.9	3	5	30	3
1985—Cincinnati NFL	16	31	92	3.0	1	12	101	8.4	3	4	24	1
1986—Cincinnati NFL	16	16	54	3.4	1	6	86	14.3	0	1	6	0
1987—Cincinnati NFL	12	70	314	4.5	1	35	277	7.9	2	3	18	0
Pro Totals—4 Years	59	196	839	4.3	5	88	810	9.2	8	13	78	4

Year Club	G.	KICKOFF RETURNS No.	Yds.	Avg.	TD.
1984—Cincinnati NFL	15	22	452	20.5	0
1985—Cincinnati NFL	16	13	218	16.8	0
1986—Cincinnati NFL	16	12	257	21.4	0
1987—Cincinnati NFL	12	2	32	16.0	0
Pro Totals—4 Years	59	49	959	19.6	0

Additional pro statistics: Recovered two fumbles, 1984; recovered one fumble, 1985 and 1987.

JAMES CHRISTOPHER JENSEN
(Jim)
Wide Receiver—Miami Dolphins
Born November 14, 1958, at Abington, Pa.
Height, 6.04. Weight, 215.
High School—Doylestown, Pa., Central Bucks.
Received bachelor of science degree in special education from Boston University in 1981.

Selected by Miami in 11th round (291st player selected) of 1981 NFL draft.
On inactive list, September 12 and September 19, 1982.
Granted free agency, February 1, 1985; re-signed by Dolphins, August 31, 1985; activated, September 7, 1985.

Year Club	G.	——PASS RECEIVING—— P.C.	Yds.	Avg.	TD.
1981—Miami NFL	16		None		
1982—Miami NFL	6		None		
1983—Miami NFL	16		None		
1984—Miami NFL	16	13	139	10.7	2
1985—Miami NFL	16	1	4	4.0	1
1986—Miami NFL	16	5	50	10.0	1
1987—Miami NFL	12	26	221	8.5	1
Pro Totals—7 Years	98	45	414	9.2	5

Additional pro statistics: Attempted one pass with no completions, 1982; attempted one pass with one completion for 35 yards and a touchdown, 1984; attempted two passes with no completions, 1986; rushed four times for 18 yards, recovered three fumbles for two yards and fumbled once, 1987.
Played in AFC Championship Game following 1982, 1984 and 1985 seasons.
Played in NFL Championship Game following 1982 and 1984 seasons.

MARK DARRELL JERUE
Linebacker—Los Angeles Rams
Born January 15, 1960, at Seattle, Wash.
Height, 6.03. Weight, 229.
High School—Mercer Island, Wash.
Attended University of Washington.

Selected by New York Jets in 5th round (135th player selected) of 1982 NFL draft.
On injured reserve with heart irregularity, August 24 through entire 1982 season.
Released by New York Jets, August 29, 1983; awarded on waivers to Baltimore Colts, August 30, 1983.
Traded by Baltimore Colts to Los Angeles Rams for quarterback Mark Reed, August 30, 1983.
USFL rights traded with rights to running back Ted McKnight and 1st and 5th round picks in 1984 draft by Jacksonville Bulls to Oakland Invaders for rights to quarterback Turk Schonert, October 24, 1983.
On injured reserve with knee injury, September 8 through October 23, 1987; activated, October 24, 1987.
On injured reserve with knee injury, November 16 through remainder of 1987 season.
Los Angeles Rams NFL, 1983 through 1987.
Games: 1983 (16), 1984 (16), 1985 (16), 1986 (16), 1987 (4). Total—68.
Pro statistics: Recovered one fumble, 1985; intercepted two passes for 23 yards and a touchdown and fumbled once, 1986.
Played in NFC Championship Game following 1985 season.

TIMOTHY LaWAYNE JESSIE
(Tim)
Running Back—Washington Redskins
Born March 1, 1963, at Opp, Ala.
Height, 6.00. Weight, 198.
High School—Opp, Ala.
Attended Auburn University.

Selected by Chicago in 11th round (305th player selected) of 1987 NFL draft.
Signed by Chicago Bears, July 27, 1987.
Released by Chicago Bears, September 7, 1987; signed as free agent replacement player by Washington Redskins, September 23, 1987.
On injured reserve with knee injury, December 19 through remainder of 1987 season.

| | | —RUSHING— | | | | PASS RECEIVING | | | | —TOTAL— | | |
Year	Club	G.	Att.	Yds.	Avg.	TD.	P.C.	Yds.	Avg.	TD.	TD.	Pts.	F.
1987—Washington NFL		3	10	37	3.7	1	1	8	8.0	0	1	6	0

Additional pro statistics: Returned four kickoffs for 73 yards, 1987.

GARY MICHAEL JETER
Defensive End—Los Angeles Rams
Born January 24, 1955, at Weirton, W. Va.
Height, 6.04. Weight, 260.
High School—Cleveland, O., Cathedral Latin.
Attended University of Southern California.
Nephew of Bob Jeter, back with Green Bay Packers and Chicago Bears, 1963 through 1973;
and Tony Jeter, end with Pittsburgh Steelers, 1966 and 1968.

Selected by New York Giants in 1st round (5th player selected) of 1977 NFL draft.
On injured reserve with knee injury, December 8 through remainder of 1978 season.
On injured reserve with knee injury, September 1 through October 1, 1981; activated, October 2, 1981.
On inactive list, September 20, 1982.
On injured reserve with knee injury, November 24 through December 23, 1982; activated, December 24, 1982.
Traded by New York Giants to Los Angeles Rams for 3rd and 6th round picks in 1983 draft, April 13, 1983.
On injured reserve with herniated disc, August 28 through November 8, 1984; activated, November 9, 1984.
New York Giants NFL, 1977 through 1982; Los Angeles Rams NFL, 1983 through 1987.
Games: 1977 (14), 1978 (13), 1979 (16), 1980 (16), 1981 (12), 1982 (4), 1983 (16), 1984 (5), 1985 (16), 1986 (15), 1987 (12). Total—139.
Pro statistics: Recovered one fumble, 1978, 1979 and 1985; recovered three fumbles for seven yards, 1980; credited with a safety, 1986.
Played in NFC Championship Game following 1985 season.

DWAYNE JILES
Linebacker—Philadelphia Eagles
Born November 23, 1961, at Linden, Tex.
Height, 6.04. Weight, 250.
High School—Linden, Tex., Kildare.
Attended Texas Tech University.

Selected by Denver in 1985 USFL territorial draft.
Selected by Philadelphia in 5th round (121st player selected) of 1985 NFL draft.
Signed by Philadelphia Eagles, July 23, 1985.
On injured reserve with cracked vertebra, August 27 through October 17, 1985; activated, October 18, 1985.
Philadelphia NFL, 1985 through 1987.
Games: 1985 (10), 1986 (16), 1987 (9). Total—35.
Pro statistics: Recovered one fumble, 1986.

ALONZO JOHNSON
Linebacker—Philadelphia Eagles
Born April 4, 1963, at Panama City, Fla.
Height, 6.03. Weight, 222.
High School—Panama City, Fla., Rutherford.
Attended University of Florida.

Named as linebacker on THE SPORTING NEWS College All-America Team, 1984 and 1985.
Selected by Philadelphia in 2nd round (48th player selected) of 1986 NFL draft.
Signed by Philadelphia Eagles, July 25, 1986.
On non-football injury list with drug problem, September 1 through October 23, 1987; activated, October 24, 1987.
On injured reserve with hamstring injury, November 12 through December 3, 1987; transferred to non-football injury list, December 4 through remainder of 1987 season.
Philadelphia NFL, 1986 and 1987.
Games: 1986 (15), 1987 (3). Total—18.
Pro statistics: Intercepted three passes for six yards and recovered one fumble, 1986; returned one punt for no yards and fumbled once, 1987.

DAMIAN JOHNSON
Offensive Tackle—New York Giants
Born December 18, 1962, at Great Bend, Kan.
Height, 6.05. Weight, 290.
High School—Great Bend, Kan.
Attended Kansas State University.

Selected by Jacksonville in 15th round (205th player selected) of 1985 USFL draft.
Signed as free agent by New York Giants, May 7, 1985.
On injured reserve with knee injury, September 2 through entire 1985 season.
New York Giants NFL, 1986 and 1987.
Games: 1986 (16), 1987 (12). Total—28.
Played in NFC Championship Game following 1986 season.
Played in NFL Championship Game following 1986 season.

DAMONE JOHNSON
Tight End—Los Angeles Rams
Born March 2, 1962, at Los Angeles, Calif.
Height, 6.04. Weight, 230.
High School—Santa Monica, Calif.
Attended California Poly State University (SLO).

Selected by Oakland in 1985 USFL territorial draft.
Selected by Los Angeles Rams in 6th round (162nd player selected) of 1985 NFL draft.
Signed by Los Angeles Rams, July 9, 1985.
Released by Los Angeles Rams, August 10, 1985; re-signed by Rams, March 21, 1986.
On injured reserve with knee injury, September 2 through November 20, 1986, activated, November 21, 1986.

| | | —PASS RECEIVING— | | | |
Year Club	G.	P.C.	Yds.	Avg.	TD.
1986—L. A. Rams NFL	5		None		
1987—L. A. Rams NFL	12	21	198	9.4	2
Pro Totals—2 Years............	17	21	198	9.4	2

DANIEL JEROME JOHNSON
(Dan)
Tight End—Miami Dolphins
Born May 17, 1960, at Minneapolis, Minn.
Height, 6.03. Weight, 245.
High School—New Hope, Minn., Cooper.
Attended Golden Valley Lutheran Junior College and Iowa State University.

Selected by Miami in 7th round (170th player selected) of 1982 NFL draft.
On injured reserve with shin splints, September 6 through entire 1982 season.
Granted free agency, February 1, 1985; re-signed by Dolphins, August 25, 1985.
Granted roster exemption, August 25 and August 26, 1985.
On non-football injury list with appendectomy, August 27 through October 4, 1985; activated, October 5, 1985.
On injured reserve with arch injury, September 8 through November 13, 1987; activated, November 14, 1987.

| | | —PASS RECEIVING— | | | |
Year Club	G.	P.C.	Yds.	Avg.	TD.
1983—Miami NFL	16	24	189	7.9	4
1984—Miami NFL	16	34	426	12.5	3
1985—Miami NFL	12	13	192	14.8	3
1986—Miami NFL	15	19	170	8.9	4
1987—Miami NFL	7	4	35	8.8	2
Pro Totals—5 Years............	66	94	1012	10.8	16

Additional pro statistics: Fumbled once, 1983 and 1987; returned one kickoff for no yards, 1986.
Played in AFC Championship Game following 1984 and 1985 seasons.
Played in NFL Championship Game following 1984 season.

DEMETRIOUS JOHNSON
Safety—San Diego Chargers
Born July 21, 1961, at St. Louis, Mo.
Height, 5.11. Weight, 190.
High School—St. Louis, Mo., McKinley.
Received degree in counseling psychology from University of Missouri.

Selected by Denver in 1st round (9th player selected) of 1983 USFL draft.
Selected by Detroit in 5th round (115th player selected) of 1983 NFL draft.
Signed by Detroit Lions, June 1, 1983.
Traded by Detroit Lions to Indianapolis Colts for conditional 12th round pick in 1989 draft, August 24, 1987.
Released by Indianapolis Colts, September 7, 1987; signed as free agent replacement player by Miami Dolphins, September 28, 1987.
Released by Miami Dolphins, November 3, 1987; signed as free agent by San Diego Chargers, March 4, 1988.
Detroit NFL, 1983 through 1986; Miami NFL, 1987.
Games: 1983 (14), 1984 (16), 1985 (16), 1986 (16), 1987 (3). Total—65.
Pro statistics: Recovered one fumble, 1983 and 1984; returned one punt for no yards, 1984; intercepted three passes for 39 yards, recovered five fumbles for 24 yards and fumbled once, 1985; intercepted two passes for 18 yards and recovered two fumbles for two yards, 1986.

EARL JOHNSON JR.
Cornerback—Detroit Lions
Born October 20, 1963, at Daytona Beach, Fla.
Height, 6.00. Weight, 190.
High School—Daytona Beach, Fla., Seabreese.
Received bachelor of arts degree in business administration from University of South Carolina.

Selected by Los Angeles in 1985 USFL territorial draft.
Selected by New Orleans in 9th round (236th player selected) of 1985 NFL draft.
Signed by New Orleans Saints, July 16, 1985.
On injured reserve with knee injury, August 20 through December 12, 1985; activated, December 13, 1985.
On injured reserve with shoulder injury, August 26 through September 30, 1986.
Released by New Orleans Saints, October 1, 1986; signed as free agent by Denver Broncos, May 1, 1987.
Released by Denver Broncos, September 7, 1987; re-signed as replacement player by Broncos, October 3, 1987.
Released by Denver Broncos, November 3, 1987; signed as free agent by Detroit Lions, November 6, 1987.
Released by Detroit Lions, November 19, 1987; re-signed by Lions, February 12, 1988.
New Orleans NFL, 1985; Denver NFL, 1987.
Games: 1985 (2), 1987 (3). Total—5.

EDDIE JOHNSON
Linebacker—Cleveland Browns
Born February 3, 1959, at Albany, Ga.
Height, 6.01. Weight, 225.
High School—Albany, Ga., Daughtery.
Attended University of Louisville.

Selected by Cleveland in 7th round (187th player selected) of 1981 NFL draft.
Cleveland NFL, 1981 through 1987.
Games: 1981 (16), 1982 (9), 1983 (16), 1984 (16), 1985 (16), 1986 (16), 1987 (12). Total—101.
Pro statistics: Returned one kickoff for seven yards, 1981; recovered one fumble, 1981 and 1987; intercepted two passes for three yards, 1984; intercepted one pass for six yards, 1985; intercepted one pass for 11 yards, 1987.
Played in AFC Championship Game following 1986 and 1987 seasons.

EZRA RAY JOHNSON
Defensive End—Indianapolis Colts
Born October 2, 1955, at Shreveport, La.
Height, 6.04. Weight, 264.
High School—Shreveport, La., Green Oaks.
Attended Morris Brown College.

Selected by Green Bay in 1st round (28th player selected) of 1977 NFL draft.
On injured reserve with knee injury, December 14 through remainder of 1984 season.
On injured reserve with knee injury, September 11 through November 6, 1987; activated, November 7, 1987.
Granted free agency with no qualifying offer, February 1, 1988; signed by Indianapolis Colts, April 27, 1988.
Green Bay NFL, 1977 through 1987.
Games: 1977 (14), 1978 (16), 1979 (11), 1980 (15), 1981 (16), 1982 (9), 1983 (16), 1984 (13), 1985 (16), 1986 (16), 1987 (6). Total—148.
Pro statistics: Recovered one fumble, 1977; recovered two fumbles, 1978 and 1985; returned one kickoff for 14 yards, 1978; recovered two fumbles, 1983.
Played in Pro Bowl (NFL All-Star Game) following 1978 season.

—DID YOU KNOW—
That in an October 13, 1985 game between the L.A. Rams and Tampa Bay, with 13:13 left to play, Tampa Bay quarterback Steve DeBerg completed his 13th pass of the game, a 13-yard touchdown to wide receiver Gerald Carter? It was Carter's 13th pass reception of the season and 13th career touchdown catch.

GREGGORY DA-MARR JOHNSON
Defensive Back—Phoenix Cardinals
Born October 20, 1958, at Houston, Tex.
Height, 6.01. Weight, 195.
High School—Houston, Tex., Ross S. Sterling.
Attended Oklahoma State University.
Cousin of Winston Hill, offensive tackle with New York Jets and Los Angeles Rams,
1963 through 1977; Ernie Holmes, defensive tackle with Pittsburgh Steelers and New England Patriots,
1972 through 1977; and Ronnie Coleman, running back with Houston Oilers, 1974 through 1981.
Signed as free agent by Seattle Seahawks, May 9, 1981.
USFL rights traded by Oklahoma Outlaws to New Jersey Generals for 5th round pick in 1984 draft, January 4, 1984.
Signed by New Jersey Generals, January 11, 1984, for contract to take effect after being granted free agency, February 1, 1984.
Granted free agency when USFL suspended operations, August 7, 1986; re-signed by Seattle Seahawks, September 1, 1986.
Granted roster exemption, September 1 through September 10, 1986; activated, September 11, 1986.
Released by Seattle Seahawks, September 1, 1987; signed as free agent by St. Louis Cardinals, November 5, 1987.
Franchise transferred to Phoenix, March 15, 1988.

		—INTERCEPTIONS—				—KICKOFF RET.—				—TOTAL—		
Year Club	G.	No.	Yds.	Avg.	TD.	No.	Yds.	Avg.	TD.	TD.	Pts.	F.
1981—Seattle NFL	16		None			13	235	18.1	0	0	0	2
1982—Seattle NFL	9		None				None			0	0	0
1983—Seattle NFL	16		None				None			0	0	1
1984—New Jersey USFL	18	4	57	14.3	0		None			1	6	0
1985—New Jersey USFL	18	5	95	19.0	0	1	0	0.0	0	0	0	0
1986—Seattle NFL	15		None				None			0	0	0
1987—St. Louis NFL	8		None				None			0	0	0
NFL Totals—5 Years	64	0	0	0.0	0	13	235	18.1	0	0	0	3
USFL Totals—2 Years	36	9	152	16.9	0	1	0	0.0	0	1	6	0
Pro Totals—7 Years	100	9	152	16.9	0	14	235	16.8	0	1	6	3

Additional NFL statistics: Returned one punt for 16 yards and recovered four fumbles for 31 yards and a touchdown, 1981; returned one punt for three yards, 1982; returned three punts for 17 yards, 1983; recovered one fumble, 1983 and 1986.
Additional USFL statistics: Recovered one fumble for eight yards and recovered blocked punt in end zone for a touchdown, 1984; recovered three fumbles for four yards, 1985.
Played in AFC Championship Game following 1983 season.

JAMES L. JOHNSON
Linebacker—Los Angeles Raiders
Born June 21, 1962, at Los Angeles, Calif.
Height, 6.02. Weight, 235.
High School—Lake Elsinore, Calif.
Attended Orange Coast College and San Diego State University.
Selected by Portland in 4th round (50th player selected) of 1985 USFL draft.
Selected by Detroit in 3rd round (62nd player selected) of 1985 NFL draft.
Signed by Detroit Lions, July 26, 1985.
On injured reserve with back injury, September 2 through entire 1985 season.
Released by Detroit Lions, October 11, 1986; re-signed by Lions, November 11, 1986.
Released by Detroit Lions, September 1, 1987; signed as free agent replacement player by San Francisco 49ers, September 24, 1987.
Traded by San Francisco 49ers to San Diego Chargers for past considerations, October 13, 1987.
Released by San Diego Chargers, October 20, 1987; signed as free agent by Los Angeles Raiders, April 22, 1988.
Detroit NFL, 1986; San Francisco (1)-San Diego (1) NFL, 1987.
Games: 1986 (11), 1987 (2). Total—13.

JOHNNIE JOHNSON JR.
Safety—Los Angeles Rams
Born October 8, 1956, at La Grange, Tex.
Height, 6.01. Weight, 183.
High School—La Grange, Tex.
Attended University of Texas.
Brother of Bobby Johnson, defensive back with New Orleans Saints
and St. Louis Cardinals, 1983 through 1986.
Named as safety on THE SPORTING NEWS College All-America Team, 1980.
Selected by Los Angeles in 1st round (17th player selected) of 1980 NFL draft.
On injured reserve with broken ankle, August 28 through October 16, 1984; activated, October 17, 1984.
On injured reserve with broken arm, November 25 through remainder of 1987 season.

		——INTERCEPTIONS——			
Year Club	G.	No.	Yds.	Avg.	TD.
1980—L.A. Rams NFL	16	3	102	34.0	1
1981—L.A. Rams NFL	16		None		
1982—L.A. Rams NFL	9	1	7	7.0	0
1983—L.A. Rams NFL	16	4	115	28.8	*2
1984—L.A. Rams NFL	9	2	21	10.5	0
1985—L.A. Rams NFL	16	5	96	19.2	*1
1986—L.A. Rams NFL	16	1	13	13.0	0
1987—L.A. Rams NFL	7	1	0	0.0	0
Pro Totals—8 Years	105	17	354	20.8	4

Additional pro statistics: Returned one punt for three yards, 1980 and 1984; recovered five fumbles for 16 yards, 1980; returned one punt for 39 yards and recovered five fumbles for five yards, 1981; recovered two fumbles for nine yards, 1982; returned 14 punts for 109 yards, recovered two fumbles for four yards and fumbled once, 1983; recovered one fumble, 1985; recovered two fumbles, 1986.; returned blocked punt 20 yards for a touchdown and returned one punt for five yards, 1987.

Played in NFC Championship Game following 1985 season.

KELLEY ANTONIO JOHNSON
Wide Receiver—Indianapolis Colts
Born June 3, 1962, at Carlsbad, N.M.
Height, 5.08. Weight, 155.
High School—Carlsbad, N.M.
Attended Los Angeles Valley College and University of Colorado.

Selected by Denver in 1985 USFL territorial draft.
Signed by Denver Gold, January 3, 1985.
On developmental squad, February 21 through March 1, 1985; activated, March 2, 1985.
Released by Denver Gold, July 31, 1985; re-signed by Gold, August 22, 1985.
Franchise merged with Jacksonville, February 19, 1986.
Granted free agency when USFL suspended operations, August 7, 1986; signed by Ottawa Rough Riders, August 27, 1986.
Released by Ottawa Rough Riders, June 20, 1987; signed as free agent by Houston Oilers, August 6, 1987.
Released by Houston Oilers, September 1, 1987; signed as free agent replacement player by Indianapolis Colts, September 24, 1987.
Released by Indianapolis Colts, October 20, 1987; re-signed by Colts, April 27, 1988.
On developmental squad for 1 game with Denver Gold in 1985.

| | | —PASS RECEIVING— | | | |
Year Club	G.	P.C.	Yds.	Avg.	TD.
1985—Denver USFL	13	10	149	14.9	1
1986—Ottawa CFL	4	5	158	31.6	1
1987—Indianapolis NFL	3	1	15	15.0	0
Pro Totals—3 Years	20	16	322	20.1	2

Additional USFL statistics: Rushed once for 28 yards, 1985.
Additional CFL statistics: Returned 13 punts for 29 yards, returned one kickoff for 10 yards and rushed once for minus eight yards, 1987.
Additional NFL statistics: Returned six kickoffs for 98 yards, returned nine punts for 42 yards and fumbled once, 1987.

KENNETH JOHNSON
(Kenny)
Cornerback—Green Bay Packers
Born December 28, 1963, at Weir, Miss.
Height, 6.00. Weight, 185.
High School—Weir, Miss.
Attended Mississippi State University.

Selected by New Jersey in 1984 USFL territorial draft.
Signed by New Jersey Generals, January 26, 1984.
On developmental squad, February 24 through March 16, 1984; activated, March 17, 1984.
On developmental squad, March 24 through April 6, 1984; activated, April 7, 1984.
On developmental squad, April 29 through May 4, 1984; activated, May 5, 1984.
On developmental squad, June 10 through June 14, 1984; activated, June 15, 1984.
On developmental squad, June 23 through remainder of 1984 season.
On developmental squad, March 30 through April 5, 1985; activated, April 6, 1985.
Granted free agency, August 1, 1985; re-signed by Generals, April 21, 1986.
Granted free agency when USFL suspended operations, August 7, 1986; signed as free agent by Green Bay Packers, May 5, 1987.
On developmental squad for 8 games with New Jersey Generals in 1984.
On developmental squad for 1 game with New Jersey Generals in 1985.
New Jersey USFL, 1984 and 1985; Green Bay NFL, 1987.
Games: 1984 (9), 1985 (17), 1987 (12). Total USFL—26. Total Pro—38.
USFL statistics: Intercepted one pass for no yards and credited with one sack for no yards, 1985.
NFL statistics: Intercepted one pass for two yards, 1987.

KENNETH RAY JOHNSON
(Kenny)
Safety—Houston Oilers
Born January 7, 1958, at Columbia, Miss.
Height, 5.10. Weight, 172.
High School—Moss Point, Miss.
Attended Mississippi State University.

Selected by Atlanta in 5th round (137th player selected) of 1980 NFL draft.
Tied NFL record for most touchdowns scored by interception, game (2), against Green Bay Packers, November 27, 1983.
On injured reserve with fractured shoulder blade, September 16 through December 6, 1985; activated, December 7, 1985.
On non-football injury list with chicken pox, October 24 through December 17, 1986; awarded on procedural waivers to Houston Oilers, December 19, 1986.
Released by Houston Oilers, September 7, 1987; re-signed as replacement player by Oilers, September 30, 1987.

Year Club	G.	No.	Yds.	INTERCEPTIONS Avg.	TD.	No.	-PUNT RETURNS- Yds. Avg.	TD.	No.	—KICKOFF RET.— Yds. Avg.	TD.	—TOTAL— TD. Pts.	F.
1980—Atlanta NFL	16	4	49	12.3	0	23	281 12.2	0		None		0 0	2
1981—Atlanta NFL	16	3	35	11.7	0	4	6 1.5	0		None		2 12	1
1982—Atlanta NFL	9	2	30	15.0	0		None			None		0 0	0
1983—Atlanta NFL	16	2	57	28.5	*2		None		11	224 20.4	0	2 12	1
1984—Atlanta NFL	16	5	75	15.0	0	10	79 7.9	0	19	359 18.9	0	0 0	2
1985—Atlanta NFL	5			None			None		1	20 20.0	0	0 0	0
1986—Atl. (7)-Hou. (1) NFL	8			None			None			None		0 0	0
1987—Houston NFL	12			None		24	196 8.2	0	2	24 12.0	0	0 0	3
Pro Totals—8 Years	98	16	246	15.4	2	61	562 9.2	0	33	627 19.0	0	4 24	9

Additional pro statistics: Recovered four fumbles for seven yards, 1980; recovered two fumbles for 55 yards and two touchdowns, 1981; recovered one fumble, 1983 and 1987.

LAWRENCE WENDELL JOHNSON
Safety—Buffalo Bills
Born September 11, 1957, at Gary, Ind.
Height, 5.11. Weight, 204.
High School—Gary, Ind., Roosevelt.
Attended University of Wisconsin.
Named as cornerback on THE SPORTING NEWS College All-America Team, 1978.
Selected by Cleveland in 2nd round (40th player selected) of 1979 NFL draft.
On injured reserve with shoulder injury, September 17 through remainder of 1980 season.
On injured reserve with knee injury, December 29 through remainder of 1982 season.
Traded by Cleveland Browns to Buffalo Bills for draft choice, October 9, 1984.
On injured reserve with calf injury, September 2 through entire 1986 season.
On injured reserve with knee injury, November 24 through remainder of 1987 season.

Year Club	G.	No.	INTERCEPTIONS Yds.	Avg.TD.
1979—Cleveland NFL	16		None	
1980—Cleveland NFL	2	1	3	3.0 0
1981—Cleveland NFL	16		None	
1982—Cleveland NFL	8	4	17	4.3 0
1983—Cleveland NFL	16	2	0	0.0 0
1984—Cle. (6)-Buf. (10) NFL	16	1	0	0.0 0
1985—Buffalo NFL	16	1	0	0.0 0
1987—Buffalo NFL	6		None	
Pro Totals—8 Years	96	9	20	2.2 0

Additional pro statistics: Recovered one fumble, 1980 and 1982.

LEE JOHNSON
Punter—Cleveland Browns
Born November 27, 1961, at Dallas, Tex.
Height, 6.02. Weight, 199.
High School—The Woodlands, Tex., McCullough.
Attended Brigham Young University.
Selected by Houston in 9th round (125th player selected) of 1985 USFL draft.
Selected by Houston in 5th round (138th player selected) of 1985 NFL draft.
Signed by Houston Oilers, June 25, 1985.
Crossed picket line during players' strike, October 14, 1987.
Released by Houston Oilers, December 1, 1987; awarded on waivers to Buffalo Bills, December 2, 1987.
Released by Buffalo Bills, December 9, 1987; awarded on waivers to Cleveland Browns, December 10, 1987.

Year Club	G.	No.	PUNTING Avg.	Blk.
1985—Houston NFL	16	83	41.7	0
1986—Houston NFL	16	88	41.2	0
1987—Hou. (9)-Cle. (3) NFL	12	50	39.4	0
Pro Totals—3 Years	44	221	40.9	0

Additional pro statistics: Rushed once for no yards, recovered one fumble for seven yards and fumbled twice, 1985.
Played in AFC Championship Game following 1987 season.

MICHAEL JOHNSON
(Mike)
Linebacker—Cleveland Browns
Born November 26, 1962, at Southport, N.C.
Height, 6.01. Weight, 228.
High School—Hyattsville, Md., DeMatha.
Attended Virginia Tech.
Selected by Pittsburgh in 1984 USFL territorial draft.
USFL rights traded with defensive end Mark Buben, rights to linebacker Al Chesley and draft choice by Pittsburgh Maulers to Philadelphia Stars for rights to linebacker Ron Crosby, February 1, 1984.
Signed by Philadelphia Stars, February 20, 1984.
Granted roster exemption, February 20 through March 1, 1984; activated, March 2, 1984.
Selected by Cleveland in 1st round (18th player selected) of 1984 NFL supplemental draft.
Franchise transferred to Baltimore, November 1, 1984.

Granted free agency when USFL suspended operations, August 7, 1986; signed by Cleveland Browns, August 12, 1986.

Granted roster exemption, August 12 through August 21, 1986; activated, August 22, 1986.

Philadelphia USFL, 1984; Baltimore USFL, 1985; Cleveland NFL, 1986 and 1987.

Games: 1984 (17), 1985 (18), 1986 (16), 1987 (11). Total USFL—35. Total NFL—27. Total Pro—62.

USFL statistics: Credited with two sacks for four yards and recovered one fumble for eight yards, 1984; credited with 3½ sacks for 25½ yards and recovered two fumbles, 1985.

NFL statistics: Recovered two fumbles, 1986; intercepted one pass for three yards and recovered one fumble, 1987.

Played in USFL Championship Game following 1984 and 1985 seasons.

Played in AFC Championship Game following 1986 and 1987 seasons.

MICHAEL LAMAR JOHNSON
(M. L.)
Linebacker—Seattle Seahawks

Born January 24, 1964, at New York, N. Y.
Height, 6.03. Weight, 225.
High School—Los Angeles, Calif., Thomas Jefferson.
Attended University of Hawaii.

Selected by Seattle in 9th round (243rd selected) of 1987 NFL draft.
Signed by Seattle Seahawks, July 21, 1987.
Seattle NFL, 1987.
Games: 1987 (8).

NORM JOHNSON
Placekicker—Seattle Seahawks

Born May 31, 1960, at Inglewood, Calif.
Height, 6.02. Weight, 198.
High School—Garden Grove, Calif., Pacifica.
Attended University of California at Los Angeles.

Named to THE SPORTING NEWS NFL All-Star Team, 1984.
Signed as free agent by Seattle Seahawks, May 4, 1982.
Crossed picket line during players' strike, October 14, 1987.

		——PLACE KICKING——					
Year	Club	G.	XP.	XPM.	FG.	FGA.	Pts.
1982—Seattle NFL		9	13	1	10	14	43
1983—Seattle NFL		16	49	1	18	25	103
1984—Seattle NFL		16	50	1	20	24	110
1985—Seattle NFL		16	40	1	14	25	82
1986—Seattle NFL		16	42	0	22	35	108
1987—Seattle NFL		13	40	0	15	20	85
Pro Totals—6 Years		86	234	4	99	143	531

Additional pro statistics: Attempted one pass with one completion for 27 yards, 1982.
Played in AFC Championship Game following 1983 season.
Played in Pro Bowl (NFL All-Star Game) following 1984 season.

RICHARD JOHNSON
Cornerback—Houston Oilers

Born September 16, 1963, at Harvey, Ill.
Height, 6.01. Weight, 190.
High School—Harvey, Ill., Thornton.
Attended University of Wisconsin.

Named as defensive back on THE SPORTING NEWS College All-America Team, 1984.
Selected by Jacksonville in 1985 USFL territorial draft.
Selected by Houston in 1st round (11th player selected) of 1985 NFL draft.
Signed by Houston Oilers, August 22, 1985.
Granted roster exemption, August 22 through August 29, 1985; activated, August 30, 1985.
On injured reserve with knee injury, November 14 through remainder of 1987 season.
Houston NFL, 1985 through 1987.
Games: 1985 (16), 1986 (16), 1987 (5). Total—37.
Pro statistics: Recovered one fumble, 1985; intercepted two passes for six yards, 1986; intercepted one pass for no yards, 1987.

RON JOHNSON
Wide Receiver—Philadelphia Eagles

Born September 21, 1958, at Monterey, Calif.
Height, 6.03. Weight, 186.
High School—Monterey, Calif.
Attended California State University at Long Beach.

Selected by Seattle in 7th round (170th player selected) of 1981 NFL draft.
Released by Seattle Seahawks, August 17, 1981; claimed on waivers by Baltimore Colts, August 19, 1981.
Released by Baltimore Colts, August 25, 1981; signed as free agent by Hamilton Tiger-Cats, March 10, 1982.
Granted free agency, March 1, 1985.
USFL rights traded by Los Angeles Express to Portland Breakers for past considerations, May 15, 1985.
Signed by Portland Breakers, May 15, 1985.
Released by Portland Breakers, June 26, 1985; signed as free agent by Philadelphia Eagles, July 22, 1985.

On injured reserve with dislocated shoulder, November 19 through remainder of 1985 season.
On injured reserve with concussion, October 29 through November 23, 1986; activated, November 24, 1986.

		—RUSHING—				PASS RECEIVING				—TOTAL—		
Year Club	G.	Att.	Yds.	Avg.	TD.	P.C.	Yds.	Avg.	TD.	TD.	Pts.	F.
1982—Hamilton CFL	11	1	—3	—3.0	0	37	505	13.6	5	5	30	1
1983—Hamilton CFL	16		None			53	914	17.2	6	6	36	1
1984—Hamilton CFL	15		None			50	684	13.6	2	2	12	0
1985—Portland USFL	6	4	15	3.8	0	22	476	21.6	2	2	12	0
1985—Philadelphia NFL	8		None			11	186	16.9	0	0	0	0
1986—Philadelphia NFL	12		None			11	207	18.8	1	1	6	0
1987—Philadelphia NFL	3		None				None			0	0	0
CFL Totals—3 Years	42	1	—3	—3.0	0	140	2103	15.0	13	13	78	2
USFL Totals—1 Year	6	4	15	3.8	0	22	476	21.6	2	2	12	0
NFL Totals—3 Years	23	0	0	0.0	0	22	393	17.9	1	1	6	0
Pro Totals—7 Years	71	5	12	2.4	0	184	2972	16.2	16	16	96	2

Additional pro statistics: Recovered one fumble, 1986.

THOMAS JOHNSON
(Pepper)
Linebacker—New York Giants
Born July 29, 1964, at Detroit, Mich.
Height, 6.03. Weight, 248.
High School—Detroit, Mich., Mackenzie.
Attended Ohio State University.
Selected by New Jersey in 1986 USFL territorial draft.
Selected by New York Giants in 2nd round (51st player selected) of 1986 NFL draft.
Signed by New York Giants, July 30, 1986.
New York Giants NFL, 1986 and 1987.
Games: 1986 (16), 1987 (12). Total—28.
Pro statistics: Intercepted one pass for 13 yards, 1986; recovered one fumble, 1987.
Played in NFC Championship Game following 1986 season.
Played in NFL Championship Game following 1986 season.

TIMOTHY JOHNSON
(Tim)
Defensive End-Defensive Tackle—Pittsburgh Steelers
Born January 29, 1965, at Sarasota, Fla.
Height, 6.03. Weight, 260.
High School—Sarasota, Fla.
Received bachelor of arts degree in hotel, restaurant and institutional management
from Penn State University in 1987.
Selected by Pittsburgh in 6th round (141st player selected) of 1987 NFL draft.
Signed by Pittsburgh Steelers, July 26, 1987.
Pittsburgh NFL, 1987.
Games: 1987 (12).

TROY DWAN JOHNSON
Wide Receiver—Phoenix Cardinals
Born October 20, 1962, at New Orleans, La.
Height, 6.01. Weight, 175.
High School—Bourg, La., South Terrebonne.
Attended Southeastern Louisiana University and Southern University.
Signed as free agent by Denver Gold, January 29, 1985.
On developmental squad, February 21 through March 15, 1985; activated, March 16, 1985.
Released by Denver Gold, July 31, 1985; awarded on waivers to Arizona Outlaws, August 1, 1985.
Granted free agency when USFL suspended operations, August 7, 1986; signed as free agent by Dallas Cowboys,
August 19, 1986.
Released by Dallas Cowboys, August 23, 1986; signed as free agent by St. Louis Cardinals, September 25, 1986.
Crossed picket line during players' strike, October 2, 1987.
Franchise transferred to Phoenix, March 15, 1988.
On developmental squad for 3 games with Denver Gold in 1985.

		—PASS RECEIVING—			
Year Club	G.	P.C.	Yds.	Avg.	TD.
1985—Denver USFL	14	14	167	11.9	0
1986—St. Louis NFL	13	14	203	14.5	0
1987—St. Louis NFL	14	15	308	20.5	2
USFL Totals—1 Year	14	14	167	11.9	0
NFL Totals—2 Years	27	29	511	17.6	2
Pro Totals—3 Years	41	43	678	15.8	2

Additional USFL statistics: Returned five kickoffs for 97 yards, rushed twice for 11 yards, recovered one fumble
and fumbled once, 1985.
Additional NFL statistics: Returned three kickoffs for 46 yards, 1986; rushed once for nine yards, 1987.

TRUMAINE JOHNSON
Wide Receiver—Buffalo Bills
Born November 16, 1960, at Bogaloosa, La.
Height, 6.01. Weight, 196.
High School—Baker, La.
Attended Grambling State University.

Named as wide receiver on THE SPORTING NEWS USFL All-Star Team, 1983 and 1984.
Selected by Chicago in 1st round (11th player selected) of 1983 USFL draft.
Signed by Chicago Blitz, January 14, 1983.
Selected by San Diego in 6th round (141st player selected) of 1983 NFL draft.
Franchise transferred to Arizona, September 30, 1983.
Protected in merger of Arizona Wranglers and Oklahoma Outlaws, December 6, 1984.
Left Arizona Outlaws camp voluntarily, January 23, 1985.
On suspended list, February 22 through entire 1985 season.
Released by Arizona Outlaws, July 10, 1985; signed by San Diego Chargers, July 12, 1985.
Traded with 7th round pick in 1988 draft by San Diego Chargers to Buffalo Bills for linebacker David Brandon and 4th round pick in 1988 draft, August 31, 1987.

Year Club	G.	Att.	Yds.	Avg.	TD.	P.C.	Yds.	Avg.	TD.	TD.	Pts.	F.
			RUSHING				PASS RECEIVING				TOTAL	
1983—Chicago USFL	18	7	40	5.7	0	★81	★1322	16.3	10	10	60	3
1984—Arizona USFL	18	1	3	3.0	0	90	1268	14.1	13	13	78	3
1985—San Diego NFL	11		None			4	51	12.8	1	1	6	0
1986—San Diego NFL	16		None			30	399	13.3	1	1	6	1
1987—Buffalo NFL	12		None			15	186	12.4	2	2	12	0
USFL Totals—2 Years	36	8	43	5.4	0	171	2590	15.1	23	23	138	6
NFL Totals—3 Years	39	0	0	0.0	0	49	636	13.0	4	4	24	1
Pro Totals—5 Years	75	8	43	5.4	0	220	3226	14.7	27	27	162	7

Additional pro statistics: Returned one punt for 26 yards, recovered two fumbles and attempted one pass with no completions, 1983; recovered one fumble and returned two punts for four yards, 1984; returned three kickoffs for 48 yards, 1986.
Played in USFL Championship Game following 1984 season.

VANCE EDWARD JOHNSON
Wide Receiver—Denver Broncos
Born March 13, 1963, at Trenton, N.J.
Height, 5.11. Weight, 174.
High School—Tucson, Ariz., Cholla.
Attended University of Arizona.

Selected by Arizona in 1985 USFL territorial draft.
Selected by Denver in 2nd round (31st player selected) of 1985 NFL draft.
Signed by Denver Broncos, July 16, 1985.
On injured reserve with knee injury, September 9 through October 9, 1986; activated, October 10, 1986.

Year Club	G.	Att.	Yds.	Avg.	TD.	P.C.	Yds.	Avg.	TD.	TD.	Pts.	F.
			RUSHING				PASS RECEIVING				TOTAL	
1985—Denver NFL	16	10	36	3.6	0	51	721	14.1	3	3	18	5
1986—Denver NFL	12	5	15	3.0	0	31	363	11.7	2	2	12	1
1987—Denver NFL	11	1	—8	—8.0	0	42	684	16.3	7	7	42	1
Pro Totals—3 Years	39	16	43	2.7	0	124	1768	14.3	12	12	72	7

Year Club	G.	No.	Yds.	Avg.	TD.	No.	Yds.	Avg.	TD.
			PUNT RETURNS				KICKOFF RET.		
1985—Denver NFL	16	30	260	8.7	0	30	740	24.7	0
1986—Denver NFL	12	3	36	12.0	0	2	21	10.5	0
1987—Denver NFL	11	1	9	9.0	0	7	140	20.0	0
Pro Totals—3 Years	39	34	305	9.0	0	39	901	23.1	0

Additional pro statistics: Attempted one pass with no completions, 1985 through 1987; recovered two fumbles, 1985.
Played in AFC Championship Game following 1986 season.
Played in NFL Championship Game following 1986 and 1987 seasons.

VAUGHAN MONROE JOHNSON
Linebacker—New Orleans Saints
Born March 24, 1962, at Morehead City, N.C.
Height, 6.03. Weight, 235.
High School—Morehead City, N.C., West Carteret.
Attended North Carolina State University.

Named as linebacker on THE SPORTING NEWS College All-America Team, 1983.
Selected by Jacksonville in 1984 USFL territorial draft.
Signed by Jacksonville Bulls, January 17, 1984.
On developmental squad, April 6 through April 12, 1984; activated, April 13, 1984.
Selected by New Orleans in 1st round (15th player selected) of 1984 NFL supplemental draft.
Granted free agency when USFL suspended operations, August 7, 1986; signed by New Orleans Saints, August 12, 1986.
Granted roster exemption, August 12 through August 24, 1986; activated, August 25, 1986.
On developmental squad for 1 game with Jacksonville Bulls in 1984.
Jacksonville USFL, 1984 and 1985; New Orleans NFL, 1986 and 1987.
Games: 1984 (17), 1985 (18), 1986 (16), 1987 (12). Total USFL—35. Total NFL—28. Total Pro—63.
USFL statistics: Credited with one sack for 13 yards, intercepted one pass for four yards and recovered blocked

kick in end zone for a touchdown, 1984; credited with three sacks for 18 yards and recovered one fumble for three yards, 1985.

NFL statistics: Intercepted one pass for 15 yards, 1986; recovered one fumble, 1986 and 1987; intercepted one pass for no yards, 1987.

WALTER ULYSSES JOHNSON
Linebacker—Houston Oilers
Born November 13, 1963, at Monroe, La.
Height, 6.00. Weight, 241.
High School—Ferriday, La.
Attended Louisiana Tech University.

Selected by Houston in 2nd round (46th player selected) of 1987 NFL draft.
Signed by Houston Oilers, July 31, 1987.
Crossed picket line during players' strike, October 14, 1987.
Houston NFL, 1987.
Games: 1987 (10).

WILLIAM ALEXANDER JOHNSON
(Will)
Linebacker—Chicago Bears
Born December 4, 1964, at Monroe, La.
Height, 6.04. Weight, 245.
High School—Monroe, La., Neville.
Attended Northeast Louisiana University.

Selected by Chicago in 5th round (138th player selected) of 1987 NFL draft.
Signed by Chicago Bears, July 30, 1987.
Chicago NFL, 1987.
Games: 1987 (11).

WILLIAM ARTHUR JOHNSON
(Billy White Shoes)
Wide Receiver—Indianapolis Colts
Born January 27, 1952, at Bouthwyn, Pa.
Height, 5.09. Weight, 170.
High School—Boothwyn, Pa., Chichester.
Attended Widener College.

Established NFL record for punt return yards, career (3,123).
Tied NFL record for most touchdowns, combined returns, season (4), 1975.
Named as punt returner to THE SPORTING NEWS NFL All-Star Team, 1983.
Selected by Houston in 15th round (365th player selected) of 1974 NFL draft.
On injured reserve with knee injury, November 10 through remainder of 1978 season.
On injured reserve with knee injury, September 11 through remainder of 1979 season.
Granted free agency, February 2, 1981; signed by Montreal Alouettes, May 19, 1981.
Released by Montreal Concordes, April 15, 1982; signed as free agent by Atlanta Falcons, July 20, 1982.
On injured reserve with knee injury, October 9 through remainder of 1984 season.
On injured reserve with foot injury, August 26 through October 17, 1986; activated, October 18, 1986.
On injured reserve with foot injury, November 1 through December 12, 1986; activated, December 13, 1986.
Granted free agency with no qualifying offer, February 1, 1988; signed by Indianapolis Colts, April 27, 1988.
Played for Philadelphia Athletics of American Professional Slo-Pitch Softball League, 1978.

Year Club	G.	—RUSHING— Att.	Yds.	Avg.	TD.	PASS RECEIVING P.C.	Yds.	Avg.	TD.	—TOTAL— TD.	Pts.	F.
1974—Houston NFL	14	5	82	16.4	1	29	388	13.4	2	3	18	1
1975—Houston NFL	14	5	17	3.4	0	37	393	10.6	1	5	30	5
1976—Houston NFL	14	6	6	1.0	0	47	495	10.5	4	4	24	3
1977—Houston NFL	14	6	102	17.0	1	20	412	20.6	3	7	42	2
1978—Houston NFL	5		None			1	10	10.0	0	0	0	0
1979—Houston NFL	2		None			6	108	18.0	1	1	6	0
1980—Houston NFL	16	2	1	0.5	0	31	343	11.1	2	2	12	1
1981—Montreal CFL	16	1	−9	−9.0	0	65	1060	16.3	5	5	30	3
1982—Atlanta NFL	9		None			2	11	5.5	0	0	0	1
1983—Atlanta NFL	16	15	83	5.5	0	64	709	11.1	4	5	30	4
1984—Atlanta NFL	6	3	8	2.7	0	24	371	15.5	3	3	18	1
1985—Atlanta NFL	16	8	−8	−1.0	0	62	830	13.4	5	5	30	4
1986—Atlanta NFL	4	6	25	4.2	0	6	57	9.5	0	0	0	0
1987—Atlanta NFL	12		None			8	84	10.5	0	0	0	2
NFL Totals—13 Years	142	56	316	5.6	2	337	4211	12.5	25	35	210	24
CFL Totals—1 Year	16	1	−9	−9.0	0	65	1060	16.3	5	5	30	3
Pro Totals—14 Years	158	57	307	5.4	2	402	5271	13.1	30	40	240	27

Year Club	G.	—PUNT RETURNS— No.	Yds.	Avg.	TD.	—KICKOFF RET.— No.	Yds.	Avg.	TD.
1974—Houston NFL	14	30	409	13.6	0	29	785	27.1	0
1975—Houston NFL	14	40	612	★15.3	★3	33	798	24.2	★1
1976—Houston NFL	14	38	403	10.6	0	26	579	22.3	0
1977—Houston NFL	14	35	539	★15.4	★2	25	630	25.2	0
1978—Houston NFL	5	8	60	7.5	0	4	73	18.3	0
1979—Houston NFL	2	4	17	4.3	0	4	37	9.3	0

Year Club	G.	—PUNT RETURNS— No.	Yds.	Avg.	TD.	—KICKOFF RET.— No.	Yds.	Avg.TD.
1980—Houston NFL	16			None				None
1981—Montreal CFL	16	59	597	10.1	0			None
1982—Atlanta NFL	9	24	273	11.4	0			None
1983—Atlanta NFL	16	46	489	10.6	*1			None
1984—Atlanta NFL	6	15	152	10.1	0	2	39	19.5 0
1985—Atlanta NFL	16	10	82	8.2	0			None
1986—Atlanta NFL	4	8	87	10.9	0			None
1987—Atlanta NFL	12	21	168	8.0	0			None
NFL Totals—13 Years	142	279	3291	11.8	6	123	2941	23.9 2
CFL Totals—1 Year	16	59	597	10.1	0	0	0	0.0 0
Pro Totals—14 Years	158	338	3888	11.5	6	123	2941	23.9 2

Additional pro statistics: Recovered one fumble, 1975 and 1976; attempted one pass with no completions and recovered two fumbles, 1983.

Played in Pro Bowl (NFL All-Star Game) following 1975, 1977 and 1983 seasons.

WILLIAM THOMAS JOHNSON
(Bill)
Running Back—Cincinnati Bengals

Born October 31, 1960, at Poughkeepsie, N.Y.
Height, 6.02. Weight, 230.
High School—Freedom Plains, N.Y., Arlington.
Attended Arkansas State University.

Selected by Denver in 17th round (343rd player selected) of 1984 USFL draft.
Signed by Denver Gold, January 29, 1984.
On developmental squad, February 24 through March 23, 1984; activated, March 24, 1984.
On developmental squad, June 8 through June 14, 1984; activated, June 15, 1984.
Selected by Cincinnati in 2nd round (35th player selected) of 1984 NFL supplemental draft.
Granted free agency, August 1, 1985; signed by Cincinnati Bengals, August 9, 1985.
On injured reserve with hamstring injury, December 20 through remainder of 1985 season.
On developmental squad for 5 games with Denver Gold in 1984.

Year Club	G.	——RUSHING—— Att.	Yds.	Avg.	TD.	PASS RECEIVING P.C.	Yds.	Avg.	TD.	—TOTAL— TD.	Pts.	F.
1984—Denver USFL	13	36	132	3.7	2	10	135	13.5	1	3	18	4
1985—Denver USFL	18	212	1261	*6.0	15	29	337	11.6	1	16	96	8
1985—Cincinnati NFL	13	8	44	5.5	0			None		0	0	0
1986—Cincinnati NFL	14	39	226	5.8	0	13	103	7.9	0	0	0	2
1987—Cincinnati NFL	11	39	205	5.3	1	3	19	6.3	0	1	6	0
USFL Totals—2 Years	31	248	1393	5.6	17	39	472	12.1	2	19	114	12
NFL Totals—3 Years	38	86	475	5.5	1	16	122	7.6	0	1	6	2
Pro Totals—5 Years	69	334	1868	5.6	18	55	594	10.8	2	20	120	14

Additional pro statistics: Recovered four fumbles, 1984.

ANTHONY JONES
Tight End—Washington Redskins

Born May 16, 1960, at Baltimore, Md.
Height, 6.03. Weight, 248.
High School—Baltimore, Md., Patterson.
Attended University of Maryland (Eastern Shore) and Wichita State University.

Selected by Oklahoma in 1984 USFL territorial draft.
Selected by Washington in 11th round (306th player selected) of 1984 NFL draft.
Signed by Washington Redskins, June 21, 1984.
On injured reserve with neck injury, December 21 through remainder of 1984 season.
On injured reserve with knee injury, December 16 through remainder of 1986 season.
On physically unable to perform/reserve with knee injury, September 1 through December 18, 1987; activated, December 19, 1987.
Washington NFL, 1984 through 1987.
Games: 1984 (16), 1985 (16), 1986 (15), 1987 (2). Total—49.
Pro statistics: Caught one pass for six yards, 1984; returned one kickoff for no yards, 1985; recovered one fumble, 1986.
Played in NFC Championship Game following 1987 season.
Played in NFL Championship Game following 1987 season.

BRENT MICHAEL JONES
Tight End—San Francisco 49ers

Born February 12, 1963, at Santa Clara, Calif.
Height, 6.04. Weight, 230.
High School—San Jose, Calif., Leland.
Received bachelor of science degree in economics from University of Santa Clara in 1986.
Son of Mike Jones, selected by Oakland Raiders in 21st round of 1961 AFL draft
and by Pittsburgh Steelers in 20th round of 1961 NFL draft.

Selected by Pittsburgh in 5th round (135th player selected) of 1986 NFL draft.
Signed by Pittsburgh Steelers, July 30, 1986.
On injured reserve with neck injury, August 19 through September 23, 1986.

Released by Pittsburgh Steelers, September 24, 1986; signed as free agent by San Francisco 49ers for 1987, December 24, 1986.
On injured reserve with neck injury, September 1, through December 4, 1987, activated, December 5, 1987.
Crossed picket line during players' strike, October 14, 1987.
San Francisco NFL, 1987.
Games: 1987 (4).
Pro statistics: Caught two passes for 35 yards, 1987.

BRUCE WAYNE JONES
Defensive Back—Tampa Bay Buccaneers
Born December 26, 1962, at Courtland, Ala.
Height, 6.01. Weight, 197.
High School—Courtland, Ala.
Attended University of North Alabama.

Selected by Birmingham in 1986 USFL territorial draft.
Selected by Chicago in 7th round (194th player selected) of 1986 NFL draft.
Signed by Chicago Bears, June 27, 1986.
Released by Chicago Bears, August 18, 1986; signed as free agent by Pittsburgh Steelers, March 20, 1987.
Released by Pittsburgh Steelers, October 26, 1987; signed as free agent by Tampa Bay Buccaneers, February 18, 1988.
Pittsburgh NFL, 1987.
Games: 1987 (2).

CEDRIC DECORRUS JONES
First name pronounced SEED-ric.
Wide Receiver—New England Patriots
Born June 1, 1960, at Norfolk, Va.
Height, 6.01. Weight, 184.
High School—Weldon, N.C.
Received bachelor of arts degree in history and political science from
Duke University in 1982.

Selected by New England in 3rd round (56th player selected) of 1982 NFL draft.
On inactive list, September 19, 1982.

| | | —PASS RECEIVING— | | | |
Year Club	G.	P.C.	Yds.	Avg.	TD.
1982—New England NFL.......	2	1	5	5.0	0
1983—New England NFL.......	15	20	323	16.2	1
1984—New England NFL.......	14	19	244	12.8	2
1985—New England NFL.......	16	21	237	11.3	2
1986—New England NFL.......	16	14	222	15.9	1
1987—New England NFL.......	12	25	388	15.5	3
Pro Totals—6 Years............	75	100	1419	14.2	9

Additional pro statistics: Returned four kickoffs for 63 yards, 1983; fumbled once, 1983, 1984 and 1986; returned one kickoff for 20 yards and recovered fumble in end zone for a touchdown, 1984; returned three kickoffs for 37 yards and recovered one fumble for 15 yards and a touchdown, 1985; returned four kickoffs for 63 yards and rushed once for minus seven yards, 1986; attempted one pass with no completions, 1987.
Played in AFC Championship Game following 1985 season.
Played in NFL Championship Game following 1985 season.

DARYLL KEITH JONES
Defensive Back—Denver Broncos
Born March 23, 1962, at Columbia, Ga.
Height, 6.00. Weight, 190.
High School—Columbus, Ga., Carver.
Attended University of Georgia.

Selected by Jacksonville in 1984 USFL territorial draft.
Selected by Green Bay in 7th round (181st player selected) of 1984 NFL draft.
Signed by Green Bay Packers, June 6, 1984.
On injured reserve with neck injury, October 30 through remainder of 1985 season.
On injured reserve with shoulder injury, August 19 through September 2, 1986.
Released by Green Bay Packers, September 3, 1986; signed as free agent by Atlanta Falcons, February 18, 1987.
Released by Atlanta Falcons, August 5, 1987; signed as free agent replacement player by Denver Broncos, September 25, 1987.
On injured reserve with ankle injury, October 16 through remainder of 1987 season.
Selected by Pittsburgh Pirates' organization in 17th round of free-agent draft, June 3, 1980.
Green Bay NFL, 1984 and 1985; Denver NFL, 1987.
Games: 1984 (16), 1985 (8), 1987 (1). Total—25.
Pro statistics: Returned one kickoff for 19 yards and recovered three fumbles, 1984; returned one kickoff for 11 yards, 1985.

DAVID J. JONES
Center—Washington Redskins
Born October 25, 1961, at Taipei, Taiwan.
Height, 6.03. Weight, 266.
High School—Austin, Tex., David Crockett.
Attended University of Texas.

Selected by Houston in 1984 USFL territorial draft.
Selected by Detroit in 8th round (214th player selected) of 1984 NFL draft.
Signed by Detroit Lions, June 4, 1984.
On injured reserve with pulled hamstring, September 8 through October 12, 1984; activated, October 13, 1984.
On injured reserve with back injury, December 14 through remainder of 1984 season.
On injured reserve with neck injury, November 8 through remainder of 1985 season.
Released by Detroit Lions, August 7, 1986; signed as free agent by Denver Broncos, May 1, 1987.
Released by Denver Broncos, August 26, 1987; re-signed as replacement player by Broncos, September 25, 1987.
Released by Denver Broncos, October 19, 1987; signed as free agent by Washington Redskins, November 25, 1987.
On injured reserve with neck injury, January 30, 1988 through remainder of 1987 season playoffs.
Detroit NFL, 1984 and 1985; Denver (3)-Washington (5) NFL, 1987.
Games: 1984 (10), 1985 (9), 1987 (8). Total—27.
Pro statistics: Recovered one fumble, 1985.
Played in NFC Championship Game following 1987 season.

DWIGHT SEAN JONES
(Known by middle name.)
Defensive End—Houston Oilers
Born December 19, 1962, at Kingston, Jamaica.
Height, 6.07. Weight, 265.
High School—Montclair, N.J., Kimberly Academy.
Attended Northeastern University.
Brother of Max Jones, linebacker with Birmingham Stallions, 1984.

Selected by Washington in 5th round (91st player selected) of 1984 USFL draft.
Selected by Los Angeles Raiders in 2nd round (51st player selected) of 1984 NFL draft.
Signed by Los Angeles Raiders, July 12, 1984.
Traded with 2nd and 3rd round picks in 1988 draft by Los Angeles Raiders to Houston Oilers for 1st, 3rd and 4th round picks in 1988 draft, April 21, 1988.
Los Angeles Raiders NFL, 1984 through 1987.
Games: 1984 (16), 1985 (15), 1986 (16), 1987 (12). Total—59.
Pro statistics: Recovered one fumble, 1985; recovered two fumbles, 1987.

EDWARD LEE JONES
(Ed or Too Tall)
Defensive End—Dallas Cowboys
Born February 23, 1951, at Jackson, Tenn.
Height, 6.09. Weight, 273.
High School—Jackson, Tenn., Central-Merry.
Received degree in health and physical education from Tennessee State University.

Named as defensive end on THE SPORTING NEWS College All-America Team, 1973.
Placed on retired reserve, June 19, 1979.
Selected by Dallas in 1st round (1st player selected) of 1974 NFL draft.
Crossed picket line during players' strike, October 2, 1987.
Dallas NFL, 1974 through 1978 and 1980 through 1987.
Games: 1974 (14), 1975 (14), 1976 (14), 1977 (14), 1978 (16), 1980 (16), 1981 (16), 1982 (9), 1983 (16), 1984 (16), 1985 (16), 1986 (16), 1987 (15). Total—192.
Pro statistics: Intercepted one pass for two yards, 1975; recovered one fumble, 1975, 1976, 1982 and 1987; recovered three fumbles, 1980, 1981 and 1986; intercepted one pass for no yards, 1982; intercepted one pass for 12 yards, 1983; recovered two fumbles, 1983 and 1984.
Played in NFC Championship Game following 1975, 1977, 1978 and 1980 through 1982 seasons.
Played in NFL Championship Game following 1975, 1977 and 1978 seasons.
Played in Pro Bowl (NFL All-Star Game) following 1981 through 1983 seasons.

HASSAN AMEER JONES
Wide Receiver—Minnesota Vikings
Born July 2, 1964, at Clearwater, Fla.
Height, 6.00. Weight, 195.
High School—Clearwater, Fla.
Attended Florida State University.

Selected by Tampa Bay in 1986 USFL territorial draft.
Selected by Minnesota in 5th round (120th player selected) of 1986 NFL draft.
Signed by Minnesota Vikings, July 9, 1986.

		—PASS RECEIVING—			
Year Club	G.	P.C.	Yds.	Avg.	TD.
1986—Minnesota NFL............	16	28	570	20.4	4
1987—Minnesota NFL............	12	7	189	27.0	2
Pro Totals—2 Years...........	28	35	759	21.7	6

Additional pro statistics: Rushed once for 14 yards and fumbled once, 1986.
Played in NFC Championship Game following 1987 season.

JAMES ROOSEVELT JONES
Fullback—Detroit Lions
Born March 21, 1961, at Pompano Beach, Fla.
Height, 6.02. Weight, 228.
High School—Pompano Beach, Fla., Ely.
Attended University of Florida.

Selected by Tampa Bay in 1983 USFL territorial draft.
Selected by Detroit in 1st round (13th player selected) of 1983 NFL draft.
Signed by Detroit Lions, May 12, 1983.

		—RUSHING—			PASS RECEIVING				—TOTAL—		
Year Club	G.	Att.	Yds.	Avg.	TD.	P.C.	Yds.	Avg.	TD.	TD.	Pts.	F.
1983—Detroit NFL	14	135	475	3.5	6	46	467	10.2	1	7	42	4
1984—Detroit NFL	16	137	532	3.9	3	77	662	8.6	5	8	48	6
1985—Detroit NFL	14	244	886	3.6	6	45	334	7.4	3	9	54	7
1986—Detroit NFL	16	252	903	3.6	8	54	334	6.2	1	9	54	6
1987—Detroit NFL	11	96	342	3.6	0	34	262	7.7	0	0	0	2
Pro Totals—5 Years	71	864	3138	3.6	23	256	2059	8.0	10	33	198	25

Additional pro statistics: Recovered one fumble, 1983 and 1985; attempted two passes with no completions, 1983; attempted five passes with three completions for 62 yards and a touchdown and recovered three fumbles, 1984; attempted one pass with no completions, 1985; recovered two fumbles, 1986; attempted one pass with one interception, 1987.

JOSEPH RUSSELL JONES
(Joey)
Wide Receiver—Atlanta Falcons
Born October 29, 1962, at Mobile, Ala.
Height, 5.08. Weight, 165.
High School—Mobile, Ala., Murphy.
Attended University of Alabama.

Selected by Birmingham in 1984 USFL territorial draft.
Signed by Birmingham Stallions, January 23, 1984.
Selected by Atlanta in 1st round (9th player selected) of 1984 NFL supplemental draft.
Granted free agency when USFL suspended operations, August 7, 1986; signed by Atlanta Falcons, August 18, 1986.
Granted roster exemption, August 18 through August 21, 1986; activated, August 22, 1986.
On injured reserve with hamstring injury, November 28 through remainder of 1986 season.
On injured reserve with knee injury, September 8 through entire 1987 season.

		—RUSHING—			PASS RECEIVING				—TOTAL—		
Year Club	G.	Att.	Yds.	Avg.	TD.	P.C.	Yds.	Avg.	TD.	TD.	Pts.	F.
1984—Birmingham USFL	18	7	59	8.4	1	26	584	22.5	6	7	†44	0
1985—Birmingham USFL	17	1	9	9.0	0	43	751	17.5	7	7	42	0
1986—Atlanta NFL	11	1	7	7.0	0	7	141	20.1	0	0	0	0
USFL Totals—2 Years	35	8	68	8.5	1	69	1335	19.3	13	14	86	0
NFL Totals—1 Year	11	1	7	7.0	0	7	141	20.1	0	0	0	0
Pro Totals—3 Years	46	9	75	8.3	1	76	1476	19.4	13	14	86	0

†Includes one 2-point conversion.
Additional USFL statistics: Returned one punt for seven yards, 1984.
Additional NFL statistics: Returned seven punts for 36 yards, 1986.

KENNETH EUGENE JONES
(Ken)
Offensive Tackle—New York Jets
Born December 1, 1952, at St. Louis, Mo.
Height, 6.05. Weight, 285.
High School—Bridgeton, Mo., Pattonville.
Attended Arkansas State University.

Named as guard on THE SPORTING NEWS College All-America Team, 1975.
Selected by Buffalo in 2nd round (45th player selected) of 1976 NFL draft.
Released by Buffalo Bills, September 7, 1987; signed as free agent replacement player by New York Jets, September 30, 1987.
Released by New York Jets, November 9, 1987; re-signed by Jets for 1988, November 24, 1987.
Buffalo NFL, 1976 through 1986; New York Jets NFL, 1987.
Games: 1976 (12), 1977 (14), 1978 (16), 1979 (16), 1980 (16), 1981 (15), 1982 (9), 1983 (16), 1984 (16), 1985 (16), 1986 (12), 1987 (5). Total—163.
Pro statistics: Recovered two fumbles, 1976 and 1981; recovered one fumble, 1978 through 1980 and 1983.

MARLON JONES
Defensive End—Cleveland Browns
Born July 1, 1964, at Baltimore, Md.
Height, 6.04. Weight, 260.
High School—Baltimore, Md., Milford Mill.
Attended Central State University (O.).

Signed as free agent by Toronto Argonauts, February, 1986.
Released by Toronto Argonauts, October 19, 1987; signed by Cleveland Browns, November 19, 1987.
Toronto CFL, 1986 and 1987; Cleveland NFL, 1987.
Games: 1986 CFL (14), 1987 CFL (10), 1987 NFL (1). Total CFL—24. Total Pro—25.
CFL statistics: Intercepted one pass for 35 yards, recovered one fumble and credited with nine sacks, 1986; credited with three sacks, 1987.

MICHAEL ANTHONY JONES
(Mike)
Wide Receiver—New Orleans Saints
Born April 14, 1960, at Chattanooga, Tenn.
Height, 5.11. Weight, 180.
High School—Chattanooga, Tenn., Riverside.
Attended Tennessee State University.

Selected by Minnesota in 6th round (159th player selected) of 1983 NFL draft.
Traded by Minnesota Vikings to New Orleans Saints for fullback Wayne Wilson, September 2, 1986.

Year Club	G.	P.C.	Yds.	Avg.	TD.
1983—Minnesota NFL............	16	6	95	15.8	0
1984—Minnesota NFL............	16	38	591	15.6	1
1985—Minnesota NFL............	16	46	641	13.9	4
1986—New Orleans NFL........	16	48	625	13.0	3
1987—New Orleans NFL........	12	27	420	15.6	3
Pro Totals—5 Years............	76	165	2372	14.4	11

Additional pro statistics: Rushed once for nine yards and returned two kickoffs for 31 yards, 1983; rushed four times for 45 yards and recovered two fumbles, 1984; fumbled once, 1984 and 1987; rushed twice for six yards, 1985; recovered one fumble and fumbled twice, 1986.

RODERICK WAYNE JONES
(Rod)
Defensive Back—Tampa Bay Buccaneers
Born March 31, 1964, at Dallas, Tex.
Height, 6.00. Weight, 175.
High School—Dallas, Tex., South Oak Cliff.
Attended Southern Methodist University.

Selected by Tampa Bay in 1st round (25th player selected) of 1986 NFL draft.
Signed by Tampa Bay Buccaneers, June 19, 1986.

Year Club	G.	No.	Yds.	Avg.	TD.
1986—Tampa Bay NFL	16	1	0	0.0	0
1987—Tampa Bay NFL	11	2	9	4.5	0
Pro Totals—2 Years...........	27	3	9	3.0	0

Additional pro statistics: Recovered one fumble, 1986; recovered one fumble for eight yards, 1987.

RULON KENT JONES
Defensive End—Denver Broncos
Born March 25, 1958, at Salt Lake City, Utah.
Height, 6.06. Weight, 260.
High School—Ogden, Utah, Weber.
Attended Utah State University.

Named to THE SPORTING NEWS NFL All-Star Team, 1985 and 1986.
Named as defensive tackle on THE SPORTING NEWS College All-America Team, 1979.
Selected by Denver in 2nd round (42nd player selected) of 1980 NFL draft.
On injured reserve with knee injury, September 21 through October 20, 1983; activated, October 21, 1983.
Denver NFL, 1980 through 1987.
Games: 1980 (16), 1981 (16), 1982 (9), 1983 (12), 1984 (16), 1985 (16), 1986 (16), 1987 (12). Total—113.
Pro statistics: Credited with a safety, 1980, 1983 and 1986; recovered one fumble, 1980, 1981 and 1986; recovered two fumbles for four yards, 1983; recovered two fumbles for five yards and a touchdown, 1984; recovered three fumbles, 1985.
Played in AFC Championship Game following 1986 and 1987 seasons.
Played in NFL Championship Game following 1986 and 1987 seasons.
Played in Pro Bowl (NFL All-Star Game) following 1985 and 1986 seasons.

TYRONE JONES
Linebacker—Phoenix Cardinals
Born August 3, 1961, at St. Marys, Ga.
Height, 6.00. Weight, 220.
High School—St. Marys, Ga., Camden.
Attended Southern University & A&M.

Signed as free agent by Winnipeg Blue Bombers, April 12, 1983.
Granted free agency, March 1, 1988; signed by Phoenix Cardinals, April 6, 1988.

Year Club	G.	No.	Yds.	Avg.	TD.
1983—Winnipeg CFL..............	16	1	22	22.0	0
1984—Winnipeg CFL..............	16	3	10	3.3	0
1985—Winnipeg CFL..............	16	1	5	5.0	0
1986—Winnipeg CFL..............	16	1	2	2.0	0
1987—Winnipeg CFL..............	18	1	0	0.0	0
CFL Totals—5 Years	82	7	39	5.6	0

Additional CFL statistics: Credited with 17½ sacks, 1983; credited with 20½ sacks and returned one punt for 23

yards, 1984; credited with 11 sacks, 1985; credited with 10 sacks, caught one pass for seven yards and recovered two fumbles, 1986; credited with 15 sacks, caught one pass for one yard and a touchdown and recovered two fumbles for 92 yards and a touchdown, 1987.
Played in CFL Championship Game following 1984 season.

DAVID TURNER JORDAN
Guard—Denver Broncos
Born July 14, 1962, at Birmingham, Ala.
Height, 6.06. Weight, 276.
High School—Vestavia Hills, Ala.
Attended Auburn University.

Selected by Birmingham in 1984 USFL territorial draft.
Selected by New York Giants in 10th round (255th player selected) of 1984 NFL draft.
Signed by New York Giants, June 3, 1984.
On injured reserve with sprained foot, September 2 through entire 1986 season.
Released by New York Giants, September 7, 1987; signed as free agent replacement player by Tampa Bay Buccaneers, September 24, 1987.
Released by Tampa Bay Buccaneers, November 3, 1987; signed as free agent by Denver Broncos, April 5, 1988.
New York Giants NFL, 1984 and 1985; Tampa Bay NFL, 1987.
Games: 1984 (14), 1985 (16), 1987 (3). Total—33.
Pro statistics: Recovered one fumble, 1987.

PAUL BUFORD JORDAN
(Known by middle name.)
Fullback—New Orleans Saints
Born June 26, 1962, at Lafayette, La.
Height, 6.00. Weight, 222.
High School—Iota, La.
Attended McNeese State University.

Selected by New Orleans in 1st round (13th player selected) of 1984 USFL draft.
Signed by New Orleans Breakers, January 9, 1984.
Selected by Green Bay in 1st round (12th player selected) of 1984 NFL supplemental draft.
Franchise transferred to Portland, November 13, 1984.
On developmental squad, April 6 through April 20, 1985; activated, April 21, 1985.
Released, July 31, 1985; signed by Green Bay Packers, September 2, 1985.
Granted roster exemption, September 2 through September 15, 1985.
Released by Green Bay Packers, September 16, 1985; signed as free agent by New Orleans Saints, March 6, 1986.
On developmental squad for 2 games with Portland Breakers in 1985.

| | | —RUSHING— | | | PASS RECEIVING | | | —TOTAL— | | |
Year Club	G.	Att.	Yds.	Avg. TD.	P.C.	Yds.	Avg. TD.	TD.	Pts.	F.
1984—New Orleans USFL	18	214	1276	*6.0 8	45	427	9.5 4	12	72	9
1985—Portland USFL	15	165	817	5.0 5	12	192	16.0 1	6	†38	11
1986—New Orleans NFL	16	68	207	3.0 1	11	127	11.5 0	1	6	2
1987—New Orleans NFL	12	12	36	3.0 2	2	13	6.5 0	2	12	0
USFL Totals—2 Years	33	379	2093	5.5 13	57	619	10.9 5	18	110	20
NFL Totals—2 Years	28	80	243	3.0 3	13	140	10.8 0	3	18	2
Pro Totals—4 Years	61	459	2336	5.1 16	70	759	10.8 5	21	128	22

†Includes one 2-point conversion.
Additional USFL statistics: Recovered four fumbles, 1984 and 1985.
Additional NFL statistics: Returned one punt for 13 yards and returned two kickoffs for 28 yards, 1987.

SHELBY LEWIS JORDAN
Offensive Tackle—Los Angeles Raiders
Born January 23, 1952, at East St. Louis, Ill.
Height, 6.07. Weight, 280.
High School—East St. Louis, Ill.
Received degree from Washington (Mo.) University and attending
Bryant College for master's degree in marketing.

Selected by Houston in 7th round (157th player selected) of 1973 NFL draft.
Released by Houston Oilers, 1973; signed as free agent by New England Patriots, April 2, 1974.
Missed entire 1974 and 1976 seasons due to injury.
On reserve/did not report, August 16 through August 28, 1983; reinstated, August 29, 1983.
Granted roster exemption, August 29 through September 5, 1983.
Traded by New England Patriots to Los Angeles Raiders for 4th round pick in 1985 draft, September 6, 1983.
Granted roster exemption, September 6 through September 19, 1983; activated, September 20, 1983.
On injured reserve with knee injury, November 15 through remainder of 1984 season.
On injured reserve with torn triceps, September 1 through entire 1987 season.
Crossed picket line during players' strike, September 30, 1987.
New England NFL, 1975 and 1977 through 1982; Los Angeles Raiders NFL, 1983 through 1986.
Games: 1975 (14), 1977 (10), 1978 (16), 1979 (14), 1980 (16), 1981 (16), 1982 (9), 1983 (13), 1984 (11), 1985 (16), 1986 (16).
Total—151.
Pro statistics: Recovered two fumbles for 12 yards, 1975; recovered one fumble, 1979.
Played in AFC Championship Game following 1983 season.
Played in NFL Championship Game following 1983 season.

— 233 —

STEVEN RUSSELL JORDAN
(Steve)
Tight End—Minnesota Vikings
Born January 10, 1961, at Phoenix, Ariz.
Height, 6.03. Weight, 235.
High School—Phoenix, Ariz., South Mountain.
Received bachelor of science degree in civil engineering from Brown University in 1982.
Selected by Minnesota in 7th round (179th player selected) of 1982 NFL draft.

		——PASS RECEIVING——				
Year	Club	G.	P.C.	Yds.	Avg.	TD.
1982—Minnesota NFL............		9	3	42	14.0	0
1983—Minnesota NFL............		13	15	212	14.1	2
1984—Minnesota NFL............		14	38	414	10.9	2
1985—Minnesota NFL............		16	68	795	11.7	0
1986—Minnesota NFL............		16	58	859	14.8	6
1987—Minnesota NFL............		12	35	490	14.0	2
Pro Totals—6 Years............		80	217	2812	13.0	12

Additional pro statistics: Rushed once for four yards and a touchdown, 1984; recovered one fumble, 1984 and 1986; fumbled twice, 1985; fumbled once, 1987.
Played in NFC Championship Game following 1987 season.
Played in Pro Bowl (NFL All-Star Game) following 1986 and 1987 seasons.

TIMOTHY JORDAN
(Tim)
Linebacker—New England Patriots
Born April 26, 1964, at Madison, Wis.
Height, 6.03. Weight, 226.
High School—Madison, Wis., Robert M. LaFollette.
Attended University of Wisconsin.
Selected by New England in 4th round (107th player selected) of 1987 NFL draft.
Signed by New England Patriots, July 24, 1987.
On injured reserve with hamstring injury, September 1 through November 6, 1987; activated, November 7, 1987.
New England NFL, 1987.
Games: 1987 (5).

SETH JOYNER
Linebacker—Philadelphia Eagles
Born November 18, 1964, at Spring Valley, N. Y.
Height, 6.02. Weight, 248.
High School—Spring Valley, N. Y.
Attended University of Texas at El Paso.
Selected by Philadelphia in 8th round (208th player selected) of 1986 NFL draft.
Signed by Philadelphia Eagles, July 17, 1986.
Released by Philadelphia Eagles, September 1, 1986; re-signed by Eagles, September 17, 1986.
Philadelphia NFL, 1986 and 1987.
Games: 1986 (14), 1987 (12). Total—26.
Pro statistics: Intercepted one pass for four yards, 1986; intercepted two passes for 42 yards and recovered two fumbles for 18 yards and a touchdown, 1987.

BRIAN JOSEPH JOZWIAK
Name pronounced JOEZ-we-ak.
Guard—Kansas City Chiefs
Born June 20, 1963, at Baltimore, Md.
Height, 6.05. Weight, 308.
High School—Baltimore, Md., Catonsville.
Attended West Virginia University.
Selected by Kansas City in 1st round (7th player selected) of 1986 NFL draft.
Signed by Kansas City Chiefs, August 5, 1986.
Kansas City NFL, 1986 and 1987.
Games: 1986 (15), 1987 (10). Total—25.

WILLIAM THADIUS JUDSON
Cornerback—Miami Dolphins
Born March 26, 1959, at Detroit, Mich.
Height, 6.02. Weight, 187.
High School—Atlanta, Ga., Sylvan Hills.
Received bachelor of science degree in business administration
from South Carolina State College in 1981.
Selected by Miami in 8th round (208th player selected) of 1981 NFL draft.
On injured reserve with hamstring injury, August 31 through entire 1981 season.

Year Club		G.	No.	Yds.	Avg.TD.	
1982—Miami NFL		9		None		
1983—Miami NFL		16	6	60	10.0	0
1984—Miami NFL		16	4	121	30.3	1
1985—Miami NFL		16	4	88	22.0	★1
1986—Miami NFL		16	2	0	0.0	0
1987—Miami NFL		12	2	11	5.5	0
Pro Totals—6 Years		85	18	280	15.6	2

Additional pro statistics: Recovered two fumbles for 37 yards, 1984.
Played in AFC Championship Game following 1982, 1984 and 1985 seasons.
Played in NFL Championship Game following 1982 and 1984 seasons.

ESTER JAMES JUNIOR III
(E.J.)
Linebacker—Phoenix Cardinals

Born December 8, 1959, at Sallsburg, N.C.
Height, 6.03. Weight, 235.
High School—Nashville, Tenn., Maplewood.
Received degree in public relations from University of Alabama.

Named as defensive end on THE SPORTING NEWS College All-America Team, 1980.
Selected by St. Louis in 1st round (5th player selected) of 1981 NFL draft.
On suspended list for drug use, July 25 through September 25, 1983; reinstated, September 26, 1983.
Crossed picket line during players' strike, October 2, 1987.
Franchise transferred to Phoenix, March 15, 1988.

Year Club		G.	No.	Yds.	Avg.TD.	
1981—St. Louis NFL		16	1	5	5.0	0
1982—St. Louis NFL		9		None		
1983—St. Louis NFL		12	3	27	9.0	0
1984—St. Louis NFL		16	1	18	18.0	0
1985—St. Louis NFL		16	5	109	21.8	0
1986—St. Louis NFL		13		None		
1987—St. Louis NFL		13	1	25	25.0	0
Pro Totals—7 Years		95	11	184	16.7	0

Additional pro statistics: Recovered one fumble, 1982 and 1986; recovered one fumble for one yard, 1983; recovered two fumbles for five yards and fumbled once, 1987.
Played in Pro Bowl (NFL All-Star Game) following 1984 and 1985 seasons.

ABNER KIRK JUNKIN
(Trey)
Tight End—Los Angeles Raiders

Born January 23, 1961, at Conway, Ark.
Height, 6.02. Weight, 230.
High School—North Little Rock, Ark., Northeast.
Attended Louisiana Tech University.
Brother of Mike Junkin, linebacker with Cleveland Browns.

Selected by Buffalo in 4th round (93rd player selected) of 1983 NFL draft.
Released by Buffalo Bills, September 12, 1984; signed as free agent by Washington Redskins, September 25, 1984.
Granted free agency after not receiving qualifying offer, February 1, 1985; signed by Los Angeles Raiders, March 10, 1985.
On injured reserve with knee injury, September 24 through remainder of 1986 season.
Buffalo NFL, 1983; Buffalo (2)-Washington (12) NFL, 1984; Los Angeles Raiders NFL, 1985 through 1987.
Games: 1983 (16), 1984 (14), 1985 (16), 1986 (3), 1987 (12). Total—61.
Pro statistics: Recovered one fumble, 1983 and 1984; caught two passes for eight yards and a touchdown, 1985; caught two passes for 38 yards, 1986; caught two passes for 15 yards, 1987.

MICHAEL WAYNE JUNKIN
(Mike)
Linebacker—Cleveland Browns

Born November 21, 1964, at North Little Rock, Ark.
Height, 6.03. Weight, 238.
High School—Belvidere, Ill.
Attended Duke University.
Brother of Trey Junkin, tight end with Los Angeles Raiders.

Selected by Cleveland in 1st round (5th player selected) of 1987 NFL draft.
Signed by Cleveland Browns, August 11, 1987.
On injured reserve with fractured wrist, November 13 through remainder of 1987 season.
Cleveland NFL, 1987.
Games: 1987 (4).

KERRY AUGUST JUSTIN
Cornerback—Seattle Seahawks
Born May 3, 1955, at New Orleans, La.
Height, 5.11. Weight, 175.
High School—Los Angeles, Calif., Crenshaw.
Attended East Los Angeles Junior College and Oregon State University.
Brother of Sid Justin, cornerback with Los Angeles Rams, Winnipeg Blue Bombers
and Baltimore Colts, 1979, 1980 and 1982; Tyrone Justin, defensive back
with Los Angeles Express, 1983 and 1984; and Solomon Justin, lead singer with Shalamar.

Signed as free agent by Seattle Seahawks, May 10, 1978.
USFL rights traded by Pittsburgh Maulers to New Jersey Generals for rights to guard Joe Lukens and territorial pick (tight end John Frank) in 1984 draft, November 15, 1983.
Signed by New Jersey Generals, November 15, 1983; for contract to take effect after being granted free agency, February 1, 1984.
On exempt/left squad, February 22 through March 9, 1984; activated, March 10, 1984.
On developmental squad, June 15 through June 22, 1984; activated, June 23, 1984.
On developmental squad, April 13 through April 18, 1985; activated, April 19, 1985.
Released by New Jersey Generals, July 31, 1985; re-signed by Generals, August 1, 1985.
Granted free agency when USFL suspended operations, August 7, 1986; re-signed by Seattle Seahawks, August 24, 1986.
Granted roster exemption, August 24 through August 27, 1986; activated, August 28, 1986.
On injured reserve with knee injury, November 24 through remainder of 1987 season.
On developmental squad for 1 game with New Jersey Generals in 1984 and 1985.

Year Club	G.	No.	Yds.	Avg.TD.		Year Club	G.	No.	Yds.	Avg.TD.
1978—Seattle NFL	16		None			1985—New Jersey USFL	17	8	65	8.1 ⋆1
1979—Seattle NFL	14	1	0	0.0	0	1986—Seattle NFL	16	4	29	7.3 0
1980—Seattle NFL	11	1	0	0.0	0	1987—Seattle NFL	7		None	
1981—Seattle NFL	15		None							
1982—Seattle NFL	9		None			NFL Totals—8 Years	104	7	31	4.4 0
1983—Seattle NFL	16	1	2	2.0	0	USFL Totals—2 Years	31	10	97	9.7 1
1984—New Jersey USFL	14	2	32	16.0	0	Pro Totals—10 Years	135	17	128	7.5 1

Additional NFL statistics: Recovered one fumble, 1978 and 1987; recovered three fumbles, 1979; recovered one fumble for 43 yards, 1981; recovered two fumbles, 1986.
Additional USFL statistics: Recovered one fumble for 20 yards, 1984; recovered one fumble, 1985.
Played in AFC Championship Game following 1983 season.

VYTO KAB
Tight End—Detroit Lions
Born December 23, 1959, at Albany, Ga.
Height, 6.05. Weight, 240.
High School—Wayne, N.J., DePaul.
Received degree in food service and housing administration from Penn State University.

Selected by Philadelphia in 3rd round (78th player selected) of 1982 NFL draft.
On injured reserve with ankle injury, December 14 through remainder of 1983 season.
On injured reserve with hamstring injury, September 13 through October 7, 1985.
Released by Philadelphia Eagles, October 8, 1985; awarded on waivers to New York Giants, October 9, 1985.
(Philadelphia subsequently acquired 12th round pick in 1986 draft from New York Giants for past consideration for waiving Kab).
On injured reserve with foot injury, December 28 through remainder of 1985 season playoffs.
Released by New York Giants, August 26, 1986; signed as free agent by Cleveland Browns, March 18, 1987.
On injured reserve with back injury, September 7 through October 26, 1987.
Released by Cleveland Browns, October 27, 1987; re-signed by Browns after clearing procedural waivers, November 5, 1987.
Released by Cleveland Browns, November 7, 1987; awarded on waivers to Detroit Lions, November 9, 1987.

Year Club	G.	P.C.	Yds.	Avg.	TD.
1982—Philadelphia NFL	9	4	35	8.8	1
1983—Philadelphia NFL	14	18	195	10.8	1
1984—Philadelphia NFL	16	9	102	11.3	3
1985—Phi.(1)-NYG(11) NFL..	12		None		
1987—Detroit NFL	7	5	54	10.8	0
Pro Totals—5 Years	58	36	386	10.7	5

Additional pro statistics: Recovered one fumble, 1987.

JOHN FREDERICK KAISER
Linebacker—Buffalo Bills
Born June 6, 1962, at Oconomowoc, Wis.
Height, 6.03. Weight, 227.
High School—Hartland, Wis., Arrowhead.
Attended College of the Sequoias and University of Arizona.
Cousin of Billy McCool, pitcher with Cincinnati Reds, San Diego Padres
and St. Louis Cardinals, 1964 through 1970.

Selected by Arizona in 1984 USFL territorial draft.
Selected by Seattle in 6th round (162nd player selected) of 1984 NFL draft.
Signed by Seattle Seahawks, June 15, 1984.
Released by Seattle Seahawks, September 7, 1987; awarded on waivers to Buffalo Bills, September 8, 1987.

Seattle NFL, 1984 through 1986; Buffalo NFL, 1987.
Games: 1984 (16), 1985 (16), 1986 (16), 1987 (12). Total—60.
Pro statistics: Recovered one fumble, 1987.

KENNETH SCOTT KAPLAN
(Ken)
Offensive Tackle—New Orleans Saints
Born January 12, 1960, at Boston, Mass.
Height, 6.04. Weight, 275.
High School—Brockton, Mass.
Attended University of New Hampshire.

Selected by Tampa Bay in 6th round (158th player selected) of 1983 NFL draft.
On injured reserve with back injury, August 29 through entire 1983 season.
On injured reserve with elbow injury, August 22 through September 29, 1986.
Released by Tampa Bay Buccaneers, September 30, 1986; signed as free agent by Green Bay Packers, April 6, 1987.
Released by Green Bay Packers, August 10, 1987; signed as free agent replacement player by New Orleans Saints, September 24, 1987.
Released by New Orleans Saints, October 27, 1987; re-signed by Saints, February 22, 1988.
Tampa Bay NFL, 1984 and 1985; New Orleans NFL, 1987.
Games: 1984 (16), 1985 (16), 1987 (3). Total—35.

RICHARD JOHN KARLIS
(Rich)
Placekicker—Denver Broncos
Born May 23, 1959, at Salem, O.
Height, 6.00. Weight, 180.
High School—Salem, O.
Received degree in economics from University of Cincinnati.

Signed as free agent by Houston Oilers, June 5, 1981.
Released by Houston Oilers, July 31, 1981; signed as free agent by Denver Broncos, June 4, 1982.

| | | ——PLACE KICKING—— | | | | |
Year Club	G.	XP.	XPM.	FG.	FGA.	Pts.
1982—Denver NFL	9	15	1	11	13	48
1983—Denver NFL	16	33	1	21	25	96
1984—Denver NFL	16	38	3	21	28	101
1985—Denver NFL	16	41	3	23	38	110
1986—Denver NFL	16	44	1	20	28	104
1987—Denver NFL	12	37	0	18	25	91
Pro Totals—6 Years.......	85	208	9	114	157	550

Played in AFC Championship Game following 1986 and 1987 seasons.
Played in NFL Championship Game following 1986 and 1987 seasons.

KEITH LEONARD KARTZ
Offensive Tackle—Denver Broncos
Born May 5, 1963, at Las Vegas, Nev.
Height, 6.04. Weight, 270.
High School—Encinitas, Calif., San Dieguito.
Received bachelor of science degree in social science
from University of California at Berkeley in 1986.

Signed as free agent by Seattle Seahawks, May 9, 1986.
Released by Seattle Seahawks, August 18, 1986; signed as free agent by Denver Broncos, May 1, 1987.
On injured reserve with back injury, September 7 through September 29, 1987; activated, September 30, 1987.
Crossed picket line during players' strike, September 30, 1987.
Denver NFL, 1987.
Games: 1987 (12).
Played in AFC Championship Game following 1987 season.
Played in NFL Championship Game following 1987 season.

JOHN ERIC KATTUS
(Known by middle name.)
Tight End—Cincinnati Bengals
Born March 4, 1963, at Cincinnati, O.
Height, 6.05. Weight, 235.
High School—Cincinnati, O., Colerain.
Attended University of Michigan.

Selected by Baltimore in 1986 USFL territorial draft.
Selected by Cincinnati in 4th round (91st player selected) of 1986 NFL draft.
Signed by Cincinnati Bengals, July 18, 1986.

| | | ——PASS RECEIVING—— | | |
Year Club	G.	P.C.	Yds.	Avg.	TD.
1986—Cincinnati NFL	16	11	99	9.0	1
1987—Cincinnati NFL	11	18	217	12.1	2
Pro Totals—2 Years............	27	29	316	10.9	3

Additional pro statistics: Returned two kickoffs for 22 yards, 1987.

MEL KAUFMAN
Linebacker—Washington Redskins
Born February 24, 1958, at Los Angeles, Calif.
Height, 6.02. Weight, 230.
High School—Santa Monica, Calif.
Attended California Poly State University at San Luis Obispo.
Son-in-law of Billie Matthews, assistant coach with University of Kansas, 1970;
University of California at Los Angeles, 1971 through 1978; San Francisco 49ers,
1979 through 1982; Philadelphia Eagles, 1983 and 1984; Indianapolis
Colts, 1985 and 1986; and with Kansas City Chiefs since 1987.
Signed as free agent by Washington Redskins, May 6, 1981.
On injured reserve with shoulder injury, November 19 through remainder of 1981 season.
On injured reserve with torn Achilles tendon, September 16 through remainder of 1986 season.

Year Club	G.	No.	Yds.	Avg.	TD.
		—INTERCEPTIONS—			
1981—Washington NFL	11	2	25	12.5	0
1982—Washington NFL	9	None			
1983—Washington NFL	16	2	93	46.5	1
1984—Washington NFL	15	None			
1985—Washington NFL	15	3	10	3.3	0
1986—Washington NFL	2	None			
1987—Washington NFL	12	None			
Pro Totals—7 Years	80	7	128	18.3	1

Additional pro statistics: Recovered one fumble, 1982 and 1984; recovered one fumble for 30 yards and a touchdown, 1983; recovered two fumbles, 1985.
Played in NFC Championship Game following 1982, 1983 and 1987 seasons.
Played in NFL Championship Game following 1982, 1983 and 1987 seasons.

CLARENCE HUBERT KAY
Tight End—Denver Broncos
Born July 30, 1961, at Seneca, S.C.
Height, 6.02. Weight, 237.
High School—Seneca, S.C.
Attended University of Georgia.
Selected by Jacksonville in 1984 USFL territorial draft.
Selected by Denver in 7th round (186th player selected) of 1984 NFL draft.
Signed by Denver Broncos, May 17, 1984.
On suspended list, November 15 through November 18, 1986; activated, November 19, 1986.
On suspended list, December 12, 1986 through January 9, 1987; activated, January 10, 1987.

Year Club	G.	P.C.	Yds.	Avg.	TD.
		—PASS RECEIVING—			
1984—Denver NFL	16	16	136	8.5	3
1985—Denver NFL	16	29	339	11.7	3
1986—Denver NFL	13	15	195	13.0	1
1987—Denver NFL	12	31	440	14.2	0
Pro Totals—4 Years	57	91	1110	12.2	7

Additional pro statistics: Fumbled once, 1984 and 1985; recovered one fumble, 1985; fumbled three times, 1987.
Played in AFC Championship Game following 1986 and 1987 seasons.
Played in NFL Championship Game following 1986 and 1987 seasons.

TIM ALLYNN KEARSE
Wide Receiver—Indianapolis Colts
Born October 24, 1959, at York, Pa.
Height, 5.10. Weight, 193.
High School—York, Pa.
Attended San Jose State University.
Selected by Oakland in 1983 USFL territorial draft.
Selected by San Diego in 11th round (303rd player selected) of 1983 NFL draft.
Signed with British Columbia Lions, June 1, 1983.
Traded with defensive back Ken Hinton by British Columbia Lions to Saskatchewan Roughriders for draft pick, August 28, 1983.
Released by Saskatchewan Roughriders, April 29, 1985; signed by San Diego Chargers, May 7, 1985.
Released by San Diego Chargers, July 28, 1985; signed as free agent by Detroit Lions, May 29, 1986.
On injured reserve with thumb injury, August 30 through December 16, 1986; activated after clearing procedural waivers, December 18, 1986.
Released by Detroit Lions, December 20, 1986; signed as free agent replacement player by Indianapolis Colts, September 23, 1987.
Released by Indianapolis Colts, October 20, 1987; re-signed by Colts, April 27, 1988.

Year Club	G.	P.C.	Yds.	Avg.	TD.	No.	Yds.	Avg.	TD.	TD.	Pts.	F.
		—PASS RECEIVING—				—PUNT RETURNS—				—TOTAL—		
1983—B.C. (1)-Sask. (6) CFL	7	9	144	16.0	1	15	201	13.4	1	2	12	0
1984—Saskatchewan CFL	8	19	240	12.6	0	11	125	11.4	1	1	6	3
1987—Indianapolis NFL	3	3	56	18.7	0	None				0	0	0
CFL Totals—2 Years	15	28	384	13.7	1	26	326	12.5	2	3	18	3
NFL Totals—1 Year	3	3	56	18.7	0	0	0	0.0	0	0	0	0
Pro Totals—3 Years	18	31	440	14.2	1	26	326	12.5	2	3	18	3

Additional CFL statistics: Returned one kickoff for 24 yards, 1983; rushed once for five yards and ran for seven yards with lateral on kickoff return, 1984.

MARK ANTHONY KEEL
Tight End—Kansas City Chiefs
Born October 1, 1961, at Fort Worth, Tex.
Height, 6.04. Weight, 228.
High School—Tacoma, Wash., Clover Park.
Attended Olympic College and University of Arizona.

Selected by Arizona in 1983 USFL territorial draft.
Signed by Arizona Wranglers, February 25, 1983.
Selected by New England in 9th round (240th player selected) of 1983 NFL draft.
Franchise transferred to Chicago, September 30, 1983.
On developmental squad, June 15 through remainder of 1984 season.
Franchise disbanded, November 20, 1984.
Selected by Jacksonville Bulls in USFL dispersal draft, December 6, 1984.
On developmental squad, June 14 through remainder of 1985 season.
Traded by Jacksonville Bulls to Arizona Outlaws for draft choice, February 28, 1986.
Granted free agency when USFL suspended operations, August 7, 1986; signed by New England Patriots, September 8, 1986.
On non-football injury list, September 8 through remainder of 1986 season.
Released by New England Patriots, September 7, 1987; signed as free agent replacement player by Seattle Seahawks, September 29, 1987.
Released by Seattle Seahawks, October 20, 1987; signed as free agent by Kansas City Chiefs, October 30, 1987.
On developmental squad for 2 games with Chicago Blitz in 1984.
On developmental squad for 2 games with Jacksonville Bulls in 1985.

			—PASS RECEIVING—			
Year	Club	G.	P.C.	Yds.	Avg.	TD.
1983—Arizona USFL...............		18	65	802	12.3	2
1984—Chicago USFL		16	23	263	11.4	2
1985—Jacksonville USFL.......		16	53	585	11.0	0
1987—Sea. (3)-K.C. (7) NFL...		10	8	97	12.1	1
USFL Totals—3 Years........		50	141	1650	11.7	4
NFL Totals—1 Year...........		10	8	97	12.1	1
Pro Totals—4 Years............		60	149	1747	11.7	5

Additional USFL statistics: Fumbled once, recovered one fumble and credited with one 2-point conversion, 1983; scored one 2-point conversion, 1984; fumbled three times, 1985.
Additional NFL statistics: Recovered two fumbles, 1987.

KARL RICHARD KEHR
(Rich)
Guard—Washington Redskins
Born June 18, 1959, at Phoenixville, Pa.
Height, 6.03. Weight, 285.
High School—Elgin, Ill., Larkin.
Received bachelor of arts degree in international business
and geography from Carthage College in 1981.

Signed as free agent by Green Bay Packers, May, 1981.
Released by Green Bay Packers, August 18, 1981; claimed on procedural waivers by St. Louis Cardinals, March 25, 1982.
On injured reserve with knee injury, August 13 through entire 1982 season.
On injured reserve with knee injury, August 16 through September 5, 1983.
Released by St. Louis Cardinals, September 6, 1983; signed by Oklahoma Outlaws, October 7, 1983.
Released by Oklahoma Outlaws, January 21, 1984; awarded on waivers to Arizona Wranglers, January 23, 1984.
On developmental squad, March 2 through March 8, 1984.
Released by Arizona Wranglers, March 9, 1984; signed as free agent by Houston Gamblers, June 1, 1984.
On developmental squad, June 1 through remainder of 1984 season.
On developmental squad, May 4 through May 11, 1985; activated, May 12, 1985.
Traded with defensive backs Luther Bradley, Will Lewis, Mike Mitchell and Durwood Roquemore, defensive end Pete Catan, quarterbacks Jim Kelly and Todd Dillon, defensive tackles Tony Fitzpatrick, Van Hughes and Hosea Taylor, running back Sam Harrell, linebackers Andy Hawkins and Ladell Wills, wide receivers Richard Johnson, Scott McGhee, Gerald McNeil, Ricky Sanders and Clarence Verdin, center Billy Kidd and offensive tackles Chris Riehm and Tommy Robison by Houston Gamblers to New Jersey Generals for past considerations, March 7, 1986.
Granted free agency when USFL suspended operations, August 7, 1986; signed as free agent by Miami Dolphins, August 12, 1986.
Released by Miami Dolphins after failing physical, August 13, 1986; signed as free agent by Washington Redskins, April 30, 1987.
Active for 1 game with Arizona Wranglers in 1984; did not play.
On injured reserve with knee injury, October 27 through November 27, 1987; activated, November 28, 1987.
On developmental squad for 1 game with Arizona Wranglers and 4 games with Houston Gamblers in 1984.
On developmental squad for 1 game with Houston Gamblers in 1985.
Arizona USFL, 1984; Houston USFL, 1985; Washington NFL, 1987.
Games: 1985 (16), 1987 (5). Total—21.
Played in NFC Championship Game following 1987 season.
Played in NFL Championship Game following 1987 season.

SCOTT JEFFERY KELLAR
Nose Tackle—Indianapolis Colts
Born December 31, 1963, at Elgin, Ill.
Height, 6.03. Weight, 278.
High School—Roselle, Ill., Lake Park.
Attended Northern Illinois University.
Brother of Mark Kellar, running back with Chicago Fire (WFL),
San Antonio Wings (WFL) and Minnesota Vikings, 1974 through 1978.

Selected by Indianapolis in 5th round (117th player selected) of 1986 NFL draft.
Signed by Indianapolis Colts, July 17, 1986.
Crossed picket line during players' strike, October 7, 1987.
On injured reserve with knee injury, November 2 through remainder of 1987 season.
Indianapolis NFL, 1986 and 1987.
Games: 1986 (14), 1987 (3). Total—17.

MICHAEL DENNIS KELLEY
(Mike)
Quarterback—San Diego Chargers
Born December 31, 1959, at Sonora, Calif.
Height, 6.03. Weight, 192.
High School—Augusta, Ga., Westside.
Attended Georgia Tech.

Selected by Atlanta in 6th round (149th player selected) of 1982 NFL draft.
Released by Atlanta Falcons, September 4, 1982.
USFL rights traded with 5th round pick in 1984 draft by Arizona Wranglers to Birmingham Stallions for rights to tight end Robert Hubble and defensive back Eddie Ray Walker, January 31, 1983.
Signed by Birmingham Stallions, January 31, 1983.
Released by Birmingham Stallions, February 20, 1983; awarded on waivers to Oakland Invaders, February 22, 1983.
On developmental squad, March 4 through March 13, 1983.
Released by Oakland Invaders, March 14, 1983; signed as free agent by Tampa Bay Bandits, April 20, 1983.
On developmental squad, April 20 through May 14, 1983; activated, May 15, 1983.
On developmental squad, June 21 through remainder of 1983 season.
Selected by Memphis Steamboats in 6th round (31st player selected) of USFL expansion draft, September 6, 1983.
On developmental squad, February 24 through May 23, 1984; activated, May 24, 1984.
Granted free agency when USFL suspended operations, August 7, 1986; signed by Saskatchewan Roughriders, October 8, 1986.
Released by Saskatchewan Roughriders, June 20, 1987; signed as free agent replacement player by San Diego Chargers, September 24, 1987.
Released by San Diego Chargers, October 21, 1987; re-signed by Chargers, February 22, 1988.
On developmental squad for 2 games with Oakland Invaders and 5 games with Tampa Bay Bandits in 1983.
On developmental squad for 13 games with Memphis Showboats in 1984.

| | | —————PASSING————— | | | | | | | ————RUSHING———— | | | | —TOTAL— | | |
Year Club	G.	Att.	Cmp.	Pct.	Gain	T.P.	P.I.	Avg.	Att.	Yds.	Avg.	TD.	TD.	Pts.	F.
1983—Tampa Bay USFL	6	166	81	48.8	1003	4	5	6.04	5	13	2.6	0	0	0	6
1984—Memphis USFL	5	120	82	68.3	1014	8	6	8.45	7	46	6.6	0	0	0	2
1985—Memphis USFL	13	260	165	*63.5	2186	9	14	*8.41	15	76	5.1	6	6	†38	4
1986—Saskatchewan CFL	5	24	8	33.3	77	0	1	3.21	2	5	2.5	0	0	0	0
1987—San Diego NFL	3	29	17	58.6	305	1	0	10.52	4	17	4.3	0	0	0	0
USFL Totals—3 Years	24	546	328	60.1	4203	21	25	7.70	27	135	5.0	6	6	38	12
CFL Totals—1 Year	5	24	8	33.3	77	0	1	3.21	2	5	2.5	0	0	0	0
NFL Totals—1 Year	3	29	17	58.6	305	1	0	10.52	4	17	4.3	0	0	0	0
Pro Totals—5 Years	32	599	353	58.9	4585	22	26	7.65	33	157	4.8	6	6	38	12

†Scored one 2-point conversion.
USFL Quarterback Rating Points: 1983 (63.4), 1984 (95.6), 1985 (79.1). Total—77.8.
NFL Quarterback Rating Points: 1987 (106.3).
Additional pro statistics: Recovered three fumbles, 1985.

MIKE KELLEY
Center-Guard—Philadelphia Eagles
Born August 27, 1962, at Westfield, Mass.
Height, 6.05. Weight, 280.
High School—Westfield, Mass.
Attended University of Notre Dame.

Selected by Jacksonville in 4th round (47th player selected) of 1985 USFL draft.
Selected by Houston in 3rd round (82nd player selected) of 1985 NFL draft.
Signed by Houston Oilers, July 25, 1985.
On injured reserve with neck injury, September 1 through entire 1986 season.
Left Houston Oilers camp voluntarily, July 30, 1987; returned, August 6, 1987.
Released by Houston Oilers, September 7, 1987; re-signed by Oilers, September 11, 1987.
Released by Houston Oilers, November 3, 1987; signed as free agent by Philadelphia Eagles, December 12, 1987.
Houston NFL, 1985 and 1987.
Games: 1985 (16), 1987 (1). Total—17.

KEVIN ROBERT KELLIN
Defensive End—Tampa Bay Buccaneers
Born November 16, 1959, at Hampton, Ia.
Height, 6.06. Weight, 265.
High School—Grand Rapids, Minn.
Attended University of Minnesota.

Signed as free agent by Washington Redskins, April 28, 1983.
Released by Washington Redskins, July 26, 1983; signed by Washington Federals, November 12, 1983.
On developmental squad, February 24 through March 1, 1984; activated, March 2, 1984.
On developmental squad, May 6 through May 9, 1984; activated, May 10, 1984.
Franchise transferred to Orlando, October 12, 1984.
Granted free agency, August 1, 1985; re-signed by Renegades, November 4, 1985.
Granted free agency when USFL suspended operations, August 7, 1986; signed as free agent by Tampa Bay Buccaneers, August 12, 1986.
On injured reserve with shoulder injury, September 2 through October 23, 1986, activated, October 24, 1986.
On injured reserve with knee injury, November 28 through remainder of 1987 season.
On developmental squad for 2 games with Washington Federals in 1984.
Washington USFL, 1984; Orlando USFL, 1985; Tampa Bay NFL, 1986 and 1987.
Games: 1984 (16), 1985 (17), 1986 (9), 1987 (7). Total USFL—33. Total NFL—16. Total Pro—49.
Pro statistics: Credited with five sacks for 32 yards, 1984; credited with three sacks for 18 yards, 1985.

JAMES EDWARD KELLY
(Jim)
Quarterback—Buffalo Bills
Born February 14, 1960, at Pittsburgh, Pa.
Height, 6.03. Weight, 215.
High School—East Brady, Pa.
Received bachelor of business management degree from University of Miami (Fla.) in 1982.
Brother of Pat Kelly, linebacker with Birmingham Vulcans (WFL), 1975.

Named THE SPORTING NEWS USFL Rookie of the Year, 1984.
Named as quarterback on THE SPORTING NEWS USFL All-Star Team, 1985.
Led USFL quarterbacks in passing with 97.9 points in 1985.
Selected by Chicago in 14th round (163rd player selected) of 1983 USFL draft.
Selected by Buffalo in 1st round (14th player selected) of 1983 NFL draft.
USFL rights traded with running back Mark Rush by Chicago Blitz to Houston Gamblers for 1st, 3rd, 8th and 10th round picks in 1984 draft, June 9, 1983.
Signed by Houston Gamblers, June 9, 1983.
On developmental squad, June 1 through June 28, 1985; activated, June 29, 1985.
Traded with defensive backs Luther Bradley, Will Lewis, Mike Mitchell and Durwood Roquemore, defensive end Pete Catan, quarterback Todd Dillon, defensive tackles Tony Fitzpatrick, Van Hughes and Hosea Taylor, running back Sam Harrell, linebackers Andy Hawkins and Ladell Wills, wide receivers Richard Johnson, Scott McGhee, Gerald McNeil, Ricky Sanders and Clarence Verdin, guard Rich Kehr, center Billy Kidd and offensive tackles Chris Riehm and Tommy Robison by Houston Gamblers to New Jersey Generals for past considerations, March 7, 1986.
Granted free agency when USFL suspended operations, August 7, 1986; signed by Buffalo Bills, August 18, 1986.
Granted roster exemption, August 18 through August 28, 1986; activated, August 29, 1986.
On developmental squad for 4 games with Houston Gamblers in 1985.

Year Club	G.	Att.	Cmp.	Pct.	Gain	T.P.	P.I.	Avg.	Att.	Yds.	Avg.	TD.	TD.	Pts.	F.
				PASSING						RUSHING			TOTAL		
1984—Houston USFL	18	*587	*370	63.0	*5219	*44	*26	*8.89	85	493	5.8	5	5	†32	9
1985—Houston USFL	14	*567	*360	*63.5	*4623	*39	19	8.15	28	170	6.1	1	1	6	10
1986—Buffalo NFL	16	480	285	59.4	3593	22	17	7.49	41	199	4.9	0	0	0	7
1987—Buffalo NFL	12	419	250	59.7	2798	19	11	6.68	29	133	4.6	0	0	0	6
USFL Totals—2 Years	32	1154	730	63.3	9842	83	45	8.53	113	663	5.9	6	6	38	19
NFL Totals—2 Year	28	899	535	59.5	6391	41	28	7.11	70	332	4.7	0	0	0	13
Pro Totals—4 Years	60	2053	1265	61.6	16233	124	73	7.91	183	995	5.4	6	6	38	32

†Includes one 2-point conversion.
USFL Quarterback Rating Points: 1984 (98.2), 1985 (97.9). Total—98.1.
NFL Quarterback Rating Points: 1986 (83.3), 1987 (83.8). Total—83.7.
Additional USFL statistics: Caught one pass for minus 13 yards and recovered four fumbles, 1984; caught one pass for three yards and recovered three fumbles, 1985.
Additional NFL statistics: Recovered two fumbles, 1986 and 1987; caught one pass for 35 yards, 1987.
Played in Pro Bowl (NFL All-Star Game) following 1987 season.

JOSEPH WINSTON KELLY
(Joe)
Linebacker—Cincinnati Bengals
Born December 11, 1964, at Sun Valley, Calif.
Height, 6.02. Weight, 227.
High School—Los Angeles, Calif., Jefferson.
Received degree from University of Washington in 1986.
Son of Joe Kelly Sr., former player with Montreal Argonauts (CFL); and nephew of Bob Kelly, tackle with Houston Oilers, Kansas City Chiefs, Cincinnati Bengals and Atlanta Falcons, 1961 through 1964 and 1967 through 1969.

Selected by Cincinnati in 1st round (11th player selected) of 1986 NFL draft.
Signed by Cincinnati Bengals, August 29, 1986.
Granted roster exemption, August 29 through September 2, 1986; activated, September 3, 1986.

Cincinnati NFL, 1986 and 1987.
Games: 1986 (16), 1987 (10). Total—26.
Pro statistics: Intercepted one pass for six yards and recovered one fumble, 1986.

LARRY DEAN KELM
Linebacker—Los Angeles Rams
Born November 29, 1964, at Corpus Christi, Tex.
Height, 6.04. Weight, 226.
High School—Corpus Christi, Tex., Richard King.
Attended Texas A&M University.

Selected by Los Angeles Rams in 4th round (108th player selected) of 1987 NFL draft.
Signed by Los Angeles Rams, July 23, 1987.
Crossed picket line during players' strike, October 14, 1987.
Los Angeles Rams NFL, 1987.
Games: 1987 (12).

MARK ALAN KELSO
Safety—Buffalo Bills
Born July 23, 1963, at Pittsburgh, Pa.
Height, 5.11. Weight, 177.
High School—Pittsburgh, Pa., North Hills.
Attended College of William & Mary.

Selected by Baltimore in 6th round (84th player selected) of 1985 USFL draft.
Selected by Philadelphia in 10th round (261st player selected) of 1985 NFL draft.
Signed by Philadelphia Eagles, July 19, 1985.
Released by Philadelphia Eagles, August 27, 1985; signed as free agent by Buffalo Bills, April 17, 1986.
On injured reserve with knee injury, September 22 through remainder of 1986 season.

		—INTERCEPTIONS—			
Year	Club	G.	No.	Yds.	Avg.TD.
1986—Buffalo NFL		3	None		
1987—Buffalo NFL		12	6	25	4.2 0
Pro Totals—2 Years		15	6	25	4.2 0

Additional pro statistics: Recovered two fumbles for 56 yards and a touchdown, 1987.

JEFFREY ALLAN KEMP
(Jeff)
Quarterback—Seattle Seahawks
Born July 11, 1959, at Santa Ana, Calif.
Height, 6.00. Weight, 201.
High School—Potomac, Md., Winston Churchill.
Received bachelor of arts degree in economics from Dartmouth College in 1981;
and received master's in business administration degree from Pepperdine University in 1986.
Son of Jack Kemp, quarterback with Pittsburgh Steelers, Los Angeles-San Diego Chargers and
Buffalo Bills, 1957, 1960 through 1967 and 1969; and currently Republican Congressman from New York.

Signed as free agent by Los Angeles Rams, May 11, 1981.
Released by Los Angeles Rams, August 31, 1981; re-signed by Rams, September 1, 1981.
On injured reserve with back injury, October 3 through December 1, 1981; activated, December 2, 1981.
On inactive list, September 12 and September 19, 1982.
Granted free agency, February 1, 1986; re-signed by Rams and traded to San Francisco 49ers, May 26, 1986. (This completed deal of April 29, 1986 in which 49ers traded 3rd round pick in 1986 draft to Rams for two 4th round picks in 1986 draft.)
Traded by San Francisco 49ers to Seattle Seahawks for 5th round pick in 1988 draft, May 19, 1987.
Crossed picket line during players' strike, October 14, 1987.
Active for 7 games with Los Angeles Rams in 1982; did not play.

			—PASSING—							—RUSHING—				—TOTAL—		
Year Club	G.	Att.	Cmp.	Pct.	Gain	T.P.	P.I.	Avg.	Att.	Yds.	Avg.	TD.	TD.	Pts.	F.
1981—L.A. Rams NFL	1	6	2	33.3	25	0	1	4.17	2	9	4.5	0	0	0	0
1983—L.A. Rams NFL	4	25	12	48.0	135	1	0	5.40	3	−2	−0.7	0	0	0	2
1984—L.A. Rams NFL	14	284	143	50.4	2021	13	7	7.12	34	153	4.5	1	1	6	8
1985—L.A. Rams NFL	5	38	16	42.1	214	0	1	5.63	5	0	0.0	0	0	0	2
1986—San Francisco NFL	10	200	119	59.5	1554	11	8	7.77	15	49	3.3	0	0	0	3
1987—Seattle NFL	13	33	23	69.7	396	5	1	12.00	5	9	1.8	0	0	0	2
Pro Totals—7 Years	47	586	315	53.8	4345	30	18	7.41	64	218	3.4	1	1	6	17

Quarterback Rating Points: 1981 (7.6), 1983 (77.9), 1984 (78.7), 1985 (49.7), 1986 (85.7), 1987 (137.1). Total—81.9.
Additional pro statistics: Recovered three fumbles and fumbled eight times for minus 16 yards, 1984; recovered one fumble and fumbled three times for minus three yards, 1986; recovered one fumble and fumbled twice for minus eight yards, 1987.
Member of Los Angeles Rams for 1985 Championship Game following 1985 season; did not play.

PERRY COMMODORE KEMP
Wide Receiver—Green Bay Packers
Born December 31, 1961, at Canonsburg, Pa.
Height, 5.11. Weight, 170.
High School—McDonald, Pa., Fort Cherry.
Attended California State College (Pa.).

Selected by Jacksonville in 11th round (208th player selected) of 1984 USFL draft.
Signed by Jacksonville Bulls, January 21, 1984.
Released by Jacksonville Bulls, February 20, 1986; awarded on waivers to Memphis Showboats, February 21, 1986.
Granted free agency when USFL suspended operations, August 7, 1986; signed as free agent by Dallas Cowboys, August 12, 1986.
Granted roster exemption, August 12 through August 22, 1986; activated, August 23, 1986.
Released by Dallas Cowboys, August 26, 1986; signed as free agent by Cleveland Browns, April 22, 1987.
Released by Cleveland Browns, August 25, 1987; signed as free agent replacement player by Cleveland Browns, October 1, 1987.
Released by Cleveland Browns, November 3, 1987; signed as free agent by Green Bay Packers, April 15, 1988.

Year Club	G.	P.C.	Yds.	Avg.	TD.	No.	Yds.	Avg.	TD.	TD.	Pts.	F.
			-PASS RECEIVING-			-PUNT RETURNS-				-TOTAL-		
1984—Jacksonville USFL	18	44	730	16.6	2	3	7	2.3	0	2	12	1
1985—Jacksonville USFL	18	59	915	15.5	4	13	116	8.9	0	4	†26	2
1987—Cleveland NFL	3	12	224	18.7	2			None		2	12	0
USFL Totals—2 Years	36	103	1645	16.0	6	16	123	7.7	0	6	38	3
NFL Totals—1 Year	3	12	224	18.7	2	0	0	0.0	0	2	12	0
Pro Totals—3 Years	39	115	1869	16.3	8	16	123	7.7	0	8	50	3

†Includes one 2-point conversion.
Additional pro statistics: Returned four kickoffs for 84 yards, 1984; recovered one fumble, 1984 and 1985; rushed once for minus one yard, 1985.

MICHAEL LEE KENN
(Mike)
Offensive Tackle—Atlanta Falcons
Born February 9, 1956, at Evanston, Ill.
Height, 6.07. Weight, 277.
High School—Evanston, Ill.
Received bachelor of arts degree in general studies from University of Michigan in 1978.

Named to THE SPORTING NEWS NFL All-Star Team, 1980.
Selected by Atlanta in 1st round (13th player selected) of 1978 NFL draft.
On injured reserve with knee injury, November 18 through remainder of 1985 season.
Atlanta NFL, 1978 through 1987.
Games: 1978 (16), 1979 (16), 1980 (16), 1981 (16), 1982 (9), 1983 (16), 1984 (14), 1985 (11), 1986 (16), 1987 (12). Total—142.
Pro statistics: Recovered two fumbles, 1978 and 1979; recovered three fumbles, 1980; recovered one fumble, 1981 through 1983.
Played in Pro Bowl (NFL All-Star Game) following 1980 through 1984 seasons.

DEREK KENNARD
Guard-Center—Phoenix Cardinals
Born September 9, 1962, at Stockton, Calif.
Height, 6.03. Weight, 285.
High School—Stockton, Calif., Edison.
Attended University of Nevada at Reno.

Selected by Los Angeles in 3rd round (52nd player selected) of 1984 USFL draft.
Signed by Los Angeles Express, March 22, 1984.
Granted roster exemption, March 22, 1984; activated, April 13, 1984.
On developmental squad, April 13 through April 27, 1984; activated, April 28, 1984.
Selected by St. Louis in 2nd round (45th player selected) of 1984 NFL supplemental draft.
On developmental squad, March 15 through April 12, 1985; activated, April 13, 1985.
Released by Los Angeles Express, August 1, 1985; re-signed by Express, August 2, 1985.
Released by Los Angeles Express, April 29, 1986; signed by St. Louis Cardinals, May 29, 1986.
Franchise transferred to Phoenix, March 15, 1988.
On developmental squad for 2 games with Los Angeles Express in 1984.
On developmental squad for 4 games with Los Angeles Express in 1985.
Los Angeles USFL, 1984 and 1985; St. Louis NFL, 1986 and 1987.
Games: 1984 (6), 1985 (14), 1986 (15), 1987 (12). Total USFL—20. Total NFL—27. Total Pro—47.
USFL statistics: Returned one kickoff for no yards and recovered one fumble, 1985.
NFL statistics: Fumbled twice for minus four yards, 1987.

WILLIAM PATRICK KENNEY
(Bill)
Quarterback—Kansas City Chiefs
Born January 20, 1955, at San Francisco, Calif.
Height, 6.04. Weight, 207.
High School—San Clemente, Calif.
Attended Arizona State University, Saddleback Community College and received bachelor of science degree in business management from University of Northern Colorado in 1978.
Son of Charles Kenney, guard with San Francisco 49ers, 1947.

Selected by Miami in 12th round (333rd player selected) of 1978 NFL draft.
Traded by Miami Dolphins to Washington Redskins for 6th round pick in 1979 draft, August 1, 1978.
Released by Washington Redskins, August 21, 1978; signed as free agent by Kansas City Chiefs, January 19, 1979.
On injured reserve with broken thumb, August 28 through October 5, 1984; activated, October 6, 1984.
Active for 16 games with Kansas City Chiefs in 1979; did not play.

Year Club	G.	Att.	Cmp.	Pct.	Gain	T.P.	P.I.	Avg.	Att.	Yds.	Avg.	TD.	TD.	Pts.	F.
1980—Kansas City NFL	3	69	37	53.6	542	5	2	7.86	8	8	1.0	0	0	0	1
1981—Kansas City NFL	13	274	147	53.6	1983	9	16	7.24	24	89	3.7	1	1	6	4
1982—Kansas City NFL	7	169	95	56.2	1192	7	6	7.05	13	40	3.1	0	0	0	3
1983—Kansas City NFL	16	*603	*346	57.4	4348	24	18	7.21	23	59	2.6	3	3	18	7
1984—Kansas City NFL	9	282	151	53.5	2098	15	10	7.44	9	—8	—0.9	0	0	0	8
1985—Kansas City NFL	16	338	181	53.6	2536	17	9	7.50	14	1	0.1	1	1	6	6
1986—Kansas City NFL	15	308	161	52.3	1922	13	11	6.24	18	0	0.0	0	0	0	5
1987—Kansas City NFL	11	273	154	56.4	2107	15	9	7.72	12	—2	—0.2	0	0	0	8
Pro Totals—9 Years	90	2316	1272	54.9	16728	105	81	7.22	121	187	1.5	5	5	30	42

Quarterback Rating Points: 1980 (91.4), 1981 (63.8), 1982 (77.0), 1983 (80.8), 1984 (80.7), 1985 (83.6), 1986 (70.8), 1987 (85.8). Total—78.3.

Additional pro statistics: Fumbled once for minus six yards, 1980; fumbled four times for minus two yards, 1981; recovered two fumbles, 1982; caught one pass for no yards, 1983 and 1986; recovered four fumbles, 1983; recovered three fumbles and fumbled eight times for minus 34 yards, 1984; recovered five fumbles and fumbled six times for minus 18 yards, 1985; recovered one fumble and fumbled five times for minus six yards, 1986; recovered two fumbles and fumbled eight times for minus eight yards, 1987.

Played in Pro Bowl (NFL All-Star Game) following 1983 season.

CRAWFORD FRANCIS KER
Guard—Dallas Cowboys
Born May 5, 1962, at Philadelphia, Pa.
Height, 6.03. Weight, 285.
High School—Dunedin, Fla.
Attended Arizona Western College and University of Florida.

Selected by Tampa Bay in 1985 USFL territorial draft.
Selected by Dallas in 3rd round (76th player selected) of 1985 NFL draft.
Signed by Dallas Cowboys, July 12, 1985.
On injured reserve with back injury, October 23 through remainder of 1985 season.
Dallas NFL, 1985 through 1987.
Games: 1985 (5), 1986 (16), 1987 (12). Total—33.

TYRONE P. KEYS
Defensive End—San Diego Chargers
Born October 24, 1959, at Brookhaven, Miss.
Height, 6.07. Weight, 267.
High School—Jackson, Miss., Callaway.
Received bachelor of science degree in physical education from Mississippi State University.

Selected by New York Jets in 5th round (113th player selected) of 1981 NFL draft.
Signed as free agent by British Columbia Lions, May 20, 1981.
On reserve list, July 12 through July 18, 1981; activated, July 19, 1981.
On reserve list, July 25 through August 2, 1981; activated, August 3, 1981.
On reserve list, August 16 through September 12, 1981; activated, September 13, 1981.
On reserve list, September 21 through remainder of 1981 season.
On reserve list, July 2 through July 17, 1982; activated, July 18, 1982.
On reserve list, August 15 through August 31, 1982; activated, September 1, 1982.
On reserve list, September 12 through September 18, 1982; activated, September 19, 1982.
On reserve list, October 17 through October 23, 1982; activated, October 24, 1982.
Traded by British Columbia Lions to Toronto Argonauts for defensive back Jo Jo Heath, April 25, 1983.
Released by Toronto Argonauts, July 2, 1983.
NFL rights traded by New York Jets to Chicago Bears for 5th round pick in 1985 draft, July 13, 1983.
Signed by Chicago Bears, July 10, 1983.
Released by Chicago Bears, September 1, 1986; awarded on waivers to Tampa Bay Buccaneers, September 2, 1986.
On injured reserve with abdomen injury, December 12 through remainder of 1986 season.
On injured reserve with back injury, November 3 through November 9, 1987.
Released by Tampa Bay Buccaneers, November 10, 1987; signed as free agent by Miami Dolphins, March 10, 1988.
Released by Miami Dolphins, March 23, 1988; signed as free agent by San Diego Chargers, May 12, 1988.
British Columbia CFL, 1981 and 1982; Chicago NFL, 1983 through 1985; Tampa Bay NFL, 1986 and 1987.
Games: 1981 (5), 1982 (10), 1983 (14), 1984 (15), 1985 (16), 1986 (14), 1987 (3). Total CFL—15. Total NFL—62. Total Pro—77.
Played in NFC Championship Game following 1984 and 1985 seasons.
Played in NFL Championship Game following 1985 season.

MAX JOHN KIDD
(Known by middle name.)
Punter—Buffalo Bills
Born August 22, 1961, at Springfield, Ill.
Height, 6.03. Weight, 208.
High School—Findlay, O.
Received bachelor of science degree in industrial engineering and management science from Northwestern University in 1984.

Selected by Chicago in 1984 USFL territorial draft.
Selected by Buffalo in 5th round (128th player selected) of 1984 NFL draft.
Signed by Buffalo Bills, June 1, 1984.

Year	Club	G.	PUNTING No.	Avg.	Blk.
1984—Buffalo NFL		16	88	42.0	2
1985—Buffalo NFL		16	92	41.5	0
1986—Buffalo NFL		16	75	40.4	0
1987—Buffalo NFL		12	64	39.0	0
Pro Totals—4 Years		60	319	40.8	2

Additional pro statistics: Rushed once for no yards and recovered one fumble, 1986; attempted one pass with no completions, 1987.

BLAIR ARMSTRONG KIEL
Quarterback—Green Bay Packers
Born November 29, 1961, at Columbus, Ind.
Height, 6.00. Weight, 200.
High School—Columbus, Ind., East.
Received degree in marketing from University of Notre Dame in 1984.

Selected by Chicago in 1984 USFL territorial draft.
Selected by Tampa Bay in 11th round (281st player selected) of 1984 NFL draft.
Signed by Tampa Bay Buccaneers, June 5, 1984.
On non-football injury list with ulcerative colitis, November 13 through remainder of 1984 season.
On non-football injury with Crohn's Disease, August 12 through September 30, 1985.
Released by Tampa Bay Buccaneers, October 1, 1985; signed as free agent by Indianapolis Colts, February 13, 1986.
Released by Indianapolis Colts, September 1, 1986; re-signed by Colts, September 16, 1986.
Crossed picket line during players' strike, October 7, 1987.
Released by Indianapolis Colts, November 24, 1987; signed as free agent by Green Bay Packers, May 10, 1988.

Year	Club	G.	Att.	Cmp.	Pct.	PASSING Gain	T.P.	P.I.	Avg.	Att.	RUSHING Yds.	Avg.	TD.	TD.	TOTAL Pts.	F.
1984—Tampa Bay NFL		10				None					None			0	0	0
1986—Indianapolis NFL		3	25	11	44.0	236	2	0	9.44	3	20	6.7	0	0	0	0
1987—Indianapolis NFL		4	33	17	51.5	195	1	3	5.91	4	30	7.5	0	0	0	0
Pro Totals—3 Years		17	58	28	48.3	431	3	3	7.43	7	50	7.1	0	0	0	0

Quarterback Rating Points: 1986 (104.8), 1987 (41.9). Total—69.0.
Additional pro statistics: Punted five times for 38.0 average, 1986; punted 12 times for a 36.7 average, 1987.

JAMIE KIMMEL
Linebacker—Los Angeles Raiders
Born March 28, 1962, at Johnson City, N.Y.
Height, 6.03. Weight, 235.
High School—Conklin, N.Y., Susquehanna Valley.
Attended Syracuse University.

Selected by New Jersey in 1985 USFL territorial draft.
Selected by Los Angeles Raiders in 4th round (107th player selected) of 1985 NFL draft.
Signed by Los Angeles Raiders, July 22, 1985.
On injured reserve with hamstring injury, August 27 through entire 1985 season.
Crossed picket line during players' strike, October 2, 1987.
Los Angeles Raiders NFL, 1986 and 1987.
Games: 1986 (16), 1987 (15). Total—31.
Pro statistics: Recovered one fumble, 1987.

ALFRED TERANCE KINARD
(Terry)
Safety—New York Giants
Born November 24, 1959, at Bitburg, West Germany.
Height, 6.01. Weight, 200.
High School—Sumter, S.C.
Attended Clemson University.

Named as defensive back on THE SPORTING NEWS College All-America Team, 1982.
Selected by Washington in 1983 USFL territorial draft.
Selected by New York Giants in 1st round (10th player selected) of 1983 NFL draft.
Signed by New York Giants, May 17, 1983.
On injured reserve with knee injury, December 9 through remainder of 1986 season.

Year	Club	G.	INTERCEPTIONS No.	Yds.	Avg.	TD.
1983—N.Y. Giants NFL		16	3	49	16.3	0
1984—N.Y. Giants NFL		15	2	29	14.5	0
1985—N.Y. Giants NFL		16	5	100	20.0	0
1986—N.Y. Giants NFL		14	4	52	13.0	0
1987—N.Y. Giants NFL		12	5	163	32.6	1
Pro Totals—5 Years		73	19	393	20.7	1

Additional pro statistics: Recovered one fumble for 10 yards, 1983; returned one punt for no yards and fumbled once, 1984; recovered one fumble, 1984 and 1985; recovered two fumbles, 1986.

EMANUEL KING
Linebacker—Cincinnati Bengals
Born August 15, 1963, at Leroy, Ala.
Height, 6.04. Weight, 251.
High School—Leroy, Ala.
Attended University of Alabama.

Selected by Birmingham in 1985 USFL territorial draft.
Selected by Cincinnati in 1st round (25th player selected) of 1985 NFL draft.
Signed by Cincinnati Bengals, May 30, 1985.
Cincinnati NFL, 1985 through 1987.
Games: 1985 (16), 1986 (16), 1987 (12). Total—44.
Pro statistics: Recovered one fumble, 1985; recovered one fumble for one yard, 1986.

LINDEN KEITH KING
Linebacker—Los Angeles Raiders
Born June 28, 1955, at Memphis, Tenn.
Height, 6.04. Weight, 250.
High School—Colorado Springs, Colo., Air Academy.
Attended Colorado State University.

Selected by San Diego in 3rd round (77th player selected) of 1977 NFL draft.
On injured reserve, September 12 through 1977 season.
On injured reserve with ankle injury, November 5, 1980, through January 9, 1981; activated, January 10, 1981.
Released by San Diego Chargers, July 25, 1986; signed as free agent by Los Angeles Raiders, August 2, 1986.
San Diego NFL, 1978 through 1985; Los Angeles Raiders NFL, 1986 and 1987.
Games: 1978 (14), 1979 (16), 1980 (5), 1981 (16), 1982 (9), 1983 (16), 1984 (16), 1985 (16), 1986 (16), 1987 (12).
Total—136.
Pro statistics: Intercepted one pass for three yards and recovered one fumble for 14 yards, 1978; recovered two fumbles, 1979, 1983 and 1984; intercepted one pass for 28 yards, 1981; recovered one fumble, 1982 and 1987; intercepted one pass for 19 yards, 1983; intercepted two passes for 52 yards and fumbled once, 1984; intercepted two passes for eight yards, 1985; intercepted one pass for eight yards, 1987.
Played in AFC Championship Game following 1980 and 1981 seasons.

LARRY D. KINNEBREW
Running Back—Cincinnati Bengals
Born June 11, 1959, at Rome, Ga.
Height, 6.01. Weight, 258.
High School—Rome, Ga., East.
Attended Tennessee State University.

Selected by Cincinnati in 6th round (165th player selected) of 1983 NFL draft.
On injured reserve with broken hand, September 24 through October 25, 1985; activated, October 26, 1985.

| | | —————RUSHING————— | | | | PASS RECEIVING | | | | —TOTAL— | | |
Year Club	G.	Att.	Yds.	Avg.	TD.	P.C.	Yds.	Avg.	TD.	TD.	Pts.	F.
1983—Cincinnati NFL	16	39	156	4.0	3	2	4	2.0	0	3	18	3
1984—Cincinnati NFL	16	154	623	4.0	9	19	159	8.4	1	10	60	4
1985—Cincinnati NFL	12	170	714	4.2	9	22	187	8.5	1	10	60	4
1986—Cincinnati NFL	16	131	519	4.0	8	13	136	10.5	1	9	54	6
1987—Cincinnati NFL	11	145	570	3.9	8	9	114	12.7	0	8	48	1
Pro Totals—5 Years	71	639	2582	4.0	37	65	600	9.2	3	40	240	18

Additional pro statistics: Recovered one fumble, 1983, 1985 and 1986; returned one kickoff for seven yards, 1984.

RANDALL SCOTT KIRK
(Randy)
Linebacker—San Diego Chargers
Born December 27, 1964, at San Jose, Calif.
Height, 6.02. Weight, 235.
High School—San Jose, Calif., Bellarmine College Prep.
Attended De Anza College and San Diego State University.

Signed as free agent by New York Giants, May 10, 1987.
Released by New York Giants, August 31, 1987; signed as free agent replacement player by San Diego Chargers, September 24, 1987.
San Diego NFL, 1987.
Games: 1987 (13).

JOSEPH EDWARD KLECKO
(Joe)
Defensive Tackle-Defensive End—Indianapolis Colts
Born October 15, 1953, at Chester, Pa.
Height, 6.03. Weight, 263.
High School—Chester, Pa., St. James.
Received bachelor of arts degree in history from Temple University in 1977.

Named to THE SPORTING NEWS NFL All-Star Team, 1981.
Selected by New York Jets in 6th round (144th player selected) of 1977 NFL draft.
On injured reserve with knee injury, November 26, 1982 through January 4, 1983; activated, January 5, 1983.

On injured reserve with knee injury, December 17 through remainder of 1986 season.
On physically unable to perform/reserve with knee injury, August 31 through November 13, 1987; activated, November 14, 1987.
Crossed picket line during players' strike, October 2, 1987.
Released by New York Jets, February 18, 1988; signed as free agent by Indianapolis Colts, April 22, 1988.
Played semi-pro football with Ridley Township Green Knights, 1971 and 1972.
New York Jets NFL, 1977 through 1987.
Games: 1977 (13), 1978 (16), 1979 (16), 1980 (15), 1981 (16), 1982 (2), 1983 (16), 1984 (12), 1985 (16), 1986 (11), 1987 (7). Total—140.
Pro statistics: Recovered one fumble, 1978, 1983, 1985 and 1987; recovered two fumbles, 1981 and 1984.
Played in AFC Championship Game following 1982 season.
Played in Pro Bowl (NFL All-Star Game) following 1981 and 1983 through 1985 seasons.

VICTOR K. KLEVER
(Rocky)
Tight End—New York Jets
Born July 10, 1959, at Portland, Ore.
Height, 6.03. Weight, 230.
High School—Anchorage, Alaska, West.
Received degree in business management from University of Montana in 1982.

Selected by New York Jets in 9th round (247th player selected) of 1982 NFL draft.
On injured reserve with broken hand, August 24 through entire 1982 season.
Released by New York Jets, August 29, 1983; re-signed by Jets after clearing procedural waivers, November 3, 1983.

		—PASS RECEIVING—			
Year Club	G.	P.C.	Yds.	Avg.	TD.
1983—New York Jets NFL....	5		None		
1984—New York Jets NFL....	16	3	29	9.7	1
1985—New York Jets NFL....	16	14	183	13.1	2
1986—New York Jets NFL....	16	15	150	10.0	0
1987—New York Jets NFL....	12	14	152	10.9	2
Pro Totals—5 Years............	65	46	514	11.2	3

Additional pro statistics: Returned one kickoff for three yards and recovered one fumble, 1985; returned five kickoffs for 85 yards, 1987.

JOHN KLINGEL
Defensive End—Philadelphia Eagles
Born December 21, 1963, at Marion, O.
Height, 6.03. Weight, 267.
High School—Cardington, O., Lincoln.
Attended Eastern Kentucky University.

Signed as free agent by Philadelphia Eagles, May 1, 1987.
On injured reserve with ankle and back injuries, September 6 through November 26, 1987; activated, November 27, 1987.
Philadelphia NFL, 1987.
Games: 1987 (5).
Pro statistics: Recovered one fumble, 1987.

BRUCE DONALD KLOSTERMANN
Linebacker—Denver Broncos
Born April 17, 1963, at Dubuque, Ia.
Height, 6.04. Weight, 225.
High School—Dyersville, Ia., Beckman.
Attended Waldorf College, University of Iowa and received bachelor of science degree in agricultural business from South Dakota State University in 1986.

Selected by Denver in 8th round (217th player selected) of 1986 NFL draft.
Signed by Denver Broncos, July 14, 1986.
On injured reserve with knee injury, August 25 through entire 1986 season.
Denver NFL, 1987.
Games: 1987 (9).
Played in AFC Championship Game following 1987 season.
Played in NFL Championship Game following 1987 season.

SHAWN MATT KNIGHT
Defensive End—New Orleans Saints
Born June 4, 1964, at Provo, Utah.
Height, 6.06. Weight, 290.
High School—Sparks, Nev., Edward C. Reed.
Attended Brigham Young University.

Selected by New Orleans in 1st round (11th player selected) of 1987 NFL draft.
Signed by New Orleans Saints, August 31, 1987.
Granted roster exemption, August 31 and September 1, 1987; activated, September 2, 1987.
On injured reserve with ankle injury, December 26 through remainder of 1987 season.
New Orleans NFL, 1987.
Games: 1987 (10).

GREGORY MICHAEL KOCH

Name pronounced Cook.

(Greg)
Offensive Tackle—Minnesota Vikings

Born June 14, 1955, at Bethesda, Md.
Height, 6.04. Weight, 276.
High School—Houston, Tex., Spring Woods.
Attended University of Arkansas.

Selected by Green Bay in 2nd round (39th player selected) of 1977 NFL draft.
Left Green Bay Packers camp voluntarily, August 19 through September 4, 1985; activated, September 5, 1985.
Released by Green Bay Packers, August 4, 1986; signed as free agent by Miami Dolphins, August 11, 1986.
Granted free agency, February 1, 1987; re-signed by Dolphins, September 6, 1987.
Granted roster exemption, September 6 through September 18, 1987; activated, September 19, 1987.
Traded by Miami Dolphins to Minnesota Vikings for 6th round pick in 1988 draft and 1989 draft choice, October 20, 1987.
Green Bay NFL, 1977 through 1985; Miami NFL, 1986; Miami (1)-Minnesota (9) NFL, 1987.
Games: 1977 (14), 1978 (16), 1979 (16), 1980 (16), 1981 (16), 1982 (9), 1983 (15), 1984 (15), 1985 (16), 1986 (16), 1987 (10). Total—159.
Pro statistics: Recovered one fumble, 1985.
Played in NFC Championship Game following 1987 season.

MARKUS KOCH
Defensive End—Washington Redskins

Born February 13, 1963, at Niedermarsberg, W. Germany.
Height, 6.05. Weight, 275.
High School—Kitchener, Ontario, Can., Eastwood Collegiate.
Attended Boise State University.

Selected by Washington in 2nd round (30th player selected) of 1986 NFL draft.
Signed by Washington Redskins, July 22, 1986.
Washington NFL, 1986 and 1987.
Games: 1986 (16), 1987 (12). Total—28.
Played in NFC Championship Game following 1986 and 1987 seasons.
Played in NFL Championship Game following 1987 season.

PETER ALAN KOCH
(Pete)
Defensive Tackle—Kansas City Chiefs

Born January 23, 1962, at Nassau County, N.Y.
Height, 6.06. Weight, 275.
High School—New Hyde Park, N.Y., Memorial.
Attended University of Maryland.

Brother of Larry Koch, pitcher in St. Louis Cardinals' organization, 1967, 1968, 1970 and 1971.
Selected by Washington in 1984 USFL territorial draft.
Selected by Cincinnati in 1st round (16th player selected) of 1984 NFL draft.
Signed by Cincinnati Bengals, July 30, 1984.
Released by Cincinnati Bengals, September 2, 1985; awarded on waivers to Kansas City Chiefs, September 3, 1985.
On injured reserve with knee injury, November 18 through remainder of 1987 season.
Cincinnati NFL, 1984; Kansas City NFL, 1985 through 1987.
Games: 1984 (16), 1985 (16), 1986 (16), 1987 (6). Total—54.

JOE KOHLBRAND
Linebacker—New Orleans Saints

Born March 18, 1963, at Merritt Island, Fla.
Height, 6.04. Weight, 242.
High School—Merritt Island, Fla.
Attended University of Miami (Fla.).

Selected by New Orleans in 8th round (206th player selected) of 1985 NFL draft.
Signed by New Orleans Saints, July 25, 1985.
On injured reserve with knee injury, August 28 through October 3, 1985; activated after clearing procedural waivers, October 4, 1985.
New Orleans NFL, 1985 through 1987.
Games: 1985 (12), 1986 (16), 1987 (12). Total—40.

LAWRENCE VINCENT KOLIC
Linebacker—Miami Dolphins

Born August 31, 1963, at Cleveland, O.
Height, 6.01. Weight, 238.
High School—Smithville, O.
Attended Ohio State University.

Selected by Miami in 7th round (193rd player selected) of 1986 NFL draft.
Selected by Arizona in 6th round (39th player selected) of 1986 USFL draft.
Signed by Miami Dolphins, July 11, 1986.
On injured reserve with torn groin, August 25 through December 12, 1986; activated, December 13, 1986.
Miami NFL, 1986 and 1987.
Games: 1986 (2), 1987 (7). Total—9.
Pro statistics: Recovered one fumble for four yards, 1986.

STEVE KORTE
Name pronounced Court.
Center—New Orleans Saints
Born January 15, 1960, at Denver, Colo.
Height, 6.02. Weight, 260.
High School—Littleton, Colo., Arapahoe.
Received degree in physical education from University of Arkansas.
Named as guard on THE SPORTING NEWS College All-America Team, 1982.
Selected by Birmingham in 2nd round (20th player selected) of 1983 USFL draft.
Selected by New Orleans in 2nd round (38th player selected) of 1983 NFL draft.
Signed by New Orleans Saints, June 20, 1983.
USFL rights traded by Birmingham Stallions to Memphis Showboats for offensive tackle Phil McKinnely, January 22, 1985.
On injured reserve with knee injury, September 25 through October 24, 1985; activated, October 25, 1985.
Crossed picket line during players' strike, September 23, 1987.
On injured reserve with shoulder injury, September 7 through November 27, 1987; activated, November 28, 1987.
New Orleans NFL, 1983 through 1987.
Games: 1983 (16), 1984 (15), 1985 (12), 1986 (16), 1987 (3). Total—62.
Pro statistics: Recovered one fumble in end zone for a touchdown, 1983; recovered one fumble, 1984 and 1986; fumbled once for minus 18 yards, 1985.

BERNIE KOSAR
Quarterback—Cleveland Browns
Born November 25, 1963, at Boardman, O.
Height, 6.05. Weight, 210.
High School—Boardman, O.
Received degree in finance and economics from University of Miami (Fla.) in 1985.
Selected by Cleveland in 1st round of NFL supplemental draft, July 2, 1985.
Signed by Cleveland Browns, July 2, 1985.

Year	Club	G.	Att.	Cmp.	Pct.	Gain	T.P.	P.I.	Avg.	Att.	Yds.	Avg.	TD.	TD.	Pts.	F.
					PASSING						RUSHING			TOTAL		
1985—Cleveland NFL		12	248	124	50.0	1578	8	7	6.36	26	—12	—0.5	1	1	6	14
1986—Cleveland NFL		16	531	310	58.4	3854	17	10	7.26	24	19	0.8	0	0	0	7
1987—Cleveland NFL		12	389	241	62.0	3033	22	9	7.80	15	22	1.5	1	1	6	2
Pro Totals—3 Years		40	1168	675	57.8	8465	47	26	7.25	65	29	0.4	2	2	12	23

Quarterback Rating Points: 1985 (69.3), 1986 (83.8), 1987 (95.4). Total—84.6.
Additional pro statistics: Recovered two fumbles and fumbled 14 times for minus 25 yards, 1985; caught one pass for one yard, recovered three fumbles and fumbled seven times for minus 15 yards, 1986; recovered one fumble and fumbled twice for minus three yards, 1987.
Played in AFC Championship Game following 1986 and 1987 seasons.
Played in Pro Bowl (NFL All-Star Game) following 1987 season.

GARY STUART KOWALSKI
Guard-Offensive Tackle—San Diego Chargers
Born July 2, 1960, at New Haven, Conn.
Height, 6.06. Weight, 273.
High School—Clinton, Conn., Morgan.
Attended Boston College.
Selected by Boston in 1983 USFL territorial draft.
Selected by Los Angeles Rams in 6th round (144th player selected) of 1983 NFL draft.
Signed by Los Angeles Rams, June 3, 1983.
On injured reserve with knee injury, August 28 through entire 1984 season.
Traded with 5th round pick in 1986 draft by Los Angeles Rams to San Diego Chargers for wide receiver Bobby Duckworth, September 2, 1985.
On injured reserve with knee injury, December 7 through remainder of 1985 season.
Los Angeles Rams NFL, 1983; San Diego NFL, 1985 through 1987.
Games: 1983 (15), 1985 (13), 1986 (16), 1987 (12). Total—56.
Pro statistics: Recovered one fumble, 1987.

BRUCE KOZERSKI
Guard—Cincinnati Bengals
Born April 2, 1962, at Plains, Pa.
Height, 6.04. Weight, 275.
High School—Wilkes-Barre, Pa., James M. Coughlin.
Attended Holy Cross College.
Selected by Houston in 12th round (245th player selected) of 1984 USFL draft.
Selected by Cincinnati in 9th round (231st player selected) of 1984 NFL draft.
Signed by Cincinnati Bengals, June 10, 1984.
On injured reserve with pinched neck, November 14 through December 10, 1987; activated, December 11, 1987.
Cincinnati NFL, 1984 through 1987.
Games: 1984 (16), 1985 (14), 1986 (16), 1987 (8). Total—54.
Pro statistics: Recovered one fumble, 1987.

GREG JOHN KRAGEN
Nose Tackle—Denver Broncos
Born March 4, 1962, at Chicago, Ill.
Height, 6.03. Weight, 245.
High School—Pleasanton, Calif., Amador.
Attended Utah State University.

Selected by Oklahoma in 15th round (296th player selected) of 1984 USFL draft.
Signed as free agent by Denver Broncos, May 2, 1984.
Released by Denver Broncos, August 27, 1984; re-signed by Broncos, January 20, 1985.
Denver NFL, 1985 through 1987.
Games: 1985 (16), 1986 (16), 1987 (12). Total—44.
Pro statistics: Recovered three fumbles, 1986; recovered one fumble, 1987.
Played in AFC Championship Game following 1986 and 1987 seasons.
Played in NFL Championship Game following 1986 and 1987 seasons.

THOMAS FRANCIS KRAMER
(Tommy)
Quarterback—Minnesota Vikings
Born March 7, 1955, at San Antonio, Tex.
Height, 6.02. Weight, 192.
High School—San Antonio, Tex., Robert E. Lee.
Received bachelor of business administration degree from Rice University.
Son of Colonel John J. Kramer, head coach at Texas Lutheran College, 1953 through 1958.

Led NFL quarterback in passing with 92.6 points in 1986.
Selected by Minnesota in 1st round (27th player selected) of 1977 NFL draft.
On injured reserve with knee injury, September 20 through remainder of 1983 season.

| | | | | | | | | | | | RUSHING | | | TOTAL | | |
Year	Club	G.	Att.	Cmp.	Pct.	Gain	T.P.	P.I.	Avg.	Att.	Yds.	Avg.	TD.	TD.	Pts.	F.
1977—Minnesota NFL		6	57	30	52.6	425	5	4	7.46	10	3	0.3	0	0	0	3
1978—Minnesota NFL		4	16	5	31.3	50	0	1	3.13	1	10	10.0	0	0	0	0
1979—Minnesota NFL		16	566	315	55.7	3397	23	24	6.00	32	138	4.3	1	1	6	9
1980—Minnesota NFL		15	522	299	57.3	3582	19	23	6.86	31	115	3.7	1	1	6	2
1981—Minnesota NFL		14	593	322	54.3	3912	26	24	6.60	10	13	1.3	0	0	0	8
1982—Minnesota NFL		9	308	176	57.1	2037	15	12	6.61	21	77	3.7	3	3	18	3
1983—Minnesota NFL		3	82	55	67.1	550	3	4	6.71	8	3	0.4	0	0	0	2
1984—Minnesota NFL		9	236	124	52.5	1678	9	10	7.11	15	9	0.6	0	1	6	10
1985—Minnesota NFL		15	506	277	54.7	3522	19	⋆26	6.96	27	54	2.0	0	0	0	9
1986—Minnesota NFL		13	372	208	55.9	3000	24	10	8.06	23	48	2.1	1	1	6	7
1987—Minnesota NFL		6	81	40	49.4	452	4	3	5.58	10	44	4.4	2	2	12	2
Pro Totals—11 Years		110	3339	1851	55.4	22605	147	141	6.77	188	514	2.7	8	9	54	55

Quarterback Rating Points: 1977 (77.2), 1978 (15.0), 1979 (69.7), 1980 (72.1), 1981 (72.8), 1982 (77.3), 1983 (77.8), 1984 (70.6), 1985 (67.8), 1986 (92.6), 1987 (67.5). Total—73.6.

Additional pro statistics: Fumbled three times for minus three yards, 1977; ran three yards with lateral on pass reception and fumbled nine times for minus six yards, 1979; recovered two fumbles, 1979 and 1980; recovered three fumbles, 1981; recovered one fumble and fumbled three times for minus 21 yards, 1982; recovered one fumble, 1983; caught one pass for 20 yards and a touchdown, recovered three fumbles and fumbled 10 times for minus five yards, 1984; fumbled nine times for minus 16 yards, 1985; recovered three fumbles and fumbled seven times for minus three yards, 1986.

Member of Minnesota Vikings for NFC Championship Game following 1977 and 1987 seasons; did not play.
Played in Pro Bowl (NFL All-Star Game) following 1986 season.

RICHARD BARRY KRAUSS
(Known by middle name.)
Linebacker—Indianapolis Colts
Born March 17, 1957, at Pompano Beach, Fla.
Height, 6.03. Weight, 269.
High School—Pompano Beach, Fla.
Received bachelor of science degree in education from University of Alabama.

Named as linebacker on THE SPORTING NEWS College All-America Team, 1978.
Selected by Baltimore in 1st round (6th player selected) of 1979 NFL draft.
Franchise transferred to Indianapolis, March 31, 1984.
On injured reserve with knee injury, September 29 through remainder of 1986 season.
Baltimore NFL, 1979 through 1983; Indianapolis NFL, 1984 through 1987.
Games: 1979 (15), 1980 (16), 1981 (16), 1982 (9), 1983 (16), 1984 (16), 1985 (16), 1986 (4), 1987 (12). Total—120.
Pro statistics: Recovered two fumbles, 1979, 1981, 1983, 1985 and 1987; recovered one fumble, 1980 and 1986; intercepted one pass for 10 yards, 1981; caught one pass for five yards and a touchdown, 1982; rushed once for minus one yard, 1983; intercepted three passes for 20 yards, recovered two fumbles for minus five yards and fumbled once, 1984; intercepted one pass for no yards, 1985.

RICH KRAYNAK
Linebacker—Atlanta Falcons
Born January 20, 1961, at Phoenixville, Pa.
Height, 6.01. Weight, 230.
High School—Phoenixville, Pa.
Attended University of Pittsburgh.

Selected by Philadelphia in 8th round (93rd player selected) of 1983 USFL draft.

Selected by Philadelphia in 8th round (201st player selected) of 1983 NFL draft.
Signed by Philadelphia Eagles, May 25, 1983.
On injured reserve with finger injury, October 15 through remainder of 1986 season.
Released by Philadelphia Eagles, September 6, 1987; signed as free agent replacement player by Atlanta Falcons, October 1, 1987.
On injured reserve with ankle injury, October 19 through November 16, 1987; activated, November 17, 1987.
Philadelphia NFL, 1983 through 1986; Atlanta NFL, 1987.
Games: 1983 (16), 1984 (14), 1985 (16), 1986 (6), 1987 (9). Total—61.
Pro statistics: Recovered one fumble, 1983; returned blocked punt eight yards for a touchdown, 1984; intercepted one pass for 26 yards, 1985.

MARK KREROWICZ
Guard—New York Jets
Born March 1, 1963, at Toledo, O.
Height, 6.04. Weight, 282.
High School—Toledo, O., St. John's.
Attended Ohio State University.

Selected by New Jersey in 1985 USFL territorial draft.
Selected by Cleveland in 6th round (147th player selected) of 1985 NFL draft.
Signed by Cleveland Browns, July 15, 1985.
Released by Cleveland Browns, October 19, 1985; signed as free agent by Buffalo Bills, May 6, 1986.
Left Buffalo Bills camp voluntarily and released, July 19, 1986; signed as free agent replacement player by Cleveland Browns, September 24, 1987.
Released by Cleveland Browns, October 19, 1987; signed as free agent by New York Jets, April 15, 1988.
Active for 6 games with Cleveland Browns in 1985; did not play.
Cleveland NFL, 1985 and 1987.
Games: 1987 (3).

DAVID M. KRIEG
Name pronounced Craig.
(Dave)
Quarterback—Seattle Seahawks
Born October 20, 1958, at Iola, Wis.
Height, 6.01. Weight, 196.
High School—Schofield, Wis., D.C. Everest.
Received bachelor of science degree in marketing management from Milton College in 1980.

Signed as free agent by Seattle Seahawks, May 6, 1980.

Year Club	G.	Att.	Cmp.	Pct.	Gain	T.P.	P.I.	Avg.	Att.	Yds.	Avg.	TD.	TD.	Pts.	F.
1980—Seattle NFL	1	2	0	0.0	0	0	0	0.00		None			0	0	0
1981—Seattle NFL	7	112	64	57.1	843	7	5	7.53	11	56	5.1	1	1	6	4
1982—Seattle NFL	3	78	49	62.8	501	2	2	6.42	6	—3	—0.5	0	0	0	5
1983—Seattle NFL	9	243	147	60.5	2139	18	11	8.80	16	55	3.4	2	2	12	10
1984—Seattle NFL	16	480	276	57.5	3671	32	*24	7.65	46	186	4.0	3	3	18	11
1985—Seattle NFL	16	532	285	53.6	3602	27	20	6.77	35	121	3.5	1	1	6	11
1986—Seattle NFL	15	375	225	60.0	2921	21	11	7.79	35	122	3.5	1	1	6	10
1987—Seattle NFL	12	294	178	60.5	2131	23	15	7.25	36	155	4.3	2	2	12	11
Pro Totals—8 Years	79	2116	1224	57.8	15808	130	88	7.47	185	692	3.7	10	10	60	62

Quarterback Rating Points: 1980 (39.6), 1981 (83.3), 1982 (79.0), 1983 (95.0), 1984 (83.3), 1985 (76.2), 1986 (91.0), 1987 (87.6). Total—84.2.
Additional pro statistics: Recovered one fumble and fumbled twice for minus 14 yards, 1982; caught one pass for 11 yards and recovered two fumbles, 1983; recovered three fumbles and fumbled 11 times for minus 24 yards, 1984; recovered three fumbles and fumbled 11 times for minus two yards, 1985; recovered one fumble and fumbled 10 times for minus five yards, 1986; recovered five fumbles and fumbled 11 times for minus two yards, 1987.
Played in AFC Championship Game following 1983 season.
Played in Pro Bowl (NFL All-Star Game) following 1984 season.

TIMOTHY A. KRUMRIE
Name pronounced KRUM-RYE.
(Tim)
Nose Tackle—Cincinnati Bengals
Born May 20, 1960, at Eau Claire, Wis.
Height, 6.02. Weight, 262.
High School—Mondovi, Wis.
Attended University of Wisconsin.

Selected by Tampa Bay in 7th round (84th player selected) of 1983 USFL draft.
Selected by Cincinnati in 10th round (276th player selected) of 1983 NFL draft.
Signed by Cincinnati Bengals, May 19, 1983.
Cincinnati NFL, 1983 through 1987.
Games: 1983 (16), 1984 (16), 1985 (16), 1986 (16), 1987 (12). Total—76.
Pro statistics: Recovered one fumble, 1983; recovered one fumble for eight yards, 1984; recovered two fumbles, 1985; recovered two fumbles for 18 yards, 1986.
Played in Pro Bowl (NFL All-Star Game) following 1987 season.

GARY WAYNE KUBIAK

Quarterback—Denver Broncos

Born August 15, 1961, at Houston, Tex.
Height, 6.00. Weight, 192.
High School—Houston, Tex., Saint Pius X.
Received degree in physical education from Texas A&M University.

Selected by Denver in 8th round (197th player selected) of 1983 NFL draft.

Year	Club	G.	Att.	Cmp.	Pct.	Gain	T.P.	P.I.	Avg.	Att.	Yds.	Avg.	TD.	TD.	Pts.	F.
			—PASSING—							—RUSHING—				—TOTAL—		
1983—Denver NFL		4	22	12	54.5	186	1	1	8.45	4	17	4.3	1	1	6	0
1984—Denver NFL		7	75	44	58.7	440	4	1	5.87	9	27	3.0	1	1	6	1
1985—Denver NFL		16	5	2	40.0	61	1	0	12.20	1	6	6.0	0	0	0	0
1986—Denver NFL		16	38	23	60.5	249	1	3	6.55	6	22	3.7	0	0	0	0
1987—Denver NFL		12	7	3	42.9	25	0	2	3.57	1	3	3.0	0	0	0	0
Pro Totals—5 Years		55	147	84	57.1	961	7	7	6.54	21	75	3.6	2	2	12	1

Quarterback Rating Points: 1983 (78.9), 1984 (87.6), 1985 (125.8), 1986 (55.7), 1987 (13.1). Total—72.9.
Additional pro statistics: Caught one pass for 20 yards, 1984.
Played in AFC Championship Game following 1986 and 1987 seasons.
Played in NFL Championship Game following 1986 and 1987 seasons.

PETE DAVID KUGLER

Nose Tackle-Defensive End—San Francisco 49ers

Born August 9, 1959, at Philadelphia, Pa.
Height, 6.04. Weight, 255.
High School—Cherry Hill, N.J.
Received degree from Penn State University.

Selected by San Francisco in 6th round (147th player selected) of 1981 NFL draft.
On injured reserve with pulled hamstring, December 3 through remainder of 1981 season.
On inactive list, September 12, 1982.
Granted free agency, February 1, 1984; signed by Philadelphia Stars, February 16, 1984.
On developmental squad, March 23 through March 30, 1984; activated, March 31, 1984.
On developmental squad, May 18 through May 24, 1984; activated, May 25, 1984.
Franchise transferred to Baltimore, November 1, 1984.
On developmental squad, April 6 through April 12, 1985; activated, April 13, 1985.
On developmental squad, May 15 through June 27, 1985; activated, June 28, 1985.
Granted free agency when USFL suspended operations, August 7, 1986; re-signed by San Francisco 49ers, September 4, 1986.
Granted roster exemption, September 4 through September 14, 1986; activated, September 15, 1986.
On injured reserve with rib injury, October 18, 1986 through January 1, 1987; activated, January 2, 1987.
Crossed picket line during players' strike, October 7, 1987.
On developmental squad for 2 games with Philadelphia Stars in 1984.
On developmental squad for 7 games with Baltimore Stars in 1985.
San Francisco NFL, 1981 through 1983, 1986 and 1987; Philadelphia USFL, 1984; Baltimore USFL, 1985.
Games: 1981 (13), 1982 (7), 1983 (16), 1984 (16), 1985 (11), 1986 (3), 1987 (11). Total NFL—50. Total USFL—27. Total Pro—77.
Pro statistics: Credited with three sacks for 21 yards and recovered two fumbles, 1984; credited with two sacks for 12 yards, 1985.
Played in NFC Championship Game following 1983 season.
Played in USFL Championship Game following 1984 and 1985 seasons.

JAMES MICHAEL LACHEY

Name pronounced Luh-SHAY.

(Jim)

Offensive Tackle—San Diego Chargers

Born June 4, 1963, at St. Henry, O.
Height, 6.06. Weight, 288.
High School—St. Henry, O.
Received degree in marketing from Ohio State University in 1985.

Selected by New Jersey in 1985 USFL territorial draft.
Selected by San Diego in 1st round (12th player selected) of 1985 NFL draft.
Signed by San Diego Chargers, July 28, 1985.
San Diego NFL, 1985 through 1987.
Games: 1985 (16), 1986 (16), 1987 (12). Total—44.
Played in Pro Bowl (NFL All-Star Game) following 1987 season.

—DID YOU KNOW—

That four wide receivers made their first NFL pass receptions in the same game in 1986? In the St. Louis-Tampa Bay game on October 12, Cardinal rookies Chas Fox and Troy Johnson and Buc rookie David Williams and second-year player Phil Freeman all caught at least one pass. Fox and Freeman caught touchdown passes.

MICHAEL JAMES LAMBRECHT
(Mike)
Nose Tackle—Miami Dolphins
Born May 2, 1963, at Watertown, Minn.
Height, 6.01. Weight, 271.
High School—Watertown, Minn.
Attended St. Cloud State University.

Signed as free agent by Miami Dolphins, March 31, 1987.
Released by Miami Dolphins, September 7, 1987; re-signed as replacement player by Dolphins, September 23, 1987.
On injured reserve with sprained ankle, November 9 through remainder of 1987 season.
Miami NFL, 1987.
Games: 1987 (5).

SEAN EDWARD LANDETA
Punter—New York Giants
Born January 6, 1962, at Baltimore, Md.
Height, 6.00. Weight, 200.
High School—Baltimore, Md., Loch Raven.
Attended Towson State University.

Named to THE SPORTING NEWS NFL All-Star Team, 1986.
Named as punter on THE SPORTING NEWS USFL All-Star Team, 1983 and 1984.
Led USFL in net punting average with 38.1 in 1984.
Selected by Philadelphia in 14th round (161st player selected) of 1983 USFL draft.
Signed by Philadelphia Stars, January 24, 1983.
Franchise transferred to Baltimore, November 1, 1984.
Granted free agency, August 1, 1985; signed by New York Giants, August 5, 1985.

		——PUNTING——		
Year Club	G.	No.	Avg.	Blk.
1983—Philadelphia USFL	18	86	41.9	....
1984—Philadelphia USFL	18	53	41.0	....
1985—Baltimore USFL	18	65	41.8	....
1985—New York Giants NFL	16	81	42.9	0
1986—New York Giants NFL	16	79	44.8	0
1987—New York Giants NFL	12	65	42.7	1
USFL Totals—3 Years..................	54	204	41.6	....
NFL Totals—3 Years....................	44	225	43.5	1
Pro Totals—6 Years....................	98	429	42.6	....

Additional USFL statistics: Rushed once for minus five yards and fumbled once, 1983; recovered one fumble, 1983 and 1984.
Additional NFL statistics: Attempted one pass with no completions, 1985.
Played in NFC Championship Game following 1986 season.
Played in NFL Championship Game following 1986 season.
Played in USFL Championship Game following 1983 through 1985 seasons.
Played in Pro Bowl (NFL All-Star Game) following 1986 season.

BOB LANDSEE
(Name pronounced LANDS-ee.)
Guard-Center—Philadelphia Eagles
Born March 21, 1964, at Iron Mountain, Mich.
Height, 6.04. Weight, 273.
High School—Iron Mountain, Mich.
Attended University of Wisconsin.

Selected by Philadelphia in 6th round (149th player selected) of 1986 NFL draft.
Signed by Philadelphia Eagles, July 20, 1986.
On injured reserve with broken leg, August 19 through November 3, 1986; activated, November 4, 1986.
Philadelphia NFL, 1986 and 1987.
Games: 1986 (7), 1987 (2). Total—9.

ERIC LANE
Fullback—Seattle Seahawks
Born January 6, 1959, at Oakland, Calif.
Height, 6.00. Weight, 201.
High School—Hayward, Calif.
Attended Chabot Junior College and Brigham Young University.
Nephew of MacArthur Lane, running back with St. Louis Cardinals,
Green Bay Packers and Kansas City Chiefs, 1968 through 1978.

Selected by Seattle in 8th round (196th player selected) of 1981 NFL draft.
Released by Seattle Seahawks, September 7, 1987; re-signed as replacement player by Seahawks, October 9, 1987.

		——RUSHING——			PASS RECEIVING				—TOTAL—		
Year Club	G.	Att.	Yds.	Avg.	TD.	P.C.	Yds.	Avg.	TD.	TD.	Pts.	F.
1981—Seattle NFL...............................	14	8	22	2.8	0	7	58	8.3	0	0	0	0
1982—Seattle NFL...............................	9		None				None			0	0	1
1983—Seattle NFL...............................	16	3	1	0.3	0	2	9	4.5	0	0	0	2
1984—Seattle NFL...............................	15	80	299	3.7	4	11	101	9.2	1	5	30	1

Year Club	G.	RUSHING Att.	Yds.	Avg.	TD.	PASS RECEIVING P.C.	Yds.	Avg.	TD.	—TOTAL— TD.	Pts.	F.
1985—Seattle NFL	16	14	32	2.3	0	15	153	10.2	0	0	0	0
1986—Seattle NFL	15	6	11	1.8	0	3	6	2.0	1	2	12	0
1987—Seattle NFL	12	13	40	3.1	0	4	30	7.5	0	0	0	0
Pro Totals—7 Years	97	124	405	3.3	4	42	357	8.5	2	7	42	4

KICKOFF RETURNS

Year Club	G.	No.	Yds.	Avg.	TD.
1981—Seattle NFL	14	10	208	20.8	0
1982—Seattle NFL	9	11	172	15.6	0
1983—Seattle NFL	16	4	58	14.5	0
1984—Seattle NFL	15		None		
1985—Seattle NFL	16	1	1	1.0	0
1986—Seattle NFL	15	1	3	3.0	0
1987—Seattle NFL	12	2	34	17.0	0
Pro Totals—7 Years	97	29	476	16.4	0

Additional pro statistics: Recovered one fumble, 1981 through 1983 and 1986; attempted one pass with no completions, 1982; recovered three fumbles, 1984; recovered two fumbles, 1985; returned blocked punt 12 yards for a touchdown, 1986.

Played in AFC Championship Game following 1983 season.

GENE ERIC LANG
Running Back—Denver Broncos
Born March 15, 1962, at Pass Christian, Miss.
Height, 5.10. Weight, 196.
High School—Pass Christian, Miss.
Attended Louisiana State University.

Selected by Denver in 11th round (298th player selected) of 1984 NFL draft.
On injured reserve with broken hand, December 3 through remainder of 1985 season.

Year Club	G.	RUSHING Att.	Yds.	Avg.	TD.	PASS RECEIVING P.C.	Yds.	Avg.	TD.	—TOTAL— TD.	Pts.	F.
1984—Denver NFL	16	42	5.3	2		4	24	6.0	1	3	18	0
1985—Denver NFL	12	84	318	3.8	5	23	180	7.8	2	7	42	3
1986—Denver NFL	15	29	94	3.2	1	13	105	8.1	2	3	18	0
1987—Denver NFL	12	89	303	3.4	2	17	130	7.6	2	4	24	0
Pro Totals—4 Years	55	210	757	3.6	10	57	439	7.7	7	17	102	3

KICKOFF RETURNS

Year Club	G.	No.	Yds.	Avg.	TD.
1984—Denver NFL	16	19	404	21.3	0
1985—Denver NFL	12	17	361	21.2	0
1986—Denver NFL	15	21	480	22.9	0
1987—Denver NFL	12	4	78	19.5	0
Pro Totals—4 Years	55	61	1323	21.7	0

Additional pro statistics: Recovered one fumble for six yards, 1984; recovered one fumble, 1985; attempted one pass with no completions, 1987.

Played in AFC Championship Game following 1986 and 1987 seasons.
Played in NFL Championship Game following 1986 and 1987 seasons.

REGINALD DEVAN LANGHORNE
(Reggie)
Wide Receiver—Cleveland Browns
Born April 7, 1963, at Suffolk, Va.
Height, 6.02. Weight, 195.
High School—Smithfield, Va.
Attended Elizabeth City State University.

Selected by Oakland in 4th round (52nd player selected) of 1985 USFL draft.
Selected by Cleveland in 7th round (175th player selected) of 1985 NFL draft.
Signed by Cleveland Browns, July 15, 1985.

Year Club	G.	PASS RECEIVING P.C.	Yds.	Avg.	TD.
1985—Cleveland NFL	16	1	12	12.0	0
1986—Cleveland NFL	16	39	678	17.4	1
1987—Cleveland NFL	12	20	288	14.4	1
Pro Totals—3 Years	44	60	978	16.3	2

Additional pro statistics: Returned three kickoffs for 46 yards, recovered one fumble and fumbled once, 1985; rushed once for minus 11 yards, returned four kickoffs for 57 yards and fumbled twice, 1986; returned one kickoff for eight yards, 1987.

Played in AFC Championship Game following 1986 and 1987 seasons.

—DID YOU KNOW—

That the Philadelphia Eagles set an NFL record in 1986 by allowing 104 quarterback sacks? The old record of 70 was set by Atlanta in 1968. Randall Cunningham was sacked 72 times.

KENNETH WAYNE LANIER
(Ken)
Offensive Tackle—Denver Broncos
Born July 8, 1959, at Columbus, O.
Height, 6.03. Weight, 269.
High School—Columbus, O., Marion Franklin.
Received degree in industrial arts from Florida State University in 1981.
Selected by Denver in 5th round (125th player selected) of 1981 NFL draft.
Denver NFL, 1981 through 1987.
Games: 1981 (8), 1982 (9), 1983 (16), 1984 (16), 1985 (16), 1986 (16), 1987 (12). Total—93.
Pro statistics: Recovered one fumble, 1982 and 1984.
Played in AFC Championship Game following 1986 and 1987 seasons.
Played in NFL Championship Game following 1986 and 1987 seasons.

PAUL JAY LANKFORD
Cornerback—Miami Dolphins
Born June 15, 1958, at New York, N.Y.
Height, 6.02. Weight, 182.
High School—Farmingdale, N.Y.
Received bachelor of science degree in health planning and administration
from Penn State University in 1982.
Selected by Miami in 3rd round (80th player selected) of 1982 NFL draft.
On inactive list, September 12 and September 19, 1982.
On injured reserve with cracked tibia, November 28 through remainder of 1986 season.

Year Club	G.	No.	Yds.	Avg.	TD.
1982—Miami NFL	7			None	
1983—Miami NFL	16	1	10	10.0	0
1984—Miami NFL	16	3	25	8.3	0
1985—Miami NFL	16	4	10	2.5	0
1986—Miami NFL	12			None	
1987—Miami NFL	12	3	44	14.7	0
Pro Totals—6 Years	79	11	89	8.1	0

Additional pro statistics: Recovered one fumble, 1984 and 1986; recovered one fumble for four yards, 1987.
Played in AFC Championship Game following 1982, 1984 and 1985 seasons.
Played in NFL Championship Game following 1982 and 1984 seasons.

MICHAEL JOHN LANSFORD
(Mike)
Placekicker—Los Angeles Rams
Born July 20, 1958, at Monterrey Park, Calif.
Height, 6.00. Weight, 190.
High School—Arcadia, Calif.
Attended Pasadena City College and University of Washington.
Selected by New York Giants in 12th round (312th player selected) of 1980 NFL draft.
Released by New York Giants, August 3, 1980; claimed on waivers by San Francisco 49ers, August 5, 1980.
Released by San Francisco 49ers, August 18, 1980; signed as free agent by Oakland Raiders, June, 1981.
Released by Oakland Raiders, August 18, 1981; signed as free agent by Los Angeles Rams, July 1, 1982.
On injured reserve with knee injury, August 24 through November 23, 1983; activated after clearing procedural waivers, November 25, 1983.
Crossed picket line during players' strike, October 2, 1987.

Year Club	G.	XP.	XPM.	FG.	FGA.	Pts.
1982—L.A. Rams NFL	9	23	1	9	15	50
1983—L.A. Rams NFL	4	9	0	6	9	27
1984—L.A. Rams NFL	16	37	1	25	33	112
1985—L.A. Rams NFL	16	38	1	22	29	104
1986—L.A. Rams NFL	16	34	1	17	24	85
1987—L.A. Rams NFL	15	36	2	17	21	87
Pro Totals—6 Years	76	177	6	96	131	465

Played in NFC Championship Game following 1985 season.

STEVE M. LARGENT
Wide Receiver—Seattle Seahawks
Born September 28, 1954, at Tulsa, Okla.
Height, 5.11. Weight, 191.
High School—Oklahoma City, Okla., Putnam.
Received bachelor of science degree in biology from University of Tulsa in 1976.

Established NFL records for most seasons, 50 or more pass receptions (9); most seasons, 1,000 or more yards in pass receptions (8).
Named to THE SPORTING NEWS NFL All-Star Team, 1983.
Named to THE SPORTING NEWS AFC All-Star Team, 1978.
Selected by Houston in 4th round (117th player selected) of 1976 NFL draft.
Traded by Houston Oilers to Seattle Seahawks for 8th round pick in 1977 draft, August 26, 1976.

On injured reserve with broken wrist, December 16 through remainder of 1979 season.
Crossed picket line during players' strike, October 14, 1987.

			—RUSHING—			PASS RECEIVING				—TOTAL—		
Year	Club	G.	Att.	Yds.	Avg.	TD.	P.C.	Yds.	Avg.	TD.	TD.	Pts.	F.
1976—Seattle NFL	14	4	—14	—3.5	0	54	705	13.0	4	4	24	2
1977—Seattle NFL	14		None			33	643	19.5	10	10	60	0
1978—Seattle NFL	16		None			71	1168	16.5	8	8	48	0
1979—Seattle NFL	15		None			66	1237	18.7	9	9	54	0
1980—Seattle NFL	16	1	2	2.0	0	66	1064	16.1	6	6	36	1
1981—Seattle NFL	16	6	47	7.8	1	75	1224	16.3	9	10	60	2
1982—Seattle NFL	8	1	8	8.0	0	34	493	14.5	3	3	18	0
1983—Seattle NFL	15		None			72	1074	14.9	11	11	66	3
1984—Seattle NFL	16	2	10	5.0	0	74	1164	15.7	12	12	72	1
1985—Seattle NFL	16		None			79	*1287	16.3	6	6	†37	0
1986—Seattle NFL	16		None			70	1070	15.3	9	9	54	3
1987—Seattle NFL	13	2	33	16.5	0	58	912	15.7	8	8	48	2
Pro Totals—12 Years	175	16	86	5.4	1	752	12041	16.0	95	96	577	14

†Scored an extra point.
Additional pro statistics: Returned eight kickoffs for 156 yards and returned four punts for 36 yards, 1976; returned four punts for 32 yards, 1977; recovered one fumble, 1978; recovered two fumbles, 1980; attempted one pass with no completions, 1981 and 1985; attempted one pass with one completion for 11 yards, 1983; attemped one pass with one completion for 18 yards, 1986; attempted two passes with no completions, 1987.
Played in AFC Championship Game following 1983 season.
Played in Pro Bowl (NFL All-Star Game) following 1978, 1981 and 1984 through 1987 seasons.
Named in Pro Bowl following 1979 season; replaced due to wrist injury.

GREG LASKER
Safety—New York Giants
Born September 28, 1964, at St. Louis, Mo.
Height, 6.00. Weight, 200.
High School—Conway, Ark.
Attended University of Arkansas.

Selected by New York Giants in 2nd round (53rd player selected) of 1986 NFL draft.
Signed by New York Giants, July 21, 1986.
New York Giants NFL, 1986 and 1987.
Games: 1986 (16), 1987 (11). Total—27.
Pro statistics: Intercepted one pass for no yards and returned one kickoff for no yards, 1986.
Played in NFC Championship Game following 1986 season.
Played in NFL Championship Game following 1986 season.

ROBERT L. LAVETTE
Running Back—Atlanta Falcons
Born September 8, 1963, at Cartersville, Ga.
Height, 5.11. Weight, 190.
High School—Cartersville, Ga.
Attended Georgia Tech.
Cousin of Ray Donaldson, center with Indianapolis Colts.

Selected by Jacksonville in 1985 USFL territorial draft.
Selected by Dallas in 4th round (103rd player selected) of 1985 NFL draft.
Signed by Dallas Cowboys, July 14, 1985.
On injured reserve with knee injury, December 5 through remainder of 1985 season.
Crossed picket line during players' strike, October 7, 1987.
Released by Dallas Cowboys, November 3, 1987; awarded on waivers to Philadelphia Eagles, November 4, 1987.
Released by Philadelphia Eagles, December 11, 1987; signed as free agent by Atlanta Falcons, March 21, 1988.

			—RUSHING—			PASS RECEIVING				—TOTAL—		
Year	Club	G.	Att.	Yds.	Avg.	TD.	P.C.	Yds.	Avg.	TD.	TD.	Pts.	F.
1985—Dallas NFL	12	13	34	2.6	0	1	8	8.0	0	0	0	0
1986—Dallas NFL	16	10	6	0.6	0	5	31	6.2	1	1	6	3
1987—Dallas (4)-Philadelphia (1) NFL	5		None			1	6	6.0	0	0	0	0
Pro Totals—3 Years	33	23	40	1.7	0	7	45	6.4	1	1	6	3

			—PUNT RETURNS—				—KICKOFF RET.—		
Year	Club	G.	No.	Yds.	Avg.	TD.	No.	Yds.	Avg.TD.
1985—Dallas NFL	12		None			34	682	20.1	0
1986—Dallas NFL	16	18	92	5.1	0	36	699	19.4	0
1987—Dallas (4)-Philadelphia (1) NFL	5		None			6	109	18.2	0
Pro Totals—3 Years	33	18	92	5.1	0	76	1490	19.6	0

Additional pro statistics: Recovered three fumbles, 1986.

—DID YOU KNOW—

When the Los Angeles Rams finished 6-9 in 1987, it marked the first time in John Robinson's coaching career (college or pro) that his team had a losing record? It was also the first time in his five years in the NFL that the Rams failed to make the playoffs.

PATRICK JOSEPH LEAHY
(Pat)
Placekicker—New York Jets

Born March 19, 1951, at St. Louis, Mo.
Height, 6.00. Weight, 193.
High School—St. Louis, Mo., Augustinian Academy.
Received degree in marketing and business administration from St. Louis University
(did not play college football).
Named to THE SPORTING NEWS AFC All-Star Team, 1978.
Signed as free agent by St. Louis Cardinals, 1974.
Released by St. Louis Cardinals and signed as free agent by New York Jets, November 8, 1974.
On injured reserve with knee injury, October 13 through remainder of 1979 season.

Year Club	——PLACE KICKING——						Year Club	——PLACE KICKING——				
	G.	XP.	XPM.	FG.	FGA.	Pts.		G.	XP.	XPM.	FG.	FGA.	Pts.
1974—N.Y. Jets NFL	6	18	1	6	11	36	1982—N.Y. Jets NFL	9	26	*5	11	17	59
1975—N.Y. Jets NFL	14	27	3	13	21	66	1983—N.Y. Jets NFL	16	36	1	16	24	84
1976—N.Y. Jets NFL	14	16	4	11	16	49	1984—N.Y. Jets NFL	16	38	1	17	24	89
1977—N.Y. Jets NFL	14	18	3	15	25	63	1985—N.Y. Jets NFL	16	43	2	26	34	121
1978—N.Y. Jets NFL	16	41	1	22	30	107	1986—N.Y. Jets NFL	16	44	0	16	19	92
1979—N.Y. Jets NFL	6	12	3	8	13	36	1987—N.Y. Jets NFL	12	31	0	18	22	85
1980—N.Y. Jets NFL	16	36	0	14	22	78	Pro Totals—14 Years	187	424	25	218	314	1078
1981—N.Y. Jets NFL	16	38	1	25	36	113							

Additional pro statistics: Recovered one fumble, 1975.
Played in AFC Championship Game following 1982 season.

BYRON LEE
Linebacker—Los Angeles Raiders

Born September 8, 1964, at Columbus, O.
Height, 6.02. Weight, 230.
High School—Columbus, O., Eastmoor.
Attended Ohio State University.
Nephew of Joe Roberts, player with Syracuse Nationals of NBA, 1960-61 through 1962-63; and
Kentucky Colonels of ABA, 1967-68; and assistant coach with Golden State Warriors, 1974-75 through 1978-79.
Selected by New Jersey in 1986 USFL territorial draft.
Selected by Philadelphia in 7th round (176th player selected) of 1986 NFL draft.
Signed by Philadelphia Eagles, July 22, 1986.
Released by Philadelphia Eagles, August 19, 1986; re-signed by Eagles, October 15, 1986.
On injured reserve with knee injury, October 30 through December 18, 1986; activated, December 19, 1986.
Released by Philadelphia Eagles, September 6, 1987; re-signed as replacement player by Eagles, September 24, 1987.
Released by Philadelphia Eagles, October 19, 1987; signed as free agent by Los Angeles Raiders, April 22, 1988.
Philadelphia NFL, 1986 and 1987.
Games: 1986 (3), 1987 (3). Total—6.

CARL LEE III
Defensive Back—Minnesota Vikings

Born April 6, 1961, at South Charleston, W. Va.
Height, 5.11. Weight, 185.
High School—South Charleston, W. Va.
Attended Marshall University.
Selected by Minnesota in 7th round (186th player selected) of 1983 NFL draft.
Released by Minnesota Vikings, August 27, 1985; re-signed by Vikings, September 2, 1985.

Year Club	——INTERCEPTIONS——				
	G.	No.	Yds.	Avg.	TD.
1983—Minnesota NFL	16	1	31	31.0	0
1984—Minnesota NFL	16	1	0	0.0	0
1985—Minnesota NFL	15	3	68	22.7	0
1986—Minnesota NFL	16	3	10	3.3	0
1987—Minnesota NFL	12	3	53	17.7	0
Pro Totals—5 Years	75	11	162	14.7	0

Additional pro statistics: Recovered one fumble, 1984.
Played in NFC Championship Game following 1987 season.

DANZELL IVAN LEE
Tight End—Pittsburgh Steelers

Born March 16, 1963, at Corsicana, Tex.
Height, 6.02. Weight, 229.
High School—Corsicana, Tex.
Attended Lamar University.
Selected by Washington in 6th round (163rd player selected) of 1985 NFL draft.
Signed by Washington Redskins, July 18, 1985.
On injured reserve with sprained back, August 27 through entire 1985 season.
Released by Washington Redskins, August 19, 1986; signed as free agent by Pittsburgh Steelers, March 29, 1987.
Released by Pittsburgh Steelers, September 7, 1987; re-signed as replacement player by Steelers, September 24, 1987.

		—PASS RECEIVING—			
Year	Club	G.	P.C.	Yds.	Avg.	TD.
1987—Pittsburgh NFL.............		13	12	124	10.3	0

Additional pro statistics: Recovered one fumble, 1987.

GARY DeWAYNE LEE
Wide Receiver-Safety—Detroit Lions
Born February 12, 1965, at Albany, Ga.
Height, 6.01. Weight, 202.
High School—Albany, Ga., Westover.
Attended Georgia Tech.

Selected by Detroit in 12th round (315th player selected) of 1987 NFL draft.
Signed by Detroit Lions, July 25, 1987.

		PASS RECEIVING				—KICKOFF RET.—				—TOTAL—		
Year	Club	G.	P.C.	Yds.	Avg.	TD.	No.	Yds.	Avg.	TD.	TD.	Pts.	F.
1987—Detroit NFL............................		12	19	308	16.2	0	32	719	22.5	0	0	0	1

JOHN MIN LEE
(Korean name is Min Jong Lee.)
Placekicker—Los Angeles Raiders
Born May 19, 1964, at Seoul, South Korea.
Height, 5.11. Weight, 182.
High School—Downey, Calif.
Attended University of California at Los Angeles.

Named as placekicker on THE SPORTING NEWS College All-America Team, 1984 and 1985.
Selected by Arizona in 1986 USFL territorial draft.
Selected by St. Louis in 2nd round (32nd player selected) of 1986 NFL draft.
Signed by St. Louis Cardinals, July 28, 1986.
On injured reserve with knee injury, November 19 through remainder of 1986 season.
Released by St. Louis Cardinals, September 8, 1987; signed as free agent by Los Angeles Raiders, April 15, 1988.

		——PLACE KICKING——					
Year	Club	G.	XP.	XPM.	FG.	FGA.	Pts.
1986—St. Louis NFL............		11	14	3	8	13	38

LARRY DWAYNE LEE
Guard-Center—Miami Dolphins
Born September 10, 1959, at Dayton, O.
Height, 6.02. Weight, 260.
High School—Dayton, O., Roth.
Attended University of California at Los Angeles.
Cousin of Rick Porter, running back with Detroit Lions, Baltimore Colts
and Memphis Showboats, 1982, 1983 and 1985.

Selected by Detroit in 5th round (129th player selected) of 1981 NFL draft.
Released by Detroit Lions, September 2, 1985; re-signed by Lions, September 10, 1985.
Released by Detroit Lions, November 16, 1985; awarded on waivers to Miami Dolphins, November 18, 1985.
Left Miami Dolphins camp voluntarily and retired, August 12, 1987.
Rights traded by Miami Dolphins to Denver Broncos for 8th round pick in 1988 draft, August 19, 1987.
Detroit NFL, 1981 through 1984; Detroit (5)-Miami (5) NFL, 1985; Miami NFL, 1986; Denver NFL, 1987.
Games: 1981 (16), 1982 (9), 1983 (16), 1984 (15), 1985 (11), 1986 (16), 1987 (9). Total—92.
Pro statistics: Returned one kickoff for no yards, 1981; returned one kickoff for 14 yards, 1982; returned one kickoff for 11 yards, 1983; recovered one fumble, 1984 and 1987; fumbled twice for minus 24 yards, 1984; returned one kickoff for five yards and fumbled once, 1986.
Played in AFC Championship Game following 1985 season.
Member of Denver Broncos for AFC and NFL Championship Games following 1987 season; did not play.

MARK ANTHONY LEE
Defensive Back—Green Bay Packers
Born March 20, 1958, at Hanford, Calif.
Height, 5.11. Weight, 187.
High School—Hanford, Calif.
Attended University of Washington.

Selected by Green Bay in 2nd round (34th player selected) of 1980 NFL draft.

			INTERCEPTIONS			-PUNT RETURNS-				—KICKOFF RET.—				—TOTAL—		
Year	Club	G.	No.	Yds.	Avg.	TD.	No.	Yds.	Avg.	TD.	No.	Yds.	Avg.	TD.	TD.	Pts.	F.
1980—Green Bay NFL...........		15		None			5	32	6.4	0	30	589	19.6	0	0	0	1
1981—Green Bay NFL...........		16	6	50	8.3	0	20	187	9.4	1	14	270	19.3	0	1	6	0
1982—Green Bay NFL...........		9	1	40	40.0	0		None				None			0	0	0
1983—Green Bay NFL...........		16	4	23	5.8	0	1	—4	—4.0	0	1	0	0	0	0	0	1
1984—Green Bay NFL...........		16	3	33	11.0	0		None				None			0	0	0
1985—Green Bay NFL...........		14	1	23	23.0	0		None				None			0	0	0
1986—Green Bay NFL...........		16	9	33	3.7	0		None				None			0	0	0
1987—Green Bay NFL...........		12	1	0	0.0	0		None				None			0	0	0
Pro Totals—8 Years.......		114	25	202	8.1	0	26	215	8.3	1	45	859	19.1	0	1	6	2

Additional pro statistics: Recovered one fumble, 1981 and 1986; recovered one fumble for 15 yards, 1983; recovered two fumbles, 1984.

RONALD VAN LEE
(Ronnie)
Offensive Tackle—Miami Dolphins
Born December 24, 1956, at Pine Bluff, Ark.
Height, 6.04. Weight, 265.
High School—Tyler, Tex.
Attended Baylor University.

Selected by Miami in 3rd round (65th player selected) of 1979 NFL draft.
Released by Miami Dolphins, August 29, 1983; signed as free agent by Atlanta Falcons, September 14, 1983.
Traded with 6th round pick in 1985 draft by Atlanta Falcons to Miami Dolphins for cornerback Gerald Small, August 26, 1984.
On injured reserve with groin injury, October 18 through November 23, 1986; activated, November 24, 1986.

Year Club	G.	P.C.	Yds.	Avg.	TD.
		—PASS RECEIVING—			
1979—Miami NFL	16	2	14	7.0	0
1980—Miami NFL	16	7	83	11.9	2
1981—Miami NFL	16	14	64	4.6	1
1982—Miami NFL	9	2	6	3.0	0
1983—Atlanta NFL	14		None		
1984—Miami NFL	16		None		
1985—Miami NFL	15		None		
1986—Miami NFL	10		None		
1987—Miami NFL	9		None		
Pro Totals—9 Years	121	25	167	6.7	3

Played in AFC Championship Game following 1982, 1984 and 1985 seasons.
Played in NFL Championship Game following 1982 and 1984 seasons.

ZEPHRINI LEE
(First name pronounced Zef-ren-EYE.)
(Zeph)
Running Back—Los Angeles Raiders
Born June 17, 1963, at San Francisco, Calif.
Height, 6.03. Weight, 210.
High School—San Francisco, Calif., Abraham Lincoln.
Received bachelor of science degree in exercise science
from University of Southern California in 1986.
Cousin of Ricky Bell, running back with Tampa Bay Buccaneers and San Diego Chargers,
1977 through 1982; and Archie Bell, lead singer of Archie Bell and the Drells.

Selected by New Jersey in 1986 USFL territorial draft.
Selected by Los Angeles Raiders in 9th round (246th player selected) of 1986 NFL draft.
Signed by Los Angeles Raiders, July 14, 1986.
On injured reserve with groin injury, August 26 through entire 1986 season.
Released by Los Angeles Raiders, September 1, 1987; signed as free agent replacement player by Denver Broncos, September 25, 1987.
Released by Denver Broncos, October 6, 1987; signed as free agent replacement player by Los Angeles Raiders, October 10, 1987.
Released by Los Angeles Raiders, November 3, 1987; re-signed by Raiders, November 9, 1987.
On injured reserve with groin injury, November 9 through December 18, 1987; activated, December 19, 1987.
Denver (1)-Los Angeles Raiders (2) NFL, 1987.
Games: 1987 (3).

JEFF JAMES LEIDING
Linebacker—Indianapolis Colts
Born October 28, 1961, at Kansas City, Mo.
Height, 6.03. Weight, 239.
High Schools—Tulsa, Okla., Union; and Kansas City, Mo., Hickman Mills.
Attended University of Texas.

Selected by San Antonio in 1984 USFL territorial draft.
Selected by St. Louis in 5th round (129th player selected) of 1984 NFL draft.
Signed by St. Louis Cardinals, July 16, 1984.
Released by St. Louis Cardinals, August 27, 1984; signed by San Antonio Gunslingers, January 21, 1985.
On developmental squad, March 9 through April 5, 1985; activated, April 6, 1985.
On developmental squad, May 30 through July 22, 1985.
Released by San Antonio Gunslingers, July 23, 1985; signed as free agent by Indianapolis Colts, May 12, 1986.
Released by Indianapolis Colts, August 26, 1986; re-signed by Colts, September 30, 1986.
Released by Indianapolis Colts, August 19, 1987; re-signed as replacement player by Colts, September 23, 1987.
On injured reserve with knee injury, December 1 through remainder of 1987 season.
On developmental squad for 8 games with San Antonio Gunslingers in 1985.
San Antonio USFL, 1985; Indianapolis NFL, 1986 and 1987.
Games: 1985 (10), 1986 (12), 1987 (9). Total NFL—22. Total Pro—31.
Pro statistics: Credited with a safety, 1986 and 1987.

ALBERT RAY LEWIS
Cornerback—Kansas City Chiefs
Born October 6, 1960, at Mansfield, La.
Height, 6.02. Weight, 190.
High School—Mansfield, La., DeSoto.
Attended Grambling State University.
Selected by Philadelphia in 15th round (175th player selected) of 1983 USFL draft.
Selected by Kansas City in 3rd round (61st player selected) of 1983 NFL draft.
Signed by Kansas City Chiefs, May 19, 1983.
On injured reserve with knee injury, December 10 through remainder of 1984 season.

			—INTERCEPTIONS—			
Year	Club	G.	No.	Yds.	Avg.	TD.
1983—Kansas City NFL		16	4	42	10.5	0
1984—Kansas City NFL		15	4	57	14.3	0
1985—Kansas City NFL		16	8	59	7.4	0
1986—Kansas City NFL		15	4	18	4.5	0
1987—Kansas City NFL		12	1	0	0.0	0
Pro Totals—5 Years		74	21	176	8.4	0

Additional pro statistics: Recovered two fumbles, 1983 and 1986; recovered one fumble in end zone for a touchdown, 1985; recovered one fumble, 1987.
Played in Pro Bowl (NFL All-Star Game) following 1987 season.

DAVID WAYNE LEWIS
Tight End—San Francisco 49ers
Born June 8, 1961, at Portland, Ore.
Height, 6.03. Weight, 235.
High School—Portland, Ore., U.S. Grant.
Received bachelor of science degree in political science
from University of California at Berkeley in 1984.
Selected by Oakland in 1984 USFL territorial draft.
Selected by Detroit in 1st round (20th player selected) of 1984 NFL draft.
Signed by Detroit Lions, July 19, 1984.
Released by Detroit Lions, September 7, 1987; signed as free agent replacement player by Miami Dolphins, October 7, 1987.
Released by Miami Dolphins, November 14, 1987; re-signed by Dolphins, December 9, 1987.
Released by Miami Dolphins, December 12, 1987; signed as free agent by San Francisco 49ers, April 5, 1988.

			—PASS RECEIVING—			
Year	Club	G.	P.C.	Yds.	Avg.	TD.
1984—Detroit NFL		16	16	236	14.8	3
1985—Detroit NFL		15	28	354	12.6	3
1986—Detroit NFL		11	10	88	8.8	1
1987—Miami NFL		5	6	53	8.8	1
Pro Totals—4 Years		47	60	731	12.2	8

Additional pro statistics: Recovered two fumbles and fumbled twice, 1984; fumbled once, 1985; returned one kickoff for no yards, 1987.

LEO E. LEWIS III
Wide Receiver—Minnesota Vikings
Born September 17, 1956, at Columbia, Mo.
Height, 5.08. Weight, 170.
High School—Columbia, Mo., Hickman.
Received degree in education from University of Missouri, received master's degree from
University of Tennessee and accepted at University of Minnesota for doctorate in physical education.
Son of Leo Lewis, member of Canadian Football League Hall of Fame and
running back with Winnipeg Blue Bombers, 1955 through 1966; and brother of
Marc Lewis, wide receiver with Oakland Invaders and Denver Gold, 1983 through 1985.
Signed as free agent by St. Louis Cardinals, May 21, 1979.
On injured reserve with ankle injury, August 21 through November 15, 1979.
Released by St. Louis Cardinals, November 16, 1979; signed as free agent by Calgary Stampeders, March, 1980.
Released by Calgary Stampeders, August 7, 1980; signed as free agent by Hamilton Tiger-Cats, August 13, 1980.
Released by Hamilton Tiger-Cats, August 20, 1980; signed as free agent by Minnesota Vikings, May 10, 1981.
Released by Minnesota Vikings, August 25, 1981; re-signed after clearing procedural waivers, November 11, 1981.

			—RUSHING—				PASS RECEIVING				—TOTAL—		
Year	Club	G.	Att.	Yds.	Avg.	TD.	P.C.	Yds.	Avg.	TD.	TD.	Pts.	F.
1980—Calgary (5)-Hamilton (1) CFL		6	1	62	62.0	1	8	91	11.4	1	2	12	0
1981—Minnesota NFL		4	1	16	16.0	0	2	58	29.0	0	0	0	0
1982—Minnesota NFL		9		None			8	150	18.8	3	3	18	0
1983—Minnesota NFL		14	1	2	2.0	0	12	127	10.6	0	0	0	0
1984—Minnesota NFL		16	2	11	5.5	0	47	830	17.7	4	4	24	1
1985—Minnesota NFL		10	1	2	2.0	0	29	442	15.2	3	3	18	1
1986—Minnesota NFL		16	3	−16	−5.3	0	32	600	18.8	2	2	12	3
1987—Minnesota NFL		12	5	−7	−1.4	0	24	383	16.0	2	3	18	1
CFL Total—1 Year		6	1	62	62.0	1	8	91	11.4	1	2	12	0
NFL Totals—7 Years		81	13	8	0.6	0	154	2590	16.8	14	15	90	6
Pro Totals—8 Years		87	14	70	5.0	1	162	2681	16.5	15	17	102	6

Year Club	G.	—PUNT RETURNS— No.	Yds.	Avg.	TD.	—KICKOFF RET.— No.	Yds.	Avg.	TD.
1980—Calgary (5)-Hamilton (1) CFL	6	22	163	7.4	0	15	345	23.0	0
1981—Minnesota NFL	4		None				None		
1982—Minnesota NFL	9		None				None		
1983—Minnesota NFL	14	3	52	17.3	0	1	25	25.0	0
1984—Minnesota NFL	16	4	31	7.8	0	1	31	31.0	0
1985—Minnesota NFL	10		None				None		
1986—Minnesota NFL	16	7	53	7.6	0		None		
1987—Minnesota NFL	12	22	275	12.5	1		None		
CFL Total—1 Year	6	22	163	7.4	0	15	345	23.0	0
NFL Totals—7 Years	81	36	411	11.4	1	2	56	28.0	0
Pro Totals—8 Years	87	58	574	9.9	1	17	401	23.6	0

Additional pro statistics: Recovered three fumbles, 1984; recovered one fumble, 1985 and 1986; recovered two fumbles, 1987.

Played in NFC Championship Game following 1987 season.

MARK JOSEPH LEWIS
Tight End—Detroit Lions
Born May 5, 1961, at Houston, Tex.
Height, 6.02. Weight, 250.
High School—Houston, Tex., Kashmere.
Attended Texas A&M University.

Selected by Houston in 1985 USFL territorial draft.
Selected by Green Bay in 6th round (155th player selected) of 1985 NFL draft.
Signed by Green Bay Packers, July 19, 1985.
On injured reserve with knee injury, August 27 through December 20, 1985; activated, December 21, 1985.
Released by Green Bay Packers, September 15, 1987; signed as free agent replacement player by Detroit Lions, October 16, 1987.
Green Bay NFL, 1985 and 1986; Green Bay (1)-Detroit (9) NFL, 1987.
Games: 1985 (1), 1986 (16), 1987 (10). Total—27.
Pro statistics: Caught two passes for seven yards and two touchdowns, 1986.

SIDNEY LEWIS
(Sid)
Cornerback—New York Jets
Born May 30, 1964, at Canton, O.
Height, 5.11. Weight, 180.
High School—Canton, O., McKinley.
Received degree in finance from Penn State University in 1987.

Selected by New York Jets in 10th round (268th player selected) of 1987 NFL draft.
Signed by New York Jets, July 24, 1987.
On injured reserve with dislocated finger, August 31 through December 11, 1987; activated, December 12, 1987.
New York Jets NFL, 1987.
Games: 1987 (2).

WALTER DeWAYNE LEWIS
Quarterback—New England Patriots
Born April 26, 1962, at Brewton, Ala.
Height, 6.00. Weight, 198.
High School—Brewton, Ala., T.R. Miller.
Attended University of Alabama.
Cousin of Cliff Lewis, linebacker with Green Bay Packers, 1981 through 1984.

Selected by Birmingham in 1984 USFL territorial draft.
USFL rights traded by Birmingham Stallions to Memphis Showboats for rights to defensive back Ernest Gibson, January 16, 1984.
Signed by Memphis Showboats, February 5, 1984.
On developmental squad, May 24 through remainder of 1984 season.
Selected by New England in 3rd round (70th player selected) of 1984 NFL supplemental draft.
Granted free agency when USFL suspended operations, August 7, 1986; signed by Montreal Alouettes, August 19, 1986.
Granted free agency when Montreal Alouettes suspended operations, June 24, 1987; signed by New England Patriots, July 25, 1987.
On injured reserve with thumb injury, September 1 through entire 1987 season.
On developmental squad for 5 games with Memphis Showboats in 1984.

Year Club	G.	—PASSING— Att.	Cmp.	Pct.	Gain	T.P.	P.I.	Avg.	—RUSHING— Att.	Yds.	Avg.	TD.	—TOTAL— TD.	Pts.	F.
1984—Memphis USFL	13	276	161	58.3	1862	15	10	6.75	60	552	9.2	5	5	30	9
1985—Memphis USFL	14	184	97	52.7	1593	16	5	8.66	65	591	9.1	4	4	24	7
1986—Montreal CFL	11	134	65	48.5	833	3	8	6.22	46	281	6.1	1	1	6	7
USFL Totals—2 Years	27	460	258	56.1	3455	31	15	7.51	125	1143	9.1	9	9	54	16
CFL Totals—1 Year	11	134	65	48.5	833	3	8	6.22	46	281	6.1	1	1	6	7
Pro Totals—3 Years	38	594	323	54.3	4288	34	23	7.22	171	1424	8.3	10	10	60	23

USFL Quarterback Rating Points: 1984 (81.8), 1985 (99.8). Total—88.7.
Additional USFL statistics: Recovered three fumbles, 1984; recovered one fumble, 1985.

WILLIAM GLENN LEWIS
(Bill)
Guard—Los Angeles Raiders
Born July 12, 1963, at Sioux City, Ia.
Height, 6.07. Weight, 275.
High School—Sioux City, Ia., East.
Attended University of Nebraska.

Selected by Memphis in 1986 USFL territorial draft.
Selected by Los Angeles Raiders in 7th round (191st player selected) of 1986 NFL draft.
Signed by Los Angeles Raiders, July 14, 1986.
On non-football injury list with appendectomy, September 22 through October 23, 1987; activated, October 24, 1987.
Los Angeles Raiders NFL, 1986 and 1987.
Games: 1986 (4), 1987 (8). Total—12.

GEORGE VINCENT LILJA
Center—Dallas Cowboys
Born March 3, 1958, at Evergreen Park, Ill.
Height, 6.04. Weight, 282.
High School—Orland Park, Ill., Carl Sandburg.
Received bachelor of arts degree in general studies from University of Michigan in 1981.
Brother of Larry Lilja, strength coach at Northwestern University.

Selected by Los Angeles in 4th round (104th player selected) of 1981 NFL draft.
On injured reserve with ankle injury, August 31 through entire 1981 season.
Released by Los Angeles Rams, September 8, 1983; signed as free agent by New York Jets, September 27, 1983.
Released by New York Jets, November 15, 1984; signed as free agent by Cleveland Browns, November 21, 1984.
Released by Cleveland Browns, September 7, 1987; signed as free agent replacement player by Dallas Cowboys, October 14, 1987.
Active for 1 game with Los Angeles Rams in 1983; did not play.
Los Angeles Rams NFL, 1982; Los Angeles Rams (0)-New York Jets (1) NFL, 1983; New York Jets (3)-Cleveland (4) NFL, 1984; Cleveland NFL, 1985 and 1986; Dallas NFL, 1987.
Games: 1982 (9), 1983 (1), 1984 (7), 1985 (16), 1986 (16), 1987 (5). Total—54.
Pro statistics: Recovered one fumble, 1985; fumbled once, 1987.
Played in AFC Championship Game following 1986 season.

ROBERT ANTHONEY LILLY
(Tony)
Safety—Denver Broncos
Born February 16, 1962, at Alexandria, Va.
Height, 6.00. Weight, 199.
High School—Woodbridge, Va.
Attended University of Florida.

Selected by Tampa Bay in 1984 USFL territorial draft.
Selected by Denver in 3rd round (78th player selected) of 1984 NFL draft.
Signed by Denver Broncos, May 23, 1984.
Crossed picket line during players' strike, October 14, 1987.

| | | —INTERCEPTIONS— | | | |
Year Club	G.	No.	Yds.	Avg.	TD.
1984—Denver NFL	13	1	5	5.0	0
1985—Denver NFL	16	2	4	2.0	0
1986—Denver NFL	16	3	22	7.3	0
1987—Denver NFL	13	3	29	9.7	0
Pro Totals—4 Years	58	9	60	6.7	0

Additional pro statistics: Recovered one fumble for three yards and fumbled once, 1984; recovered one fumble, 1985 and 1987; returned two punts for six yards, 1987.
Played in AFC Championship Game following 1986 and 1987 seasons.
Played in NFL Championship Game following 1986 and 1987 seasons.

CHRISTOPHER ANDREW LINDSTROM
(Chris)
Defensive End—New York Jets
Born August 3, 1960, at Weymouth, Mass.
Height, 6.07. Weight, 260.
High School—Weymouth, Mass., South.
Received bachelor of science degree in physical education
from Boston University in 1982.
Brother of Dave Lindstrom, defensive end with Kansas City Chiefs, 1978 through 1985.

Selected by St. Louis in 8th round (205th player selected) of 1982 NFL draft.
Left St. Louis Cardinals' camp voluntarily, July 22, 1982; returned, July 27, 1982.
Left St. Louis Cardinals' camp voluntarily and released, July 28, 1982; claimed on procedural waivers by Baltimore Colts, May 10, 1983.
Released by Baltimore Colts, August 22, 1983; signed as free agent by Cincinnati Bengals, September 6, 1983.
Released by Cincinnati Bengals, September 27, 1983.
USFL rights traded by New Orleans Breakers to Chicago Blitz for draft pick, December 1, 1983.
Signed as free agent by San Francisco 49ers, December 21, 1983.

Released by San Francisco 49ers, February 8, 1984; awarded on procedural waivers to Houston Oilers, April 6, 1984.

Signed by Chicago Blitz, April 27, 1984, after restraining order issued negating option year in NFL contract.

On developmental squad, May 25 through May 30, 1984; activated, May 31, 1984.

Franchise disbanded, November 20, 1984; signed as free agent by Tampa Bay Buccaneers, March 23, 1985.

Placed on retired/reserve list, August 5 through entire 1986 season.

Released by Tampa Bay Buccaneers, February 10, 1987; signed as free agent replacement player by Kansas City Chiefs, September 24, 1987.

Released by Kansas City Chiefs, October 20, 1987; signed as free agent by New York Jets, April 15, 1988.

On developmental squad for 1 game with Chicago Blitz in 1984.

Cincinnati NFL, 1983; Chicago USFL, 1984; Tampa Bay NFL, 1985; Kansas City NFL, 1987.

Games: 1983 (1), 1984 (8), 1985 (15), 1987 (3). Total NFL—19. Total Pro—27.

Pro statistics: Recovered one fumble, 1985.

COACHING RECORD

Assistant coach at Colby College, 1982.

ADAM JAMES LINGNER
Center—Buffalo Bills
Born November 2, 1960, at Indianapolis, Ind.
Height, 6.04. Weight, 260.
High School—Rock Island, Ill., Alleman.
Attended University of Illinois.

Selected by Chicago in 1983 USFL territorial draft.

Selected by Kansas City in 9th round (231st player selected) of 1983 NFL draft.

Signed by Kansas City Chiefs, June 1, 1983.

Released by Kansas City Chiefs, November 24, 1986; signed as free agent by New England Patriots, November 28, 1986.

Released by New England Patriots, December 2, 1986; signed as free agent by Denver Broncos, May 1, 1987.

Released by Denver Broncos, August 26, 1987; awarded on waivers to Buffalo Bills, August 27, 1987.

Active for 1 game with New England Patriots in 1986; did not play.

Kansas City NFL, 1983 through 1985; Kansas City (12)-New England (0) NFL, 1986; Buffalo NFL, 1987.

Games: 1983 (16), 1984 (16), 1985 (16), 1986 (12), 1987 (12). Total—72.

Pro statistics: Recovered one fumble, 1987.

RONNIE LEON LIPPETT
Name pronounced Lip-PET.
Cornerback—New England Patriots
Born December 10, 1960, at Melborne, Fla.
Height, 5.11. Weight, 180.
High School—Sebring, Fla.
Attended University of Miami (Fla.).

Selected by New England in 8th round (214th player selected) of 1983 NFL draft.

Year Club	G.	—INTERCEPTIONS—			
		No.	Yds.	Avg.	TD.
1983—New England NFL	16		None		
1984—New England NFL	16	3	23	7.7	0
1985—New England NFL	16	3	93	31.0	0
1986—New England NFL	15	8	76	9.5	0
1987—New England NFL	12	3	103	34.3	*2
Pro Totals—5 Years	75	17	295	17.4	2

Additional pro statistics: Recovered one fumble, 1983 and 1984; fumbled once, 1984.

Played in AFC Championship Game following 1985 season.

Played in NFL Championship Game following 1985 season.

LOUIS ADAM LIPPS
Wide Receiver—Pittsburgh Steelers
Born August 9, 1962, at New Orleans, La.
Height, 5.10. Weight, 190.
High School—Reserve, La., East St. John's.
Attended University of Southern Mississippi.
Cousin of Garry James, running back with Detroit Lions.

Named THE SPORTING NEWS NFL Rookie of the Year, 1984.

Selected by Arizona in 8th round (155th player selected) of 1984 USFL draft.

Selected by Pittsburgh in 1st round (23rd player selected) of 1984 NFL draft.

Signed by Pittsburgh Steelers, May 19, 1984.

On injured reserve with hamstring injury, November 21 through December 18, 1987; activated, December 19, 1987.

Year Club	G.	—RUSHING—				PASS RECEIVING				—TOTAL—		
		Att.	Yds.	Avg.	TD.	P.C.	Yds.	Avg.	TD.	TD.	Pts.	F.
1984—Pittsburgh NFL	14	3	71	23.7	1	45	860	19.1	9	11	66	8
1985—Pittsburgh NFL	16	2	16	8.0	1	59	1134	19.2	12	15	90	5
1986—Pittsburgh NFL	13	4	—3	−0.8	0	38	590	15.5	3	3	18	2
1987—Pittsburgh NFL	4		None			11	164	14.9	0	0	0	0
Pro Totals—4 Years	47	9	84	9.3	2	153	2748	18.0	24	29	174	15

Year Club	G.	—PUNT RETURNS—				—KICKOFF RET.—			
		No.	Yds.	Avg.	TD.	No.	Yds.	Avg.	TD.
1984—Pittsburgh NFL	14	53	*656	12.4	1			None	
1985—Pittsburgh NFL	16	36	437	12.1	*2	13	237	18.2	0
1986—Pittsburgh NFL	13	3	16	5.3	0			None	
1987—Pittsburgh NFL	4	7	46	6.6	0			None	
Pro Totals—4 Years	47	99	1155	11.7	3	13	237	18.2	0

Additional pro statistics: Recovered two fumbles, 1984; recovered four fumbles for three yards, 1985; recovered one fumble, 1986.

Played in AFC Championship Game following 1984 season.

Played in Pro Bowl (NFL All-Star Game) following 1984 and 1985 seasons.

DAVID GENE LITTLE
(Dave)
Tight End—Philadelphia Eagles
Born April 18, 1961, at Selma, Calif.
Height, 6.02. Weight, 226.
High School—Fresno, Calif., Roosevelt.
Attended Kings River College and Middle Tennessee State University.

Signed as free agent by Memphis Showboats, January 11, 1984.
Released by Memphis Showboats, February 20, 1984; signed as free agent by Kansas City Chiefs, June 21, 1984.
On injured reserve with knee injury, November 6 through remainder of 1984 season.
Released by Kansas City Chiefs, August 19, 1985; signed as free agent by Philadelphia Eagles, September 11, 1985.

Year Club	G.	——PASS RECEIVING——			
		P.C.	Yds.	Avg.	TD.
1984—Kansas City NFL	10	1	13	13.0	0
1985—Philadelphia NFL	15	7	82	11.7	0
1986—Philadelphia NFL	16	14	132	9.4	0
1987—Philadelphia NFL	12	1	8	8.0	0
Pro Totals—4 Years	53	23	235	10.2	0

Additional pro statistics: Recovered fumble in end zone for a touchdown, 1985; fumbled once, 1986.

DAVID LAMAR LITTLE
Linebacker—Pittsburgh Steelers
Born January 3, 1959, at Miami, Fla.
Height, 6.01. Weight, 230.
High School—Miami, Fla., Jackson.
Received degree in sociology from University of Florida.
Brother of Larry Little, guard with San Diego Chargers
and Miami Dolphins, 1967 through 1980; and currently head coach at Bethune-Cookman College.

Selected by Pittsburgh in 7th round (183rd player selected) of 1981 NFL draft.
Pittsburgh NFL, 1981 through 1987.
Games: 1981 (16), 1982 (9), 1983 (16), 1984 (16), 1985 (16), 1986 (16), 1987 (12). Total—101.
Pro statistics: Recovered one fumble 1981 and 1987; recovered one fumble for two yards, 1982; intercepted two passes for no yards and recovered two fumbles for 11 yards, 1985.
Played in AFC Championship Game following 1984 season.

GEORGE WILLARD LITTLE
Defensive End—Miami Dolphins
Born June 27, 1963, at Duquesne, Pa.
Height, 6.04. Weight, 270.
High School—Duquesne, Pa.
Attended University of Iowa.

Selected by Oakland in 1985 USFL territorial draft.
Selected by Miami in 3rd round (65th player selected) of 1985 NFL draft.
Signed by Miami Dolphins, July 18, 1985.
Miami NFL, 1985 through 1987.
Games: 1985 (14), 1986 (16), 1987 (9). Total—39.
Pro statistics: Recovered one fumble for four yards, 1986.
Played in AFC Championship Game following 1985 season.

CHARLES EDWARD LOCKETT
Wide Receiver—Pittsburgh Steelers
Born October 1, 1965, at Los Angeles, Calif.
Height, 6.00. Weight, 179.
High School—Los Angeles, Calif., Crenshaw.
Attended California State University at Long Beach.

Selected by Pittsburgh in 3rd round (66th player selected) of 1987 NFL draft.
Signed by Pittsburgh Steelers, July 20, 1987.
Crossed picket line during players' strike, October 14, 1987.

Year Club	G.	——PASS RECEIVING——			
		P.C.	Yds.	Avg.	TD.
1987—Pittsburgh NFL	11	7	116	16.6	1

Additional pro statistics: Returned two punts for three yards, recovered one fumble and fumbled once, 1987.

DANNY KEY LOCKETT
Linebacker—Detroit Lions
Born July 11, 1964, at Fort Valley, Ga.
Height, 6.02. Weight, 228.
High School—Fort Valley, Ga., Peach County.
Attended College of the Sequoias and University of Arizona.
Selected by Detroit in 6th round (148th player selected) of 1987 NFL draft.
Signed by Detroit Lions, July 25, 1987.
Crossed picket line during players' strike, October 14, 1987.
Detroit NFL, 1987.
Games: 1987 (13).
Pro statistics: Recovered one fumble, 1987.

EUGENE LOCKHART JR.
Linebacker—Dallas Cowboys
Born March 8, 1961, at Crockett, Tex.
Height, 6.02. Weight, 233.
High School—Crockett, Tex.
Received bachelor of arts degree in marketing from University of Houston in 1983.
Selected by Houston in 1984 USFL territorial draft.
Selected by Dallas in 6th round (152nd player selected) of 1984 NFL draft.
Signed by Dallas Cowboys, May 8, 1984.
On injured reserve with broken leg, December 8 through remainder of 1987 season.
Dallas NFL, 1984 through 1987.
Games: 1984 (15), 1985 (16), 1986 (16), 1987 (9). Total—56.
Pro statistics: Intercepted one pass for 32 yards, 1984; recovered one fumble, 1984, 1986 and 1987; intercepted one pass for 19 yards and a touchdown and recovered four fumbles for 17 yards, 1985; intercepted one pass for five yards, 1986; intercepted one pass for 13 yards, 1987.

JAMES DAVID LOFTON
Wide Receiver—Los Angeles Raiders
Born July 5, 1956, at Fort Ord, Calif.
Height, 6.03. Weight, 190.
High School—Los Angeles, Calif., Washington.
Received bachelor of science degree in industrial engineering from
Stanford University in 1978.
Cousin of Kevin Bass, outfielder with Houston Astros.
Named to THE SPORTING NEWS NFL All-Star Team, 1980 and 1981.
Selected by Green Bay in 1st round (6th player selected) of 1978 NFL draft.
On suspended list, December 18 through remainder of 1986 season.
Traded by Green Bay Packers to Los Angeles Raiders for 3rd round pick in 1987 draft and 4th round pick in 1988 draft, April 13, 1987.

Year Club	G.	Att.	Yds.	Avg.	TD.	P.C.	Yds.	Avg.	TD.	TD.	Pts.	F.
1978—Green Bay NFL	16	3	13	4.3	0	46	818	17.8	6	6	36	2
1979—Green Bay NFL	15	1	—1	—1.0	0	54	968	17.9	4	4	24	5
1980—Green Bay NFL	16			None		71	1226	17.3	4	4	24	0
1981—Green Bay NFL	16			None		71	1294	18.2	8	8	48	0
1982—Green Bay NFL	9	4	101	25.3	1	35	696	19.9	4	5	30	0
1983—Green Bay NFL	16	9	36	4.0	0	58	1300	★22.4	8	8	48	0
1984—Green Bay NFL	16	10	82	8.2	0	62	1361	★22.0	7	7	42	1
1985—Green Bay NFL	16	4	14	3.5	0	69	1153	16.7	4	4	24	3
1986—Green Bay NFL	15			None		64	840	13.1	4	4	24	3
1987—Los Angeles Raiders NFL	12	1	1	1.0	0	41	880	21.5	5	5	30	0
Pro Totals—10 Years	147	32	246	7.7	1	571	10536	18.5	54	55	330	14

Additional pro statistics: Returned one kickoff for no yards and attempted two passes with no completions, 1978; attempted one pass with no completions, 1979 and 1986; recovered one fumble, 1981; attempted one pass with one completion for 43 yards, 1982; recovered two fumbles for eight yards, 1986.
Played in Pro Bowl (NFL All-Star Game) following 1978 and 1980 through 1985 seasons.

NEIL VINCENT LOMAX
Quarterback—Phoenix Cardinals
Born February 17, 1959, at Portland, Ore.
Height, 6.03. Weight, 215.
High School—Lake Oswego, Ore.
Received degree in communications from Portland State University.
Selected by St. Louis in 2nd round (33rd player selected) of 1981 NFL draft.
Franchise transferred to Phoenix, March 15, 1988.

Year Club	G.	Att.	Cmp.	Pct.	Gain	T.P.	P.I.	Avg.	Att.	Yds.	Avg.	TD.	TD.	Pts.	F.
1981—St. Louis NFL	14	236	119	50.4	1575	4	10	6.67	19	104	5.5	2	2	12	6
1982—St. Louis NFL	9	205	109	53.2	1367	5	6	6.67	28	119	4.3	1	1	6	8
1983—St. Louis NFL	13	354	209	59.0	2636	24	11	7.45	27	127	4.7	2	2	12	9
1984—St. Louis NFL	16	560	345	61.6	4614	28	16	8.24	35	184	5.3	3	3	18	11
1985—St. Louis NFL	16	471	265	56.3	3214	18	12	6.82	32	125	3.9	0	0	0	10
1986—St. Louis NFL	14	421	240	57.0	2583	13	12	6.14	35	148	4.2	1	1	6	7

Year Club	G.	Att.	Cmp.	Pct.	Gain	T.P.	P.I.	Avg.	Att.	Yds.	Avg.	TD.	TD.	Pts.	F.
			PASSING							RUSHING				TOTAL	
1987—St. Louis NFL	12	*463	*275	59.4	*3387	24	12	7.32	29	107	3.7	0	0	0	7
Pro Totals—7 Years	94	2710	1562	57.6	19376	116	79	7.15	205	914	4.5	9	9	54	58

Quarterback Rating Points: 1981 (60.1), 1982 (70.1), 1983 (92.0), 1984 (92.5), 1985 (79.5), 1986 (73.6), 1987 (88.5). Total—82.1.

Additional pro statistics: Caught one pass for 10 yards, recovered one fumble and fumbled eight times for minus one yard, 1982; recovered three fumbles, 1983; recovered two fumbles and fumbled 11 times for minus five yards, 1984; recovered four fumbles and fumbled 10 times for minus one yard, 1985; recovered six fumbles, 1986; recovered three fumbles and fumbled seven times for minus three yards, 1987.

Played in Pro Bowl (NFL All-Star Game) following 1984 and 1987 seasons.

CHARLES FRANKLIN LONG II
(Chuck)
Quarterback—Detroit Lions

Born February 18, 1963, at Norman, Okla.
Height, 6.04. Weight, 211.
High School—Wheaton, Ill., North.
Received degree in marketing from University of Iowa in 1985.

Named as quarterback on THE SPORTING NEWS College All-America Team, 1985.
Selected by Detroit in 1st round (12th player selected) of 1986 NFL draft.
Selected by Baltimore in 10th round (75th player selected) of 1986 USFL draft.
Signed by Detroit Lions, August 18, 1986.
Granted roster exemption, August 18 through August 29, 1986; activated, August 30, 1986.

Year Club	G.	Att.	Cmp.	Pct.	Gain	T.P.	P.I.	Avg.	Att.	Yds.	Avg.	TD.	TD.	Pts.	F.
			PASSING							RUSHING				TOTAL	
1986—Detroit NFL	3	40	21	52.5	247	2	2	6.18	2	0	0.0	0	0	0	1
1987—Detroit NFL	12	416	232	55.8	2598	11	*20	6.25	22	64	2.9	0	0	0	8
Pro Totals—2 Years	15	456	253	55.5	2845	13	22	6.24	24	64	2.7	0	0	0	9

Quarterback Rating Points: 1986 (67.4), 1987 (63.4). Total—64.0.
Additional pro statistics: Recovered three fumbles and fumbled eight times for minus eight yards, 1987.

HOWARD M. LONG
(Howie)
Defensive End—Los Angeles Raiders

Born January 6, 1960, at Somerville, Mass.
Height, 6.05. Weight, 265.
High School—Milford, Mass.
Received bachelor of arts degree in communications from Villanova University in 1981.

Named to THE SPORTING NEWS NFL All-Star Team, 1983.
Selected by Oakland in 2nd round (48th player selected) of 1981 NFL draft.
Franchise transferred to Los Angeles, May 7, 1982.
Left Los Angeles Raiders camp voluntarily, July 30 through August 2, 1984; returned, August 3, 1984.
Crossed picket line during players' strike, October 6, 1987.
Oakland NFL, 1981; Los Angeles Raiders NFL, 1982 through 1987.
Games: 1981 (16), 1982 (9), 1983 (16), 1984 (16), 1985 (16), 1986 (13), 1987 (14). Total—100.
Pro statistics: Recovered two fumbles, 1983, 1986 and 1987; recovered two fumbles for four yards, 1984.
Played in AFC Championship Game following 1983 season.
Played in NFL Championship Game following 1983 season.
Played in Pro Bowl (NFL All-Star Game) following 1983 through 1987 seasons.

TERRY LUTHER LONG
Guard—Pittsburgh Steelers

Born July 21, 1959, at Columbia, S.C.
Height, 5.11. Weight, 275.
High School—Columbia, S.C., Eau Claire.
Attended East Carolina University.
Spent two years in Army before entering college.

Selected by Washington in 4th round (76th player selected) of 1984 USFL draft.
Selected by Pittsburgh in 4th round (111th player selected) of 1984 NFL draft.
Signed by Pittsburgh Steelers, July 10, 1984.
Crossed picket line during players' strike, October 14, 1987.
Pittsburgh NFL, 1984 through 1987.
Games: 1984 (12), 1985 (15), 1986 (16), 1987 (13). Total—56.
Pro statistics: Returned one punt for no yards and fumbled once, 1984; recovered one fumble, 1986.
Played in AFC Championship Game following 1984 season.

RONALD MANDEL LOTT
(Ronnie)
Safety—San Francisco 49ers

Born May 8, 1959, at Albuquerque, N.M.
Height, 6.00. Weight, 199.
High School—Rialto, Calif., Eisenhower.
Received bachelor of science degree in public administration from University of Southern California in 1981.

Named as defensive back on THE SPORTING NEWS College All-America Team, 1980.
Named to THE SPORTING NEWS NFL All-Star Team, 1981 and 1987.
Selected by San Francisco in 1st round (8th player selected) of 1981 NFL draft.

		—INTERCEPTIONS—					—INTERCEPTIONS—		
Year Club	G.	No.	Yds.	Avg.TD.	Year Club	G.	No.	Yds.	Avg.TD.
1981—San Francisco NFL.....	16	7	117	16.7 *3	1985—San Francisco NFL.....	16	6	68	11.3 0
1982—San Francisco NFL.....	9	2	95	47.5 *1	1986—San Francisco NFL.....	14	*10	134	13.4 1
1983—San Francisco NFL.....	15	4	22	5.5 0	1987—San Francisco NFL.....	12	5	62	12.4 0
1984—San Francisco NFL.....	12	4	26	6.5 0	Pro Totals—7 Years............	94	38	524	13.8 5

Additional pro statistics: Returned seven kickoffs for 111 yards and fumbled once, 1981; recovered two fumbles, 1981 and 1985; recovered one fumble, 1983; returned one kickoff for two yards, 1985; recovered two fumbles for 33 yards, 1987.
Played in NFC Championship Game following 1981, 1983 and 1984 seasons.
Played in NFL Championship Game following 1981 and 1984 seasons.
Played in Pro Bowl (NFL All-Star Game) following 1981 through 1984, 1986 and 1987 seasons.

FLETCHER ALLISON LOUALLEN
Defensive Back—Minnesota Vikings
Born September 12, 1962, at Jefferson, S.C.
Height, 6.00. Weight, 190.
High School—Pageland, S.C., Central.
Attended Livingston State University.

Selected by Birmingham in 14th round (279th player selected) of 1984 USFL draft.
Signed as free agent by Winnipeg Blue Bombers, February 18, 1984.
Released by Winnipeg Blue Bombers, June 10, 1984; signed by Birmingham Stallions, September 20, 1984.
Released by Birmingham Stallions, February 18, 1985; re-signed by Stallions, February 19, 1985.
On developmental squad, February 21 through March 1, 1985; activated, March 2, 1985.
On developmental squad, March 8 through May 1, 1985; activated, May 2, 1985.
On developmental squad, June 22 through July 5, 1985; activated, July 6, 1985.
Granted free agency when USFL suspended operations, August 7, 1986; signed as free agent by St. Louis Cardinals, May 20, 1987.
Released by St. Louis Cardinals, August 17, 1987; signed as free agent replacement player by Minnesota Vikings, September 24, 1987.
Released by Minnesota Vikings, October 19, 1987; re-signed by Vikings, March 22, 1988.
On developmental squad for 10 games with Birmingham Stallions in 1985.
Birmingham USFL, 1985; Minnesota NFL, 1987.
Games: 1985 (9), 1987 (3). Total—12.

DUVAL LEE LOVE
Guard—Los Angeles Rams
Born June 24, 1963, at Los Angeles, Calif.
Height, 6.03. Weight, 280.
High School—Fountain Valley, Calif.
Attended University of California at Los Angeles.

Selected by Memphis in 1985 USFL territorial draft.
Selected by Los Angeles Rams in 11th round (274th player selected) of 1985 NFL draft.
Signed by Los Angeles Rams, July 16, 1985.
On injured reserve with shoulder injury, September 2 through October 3, 1985; activated, October 4, 1985.
On injured reserve with pinched nerve in neck, November 15 through remainder of 1985 season.
On injured reserve with knee injury, September 8 through October 23, 1987; activated, October 24, 1987.
Crossed picket line during players' strike, October 14, 1987.
Los Angeles Rams NFL, 1985 through 1987.
Games: 1985 (6), 1986 (16), 1987 (10). Total—32.
Pro statistics: Returned one kickoff for minus six yards and fumbled once, 1986.

CALVIN E. LOVEALL
Defensive Back—Houston Oilers
Born July 23, 1962, at Kennewick, Wash.
Height, 5.09. Weight, 182.
High School—Kennewick, Wash.
Attended University of Idaho.

Selected by Denver in 4th round (51st player selected) of 1985 USFL draft.
Signed by Denver Gold, January 21, 1985.
Franchise merged with Jacksonville, February 19, 1986.
Granted free agency when USFL suspended operations, August 7, 1986; signed as free agent by Ottawa Rough Riders, August 26, 1986.
Released by Ottawa Rough Riders, November 5, 1987; signed as free agent by Houston Oilers, May 18, 1988.

		—INTERCEPTIONS—		
Year Club	G.	No.	Yds.	Avg.TD.
1985—Denver USFL................	18	None		
1986—Ottawa CFL.................	10	2	18	9.0 0
1987—Ottawa CFL.................	18	5	45	9.0 0
USFL Totals—1 Year..........	18	0	0	0.0 0
CFL Totals—2 Years	28	7	63	9.0 0
Pro Totals—3 Years............	46	7	63	9.0 0

Additional USFL statistics: Caught two passes for 57 yards and returned one punt for no yards, 1985.
Additional CFL statistics: Recovered one fumble for six yards and credited with one sack, 1987.

ROBERT KIRK LOWDERMILK
(Known by middle name.)
Center—Minnesota Vikings
Born April 10, 1963, at Canton, O.
Height, 6.03. Weight, 265.
High School—Salem, O.
Attended Ohio State University.
Selected by New Jersey in 1985 USFL territorial draft.
Selected by Minnesota in 3rd round (59th player selected) of 1985 NFL draft.
Signed by Minnesota Vikings, August 12, 1985.
On injured reserve with knee injury, September 2 through October 10, 1986; activated, October 11, 1986.
Minnesota NFL, 1985 through 1987.
Games: 1985 (16), 1986 (11), 1987 (12). Total—39.
Played in NFC Championship Game following 1987 season.

DOMINIC GERALD LOWERY
(Nick)
Placekicker—Kansas City Chiefs
Born May 27, 1956, at Munich, Germany
Height, 6.04. Weight, 189.
High School—Washington, D. C., St. Albans.
Received bachelor of arts degree in government from Dartmouth College in 1978.
Signed as free agent by New York Jets, May 17, 1978.
Released by New York Jets, August 21, 1978; signed as free agent by New England Patriots, September 19, 1978.
Released by New England Patriots, October 6, 1978; signed as free agent by Cincinnati Bengals, July 2, 1979.
Released by Cincinnati Bengals, August 13, 1979; signed as free agent by Washington Redskins, August 18, 1979.
Released by Washington Redskins, August 20, 1979; re-signed by Redskins, August 25, 1979.
Released by Washington Redskins, August 27, 1979; signed as free agent by Kansas City Chiefs, February 16, 1980.

| | | | ——PLACE KICKING—— | | | | |
Year	Club	G.	XP.	XPM.	FG.	FGA.	Pts.
1978—New England NFL..		2	7	0	0	1	7
1980—Kansas City NFL.....		16	37	0	20	26	97
1981—Kansas City NFL.....		16	37	1	26	36	115
1982—Kansas City NFL.....		9	17	0	19	*24	74
1983—Kansas City NFL.....		16	44	1	24	30	116
1984—Kansas City NFL.....		16	35	0	23	33	104
1985—Kansas City NFL.....		16	35	0	24	27	107
1986—Kansas City NFL.....		16	43	0	19	26	100
1987—Kansas City NFL.....		12	26	0	19	23	83
Pro Totals—9 Years.......		119	281	2	174	226	803

Additional pro statistics: Recovered one fumble, 1981.
Played in Pro Bowl (NFL All-Star Game) following 1981 season.

ORLANDO DEWEY LOWRY
Linebacker—Indianapolis Colts
Born August 14, 1961, at Cleveland, O.
Height, 6.04. Weight, 234.
High School—Shaker Heights, O.
Attended Ohio State University.
Brother of Quentin Lowry, linebacker with Washington Redskins
and Tampa Bay Buccaneers, 1981 through 1983.
Selected by New Jersey in 1984 USFL territorial draft.
USFL rights traded with rights to defensive back Garcia Lane by New Jersey Generals to Philadelphia Stars for past considerations involving linebacker Lawrence Taylor, January 9, 1984.
Signed as free agent by Washington Redskins, May 3, 1984.
Released by Washington Redskins, August 27, 1984; signed as free agent by Indianapolis Colts, March 20, 1985.
On injured reserve with finger injury, October 26 through November 26, 1987; activated, November 27, 1987.
Indianapolis NFL, 1985 through 1987.
Games: 1985 (16), 1986 (16), 1987 (8). Total—40.
Pro statistics: Returned one punt for no yards, 1985; recovered one fumble, 1987.

TIMOTHY BRIAN LUCAS
(Tim)
Linebacker—Denver Broncos
Born April 3, 1961, at Stockton, Calif.
Height, 6.03. Weight, 230.
High School—Rio Vista, Calif.
Received bachelor of arts degree in economics from University of California.
Selected by Oakland in 1983 USFL territorial draft.
Selected by St. Louis in 10th round (269th player selected) of 1983 NFL draft.
Signed by Oakland Invaders, May 6, 1983.
On developmental squad, May 6 through May 28, 1983; activated, May 29, 1983.
Protected in merger of Oakland Invaders and Michigan Panthers, December 6, 1984.
On developmental squad, April 6 through remainder of 1985 season.

Granted free agency, August 1, 1985; signed by St. Louis Cardinals, July 22, 1986.
Left St. Louis Cardinals camp and placed on reserve/left camp, July 30, 1986.
Traded by St. Louis Cardinals to San Diego Chargers for draft pick, July 18, 1987.
Released by San Diego Chargers, August 29, 1987; signed as free agent replacement player by Denver Broncos, September 25, 1987.
On developmental squad for 3 games with Oakland Invaders in 1983.
On developmental squad for 12 games with Oakland Invaders in 1985.
Oakland USFL, 1983 through 1985; Denver NFL, 1987.
Games: 1983 (6), 1984 (18), 1985 (6), 1987 (11). Total USFL—30. Total Pro—41.
USFL statistics: Credited with 5½ sacks for 47½ yards, 1984; intercepted one pass for 18 yards and credited with two sacks for six yards, 1985.
NFL statistics: Intercepted one pass for 11 yards and recovered one fumble, 1987.
On developmental squad for USFL Championship Game following 1985 season.
Played in AFC Championship Game following 1987 season.
Played in NFL Championship Game following 1987 season.

DAVID GRAHAM LUTZ
Name pronounced Loots.
Offensive Tackle—Kansas City Chiefs
Born December 30, 1959, at Monroe, N.C.
Height, 6.06. Weight, 290.
High School—Wadesboro, N.C., Bowman.
Attended Georgia Tech.

Selected by Oakland in 3rd round (31st player selected) of 1983 USFL draft.
Selected by Kansas City in 2nd round (34th player selected) of 1983 NFL draft.
Signed by Kansas City Chiefs, June 1, 1983.
On injured reserve with knee injury, September 4 through November 8, 1984; activated, November 9, 1984.
On injured reserve with knee injury, October 7 through November 27, 1986; activated, November 28, 1986.
Kansas City NFL, 1983 through 1987.
Games: 1983 (16), 1984 (7), 1985 (16), 1986 (9), 1987 (12). Total—60.
Pro statistics: Recovered one fumble, 1985.

LESTER EVERETT LYLES
Safety—New York Jets
Born December 27, 1962, at Washington, D.C.
Height, 6.03. Weight, 218.
High School—Washington, D.C., St. Albans.
Attended University of Virginia.

Selected by Orlando in 1985 USFL territorial draft.
Selected by New York Jets in 2nd round (40th player selected) of 1985 NFL draft.
Signed by New York Jets, July 3, 1985.
On injured reserve with hip injury, August 27 through November 15, 1985; activated, November 16, 1985.
On injured reserve with knee injury, September 14 through November 8, 1987; activated, November 9, 1987.
On injured reserve with ankle injury, November 27 through remainder of 1987 season.

			—INTERCEPTIONS—		
Year Club	G.	No.	Yds.	Avg.	TD.
1985—N.Y. Jets NFL	6		None		
1986—N.Y. Jets NFL	16	5	36	7.2	0
1987—N.Y. Jets NFL	4		None		
Pro Totals—3 Years	26	5	36	7.2	0

Additional pro statistics: Recovered one fumble for 13 yards, 1985; recovered one fumble for 16 yards, 1986.

ROBERT LYLES
Linebacker—Houston Oilers
Born March 21, 1961, at Los Angeles, Calif.
Height, 6.01. Weight, 223.
High School—Los Angeles, Calif., Belmont.
Attended Texas Christian University.

Selected by Houston in 5th round (114th player selected) of 1984 NFL draft.
On injured reserve with knee injury, September 25 through December 6, 1984; activated, December 7, 1984.
Houston NFL, 1984 through 1987.
Games: 1984 (6), 1985 (16), 1986 (16), 1987 (12). Total—50.
Pro statistics: Recovered one fumble for 93 yards and a touchdown and intercepted two passes for no yards, 1986; intercepted two passes for 42 yards and recovered three fumbles for 55 yards and a touchdown, 1987.

MARTY LYONS
Defensive End-Defensive Tackle—New York Jets
Born January 15, 1957, at Tokoma Park, Md.
Height, 6.05. Weight, 269.
High School—St. Petersburg, Fla., Catholic.
Attended University of Alabama.

Named as defensive lineman on THE SPORTING NEWS College All-America Team, 1978.
Selected by New York Jets in 1st round (14th player selected) of 1979 NFL draft.
On injured reserve with shoulder injury, November 12 through December 11, 1986; activated, December 12, 1986.
Crossed picket line during players' strike, October 2, 1987.

New York Jets NFL, 1979 through 1987.
Games: 1979 (16), 1980 (16), 1981 (12), 1982 (7), 1983 (16), 1984 (13), 1985 (16), 1986 (12), 1987 (13). Total—121.
Pro statistics: Recovered three fumbles, 1979; recovered one fumble, 1981 and 1986; recovered one fumble for 10 yards, 1982; credited with a safety, 1987.
Played in AFC Championship Game following 1982 season.

JOHN DAVID MAARLEVELD
(Name pronounced MARLEY-veld.)
(J. D.)
Offensive Tackle—Tampa Bay Buccaneers
Born October 24, 1961, at Jersey City, N.J.
Height, 6.06. Weight, 300.
High School—West New York, N.J., Saint Joseph's of the Palisades.
Attended University of Notre Dame and University of Maryland.

Selected by Baltimore in 1986 USFL territorial draft.
Selected by Tampa Bay in 5th round (112th player selected) of 1986 NFL draft.
Signed by Tampa Bay Buccaneers, July 25, 1986.
Tampa Bay NFL, 1986 and 1987.
Games: 1986 (14), 1987 (11). Total—25.

WILLIAM THOMAS MAAS
(Bill)
Defensive Tackle—Kansas City Chiefs
Born March 2, 1962, at Newton Square, Pa.
Height, 6.05. Weight, 268.
High School—Newton Square, Pa., Marple Newtown.
Attended University of Pittsburgh.
Brother-in-law of Dan Marino, quarterback with Miami Dolphins.

Selected by Pittsburgh in 1984 USFL territorial draft.
Selected by Kansas City in 1st round (5th player selected) of 1984 NFL draft.
Signed by Kansas City Chiefs, July 13, 1984.
Kansas City NFL, 1984 through 1987.
Games: 1984 (14), 1985 (16), 1986 (16), 1987 (11). Total—57.
Pro statistics: Recovered one fumble, 1985; recovered two fumbles, 1986; recovered one fumble for six yards and a touchdown, 1987.
Played in Pro Bowl (NFL All-Star Game) following 1986 and 1987 seasons.

MARK GOODWIN MacDONALD
Guard—Minnesota Vikings
Born April 30, 1961, at West Roxbury, Mass.
Height, 6.04. Weight, 267.
High School—Boston, Mass., Catholic Memorial.
Attended Boston College.

Selected by Pittsburgh in 4th round (84th player selected) of 1984 USFL draft (elected to return to college for final year of eligibility).
Selected by Minnesota in 5th round (115th player selected) of 1985 NFL draft.
Signed by Minnesota Vikings, July 25, 1985.
On injured reserve with knee injury, November 12 through remainder of 1986 season.
Minnesota NFL, 1985 through 1987.
Games: 1985 (16), 1986 (10), 1987 (12). Total—38.
Played in NFC Championship Game following 1987 season.

DONALD MATTHEW MACEK
Name pronounced MAY-sick.
(Don)
Center—San Diego Chargers
Born July 2, 1954, at Manchester, N. H.
Height, 6.02. Weight, 270.
High School—Manchester, N. H., Central.
Received bachelor of science degree in marketing from Boston College and attending National University for master's degree in marketing.

Selected by San Diego in 2nd round (31st player selected) of 1976 NFL draft.
On injured reserve with neck injury, December 7 through remainder of 1979 season.
Left San Diego Chargers camp voluntarily, August 7 through August 21, 1984; returned, August 22, 1984.
San Diego NFL, 1976 through 1987.
Games: 1976 (14), 1977 (14), 1978 (14), 1979 (10), 1980 (16), 1981 (15), 1982 (9), 1983 (11), 1984 (13), 1985 (15), 1986 (13), 1987 (11). Total—155.
Pro statistics: Recovered one fumble, 1976, 1977, 1980, 1981, 1983, 1986 and 1987; returned one kickoff for six yards, 1978; fumbled once, 1978, 1982 and 1987; fumbled twice for minus 23 yards, 1980.
Played in AFC Championship Game following 1980 and 1981 seasons.

CEDRIC MANUEL MACK
Cornerback—Phoenix Cardinals

Born September 14, 1960, at Freeport, Tex.
Height, 6.00. Weight, 194.
High School—Freeport, Tex., Brazosport.
Attended Baylor University.
Cousin of Phillip Epps, wide receiver with Green Bay Packers; and Milton Mack,
cornerback with New Orleans Saints.

Selected by Oakland in 12th round (138th player selected) of 1983 USFL draft.
Selected by St. Louis in 2nd round (44th player selected) of 1983 NFL draft.
Signed by St. Louis Cardinals, July 11, 1983.
On injured reserve with dislocated shoulder, September 28 through October 25, 1984; activated, October 26, 1984.
Franchise transferred to Phoenix, March 15, 1988.
Selected by New York Yankees' organization in 22nd round of free-agent draft, June 5, 1979.

			—INTERCEPTIONS—			-PASS RECEIVING-				—TOTAL—		
Year	Club	G.	No.	Yds.	Avg.	TD.	P.C.	Yds.	Avg.	TD.	TD.	Pts.	F.
1983—St. Louis NFL		16	3	25	8.3	0		None			0	0	0
1984—St. Louis NFL		12		None			5	61	12.2	0	0	0	0
1985—St. Louis NFL		16	2	10	5.0	0	1	16	16.0	0	0	0	0
1986—St. Louis NFL		15	4	42	10.5	0		None			0	0	0
1987—St. Louis NFL		10	2	0	0.0	0		None			0	0	0
Pro Totals—5 Years		69	11	77	7.0	0	6	77	12.8	0	0	0	0

Additional pro statistics: Recovered two fumbles, 1985 and 1987; recovered one fumble, 1986.

KEVIN MACK
Fullback—Cleveland Browns

Born August 9, 1962, at Kings Mountain, N.C.
Height, 6.00. Weight, 225.
High School—Kings Mountain, N.C.
Attended Clemson University.

Selected by Washington in 1984 USFL territorial draft.
Rights traded with rights to defensive tackle James Robinson by Washington Federals to Los Angeles Express for
draft choices, March 16, 1984.
Signed by Los Angeles Express, March 16, 1984.
Granted roster exemption, March 16, 1984; activated, March 23, 1984.
On developmental squad, March 30 through April 6, 1984; activated, April 7, 1984.
On developmental squad, April 28 through May 10, 1984; activated, May 11, 1984.
Selected by Cleveland in 1st round (11th player selected) of 1984 NFL supplemental draft.
Released by Los Angeles Express, January 31, 1985; signed by Cleveland Browns, February 1, 1985.
On developmental squad for 3 games with Los Angeles Express in 1984.

			——RUSHING——				PASS RECEIVING				—TOTAL—		
Year	Club	G.	Att.	Yds.	Avg.	TD.	P.C.	Yds.	Avg.	TD.	TD.	Pts.	F.
1984—Los Angeles USFL		12	73	330	4.5	4	6	38	6.3	0	4	24	3
1985—Cleveland NFL		16	222	1104	5.0	7	29	297	10.2	3	10	60	4
1986—Cleveland NFL		12	174	665	3.8	10	28	292	10.4	0	10	60	6
1987—Cleveland NFL		12	201	735	3.7	5	32	223	7.0	1	6	36	6
USFL Totals—1 Year		12	73	330	4.5	4	6	38	6.3	0	4	24	3
NFL Totals—3 Years		40	597	2504	4.2	22	89	812	9.1	4	26	156	16
Pro Totals—4 Years		52	670	2834	4.2	26	95	850	8.9	4	30	180	19

Additional USFL statistics: Returned three kickoffs for 20 yards and recovered four fumbles, 1984.
Additional NFL statistics: Recovered three fumbles, 1985; recovered one fumble, 1986 and 1987.
Played in AFC Championship Game following 1986 and 1987 seasons.
Played in Pro Bowl (NFL All-Star Game) following 1985 and 1987 seasons.

MILTON JEROME MACK
Cornerback—New Orleans Saints

Born September 20, 1963, at Jackson, Miss.
Height, 5.11. Weight, 182.
High School—Jackson, Miss., Callaway.
Attended Alcorn State University.
Cousin of Cedric Mack, cornerback with Phoenix Cardinals.

Selected by New Orleans in 5th round (123rd player selected) of 1987 NFL draft.
Signed by New Orleans Saints, July 24, 1987.
Crossed picket line during players' strike, October 14, 1987.

			——INTERCEPTIONS——			
Year	Club	G.	No.	Yds.	Avg.	TD.
1987—New Orleans NFL		13	4	32	8.0	0

TERENCE MACK
Linebacker—Phoenix Cardinals

Born September 9, 1964, at Winnsboro, S.C.
Height, 6.03. Weight, 230.
High School—Winnsboro, S.C.
Attended Clemson University.

Signed as free agent by Cincinnati Bengals, May 1, 1987.

Released by Cincinnati Bengals, August 2, 1987; signed as free agent replacement player by St. Louis Cardinals, September 25, 1987.
Released by St. Louis Cardinals, December 8, 1987; re-signed by Cardinals, April 1, 1988.
St. Louis NFL, 1987.
Games: 1987 (5).

KYLE ERICKSON MACKEY
Quarterback—New York Jets
Born March 2, 1962, at Alpine, Tex.
Height, 6.03. Weight, 220.
High School—Alpine, Tex.
Attended East Texas State University.
Son of Dee Mackey, tight end with San Francisco 49ers, Baltimore Colts
and New York Jets, 1960 through 1965.

Selected by Washington in 11th round (215th player selected) of 1984 USFL draft.
Selected by St. Louis in 11th round (296th player selected) of 1984 NFL draft.
Signed by St. Louis Cardinals, July 16, 1984.
Released by St. Louis Cardinals, August 26, 1985; signed as free agent by Philadelphia Eagles, March 10, 1986.
Released by Philadelphia Eagles, August 19, 1986; re-signed by Eagles, December 8, 1986.
Released by Philadelphia Eagles, April 15, 1987; signed as free agent by New Orleans Saints, May 7, 1987.
Released by New Orleans Saints, August 3, 1987; signed as free agent replacement player by Miami Dolphins, September 23, 1987.
On injured reserve with mouth injury, October 20 through November 2, 1987.
Released by Miami Dolphins, November 3, 1987; signed as free agent by New York Jets, April 29, 1988.
Active for 16 games with St. Louis Cardinals in 1984; did not play.
Active for 2 games with Philadelphia Eagles in 1986; did not play.

		—————PASSING—————							—RUSHING—				—TOTAL—		
Year Club	G.	Att.	Cmp.	Pct.	Gain	T.P.	P.I.	Avg.	Att.	Yds.	Avg.	TD.	TD.	Pts.	F.
1987—Miami NFL	3	109	57	52.3	604	3	5	5.54	17	98	5.8	2	2	12	3

Quarterback Rating Points: 1987 (58.8).
Additional pro statistics: Fumbled three times for minus six yards, 1987.

CALVIN MAGEE
Tight End—Tampa Bay Buccaneers
Born April 23, 1963, at New Orleans, La.
Height, 6.03. Weight, 240.
High School—New Orleans, La., Booker T. Washington.
Attended Southern University.

Selected by Portland in 1985 USFL territorial draft.
Signed as free agent by Tampa Bay Buccaneers, May 9, 1985.

		—————PASS RECEIVING—————			
Year Club	G.	P.C.	Yds.	Avg.	TD.
1985—Tampa Bay NFL	16	26	288	11.1	3
1986—Tampa Bay NFL	16	45	564	12.5	5
1987—Tampa Bay NFL	11	34	424	12.5	3
Pro Totals—3 Years	43	105	1276	12.2	11

Additional pro statistics: Returned two kickoffs for 20 yards, 1985; fumbled once, 1985 and 1986; returned two kickoffs for 21 yards, 1986.

DONALD JAMES MAGGS
(Don)
Offensive Tackle-Guard—Houston Oilers
Born November 1, 1961, at Youngstown, O.
Height, 6.05. Weight, 279.
High School—Youngstown, O., Cardinal Mooney.
Attended Tulane University.

Selected by Pittsburgh in 2nd round (28th player selected) of 1984 USFL draft.
Signed by Pittsburgh Maulers, January 10, 1984.
On developmental squad, March 3 through March 17, 1984; activated, March 18, 1984.
Selected by Houston in 2nd round (29th player selected) of 1984 NFL supplemental draft.
Franchise disbanded, October 25, 1984.
Selected by New Jersey Generals in USFL dispersal draft, December 6, 1984.
Granted free agency when USFL suspended operations, August 7, 1986; signed by Houston Oilers, August 13, 1986.
Granted roster exemption, August 13 through August 24, 1986; activated, August 25, 1986.
On injured reserve with knee injury, August 31 through December 18, 1987; activated, December 19, 1987.
On developmental squad for 2 games with Pittsburgh Maulers in 1984.
Active for 1 game with Houston Oilers in 1987; did not play.
Pittsburgh USFL, 1984; New Jersey USFL, 1985; Houston NFL, 1986.
Games: 1984 (16), 1985 (18), 1986 (14). Total USFL—34. Toal Pro—48.
Pro statistics: Recovered one fumble, 1984.

—DID YOU KNOW—
That the Washington Redskins and Denver Broncos combined for 45 points in the first half of the 1988 Super Bowl to establish a new record? The old record of 44 points was set in 1985 by San Francisco and Miami.

DONALD VINCENT MAJKOWSKI
(Name pronounced Muh-KOW-skee.)
(Don)
Quarterback—Green Bay Packers
Born February 25, 1964, at Buffalo, N.Y.
Height, 6.02. Weight, 197.
High Schools—Depew, N.Y.; and Fork Union, Vir., Military Academy.
Received degree in sports management from University of Virginia in 1987.
Grandson of Edward Majkowski, minor league pitcher, 1931 and 1940.
Selected by Green Bay in 10th round (255th player selected) of 1987 NFL draft.
Signed by Green Bay Packers, July 25, 1987.

			—————PASSING—————						—RUSHING—				—TOTAL—		
Year	Club	G.	Att.	Cmp.	Pct.	Gain	T.P.	P.I.	Avg.	Att.	Yds.	Avg.	TD.	TD.	Pts.	F.
1987—Green Bay NFL		7	127	55	43.3	875	5	3	6.89	15	127	8.5	0	0	0	5

Quarterback Rating Points: 1987 (70.2).

RICK LEROY MALLORY
Guard—Tampa Bay Buccaneers
Born October 21, 1960, at Seattle, Wash.
Height, 6.02. Weight, 265.
High School—Renton, Wash., Lindbergh.
Attended University of Washington.
Selected by Arizona in 11th round (221st player selected) of 1984 USFL draft.
Selected by Tampa Bay in 9th round (225th player selected) of 1984 NFL draft.
Signed by Tampa Bay Buccaneers, June 21, 1984.
On injured reserve with ankle injury, August 27 through entire 1984 season.
Tampa Bay NFL, 1985 through 1987.
Games: 1985 (13), 1986 (16), 1987 (12). Total—41.
Pro statistics: Caught one pass for nine yards, 1986.

MARK M. MALONE
Quarterback—San Diego Chargers
Born November 22, 1958, at El Cajon, Calif.
Height, 6.04. Weight, 222.
High School—El Cajon, Calif., Valley.
Attended Arizona State University.
Selected by Pittsburgh in 1st round (28th player selected) of 1980 NFL draft.
On physically unable to perform/active with knee injury, July 29 through August 23, 1982.
On reserve, August 24 through December 13, 1982; activated, December 14, 1982.
Traded by Pittsburgh Steelers to San Diego Chargers for 8th round pick in 1988 draft and conditional future considerations, April 12, 1988.
Active for 3 games with Pittsburgh Steelers in 1982; did not play.

			—————PASSING—————						—RUSHING—				—TOTAL—		
Year	Club	G.	Att.	Cmp.	Pct.	Gain	T.P.	P.I.	Avg.	Att.	Yds.	Avg.	TD.	TD.	Pts.	F.
1980—Pittsburgh NFL		1	None							None				0	0	0
1981—Pittsburgh NFL		8	88	45	51.1	553	3	5	6.28	16	68	4.3	2	3	18	2
1983—Pittsburgh NFL		2	20	9	45.0	124	1	2	6.20	None				0	0	0
1984—Pittsburgh NFL		13	272	147	54.0	2137	16	17	7.86	25	42	1.7	3	3	18	4
1985—Pittsburgh NFL		10	233	117	50.2	1428	13	7	6.13	15	80	5.3	1	1	6	3
1986—Pittsburgh NFL		14	425	216	50.8	2444	15	18	5.75	31	107	3.5	5	5	30	7
1987—Pittsburgh NFL		12	336	156	46.4	1896	6	19	5.64	34	162	4.8	3	3	18	10
Pro Totals—8 Years		60	1374	690	50.2	8582	54	68	6.25	121	459	3.8	14	15	90	26

Quarterback Rating Points: 1981 (58.4), 1983 (42.5), 1984 (73.4), 1985 (75.5), 1986 (62.5), 1987 (46.7). Total—62.6.
Additional pro statistics: Caught one pass for 90 yards and a touchdown and returned one kickoff for three yards, 1981; recovered one fumble, 1983; recovered two fumbles, 1984; recovered three fumbles and fumbled three times for minus five yards, 1985; recovered one fumble and fumbled seven times for minus eight yards, 1986; recovered five fumbles and fumbled 10 times for minus three yards, 1987.
Played in AFC Championship Game following 1984 season.

RALPH DeVAUGHN MALONE
Defensive End—Los Angeles Raiders
Born January 12, 1964, at Huntsville, Ala.
Height, 6.05. Weight, 225.
High School—Madison, Ala., Bob Jones.
Received degree from Georgia Tech in 1987.
Signed as free agent by Cleveland Browns, May 4, 1986.
On injured reserve with knee injury, January 10, 1987 through 1986 playoffs.
On injured reserve with finger injury, August 11 through November 9, 1987.
Released by Cleveland Browns, November 10, 1987; signed as free agent by Los Angeles Raiders, April 28, 1988.
Cleveland NFL, 1986.
Games 1986 (16).

JOHN MANDARICH
Nose Tackle—New Orleans Saints
Born August 1, 1961, at Thunder Bay, Ont., Canada.
Height, 6.04. Weight, 281.
High School—Ontario, Can., White Oak.
Attended Kent State University.

Selected by Edmonton in 1st round (8th player selected) of 1984 CFL draft.
Granted free agency, March 1, 1988; signed as free agent by New Orleans Saints, May 3, 1988.
Edmonton CFL, 1984 through 1987.
Games: 1984 (15), 1985 (16), 1986 (17), 1987 (12). Total—60.
CFL statistics: Recovered two fumbles, 1984; returned two kickoffs for three yards, 1985; recovered two fumbles for one yard, 1986.

CHRIS SCOTT MANDEVILLE
Safety—Green Bay Packers
Born February 1, 1965, at Santa Barbara, Calif.
Height, 6.01. Weight, 213.
High School—Irvine, Calif.
Attended University of California at Davis.

Signed as free agent by Green Bay Packers, May 18, 1987.
On injured reserve with thigh injury, November 17 through December 25, 1987; activated, December 26, 1987.
Green Bay NFL, 1987.
Games: 1987 (4).

WILLIAM H. MANDLEY
(Pete)
Wide Receiver-Punt Returner—Detroit Lions
Born July 29, 1961, at Mesa, Ariz.
Height, 5.10. Weight, 191.
High School—Mesa, Ariz., Westwood.
Attended Northern Arizona University.

Selected by Arizona in 1984 USFL territorial draft.
Selected by Detroit in 2nd round (47th player selected) of 1984 NFL draft.
Signed by Detroit Lions, July 10, 1984.

		PASS RECEIVING				–PUNT RETURNS–				—KICKOFF RET.—				—TOTAL—		
Year Club	G.	P.C.	Yds.	Avg.	TD.	No.	Yds.	Avg.	TD.	No.	Yds.	Avg.	TD.	TD.	Pts.	F.
1984—Detroit NFL	15	3	38	12.7	0	2	0	0.0	0	22	390	17.7	0	0	0	2
1985—Detroit NFL	16	18	316	17.6	0	38	403	10.6	1	6	152	25.3	0	1	6	3
1986—Detroit NFL	16	7	106	15.1	0	43	420	9.8	1	2	37	18.5	0	1	6	3
1987—Detroit NFL	12	58	720	12.4	7	23	250	10.9	0			None		7	42	0
Pro Totals—4 Years	59	86	1180	13.7	7	106	1073	10.1	2	30	579	19.3	0	9	54	8

Additional pro statistics: Recovered two fumbles, 1984 and 1985; recovered one fumble, 1986 and 1987; rushed once for three yards, 1987.

DEXTER MANLEY
Defensive End—Washington Redskins
Born February 2, 1959, at Houston, Tex.
Height, 6.03. Weight, 257.
High School—Houston, Tex., Yates.
Attended Oklahoma State University.
Cousin of Eric Dickerson, running back with Indianapolis Colts.

Named to THE SPORTING NEWS NFL All-Star Team, 1986.
Selected by Washington in 5th round (119th player selected) of 1981 NFL draft.
Granted free agency, February 1, 1986; re-signed by Redskins, August 27, 1986.
Granted roster exemption, August 27 through September 4, 1986; activated, Septmber 5, 1986.
Washington NFL, 1981 through 1987.
Games: 1981 (16), 1982 (9), 1983 (16), 1984 (15), 1985 (16), 1986 (16), 1987 (11). Total—99.
Pro statistics: Intercepted one pass for minus two yards and recovered three fumbles for three yards, 1982; intercepted one pass for one yard, 1983; recovered one fumble, 1984; recovered one fumble for 26 yards and a touchdown, 1986.
Played in NFC Championship Game following 1982, 1983, 1986 and 1987 seasons.
Played in NFL Championship Game following 1982, 1983 and 1987 seasons.
Played in Pro Bowl (NFL All-Star Game) following 1986 season.

CHARLES MANN
Defensive End—Washington Redskins
Born April 12, 1961, at Sacramento, Calif.
Height, 6.06. Weight, 270.
High School—Sacramento, Calif., Valley.
Attended University of Nevada at Reno.

Selected by Oakland in 18th round (210th player selected) of 1983 USFL draft.
Selected by Washington in 3rd round (84th player selected) of 1983 NFL draft.
Signed by Washington Redskins, May 9, 1983.
Washington NFL, 1983 through 1987.

Games: 1983 (16), 1984 (16), 1985 (16), 1986 (15), 1987 (12). Total—75.
Pro statistics: Credited with one safety, 1983; recovered one fumble, 1984, 1985 and 1987.
Played in NFC Championship Game following 1983, 1986 and 1987 seasons.
Played in NFL Championship Game following 1983 and 1987 seasons.
Played in Pro Bowl (NFL All-Star Game) following 1987 season.

TIM MANOA
Fullback—Cleveland Browns
Born September 9, 1964, at Tonga.
Height, 6.01. Weight, 227.
High Schools—Kahuka, Haw.; and Wexford, Pa., North Allegheny.
Attended Penn State University.

Selected by Cleveland in 3rd round (80th player selected) of 1987 NFL draft.
Signed by Cleveland Browns, July 26, 1987.

		——RUSHING——				PASS RECEIVING				—TOTAL—		
Year	Club	G.	Att.	Yds.	Avg.	TD.	P.C.	Yds.	Avg.	TD.	TD.	Pts.	F.
1987—Cleveland NFL		12	23	116	5.0	0	1	8	8.0	0	0	0	1

Additional pro statistics: Returned two kickoffs for 14 yards and recovered one fumble, 1987.
Played in AFC Championship Game following 1987 season.

LIONEL MANUEL JR.
Wide Receiver—New York Giants
Born April 13, 1962, at Rancho Cucamonga, Calif.
Height, 5.11. Weight, 180.
High School—La Puente, Calif., Bassett.
Attended Citrus College and University of The Pacific.

Selected by Los Angeles in 1984 USFL territorial draft.
Selected by New York Giants in 7th round (171st player selected) of 1984 NFL draft.
Signed by New York Giants, June 4, 1984.
On injured reserve with pulled hamstring, November 30 through December 27, 1985; activated, December 28, 1985.
On injured reserve with knee injury, September 29, 1986 through January 2, 1987; activated, January 3, 1987.
On injured reserve with thumb injury, September 21 through October 23, 1987; activated, October 24, 1987.

		-PASS RECEIVING-				-PUNT RETURNS-				—TOTAL—		
Year	Club	G.	P.C.	Yds.	Avg.	TD.	No.	Yds.	Avg.	TD.	TD.	Pts.	F.
1984—New York Giants NFL		16	33	619	18.8	4	8	62	7.8	0	4	24	2
1985—New York Giants NFL		12	49	859	17.5	5		None			5	30	1
1986—New York Giants NFL		4	11	181	16.5	3	3	22	7.3	0	3	18	0
1987—New York Giants NFL		12	30	545	18.2	6		None			6	36	1
Pro Totals—4 Years		44	123	2204	17.9	18	11	84	7.6	0	18	108	4

Additional pro statistics: Rushed three times for two yards, 1984; rushed once for 25 yards, 1986; rushed once for minus 10 yards, 1987.
Played in NFC Championship Game following 1986 season.
Played in NFL Championship Game following 1986 season.

KENNETH MARGERUM
(Ken)
Wide Receiver—San Francisco 49ers
Born October 5, 1958, at Fountain Valley, Calif.
Height, 6.00. Weight, 180.
High School—Fountain Valley, Calif.
Received bachelor of arts degree in communications and psychology
from Stanford University.

Named as wide receiver on THE SPORTING NEWS College All-America Team, 1979.
Selected by Chicago in 3rd round (67th player selected) of 1981 NFL draft.
On physically unable to perform/reserve with knee injury, July 20 through entire 1984 season.
On injured reserve with calf injury, September 11 through October 21, 1986.
Released by Chicago Bears, October 22, 1986; signed as free agent by San Francisco 49ers for 1987, November 7, 1986.
Signed for 1986 season, November 21, 1986.
On injured reserve with leg injury, September 7 through December 17, 1987; activated, December 18, 1987.

	——PASS RECEIVING——				
Year	Club	G.	P.C.	Yds.	Avg.	TD.
1981—Chicago NFL		16	39	584	15.0	1
1982—Chicago NFL		9	14	207	14.8	3
1983—Chicago NFL		15	21	336	16.0	2
1985—Chicago NFL		16	17	190	11.2	2
1986—Chi. (1)-S.F. (5) NFL		6	2	12	6.0	0
1987—San Francisco NFL		2	1	7	7.0	0
Pro Totals—6 Years		64	94	1336	14.2	8

Additional pro statistics: Rushed once for 11 yards and recovered one fumble, 1981; fumbled once, 1982, 1983 and 1985; rushed once for seven yards, 1983; rushed once for minus seven yards, 1985.
Played in NFC Championship Game following 1985 season.
Played in NFL Championship Game following 1985 season.

DANIEL CONSTANTINE MARINO JR.
(Dan)
Quarterback—Miami Dolphins

Born September 15, 1961, at Pittsburgh, Pa.
Height, 6.04. Weight, 214.
High School—Pittsburgh, Pa., Central Catholic.
Received bachelor of arts degree in communications from University of Pittsburgh.
Brother-in-law of Bill Maas, defensive tackle with Kansas City Chiefs.

Named THE SPORTING NEWS NFL Player of the Year, 1984.
Named to THE SPORTING NEWS NFL All-Star Team, 1984 through 1986.
Named THE SPORTING NEWS NFL Rookie of the Year, 1983.
Named as quarterback on THE SPORTING NEWS College All-America Team, 1981.
Established NFL records for completion percentage by rookie (58.45), 1983; most touchdowns passing, season (48), 1984; most passing yards gained, season (5,084), 1984; most passes completed, season (378), 1984; most games, 300 yards passing, season (9), 1984; most games, 400 yards passing, season (4), 1984; most passes attempted, season (623), 1986; most 400-yard passing games, career (7); highest passer rating, career (94.1).
Tied NFL record for most consecutive games, 400 yards passing (2), 1984; most 4,000-yard seasons (3); most consecutive seasons leading league in completions (3).
Led NFL quarterbacks in passing with 108.9 points in 1984.
Selected by Los Angeles in 1st round (1st player selected) of 1983 USFL draft.
Selected by Miami in 1st round (27th player selected) of 1983 NFL draft.
Signed by Miami Dolphins, July 9, 1983.
Left Miami Dolphins camp voluntarily, July 25 through August 31, 1985.
Reported and granted roster exemption, September 1 through September 4, 1985; activated, September 5, 1985.
Selected by Kansas City Royals' organization in 4th round of free-agent draft, June 5, 1979.

				—————PASSING—————						——RUSHING——			—TOTAL—		
Year	Club	G.	Att.	Cmp.	Pct.	Gain	T.P.	P.I.	Avg.	Att.	Yds.	Avg.	TD.	TD.	Pts.	F.
1983—Miami NFL		11	296	173	58.4	2210	20	6	7.47	28	45	1.6	2	2	12	5
1984—Miami NFL		16	*564	*362	64.2	*5084	*48	17	*9.01	28	—7	—0.3	0	0	0	6
1985—Miami NFL		16	567	*336	59.3	*4137	*30	21	7.30	26	—24	—0.9	0	0	0	9
1986—Miami NFL		16	*623	*378	60.7	*4746	*44	23	7.62	12	—3	—0.3	0	0	0	8
1987—Miami NFL		12	444	263	59.2	3245	26	13	7.31	12	—5	—0.4	1	1	6	5
Pro Totals—5 Years		71	2494	1512	60.6	19422	168	80	7.79	106	6	0.1	3	3	18	33

Quarterback Rating Points: 1983 (96.0), 1984 (108.9), 1985 (84.1), 1986 (92.5), 1987 (89.2). Total—94.1.
Additional pro statistics: Recovered two fumbles, 1983; recovered two fumbles and fumbled six times for minus three yards, 1984; recovered two fumbles and fumbled nine times for minus four yards, 1985; recovered four fumbles and fumbled eight times for minus 12 yards, 1986; recovered four fumbles and fumbled five times for minus 25 yards, 1987.
Played in AFC Championship Game following 1984 and 1985 seasons.
Played in NFL Championship Game following 1984 season.
Played in Pro Bowl (NFL All-Star Game) following 1984 season.
Named to play in Pro Bowl following 1983 season; replaced due to injury by Bill Kenney.
Named to play in Pro Bowl following 1985 season; replaced due to injury by Ken O'Brien.
Named to play in Pro Bowl following 1986 season; replaced due to injury by Boomer Esiason.
Named to play in Pro Bowl following 1987 season; replaced due to injury by Jim Kelly.

FRED D. MARION
Safety—New England Patriots

Born August 2, 1959, at Gainesville, Fla.
Height, 6.02. Weight, 191.
High School—Gainesville, Fla., Buchholz.
Attended University of Miami (Fla.).
Brother of Frank Marion, linebacker with Memphis Southmen (WFL) and New York Giants, 1975 and 1977 through 1983.

Selected by New England in 5th round (112th player selected) of 1982 NFL draft.

			——INTERCEPTIONS——			
Year	Club	G.	No.	Yds.	Avg.	TD.
1982—New England NFL	9		None			
1983—New England NFL	16	2	4	2.0	0	
1984—New England NFL	16	2	39	19.5	0	
1985—New England NFL	16	7	*189	27.0	0	
1986—New England NFL	16	2	56	28.0	1	
1987—New England NFL	12	4	53	13.3	0	
Pro Totals—6 Years	85	17	341	20.1	1	

Additional pro statistics: Recovered one fumble, 1982, 1984 and 1987; recovered three fumbles for nine yards, 1985; returned one punt for 12 yards, 1986; returned one punt for no yards, 1987.
Played in AFC Championship Game following 1985 season.
Played in NFL Championship Game following 1985 season.
Played in Pro Bowl (NFL All-Star Game) following 1985 season.

DOUGLAS CHARLES MARRONE
(Doug)
Guard—Miami Dolphins

Born July 25, 1964, at Bronx, N.Y.
Height, 6.05. Weight, 269.
High School—Bronx, N.Y., Herbert H. Lehman.
Attended Syracuse University.

Selected by New Jersey in 1986 USFL territorial draft.
Selected by Los Angeles Raiders in 6th round (164th player selected) of 1986 NFL draft.
Signed by Los Angeles Raiders, July 14, 1986.
Released by Los Angeles Raiders, August 19, 1986; signed as free agent by Miami Dolphins for 1987, October 16, 1986.
Released by Miami Dolphins, September 7, 1987; re-signed by Dolphins, September 8, 1987.
On injured reserve with thigh injury, September 19 through December 11, 1987; activated, December 12, 1987.
Miami NFL, 1987.
Games: 1987 (4).

DOUG MARSH
Tight End—Indianapolis Colts
Born June 18, 1958, at Akron, O.
Height, 6.03. Weight, 240.
High School—Akron, O., Central.
Attended University of Michigan.

Selected by St. Louis in 2nd round (33rd player selected) of 1980 NFL draft.
On injured reserve with knee injury, September 1 through October 1, 1981; activated, October 2, 1981.
On injured reserve with dislocated hip, October 28 through remainder of 1981 season.
Granted free agency, February 1, 1987; St. Louis Cardinals exercised option not to re-sign, June 1, 1987.
Signed by Atlanta Falcons, July 24, 1987.
Released by Atlanta Falcons, September 7, 1987; signed as free agent by Indianapolis Colts, February 10, 1988.

		—PASS RECEIVING—			
Year Club	G.	P.C.	Yds.	Avg.	TD.
1980—St. Louis NFL	16	22	269	12.2	4
1981—St. Louis NFL	4	6	80	13.3	1
1982—St. Louis NFL	8	5	83	16.6	0
1983—St. Louis NFL	16	32	421	13.2	8
1984—St. Louis NFL	16	39	608	15.6	5
1985—St. Louis NFL	16	37	355	9.6	1
1986—St. Louis NFL	16	25	313	12.5	0
Pro Totals—7 Years	92	166	2129	12.8	19

Additional pro statistics: Fumbled once, 1980, 1981 and 1983; rushed once for minus five yards, 1984; rushed once for five yards, 1986.

HENRY H. MARSHALL
Wide Receiver—Kansas City Chiefs
Born August 9, 1954, at Broxton, Ga.
Height, 6.02. Weight, 213.
High School—Dalzell, S.C., Hillcrest.
Attended University of Missouri.

Selected by Kansas City in 3rd round (79th player selected) of 1976 NFL draft.
On injured reserve with knee injury, November 25 through remainder of 1981 season.
On injured reserve with broken arm, December 7 through remainder of 1983 season.
On injured reserve with separated shoulder, November 5 through December 12, 1985; activated, December 13, 1985.

		—RUSHING—				PASS RECEIVING				—TOTAL—		
Year Club	G.	Att.	Yds.	Avg.	TD.	P.C.	Yds.	Avg.	TD.	TD.	Pts.	F.
1976—Kansas City NFL	14	5	101	20.2	1	28	443	15.8	2	3	18	1
1977—Kansas City NFL	14	7	11	1.6	0	23	445	19.3	4	4	24	2
1978—Kansas City NFL	16	1	−5	−5.0	0	26	433	16.7	2	2	12	0
1979—Kansas City NFL	16	2	34	17.0	1	21	332	15.8	1	2	12	0
1980—Kansas City NFL	16	3	22	7.3	0	47	799	17.0	6	6	36	0
1981—Kansas City NFL	12	3	69	23.0	0	38	620	16.3	4	4	24	2
1982—Kansas City NFL	9	3	25	8.3	0	40	549	13.7	3	3	18	0
1983—Kansas City NFL	13		None			50	788	15.8	6	6	36	0
1984—Kansas City NFL	16		None			62	912	14.7	4	4	24	2
1985—Kansas City NFL	11		None			25	446	17.8	0	0	0	1
1986—Kansas City NFL	16		None			46	652	14.2	1	1	6	0
1987—Kansas City NFL	12		None			10	126	12.6	0	0	0	0
Pro Totals—12 Years	165	24	257	10.7	2	416	6545	15.7	33	35	210	8

Additional pro statistics: Returned one kickoff for no yards, 1976; returned six punts for 51 yards, 1978; attempted one pass with one interception, 1981; attempted one pass with no completions, 1982 and 1986.

LEONARD ALLEN MARSHALL
Defensive End—New York Giants
Born October 22, 1961, at Franklin, La.
Height, 6.03. Weight, 285.
High School—Franklin, La.
Attended Louisiana State University.
Brother of Chris Marshall, linebacker at Tulane University; and related
to Eddie Robinson, head coach at Grambling State University; Ernie Ladd,
defensive lineman with San Diego Chargers, Houston Oilers and Kansas City Chiefs,
1961 through 1968; and Warren Wells, wide receiver with Detroit Lions and Oakland
Raiders, 1964 and 1967 through 1970.

Selected by Tampa Bay in 10th round (109th player selected) of 1983 USFL draft.

Selected by New York Giants in 2nd round (37th player selected) of 1983 NFL draft.
Signed by New York Giants, June 13, 1983.
On injured reserve with dislocated wrist, December 15 through remainder of 1987 season.
New York Giants NFL, 1983 through 1987.
Games: 1983 (14), 1984 (16), 1985 (16), 1986 (16), 1987 (10). Total—72.
Pro statistics: Credited with one safety, 1983; intercepted one pass for three yards, 1985; intercepted one pass for no yards and recovered three fumbles, 1986.
Played in NFC Championship Game following 1986 season.
Played in NFL Championship Game following 1986 season.
Played in Pro Bowl (NFL All-Star Game) following 1985 and 1986 seasons.

WARREN KEITH MARSHALL
Running Back—Denver Broncos
Born July 24, 1964, at High Point, N.C.
Height, 6.00. Weight, 216.
High School—High Point, N.C., T. Wingate Andrews.
Received bachelor of science degree in education from James Madison University in 1987.

Selected by Denver in 6th round (167th player selected) of 1987 NFL draft.
Signed by Denver Broncos, July 21, 1987.
On injured reserve with eye injury, September 1 through November 27, 1987; activated, November 28, 1987.
On injured reserve with knee injury, January 16, 1988 through remainder of 1987 season playoffs.
Denver NFL, 1987.
Games: 1987 (1).

WILBER BUDDYHIA MARSHALL
Linebacker—Washington Redskins
Born April 18, 1962, at Titusville, Fla.
Height, 6.01. Weight, 230.
High School—Titusville, Fla., Astronaut.
Attended University of Florida.

Named to THE SPORTING NEWS NFL All-Star Team, 1986.
Selected by Tampa Bay in 1984 USFL territorial draft.
Selected by Chicago in 1st round (11th player selected) of 1984 NFL draft.
Signed by Chicago Bears, June 19, 1984.
Granted free agency, February 1, 1988; signed by Washington Redskins, March 15, 1988 when Chicago Bears elected not to match offer; Chicago received 1st round picks in 1988 and 1989 drafts in compensation.

Year Club	G.	No.	Yds.	Avg.	TD.
			—INTERCEPTIONS—		
1984—Chicago NFL	15		None		
1985—Chicago NFL	16	4	23	5.8	0
1986—Chicago NFL	16	5	68	13.6	1
1987—Chicago NFL	12		None		
Pro Totals—4 Years	59	9	91	10.1	1

Additional pro statistics: Ran two yards with lateral on kickoff return and recovered one fumble for eight yards, 1985; recovered three fumbles for 12 yards and a touchdown, 1986; ran once for one yard and recovered one fumble, 1987.
Played in NFC Championship Game following 1984 and 1985 seasons.
Played in NFL Championship Game following 1985 season.
Played in Pro Bowl (NFL All-Star Team) following 1986 and 1987 seasons.

CHARLES M. MARTIN
Nose Tackle—Houston Oilers
Born August 31, 1959, at Canton, Ga.
Height, 6.04. Weight, 280.
High School—Canton, Ga., Cherokee.
Attended Livingston University.

Selected by Birmingham in 15th round (173rd player selected) of 1983 USFL draft.
Signed by Birmingham Stallions, January 22, 1983.
On developmental squad, March 26 through April 9, 1983; activated, April 10, 1983.
On developmental squad, June 17 through July 1, 1983; activated, July 2, 1983.
Released by Birmingham Stallions, February 13, 1984; signed as free agent by Green Bay Packers, July 7, 1984.
On suspended list, December 2 through December 14, 1986; activated, December 15, 1986.
Released by Green Bay Packers, September 22, 1987; awarded on waivers to Houston Oilers, September 23, 1987.
Crossed picket line during players' strike, October 8, 1987.
On developmental squad for 4 games with Birmingham Stallions in 1983.
Birmingham USFL, 1983; Green Bay NFL, 1984 through 1986; Green Bay (2)-Houston (12) NFL, 1987.
Games: 1983 (14), 1984 (16), 1985 (16), 1986 (14), 1987 (14). Total NFL—60. Total Pro—74.
USFL statistics: Recovered one fumble, 1983.
NFL statistics: Recovered one fumble, 1985 through 1987.

CHRISTOPHER MARTIN
(Chris)
Linebacker—Minnesota Vikings
Born December 19, 1960, at Huntsville, Ala.
Height, 6.02. Weight, 231.
High School—Huntsville, Ala., J. O. Johnson.
Attended Auburn University.

Selected by Birmingham in 1983 USFL territorial draft.
Signed as free agent by New Orleans Saints, May 5, 1983.
On injured reserve with ankle injury, December 17 through remainder of 1983 season.
Released by New Orleans Saints, August 27, 1984; awarded on waivers to Minnesota Vikings, August 28, 1984.
New Orleans NFL, 1983; Minnesota NFL, 1984 through 1987.
Games: 1983 (15), 1984 (16), 1985 (12), 1986 (16), 1987 (12). Total—71.
Pro statistics: Recovered one fumble for eight yards and a touchdown, 1984; recovered one fumble, 1986 and 1987.
Played in NFC Championship Game following 1987 season.

DOUG MARTIN
Defensive End—Minnesota Vikings
Born May 22, 1957, at Fairfield, Calif.
Height, 6.03. Weight, 258.
High School—Fairfield, Calif., Armijo.
Attended University of Washington.
Brother of George Martin, defensive end with New York Giants.

Selected by Minnesota in 1st round (9th player selected) of 1980 NFL draft.
Placed on did not report list, August 15, 1980; activated, September 13, 1980.
Granted free agency, February 1, 1984.
Placed on did not report list, August 14 through August 17, 1984; re-signed by Vikings, August 18, 1984.
Granted roster exemption, August 21 through August 31, 1984; activated, September 1, 1984.
Minnesota NFL, 1980 through 1987.
Games: 1980 (11), 1981 (16), 1982 (9), 1983 (16), 1984 (13), 1985 (16), 1986 (15), 1987 (12). Total—108.
Pro statistics: Recovered one fumble, 1981; intercepted one pass for no yards, 1982; recovered two fumbles, 1983 and 1986; recovered two fumbles for 29 yards, 1985.
Played in NFC Championship Game following 1987 season.

ERIC MARTIN
Wide Receiver—New Orleans Saints
Born November 8, 1961, at Van Vleck, Tex.
Height, 6.01. Weight, 207.
High School—Van Vleck, Tex.
Attended Louisiana State University.

Named as wide receiver on THE SPORTING NEWS College All-America Team, 1983.
Selected by Portland in 1985 USFL territorial draft.
Selected by New Orleans in 7th round (179th player selected) of 1985 NFL draft.
Signed by New Orleans Saints, June 21, 1985.
Crossed picket line during players' strike, September 30, 1987.

		PASS RECEIVING			-PUNT RETURNS-				—KICKOFF RET.—				—TOTAL—		
Year Club	G.	P.C.	Yds.	Avg.	TD.	No.	Yds.	Avg.	TD.	No.	Yds.	Avg.	TD.	TD.	Pts.	F.
1985—New Orleans NFL	16	35	522	14.9	4	8	53	6.6	0	15	384	25.6	0	4	24	1
1986—New Orleans NFL	16	37	675	18.2	5	24	227	9.5	0	3	64	21.3	0	5	30	5
1987—New Orleans NFL	15	44	778	17.7	7	14	88	6.3	0	1	15	15.0	0	7	42	3
Pro Totals—3 Years	47	116	1975	17.0	16	46	368	8.0	0	19	463	24.4	0	16	96	9

Additional pro statistics: Rushed twice for minus one yard, 1985; recovered one fumble, 1987.

GEORGE DWIGHT MARTIN
Defensive End—New York Giants
Born February 16, 1953, at Greenville, S. C.
Height, 6.04. Weight, 255.
High School—Fairfield, Calif., Armijo.
Attended University of Oregon.
Brother of Doug Martin, defensive end with Minnesota Vikings.

Established NFL record for touchdowns by down lineman, career (6).
Selected by New York Giants in 11th round (262nd player selected) of 1975 NFL draft.
New York Giants NFL, 1975 through 1987.
Games: 1975 (14), 1976 (14), 1977 (10), 1978 (16), 1979 (16), 1980 (16), 1981 (16), 1982 (9), 1983 (14), 1984 (16), 1985 (16), 1986 (16), 1987 (12). Total—185.
Pro statistics: Recovered two fumbles, 1976; intercepted one pass for 30 yards and one touchdown, 1977; recovered one fumble, 1977, 1980 and 1984 through 1986; ran 83 yards with blocked field goal for a touchdown, 1978; recovered three fumbles, 1979; caught one pass for four yards and a touchdown, 1980; recovered three fumbles for 28 yards and two touchdowns, 1981; intercepted one pass for 56 yards and a touchdown, 1985; intercepted one pass for 78 yards and a touchdown, 1986.
Played in NFC Championship Game following 1986 season.
Played in NFL Championship Game following 1986 season.

KELVIN BRIAN MARTIN
Wide Receiver—Dallas Cowboys
Born May 14, 1965, at San Diego, Calif.
Height, 5.09. Weight, 163.
High School—Jacksonville, Fla., Ribault.
Received bachelor of arts degree in speech communication from Boston College in 1987.

Selected by Dallas in 4th round (95th player selected) of 1987 NFL draft.
Signed by Dallas Cowboys, July 13, 1987.
On injured reserve with leg injury, September 15 through November 13, 1987; activated, November 14, 1987.
Crossed picket line during players' strike, October 14, 1987.

Year Club	G.	P.C.	Yds.	Avg.	TD.	No.	Yds.	Avg.	TD.	No.	Yds.	Avg.	TD.	TD.	Pts.	F.
		PASS RECEIVING				-PUNT RETURNS-				—KICKOFF RET.—				—TOTAL—		
1987—Dallas NFL	7	5	103	20.6	0	22	216	9.8	0	12	237	19.8	0	0	0	1

MICHAEL MARTIN
(Mike)
Wide Receiver—Cincinnati Bengals
Born November 18, 1960, at Washington, D.C.
Height, 5.10. Weight, 186.
High School—Washington, D.C., Eastern.
Attended University of Illinois.

Selected by Chicago in 1983 USFL territorial draft.
Selected by Cincinnati in 8th round (221st player selected) of 1983 NFL draft.
Signed by Cincinnati Bengals, May 19, 1983.
On injured reserve with broken fibula, November 17 through remainder of 1983 season.
On injured reserve with hamstring injury, October 13 through December 18, 1986; activated, December 19, 1986.

Year Club	G.	P.C.	Yds.	Avg.	TD.	No.	Yds.	Avg.	TD.	No.	Yds.	Avg.	TD.	TD.	Pts.	F.
		PASS RECEIVING				-PUNT RETURNS-				—KICKOFF RET.—				—TOTAL—		
1983—Cincinnati NFL............	10	2	22	11.0	0	23	227	9.9	0	1	19	19.0	0	0	0	2
1984—Cincinnati NFL............	15	11	164	14.9	0	24	376	*15.7	0	19	386	20.3	0	0	0	4
1985—Cincinnati NFL............	16	14	187	13.4	0	32	268	8.4	0	48	1104	23.0	0	0	0	4
1986—Cincinnati NFL............	7	3	68	22.7	0	13	96	7.4	0	4	83	20.8	0	0	0	0
1987—Cincinnati NFL............	12	20	394	19.7	3	28	277	9.9	0	3	51	17.0	0	3	18	1
Pro Totals—5 Years.......	60	50	835	16.7	3	120	1244	10.4	0	75	1643	21.9	0	3	18	11

Additional pro statistics: Rushed twice for 21 yards, 1983; rushed once for three yards and recovered two fumbles, 1984.

ROD MARTIN
Linebacker—Los Angeles Raiders
Born April 7, 1954, at Welch, W. Va.
Height, 6.02. Weight, 225.
High School—Los Angeles, Calif., Hamilton.
Attended Los Angeles City College and University of Southern California.
Brother of Ricky Martin, wide receiver with Winnipeg Blue Bombers
and Pittsburgh Maulers, 1982 through 1984.

Named to THE SPORTING NEWS NFL All-Star Team, 1983.
Selected by Oakland in 12th round (317th player selected) of 1977 NFL draft.
Traded with defensive back Steve Jackson by Oakland Raiders to San Francisco 49ers for future considerations, August 30, 1977.
Released by San Francisco 49ers, September 14, 1977; signed as free agent by Oakland Raiders, November 7, 1977.
Franchise transferred to Los Angeles, May 7, 1982.

Year Club	G.	No.	Yds.	Avg.	TD.
		——INTERCEPTIONS——			
1977—Oakland NFL.................	1		None		
1978—Oakland NFL.................	15		None		
1979—Oakland NFL.................	16		None		
1980—Oakland NFL.................	16	2	15	7.5	0
1981—Oakland NFL.................	16	1	7	7.0	0
1982—L.A. Raiders NFL........	9	3	60	20.0	*1
1983—L.A. Raiders NFL........	16	4	81	20.3	*2
1984—L.A. Raiders NFL........	16	2	31	15.5	1
1985—L.A. Raiders NFL........	16	1	16	16.0	0
1986—L.A. Raiders NFL........	16	1	15	15.0	0
1987—L.A. Raiders NFL........	12		None		
Pro Totals—11 Years.........	149	14	225	16.1	4

Additional pro statistics: Recovered one fumble, 1979; recovered two fumbles for 42 yards and a touchdown, 1980; recovered three fumbles, 1981; returned one kickoff for no yards, 1983; recovered one fumble for 77 yards and a touchdown and credited with one safety, 1984; recovered three fumbles for three yards and fumbled once, 1985.
Played in AFC Championship Game following 1977, 1980 and 1983 seasons.
Played in NFL Championship Game following 1980 and 1983 seasons.
Played in Pro Bowl (NFL All-Star Team) following 1983 and 1984 seasons.

TRACY MARTIN
Wide Receiver-Kick Returner—New York Jets
Born December 4, 1964, at Minneapolis, Minn.
Height, 6.03. Weight, 205.
High School—Brooklyn Center, Minn.
Attended University of North Dakota.
Son of Bill Lordan, former drummer for Sly and The Family Stone, Jimi Hendrix and James Brown.

Selected by New York Jets in 6th round (161st player selected) of 1987 NFL draft.
Signed by New York Jets, July 24, 1987.

Year Club	G.	No.	Yds.	Avg.	TD.
		KICKOFF RETURNS			
1987—New York Jets NFL....	12	8	180	22.5	0

EUGENE RAYMOND MARVE
Linebacker—Buffalo Bills
Born August 14, 1960, at Flint, Mich.
Height, 6.02. Weight, 240.
High School—Flint, Mich., Northern.
Attended Saginaw Valley State College.

Selected by Buffalo in 3rd round (59th player selected) of 1982 NFL draft.
On injured reserve with dislocated elbow, November 14 through remainder of 1987 season.
Buffalo NFL, 1982 through 1987.
Games: 1982 (9), 1983 (16), 1984 (16), 1985 (14), 1986 (16), 1987 (5). Total—76.
Pro statistics: Intercepted one pass for no yards, 1982; recovered one fumble, 1982 and 1985; recovered three fumbles, 1984.

MICKEY MARVIN
Guard—Los Angeles Raiders
Born October 5, 1955, at Hendersonville, N.C.
Height, 6.04. Weight, 265.
High School—Hendersonville, N.C., Brevard.
Attended University of Tennessee.

Selected by Oakland in 4th round (112th player selected) of 1977 NFL draft.
On injured reserve with knee injury, September 12 through December 6, 1979; activated, December 7, 1979.
Franchise transferred to Los Angeles, May 7, 1982.
On injured reserve with knee injury, August 27 through December 25, 1987; activated, December 26, 1987.
Crossed picket line during players' strike, September 24, 1987.
Oakland NFL, 1977 through 1981; Los Angeles Raiders NFL, 1982 through 1987.
Games: 1977 (8), 1978 (14), 1979 (2), 1980 (16), 1981 (16), 1982 (9), 1983 (14), 1984 (9), 1985 (15), 1986 (16), 1987 (1). Total—120.
Pro statistics: Recovered one fumble, 1978, 1980, 1981 and 1984.
Played in AFC Championship Game following 1977, 1980 and 1983 seasons.
Played in NFL Championship Game following 1980 and 1983 seasons.

RICHARD RAY MASSIE
(Rick)
Wide Receiver—Denver Broncos
Born January 16, 1960, at Paris, Ky.
Height, 6.01. Weight, 190.
High School—Paris, Ky., Bourbon County.
Received bachelor of arts degree in education from University of Kentucky in 1983.

Signed as free agent by Calgary Stampeders, March 27, 1984.
Selected by Denver in 2nd round (46th player selected) of 1984 NFL supplemental draft.
Released by Calgary Stampeders, August 18, 1984; re-signed by Stampeders, September 16, 1984.
On injured reserve, October 14 through remainder of 1984 season.
Released by Calgary Stampeders, June 20, 1985; signed by Denver Broncos, February 6, 1986.
Released by Denver Broncos, August 4, 1986; re-signed by Broncos, May 1, 1987.
Released by Denver Broncos, August 26, 1987; re-signed as replacement player by Broncos, September 25, 1987.
On injured reserve with broken leg, December 18 through remainder of 1987 season.

| | | —PASS RECEIVING— | | | |
Year Club	G.	P.C.	Yds.	Avg.	TD.
1984—Calgary CFL	9	15	233	15.5	0
1987—Denver NFL	9	13	244	18.8	4
Pro Totals—2 Years	18	28	477	17.0	4

BRUCE MARTIN MATHISON
Quarterback—Seattle Seahawks
Born April 25, 1959, at Superior, Wis.
Height, 6.03. Weight, 203.
High School—Superior, Wis.
Attended University of Nebraska.

Selected by Boston in 1983 USFL territorial draft.
Selected by San Diego in 10th round (272nd player selected) of 1983 NFL draft.
Signed by San Diego Chargers, May 26, 1983.
Released by San Diego Chargers, September 2, 1985; signed as free agent by Buffalo Bills, September 10, 1985.
Released by Buffalo Bills, August 26, 1986; signed as free agent by San Diego Chargers, October 28, 1986.
Released by San Diego Chargers, November 12, 1986; signed as free agent by Los Angeles Raiders, March 4, 1987.
Released by Los Angeles Raiders, July 31, 1987; signed as free agent replacement player by Houston Oilers, September 23, 1987.
Left Houston Oilers camp voluntarily and released, September 25, 1987; signed as free agent replacement player by Seattle Seahawks, September 30, 1987.
On injured reserve with back injury, December 4 through remainder of 1987 season.

| | | ——————PASSING—————— | | | | | | | ——RUSHING—— | | | —TOTAL— | | |
Year Club	G.	Att.	Cmp.	Pct.	Gain	T.P.	P.I.	Avg.	Att.	Yds.	Avg.	TD.	TD.	Pts.	F.
1983—San Diego NFL	1	5	3	60.0	41	0	1	8.20	1	0	0.0	0	0	0	1
1984—San Diego NFL	2			None						None			0	0	0
1985—Buffalo NFL	10	228	113	49.6	1635	4	14	7.17	27	231	8.6	1	1	6	8
1986—San Diego NFL	2			None					1	—1	—1.0	0	0	0	0

— 281 —

Year Club		G.	PASSING						RUSHING				TOTAL		
			Att.	Cmp.	Pct.	Gain	T.P.	P.I.	Avg.	Att.	Yds.	Avg.	TD.	TD.	Pts.	F.

Year Club	G.	Att.	Cmp.	Pct.	Gain	T.P.	P.I.	Avg.	Att.	Yds.	Avg.	TD.	TD.	Pts.	F.
1987—Seattle NFL	3	76	36	47.4	501	3	5	6.59	5	15	3.0	0	0	0	0
Pro Totals—5 Years	18	309	152	49.2	2177	7	20	7.05	34	245	7.2	1	1	6	9

Quarterback Rating Points: 1985 (53.5), 1987 (54.8). Total—53.1.
Additional pro statistics: Recovered two fumbles and fumbled eight times for minus nine yards, 1985.

TREVOR ANTHONY MATICH
Center—New England Patriots
Born October 9, 1961, at Sacramento, Calif.
Height, 6.04. Weight, 270.
High School—Sacramento, Calif., Rio Americano.
Attended Brigham Young University.

Selected by Houston in 10th round (139th player selected) of 1985 USFL draft.
Selected by New England in 1st round (28th player selected) of 1985 NFL draft.
Signed by New England Patriots, July 30, 1985.
On injured reserve with ankle injury, October 12 through remainder of 1985 season.
On injured reserve with broken foot, September 7 through November 6, 1987; activated, November 7, 1987.
New England NFL, 1985 through 1987.
Games: 1985 (1), 1986 (11), 1987 (6). Total—18.

RONALD ANTHONY MATTES
(Ron)
Offensive Tackle—Seattle Seahawks
Born August 8, 1963, at Shenandoah, Pa.
Height, 6.06. Weight, 306.
High School—Ashland, Pa., North Schuylkill.
Attended University of Virginia.

Selected by Orlando in 1985 USFL territorial draft.
Selected by Seattle in 7th round (193rd player selected) of 1985 NFL draft.
Signed by Seattle Seahawks, July 19, 1985.
On injured reserve with back injury, August 27 through entire 1985 season.
Seattle NFL, 1986 and 1987.
Games: 1986 (16), 1987 (12). Total—28.

AUBREY DERRON MATTHEWS
Wide Receiver—Atlanta Falcons
Born September 15, 1962, at Pasaqoula, Miss.
Height, 5.07. Weight, 165.
High School—Moss Point, Miss.
Attended Gulf Coast Junior College and Delta State University.

Signed by Jacksonville Bulls, January 10, 1984.
On developmental squad, April 10 through April 24, 1984; activated, April 25, 1984.
On developmental squad, June 10 through June 14, 1985; activated, June 15, 1985.
Granted free agency when USFL suspended operations, August 7, 1986; signed as free agent by Atlanta Falcons, August 18, 1986.
Granted roster exemption, August 18 through August 21, 1986; activated, August 22, 1986.
On injured reserve with hamstring injury, August 26 through November 26, 1986; activated after clearing procedural waivers, November 28, 1986.
On developmental squad for 2 games with Jacksonville Bulls in 1984.
On developmental squad for 1 game with Jacksonville Bulls in 1985.

Year Club	G.	PASS RECEIVING				KICKOFF RET.				TOTAL		
		P.C.	Yds.	Avg.	TD.	No.	Yds.	Avg.	TD.	TD.	Pts.	F.
1984—Jacksonville USFL	16	27	406	15.0	1	29	623	21.5	0	1	6	5
1985—Jacksonville USFL	16	25	271	10.8	5	19	366	19.3	0	5	30	2
1986—Atlanta NFL	4	1	25	25.0	0	3	42	14.0	0	0	0	0
1987—Atlanta NFL	12	32	537	16.8	3		None			3	18	2
USFL Totals—2 Years	32	52	677	13.0	6	48	989	20.6	0	6	36	7
NFL Totals—2 Years	16	33	562	17.0	3	3	42	14.0	0	3	18	2
Pro Totals—4 Years	48	85	1239	14.6	9	51	1031	20.2	0	9	54	9

Additional USFL statistics: Rushed three times for five yards and recovered four fumbles, 1984; recovered two fumbles, 1985.
Additional NFL statistics: Rushed once for 12 yards, 1986; rushed once for minus four yards and recovered one fumble, 1987.

BRUCE MATTHEWS
Offensive Tackle-Guard—Houston Oilers
Born August 8, 1961, at Arcadia, Calif.
Height, 6.05. Weight, 280.
High School—Arcadia, Calif.
Received degree in industrial engineering from University of Southern California in 1983.
Son of Clay Matthews Sr., end with San Francisco 49ers, 1950 and 1953 through 1955;
brother of Clay Matthews Jr., linebacker with Cleveland Browns.
Named as guard on THE SPORTING NEWS College All-America Team, 1982.

Selected by Los Angeles in 1983 USFL territorial draft.
Selected by Houston in 1st round (9th player selected) of 1983 NFL draft.
Signed by Houston Oilers, July 24, 1983.
Granted free agency, February 1, 1987.
Placed on reserve/unsigned list, August 31 through November 3, 1987.
Re-signed by Houston Oilers, November 4, 1987.
Granted roster exemption, November 4 through November 6, 1987; activated, November 7, 1987.
Houston NFL, 1983 through 1987.
Games: 1983 (16); 1984 (16), 1985 (16), 1986 (16), 1987 (8). Total—72.
Pro statistics: Recovered three fumbles, 1985; recovered one fumble for seven yards, 1986.

WILLIAM CLAY MATTHEWS JR.
(Known by middle name.)
Linebacker—Cleveland Browns
Born March 15, 1956, at Palo Alto, Calif.
Height, 6.02. Weight, 235.
High Schools—Arcadia, Calif.; and Winnetka, Ill., New Trier East.
Received bachelor of science degree in business administration from University of Southern California
in 1978; and attending Southern California for master's in business administration.
Son of Clay Matthews Sr., end with San Francisco 49ers, 1950 and 1953 through 1955;
brother of Bruce Matthews, offensive tackle-guard with Houston Oilers.
Named to THE SPORTING NEWS NFL All-Star Team, 1984.
Named as linebacker on THE SPORTING NEWS College All-America Team, 1977.
Selected by Cleveland in 1st round (12th player selected) of 1978 NFL draft.
On injured reserve with broken ankle, September 16 through December 30, 1982; activated, December 31, 1982.

Year Club	G.	No.	Yds.	Avg.	TD.
			—INTERCEPTIONS—		
1978—Cleveland NFL.............	15	1	5	5.0	0
1979—Cleveland NFL.............	16	1	30	30.0	0
1980—Cleveland NFL.............	14	1	6	6.0	0
1981—Cleveland NFL.............	16	2	14	7.0	0
1982—Cleveland NFL.............	2		None		
1983—Cleveland NFL.............	16		None		
1984—Cleveland NFL.............	16		None		
1985—Cleveland NFL.............	14		None		
1986—Cleveland NFL.............	16	2	12	6.0	0
1987—Cleveland NFL.............	12	3	62	20.7	1
Pro Totals—10 Years.........	137	10	129	12.9	1

Additional pro statistics: Recovered two fumbles, 1979 and 1987; recovered one fumble, 1980 and 1984; recovered
two fumbles for 16 yards, 1981; recovered one fumble for 15 yards, 1985.
Played in AFC Championship Game following 1986 and 1987 seasons.
Played in Pro Bowl (NFL All-Star Game) following 1985 and 1987 seasons.

BRETT DERRELL MAXIE
Safety—New Orleans Saints
Born January 13, 1962, at Dallas, Tex.
Height, 6.02. Weight, 194.
High School—Dallas, Tex., James Madison.
Attended Texas Southern University.
Signed as free agent by New Orleans Saints, June 21, 1985.
Released by New Orleans Saints, September 2, 1985; re-signed by Saints, September 3, 1985.
New Orleans NFL, 1985 through 1987.
Games: 1985 (16), 1986 (15), 1987 (12). Total—43.
Pro statistics: Recovered one fumble, 1985 and 1986; intercepted two passes for 15 yards, 1986; intercepted three
passes for 17 yards, returned one punt for 12 yards and credited with a safety, 1987.

VERNON LEROY MAXWELL
Linebacker—Detroit Lions
Born October 25, 1961, at Birmingham, Ala.
Height, 6.02. Weight, 238.
High School—Los Angeles, Calif., Verbum Dei.
Attended Arizona State University.
Named as linebacker on THE SPORTING NEWS College All-America Team, 1982.
Selected by Arizona in 1983 USFL territorial draft.
Selected by Baltimore in 2nd round (29th player selected) of 1983 USFL draft.
Signed by Baltimore Colts, July 21, 1983.
Franchise transferred to Indianapolis, March 31, 1984.
Traded by Indianapolis Colts to San Diego Chargers for 5th round pick in 1986 draft, August 1, 1985.
Released by San Diego Chargers, August 27, 1985; signed as free agent by Detroit Lions, October 25, 1985.
Baltimore NFL, 1983; Indianapolis NFL, 1984; Detroit NFL, 1985 through 1987.
Games: 1983 (16), 1984 (16), 1985 (9), 1986 (15), 1987 (12). Total—68.
Pro statistics: Intercepted one pass for 31 yards, 1983; recovered two fumbles, 1983 and 1984; recovered four
fumbles, 1986.

MARK MAY
Offensive Tackle—Washington Redskins
Born November 2, 1959, at Oneonta, N.Y.
Height, 6.06. Weight, 295.
High School—Oneonta, N.Y.
Attended University of Pittsburgh.

Outland Trophy winner, 1980.
Named as offensive tackle on THE SPORTING NEWS College All-America Team, 1980.
Selected by Washington in 1st round (20th player selected) of 1981 NFL draft.
On injured reserve with knee injury, September 8 through October 23, 1987; activated, October 24, 1987.
Washington NFL, 1981 through 1987.
Games: 1981 (16), 1982 (9), 1983 (15), 1984 (16), 1985 (16), 1986 (16), 1987 (10). Total—98.
Pro statistics: Recovered one fumble, 1983 and 1985 through 1987.
Played in NFC Championship Game following 1982, 1983, 1986 and 1987 seasons.
Played in NFL Championship Game following 1982, 1983 and 1987 seasons.

RUEBEN MAYES
Running Back—New Orleans Saints
Born June 16, 1963, at North Battleford, Saskatchewan, Can.
Height, 5.11. Weight, 200.
High School—North Battleford, Saskatchewan, Can., Comprehensive.
Attended Washington State University.

Named THE SPORTING NEWS Rookie of the Year, 1986.
Selected by Memphis in 1986 USFL territorial draft.
Selected by New Orleans in 3rd round (57th player selected) of 1986 NFL draft.
Signed by New Orleans Saints, June 20, 1986.

		—RUSHING—				PASS RECEIVING				—TOTAL—		
Year Club	G.	Att.	Yds.	Avg.	TD.	P.C.	Yds.	Avg.	TD.	TD.	Pts.	F.
1986—New Orleans NFL	16	286	1353	4.7	8	17	96	5.6	0	8	48	4
1987—New Orleans NFL	12	243	917	3.8	5	15	68	4.5	0	5	30	8
Pro Totals—2 Years	28	529	2270	4.3	13	32	164	5.1	0	13	78	12

Additional pro statistics: Returned 10 kickoffs for 213 yards (21.3 avg.), 1986; recovered one fumble, 1987.
Named to play in Pro Bowl (NFL All-Star Game) following 1986 season; replaced due to injury by Gerald Riggs.
Named to play in Pro Bowl following 1987 season; replaced due to injury by Gerald Riggs.

STAFFORD EARL MAYS
Defensive End—Minnesota Vikings
Born March 13, 1958, at Lawrence, Kan.
Height, 6.02. Weight, 264.
High School—Tacoma, Wash., Lincoln.
Attended Mt. Hood Junior College and received degree in sociology
from University of Washington in 1981.

Selected by St. Louis in 9th round (225th player selected) of 1980 NFL draft.
Released by St. Louis Cardinals, August 17, 1987; signed as free agent by Minnesota Vikings, August 19, 1987.
Released by Minnesota Vikings, September 7, 1987; re-signed as replacement player by Vikings, October 8, 1987.
St. Louis NFL, 1980 through 1986; Minnesota NFL, 1987.
Games: 1980 (16), 1981 (16), 1982 (8), 1983 (16), 1984 (16), 1985 (16), 1986 (16), 1987 (12). Total—116.
Pro statistics: Recovered one fumble, 1981 and 1982; recovered two fumbles, 1983 and 1987.
Played in NFC Championship Game following 1987 season.

DERRICK MARK McADOO
Running Back—Phoenix Cardinals
Born April 2, 1965, at Pensacola, Fla.
Height, 5.10. Weight, 198.
High School—Houston, Tex., Northwest Academy.
Attended Baylor University.
Cousin of Bob McAdoo, forward with Buffalo, New York Knicks, Boston, Detroit,
New Jersey, Los Angeles Lakers and Philadelphia, 1972-73 through 1985-86.

Signed as free agent by St. Louis Cardinals, May 19, 1987.
Crossed picket line during players' strike, October 2, 1987.
Franchise transferred to Phoenix, March 15, 1988.

		—RUSHING—				PASS RECEIVING				—TOTAL—		
Year Club	G.	Att.	Yds.	Avg.	TD.	P.C.	Yds.	Avg.	TD.	TD.	Pts.	F.
1987—St. Louis NFL	15	53	230	4.3	3	2	12	6.0	0	4	24	2

		KICKOFF RETURNS			
Year Club	G.	No.	Yds.	Avg.TD.	
1987—St. Louis NFL	15	23	444	19.3	0

Additional pro statistics: Recovered three fumbles (including one in end zone for a touchdown), 1987.

—DID YOU KNOW—

That in the Seattle-Pittsburgh game on December 6, both starting quarterbacks had fewer than 100 yards passing? The Steelers' Mark Malone threw for 99 yards and the Seahawks' Dave Krieg 91 in Pittsburgh's 13-9 victory.

KEVIN LEE McARTHUR
Linebacker—New York Jets
Born May 11, 1963, at Cameron, La.
Height, 6.02. Weight, 245.
High School—Lake Charles, La.
Attended Lamar University.

Signed as free agent by Los Angeles Raiders, May 20, 1984.
Released by Los Angeles Raiders, July 22, 1984; awarded on waivers to New York Jets, July 23, 1984.
Released by New York Jets, August 20, 1984; re-signed by Jets, May 7, 1985.
Released by New York Jets, August 27, 1985; re-signed by Jets, March 21, 1986.
Released by New York Jets, August 19, 1986; re-signed by Jets, October 29, 1986.
New York Jets NFL, 1986 and 1987.
Games: 1986 (8), 1987 (12). Total—20.

KENNETH CHRISTOPHER McCLENDON
(Skip)
Defensive End—Cincinnati Bengals
Born April 9, 1964, at Detroit, Mich.
Height, 6.06. Weight, 270.
High School—Detroit, Mich., Redford.
Attended Northwestern University, Butler County Community College
and Arizona State University.

Selected by Cincinnati in 3rd round (77th player selected) of 1987 NFL draft.
Signed by Cincinnati Bengals, May 29, 1987.
Cincinnati NFL, 1987.
Games: 1987 (12).

MIKE J. McCLOSKEY
Tight End—Indianapolis Colts
Born February 2, 1961, at Philadelphia, Pa.
Height, 6.05. Weight, 246.
High School—Philadelphia, Pa., Father Judge.
Received bachelor of science degree from Penn State University.

Selected by Philadelphia in 1983 USFL territorial draft.
Selected by Houston in 4th round (88th player selected) of 1983 NFL draft.
Signed by Houston Oilers, June 22, 1983.
Released by Houston Oilers, August 26, 1986; signed as free agent by Los Angeles Raiders, March 21, 1987.
Released by Los Angeles Raiders, August 17, 1987; awarded on waivers to Philadelphia Eagles, August 18, 1987.
On injured reserve with hamstring injury, September 6 through November 11, 1987; activated, November 12, 1987.
Released by Philadelphia Eagles, November 23, 1987; awarded on waivers to Indianapolis Colts, November 24, 1987.

| | | —PASS RECEIVING— | | | |
Year Club	G.	P.C.	Yds.	Avg.	TD.
1983—Houston NFL	16	16	137	8.6	1
1984—Houston NFL	15	9	152	16.9	1
1985—Houston NFL	16	4	29	7.3	1
1987—Philadelphia NFL	1		None		
Pro Totals—4 Years	48	29	318	11.0	3

Additional pro statistics: Returned one kickoff for 11 yards, 1983; recovered one fumble, 1985.

MILT B. McCOLL
Linebacker—San Francisco 49ers
Born August 28, 1959, at Oak Park, Ill.
Height, 6.06. Weight, 230.
High School—Covina, Calif., South Hills.
Received degree in human biology from Stanford University and studied
at Stanford's overseas campus at Cliveden, England, 1980;
and currently attending medical school at Stanford University.
Son of Bill McColl, end with Chicago Bears, 1952 through 1959.

Signed as free agent by San Francisco 49ers, July 1, 1981.
On injured reserve with pulled hamstring, October 22 through November 17, 1983; activated, November 18, 1983.
San Francisco NFL, 1981 through 1987.
Games: 1981 (16), 1982 (9), 1983 (12), 1984 (16), 1985 (16), 1986 (16), 1987 (12). Total—97.
Pro statistics: Intercepted one pass for 22 yards, 1981; recovered one fumble for 28 yards and a touchdown, 1985; intercepted one pass for no yards, 1987.
Played in NFC Championship Game following 1981 and 1984 seasons.
Member of San Francisco 49ers for NFC Championship Game following 1983 season; did not play.
Played in NFL Championship Game following 1981 and 1984 seasons.

—DID YOU KNOW—
That the 1987 Super Bowl champion New York Giants didn't score a touchdown in the first quarter of a game that season until Joe Morris' 2-yard touchdown run a 27-7 victory over St. Louis in Week 15?

PHILIP JOSEPH McCONKEY
(Phil)
Wide Receiver—New York Giants
Born February 24, 1957, at Buffalo, N.Y.
Height, 5.10. Weight, 170.
High School—Buffalo, N.Y., Caniaius.
Attended U.S. Naval Academy.

Signed as free agent by New York Giants, May 6, 1983.
On military reserve, August 29 through entire 1983 season.
On injured reserve with broken ribs, November 26 through remainder of 1984 season.
Released by New York Giants, September 1, 1986; awarded on waivers to Green Bay Packers, September 2, 1986.
Traded by Green Bay Packers to New York Giants for 12th round pick in 1987 draft, September 30, 1986.

Year Club	G.	PASS RECEIVING P.C.	Yds.	Avg.	TD.	–PUNT RETURNS– No.	Yds.	Avg.	TD.	–KICKOFF RET.– No.	Yds.	Avg.	TD.	–TOTAL– TD.	Pts.	F.
1984—N.Y. Giants NFL	13	8	154	19.3	0	46	306	6.7	0	28	541	19.3	0	1	6	2
1985—N.Y. Giants NFL	16	25	404	16.2	1	53	442	8.3	0	12	234	19.5	0	1	6	1
1986—GB (4)-NYG (12) NFL.	16	16	279	17.4	1	32	253	7.9	0	24	471	19.6	0	1	6	1
1987—N.Y. Giants NFL	12	11	186	16.9	0	42	394	9.4	0	1	8	8.0	0	0	0	2
Pro Totals—4 Years.......	57	60	1023	17.1	2	173	1395	8.1	0	65	1254	19.3	0	3	18	6

Additional pro statistics: Recovered kickoff in end zone for a touchdown, 1984; recovered one fumble, 1984, 1986 and 1987; recovered two fumbles, 1985.
Played in NFC Championship Game following 1986 season.
Played in NFL Championship Game following 1986 season.

MIKE McDONALD
Linebacker—Los Angeles Rams
Born June 22, 1958, at North Hollywood, Calif.
Height, 6.01. Weight, 235.
High School—Burbank, Calif., John Burroughs.
Attended University of Southern California.

Signed as free agent by Los Angeles Rams, December 21, 1983.
Released by Los Angeles Rams, August 27, 1984; re-signed by Rams, August 28, 1984.
Released by Los Angeles Rams, August 17, 1986; re-signed by Rams, September 24, 1986.
Released by Los Angeles Rams, February 1, 1987; signed as free agent by Kansas City Chiefs, August 28, 1987.
Released by Kansas City Chiefs, August 31, 1987; signed as free agent replacement player by Los Angeles Rams, October 15, 1987.
Los Angeles Rams NFL, 1984, 1986 and 1987.
Games: 1984 (16), 1986 (13), 1987 (10). Total—39.

COACHING RECORD
Graduate assistant coach at University of Southern California, 1980 and 1981.
Assistant coach at Burroughs (Calif.) High School, 1982, 1983 and 1985.

PAUL McDONALD
Quarterback—Dallas Cowboys
Born February 23, 1958, at Montebello, Calif.
Height, 6.02. Weight, 185.
High School—La Puente, Calif., Bishop Amat.
Received business degree from University of Southern California; and
attending Case Western Reserve for master's degree in business.

Selected by Cleveland in 4th round (109th player selected) of 1980 NFL draft.
Released by Cleveland Browns, June 23, 1986; signed as free agent by Seattle Seahawks, July 16, 1986.
Released by Seattle Seahawks, August 26, 1986; signed as free agent by Dallas Cowboys, November 4, 1986.
Active for 12 games with Dallas Cowboys in 1987; did not play.

Year Club	G.	PASSING Att.	Cmp.	Pct.	Gain	T.P.	P.I.	Avg.	RUSHING Att.	Yds.	Avg.	TD.	–TOTAL– TD.	Pts.	F.
1980—Cleveland NFL..................	15			None					3	2	0.7	0	0	0	2
1981—Cleveland NFL..................	12	57	35	61.4	463	4	2	8.12	2	0	0.0	0	0	0	4
1982—Cleveland NFL..................	9	149	73	49.0	993	5	8	6.66	7	–13	–1.9	0	0	0	3
1983—Cleveland NFL..................	16	68	32	47.1	341	1	4	5.01	3	17	5.7	0	0	0	1
1984—Cleveland NFL..................	16	493	271	55.0	3472	14	23	7.04	22	4	0.2	1	1	6	16
1985—Cleveland NFL..................	16			None							None		0	0	0
1986—Dallas NFL	1			None							None		0	0	0
Pro Totals—8 Years...........	85	767	411	53.6	5269	24	37	6.87	37	10	0.3	1	1	6	26

Quarterback Rating Points: 1981 (95.8), 1982 (59.5), 1983 (42.6), 1984 (67.3). Total—65.7.
Additional pro statistics: Fumbled twice for minus nine yards, 1980; recovered one fumble, 1983; caught one pass for minus four yards, recovered five fumbles and fumbled 16 times for minus five yards, 1984.

TIM McDONALD
Defensive Back—Phoenix Cardinals
Born January 6, 1965, at Fresno, Calif.
Height, 6.02. Weight, 207.
High School—Edison, Calif.
Attended University of Southern California.

Selected by St. Louis in 2nd round (34th player selected) of 1987 NFL draft.
Signed by St. Louis Cardinals, August 2, 1987.
On injured reserve with broken ankle, September 1 through December 11, 1987; activated, December 12, 1987.
Franchise transferred to Phoenix, March 15, 1988.
St. Louis NFL, 1987.
Games: 1987 (3).

REGINALD LEE McELROY
(Reggie)
Offensive Tackle—New York Jets
Born March 4, 1960, at Beaumont, Tex.
Height, 6.06. Weight, 275.
High School—Beaumont, Tex., Charlton Pollard.
Received degree in physical education from West Texas State University.

Selected by New York Jets in 2nd round (51st player selected) of 1982 NFL draft.
On injured reserve with knee injury, August 24 through entire 1982 season.
Granted free agency, February 1, 1985; re-signed by Jets, September 10, 1985.
Granted roster exemption, September 10 through September 13, 1985; activated, September 14, 1985.
On injured reserve with knee injury, October 22 through December 11, 1986; activated, December 12, 1986.
On injured reserve with knee injury, December 17 through remainder of 1986 season.
On physically unable to perform/reserve with knee injury, September 6 through November 8, 1987; activated, November 9, 1987.
New York Jets NFL, 1983 through 1987.
Games: 1983 (16), 1984 (16), 1985 (13), 1986 (8), 1987 (8). Total—61.
Pro statistics: Returned one kickoff for seven yards, 1983; recovered one fumble for minus two yards, 1986.

VANN WILLIAM McELROY
Safety—Los Angeles Raiders
Born January 13, 1960, at Birmingham, Ala.
Height, 6.02. Weight, 195.
High School—Uvalde, Tex.
Received bachelor of business administration degree in marketing management
from Baylor University in 1983.

Selected by Los Angeles Raiders in 3rd round (64th player selected) of 1982 NFL draft.
On inactive list, September 12 and September 19, 1982.

| | | —INTERCEPTIONS— | | | |
Year Club	G.	No.	Yds.	Avg.	TD.
1982—L.A. Raiders NFL.........	7		None		
1983—L.A. Raiders NFL.........	16	8	68	8.5	0
1984—L.A. Raiders NFL.........	16	4	42	10.5	0
1985—L.A. Raiders NFL.........	12	2	23	11.5	0
1986—L.A. Raiders NFL.........	16	7	105	15.0	0
1987—L.A. Raiders NFL.........	12	4	41	10.3	1
Pro Totals—6 Years............	79	25	279	11.2	1

Additional pro statistics: Intercepted one pass for no yards, 1982; recovered three fumbles for five yards, 1983; recovered four fumbles for 12 yards, 1984; recovered one fumble, 1985.
Played in AFC Championship Game following 1983 season.
Played in NFL Championship Game following 1983 season.
Played in Pro Bowl (NFL All-Star Game) following 1983 and 1984 seasons.

CRAIG McEWEN
Tight End—Washington Redskins
Born December 16, 1965, at Northport, N.Y.
Height, 6.01. Weight, 207.
High School—Northport, N.Y.
Attended University of Utah.

Signed as free agent by Washington Redskins, May 4, 1987.
Released by Washington Redskins, September 7, 1987; re-signed as replacement player by Redskins, September 23, 1987.
On injured reserve with back injury, November 3 through remainder of 1987 season.

| | | —PASS RECEIVING— | | | |
Year Club	G.	P.C.	Yds.	Avg.	TD.
1987—Washington..................	4	12	164	13.7	0

PAUL McFADDEN
Placekicker—Philadelphia Eagles
Born September 24, 1961, at Cleveland, O.
Height, 5.11. Weight, 163.
High School—Euclid, O.
Received bachelor of science degree in general administration
from Youngstown State University in 1984.

Selected by Chicago in 9th round (174th player selected) of 1984 USFL draft.
Selected by Philadelphia in 12th round (312th player selected) of 1984 NFL draft.
Signed by Philadelphia Eagles, July 15, 1984.

Year	Club	G.	XP.	XPM.	FG.	FGA.	Pts.
		PLACE KICKING					
1984—Philadelphia NFL		16	26	1	*30	*37	116
1985—Philadelphia NFL		16	29	0	25	30	104
1986—Philadelphia NFL		16	26	1	20	31	86
1987—Philadelphia NFL		12	36	0	16	26	84
Pro Totals—4 Years		60	117	2	91	124	390

BUFORD LAMAR McGEE

Running Back—Los Angeles Rams

Born August 16, 1960, at Durant, Miss.
Height, 6.00. Weight, 206.
High School—Durant, Miss.
Received bachelor of science degree in business from University of Mississippi in 1984.

Selected by Birmingham in 1984 USFL territorial draft.
Selected by San Diego in 11th round (286th player selected) of 1984 NFL draft.
Signed by San Diego Chargers, June 2, 1984.
On injured reserve with hamstring injury, September 3 through October 4, 1985; activated, October 5, 1985.
On injured reserve with knee injury, November 8 through remainder of 1986 season.
Granted free agency, February 1, 1987; re-signed by Chargers and traded with 2nd round pick in 1988 draft and conditional 4th or 5th round pick in 1989 draft to Los Angeles Rams for running back Barry Redden, June 9, 1987.
On injured reserve with ruptured Achilles tendon, October 28 through remainder of 1987 season.

		RUSHING				PASS RECEIVING				TOTAL		
Year Club	G.	Att.	Yds.	Avg.	TD.	P.C.	Yds.	Avg.	TD.	TD.	Pts.	F.
1984—San Diego NFL	16	67	226	3.4	4	9	76	8.4	2	6	36	1
1985—San Diego NFL	11	42	181	4.3	3	3	15	5.0	0	3	18	4
1986—San Diego NFL	9	63	187	3.0	7	10	105	10.5	0	7	42	4
1987—Los Angeles Rams NFL	3	3	6	2.0	1	7	40	5.7	0	1	6	0
Pro Totals—4 Years	39	175	600	3.4	15	29	236	8.1	2	17	102	9

		KICKOFF RETURNS			
Year Club	G.	No.	Yds.	Avg.	TD.
1984—San Diego NFL	16	14	315	22.5	0
1985—San Diego NFL	11	7	135	19.3	0
1986—San Diego NFL	9	1	15	15.0	0
1987—L.A. Rams NFL	3			None	
Pro Totals—4 Years	39	22	465	21.0	0

Additional pro statistics: Recovered one fumble, 1984; recovered two fumbles, 1985; attempted one pass with one completion for one yard, 1986.

TIMOTHY DWANYE McGEE

(Tim)

Wide Receiver—Cincinnati Bengals

Born August 7, 1964, at Cleveland, O.
Height, 5.10. Weight, 175.
High School—Cleveland, O., John Hay.
Attended University of Tennessee.

Selected by Memphis in 1986 USFL territorial draft.
Selected by Cincinnati in 1st round (21st player selected) of 1986 NFL draft.
USFL rights traded by Memphis Showboats to Jacksonville Bulls for rights to center Leonard Burton and offensive tackle Doug Williams, May 6, 1986.
Signed by Cincinnati Bengals, July 26, 1986.
On injured reserve with hamstring injury, September 19 through October 20, 1987; activated, October 21, 1987.

		PASS RECEIVING				KICKOFF RET.				TOTAL		
Year Club	G.	P.C.	Yds.	Avg.	TD.	No.	Yds.	Avg.	TD.	TD.	Pts.	F.
1986—Cincinnati NFL	16	16	276	17.3	1	43	*1007	23.4	0	1	6	0
1987—Cincinnati NFL	11	23	408	17.7	1	15	242	16.1	0	1	6	0
Pro Totals—2 Years	27	39	684	17.5	2	58	1249	21.5	0	2	12	0

Additional pro statistics: Rushed four times for 10 yards, returned three punts for 21 yards and recovered one fumble, 1986; rushed once for minus 10 yards, 1987.

LAWRENCE McGREW

Linebacker—New England Patriots

Born July 23, 1957, at Berkeley, Calif.
Height, 6.05. Weight, 233.
High School—Berkeley, Calif.
Attended Contra Costa Junior College and received degree in speech communications from University of Southern California in 1980.

Selected by New England in 2nd round (45th player selected) of 1980 NFL draft.
On injured reserve with knee and elbow injuries, December 19 through remainder of 1980 season.
On injured reserve with knee injury, August 31 through entire 1981 season.
New England NFL, 1980 and 1982 through 1987.
Games: 1980 (11), 1982 (8), 1983 (16), 1984 (16), 1985 (13), 1986 (14), 1987 (12). Total—90.
Pro statistics: Intercepted one pass for three yards, 1983; recovered one fumble, 1983 and 1987; intercepted one pass for no yards and recovered two fumbles, 1985; intercepted two passes for 44 yards, 1986.
Played in AFC Championship Game following 1985 season.
Played in NFL Championship Game following 1985 season.

THOMAS McHALE
(Tom)
Defensive End—Tampa Bay Buccaneers
Born February 25, 1963, at Gaithersburg, Md.
Height, 6.04. Weight, 275.
High School—Gaithersburg, Md.
Attended Cornell University.

Signed as free agent by Tampa Bay Buccaneers, May 4, 1987.
On injured reserve with back injury, September 7 through November 27, 1987; activated, November 28, 1987.
Tampa Bay NFL, 1987.
Games: 1987 (3).
Pro statistics: Recovered one fumble, 1987.

GUY MAURICE McINTYRE
Guard—San Francisco 49ers
Born Feburary 17, 1961, at Thomasville, Ga.
Height, 6.03. Weight, 264.
High School—Thomasville, Ga.
Attended University of Georgia.
Cousin of Lomas Brown, offensive tackle with Detroit Lions.

Selected by Jacksonville in 1984 USFL territorial draft.
Selected by San Francisco in 3rd round (73rd player selected) of 1984 NFL draft.
Signed by San Francisco 49ers, May 8, 1984.
On injured reserve with foot injury, October 31 through remainder of 1987 season.
San Francisco NFL, 1984 through 1987.
Games: 1984 (15), 1985 (15), 1986 (16), 1987 (3). Total—49.
Pro statistics: Returned one kickoff for no yards, 1984; recovered one fumble in end zone for a touchdown, 1985.
Played in NFC Championship Game following 1984 season.
Played in NFL Championship Game following 1984 season.

RALEIGH McKENZIE
Guard—Washington Redskins
Born February 8, 1963, at Knoxville, Tenn.
Height, 6.02. Weight, 275.
High School—Knoxville, Tenn., Austin-East.
Twin brother of Reggie McKenzie, linebacker with Los Angeles Raiders.

Selected by Washington in 11th round (290th player selected) of 1985 NFL draft.
Signed by Washington Redskins, June 20, 1985.
Washington NFL, 1985 through 1987.
Games: 1985 (6), 1986 (15), 1987 (12). Total—33.
Played in NFC Championship Game following 1986 and 1987 seasons.
Played in NFL Championship Game following 1987 season.

REGINALD McKENZIE
(Reggie)
Linebacker—Los Angeles Raiders
Born February 8, 1963, at Knoxville, Tenn.
Height, 6.01. Weight, 235.
High School—Knoxville, Tenn., Austin-East.
Attended University of Tennessee.
Twin brother of Raleigh McKenzie, guard with Washington Redskins.

Selected by Los Angeles Raiders in 10th round (275th player selected) of 1985 NFL draft.
Signed by Los Angeles Raiders, June 26, 1985.
Los Angeles Raiders NFL, 1985 through 1987.
Games: 1985 (16), 1986 (16), 1987 (10). Total—42.
Pro statistics: Recovered one fumble, 1985; intercepted one pass for nine yards, 1986.

DENNIS LEWIS McKINNON
Wide Receiver—Chicago Bears
Born August 22, 1961, at Quitman, Ga.
Height, 6.01. Weight, 185.
High School—Miami, Fla., South Miami Senior.
Received bachelor of arts degree in criminology from Florida State University in 1983.

Signed as free agent by Chicago Bears, May 4, 1983.
On physically unable to perform/reserve with knee injury, August 18 through entire 1986 season.

Year Club	G.	PASS RECEIVING				-PUNT RETURNS-				—KICKOFF RET.—				—TOTAL—		
		P.C.	Yds.	Avg.	TD.	No.	Yds.	Avg.	TD.	No.	Yds.	Avg.	TD.	TD.	Pts.	F.
1983—Chicago NFL	16	20	326	16.3	4	34	316	9.3	⋆1	2	42	21.0	0	5	30	2
1984—Chicago NFL	12	29	431	14.9	3	5	62	12.4	0		None			3	18	1
1985—Chicago NFL	14	31	555	17.9	7	4	44	11.0	0	1	16	16.0	0	7	42	1
1987—Chicago NFL	12	27	406	15.0	1	40	405	10.1	⋆2		None			3	18	6
Pro Totals—4 Years	54	107	1718	16.1	15	83	827	10.0	3	3	58	19.3	0	18	108	10

Additional pro statistics: Recovered one fumble, 1983; rushed twice for 12 yards, 1984; rushed once for no yards, 1985; recovered three fumbles, 1987.

Played in NFC Championship Game following 1984 and 1985 seasons.
Played in NFL Championship Game following 1985 season.

DENNIS N. McKNIGHT
Center-Guard—San Diego Chargers
Born September 12, 1959, at Dallas, Tex.
Height, 6.03. Weight, 273.
High School—Staten Island, N.Y., Wagner.
Received degree from Drake University in 1981.

Signed as free agent by Cleveland Browns, May 3, 1981.
Released by Cleveland Browns, August 18, 1981; signed as free agent by San Diego Chargers, March 30, 1982.
On inactive list, September 12 and September 19, 1982.
San Diego NFL, 1982 through 1987.
Games: 1982 (7), 1983 (16), 1984 (16), 1985 (16), 1986 (16), 1987 (12). Total—83.
Pro statistics: Recovered two fumbles, 1983 and 1984.

TIM B. McKYER
Cornerback—San Francisco 49ers
Born September 5, 1963, at Orlando, Fla.
Height, 6.00. Weight, 174.
High School—Port Arthur, Tex., Lincoln.
Attended University of Texas at Arlington.

Selected by San Francisco in 3rd round (64th player selected) of 1986 NFL draft.
Signed by San Francisco 49ers, July 20, 1986.

		—INTERCEPTIONS—			
Year Club	G.	No.	Yds.	Avg.	TD.
1986—San Francisco NFL	16	6	33	5.5	1
1987—San Francisco NFL	12	2	0	0.0	0
Pro Totals—2 Years............	28	8	33	4.1	1

Additional pro statistics: Returned one kickoff for 15 yards and returned one punt for five yards, 1986.

CHRIS McLEMORE
Running Back—Los Angeles Raiders
Born December 31, 1963, at Las Vegas, Nev.
Height, 6.01. Weight, 235.
High School—Las Vegas, Nev., Valley.
Attended University of Colorado and University of Arizona.

Selected by Los Angeles Raiders in 11th round (288th player selected) of 1987 NFL draft.
Signed by Los Angeles Raiders, July 10, 1987.
Released by Los Angeles Raiders, September 7, 1987; signed as free agent replacement player by Indianapolis Colts, September 23, 1987.
Released by Indianapolis Colts, October 27, 1987; signed as free agent by Los Angeles Raiders, November 11, 1987.
On injured reserve with elbow injury, December 26 through remainder of 1987 season.

		—RUSHING—			PASS RECEIVING			—TOTAL—		
Year Club	G.	Att.	Yds.	Avg.	TD.	P.C.	Yds.	Avg. TD.	TD. Pts. F.	
1987—Ind.(2)-L.A. Raid.(3) NFL......................	5	17	58	3.4	0	2	9	4.5 0	0 0 1	

JAMES ROBERT McMAHON
(Jim)
Quarterback—Chicago Bears
Born August 21, 1959, at Jersey City, N.J.
Height, 6.01. Weight, 187.
High School—Roy, Utah.
Attended Brigham Young University.

Selected by Chicago in 1st round (5th player selected) of 1982 NFL draft.
On injured reserve with lacerated kidney, November 9 through remainder of 1984 season.
On injured reserve with shoulder injury, November 28 through remainder of 1986 season.
On injured reserve with shoulder injury, September 7 through October 21, 1987; activated, October 22, 1987.

		—PASSING—							—RUSHING—				—TOTAL—		
Year Club	G.	Att.	Cmp.	Pct.	Gain	T.P.	P.I.	Avg.	Att.	Yds.	Avg.	TD.	TD.	Pts.	F.
1982—Chicago NFL....................	8	210	120	57.1	1501	9	7	7.15	24	105	4.4	1	1	6	1
1983—Chicago NFL....................	14	295	175	59.3	2184	12	13	7.40	55	307	5.6	2	3	18	4
1984—Chicago NFL....................	9	143	85	59.4	1146	8	2	8.01	39	276	7.1	2	2	12	1
1985—Chicago NFL....................	13	313	178	56.9	2392	15	11	7.64	47	252	5.4	3	4	24	4
1986—Chicago NFL....................	6	150	77	51.3	995	5	8	6.63	22	152	6.9	1	1	6	1
1987—Chicago NFL....................	7	210	125	59.5	1639	12	8	7.80	22	88	4.0	2	2	12	2
Pro Totals—6 Years..........	57	1321	760	57.5	9857	61	49	7.46	209	1180	5.6	11	13	78	13

Quarterback Rating Points: 1982 (80.1), 1983 (77.6), 1984 (97.8), 1985 (82.6), 1986 (61.4), 1987 (87.4). Total—81.0.
Additional pro statistics: Punted once for 59 yards, 1982; caught one pass for 18 yards and a touchdown, punted once for 36 yards and recovered three fumbles, 1983; caught one pass for 42 yards, 1984; caught one pass for 13 yards and a touchdown, 1985.
Played in NFC Championship Game following 1985 season.
Played in NFL Championship Game following 1985 season.
Played in Pro Bowl (NFL All-Star Game) following 1985 season.

STEVE DOUGLAS McMICHAEL
Defensive Tackle—Chicago Bears
Born October 17, 1957, at Houston, Tex.
Height, 6.02. Weight, 265.
High School—Freer, Tex.
Attended University of Texas.

Named to THE SPORTING NEWS NFL All-Star Team, 1986 and 1987.
Selected by New England in 3rd round (73rd player selected) of 1980 NFL draft.
On injured reserve with back injury, November 3 through remainder of 1980 season.
Released by New England Patriots, August 24, 1981; signed as free agent by Chicago Bears, October 15, 1981.
New England NFL, 1980; Chicago NFL, 1981 through 1987.
Games: 1980 (6), 1981 (10), 1982 (9), 1983 (16), 1984 (16), 1985 (16), 1986 (16), 1987 (12). Total—101.
Pro statistics: Recovered one fumble, 1981 and 1985; recovered one fumble for 64 yards, 1982; recovered two fumbles, 1983 and 1986; credited with one safety, 1985 and 1986; intercepted one pass for five yards, 1986.
Played in NFC Championship Game following 1984 and 1985 seasons.
Played in NFL Championship Game following 1985 season.
Played in Pro Bowl (NFL All-Star Team) following 1986 and 1987 seasons.

LEWIS LORANDO McMILLAN
(Randy)
Fullback—Indianapolis Colts
Born December 17, 1958, at Havre de Grace, Md.
Height, 6.00. Weight, 212.
High School—Belair, Md., North Hartford.
Attended Hartford Community College and University of Pittsburgh.

Selected by Baltimore in 1st round (12th player selected) of 1981 NFL draft.
Franchise transferred to Indianapolis, March 31, 1984.
On non-football injury list with broken leg, August 1 through entire 1987 season.

Year Club	G.	Att.	Yds.	Avg.	TD.	P.C.	Yds.	Avg.	TD.	TD.	Pts.	F.
1981—Baltimore NFL	16	149	597	4.0	3	50	466	9.3	1	4	24	1
1982—Baltimore NFL	9	101	305	3.0	1	15	90	6.0	0	1	6	1
1983—Baltimore NFL	16	198	802	4.1	5	24	195	8.1	1	6	36	5
1984—Indianapolis NFL	16	163	705	4.3	5	19	201	10.6	0	5	30	1
1985—Indianapolis NFL	15	190	858	4.5	7	22	115	5.2	0	7	42	0
1986—Indianapolis NFL	16	189	609	3.2	3	34	289	8.5	0	3	18	5
Pro Totals—6 Years	88	990	3876	3.9	24	164	1356	8.3	2	26	156	13

Additional pro statistics: Recovered one fumble, 1982; recovered three fumbles, 1983; recovered two fumbles, 1986.

AUDREY GLENN McMILLIAN
Cornerback—Houston Oilers
Born August 13, 1962, at Carthage, Tex.
Height, 6.00. Weight, 190.
High School—Carthage, Tex.
Received bachelor of science degree in industrial distribution
from Purdue University in 1985.

Selected by Houston in 1985 USFL territorial draft.
Selected by New England in 3rd round (84th player selected) of 1985 NFL draft.
Signed by New England Patriots, July 1, 1985.
Released by New England Patriots, September 2, 1985; awarded on waivers to Houston Oilers, September 3, 1985.
Released by Houston Oilers, September 22, 1986; re-signed by Oilers, September 24, 1986.
Houston NFL, 1985 through 1987.
Games: 1985 (16), 1986 (16), 1987 (12). Total—44.
Pro statistics: Recovered two fumbles for four yards, 1986.

SEAN McNANIE
Defensive End—Buffalo Bills
Born September 9, 1961, at Mundelein, Ill.
Height, 6.05. Weight, 270.
High School—Mundelein, Ill.
Attended Arizona State University and San Diego State University.

Selected by Oakland in 2nd round (30th player selected) of 1984 USFL draft.
Selected by Buffalo in 3rd round (79th player selected) of 1984 NFL draft.
Signed by Buffalo Bills, June 1, 1984.
Buffalo NFL, 1984 through 1987.
Games: 1984 (15), 1985 (16), 1986 (16), 1987 (12). Total—59.
Pro statistics: Recovered one fumble, 1986; recovered one fumble for 14 yards and a touchdown, 1987.

DONALD McNEAL
(Don)
Cornerback—Miami Dolphins
Born May 6, 1958, at Atmore, Ala.
Height, 5.11. Weight, 192.
High School—Atmore, Ala., Escambia County.
Received bachelor of science degree in social welfare from University of Alabama.
Cousin of Mike Williams, running back with Philadelphia Eagles, 1983 and 1984.

Named as cornerback on THE SPORTING NEWS College All-America Team, 1979.
Selected by Miami in 1st round (21st player selected) of 1980 NFL draft.
On injured reserve with wrist injury, December 11 through remainder of 1980 season.
On injured reserve with Achilles tendon injury, August 29 through entire 1983 season.
On injured reserve with knee injury, August 19 through October 18, 1985; activated, October 19, 1985.

| | | —INTERCEPTIONS— | | | |
Year Club	G.	No.	Yds.	Avg.	TD.
1980—Miami NFL	13	5	17	3.4	0
1981—Miami NFL	12	None			
1982—Miami NFL	9	4	42	10.5	*1
1984—Miami NFL	11	3	41	13.7	1
1985—Miami NFL	10	None			
1986—Miami NFL	15	2	46	23.0	0
1987—Miami NFL	12	None			
Pro Totals—7 Years	82	14	146	10.4	2

Additional pro statistics: Recovered one fumble, 1980 and 1981; recovered two fumbles for five yards, 1984.
Played in AFC Championship Game following 1982, 1984 and 1985 seasons.
Played in NFL Championship Game following 1982 and 1984 seasons.

FREEMAN McNEIL
Running Back—New York Jets
Born April 22, 1959, at Jackson, Miss.
Height, 5.11. Weight, 212.
High School—Wilmington, Calif., Banning.
Attended University of California at Los Angeles.

Selected by New York Jets in 1st round (3rd player selected) of 1981 NFL draft.
On injured reserve with foot injury, October 10 through November 13, 1981; activated, November 14, 1981.
On injured reserve with separated shoulder, September 27 through November 10, 1983; activated, November 11, 1983.
On injured reserve with broken ribs, December 6 through remainder of 1984 season.
On injured reserve with dislocated elbow, September 14 through October 19, 1986; activated, October 20, 1986.

| | | —RUSHING— | | | | PASS RECEIVING | | | | —TOTAL— | | |
Year Club	G.	Att.	Yds.	Avg.	TD.	P.C.	Yds.	Avg.	TD.	TD.	Pts.	F.
1981—New York Jets NFL	11	137	623	4.5	2	18	171	9.5	1	3	18	5
1982—New York Jets NFL	9	151	*786	*5.2	6	16	187	11.7	1	7	42	7
1983—New York Jets NFL	9	160	654	4.1	1	21	172	8.2	3	4	24	4
1984—New York Jets NFL	12	229	1070	4.7	5	25	294	11.8	1	6	36	4
1985—New York Jets NFL	14	294	1331	4.5	3	38	427	11.2	2	5	30	9
1986—New York Jets NFL	12	214	856	4.0	5	49	410	8.4	1	6	36	8
1987—New York Jets NFL	9	121	530	4.4	0	24	262	10.9	1	1	6	1
Pro Totals—7 Years	76	1306	5850	4.5	22	191	1923	10.1	10	32	192	38

Additional pro statistics: Attempted one pass with one completion for five yards and a touchdown, 1983; recovered one fumble, 1983 and 1984.
Played in AFC Championship Game following 1982 season.
Played in Pro Bowl (NFL All-Star Game) following 1982 and 1985 seasons.
Named to Pro Bowl following 1984 season; replaced due to injury by Greg Bell.

GERALD LYNN McNEIL
Wide Receiver-Punt Returner—Cleveland Browns
Born March 27, 1962, at Frankfurt, West Germany.
Height, 5.07. Weight, 147.
High School—Killeen, Tex.
Attended Baylor University.

Named as punt returner on THE SPORTING NEWS USFL All-Star Team, 1985.
Selected by San Antonio in 1984 USFL territorial draft.
Signed by Houston Gamblers, February 16, 1984.
USFL rights traded by San Antonio Gunslingers to Houston Gamblers for 2nd round pick in 1985 draft, February 23, 1984.
On developmental squad, March 23 through April 13, 1984; activated, April 14, 1984.
Selected by Cleveland in 2nd round (44th player selected) of 1984 NFL supplemental draft.
Traded with defensive backs Luther Bradley, Will Lewis, Mike Mitchell and Durwood Roquemore, defensive end Pete Catan, quarterbacks Jim Kelly and Todd Dillon, defensive tackles Tony Fitzpatrick, Van Hughes and Hosea Taylor, running back Sam Harrell, linebackers Andy Hawkins and Ladell Wills, wide receivers Richard Johnson, Scott McGhee, Ricky Sanders and Clarence Verdin, guard Rich Kehr, center Billy Kidd and offensive tackles Chris Riehm and Tommy Robison by Houston Gamblers to New Jersey Generals for past considerations, March 7, 1986.
Granted free agency when USFL suspended operations, August 7, 1986; signed by Cleveland Browns, August 12, 1986.
Granted roster exemption, August 12 through August 21, 1986; activated, August 22, 1986.
On developmental squad for 3 games with Houston Gamblers in 1984.

| | | PASS RECEIVING | | | | -PUNT RETURNS- | | | | —KICKOFF RET.— | | | | —TOTAL— | | |
Year Club	G.	P.C.	Yds.	Avg.	TD.	No.	Yds.	Avg.	TD.	No.	Yds.	Avg.	TD.	TD.	Pts.	F.
1984—Houston USFL	15	33	501	15.2	1	31	323	10.4	*1	None				2	12	4
1985—Houston USFL	18	58	1017	17.5	6	39	*505	*13.0	*2	2	62	31.0	0	8	48	4
1986—Cleveland NFL	16	1	9	9.0	0	40	348	8.7	1	47	997	21.2	*1	2	12	3
1987—Cleveland NFL	12	8	120	15.0	0	34	386	11.4	0	11	205	18.6	0	2	12	2
USFL Totals—2 Years	33	91	1518	16.7	7	70	828	11.8	3	2	62	31.0	0	10	60	8
NFL Totals—2 Years	28	9	129	14.3	2	74	734	9.9	1	58	1202	20.7	1	4	24	5
Pro Totals—4 Years	61	100	1647	16.5	9	144	1562	10.8	4	60	1264	21.1	1	14	84	13

Additional USFL statistics: Rushed once for 11 yards and recovered two fumbles, 1984; recovered one fumble, 1985.
Additional NFL statistics: Rushed once for 12 yards, 1986; rushed once for 17 yards, 1987.
Played in AFC Championship Game following 1986 and 1987 seasons.
Played in Pro Bowl (NFL All-Star Game) following 1987 season.

MARK ANTHONY McNEIL
Defensive Back—Miami Dolphins
Born August 25, 1961, at San Antonio, Tex.
Height, 6.00. Weight, 195.
High School—San Antonio, Tex., Sam Houston.
Attended University of Nevada at Las Vegas, Mt. San Antonio College and University of Houston.
Signed as free agent by San Antonio Gunslingers, April 6, 1985.
On developmental squad, April 6 through April 10, 1985; activated, April 11, 1985.
Released by San Antonio Gunslighter, July 23, 1985; signed as free agent by Los Angeles Rams, March 21, 1986.
Released by Los Angeles Rams, August 14, 1986; signed as free agent by Miami Dolphins, April 15, 1988.
On developmental squad for 1 game with San Antonio Gunslingers in 1985.
San Antonio USFL, 1985.
Games: 1985 (6).

BRUCE EDWARD McNORTON
Cornerback—Detroit Lions
Born February 28, 1959, at Daytona Beach, Fla.
Height, 5.11. Weight, 175.
High School—Daytona Beach, Fla., Spruce Creek.
Received bachelor of arts degree in social work from Georgetown (Ky.) College in 1982.
Selected by Detroit in 4th round (96th player selected) of 1982 NFL draft.
On injured reserve with knuckle injury, September 10 through December 10, 1982; activated, December 11, 1982.

| | | ——INTERCEPTIONS—— | | | |
Year Club	G.	No.	Yds.	Avg.	TD.
1982—Detroit NFL	4			None	
1983—Detroit NFL	16	7	30	4.3	0
1984—Detroit NFL	16	2	0	0.0	0
1985—Detroit NFL	16	2	14	7.0	0
1986—Detroit NFL	16	4	10	2.5	0
1987—Detroit NFL	12	3	20	6.7	0
Pro Totals—6 Years	80	18	74	4.1	0

Additional pro statistics: Recovered two fumbles, 1986.

DAN McQUAID
Offensive Tackle—Minnesota Vikings
Born October 4, 1960, at Cortland, Calif.
Height, 6.07. Weight, 278.
High School—Clarksburg, Calif., Delta.
Attended University of Nevada at Las Vegas.
Selected by New Jersey in 16th round (318th player selected) of 1984 USFL draft.
Signed as free agent by Los Angeles Rams, May 4, 1984.
On injured reserve with back injury, August 21 through entire 1984 season.
Traded by Los Angeles Rams to Washington Redskins for 4th round pick in 1986 draft, August 24, 1985.
On injured reserve with ankle injury, October 27 through remainder of 1987 season.
Released by Washington Redskins, May 9, 1988; awarded on waivers to Minnesota Vikings, May 24, 1988.
Washington NFL, 1985 through 1987.
Games: 1985 (16), 1986 (13), 1987 (1). Total—30.
Played in NFC Championship Game following 1986 season.

RODNEY McSWAIN
(Rod)
Cornerback—New England Patriots
Born January 28, 1962, at Caroleen, N.C.
Height, 6.01. Weight, 198.
High School—Forest City, N.C., Chase.
Attended Clemson University.
Brother of Chuck McSwain, running back with Dallas Cowboys and New England Patriots, 1983, 1984 and 1987.
Selected by Washington in 1984 USFL territorial draft.
Selected by Atlanta in 3rd round (63rd player selected) of 1984 NFL draft.
Signed by Atlanta Falcons, May 16, 1984.
Traded by Atlanta Falcons to New England Patriots for 8th round pick in 1985 draft, August 27, 1984.
On injured reserve with shoulder separation, September 2 through October 2, 1986; activated, October 3, 1986.
New England NFL, 1984 through 1987.
Games: 1984 (15), 1985 (16), 1986 (9), 1987 (12). Total—52.
Pro statistics: Recovered one fumble, 1984; intercepted one pass for no yards, 1985; returned blocked punt 31 yards
for a touchdown and intercepted one pass for three yards, 1986; intercepted one pass for 17 yards, 1987.
Played in AFC Championship Game following 1985 season.
Played in NFL Championship Game following 1985 season.

JOHNNY MEADS
Linebacker—Houston Oilers
Born June 25, 1961, at Labadieville, La.
Height, 6.02. Weight, 230.
High School—Napoleonville, La., Assumption.
Attended Nicholls State University.
Selected by New Orleans in 3rd round (55th player selected) of 1984 USFL draft.
Selected by Houston in 3rd round (58th player selected) of 1984 NFL draft.
Signed by Houston Oilers, July 17, 1984.
On injured reserve with knee injury, October 8 through remainder of 1985 season.
Houston NFL, 1984 through 1987.
Games: 1984 (16), 1985 (5), 1986 (16), 1987 (12). Total—49.
Pro statistics: Recovered one fumble, 1986.

KARL BERNARD MECKLENBURG
Defensive End-Linebacker—Denver Broncos
Born September 1, 1960, at Seattle, Wash.
Height, 6.03. Weight, 230.
High School—Edina, Minn., West.
Attended Augustana College (S.D.) and received bachelor of
science degree in biology from University of Minnesota in 1983.
Named to THE SPORTING NEWS NFL All-Star Team, 1986.
Selected by Chicago in 21st round (246th player selected) of 1983 USFL draft.
Selected by Denver in 12th round (310th player selected) of 1983 NFL draft.
Signed by Denver Broncos, May 14, 1983.
Denver NFL, 1983 through 1987.
Games: 1983 (16), 1984 (16), 1985 (16), 1986 (16), 1987 (12). Total—76.
Pro statistics: Intercepted two passes for 105 yards, 1984; recovered one fumble, 1984 through 1987; intercepted
three passes for 23 yards, 1987.
Played in AFC Championship Game following 1986 and 1987 seasons.
Played in NFL Championship Game following 1986 and 1987 seasons.
Played in Pro Bowl (NFL All-Star Game) following 1985 through 1987 seasons.

LANCE ALAN MEHL
Name pronounced Mell.
Linebacker—New York Jets
Born February 14, 1958, at Bellaire, O.
Height, 6.03. Weight, 235.
High School—Bellaire, O.
Received bachelor of science degree in industrial arts education from
Pennsylvania State University in 1980.
Selected by New York Jets in 3rd round (69th player selected) of 1980 NFL draft.
On injured reserve with knee injury, October 29 through remainder of 1986 season.
On physically unable to perform/reserve with knee injury, August 31 through November 15, 1987; activated,
November 16, 1987.
On injured reserve with knee injury, December 9 through remainder of 1987 season.

| Year Club | G. | —INTERCEPTIONS— | | | |
		No.	Yds.	Avg.	TD.
1980—New York Jets NFL....	14	None			
1981—New York Jets NFL....	15	3	17	5.7	0
1982—New York Jets NFL....	9	2	38	19.0	0
1983—New York Jets NFL....	16	7	57	8.1	1
1984—New York Jets NFL....	16	None			
1985—New York Jets NFL....	16	3	33	11.0	0
1986—New York Jets NFL....	8	None			
1987—New York Jets NFL....	3	None			
Pro Totals—8 Years............	97	15	145	9.7	1

Additional pro statistics: Recovered one fumble, 1981 through 1984 and 1986; fumbled once, 1985.
Played in AFC Championship Game following 1982 season.
Played in Pro Bowl (NFL All-Star Game) following 1985 season.

GREGORY PAUL MEISNER
(Greg)
Nose Tackle—Los Angeles Rams
Born April 23, 1959, at New Kensington, Pa.
Height, 6.03. Weight, 265.
High School—New Kensington, Pa., Valley.
Received bachelor of arts degree in psychology from University of Pittsburgh in 1981.
Selected by Los Angeles in 3rd round (63rd player selected) of 1981 NFL draft.
On non-football injury list with head injuries suffered in bar fight, August 18 through October 23, 1981; activated,
October 24, 1981.
On injured reserve with knee injury, December 16 through remainder of 1982 season.
Granted free agency, February 1, 1985; re-signed by Rams, September 18, 1985.
Granted roster exemption, September 18 and September 19, 1985; activated, September 20, 1985.
Crossed picket line during players' strike, October 2, 1987.
Los Angeles Rams NFL, 1981 through 1987.

Games: 1981 (9), 1982 (6), 1983 (16), 1984 (16), 1985 (14), 1986 (15), 1987 (15). Total—91.
Pro statistics: Returned one kickoff for 17 yards, 1981; recovered one fumble, 1984; recovered one fumble for 15 yards, 1986.
Played in NFC Championship Game following 1985 season.

SAM MERRIMAN
Linebacker—Seattle Seahawks
Born May 5, 1961, at Tucson, Ariz.
Height, 6.03. Weight, 232.
High School—Tucson, Ariz., Amphitheater.
Attended University of Idaho.

Selected by Arizona in 12th round (143rd player selected) of 1983 USFL draft.
Selected by Seattle in 7th round (177th player selected) of 1983 NFL draft.
Signed by Seattle Seahawks, May 22, 1983.
On injured reserve with ankle injury, September 7 through October 30, 1987. activated, October 31, 1987.
Seattle NFL, 1983 through 1987.
Games: 1983 (16), 1984 (16), 1985 (14), 1986 (16), 1987 (9). Total—71.
Pro statistics: Recovered one fumble, 1983 and 1986; recovered blocked punt in end zone for a touchdown, 1985.
Played in AFC Championship Game following 1983 season.

MICHAEL LAMAR MERRIWEATHER
(Mike)
Linebacker—Pittsburgh Steelers
Born November 26, 1960, at Albans, N.Y.
Height, 6.02. Weight, 221.
High School—Vallejo, Calif.
Received bachelor of arts degree in history from University of the Pacific in 1982.

Selected by Pittsburgh in 3rd round (70th player selected) of 1982 NFL draft.

			—INTERCEPTIONS—			
Year	Club	G.	No.	Yds.	Avg.TD.	
1982—Pittsburgh NFL.............		9		None		
1983—Pittsburgh NFL.............		16	3	55	18.3	1
1984—Pittsburgh NFL.............		16	2	9	4.5	0
1985—Pittsburgh NFL.............		16	2	36	18.0	*1
1986—Pittsburgh NFL.............		16	2	14	7.0	0
1987—Pittsburgh NFL.............		12	2	26	13.0	0
Pro Totals—6 Years............		85	11	140	12.7	2

Additional pro statistics: Returned one punt for three yards, 1982; recovered two fumbles, 1983; recovered one fumble, 1984; fumbled once, 1985; returned one kickoff for 27 yards and recovered two fumbles for 18 yards, 1986; recovered four fumbles for four yards, 1987.
Played in AFC Championship Game following 1984 season.
Played in Pro Bowl (NFL All-Star Game) following 1984 through 1986 seasons.

SCOTT MERSEREAU
Defensive End—New York Jets
Born April 8, 1965, at Riverhead, N.Y.
Height, 6.03. Weight, 278.
High School—Riverhead, N.Y.
Attended Southern Connecticut State University.

Selected by Los Angeles Rams in 5th round (136th player selected) of 1987 NFL draft.
Signed by Los Angeles Rams, July 25, 1987.
Released by Los Angeles Rams, September 7, 1987; signed as replacement player by New York Jets, September 24, 1987.
New York Jets NFL, 1987.
Games: 1987 (13).
Pro statistics: Recovered one fumble, 1987.

BRUCE M. MESNER
Nose Tackle—Buffalo Bills
Born March 21, 1964, at New York, N.Y.
Height, 6.05. Weight, 280.
High School—Harrison, N.Y.
Attended University of Maryland.

Selected by Buffalo in 8th round (209th player selected) of 1987 NFL draft.
Signed by Buffalo Bills, July 24, 1987.
Buffalo NFL, 1987.
Games: 1987 (11).

PETER HENRY METZELAARS
(Pete)
Tight End—Buffalo Bills
Born May 24, 1960, at Three Rivers, Mich.
Height, 6.07. Weight, 240.
High School—Portage, Mich., Central.
Received bachelor of science degree in economics from Wabash College in 1982.

Selected by Seattle in 3rd round (75th player selected) of 1982 NFL draft.
On injured reserve with knee injury, October 17 through November 30, 1984; activated, December 1, 1984.
Traded by Seattle Seahawks to Buffalo Bills for wide receiver Byron Franklin, August 20, 1985.

			——PASS RECEIVING——			
Year Club		G.	P.C.	Yds.	Avg.	TD.
1982—Seattle NFL		9	15	152	10.1	0
1983—Seattle NFL		16	7	72	10.3	1
1984—Seattle NFL		9	5	80	16.0	0
1985—Buffalo NFL		16	12	80	6.7	1
1986—Buffalo NFL		16	49	485	9.9	3
1987—Buffalo NFL		12	28	290	10.4	0
Pro Totals—6 Years		78	116	1159	10.0	5

Additional pro statistics: Recovered one fumble, 1982 and 1987; fumbled twice, 1982 and 1986; returned one kickoff for no yards, 1983; fumbled once, 1984; recovered one fumble for two yards, 1985; recovered one fumble in end zone for a touchdown, 1986; fumbled three times, 1987.
Played in AFC Championship Game following 1983 season.

RICHARD JAMES MIANO

Name pronounced Mee-AN-oh.

(Rich)

Safety—New York Jets

Born September 3, 1962, at Newton, Mass.
Height, 6.00. Weight, 200.
High School—Honolulu, Haw., Kaiser.
Attended University of Hawaii.

Selected by Denver in 9th round (132nd player selected) of 1985 USFL draft.
Selected by New York Jets in 6th round (166th player selected) of 1985 NFL draft.
Signed by New York Jets, July 16, 1985.
Released by New York Jets, September 2, 1985; re-signed by Jets, September 3, 1985.
New York Jets NFL, 1985 through 1987.
Games: 1985 (16), 1986 (14), 1987 (12). Total—42.
Pro statistics: Intercepted two passes for nine yards, 1985; intercepted three passes for 24 yards and returned blocked field goal attempt 67 yards for a touchdown, 1987.

ROBERT ANTHONY MICHO

(Bob)

Running Back-Tight End—Denver Broncos

Born March 7, 1962, at Omaha, Neb.
Height, 6.03. Weight, 240.
High School—Austin, Tex., L.C. Anderson.
Attended University of Texas.

Selected by Houston in 1984 USFL territorial draft.
Selected by Denver in 10th round (272nd player selected) of 1984 NFL draft.
Signed by Denver Broncos, May 12, 1984.
On injured reserve with toe injury, August 13 through November 7, 1984.
Awarded on procedural waivers to San Diego Chargers, November 9, 1984.
On injured reserve with foot injury, August 26 through entire 1985 season.
On injured reserve with hamstring injury, August 26 through November 12, 1986.
Released by San Diego Chargers, November 13, 1986; awarded on waivers to Denver Broncos, November 14, 1986.
Crossed picket line during players' strike, October 2, 1987.

		——RUSHING——				PASS RECEIVING				—TOTAL—		
Year Club	G.	Att.	Yds.	Avg.	TD.	P.C.	Yds.	Avg.	TD.	TD.	Pts.	F.
1984—San Diego NFL	6		None				None			0	0	0
1986—Denver NFL	5		None				None			0	0	0
1987—Denver NFL	15	4	8	2.0	0	25	242	9.7	2	2	12	1
Pro Totals—3 Years	26	4	8	2.0	0	25	242	9.7	2	2	12	1

Played in AFC Championship Game following 1986 and 1987 seasons.
Played in NFL Championship Game following 1986 and 1987 seasons.

FRANKLIN MIDDLETON JR.

(Frank)

Running Back—Miami Dolphins

Born October 28, 1960, at Savannah, Ga.
Height, 5.11. Weight, 201.
High School—Savannah, Ga., Sol C. Johnson.
Attended Florida A&M University.

Selected by Tampa Bay in 1983 USFL territorial draft.
Signed as free agent by Seattle Seahawks, April 28, 1983.
Released by Seattle Seahawks, July 25, 1983; signed as free agent by Tampa Bay Bandits, September 30, 1983.
Released by Tampa Bay Bandits, January 17, 1984; signed as free agent by Indianapolis Colts, June 21, 1984.
Released by Indianapolis Colts, October 16, 1985; signed as free agent by Tampa Bay Buccaneers, March 22, 1986.
Released by Tampa Bay Buccaneers, August 25, 1986; signed as free agent by San Diego Chargers, April 13, 1987.
On injured reserve with knee injury, September 1 through September 7, 1987.

Released by San Diego Chargers, September 8, 1987; re-signed as replacement player by Chargers, September 28, 1987.

Released by San Diego Chargers, October 21, 1987; signed as free agent by Miami Dolphins, March 22, 1988.

Year Club	G.	RUSHING				PASS RECEIVING				TOTAL		
		Att.	Yds.	Avg.	TD.	P.C.	Yds.	Avg.	TD.	TD.	Pts.	F.
1984—Indianapolis NFL	16	92	275	3.0	1	15	112	7.5	1	2	12	2
1985—Indianapolis NFL	5	13	35	2.7	1	5	54	10.8	0	1	6	0
1987—San Diego NFL	3	28	74	2.6	1	8	43	5.4	0	1	6	0
Pro Totals—3 Years	24	133	384	2.9	3	28	209	7.5	1	4	24	2

Additional pro statistics: Returned one kickoff for 11 yards and recovered two fumbles, 1984; returned one kickoff for 20 yards, 1985.

RONALD ALLEN MIDDLETON
(Ron)
Tight End—Atlanta Falcons
Born July 17, 1965, at Atmore, Ala.
Height, 6.02. Weight, 252.
High School—Atmore, Ala., Escambia County.
Attended Auburn University.

Selected by Birmingham in 1986 USFL territorial draft.
Signed as free agent by Atlanta Falcons, May 3, 1986.

Year Club	G.	PASS RECEIVING			
		P.C.	Yds.	Avg.	TD.
1986—Atlanta NFL	16	6	31	5.2	0
1987—Atlanta NFL	12	1	1	1.0	0
Pro Totals—2 Years	28	7	32	4.6	0

PAUL SALVATORE MIGLIAZZO
(Name pronounced Mill-YAUZ-oh.)
Linebacker—Indianapolis Colts
Born March 11, 1964, at Kansas City, Mo.
Height, 6.01. Weight, 228.
High School—Kansas City, Mo., Rockhurst.
Received bachelor of business administration degree
from University of Oklahoma in 1987.

Selected by Chicago in 8th round (221st player selected) of 1987 NFL draft.
Signed by Chicago Bears, July 31, 1987.
On injured reserve with dislocated shoulder, August 27 through November 10, 1987; activated November 11, 1987.
Released by Chicago Bears, December 7, 1987; signed as free agent by Indianapolis Colts, May 3, 1988.
Chicago NFL, 1987.
Games: 1987 (3).

DOUG ADOLPH MIKOLAS
Nose Tackle—San Francisco 49ers
Born June 7, 1962, at Manteca, Calif.
Height, 6.01. Weight, 270.
High School—Scio, Ore.
Attended Portland State University and Oregon Tech.

Selected by Denver in 7th round (94th player selected) of 1985 USFL draft.
Signed by Denver Gold, January 21, 1985.
On developmental squad, April 20 through May 2, 1985; activated, May 3, 1985.
Franchise merged with Jacksonville, February 19, 1986.
Granted free agency when USFL suspended operations, August 7, 1986; signed as free agent by Toronto Argonauts, August 26, 1986.
Released by Toronto Argonauts, September 22, 1986; signed as free agent by San Francisco 49ers, April 8, 1987.
Released by San Francisco 49ers, September 7, 1987; re-signed by 49ers, September 8, 1987.
Released by San Francisco 49ers, September 12, 1987; re-signed as replacement player by 49ers, September 30, 1987.
On developmental squad for 2 games with Denver Gold in 1985.
Denver USFL, 1985; Toronto CFL, 1986; San Francisco NFL, 1987.
Games: 1985 (16), 1986 (3), 1987 (8). Total—27.
Pro statistics: Credited with 4½ sacks for 27½ yards and recovered one fumble, 1985.

JOSEPH MICHAEL MILINICHIK
(Joe)
(Name pronounced Mah-lynn-check.)
Guard-Offensive Tackle—Detroit Lions
Born March 30, 1963, at Allentown, Pa.
Height, 6.05. Weight, 275.
High School—Emmaus, Pa.
Received bachelor of science degree in vocational industrial education
from North Carolina State University in 1985.

Selected by Jacksonville in 1986 USFL territorial draft.
Selected by Detroit in 3rd round (69th player selected) of 1986 NFL draft.

Signed by Detroit Lions, July 15, 1986.
On injured reserve with dislocated elbow, September 2 through entire 1986 season.
Detroit NFL, 1987.
Games: 1987 (11).

BRYAN MILLARD
Name pronounced Mill-ARD.
Guard—Seattle Seahawks
Born December 2, 1960, at Sioux City, Ia.
Height, 6.05. Weight, 282.
High School—Dumas, Tex.
Attended University of Texas.

Selected by New Jersey in 12th round (142nd player selected) of 1983 USFL draft.
Signed by New Jersey Generals, February 4, 1983.
On injured reserve with knee injury, April 18 through remainder of 1983 season.
On developmental squad, May 6 through May 10, 1984; activated, May 11, 1984.
Granted free agency, July 15, 1984; signed as free agent by Seattle Seahawks, July 31, 1984.
On injured reserve with knee injury, December 8 through remainder of 1984 season.
On developmental squad for 1 game with New Jersey Generals in 1984.
New Jersey USFL, 1983 and 1984; Seattle NFL, 1984 through 1987.
Games: 1983 (7), 1984 USFL (17), 1984 NFL (14), 1985 (16), 1986 (16), 1987 (12). Total USFL—24. Total NFL—58.
Total Pro—82.
Pro statistics: Recovered one fumble, 1986; caught one pass for minus five yards and recovered two fumbles, 1987.

KEITH MILLARD
Name pronounced Mill-ARD.
Defensive Tackle—Minnesota Vikings
Born March 18, 1962, at Pleasanton, Calif.
Height, 6.05. Weight, 260.
High School—Pleasanton, Calif., Foothill.
Attended Washington State University.

Selected by Arizona in 1st round (5th player selected) of 1984 USFL draft.
Selected by Minnesota in 1st round (13th player selected) of 1984 NFL draft.
USFL rights traded by Arizona Wranglers to Jacksonville Bulls for 1st round pick in 1985 draft, July 5, 1984.
Signed by Jacksonville Bulls, July 5, 1984.
On developmental squad, March 2 through March 8, 1985; activated, March 9, 1985.
On suspended list, May 23 through May 29, 1985; reinstated, May 30, 1985.
Released by Jacksonville Bulls, August 5, 1985; signed by Minnesota Vikings, August 6, 1985.
On developmental squad for 1 game with Jacksonville Bulls in 1985.
Jacksonville USFL, 1985; Minnesota NFL, 1985 through 1987.
Games: 1985 USFL (17), 1985 NFL (16), 1986 (15), 1987 (9). Total NFL—40. Total Pro—57.
USFL statistics: Credited with 12 sacks for 86½ yards and recovered one fumble, 1985.
NFL statistics: Recovered one fumble, 1985; intercepted one pass for 17 yards and recovered one fumble for three
yards, 1986; recovered two fumbles for eight yards, 1987.
Played in NFC Championship Game following 1987 season.

HUGH MILLEN
Quarterback—Los Angeles Rams
Born November 22, 1963, at Des Moines, Ia.
Height, 6.05. Weight, 216.
High School—Seattle, Wash., Roosevelt.
Attended Santa Rosa Junior College and University of Washington.

Selected by Los Angeles Rams in 3rd round (71st player selected) of 1986 NFL draft.
Signed by Los Angeles Rams, July 17, 1986.
On injured reserve with broken ankle, August 19 through entire 1986 season.
On injured reserve with knee injury, September 7 through December 3, 1987; activated, December 4, 1987.
Los Angeles Rams NFL, 1987.
Games: 1987 (1).
Pro statistics: Completed only pass attempt for no yards, 1987.

MATT G. MILLEN
Linebacker—Los Angeles Raiders
Born March 12, 1958, at Hokendauqua, Pa.
Height, 6.02. Weight, 245.
High School—Whitehall, Pa.
Received bachelor of business administration degree in marketing from
Pennsylvania State University in 1980.
Nephew of Andy Tomasic, back with Pittsburgh Steelers, 1942 and 1946 and
pitcher with New York Giants, 1949.

Selected by Oakland in 2nd round (43rd player selected) of 1980 NFL draft.
Franchise transferred to Los Angeles, May 7, 1982.

Year Club		—INTERCEPTIONS—			
Year Club	G.	No.	Yds.	Avg.	TD.
1980—Oakland NFL..............	16	2	17	8.5	0
1981—Oakland NFL..............	16		None		
1982—L.A. Raiders NFL........	9	3	77	25.7	0
1983—L.A. Raiders NFL........	16	1	14	14.0	0
1984—L.A. Raiders NFL........	16		None		
1985—L.A. Raiders NFL........	16		None		
1986—L.A. Raiders NFL........	16		None		
1987—L.A. Raiders NFL........	12	1	6	6.0	0
Pro Totals—8 Years...........	117	7	114	16.3	0

Additional pro statistics: Recovered one fumble, 1981; returned one kickoff for 13 yards and recovered two fumbles, 1982; returned two kickoffs for 19 yards, 1983; returned three kickoffs for 40 yards, 1986; returned one kickoff for no yards and fumbled once, 1987.
Played in AFC Championship Game following 1980 and 1983 seasons.
Played in NFL Championship Game following 1980 and 1983 seasons.

BRETT MILLER
Offensive Tackle—Atlanta Falcons
Born October 2, 1958 at Lynwood, Calif.
Height, 6.07. Weight, 300.
High School—Glendale, Calif.
Attended Glendale Community College and University of Iowa.

Selected by Washington in 5th round (57th player selected) of 1983 USFL draft.
Selected by Atlanta in 5th round (129th player selected) of 1983 NFL draft.
Signed by Atlanta Falcons, May 25, 1983.
On injured reserve with sprained ankle, November 12 through December 9, 1985; activated, December 10, 1985.
On injured reserve with knee injury, October 16 through November 14, 1986; activated, November 15, 1986.
On injury reserve with knee injury, November 28 through remainder of 1986 season.
On injured reserve with injured arch in foot, September 8 through October 30, 1987; activated, October 31, 1987.
Atlanta NFL, 1983 through 1987.
Games: 1983 (16), 1984 (15), 1985 (12), 1986 (8), 1987 (2). Total—53.
Pro statistics: Recovered one fumble, 1986.

CHRISTOPHER JAMES MILLER
(Chris)
Quarterback—Atlanta Falcons
Born August 9, 1965, at Pomona, Calif.
Height, 6.02. Weight, 195.
High School—Eugene, Ore., Sheldon.
Attended University of Oregon.

Selected by Atlanta in 1st round (13th player selected) of 1987 NFL draft.
Signed by Atlanta Falcons, October 30, 1987.
Granted roster exemption, October 30 through November 8, 1987; activated, November 9, 1987.

Year Club		—————PASSING—————							———RUSHING———				—TOTAL—		
Year Club	G.	Att.	Cmp.	Pct.	Gain	T.P.	P.I.	Avg.	Att.	Yds.	Avg.	TD.	TD.	Pts.	F.
1987—Atlanta NFL	3	92	39	42.4	552	1	9	6.00	4	21	5.3	0	0	0	0

Quarterback Rating Points: 1987 (26.4).

RECORD AS BASEBALL PLAYER

Year Club	League	Pos.	G.	AB.	R.	H.	2B.	3B.	HR.	RBI.	B.A.	PO.	A.	E.	F.A.
1985—Bellingham† .... N'west				(Did not play)											
1986—Bellingham .... N'west		SS	3	9	5	5	0	1	0	1	.556	5	5	1	.909
1986—Salinas .... Calif.		SS	27	79	8	8	2	1	0	3	.101	38	74	8	.933

Selected by Toronto Blue Jays' organization in 17th round of free-agent draft, June 6, 1983.
Selected by Toronto Blue Jays' organization in secondary phase of free-agent draft, January 17, 1984.
Selected by Seattle Mariners' organization in 5th round of free-agent draft, January 9, 1985.
†On disabled list, June 1, 1985 through entire season.

LES P. MILLER
Defensive End—San Diego Chargers
Born March 1, 1965, at Arkansas City, Kan.
Height, 6.07. Weight, 285.
High School—Arkansas City, Kan.
Attended Fort Hays Kansas State University.

Signed as free agent by New Orleans Saints, May 11, 1987.
Released by New Orleans Saints, September 7, 1987; signed as free agent replacement player by San Diego Chargers, September 24, 1987.
San Diego NFL, 1987.
Games: 1987 (9).
Pro statistics: Recovered two fumbles (including one in end zone for a touchdown), 1987.

NICHOLAS GALEN MILLER
(Nick)
Linebacker—Cleveland Browns
Born October 26, 1963, at Brunswick, Me.
Height, 6.02. Weight, 238.
High School—Clute, Tex., Brazoswood.
Attended University of Arkansas.

Selected by Memphis in 1986 USFL territorial draft.
Selected by Cleveland in 5th round (127th player selected) of 1986 NFL draft.
Signed by Cleveland Browns, July 18, 1986.
On injured reserve with knee injury, August 22 through entire 1986 season.
On injured reserve with arm and hand injuries, September 7 through September 13, 1987.
Released by Cleveland Browns, September 14, 1987; re-signed as replacement player by Browns, October 16, 1987.
Cleveland NFL, 1987.
Games: 1987 (9).
Played in AFC Championship Game following 1987 season.

SHAWN MILLER
Defensive End—Los Angeles Rams
Born March 14, 1961, at Ogden, Utah.
Height, 6.04. Weight, 255.
High School—Ogden, Utah, Weber.
Attended Utah State University.

Signed as free agent by Los Angeles Rams, May 5, 1984.
Released by Los Angeles Rams, August 27, 1984; re-signed by Rams, August 28, 1984.
On injured reserve with back injury, November 9 through remainder of 1984 season.
Crossed picket line during players' strike, October 2, 1987.
Los Angeles Rams NFL, 1984 through 1987.
Games: 1984 (8), 1985 (16), 1986 (16), 1987 (6). Total—46.
Pro statistics: Returned one kickoff for 10 yards, 1985; recovered two fumbles for 29 yards, 1986.
Played in NFC Championship Game following 1985 season.

SOLOMON MILLER
Wide Receiver—Tampa Bay Buccaneers
Born December 6, 1964, at Los Angeles, Calif.
Height, 6.01. Weight, 185.
High School—Carson, Calif.
Attended Utah State University.

Selected by New York Giants in 6th round (157th player selected) of 1986 NFL draft.
Signed by New York Giants, July 16, 1986.
Released by New York Giants, September 7, 1987; signed as free agent by Tampa Bay Buccaneers, September 22, 1987.

| | | —PASS RECEIVING— | | |
Year Club	G.	P.C.	Yds.	Avg.	TD.
1986—New York Giants NFL	16	9	144	16.0	2
1987—Tampa Bay NFL	8	5	97	19.4	0
Pro Totals—2 Years	24	14	241	17.2	2

Additional pro statistics: Rushed once for three yards, returned seven kickoffs for 111 yards, recovered four fumbles and fumbled once, 1986; returned three kickoffs for 68 yards, 1987.
Played in NFC Championship Game following 1986 season.
Played in NFL Championship Game following 1986 season.

SAMUEL DAVIS MILLS JR.
(Sam)
Linebacker—New Orleans Saints
Born June 3, 1959, Neptune, N.J.
Height, 5.09. Weight, 225.
High School—Long Branch, N.J.
Attended Montclair State College.

Named as inside linebacker on THE SPORTING NEWS USFL All-Star Team, 1983 and 1985.
Signed as free agent by Cleveland Browns, May 3, 1981.
Released by Cleveland Browns, August 24, 1981; signed as free agent by Toronto Argonauts, March, 1982.
Released by Toronto Argonauts, June 30, 1982; signed by Philadelphia Stars, October 21, 1982.
Franchise transferred to Baltimore, November 1, 1984.
Granted free agency, August 1, 1985; re-signed by Stars, August 7, 1985.
Granted free agency when USFL suspended operations, August 7, 1986; signed as free agent by New Orleans Saints, August 12, 1986.
Granted roster exemption, August 12 through August 21, 1986; activated, August 22, 1986.

Year Club	G.	—INTERCEPTIONS— No.	Yds.	Avg.	TD.	Year Club	G.	—INTERCEPTIONS— No.	Yds.	Avg.	TD.
1983—Philadelphia USFL	18	3	13	4.3	0	1987—New Orleans NFL	12		None		
1984—Philadelphia USFL	18	3	24	8.0	0	USFL Totals—3 Years	54	9	69	7.7	1
1985—Baltimore USFL	18	3	32	10.7	*1	NFL Totals—2 Years	28	0	0	0.0	0
1986—New Orleans NFL	16		None			Pro Totals—5 Years	82	9	69	7.7	1

Additional USFL statistics: Credited with 3½ sacks for 37 yards and recovered five fumbles for eight yards, 1983; credited with five sacks for 39 yards and recovered three fumbles for two yards, 1984; credited with 5½ sacks for 41 yards and recovered two fumbles, 1985.
Additional NFL statistics: Recovered one fumble, 1986; recovered three fumbles, 1987.
Played in USFL Championship Game following 1983 through 1985 seasons.
Played in Pro Bowl (NFL All-Star Game) following 1987 season.

RICHARD MILOT
(Rich)
Linebacker
Born May 28, 1957, at Coraopolis, Pa.
Height, 6.04. Weight, 237.
High School—Coraopolis, Pa., Moon.
Received bachelor of business administration degree in marketing from
Pennsylvania State University in 1979.
Selected by Washington in 7th round (182nd player selected) of 1979 NFL draft.
On injured reserve with knee injury, October 20 through November 20, 1981; activated, November 21, 1981.
Released by Washington Redskins, May 17, 1988.

| | | —INTERCEPTIONS— | | | |
Year Club	G.	No.	Yds.	Avg.	TD.
1979—Washington NFL	14		None		
1980—Washington NFL	16	4	—8	—2.0	0
1981—Washington NFL	11		None		
1982—Washington NFL	9		None		
1983—Washington NFL	16	2	20	10.0	0
1984—Washington NFL	14	3	42	14.0	0
1985—Washington NFL	16	2	33	16.5	0
1986—Washington NFL	16	2	33	16.5	0
1987—Washington NFL	9		None		
Pro Totals—9 Years	121	13	120	9.2	0

Additional pro statistics: Recovered one fumble, 1980 and 1987; recovered one fumble for 18 yards, 1981; fumbled once, 1981 and 1986; returned one punt for three yards and recovered two fumbles, 1986.
Played in NFC Championship Game following 1982, 1983 and 1986 seasons.
Played in NFL Championship Game following 1982, 1983 and 1987 seasons.

FRANKY LyDALE MINNIFIELD
(Frank)
Cornerback—Cleveland Browns
Born January 1, 1960, at Lexington, Ky.
Height, 5.09. Weight, 180.
High School—Lexington, Ky., Henry Clay.
Attended University of Louisville.
Cousin to Dirk Minniefield, guard with Boston Celtics.
Named to THE SPORTING NEWS NFL All-Star Team, 1987.
Selected by Chicago in 3rd round (30th player selected) of 1983 USFL draft.
Signed by Chicago Blitz, January 28, 1983.
On injured reserve with knee injury, March 8 through remainder of 1983 season.
Franchise transferred to Arizona, September 30, 1983.
On developmental squad, March 4 through March 21, 1984; activated, March 22, 1984.
On developmental squad, April 27 through May 6, 1984; activated, May 7, 1984.
Signed by Cleveland Browns, May 20, 1984.
Released by Arizona Wranglers, August 23, 1984.
Cleveland Browns contract approved by NFL, August 25, 1984.
Granted roster exemption, August 25 through August 30, 1984; activated, August 31, 1984.
On developmental squad for 3 games with Arizona Wranglers in 1984.

| | | —INTERCEPTIONS— | | | |
Year Club	G.	No.	Yds.	Avg.	TD.
1983—Chicago USFL	1		None		
1984—Arizona USFL	15	4	74	18.5	1
1984—Cleveland NFL	15	1	26	26.0	0
1985—Cleveland NFL	16	1	3	3.0	0
1986—Cleveland NFL	15	3	20	6.7	0
1987—Cleveland NFL	12	4	24	6.0	0
USFL Totals—2 Years	16	4	74	18.5	1
NFL Totals—4 Years	58	9	73	8.1	0
Pro Totals—6 Years	74	13	147	11.3	1

Additional USFL statistics: Recovered two fumbles for minus six yards, 1984.
Additional NFL statistics: Recovered two fumbles for 10 yards, 1984; recovered one fumble for six yards, 1985; recovered blocked punt in end zone for a touchdown and recovered two fumbles, 1986.
Played in USFL Championship Game following 1984 season.
Played in AFC Championship Game following 1986 and 1987 seasons.
Played in Pro Bowl (NFL All-Star Game) following 1986 and 1987 seasons.

DEAN MARTIN MIRALDI
Guard—Los Angeles Raiders
Born April 8, 1958, at Culver City, Calif.
Height, 6.06. Weight, 280.
High School—Rosemead, Calif.
Attended California State University at Long Beach and University of Utah.

Selected by Philadelphia in 2nd round (55th player selected) of 1981 NFL draft.
On injured reserve with pulled hamstring, September 1 through entire 1981 season.
On inactive list, September 12 and September 19, 1982.
On injured reserve with knee injury, November 19 through December 23, 1982; activated, December 24, 1982.
Released by Philadelphia Eagles, August 20, 1985; signed as free agent by Denver Broncos, August 26, 1985.
Released by Denver Broncos, August 18, 1986; signed as free agent by Los Angeles Raiders, March 4, 1987.
Released by Los Angeles Raiders, September 7, 1987; re-signed by Raiders, September 9, 1987.
Philadelphia NFL, 1982 through 1984; Denver NFL, 1985; Los Angeles Raiders NFL, 1987.
Games: 1982 (1), 1983 (13), 1984 (16), 1985 (10), 1987 (10). Total—50.

DEVON D. MITCHELL
Safety—Detroit Lions
Born December 30, 1962, at Kingston, Jamaica.
Height, 6.01. Weight, 194.
High School—Brooklyn, N.Y., Samuel J. Tilden.
Attended University of Iowa.

Selected by Detroit in 4th round (92nd player selected) of 1986 NFL draft.
Signed by Detroit Lions, June 17, 1986.
On injured reserve with knee injury, September 7 through entire 1987 season.
Crossed picket line during players' strike, October 14, 1987.

		—INTERCEPTIONS—			
Year	Club	G.	No.	Yds.	Avg.TD.
1986—Detroit NFL		16	5	41	8.2 0

LEONARD BOYD MITCHELL
Offensive Tackle—Atlanta Falcons
Born October 12, 1958, at Houston, Tex.
Height, 6.07. Weight, 295.
High School—Houston, Tex., Booker T. Washington.
Attended University of Houston.

Named as defensive tackle on THE SPORTING NEWS College All-America Team, 1980.
Selected by Philadelphia in 1st round (27th player selected) of 1981 NFL draft.
On injured reserve with knee injury, November 26 through remainder of 1986 season.
Traded by Philadelphia Eagles to Houston Oilers for draft pick, August 3, 1987; returned to Eagles after failing physical, August 6, 1987.
Traded by Philadelphia Eagles to Atlanta Falcons for 4th round pick in 1988 draft, August 7, 1987.
Philadelphia NFL, 1981 through 1986; Atlanta NFL, 1987.
Games: 1981 (16), 1982 (9), 1983 (10), 1984 (16), 1985 (16), 1986 (10), 1987 (12). Total—89.

LYVONIA ALBERT MITCHELL
(Stump)
Running Back—Phoenix Cardinals
Born March 15, 1959, at St. Mary's, Ga.
Height, 5.09. Weight, 188.
High School—St. Mary's, Ga., Camden County.
Attended The Citadel.

Established NFL record for most yards, combined kick returns, season (1,737), 1981; most kickoff returns, rookie season (55), 1981; most combined kick returns, game, 13 vs. Atlanta Falcons, October 10, 1981.
Selected by St. Louis in 9th round (226th player selected) of 1981 NFL draft.
Franchise transferred to Phoenix, March 15, 1988.

			—RUSHING—				PASS RECEIVING				—TOTAL—		
Year	Club	G.	Att.	Yds.	Avg.	TD.	P.C.	Yds.	Avg.	TD.	TD.	Pts.	F.
1981—St. Louis NFL		16	31	175	5.6	0	6	35	5.8	1	2	12	3
1982—St. Louis NFL		9	39	189	4.8	1	11	149	13.5	0	1	6	3
1983—St. Louis NFL		15	68	373	5.5	3	7	54	7.7	0	3	18	5
1984—St. Louis NFL		16	81	434	5.4	9	26	318	12.2	2	11	66	6
1985—St. Louis NFL		16	183	1006	*5.5	7	47	502	10.7	3	10	60	6
1986—St. Louis NFL		15	174	800	4.6	5	41	276	6.7	0	5	30	4
1987—St. Louis NFL		12	203	781	3.8	3	45	397	8.8	2	5	30	3
Pro Totals—7 Years		99	779	3758	4.8	28	183	1731	9.5	8	37	222	30

			—PUNT RETURNS—				—KICKOFF RET.—		
Year	Club	G.	No.	Yds.	Avg.	TD.	No.	Yds.	Avg.TD.
1981—St. Louis NFL		16	42	445	10.6	1	55	*1292	23.5 0
1982—St. Louis NFL		9	27	165	6.1	0	16	364	22.8 0
1983—St. Louis NFL		15	38	337	8.9	0	36	778	21.6 0
1984—St. Louis NFL		16	38	333	8.8	0	35	804	23.0 0

Year Club	G.	No.	Yds.	Avg.	TD.	No.	Yds.	Avg.	TD.
		—PUNT RETURNS—				—KICKOFF RET.—			
1985—St. Louis NFL	16	11	97	8.8	0	19	345	18.2	0
1986—St. Louis NFL	15			None		6	203	33.8	0
1987—St. Louis NFL	12			None				None	
Pro Totals—7 Years	99	156	1377	8.8	1	167	3786	22.7	0

Additional pro statistics: Recovered one fumble, 1982, 1983, 1986 and 1987; recovered two fumbles, 1984 and 1985; attempted one pass with one completion for 20 yards, 1984; attempted two passes with one completion for 31 yards, 1985; attempted three passes with one completion for 15 yards and a touchdown, 1986; attempted three passes with one completion for 17 yards, 1987.

MICHAEL G. MITCHELL
(Mike)
Cornerback—New York Jets
Born October 18, 1961, at Waco, Tex.
Height, 5.10. Weight, 175.
High School—Waco, Tex., Richfield.
Attended Howard Payne University.

Signed as free agent by Houston Oilers, June 2, 1983.
Released by Houston Oilers, July 27, 1983.
USFL rights traded by San Antonio Gunslingers to Houston Gamblers for rights to wide receiver Glenn Starks, August 26, 1983.
Signed by Houston Gamblers, September 5, 1983.
Traded with defensive backs Luther Bradley, Will Lewis and Durwood Roquemore, defensive end Pete Catan, quarterbacks Jim Kelly and Todd Dillon, defensive tackles Tony Fitzpatrick, Van Hughes and Hosea Taylor, running back Sam Harrell, linebackers Andy Hawkins and Ladell Wills, wide receivers Richard Johnson, Scott McGhee, Gerald McNeil, Ricky Sanders and Clarence Verdin, guard Rich Kehr, center Billy Kidd and offensive tackles Chris Riehm and Tommy Robison by Houston Gamblers to New Jersey Generals for past considerations, March 7, 1986.
Granted free agency when USFL suspended operations, August 7, 1986; signed as free agent by Washington Redskins, April 30, 1987.
Released by Washington Redskins, August 17, 1987; re-signed as replacement player by Redskins, September 23, 1987.
Released by Washington Redskins, October 20, 1987; signed as free agent by New York Jets, April 8, 1988.

Year Club	G.	No.	Yds.	Avg.	TD.
		—INTERCEPTIONS—			
1984—Houston USFL	18	4	43	10.8	0
1985—Houston USFL	18	3	37	12.3	0
1987—Washington NFL	3	1	17	17.0	0
USFL Totals—2 Years	36	7	80	11.4	0
NFL Totals—1 Year	3	1	17	17.0	0
Pro Totals—3 Years	39	8	97	12.1	0

Additional pro statistics: Credited with one sack for four yards and recovered one fumble, 1984.

ROLAND EARL MITCHELL
Cornerback—Buffalo Bills
Born March 15, 1964, at Columbus, Tex.
Height, 5.11. Weight, 180.
High School—Bay City, Tex.
Attended Texas Tech University.

Selected by Buffalo in 2nd round (33rd player selected) of 1987 NFL draft.
Signed by Buffalo Bills, July 24, 1987.
Buffalo NFL, 1987.
Games: 1987 (11).

ALONZO MITZ
Defensive End—Seattle Seahawks
Born June 5, 1963, at Henderson, N. C.
Height, 6.03. Weight, 275.
High School—Fort Pierce, Fla., Central.
Attended University of Florida.

Selected by Tampa Bay in 1986 USFL territorial draft.
Selected by Seattle in 8th round (211th player selected) of 1986 NFL draft.
Signed by Seattle Seahawks, June 15, 1986.
On injured reserve with shoulder injury, September 1 through November 13, 1986; activated, November 14, 1986.
On injured reserve with elbow injury, September 7 through October 23, 1987; activated, October 24, 1987.
Seattle NFL, 1986 and 1987.
Games: 1986 (6), 1987 (6). Total—12.

ORSON ODELL MOBLEY
Tight End—Denver Broncos
Born March 4, 1963, at Brookeville, Fla.
Height, 6.05. Weight, 256.
High School—Miami, Fla., Palmetto.
Attended Florida State University and Salem College.

Selected by Denver in 6th round (151st player selected) of 1986 NFL draft.
Signed by Denver Broncos, July 17, 1986.

Year Club	G.	P.C.	Yds.	Avg.	TD.
		—PASS RECEIVING—			
1986—Denver NFL	14	22	332	15.1	1
1987—Denver NFL	10	16	228	14.3	1
Pro Totals—2 Years	24	38	560	14.7	2

Additional pro statistics: Rushed once for minus one yard, 1986; fumbled once, 1986 and 1987.
Played in AFC Championship Game following 1986 and 1987 seasons.
Played in NFL Championship Game following 1986 and 1987 seasons.

TIMOTHY MOFFETT
(Tim)
Wide Receiver—San Diego Chargers
Born February 8, 1962, at Laurel, Miss.
Height, 6.02. Weight, 180.
High School—Taylorsville, Miss.
Attended University of Mississippi.

Selected by Birmingham in 1985 USFL territorial draft.
Selected by Los Angeles Raiders in 3rd round (79th player selected) of 1985 NFL draft.
Signed by Los Angeles Raiders, July 16, 1985.
Released by Los Angeles Raiders, September 1, 1987; signed as free agent replacement player by San Diego Chargers, September 24, 1987.
Released by San Diego Chargers, October 21, 1987; re-signed by Chargers, April 15, 1988.

Year Club	G.	P.C.	Yds.	Avg.	TD.
		—PASS RECEIVING—			
1985—L.A. Raiders NFL	13	5	90	18.0	0
1986—L.A. Raiders NFL	16	6	77	12.8	0
1987—San Diego NFL	2	5	80	16.0	1
Pro Totals—3 Years	31	16	247	15.4	1

Additional pro statistics: Fumbled once, 1985; recovered one fumble, 1986.

MICHAEL JEROME MOFFITT
(Mike)
Tight End—Indianapolis Colts
Born July 28, 1963, at Los Angeles, Calif.
Height, 6.04. Weight, 211.
High School—Los Angeles, Calif.
Attended Fresno State University.

Signed as free agent by Green Bay Packers, May 3, 1986.
On injured reserve with disclosed jaw, August 19 through November 24, 1986; activated after clearing procedural waivers, November 26, 1986.
Released by Green Bay Packers, August 31, 1987; signed as free agent by Indianapolis Colts, March 30, 1988.

Year Club	G.	P.C.	Yds.	Avg.	TD.
		—PASS RECEIVING—			
1986—Green Bay NFL	4	4	87	21.8	0

RALF MOJSIEJENKO
Name pronounced Mose-YEN-ko.
Punter—San Diego Chargers
Born January 28, 1963, at Salzgitter Lebenstadt, West Germany.
Height, 6.03. Weight, 210.
High School—Bridgman, Mich.
Attended Michigan State University.

Named as punter on THE SPORTING NEWS College All-America Team, 1983.
Selected by Jacksonville in 9th round (118th player selected) of 1985 USFL draft.
Selected by San Diego in 4th round (96th player selected) of 1985 NFL draft.
Signed by San Diego Chargers, July 23, 1985.

Year Club	G.	No.	Avg.	Blk.
		—PUNTING—		
1985—San Diego NFL	16	68	42.4	0
1986—San Diego NFL	16	72	42.0	2
1987—San Diego NFL	12	67	42.9	0
Pro Totals—3 Years	44	207	42.4	2

Additional pro statistics: Rushed once for no yards and fumbled once for 13-yard loss, 1985.
Played in Pro Bowl (NFL All-Star Game) following 1987 season.

RONNIE CARL MONACO
(Ron)
Linebacker—Kansas City Chiefs
Born May 3, 1963, at New Haven, Conn.
Height, 6.01. Weight, 225.
High School—Hamden, Conn.

Attended San Diego State University, Vanderbilt University, Northwest Mississippi Junior College and received bachelor of science degree in sociology from University of South Carolina in 1986.
Brother of Rob Monaco, offensive tackle with St. Louis Cardinals, 1985.
Signed as free agent by St. Louis Cardinals, July 7, 1986.
Released by St. Louis Cardinals, September 7, 1987; signed as free agent replacement player by Green Bay Packers, September 25, 1987.
Released by Green Bay Packers, October 20, 1987; signed as free agent by Kansas City Chiefs, March 28, 1988.
St. Louis NFL, 1986; Green Bay NFL, 1987.
Games: 1986 (15), 1987 (2). Total—17.
Pro statistics: Recovered one fumble, 1986.

MATTHEW L. MONGER
(Matt)
Linebacker—New York Jets
Born November 15, 1961, at Denver, Colo.
Height, 6.01. Weight, 235.
High School—Miami, Okla.
Received bachelor of science degree in marketing
from Oklahoma State University in 1985.
Selected by New York Jets in 8th round (208th player selected) of 1985 NFL draft.
Signed by New York Jets, July 23, 1985.
New York Jets NFL, 1985 through 1987.
Games: 1985 (15), 1986 (16), 1987 (12). Total—43.
Pro statistics: Recovered two fumbles, 1985; recovered one fumble, 1986.

ART MONK
Wide Receiver—Washington Redskins
Born December 5, 1957, at White Plains, N.Y.
Height, 6.03. Weight, 209.
High School—White Plains, N.Y.
Attended Syracuse University.
Established NFL record for most pass receptions, season (106), 1984.
Named to THE SPORTING NEWS NFL All-Star Team, 1984 and 1985.
Selected by Washington in 1st round (18th player selected) of 1980 NFL draft.
On injured reserve with broken foot, January 7, 1983 through remainder of 1982 season playoffs.
On injured reserve with knee injury, September 2 through September 29, 1983; activated, September 30, 1983.
On injured reserve with knee injury, December 9, 1987 through January 29, 1988; activated, January 30, 1988.

| | | —RUSHING— | | | | PASS RECEIVING | | | | —TOTAL— | | |
Year Club	G.	Att.	Yds.	Avg.	TD.	P.C.	Yds.	Avg.	TD.	TD.	Pts.	F.
1980—Washington NFL	16			None		58	797	13.7	3	3	18	0
1981—Washington NFL	16	1	—5	—5.0	0	56	894	16.0	6	6	36	0
1982—Washington NFL	9	7	21	3.0	0	35	447	12.8	1	1	6	3
1983—Washington NFL	12	3	—19	—6.3	0	47	746	15.9	5	5	30	0
1984—Washington NFL	16	2	18	9.0	0	*106	1372	12.9	7	7	42	0
1985—Washington NFL	15	7	51	7.3	0	91	1226	13.5	2	2	12	2
1986—Washington NFL	16	4	27	6.8	0	73	1068	14.6	4	4	24	2
1987—Washington NFL	9	6	63	10.5	0	38	483	12.7	6	6	36	0
Pro Totals—8 Years	109	30	156	5.2	0	504	7033	14.0	34	34	204	7

Additional pro statistics: Returned one kickoff for 10 yards, 1980; attempted one pass with one completion for 46 yards, 1983; fumbled once, 1984; recovered two fumbles, 1986.
Played in NFC Championship Game following 1983 and 1986 seasons.
Played in NFL Championship Game following 1983 and 1987 seasons.
Played in Pro Bowl (NFL All-Star Game) following 1984 through 1986 seasons.

JOSEPH C. MONTANA
(Joe)
Quarterback—San Francisco 49ers
Born June 11, 1956, at Monongahela, Pa.
Height, 6.02. Weight, 195.
High School—Monongahela, Pa., Ringgold.
Received bachelor of business administration degree in marketing from
University of Notre Dame in 1978.
Established NFL records for highest completion percentage, career (63.61); lowest interception percentage, career (2.64); most consecutive 300-yard games, season (5), 1982.
Led NFL quarterbacks in passing with 102.1 points in 1987.
Selected by San Francisco in 3rd round (82nd player selected) of 1979 NFL draft.
On injured reserve with back injury, September 15 through November 5, 1986; activated, November 6, 1986.
Crossed picket line during players' strike, October 7, 1987.

| | | | —PASSING— | | | | | | —RUSHING— | | | | —TOTAL— | | |
Year Club	G.	Att.	Cmp.	Pct.	Gain	T.P.	P.I.	Avg.	Att.	Yds.	Avg.	TD.	TD.	Pts.	F.
1979—San Francisco NFL	16	23	13	56.5	96	1	0	4.17	3	22	7.3	0	0	0	1
1980—San Francisco NFL	15	273	176	*64.5	1795	15	9	6.58	32	77	2.4	2	2	12	4
1981—San Francisco NFL	16	488	311	*63.7	3565	19	12	7.31	25	95	3.8	2	2	12	2
1982—San Francisco NFL	9	*346	213	61.6	2613	*17	11	7.55	30	118	3.9	1	1	6	4
1983—San Francisco NFL	16	515	332	64.5	3910	26	12	7.59	61	284	4.7	2	2	12	3
1984—San Francisco NFL	16	432	279	64.6	3630	28	10	8.40	39	118	3.0	2	2	12	4

Year	Club	G.	PASSING							RUSHING				TOTAL		
			Att.	Cmp.	Pct.	Gain	T.P.	P.I.	Avg.	Att.	Yds.	Avg.	TD.	TD.	Pts.	F.
1985—San Francisco NFL		15	494	303	*61.3	3653	27	13	7.39	42	153	3.6	3	3	18	5
1986—San Francisco NFL		8	307	191	62.2	2236	8	9	7.28	17	38	2.2	0	0	0	3
1987—San Francisco NFL		13	398	266	*66.8	3054	*31	13	7.67	35	141	4.0	1	1	6	3
Pro Totals—9 Years		124	3276	2084	63.6	24552	172	89	7.49	284	1046	3.7	13	13	78	29

Quarterback Rating Points: 1979 (80.9), 1980 (87.8), 1981 (88.2), 1982 (87.9), 1983 (94.6), 1984 (102.9), 1985 (91.3), 1986 (80.7), 1987 (102.1). Total—92.7.

Additional pro statistics: Recovered one fumble, 1979 and 1980; recovered two fumbles and fumbled four times for minus two yards, 1982; recovered two fumbles and fumbled four times for minus three yards, 1984; recovered three fumbles and fumbled five times for minus 11 yards, 1985; recovered two fumbles and fumbled three times for minus five yards, 1987.

Played in NFC Championship Game following 1981, 1983 and 1984 seasons.
Played in NFL Championship Game following 1981 and 1984 seasons.
Played in Pro Bowl (NFL All-Star Game) following 1981, 1983, 1984 and 1987 seasons.
Named to play in Pro Bowl following 1985 season; replaced due to injury by Jim McMahon.

MAX MONTOYA JR.
Guard—Cincinnati Bengals
Born May 12, 1956, at Montebello, Calif.
Height, 6.05. Weight, 275.
High School—La Puente, Calif.
Attended Mt. San Jacinto Junior College and University of California at Los Angeles.

Selected by Cincinnati in 7th round (168th player selected) of 1979 NFL draft.
Cincinnati NFL, 1979 through 1987.
Games: 1979 (11), 1980 (16), 1981 (16), 1982 (9), 1983 (16), 1984 (16), 1985 (16), 1986 (16), 1987 (10). Total—126.
Pro statistics: Recovered one fumble, 1981 and 1986.
Played in AFC Championship Game following 1981 season.
Played in NFL Championship Game following 1981 season.
Played in Pro Bowl (NFL All-Star Game) following 1986 season.

WARREN MOON
Quarterback—Houston Oilers
Born November 18, 1956, at Los Angeles, Calif.
Height, 6.03. Weight, 210.
High School—Los Angeles, Calif., Hamilton.
Attended University of Washington.

Tied NFL record for most fumbles, season (17), 1984.
Signed as free agent by Edmonton Eskimos, March, 1978.
USFL rights traded by Memphis Showboats to Los Angeles Express for future draft pick, August 30, 1983.
Granted free agency, March 1, 1984; signed by Houston Oilers, March 1, 1984.

Year	Club	G.	PASSING							RUSHING				TOTAL		
			Att.	Cmp.	Pct.	Gain	T.P.	P.I.	Avg.	Att.	Yds.	Avg.	TD.	TD.	Pts.	F.
1978—Edmonton CFL		15	173	89	51.4	1112	5	7	6.43	30	114	3.8	1	1	6	1
1979—Edmonton CFL		16	274	149	54.4	2382	20	12	8.69	56	150	2.7	2	2	12	1
1980—Edmonton CFL		16	331	181	54.7	3127	25	11	9.45	55	352	6.4	3	3	18	0
1981—Edmonton CFL		15	378	237	62.7	3959	27	12	10.47	50	298	6.0	3	3	18	0
1982—Edmonton CFL		16	562	333	59.3	5000	36	16	8.90	54	259	4.8	4	4	24	1
1983—Edmonton CFL		16	664	380	57.2	5648	31	19	8.51	85	527	6.2	3	3	18	7
1984—Houston NFL		16	450	259	57.6	3338	12	14	7.42	58	211	3.6	1	1	6	*17
1985—Houston NFL		14	377	200	53.1	2709	15	19	7.19	39	130	3.3	0	0	0	12
1986—Houston NFL		15	488	256	52.5	3489	13	*26	7.15	42	157	3.7	2	2	12	11
1987—Houston NFL		12	368	184	50.0	2806	21	18	7.63	34	112	3.3	3	3	18	8
CFL Totals—6 Years		94	2382	1369	57.5	21228	144	77	8.91	330	1700	5.2	16	16	96	11
NFL Totals—4 Years		57	1683	899	53.4	12342	61	77	7.33	173	610	3.5	6	6	36	48
Pro Totals—10 Years		151	4065	2268	55.8	33570	205	154	8.26	503	2310	4.6	22	22	132	59

Quarterback Rating Points: 1984 (76.9), 1985 (68.5), 1986 (62.3), 1987 (74.2). Total—70.0.
Additional CFL statistics: Recovered one fumble, 1982.
Additional NFL statistics: Recovered seven fumbles and fumbled 17 times for minus one yard, 1984; recovered five fumbles and fumbled 12 times for minus eight yards, 1985; recovered three fumbles and fumbled 11 times for minus four yards, 1986; recovered six fumbles and fumbled eight times for minus seven yards, 1987.
Played in CFL Championship Game following 1978 through 1982 seasons.

BRENT ALLEN MOORE
Linebacker—Green Bay Packers
Born January 9, 1963, at Novato, Calif.
Height, 6.05. Weight, 242.
High School—Novato, Calif., San Marin.
Received bachelor of science degree in business administration
from University of Southern California in 1986.

Selected by Green Bay in 9th round (236th player selected) of 1986 NFL draft.
Signed by Green Bay Packers, July 17, 1986.
On injured reserve with toe injury, August 19 through entire 1986 season.
On injured reserve with foot injury, September 1 through October 30, 1987; activated, October 31, 1987.
Green Bay NFL, 1987.
Games: 1987 (4).

MALCOLM G. MOORE
Tight End—Los Angeles Rams
Born June 24, 1961, at San Fernando, Calif.
Height, 6.03. Weight, 236.
High School—San Fernando, Calif.
Attended University of Southern California.

Selected by Los Angeles in 1984 USFL territorial draft.
Signed by Los Angeles Express, January 19, 1984.
Selected by Dallas in 2nd round (54th player selected) of 1984 NFL supplemental draft.
Released by Los Angeles Express, February 11, 1985; signed by Dallas Cowboys, March 20, 1985.
Released by Dallas Cowboys, August 5, 1985; signed as free agent by San Diego Chargers, March 10, 1986.
On injured reserve with knee injury, August 18 through entire 1986 season.
Released by San Diego Chargers, September 7, 1987; signed as free agent replacement player by Los Angeles Rams, September 23, 1987.
Released by Los Angeles Rams, October 21, 1987; re-signed by Rams, December 29, 1987.

| | | | —PASS RECEIVING— | | |
Year Club	G.	P.C.	Yds.	Avg.	TD.
1984—Los Angeles USFL........	17	31	354	11.4	0
1987—L.A. Rams NFL.............	3	6	107	17.8	1
Pro Totals—2 Years............	20	37	461	12.5	1

Additional pro statistics: Fumbled once, 1984.

MARK QUENTIN MOORE
Safety—Seattle Seahawks
Born September 3, 1964, at Nacogdoches, Tex.
Height, 6.00. Weight, 194.
High School—Nacogdoches, Tex.
Attended Oklahoma State University.

Selected by Seattle in 4th round (104th player selected) of 1987 NFL draft.
Signed by Seattle Seahawks, July 22, 1987.
On injured reserve with hamstring injury, September 7 through October 23, 1987; activated, October 24, 1987.
On injured reserve with hamstring injury, October 31 through November 29, 1987; activated, November 30, 1987.
Seattle NFL, 1987.
Games: 1987 (5).

ROBERT ANTHONY MOORE
Safety—Atlanta Falcons
Born August 15, 1964, at Shreveport, La.
Height, 5.11. Weight, 190.
High School—Shreveport, La., Captain Shreve.
Attended Northwestern State University.

Signed as free agent by Atlanta Falcons, June 30, 1986.
Released by Atlanta Falcons, September 1, 1986; re-signed by Falcons, September 2, 1986.
Atlanta NFL, 1986 and 1987.
Games: 1986 (16), 1987 (12). Total—28.
Pro statistics: Intercepted one pass for no yards, 1986; intercepted two passes for 23 yards and recovered two fumbles for 20 yards and a touchdown, 1987.

STEPHEN ELLIOTT MOORE
(Steve)
Offensive Tackle—New England Patriots
Born October 1, 1960, at Memphis, Tenn.
Height, 6.05. Weight, 305.
High School—Memphis, Tenn., Fairley.
Attended Tennessee State University.
Brother of Jeffrey B. Moore, wide receiver with Los Angeles Rams, 1980 and 1981.

Selected by Birmingham in 4th round (37th player selected) of 1983 USFL draft.
Selected by New England in 3rd round (80th player selected) of 1983 NFL draft.
Signed by New England Patriots, May 25, 1983.
On injured reserve with broken ankle, November 26 through remainder of 1986 season.
On injured reserve with ankle injury, December 3 through remainder of 1987 season.
New England NFL, 1983 through 1987.
Games: 1983 (4), 1984 (16), 1985 (16), 1986 (11), 1987 (5). Total—52.
Played in AFC Championship Game following 1985 season.
Played in NFL Championship Game following 1985 season.

EMERY MATTHEW MOOREHEAD
Tight End—Chicago Bears
Born March 22, 1954, at Evanston, Ill.
Height, 6.02. Weight, 225.
High School—Evanston, Ill.
Received bachelor of arts degree in communications from University of Colorado in 1977.

Selected by New York Giants in 6th round (153rd player selected) of 1977 NFL draft.
On injured reserve with bruised kidney, November 27 through remainder of 1979 season.

Traded by New York Giants to Denver Broncos for 8th round pick in 1981 draft, May 23, 1980.
Released by Denver Broncos, September 1, 1980; re-signed by Broncos, September 2, 1980.
Released by Denver Broncos, August 3, 1981; claimed on waivers by Chicago Bears, August 4, 1981.
Released by Chicago Bears, August 29, 1981; re-signed by Bears after clearing procedural waivers, October 21, 1981.

			RUSHING			PASS RECEIVING				TOTAL		
Year Club	G.	Att.	Yds.	Avg.	TD.	P.C.	Yds.	Avg.	TD.	TD.	Pts.	F.
1977—New York Giants NFL	13	1	5	5.0	0	12	143	11.9	1	1	6	0
1978—New York Giants NFL	10		None			3	45	15.0	0	0	0	0
1979—New York Giants NFL	13	36	95	2.6	0	9	62	6.9	0	0	0	0
1980—Denver NFL	16	2	7	3.5	0		None			0	0	0
1981—Chicago NFL	9		None				None			0	0	0
1982—Chicago NFL	9	2	3	1.5	0	30	363	12.1	5	5	30	0
1983—Chicago NFL	16	5	6	1.2	0	42	597	14.2	3	3	18	0
1984—Chicago NFL	16	1	−2	−2.0	0	29	497	17.1	1	1	6	0
1985—Chicago NFL	15		None			35	481	13.7	1	1	6	0
1986—Chicago NFL	16		None			26	390	15.0	1	1	6	1
1987—Chicago NFL	12		None			24	269	11.2	1	1	6	1
Pro Totals—11 Years	145	47	114	2.4	0	210	2847	13.6	13	13	78	2

Additional pro statistics: Returned four punts for 65 yards (16.3 average), 1977; returned two punts for 52 yards (26.0 average), 1978; returned one kickoff for 16 yards, 1979; returned one kickoff for 18 yards, 1980; returned 23 kickoffs for 476 yards (20.7 average), 1981; recovered one fumble, 1986.
Played in NFC Championship Game following 1984 and 1985 seasons.
Played in NFL Championship Game following 1985 season.

RICHARD JAMES MORAN
(Rich)
Center-Guard—Green Bay Packers
Born March 19, 1962, at Boise, Ida.
Height, 6.02. Weight, 272.
High School—Pleasanton, Calif., Foothill.
Received degree in marketing from San Diego State University in 1985.
Son of Jim Moran, defensive tackle with New York Giants, 1964 through 1967; and brother of Eric Moran, offensive tackle-guard with Los Angeles Express and Houston Oilers, 1983 through 1986.
Selected by Arizona in 4th round (57th player selected) of 1985 USFL draft.
Selected by Green Bay in 3rd round (71st player selected) of 1985 NFL draft.
Signed by Green Bay Packers, July 24, 1985.
On injured reserve with knee injury, September 10 through November 25, 1986; activated, November 26, 1986.
Green Bay NFL, 1985 through 1987.
Games: 1985 (16), 1986 (5), 1987 (12). Total—33.
Pro statistics: Recovered one fumble and fumbled once for three yards, 1987.

STANLEY DOUGLAS MORGAN
Wide Receiver—New England Patriots
Born February 17, 1955, at Easley, S. C.
Height, 5.11. Weight, 181.
High School—Easley, S. C.
Received bachelor of science degree in education from University of Tennessee in 1979.
Named to THE SPORTING NEWS NFL All-Star Team, 1986.
Selected by New England in 1st round (25th player selected) of 1977 NFL draft.

			RUSHING			PASS RECEIVING				TOTAL		
Year Club	G.	Att.	Yds.	Avg.	TD.	P.C.	Yds.	Avg.	TD.	TD.	Pts.	F.
1977—New England NFL	14	1	10	10.0	0	21	443	*21.1	3	3	18	0
1978—New England NFL	16	2	11	5.5	0	34	820	24.1	5	5	30	6
1979—New England NFL	16	7	39	5.6	0	44	1002	*22.8	*12	13	78	1
1980—New England NFL	16	4	36	9.0	0	45	991	*22.0	6	6	36	0
1981—New England NFL	13	2	21	10.5	0	44	1029	*23.4	6	6	36	2
1982—New England NFL	9	2	3	1.5	0	28	584	20.9	3	3	18	0
1983—New England NFL	16	1	13	13.0	0	58	863	14.9	2	2	12	5
1984—New England NFL	13		None			38	709	18.7	5	5	30	0
1985—New England NFL	15	1	0	0.0	0	39	760	19.5	5	5	30	1
1986—New England NFL	16		None			84	1491	17.8	10	10	60	0
1987—New England NFL	10		None			40	672	16.8	3	3	18	0
Pro Totals—11 Years	154	20	133	6.7	0	475	9364	19.7	60	61	366	15

		PUNT RETURNS						PUNT RETURNS		
Year Club	G.	No.	Yds.	Avg.TD.	Year Club		G.	No.	Yds.	Avg.TD.
1977—New England NFL	14	16	220	13.8 0	1983—New England NFL		16		None	
1978—New England NFL	16	32	335	10.5 0	1984—New England NFL		13		None	
1979—New England NFL	16	29	289	10.0 1	1985—New England NFL		15		None	
1980—New England NFL	16		None		1986—New England NFL		16		None	
1981—New England NFL	13	15	116	7.7 0	1987—New England NFL		10		None	
1982—New England NFL	9		None		Pro Totals—11 Years		154	92	960	10.4 1

Additional pro statistics: Returned one kickoff for 17 yards, 1978; returned one kickoff for 12 yards, 1979; recovered one fumble for three yards, 1980; recovered two fumbles, 1981 and 1983.
Played in AFC Championship Game following 1985 season.

Played in NFL Championship Game following 1985 season.
Played in Pro Bowl (NFL All-Star Game) following 1979, 1980, 1986 and 1987 seasons.

LARRY MORIARTY
Running Back—Kansas City Chiefs
Born April 24, 1958, at Santa Barbara, Calif.
Height, 6.01. Weight, 240.
High School—Santa Barbara, Calif., Dos Pueblos.
Attended Santa Barbara City Junior College and received bachelor of arts degree
in sociology from University of Notre Dame in 1988.
Cousin of Pat Moriarty, running back with Cleveland Browns, 1979; and Tom Moriarty,
safety with Atlanta Falcons, Pittsburgh Steelers, Michigan Panthers and
Pittsburgh Maulers, 1977 through 1981, 1983 and 1984.
Selected by Chicago in 1983 USFL territorial draft.
Selected by Houston in 5th round (114th player selected) of 1983 NFL draft.
Signed by Houston Oilers, July 14, 1983.
On did not report list, August 20 through August 29, 1985.
Granted roster exemption, August 30 through September 6, 1985; activated, September 7, 1985.
Traded by Houston Oilers to Kansas City Chiefs for 6th round pick in 1987 draft, October 14, 1986.

		—RUSHING—			PASS RECEIVING				—TOTAL—		
Year Club	G.	Att.	Yds.	Avg.	TD.	P.C.	Yds.	Avg.	TD.	TD.	Pts.	F.
1983—Houston NFL	16	65	321	4.9	3	4	32	8.0	0	3	18	1
1984—Houston NFL	14	189	785	4.2	6	31	206	6.6	1	7	42	5
1985—Houston NFL	15	106	381	3.6	3	17	112	6.6	0	3	18	2
1986—Hou.(5)-K.C.(10) NFL	15	90	252	2.8	1	9	67	7.4	0	1	6	2
1987—Kansas City NFL	12	30	107	3.6	0	10	37	3.7	1	1	6	0
Pro Totals—5 Years	72	480	1846	3.8	13	71	454	6.4	2	15	90	10

Additional pro statistics: Returned two kickoffs for 25 yards and recovered one fumble, 1983; attempted one pass
with one completion for 16 yards and recovered two fumbles, 1984; returned four kickoffs for 80 yards, 1986; returned
six kickoffs for 102 yards, 1987.

JAMES ROBERT MORRIS
(Jim Bob)
Defensive Back—Green Bay Packers
Born May 17, 1961, at Burbank, Calif.
Height, 6.03. Weight, 211.
High School—Hamilton, Kan.
Attended Coffeyville Junior College and Kansas State University.
Signed as free agent by Kansas City Chiefs, May 5, 1983.
Released by Kansas City Chiefs, August 1, 1983.
USFL rights traded by Oklahoma Outlaws to San Antonio Gunslingers for past consideration, January 31, 1984.
Signed by San Antonio Gunslingers, January 31, 1984.
On developmental squad, April 26 through May 2, 1984; activated, May 3, 1984.
On developmental squad, May 17 through May 30, 1984; activated, May 31, 1984.
On developmental squad, June 22 through remainder of 1985 season.
Released by San Antonio Gunslingers, July 23, 1985; signed as free agent by Memphis Showboats, June 27, 1986.
Granted free agency when USFL suspended operations, August 7, 1986; signed as replacement player by Green
Bay Packers, September 25, 1987.
On injury reserve with knee injury, December 26 through remainder of 1987 season.
On developmental squad for 3 games with San Antonio Gunslingers in 1984.
On developmental squad for 1 game with San Antonio Gunslingers in 1985.

		—INTERCEPTIONS—			
Year Club	G.	No.	Yds.	Avg.	TD.
1984—San Antonio USFL	15	3	19	6.3	0
1985—San Antonio USFL	17	2	37	18.5	0
1987—Green Bay NFL	11	3	135	45.0	0
USFL Totals—2 Years	32	5	56	11.2	0
NFL Totals—1 Year	11	3	135	45.0	0
Pro Totals—3 Years	43	8	191	23.9	0

Additional pro statistics: Credited with four sacks for 39 yards, 1984; credited with four sacks for 45 yards,
recovered two fumbles and fumbled once, 1985.

JOSEPH MORRIS
(Joe)
Running Back—New York Giants
Born September 15, 1960, at Fort Bragg, N.C.
Height, 5.07. Weight, 195.
High Schools—Southern Pines, N.C.; and Ayer, Mass.
Attended Syracuse University.
Brother of Jamie Morris, rookie running back with Washington Redskins.
Named to THE SPORTING NEWS NFL All-Star Team, 1986.
Selected by New York Giants in 2nd round (45th player selected) of 1982 NFL draft.
Granted roster exemption, August 26 through August 28, 1986; activated, August 29, 1986.

Year Club	G.	RUSHING				PASS RECEIVING				—TOTAL—		
		Att.	Yds.	Avg.	TD.	P.C.	Yds.	Avg.	TD.	TD.	Pts.	F.
1982—New York Giants NFL	5	15	48	3.2	1	8	34	4.3	0	1	6	1
1983—New York Giants NFL	15	35	145	4.1	0	2	1	0.5	1	1	6	2
1984—New York Giants NFL	16	133	510	3.8	4	12	124	10.3	0	4	24	1
1985—New York Giants NFL	16	294	1336	4.5	*21	22	212	9.6	0	*21	126	6
1986—New York Giants NFL	15	341	1516	4.4	14	21	233	11.1	1	15	90	6
1987—New York Giants NFL	11	193	658	3.4	3	11	114	10.4	0	3	18	2
Pro Totals—6 Years	78	1011	4213	4.2	43	76	718	9.4	2	45	270	18

Year Club	G.	KICKOFF RETURNS		
		No.	Yds.	Avg.TD.
1982—New York Giants NFL	5	None		
1983—New York Giants NFL	15	14	255	18.2 0
1984—New York Giants NFL	16	6	69	11.5 0
1985—New York Giants NFL	16	2	25	12.5 0
1986—New York Giants NFL	15	None		
1987—New York Giants NFL	11	None		
Pro Totals—6 Years	78	22	349	15.9 0

Additional pro statistics: Recovered one fumble, 1982 and 1983; recovered two fumbles, 1985 and 1986.
Played in NFC Championship Game following 1986 season.
Played in NFL Championship Game following 1986 season.
Played in Pro Bowl (NFL All-Star Game) following 1985 and 1986 seasons.

LEE A. MORRIS
Wide Receiver—Green Bay Packers
Born July 14, 1964, at Oklahoma City, Okla.
Height, 5.10. Weight, 180.
High School—Del City, Okla.
Attended University of Oklahoma.

Signed as free agent by Green Bay Packers, July 10, 1987.
Released by Green Bay Packers, September 7, 1987; re-signed as replacement player by Packers, September 25, 1987.
On injured reserve with toe injury, November 3 through December 11, 1987; activated, December 12, 1987.

Year Club	G.	PASS RECEIVING			
		P.C.	Yds.	Avg.	TD.
1987—Green Bay NFL	5	16	259	16.2	1

Additional pro statistics: Rushed twice for two yards, returned one punt for one yard, returned six kickoffs for 104 yards, recovered two fumbles and fumbled once, 1987.

MICHAEL STEPHEN MORRIS
Guard—Phoenix Cardinals
Born February 22, 1961, at Centerville, Ia.
Height, 6.05. Weight, 275.
High School—Centerville, Ia.
Received degree in psychology and physical education
from Northeast Missouri State University.

Signed as free agent by Arizona Outlaws, November 1, 1984.
Released by Arizona Outlaws, February 11, 1985; signed as free agent by Denver Broncos, May 8, 1986.
Released by Denver Broncos, July 21, 1986; signed as free agent by St. Louis Cardinals, May 20, 1987.
Crossed picket line during players' strike, October 7, 1987.
Franchise transferred to Phoenix, March 15, 1988.
St. Louis NFL, 1987.
Games: 1987 (14).

RANDALL MORRIS
Running Back—Seattle Seahawks
Born April 22, 1961, at Anniston, Ala.
Height, 6.00. Weight, 200.
High School—Long Beach, Calif., Polytechnic.
Attended University of Tennessee.

Brother of Thomas Morris, safety with Tampa Bay Buccaneers, 1982 and 1983.
Selected by Memphis in 1984 USFL territorial draft.
Selected by Seattle in 10th round (270th player selected) of 1984 NFL draft.
Signed by Seattle Seahawks, May 18, 1984.
On injured reserve with neck injury, August 28 through September 27, 1984; activated, September 28, 1984.

Year Club	G.	RUSHING				PASS RECEIVING				—TOTAL—		
		Att.	Yds.	Avg.	TD.	P.C.	Yds.	Avg.	TD.	TD.	Pts.	F.
1984—Seattle NFL	10	58	189	3.3	0	9	61	6.8	0	0	0	2
1985—Seattle NFL	16	55	236	4.3	0	6	14	2.3	0	0	0	4
1986—Seattle NFL	16	19	149	7.8	1	None				1	6	2
1987—Seattle NFL	10	21	71	3.4	0	None				0	0	0
Pro Totals—4 Years	52	153	645	4.2	1	15	75	5.0	0	1	6	8

Year Club	G.	No.	Yds.	Avg.	TD.
1984—Seattle NFL....................	10	8	153	19.1	0
1985—Seattle NFL....................	16	31	636	20.5	0
1986—Seattle NFL....................	16	23	465	20.2	0
1987—Seattle NFL....................	10	9	149	16.6	0
Pro Totals—4 Years............	52	71	1403	19.8	0

Additional pro statistics: Recovered one fumble, 1984; attempted one pass with no completions, 1985 and 1986.

RONALD WAYNE MORRIS
(Ron)
Wide Receiver—Chicago Bears

Born November 14, 1964, at Cooper, Tex.
Height, 6.01. Weight, 187.
High School—Cooper, Tex.
Attended Southern Methodist University.

Selected by Chicago in 2nd round (54th player selected) of 1987 NFL draft.
Signed by Chicago Bears, July 31, 1987.

Year Club	G.	P.C.	Yds.	Avg.	TD.
		—PASS RECEIVING—			
1987—Chicago NFL	12	20	379	19.0	1

TIMOTHY MORRISON
(Tim)
Cornerback—Seattle Seahawks

Born April 3, 1963, at Raeford, N.C.
Height, 6.01. Weight, 195.
High School—Fayetteville, N.C., Terry Sanford.
Attended University of North Carolina.

Signed as free agent by Washington Redskins, May 6, 1986.
Granted free agency, February 1, 1988; withdrew qualifying offer, May 5, 1988.
Re-signed by Redskins and traded to Seattle Seahawks for future draft choice, May 23, 1988.
Washington NFL, 1986 and 1987.
Games: 1986 (16), 1987 (7). Total—23.
Pro statistics: Recovered one fumble, 1986.
Played in NFC Championship Game following 1986 and 1987 seasons.
Member of Washington Redskins for NFL Championship Game following 1987 season; inactive.

GUY WALKER MORRISS
Center-Guard—New England Patriots

Born May 13, 1951, at Colorado City, Tex.
Height, 6.04. Weight, 275.
High School—Arlington, Tex., Sam Houston.
Received bachelor of science degree in physical education from Texas Christian University in 1973.

Selected by Philadelphia in 2nd round (28th player selected) of 1973 NFL draft.
Released by Philadelphia Eagles, March 5, 1984; signed as free agent by New England Patriots, July 31, 1984.
Released by New England Patriots, September 1, 1986; re-signed by Patriots, September 2, 1986.
Released by New England Patriots, September 7, 1987; re-signed by Patriots, September 8, 1987.
Crossed picket line during players' strike, October 2, 1987.
On injured reserve with broken hand, November 30 through remainder of 1987 season.
Philadelphia NFL, 1973 through 1983; New England NFL, 1984 through 1987.
Games: 1973 (14), 1974 (14), 1975 (14), 1976 (14), 1977 (13), 1978 (16), 1979 (16), 1980 (16), 1981 (16), 1982 (9), 1983 (16), 1984 (16), 1985 (16), 1986 (16), 1987 (11). Total—217.
Pro statistics: Recovered one fumble, 1973; fumbled twice and recovered two fumbles for minus 10 yards, 1974; fumbled twice and recovered one fumble, 1975; fumbled once, 1977, 1983 and 1987; fumbled twice for minus eight yards, 1981.
Played in NFC Championship Game following 1980 season.
Played in AFC Championship Game following 1985 season.
Played in NFL Championship Game following 1980 and 1985 seasons.

JAMES MORRISSEY
(Jim)
Linebacker—Chicago Bears

Born December 24, 1962, at Flint, Mich.
Height, 6.03. Weight, 222.
High School—Flint, Mich., Powers.
Attended Michigan State University.

Selected by Baltimore in 8th round (106th player selected) of 1985 USFL draft.
Selected by Chicago in 11th round (302nd player selected) of 1985 NFL draft.
Signed by Chicago Bears, June 26, 1985.
Released by Chicago Bears, September 2, 1985; re-signed by Bears, September 10, 1985.
Chicago NFL, 1985 through 1987.
Games: 1985 (15), 1986 (16), 1987 (10). Total—41.
Played in NFC Championship Game following 1985 season.
Played in NFL Championship Game following 1985 season.

BOBBY MORSE
Running Back-Kick Returner—Philadelphia Eagles
Born October 3, 1965, at Muskegon, Mich.
Height, 5.10. Weight, 213.
High School—Muskegon, Mich., Catholic Central.
Received degree in advertisng from Michigan State University in 1987.
Selected by Philadelphia in 12th round (316th player selected) of 1987 NFL draft.
Signed by Philadelphia Eagles, August 6, 1987.

| | | —RUSHING— | | | PASS RECEIVING | | | | —TOTAL— | | |
Year Club	G.	Att.	Yds.	Avg.	TD.	P.C.	Yds.	Avg.	TD.	TD.	Pts.	F.
1987—Philadelphia NFL	11	6	14	2.3	0	1	8	8.0	0	0	0	1

| | | —PUNT RETURNS— | | | | —KICKOFF RET.— | | |
Year Club	G.	No.	Yds.	Avg.	TD.	No.	Yds.	Avg.TD.
1987—Philadelphia NFL	11	20	121	6.1	0	24	386	16.1 0

Additional pro statistics: Recovered one fumble, 1987.

DONALD HOWARD MOSEBAR
(Don)
Center—Los Angeles Raiders
Born September 11, 1961, at Yakima, Calif.
Height, 6.06. Weight, 275.
High School—Visalia, Calif., Mount Whitney.
Attended University of Southern California.
Selected by Los Angeles in 1983 USFL territorial draft.
Selected by Los Angeles Raiders in 1st round (26th player selected) of 1983 NFL draft.
Signed by Los Angeles Raiders, August 29, 1983.
Granted roster exemption, August 29, 1983; activated, September 9, 1983.
On injured reserve with back injury, November 8 through remainder of 1984 season.
Los Angeles Raiders NFL, 1983 through 1987.
Games: 1983 (14), 1984 (10), 1985 (16), 1986 (16), 1987 (12). Total—68.
Pro statistics: Recovered one fumble and fumbled once, 1986.
Played in AFC Championship Game following 1983 season.
Played in NFL Championship Game following 1983 season.

WINSTON N. MOSS
Linebacker—Tampa Bay Buccaneers
Born December 24, 1965, at Miami, Fla.
Height, 6.03. Weight, 235.
High School—Miami, Fla., Southridge.
Attended University of Miami (Fla.).
Selected by Tampa Bay in 2nd round (50th player selected) of 1987 NFL draft.
Signed by Tampa Bay Buccaneers, July 18, 1987.
Tampa Bay NFL, 1987.
Games: 1987 (12).
Pro statistics: Recovered one fumble in end zone for a touchdown, 1987.

WALTER STEPHEN MOTT III
(Steve)
Center—Detroit Lions
Born March 24, 1961, at New Orleans, La.
Height, 6.03. Weight, 270.
High School—Marrero, La., Archbishop Shaw.
Attended University of Alabama.
Selected by Birmingham in 1983 USFL territorial draft.
Selected by Detroit in 5th round (121st player selected) of 1983 NFL draft.
Signed by Detroit Lions, June 1, 1983.
On physically unable to perform/active with knee injury, July 22 through August 8, 1984; activated, August 9, 1984.
On injured reserve with dislocated ankle, October 8 through remainder of 1984 season.
Detroit NFL, 1983 through 1987.
Games: 1983 (13), 1984 (6), 1985 (16), 1986 (14), 1987 (11). Total—60.
Pro statistics: Fumbled once, 1983; recovered one fumble, 1985.

ZEKE MOWATT
Tight End—New York Giants
Born March 5, 1961, at Wauchula, Fla.
Height, 6.03. Weight, 238.
High School—Wauchula, Fla., Hardee County.
Attended Florida State University.
Selected by Tampa Bay in 1983 USFL territorial draft.
Signed as free agent by New York Giants, June 1, 1983.
On injured reserve with knee injury, August 31 through entire 1985 season.

		PASS RECEIVING			
Year Club	G.	P.C.	Yds.	Avg.	TD.
1983—New York Giants NFL	16	21	280	13.3	1
1984—New York Giants NFL	16	48	698	14.5	6
1986—New York Giants NFL	16	10	119	11.9	2
1987—New York Giants NFL	12	3	39	13.0	1
Pro Totals—4 Years............	60	82	1136	13.9	10

Additional pro statistics: Recovered one fumble and fumbled once, 1986.
Played in NFC Championship Game following 1986 season.
Played in NFL Championship Game following 1986 season.

PAUL STEWART MOYER
Safety—Seattle Seahawks
Born July 26, 1961, at Villa Park, Calif.
Height, 6.01. Weight, 201.
High School—Villa Park, Calif.
Attended Fullerton College and Arizona State University.

Signed as free agent by Seattle Seahawks, April 28, 1983.
On injured reserve with shoulder injury, September 11 through October 17, 1985; activated, October 18, 1985.

		INTERCEPTIONS			
Year Club	G.	No.	Yds.	Avg.	TD.
1983—Seattle NFL..................	16	1	19	19.0	1
1984—Seattle NFL..................	16		None		
1985—Seattle NFL..................	11		None		
1986—Seattle NFL..................	16	3	38	12.7	0
1987—Seattle NFL..................	12	1	0	0.0	0
Pro Totals—5 Years............	71	5	57	11.4	1

Additional pro statistics: Recovered three fumbles, 1983; recovered blocked punt in end zone for a touchdown, 1986; recovered three fumbles for 10 yards, 1987.
Played in AFC Championship Game following 1983 season.

MARK DAVID MRAZ
Defensive End—Atlanta Falcons
Born February 9, 1965, at Glendale, Calif.
Height, 6.04. Weight, 255.
High School—Glendora, Calif.
Attended Utah State University.

Selected by Atlanta in 5th round (125th player selected) of 1987 NFL draft.
Signed by Atlanta Falcons, July 26, 1987.
Atlanta NFL, 1987.
Games: 1987 (11).

JAMIE F. MUELLER
(Name pronounced MEW-ler.)
Fullback—Buffalo Bills
Born October 4, 1964, at Cleveland, O.
Height, 6.01. Weight, 225.
High School—Fairview Park, O., Fairview.
Attended Bendictine College.

Selected by Buffalo in 3rd round (78th player selected) of 1987 NFL draft.
Signed by Buffalo Bills, July 25, 1987.

		RUSHING			PASS RECEIVING				TOTAL		
Year Club	G.	Att.	Yds.	Avg.	TD.	P.C.	Yds.	Avg.	TD.	TD.	Pts. F.
1987—Buffalo NFL................................	12	82	354	4.3	2	3	13	4.3	0	2	12 5

Additional pro statistics: Returned five kickoffs for 74 yards and recovered one fumble, 1987.

VANCE ALAN MUELLER
Running Back—Los Angeles Raiders
Born May 5, 1964, at Tucson, Ariz.
Height, 6.00. Weight, 210.
High School—Jackson, Calif.
Received bachelor of science degree in psychology and physiology from Occidental College in 1986.

Selected by Los Angeles Raiders in 4th round (103rd player selected) of 1986 NFL draft.
Signed by Los Angeles Raiders, July 15, 1986.

		RUSHING			PASS RECEIVING				TOTAL		
Year Club	G.	Att.	Yds.	Avg.	TD.	P.C.	Yds.	Avg.	TD.	TD.	Pts. F.
1986—Los Angeles Raiders NFL	15	13	30	2.3	0	6	54	9.0	0	0	0 1
1987—Los Angeles Raiders NFL	12	37	175	4.7	1	11	95	8.6	0	1	6 3
Pro Totals—2 Years.................................	27	50	205	4.1	1	17	149	8.8	0	1	6 4

Year Club	G.	No.	Yds.	Avg.TD.
1986—L. A. Raiders NFL........	15	2	73	36.5	0
1987—L. A. Raiders NFL........	12	27	588	21.8	0
Pro Totals—2 Years............	27	29	661	22.8	0

Additional pro statistics: Recovered one fumble, 1987.

MICHAEL RENE MULARKEY
(Mike)
Tight End—Minnesota Vikings
Born November 19, 1961, at Miami, Fla.
Height, 6.04. Weight, 233.
High School—Fort Lauderdale, Fla., Northeast.
Attended University of Florida.

Selected by Tampa Bay in 1983 USFL territorial draft.
Selected by San Francisco in 9th round (229th player selected) of 1983 NFL draft.
Signed by San Francisco 49ers, June 1, 1983.
Released by San Francisco 49ers, August 29, 1983; awarded on waivers to Minnesota Vikings, August 30, 1983.
On injured reserve with ankle injury, September 30 through remainder of 1983 season.
On injured reserve with knee injury, September 8 through October 30, 1987; activated, October 31, 1987.
Crossed picket line during players' strike, October 7, 1987; returned to picket line, October 12, 1987.

			—PASS RECEIVING—		
Year Club	G.	P.C.	Yds.	Avg.	TD.
1983—Minnesota NFL............	3		None		
1984—Minnesota NFL............	16	14	134	9.6	2
1985—Minnesota NFL............	15	13	196	15.1	1
1986—Minnesota NFL............	16	11	89	8.1	2
1987—Minnesota NFL............	9	1	6	6.0	0
Pro Totals—5 Years............	59	39	425	10.9	5

Additional pro statistics: Recovered one fumble and fumbled once, 1984; ran nine yards with lateral on kickoff return, 1985; returned one kickoff for 16 yards, 1987.

MARK ALAN MULLANEY
Defensive End—Minnesota Vikings
Born April 30, 1953, at Denver, Colo.
Height, 6.06. Weight, 245.
High School—Denver, Colo., George Washington.
Received degree in humanities and social science from Colorado State University.

Selected by Minnesota in 1st round (25th player selected) of 1975 NFL draft.
On injured reserve with broken collarbone, September 30 through December 4, 1983; activated, December 5, 1983.
On injured reserve with nerve damage in neck, November 23 through remainder of 1984 season.
On injured reserve with knee injury, October 1 through October 31, 1986; activated, November 1, 1986.
On injured reserve with neck injury, September 1 through entire 1987 season.
Crossed picket line during players' strike, October 7, 1987.
Minnesota NFL, 1975 through 1986.
Games: 1975 (14), 1976 (12), 1977 (14), 1978 (15), 1979 (16), 1980 (16), 1981 (15), 1982 (9), 1983 (7), 1984 (7), 1985 (15), 1986 (11). Total—151.
Pro statistics: Recovered two fumbles for three yards, 1976; recovered one fumble, 1978, 1980, 1981 and 1983; intercepted one pass for 15 yards and recovered two fumbles, 1985.
Played in NFC Championship Game following 1976 and 1977 seasons.
Played in NFL Championship Game following 1976 season.

LLOYD ELLIS MUMPHREY
Defensive Lineman—Tampa Bay Buccaneers
Born February 14, 1961, at Memphis, Tenn.
Height, 6.03. Weight, 247.
High School—Memphis, Tenn., Westwood.
Attended Mississippi Valley State University.

Signed as free agent by San Francisco 49ers, May 20, 1985.
Released by San Francisco 49ers, August 12, 1985; signed as free agent by Edmonton Eskimos, April 10, 1987.
Released by Edmonton Eskimos, August 3, 1987; signed as free agent by Tampa Bay Buccaneers, August 14, 1987.
Released by Tampa Bay Buccaneers, August 31, 1987; signed as free agent replacement player by Kansas City Chiefs, September 29, 1987.
Released by Kansas City Chiefs, October 20, 1987; signed as free agent by Tampa Bay Bucaneers for 1988, December 10, 1987.
Edmonton CFL, 1987; Kansas City NFL, 1987.
Games: 1987 CFL (3), 1987 NFL (3). Total—6.
CFL statistics: Recovered one fumble, 1987.

MIKE MUNCHAK
Guard—Houston Oilers
Born March 5, 1960, at Scranton, Pa.
Height, 6.03. Weight, 280.
High School—Scranton, Pa., Central.
Received bachelor of business administration degree from Penn State University in 1982.

Named to THE SPORTING NEWS NFL All-Star Team, 1987.
Selected by Houston in 1st round (8th player selected) of 1982 NFL draft.
On injured reserve with broken ankle, November 24 through December 23, 1982; activated, December 24, 1982.
On injured reserve with knee injury, October 14 through remainder of 1986 season.
Houston NFL, 1982 through 1987.
Games: 1982 (4), 1983 (16), 1984 (16), 1985 (16), 1986 (6), 1987 (12). Total—70.
Pro statistics: Recovered two fumbles for three yards, 1985, recovered one fumble in end zone for a touchdown, 1986; recovered one fumble, 1987.
Played in Pro Bowl (NFL All-Star Game) following 1984, 1985 and 1987 seasons.

MARC CHRISTOPHER MUNFORD
Linebacker—Denver Broncos
Born February 14, 1965, at Lincoln, Neb.
Height, 6.02. Weight, 231.
High School—Littleton, Colo., Heritage.
Attended University of Nebraska.

Selected by Denver in 4th round (111th player selected) of 1987 NFL draft.
Signed by Denver Broncos, July 19, 1987.
On injured reserve with back injury, January 9, 1988 through remainder of 1987 season playoffs.
Denver NFL, 1987.
Games: 1987 (12).
Pro statistics: Recovered two fumbles, 1987.

MICHAEL ANTHONY MUNOZ
(Known by middle name.)
Offensive Tackle—Cincinnati Bengals
Born August 19, 1958, at Ontario, Calif.
Height, 6.06. Weight, 278.
High School—Ontario, Calif., Chaffey.
Received bachelor of science degree in public administration from
University of Southern California in 1980.

Named to THE SPORTING NEWS NFL All-Star Team, 1981 and 1984 through 1986.
Selected by Cincinnati in 1st round (3rd player selected) of 1980 NFL draft.
Granted free agency, February 1, 1987; re-signed by Bengals, September 12, 1987.
Granted roster exemption, September 12 through September 18, 1987; activated, September 19, 1987.
Cincinnati NFL, 1980 through 1987.
Games: 1980 (16), 1981 (16), 1982 (9), 1983 (16), 1984 (16), 1985 (16), 1986 (16), 1987 (11). Total—116.
Pro statistics: Caught one pass for minus six yards, 1980; caught one pass for one yard and a touchdown and recovered one fumble, 1984; caught one pass for one yard, 1985; caught two passes for seven yards and two touchdowns, 1986; caught two passes for 15 yards and a touchdown, 1987.
Played in AFC Championship Game following 1981 season.
Played in NFL Championship Game following 1981 season.
Played in Pro Bowl (NFL All-Star Game) following 1981 and 1983 through 1986 seasons.
Named to play in Pro Bowl following 1987 season; replaced due to injury by Jim Lachey.

KEVIN DION MURPHY
Linebacker—Tampa Bay Buccaneers
Born September 8, 1963, at Plano, Tex.
Height, 6.02. Weight, 230.
High School—Richardson, Tex., L. V. Berkner.
Received degree in marketing from University of Oklahoma in 1986.

Named as linebacker on THE SPORTING NEWS College All-America Team, 1985.
Selected by Los Angeles in 11th round (154th player selected) of 1985 NFL USFL draft (elected to return to college for final year of eligibility).
Selected by Tampa Bay in 2nd round (40th player selected) of 1986 NFL draft.
Signed by Tampa Bay Buccaneers, July 22, 1986.
Tampa Bay NFL, 1986 and 1987.
Games: 1986 (16), 1987 (9). Total—25.
Pro statistics: Recovered one fumble, 1986.

MARK STEVEN MURPHY
Safety—Green Bay Packers
Born April 22, 1958, at Canton, O.
Height, 6.02. Weight, 199.
High School—Canton, O., Glen Oaks.
Received bachelor of science degree in business administration from West Liberty State College.

Signed as free agent by Green Bay Packers, April 25, 1980.
On injured reserve with broken hand, August 14 through December 17, 1980; activated after clearing procedural waivers, December 19, 1980.
On injured reserve with ankle injury, September 2 through entire 1986 season.

Year Club		G.	No.	Yds.	Avg.TD.		Year Club		G.	No.	Yds.	Avg.TD.
1980—Green Bay NFL		1		None			1984—Green Bay NFL		16	1	4	4.0 0
1981—Green Bay NFL		16	3	57	19.0 0		1985—Green Bay NFL		15	2	50	25.0 *1
1982—Green Bay NFL		9		None			1987—Green Bay NFL		12		None	
1983—Green Bay NFL		16		None			Pro Totals—7 Years		85	6	111	18.5 1

— 315 —

Additional pro statistics: Recovered two fumbles, 1981 and 1987; recovered one fumble, 1983 and 1985; recovered one fumble for two yards and fumbled once, 1984; returned one punt for four yards, 1985.

EDWARD PETER MURRAY
(Ed)
Placekicker—Detroit Lions

Born August 29, 1956, at Halifax, Nova Scotia.
Height, 5.10. Weight, 175.
High School—Victoria, British Columbia, Spectrum.
Received bachelor of science degree in education from Tulane University in 1980.
Cousin of Mike Rogers, center with Edmonton Oilers, New England-Hartford Whalers and
New York Rangers, 1974-75 through 1985-86.

Selected by Detroit in 7th round (166th player selected) of 1980 NFL draft.
On suspended list, September 10 through November 19, 1982; reinstated, November 20, 1982.

		—PLACE KICKING—					
Year	Club	G.	XP.	XPM.	FG.	FGA.	Pts.
1980—Detroit NFL		16	35	1	*27	*42	116
1981—Detroit NFL		16	46	0	25	35	*121
1982—Detroit NFL		7	16	0	11	12	49
1983—Detroit NFL		16	38	0	25	32	113
1984—Detroit NFL		16	31	0	20	27	91
1985—Detroit NFL		16	31	2	26	31	109
1986—Detroit NFL		16	31	1	18	25	85
1987—Detroit NFL		12	21	0	20	32	81
Pro Totals—8 Years		115	249	4	172	236	765

Additional pro statistics: Punted once for 37 yards, 1986; punted four times for a 38.8 average, 1987.
Played in Pro Bowl (NFL All-Star Game) following 1980 season.

WALTER C. MURRAY
Wide Receiver—Indianapolis Colts

Born December 13, 1962, at Berkeley, Calif.
Height, 6.04. Weight, 200.
High School—Berkeley, Calif.
Received bachelor of arts and science degree from University of Hawaii in 1986.

Selected by Washington in 2nd round (45th player selected) of 1986 NFL draft.
NFL rights traded by Washington Redskins to Indianapolis Colts for 2nd round pick in 1987 draft, October 7, 1986.
Signed by Indianapolis Colts, October 7, 1986.
Granted roster exemption, October 7 through October 16, 1986; activated, October 17, 1986.
Crossed picket line during players' strike, September 28, 1987; returned to picket line, October 1, 1987.
Crossed picket line during players' strike, October 2, 1987.

		—PASS RECEIVING—			
Year	Club	G.	P.C.	Yds.	Avg. TD.
1986—Indianapolis NFL		5	2	34	17.0 0
1987—Indianapolis NFL		14	20	339	17.0 3
Pro Totals—2 Years		19	22	373	17.0 3

PETER MICHAEL NAJARIAN
(Pete)
Linebacker—Tampa Bay Buccaneers

Born December 22, 1963, at San Francisco, Calif.
Height, 6.02. Weight, 230.
High School—Minneapolis, Minn., Central.
Attended University of Minnesota.

Signed as free agent by Seattle Seahawks, May 2, 1986.
Released by Seattle Seahawks, August 1, 1986; signed as free agent by Minnesota Vikings, August 5, 1986.
Released by Minnesota Vikings, August 26, 1986; re-signed by Vikings, April 8, 1987.
Released by Minnesota Vikings, September 7, 1987; re-signed as replacement player by Vikings, October 1, 1987.
Released by Minnesota Vikings, October 19, 1987; re-signed by Vikings, November 5, 1987.
Released by Minnesota Vikings, November 25, 1987; re-signed by Vikings, December 2, 1987.
Released by Minnesota Vikings, December 8, 1987; signed as free agent by Tampa Bay Buccaneers, February 18, 1988.
Minnesota NFL, 1987.
Games: 1987 (5).

JOSEPH ANDREW NASH
(Joe)
Nose Tackle—Seattle Seahawks

Born October 11, 1960, at Boston, Mass.
Height, 6.02. Weight, 257.
High School—Dorchester, Mass., Boston College High.
Received bachelor of arts degree in sociology from Boston College in 1982.

Signed as free agent by Seattle Seahawks, April 30, 1982.
On inactive list, September 12 and September 19, 1982.
Seattle NFL, 1982 through 1987.

Games: 1982 (7), 1983 (16), 1984 (16), 1985 (16), 1986 (16), 1987 (12). Total—83.
Pro statistics: Recovered three fumbles (including one in end zone for a touchdown), 1984; recovered two fumbles, 1986.
Played in AFC Championship Game following 1983 season.
Played in Pro Bowl (NFL All-Star Game) following 1984 season.

RICKY RENNARD NATTIEL
(Name pronounced Na-TEEL.)
Wide Receiver—Denver Broncos
Born January 25, 1966, at Gainesville, Fla.
Height, 5.09. Weight, 180.
High School—Newberry, Fla.
Received degree in rehabilitation counseling from University of Florida in 1987.
Selected by Denver in 1st round (27th player selected) of 1987 NFL draft.
Signed by Denver Broncos, July 23, 1987.

			—PASS RECEIVING—				—PUNT RETURNS—				—TOTAL—		
Year	Club	G.	P.C.	Yds.	Avg.	TD.	No.	Yds.	Avg.	TD.	TD.	Pts.	F.
1987—Denver NFL		12	31	630	20.3	2	12	73	6.1	0	2	12	2

Additional pro statistics: Rushed twice for 13 yards, returned four kickoffs for 78 yards and recovered one fumble, 1987.
Played in AFC Championship Game following 1987 season.
Played in NFL Championship Game following 1987 season.

FRANKIE LEON NEAL
Wide Receiver—Green Bay Packers
Born October 1, 1965, at Sebring, Fla.
Height, 6.01. Weight, 202.
High School—Okeechobee, Fla.
Attended University of Florida and Fort Hays Kansas State University.
Selected by Green Bay in 3rd round (71st player selected) of 1987 NFL draft.
Signed by Green Bay Packers, August 1, 1987.

			——PASS RECEIVING——			
Year	Club	G.	P.C.	Yds.	Avg.	TD.
1987—Green Bay NFL		12	36	420	11.7	3

Additional pro statistics: Rushed once for no yards, returned four kickoffs for 44 yards, attempted one pass for no yards and fumbled once, 1987.

CHARLES LaVERNE NELSON
(Chuck)
Placekicker—Minnesota Vikings
Born February 23, 1960, at Seattle, Wash.
Height, 5.11. Weight, 175.
High School—Everett, Wash.
Attended University of Washington.
Named as placekicker on THE SPORTING NEWS College All-America Team, 1982.
Selected by Chicago in 23rd round (270th player selected) of 1983 USFL draft.
Selected by Los Angeles Rams in 4th round (87th player selected) of 1983 NFL draft.
Signed by Los Angeles Rams, July 13, 1983.
Released by Los Angeles Rams, August 27, 1984; signed as free agent by Buffalo Bills, October 30, 1984.
Released by Buffalo Bills, August 19, 1985; signed as free agent by Minnesota Vikings, March 18, 1986.
Released by Minnesota Vikings, September 1, 1986; re-signed by Vikings, September 2, 1986.

		——PLACE KICKING——					
Year	Club	G.	XP.	XPM.	FG.	FGA.	Pts.
1983—L. A. Rams NFL		12	33	*4	5	11	48
1984—Buffalo NFL		7	14	0	3	5	23
1986—Minnesota NFL		16	44	3	22	28	110
1987—Minnesota NFL		12	36	1	13	24	75
Pro Totals—4 Years		47	127	8	43	68	256

Additional pro statistics: Recovered one fumble, 1983; punted three times for a 24.0 avg., 1986.
Played in NFC Championship Game following 1987 season.

DARRIN MILO NELSON
Running Back—Minnesota Vikings
Born January 2, 1959, at Sacramento, Calif.
Height, 5.09. Weight, 185.
High School—Downey, Calif., Pius X.
Received bachelor of science degree in urban and environmental planning
from Stanford University in 1981.
Brother of Kevin Nelson, running back with Los Angeles Express, 1984 and 1985; cousin of
Ozzie Newsome, tight end with Cleveland Browns; Carlos Carson, wide receiver with Kansas City Chiefs; and
Charles Alexander, running back with Cincinnati Bengals, 1979 through 1985.
Selected by Minnesota in 1st round (7th player selected) of 1982 NFL draft.

Year Club	G.	RUSHING				PASS RECEIVING				TOTAL		
		Att.	Yds.	Avg.	TD.	P.C.	Yds.	Avg.	TD.	TD.	Pts.	F.
1982—Minnesota NFL	7	44	136	3.1	0	9	100	11.1	0	0	0	2
1983—Minnesota NFL	15	154	642	4.2	1	51	618	12.1	0	1	6	5
1984—Minnesota NFL	15	80	406	5.1	3	27	162	6.0	1	4	24	4
1985—Minnesota NFL	16	200	893	4.5	5	43	301	7.0	1	6	36	7
1986—Minnesota NFL	16	191	793	4.2	4	53	593	11.2	3	7	42	3
1987—Minnesota NFL	10	131	642	*4.9	2	26	129	5.0	0	2	12	2
Pro Totals—6 Years	79	800	3512	4.4	15	209	1903	9.1	5	20	120	23

Year Club	G.	PUNT RETURNS				KICKOFF RET.			
		No.	Yds.	Avg.	TD.	No.	Yds.	Avg.	TD.
1982—Minnesota NFL	7	None				6	132	22.0	0
1983—Minnesota NFL	15	None				18	445	24.7	0
1984—Minnesota NFL	15	23	180	7.8	0	39	891	22.8	0
1985—Minnesota NFL	16	16	133	8.3	0	3	51	17.0	0
1986—Minnesota NFL	16	None				3	105	35.0	0
1987—Minnesota NFL	10	None				7	164	23.4	0
Pro Totals—6 Years	79	39	313	8.0	0	76	1788	23.5	0

Additional pro statistics: Recovered one fumble, 1983; recovered three fumbles, 1984; recovered two fumbles for 16 yards, 1985.
Played in NFC Championship Game following 1987 season.

EDMUND CLAU-VON NELSON
Defensive End-Defensive Tackle—New Orleans Saints
Born April 30, 1960, at Live Oak, Fla.
Height, 6.03. Weight, 266.
High School—Tampa, Fla., C. Leon King.
Received bachelor of science degree in personnel management
and industrial relations from Auburn University.
Selected by Pittsburgh in 7th round (172nd player selected) of 1982 NFL draft.
On injured reserve with calf injury, November 15 through remainder of 1985 season.
Released by Pittsburgh Steelers, May 24, 1988; awarded on waivers to New Orleans Saints, June 7, 1988.
Pittsburgh NFL, 1982 through 1987.
Games: 1982 (8), 1983 (16), 1984 (16), 1985 (6), 1986 (16), 1987 (10). Total—72.
Pro statistics: Recovered one fumble, 1982 and 1987; recovered two fumbles, 1986.
Played in AFC Championship Game following 1984 season.

KARL NELSON
Offensive Tackle—New York Giants
Born June 14, 1960, at DeKalb, Ill.
Height, 6.06. Weight, 285.
High School—DeKalb, Ill.
Attended Iowa State University.
Selected by Tampa Bay in 4th round (44th player selected) of 1983 USFL draft.
Selected by New York Giants in 3rd round (70th player selected) of 1983 NFL draft.
Signed by New York Giants, June 13, 1983.
On injured reserve with foot injury, August 23 through entire 1983 season.
On injured reserve with Hodgkins disease, August 25 through entire 1987 season.
New York Giants NFL, 1984 through 1986.
Games: 1984 (16), 1985 (16), 1986 (16). Total—48.
Pro statistics: Recovered one fumble, 1985 and 1986.
Played in NFC Championship Game following 1986 season.
Played in NFL Championship Game following 1986 season.

ROBERT WILLIAM NELSON
(Bob)
Nose Tackle—Green Bay Packers
Born March 3, 1959, at Baltimore, Md.
Height, 6.03. Weight, 265.
High School—Baltimore, Md., Patapsco.
Attended University of Miami (Fla.).
Selected by Miami in 5th round (120th player selected) of 1982 NFL draft.
Released by Miami Dolphins, September 6, 1982; signed by Chicago Blitz, November 30, 1983.
Traded with running back Kevin McLee and 12th round picks in 1984 and 1985 drafts by Chicago Blitz to Arizona Wranglers for rights to guard Bruce Branch, January 13, 1983.
Franchise transferred to Chicago, September 30, 1983.
Traded by Chicago Blitz to Oklahoma Outlaws for guard Terry Crouch, January 19, 1984.
Not protected in merger of Oklahoma Outlaws and Arizona Wranglers; selected by Jacksonville Bulls in USFL dispersal draft, December 6, 1984.
Granted free agency, August 1, 1985; signed by Tampa Bay Buccaneers, August 6, 1985.
Released by Tampa Bay Buccaneers, September 2, 1985; re-signed by Buccaneers, March 21, 1986.
Released by Tampa Bay Buccaneers, September 7, 1987; signed as free agent by Green Bay Packers, May 5, 1988.
Arizona USFL, 1983; Oklahoma USFL, 1984; Jacksonville USFL, 1985; Tampa Bay NFL, 1986.
Games: 1983 (18), 1984 (18), 1985 (18), 1986 (16). Total USFL—54. Total Pro—70.
USFL statistics: Credited with six sacks for 44 yards, 1983; recovered two fumbles and credited with 6½ sacks for 43 yards, 1984; credited with 5½ sacks for 37 yards, 1985.
NFL statistics: Recovered one fumble, 1986.

THOMAS LEE NEVILLE
(Tom)
Offensive Tackle-Guard—Green Bay Packers
Born September 4, 1961, at Great Falls, Mont.
Height, 6.05. Weight, 306.
High School—Fairbanks, Alaska, Ben Eielson AFB.
Attended Weber State College and Fresno State University.

Selected by Oakland in 1985 USFL territorial draft.
Signed as free agent by Seattle Seahawks, May 7, 1985.
Released by Seattle Seahawks, August 12, 1985; signed as free agent by Green Bay Packers, March 28, 1986.
Green Bay NFL, 1986 and 1987.
Games: 1986 (16), 1987 (12). Total—28.
Additional pro statistics: Recovered one fumble, 1987.

TOM G. NEWBERRY
Guard—Los Angeles Rams
Born December 20, 1962, at Onalaska, Wis.
Height, 6.02. Weight, 279.
High School—Onalaska, Wis.
Received degree in geography from University of Wisconsin at La Crosse in 1986.

Selected by Los Angeles Rams in 2nd round (50th player selected) of 1986 NFL draft.
Signed by Los Angeles Rams, July 18, 1986.
Los Angeles Rams NFL, 1986 and 1987.
Games: 1986 (16), 1987 (12). Total—28.
Pro statistics: Recovered one fumble in end zone for a touchdown, 1986.

HARRY KENT NEWSOME JR.
Punter—Pittsburgh Steelers
Born January 25, 1963, at Cheraw, S.C.
Height, 6.00. Weight, 187.
High School—Cheraw, S.C.
Attended Wake Forest University.

Selected by New Jersey in 15th round (213th player selected) of 1985 USFL draft.
Selected by Pittsburgh in 8th round (214th player selected) of 1985 NFL draft.
Signed by Pittsburgh Steelers, July 26, 1985.

Year Club	G.	No.	Avg.	Blk.
1985—Pittsburgh NFL	16	78	39.6	1
1986—Pittsburgh NFL	16	86	40.1	*3
1987—Pittsburgh NFL	12	64	41.8	1
Pro Totals—3 Years	44	228	40.4	5

Additional pro statistics: Attempted two passes with one completion for 12 yards and a touchdown, 1986; rushed twice for 16 yards, recovered one fumble and fumble once for minus 17 yards, 1987.

OZZIE NEWSOME
Tight End—Cleveland Browns
Born March 16, 1956, at Muscle Shoals, Ala.
Height, 6.02. Weight, 232.
High School—Leighton, Ala., Colbert County.
Received bachelor of science degree in recreation and park management from University of Alabama.
Cousin of Darrin Nelson, running back with Minnesota Vikings; and Kevin Nelson,
running back with Los Angeles Express, 1984 and 1985.

Established NFL record for most pass receptions by tight end, career (541).
Named to THE SPORTING NEWS NFL All-Star Team, 1984.
Named to THE SPORTING NEWS AFC All-Star Team, 1979.
Named as wide receiver on THE SPORTING NEWS College All-America Team, 1977.
Selected by Cleveland in 1st round (23rd player selected) of 1978 NFL draft.
Crossed picket line during players' strike, October 14, 1987.

Year Club	G.	P.C.	Yds.	Avg.	TD.
1978—Cleveland NFL	16	38	589	15.5	2
1979—Cleveland NFL	16	55	781	14.2	9
1980—Cleveland NFL	16	51	594	11.6	3
1981—Cleveland NFL	16	69	1002	14.5	6
1982—Cleveland NFL	8	49	633	12.9	3
1983—Cleveland NFL	16	89	970	10.9	6
1984—Cleveland NFL	16	89	1001	11.2	5
1985—Cleveland NFL	16	62	711	11.5	5
1986—Cleveland NFL	16	39	417	10.7	3
1987—Cleveland NFL	13	34	375	11.0	0
Pro Totals—10 Years	149	575	7073	12.3	42

Additional pro statistics: Returned two punts for 29 yards, rushed 13 times for 96 yards and two touchdowns and fumbled once, 1978; rushed once for six yards, 1979; rushed twice for 13 yards and fumbled twice, 1980; rushed twice for 20 yards, 1981; recovered one fumble, 1985.
Played in AFC Championship Game following 1986 and 1987 seasons.
Played in Pro Bowl (NFL All-Star Game) following 1981, 1984 and 1985 seasons.

TIMOTHY ARTHUR NEWSOME
(Timmy)
Fullback—Dallas Cowboys
Born May 17, 1958, at Ahoskie, N. C.
Height, 6.01. Weight, 235.
High School—Ahoskie, N. C.
Received bachelor of arts degree in business administration from
Winston-Salem State University in 1980.
Selected by Dallas in 6th round (162nd player selected) of 1980 NFL draft.

Year Club	G.	RUSHING Att.	Yds.	Avg.	TD.	PASS RECEIVING P.C.	Yds.	Avg.	TD.	TOTAL TD.	Pts.	F.
1980—Dallas NFL	16	25	79	3.2	2	4	43	10.8	0	2	12	0
1981—Dallas NFL	15	13	38	2.9	0	None				0	0	1
1982—Dallas NFL	9	15	98	6.5	1	6	118	19.7	1	2	12	1
1983—Dallas NFL	16	44	185	4.2	2	18	250	13.9	4	6	36	0
1984—Dallas NFL	15	66	268	4.1	5	26	263	10.1	0	5	30	3
1985—Dallas NFL	14	88	252	2.9	2	46	361	7.8	1	3	18	2
1986—Dallas NFL	16	34	110	3.2	2	48	421	8.8	3	5	30	2
1987—Dallas NFL	11	25	121	4.8	2	34	274	8.1	2	4	24	1
Pro Totals—8 Years	112	310	1151	3.7	16	182	1730	9.5	11	27	162	10

		KICKOFF RETURNS			
Year Club	G.	No.	Yds.	Avg.	TD.
1980—Dallas NFL	16	12	293	24.4	0
1981—Dallas NFL	15	12	228	19.0	0
1982—Dallas NFL	9	5	74	14.8	0
1983—Dallas NFL	16	1	28	28.0	0
1984—Dallas NFL	15	None			
1985—Dallas NFL	14	None			
1986—Dallas NFL	16	2	32	16.0	0
1987—Dallas NFL	11	2	22	11.0	0
Pro Totals—8 Years	112	34	677	19.9	0

Additional pro statistics: Recovered two fumbles, 1980; recovered one fumble, 1982 and 1986.
Played in NFC Championship Game following 1980 through 1982 seasons.

VINCENT KARL NEWSOME
(Vince)
Safety—Los Angeles Rams
Born January 22, 1961, at Braintree, Wash.
Height, 6.01. Weight, 179.
High School—Vacaville, Calif.
Attended University of Washington.
Selected by Oakland in 4th round (42nd player selected) of 1983 USFL draft.
Selected by Los Angeles Rams in 4th round (97th player selected) of 1983 NFL draft.
Signed by Los Angeles Rams, May 22, 1983.
On injured reserve with knee injury, December 8 through remainder of 1987 season.

		INTERCEPTIONS			
Year Club	G.	No.	Yds.	Avg.	TD.
1983—L.A. Rams NFL	16	None			
1984—L.A. Rams NFL	16	1	31	31.0	0
1985—L.A. Rams NFL	16	3	20	6.7	0
1986—L.A. Rams NFL	16	3	45	15.0	0
1987—L.A. Rams NFL	8	None			
Pro Totals—5 Years	72	7	96	13.7	0

Additional pro statistics: Recovered one fumble, 1985 and 1986; recovered one fumble for seven yards, 1987.
Played in NFC Championship Game following 1985 season.

NATHANIEL NEWTON JR.
(Nate)
Guard—Dallas Cowboys
Born December 20, 1961, at Orlando, Fla.
Height, 6.03. Weight, 317.
High School—Orlando, Fla., Jones.
Attended Florida A&M University.
Brother of Tim Newton, defensive tackle with Minnesota Vikings.
Selected by Tampa Bay in 1983 USFL territorial draft.
Signed as free agent by Washington Redskins, May 5, 1983.
Released by Washington Redskins, August 29, 1983; signed by Tampa Bay Bandits, November 6, 1983.
Granted free agency when USFL suspended operations, August 7, 1986; signed as free agent by Dallas Cowboys, August 14, 1986.
Granted roster exemption, August 14 through August 20, 1986; activated, August 21, 1986.
Crossed picket line during players' strike, October 24, 1987.
Tampa Bay USFL, 1984 and 1985; Dallas NFL, 1986 and 1987.
Games: 1984 (18), 1985 (18), 1986 (11), 1987 (11). Total USFL—36. Total NFL—22. Total Pro—58.

TIMOTHY REGINALD NEWTON
(Tim)
Defensive Tackle—Minnesota Vikings
Born March 23, 1963, at Orlando, Fla.
Height, 6.00. Weight, 297.
High School—Orlando, Fla., Jones.
Attended University of Florida.
Brother of Nate Newton, guard with Dallas Cowboys.

Selected by Tampa Bay in 1985 USFL territorial draft.
Selected by Minnesota in 6th round (164th player selected) of 1985 NFL draft.
Signed by Minnesota Vikings, June 17, 1985.
Minnesota NFL, 1985 through 1987.
Games: 1985 (16), 1986 (14), 1987 (9). Total—39.
Pro statistics: Intercepted two passes for 63 yards and fumbled once, 1985; recovered one fumble, 1985 and 1986.
Played in NFC Championship Game following 1987 season.

GERALD W. NICHOLS
Defensive Tackle—New York Jets
Born February 10, 1964, at St. Louis, Mo.
Height, 6.02. Weight, 261.
High School—St. Louis, Mo., Hazelwood East.
Received degree in psychology from Florida State University in 1987.

Selected by New York Jets in 7th round (187th player selected) of 1987 NFL draft.
Signed by New York Jets, July 20, 1987.
Crossed picket line during players' strike, October 12, 1987.
New York Jets NFL, 1987.
Games: 1987 (13).

MARK STEPHEN NICHOLS
Wide Receiver—Detroit Lions
Born October 29, 1959, at Bakersfield, Calif.
Height, 6.02. Weight, 208.
High School—Bakersfield, Calif.
Attended Bakersfield Junior College and San Jose State University.

Selected by Detroit in 1st round (16th player selected) of 1981 NFL draft.
On injured reserve with broken foot, December 25 through remainder of 1982 season.
On injured reserve with knee injury, December 21 through remainder of 1985 season.
On physically unable to perform/reserve with knee injury, July 21 through entire 1986 season.

| | | —PASS RECEIVING— | | | |
Year Club	G.	P.C.	Yds.	Avg.	TD.
1981—Detroit NFL	12	10	222	22.2	1
1982—Detroit NFL	7	8	146	18.3	2
1983—Detroit NFL	16	29	437	15.1	1
1984—Detroit NFL	15	34	744	21.9	1
1985—Detroit NFL	14	36	592	16.4	4
1987—Detroit NFL	12	7	87	12.4	0
Pro Totals—6 Years	76	124	2228	18.0	9

Additional pro statistics: Rushed three times for 50 yards and returned four kickoffs for 74 yards, 1981; fumbled once, 1981 and 1985; rushed once for three yards, 1982; rushed once for 13 yards and fumbled twice, 1983; rushed three times for 27 yards and recovered one fumble, 1984; rushed once for 15 yards, 1985.

HARDY OTTO NICKERSON
Linebacker—Pittsburgh Steelers
Born September 1, 1965, at Los Angeles, Calif.
Height, 6.02. Weight, 224.
High School—Los Angeles, Calif., Verbum Dei.
Attended University of California at Berkeley.

Selected by Pittsburgh in 5th round (122nd player selected) of 1987 NFL draft.
Signed by Pittsburgh Steelers, July 26, 1987.
Pittsburgh NFL, 1987.
Games: 1987 (12).
Pro statistics: Recovered one fumble, 1987.

SCOTT STEPHEN NICOLAS
Linebacker—Miami Dolphins
Born August 7, 1960, at Wichita Falls, Tex.
Height, 6.03. Weight, 226.
High School—Clearwater, Fla.
Received bachelor of business administration degree in marketing
from University of Miami (Fla.) in 1982.

Selected by Cleveland in 12th round (310th player selected) of 1982 NFL draft.
Released by Cleveland Browns, September 7, 1987; signed as free agent replacement player by Miami Dolphins, October 10, 1987.
Cleveland NFL, 1982 through 1986; Miami NFL, 1987.

Games: 1982 (9), 1983 (16), 1984 (16), 1985 (16), 1986 (16), 1987 (12). Total—85.

Pro statistics: Returned two kickoffs for 16 yards and fumbled once for minus 14 yards, 1982; returned two kickoffs for 29 yards, 1983; recovered one fumble, 1984 and 1985; returned one kickoff for 12 yards, 1984; returned one kickoff for nine yards, 1985; returned three kickoffs for 28 yards, 1986.

Played in AFC Championship Game following 1986 season.

TORRAN BLAKE NIXON
(Tory)
Cornerback—San Francisco 49ers

Born February 24, 1962, at Eugene, Ore.
Height, 5.11. Weight, 186.
High School—Phoenix, Ariz., Shadow Mountain.
Attended Univeristy of Arizona, Phoenix College and San Diego State University.

Selected by Arizona in 1st round (2nd player selected) of 1985 USFL draft.
Selected by Washington in 2nd round (33rd player selected) of 1985 NFL draft.
Signed by Washington Redskins, August 1, 1985.
Traded by Washington Redskins to San Francisco 49ers for 6th round pick in 1986 draft, September 2, 1985.

Year Club	G.	No.	Yds.	Avg.	TD.
1985—San Francisco NFL	16		None		
1986—San Francisco NFL	16	2	106	53.0	1
1987—San Francisco NFL	12	1	5	5.0	0
Pro Totals—3 Years............	44	3	111	37.0	1

Additional pro statistics: Recovered two fumbles, 1986.

BRIAN DAVID NOBLE
Linebacker—Green Bay Packers

Born September 6, 1962, at Anaheim, Calif.
Height, 6.03. Weight, 252.
High School—Anaheim, Calif.
Attended Fullerton College and Arizona State University.

Selected by Arizona in 1985 USFL territorial draft.
Selected by Green Bay in 5th round (125th player selected) of 1985 NFL draft.
Signed by Green Bay Packers, July 19, 1985.
Green Bay NFL, 1985 through 1987.
Games: 1985 (16), 1986 (16), 1987 (12). Total—44.
Pro statistics: Returned one kickoff for one yard, 1986; intercepted one pass for 10 yards and recovered five fumbles, 1987.

FALANIKO NOGA

First name pronounced Fah-lah-NEE-koh.

(Niko)
Linebacker—Phoenix Cardinals

Born March 2, 1962, at American Samoa.
Height, 6.01. Weight, 235.
High School—Honolulu, Haw., Farrington.
Attended University of Hawaii.
Brother of Pete Noga, linebacker with Indianapolis Colts;
and Al Noga, rookie defensive tackle with Minnesota Vikings.

Selected by Oakland in 10th round (192nd player selected) of 1984 USFL draft.
Selected by St. Louis in 8th round (201st player selected) of 1984 NFL draft.
Signed by St. Louis Cardinals, July 16, 1984.
Franchise transferred to Phoenix, March 15, 1988.
St. Louis NFL, 1984 through 1987.
Games: 1984 (16), 1985 (16), 1986 (16), 1987 (12). Total—60.
Pro statistics: Recovered one fumble, 1984; recovered two fumbles, 1985 and 1986; recovered one fumble for 23 yards and a touchdown, 1987.

DANIEL NICHOLAS NOONAN
(Danny)
Defensive Tackle—Dallas Cowboys

Born July 14, 1965, at Lincoln, Neb.
Height, 6.04. Weight, 270.
High School—Lincoln, Neb., Northeast.
Attended University of Nebraska.

Selected by Dallas in 1st round (12th player selected) of 1987 NFL draft.
Signed by Dallas Cowboys, August 30, 1987.
Granted roster exemption, August 30 through September 13, 1987; activated, September 14, 1987.
Dallas NFL, 1987.
Games: 1987 (11).

FRED MARVIN NORDGREN
Defensive Tackle—Houston Oilers
Born December 11, 1959, at Hillsboro, Ore.
Height, 5.11. Weight, 245.
High School—Hillsboro, Ore.
Attended Portland State University.

Signed by Toronto Argonauts, April, 1982.
Released by Toronto Argonauts, August 4, 1982; re-signed by Argonauts, August 11, 1983.
Released by Toronto Argonauts, August 16, 1982; signed by Tampa Bay Bandits, January 10, 1983.
On developmental squad, May 16 through remainder of 1985 season.
Granted free agency when USFL suspended operations, August 7, 1986; signed as free agent replacement player by Tampa Bay Buccaneers, September 24, 1987.
Released by Tampa Bay Buccaneers, October 19, 1987; signed as free agent by Houston Oilers, May 16, 1988.
On developmental squad for 6 games with Tampa Bay Bandits in 1985.
Toronto CFL, 1982; Tampa Bay USFL, 1983 through 1985; Tampa Bay NFL, 1987.
Games: 1982 (5), 1983 (18), 1984 (18), 1985 (11), 1987 (3). Total USFL—47. Total Pro—55.
Pro statistics: Credited with 15 sacks for 105 yards, intercepted one pass for 23 yards and a touchdown and recovered two fumbles, 1983; credited with 4½ sacks for 22½ yards, 1984; intercepted one pass for two yards and credited with 10 sacks for 74 yards, 1985.

MICHAEL ADAM NORSETH
(Mike)
Quarterback—Cincinnati Bengals
Born August 22, 1964, at Hollywood, Calif.
Height, 6.02. Weight, 200.
High School—LaCrescenta, Calif., Valley.
Attended Snow College and Kansas University.

Selected by Cleveland in 7th round (174th player selected) of 1986 NFL draft.
Signed by Cleveland Browns, July 18, 1986.
On injured reserve with stomach injury, August 28 through entire 1986 season.
Released by Cleveland Browns, Setpember 7, 1987; awarded on waivers to Cincinnati Bengals, September 8, 1987.
Active for 3 games with Cincinnati Bengals in 1987; did not play.
Cincinnati NFL, 1987.

MERRITT JAY NORVELL
(Known by middle name.)
Linebacker—Chicago Bears
Born March 28, 1963, at Madison, Wis.
Height, 6.02. Weight, 232.
High School—Madison, Wis., James Madison Memorial.
Received bachelor of liberal arts degree from University of Iowa in 1986.

Signed as free agent by Denver Broncos, May 1, 1986.
Released by Denver Broncos, July 24, 1986; signed as free agent by Chicago Bears, April 20, 1987.
Released by Chicago Bears, September 7, 1987; re-signed as replacement player by Bears, September 24, 1987.
Chicago NFL, 1987.
Games: 1987 (6).

SCOTT ALLAN NORWOOD
Placekicker—Buffalo Bills
Born July 17, 1960, at Alexandria, Va.
Height, 6.00. Weight, 206.
High School—Alexandria, Va., Thomas Jefferson.
Received bachelor of business administration degree in management from James Madison University.

Signed as free agent by Atlanta Falcons, May 5, 1982.
Released by Atlanta Falcons, August 30, 1982; signed by Birmingham Stallions, January 4, 1983.
On developmental squad, March 15 through March 25, 1984.
On injured reserve with knee injury. March 26 through remainder of 1984 season.
Released by Birmingham Stallions, February 18, 1985; signed as free agent by Buffalo Bills, March 22, 1985.
Released by Buffalo Bills, September 1, 1986; re-signed by Bills, September 2, 1986.
On developmental squad for 2 games with Birmingham Stallions in 1984.

Year Club	G.	XP.	XPM.	FG.	FGA.	Pts.
1983—Birmingham USFL .	18	34	1	25	34	109
1984—Birmingham USFL .	3	4	0	3	4	13
1985—Buffalo NFL	16	23	0	13	17	62
1986—Buffalo NFL	16	32	2	17	27	83
1987—Buffalo NFL	12	31	0	10	15	61
USFL Totals—2 Years...	21	38	1	28	38	122
NFL Totals—3 Years.....	44	86	2	40	59	206
Pro Totals—5 Years.......	65	124	3	68	97	328

Additional pro statistics: Caught one pass for no yards and recovered one fumble, 1983.

JAY McKINLEY NOVACEK
Tight End—Phoenix Cardinals
Born October 24, 1962, at Martin, S.D.
Height, 6.04. Weight, 235.
High School—Gothenburg, Neb.
Received bachelor of science degree in industrial education
from University of Wyoming in 1986.

Selected by Houston in 5th round (69th player selected) of 1985 USFL draft.
Selected by St. Louis in 6th round (158th player selected) of 1985 NFL draft.
Signed by St. Louis Cardinals, July 21, 1985.
On injured reserve with broken thumb, August 19 through October 16, 1986; activated, October 17, 1986.
On injured reserve with knee injury, December 10 through remainder of 1986 season.
On injured reserve with broken bone in elbow, November 3 through December 4, 1987; activated, December 5, 1987.
Franchise transferred to Phoenix, March 15, 1988.

		—PASS RECEIVING—			
Year Club	G.	P.C.	Yds.	Avg.	TD.
1985—St. Louis NFL	16	1	4	4.0	0
1986—St. Louis NFL	8	1	2	2.0	0
1987—St. Louis NFL	7	20	254	12.7	3
Pro Totals—3 Years	31	22	260	11.8	3

Additional pro statistics: Returned one kickoff for 20 yards, 1985; fumbled once, 1987.

TERENCE JOHN NUGENT
(Terry)
Quarterback—Denver Broncos
Born December 5, 1961, at Merced, Calif.
Height, 6.04. Weight, 214.
High School—Elk Grove, Calif.
Received bachelor of science degree in physical education from Colorado State University in 1985.

Selected by Denver in 1984 USFL territorial draft.
Selected by Cleveland in 6th round (158th player selected) of 1984 NFL draft.
Signed by Cleveland Browns, June 14, 1984.
Released by Cleveland Browns, August 27, 1985; signed as free agent by Tampa Bay Buccaneers, May 20, 1986.
Released by Tampa Bay Buccaneers, August 17, 1986; signed as free agent by Indianapolis Colts, March 28, 1987.
Active for 16 games with Cleveland Browns in 1984; did not play.
Released by Indianapolis Colts, August 11, 1987; re-signed as replacement player by Colts, September 24, 1987.
On retired/reserve, October 20 through November 30, 1987.
Released by Indianapolis Colts, December 1, 1987; re-signed by Colts, December 3, 1987.
Released by Indianapolis Colts, May 9, 1988; signed as free agent by Denver Broncos, May 24, 1988.
Cleveland NFL, 1984; Indianapolis NFL, 1987.
Games: 1987 (1).
Pro statistics: Attempted five passes with three completions for 47 yards and rushed twice for one yard, 1987.

FREDDIE JOE NUNN
(Freddie Joe)
Defensive End—Phoenix Cardinals
Born April 9, 1962, at Noxubee County, Miss.
Height, 6.04. Weight, 255.
High School—Louisville, Miss., Nanih Waiya.
Attended University of Mississippi.

Selected by Birmingham in 1985 USFL territorial draft.
Selected by St. Louis in 1st round (18th player selected) of 1985 NFL draft.
Signed by St. Louis Cardinals, August 5, 1985.
Franchise transferred to Phoenix, March 15, 1988.
St. Louis NFL, 1985 through 1987.
Games: 1985 (16), 1986 (16), 1987 (12). Total—44.
Pro statistics: Recovered two fumbles, 1985; recovered one fumble, 1986.

BART STEVEN OATES
Center—New York Giants
Born December 16, 1958, at Mesa, Ariz.
Height, 6.03. Weight, 267.
High School—Albany, Ga.
Received bachelor's degree in accounting from Brigham Young University;
and attending Seton Hall Law School.
Brother of Brad Oates, offensive tackle with St. Louis Cardinals, Detroit Lions,
Kansas City Chiefs, Cincinnati Bengals, Green Bay Packers and Philadelphia Stars,
1976 through 1981, 1983 and 1984.

Named as center on THE SPORTING NEWS USFL All-Star Team, 1983.
Selected by Philadelphia in 2nd round (17th player selected) of 1983 USFL draft.
Signed by Philadelphia Stars, January 24, 1983.
On developmental squad, April 28 through May 5, 1983; activated, May 6, 1983.
Franchise transferred to Baltimore, November 1, 1984.
Released by Baltimore Stars, August 27, 1985; signed as free agent by New York Giants, August 28, 1985.

On developmental squad for 1 game with Philadelphia Stars in 1983.
Philadelphia USFL, 1983 and 1984; Baltimore USFL, 1985; New York Giants NFL, 1985 through 1987.
Games: 1983 (17), 1984 (17), 1985 USFL (18), 1985 NFL (16), 1986 (16), 1987 (12). Total USFL—52. Total NFL—44. Total Pro—96.
USFL statistics: Rushed once for five yards and recovered two fumbles, 1984; recovered one fumble for four yards, 1985.
NFL statistics: Recovered two fumbles, 1985; fumbled once for minus four yards, 1986; recovered one fumble, 1987.
Played in NFC Championship Game following 1986 season.
Played in NFL Championship Game following 1986 season.
Played in USFL Championship Game following 1983 through 1985 seasons.

KENNETH JOHN O'BRIEN JR.
(Ken)
Quarterback—New York Jets

Born November 27, 1960, at Long Island, N.Y.
Height, 6.04. Weight, 210.
High School—Sacramento, Calif., Jesuit.
Attended California State University at Sacramento and received degree in
political science from University of California at Davis in 1983.

Led NFL quarterbacks in passing with 96.2 points in 1985.
Selected by Oakland in 6th round (66th player selected) of 1983 USFL draft.
Selected by New York Jets in 1st round (24th player selected) of 1983 NFL draft.
Signed by New York Jets, July 21, 1983.
Active for 16 games with New York Jets in 1983; did not play.

				—————PASSING—————					—RUSHING—			—TOTAL—		
Year	Club	G.	Att.	Cmp.	Pct.	Gain	T.P.	P.I.	Avg.	Att.	Yds.	Avg.	TD.	TD.	Pts.	F.
1984—N.Y. Jets NFL		10	203	116	57.1	1402	6	7	6.91	16	29	1.8	0	0	0	4
1985—N.Y. Jets NFL		16	488	297	60.9	3888	25	8	7.97	25	58	2.3	0	0	0	14
1986—N.Y. Jets NFL		15	482	300	62.2	3690	25	20	7.66	17	46	2.7	0	0	0	10
1987—N.Y. Jets NFL		12	393	234	59.5	2696	13	8	6.86	30	61	2.0	0	0	0	8
Pro Totals—5 Years		53	1566	947	60.5	11676	69	43	7.46	88	194	2.2	0	0	0	36

Quarterback Rating Points: 1984 (74.0), 1985 (96.2), 1986 (85.8), 1987 (82.8). Total—87.0.
Additional pro statistics: Recovered two fumbles, 1984; recovered four fumbles, 1985; recovered five fumbles and fumbled 10 times for minus three yards, 1986; recovered one fumble and fumbled eight times for minus 10 yards, 1987.
Played in Pro Bowl (NFL All-Star Game) following 1985 season.

CLIFTON LOUIS ODOM
(Cliff)
Linebacker—Indianapolis Colts

Born August 15, 1958, at Beaumont, Tex.
Height, 6.02. Weight, 245.
High School—Beaumont, Tex., French.
Attended University of Texas at Arlington.

Selected by Cleveland in 3rd round (72nd player selected) of 1980 NFL draft.
On injured reserve with knee injury, November 3 through remainder of 1980 season.
Released by Cleveland Browns, August 18, 1981; signed as free agent by Oakland Raiders, March 1, 1982.
Franchise transferred to Los Angeles, May 7, 1982.
Released by Los Angeles Raiders, August 10, 1982; signed as free agent by Baltimore Colts, August 12, 1982.
Released by Baltimore Colts, September 6, 1982; re-signed by Colts, September 7, 1982.
Franchise transferred to Indianapolis, March 31, 1984.
Granted free agency, February 1, 1986; re-signed by Colts, August 17, 1986.
Granted roster exemption, August 17 through August 21, 1986; activated, August 22, 1986.
Cleveland NFL, 1980; Baltimore NFL, 1982 and 1983; Indianapolis NFL, 1984 through 1987.
Games: 1980 (8), 1982 (8), 1983 (15), 1984 (16), 1985 (16), 1986 (16), 1987 (12). Total—91.
Pro statistics: Recovered one fumble, 1984; recovered two fumbles, 1985 and 1986; recovered three fumbles for eight yards, 1987.

NATHANIEL BERNARD ODOMES
(Nate)
Cornerback—Buffalo Bills

Born August 25, 1965, at Columbus, Ga.
Height, 5.09. Weight, 188.
High School—Columbus, Ga., Carver.
Attended University of Wisconsin.

Selected by Buffalo in 2nd round (29th player selected) of 1987 NFL draft.
Signed by Buffalo Bills, July 22, 1987.
Buffalo NFL, 1987.
Games: 1987 (12).
Pro statistics: Recovered two fumbles, 1987.

JOHN ARNOLD OFFERDAHL
Linebacker—Miami Dolphins

Born August 17, 1964, at Wisconsin Rapids, Wis.
Height, 6.02. Weight, 232.
High School—Fort Atkinson, Wis.
Attended Western Michigan University.

Selected by Miami in 2nd round (52nd player selected) of 1986 NFL draft.
Signed by Miami Dolphins, July 29, 1986.
On injured reserve with torn bicep, September 8 through October 30, 1987; activated, October 31, 1987.
Miami NFL, 1986 and 1987.
Games: 1986 (15), 1987 (9). Total—24.
Pro statistics: Intercepted one pass for 14 yards, 1986.
Played in Pro Bowl (NFL All-Star Game) following 1986 and 1987 seasons.

CHRISTIAN E. OKOYE
(Name pronounced Oh-KOY-yea.)
Running Back—Kansas City Chiefs
Born August 16, 1961, at Enugu, Nigeria.
Height, 6.01. Weight, 253.
High School—Enugu, Nigeria, Uwani Secondary School.
Received degree in phsycial education from Azusa Pacific University in 1987.
Selected by Kansas City in 2nd round (35th player selected) of 1987 NFL draft.
Signed by Kansas City Chiefs, July 21, 1987.

		—RUSHING—				PASS RECEIVING				—TOTAL—		
Year Club	G.	Att.	Yds.	Avg.	TD.	P.C.	Yds.	Avg.	TD.	TD.	Pts.	F.
1987—Kansas City NFL	12	157	660	4.2	3	24	169	7.0	0	3	18	5

NEAL OLKEWICZ
Linebacker—Washington Redskins
Born January 30, 1957, at Phoenixville, Pa.
Height, 6.00. Weight, 233.
High School—Phoenixville, Pa.
Received bachelor of arts degree in law enforcement from University of Maryland in 1979.
Signed as free agent by Washington Redskins, May 7, 1979.
On injured reserve with knee injury, December 10 through remainder of 1981 season.
On injured reserve with knee injury, September 7 through October 23, 1987; activated, October 24, 1987.

		—INTERCEPTIONS—		
Year Club	G.	No.	Yds.	Avg.TD.
1979—Washington NFL	16	1	4	4.0 0
1980—Washington NFL	12		None	
1981—Washington NFL	14	2	22	11.0 1
1982—Washington NFL	9		None	
1983—Washington NFL	16	1	14	14.0 0
1984—Washington NFL	16		None	
1985—Washington NFL	16	1	21	21.0 0
1986—Washington NFL	16	1	15	15.0 0
1987—Washington NFL	10		None	
Pro Totals—9 Years	125	6	76	12.7 1

Additional pro statistics: Recovered one fumble, 1980 and 1985; recovered three fumbles, 1982 and 1986; recovered two fumbles, 1983 and 1984.
Played in NFC Championship Game following 1982, 1983, 1986 and 1987 seasons.
Played in NFL Championship Game following 1982, 1983 and 1987 seasons.

LESLIE CORNELIUS O'NEAL
Defensive End—San Diego Chargers
Born May 7, 1964, at Pulaski County, Ark.
Height, 6.04. Weight, 255.
High School—Little Rock, Ark., Hall.
Attended Oklahoma State University.
Named as defensive lineman on THE SPORTING NEWS College All-America Team, 1984 and 1985.
Selected by New Jersey in 1986 USFL territorial draft.
Selected by San Diego in 1st round (8th player selected) of 1986 NFL draft.
Signed by San Diego Chargers, August 5, 1986.
On injured reserve with knee injury, December 4 through remainder of 1986 season.
On physically unable to perform/reserve with knee injury, August 30 through entire 1987 season.
San Diego NFL, 1986.
Games: 1986 (13).
Pro statistics: Intercepted two passes for 22 yards and a touchdown and recovered two fumbles, 1986.

TERRY ORR
Tight End—Washington Redskins
Born September 27, 1961, at Savannah, Ga.
Height, 6.03. Weight, 227.
High School—Abilene, Tex., Cooper.
Received bachelor of science degree in speech communications
from University of Texas in 1985.
Selected by San Antonio in 1985 USFL territorial draft.
Selected by Washington in 10th round (263rd player selected) of 1985 NFL draft.
Signed by Washington Redskins, July 18, 1985.
On injured reserve with ankle injury, August 20 through entire 1985 season.
On injured reserve with shoulder injury, September 7 through October 23, 1987; activated, October 24, 1987.

Year Club		—PASS RECEIVING—			
	G.	P.C.	Yds.	Avg.	TD.
1986—Washington NFL	16	3	45	15.0	1
1987—Washington NFL	10	3	35	11.7	0
Pro Totals—2 Years	26	6	80	13.3	1

Additional pro statistics: Returned two kickoffs for 31 yards, 1986; returned four kickoffs for 62 yards, 1987.
Played in NFC Championship Game following 1986 and 1987 seasons.
Played in NFL Championship Game following 1987 season.

BRYANT KEITH ORTEGO
(Known by middle name.)
Wide Receiver—Chicago Bears
Born August 30, 1963, at Eunice, La.
Height, 6.00. Weight, 180.
High School—Eunice, La.
Attended McNeese State University.

Signed as free agent by Chicago Bears, May 3, 1985.
On injured reserve with knee injury, August 19 through November 6, 1985; activated after clearing procedural waivers, November 8, 1985.

Year Club		—PUNT RETURNS—			
	G.	No.	Yds.	Avg.	TD.
1985—Chicago NFL	7	17	158	9.3	0
1986—Chicago NFL	16	23	430	18.7	2
1987—Chicago NFL	8			None	
Pro Totals—3 Years	31	40	588	14.7	2

Additional pro statistics: Fumbled once, 1986.
Played in NFC Championship Game following 1985 season.
Played in NFL Championship Game following 1985 season.

PAUL EUGENE OSWALD
Center—Dallas Cowboys
Born April 9, 1964, at Topeka, Kan.
Height, 6.03. Weight, 273.
High School—Topeka, Kan., Hayden.
Attended University of Kansas.

Selected by Pittsburgh in 11th round (289th player selected) of 1987 NFL draft.
Signed by Pittsburgh Steelers, July 24, 1987.
Released by Pittsburgh Steelers, November 3, 1987; signed as free agent by Dallas Cowboys, April 28, 1988.
Pittsburgh NFL, 1987.
Games: 1987 (2).

MEL TYRAE OWENS
Linebacker—Los Angeles Rams
Born December 7, 1958, at Detroit, Mich.
Height, 6.02. Weight, 224.
High School—DeKalb, Ill.
Received bachelor of arts degree in political science from University of Michigan in 1981.

Selected by Los Angeles in 1st round (9th player selected) of 1981 NFL draft.
Crossed picket line during players' strike, October 14, 1987.
Los Angeles Rams NFL, 1981 through 1987.
Games: 1981 (16), 1982 (7), 1983 (16), 1984 (16), 1985 (16), 1986 (16), 1987 (12). Total—99.
Pro statistics: Recovered two fumbles, 1983 and 1984; intercepted one pass for minus four yards, 1984; recovered two fumbles for 14 yards, 1985; recovered one fumble, 1986 and 1987; intercepted one pass for 26 yards, 1987.
Played in NFC Championship Game following 1985 season.

GARY A. PADJEN
Linebacker—Atlanta Falcons
Born July 2, 1958, at Salt Lake City, Utah.
Height, 6.02. Weight, 241.
High School—Kearns, Utah.
Received degree in general business from Arizona State University.

Signed as free agent by Dallas Cowboys, May, 1980.
Released by Dallas Cowboys, August 25, 1980; signed as free agent by Washington Redskins, April 6, 1981.
Released by Washington Redskins, August 10, 1981; signed as free agent by Baltimore Colts, March 15, 1982.
On inactive list, September 19, 1982.
Franchise transferred to Indianapolis, March 31, 1984.
Released by Indianapolis Colts, August 27, 1985; signed as free agent by Arizona Outlaws, January 21, 1986.
Granted free agency when USFL suspended operations, August 7, 1986; re-signed as replacement player by Indianapolis Colts, September 23, 1987.
Placed on reserve/retired list, October 19 through November 30, 1987.
Released by Indianapolis Colts, December 1, 1987; signed as free agent by Atlanta Falcons, April 15, 1988.
Baltimore NFL, 1982 and 1983; Indianapolis NFL, 1984 and 1987.
Games: 1982 (8), 1983 (16), 1984 (16), 1987 (1). Total—41.
Pro statistics: Recovered one fumble, 1983; returned one punt for no yards and fumbled once, 1984.

MICHAEL JONATHAN PAGEL
(Mike)
Quarterback—Cleveland Browns
Born September 13, 1960, at Douglas, Ariz.
Height, 6.02. Weight, 206.
High School—Phoenix, Ariz., Washington.
Attended Arizona State University.
Brother of Karl Pagel, outfielder-first baseman with Chicago Cubs and Cleveland Indians, 1978, 1979 and 1981 through 1983; and minor league coach, Cleveland Indians' organization, 1984.
Selected by Baltimore in 4th round (84th player selected) of 1982 NFL draft.
Franchise transferred to Indianapolis, March 31, 1984.
Granted free agency, February 1, 1986; re-signed by Colts and traded to Cleveland Browns for 9th round pick in 1987 draft, May 22, 1986.

Year Club	G.	Att.	Cmp.	Pct.	Gain	T.P.	P.I.	Avg.	Att.	Yds.	Avg.	TD.	TD.	Pts.	F.
					PASSING					RUSHING				TOTAL	
1982—Baltimore NFL	9	221	111	50.2	1281	5	7	5.80	19	82	4.3	1	1	6	9
1983—Baltimore NFL	15	328	163	49.7	2353	12	17	7.17	54	441	8.2	0	0	0	4
1984—Indianapolis NFL	11	212	114	53.8	1426	8	8	6.73	26	149	5.7	1	1	6	4
1985—Indianapolis NFL	16	393	199	50.6	2414	14	15	6.14	25	160	6.4	2	2	12	6
1986—Cleveland NFL	1	3	2	66.7	53	0	0	17.67	2	0	0.0	0	0	0	2
1987—Cleveland NFL	4			None						None			0	0	0
Pro Totals—6 Years	56	1157	589	50.9	7527	39	47	6.51	126	832	6.6	4	4	24	25

Quarterback Rating Points: 1982 (62.4), 1983 (64.0), 1984 (71.8), 1985 (65.8), 1986 (109.7). Total—65.9.
Additional pro statistics: Recovered three fumbles and fumbled nine times for minus four yards, 1982; recovered one fumble, 1984; recovered two fumbles and caught one pass for six yards, 1985; recovered one fumble and fumbled twice for minus four yards, 1986.
Played in AFC Championship Game following 1987 season.
Member of Cleveland Browns for AFC Championship Game following 1986 season; did not play.

ANTHONY R. PAIGE
(Tony)
Fullback—Detroit Lions
Born October 14, 1962, at Washington, D.C.
Height, 5.10. Weight, 230.
High School—Hyattsville, Md., DeMatha Catholic.
Received degree in broadcasting from Virginia Tech.
Selected by Pittsburgh in 1984 USFL territorial draft.
Selected by New York Jets in 6th round (149th player selected) of 1984 NFL draft.
Signed by New York Jets, May 29, 1984.
Granted free agency, February 1, 1987; withdrew qualifying offer, August 25, 1987.
Signed by Detroit Lions, November 19, 1987.

Year Club	G.	Att.	Yds.	Avg.	TD.	P.C.	Yds.	Avg.	TD.	TD.	Pts.	F.
			RUSHING				PASS RECEIVING				TOTAL	
1984—New York Jets NFL	16	35	130	3.7	7	6	31	5.2	1	8	48	1
1985—New York Jets NFL	16	55	158	2.9	8	18	120	6.7	2	10	60	1
1986—New York Jets NFL	16	47	109	2.3	2	18	121	6.7	0	2	12	2
1987—Detroit NFL	5	4	13	3.3	0	2	1	0.5	0	0	0	0
Pro Totals—4 Years	53	141	410	2.9	17	44	273	6.2	3	20	120	4

Additional pro statistics: Returned three kickoffs for seven yards, 1984; recovered one fumble, 1985 and 1987.

STEPHONE PAIGE
Wide Receiver—Kansas City Chiefs
Born October 15, 1961, at Long Beach, Calif.
Height, 6.02. Weight, 183.
High School—Long Beach, Calif., Polytechnic.
Attended Saddleback College and Fresno State University.
Established NFL record for pass reception yards, game (309), against San Diego Chargers, December 22, 1985.
Selected by Oakland in 1983 USFL territorial draft.
Signed as free agent by Kansas City Chiefs, May 9, 1983.

Year Club	G.	P.C.	Yds.	Avg.	TD.	No.	Yds.	Avg.	TD.	TD.	Pts.	F.
			PASS RECEIVING				KICKOFF RET.				TOTAL	
1983—Kansas City NFL	16	30	528	17.6	6		None			6	36	1
1984—Kansas City NFL	16	30	541	18.0	4	27	544	20.1	0	4	24	0
1985—Kansas City NFL	16	43	943	*21.9	10	2	36	18.0	0	10	60	0
1986—Kansas City NFL	16	52	829	15.9	11		None			11	66	0
1987—Kansas City NFL	12	43	707	16.4	4		None			4	24	0
Pro Totals—5 Years	76	198	3548	17.9	35	29	580	20.0	0	35	210	1

Additional pro statistics: Recovered one fumble, 1983; rushed three times for 19 yards, 1984; rushed once for 15 yards, 1985; rushed twice for minus two yards, 1986.

—DID YOU KNOW—
That the Dallas Cowboys' 24-13 loss to St. Louis on September 13 was only their second loss in 23 years on opening day?

PAUL WOODROW PALMER
Running Back—Kansas City Chiefs
Born October 14, 1964, at Bethesda, Md.
Height, 5.09. Weight, 184.
High School—Potomac, Md., Winston Churchill.
Attended Temple University.

Named as running back on THE SPORTING NEWS College All-America Team, 1986.
Selected by Kansas City in 1st round (19th player selected) of 1987 NFL draft.
Signed by Kansas City Chiefs, July 17, 1987.

		—————RUSHING—————				PASS RECEIVING				—TOTAL—		
Year	Club	G.	Att.	Yds.	Avg.	TD.	P.C.	Yds.	Avg.	TD.	TD.	Pts.	F.
1987—Kansas City NFL		12	24	155	6.5	0	4	27	6.8	0	2	12	2

		KICKOFF RETURNS			
Year	Club	G.	No.	Yds.	Avg.TD.
1987—Kansas City NFL		12	⋆38	⋆923	24.3 ⋆2

Additional pro statistics: Attempted one pass with no completions, 1987.

IRVIN LEE PANKEY
(Irv)
Offensive Tackle—Los Angeles Rams
Born February 15, 1958, at Aberdeen, Md.
Height, 6.05. Weight, 280.
High School—Aberdeen, Md.
Attended Pennsylvania State University.

Selected by Los Angeles in 2nd round (50th player selected) of 1980 NFL draft.
On injured reserve with torn Achilles tendon, August 16 through entire 1983 season.
Los Angeles Rams NFL, 1980 through 1987.
Games: 1980 (16), 1981 (13), 1982 (9), 1984 (16), 1985 (16), 1986 (16), 1987 (12). Total—98.
Pro statistics: Recovered two fumbles and returned one kickoff for no yards, 1981; recovered one fumble, 1985 and 1986.
Played in NFC Championship Game following 1985 season.

WILLIAM PARIS
(Bubba)
Offensive Tackle—San Francisco 49ers
Born October 6, 1960, at Louisville, Ky.
Height, 6.06. Weight, 306.
High School—Louisville, Ky., DeSales.
Received degree from University of Michigan in 1982.

Selected by San Francisco in 2nd round (29th player selected) of 1982 NFL draft.
On injured reserve with knee injury, September 6 through entire 1982 season.
San Francisco NFL, 1983 through 1987.
Games: 1983 (16), 1984 (16), 1985 (16), 1986 (10), 1987 (11). Total—69.
Pro statistics: Recovered one fumble, 1984 and 1986.
Played in NFC Championship Game following 1983 and 1984 seasons.
Played in NFL Championship Game following 1984 season.

ANDREW JAMES PARKER
(Andy)
Tight End—Los Angeles Raiders
Born September 8, 1961, at Redlands, Calif.
Height, 6.05. Weight, 250.
High Schools—Dana Point, Calif., Dana Hills; and Encinitas, Calif., San Dieguito.
Received bachelor of science degree in physical education
from University of Utah in 1984.

Selected by Philadelphia in 5th round (100th player selected) of 1984 USFL draft.
Selected by Los Angeles Raiders in 5th round (127th player selected) of 1984 NFL draft.
Signed by Los Angeles Raiders, June 19, 1984.
On injured reserve with back injury, November 3 through remainder of 1984 season.
On injured reserve with foot injury, December 19 through remainder of 1986 season.
Los Angeles Raiders NFL, 1984 through 1987.
Games: 1984 (9), 1985 (16), 1986 (13), 1987 (12). Total—50.
Pro statistics: Caught two passes for eight yards and a touchdown, 1986; recovered one fumble, 1987.

JEFFREY DUPREE PARKS
(Jeff)
Tight End—Houston Oilers
Born September 14, 1964, at Columbia, S.C.
Height, 6.04. Weight, 240.
High School—Gardendale, Ala.
Attended Auburn University.

Selected by Birmingham in 1986 USFL territorial draft.
Selected by Houston in 5th round (114th player selected) of 1986 NFL draft.
Signed by Houston Oilers, July 23, 1986.
On injured reserve with pulled hamstring, October 8 through remainer of 1986 season.
On injured reserve with foot injury, September 6 through November 13, 1987; activated, November 14, 1987.
Houston NFL, 1986 and 1987.
Games: 1986 (5), 1987 (7). Total—12.

RICHARD BLAKE PARTRIDGE
(Rick)
Punter—Buffalo Bills
Born August 26, 1957, at Orange, Calif.
Height, 6.01. Weight, 175.
High School—Tustin, Calif.
Attended Golden West Junior College and received bachelor of science degree
in accounting from University of Utah in 1979.
Brother of Jeff Partridge, punter with Los Angeles Express, 1983 through 1985.

Selected by Green Bay in 8th round (208th player selected) of 1979 NFL draft.
Released by Green Bay Packers, August 23, 1979; signed as free agent by New Orleans Saints, September 20, 1979.
Traded by New Orleans Saints to San Diego Chargers for 8th round pick in 1981 draft, August 31, 1980.
Released by San Diego Chargers, August 17, 1981; signed as free agent by Baltimore Colts, May 5, 1982.
Released by Baltimore Colts, August 10, 1982; signed by Denver Gold, February 4, 1983.
Released by Denver Gold, February 27, 1983; signed as free agent by Michigan Panthers, April 26, 1983.
Released by Michigan Panthers, June 7, 1983; signed as free agent by Memphis Showboats, October 24, 1983.
Traded by Memphis Showboats to New Jersey Generals for draft choice, January 28, 1985.
Granted free agency with option not exercised, July 31, 1985; awarded on waivers to Baltimore Stars, August 1, 1985.
Released by Baltimore Stars, August 2, 1985; signed as free agent by Denver Broncos, April 23, 1986.
Released by Denver Broncos, August 11, 1986; signed as free agent by Buffalo Bills, May 11, 1987.
Released by Buffalo Bills, August 31, 1987; re-signed as replacement player by Bills, September 24, 1987.
Released by Buffalo Bills, October 19, 1987; re-signed by Bills, April 22, 1988.

| | | ——PUNTING—— | | |
Year Club	G.	No.	Avg.	Blk.
1979—New Orleans NFL	13	57	40.9	0
1980—San Diego NFL	16	60	39.1	1
1983—Michigan USFL	6	23	39.3	....
1984—Memphis USFL	18	80	41.3	...
1985—New Jersey USFL	18	66	41.4	....
1987—Buffalo NFL	3	18	37.7	1
NFL Totals—3 Years	32	135	39.7	2
USFL Totals—3 Years	42	169	41.1	....
Pro Totals—6 Years	74	304	40.4	....

Additional NFL statistics: Rushed three times for no yards and recovered three fumbles, 1980; rushed once for 13 yards and recovered one fumble, 1987.
Additional USFL statistics: Recovered one fumble and attempted one pass with no completions, 1983; fumbled twice, 1984; attempted one pass with one interception, rushed three times for 16 yards and a touchdown and recovered two fumbles, 1985.
Played in AFC Championship Game following 1980 season.

KEITH PAXTON PASKETT
Wide Receiver—Green Bay Packers
Born December 7, 1964, at Nashville, Tenn.
Height, 5.11. Weight, 180.
High School—Nashville, Tenn., Glencliff.
Attended Western Kentucky University.

Signed as free agent by Green Bay Packers, May 18, 1987.

| | | ——PASS RECEIVING—— | | | |
Year Club	G.	P.C.	Yds.	Avg.	TD.
1987—Green Bay NFL	12	12	188	15.7	1

JOEL PATTEN
Offensive Tackle—Indianapolis Colts
Born February 7, 1958, at Augsburg, Germany.
Height, 6.07. Weight, 307.
High School—Fairfax, Va., Robinson.
Received bachelor of arts degree in history education from Duke University.

Signed as free agent by Cleveland Browns, May 7, 1980.
On injured reserve with groin injury, September 6 through November 6, 1980; activated, November 7, 1980.
On injured reserve with knee injury, August 24 through entire 1981 season.
Released by Cleveland Browns, September 8, 1982.
USFL rights traded by Michigan Panthers to Washington Federals for past consideration, February 2, 1983.
Signed by Washington Federals, February 8, 1983.
On developmental squad, May 4 through June 2, 1984; activated, June 3, 1984.
Franchise transferred to Orlando, October 12, 1984.
Released by Orlando Renegades, August 26, 1985; signed as free agent by Dallas Cowboys, March 21, 1986.
Released by Dallas Cowboys, August 21, 1986; signed as free agent by Indianapolis Colts, May 11, 1987.

On developmental squad for 4 games with Washington Federals in 1984.
Cleveland NFL, 1980; Washington USFL, 1983 and 1984; Orlando USFL, 1985; Indianapolis NFL, 1987.
Games: 1980 (16), 1983 (18), 1984 (14), 1985 (18), 1987 (12). Total NFL—28. Total USFL—50. Total Pro—78.
Pro statistics: Recovered two fumbles, 1983.

ELVIS VERNELL PATTERSON
Cornerback—San Diego Chargers
Born October 21, 1960, at Bryan, Tex.
Height, 5.11. Weight, 198.
High School—Houston, Tex., Jack Yates.
Attended University of Kansas.

Selected by Jacksonville in 10th round (207th player selected) of 1984 USFL draft.
Signed as free agent by New York Giants, May 3, 1984.
Released by New York Giants, September 16, 1987; signed as free agent replacement player by San Diego Chargers, September 24, 1987.

		——INTERCEPTIONS——			
Year Club	G.	No.	Yds.	Avg.	TD.
1984—N.Y. Giants NFL	15		None		
1985—N.Y. Giants NFL	16	6	88	14.7	*1
1986—N.Y. Giants NFL	15	2	26	13.0	0
1987—NYG (1)-SD (13) NFL .	14	1	75	75.0	1
Pro Totals—4 Years............	60	9	189	21.0	2

Additional pro statistics: Recovered one fumble, 1985 and 1987.
Played in NFC Championship Game following 1986 season.
Played in NFL Championship Game following 1986 season.

MARK LESTER PATTISON
Wide Receiver—New Orleans Saints
Born December 13, 1961, at Seattle, Wash.
Height, 6.02. Weight, 190.
High School—Seattle, Wash., Roosevelt.
Received degree in political science from University of Washington.

Selected by Portland in 1985 USFL territorial draft.
Selected by Los Angeles Raiders in 7th round (199th player selected) of 1985 NFL draft.
Signed by Los Angeles Raiders, June 29, 1985.
On injured reserve with hamstring injury, August 27 through entire 1985 season.
Released by Los Angeles Raiders, September 1, 1986; signed as free agent by Los Angeles Rams, September 18, 1986.
Released by Los Angeles Rams, September 24, 1986; signed as free agent by Los Angeles Raiders, December 10, 1986.
Released by Los Angeles Raiders, September 9, 1987; awarded on waivers to New Orleans Saints, September 10, 1987.

		——PASS RECEIVING——			
Year Club	G.	P.C.	Yds.	Avg.	TD.
1986—Ram (1)-Raid (2) NFL	3	2	12	6.0	0
1987—New Orleans NFL........	9	9	132	14.7	0
Pro Totals—2 Years............	12	11	144	13.1	0

AARON DANTIANTO PEARSON
Linebacker—Kansas City Chiefs
Born August 22, 1964, at Gadsden, Ala.
Height, 6.00. Weight, 236.
High School—Gadsden, Ala.
Attended Itawamba Junior College and Mississippi State University.

Selected by Kansas City in 11th round (285th player selected) of 1986 NFL draft.
Signed by Kansas City Chiefs, July 23, 1986.
Kansas City NFL, 1986 and 1987.
Games: 1986 (15), 1987 (12). Total—27.
Pro statistics: Returned one kickoff for no yards, 1986; returned two kickoffs for four yards and fumbled twice, 1987.

JAYICE PEARSON
(J. C.)
Cornerback—Kansas City Chiefs
Born August 17, 1963, at Japan.
Height, 5.11. Weight, 183.
High School—Oceanside, Calif., El Camino.
Attended California State Poly University, Fullerton College and University of Washington.

Signed as free agent by Washington Redskins, May 13, 1985.
Released by Washington Redskins, August 27, 1985; signed as free agent by Kansas City Chiefs, April 14, 1986.
On injured reserve with sprained ankle, August 18 through October 29, 1986; activated after clearing procedural waivers, October 31, 1986.
Kansas City NFL, 1986 and 1987.
Games: 1986 (8), 1987 (12). Total—20.

BRENT RICHARD PEASE
Quarterback—Houston Oilers
Born October 8, 1964, at Moscow, Ida.
Height, 6.02. Weight, 200.
High School—Mountain Home, Ida.
Attended Walla Walla Community College and University of Montana.
Selected by Minnesota in 11th round (295th player selected) of 1987 NFL draft.
Signed by Minnesota Vikings, July 27, 1987.
Released by Minnesota Vikings, September 4, 1987; signed as free agent replacement player by Houston Oilers, September 24, 1987.

		—————PASSING—————							—RUSHING—			—TOTAL—		
Year	Club	G.	Att.	Cmp.	Pct.	Gain	T.P.	P.I.	Avg.	Att.	Yds.	Avg.	TD.	TD.	Pts.	F.
1987—Houston NFL		6	113	56	49.6	728	3	5	6.44	15	33	2.2	1	1	6	2

Quarterback Rating Points: 1987 (60.6).
Additional pro statistics: Recovered two fumbles, 1987.

MARION TODD PEAT
(Known by middle name.)
Guard—Phoenix Cardinals
Born May 20, 1964, at Champaign, Ill.
Height, 6.02. Weight, 294.
High School—Champaign, Ill., Central.
Received degree in criminal justice from Northern Illinois University in 1987.
Selected by St. Louis in 11th round (285th player selected) of 1987 NFL draft.
Signed by St. Louis Cardinals, July 14, 1987.
Franchise transferred to Phoenix, March 15, 1988.
St. Louis NFL, 1987.
Games: 1987 (12).

STEVEN CARL PELLUER
Name pronounced Puh-LURE.
(Steve)
Quarterback—Dallas Cowboys
Born July 29, 1962, at Yakima, Wash.
Height, 6.04. Weight, 210.
High School—Bellevue, Wash., Interlake.
Attended University of Washington.
Brother of Scott Pelluer, linebacker with New Orleans Saints, 1981 through 1985.
Selected by Oakland in 6th round (110th player selected) of 1984 USFL draft.
Selected by Dallas in 5th round (113th player selected) of 1984 NFL draft.
Signed by Dallas Cowboys, July 7, 1984.

		—————PASSING—————							—RUSHING—			—TOTAL—		
Year	Club	G.	Att.	Cmp.	Pct.	Gain	T.P.	P.I.	Avg.	Att.	Yds.	Avg.	TD.	TD.	Pts.	F.
1984—Dallas NFL		1				None						None		0	0	0
1985—Dallas NFL		2	8	5	62.5	47	0	0	5.88	3	−2	−0.7	0	0	0	0
1986—Dallas NFL		16	378	215	56.9	2727	8	17	7.21	41	255	6.2	1	1	6	9
1987—Dallas NFL		12	101	55	54.5	642	3	2	6.36	25	142	5.7	1	1	6	0
Pro Totals—4 Years		31	487	275	56.5	3416	11	19	7.01	69	395	5.7	2	2	12	9

Quarterback Rating Points: 1985 (78.6), 1986 (67.9), 1987 (75.6). Total—69.8.
Additional pro statistics: Recovered three fumbles, 1986.

JESSE ANDREW PENN II
Linebacker—Dallas Cowboys
Born September 6, 1962, at Martinsville, Va.
Height, 6.03. Weight, 224.
High School—Martinsville, Va.
Attended Virginia Tech.
Selected by New Jersey in 1st round (5th player selected) of 1985 USFL draft.
Selected by Dallas in 2nd round (44th player selected) of 1985 NFL draft.
Signed by Dallas Cowboys, May 9, 1985.
Dallas NFL, 1985 through 1987.
Games: 1985 (16), 1986 (15), 1987 (11). Total—42.
Pro statistics: Returned blocked punt 46 yards for a touchdown, 1985; recovered one fumble, 1985 and 1987; recovered three fumbles for 12 yards, 1986; intercepted one pass for 21 yards, 1987.

JAY LESLIE PENNISON
Center—Houston Oilers
Born September 9, 1961, at Houma, La.
Height, 6.01. Weight, 275.
High School—Houma, La., Terrebonne.
Attended Nicholls State University.
Selected by Jacksonville in 13th round (267th player selected) of 1984 USFL draft.

Signed by Jacksonville Bulls, January 19, 1984.
Released injured by Jacksonville Bulls, February 20, 1984; signed as free agent by Washington Redskins, May 2, 1984.
Released by Washington Redskins, August 21, 1984; re-signed by Jacksonville Bulls, October 9, 1984.
Released by Jacksonville Bulls, August 7, 1986; signed as free agent by Houston Oilers, August 12, 1986.
Jacksonville USFL, 1985; Houston NFL, 1986 and 1987.
Games: 1985 (18), 1986 (16), 1987 (12). Total NFL—28. Total Pro—46
USFL statistics: Recovered two fumbles, 1985.
NFL statistics: Fumbled once, 1986; recovered one fumble and fumbled once for minus 12 yards, 1987.

WILLIAM PERRY
Defensive Tackle—Chicago Bears
Born December 16, 1962, at Aiken, S.C.
Height, 6.02. Weight, 315.
High School—Aiken, S.C.
Attended Clemson University.
Brother of Michael Dean Perry, rookie defensive lineman with Cleveland Browns.

Selected by Orlando in 1985 USFL territorial draft.
Selected by Chicago in 1st round (22nd player selected) of 1985 NFL draft.
Signed by Chicago Bears, August 5, 1985.
Chicago NFL, 1985 through 1987.
Games: 1985 (16), 1986 (16), 1987 (12). Total—44.
Pro statistics: Rushed five times for seven yards and two touchdowns, caught one pass for four yards and a touchdown and recovered two fumbles for 66 yards, 1985; rushed once for minus one yard and fumbled once, 1986; rushed once for no yards and fumbled once, 1987.
Played in NFC Championship Game following 1985 season.
Played in NFL Championship Game following 1985 season.

JAMES T. PERRYMAN
(Jim)
Safety—Indianapolis Colts
Born December 23, 1960, at Oakland, Calif.
Height, 6.00. Weight, 187.
High School—Pittsburgh, Pa., South Hills Catholic.
Received bachelor of science degree in industrial engineering from Millikin University.

Signed as free agent by Denver Gold, January 10, 1983.
Released by Denver Gold, February 2, 1983; signed as free agent by Pittsburgh Maulers, October 5, 1983.
Released by Pittsburgh Maulers, February 16, 1984; re-signed by Maulers, May 2, 1984.
On developmental squad, May 2 through May 9, 1984; activated, May 10, 1984.
Franchise disbanded, October 25, 1984; selected by Oakland Invaders in USFL dispersal draft, December 6, 1984.
Released by Oakland Invaders, January 28, 1985; signed as free agent by Buffalo Bills, March 21, 1985.
Released by Buffalo Bills, August 27, 1985; re-signed by Bills, October 12, 1985.
On injured reserve with ankle injury, August 18 through September 23, 1986.
Released by Buffalo Bills, September 24, 1986; signed as free agent by Indianapolis Colts, May 11, 1987.
Crossed picket line during players' strike, September 28, 1987.
On developmental squad for 1 game with Pittsburgh Maulers in 1984.
Pittsburgh USFL, 1984; Buffalo NFL, 1985; Indianapolis NFL, 1987.
Games: 1984 (12), 1985 (11), 1987 (14). Total NFL—25. Total Pro—37.
Pro statistics: Intercepted one pass for no yards, returned one kickoff for four yards and recovered one fumble for five yards, 1987.

ROBERT PERRYMAN
(Bob)
Running Back—New England Patriots
Born October 16, 1964, at Raleigh, N. C.
Height, 6.01. Weight, 233.
High School—Bourne, Mass.
Received degree from University of Michigan in 1987.
Brother of Ron Perryman, linebacker at Boston College.

Selected by New England in 3rd round (79th player selected) of 1987 NFL draft.
Signed by New England Patriots, July 26, 1987.

| | | ——RUSHING—— | | | | PASS RECEIVING | | | | —TOTAL— | | |
Year Club	G.	Att.	Yds.	Avg.	TD.	P.C.	Yds.	Avg.	TD.	TD.	Pts.	F.
1987—New England NFL	9	41	187	4.6	0	3	13	4.3	0	0	0	1

Additional pro statistics: Returned three kickoffs for 43 yards and recovered two fumbles, 1987.

JOSEPH GORDON PHILLIPS
(Joe)
Defensive End—San Diego Chargers
Born July 15, 1963, at Portland, Ore.
Height, 6.05. Weight, 278.
High School—Vancouver, Wash., Columbia River.
Attended Oregon State University, Chemeketa Community College and received bachelor of arts degree in economics from Southern Methodist University of 1986.

Selected by Minnesota in 4th round (93rd player selected) of 1986 NFL draft.
Signed by Minnesota Vikings, July 28, 1986.
Released by Minnesota Vikings, September 7, 1987; signed as free agent replacement player by San Diego Chargers, September 24, 1987.
Minnesota NFL, 1986; San Diego NFL, 1987.
Games: 1986 (16), 1987 (13). Total—29.
Pro statistics: Recovered one fumble, 1986.

RAYMOND THOMAS PHILLIPS JR.
(Ray)
Defensive End—Denver Broncos
Born July 24, 1964, at Mooresville, N. C.
Height, 6.03. Weight, 240.
High School—Charlotte, N. C., North Mecklenburg.
Received bachelor of arts degree in criminal justice from
North Carolina State University in 1986.

Selected by Denver in 7th round (188th player selected) of 1986 NFL draft.
Signed by Denver Broncos, July 17, 1986.
Released by Denver Broncos, August 25, 1986; awarded on waivers to Atlanta Falcons, August 26, 1986.
Released by Atlanta Falcons, September 1, 1986; re-signed by Falcons, September 9, 1986.
Released by Atlanta Falcons, September 17, 1986; re-signed by Falcons, March 20, 1987.
Released by Atlanta Falcons, August 5, 1987; signed as free agent by Philadelphia Eagles, August 17, 1987.
Released by Philadelphia Eagles, Sepember 6, 1987; re-signed as replacement player by Eagles, September 24, 1987.
Released by Philadelphia Eagles, October 19, 1987; signed as free agent by Denver Broncos, April 5, 1988.
Atlanta NFL, 1986; Philadelphia NFL, 1987.
Games: 1986 (1), 1987 (3). Total—4.

REGGIE PHILLIPS
Defensive Back—Chicago Bears
Born December 12, 1960, at Houston, Tex.
Height, 5.10. Weight, 170.
High School—Houston, Tex., Jack Yates.
Attended Southern Methodist University.

Selected by Houston in 1985 USFL territorial draft.
Selected by Chicago in 2nd round (49th player selected) of 1985 NFL draft.
Signed by Chicago Bears, July 9, 1985.
Chicago NFL, 1985 through 1987.
Games: 1985 (16), 1986 (16), 1987 (12). Total—44.
Pro statistics: Recovered one fumble, 1985; intercepted one pass for six yards, 1986; intercepted two passes for one yard, 1987.
Played in NFC Championship Game following 1985 season.
Played in NFL Championship Game following 1985 season.

BILL PICKEL
Name pronounced Pick-ELL.
Defensive Tackle—Los Angeles Raiders
Born November 5, 1959, at Queens, N.Y.
Height, 6.05. Weight, 260.
High Schools—Milford, Conn.; and Brooklyn, N.Y., St. Francis.
Attended Rutgers University.
Brother of Chris Pickel, linebacker at Rutgers University.

Named to THE SPORTING NEWS NFL All-Star Team, 1986.
Selected by New Jersey in 1983 USFL territorial draft.
Selected by Los Angeles Raiders in 2nd round (54th player selected) of 1983 NFL draft.
Signed by Los Angeles Raiders, May 26, 1983.
Crossed picket line during players' strike, October 6, 1987.
Los Angeles Raiders NFL, 1983 through 1987.
Games: 1983 (16), 1984 (16), 1985 (16), 1986 (15), 1987 (12). Total—75.
Pro statistics: Recovered one fumble, 1983; recovered two fumbles, 1986 and 1987.
Played in AFC Championship Game following 1983 season.
Played in NFL Championship Game following 1983 season.

CLAY FLOYD PICKERING
Wide Receiver—New England Patriots
Born June 2, 1961, at Jacksonville, Fla.
Height, 6.05. Weight, 215.
High School—Akron, O., Archbishop.
Attended University of Maine.

Signed as free agent by Cincinnati Bengals, May 20, 1984.
Released by Cincinnati Bengals, August 27, 1984; re-signed by Bengals, August 28, 1984.
On injured reserve with pulled hamstring, September 21 through remainder of 1984 season.
On injured reserve with pulled hamstring, September 3 through December 19, 1985; activated, December 20, 1985.
Released by Cincinnati Bengals, August 18, 1986; awarded on waivers to Chicago Bears, August 19, 1986.
Released by Chicago Bears, August 26, 1986; re-signed by Bears, September 12, 1986.
Released by Chicago Bears, November 4, 1986; re-signed by Bears, February 27, 1987.

Released by Chicago Bears, August 12, 1987; signed as free agent replacement player by Dallas Cowboys, September 23, 1987.

Released by Dallas Cowboys, October 7, 1987; signed as free agent replacement player by New England Patriots, October 13, 1987.

Released by New England Patriots, October 23, 1987; re-signed by Patriots, May 4, 1988.

Cincinnati NFL, 1984 and 1985; Chicago NFL, 1986: New England NFL, 1987.

Games: 1984 (3), 1985 (1), 1986 (4), 1987 (1). Total—9.

MARK HAROLD PIKE
Linebacker—Buffalo Bills

Born December 27, 1963, at Elizabethtown, Ky.

Height, 6.04. Weight, 257.

High School—Edgewood, Ky., Dixie Heights.

Attended Georgia Tech.

Selected by Jacksonville in 1986 USFL territorial draft.

Selected by Buffalo in 7th round (178th player selected) of 1986 NFL draft.

Signed by Buffalo Bills, July 20, 1986.

On injured reserve with shoulder injury, August 26 through entire 1986 season.

On injured reserve with leg injury, September 16 through November 13, 1987; activated, November 14, 1987.

On injured reserve with foot injury, December 8 through remainder of 1987 season.

Buffalo NFL, 1987.

Games: 1987 (3).

ALLEN JEROME PINKETT
Running Back—Houston Oilers

Born January 25, 1964, at Washington, D.C.

Height, 5.09. Weight, 185.

High School—South Hill, Va., Parkview.

Received bachelor of business administration degree in marketing from University of Notre Dame in 1986.

Cousin of Eric Dorsey, defensive end with New York Giants.

Selected by Orlando in 1986 USFL territorial draft.

Selected by Houston in 3rd round (61st player selected) of 1986 NFL draft.

Signed by Houston Oilers, July 31, 1986.

On injured reserve with shoulder injury, October 27 through November 27, 1987; activated, November 28, 1987.

		—RUSHING—				PASS RECEIVING				—TOTAL—		
Year	Club	G.	Att.	Yds.	Avg.	TD.	P.C.	Yds.	Avg.	TD.	TD.	Pts.	F.
1986—Houston NFL		16	77	225	2.9	2	35	248	7.1	1	3	18	2
1987—Houston NFL		8	31	149	4.8	2	1	7	7.0	0	2	12	1
Pro Totals—2 Years		24	108	374	3.5	4	36	255	7.1	1	5	30	3

		KICKOFF RETURNS			
Year	Club	G.	No.	Yds.	Avg.TD.
1986—Houston NFL		16	26	519	20.0 0
1987—Houston NFL		8	17	322	18.9 0
Pro Totals—2 Years		24	43	841	19.6 0

Additional pro statistics: Returned one punt for minus one yard and recovered one fumble, 1986.

MIKE PITTS
Defensive Tackle-Defensive End—Philadelphia Eagles

Born September 25, 1960, at Baltimore, Md.

Height, 6.05. Weight, 277.

High School—Baltimore, Md., Polytechnic.

Attended University of Alabama.

Cousin of Rick Porter, running back with Detroit Lions, Baltimore Colts and Memphis Showboats, 1982, 1983 and 1985.

Named as defensive end on THE SPORTING NEWS College All-America Team, 1982.

Selected by Birmingham in 1983 USFL territorial draft.

Selected by Atlanta in 1st round (16th player selected) of 1983 NFL draft.

Signed by Atlanta Falcons, July 16, 1983.

On injured reserve with knee injury, December 6 through remainder of 1984 season.

Granted free agency, February 1, 1987; re-signed by Falcons and traded to Philadelphia Eagles for defensive end Greg Brown, September 7, 1987.

Granted roster exemption, September 7 through September 10, 1987; activated, September 11, 1987.

Atlanta NFL, 1983 through 1986; Philadelphia NFL, 1987.

Games: 1983 (16), 1984 (14), 1985 (16), 1986 (16), 1987 (12). Total—74.

Pro statistics: Recovered one fumble for 26 yards, 1983; recovered two fumbles, 1984; intercepted one pass for one yard, recovered one fumble for six yards and fumbled once, 1985; recovered two fumbles for 22 yards and a touchdown, 1986; recovered four fumbles for 21 yards, 1987.

RONALD DWAYNE PITTS
(Ron)
Cornerback-Safety—Buffalo Bills

Born October 14, 1962, at Detroit, Mich.

Height, 5.10. Weight, 175.

High School—Orchard Park, N.Y.

Received degree in communications from University of California at Los Angeles in 1985. Son of Elijah Pitts, running back with Green Bay Packers, Los Angeles Rams and New Orleans Saints, 1961 through 1971; scout, Green Bay Packers, 1972; and assistant coach with Los Angeles Rams, 1973 through 1977; Houston Oilers, 1981 through 1983; Hamilton Tiger-Cats, 1984 and Buffalo Bills, 1978 through 1980 and since 1985.

Selected by Buffalo in 7th round (169th player selected) of 1985 NFL draft.
Signed by Buffalo Bills, July 30, 1985.
On injured reserve with foot injury, August 19 through entire 1985 season.
On injured reserve with foot injury, September 2 through October 17, 1986; activated, October 18, 1986.

		-INTERCEPTIONS-				-PUNT RETURNS-				—TOTAL—		
Year	Club	G.	No.	Yds.	Avg.	TD.	No.	Yds.	Avg.	TD.	TD.	Pts.	F.
1986—Buffalo NFL	10			None			18	194	10.8	1		1	6	2
1987—Buffalo NFL	12	3	19	6.3	0		23	149	6.5	0		0	0	3
Pro Totals—2 Years	22	3	19	6.3	0		41	343	8.4	1		1	6	5

Additional pro statistics: Returned one kickoff for seven yards and recovered two fumbles, 1986; recovered one fumble, 1987.

BRUCE ELLIOTT PLUMMER
Defensive Back—Denver Broncos
Born September 1, 1964, at Bogalusa, La.
Height, 6.01. Weight, 197.
High School—Bogalusa, La.
Attended Mississippi State University.

Selected by Denver in 9th round (250th player selected) of 1987 NFL draft.
Signed by Denver Broncos, July 19, 1987.
Dallas NFL, 1987.
Games: 1987 (11).
Played in AFC Championship Game following 1987 season.
Played in NFL Championship Game following 1987 season.

GARY LEE PLUMMER
Linebacker—San Diego Chargers
Born January 26, 1960, at Fremont, Calif.
Height, 6.02. Weight, 240.
High School—Mission San Jose, Calif.
Attended Ohlone Junior College and University of California at Berkeley.

Selected by Oakland in 1983 USFL territorial draft.
Signed by Oakland Invaders, January 26, 1983.
On developmental squad, March 30 through April 5, 1984; activated, April 6, 1984.
Protected in merger of Oakland Invaders and Michigan Panthers, December 6, 1984.
Released by Oakland Invaders, August 2, 1985; awarded on waivers to Tampa Bay Bandits, August 3, 1985.
Granted free agency when USFL suspended operations, August 7, 1986; signed as free agent by San Diego Chargers, August 18, 1986.
Granted roster exemption, August 18 through August 21, 1986; activated, August 22, 1986.
On injured reserve with broken wrist, October 27 through November 27, 1987; activated, November 28, 1987.
On developmental squad for 1 game with Oakland Invaders in 1984.
Oakland USFL, 1983 through 1985; San Diego NFL, 1986 and 1987.
Games: 1983 (18), 1984 (17), 1985 (18), 1986 (15), 1987 (8). Total USFL—53. Total NFL—23. Total Pro—76.
USFL statistics: Intercepted three passes for 20 yards, 1983; recovered one fumble, 1983 through 1985; credited with one sack for eight yards and intercepted two passes for 11 yards, 1984; credited with one sack for seven yards, intercepted one pass for 46 yards and returned three kickoffs for 31 yards, 1985.
NFL statistics: Returned one kickoff for no yards and recovered two fumbles, 1986; intercepted one pass for two yards, 1987.
Played in USFL Championship Game following 1985 season.

ARTHUR SCOTT PLUNKETT
(Art)
Offensive Tackle—New England Patriots
Born March 8, 1959, at Chicago, Ill.
Height, 6.08. Weight, 282.
High Schools—Arlington Heights, Ill., Arlington; and Salt Lake City, Utah, Skyline.
Attended University of Nevada at Las Vegas.

Selected by Los Angeles in 8th round (216th player selected) of 1981 NFL draft.
On injured reserve with back injury, August 24 through October 26, 1981; claimed on procedural waivers by St. Louis Cardinals, October 28, 1981.
Released by St. Louis Cardinals, September 3, 1985, signed as free agent by New England Patriots, September 11, 1985.
On injured reserve with knee injury, August 26 through entire 1986 season.
On injured reserve with knee injury, September 16 through November 13, 1987; activated, November 14, 1987.
St. Louis NFL, 1981 through 1984; New England NFL, 1985 and 1987.
Games: 1981 (8), 1982 (9), 1983 (16), 1984 (16), 1985 (15), 1987 (7). Total—71.
Played in AFC Championship Game following 1985 season.
Played in NFL Championship Game following 1985 season.

JAMES WILLIAM PLUNKETT JR.
(Jim)
Quarterback—Los Angeles Raiders

Born December 5, 1947, at San Jose, Calif.
Height, 6.02. Weight, 220.
High Schools—San Jose, Calif., Overfeldt and James Lick.
Attended Stanford University.

Tied NFL record for longest completed passing play from scrimmage when he threw a 99-yard touchdown pass to wide receiver Cliff Branch against Washington Redskins, October 2, 1983.
Heisman Trophy winner, 1970.
Named THE SPORTING NEWS College Football Player of the Year, 1970.
Named as quarterback on THE SPORTING NEWS College All-America Team, 1970.
Named THE SPORTING NEWS AFC Rookie of the Year, 1971.
Selected by New England in 1st round (1st player selected) of 1971 NFL draft.
Traded by New England Patriots to San Francisco 49ers for quarterback Tom Owen and four draft choices (two 1st round selections in 1976 plus 1st and 2nd round picks in 1977), April 5, 1976.
Released by San Francisco 49ers, August 28, 1978; signed as free agent by Oakland Raiders, September 12, 1978.
Franchise transferred to Los Angeles, May 7, 1982.
On injured reserve with pulled abdominal muscle, October 13 through November 11, 1984; activated, November 12, 1984.
On injured reserve with dislocated shoulder, September 23 through remainder of 1985 season.
On physically unable to perform/reserve with shoulder injury, September 1 through entire 1987 season.
Active for 14 games with Oakland Raiders in 1978; did not play.

				—PASSING—						—RUSHING—				—TOTAL—		
Year	Club	G.	Att.	Cmp.	Pct.	Gain	T.P.	P.I.	Avg.	Att.	Yds.	Avg.	TD.	TD.	Pts.	F.
1971—New England NFL		14	328	158	48.2	2158	19	16	6.58	45	210	4.7	0	0	0	6
1972—New England NFL		14	355	169	47.6	2196	8	25	6.19	36	230	6.4	1	1	6	6
1973—New England NFL		14	376	193	51.3	2550	13	17	6.78	44	209	4.8	5	5	30	6
1974—New England NFL		14	352	173	49.1	2457	19	22	6.98	30	161	5.4	2	2	12	4
1975—New England NFL		5	92	36	39.1	571	3	7	6.21	4	7	1.8	1	1	6	2
1976—San Francisco NFL		12	243	126	51.9	1592	13	16	6.55	19	95	5.0	0	0	0	1
1977—San Francisco NFL		14	248	128	51.6	1693	9	14	6.83	28	71	2.5	1	1	6	2
1979—Oakland NFL		4	15	7	46.7	89	1	1	5.93	3	18	6.0	0	0	0	0
1980—Oakland NFL		13	320	165	51.6	2299	18	16	7.18	28	141	5.0	2	2	12	9
1981—Oakland NFL		9	179	94	52.5	1045	4	9	5.84	12	38	3.2	1	1	6	3
1982—L.A. Raiders NFL		9	261	152	58.2	2035	14	15	7.80	15	6	0.4	0	0	0	4
1983—L.A. Raiders NFL		14	379	230	60.7	2935	20	18	7.74	26	78	3.0	0	0	0	7
1984—L.A. Raiders NFL		8	198	108	54.5	1473	6	10	7.44	16	14	0.9	1	1	6	2
1985—L.A. Raiders NFL		3	103	71	68.9	803	3	3	7.80	5	12	2.4	0	0	0	6
1986—L.A. Raiders NFL		10	252	133	52.8	1986	14	9	7.88	12	47	3.9	0	0	0	4
Pro Totals—16 Years		157	3701	1943	52.5	25882	164	198	6.99	323	1337	4.1	14	14	84	62

Quarterback Rating Points: 1971 (68.6), 1972 (46.1), 1973 (66.0), 1974 (63.8), 1975 (39.9), 1976 (62.8), 1977 (62.2), 1979 (60.1), 1980 (72.8), 1981 (56.7), 1982 (77.3), 1983 (82.7), 1984 (67.6), 1985 (89.6), 1986 (82.5). Total—67.6.
Additional pro statistics: Recovered one fumble, 1972 through 1974, 1981, 1982 and 1984; recovered two fumbles, 1977 and 1980; fumbled three times for minus six yards, 1981; fumbled four times for minus seven yards, 1982; recovered three fumbles, 1983; recovered one fumble and fumbled six times for minus five yards, 1985; fumbled four times for minus three yards, 1986.
Played in AFC Championship Game following 1980 and 1983 seasons.
Played in NFL Championship Game following 1980 and 1983 seasons.

JOHNNIE EDWARD POE
Cornerback—San Francisco 49ers

Born August 29, 1959, at St. Louis, Mo.
Height, 6.01. Weight, 194.
High School—East St. Louis, Ill., Lincoln.
Attended University of Missouri.

Selected by New Orleans in 6th round (144th player selected) of 1981 NFL draft.
Granted free agency with no qualifying offer, February 1, 1988; signed by San Francisco 49ers, April 22, 1988.

			—INTERCEPTIONS—			
Year	Club	G.	No.	Yds.	Avg.	TD.
1981—New Orleans NFL		15	1	0	0.0	0
1982—New Orleans NFL		9		None		
1983—New Orleans NFL		16	7	146	20.9	1
1984—New Orleans NFL		16	1	16	16.0	0
1985—New Orleans NFL		16	3	63	21.0	⋆1
1986—New Orleans NFL		16	4	42	10.5	0
1987—New Orleans NFL		12	1	0	0.0	0
Pro Totals—7 Years		100	17	267	15.7	2

Additional pro statistics: Recovered one fumble for 10 yards and returned one punt for two yards, 1981; recovered one fumble, 1982, 1985 and 1986; recovered two fumbles, 1983; fumbled once, 1985; returned eight punts for 71 yards, 1986; returned blocked field goal attempt 61 yards for a touchdown, 1987.

—DID YOU KNOW—

That the New Orleans Saints had a club-record two safeties in the fourth quarter against Cleveland on September 13?

FRANK POLLARD
Running Back—Pittsburgh Steelers
Born June 15, 1957, at Clifton, Tex.
Height, 5.10. Weight, 230.
High School—Meridian, Tex.
Attended Baylor University.

Selected by Pittsburgh in 11th round (305th player selected) of 1980 NFL draft.
On injured reserve with knee injury, October 7 through remainder of 1986 season.
Crossed picket line during players' strike, October 7, 1987.

		—RUSHING—				PASS RECEIVING				—TOTAL—		
Year Club	G.	Att.	Yds.	Avg.	TD.	P.C.	Yds.	Avg.	TD.	TD.	Pts.	F.
1980—Pittsburgh NFL	16	4	16	4.0	0		None			0	0	1
1981—Pittsburgh NFL	14	123	570	4.6	2	19	156	8.2	0	2	12	5
1982—Pittsburgh NFL	9	62	238	3.8	2	6	39	6.5	0	2	12	3
1983—Pittsburgh NFL	16	135	608	4.5	4	16	127	7.9	0	4	24	5
1984—Pittsburgh NFL	15	213	851	4.0	6	21	186	8.9	0	6	36	9
1985—Pittsburgh NFL	16	233	991	4.3	3	24	250	10.4	0	3	18	2
1986—Pittsburgh NFL	3	24	86	3.6	0	2	15	7.5	0	0	0	1
1987—Pittsburgh NFL	12	128	536	4.2	3	14	77	5.5	0	3	18	3
Pro Totals—8 Years	101	922	3896	4.2	20	102	850	8.3	0	20	120	29

	KICKOFF RETURNS						KICKOFF RETURNS			
Year Club	G.	No.	Yds.	Avg.TD.	Year Club	G.	No.	Yds.	Avg.TD.
1980—Pittsburgh NFL	16	22	494	22.5 0	1985—Pittsburgh NFL	16		None	
1981—Pittsburgh NFL	14		None		1986—Pittsburgh NFL	3		None	
1982—Pittsburgh NFL	9		None		1987—Pittsburgh NFL	12		None	
1983—Pittsburgh NFL	16		None		Pro Totals—8 Years	101	22	494	22.5 0
1984—Pittsburgh NFL	15		None						

Additional pro statistics: Returned one punt for five yards, 1980; recovered one fumble, 1983 and 1985; recovered two fumbles, 1984; recovered one fumble for one yard, 1987.
Played in AFC Championship Game following 1984 season.

KERRY PORTER
Running Back—Buffalo Bills
Born September 23, 1964, at Vicenza, Italy.
Height, 6.01. Weight, 210.
High School—Great Falls, Mont.
Attended Washington State University.

Selected by Buffalo in 7th round (171st player selected) of 1987 NFL draft.
Signed by Buffalo Bills, July 23, 1987.
On injured reserve with shoulder injury, September 7 through October 22, 1987, activated, October 23, 1987.
Buffalo NFL, 1987.
Games: 1987 (6).
Pro statistics: Rushed twice for no yards, 1987.

RICHARD ANTHONY PORTER
(Rick)
Running Back—Buffalo Bills
Born January 14, 1960, at Sylacaga, Ala.
Heigh 5.10. Weight, 210.
High School—Baltimore, Md., Milford Mill.
Attended Slippery Rock State College.
Cousin of Mike Pitts, defensive end with Philadelphia Eagles.

Selected by Detroit in 12th round (319th player selected) of 1982 NFL draft.
On inactive list, September 12 and September 19, 1982.
Released by Detroit Lions, November 30, 1982; signed as free agent by Philadelphia Eagles, February 12, 1983.
Released by Philadelphia Eagles, August 11, 1983; signed as free agent by Baltimore Colts, September 14, 1983.
Franchise transferred to Indianapolis, March 31, 1984.
Released by Indianapolis Colts, August 22, 1984; signed by Baltimore Stars, December 1, 1984.
Released by Baltimore Stars, February 18, 1985; awarded on waivers to Memphis Showboats, February 19, 1985.
Granted free agency when USFL suspended operations, August 7, 1986; signed by Montreal Alouettes, October 7, 1986.
Granted free agency when Montreal Alouettes suspended operations, June 24, 1987; signed by Buffalo Bills, July 11, 1987.
Released by Buffalo Bills, September 7, 1987; re-signed as replacement player by Bills, October 14, 1987.

		—RUSHING—				PASS RECEIVING				—TOTAL—		
Year Club	G.	Att.	Yds.	Avg.	TD.	P.C.	Yds.	Avg.	TD.	TD.	Pts.	F.
1982—Detroit NFL	1		None				None			0	0	0
1983—Baltimore NFL	14		None				None			0	0	6
1985—Memphis USFL	18	43	188	4.4	0	14	210	15.0	0	0	0	2
1986—Montreal CFL	1	10	63	63.0	0	3	19	63	0	0	0	0
1987—Buffalo NFL	9	47	177	3.8	0	9	70	7.8	0	0	0	0
NFL Totals—3 Years	24	47	177	3.8	0	9	70	7.8	0	0	0	6
USFL Totals—1 Year	18	43	188	4.4	0	14	210	15.0	0	0	0	2
CFL Totals—1 Year	1	10	63	6.3	0	3	19	6.3	0	0	0	0
Pro Totals—5 Years	43	100	428	4.3	0	26	299	11.5	0	0	0	8

Year Club	G.	—PUNT RETURNS— No.	Yds.	Avg.	TD.	—KICKOFF RET.— No.	Yds.	Avg.	TD.
1982—Detroit NFL	1			None				None	
1983—Baltimore NFL	14	14	104	7.4	0	18	340	18.9	0
1985—Memphis USFL	18			None		3	52	17.3	0
1986—Montreal CFL	1			None		3	70	23.3	0
1987—Buffalo NFL	9			None		8	219	27.4	0
NFL Totals—3 Years	24	14	104	7.4	0	26	559	21.5	0
USFL Totals—1 Year	18	0	0	0.0	0	3	52	17.3	0
CFL Totals—1 Year	1	0	0	0.0	0	3	70	23.3	0
Pro Totals—5 Years	43	14	104	7.4	0	32	681	21.3	0

Additional NFL statistics: Recovered four fumbles, 1983.
Additional USFL statistics: Recovered two fumbles, 1985.

KARL ALANZO POWE
Name pronounced Poe.
Wide Receiver—Green Bay Packers
Born January 17, 1962, at Mobile, Ala.
Height, 6.02. Weight, 175.
High School—Prichard, Ala., Mattie T. Blount.
Attended Alabama State University.

Selected by Birmingham in 1985 USFL territorial draft.
Selected by Dallas in 7th round (178th player selected) of 1985 NFL draft.
Signed by Dallas Cowboys, July 2, 1985.
On injured reserve with neck injury, September 10 through remainder of 1986 season.
On injured reserved with shoulder injury, September 1 through October 19, 1987.
Crossed picket line during players' strike, October 7, 1987.
Released by Dallas Cowboys, October 20, 1987; signed as free agent by Green Bay Packers, April 15, 1988.

Year Club	G.	——PASS RECEIVING—— P.C.	Yds.	Avg.	TD.
1985—Dallas NFL	15	14	237	16.9	0
1986—Dallas NFL	1			None	
Pro Totals—2 Years	16	14	237	16.9	0

Additional pro statistics: Returned one kickoff for 17 yards and fumbled once, 1985.

ALVIN ROBERT POWELL II
Guard—Seattle Seahawks
Born November 19, 1959, at Panama.
Height, 6.05. Weight, 291.
High School—Fayetteville, N.C., Pine Forest.
Attended Winston-Salem State University.

Selected by Oklahoma in 6th round (121st player selected) of 1984 USFL draft.
Signed by Oklahoma Outlaws, January 16, 1984.
Selected by Seattle in 2nd round (49th player selected) of 1984 NFL supplemental draft.
Protected in merger of Oklahoma Outlaws and Arizona Wranglers, December 6, 1984.
Granted free agency when USFL suspended operations, August 7, 1986; signed by Seattle Seahawks, August 11, 1986.
Granted roster exemption, August 11 through August 21, 1986; activated, August 22, 1986.
On injured reserve with back injury, September 3 through entire 1986 season.
Oklahoma USFL, 1984; Arizona USFL, 1985; Seattle NFL, 1987.
Games: 1984 (18), 1985 (18), 1987 (12). Total USFL—36. Total Pro—48.
USFL statistics: Recovered two fumbles, 1984; recovered one fumble, 1985.
NFL statistics: Returned three kickoffs for 23 yards and fumbled once, 1987.

TROY DEAN PRATER
(Known by middle name.)
Defensive End—Buffalo Bills
Born September 28, 1958, at Altus, Okla.
Height, 6.04. Weight, 260.
High School—Wichita Falls, Tex., Rider.
Attended Oklahoma State University.

Selected by Cleveland in 10th round (271st player selected) of 1981 NFL draft.
Released by Cleveland Browns, August 24, 1981; signed as free agent by Kansas City Chiefs, May 10, 1982.
On commissioner's exempt list, November 20 through November 23, 1982.
On non-football injury list with knee injury, November 24 through remainder of 1982 season.
USFL rights traded with running back Darrell Smith, defensive tackle Mike Perko and placekicker Rex Robinson by Chicago Blitz to Boston Breakers for rights to quarterback Greg Landry, August 11, 1983.
USFL rights traded by New Orleans Breakers to Chicago Blitz for future draft pick, January 26, 1984.
Released by Kansas City Chiefs, August 27, 1984; signed as free agent by Buffalo Bills, September 12, 1984.
Released by Buffalo Bills, August 30, 1985; re-signed by Bills, September 3, 1985.
Kansas City NFL, 1982 and 1983; Buffalo NFL, 1984 through 1987.
Games: 1982 (2), 1983 (16), 1984 (13), 1985 (16), 1986 (16), 1987 (10). Total—73.
Pro statistics: Recovered one fumble, 1983.

JOHN STANLEY PRESTON
Safety—Green Bay Packers
Born August 28, 1962, at Dallas, Tex.
Height, 6.00. Weight, 200.
High School—Dallas, Tex., South Oak Cliff.
Attended Texas Christian University and Central State University.

Selected by New Jersey in 14th round (276th player selected) of 1984 USFL draft.
Signed by New Jersey Generals, January 13, 1984.
On developmental squad, March 10 through March 16, 1984; activated, March 17, 1984.
On developmental squad, March 16 through March 22, 1985; activated, March 23, 1985.
On developmental squad, April 29 through May 4, 1985; activated, May 5, 1985.
Released by New Jersey Generals, August 1, 1985; re-signed by Generals, April 10, 1986.
Granted free agency when USFL suspended operations, August 7, 1986; signed as free agent by St. Louis Cardinals, May 20, 1987.
Crossed picket line during players' strike, October 14, 1987.
Released by St. Louis Cardinals, November 3, 1987; signed as free agent by Green Bay Packers, May 26, 1988.
On developmental squad for 1 game with New Jersey General in 1984.
On developmental squad for 2 games with New Jersey Generals in 1985.

			—INTERCEPTIONS—		
Year Club	G.	No.	Yds.	Avg.	TD.
1984—New Jersey USFL	17	1	0	0.0	0
1985—New Jersey USFL	16	3	22	7.3	0
1987—St. Louis NFL	5		None		
USFL Totals—2 Years	33	4	22	5.5	0
NFL Totals—1 Year	5	0	0	0.0	0
Pro Totals—3 Years	38	4	22	5.5	0

Additional pro statistics: Recovered one fumble for four yards, 1985.

MITCHELL PRICE
Defensive End—Cleveland Browns
Born July 29, 1961, at Newberry, S. C.
Height, 6.03. Weight, 260.
High School—Newberry, S. C.
Attended Livingston University.

Signed as free agent by Hamilton Tiger-Cats, March 19, 1983.
Released by Hamilton Tiger-Cats, October 26, 1987; signed as free agent by Cleveland Browns, March 4, 1988.
Hamilton CFL, 1983 through 1987.
Games: 1983 (16), 1984 (12), 1985 (16), 1986 (15), 1987 (10). Total—69.
CFL statistics: Intercepted one pass for eight yards and recovered two fumbles for eight yards, 1983; intercepted two passes for 27 yards, 1985.

MICHAEL ROBERT PRIOR
(Mike)
Defensive Back—Indianapolis Colts
Born November 14, 1963, at Chicago Heights, Ill.
Height, 6.00. Weight, 200.
High School—Chicago Heights, Ill., Marion Catholic.
Received degree in business administration
from Illinois State University in 1985.

Selected by Memphis in 4th round (60th player selected) of 1985 USFL draft.
Selected by Tampa Bay in 7th round (176th player selected) of 1985 NFL draft.
Signed by Tampa Bay Buccaneers, June 10, 1985.
On injured reserve with fractured wrist, August 25 through September 28, 1986.
Released by Tampa Bay Buccaneers, September 29, 1986; signed as free agent by Indianapolis Colts, May 11, 1987.
Released by Indianapolis Colts, August 31, 1987; re-signed as replacement player by Colts, September 23, 1987.
Selected by Baltimore Orioles' organization in 18th round of free-agent draft, June 4, 1984.
Selected by Los Angeles Dodgers' organization in 4th round of free-agent draft, June 3, 1985.

		INTERCEPTIONS			–PUNT RETURNS–			—KICKOFF RET.—			—TOTAL—		
Year Club	G.	No.	Yds.	Avg. TD.	No.	Yds.	Avg. TD.	No.	Yds.	Avg. TD.	TD.	Pts.	F.
1985—Tampa Bay NFL	16		None		13	105	8.1 0	10	131	13.1 0	0	0	4
1987—Indianapolis NFL	13	6	57	9.5 0			None	3	47	15.7 0	0	0	0
Pro Totals—2 Years	29	6	57	9.5 0	13	105	8.1 0	13	178	13.7 0	0	0	4

Additional pro statistics: Recovered three fumbles, 1985 and 1987.

EUGENE ANTHONY PROFIT
Cornerback—New England Patriots
Born November 11, 1964, at Baton Rouge, La.
Height, 5.10. Weight, 175.
High School—Gardena, Calif., Junipero Serra.
Received bachelor of arts degree in economics from Yale University in 1986.

Selected by New Jersey in 11th round (83rd player selected) of 1986 USFL draft.
Signed as free agent by New England Patriots, May 10, 1986.
On injured reserve with thumb injury, August 18 through November 26, 1986; activated after clearing procedural waivers, November 28, 1986.

New England NFL, 1986 and 1987.
Games: 1986 (4), 1987 (7). Total—11.

JOE PROKOP
Punter—New York Jets
Born July 7, 1960, at St. Paul, Minn.
Height, 6.03. Weight, 225.
High School—White Bear Lake, Minn.
Attended California State Poly University at Pomona.

Signed as free agent by Los Angeles Rams, June 20, 1984.
Released by Los Angeles Rams, July 16, 1984.
USFL rights traded by Los Angeles Express to Houston Gamblers for past considerations, November 12, 1984.
Signed by Houston Gamblers, November 12, 1984.
Released by Houston Gamblers, January 28, 1985; signed as free agent by San Antonio Gunslingers, February 5, 1985.
Released by San Antonio Gunslingers, February 12, 1985; signed as free agent by New York Giants, June 21, 1985.
Released by New York Giants, August 26, 1985; signed as free agent by Green Bay Packers, September 4, 1985.
Released by Green Bay Packers, November 5, 1985; signed as free agent by New York Jets, March 25, 1986.
Released by New York Jets, August 25, 1986; signed as free agent by San Diego Chargers, April 13, 1987.
On injured reserve with quadricep injury, September 1 through September 14, 1987.
Released by San Diego Chargers, September 15, 1987; re-signed as replacement player by Chargers, September 24, 1987.
Released by San Diego Chargers, October 21, 1987; signed as free agent by New York Jets, April 8, 1988.

		—PUNTING—		
Year Club	G.	No.	Avg.	Blk.
1985—Green Bay NFL	9	56	39.5	0
1987—San Diego NFL	3	17	38.5	0
Pro Total—2 Years	12	73	39.3	0

ANDREW PROVENCE
Defensive End—Denver Broncos
Born March 8, 1961, at Savannah, Ga.
Height, 6.03. Weight, 267.
High School—Savannah, Ga., Benedictine.
Attended University of South Carolina.

Selected by Washington in 1983 USFL territorial draft.
Selected by Atlanta in 3rd round (75th player selected) of 1983 NFL draft.
Signed by Atlanta Falcons, May 30, 1983.
On injured reserve with fractured finger, September 7 through November 27, 1987; activated, November 28, 1987.
Granted free agency, February 1, 1988; re-signed by Falcons and traded to Denver Broncos for conditional 10th round pick in 1989 draft, May 10, 1988.
Atlanta NFL, 1983 through 1987.
Games: 1983 (16), 1984 (16), 1985 (16), 1986 (16), 1987 (5). Total—69.
Pro statistics: Recovered one fumble for 26 yards, 1983; recovered one fumble, 1984.

JAMES BOUBIAS PRUITT
Wide Receiver—Miami Dolphins
Born January 29, 1964, at Los Angeles, Calif.
Height, 6.02. Weight, 199.
High School—Los Angeles, Calif., Thomas Jefferson.
Attended California State University at Fullerton.

Selected by Miami in 4th round (107th player selected) of 1986 NFL draft.
Selected by New Jersey in 1st round (5th player selected) of 1986 USFL draft.
Signed by Miami Dolphins, July 24, 1986.

		-PASS RECEIVING-				-PUNT RETURNS-				—TOTAL—		
Year Club	G.	P.C.	Yds.	Avg.	TD.	No.	Yds.	Avg.	TD.	TD.	Pts.	F.
1986—Miami NFL	16	15	235	15.7	2	11	150	13.6	1	3	18	4
1987—Miami NFL	12	26	404	15.5	3		None			3	18	1
Pro Totals—2 Years	28	41	639	15.6	5	11	150	13.6	1	6	36	5

Additional pro statistics: Recovered two fumbles, 1986.

PHILLIP DAVID PUZZUOLI
Name pronounced Pa-ZOOL-ee.
(Dave)
Nose Tackle—Cleveland Browns
Born January 12, 1961, at Greenwich, Conn.
Height, 6.03. Weight, 260.
High School—Stamford, Conn., Catholic.
Attended University of Pittsburgh.

Selected by Tampa Bay in 8th round (85th player selected) of 1983 USFL draft.
Selected by Cleveland in 6th round (149th player selected) of 1983 NFL draft.
Signed by Cleveland Browns, May 31, 1983.
Cleveland NFL, 1983 through 1987.

Games: 1983 (16), 1984 (16), 1985 (16), 1986 (16), 1987 (12). Total—76.

Pro statistics: Recovered one fumble for two yards, 1983; recovered one fumble, 1984; returned two kickoffs for eight yards, 1985; returned one kickoff for 32 yards, 1986.

Played in AFC Championship Game following 1986 and 1987 seasons.

BERNARD QUARLES
Quarterback—Los Angeles Rams
Born January 4, 1960, at Los Angeles, Calif.
Height, 6.01. Weight, 205.
High School—Los Angeles, Calif., Jefferson.
Attended University of California at Los Angeles and University of Hawaii.

Selected by Los Angeles in 22nd round (264th player selected) of 1983 USFL draft.

Signed as free agent by Calgary Stampeders, May, 1983.

Traded with wide receiver Phil Charron by Calgary Stampeders to Ottawa Rough Riders for wide receiver Dwight Edwards and linebacker Dan Rashovich, May, 1985.

Traded by Ottawa Rough Riders to Saskatchewan Roughriders for wide receiver Stewart Fraser and 4th round pick in 1986 draft, October, 1985.

Released by Saskatchewan Roughriders, May 17, 1988; signed as free agent replacement player by Los Angeles Rams, September 23, 1987.

Released by Los Angeles Rams, October 21, 1987; re-signed by Rams, March 8, 1988.

					PASSING					RUSHING			TOTAL		
Year Club	G.	Att.	Cmp.	Pct.	Gain	T.P.	P.I.	Avg.	Att.	Yds.	Avg.	TD.	TD.	Pts.	F.
1983—Calgary CFL	16	323	179	55.4	2841	17	19	8.80	57	438	7.7	2	2	12	7
1984—Calgary CFL	13	177	92	52.0	1341	6	9	7.58	45	322	7.2	1	1	6	5
1985—Ottawa CFL	11	101	50	49.5	635	1	6	6.29	26	178	6.8	0	0	0	2
1986—Saskatchewan CFL	18	201	109	54.2	1672	6	6	8.32	33	247	7.5	0	0	0	3
1987—Los Angeles Rams NFL..	1	3	1	33.3	40	1	1	13.33	1	8	8.0	0	0	0	0
CFL Totals—4 Years	58	802	430	53.6	6489	30	40	8.09	161	1185	7.4	3	3	18	17
NFL Totals—1 Year	1	3	1	33.3	40	1	1	13.33	1	8	8.0	0	0	0	0
Pro Totals—5 Years	59	805	431	53.5	6529	31	41	8.11	162	1193	7.4	3	3	18	17

NFL Quarterback Rating Points: 1987 (81.9).

Additional pro statistics: Recovered two fumbles, 1983; recovered one fumble, 1985 and 1986.

JERRY DEAN QUICK
Offensive Lineman—Pittsburgh Steelers
Born December 30, 1963, at Anthony, Kan.
Height, 6.05. Weight, 273.
High School—Harper, Kan., Chaparral.
Attended Butler County Community College and Wichita State University.

Signed as free agent by Pittsburgh Steelers, May 21, 1986.

On injured reserve with groin injury, August 19 through entire 1986 season.

On injured reserve with ankle injury, September 7 through September 14, 1987.

Released by Pittsburgh Steelers, September 15, 1987; re-signed by Steelers after clearing procedural waivers, September 18, 1987.

Crossed picket line during players' strike, October 13, 1987.

Pittsburgh NFL, 1987.

Games: 1987 (1).

MICHAEL ANTHONY QUICK
(Mike)
Wide Receiver—Philadelphia Eagles
Born May 14, 1959, at Hamlet, N.C.
Height, 6.02. Weight, 190.
High School—Rockingham, N.C., Richmond.
Attended Fork Union Military Academy and North Carolina State University.

Named to THE SPORTING NEWS NFL All-Star Team, 1985.

Tied NFL record for longest passing play from scrimmage when he caught a 99-yard touchdown pass from quarterback Ron Jaworski against Atlanta Falcons, November 10, 1985.

Selected by Philadelphia in 1st round (20th player selected) of 1982 NFL draft.

On did not report list, August 20 through September 1, 1985.

Reported and granted roster exemption, September 2 through September 4, 1985; activated, September 5, 1985.

		PASS RECEIVING			
Year Club	G.	P.C.	Yds.	Avg.	TD.
1982—Philadelphia NFL	9	10	156	15.6	1
1983—Philadelphia NFL	16	69	*1409	20.4	13
1984—Philadelphia NFL	14	61	1052	17.2	9
1985—Philadelphia NFL	16	73	1247	17.1	11
1986—Philadelphia NFL	16	60	939	15.7	9
1987—Philadelphia NFL	12	46	790	17.2	11
Pro Totals—6 Years	83	319	5593	17.5	54

Additional pro statistics: Recovered one fumble, 1982 and 1985 through 1987; fumbled once, 1983, 1985 and 1986; rushed once for minus five yards, 1984; returned two kickoffs for six yards, 1986; fumbled three times, 1987.

Played in Pro Bowl (NFL All-Star Game) following 1983 through 1985 and 1987 seasons.

Member of Pro Bowl following 1986 season; did not play.

FRED QUILLAN
Center—San Diego Chargers
Born January 27, 1956, at Portland, Ore.
Height, 6.05. Weight, 266.
High School—Portland, Ore., Central Catholic.
Attended University of Oregon.

Selected by San Francisco in 7th round (175th player selected) of 1978 NFL draft.
Granted free agency, February 1, 1988; re-signed by 49ers and traded with conditional 1989 draft pick to San Diego Chargers for wide receiver Wes Chandler and conditional 1989 draft pick, June 3, 1988.
San Francisco NFL, 1978 through 1987.
Games: 1978 (14), 1979 (16), 1980 (16), 1981 (16), 1982 (9), 1983 (14), 1984 (16), 1985 (15), 1986 (16), 1987 (11). Total—143.
Pro statistics: Returned one kickoff for eight yards, 1978; fumbled twice for minus 34 yards, 1979; fumbled once for minus 42 yards, 1980; fumbled once, 1981; recovered one fumble, 1983.
Played in NFC Championship Game following 1981, 1983 and 1984 seasons.
Played in NFL Championship Game following 1981 and 1984 seasons.
Played in Pro Bowl (NFL All-Star Game) following 1984 and 1985 seasons.

MARCUS QUINN
Safety—Tampa Bay Buccaneers
Born June 27, 1959, at Tylertown, Miss.
Height, 6.01. Weight, 207.
High School—New Orleans, La., St. Augustine.
Received degree in criminal justice from Louisiana State University.

Named as safety on THE SPORTING NEWS USFL All-Star Team, 1984.
Signed as free agent by Ottawa Rough Riders, March, 1981.
Released by Ottawa Rough Riders, June 20, 1981; signed as free agent by New Orleans Saints, April 8, 1982.
Released by New Orleans Saints, August 31, 1982; signed by Oakland Invaders, February 6, 1983.
Protected in merger of Oakland Invaders and Michigan Panthers, December 6, 1984.
Traded by Oakland Invaders to Tampa Bay Bandits for draft choices, March 7, 1985.
Granted free agency when USFL suspended operations, August 7, 1986; signed as free agent replacement player by Tampa Bay Buccaneers, September 24, 1987.
Released by Tampa Bay Buccaneers, October 19, 1987; re-signed by Buccaneers for 1988, December 7, 1987.

| | | —INTERCEPTIONS— | | | |
Year Club	G.	No.	Yds.	Avg.	TD.
1983—Oakland USFL..............	18	4	46	11.5	0
1984—Oakland USFL..............	18	*12	244	20.3	0
1985—Oak (2)-TB (15) USFL.	17	7	41	5.9	0
1987—Tampa Bay NFL..........	3		None		
USFL Totals—3 Years........	53	23	331	14.4	0
NFL Totals—1 Year...........	3	0	0	0.0	0
Pro Totals—4 Years............	56	23	331	14.4	0

Additional USFL statistics: Recovered three fumbles, returned three punts for 11 yards and credited with one sack for 13 yards, 1983; credited with one sack for seven yards and recovered two fumbles for 22 yards, 1984; returned one punt for no yards, recovered three fumbles for one yard and fumbled once, 1985.
Additional NFL statistics: Recovered one fumble, 1987.

COACHING RECORD
Graduate assistant at Louisiana State University, 1981.

GEORGE JOSEPH RADACHOWSKY JR.
Safety—New York Jets
Born September 7, 1962, at Danbury, Conn.
Height, 5.11. Weight, 190.
High School—Danbury, Conn.
Attended Boston College.

Selected by Philadelphia in 5th round (84th player selected) of 1984 USFL draft.
Selected by Los Angeles Rams in 7th round (188th player selected) of 1984 NFL draft.
Signed by Los Angeles Rams, July 9, 1984.
Traded by Los Angeles Rams to Indianapolis Colts for 11th round pick in 1985 draft, August 27, 1984.
Released by Indianapolis Colts, September 30, 1985; re-signed by Colts, April 1, 1986.
Released by Indianapolis Colts, August 18, 1986; signed as free agent by New York Jets, May 10, 1987.
Released by New York Jets, August 31, 1987; re-signed as replacement player by Jets, September 24, 1987.
Released by New York Jets, October 26, 1987; re-signed by Jets, October 28, 1987.
Released by New York Jets, November 3, 1987; re-signed by Jets, November 27, 1987.
Indianapolis NFL, 1984 and 1985; New York Jets NFL, 1987.
Games: 1984 (16), 1985 (3), 1987 (8). Total—27.
Pro statistics: Returned one kickoff for no yards and fumbled once, 1984; intercepted two passes for 45 yards, 1987.

JOHN RADE
Name pronounced RAY-dee.
Linebacker—Atlanta Falcons
Born August 31, 1960, at Ceres, Calif.
Height, 6.01. Weight, 240.
High School—Sierra Vista, Ariz., Buena.
Attended Modesto Junior College and Boise State University.

Signed as free agent by Boston Breakers, February 10, 1983.
Released by Boston Breakers, February 12, 1983.
Selected by Atlanta in 8th round (215th player selected) of 1983 NFL draft.
Signed by Atlanta Falcons, May 16, 1983.
On injured reserve with pinched nerve in neck, October 24 through remainder of 1984 season.
On injured reserve with ankle injury, December 18 through remainder of 1986 season.
Atlanta NFL, 1983 through 1987.
Games: 1983 (16), 1984 (7), 1985 (16), 1986 (15), 1987 (11). Total—65.
Pro statistics: Recovered two fumbles for 16 yards and a touchdown, 1983; recovered one fumble, 1984; intercepted two passes for 42 yards and a touchdown, 1985; intercepted one pass for six yards, 1986.

J. SCOTT RADECIC

Name pronounced RADD-ah-seck.

(Known by middle name.)

Linebacker—Buffalo Bills

Born June 14, 1962, at Pittsburgh, Pa.
Height, 6.03. Weight, 242.
High School—Pittsburgh, Pa., Brentwood.
Attended Penn State University.
Brother of Keith Radecic, center with St. Louis Cardinals, 1987.

Selected by Philadelphia in 1984 USFL territorial draft.
Selected by Kansas City in 2nd round (34th player selected) of 1984 NFL draft.
Signed by Kansas City Chiefs, July 12, 1984.
Released by Kansas City Chiefs, September 7, 1987; awarded on waivers to Buffalo Bills, September 8, 1987.

| | | —INTERCEPTIONS— | | | |
Year Club	G.	No.	Yds.	Avg.	TD.
1984—Kansas City NFL	16	2	54	27.0	1
1985—Kansas City NFL	16	1	21	21.0	0
1986—Kansas City NFL	16	1	20	20.0	0
1987—Buffalo NFL	12	2	4	2.0	0
Pro Totals—4 Years	60	6	99	16.5	1

Additional pro statistics: Recovered one fumble, 1985 and 1986; returned one kickoff for 14 yards and recovered two fumbles, 1987.

WAYNE R. RADLOFF

Center—Atlanta Falcons

Born May 17, 1961, at London, England.
Height, 6.05. Weight, 277.
High School—Winter Park, Fla.
Attended University of Georgia.

Named center on THE SPORTING NEWS USFL All-Star Team, 1984.
Selected by Michigan in 2nd round (15th player selected) of 1983 USFL draft.
Signed by Michigan Panthers, January 22, 1983.
On developmental squad, April 4 through April 9, 1983; activated, April 10, 1983.
Not protected an merger of Michigan Panthers and Oakland Invaders; not selected in USFL dispersal draft, December 6, 1984.
Signed as free agent by Atlanta Falcons, March 1, 1985.
On developmental squad for 1 game with Michigan Panthers in 1983.
Michigan USFL, 1983 and 1984; Atlanta NFL, 1985 through 1987.
Games: 1983 (17), 1984 (18), 1985 (16), 1986 (16), 1987 (12). Total USFL—35. Total NFL—44. Total Pro—79.
USFL statistics: Recovered one fumble, 1983.
NFL statistics: Recovered one fumble for minus three yards, 1986.
Played in USFL Championship Game following 1983 season.

THOMAS MICHAEL RAFFERTY

(Tom)

Center—Dallas Cowboys

Born August 2, 1954, at Syracuse, N. Y.
Height, 6.03. Weight, 264.
High School—Manlius, N. Y.
Received bachelor of science degree in physical education from Penn State University;
attending University of Dallas for master's degree.

Selected by Dallas in 4th round (119th player selected) of 1976 NFL draft.
Dallas NFL, 1976 through 1987.
Games: 1976 (13), 1977 (14), 1978 (16), 1979 (16), 1980 (16), 1981 (16), 1982 (9), 1983 (16), 1984 (16), 1985 (16), 1986 (16), 1987 (12). Total—176.
Pro statistics: Fumbled once, 1977; recovered one fumble, 1979, 1981, 1986 and 1987; recovered one fumble for six yards, 1980; fumbled twice for minus 30 yards, 1981; recovered two fumbles, 1982, 1984 and 1985; caught one pass for eight yards, 1983.
Played in NFC Championship Game following 1977, 1978 and 1980 through 1982 seasons.
Played in NFL Championship Game following 1977 and 1978 seasons.

GREGG ADAM RAKOCZY

(Name pronounced Ra-KOZE-e.)

Offensive Tackle—Cleveland Browns

Born May 18, 1965, at Medford Lakes, N.J.
Height, 6.06. Weight, 290.
High School—Medford, N.J., Shawnee.
Attended University of Miami (Fla.).
Selected by Cleveland in 2nd round (32nd player selected) of 1987 NFL draft.
Signed by Cleveland Browns, July 29, 1987.
Cleveland NFL, 1987.
Games: 1987 (12).
Played in AFC Championship Game following 1987 season.

THOMAS LLOYD RAMSEY

(Tom)

Quarterback—New England Patriots

Born July 9, 1961, at Encino, Calif.
Height, 6.01. Weight, 188.
High School—Granada Hills, Calif., Kennedy.
Received bachelor of science degree in sociology
from University of California at Los Angeles in 1983.
Selected by Los Angeles in 5th round (49th player selected) of 1983 USFL draft.
Signed by Los Angeles Express, February 10, 1983.
Selected by New England in 10th round (267th player selected) of 1983 NFL draft.
On developmental squad, July 2 through remainder of 1983 season.
Traded by Los Angeles Express to Oakland Invaders for 3rd round pick in 1985 draft, March 29, 1984.
On developmental squad, March 30 through April 28, 1984; activated, April 29, 1984.
Released by Oakland Invaders, July 17, 1984; signed by New England Patriots, July 25, 1984.
On injured reserve with thumb injury, August 21 through entire 1984 season.
Released by New England Patriots, September 11, 1985; re-signed by Patriots, October 17, 1985.
On developmental squad for 1 game with Los Angeles Express in 1983.
On developmental squad for 4 games with Oakland Invaders in 1984.
Active for 11 games with New England Patriots in 1985; did not play.

		PASSING							RUSHING				TOTAL		
Year Club	G.	Att.	Cmp.	Pct.	Gain	T.P.	P.I.	Avg.	Att.	Yds.	Avg.	TD.	TD.	Pts.	F.
1983—Los Angeles USFL	17	307	160	52.1	1975	13	14	6.43	28	80	2.9	1	1	6	4
1984—L.A. (5)-Oak. (5) USFL	10	91	54	59.3	512	2	7	5.63	8	38	4.8	0	0	0	1
1986—New England NFL	5	3	1	33.3	7	0	0	2.33	1	—6	—6.0	0	0	0	0
1987—New England NFL	9	134	71	53.0	898	6	6	6.70	13	75	5.8	1	1	6	4
USFL Totals—2 Years	27	398	214	53.8	2487	15	21	6.25	36	118	3.3	1	1	6	5
NFL Totals—3 Years	14	137	72	52.6	905	6	6	6.61	14	69	4.9	1	1	6	4
Pro Totals—5 Years	41	535	286	53.5	3392	21	27	6.34	50	187	3.7	2	2	12	9

USFL Quarterback Rating Points: 1983 (67.1), 1984 (50.3). Total—63.6.
NFL Quarterback Rating Points: 1986 (42.4), 1987 (70.4). Total—69.8.
Additional pro statistics: Recovered one fumble, 1987.
Member of New England Patriots for AFC Championship Game following 1985 season; did not play.
Member of New England Patriots for NFL Championship Game following 1985 season; did not play.

ERVIN RANDLE

Linebacker—Tampa Bay Buccaneers

Born October 12, 1962, at Hearne, Tex.
Height, 6.01. Weight, 250.
High School—Hearne, Tex.
Attended Baylor University.
Selected by San Antonio in 1985 USFL territorial draft.
Selected by Tampa Bay in 3rd round (64th player selected) of 1985 NFL draft.
Signed by Tampa Bay Buccaneers, July 18, 1985.
Tampa Bay NFL, 1985 through 1987.
Games: 1985 (16), 1986 (16), 1987 (12). Total—44.
Pro statistics: Intercepted one pass for no yards and recovered two fumbles, 1985; recovered one fumble, 1987.

RANDY ROBERT RASMUSSEN

Center-Guard—Minnesota Vikings

Born September 27, 1960, at Minneapolis, Minn.
Height, 6.01. Weight, 253.
High School—St. Paul, Minn., Irondale.
Received bachelor of applied studies degree in business and marketing from
University of Minnesota in 1984.
Selected by Chicago in 12th round (241st player selected) of 1984 USFL draft.
Selected by Pittsburgh in 8th round (220th player selected) of 1984 NFL draft.
Signed by Pittsburgh Steelers, June 18, 1984.
On injured reserve with knee injury, August 20 through October 2, 1985; activated after clearing procedural waivers, October 4, 1985.
On injured reserve with knee injury, October 24 through remainder of 1986 season.

Released by Pittsburgh Steelers, September 7, 1987; signed as free agent by Minnesota Vikings, October 20, 1987.
Released by Minnesota Vikings, October 21, 1987; re-signed by Vikings, November 16, 1987.
Pittsburgh NFL, 1984 through 1986; Minnesota NFL, 1987.
Games: 1984 (16), 1985 (11), 1986 (4), 1987 (5). Total—36.
Played in AFC Championship Game following 1984 season.
Played in NFC Championship Game following 1987 season.

THOMAS DEAN RATHMAN
(Tom)
Fullback—San Francisco 49ers

Born October 7, 1962, at Grand Island, Neb.
Height, 6.01. Weight, 232.
High School—Grand Island, Neb.
Attended University of Nebraska.

Selected by Memphis in 1986 USFL territorial draft.
Selected by San Francisco in 3rd round (56th player selected) of 1986 NFL draft.
Signed by San Francisco 49ers, July 16, 1986.

Year Club	G.	Att.	Yds.	Avg.	TD.	P.C.	Yds.	Avg.	TD.	TD.	Pts.	F.
		RUSHING				PASS RECEIVING				TOTAL		
1986—San Francisco NFL	16	33	138	4.2	1	13	121	9.3	0	1	6	0
1987—San Francisco NFL	12	62	257	4.1	1	30	329	11.0	3	4	24	1
Pro Totals—2 Years	28	95	395	4.2	2	43	450	10.5	3	5	30	1

Additional pro statistics: Returned three kickoffs for 66 yards, 1986; returned two kickoffs for 37 yards, 1987.

GARY PHILLIP REASONS
Linebacker—New York Giants

Born February 18, 1962, at Crowley, Tex.
Height, 6.04. Weight, 234.
High School—Crowley, Tex.
Received bachelor of science degree in business administration
from Northwestern State University.

Selected by New Jersey in 2nd round (26th player selected) of 1984 USFL draft.
USFL rights traded by New Jersey Generals to Tampa Bay Bandits for rights to linebacker Jim LeClair, January 30, 1984.
Selected by New York Giants in 4th round (105th player selected) of 1984 NFL draft.
Signed by New York Giants, July 12, 1984.
Granted free agency, February 1, 1987; re-signed by Giants, September 10, 1987.
Granted roster exemption, September 10 through September 20, 1987; activated, September 21, 1987.

Year Club	G.	No.	Yds.	Avg.	TD.
		INTERCEPTIONS			
1984—N.Y. Giants NFL	16	2	26	13.0	0
1985—N.Y. Giants NFL	16	1	10	10.0	0
1986—N.Y. Giants NFL	16	2	28	14.0	0
1987—N.Y. Giants NFL	10			None	
Pro Totals—4 Years	58	5	64	12.8	0

Additional pro statistics: Recovered three fumbles, 1984.
Played in NFC Championship Game following 1986 season.
Played in NFL Championship Game following 1986 season.

BARRY REDDEN
Fullback—San Diego Chargers

Born July 21, 1960, at Sarasota, Fla.
Height, 5.10. Weight, 219.
High School—Sarasota, Fla.
Received degree in psychology from University of Richmond in 1982.

Selected by Los Angeles Rams in 1st round (14th player selected) of 1982 NFL draft.
Granted free agency, February 1, 1987; re-signed by Rams and traded to San Diego Chargers for running back Buford McGee, 2nd round pick in 1988 draft and conditional 4th or 5th round pick in 1989 draft, June 9, 1987.

Year Club	G.	Att.	Yds.	Avg.	TD.	P.C.	Yds.	Avg.	TD.	TD.	Pts.	F.
		RUSHING				PASS RECEIVING				TOTAL		
1982—Los Angeles Rams NFL	9	8	24	3.0	0	4	16	4.0	0	0	0	2
1983—Los Angeles Rams NFL	15	75	372	5.0	2	4	30	7.5	0	2	12	2
1984—Los Angeles Rams NFL	14	45	247	5.5	0	4	39	9.8	0	0	0	0
1985—Los Angeles Rams NFL	14	87	380	4.4	0	16	162	10.1	0	0	0	1
1986—Los Angeles Rams NFL	15	110	467	4.2	4	28	217	7.8	1	5	30	1
1987—San Diego NFL	12	11	36	3.3	0	7	46	6.6	0	0	0	0
Pro Totals—6 Years	79	336	1526	4.5	6	63	510	8.1	1	7	42	6

Year Club	G.	No.	Yds.	Avg.	TD.
		KICKOFF RETURNS			
1982—L.A. Rams NFL	9	22	502	22.8	0
1983—L.A. Rams NFL	15	19	358	18.8	0
1984—L.A. Rams NFL	14	23	530	23.0	0
1985—L.A. Rams NFL	14			None	

Year Club	G.	No.	Yds.	Avg.	TD.
		KICKOFF RETURNS			
1986—L.A. Rams NFL	15			None	
1987—San Diego NFL	12			None	
Pro Totals—6 Years	79	64	1390	21.7	0

Additional pro statistics: Recovered one fumble, 1982.
Played in NFC Championship Game following 1985 season.

ANDRE DARNELL REED
Wide Receiver—Buffalo Bills

Born January 29, 1964, at Allentown, Pa.
Height, 6.00. Weight, 190.
High School—Allentown Pa., Louis E. Dieruff.
Attended Kutztown State College.

Selected by Orlando in 3rd round (39th player selected) of 1985 USFL draft.
Selected by Buffalo in 4th round (86th player selected) of 1985 NFL draft.
Signed by Buffalo Bills, July 19, 1985.

			—PASS RECEIVING—			
Year	Club	G.	P.C.	Yds.	Avg.	TD.
1985—Buffalo NFL		16	48	637	13.3	4
1986—Buffalo NFL		15	53	739	13.9	7
1987—Buffalo NFL		12	57	752	13.2	5
Pro Totals—3 Years		43	158	2128	13.5	16

Additional pro statistics: Rushed three times for minus one yard and a touchdown, returned five punts for 12 yards, recovered two fumbles and fumbled once, 1985; rushed three times for minus eight yards, recovered two fumbles for two yards and fumbled twice, 1986; rushed once for one yard, 1987.

DOUG REED
Defensive End—Los Angeles Rams

Born July 16, 1960, at San Diego, Calif.
Height, 6.03. Weight, 250.
High School—San Diego, Calif., Abraham Lincoln.
Attended San Diego City College and San Diego State University.

Selected by Los Angeles in 17th round (193rd player selected) of 1983 USFL draft.
Selected by Los Angeles Rams in 4th round (111th player selected) of 1983 NFL draft.
Signed by Los Angeles Rams, June 3, 1983.
On injured reserve with leg injury, August 29 through entire 1983 season.
Los Angeles Rams NFL, 1984 through 1987.
Games: 1984 (9), 1985 (16), 1986 (16), 1987 (12). Total—53.
Pro statistics: Recovered one fumble for two yards, 1984.
Played in NFC Championship Game following 1985 season.

KEN REEVES
Offensive Tackle-Guard—Philadelphia Eagles

Born October 4, 1961, at Pittsburg, Tex.
Height, 6.05. Weight, 270.
High School—Pittsburg, Tex.
Attended Texas A&M University.

Selected by Houston in 1985 USFL territorial draft.
Selected by Philadelphia in 6th round (156th player selected) of 1985 NFL draft.
Signed by Philadelphia Eagles, July 23, 1985.
Philadelphia NFL, 1985 through 1987.
Games: 1985 (15), 1986 (15), 1987 (10). Total—40.
Pro statistics: Recovered one fumble, 1985 and 1986; ran one yard with lateral on kickoff return, 1987.

FRANK MICHAEL REICH

Name pronounced Rike.

Quarterback—Buffalo Bills

Born December 4, 1961, at Freeport, N.Y.
Height, 6.03. Weight, 208.
High School—Lebanon, Pa., Cedar Crest.
Received bachelor of science degree in finance from University of Maryland in 1984.

Selected by Tampa Bay in 1985 USFL territorial draft.
Selected by Buffalo in 3rd round (57th player selected) of 1985 NFL draft.
Signed by Buffalo Bills, August 1, 1985.
On injured reserve with Achilles heel injury, September 3 to December 5, 1985; activated, December 6, 1985.
Active for 12 games with Buffalo Bills in 1987; did not play.

			—————PASSING—————							—RUSHING—			—TOTAL—		
Year	Club	G.	Att.	Cmp.	Pct.	Gain	T.P.	P.I.	Avg.	Att.	Yds.	Avg.	TD.	TD.	Pts.	F.
1985—Buffalo NFL		1	1	1	100.0	19	0	0	19.00	None				0	0	0
1986—Buffalo NFL		3	19	9	47.4	104	0	2	5.47	1	0	0.0	0	0	0	1
Pro Totals—3 Years		4	20	10	50.0	123	0	2	6.15	1	0	0.0	0	0	0	1

Quarterback Rating Points: 1985 (118.8), 1986 (24.8). Total—29.8

MIKE REICHENBACH
Linebacker—Philadelphia Eagles

Born September 14, 1961, at Fort Meade, Md.
Height, 6.02. Weight, 230.
High School—Bethlehem, Pa., Liberty.
Attended East Stroudsburg University.

Signed as free agent by Philadelphia Eagles, June 18, 1984.

Released by Philadelphia Eagles, August 27, 1984; re-signed by Eagles, September 25, 1984.
Philadelphia NFL, 1984 through 1987.
Games: 1984 (12), 1985 (16), 1986 (16), 1987 (11). Total—55.
Pro statistics: Recovered two fumbles, 1984; intercepted one pass for 10 yards, 1985.

ALAN DeWITT REID
Running Back—Philadelphia Eagles
Born September 6, 1960, at Wruzburg, Germany.
Height, 5.08. Weight, 197.
High School—El Paso, Tex.
Attended Los Angeles Pierce Junior College, Texas Christian University and University of Minnesota.

Selected by Memphis in 19th round (382nd player selected) of 1984 USFL draft.
Signed by Memphis Showboats, January 19, 1984.
Released by Memphis Showboats, February 21, 1985; signed as free agent by Montreal Concordes, March 10, 1985.
Released by Montreal Alouettes, August 18, 1986; signed as free agent by Philadelphia Eagles, February 9, 1987.
On injured reserve with pulled thigh muscle, August 26 through November 22, 1987; activated, November 23, 1987.

Year Club	G.	RUSHING				PASS RECEIVING				TOTAL		
		Att.	Yds.	Avg.	TD.	P.C.	Yds.	Avg.	TD.	TD.	Pts.	F.
1984—Memphis USFL	17	191	723	3.8	3	37	302	8.2	2	5	30	5
1985—Montreal CFL	10	75	373	5.0	3	56	465	8.3	0	3	18	2
1986—Montreal CFL	7	46	191	4.2	1	24	188	7.8	0	1	6	2
1987—Philadelphia NFL	1	None				None				0	0	0
USFL Totals—1 Year	17	191	723	3.8	3	37	302	8.2	2	5	30	5
CFL Totals—2 Years	17	121	564	4.7	4	80	653	8.2	0	4	24	4
NFL Totals—1 Year	1	0	0	0.0	0	0	0	0.0	0	0	0	0
Pro Totals—4 Years	35	312	1287	4.1	7	117	955	8.2	2	9	54	9

Additional CFL statistics: Returned six kickoffs for 92 yards, 1984; returned three punts for four yards, 1985.
Additional NFL statistics: Returned four kickoffs for 58 yards, 1987.

MICHAEL EDWARD REID
Linebacker—Atlanta Falcons
Born June 25, 1964, at Albany, Ga.
Height, 6.02. Weight, 226.
High School—Albany, Ga., Dougherty.
Attended University of Wisconsin.

Selected by Atlanta in 7th round (181st player selected) of 1987 NFL draft.
Signed by Atlanta Falcons, July 26, 1987.
Atlanta NFL, 1987.
Games: 1987 (11).

BRUCE MICHAEL REIMERS
Offensive Tackle—Cincinnati Bengals
Born September 18, 1960, at Algona, Ia.
Height, 6.07. Weight, 280.
High School—Humboldt, Ia.
Attended Iowa State University.

Selected by Los Angeles in 7th round (136th player selected) of 1984 USFL draft.
Selected by Cincinnati in 8th round (204th player selected) of 1984 NFL draft.
Signed by Cincinnati Bengals, June 20, 1984.
Cincinnati NFL, 1984 through 1987.
Games: 1984 (15), 1985 (14), 1986 (16), 1987 (10). Total—55.
Pro statistics: Recovered one fumble, 1987.

JOHNNY REMBERT
Linebacker—New England Patriots
Born January 19, 1961, at Hollandale, Miss.
Height, 6.03. Weight, 234.
High School—Arcadia, Fla., DeSoto.
Attended Cowley County Community College and Clemson University.

Selected by Washington in 1983 USFL territorial draft.
Selected by New England in 4th round (101st player selected) of 1983 NFL draft.
Signed by New England Patriots, May 16, 1983.
On injured reserve with knee injury, August 28 through November 2, 1984; activated, November 3, 1984.
New England NFL, 1983 through 1987.
Games: 1983 (15), 1984 (7), 1985 (16), 1986 (16), 1987 (11). Total—65.
Pro statistics: Recovered one fumble, 1983; recovered three fumbles for nine yards (including one in end zone for a touchdown), 1985; intercepted one pass for 37 yards, recovered three fumbles (including one in end zone for a touchdown) and returned three kickoffs for 27 yards, 1986; intercepted one pass for one yard, 1987.
Played in AFC Championship Game following 1985 season.
Played in NFL Championship Game following 1985 season.

—DID YOU KNOW—
That there were no fumbles in last year's National Football Conference championship game?

DANIEL LLOYD REMSBERG
(Dan)
Offensive Tackle—Denver Broncos
Born April 7, 1962, at Temple, Tex.
Height, 6.06. Weight, 275.
High School—Temple, Tex.
Received degree in Pre-law and accounting from Abilene Christian University in 1986.

Selected by Houston in 4th round (53rd player selected) of 1985 USFL draft.
Selected by San Diego in 9th round (252nd player selected) of 1985 NFL draft.
Signed by San Diego Chargers, July 10, 1986.
Released by San Diego Chargers, August 14, 1986; signed as free agent by Denver Broncos, December 30, 1985.
Denver NFL, 1986 and 1987.
Games: 1986 (16), 1987 (5). Total—21.
Played in AFC Championship Game following 1986 season.
Played in NFL Championship Game following 1986 season.
Member of Denver Broncos for NFL Championship Game following 1987 season; inactive.

MICHAEL RAY RENFRO
(Mike)
Wide Receiver—Dallas Cowboys
Born June 19, 1955, at Fort Worth, Tex.
Height, 6.00. Weight, 184.
High School—Fort Worth, Tex., Arlington Heights.
Received degree in business management from Texas Christian University.
Son of Ray Renfro, back with Cleveland Browns, 1952 through 1963; and
assistant coach with Detroit Lions and Dallas Cowboys, 1965 and 1968 through 1972.

Selected by Houston in 4th round (98th player selected) of 1978 NFL draft.
On injured reserve with knee injury, December 5 through remainder of 1978 season.
On injured reserve with pulled hamstring, November 27 through remainder of 1981 season.
On injured reserve with hepatitis, August 30 through September 29, 1983; activated, September 30, 1983.
On injured reserve with knee injury, November 28 through remainder of 1983 season.
Traded with 2nd round pick in 1984 draft and 5th round pick in 1985 draft by Houston Oilers to Dallas Cowboys for wide receiver Butch Johnson and 2nd round pick in 1984 draft, April 13, 1984.
On injured reserve with separated shoulder, September 8 through October 3, 1986; activated, October 4, 1986.
Crossed picket line during players' strike, October 2, 1987.

		—PASS RECEIVING—				
Year	Club	G.	P.C.	Yds.	Avg.	TD.
1978—Houston NFL		14	26	339	13.0	2
1979—Houston NFL		15	16	323	20.2	2
1980—Houston NFL		16	35	459	13.1	1
1981—Houston NFL		12	39	451	11.6	1
1982—Houston NFL		9	21	295	14.0	1
1983—Houston NFL		9	23	316	13.7	2
1984—Dallas NFL		16	35	583	16.7	2
1985—Dallas NFL		16	60	955	15.9	8
1986—Dallas NFL		12	22	325	14.8	3
1987—Dallas NFL		14	46	662	14.4	4
Pro Totals—10 Years		133	323	4708	14.6	28

Additional pro statistics: Rushed once for nine yards, 1978; fumbled once, 1978, 1979, 1983 and 1987; rushed once for 12 yards, 1980; recovered two fumbles for 12 yards and fumbled twice, 1981; rushed once for three yards, 1983; attempted two passes with one completion for 49 yards and a touchdown, 1984; recovered one fumble and fumbled three times, 1985; attenpted one pass with one completion for 23 yards, 1986.
Played in AFC Championship Game following 1979 season.

WILLIAM ARTHUR RENNER JR.
(Bill)
Punter—New York Jets
Born May 23, 1959, at Quantico, Va.
Height, 6.00. Weight, 198.
High School—Springfield, Va., Robert E. Lee.
Received bachelor of science degree in education from Virginia Tech in 1982;
and received master's degree in education from Virginia Tech in 1983.

Signed as free agent by Minnesota Vikings, June 6, 1983.
Released by Minnesota Vikings, August 22, 1983; signed as free agent by Pittsburgh Maulers, September 10, 1983.
Released by Pittsburgh Maulers, December 16, 1983; signed as free agent by Chicago Bears, February 6, 1984.
Released by Chicago Bears, August 14, 1984; signed as free agent by Green Bay Packers, May 27, 1986.
Released by Green Bay Packers, August 25, 1986; re-signed by Packers, December 5, 1986.
Released by Green Bay Packers, August 17, 1987; re-signed as replacement player by Packers, September 25, 1987.
Released by Green Bay Packers, October 20, 1987; signed as free agent by New York Jets, March 30, 1988.

		—PUNTING—			
Year	Club	G.	No.	Avg.	Blk.
1986—Green Bay NFL		3	15	41.5	*3
1987—Green Bay NFL		3	20	35.6	0
Pro Totals—2 Years		6	35	38.1	3

Additional pro statistics: Rushed once for no yards, 1986.

FUAD REVEIZ
Placekicker—Miami Dolphins

Born February 24, 1963, at Bogota, Columbia.
Height, 5.11. Weight, 217.
High School—Miami, Fla., Sunset.
Attended University of Tennessee.
Brother of Carlos Reveiz, placekicker with New England Patriots.

Selected by Memphis in 1985 USFL territorial draft.
Selected by Miami in 7th round (195th player selected) of 1985 NFL draft.
Signed by Miami Dolphins, July 20, 1985.

		—————PLACE KICKING—————					
Year	Club	G.	XP.	XPM.	FG.	FGA.	Pts.
1985—Miami NFL		16	50	2	22	27	116
1986—Miami NFL		16	*52	3	14	22	94
1987—Miami NFL		11	28	2	9	11	55
Pro Totals—3 Years		43	130	7	45	60	265

Played in AFC Championship Game following 1985 season.

DERRICK SCOTT REYNOLDS
(Ricky)
Defesive Back—Tampa Bay Buccaneers

Born January 19, 1965, at Sacramento, Calif.
Height, 5.11. Weight, 182.
High School—Sacramento, Calif., Luther Burbank.
Attended Washington State University.
Cousin of Jerry Royster, infielder with New York Yankees.

Selected by Tampa Bay in 2nd round (36th player selected) of 1987 NFL draft.
Signed by Tampa Bay Buccaneers, July 18, 1987.
Tampa Bay NFL, 1987.
Games. 1987 (12).

EDWARD RANNELL REYNOLDS
(Ed)
Linebacker—New England Patriots

Born September 23, 1961, at Stuttgart, West Germany.
Height, 6.05. Weight, 242.
High School—Ridgeway, Va., Drewry Mason.
Received bachelor of science degree in elementary education from University of Virginia in 1983.

Signed as free agent by New England Patriots, May 10, 1983.
Released by New England Patriots, August 29, 1983; re-signed by Patriots, September 28, 1983.
Released by New England Patriots, August 27, 1984; re-signed by Patriots, August 28, 1984.
On injured reserve with knee injury, September 11 through October 11, 1985; activated, October 12, 1985.
New England NFL, 1983 through 1987.
Games: 1983 (12), 1984 (16), 1985 (16), 1986 (16), 1987 (12). Total—68.
Pro statistics: Recovered two fumbles, 1983; recovered one fumble, 1986.
Played in AFC Championship Game following 1985 season.
Played in NFL Championship Game following 1985 season.

ALLEN TROY RICE
Running Back—Minnesota Vikings

Born April 5, 1962, at Houston, Tex.
Height, 5.10. Weight, 204.
High School—Houston, Tex., Klein.
Attended Wharton County Junior College, Ranger Junior College and Baylor University.

Selected by Houston in 1984 USFL territorial draft.
Selected by Minnesota in 5th round (140th player selected) of 1984 NFL draft.
Signed by Minnesota Vikings, July 20, 1984.

			————RUSHING————				PASS RECEIVING				—TOTAL—		
Year	Club	G.	Att.	Yds.	Avg.	TD.	P.C.	Yds.	Avg.	TD.	TD.	Pts.	F.
1984—Minnesota NFL		14	14	58	4.1	1	4	59	14.8	1	2	12	1
1985—Minnesota NFL		14	31	104	3.4	3	9	61	6.8	1	4	24	0
1986—Minnesota NFL		14	73	220	3.0	2	30	391	13.0	3	5	30	5
1987—Minnesota NFL		12	51	131	2.6	1	19	201	10.6	1	2	12	1
Pro Totals—4 Years		54	169	513	3.0	7	62	712	11.5	6	13	78	7

Additional pro statistics: Returned three kickoffs for 34 yards, 1984; recovered two fumbles, 1984 and 1986; returned four kickoffs for 70 yards, 1985; recovered one fumble, 1985 and 1987; returned five kickoffs for 88 yards, returned one punt for no yards and attempted one pass with no completions, 1986; returned two kickoffs for 29 yards, 1987.
Played in NFC Championship Game following 1987 season.

—DID YOU KNOW—

That the Pittsburgh Steelers failed to put a linebacker in the Pro Bowl for the first time since 1970 last season?

JERRY LEE RICE
Wide Receiver—San Francisco 49ers
Born October 13, 1962, at Starkville, Miss.
Height, 6.02. Weight, 200.
High School—Crawford, Miss., B.L. Moor.
Attended Mississippi Valley State University.

Named THE SPORTING NEWS NFL Player of the Year, 1987.
Named to THE SPORTING NEWS NFL All-Star Team, 1986 and 1987.
Named as wide receiver on THE SPORTING NEWS College All-America Team, 1984.
Selected by Birmingham in 1st round (1st player selected) of 1985 USFL draft.
Selected by San Francisco in 1st round (16th player selected) of 1985 NFL draft.
Signed by San Francisco 49ers, July 23, 1985.

| | | —RUSHING— | | | | PASS RECEIVING | | | | —TOTAL— | |
Year	Club	G.	Att.	Yds.	Avg.	TD.	P.C.	Yds.	Avg.	TD.	TD.	Pts.	F.
1985—San Francisco NFL		16	6	26	4.3	1	49	927	18.9	3	4	24	1
1986—San Francisco NFL		16	10	72	7.2	1	86	*1570	18.3	*15	16	96	2
1987—San Francisco NFL		12	8	51	6.4	1	65	1078	16.6	*22	*23	*138	2
Pro Totals—3 Years		44	24	149	6.2	3	200	3575	17.9	40	43	258	5

Additional pro statistics: Returned one kickoff for six yards, 1985; attempted two passes with one completion for 16 yards and recovered three fumbles, 1986; recovered one fumble, 1987.
Played in Pro Bowl (NFL All-Star Game) following 1986 and 1987 seasons.

ERIC RICHARDSON
Wide Receiver—San Francisco 49ers
Born April 18, 1962, at San Francisco, Calif.
Height, 6.01. Weight, 183.
High School—Novato, Calif.
Attended Monterey Peninsula College and San Jose State University.

Selected by Oakland in 1984 USFL territorial draft.
Selected by Buffalo in 2nd round (41st player selected) of 1984 NFL draft.
Signed by Buffalo Bills, May 17, 1984.
On injured reserve with knee injury, August 28 through entire 1984 season.
Released by Buffalo Bills, September 8, 1987; signed as free agent by San Francisco 49ers, March 10, 1988.

| | | —PASS RECEIVING— | | | |
Year	Club	G.	P.C.	Yds.	Avg.	TD.
1985—Buffalo NFL		16	12	201	16.8	0
1986—Buffalo NFL		14	3	49	16.3	0
Pro Totals—2 Years		30	15	250	16.7	0

Additional pro statistics: Returned three kickoffs for 69 yards, 1985; returned six kickoffs for 123 yards and returned one punt for no yards, recovered one fumble and fumbled four times, 1986.

GREGORY LAMAR RICHARDSON
(Greg)
Wide Receiver-Kick Returner—Minnesota Vikings
Born October 6, 1964, at Mobile, Ala.
Height, 5.07. Weight, 172.
High School—Mobile, Ala., Williamson.
Attended University of Alabama.

Selected by Minnesota in 6th round (156th player selected) of 1987 NFL draft.
Signed by Minnesota Vikings, July 30, 1987.
Minnesota NFL, 1987.
Games: 1987 (2).
Pro statistics: Returned four kickoffs for 76 yards, returned four punts for 19 yards and fumbled once, 1987.

MICHAEL CALVIN RICHARDSON
(Mike)
Cornerback—Chicago Bears
Born May 23, 1961, at Compton, Calif.
Height, 6.00. Weight, 188.
High School—Compton, Calif.
Attended Arizona State University.

Named as defensive back on THE SPORTING NEWS College All-America Team, 1981 and 1982.
Selected by Arizona in 1983 USFL territorial draft.
Selected by Chicago in 2nd round (33rd player selected) of 1983 NFL draft.
Signed by Chicago Bears, July 20, 1983.

| | | —INTERCEPTIONS— | | | |
Year	Club	G.	No.	Yds.	Avg.	TD.
1983—Chicago NFL		16	5	9	1.8	0
1984—Chicago NFL		15	2	7	3.5	0
1985—Chicago NFL		14	4	174	43.5	*1
1986—Chicago NFL		16	7	69	9.9	0
1987—Chicago NFL		11		None		
Pro Totals—5 Years		72	18	259	14.4	1

Additional pro statistics: Returned one kickoff for 17 yards and recovered two fumbles for seven yards, 1983;

recovered one fumble, 1984; recovered one fumble for four yards and fumbled once, 1985; fumbled three times for minus five yards, 1986.
Played in NFC Championship Game following 1984 and 1985 seasons.
Played in NFL Championship Game following 1985 season.

ROBBERT LEE RIDDICK
(Robb)
Running Back—Buffalo Bills
Born April 26, 1957, at Quakertown, Pa.
Height, 6.00. Weight, 195.
High School—Perkasie, Pa., Pennridge.
Attended Millersville State College.
Cousin of Will Lewis, cornerback with Seattle Seahawks, Kansas City Chiefs,
Denver Gold and Houston Gamblers, 1980, 1981, 1983 and 1984;
and Tim Lewis, defensive back with Green Bay Packers, 1983 through 1986.
Selected by Buffalo in 9th round (241st player selected) of 1981 NFL draft.
On injured reserve with ankle injury, September 3 through October 16, 1981; activated, October 17, 1981.
On injured reserve with knee injury, September 7 through entire 1982 season.
On injured reserve with knee injury, August 19 through entire 1985 season.
Crossed picket line during players' strike, October 14, 1987.
On injured reserve with broken collarbone, November 13 through remainder of 1987 season.

Year Club	G.	Att.	Yds.	Avg.	TD.	P.C.	Yds.	Avg.	TD.	TD.	Pts.	F.
		——RUSHING——				PASS RECEIVING				—TOTAL—		
1981—Buffalo NFL	10	3	29	9.7	0	None				0	0	1
1983—Buffalo NFL	16	4	18	4.5	0	3	43	14.3	0	0	0	7
1984—Buffalo NFL	16	3	3	1.0	0	23	276	12.0	0	0	0	1
1986—Buffalo NFL	15	150	632	4.2	4	49	468	9.6	1	5	30	8
1987—Buffalo NFL	6	59	221	3.7	5	15	96	6.4	3	8	†50	2
Pro Totals—5 Years	63	219	903	4.1	9	90	883	9.8	4	13	80	19

Year Club	G.	No.	Yds.	Avg.	TD.	No.	Yds.	Avg.TD.
		—PUNT RETURNS—				—KICKOFF RET.—		
1981—Buffalo NFL	10	4	48	12.0	0	14	257	18.4	0
1983—Buffalo NFL	16	42	241	5.7	0	28	568	20.3	0
1984—Buffalo NFL	16	None				None		
1986—Buffalo NFL	15	None				8	200	25.0	0
1987—Buffalo NFL	6	None				7	151	21.6	0
Pro Totals—5 Years	63	46	289	6.3	0	57	1176	20.6	0

†Includes one safety.
Additional pro statistics: Recovered one fumble, 1983 and 1987; attempted one pass with one completion for 35 yards, 1987.

CHRISTOPHER ALAN RIEHM
(Chris)
Offensive Tackle—Los Angeles Raiders
Born April 14, 1961, at Columbus, O.
Height, 6.06. Weight, 275.
High School—Medina, O., Highland.
Attended Ohio State University.
Signed as free agent by Kansas City Chiefs, May 5, 1983.
Released by Kansas City Chiefs after failing physical, May 12, 1983; signed as free agent by Baltimore Colts, July 1, 1983.
Left Baltimore Colts camp voluntarily and released, August 2, 1983.
USFL rights traded by Washington Federals to Oakland Invaders for rights to linebacker Bernard West, October 26, 1983.
Signed by Oakland Invaders, November 6, 1983.
Released by Oakland Invaders, February 13, 1984; re-signed by Invaders, March 30, 1984.
On developmental squad, April 21 through May 3, 1984; activated, May 4, 1984.
Not protected in merger of Oakland Invaders and Michigan Panthers; selected by Houston Gamblers in USFL dispersal draft, December 6, 1984.
On developmental squad, March 3 through March 30, 1985; activated, March 31, 1985.
On developmental squad, June 3 through remainder of 1985 season.
Traded with defensive backs Luther Bradley, Will Lewis, Mike Mitchell and Durwood Roquemore, defensive end Pete Catan, quarterbacks Jim Kelly and Todd Dillon, defensive tackles Tony Fitzpatrick, Van Hughes and Hosea Taylor, running back Sam Harrell, linebackers Andy Hawkins and Ladell Wills, wide receivers Richard Johnson, Scott McGhee, Gerald McNeil, Ricky Sanders and Clarence Verdin, guard Rich Kehr, center Billy Kidd and offensive tackle Tommy Robison by Houston Gamblers to New Jersey Generals for past considerations, March 7, 1986.
Granted free agency when USFL suspended operations, August 7, 1986; signed as free agent by Los Angeles Raiders, August 12, 1986.
On injured reserve with pinched nerve in neck, September 1 through November 29, 1987; activated, November 30, 1987.
Crossed picket line during players' strike, September 24, 1987.
On injured reserve with knee injury, December 3 through remainder of 1987 season.
On developmental squad for 2 games with Oakland Invaders in 1984.
On developmental squad for 8 games with Houston Gamblers in 1985.
Oakland USFL, 1984; Houston USFL, 1985; Los Angeles Raiders NFL, 1986 and 1987.
Games: 1984 (7), 1985 (8), 1986 (12), 1987 (1). Total USFL—15. Total NFL—13. Total Pro—28.
Pro statistics: Caught one pass for eight yards, 1985.

JOHN WILLIAM RIENSTRA
Name pronounced REEN-struh.
Guard—Pittsburgh Steelers
Born March 22, 1963, at Grand Rapids, Mich.
Height, 6.05. Weight, 269.
High School—Bryn Athyn, Pa., Academy of the New Church.
Attended Temple University.
Selected by Baltimore in 1986 USFL territorial draft.
Selected by Pittsburgh in 1st round (9th player selected) of 1986 NFL draft.
Signed by Pittsburgh Steelers, August 12, 1986.
On injured reserve with broken foot, October 9 through remainder of 1986 season.
Pittsburgh NFL, 1986 and 1987.
Games: 1986 (4), 1987 (12). Total—16.

DOUG RIESENBERG
Offensive Tackle—New York Giants
Born July 22, 1965, at Moscow, Ida.
Height, 6.05. Weight, 275.
High School—Moscow, Ida.
Attended University of California at Berkeley.
Selected by New York Giants in 6th round (168th player selected) of 1987 NFL draft.
Signed by New York Giants, July 27, 1987.
New York Giants NFL, 1987.
Games: 1987 (8).

GERALD ANTONIO RIGGS
Running Back—Atlanta Falcons
Born November 6, 1960, at Tullos, La.
Height, 6.01. Weight, 230.
High School—Las Vegas, Nev., Bonanza.
Attended Arizona State University.
Selected by Atlanta in 1st round (9th player selected) of 1982 NFL draft.
On did not report list, August 19 through September 1, 1986.
Granted roster exemption, September 2 through September 5, 1986; activated, September 6, 1986.

		—RUSHING—				PASS RECEIVING				—TOTAL—		
Year Club	G.	Att.	Yds.	Avg.	TD.	P.C.	Yds.	Avg.	TD.	TD.	Pts.	F.
1982—Atlanta NFL	9	78	299	3.8	5	23	185	8.0	0	5	30	1
1983—Atlanta NFL	14	100	437	4.4	8	17	149	8.8	0	8	48	7
1984—Atlanta NFL	15	353	1486	4.2	13	42	277	6.6	0	13	78	11
1985—Atlanta NFL	16	*397	1719	4.3	10	33	267	8.1	0	10	60	0
1986—Atlanta NFL	16	343	1327	3.9	9	24	136	5.7	0	9	54	6
1987—Atlanta NFL	12	203	875	4.3	2	25	199	8.0	0	2	12	4
Pro Totals—6 Years	82	1474	6143	4.2	47	164	1213	7.4	0	47	282	29

		KICKOFF RETURNS			
Year Club	G.	No.	Yds.	Avg.	TD.
1982—Atlanta NFL	9		None		
1983—Atlanta NFL	14	17	330	19.4	0
1984—Atlanta NFL	15		None		
1985—Atlanta NFL	16		None		
1986—Atlanta NFL	16		None		
1987—Atlanta NFL	12		None		
Pro Totals—6 Years	82	17	330	19.4	0

Additional pro statistics: Recovered one fumble, 1983, 1986 and 1987; recovered two fumbles, 1984; attempted one pass with no completions, 1986.
Played in Pro Bowl (NFL All-Star Game) following 1985 through 1987 seasons.

JIM THOMAS RIGGS
Tight End—Cincinnati Bengals
Born September 29, 1963, at Fort Knox, Ky.
Height, 6.05. Weight, 245.
High School—Laurinburg, N.C., Scotland.
Received bachelor of science degree in economics and marketing
from Clemson University in 1987.
Selected by Cincinnati in 4th round (103rd player selected) of 1987 NFL draft.
Signed by Cincinnati Bengals, July 26, 1987.
Cincinnati NFL, 1987.
Games: 1987 (9).

DAVE BRIAN RIMINGTON
Center—Cincinnati Bengals
Born May 22, 1960, at Omaha, Neb.
Height, 6.03. Weight, 288.
High School—Omaha, Neb., South.
Received degree from University of Nebraska.

Outland Trophy winner, 1981 and 1982.
Named as center on THE SPORTING NEWS College All-America Team, 1982.
Selected by Boston in 1983 USFL territorial draft.
Selected by Cincinnati in 1st round (25th player selected) of 1983 NFL draft.
Signed by Cincinnati Bengals, June 6, 1983.
Cincinnati NFL, 1983 through 1987.
Games: 1983 (12), 1984 (16), 1985 (16), 1986 (12), 1987 (8). Total—64.
Pro statistics: Recovered one fumble and fumbled once, 1983; recovered three fumbles, 1985; fumbled twice for minus 23 yards, 1986; fumbled twice for minus 18 yards, 1987.

CODY LEWIS RISIEN
Name pronounced RISE-un.
Offensive Tackle—Cleveland Browns
Born March 22, 1957, at Bryan, Tex.
Height, 6.07. Weight, 280.
High School—Houston, Tex., Cypress Fairbanks.
Received bachelor of science degree in building construction from Texas A&M University in 1982.
Selected by Cleveland in 7th round (183rd player selected) of 1979 NFL draft.
On injured reserve with knee injury, August 27 through entire 1984 season.
On injured reserve with knee injury, September 27 through October 22, 1985; activated, October 23, 1985.
Granted free agency, February 1, 1987; re-signed by Browns, August 31, 1987.
Granted roster exemption, August 31 through September 4, 1987; activated, September 5, 1987.
Crossed picket line during players' strike, October 14, 1987.
Cleveland NFL, 1979 through 1983 and 1985 through 1987.
Games: 1979 (15), 1980 (16), 1981 (16), 1982 (9), 1983 (16), 1985 (12), 1986 (16), 1987 (13). Total—113.
Pro statistics: Recovered two fumbles, 1986.
Played in AFC Championship Game following 1986 and 1987 seasons.
Played in Pro Bowl (NFL All-Star Game) following 1986 and 1987 seasons.

JAMES ALEXANDER RITCHER
(Jim)
Guard—Buffalo Bills
Born May 21, 1958, at Berea, O.
Height, 6.03. Weight, 265.
High School—Granger, O., Highland.
Attended North Carolina State University.
Named as center on THE SPORTING NEWS College All-America Team, 1979.
Outland Trophy winner, 1979.
Selected by Buffalo in 1st round of (16th player selected) 1980 NFL draft.
Buffalo NFL, 1980 through 1987.
Games: 1980, (14), 1981 (14), 1982 (9), 1983 (16), 1984 (14), 1985 (16), 1986 (16), 1987 (12). Total—111.
Pro statistics: Recovered one fumble, 1986.

RONALD EUGENE RIVERA
(Ron)
Linebacker—Chicago Bears
Born January 7, 1962, at Fort Ord, Calif.
Height, 6.03. Weight, 235.
High School—Seaside, Calif.
Attended University of California at Berkeley.
Named as linebacker on THE SPORTING NEWS College All-America Team, 1983.
Selected by Oakland in 1984 USFL territorial draft.
Selected by Chicago in 2nd round (44th player selected) of 1984 NFL draft.
Signed by Chicago Bears, July 2, 1984.
Chicago NFL, 1984 through 1987.
Games: 1984 (15), 1985 (16), 1986 (16), 1987 (12). Total—59.
Pro statistics: Intercepted one pass for four yards and recovered one fumble for five yards and a touchdown, 1985; intercepted two passes for 19 yards, 1987.
Played in NFC Championship Game following 1984 and 1985 seasons.
Played in NFL Championship Game following 1985 season.

JAMES ELBERT ROBBINS
(Tootie)
Offensive Tackle—Phoenix Cardinals
Born June 2, 1958, at Windsor, N.C.
Height, 6.05. Weight, 302.
High School—Bertie County, N.C.
Attended East Carolina University.
Selected by St. Louis in 4th round (90th player selected) of 1982 NFL draft.
Granted free agency, February 1, 1986; re-signed by Cardinals, September 4, 1986.
Granted roster exemption, September 4 through September 11, 1986; activated, September 12, 1986.
Crossed picket line during players' strike, October 7, 1987.
Franchise transferred to Phoenix, March 15, 1988.
St. Louis NFL, 1982 through 1987.

Games: 1982 (9), 1983 (13), 1984 (16), 1985 (12), 1986 (12), 1987 (14). Total—76.
Pro statistics: Recovered one fumble, 1983 and 1985.

RANDY ROBBINS
Safety—Denver Broncos
Born September 14, 1962, at Casa Grande, Ariz.
Height, 6.02. Weight, 189.
High School—Casa Grande, Ariz., Union.
Attended University of Arizona.

Selected by Arizona in 1984 USFL territorial draft.
Selected by Denver in 4th round (89th player selected) of 1984 NFL draft.
Signed by Denver Broncos, July 6, 1984.
On injured reserve with fractured forearm, August 20 through October 15, 1985; activated, October 16, 1985.
On injured reserve with knee injury, December 18, 1987 through January 15, 1988; activated, January 16, 1988.

			—INTERCEPTIONS—		
Year Club	G.	No.	Yds.	Avg.	TD.
1984—Denver NFL	16	2	62	31.0	1
1985—Denver NFL	10	1	3	3.0	0
1986—Denver NFL	16		None		
1987—Denver NFL	10	3	9	3.0	0
Pro Totals—4 Years	52	6	74	12.3	1

Additional pro statistics: Recovered one fumble, 1984; recovered two fumbles, 1986.
Played in AFC Championship Game following 1986 season.
Played in NFL Championship Game following 1986 and 1987 seasons.

LARRY ROBERTS
Defensive End—San Francisco 49ers
Born June 2, 1963, at Dothan, Ala.
Height, 6.03. Weight, 264.
High School—Dothan, Ala., Northview.
Attended University of Alabama.

Selected by Birmingham in 1986 USFL territorial draft.
Selected by San Francisco in 2nd round (39th player selected) of 1986 NFL draft.
Signed by San Francisco 49ers, August 5, 1986.
San Franciso NFL, 1986 and 1987.
Games: 1986 (16), 1987 (11). Total—27.
Pro statistics: Recovered one fumble, 1986.

WILLIAM HAROLD ROBERTS
Offensive Tackle—New York Giants
Born August 5, 1962, at Miami, Fla.
Height, 6.05. Weight, 280.
High School—Miami, Fla., Carol City.
Attended Ohio State University.
Cousin of Reggie Sandilands, wide receiver with Memphis Showboats, 1984.

Selected by New Jersey in 1984 USFL territorial draft.
Selected by New York Giants in 1st round (27th player selected) of 1984 NFL draft.
Signed by New York Giants, June 4, 1984.
On injured reserve with knee injury, July 20 through entire 1985 season.
New York Giants NFL, 1984, 1986 and 1987.
Games: 1984 (11), 1986 (16), 1987 (12). Total—39.
Pro statistics: Recovered one fumble, 1984.
Played in NFC Championship Game following 1986 season.
Played in NFL Championship Game following 1986 season.

EUGENE ROBINSON
Safety—Seattle Seahawks
Born May 28, 1963, at Hartford, Conn.
Height, 6.00. Weight, 186.
High School—Hartford, Conn., Weaver.
Attended Colgate University.

Selected by New Jersey in 1985 USFL territorial draft.
Signed as free agent by Seattle Seahawks, May 15, 1985.

			—INTERCEPTIONS—		
Year Club	G.	No.	Yds.	Avg.	TD.
1985—Seattle NFL	16	2	47	23.5	0
1986—Seattle NFL	16	3	39	13.0	0
1987—Seattle NFL	12	3	75	25.0	0
Pro Totals—3 Years	44	8	161	20.1	0

Additional pro statistics: Returned one kickoff for 10 yards, 1985; recovered three fumbles for six yards, 1986; returned blocked punt eight yards for a touchdown and recovered one fumble, 1987.

FREDDIE ROBINSON
Defensive Back—Indianapolis Colts
Born February 1, 1964, at Mobile, Ala
Height, 6.01. Weight, 191.
High School—Mobile, Ala., Davidson.
Attended University of Alabama.
Selected by Indianapolis in 6th round (142nd player selected) of 1987 NFL draft.
Signed by Indianapolis Colts, July 23, 1987.
Indianapolis NFL, 1987
Game: 1987 (9).
Pro statistics: Intercepted two passes for 86 yards and recovered one fumble, 1987.

GERALD ROBINSON
Defensive End—Minnesota Vikings
Born May 4, 1963, at Tuskegee, Ala.
Height, 6.03. Weight, 261.
High School—Notasulga, Ala.
Attended Auburn University.
Selected by Birmingham in 1986 USFL territorial draft.
Selected by Minnesota in 1st round (14th player selected) of 1986 NFL draft.
Signed by Minnesota Vikings, July 27, 1986.
On injured reserve with broken leg, November 1 through November 27, 1986; activated, November 28, 1986.
On injured reserve with knee injury, October 20 through November 24, 1987; activated, November 25, 1987.
Minnesota NFL, 1986 and 1987.
Games: 1986 (12), 1987 (4). Total—16.

GREGORY LOUIS ROBINSON
(Greg)
Offensive Tackle—San Francisco 49ers
Born December 25, 1962, at Sacramento, Calif.
Height, 6.05. Weight, 285.
High School—Elk Grove, Calif.
Attended University of Nevada at Reno and California State University at Sacramento.
Selected by New England in 5th round (137th player selected) of 1986 NFL draft.
Signed by New England Patriots, July 18, 1986.
Released by New England Patriots, August 26, 1986; signed as free agent by Tampa Bay Buccaneers, October 14, 1986.
Released by Tampa Bay Buccaneers, August 17, 1987; awarded on waivers to Houston Oilers, August 18, 1987.
Released by Houston Oilers, September 1, 1987; signed as free agent replacement player by New England Patriots, September 24, 1987.
Released by New England Patriots, November 7, 1987; signed as free agent by San Francisco 49ers, February 10, 1988.
Tampa Bay NFL, 1986; New England NFL, 1987.
Games: 1986 (3), 1987 (3). Total—6.
Pro statistics: Recovered one fumble, 1987.

JERRY DEWAYNE ROBINSON
Linebacker—Los Angeles Raiders
Born December 18, 1956, at San Francisco, Calif.
Height, 6.02. Weight, 225.
High School—Santa Rosa, Calif., Cardinal Newman.
Attended University of California at Los Angeles.
Named as linebacker on THE SPORTING NEWS College All-America Team, 1978.
Selected by Philadelphia in 1st round (21st player selected) of 1979 NFL draft.
On did not report list, August 20 through September 25, 1985.
Reported and granted roster exemption, September 26 through October 7, 1985; activated, October 8, 1985.
Traded by Philadelphia Eagles to Los Angeles Raiders for 2nd round pick in 1986 draft, September 30, 1985.
Crossed picket line during players' strike, October 14, 1987.

| | | | —INTERCEPTIONS— | | |
Year Club	G.	No.	Yds.	Avg.	TD.
1979—Philadelphia NFL	16		None		
1980—Philadelphia NFL	16	2	13	6.5	0
1981—Philadelphia NFL	15	1	3	3.0	0
1982—Philadelphia NFL	9	3	19	6.3	0
1983—Philadelphia NFL	16		None		
1984—Philadelphia NFL	15		None		
1985—L.A. Raiders NFL	11		None		
1986—L.A. Raiders NFL	16	4	42	10.5	1
1987—L.A. Raiders NFL	12		None		
Pro Totals—9 Years	126	10	77	7.7	1

Pro statistics: Recovered two fumbles, 1979, 1981, 1983 and 1986; recovered four fumbles for 59 yards and one touchdown and fumbled once, 1980; recovered one fumble, 1984; returned blocked punt two yards for a touchdown, 1986.
Played in NFC Championship Game following 1980 season.
Played in NFL Championship Game following 1980 season.
Played in Pro Bowl (NFL All-Star Game) following 1981 season.

MARK LEON ROBINSON
Safety—Tampa Bay Buccaneers
Born September 13, 1962, at Washington, D.C.
Height, 5.11. Weight, 206.
High School—Silver Spring, Md., John F. Kennedy.
Received degree in business administration from Penn State University in 1988.
Brother of Eric Robinson, running back with Washington Federal, 1983 and 1984.
Selected by Philadelphia in 1984 USFL territorial draft.
Selected by Kansas City in 4th round (90th player selected) of 1984 NFL draft.
Signed by Kansas City Chiefs, July 12, 1984.
On injured reserve with sprained ankle, September 3 through October 11, 1985; activated, October 12, 1985.
On injured reserve with thigh injury, October 24 through December 4, 1986; activated, December 5, 1986.
Traded with 4th and 8th round picks in 1988 draft by Kansas City Chiefs to Tampa Bay Buccaneers for quarterback Steve DeBerg, March 30, 1988.
Kansas City NFL, 1984 through 1987.
Games: 1984 (16), 1985 (11), 1986 (9), 1987 (12). Total—48.
Pro statistics: Intercepted one pass for 20 yards and recovered one fumble, 1985; intercepted two passes for 42 yards, returned five kickoffs for 97 yards and recovered two fumbles, 1987.

SHELTON ROBINSON
Linebacker—Detroit Lions
Born September 14, 1960, at Goldsboro, N.C.
Height, 6.02. Weight, 233.
High School—Pikeville, N.C., Aycock.
Received bachelor of science degree in industrial relations from
University of North Carolina in 1982.
Signed as free agent by Seattle Seahawks, April 30, 1982.
Traded by Seattle Seahawks to Detroit Lions for 5th round pick in 1987 draft, September 1, 1986.
Seattle NFL, 1982 through 1985; Detroit NFL, 1986 and 1987.
Games: 1982 (9), 1983 (16), 1984 (16), 1985 (15), 1986 (16), 1987 (12). Total—84.
Pro statistics: Intercepted one pass for 18 yards and recovered four fumbles for 21 yards and two touchdowns, 1983; recovered four fumbles for three yards, 1984; recovered one fumble for six yards, 1985; recovered two fumbles, 1987.
Played in AFC Championship Game following 1983 season.

STACY ROBINSON
Wide Receiver—New York Giants
Born February 19, 1962, at St. Paul, Minn.
Height, 5.11. Weight, 186.
High School—St. Paul, Minn., Central.
Attended Prairie View A&M University and North Dakota State University.
Selected by Portland in 3rd round (34th player selected) of 1985 USFL draft.
Selected by New York Giants in 2nd round (46th player selected) of 1985 NFL draft.
Signed by New York Giants, July 17, 1985.
On injured reserve with broken hand, September 4 through November 29, 1985; activated, November 30, 1985.
On injured reserve with ankle injury, October 18 through November 14, 1986; activated, November 15, 1986.
On injured reserve with hairline fracture in leg, December 1 through remainder of 1987 season.

Year Club	G.	P.C.	—PASS RECEIVING— Yds.	Avg.	TD.
1985—N.Y. Giants NFL	4		None		
1986—N.Y. Giants NFL	12	29	494	17.0	2
1987—N.Y. Giants NFL	5	6	58	9.7	2
Pro Totals—3 Years...........	21	35	552	15.8	4

Additional pro statistics: Fumbled once, 1986.
Played in NFC Championship Game following 1986 season.
Played in NFL Championship Game following 1986 season.

TOMMY L. ROBISON
Offensive Tackle—Green Bay Packers
Born November 17, 1961, at Merkle, Tex.
Height, 6.04. Weight, 290.
High School—Gregory, Tex., Gregory-Portland.
Received bachelor of science degree in business management from Texas A&M University.
Selected by Houston in 1984 USFL territorial draft.
Signed by Houston Gamblers, January 22, 1984.
On developmental squad, June 10 through June 17, 1984; activated, June 18, 1984.
Selected by Cleveland in 2nd round (50th player selected) of 1984 NFL supplemental draft.
Traded with defensive backs Luther Bradley, Will Lewis, Mike Mitchell and Durwood Roquemore, defensive end Pete Catan, quarterbacks Jim Kelly and Todd Dillon, defensive tackles Tony Fitzpatrick, Van Hughes and Hosea Taylor, running back Sam Harrell, linebackers Andy Hawkins and Ladell Wills, wide receivers Richard Johnson, Scott McGhee, Gerald McNeil, Ricky Sanders and Clarence Verdin, guard Rich Kehr, center Billy Kidd and offensive tackle Chris Riehm by Houston Gamblers to New Jersey Generals for past considerations, March 7, 1986.
NFL rights traded with 7th round pick in 1987 draft by Cleveland Browns to Green Bay Packers for wide receiver John Jefferson, September 19, 1985.
Granted free agency when USFL suspended operations, August 7, 1986; signed by Green Bay Packers, April 13, 1987.

On developmental squad for 1 game with Houston Gamblers in 1984.
Houston USFL, 1984 and 1985; Green Bay NFL, 1987.
Games: 1984 (17), 1985 (18), 1987 (3). Total USFL—35. Total Pro—38.

REGINALD HENRY ROBY
(Reggie)
Punter—Miami Dolphins

Born July 30, 1961, at Waterloo, Ia.
Height, 6.02. Weight, 243.
High School—Waterloo, Ia., East.
Attended University of Iowa.
Brother of Mike Roby, first baseman-outfielder in San Francisco Giants' organization, 1967 and 1968.
Named to THE SPORTING NEWS NFL All-Star Team, 1984.
Led NFL in net punting average with 38.1 in 1984 and 37.4 in 1986.
Selected by Chicago in 16th round (187th player selected) of 1983 USFL draft.
Selected by Miami in 6th round (167th player selected) of 1983 NFL draft.
Signed by Miami Dolphins, July 9, 1983.
On injured reserve with knee, ankle and groin injuries, September 16 through October 30, 1987; activated, October 31, 1987.
Crossed picket line during players' strike, October 14, 1987.

| | | ——PUNTING—— | | |
Year Club	G.	No.	Avg.	Blk.
1983—Miami NFL	16	74	43.1	1
1984—Miami NFL	16	51	44.7	0
1985—Miami NFL	16	59	43.7	0
1986—Miami NFL	15	56	44.2	0
1987—Miami NFL	10	32	42.8	0
Pro Totals—5 Years	73	272	43.8	1

Additional pro statistics: Rushed twice for minus eight yards, recovered two fumbles and fumbled twice for minus 11 yards, 1986; rushed once for no yards and recovered one fumble, 1987.
Played in AFC Championship Game following 1984 and 1985 seasons.
Played in NFL Championship Game following 1984 season.
Played in Pro Bowl (NFL All-Star Game) following 1984 season.

CHRIS ROCKINS
Safety—Cleveland Browns

Born May 18, 1962, at Sherman, Tex.
Height, 6.00. Weight, 195.
High School—Sherman, Tex.
Attended Oklahoma State University.
Selected by Oklahoma in 1984 USFL territorial draft.
Selected by Cleveland in 2nd round (48th player selected) of 1984 NFL draft.
Signed by Cleveland Browns, May 17, 1984.

| | | ——INTERCEPTIONS—— | | |
Year Club	G.	No.	Yds.	Avg.TD.
1984—Cleveland NFL	16	1	0	0.0 0
1985—Cleveland NFL	16	1	8	8.0 0
1986—Cleveland NFL	16	2	41	20.5 0
1987—Cleveland NFL	12	2	25	12.5 0
Pro Totals—4 Years	60	6	74	12.3 0

Additional pro statistics: Recovered three fumbles and fumbled once, 1986; recovered one fumble, 1987.
Played in AFC Championship Game following 1986 and 1987 seasons.

MARK RODENHAUSER
Center—Chicago Bears

Born June 1, 1961, at Addision, Ill.
Height, 6.05. Weight, 260.
High School—Addison, Ill., Addison Trail.
Attended Illinois State University.
Signed as free agent by Michigan Panthers, January 15, 1984.
Released by Michigan Panthers, February 13, 1984; signed as free agent by Memphis Showboats, December 3, 1984.
Released by Memphis Showboats, January 22, 1985; signed as free agent by Chicago Bruisers of Arena Football League, June 29, 1987.
Granted free agency, August 15, 1987; signed as replacement player by Chicago Bears, September 24, 1987.
Chicago Bruisers Arena Football, 1987; Chicago NFL, 1987.
Games: 1987 Chicago Arena Football (4), 1987 NFL (9). Total Pro—9.

RODERICK DEL RODGERS
(Known by middle name.)
Running Back—San Francisco 49ers

Born June 22, 1960, at Tacoma, Wash.
Height, 5.10. Weight, 202.
High School—Salinas, Calif., North.
Received bachelor of science degree in consumer education from University of Utah.
Cousin of Anthony Toney, running back with Philadelphia Eagles.

Selected by Green Bay in 3rd round (71st player selected) of 1982 NFL draft.
On injured reserve with neck injury, August 29 through entire 1983 season.
On injured reserve with broken fibula, August 12 through entire 1985 season.
Granted free agency with no qualifying offer, February 1, 1986; signed by San Francisco 49ers, April 8, 1987.
Released by San Francisco 49ers, August 28, 1987; re-signed as replacement player by 49ers, September 24, 1987.
Released by San Francisco 49ers, November 21, 1987; re-signed by 49ers, April 15, 1988.

		—RUSHING—				PASS RECEIVING				—TOTAL—		
Year Club	G.	Att.	Yds.	Avg.	TD.	P.C.	Yds.	Avg.	TD.	TD.	Pts.	F.
1982—Green Bay NFL	9	46	175	3.8	1	3	23	7.7	0	3	18	2
1984—Green Bay NFL	14	25	94	3.8	0	5	56	11.2	0	1	6	1
1987—San Francisco NFL	7	11	46	4.2	1	2	45	22.5	0	1	6	1
Pro Totals—3 Years	30	82	315	3.8	2	10	124	12.4	0	5	30	4

		KICKOFF RETURNS			
Year Club	G.	No.	Yds.	Avg.	TD.
1982—Green Bay NFL	9	20	436	21.8	0
1984—Green Bay NFL	14	39	843	21.6	*1
1987—San Francisco NFL	7	17	358	21.1	0
Pro Totals—3 Years	30	76	1637	21.5	1

Additional pro statistics: Recovered two fumbles in end zone for two touchdowns, 1982.

RUBEN ANGEL RODRIGUEZ
Punter—Seattle Seahawks
Born March 3, 1965, at Visalia, Calif.
Height, 6.02. Weight, 220.
High School—Woodlake, Calif.
Attended College of the Sequoias and University of Arizona.

Selected by Seattle in 5th round (131st player selected) of 1987 NFL draft.
Signed by Seattle Seahawks, July 21, 1987.
Released by Seattle Seahawks, September 7, 1987; re-signed by Seahawks, September 8, 1987.

		—PUNTING—		
Year Club	G.	No.	Avg.	Blk.
1987—Seattle NFL	12	47	40.0	0

Additional pro statistics: Rushed once for no yards, 1987.

GEORGE WASHINGTON ROGERS JR.
Running Back
Born December 8, 1958, at Duluth, Ga.
Height, 6.02. Weight, 229.
High School—Duluth, Ga.
Attended University of South Carolina.

Heisman Trophy winner, 1980.
Named as running back on THE SPORTING NEWS College All-America Team, 1980.
Tied NFL record for most 100-yard games, rushing by rookie (9), 1981.
Named THE SPORTING NEWS NFL Rookie of the Year, 1981.
Named to THE SPORTING NEWS NFL All-Star Team, 1981.
Selected by New Orleans in 1st round (1st player selected) of 1981 NFL draft.
On inactive list, September 19, 1982.
Traded with 5th, 10th and 11th round picks in 1985 draft by New Orleans Saints to Washington Redskins for 1st round pick in 1985 draft, April 26, 1985.
On injured reserve with shoulder injury, September 16 through October 23, 1987; activated, October 24, 1987.
Released by Washington Redskins, May 17, 1988.

		—RUSHING—				PASS RECEIVING				—TOTAL—		
Year Club	G.	Att.	Yds.	Avg.	TD.	P.C.	Yds.	Avg.	TD.	TD.	Pts.	F.
1981—New Orleans NFL	16	*378	*1674	4.4	13	16	126	7.9	0	13	78	13
1982—New Orleans NFL	6	122	535	4.4	3	4	21	5.3	0	3	18	4
1983—New Orleans NFL	13	256	1144	4.5	5	12	69	5.8	0	5	30	8
1984—New Orleans NFL	16	239	914	3.8	2	12	76	6.3	0	2	12	2
1985—Washington NFL	15	231	1093	4.7	7	4	29	7.3	0	7	42	9
1986—Washington NFL	15	303	1203	4.0	*18	3	24	8.0	0	*18	108	7
1987—Washington NFL	11	163	613	3.8	6	4	23	5.8	0	6	36	2
Pro Totals—7 Years	92	1692	7176	4.2	54	55	368	6.7	0	54	324	45

Additional pro statistics: Recovered one fumble, 1981 and 1984; recovered two fumbles, 1983, 1985 and 1986.
Played in NFC Championship Game following 1986 and 1987 seasons.
Played in NFL Championship Game following 1987 season.
Played in Pro Bowl (NFL All-Star Game) following 1981 and 1982 seasons.

REGINALD O'KEITH ROGERS
(Reggie)
Defensive End—Detroit Lions
Born January 21, 1964, at Sacramento, Calif.
Height, 6.06. Weight, 272.
High School—Sacramento, Calif., Norte Del Rio.
Attended University of Washington.
Brother of Don Rogers, safety with Cleveland Browns, 1984 and 1985.

Selected by Detroit in 1st round (7th player selected) of 1987 NFL draft.

Signed by Detroit Lions, July 24, 1987.
On non-football injury list, November 6 through December 6, 1987; activated, December 7, 1987.
Detroit NFL, 1987.
Games: 1987 (6).

JEFFREY CHARLES ROHRER
(Jeff)
Linebacker—Dallas Cowboys
Born December 25, 1958, at Inglewood, Calif.
Height, 6.02. Weight, 222.
High School—Manhattan Beach, Calif., Mira Costa.
Received bachelor of science degree in administrative sciences from
Yale University in 1982.

Selected by Dallas in 2nd round (53rd player selected) of 1982 NFL draft.
Dallas NFL, 1982 through 1987.
Games: 1982 (8), 1983 (16), 1984 (16), 1985 (15), 1986 (16), 1987 (12). Total—83.
Pro statistics: Recovered one fumble for five yards and fumbled once, 1984; recovered one fumble, 1986; recovered two fumbles, 1987.
Played in NFC Championship Game following 1982 season.

DONALD DEMETRIUS ROLLE
(Butch)
Tight End—Buffalo Bills
Born August 19, 1964, at Miami, Fla.
Height, 6.03. Weight, 242.
High School—Hallandale, Fla.
Attended Michigan State University.

Selected by Buffalo in 7th round (180th player selected) of 1986 NFL draft.
Signed by Buffalo Bills, July 23, 1986.

		—PASS RECEIVING—			
Year Club	G.	P.C.	Yds.	Avg.	TD.
1986—Buffalo NFL..................	16	4	56	14.0	0
1987—Buffalo NFL..................	12	2	6	3.0	2
Pro Totals—2 Years............	28	6	62	10.3	2

Additional pro statistics: Returned one kickoff for six yards, 1987.

CHARLES MICHAEL ROMES
Cornerback—Seattle Seahawks
Born December 16, 1954, at Verdun, France.
Height, 6.01. Weight, 190.
High School—Durham, N. C., Hillside.
Attended Lake City Junior College and North Carolina Central University.

Selected by Buffalo in 12th round (309th player selected) of 1977 NFL draft.
Granted free agency, February 1, 1987; re-signed by Bills and traded to Kansas City Chiefs for 12th round pick in 1988 draft, July 14, 1987.
Released by Kansas City Chiefs, September 7, 1987; signed as free agent by San Diego Chargers, September 15, 1987.
Released by San Diego Chargers, November 17, 1987; signed as free agent by Seattle Seahawks, December 30, 1987.

		—INTERCEPTIONS—			
Year Club	G.	No.	Yds.	Avg.	TD.
1977—Buffalo NFL..................	14		None		
1978—Buffalo NFL..................	16	2	95	47.5	1
1979—Buffalo NFL..................	16	1	0	0.0	0
1980—Buffalo NFL..................	16	2	41	20.5	0
1981—Buffalo NFL..................	16	4	113	28.3	0
1982—Buffalo NFL..................	9	1	8	8.0	0
1983—Buffalo NFL..................	16	2	27	13.5	0
1984—Buffalo NFL..................	16	5	130	26.0	0
1985—Buffalo NFL..................	16	7	56	8.0	0
1986—Buffalo NFL..................	16	4	23	5.8	0
1987—San Diego NFL............	5		None		
Pro Totals—11 Years.........	156	28	493	17.6	1

Additional pro statistics: Returned one kickoff for 18 yards, 1977; fumbled once, 1977, 1978 and 1981; recovered two fumbles, 1978; ran 76 yards with blocked field goal for a touchdown and recovered one fumble for minus 10 yards, 1979; recovered two fumbles for 11 yards, 1981; recovered one fumble, 1984 and 1985; recovered one fumble for six yards, 1986.

DANIEL PETER ROSADO
(Dan)
Guard-Offensive Tackle—San Diego Chargers
Born July 6, 1959, at Lawton, Okla.
Height, 6.03. Weight, 280.
High School—Canton, Ga., Cherokee.
Attended Northern Illinois University.

Signed as free agent by Houston Gamblers, October 21, 1984.
On developmental squad, April 12 through May 3, 1985; activated, May 4, 1985.
On developmental squad, May 12 through May 17, 1985; activated, May 18, 1985.
Released by Houston Gamblers, July 31, 1985; awarded on waivers to Arizona Outlaws, August 1, 1985.
Granted free agency when USFL suspended operations, August 7, 1986; signed as free agent by Miami Dolphins, August 12, 1986.
Released by Miami Dolphins, September 1, 1986; re-signed by Dolphins for 1987, November 7, 1986.
Released by Miami Dolphins, September 7, 1987; signed as free agent replacement player by San Diego Chargers, September 24, 1987.
On injured reserve with pinched nerve in neck, November 3 through remainder of 1987 season.
On developmental squad for 4 games with Houston Gamblers in 1985.
Houston USFL, 1985; San Diego NFL, 1987.
Games: 1985 (14), 1987 (4). Total Pro—18.
Pro statistics: Caught one pass for no yards and recovered one fumble, 1985.

CARLTON ROSE
Linebacker—Washington Redskins
Born February 8, 1962, at Pompano, Fla.
Height, 6.01. Weight, 218.
High School—Fort Lauderdale, Fla., Stranahan.
Attended University of Michigan.

Selected by Michigan in 17th round (351st player selected) of 1984 USFL draft.
Signed by Michigan Panthers, January 21, 1984.
On developmental squad, February 24 through March 17, 1984; activated, March 18, 1984.
On developmental squad, March 26 through April 28, 1984; activated, April 29, 1984.
Not protected in merger of Michigan Panthers and Oakland Invaders; selected by Los Angeles Express in USFL disperal draft, December 6, 1984.
On developmental squad, February 21 through February 25, 1985.
Released by Los Angeles Express, February 26, 1985; awarded on waivers to Memphis Showboats, February 27, 1985.
Granted free agency when USFL suspended operations, August 7, 1986; signed as free agent by Washington Redskins, June 22, 1987.
Released by Washington Redskins, August 3, 1987; re-signed as replacement player by Redskins, September 23, 1987.
Released by Washington Redskins, October 20, 1987; re-signed by Redskins for 1988, December 17, 1987.
On developmental squad for 8 games with Michigan Panthers in 1984.
On developmental squad for 1 game with Los Angeles Express in 1985.
Michigan USFL, 1984; Memphis USFL, 1985; Washington NFL, 1987.
Games: 1984 (10), 1985 (17), 1987 (2). Total USFL—27. Total Pro—29.
Pro statistics: Credited with four sacks for 30 yards, 1984; credited with two sacks for 16 yards and recovered one fumble for 55 yards and a touchdown, 1985.

DONOVAN ROSE
Safety—Indianapolis Colts
Born March 9, 1957, at Norfolk, Va.
Height, 6.01. Weight, 190.
High School—Norfolk, Va., Norview.
Attended Hampton Institute.

Signed as free agent by Kansas City Chiefs, May 10, 1980.
Released by Kansas City Chiefs, September 1, 1980; re-signed by Chiefs after clearing procedural waivers, October 25, 1980.
Released by Kansas City Chiefs, August 25, 1981; signed as free agent by Toronto Argonauts, September 5, 1981.
Traded by Toronto Argonauts to Winnipeg Blue Bombers for draft choice, October 10, 1983.
Traded by Winnipeg Blue Bombers to Toronto Argonauts for draft choice, January 7, 1984.
Traded with 1985 draft choice by Toronto Argonauts to Winnipeg Blue Bombers for defensive back Paul Bennett, June 13, 1984.
Traded by Winnipeg Blue Bombers to Hamilton Tiger-Cats for draft choice, July 2, 1985.
Granted free agency, March 1, 1986; signed as free agent by Miami Dolphins, April 2, 1986.
On injured reserve with ankle injury, September 11 through October 10, 1986; activated, October 11, 1986.
Released by Miami Dolphins, September 7, 1987; re-signed by Dolphins, September 8, 1987.
Released by Miami Dolphins, February 22, 1988; awarded on waivers to Indianapolis Colts, March 4, 1988.

Year Club	G.	No.	Yds.	Avg.	TD.
1980—Kansas City NFL..........	7	None			
1981—Toronto CFL.................	8	None			
1982—Torono CFL.................	9	1	34	34.0	0
1983—Tor (5)-Wpg (3) CFL ...	8	4	98	24.5	1
1984—Winnipeg CFL..............	16	8	39	4.9	0
1985—Hamilton CFL	13	6	151	25.2	0
1986—Miami NFL..................	12	2	63	31.5	0
1987—Miami NFL..................	12	None			
NFL Totals—3 Years..........	31	2	63	31.5	0
CFL Totals—5 Years	54	19	322	16.9	1
Pro Totals—8 Years..........	85	21	385	18.3	1

Additional CFL statistics: Returned six kickoffs for 122 yards, returned two punts for 33 yards and recovered two fumbles for four yards, 1981; recovered one fumble for 28 yards, 1983; recovered one fumble, 1984.
Additional NFL statistics: Recovered one fumble, 1987.

KENNY FRANK ROSE
(Ken)
Linebacker—New York Jets
Born June 9, 1961, at Sacramento, Calif.
Height, 6.01. Weight, 215.
High School—Sacramento, Calif., Christian Brothers.
Attended University of Nevada at Las Vegas.
Signed as free agent by Saskatchewan Roughriders, May 5, 1985.
Released by Saskatchewan Roughriders, June 16, 1985; re-signed by Roughriders, June 23, 1985.
Released by Saskatchewan Roughriders, July 3, 1985; signed as free agent by Los Angeles Raiders, July 10, 1985.
Released by Los Angeles Raiders, August 13, 1985; re-signed by Raiders, August 16, 1985.
Released by Los Angeles Raiders, August 20, 1985.
USFL rights traded by Oakland Invaders to Tampa Bay Bandits for past considerations, September 6, 1985.
Signed by Tampa Bay Bandits, May 21, 1986.
Granted free agency when USFL suspended operations, August 7, 1986; signed as free agent by New York Jets, April 8, 1987.
Released by New York Jets, September 6, 1987; re-signed as replacement player by Jets, September 24, 1987.
New York Jets NFL, 1987.
Games: 1987 (10).
Pro statistics: Intercepted one pass for one yard, 1987.

KEVIN LESLEY ROSS
Cornerback—Kansas City Chiefs
Born January 16, 1962, at Camden, N.J.
Height, 5.09. Weight, 180.
High School—Paulsboro, N.J.
Attended Temple University.
Selected by Philadelphia in 1984 USFL territorial draft.
Selected by Kansas City in 7th round (173rd player selected) of 1984 NFL draft.
Signed by Kansas City Chiefs, June 21, 1984.
Crossed picket line during players' strike, October 14, 1987.

| | | | —INTERCEPTIONS— | | |
Year Club	G.	No.	Yds.	Avg.	TD.
1984—Kansas City NFL..........	16	6	124	20.7	1
1985—Kansas City NFL..........	16	3	47	15.7	0
1986—Kansas City NFL..........	16	4	66	16.5	0
1987—Kansas City NFL..........	12	3	40	13.3	0
Pro Totals—4 Years..........	60	16	277	17.3	1

Additional pro statistics: Recovered one fumble, 1984 and 1985; recovered three fumbles for 33 yards and a touchdown, 1986; returned blocked field goal attempt 65 yards for a touchdown, 1987.

CURTIS LAMAR ROUSE
Guard-Offensive Tackle—San Diego Chargers
Born July 13, 1960, at Augusta, Ga.
Height, 6.03. Weight, 340.
High School—Augusta, Ga., Lucy C. Laney.
Attended University of Tennessee at Chattanooga.
Selected by Minnesota in 11th round (286th player selected) of 1982 NFL draft.
Released by Minnesota Vikings, September 1, 1986; re-signed by Vikings, November 12, 1986.
On non-football injury list with head injury, November 20 through November 27, 1986; activated after clearing procedural waivers, November 29, 1986.
Released by Minnesota Vikings, September 7, 1987; signed as free agent replacement player by San Diego Chargers, September 28, 1987.
Minnesota NFL, 1982 through 1986; San Diego NFL, 1987.
Games: 1982 (5), 1983 (16), 1984 (16), 1985 (16), 1986 (5), 1987 (10). Total—68.
Pro statistics: Recovered two fumbles, 1983; returned two kickoffs for 22 yards, 1984; recovered one fumble, 1984 and 1985.

LEE ROUSON
Running Back—New York Giants
Born October 18, 1962, at Elizabeth City, N.C.
Height, 6.01. Weight, 222.
High School—Greensboro, N.C., Page.
Attended Colorado University.
Cousin of Johnny Walton, quarterback with San Antonio Wings (WFL), Philadelphia Eagles and Boston-New Orleans Breakers, 1975, 1976, 1978, 1979, 1983 and 1984; and head coach at Elizabeth City State University, 1980 through 1982.
Selected by New Jersey in 1st round (11th player selected) of 1985 USFL draft.
Selected by New York Giants in 8th round (213th player selected) of 1985 NFL draft.
Signed by New York Giants, July 2, 1985.
On injured reserve with hamstring injury, September 2 through December 13, 1985; activated, December 14, 1985.

| | | —RUSHING— | | | | PASS RECEIVING | | | | —TOTAL— | | |
Year Club	G.	Att.	Yds.	Avg.	TD.	P.C.	Yds.	Avg.	TD.	TD.	Pts.	F.
1985—New York Giants NFL............	2	1	1	1.0	0	None				0	0	0
1986—New York Giants NFL............	14	54	179	3.3	2	8	121	15.1	1	3	18	0
1987—New York Giants NFL............	12	41	155	3.8	0	11	129	11.7	1	1	6	3
Pro Totals—3 Years.................	28	96	335	3.5	2	19	250	13.2	2	4	24	3

Year Club	G.	No.	Yds.	Avg.	TD.
1985—N. Y. Giants NFL.........	2	2	35	17.5	0
1986—N. Y. Giants NFL.........	14	2	21	10.5	0
1987—N. Y. Giants NFL.........	12	22	497	22.6	0
Pro Totals—3 Years............	28	26	553	21.3	0

Additional pro statistics: Recovered one fumble, 1987.
Played in NFC Championship Game following 1986 season.
Played in NFL Championship Game following 1986 season.

MIKE ROZIER
Running Back—Houston Oilers
Born March 1, 1961, at Camden, N.J.
Height, 5.10. Weight, 211.
High School—Camden, N.J., Wilson.
Attended Coffeyville Community College and University of Nebraska.
Named THE SPORTING NEWS College Football Player of the Year, 1983.
Heisman Trophy winner, 1983.
Named as running back on THE SPORTING NEWS College All-America Team, 1983.
Selected by Pittsburgh in 1st round (1st player selected) of 1984 USFL draft.
Signed by Pittsburgh Maulers, January 3, 1984.
On developmental squad, May 18 through June 15, 1984; activated, June 16, 1984.
Selected by Houston in 1st round (2nd player selected) of 1984 NFL supplemental draft.
Franchise disbanded, October 25, 1984.
Personal services contract assigned to Baltimore Stars, November 1, 1984.
Signed as free agent with Jacksonville Bulls, February 1, 1985.
Granted roster exemption, February 1 through February 13, 1985; activated, February 14, 1985.
Granted free agency, July 1, 1985; signed by Houston Oilers, July 1, 1985.
On injured reserve with knee injury, December 2 through remainder of 1986 season.
On developmental squad for 4 games with Pittsburgh Maulers in 1984.

Year Club	G.	RUSHING Att.	Yds.	Avg.	TD.	PASS RECEIVING P.C.	Yds.	Avg.	TD.	—TOTAL— TD.	Pts.	F.
1984—Pittsburgh USFL....................	14	223	792	3.6	3	32	259	8.1	0	3	18	8
1985—Jacksonville USFL..................	18	320	1361	4.3	12	50	366	7.3	3	15	90	10
1985—Houston NFL........................	14	133	462	3.5	8	9	96	10.7	0	8	48	3
1986—Houston NFL........................	13	199	662	3.3	4	24	180	7.5	0	4	24	6
1987—Houston NFL........................	11	229	957	4.2	3	27	192	7.1	0	3	18	5
USFL Totals—2 Years.......................	32	543	2153	4.0	15	82	625	7.6	3	18	108	18
NFL Totals—3 Years........................	38	561	2081	3.7	15	60	468	7.8	0	15	90	14
Pro Totals—5 Years........................	70	1104	4234	3.8	30	142	1093	7.7	3	33	198	32

Additional USFL statistics: Recovered eight fumbles, 1984; recovered four fumbles, 1985.
Additional NFL statistics: Recovered three fumbles, 1985; attempted one pass with one completion for 13 yards, 1986; recovered two fumbles, 1986 and 1987.
Played in Pro Bowl (NFL All-Star Game) following 1987 season.

LARRY DUANE RUBENS
Center—Chicago Bears
Born January 25, 1959, at Spokane, Wash.
Height, 6.02. Weight, 262.
High School—Spokane, Wash., Mead.
Attended Montana State University.
Signed as free agent by Green Bay Packers, May 14, 1982.
Released by Green Bay Packers, August 27, 1984.
USFL rights traded by Tampa Bay Bandits to Memphis Showboats for rights to cornerback Renard Young, November 26, 1984.
Signed by Memphis Showboats, December 20, 1984.
Granted free agency when USFL suspended operations, August 7, 1986; signed as free agent by Chicago Bears, August 13, 1986.
On injured reserve with knee injury, September 7 through entire 1987 season.
Green Bay NFL, 1982 and 1983; Memphis USFL, 1985; Chicago NFL, 1986.
Games: 1982 (9), 1983 (16), 1985 (18), 1986 (16). Total NFL—41. Total Pro—59.
Pro statistics: Fumbled once for minus 15 yards, 1982; recovered one fumble, 1983.

ROBIN JAMES RUBICK
(Rob)
Tight End—Detroit Lions
Born September 27, 1960, at Newberry, Mich.
Height, 6.03. Weight, 234.
High School—Newberry, Mich.
Received degree in physical educaton from Grand Valley State College.
Nephew of Tom Villemure, head basketball coach at Grand Valley State College.
Selected by Detroit in 12th round (326th player selected) of 1982 NFL draft.
On physically unable to perform/active with back injury, July 27 through October 16, 1985; activated, October 17, 1985.

	——PASS RECEIVING——				
Year Club	G.	P.C.	Yds.	Avg.	TD.
1982—Detroit NFL..................	7		None		
1983—Detroit NFL..................	16	10	81	8.1	1
1984—Detroit NFL..................	16	14	188	13.4	1
1985—Detroit NFL..................	9	2	33	16.5	0
1986—Detroit NFL..................	16	5	62	12.4	0
1987—Detroit NFL..................	9	13	147	11.3	1
Pro Totals—6 Years............	73	44	511	11.6	3

Additional pro statistics: Rushed once for one yard and a touchdown, 1982.

MIKE ALAN RUETHER
Guard-Center—Phoenix Cardinals
Born September 20, 1962, at Inglewood, Calif.
Height, 6.04. Weight, 275.
High School—Shawnee Mission, Kan., Bishop Miege.
Attended University of Texas.

Selected by Houston in 1984 USFL territorial draft.
USFL rights traded with rights to offensive tackle Mark Adickes by Houston Gamblers to Los Angeles Express for 2nd round pick in 1985 and 1986 drafts, February 13, 1984.
Signed by Los Angeles Express, February 13, 1984.
Granted roster exemption, February 13 through February 23, 1984; activated, February 24, 1984.
Selected by St. Louis in 1st round (17th player selected) of 1984 NFL supplemental draft.
On developmental squad, February 21 through March 7, 1985; activated, March 8, 1985.
Granted free agency when USFL suspended operations, August 7, 1986; signed by St. Louis Cardinals, September 30, 1986.
Granted roster exemption, September 30 through October 9, 1986; activated, October 10, 1986.
Franchise transferred to Phoenix, March 15, 1988.
On developmental squad for 2 games with Los Angeles Express in 1985.
Los Angeles USFL, 1984 and 1985; St. Louis NFL, 1986 and 1987.
Games: 1984 (17), 1985 (17), 1986 (10), 1987 (12). Total USFL—34. Total NFL—22. Total Pro—56.
Pro statistics: Recovered two fumbles, 1984.

KENNETH F. RUETTGERS
Name pronounced RUTT-gers.
(Ken)
Offensive Tackle—Green Bay Packers
Born August 20, 1962, at Bakersfield, Calif.
Height, 6.05. Weight, 280.
High School—Bakersfield, Calif., Garces Memorial.
Received bachelor of business administration degree from University of Southern California in 1985.

Selected by Green Bay in 1st round (7th player selected) of 1985 NFL draft.
Signed by Green Bay Packers, August 12, 1985.
Green Bay NFL, 1985 through 1987.
Games: 1985 (15), 1986 (16), 1987 (12). Total—43.
Pro statistics: Recovered one fumble, 1986.

MAX CULP RUNAGER
Punter—San Francisco 49ers
Born March 24, 1956, at Greenwood, S.C.
Height, 6.01. Weight, 189.
High School—Orangeburg, S.C., Wilkinson.
Received bachelor of science degree in health and physical education from University of South Carolina.

Selected by Philadelphia in 8th round (211th player selected) of 1979 NFL draft.
Released by Philadelphia Eagles, September 28, 1983; re-signed by Eagles, October 26, 1983.
Released by Philadelphia Eagles, August 27, 1984; signed as free agent by San Francisco 49ers, September 12, 1984.

	——PUNTING——			
Year Club	G.	No.	Avg.	Blk.
1979—Philadelphia NFL	16	74	39.6	1
1980—Philadelphia NFL	16	75	39.3	1
1981—Philadelphia NFL	15	63	40.7	0
1982—Philadelphia NFL	9	44	40.5	0
1983—Philadelphia NFL	12	59	41.7	0
1984—San Francisco NFL	14	56	41.8	1
1985—San Francisco NFL	16	86	39.8	1
1986—San Francisco NFL	16	83	41.6	2
1987—San Francisco NFL	12	55	39.2	1
Pro Totals—9 Years....................	126	595	40.5	7

Additional pro statistics: Recovered one fumble and fumbled once, 1979; rushed once for six yards, 1983; rushed once for minus five yards, 1984.
Played in NFC Championship Game following 1980 and 1984 seasons.
Played in NFL Championship Game following 1980 and 1984 seasons.

MICHAEL JOSEPH RUTH
(Mike)
Nose Tackle—New England Patriots

Born June 25, 1964, at Norristown, Pa.
Height, 6.01. Weight, 266.
High School—Fairview Village, Pa., Methacton.
Attended Boston College.

Selected by New England in 2nd round (42nd player selected) of 1986 NFL draft.
Signed by New England Patriots, August 4, 1986.
On injured reserve with hip injury, October 24, 1986 through January 1, 1987; activated, January 2, 1987.
On injured reserve with knee injury, September 1 through November 20, 1987; activated, November 21, 1987.
New England NFL, 1986 and 1987.
Games: 1986 (6), 1987 (2). Total—8.
Pro statistics: Recovered one fumble, 1986.

REGINALD BERNARD RUTLAND
(Reggie)
Safety—Minnesota Vikings

Born June 20, 1964, at East Point, Ga.
Height, 6.01. Weight, 195.
High School—East Point, Ga., Russell.
Attended Georgia Tech.

Selected by Minnesota in 4th round (100th player selected) of 1987 NFL draft.
Signed by Minnesota Vikings, July 17, 1987.
On injured reserve with ankle injury, November 18 through December 24, 1987; activated, December 25, 1987.
Minnesota NFL, 1987.
Games: 1987 (7).
Played in NFC Championship Game following 1987 season.

JEFFREY RONALD RUTLEDGE
(Jeff)
Quarterback—New York Giants

Born January 22, 1957, at Birmingham, Ala.
Height, 6.01. Weight, 195.
High School—Birmingham, Ala., Banks.
Received degree in business education from University of Alabama.
Son of Paul E. (Jack) Rutledge, minor league infielder, 1950 through 1952.

Selected by Los Angeles in 9th round (246th player selected) of 1979 NFL draft.
On injured reserve with mononucleosis, October 22 through remainder of 1980 season.
On injured reserve with broken thumb, November 2 through remainder of 1981 season.
Traded to New York Giants for 4th round pick in 1983 draft, September 5, 1982.
Crossed picket line during players' strike, October 14, 1987.
Active for 9 games with New York Giants in 1982; did not play.

Year	Club	G.	Att.	Cmp.	Pct.	Gain	T.P.	P.I.	Avg.	Att.	Yds.	Avg.	TD.	TD.	Pts.	F.
						PASSING						RUSHING			TOTAL	
1979—Los Angeles NFL		3	32	13	40.6	125	1	4	3.91	5	27	5.4	0	0	0	0
1980—Los Angeles NFL		1	4	1	25.0	26	0	0	6.50		None			0	0	0
1981—Los Angeles NFL		4	50	30	60.0	442	3	4	8.84	5	—3	—0.6	0	0	0	0
1983—New York Giants NFL		4	174	87	50.0	1208	3	8	6.94	7	27	3.9	0	0	0	6
1984—New York Giants NFL		16	1	1	100.0	9	0	0	9.00		None			0	0	0
1985—New York Giants NFL		16				None				2	—6	—3.0	0	0	0	1
1986—New York Giants NFL		16	3	1	33.3	13	1	0	4.33	3	19	6.3	0	0	0	0
1987—New York Giants NFL		13	155	79	51.0	1048	5	11	6.76	15	31	2.1	0	0	0	7
Pro Totals—9 Years		73	419	212	50.6	2871	13	27	6.85	37	95	2.6	0	0	0	14

Quarterback Rating Points: 1979 (23.0), 1980 (54.2), 1981 (75.6), 1983 (59.3), 1984 (104.2), 1986 (87.5), 1987 (53.9). Total—56.5.
Additional pro statistics: Recovered three fumbles and fumbled seven times for minus three yards, 1987.
Played in NFC Championship Game following 1986 season.
Played in NFL Championship Game following 1986 season.
Member of Los Angeles Rams for NFC and NFL Championship Game following 1979 season; did not play.

ROGER BRIAN RUZEK
Placekicker—Dallas Cowboys

Born December 17, 1960, at San Francisco, Calif.
Height, 6.01. Weight, 190.
High School—San Francisco, Calif., El Camino.
Received degree from Weber State College.

Signed as free agent by Cleveland Browns, May 5, 1983.
Released by Cleveland Browns, August 16, 1983; signed by Pittsburgh Maulers, October 10, 1983.
Released by Pittsburgh Maulers, December 16, 1983; signed as free agent by New Jersey Generals, January 7, 1984.
Released by New Jersey Generals, July 31, 1985; awarded on waivers to Memphis Showboats, August 1, 1985.
Granted free agency when USFL suspended operations, August 7, 1986; signed as free agent by Dallas Cowboys, April 10, 1987.
Released by Dallas Cowboys, August 6, 1987; re-signed by Cowboys, August 20, 1987.

		——PLACE KICKING——					
Year	Club	G.	XP.	XPM.	FG.	FGA.	Pts.
1984—New Jersey USFL ...		18	51	2	17	23	102
1985—New Jersey USFL ...		18	49	3	17	25	100
1987—Dallas NFL		12	26	0	22	25	92
USFL Totals—2 Years...		36	100	5	34	48	202
NFL Totals—1 Year.......		12	26	0	22	25	92
Pro Totals—3 Years.......		48	126	5	56	73	294

Additional pro statistics: Punted once for 36 yards, 1985.

JAMES JOSEPH RYAN
(Jim)
Linebacker—Denver Broncos

Born May 18, 1957, at Camden, N.J.
Height, 6.01. Weight, 225.
High School—Pennsauken, N.J., Bishop Eustace.
Received bachelor of administration degree in management from College of William & Mary in 1979 and received master's degree in business administration from University of Denver.

Signed as free agent by Denver Broncos, May 12, 1979.
Crossed picket line during players' strike, October 2, 1987.
Denver NFL, 1979 through 1987.
Games: 1979 (16), 1980 (16), 1981 (16), 1982 (9), 1983 (15), 1984 (16), 1985 (16), 1986 (16), 1987 (14). Total—134.
Pro statistics: Recovered one fumble, 1979, 1983, 1984 and 1985; intercepted one pass for 21 yards, 1980; returned one kickoff for no yards, 1980 and 1986; returned one kickoff for two yards, 1981; intercepted one pass for 13 yards, 1984; intercepted three passes for seven yards, returned two kickoffs for nine yards, credited with a safety, recovered two fumbles and fumbled once, 1987.
Played in AFC Championship Game following 1986 and 1987 seasons.
Played in NFL Championship Game following 1986 and 1987 seasons.

PATRICK LEE RYAN
(Pat)
Quarterback—New York Jets

Born September 16, 1955, at Hutchinson, Kan.
Height, 6.03. Weight, 210.
High School—Oklahoma City, Okla., Putnam.
Received degree in transportation from University of Tennessee in 1978.

Selected by New York Jets in 11th round (281st player selected) of 1978 NFL draft.
Crossed picket line during players' strike, October 14, 1987.

			—————PASSING—————							——RUSHING——				—TOTAL—		
Year	Club	G.	Att.	Cmp.	Pct.	Gain	T.P.	P.I.	Avg.	Att.	Yds.	Avg.	TD.	TD.	Pts.	F.
1978—New York Jets NFL........		2	14	9	64.3	106	0	2	7.57	None				0	0	0
1979—New York Jets NFL........		1	4	2	50.0	13	0	1	3.25	None				0	0	1
1980—New York Jets NFL........		14			None					None				0	0	0
1981—New York Jets NFL........		15	10	4	40.0	48	1	1	4.80	3	—5	—1.7	0	0	0	0
1982—New York Jets NFL........		9	18	12	66.7	146	2	1	8.11	1	—1	—1.0	0	0	0	0
1983—New York Jets NFL........		16	40	21	52.5	259	2	2	6.48	4	23	5.8	0	0	†1	2
1984—New York Jets NFL........		16	285	156	54.7	1939	14	14	6.80	23	92	4.0	0	0	†1	4
1985—New York Jets NFL........		16	9	6	66.7	95	0	0	10.56	3	—5	—1.7	0	0	0	0
1986—New York Jets NFL........		16	55	34	61.8	342	2	1	6.22	8	28	3.5	0	0	0	0
1987—New York Jets NFL........		13	53	32	60.4	314	4	2	5.92	4	5	1.3	1	1	6	0
Pro Totals—10 Years.........		118	488	276	56.6	3262	25	24	6.68	46	137	3.0	1	1	8	7

†Scored one extra point.
Quarterback Rating Points: 1978 (47.6), 1979 (17.7), 1981 (49.2), 1982 (105.1), 1983 (68.6), 1984 (72.0), 1985 (101.6), 1986 (84.1), 1987 (86.5). Total—73.7.
Additional pro statistics: Recovered one fumble, 1983 and 1984.
Member of New York Jets for AFC Championship Game following 1982 season; did not play.

MARK ROBERT RYPIEN
Quarterback—Washington Redskins

Born October 2, 1962, at Calgary, Alberta, Can.
Height, 6.04. Weight, 234.
High School—Spokane, Wash., Shadle Park.
Attended Washington State University.
Brother of Tim Rypien, catcher in Toronto Blue Jays' organization, 1984 through 1986; and cousin of Shane Churla, forward with Hartford Whalers.

Selected by Washington in 6th round (146th player selected) of 1986 NFL draft.
Signed by Washington Redskins, July 18, 1986.
On injured reserve with knee injury, September 5 through entire 1986 season.
On injured reserve with back injury, September 7 through November 27, 1987; activated, November 28, 1987.
Active for 1 game with Washington Redskins in 1987; did not play.
Washington NFL, 1987.
Member of Washington Redskins for NFL Championship Game following 1987 season; inactive.

RODERICK SADDLER
(Rod)
Defensive End—Phoenix Cardinals
Born September 26, 1965, at Atlanta, Ga.
Height, 6.05. Weight, 276.
High School—Decatur, Ga., Columbia.
Attended Texas A&M University.
Cousin of Clark Gaines, running back with New York Jets and Kansas City Chiefs, 1976 though 1982.
Selected by St. Louis in 4th round (90th player selected) of 1987 NFL draft.
Signed by St. Louis Cardinals, July 21, 1987.
Franchise transferred to Phoenix, March 15, 1988.
St. Louis NFL, 1987.
Games: 1987 (12).
Pro statistics: Intercepted one pass for no yards, 1987.

RAYMOND DANIEL SALEAUMUA
(Name pronounced SAL-uh-MOO-uh.)
(Dan)
Nose Tackle—Detroit Lions
Born November 11, 1964, at San Diego, Calif.
Height, 6.00. Weight, 285.
High School—National City, Calif., Sweetwater.
Attended Arizona State University.
Selected by Detroit in 7th round (175th player selected) of 1987 NFL draft.
Signed by Detroit Lions, July 25, 1987.
On injured reserve with hamstring injury, September 7 through October 30, 1987; activated, October 31, 1987.
Detroit NFL, 1987.
Games: 1987 (9).
Pro statistics: Returned three kickoffs for 57 yards, 1987.

HARVEY SALEM
Guard—Detroit Lions
Born January 15, 1961, at Berkeley, Calif.
Height, 6.06. Weight, 285.
High School—El Cerrito, Calif.
Received degree from University of California at Berkeley.
Named as offensive tackle on THE SPORTING NEWS College All-America Team, 1982.
Selected by Oakland in 1983 USFL territorial draft.
Selected by Houston in 2nd round (30th player selected) of 1983 NFL draft.
Signed by Houston Oilers, July 14, 1983.
On did not report list, August 19 through September 7, 1986.
Granted roster exemption, September 8 through September 18, 1986; activated, September 19, 1986.
Traded by Houston Oilers to Detroit Lions for 2nd round pick in 1987 draft, September 23, 1986.
Granted free agency, February 1, 1987; re-signed by Lions, September 12, 1987.
Granted roster exemption, September 12 through September 18, 1987; activated, September 19, 1987.
Houston NFL, 1983 through 1985; Houston (1)-Detroit (13) NFL, 1986; Detroit NFL, 1987.
Games: 1983 (16), 1984 (16), 1985 (14), 1986 (14), 1987 (11). Total—71.

RICHARD SEAN SALISBURY
(Known by middle name.)
Quarterback—Indianapolis Colts
Born March 9, 1963, at Long Beach, Calif.
Height, 6.05. Weight, 215.
High School—Escondido, Calif., Orange Glen.
Received bachelor's degree in broadcasting from University of Southern California in 1986.
Selected by New Jersey in 1986 USFL territorial draft.
Signed as free agent by Seattle Seahawks, May 12, 1986.
On injured reserve with shoulder injury, October 22 through remainder of 1986 season.
Released by Seattle Seahawks, September 1, 1987; signed as free agent replacement player by Indianapolis Colts, October 14, 1987.
Active for 7 games with Seattle Seahawks in 1986; did not play.

					—PASSING—				—RUSHING—			—TOTAL—		
Year	Club	G.	Att.	Cmp.	Pct.	Gain	T.P.	P.I.	Avg.	Att.	Yds.	Avg. TD.	TD.	Pts.	F.
1987—Indianapolis NFL		2	12	8	66.7	68	0	2	5.67	None			0	0	1

Quarterback Rating Points: 1987 (41.7).

JEROME ELI SALLY
Nose Tackle—Indianapolis Colts
Born February 24, 1959, at Chicago, Ill.
Height, 6.03. Weight, 270.
High School—Maywood, Ill., Proviso East.
Received bachelor of science degree in industrial engineering from University of Missouri.
Signed as free agent by New Orleans Saints, May 27, 1982.
Released by New Orleans Saints, August 31, 1982; signed as free agent by New York Giants, December 1, 1982.

Traded by New York Giants to Indianapolis Colts for 7th round pick in 1988 draft, September 2, 1987.
New York Giants NFL, 1982 through 1986; Indianapolis NFL, 1987.
Games: 1982 (4), 1983 (16), 1984 (16), 1985 (16), 1986 (16), 1987 (12). Total—80.
Pro statistics: Recovered one fumble, 1983; returned one kickoff for four yards, 1985.
Played in NFC Championship Game following 1986 season.
Played in NFL Championship Game following 1986 season.

CLINTON BERNARD SAMPSON
(Clint)
Wide Receiver—Buffalo Bills
Born January 4, 1961, at Los Angeles, Calif.
Height, 5.11. Weight, 183.
High School—Los Angeles, Calif., Crenshaw.
Attended Mt. San Antonio College and received degree in public administration
and business management from San Diego State University in 1983.
Selected by Boston in 3rd round (35th player selected) of 1983 USFL draft.
Selected by Denver in 3rd round (60th player selected) of 1983 NFL draft.
Signed by Denver Broncos, July 13, 1983.
On injured reserve with concussion, October 26 through November 19, 1984; activated, November 20, 1984.
Traded by Denver Broncos to Buffalo Bills for conditional 7th round pick in 1988 draft, July 14, 1987.
On injured reserve with knee injury, September 1 through entire 1987 season.

| | | —PASS RECEIVING— | | | |
Year Club	G.	P.C.	Yds.	Avg.	TD.
1983—Denver NFL	16	10	200	20.0	3
1984—Denver NFL	12	9	123	13.7	1
1985—Denver NFL	16	26	432	16.6	4
1986—Denver NFL	15	21	259	12.3	0
Pro Totals—4 Years	59	66	1014	15.4	8

Additional pro statistics: Fumbled once, 1984 and 1986.
Played in AFC Championship Game following 1986 season.
Played in NFL Championship Game following 1986 season.

LUPE SANCHEZ
First name pronounced Loop.
Safety-Kick Returner—Pittsburgh Steelers
Born October 28, 1961, at Tulare, Calif.
Height, 5.10. Weight, 192.
High School—Visalia, Calif., Mount Whitney.
Attended University of California at Los Angeles.
Selected by Arizona in 1st round (15th player selected) of 1984 USFL draft.
Signed by Arizona Wranglers, February 20, 1984.
Granted roster exemption, February 20 through March 9, 1984; activated, March 10, 1984.
On developmental squad, April 15 through April 26, 1984; activated, April 27, 1984.
On developmental squad, May 7 through June 7, 1984; activated, June 8, 1984.
Selected by Kansas City in 2nd round (33rd player selected) of 1984 NFL supplemental draft.
Franchise renamed Outlaws, December 4, 1984.
Traded by Arizona Outlaws to Orlando Renegades for past considerations, December 6, 1984.
Granted free agency when USFL suspended operations, August 7, 1986; signed by Kansas City Chiefs, August 12, 1986.
Released by Kansas City Chiefs, September 1, 1986; signed as free agent by Pittsburgh Steelers, October 7, 1986.
On developmental squad for 7 games with Arizona Wranglers in 1984.

| | | INTERCEPTIONS | | | | —KICKOFF RET.— | | | | —TOTAL— | | |
Year Club	G.	No.	Yds.	Avg.	TD.	No.	Yds.	Avg.	TD.	TD.	Pts.	F.
1984—Arizona USFL	9	1	14	14.0	0		None			0	0	0
1985—Orlando USFL	17	2	88	44.0	⋆1	2	30	15.0	0	1	6	1
1986—Pittsburgh NFL	11	3	71	23.7	1	25	591	23.6	0	1	6	2
1987—Pittsburgh NFL	12		None			6	116	19.3	0	0	0	1
USFL Totals—2 Years	26	3	102	34.0	1	2	30	15.0	0	1	6	1
NFL Totals—2 Year	23	3	71	23.7	1	31	707	22.8	0	1	6	3
Pro Totals—4 Years	49	6	173	28.8	2	33	737	22.3	0	2	12	4

Additional USFL statistics: Returned one punt for two yards, 1984; returned one punt for no yards and recovered one fumble, 1985.
Additional NFL statistics: Recovered one fumble, 1986.
Played in USFL Championship Game following 1984 season.

CHARLES SAMUEL SANDERS
(Chuck)
Running Back—New York Giants
Born April 24, 1964, at Pittsburgh, Pa.
Height, 6.01. Weight, 233.
High School—Pittsburgh, Pa., Penn Hills.
Received bachelor of science degree in management from
Slippery Rock University of Pennsylvania in 1986.
Selected by San Diego in 11th round (293rd player selected) of 1986 NFL draft.
Selected by Orlando in 6th round (37th player selected) of 1986 USFL draft.

Signed by San Diego Chargers, July 17, 1986.
Released by San Diego Chargers, August 26, 1986; signed as free agent by Pittsburgh Steelers, September 9, 1986.
Released by Pittsburgh Steelers, August 31, 1987; re-signed as replacement player by Steelers, September 24, 1987.
Released by Pittsburgh Steelers, November 3, 1987; signed as free agent by New York Giants, February 29, 1988.

		—RUSHING—				PASS RECEIVING				—TOTAL—		
Year Club	G.	Att.	Yds.	Avg.	TD.	P.C.	Yds.	Avg.	TD.	TD.	Pts.	F.
1986—Pittsburgh NFL	14	4	12	3.0	0	2	19	9.5	0	0	0	0
1987—Pittsburgh NFL	5	11	65	5.9	1	1	11	11.0	0	1	6	0
Pro Totals—2 Years	19	15	77	5.1	1	3	30	10.0	0	1	6	0

		KICKOFF RETURNS		
Year Club	G.	No.	Yds.	Avg.TD.
1986—Pittsburgh NFL	14	8	148	18.5 0
1987—Pittsburgh NFL	5		None	
Pro Totals—2 Years	19	8	148	18.5 0

ERIC DOWNER SANDERS
Offensive Tackle-Guard—Detroit Lions
Born October 22, 1958, at Reno, Nev.
Height, 6.07. Weight, 280.
High School—Reno, Nev., Wooster.
Attended University of Nevada at Reno.

Selected by Atlanta in 5th round (136th player selected) of 1981 NFL draft.
On injured reserve with knee injury, November 10 through remainder of 1984 season.
On injured reserve with back injury, October 31 through November 26, 1986; awarded on procedural waivers to Detroit Lions, November 28, 1986.
Atlanta NFL, 1981 through 1985; Atlanta (8)-Detroit (3) NFL, 1986; Detroit NFL, 1987.
Games: 1981 (16), 1982 (9), 1983 (15), 1984 (10), 1985 (16), 1986 (11), 1987 (12). Total—89.
Pro statistics: Recovered one fumble, 1982; recovered one fumble for minus 23 yards, 1985.

RICKY WAYNE SANDERS
Running Back—Washington Redskins
Born September 30, 1962, at Temple, Tex.
Height, 5.11. Weight, 180.
High School—Belton, Tex.
Attended Southwest Texas State University.

Selected by Houston in 1984 USFL territorial draft.
Signed by Houston Gamblers, January 26, 1984.
Selected by New England in 1st round (16th player selected) of 1984 NFL supplemental draft.
On developmental squad, March 7 through May 5, 1985; activated, May 6, 1985.
Traded with defensive backs Luther Bradley, Will Lewis, Mike Mitchell and Durwood Roquemore, defensive end Pete Catan, quarterbacks Jim Kelly and Todd Dillon, defensive tackles Tony Fitzpatrick, Van Hughes and Hosea Taylor, running back Sam Harrell, linebackers Andy Hawkins and Ladell Wills, wide receivers Richard Johnson, Scott McGhee, Gerald McNeil and Clarence Verdin, guard Rich Kehr, center Billy Kidd and offensive tackles Chris Riehm and Tommy Robison by Houston Gamblers to New Jersey Generals for past considerations, March 7, 1986.
Granted free agency when USFL suspended operations, August 7, 1986.
NFL rights traded by New England Patriots to Washington Redskins for 3rd round pick in 1987 draft, August 11, 1986.
Signed by Washington Redskins, August 13, 1986.
Granted roster exemption, August 13 through August 24, 1986; activated, August 25, 1986.
On injured reserve with pulled calf and hamstring, September 2 through October 10, 1986; activated, October 11, 1986.
On developmental squad for 8 games with Houston Gamblers in 1985.

		—RUSHING—				PASS RECEIVING				—TOTAL—		
Year Club	G.	Att.	Yds.	Avg.	TD.	P.C.	Yds.	Avg.	TD.	TD.	Pts.	F.
1984—Houston USFL	18	10	58	5.8	0	101	1378	13.6	11	11	66	3
1985—Houston USFL	10	5	32	6.4	0	48	538	11.2	7	7	†44	0
1986—Washington NFL	10		None			14	286	20.4	2	2	12	0
1987—Washington NFL	12	1	—4	—4.0	0	37	630	17.0	3	3	18	0
USFL Totals—2 Years	28	15	90	6.0	0	149	1916	12.9	18	18	110	3
NFL Totals—2 Years	22	1	—4	—4.0	0	51	916	18.0	5	5	30	0
Pro Totals—4 Years	50	16	86	5.4	0	200	2832	14.2	23	23	140	3

		—PUNT RETURNS—				—KICKOFF RET.—		
Year Club	G.	No.	Yds.	Avg.	TD.	No.	Yds.	Avg.TD.
1984—Houston USFL	18	19	148	7.8	0	2	28	14.0 0
1985—Houston USFL	10		None				None	
1986—Washington NFL	10		None				None	
1987—Washington NFL	12		None			4	118	29.5 0
USFL Totals—2 Years	28	19	148	7.8	0	2	28	14.0 0
NFL Totals—2 Years	22	0	0	0.0	0	4	118	29.5 0
Pro Totals—4 Years	50	19	148	7.8	0	6	146	24.3 0

†Includes one 2-point conversion.

Additional pro statistics: Recovered two fumbles, 1984; attempted one pass with no completions, 1985.
Played in NFC Championship Game following 1986 and 1987 seasons.
Played in NFL Championship Game following 1987 season.

THOMAS SANDERS
Running Back—Chicago Bears
Born January 4, 1962, at Giddings, Tex.
Height, 5.11. Weight, 203.
High School—Giddings, Tex.
Attended Texas A&M University.

Selected by Houston in 1985 USFL territorial draft.
Selected by Chicago in 9th round (250th player selected) of 1985 NFL draft.
Signed by Chicago Bears, July 10, 1985.

		—RUSHING—				PASS RECEIVING				—TOTAL—		
Year	Club	G.	Att.	Yds.	Avg.	TD.	P.C.	Yds.	Avg.	TD.	TD.	Pts.	F.
1985—Chicago NFL		15	25	104	4.2	1	1	9	9.0	0	1	6	1
1986—Chicago NFL		16	27	224	8.3	5	2	18	9.0	0	5	30	2
1987—Chicago NFL		12	23	122	5.3	1	3	53	17.7	0	1	6	1
Pro Totals—3 Years		43	75	450	6.0	7	6	80	13.3	0	7	42	4

		KICKOFF RETURNS			
Year	Club	G.	No.	Yds.	Avg.TD.
1985—Chicago NFL	15	1	10	10.0	0
1986—Chicago NFL	16	22	399	18.1	0
1987—Chicago NFL	12	20	349	17.5	0
Pro Totals—3 Years	43	43	758	17.6	0

Played in NFC Championship Game following 1985 season.
Played in NFL Championship Game following 1985 season.

JESSE SAPOLU
Name pronounced SA-pole-low.
Guard-Center—San Francisco 49ers
Born March 10, 1961, at Laie, Western Samoa.
Height, 6.04. Weight, 260.
High School—Honolulu, Haw., Farrington.
Attended University of Hawaii.

Selected by Oakland in 17th round (199th player selected) of 1983 USFL draft.
Selected by San Francisco in 11th round (289th player selected) of 1983 NFL draft.
Signed by San Francisco 49ers, July 10, 1983.
On physically unable to perform/active with fractured foot, July 19 through August 12, 1984.
On physically unable to perform/reserve with fractured foot, August 13 through November 7, 1984; activated, November 8, 1984.
On injured reserve with fractured foot, November 16 through remainder of 1984 season.
On injured reserve with broken foot, August 12 through entire 1985 season.
On injured reserve with broken leg, July 30 through entire 1986 season.
San Francisco NFL, 1983, 1984 and 1987.
Games: 1983 (16), 1984 (1), 1987 (12). Total—29.
Played in NFC Championship Game following 1983 season.

BRODERICK LAWRENCE SARGENT
Fullback—Phoenix Cardinals
Born September 16, 1962, at Waxahachie, Tex.
Height, 5.10. Weight, 215.
High School—Waxahachie, Tex.
Attended Baylor University.

Signed as free agent by St. Louis Cardinals, May 13, 1986.
Crossed picket line during players' strike, October 1, 1987.
Franchise transferred to Phoenix, March 15, 1988.

		—RUSHING—				PASS RECEIVING				—TOTAL—		
Year	Club	G.	Att.	Yds.	Avg.	TD.	P.C.	Yds.	Avg.	TD.	TD.	Pts.	F.
1986—St. Louis NFL		16		None			1	8	8.0	0	0	0	0
1987—St. Louis NFL		15	18	90	5.0	0	2	19	9.5	0	0	0	1
Pro Totals—2 Years		31	18	90	5.0	0	3	27	9.0	0	0	0	1

Additional pro statistics: Returned two kickoffs for 27 yards, 1986; returned three kickoffs for 37 yards, 1987.

ALVIS SATELE
Linebacker—San Diego Chargers
Born April 30, 1963, at Honolulu, Haw.
Height, 6.01. Weight, 230.
High School—Kaneoag, Haw., Castle.
Attended University of Hawaii.

Signed as free agent by Washington Redskins, May 6, 1985.
Released by Washington Redskins, July 29, 1985; signed as free agent by Calgary Stampeders, April 12, 1986.
Released by Calgary Stampeders, June 17, 1987; signed as free agent by British Columbia Lions, June 23, 1987.
Released by British Columbia Lions, October 19, 1987; signed as free agent by San Diego Chargers, May 4, 1988.
Calgary CFL, 1986; British Columbia CFL, 1987.
Games: 1986 (6), 1987 (9). Total—15.
Pro statistics: Recovered two fumbles, 1986.

MIKE SAXON
Punter—Dallas Cowboys
Born July 10, 1962, at Arcadia, Calif.
Height, 6.03. Weight, 193.
High School—Arcadia, Calif.
Attended Pasadena City College and San Diego State University.
Selected by Arizona in 13th round (265th player selected) of 1984 USFL draft.
Selected by Detroit in 11th round (300th player selected) of 1984 NFL draft.
Signed by Detroit Lions, May 29, 1984.
Released by Detroit Lions, August 27, 1984; signed by Arizona Wranglers, November 7, 1984.
Released by Arizona Wranglers, February 11, 1985; signed as free agent by Dallas Cowboys, March 27, 1985.

			—PUNTING—		
Year Club	G.	No.	Avg.	Blk.	
1985—Dallas NFL	16	81	41.9	1	
1986—Dallas NFL	16	86	40.7	1	
1987—Dallas NFL	12	68	39.5	0	
Pro Totals—3 Years	44	235	40.8	2	

MIKE SCHAD
Guard—Los Angeles Rams
Born October 2, 1963, at Trenton, Ontario, Can.
Height, 6.05. Weight, 290.
High School—Bellville, Ontario, Can., Moira Secondary.
Received degrees in geography and physiology from Queens College (Canada) in 1986.
Selected by Los Angeles Rams in 1st round (23rd player selected) of 1986 NFL draft.
Signed by Los Angeles Rams, August 4, 1986.
On injured reserve with back injury, September 4 through entire 1986 season.
On injured reserve with pinched nerve in neck, September 7 through December 3, 1987; activated, December 4, 1987.
Los Angeles Rams NFL, 1987.
Games: 1987 (1).

BRUCE DANIEL SCHOLTZ
Linebacker—Seattle Seahawks
Born September 26, 1958, at La Grange, Tex.
Height, 6.06. Weight, 240.
High School—Austin, Tex., Crockett.
Attended University of Texas.
Selected by Seattle in 2nd round (33rd player selected) of 1982 NFL draft.
On injured reserve with sprained ankle, November 3 through December 4, 1987; activated, December 5, 1987.

		—INTERCEPTIONS—			
Year Club	G.	No.	Yds.	Avg.	TD.
1982—Seattle NFL	9	1	31	31.0	1
1983—Seattle NFL	16	1	8	8.0	0
1984—Seattle NFL	16	1	15	15.0	0
1985—Seattle NFL	16		None		
1986—Seattle NFL	16	2	10	5.0	0
1987—Seattle NFL	8		None		
Pro Totals—6 Years	81	5	64	12.8	1

Additional pro statistics: Recovered one fumble, 1982 through 1985; returned three kickoffs for 39 yards, 1986; returned one kickoff for 11 yards, 1987.
Played in AFC Championship Game following 1983 season.

TURK LEROY SCHONERT
Quarterback—Cincinnati Bengals
Born January 15, 1957, at Torrance, Calif.
Height, 6.01. Weight, 196.
High School—Anaheim, Calif., Servite.
Attended Stanford University.
Selected by Chicago in 9th round (242nd player selected) of 1980 NFL draft.
Released by Chicago Bears, August 25, 1980; claimed on waivers by Cincinnati Bengals, August 26, 1980.
USFL rights traded by Oakland Invaders to Jacksonville Bulls for rights to running back Ted McKnight, linebacker Mark Jerue and 1st and 5th round picks in 1984 draft, October 24, 1983.
On injured reserve with separated shoulder, December 5 through remainder of 1984 season.
Granted free agency, February 1, 1985; re-signed by Bengals, April 4, 1985.
Traded by Cincinnati Bengals to Atlanta Falcons for 3rd round pick in 1986 draft, April 4, 1986.
Released by Atlanta Falcons, September 8, 1987; signed as free agent by Cincinnati Bengals, September 10, 1987.
Active for 16 games with Cincinnati Bengals in 1980; did not play.

		—PASSING—							—RUSHING—				—TOTAL—		
Year Club	G.	Att.	Cmp.	Pct.	Gain	T.P.	P.I.	Avg.	Att.	Yds.	Avg.	TD.	TD.	Pts.	F.
1981—Cincinnati NFL	4	19	10	52.6	166	0	0	8.74	7	41	5.9	0	0	0	1
1982—Cincinnati NFL	2	1	1	100.0	6	0	0	6.00	3	—8	—2.7	0	0	0	1
1983—Cincinnati NFL	9	156	92	59.0	1159	2	5	7.43	29	117	4.0	2	2	12	6
1984—Cincinnati NFL	8	117	78	66.7	945	4	7	8.08	13	77	5.9	1	1	6	2
1985—Cincinnati NFL	7	51	33	64.7	460	1	0	9.02	8	39	4.9	0	0	0	3

Year Club	G.	Att.	Cmp.	Pct.	Gain	T.P.	P.I.	Avg.	Att.	Yds.	Avg.	TD.	TD.	Pts.	F.
				PASSING						RUSHING				TOTAL	
1986—Atlanta NFL	8	154	95	61.7	1032	4	8	6.70	11	12	1.1	1	1	6	5
1987—Cincinnati NFL	11				None						None		0	0	0
Pro Totals—8 Years	49	498	309	62.0	3768	11	20	7.57	71	278	3.9	4	4	24	18

Quarterback Rating Points: 1981 (82.3), 1982 (91.7), 1983 (73.1), 1984 (77.8), 1985 (100.1), 1986 (68.4). Total—76.0.
Additional pro statistics: Recovered one fumble, 1982; recovered four fumbles, 1983; recovered two fumbles and fumbled three times for minus two yards, 1985; recovered one fumble and fumbled five times for minus two yards, 1986.
Member of Cincinnati Bengals for AFC and NFL Championship Games following 1981 season; did not play.

ADAM SCHREIBER
Guard—Philadelphia Eagles
Born February 20, 1962, at Galveston, Tex.
Height, 6.04. Weight, 277.
High School—Huntsville, Ala., Butler.
Attended University of Texas.

Selected by Houston in 1984 USFL territorial draft.
Selected by Seattle in 9th round (243rd player selected) of 1984 NFL draft.
Signed by Seattle Seahawks, June 20, 1984.
Released by Seattle Seahawks, August 27, 1984; re-signed by Seahawks, October 10, 1984.
Released by Seattle Seahawks, August 29, 1985; signed as free agent by New Orleans Saints, November 20, 1985.
Released by New Orleans Saints, September 1, 1986; signed as free agent by Philadelphia Eagles, October 16, 1986.
Seattle NFL, 1984; New Orleans NFL, 1985; Philadelphia NFL, 1986 and 1987.
Games: 1984 (6), 1985 (1), 1986 (9), 1987 (12). Total—28.

JAY BRIAN SCHROEDER
Name pronounced SCHRAY-der.
Quarterback—Washington Redskins
Born June 28, 1961, at Milwaukee, Wis.
Height, 6.04. Weight, 215.
High School—Pacific Palisades, Calif.
Attended University of California at Los Angeles.

Selected by Washington in 3rd round (83rd player selected) of 1984 NFL draft.
Active for 16 games with Washington Redskins in 1984; did not play.

Year Club	G.	Att.	Cmp.	Pct.	Gain	T.P.	P.I.	Avg.	Att.	Yds.	Avg.	TD.	TD.	Pts.	F.
				PASSING						RUSHING				TOTAL	
1985—Washington NFL	9	209	112	53.6	1458	5	5	6.98	17	30	1.8	0	0	0	5
1986—Washington NFL	16	541	276	51.0	4109	22	22	7.60	36	47	1.3	1	1	6	9
1987—Washington NFL	11	267	129	48.3	1878	12	10	7.03	26	120	4.6	3	3	18	5
Pro Totals—4 Years	36	1017	517	50.8	7445	39	37	7.32	79	197	2.5	4	4	24	19

Quarterback Rating Points: 1985 (73.8), 1986 (72.9), 1987 (71.0). Total—72.6.
Additional pro statistics: Punted four times for 33.0 average, recovered one fumble and fumbled five times for minus three yards, 1985; recovered five fumbles and fumbled nine times for minus 19 yards, 1986.
Played in NFC Championship Game following 1986 and 1987 seasons.
Played in NFL Championship Game following 1987 season.
Played in Pro Bowl (NFL All-Star Game) following 1986 season.

RECORD AS BASEBALL PLAYER
Led Carolina League batters in strikeouts with 172 in 1982.
Led South Atlantic League batters in strikeouts with 142 in 1981.
Received reported $100,000 bonus to sign with Toronto Blue Jays, 1979.

Year Club	League	Pos.	G.	AB.	R.	H.	2B.	3B.	HR.	RBI.	B.A.	PO.	A.	E.	F.A.
1979—Utica†	NYP						(Did not play)								
1980—Medicine Hat‡	Pion.	OF	52	171	27	40	6	2	2	21	.234	93	6	5	.952
1981—Florence	S. Atl.	3B-OF	131	417	51	85	17	1	10	47	.204	112	101	28	.884
1982—Kinston	Carol.	OF	132	435	59	95	17	1	15	55	.218	178	17	15	.929
1983—Kinston§	Carol.	C-OF-1B	92	281	30	58	9	2	9	43	.206	519	53	20	.966

Selected by Toronto Blue Jays' organization in 1st round (third player selected) of free-agent draft, June 5, 1979.
†On temporary inactive list, June 30, 1979 through remainder of season.
‡On temporary inactive list, August 14 to September 3, 1980.
§Released, February 28, 1984.

ERIC JON SCHUBERT
Placekicker—Los Angeles Raiders
Born May 28, 1962, at Abington, Pa.
Height, 5.08. Weight, 193.
High School—Wanaque, N.J., Lakeland Regional.
Attended University of Pittsburgh.

Selected by Pittsburgh in 1984 USFL territorial draft.
Signed by Pittsburgh Maulers, May 17, 1984.
Franchise disbanded, October 25, 1984; not selected in USFL dispersal draft, December 6, 1984.
Signed as free agent by New Jersey Generals, January 21, 1985.
Released by New Jersey Generals, February 18, 1985; signed as free agent by New England Patriots, April 16, 1985.
Released by New England Patriots, August 12, 1985; signed as free agent by New York Giants, August 20, 1985.
Released by New York Giants, August 26, 1985; re-signed by Giants, November 1, 1985.
Released by New York Giants, August 20, 1986; signed as free agent by St. Louis Cardinals, November 19, 1986.

Released by St. Louis Cardinals, April 2, 1987; signed as free agent by Kansas City Chiefs, May 14, 1987.
Released by Kansas City Chiefs, July 27, 1987; signed as free agent replacement player by New England Patriots, September 24, 1987.
Released by New England Patriots, October 15, 1987; re-signed by Patriots, October 23, 1987.
Released by New England Patriots, October 26, 1987; signed as free agent by Los Angeles Raiders for 1988, December 24, 1987.

			—PLACE KICKING—			
Year	Club	G.	XP.	XPM.	FG.	FGA.	Pts.
1984—Pittsburgh USFL......		6	4	2	4	10	16
1985—N.Y. Giants NFL		8	26	1	10	13	56
1986—St. Louis NFL............		5	9	0	3	11	18
1987—New England NFL..		1	1	0	1	2	4
USFL Totals—1 Year.....		6	4	2	4	10	16
NFL Totals—3 Years.....		14	36	1	14	26	78
Pro Totals—4 Years.......		20	40	3	18	36	94

COACHING RECORD

Assistant coach at Lakeland Regional High School, Wanaque, N.J., 1985.

SCOTT ANDREW SCHWEDES
Wide Receiver—Miami Dolphins
Born June 30, 1965, at Syracuse, N. Y.
Height, 6.00. Weight, 174.
High School—Dewitt, N. Y., Jamesville-DeWitt.
Received bachelor of science degree in marketing
from Syracuse University in 1987.

Selected by Miami in 2nd round (56th player selected) of 1987 NFL draft.
Signed by Miami Dolphins, August 4, 1987.

			-PUNT RETURNS-				—KICKOFF RET.—				—TOTAL—		
Year	Club	G.	No.	Yds.	Avg.	TD.	No.	Yds.	Avg.	TD.	TD.	Pts.	F.
1987—Miami NFL..............................		12	24	203	8.5	0	9	177	19.7	0	0	0	7

Additonal pro statistics: Recovered three fumbles, 1987.

CARLOS B. SCOTT
Offensive Tackle—Denver Broncos
Born July 2, 1960, at Hempstead, Tex.
Height, 6.04. Weight, 285.
High School—Waller, Tex.
Attended University of Texas at El Paso.

Selected by Arizona in 18th round (215th player selected) of 1983 USFL draft.
Selected by St. Louis in 7th round (184th player selected) of 1983 NFL draft.
Signed by St. Louis Cardinals, July 13, 1983.
Released by St. Louis Cardinals, August 21, 1986; signed as free agent by New York Jets, March 11, 1987.
Released by New York Jets, September 6, 1987; signed as free agent by Denver Broncos, September 25, 1987.
Released by Denver Broncos, October 19, 1987; re-signed by Broncos, April 5, 1988.
Active for 1 game with Denver Broncos in 1987; did not play.
St. Louis NFL, 1983 through 1985; Denver NFL, 1987.
Games: 1983 (13), 1984 (16), 1985 (16). Total—45.
Pro statistics: Fumbled once, 1985.

CHRISTOPHER STERLING SCOTT
(Chris)
Defensive End—Miami Dolphins
Born December 11, 1961, at Berea, O.
Height, 6.05. Weight, 271.
High School—Berea, O.
Attended Purdue University.

Selected by Indianapolis in 3rd round (66th player selected) of 1984 NFL draft.
Released by Indianapolis Colts, September 1, 1986; re-signed by Colts, July 22, 1987.
Released by Indianapolis Colts, August 11, 1987; re-signed as replacement player by Colts, September 28, 1987.
Released by Indianapolis Colts, October 19, 1987; signed as free agent by Miami Dolphins for 1988, December 18, 1987.
Indianapolis NFL, 1984, 1985 and 1987.
Games: 1984 (14), 1985 (16), 1987 (3). Total—33.

CHUCK SCOTT
Wide Receiver—San Francisco 49ers
Born May 24, 1963, at Jacksonville, Fla.
Height, 6.02. Weight, 202.
High School—Maitland, Fla., Lake Howell.
Attended Vanderbilt University.

Named as tight end on THE SPORTING NEWS College All-America Team, 1983.
Selected by Memphis in 1985 USFL territorial draft.
Selected by Los Angeles Rams in 2nd round (50th player selected) of 1985 NFL draft.

Signed by Los Angeles Rams, July 26, 1985.
On injured reserve with rotator cuff injury, September 2 through entire 1985 season.
Released by Los Angeles Rams, September 1, 1986; re-signed by Rams, September 2, 1986.
On injured reserve with shoulder injury, November 13 through remainder of 1986 season.
Released by Los Angeles Rams, September 7, 1987; signed as free agent by Dallas Cowboys, September 30, 1987.
Released by Dallas Cowboys, October 26, 1987; signed as free agent by San Francisco 49ers, April 22, 1988.

		—PASS RECEIVING—				
Year	Club	G.	P.C.	Yds.	Avg.	TD.
1986—L.A. Rams NFL............		9	5	76	15.2	0
1987—Dallas NFL		2	1	11	11.0	0
Pro Totals—2 Years...........		11	6	87	14.5	0

PATRICK S. SCOTT
Wide Receiver—Green Bay Packers
Born September 13, 1964, at Shreveport, La.
Height, 5.10. Weight, 170.
High School—Ringgold, La.
Received bachelor of science degree from Grambling State University in 1987.

Selected by Green Bay in 11th round (282nd player selected) of 1987 NFL draft.
Signed by Green Bay Packers, July 28, 1987.
Released by Green Bay Packers, September 7, 1987; re-signed as replacement by Packers, September 25, 1987.

		—PASS RECEIVING—				
Year	Club	G.	P.C.	Yds.	Avg.	TD.
1987—Green Bay NFL............		8	8	79	9.9	0

Additional pro statistics: Rushed once for two yards, returned six punts for 71 yards, returned two kickoffs for 32 yards, recovered two fumbles and fumbled twice, 1987.

VICTOR RAMONE SCOTT
Safety—Dallas Cowboys
Born June 1, 1962, at East St. Louis, Ill.
Height, 6.00. Weight, 203.
High School—East St. Louis, Ill.
Attended University of Colorado.

Selected by Denver in 1984 USFL territorial draft.
Selected by Dallas in 2nd round (40th player selected) of 1984 NFL draft.
Signed by Dallas Cowboys, June 27, 1984.
On injured reserve with dislocated wrist, October 11 through December 19, 1986; activated, December 20, 1986.
On non-football injury list with drug problem, October 30 through November 30, 1987; activated, December 1, 1987.

		—INTERCEPTIONS—				
Year	Club	G.	No.	Yds.	Avg.	TD.
1984—Dallas NFL		16	1	5	5.0	0
1985—Dallas NFL		16	2	26	13.0	*1
1986—Dallas NFL		5	1	31	31.0	0
1987—Dallas NFL		6	1	1	1.0	0
Pro Totals—4 Years...........		43	5	63	12.6	1

Additional pro statistics: Recovered two fumbles, 1984; fumbled once, 1985; recovered one fumble for three yards, 1987.

COLIN ROBERT SCOTTS
Defensive Tackle—Phoenix Cardinals
Born April 26, 1963, at Sydney, Australia.
Height, 6.05. Weight, 263.
High School—Sydney, Australia, Scots College.
Attended University of Hawaii.

Selected by St. Louis in 3rd round (70th player selected) of 1987 NFL draft.
Signed by St. Louis Cardinals, July 18, 1987.
Franchise transferred to Phoenix, March 15, 1988.
St. Louis NFL, 1987.
Games: 1987 (7).

WILLIAM CHARLES SCRIBNER
(Bucky)
Punter—Minnesota Vikings
Born July 11, 1960, at Lawrence, Kan.
Height, 6.00. Weight, 205.
High School—Lawrence, Kan.
Attended Pratt Community College and received bachelor of
arts degree in personnel administration from Kansas University.

Selected by Green Bay in 11th round (299th player selected) of 1983 NFL draft.
Released by Green Bay Packers, September 4, 1985; signed as free agent by Seattle Seahawks, May 14, 1986.
Released by Seattle Seahawks, August 11, 1986; signed as free agent replacement player by Minnesota Vikings, October 14, 1987.
Released by Minnesota Vikings, October 19, 1987; re-signed by Vikings, November 4, 1987.
Released by Minnesota Vikings, November 10, 1987; re-signed by Vikings for 1988, November 13, 1987.

Signed for 1987 season, December 8, 1987.

Year Club	—PUNTING—		
	G.	No.	Avg. Blk.
1983—Green Bay NFL	16	69	41.6 1
1984—Green Bay NFL	16	85	42.3 0
1987—Minnesota NFL	4	20	41.3 0
Pro Totals—3 Years	36	174	41.9 1

Additional pro statistics: Attemped one pass with no completions, 1984; rushed once for minus seven yards and fumbled once, 1987.
Played in NFC Championship Game following 1987 season.

JOHN SCULLY
Guard—Atlanta Falcons
Born August 2, 1958, at Huntington, N.Y.
Height, 6.06. Weight, 270.
High School—Huntington, N.Y., Holy Family.
Received bachelor of arts degree in sociology from University of Notre Dame in 1980.
Brother-in-law of Tom Thayer, guard with Chicago Bears.
Named as center on THE SPORTING NEWS College All-America Team, 1980.
Selected by Atlanta in 4th round (109th player selected) of 1981 NFL draft.
On injured reserve with broken leg, October 29 through remainder of 1985 season.
On injured reserve with broken leg, December 13 through remainder of 1986 season.
Atlanta NFL, 1981 through 1987.
Games: 1981 (16), 1982 (9), 1983 (16), 1984 (16), 1985 (8), 1986 (14), 1987 (12). Total—91.
Pro statistics: Returned one kickoff for no yards, 1982; recovered one fumble, 1984; recovered two fumbles, 1986.

EUGENE SEALE
Linebacker—Houston Oilers
Born June 3, 1964, at Jasper, Tex.
Height, 5.10. Weight, 250.
High School—Jasper, Tex.
Attended Lamar University.
Selected by New Jersey in 5th round (34th player selected) of 1986 USFL draft.
Signed by New Jersey Generals, May 28, 1986.
Granted free agency when USFL suspended operations, August 7, 1986; signed as replacement player by Houston Oilers, September 23, 1987.
Released by Houston Oilers, November 3, 1987; re-signed by Oilers, November 24, 1987.
Houston NFL, 1987.
Games: 1987 (9).
Pro statistics: Intercepted one pass for 73 yards and a touchdown, 1987.

SAMUEL RICARDO SEALE
(Sam)
Cornerback—Los Angeles Raiders
Born October 6, 1962, at Barbados, West Indies.
Height, 5.09. Weight, 185.
High School—Orange, N.J.
Attended Western State College.
Selected by Memphis in 15th round (309th player selected) of 1984 USFL draft.
Selected by Los Angeles Raiders in 8th round (224th player selected) of 1984 NFL draft.
Signed by Los Angeles Raiders, June 6, 1984.

Year Club	G.	-INTERCEPTIONS-				—KICKOFF RET.—				—TOTAL—		
		No.	Yds.	Avg.	TD.	No.	Yds.	Avg.	TD.	TD.	Pts.	F.
1984—Los Angeles Raiders NFL	12	None				None				0	0	0
1985—Los Angeles Raiders NFL	16	1	38	38.0	1	23	482	21.0	0	1	6	0
1986—Los Angeles Raiders NFL	16	4	2	0.5	0	None				0	0	0
1987—Los Angeles Raiders NFL	12	None				None				0	0	0
Pro Totals—4 Years	56	5	40	8.0	1	23	482	21.0		1	6	0

Additional pro statistics: Recovered one fumble, 1986; recovered one fumble for minus nine yards, 1987.

LEON SEALS
Defensive End—Buffalo Bills
Born January 30, 1964, at New Orleans, La.
Height, 6.04. Weight, 265.
High School—Baton Rouge, La., Scotlandville.
Attended Jackson State University.
Selected by Buffalo in 4th round (109th player selected) of 1987 NFL draft.
Signed by Buffalo Bills, July 26, 1987.
Crossed picket line during players' strike, October 14, 1987.
Buffalo NFL, 1987.
Games: 1987 (13).

JOHN R. SETTLE
Running Back—Atlanta Falcons
Born June 2, 1965, at Reidsville, N.C.
Height, 5.09. Weight, 207.
High School—Ruffin, N.C., Rockingham County.
Attended Appalachian State University.
Signed as free agent by Atlanta Falcons, May 1, 1987.

			—RUSHING—			PASS RECEIVING			—TOTAL—		
Year	Club	G.	Att.	Yds.	Avg.	TD.	P.C.	Yds.	Avg.	TD.	TD.	Pts.	F.
1987—Atlanta NFL		9	19	72	3.8	0	11	153	13.9	0	0	0	2

			KICKOFF RETURNS			
Year	Club	G.	No.	Yds.	Avg.TD.
1987—Atlanta NFL		9	10	158	15.8	0

Additional pro statistics: Recovered one fumble, 1987.

FRANK SEURER
Name pronounced SIGH-er.
Quarterback—Kansas City Chiefs
Born August 16, 1962, at Huntington Beach, Calif.
Height, 6.01. Weight, 195.
High School—Huntington Beach, Calif., Edison.
Attended University of Kansas.
Selected by Los Angeles in 5th round (94th player selected) of 1984 USFL draft.
Signed by Los Angeles Express, January 16, 1984.
Selected by Seattle in 3rd round (76th player selected) of 1984 NFL supplemental draft.
Released by Los Angeles Express, July 22, 1985; signed by Seattle Seahawks, July 25, 1985.
Released by Seattle Seahawks, August 20, 1985; signed as free agent by Kansas City Chiefs, April 14, 1986.
On non-football injury list with ankle injury, September 7 through October 22, 1987; activated, October 23, 1987.

			—————PASSING—————							—RUSHING—			—TOTAL—		
Year	Club	G.	Att.	Cmp.	Pct.	Gain	T.P.	P.I.	Avg.	Att.	Yds.	Avg.	TD.	TD.	Pts.	F.
1984—Los Angeles USFL		7	132	64	48.5	658	3	8	4.98	11	32	2.9	0	0	0	1
1985—Los Angeles USFL		13	242	120	49.6	1479	7	18	6.11	16	96	6.0	0	0	0	3
1986—Kansas City NFL		1				None						None		0	0	0
1987—Kansas City NFL		8	55	26	47.3	340	0	4	6.18	9	33	3.7	0	0	0	2
USFL Totals—2 Years		20	374	184	49.2	2137	10	26	5.71	27	128	4.7	0	0	0	4
NFL Totals—2 Years		9	55	26	47.3	340	0	4	6.18	9	33	3.7	0	0	0	2
Pro Totals—4 Years		29	429	210	49.0	2477	10	30	5.77	36	161	4.5	0	0	0	6

USFL Quarterback Rating Points: 1984 (45.6), 1985 (47.5). Total—46.7.
NFL Quarterback Rating Points: 1987 (36.9).
Additional USFL statistics: Recovered two fumbles for six yards, 1984; recovered one fumble, 1985.
Additional NFL statistics: Recovered one fumble, 1987.

STEVEN EDWARD SEWELL
(Steve)
Running Back-Wide Receiver—Denver Broncos
Born April 2, 1963, at San Francisco, Calif.
Height, 6.03. Weight, 210.
High School—San Francisco, Calif., Riordan.
Attended University of Oklahoma.
Selected by Los Angeles in 1st round (16th player selected) of 1985 USFL draft.
Selected by Denver in 1st round (26th player selected) of 1985 NFL draft.
Signed by Denver Broncos, July 22, 1985.
On injured reserve with separated shoulder, November 14 through December 16, 1986; activated, December 17, 1986.
On injured reserve with broken jaw, November 24, 1987 through January 8, 1988; activated, January 9, 1988.

			—RUSHING—			PASS RECEIVING			—TOTAL—		
Year	Club	G.	Att.	Yds.	Avg.	TD.	P.C.	Yds.	Avg.	TD.	TD.	Pts.	F.
1985—Denver NFL		16	81	275	3.4	4	24	224	9.3	1	5	30	0
1986—Denver NFL		11	23	123	5.3	1	23	294	12.8	1	2	12	0
1987—Denver NFL		7	19	83	4.4	2	13	209	16.1	1	3	18	1
Pro Totals—3 Years		34	123	481	3.9	7	60	727	12.1	3	10	60	1

Additional pro statistics: Returned one kickoff for 29 yards, attempted one pass with no completions and recovered one fumble, 1985; attempted one pass with one completion for 23 yards and a touchdown, 1986.
Played in AFC Championship Game following 1986 and 1987 seasons.
Played in NFL Championship Game following 1986 and 1987 seasons.

LUIS ERNESTO SHARPE JR.
Offensive Tackle—Phoenix Cardinals
Born June 16, 1960, at Havana, Cuba.
Height, 6.04. Weight, 260.
High School—Detroit, Mich., Southwestern.
Attended University of California at Los Angeles.
Named as offensive tackle on THE SPORTING NEWS College All-America Team, 1981.

Selected by St. Louis in 1st round (16th player selected) of 1982 NFL draft.
Granted free agency, February 1, 1985.
USFL rights traded by Houston Gamblers to Memphis Showboats for draft picks, April 18, 1985.
Signed by Memphis Showboats, April 18, 1985.
Released by Memphis Showboats, August 25, 1985; re-signed by St. Louis Cardinals, August 31, 1985.
Granted roster exemption, August 31 through September 2, 1985; activated, September 3, 1985.
Franchise transferred to Phoenix, March 15, 1988.
St. Louis NFL, 1982 through 1987; Memphis USFL, 1985.
Games: 1982 (9), 1983 (16), 1984 (16), 1985 USFL (10), 1985 NFL (16), 1986 (16), 1987 (12). Total NFL—85. Total Pro—95.
Pro statistics: Recovered one fumble, 1982, 1984 and 1987; rushed once for 11 yards and recovered two fumbles, 1983.
Played in Pro Bowl (NFL All-Star Game) following 1987 season.

CHRISTOPHER JONATHAN SHEFFIELD
(Chris)
Cornerback—Detroit Lions
Born January 9, 1963, at Cairo, Ga.
Height, 6.01. Weight, 200.
High School—Cairo, Ga.
Attended Albany State College.

Signed as free agent by Pittsburgh Steelers, May 1, 1986.
On injured reserve with ankle and shoulder injuries, October 17 through November 27, 1986; activated, November 28, 1986.
Crossed picket line during players' strike, October 14, 1987.
Released by Pittsburgh Steelers, November 3, 1987; signed as free agent by Detroit Lions, November 6, 1987.
Pittsburgh NFL, 1986; Pittsburgh (5)-Detroit (6) NFL, 1987.
Games: 1986 (10), 1987 (11). Total—21.
Pro statistics: Intercepted one pass for two yards, 1987.

TODD ANDREW SHELL
Linebacker—San Francisco 49ers
Born June 24, 1962, at Mesa, Ariz.
Height, 6.04. Weight, 225.
High School—Mesa, Ariz., Mountain View.
Attended Brigham Young University.

Selected by Denver in 3rd round (51st player selected) of 1984 USFL draft.
Selected by San Francisco in 1st round (24th player selected) of 1984 NFL draft.
Signed by San Francisco 49ers, June 12, 1984.
On injured reserve with groin injury, September 3 through October 24, 1986; activated, October 25, 1986.
On injured reserve with thigh injury, October 29 through remainder of 1986 season.
On injured reserve with knee injury, September 7 through November 20, 1987; activated, November 21, 1987.

| | | | —INTERCEPTIONS— | | |
Year Club	G.	No.	Yds.	Avg.	TD.
1984—San Francisco NFL	16	3	81	27.0	1
1985—San Francisco NFL	15	1	33	33.0	0
1986—San Francisco NFL	1		None		
1987—San Francisco NFL	6	1	1	1.0	0
Pro Totals—4 Years............	38	5	115	23.0	1

Additional pro statistics: Recovered one fumble, 1984 and 1985.
Played in NFC Championship Game following 1984 season.
Played in NFL Championship Game following 1984 season.

ELBERT VERNELL SHELLEY
Safety—Atlanta Falcons
Born December 24, 1964, at Tyronza, Ark.
Height, 5.11. Weight, 180.
High School—Trumann, Ark.
Attended Arkansas State University.

Selected by Atlanta in 11th round (292nd player selected) of 1987 NFL draft.
Signed by Atlanta Falcons, July 27, 1987.
On injured reserve with neck injury, September 2 through November 27, 1987; activated, November 28, 1987.
Atlanta NFL, 1987.
Games: 1987 (4).

MICHAEL WATSON SHERRARD
(Mike)
Wide Receiver—Dallas Cowboys
Born June 21, 1963, at Oakland, Calif.
Height, 6.02. Weight, 194.
High School—Chino, Calif.
Received bachelor of arts degree in history from University of California at Los Angeles in 1986.
Son of Cherrie Sherrard, sprinter in 100-meter hurdles for 1964 U.S. Olympic Team.

Selected by Arizona in 1986 USFL territorial draft.
Selected by Dallas in 1st round (18th player selected) of 1986 NFL draft.

Signed by Dallas Cowboys, August 7, 1986.
On injured reserve with broken leg, September 1 through entire 1987 season.

Year Club	G.	P.C.	Yds.	Avg.	TD.
		—PASS RECEIVING—			
1986—Dallas NFL	16	41	744	18.1	5

Additional pro statistics: Rushed twice for 11 yards, 1986.

TIMOTHY THOMAS SHERWIN
(Tim)
Tight End—Indianapolis Colts
Born May 4, 1958, at Troy, N.Y.
Height, 6.05. Weight, 252.
High School—Watervliet, N.Y.
Received bachelor of arts degree in sociology from Boston College in 1981.

Selected by Baltimore in 4th round (94th player selected) of 1981 NFL draft.
Franchise transferred to Indianapolis, March 31, 1984.
On injured reserve with knee injury, November 6 through remainder of 1985 season.
Released by Indianapolis Colts, October 8, 1986; re-signed by Colts, December 10, 1986.
On injured reserve with wrist injury, December 3 through remainder of 1987 season.

Year Club	G.	P.C.	Yds.	Avg.	TD.
		—PASS RECEIVING—			
1981—Baltimore NFL	16	2	19	9.5	0
1982—Baltimore NFL	9	21	280	13.3	0
1983—Baltimore NFL	15	25	358	14.3	0
1984—Indianapolis NFL	16	11	169	15.4	0
1985—Indianapolis NFL	8	5	64	12.8	0
1986—Indianapolis NFL	7	3	26	8.7	1
1987—Indianapolis NFL	8	9	86	9.6	1
Pro Totals—7 Years	79	76	1002	13.2	2

Additional pro statistics: Recovered one fumble for a touchdown, 1982; returned one kickoff for two yards, 1984; fumbled once, 1985.

JACKIE RENARDO SHIPP
Linebacker—Miami Dolphins
Born March 19, 1962, at Muskogee, Okla.
Height, 6.02. Weight, 236.
High School—Stillwater, Okla., C.E. Donart.
Attended Oklahoma University.

Selected by Oklahoma in 1984 USFL territorial draft.
Selected by Miami in 1st round (14th player selected) of 1984 NFL draft.
Signed by Miami Dolphins, July 14, 1984.
Miami NFL, 1984 through 1987.
Games: 1984 (16), 1985 (16), 1986 (16), 1987 (12). Total—60.
Pro statistics: Intercepted one pass for seven yards and recovered two fumbles, 1985; recovered one fumble, 1986.
Played in AFC Championship Game following 1984 and 1985 seasons.
Played in NFL Championship Game following 1984 season.

MICKEY CHARLES SHULER
Tight End—New York Jets
Born August 21, 1956, at Harrisburg, Pa.
Height, 6.03. Weight, 231.
High School—Enola, Pa., East Pennsboro.
Received degree in health and physical education from Pennsylvania State University.

Selected by New York Jets in 3rd round (61st player selected) of 1978 NFL draft.
On injured reserve with shoulder separation, September 1 through November 13, 1981; activated, November 14, 1981.

Year Club	G.	P.C.	Yds.	Avg.	TD.
		—PASS RECEIVING—			
1978—N.Y. Jets NFL	16	11	67	6.1	3
1979—N.Y. Jets NFL	16	16	225	14.1	3
1980—N.Y. Jets NFL	16	22	226	10.3	2
1981—N.Y. Jets NFL	6		None		
1982—N.Y. Jets NFL	9	8	132	16.5	3
1983—N.Y. Jets NFL	16	26	272	10.5	1
1984—N.Y. Jets NFL	16	68	782	11.5	6
1985—N.Y. Jets NFL	16	76	879	11.6	7
1986—N.Y. Jets NFL	16	69	675	9.8	4
1987—N.Y. Jets NFL	11	43	434	10.1	3
Pro Totals—10 Years	138	339	3692	10.9	32

Additional pro statistics: Fumbled once, 1978 through 1980, 1984 and 1985; returned one kickoff for 12 yards, 1978; returned one kickoff for 15 yards, 1979; returned two kickoffs for 25 yards, 1980; returned one kickoff for three yards, 1983; returned one kickoff for no yards, 1984; recovered one fumble, 1985 and 1986; returned two kickoffs for minus three yards, 1986; fumbled twice, 1987.
Played in AFC Championship Game following 1982 season.
Played in Pro Bowl (NFL All-Star Game) following 1986 season.

ERIC SCOTT SIEVERS
Tight End—San Diego Chargers
Born November 9, 1958, at Urbana, Ill.
Height, 6.04. Weight, 230.
High School—Arlington, Va., Washington & Lee.
Attended University of Maryland.
Selected by San Diego in 4th round (107th player selected) of 1981 NFL draft.
On injured reserve with knee injury, November 19 through remainder of 1986 season.

		—PASS RECEIVING—			
Year Club	G.	P.C.	Yds.	Avg.	TD.
1981—San Diego NFL	16	22	276	12.5	3
1982—San Diego NFL	9	12	173	14.4	1
1983—San Diego NFL	16	33	452	13.7	3
1984—San Diego NFL	14	41	438	10.7	3
1985—San Diego NFL	16	41	438	10.7	6
1986—San Diego NFL	9	2	14	7.0	0
1987—San Diego NFL	12			None	
Pro Totals—7 Years...........	92	151	1791	11.9	16

Additional pro statistics: Returned two kickoffs for four yards, 1981; recovered one fumble and fumbled once, 1981 and 1984; returned one kickoff for 17 yards, 1982; returned one kickoff for six yards and rushed once for minus seven yards, 1983; returned one kickoff for three yards, 1985.
Played in AFC Championship Game following 1981 season.

VAI SIKAHEMA
Running Back-Kick Returner—Phoenix Cardinals
Born August 29, 1962, at Nuku'Alofa, Tonga.
Height, 5.09. Weight, 191.
High School—Mesa, Ariz.
Attended Brigham Young University.
Tied NFL record for most touchdowns, punt returns, game (2), against Tampa Bay Buccaneers, December 21, 1986.
Selected by St. Louis in 10th round (254th player selected) of 1986 NFL draft.
Selected by Arizona in 7th round (47th player selected) of 1986 USFL draft.
Signed by St. Louis Cardinals, July 11, 1986.
Crossed picket line during players' strike, October 2, 1987.
Franchise transferred to Phoenix, March 15, 1988.

		—RUSHING—				PASS RECEIVING				—TOTAL—		
Year Club	G.	Att.	Yds.	Avg.	TD.	P.C.	Yds.	Avg.	TD.	TD.	Pts.	F.
1986—St. Louis NFL..	16	16	62	3.9	0	10	99	9.9	1	3	18	2
1987—St. Louis NFL..	15			None				None		1	6	0
Pro Totals—2 Years...................................	31	16	62	3.9	0	10	99	9.9	1	4	24	2

		—PUNT RETURNS—				—KICKOFF RET.—		
Year Club	G.	No.	Yds.	Avg.	TD.	No.	Yds.	Avg.TD.
1986—St. Louis NFL..	16	43	*522	12.1	*2	37	847	22.9 0
1987—St. Louis NFL..	15	*44	*550	12.5	1	34	761	22.4 0
Pro Totals—2 Years...................................	31	87	1072	12.3	3	71	1608	22.6 0

Played in Pro Bowl (NFL All-Star Game) following 1986 and 1987 seasons.

DANIEL WILLIAM SILEO
(Dan)
Nose Tackle—Tampa Bay Buccaneers
Born January 3, 1964, at Stamford, Conn.
Height, 6.02. Weight, 282.
High School—Stamford, Conn., Stamford Catholic.
Attended University of Maryland, University of Cincinnati and University of Miami (Fla.).
Signed as free agent by Tampa Bay Bucaneers, September 6, 1987.
Contract voided by NFL, September 11, 1987.
Selected by Tampa Bay in 3rd round of 1987 NFL supplemental draft, September 16, 1987.
Signed by Tampa Bay Bucaneers, September 16, 1987.
Granted roster exemption, September 16 through October 23, 1987; activated, October 24, 1987.
Tampa Bay NFL, 1987.
Games: 1987 (10).

ANTHONY EARL SIMMONS
(Tony)
Defensive End—Buffalo Bills
Born December 18, 1962, at Oakland, Calif.
Height, 6.04. Weight, 270.
High School—Oakland, Calif., McClymonds.
Attended University of Tennessee.
Selected by Memphis in 1985 USFL territorial draft.
Selected by San Diego in 12th round (318th player selected) of 1985 NFL draft.
Signed by San Diego Chargers, July 10, 1985.

On injured reserve with knee injury, August 25 through entire 1986 season.
Released by San Diego Chargers, August 29, 1987; re-signed as replacement player by Chargers, September 28, 1987.
Released by San Diego Chargers, October 21, 1987; signed as free agent by Buffalo Bills, May 12, 1988.
San Diego NFL, 1985 and 1987.
Games: 1985 (13), 1987 (3). Total—16.

CLYDE SIMMONS
Defensive End—Philadelphia Eagles
Born August 4, 1964, at Lanes, S. C.
Height, 6.06. Weight, 276.
High School—Wilmington, N. C., New Hanover.
Attended Western Carolina University.

Selected by Philadelphia in 9th round (233rd player selected) of 1986 NFL draft.
Signed by Philadelphia Eagles, July 3, 1986.
Philadelphia NFL, 1986 and 1987.
Games: 1986 (16), 1987 (12). Total—28.
Pro statistics: Returned one kickoff for no yards, 1986; recovered one fumble, 1987.

ED SIMMONS
Offensive Tackle—Washington Redskins
Born December 31, 1963, at Seattle, Wash.
Height, 6.05. Weight, 275.
High School—Seattle, Wash., Nathan Hale.
Attended Eastern Washington University.

Selected by Washington in 6th round (164th player selected) of 1987 NFL draft.
Signed by Washington Redskins, July 24, 1987.
On injured reserve with knee injury, November 23 through remainder of 1987 season.
Washington NFL, 1987.
Games: 1987 (5).

PHILLIP SIMMS
(Phil)
Quarterback—New York Giants
Born November 3, 1956, at Lebanon, Ky.
Height, 6.03. Weight, 216.
High School—Louisville, Ky., Southern.
Attended Morehead State University.

Selected by New York Giants in 1st round (7th player selected) of 1979 NFL draft.
On injured reserve with separated shoulder, November 18 through December 25, 1981; activated, December 26, 1981.
On injured reserve with knee injury, August 30 through entire 1982 season.
On injured reserve with dislocated thumb, October 13 through remainder of 1983 season.

			—————PASSING—————							——RUSHING——				—TOTAL—		
Year	Club	G.	Att.	Cmp.	Pct.	Gain	T.P.	P.I.	Avg.	Att.	Yds.	Avg.	TD.	TD.	Pts.	F.
1979—N.Y. Giants NFL		12	265	134	50.6	1743	13	14	6.58	29	166	5.7	1	1	6	9
1980—N.Y. Giants NFL		13	402	193	48.0	2321	15	19	5.77	36	190	5.3	1	1	6	6
1981—N.Y. Giants NFL		10	316	172	54.4	2031	11	9	6.43	19	42	2.2	0	0	0	7
1983—N.Y. Giants NFL		2	13	7	53.8	130	0	1	10.00		None			0	0	0
1984—N.Y. Giants NFL		16	533	286	53.7	4044	22	18	7.59	42	162	3.9	0	0	0	8
1985—N.Y. Giants NFL		16	495	275	55.6	3829	22	20	7.74	37	132	3.6	0	0	0	*16
1986—N.Y. Giants NFL		16	468	259	55.3	3487	21	22	7.45	43	72	1.7	1	1	6	9
1987—N.Y. Giants NFL		9	282	163	57.8	2230	17	9	7.91	14	44	3.1	0	0	0	4
Pro Totals—8 Years		94	2774	1489	53.7	19815	121	112	7.14	220	808	3.7	3	3	18	59

Quarterback Rating Points: 1979 (65.9), 1980 (58.9), 1981 (74.2), 1983 (56.6), 1984 (78.1), 1985 (78.6), 1986 (74.6), 1987 (90.0). Total—74.6.
Additional pro statistics: Fumbled nine times for minus two yards, 1979; recovered two fumbles, 1980 and 1981; fumbled six times for minus five yards, 1980; fumbled seven times for minus 15 yards, 1981; caught one pass for 13 yards, recovered four fumbles and fumbled eight times for minus five yards, 1984; recovered five fumbles and fumbled 16 times for minus 22 yards, 1985; recovered three fumbles and fumbled nine times for minus two yards, 1986; recovered one fumble, 1987.
Played in NFC Championship Game following 1986 season.
Played in NFL Championship Game following 1986 season.
Played in Pro Bowl (NFL All-Star Game) following 1985 season.

RONALD BERNARD SIMPKINS
(Ron)
Linebacker—Green Bay Packers
Born April 2, 1958, at Detroit, Mich.
Height, 6.01. Weight, 235.
High School—Detroit, Mich., Western.
Received bachelor of general studies degree from University of Michigan in 1980.

Selected by Cincinnati in 7th round (167th player selected) of 1980 NFL draft.
On injured reserve with pulled hamstring, August 31 through entire 1981 season.
Released by Cincinnati Bengals, September 6, 1982; re-signed by Bengals, September 14, 1982.

On inactive list, September 19, 1982.
Released by Cincinnati Bengals, September 7, 1987; signed as free agent by Green Bay Packers, May 27, 1988.
Cincinnati NFL, 1980 and 1982 through 1986.
Games: 1980 (16), 1982 (5), 1983 (15), 1984 (16), 1985 (16), 1986 (16). Total—84.
Pro statistics: Returned three kickoffs for eight yards and fumbled once, 1980; recovered one fumble, 1980, 1983 and 1984; recovered one fumble for four yards, 1985; returned two kickoffs for 24 yards, 1986.

DARRYL LEON SIMS
Defensive End—Cleveland Browns
Born July 23, 1961, at Winston-Salem, N.C.
Height, 6.03. Weight, 282.
High School—Bridgeport, Conn., Basick.
Attended University of Wisconsin.

Selected by Jacksonville in 1985 USFL territorial draft.
Selected by Pittsburgh in 1st round (20th player selected) of 1985 NFL draft.
Signed by Pittsburgh Steelers, July 18, 1985.
Released by Pittsburgh Steelers, September 7, 1987; signed as free agent replacement player by Cleveland Browns, September 23, 1987.
Pittsburgh NFL, 1985 and 1986; Cleveland NFL, 1987.
Games: 1985 (16), 1986 (16), 1987 (10). Total—42.
Pro statistics: Recovered one fumble for two yards, 1986.
Played in AFC Championship Game following 1987 season.

KENNETH W. SIMS
(Ken)
Defensive End—New England Patriots
Born October 31, 1959, at Kosse, Tex.
Height, 6.05. Weight, 271.
High School—Groesbeck, Tex.
Attended University of Texas.

Named as defensive end on THE SPORTING NEWS College All-America Team, 1981.
Selected by New England in 1st round (1st player selected) of 1982 NFL draft.
On injured reserve with broken leg, December 3 through remainder of 1985 season.
On injured reserve with back and hip injuries, September 2 through October 16, 1986; activated, October 17, 1986.
On injured reserve with back injury, November 26 through remainder of 1986 season.
New England NFL, 1982 through 1987.
Games: 1982 (9), 1983 (5), 1984 (16), 1985 (13), 1986 (3), 1987 (12). Total—58.
Pro statistics: Recovered two fumbles, 1985; recovered one fumble for six yards, 1986; recovered one fumble, 1987.

CURT EDWARD SINGER
Offensive Tackle—Seattle Seahawks
Born November 4, 1961, at Aliquippa, Pa.
Height, 6.05. Weight, 279.
High School—Aliquippa, Pa., Hopewell.
Attended University of Tennessee.

Selected by Memphis in 1984 USFL territorial draft.
Selected by Washington in 6th round (167th player selected) of 1984 NFL draft.
Signed by Washington Redskins, June 26, 1984.
Released by Washington Redskins, August 27, 1984; re-signed by Redskins, August 28, 1984.
On injured reserve with back injury, August 30 through entire 1984 season.
Released by Washington Redskins, August 20, 1985; signed as free agent by Seattle Seahawks, April 15, 1986.
On injured reserve with ankle injury, September 8 through entire 1987 season.
Seattle NFL, 1986.
Games: 1986 (11).

MICHAEL SINGLETARY
(Mike)
Linebacker—Chicago Bears
Born October 9, 1958, at Houston, Tex.
Height, 6.00. Weight, 235.
High School—Houston, Tex., Worthing.
Received bachelor of arts degree in management from Baylor University.

Named to THE SPORTING NEWS NFL All-Star Team, 1984 through 1987.
Named as linebacker on THE SPORTING NEWS College All-America Team, 1980.
Selected by Chicago in 2nd round (38th player selected) of 1981 NFL draft.
Placed on did not report list, August 19 and August 20, 1985.
Granted roster exemption, August 21 through August 25, 1985; activated, August 26, 1985.
Chicago NFL, 1981 through 1987.
Games: 1981 (16), 1982 (9), 1983 (16), 1984 (16), 1985 (16), 1986 (14), 1987 (12). Total—99.
Pro statistics: Intercepted one pass for minus three yards, 1981; recovered one fumble, 1982, 1984 and 1987; intercepted one pass for no yards and recovered four fumbles for 15 yards, 1983; intercepted one pass for four yards, 1984; intercepted one pass for 23 yards and recovered three fumbles for 11 yards, 1985; intercepted one pass for three yards, 1986.
Played in NFC Championship Game following 1984 and 1985 seasons.
Played in NFL Championship Game following 1985 season.
Played in Pro Bowl (NFL All-Star Game) following 1983 through 1987 seasons.

REGGIE SINGLETARY
Guard—Philadelphia Eagles
Born January 17, 1964, at Whiteville, N. C.
Height, 6.03. Weight, 280.
High School—Cerro Gordo, N. C., West Columbus.
Attended North Carolina State University.
Selected by Jacksonville in 1986 USFL territorial draft.
Selected by Philadelphia in 12th round (315th player selected) of 1986 NFL draft.
Signed by Philadelphia Eagles, May 27, 1986.
Philadelphia NFL, 1986 and 1987.
Games: 1986 (16), 1987 (12). Total—28.
Pro statistics: Recovered one fumble, 1986; caught one pass for minus 11 yards, 1987.

PAUL ANTHONY SKANSI
Wide Receiver—Seattle Seahawks
Born January 11, 1961, at Tacoma, Wash.
Height, 5.11. Weight, 183.
High School—Gig Harbor, Wash., Peninsula.
Attended University of Washington.
Selected by Michigan in 4th round (39th player selected) of 1983 USFL draft.
Selected by Pittsburgh in 5th round (133rd player selected) of 1983 NFL draft.
Signed by Pittsburgh Steelers, June 5, 1983.
Released by Pittsburgh Steelers, August 27, 1984; signed as free agent by Seattle Seahawks, October 25, 1984.
Released by Seattle Seahawks, September 2, 1985; re-signed by Seahawks, October 2, 1985.

		PASS RECEIVING				-PUNT RETURNS-				—KICKOFF RET.—				—TOTAL—		
Year Club	G.	P.C.	Yds.	Avg.	TD.	No.	Yds.	Avg.	TD.	No.	Yds.	Avg.	TD.	TD.	Pts.	F.
1983—Pittsburgh NFL............	15	3	39	13.0	0	43	363	8.4	0		None			0	0	5
1984—Seattle NFL..................	7	7	85	12.1	0	16	145	9.1	0		None			0	0	1
1985—Seattle NFL..................	12	21	269	12.8	1	31	312	10.1	0	19	358	18.8	0	1	6	1
1986—Seattle NFL..................	16	22	271	12.3	0	5	38	7.6	0	1	21	21.0	0	0	0	1
1987—Seattle NFL..................	12	19	207	10.9	1		None				None			1	6	1
Pro Totals—5 Years.......	62	72	871	12.1	2	95	858	9.0	0	20	379	19.0	0	2	12	8

Additional pro statistics: Recovered two fumbles, 1983; recovered one fumble, 1985.

JAMES JEFFREY SKOW
(Jim)
Defensive End—Cincinnati Bengals
Born June 29, 1963, at Omaha, Neb.
Height, 6.03. Weight, 250.
High School—Omaha, Neb., Roncalli.
Received degree from University of Nebraska in 1987.
Selected by Cincinnati in 3rd round (58th player selected) of 1986 NFL draft.
Signed by Cincinnati Bengals, August 9, 1986.
Cincinnati NFL, 1986 and 1987.
Games: 1986 (16), 1987 (12). Total—28.

JACKIE RAY SLATER
Offensive Tackle—Los Angeles Rams
Born May 27, 1954, at Jackson, Miss.
Height, 6.04. Weight, 275.
High School—Jackson, Miss., Wingfield.
Received bachelor of arts degree from Jackson State University;
attending Livingston University for master's degree in physical education.
Selected by Los Angeles in 3rd round (86th player selected) of 1976 NFL draft.
On injured reserve with knee injury, October 17 through remainder of 1984 season.
Crossed picket line during players' strike, October 14, 1987.
Los Angeles Rams NFL, 1976 through 1986.
Games: 1976 (14), 1977 (14), 1978 (16), 1979 (16), 1980 (15), 1981 (11), 1982 (9), 1983 (16), 1984 (7), 1985 (16), 1986 (16), 1987 (12). Total—162.
Pro statistics: Recovered one fumble, 1978, 1980 and 1985; recovered one fumble for 13 yards, 1983.
Played in NFC Championship Game following 1976, 1978, 1979 and 1985 seasons.
Played in NFL Championship Game following 1979 season.
Played in Pro Bowl (NFL All-Star Game) following 1983 and 1985 through 1987 seasons.

TONY TYRONE SLATON
Center—Los Angeles Rams
Born April 12, 1961, at Merced, Calif.
Height, 6.03. Weight, 265.
High School—Merced, Calif.
Received bachelor of science degree from University of Southern California in 1984.
Selected by Los Angeles in 1984 USFL territorial draft.
Selected by Buffalo in 6th round (155th player selected) of 1984 NFL draft.
Signed by Buffalo Bills, June 1, 1984.
Released by Buffalo Bills, August 20, 1984; signed as free agent by Los Angeles Rams, August 23, 1984.

On injured reserve with strained abdominal muscles, September 21 through remainder of 1984 season.
Released by Los Angeles Rams, August 20, 1985; re-signed by Rams, September 19, 1985.
Active for 3 games with Los Angeles Rams in 1984; did not play.
Los Angeles Rams NFL, 1984 through 1987.
Games: 1985 (13), 1986 (14), 1987 (11). Total—38.
Pro statistics: Returned one kickoff for 18 yards and recovered one fumble, 1985.
Played in NFC Championship Game following 1985 season.

WEBSTER M. SLAUGHTER
Wide Receiver—Cleveland Browns
Born October 19, 1964, at Stockton, Calif.
Height, 6.00. Weight, 170.
High School—Stockton, Calif., Franklin.
Attended San Diego State University.

Selected by Cleveland in 2nd round (43rd player selected) of 1986 NFL draft.
Signed by Cleveland Browns, July 24, 1986.

| | | —PASS RECEIVING— | | | |
Year	Club	G.	P.C.	Yds.	Avg.	TD.
1986—Cleveland NFL.............		16	40	577	14.4	4
1987—Cleveland NFL.............		12	47	806	17.1	7
Pro Totals—2 Years...........		28	87	1383	15.9	11

Additional pro statistics: Rushed once for one yard, returned one punt for two yards, recovered fumble in end zone for a touchdown, 1986; fumbled once, 1986 and 1987.
Played in AFC Championship Game following 1986 and 1987 seasons.

JOHN FREDRICK SMALL
(Fred)
Linebacker—Atlanta Falcons
Born July 15, 1963, at Los Angeles, Calif.
Height, 5.11. Weight, 227.
High School—Los Angeles, Calif., John C. Fremont.
Attended University of Washington.

Selected by Portland in 1985 USFL territorial draft.
Selected by Pittsburgh in 9th round (241st player selected) of 1985 NFL draft.
Signed by Pittsburgh Steelers, July 19, 1985.
On injured reserve with hamstring injury, August 19 through September 2, 1986.
Released by Pittsburgh Steelers, September 3, 1986; signed as free agent by San Francisco 49ers, February 25, 1987.
On injured reserve with hamstring injury, August 28 through October 25, 1987.
Released by San Francisco 49ers, October 26, 1987; signed as free agent by Atlanta Falcons, April 15, 1988.
Pittsburgh NFL, 1985.
Games: 1985 (16).

DONALD FREDRICK SMEREK
(Don)
Defensive Lineman—Dallas Cowboys
Born December 10, 1957, at Waterford, Mich.
Height, 6.07. Weight, 265.
High School—Henderson, Nev., Basic.
Received degree in physical education from University of Nevada at Reno.

Signed as free agent by Dallas Cowboys, May, 1980.
On injured reserve with rib injury entire 1980 season.
On injured reserve with knee injury, September 19 through remainder of 1981 season.
USFL rights traded by San Antonio Gunslingers to Michigan Panthers for rights to wide receiver Stanley Washington, October 13, 1983.
On injured reserve with shoulder injury, September 10 through October 25, 1985; activated, October 26, 1985.
On injured reserve with knee injury, September 3 through October 10, 1986; activated, October 11, 1986.
On injured reserve with torn hamstring, September 7 through entire 1987 season.
Crossed picket line during players' strike, September 23, 1987.
Dallas NFL, 1981 through 1986.
Games: 1981 (2), 1982 (7), 1983 (15), 1984 (16), 1985 (10), 1986 (11). Total—61.
Played in NFC Championship Game following 1982 season.

FREDERICK C. SMERLAS
(Fred)
Nose Tackle—Buffalo Bills
Born April 8, 1957, at Waltham, Mass.
Height, 6.03. Weight, 280.
High School—Waltham, Mass.
Attended Boston College.

Selected by Buffalo in 2nd round (32nd player selected) of 1979 NFL draft.
On injured reserve with knee injury, November 29 through remainder of 1979 season.
Buffalo NFL, 1979 through 1987.
Games: 1979 (13), 1980 (16), 1981 (16), 1982 (9), 1983 (16), 1984 (16), 1985 (16), 1986 (16), 1987 (12). Total—130.
Pro statistics: Recovered three fumbles for 23 yards and one touchdown, 1979; recovered one fumble for 17 yards,

1981; recovered two fumbles, 1982 and 1984; intercepted one pass for 25 yards, 1984; recovered one fumble, 1985; intercepted one pass for three yards, 1986.
Played in Pro Bowl (NFL All-Star Game) following 1980 through 1983 seasons.

AL FREDRICK SMITH
Linebacker—Houston Oilers
Born November 26, 1964, at Los Angeles, Calif.
Height, 6.01. Weight, 230.
High School—Playa Del Rey, Calif., St. Bernard.
Attended California State Poly University and received bachelor of science degree
in sociology from Utah State University in 1987.
Brother of Aaron Smith, linebacker with Denver Broncos, 1984.
Selected by Houston in 6th round (147th player selected) of 1987 NFL draft.
Signed by Houston Oilers, July 31, 1987.
Houston NFL, 1987.
Games: 1987 (12).

BILLY RAY SMITH JR.
(Billy Ray)
Linebacker—San Diego Chargers
Born August 10, 1961, at Fayetteville, Ark.
Height, 6.03. Weight, 236.
High School—Plano, Tex.
Attended University of Arkansas.
Son of Billy Ray Smith, Sr., defensive tackle with Los Angeles Rams, Pittsburgh
Steelers and Baltimore Colts, 1957 through 1962 and 1964 through 1970.
Named as defensive end on THE SPORTING NEWS College All-America Team, 1981 and 1982.
Selected by Oakland in 1st round (7th player selected) of 1983 USFL draft.
Selected by San Diego in 1st round (5th player selected) of 1983 NFL draft.
Signed by San Diego Chargers, May 19, 1983.
On injured reserve with back injury, December 20 through remainder of 1985 season.

| | | | —INTERCEPTIONS— | | |
Year	Club	G.	No.	Yds.	Avg.TD.
1983—San Diego NFL		16		None	
1984—San Diego NFL		16	3	41	13.7	0
1985—San Diego NFL		15	1	0	0.0	0
1986—San Diego NFL		16		None	
1987—San Diego NFL		12	5	28	5.6	0
Pro Totals—5 Years		75	9	69	7.7	0

Additional pro statistics: Returned one kickoff for 10 yards, 1983; recovered one fumble, 1983 and 1986; recovered three fumbles, 1984, 1985 and 1987; had only pass attempt intercepted, 1987.

BRUCE BERNARD SMITH
Defensive End—Buffalo Bills
Born June 18, 1963, at Norfolk, Va.
Height, 6.04. Weight, 285.
High School—Norfolk, Va., Booker T. Washington.
Attended Virginia Tech.
Named to THE SPORTING NEWS NFL All-Star Team, 1987.
Outland Trophy winner, 1984.
Selected by Baltimore in 1985 USFL territorial draft.
Signed by Buffalo Bills, February 28, 1985.
Selected officially by Buffalo in 1st round (1st player selected) of 1985 NFL draft.
Buffalo NFL, 1985 through 1987.
Games: 1985 (16), 1986 (16), 1987 (12). Total—44.
Pro statistics: Rushed once for no yards and recovered four fumbles, 1985; recovered two fumbles for 15 yards and a touchdown, 1987.
Played in Pro Bowl (NFL All-Star Game) following 1987 season.

CARL DOUGLAS SMITH
(Doug)
Center—Los Angeles Rams
Born November 25, 1956, at Columbus, O.
Height, 6.03. Weight, 260.
High School—Columbus, O., Northland.
Received bachelor of science degree in education from Bowling Green State University in 1978
and attending California State University at Fullerton for master's degree in exercise physiology.
Signed as free agent by Los Angeles Rams, May 16, 1978.
On injured reserve with knee injury, September 28 through remainder of 1979 season.
On injured reserve with knee injury, October 30 through remainder of 1980 season.
On injured reserve with concussion, December 14 through remainder of 1985 season.
Los Angeles Rams NFL, 1978 through 1987.
Games: 1978 (16), 1979 (4), 1980 (8), 1981 (16), 1982 (9), 1983 (14), 1984 (16), 1985 (13), 1986 (16), 1987 (12). Total—124.
Pro statistics: Recovered one fumble, 1978 and 1985; returned one kickoff for eight yards, 1978; fumbled once, 1981 and 1983; recovered two fumbles, 1982.

Played in NFC Championship Game following 1978 season.
Played in Pro Bowl (NFL All-Star Game) following 1984, 1986 and 1987 seasons.
Named to play in Pro Bowl following 1985 season; replaced due to injury by Fred Quillan.

DARYLE RAY SMITH
Offensive Tackle—Dallas Cowboys
Born January 18, 1964, at Knoxville, Tenn.
Height, 6.05. Weight, 278.
High School—Knoxville, Tenn., Powell.
Attended University of Tennessee.

Signed as free agent by Seattle Seahawks, May 5, 1987.
Released by Seattle Seahawks, September 7, 1987; signed as free agent replacement player by Dallas Cowboys,
September 23, 1987.
Dallas NFL, 1987.
Games: 1987 (9).

DENNIS SMITH
Safety—Denver Broncos
Born February 3, 1959, at Santa Monica, Calif.
Height, 6.03. Weight, 200.
High School—Santa Monica, Calif.
Attended University of Southern California.

Selected by Denver in 1st round (15th player selected) of 1981 NFL draft.
On injured reserve with broken arm, November 24, 1987 through January 15, 1988; activated, January 16, 1988.

| | | —INTERCEPTIONS— | | | |
Year Club	G.	No.	Yds.	Avg.	TD.
1981—Denver NFL	16	1	65	65.0	0
1982—Denver NFL	8	1	29	29.0	0
1983—Denver NFL	14	4	39	9.8	0
1984—Denver NFL	15	3	13	4.3	0
1985—Denver NFL	13	3	46	15.3	0
1986—Denver NFL	14	1	0	0.0	0
1987—Denver NFL	6	2	21	10.5	0
Pro Totals—7 Years	86	15	213	14.2	0

Additional pro statistics: Recovered two fumbles, 1981 and 1987; recovered one fumble for 64 yards and a touch-
down, 1984; recovered one fumble, 1986.
Played in AFC Championship Game following 1986 and 1987 seasons.
Played in NFL Championship Game following 1986 and 1987 seasons.
Played in Pro Bowl (NFL All-Star Game) following 1985 and 1986 seasons.

DOUGLAS ARTHUR SMITH
(Doug)
Nose Tackle—Houston Oilers
Born June 13, 1960, at Mesic, N.C.
Height, 6.05. Weight, 285.
High School—Bayboro, N.C., Pamlico Central.
Attended Auburn University.

Named as defensive tackle on THE SPORTING NEWS USFL All-Star Team, 1985.
Selected by Birmingham in 1984 USFL territorial draft.
Selected by Houston in 2nd round (29th player selected) of 1984 NFL draft.
Signed by Birmingham Stallions, August 2, 1984.
On developmental squad, March 2 through March 7, 1985; activated, March 8, 1985.
Released by Birmingham Stallions, October 7, 1985; signed by Houston Oilers, October 10, 1985.
Granted roster exemption, October 10, 1985.
On injured reserve with hamstring injury, December 16 through remainder of 1986 season.
Crossed picket line during players' strike, September 29, 1987.
On developmental squad for 1 game with Birmingham Stallions in 1985.
Birmingham USFL, 1985; Houston NFL, 1985 through 1987.
Games: 1985 USFL (17), 1985 NFL (11), 1986 (13), 1987 (14). Total NFL—38. Total Pro—55.
USFL statistics: Credited with five sacks and recovered one fumble, 1985.

JEFF K. SMITH
Running Back—Tampa Bay Buccaneers
Born March 22, 1962, at Wichita, Kan.
Height, 5.09. Weight, 201.
High School—Wichita, Kan., Southeast.
Attended University of Nebraska.

Selected by Baltimore in 7th round (101st player selected) of 1985 USFL draft.
Selected by Kansas City in 10th round (267th player selected) of 1985 NFL draft.
Signed by Kansas City Chiefs, July 18, 1985.
On injured reserve with sprained ankle, December 4 through remainder of 1985 season.
Traded by Kansas City Chiefs to Tampa Bay Buccaneers for 8th round pick in 1988 draft, September 3, 1987.

Year Club	G.	Att.	Yds.	Avg.	TD.	P.C.	Yds.	Avg.	TD.	TD.	Pts.	F.
		RUSHING				PASS RECEIVING				−TOTAL−		
1985—Kansas City NFL	13	30	118	3.9	0	18	157	8.7	2	2	12	1
1986—Kansas City NFL	15	54	238	4.4	3	33	230	7.0	3	6	36	4
1987—Tampa Bay NFL	12	100	309	3.1	2	20	197	9.9	2	4	24	2
Pro Totals—3 Years	40	184	665	3.6	5	71	584	8.2	7	12	72	7

Year Club	G.	No.	Yds.	Avg.	TD.	No.	Yds.	Avg.	TD.
		−PUNT RETURNS−				−KICKOFF RET.−			
1985—Kansas City NFL	13	None				33	654	19.8	0
1986—Kansas City NFL	15	29	245	8.4	0	29	557	19.2	0
1987—Tampa Bay NFL	12	None				5	84	16.8	0
Pro Totals—3 Years	40	29	245	8.4	0	67	1295	19.3	0

Additional pro statistics: Recovered one fumble, 1985.

JOHN THOMAS SMITH
(J. T.)
Wide Receiver—Phoenix Cardinals

Born October 29, 1955, at Leonard, Tex.
Height, 6.02. Weight, 185.
High School—Leonard, Tex., Big Spring.
Attended North Texas State University.

Named to THE SPORTING NEWS NFL All-Star Team, 1987.
Named as punt returner on THE SPORTING NEWS NFL All-Star Team, 1980.
Signed as free agent by Washington Redskins, May, 1978.
Released by Washington Redskins, September 21, 1978; signed as free agent by Kansas City Chiefs, November 7, 1978.
On inactive list, September 19, 1982.
On injured reserve with knee injury, August 30 through October 13, 1983; activated, October 14, 1983.
On injured reserve with separated shoulder, December 10 through remainder of 1984 season.
Released by Kansas City Chiefs, August 26, 1985; signed as free agent by St. Louis Cardinals, September 17, 1985.
Crossed picket line during players' strike, October 2, 1987.
Franchise transferred to Phoenix, March 15, 1988.

Year Club	G.	P.C.	Yds.	Avg.	TD.	No.	Yds.	Avg.	TD.	No.	Yds.	Avg.	TD.	TD.	Pts.	F.
		PASS RECEIVING				−PUNT RETURNS−				−KICKOFF RET.−				−TOTAL−		
1978—Wash(6)-KC(6) NFL	12	None				4	33	8.3	0	1	18	18.0	0	0	0	0
1979—Kansas City NFL	16	33	444	13.5	3	58	*612	10.6	2	None				5	30	3
1980—Kansas City NFL	16	46	655	14.2	2	40	*581	*14.5	*2	None				4	24	1
1981—Kansas City NFL	16	63	852	13.5	2	50	528	10.6	0	None				2	12	2
1982—Kansas City NFL	5	10	168	16.8	1	3	26	8.7	0	None				1	6	0
1983—Kansas City NFL	9	7	85	12.1	0	26	210	8.1	0	1	5	5.0	0	0	0	0
1984—Kansas City NFL	15	8	69	8.6	0	39	332	8.5	0	19	391	20.6	0	0	0	0
1985—St. Louis NFL	14	43	581	13.5	1	26	283	10.9	0	4	59	14.8	0	1	6	3
1986—St. Louis NFL	16	80	1014	12.7	6	1	6	6.0	0	None				6	36	1
1987—St. Louis NFL	15	*91	*1117	12.3	8	None				None				8	48	2
Pro Totals—10 Years	134	381	4985	13.1	23	247	2611	10.6	4	25	473	18.9	0	27	162	13

Additional pro statistics: Recovered one fumble for one yard, 1979; recovered two fumbles, 1980; recovered one fumble for 19 yards, 1981; rushed three times for 36 yards, 1985; recovered three fumbles, 1986.
Played in Pro Bowl (NFL All-Star Game) following 1980 season.

LANCE SMITH
Offensive Tackle-Guard—Phoenix Cardinals

Born January 1, 1963, at Kannapolis, N.C.
Height, 6.02. Weight, 262.
High School—Kannapolis, N.C., A.L. Brown.
Attended Louisiana State University.

Selected by Portland in 1985 USFL territorial draft.
Selected by St. Louis in 3rd round (72nd player selected) of 1985 NFL draft.
Signed by St. Louis Cardinals, July 21, 1985.
Crossed picket line during players' strike, October 2, 1987.
Franchise transferred to Phoenix, March 15, 1988.
St. Louis NFL, 1985 through 1987.
Games: 1985 (14), 1986 (15), 1987 (15). Total—44.
Pro statistics: Recovered one fumble, 1985.

LEONARD PHILLIP SMITH
Safety—Phoenix Cardinals

Born September 2, 1960, at New Orleans, La.
Height, 5.11. Weight, 202.
High School—Baton Rouge, La., Robert E. Lee.
Attended McNeese State University.

Selected by Boston in 2nd round (14th player selected) of 1983 USFL draft.
Selected by St. Louis in 1st round (17th player selected) of 1983 NFL draft.
Signed by St. Louis Cardinals, May 3, 1983.
Crossed picket line during players' strike, September 23, 1987.
Franchise transferred to Phoenix, March 15, 1988.

| | | —INTERCEPTIONS— | | |
Year Club	G.	No.	Yds.	Avg.	TD.
1983—St. Louis NFL................	16		None		
1984—St. Louis NFL................	12	2	31	15.5	1
1985—St. Louis NFL................	16	2	73	36.5	0
1986—St. Louis NFL................	16	1	13	13.0	0
1987—St. Louis NFL................	15		None		
Pro Totals—5 Years...........	75	5	117	23.4	1

Additional pro statistics: Returned one kickoff for 19 yards, 1983; recovered one fumble, 1984; returned five kickoffs for 68 yards and recovered three fumbles and fumbled once, 1985; recoveed one fumble for 29 yards and a touchdown, 1987.

LERNARD SMITH
(Reggie)
Offensive Tackle—Indianapolis Colts
Born August 29, 1961, at Chicago, Ill.
Height, 6.04. Weight, 285.
High School—Chicago, Ill., Vocational.
Attended University of Kansas.

Selected by Tampa Bay in 4th round (70th player selected) of 1984 USFL draft.
Signed by Tampa Bay Bandits, March 7, 1984.
Granted roster exemption, March 7 through March 13, 1984; activated, March 14, 1984.
Selected by Denver in 3rd round (78th player selected) of 1984 NFL supplemental draft.
Granted free agency when USFL suspended operations, August 7, 1986; signed by Denver Broncos, September 3, 1986.
Granted roster exemption, September 3 through September 15, 1986.
Released by Denver Broncos, September 16, 1986; signed as free agent by Dallas Cowboys and placed on reserve/future list, December 18, 1986.
Released by Dallas Cowboys, September 7, 1987; signed as free agent replacement player by Tampa Bay Buccaneers, September 24, 1987.
Released by Tampa Bay Buccaneers, October 19, 1987; signed as free agent by Indianapolis Colts, May 3, 1988.
Tampa Bay USFL, 1984 and 1985; Tampa Bay NFL, 1987.
Games: 1984 (15), 1985 (18), 1987 (3). Total USFL—33. Total Pro—36.
Pro statistics: Recovered one fumble, 1985.

MICHAEL WAYNE SMITH
(Mike)
Cornerback—Miami Dolphins
Born October 24, 1962, at Houston, Tex.
Height, 6.00. Weight, 175.
High School—Houston, Tex., Booker T. Washington.
Attended University of Texas at El Paso.

Selected by Arizona in 4th round (49th player selected) of 1985 USFL draft.
Selected by Miami in 4th round (91st player selected) of 1985 NFL draft.
Signed by Miami Dolphins, May 30, 1985.
Released by Miami Dolphins, October 5, 1985; re-signed by Dolphins, November 13, 1985.
On injured reserve with ankle injury, December 9 through remainder of 1986 season.
Miami NFL, 1985 through 1987.
Games: 1985 (7), 1986 (14), 1987 (8). Total—29.
Pro statistics: Recovered one fumble, 1986.
Played in AFC Championship Game following 1985 season.

RICKY SMITH
Wide Receiver-Cornerback—Detroit Lions
Born July 20, 1960, at Quincy, Fla.
Height, 6.00. Weight, 188.
High School—Quincy, Fla., James A. Shanks.
Received bachelor of science degree in human services from
Alabama State University in 1982.

Selected by New England in 6th round (141st player selected) on 1982 NFL draft.
Traded by New England Patriots to Washington Redskins for 7th round pick in 1985 draft, September 11, 1984.
Released by Washington Redskins, July 29, 1985; awarded on waivers to Indianapolis Colts, July 30, 1985.
Released by Indianapolis Colts, September 2, 1985; signed as free agent by Miami Dolphins for 1986, December 20, 1985.
Released by Miami Dolphins, August 18, 1986; signed as free agent by Detroit Lions, March 9, 1987.
Released by Detroit Lions, September 7, 1987; re-signed by Lions, September 11, 1987.

| | | -PUNT RETURNS- | | | | —KICKOFF RET.— | | | | —TOTAL— | | |
Year Club	G.	No.	Yds.	Avg.	TD.	No.	Yds.	Avg.	TD.	TD.	Pts.	F.
1982—New England NFL....................	9	16	139	8.7	0	24	567	23.6	*1	1	6	3
1983—New England NFL....................	16	38	398	10.5	0	42	916	21.8	0	0	0	11
1984—N.E. (1)-Wash. (11) NFL..........	12		None			1	22	22.0	0	0	0	0
1987—Detroit NFL............................	12		None				None			0	0	0
Pro Totals—4 Years.....................	49	54	537	9.9	0	67	1505	22.5	1	1	6	14

Additional pro statistics: Recovered two fumbles, 1982; recovered six fumbles, 1983; intercepted one pass for 37 yards, 1984; intercepted one pass for 34 yards and a touchdown, 1987.

ROBERT BENJAMIN SMITH
Defensive End—Dallas Cowboys
Born December 3, 1962, at Bogalusa, La.
Height, 6.07. Weight, 270.
High School—Bogalusa, La.
Attended Grambling State University.
Brother of Sean Smith, defensive end with Chicago Bears.

Selected by New Orleans in 1984 USFL territorial draft.
USFL rights traded by New Orleans Breakers to Arizona Wranglers for defensive end Junior Ah You and past considerations, January 9, 1984.
Signed by Arizona Wranglers, January 9, 1984.
On developmental squad, February 24 through April 20, 1984.
On injured reserve with knee injury, April 21 through June 25, 1984; activated, June 26, 1984.
Selected by Minnesota in 2nd round (40th player selected) of 1984 NFL supplemental draft.
Not protected in merger of Arizona Wranglers and Oklahoma Outlaws, December 6, 1984; signed by Minnesota Vikings, March 21, 1985.
Released by Minnesota Vikings, August 26, 1986; signed as free agent by Dallas Cowboys, April 30, 1987.
On injured reserve with broken arm, September 7 through entire 1987 season.
Crossed picket line during players' strike, October 1, 1987.
On developmental squad for 8 games with Arizona Wranglers in 1984.
On developmental squad for USFL Championship Game following 1984 season.
Minnesota NFL, 1985.
Games: 1985 (16).

SEAN LAMAR SMITH
Defensive End—Chicago Bears
Born March 27, 1965, at Bogalusa, La.
Height, 6.04. Weight, 275.
High School—Bogalusa, La.
Attended Grambling State University.
Brother of Robert Smith, defensive end with Dallas Cowboys.

Selected by Chicago in 4th round (101st player selected) of 1987 NFL draft.
Signed by Chicago Bears, August 3, 1987.
Chicago NFL, 1987.
Games: 1987 (10).
Pro statistics: Recovered one fumble, 1987.

STEVEN ANTHONY SMITH
(Steve)
Running Back—Los Angeles Raiders
Born August 30, 1964, at Washington, D. C.
Height, 6.01. Weight, 235.
High School—Hyattsville, Md., DeMatha Catholic.
Received degree in hotel, restaurant and institutional management
from Penn State University in 1987.

Selected by Los Angeles Raiders in 3rd round (81st player selected) of 1987 NFL draft.
Signed by Los Angeles Raiders, July 22, 1987.
On injured reserve with knee injury, September 16 through October 23, 1987; activated, October 24, 1987.
On injured reserve with knee and ankle injuries, December 3 through remainder of 1987 season.

Year Club	G.	Att.	Yds.	Avg.	TD.	P.C.	Yds.	Avg.	TD.	TD.	Pts.	F.
1987—Los Angeles Raiders NFL	7	5	18	3.6	0	3	46	15.3	0	0	0	0

Additional pro statistics: Recovered one fumble, 1987.

TIMMY SMITH
Running Back—Washington Redskins
Born January 21, 1964, at Hobbs, N. M.
Height, 5.11. Weight, 216.
High School—Hobbs, N. M.
Attended Texas Tech University.

Selected by Washington in 5th round (117th player selected) of 1987 NFL draft.
Signed by Washington Redskins, July 24, 1987.

Year Club	G.	Att.	Yds.	Avg.	TD.	P.C.	Yds.	Avg.	TD.	TD.	Pts.	F.
1987—Washington NFL	7	29	126	4.3	0	1	−2	−2.0	0	0	0	0

Played in NFC Championship Game following 1987 season.
Played in NFL Championship Game following 1987 season.

WAYNE LESTER SMITH
Cornerback—Minnesota Vikings
Born May 9, 1957, at Chicago, Ill.
Height, 6.00. Weight, 170.
High School—Chicago, Ill., Harper.
Attended University of Wisconsin at LaCrosse, Loop Junior College and received bachelor
of arts degree in sociology and management from Purdue University in 1980.

Selected by Detroit in 11th round (278th player selected) of 1980 NFL draft.
Released by Detroit Lions, December 7, 1982; claimed on waivers by St. Louis Cardinals, December 8, 1982.
On injured reserve with knee injury, December 16 through remainder of 1982 season.
Released by St. Louis Cardinals, August 10, 1987; signed as free agent by Indianapolis Colts, August 17, 1987.
Released by Indianapolis Colts, August 25, 1987; signed as free agent replacement player by Minnesota Vikings,)ctober 14, 1987.
Released by Minnesota Vikings, October 19, 1987; re-signed by Vikings, November 11, 1987.

| | | | —INTERCEPTIONS— | | |
Year Club	G.	No.	Yds.	Avg.	TD.
1980—Detroit NFL..................	16	1	23	23.0	0
1981—Detroit NFL..................	16		None		
1982—Det. (5)-St.L. (1) NFL ..	6	1	10	10.0	0
1983—St. Louis NFL.................	16	2	3	1.5	0
1984—St. Louis NFL.................	16	4	35	8.8	0
1985—St. Louis NFL.................	16		None		
1986—St. Louis NFL.................	16	1	35	35.0	0
1987—Minnesota NFL.............	6	1	24	24.0	0
Pro Totals—8 Years............	108	10	130	13.0	0

Additional pro statistics: Recovered two fumbles, 1980; recovered one fumble for four yards, 1981; recovered one umble, 1983, 1985 and 1986; recovered three fumbles for 12 yards, 1984.

ANGELO SNIPES
Linebacker—Kansas City Chiefs
Born January 11, 1963, at Atlanta, Ga.
Height, 6.00. Weight, 215.
High School—Atlanta, Ga., Walker.
Attended West Georgia College.

Selected by Oakland in 14th round (196th player selected) of 1985 USFL draft.
Signed by Oakland Invaders, Jaunary 23, 1985.
Traded with guard Reggie Irving and defensive tackle Bob Standifer by Oakland Invaders to Memphis Showboats 'or past considerations, February 28, 1986.
Granted free agency when USFL suspended operations, August 7, 1986; signed as free agent by Washington Redskins, August 11, 1986.
Granted roster exemption, August 11 through August 22, 1986; activated, Augut 23, 1986.
Released by Washington Redskins, November 11, 1986; awarded on waivers to San Diego Chargers, November 12, 1986.
Released by San Diego Chargers, October 27, 1987; signed as free agent by Kansas City Chiefs, December 2, 1987.
Oakland USFL, 1985; Washington (10)-San Diego (6) NFL, 1986; San Diego (2)-Kansas City (4) NFL, 1987.
Games: 1985 (18), 1986 (16), 1987 (6). Total NFL—22. Total Pro—40.
USFL statistics: Credited with 11½ sacks for 93 yards, returned one kickoff for 10 yards and recovered one fumble, 1985.
NFL statistics: Recovered one fumble, 1986.
Played in USFL Championship Game following 1985 season.

BRYAN SOCHIA
Name pronounced So-SHAY.
Nose Tackle—Miami Dolphins
Born July 21, 1961, at Massena, N.Y.
Height, 6.03. Weight, 274.
High School—Brasher Falls, N.Y., St. Lawrence Central.
Attended Northwestern Oklahoma State University.

Signed as free agent by Houston Oilers, June 2, 1983.
On injured reserve with knee and ankle injuries, August 29 through September 26, 1983; activated after clearing procedural waivers, September 27, 1983.
Granted free agency, February 1, 1986; re-signed by Oilers, October 21, 1986.
Granted roster exemption, October 21 through November 2, 1986.
Released by Houston Oilers, November 3, 1986; signed as free agent by Miami Dolphins, November 12, 1986.
Houston NFL, 1983 through 1985; Miami NFL, 1986 and 1987.
Games: 1983 (12), 1984 (16), 1985 (16), 1986 (6), 1987 (12). Total—62.

KURT SOHN
Name pronounced Sewn.
Wide Receiver-Kick Returner—New York Jets
Born June 26, 1957, at Ithaca, N.Y.
Height, 5.11. Weight, 180.
High School—Huntington, N.Y.
Attended Nassau Community College, North Carolina State and Fordham University.

Signed as free agent by Los Angeles Rams, May 29, 1980.
Released by Los Angeles Rams, August 18, 1980; signed as free agent by New York Jets, June 16, 1981.
On injured reserve with knee injury, August 19 through remainder of 1983 season.
On physically unable to perform/active with knee injury, July 14 through August 12, 1984; activated, August 13, 1984.
On injured reserve with knee injury, October 26 through November 29, 1984; activated, November 30, 1984.

Year Club	G.	PASS RECEIVING				-PUNT RETURNS-				-KICKOFF RET.-				-TOTAL-		
		P.C.	Yds.	Avg.	TD.	No.	Yds.	Avg.	TD.	No.	Yds.	Avg.	TD.	TD.	Pts.	F.
1981—New York Jets NFL....	16	None				13	66	5.1	0	26	528	20.3	0	0	0	5
1982—New York Jets NFL....	9	None				None				15	299	19.9	0	0	0	0
1984—New York Jets NFL....	5	2	28	14.0	0	None				None				0	0	0
1985—New York Jets NFL....	15	39	534	13.7	4	16	149	9.3	0	3	7	2.3	0	4	24	0
1986—New York Jets NFL....	15	8	129	16.1	2	35	289	8.3	0	7	124	17.7	0	2	12	3
1987—New York Jets NFL....	12	23	261	11.3	2	1	6	6.0	0	3	47	15.7	0	2	12	0
Pro Totals—6 Years.......	72	72	952	13.2	8	65	510	7.8	0	54	1005	18.6	0	8	48	8

Additional pro statistics: Recovered two fumbles, 1981; rushed once for 12 yards, 1985; rushed twice for minus 11 yards and recovered one fumble, 1986.
Played in AFC Championship Game following 1982 season.

JESSE WILLIAM SOLOMON
Linebacker—Minnesota Vikings

Born November 4, 1963, at Madison, Fla.
Height, 6.00. Weight, 235.
High School—Madison, Fla.
Attended North Florida Junior College and received bachelor of science degree in political science from Florida State University in 1986.

Selected by Tampa Bay in 1986 USFL territorial draft.
Selected by Minnesota in 12th round (318th player selected) of 1986 NFL draft.
Signed by Minnesota Vikings, July 27, 1986.
Minnesota NFL, 1986 and 1987.
Games: 1986 (13), 1987 (12). Total—25.
Pro statistics: Intercepted two passes for 34 yards and recovered two fumbles, 1986; intercepted one pass for 30 yards and recovered one fumble for 33 yards, 1987.
Played in NFC Championship Game following 1987 season.

RONALD MATTHEW SOLT
(Ron)
Guard—Indianapolis Colts

Born May 19, 1962, at Bainebridge, Md.
Height, 6.03. Weight, 285.
High School—Wilkes-Barre, Pa., James M. Coughlin.
Attended University of Maryland.

Selected by Washington in 1984 USFL territorial draft.
Selected by Indianapolis in 1st round (19th player selected) of 1984 NFL draft.
Signed by Indianapolis Colts, August 11, 1984.
On injured reserve with knee injury, December 17 through remainder of 1985 season.
Indianapolis NFL, 1984 through 1987.
Games: 1984 (16), 1985 (15), 1986 (16), 1987 (12). Total—59.
Pro statistics: Recovered one fumble, 1984.
Played in Pro Bowl (NFL All-Star Game) following 1987 season.

JOHN STEPHEN SPAGNOLA
Tight End—Philadelphia Eagles

Born August 1, 1957, at Bethlehem, Pa.
Height, 6.04. Weight, 240.
High School—Bethlehem, Pa., Catholic.
Received bachelor of arts degree in political science from Yale University in 1980.

Selected by New England in 9th round (245th player selected) of 1979 NFL draft.
Released by New England Patriots, August 20, 1979; signed as free agent by Philadelphia Eagles, August 27, 1979.
On injured reserve with back injury, August 30 through entire 1983 season.

Year Club	G.	PASS RECEIVING			
		P.C.	Yds.	Avg.	TD.
1979—Philadelphia NFL	16	2	24	12.0	0
1980—Philadelphia NFL	16	18	193	10.7	3
1981—Philadelphia NFL	11	6	83	13.8	0
1982—Philadelphia NFL	9	26	313	12.0	2
1984—Philadelphia NFL	16	65	701	10.8	1
1985—Philadelphia NFL	16	64	772	12.1	5
1986—Philadelphia NFL	15	39	397	10.2	1
1987—Philadelphia NFL	12	36	350	9.7	2
Pro Totals—8 Years...........	111	256	2833	11.1	14

Additional pro statistics: Recovered one fumble, 1979 through 1981 and 1986; returned one kickoff for no yards, 1980; fumbled twice, 1980, 1984, 1986 and 1987; fumbled once, 1985.
Played in NFC Championship Game following 1980 season.
Played in NFL Championship Game following 1980 season.

—DID YOU KNOW—

That the New England Patriots have lost 12 consecutive games to NFC East opponents? Their last win against an NFC East team was on October 8, 1978, against Philadelphia.

TIM SPENCER
Fullback—San Diego Chargers
Born December 10, 1960, at Martins Ferry, O.
Height, 6.01. Weight, 227.
High School—St. Clairsville, O., Richland.
Attended Ohio State University.
Selected by Chicago in 1st round (2nd player selected) of 1983 USFL draft.
Signed by Chicago Blitz, January 7, 1983.
Selected by San Diego in 11th round (307th player selected) of 1983 NFL draft.
Franchise transferred to Arizona, September 30, 1983.
Not protected in merger of Arizona Wranglers and Oklahoma Outlaws; selected by Memphis Showboats in USFL dispersal draft, December 6, 1984.
On developmental squad, February 21 through March 8, 1985; activated, March 9, 1985.
Granted free agency, August 1, 1985; signed by San Diego Chargers, August 2, 1985.
On developmental squad for 2 games with Memphis Showboats in 1985.

Year	Club	G.	Att.	Yds.	Avg.	TD.	P.C.	Yds.	Avg.	TD.	TD.	Pts.	F.
				RUSHING			PASS RECEIVING				—TOTAL—		
1983—Chicago USFL		18	300	1157	3.9	6	38	362	9.5	2	8	48	2
1984—Arizona USFL		18	227	1212	5.3	17	46	589	12.8	2	19	114	3
1985—Memphis USFL		16	198	789	4.0	3	14	96	6.9	0	3	18	3
1985—San Diego NFL		16	124	478	3.9	10	11	135	12.3	0	10	60	1
1986—San Diego NFL		14	99	350	3.5	6	6	48	8.0	0	6	36	2
1987—San Diego NFL		12	73	228	3.1	0	17	123	7.2	0	0	0	1
USFL Totals—3 Years		52	725	3158	4.4	26	98	1047	10.7	4	30	180	8
NFL Totals—3 Years		42	296	1056	3.6	16	34	306	9.0	0	16	96	4
Pro Totals—6 Years		94	1021	4214	4.1	42	132	1353	10.3	4	46	276	12

Additional USFL statistics: Attempted one pass with no completions, 1983; recovered one fumble, 1983 and 1985.
Additional NFL statistics: Returned five kickoffs for 81 yards and recovered one fumble, 1986.
Played in USFL Championship Game following 1984 season.

JOHN STEVEN STADNIK
Offensive Tackle—San Diego Chargers
Born February 18, 1959, at Chicago, Ill.
Height, 6.04. Weight, 273.
High School—Blue Island, Ill., Dwight D. Eisenhower.
Received bachelor of science degree in commercial recreation
and park administration from Western Illinois University.
Selected by Chicago in 1983 USFL territorial draft.
Signed as free agent by Seattle Seahawks, April 28, 1983.
Released by Seattle Seahawks, July 18, 1983; signed by Arizona Wranglers, October 12, 1983.
On developmental squad, March 18 through March 31, 1984; activated, April 1, 1984.
Protected in merger of Arizona Wranglers and Oklahoma Outlaws, December 6, 1984.
Granted free agency when USFL suspended operations, August 7, 1986; signed as free agent by San Diego Chargers, April 13, 1987.
Released by San Diego Chargers, August 29, 1987; re-signed as replacement player by Chargers, September 24, 1987.
Released by San Diego Chargers, October 20, 1987; re-signed by Chargers, March 4, 1988.
On developmental squad for 2 games with Arizona Wranglers in 1984.
Arizona USFL, 1984 and 1985; San Diego NFL, 1987.
Games: 1984 (13), 1985 (17), 1987 (3). Total USFL—30. Total Pro—33.
Pro statistics: Recovered two fumbles, 1985.
Played in USFL Championship Game following 1984 season.

SYLVESTER STAMPS
Running Back—Atlanta Falcons
Born February 24, 1961, at Vicksburg, Miss.
Height, 5.07. Weight, 171.
High School—Vicksburg, Miss.
Attended Jackson State University.
Named as kickoff returner to THE SPORTING NEWS NFL All-Star Team, 1987.
Selected by Birmingham in 18th round (370th player selected) of 1984 USFL draft.
Signed by Birmingham Stallions, January 12, 1984.
Released by Birmingham Stallions, February 8, 1984; signed as free agent by Atlanta Falcons, May 2, 1984.
On injured reserve with hamstring injury, November 29 through remainder of 1984 season.
Released by Atlanta Falcons, September 2, 1985; re-signed by Falcons, December 6, 1985.
Released by Atlanta Falcons, December 7, 1985; re-signed by Falcons, December 10, 1985.
On injured reserve with hamstring injury, December 13 through remainder of 1986 season.
On injured reserve with foot injury, November 9 through December 11, 1987; activated, December 12, 1987.

Year	Club	G.	Att.	Yds.	Avg.	TD.	P.C.	Yds.	Avg.	TD.	TD.	Pts.	F.
				RUSHING			PASS RECEIVING				—TOTAL—		
1984—Atlanta NFL		10	3	15	5.0	0	4	48	12.0	0	0	0	2
1985—Atlanta NFL		2		None				None			0	0	0
1986—Atlanta NFL		14	30	220	7.3	0	20	221	11.1	1	1	6	4
1987—Atlanta NFL		7	1	6	6.0	0	4	40	10.0	0	1	6	1
Pro Totals—4 Years		33	34	241	7.1	0	28	309	11.0	1	2	12	7

Year	Club	G.	No.	Yds.	Avg.TD.	
1984—Atlanta NFL		10	19	452	23.8	0
1985—Atlanta NFL		2	4	89	22.3	0
1986—Atlanta NFL		14	24	514	21.4	0
1987—Atlanta NFL		7	24	660	*27.5	1
Pro Totals—4 Years		33	71	1715	24.2	1

Additional pro statistics: Returned one punt for eight yards, 1986; recovered one fumble, 1986 and 1987.

BOB EUGENE STANDIFER
Defensive Tackle—Kansas City Chiefs
Born June 3, 1963, at Chattanooga, Tenn.
Height, 6.05. Weight, 277.
High School—Chattanooga, Tenn., Central.
Received bachelor of science degree in business management
from University of Tennessee at Chattanooga.

Selected by Oakland in 1st round (7th player selected) of 1985 USFL draft.
Signed by Oakland Invaders, January 23, 1985.
Released by Oakland Invaders, February 11, 1985; re-signed by Invaders, February 21, 1985.
On developmental squad, February 21 through May 10, 1985; activated, May 11, 1985.
On developmental squad, May 23 through June 14, 1985; activated, June 15, 1985.
Traded with guard Reggie Irving and linebacker Angelo Snipes by Oakland Invaders to Memphis Showboats for past considerations, February 28, 1986.
Granted free agency when USFL suspended operations, August 7, 1986; signed as free agent by San Francisco 49ers, March 17, 1987.
Released by San Francisco 49ers, August 24, 1987; re-signed by 49ers, September 24, 1987.
On injured reserve with pulled abdomen muscle, October 12 through December 14, 1987.
Released by San Francisco 49ers, December 15, 1987; signed as free agent by Kansas City Chiefs, March 28, 1988.
On developmental squad for 14 games with Oakland Invaders in 1985.
Oakland USFL, 1985.
Games: 1985 (4).
On developmental squad for USFL Championship Game following 1985 season.

WALTER STANLEY
Wide Receiver-Punt Returner—Green Bay Packers
Born November 5, 1962, at Chicago, Ill.
Height, 5.09. Weight, 180.
High School—Chicago, Ill., South Shore.
Attended University of Colorado and Mesa College (Colo.).

Selected by Memphis in 4th round (54th player selected) of 1985 USFL draft.
Selected by Green Bay in 4th round (98th player selected) of 1985 NFL draft.
Signed by Green Bay Packers, July 19, 1985.

			PASS RECEIVING				–PUNT RETURNS–				—KICKOFF RET.—				—TOTAL—		
Year	Club	G.	P.C.	Yds.	Avg.	TD.	No.	Yds.	Avg.	TD.	No.	Yds.	Avg.	TD.	TD.	Pts.	F.
1985—Green Bay NFL		13			None		14	179	12.8	0	9	212	23.6	0	0	0	0
1986—Green Bay NFL		16	35	723	20.7	2	33	316	9.6	1	28	559	20.0	0	3	18	1
1987—Green Bay NFL		12	38	672	17.7	3	28	173	6.2	0	3	47	15.7	0	3	18	5
Pro Totals—3 Years		41	73	1395	19.1	5	75	668	8.9	1	40	818	20.5	0	6	36	8

Additional pro statistics: Rushed once for 19 yards, 1986; rushed four times for 38 yards and recovered three fumbles, 1987.

ROHN TAYLOR STARK
(First name pronounced Ron).
Punter—Indianapolis Colts
Born May 4, 1959, at Minneapolis, Minn.
Height, 6.03. Weight, 204.
High School—Pine River, Minn.
Attended United States Air Force Academy Prep School and received degree
in finance from Florida State University.

Established NFL record for highest average, punting, career, 300 or more attempts (45.16).
Named as punter on THE SPORTING NEWS College All-America Team, 1981.
Led NFL in punting yards with 4,124 in 1983.
Selected by Baltimore in 2nd round (34th player selected) of 1982 NFL draft.
Franchise transferred to Indianapolis, March 31, 1984.

			——PUNTING——		
Year	Club	G.	No.	Avg.	Blk.
1982—Baltimore NFL		9	46	44.4	0
1983—Baltimore NFL		16	91	*45.3	0
1984—Indianapolis NFL		16	*98	44.7	0
1985—Indianapolis NFL		16	78	*45.9	*2
1986—Indianapolis NFL		16	76	*45.2	0
1987—Indianapolis NFL		12	61	40.0	*2
Pro Totals—6 Years		85	450	44.5	4

Additional pro statistics: Rushed once for eight yards, 1982 and 1983; attempted one pass with no completions, 1982, 1983 and 1985; fumbled once, 1982 and 1986; rushed twice for no yards and attempted one pass with one

interception, 1984; recovered one fumble, 1984 through 1986.
Played in Pro Bowl (NFL All-Star Game) following 1985 and 1986 seasons.

STEPHEN DALE STARRING
First name pronounced Steff-in.
Wide Receiver-Kick Returner—New England Patriots
Born July 30, 1961, at Baton Rouge, La.
Height, 5.10. Weight, 172.
High School—Vinton, La.
Received degree in physical education from McNeese State University in 1985.

Selected by Washington in 3rd round (28th player selected) of 1983 USFL draft.
Selected by New England in 3rd round (74th player selected) of 1983 NFL draft.
Signed by New England Patriots, May 16, 1983.

Year Club	G.	P.C.	-PASS RECEIVING- Yds.	Avg.	TD.	No.	-PUNT RETURNS- Yds.	Avg.	TD.	TD.	—TOTAL— Pts.	F.
1983—New England NFL	15	17	389	22.9	2		None			2	12	1
1984—New England NFL	16	46	657	14.3	4	10	73	7.3	0	4	24	1
1985—New England NFL	16	16	235	14.7	0	2	0	0.0	0	0	0	4
1986—New England NFL	14	16	295	18.4	2	6	18	3.0	0	2	12	4
1987—New England NFL	11	17	289	17.0	3	1	17	17.0	0	3	18	2
Pro Totals—5 Years	72	112	1865	16.7	11	19	108	5.7	0	11	66	12

Year Club	G.	No.	KICKOFF RETURNS Yds.	Avg.	TD.
1983—New England NFL	15		None		
1984—New England NFL	16		None		
1985—New England NFL	16	48	1012	21.1	0
1986—New England NFL	14	36	802	22.3	0
1987—New England NFL	11	23	445	19.3	0
Pro Totals—5 Years	72	107	2259	21.1	0

Additional pro statistics: Recovered one fumble for eight yards and rushed twice for minus 16 yards, 1984; recovered one fumble, 1985 and 1987; rushed once for no yards and recovered two fumbles for minus five yards, 1986; rushed twice for 13 yards, 1987.
Played in AFC Championship Game following 1985 season.
Played in NFL Championship Game following 1985 season.

DEAN STEINKUHLER
Name pronounced Stine-cooler.
Offensive Tackle-Guard—Houston Oilers
Born January 27, 1961, at Burr, Neb.
Height, 6.03. Weight, 278.
High School—Sterling, Neb.
Attended University of Nebraska.

Outland Trophy winner, 1983.
Named as guard on THE SPORTING NEWS College All-America Team, 1983.
Selected by Arizona in 6th round (116th player selected) of 1984 USFL draft.
Signed by Houston Oilers, April 30, 1984.
Selected officially by Houston in 1st round (2nd player selected) of 1984 NFL draft.
On injured reserve with knee injury, November 5 through remainder of 1984 season.
On injured reserve with knee injury, October 11 through December 19, 1985; activated, December 20, 1985.
Active for 6 games with Houston Oilers in 1985; did not play.
Houston NFL, 1984 through 1987.
Games: 1984 (10), 1986 (16), 1987 (11). Total—37.
Pro statistics: Recovered two fumbles, 1986.

SCOTT STEPHEN
Linebacker—Green Bay Packers
Born June 18, 1964, at Los Angeles, Calif.
Height, 6.02. Weight, 232.
High School—Los Angeles, Calif., Manual Arts.
Attended Arizona State University.

Selected by Green Bay in 3rd round (69th player selected) of 1987 NFL draft.
Signed by Green Bay Packers, July 29, 1987.
Green Bay NFL, 1987.
Games: 1987 (8).

DWIGHT EUGENE STEPHENSON
Center—Miami Dolphins
Born November 20, 1957, at Murfreesboro, N.C.
Height, 6.02. Weight, 255.
High School—Hampton, Va.
Attended University of Alabama.

Named to THE SPORTING NEWS NFL All-Star Team, 1984 through 1986.
Selected by Miami in 2nd round (48th player selected) of 1980 NFL draft.
On injured reserve with knee injury, December 9 through remainder of 1987 season.

— 393 —

Miami NFL, 1980 through 1987.
Games: 1980 (16), 1981 (16), 1982 (9), 1983 (16), 1984 (16), 1985 (16), 1986 (16), 1987 (9). Total—114.
Pro statistics: Recovered one fumble, 1980, 1984 and 1986; fumbled once, 1987.
Played in AFC Championship Game following 1982, 1984 and 1985 seasons.
Played in NFL Championship Game following 1982 and 1984 seasons.
Played in Pro Bowl (NFL All-Star Game) following 1983 through 1986 seasons.
Named to play in Pro Bowl following 1987 season; replaced due to injury by Mike Webster.

MICHAEL STEWART
Safety—Los Angeles Rams
Born July 12, 1965, at Atascadero, Calif.
Height, 5.11. Weight, 195.
High School—Bakersfield, Calif.
Attended Bakersfield College and Fresno State University.
Selected by Los Angeles Rams in 8th round (213th player selected) of 1987 NFL draft.
Signed by Los Angeles Rams, July 6, 1987.
Selected by Milwaukee Brewers' organization in 29th round of free-agent draft, June 4, 1984.
Selected by Minnesota Twins' organization in 26th round of free-agent draft, June 2, 1986.
Selected by Toronto Blue Jays' organization in 49th round of free-agent draft, June 2, 1987.
Los Angeles Rams NFL, 1987.
Games: 1987 (12).
Pro statistics: Credited with a safety, 1987.

ARTHUR BARRY STILL
(Art)
Defensive End—Kansas City Chiefs
Born December 5, 1955, at Camden, N.J.
Height, 6.07. Weight, 257.
High School—Camden, N.J.
Received bachelor of arts degree in general studies from University of Kentucky in 1978.
Named as defensive end on THE SPORTING NEWS College All-America Team, 1977.
Named to THE SPORTING NEWS NFL All-Star Team, 1980.
Selected by Kansas City in 1st round (2nd player selected) of 1978 NFL draft.
On injured reserve with knee injury, September 23 through October 30, 1981; activated, October 31, 1981.
On injured reserve with knee injury, November 5 through remainder of 1985 season.
Kansas City NFL, 1978 through 1987.
Games: 1978 (16), 1979 (16), 1980 (16), 1981 (11), 1982 (9), 1983 (15), 1984 (16), 1985 (9), 1986 (16), 1987 (12). Total—136.
Pro statistics: Recovered one fumble, 1978, 1980, 1981 and 1983; recovered one fumble for 13 yards, 1979; recovered one fumble for four yards, 1982; recovered one fumble for three yards, 1984; recovered two fumbles, 1985 and 1986.
Played in Pro Bowl (NFL All-Star Game) following 1980 through 1982 and 1984 seasons.

KENNETH LEE STILLS
(Ken)
Defensive Back—Green Bay Packers
Born September 6, 1963, at Oceanside, Calif.
Height, 5.10. Weight, 185.
High School—Oceanside, Calif., El Camino.
Attended El Camino College and University of Wisconsin.
Selected by Jacksonville in 1985 USFL territorial draft.
Selected by Green Bay in 8th round (209th player selected) of 1985 NFL draft.
Signed by Green Bay Packers, July 19, 1985.
Released by Green Bay Packers, September 2, 1985; re-signed by Packers, October 30, 1985.

| | | KICKOFF RETURNS | | | |
Year Club	G.	No.	Yds.	Avg.	TD.
1985—Green Bay NFL............	8	1	14	14.0	0
1986—Green Bay NFL............	16	10	209	20.9	0
1987—Green Bay NFL............	11			None	
Pro Totals—3 Years............	35	11	223	20.3	0

Additional pro statistics: Intercepted one pass for 58 yards and a touchdown and fumbled once, 1986; recovered one fumble, 1987.

LOUIS FRED STOKES
(Known by middle name.)
Defensive End—Los Angeles Rams
Born March 14, 1964, at Vidalia, Ga.
Height, 6.03. Weight, 262.
High School—Vidalia, Ga.
Attended Georgia Southern College.
Selected by Los Angeles Rams in 12th round (332nd player selected) of 1987 NFL draft.
Signed by Los Angeles Rams, July 18, 1987.
On injured reserve with shoulder injury, September 7 through November 6, 1987; activated, November 7, 1987.
Los Angeles Rams NFL, 1987.
Games: 1987 (8).

DWIGHT STONE
Running Back-Kick Returner—Pittsburgh Steelers
Born January 28, 1964, at Florala, Ala.
Height, 6.00. Weight, 188.
High School—Florala, Ala.
Attended Marion Military Institute and Middle Tennessee State University.

Signed as free agent by Pittsburgh Steelers, May 19, 1987.
Crossed picket line during players' strike, October 7, 1987.

		——RUSHING——				PASS RECEIVING				—TOTAL—		
Year Club	G.	Att.	Yds.	Avg.	TD.	P.C.	Yds.	Avg.	TD.	TD.	Pts.	F.
1987—Pittsburgh NFL	14	17	135	7.9	0	1	22	22.0	0	0	0	0

		KICKOFF RETURNS			
Year Club	G.	No.	Yds.	Avg.	TD.
1987—Pittsburgh NFL	14	28	568	20.3	0

Additional pro statistics: Recovered one fumble, 1987.

CLIFFORD LEWIS STOUDT
(Cliff)
Quarterback—Phoenix Cardinals
Born March 27, 1955, at Oberlin, O.
Height, 6.04. Weight, 218.
High School—Oberlin, O.
Attended Youngstown State University.

Selected by Pittsburgh in 5th round (121st player selected) of 1977 NFL draft.
On injured reserve with broken arm, November 12 through remainder of 1981 season.
On inactive list, September 13, 1982.
Signed by Birmingham Stallions, January 10, 1984, for contract to take effect after being granted free agency, February 1, 1984.
Granted free agency when USFL suspended operations, August 7, 1986; re-signed by Pittsburgh Steelers and traded to St. Louis Cardinals for 5th round pick in 1988 draft, September 2, 1986.
Franchise transferred to Phoenix, March 15, 1988.
Active for 11 games with Pittsburgh Steelers in 1977; did not play.
Active for 16 games with Pittsburgh Steelers in 1978 and 1979; did not play.

		——————PASSING——————							——RUSHING——				—TOTAL—		
Year Club	G.	Att.	Cmp.	Pct.	Gain	T.P.	P.I.	Avg.	Att.	Yds.	Avg.	TD.	TD.	Pts.	F.
1980—Pittsburgh NFL	6	60	32	53.3	493	2	2	8.22	9	35	3.9	0	0	0	1
1981—Pittsburgh NFL	2	3	1	33.3	17	0	0	5.67	3	11	3.7	0	0	0	0
1982—Pittsburgh NFL	6	35	14	40.0	154	0	5	4.40	11	28	2.5	0	0	0	1
1983—Pittsburgh NFL	16	381	197	51.7	2553	12	21	6.70	77	479	6.2	4	4	24	10
1984—Birmingham USFL	17	366	212	57.9	3121	26	7	8.53	68	440	6.5	9	9	†56	1
1985—Birmingham USFL	18	444	266	59.9	3358	34	19	7.56	80	437	5.5	5	5	30	9
1986—St. Louis NFL	5	91	52	57.1	542	3	7	5.96	7	53	7.6	0	0	0	1
1987—St. Louis NFL	12	1	0	0.0	0	0	0	0.00	1	−2	−2.0	0	0	0	0
NFL Totals—9 Years	47	571	296	51.8	3759	17	35	6.58	108	604	5.6	4	4	24	13
USFL Totals— 2 Years	35	810	478	59.0	6479	60	26	8.00	148	877	5.9	14	14	86	10
Pro Totals—11 Years	82	1381	774	56.0	10238	77	61	7.41	256	1481	5.8	18	18	110	23

†Includes one 2-point conversion.
NFL Quarterback Rating Points: 1980 (78.0), 1981 (53.5), 1982 (14.2), 1983 (60.6), 1986 (53.5), 1987 (39.6). Total—57.3.
USFL Quarterback Rating Points: 1984 (101.6), 1985 (91.2). Total—95.9.
Additional NFL statistics: Recovered one fumble and fumbled once for minus two yards, 1980; recovered two fumbles, 1983.
Additional USFL statistics: Recovered two fumbles, 1985.
Member of Pittsburgh Steelers for AFC and NFL Championship Game following 1978 and 1979 seasons; did not play.

JEFF OWEN STOVER
Defensive End—San Francisco 49ers
Born May 22, 1958, at Corning, Calif.
Height, 6.05. Weight, 275.
High School—Corning, Calif., Union.
Attended University of Oregon.

Signed as free agent by San Francisco 49ers, April 20, 1982.
On injured reserve with knee injury, September 4 through November 15, 1984; activated, November 16, 1984.
Granted free agency, February 1, 1987; re-signed by 49ers, September 9, 1987.
Granted roster exemption, September 9 through September 11, 1987; activated, September 12, 1987.
San Francisco NFL, 1982 through 1987.
Games: 1982 (9), 1983 (16), 1984 (6), 1985 (16), 1986 (15), 1987 (12). Total—74.
Pro statistics: Recovered one fumble, 1982, 1983 and 1985.
Played in NFC Championship Game following 1983 and 1984 seasons.
Played in NFL Championship Game following 1984 season.

—DID YOU KNOW—
That Washington's 17-10 victory over Minnesota in the 1987 NFC title game marked the first time since 1983 that both teams scored in the conference championship game?

TYRONNE KEVIN STOWE
Linebacker—Pittsburgh Steelers
Born May 30, 1965, at Passaic, N.J.
Height, 6.01. Weight, 232.
High School—Passaic, N.J.
Attended Rutgers University.
Signed as free agent by San Diego Chargers, April 30, 1987.
Released by San Diego Chargers, September 7, 1987; signed as replacement player by Pittsburgh Steelers, September 24, 1987.
Pittsburgh NFL, 1987.
Games: 1987 (13).

STEPHEN MICHAEL STRACHAN
(Steve)
Running Back—Los Angeles Raiders
Born March 22, 1963, at Everett, Mass.
Height, 6.01. Weight, 220.
High School—Burlington, Mass.
Received bachelor of science degree in finance from Boston College in 1985.
Selected by Los Angeles Raiders in 11th round (303rd player selected) of 1985 NFL draft.
Signed by Los Angeles Raiders, June 28, 1985.
Released by Los Angeles Raiders, August 27, 1985; re-signed by Raiders, September 23, 1985.
On injured reserve with hamstring injury, October 23 through remainder of 1985 season.
Crossed picket line during players' strike, October 14, 1987.

Year Club	G.	Att.	Yds.	Avg.	TD.	P.C.	Yds.	Avg.	TD.	TD.	Pts.	F.
		—RUSHING—				PASS RECEIVING				—TOTAL—		
1985—Los Angeles Raiders NFL	4	2	1	0.5	0	None				0	0	0
1986—Los Angeles Raiders NFL	16	18	53	2.9	0	None				0	0	0
1987—Los Angeles Raiders NFL	11	28	108	3.9	0	4	42	10.5	0	0	0	1
Pro Totals—3 Years	31	48	162	3.4	0	4	42	10.5	0	0	0	1

TROY EDWIN STRADFORD
Running Back—Miami Dolphins
Born September 11, 1964, at Elizabeth, N.J.
Height, 5.09. Weight, 191.
High School—Linden, N.J.
Received bachelor of arts degree in communications from Boston College in 1987.
Selected by Miami in 4th round (99th player selected) of 1987 NFL draft.
Signed by Miami Dolphins, July 24, 1987.

Year Club	G.	Att.	Yds.	Avg.	TD.	P.C.	Yds.	Avg.	TD.	TD.	Pts.	F.
		—RUSHING—				PASS RECEIVING				—TOTAL—		
1987—Miami NFL	12	145	619	4.3	6	48	457	9.5	1	7	42	6

Year Club	G.	No.	Yds.	Avg.	TD.
		KICKOFF RETURNS			
1987—Miami NFL	12	14	258	18.4	0

Additional pro statistics: Attempted one pass with one completion for six yards and recovered two fumbles, 1987.

THOMAS STRAUTHERS
(Tom)
Defensive End—Atlanta Falcons
Born April 6, 1961, at Wesson, Miss.
Height, 6.04. Weight, 265.
High School—Brookhaven, Miss.
Attended Jackson State University.
Selected by Oakland in 21st round (247th player selected) of 1983 USFL draft.
Selected by Philadelphia in 10th round (258th player selected) of 1983 NFL draft.
Signed by Philadelphia Eagles, June 15, 1983.
On injured reserve with broken hand, August 16 through November 23, 1983; activated by Philadelphia Eagles after clearing procedural waivers, November 25, 1983.
Granted free agency, Feburary 1, 1987; re-signed by Eagles, August 11, 1987.
Released by Philadelphia Eagles after failing physical, August 12, 1987; signed as free agent by Miami Dolphins, August 21, 1987.
Released by Miami Dolphins, September 7, 1987; signed as free agent by Atlanta Falcons, February 22, 1988.
Philadelphia NFL, 1983 through 1986.
Games: 1983 (4), 1984 (16), 1985 (16), 1986 (11). Total—47.
Pro statistics: Returned one kickoff for 12 yards, 1984.

RICHARD GENE STRENGER
(Rich)
Offensive Tackle—Buffalo Bills
Born March 10, 1960, at Port Washington, Wis.
Height, 6.07. Weight, 285.
High School—Grafton, Wis.
Received bachelor of science degree in literature science and art from University of Michigan in 1983.

Selected by Michigan in 1983 USFL territorial draft.
Selected by Detroit in 2nd round (40th player selected) of 1983 NFL draft.
Signed by Detroit Lions, July 4, 1983.
On injured reserve with knee injury, September 4 through remainder of 1984 season.
On injured reserve with knee injury, October 31 through remainder of 1987 season.
Granted free agency with no qualifying offer, February 1, 1988; signed by Buffalo Bills, May 27, 1988.
Detroit NFL, 1983 through 1987.
Games: 1983 (16), 1984 (1), 1985 (13), 1986 (16), 1987 (3). Total—49.

DONALD JOSEPH STROCK
(Don)
Quarterback—Miami Dolphins
Born November 27, 1950, at Pottstown, Pa.
Height, 6.05. Weight, 225.
High School—Pottstown, Pa., Owen J. Roberts.
Received bachelor of science degree in distributive direction from
Virginia Technical University in 1973.
Brother of Dave Strock, placekicker with Florida Blazers (WFL), 1974.
Selected by Miami in 5th round (111th player selected) of 1973 NFL draft.
On did not report list, August 16 through September 4, 1983.
Reported and granted roster exemption, September 5, 1983; activated, September 9, 1983.
Member of Miami Dolphins' taxi squad, 1973.

Year	Club	G.	Att.	Cmp.	Pct.	Gain	T.P.	P.I.	Avg.	Att.	Yds.	Avg.	TD.	TD.	Pts.	F.
						PASSING					RUSHING			TOTAL		
1974—Miami NFL		1				None				1	—7	—7.0	0	0	0	0
1975—Miami NFL		6	45	26	57.8	230	2	2	5.11	6	38	6.3	1	1	6	1
1976—Miami NFL		4	47	21	44.7	359	3	2	7.64	2	13	6.5	1	1	6	1
1977—Miami NFL		4	4	2	50.0	12	0	1	3.00		None			0	0	0
1978—Miami NFL		16	135	72	53.3	825	12	6	6.11	10	23	2.3	0	0	0	4
1979—Miami NFL		16	100	56	56.0	830	6	6	8.30	3	18	6.0	0	0	0	3
1980—Miami NFL		16	62	30	48.4	313	1	5	5.05	1	—3	—3.0	0	0	0	1
1981—Miami NFL		16	130	79	60.8	901	6	8	6.93	14	—26	—1.9	0	0	0	0
1982—Miami NFL		9	55	30	54.5	306	2	5	5.56	3	—9	—3.0	0	0	0	1
1983—Miami NFL		15	52	34	65.4	403	4	1	7.75	6	—16	—2.7	0	0	0	0
1984—Miami NFL		16	6	4	66.7	27	0	0	4.50	2	—5	—2.5	0	0	0	1
1985—Miami NFL		16	9	7	77.8	141	1	0	15.67	2	—6	—3.0	0	0	0	0
1986—Miami NFL		16	20	14	70.0	152	2	0	7.60	1	0	0.0	0	0	0	1
1987—Miami NFL		12	23	13	56.5	114	0	1	4.96		None			0	0	0
Pro Totals—14 Years		163	688	388	56.4	4613	39	37	6.70	51	20	0.4	2	2	12	13

Quarterback Rating Points: 1975 (67.9), 1976 (74.6), 1977 (16.7), 1978 (83.3), 1979 (78.3), 1980 (35.1), 1981 (71.1), 1982 (44.8), 1983 (106.5), 1984 (76.4), 1985 (155.8), 1986 (125.4), 1987 (51.7). Total—73.5.
Additional pro statistics: Recovered one fumble, 1975, 1978 and 1983; fumbled four times for minus five yards, 1978; fumbled once for minus three yards, 1982; fumbled once for minus two yards, 1984; recovered one fumble and fumbled once for minus four yards, 1986; punted nine times for a 30.8 average, 1987.
Played in AFC Championship Game following 1982, 1984 and 1985 seasons.
Played in NFL Championship Game following 1982 and 1984 seasons.

VINCE M. STROTH
Offensive Tackle—New York Jets
Born November 25, 1960, at San Jose, Calif.
Height, 6.03. Weight, 259.
High School—San Jose, Calif., Bellarmine.
Received degree in art history from Brigham Young University.
Selected by Arizona in 13th round (146th player selected) of 1983 USFL draft.
Signed by Arizona Wranglers, January 27, 1983.
On developmental squad, March 4 through March 31, 1983; activated, April 1, 1983.
Franchise transferred to Chicago, September 30, 1983.
Franchise disbanded, November 20, 1984.
Selected by New Jersey Generals in USFL dispersal draft, December 6, 1984.
Granted free agency, August 1, 1985; signed by San Francisco 49ers, December 18, 1985.
Released by San Francisco 49ers, August 19, 1986; signed as free agent by Kansas City Chiefs, April 27, 1987.
Released by Kansas City Chiefs, August 31, 1987; signed as free agent replacement player by Houston Oilers, October 1, 1987.
On injured reserve with knee injury, December 2 through remainder of 1987 season.
Granted free agency with no qualifying offer, February 1, 1988; signed by New York Jets, May 23, 1988.
On developmental squad for 4 games with Arizona Wranglers in 1983.
Arizona USFL 1983; Chicago USFL, 1984; New Jersey USFL, 1985; San Francisco NFL, 1985; Houston NFL, 1987.
Games: 1983 (14), 1984 (6), 1985 USFL (18), 1985 NFL (1), 1987 (9). Total USFL—38. Total NFL—10. Total Pro—48.
Pro statistics: Returned two kickoffs for 25 yards and recovered one fumble for four yards, 1984.

WILBUR LAMAR STROZIER
Tight End—Seattle Seahawks
Born November 12, 1964, at LaGrange, Ga.
Height, 6.04. Weight, 255.
High School—LaGrange, Ga.
Attended University of Georgia.

Selected by Denver in 7th round (194th player selected) of 1987 NFL draft.
Signed by Denver Broncos, July 18, 1987.
Released by Denver Broncos, September 1, 1987; signed as free agent by Seattle Seahawks, September 8, 1987.
Seattle NFL, 1987.
Games: 1987 (12).

DAVID DERALD STUDDARD
(Dave)
Offensive Tackle—Denver Broncos

Born November 22, 1955, at San Antonio, Tex.
Height, 6.04. Weight, 260.
High School—Pearsall, Tex.
Received degree in physical education from University of Texas.
Brother of Les Studdard, center with Kansas City Chiefs and Houston Oilers, 1982 and 1983; and nephew of Howard Fest, guard with Cincinnati Bengals and Tampa Bay Buccaneers, 1968 through 1976.
Selected by Baltimore in 9th round (245th player selected) of 1978 NFL draft.
Released by Baltimore Colts, August 30, 1978; signed as free agent by Denver Broncos, January 31, 1979.
Crossed picket line during players' strike, October 1, 1987.
Denver NFL, 1979 through 1987.
Games: 1979 (16), 1980 (16), 1981 (16), 1982 (9), 1983 (16), 1984 (16), 1985 (16), 1986 (15), 1987 (14). Total—134.
Pro statistics: Caught one pass for two yards and a touchdown, 1979 and 1986; recovered one fumble, 1980, 1983 and 1986; caught one pass for 10 yards, 1981; returned two kickoffs for eight yards, 1983; caught one pass for minus four yards, 1984; recovered two fumbles, 1985.
Played in AFC Championship Game following 1986 and 1987 seasons.
Played in NFL Championship Game following 1986 and 1987 seasons.

JOHN SCOTT STUDWELL
(Known by middle name.)
Linebacker—Minnesota Vikings

Born August 27, 1954, at Evansville, Ind.
Height, 6.02. Weight, 230.
High School—Evansville, Ind., Harrison.
Attended University of Illinois.
Selected by Minnesota in 9th round (250th player selected) of 1977 NFL draft.

| | | | —INTERCEPTIONS— | | | |
Year	Club	G.	No.	Yds.	Avg.	TD.
1977—Minnesota NFL		14	1	4	4.0	0
1978—Minnesota NFL		13		None		
1979—Minnesota NFL		14	1	18	18.0	0
1980—Minnesota NFL		16	1	4	4.0	0
1981—Minnesota NFL		16		None		
1982—Minnesota NFL		8	1	3	3.0	0
1983—Minnesota NFL		16		None		
1984—Minnesota NFL		16	1	20	20.0	0
1985—Minnesota NFL		14	2	20	10.0	0
1986—Minnesota NFL		15	1	2	2.0	0
1987—Minnesota NFL		12	2	26	13.0	0
Pro Totals—11 Years		154	10	97	9.7	0

Additional pro statistics: Recovered one fumble for six yards and returned one kickoff for no yards, 1979; recovered one fumble, 1980, 1982, 1983 and 1987; recovered three fumbles, 1981; recovered four fumbles, 1986.
Played in NFC Championship Game following 1977 and 1987 seasons.
Played in Pro Bowl (NFL All-Star Game) following 1987 season.

MATTHEW JEROME SUHEY
(Matt)
Fullback—Chicago Bears

Born July 7, 1958, at Bellefonte, Pa.
Height, 5.11. Weight, 217.
High School—State College, Pa.
Received bachelor of science degree in marketing from Penn State University in 1980.
Grandson of Bob Higgins, end with Canton Bulldogs, 1920 and 1921; and son of Steve Suhey, guard with Pittsburgh Steelers, 1948 and 1949.
Selected by Chicago in 2nd round (46th player selected) of 1980 NFL draft.

| | | | ——RUSHING—— | | | | PASS RECEIVING | | | | —TOTAL— | | |
Year	Club	G.	Att.	Yds.	Avg.	TD.	P.C.	Yds.	Avg.	TD.	TD.	Pts.	F.
1980—Chicago NFL		16	22	45	2.0	0	7	60	8.6	0	0	0	1
1981—Chicago NFL		15	150	521	3.5	3	33	168	5.1	0	3	18	3
1982—Chicago NFL		9	70	206	2.9	3	36	333	9.3	0	3	18	2
1983—Chicago NFL		16	149	681	4.6	4	49	429	8.8	1	5	30	5
1984—Chicago NFL		16	124	424	3.4	4	42	312	7.4	2	6	36	6
1985—Chicago NFL		16	115	471	4.1	1	33	295	8.9	1	2	12	2
1986—Chicago NFL		16	84	270	3.2	2	24	235	9.8	0	2	12	1
1987—Chicago NFL		12	7	24	3.4	0	7	54	7.7	0	0	0	0
Pro Totals—8 Years		116	721	2642	3.7	17	231	1886	8.2	4	21	126	20

KICKOFF RETURNS

Year Club	G.	No.	Yds.	Avg.	TD.
1980—Chicago NFL	16	19	406	21.4	0
1981—Chicago NFL	15		None		
1982—Chicago NFL	9		None		
1983—Chicago NFL	16		None		
1984—Chicago NFL	16		None		
1985—Chicago NFL	16		None		
1986—Chicago NFL	16		None		
1987—Chicago NFL	12	1	9	9.0	0
Pro Totals—8 Years	116	20	415	20.8	0

Additional pro statistics: Returned one punt for four yards, 1980; recovered three fumbles, 1981; recovered one fumble, 1982 and 1985; attempted one pass with one completion for 74 yards and a touchdown, 1983; attempted one pass with no completions and recovered two fumbles, 1984.
Played in NFC Championship Game following 1984 and 1985 seasons.
Played in NFL Championship Game following 1985 season.

JOHN LLOYD SULLIVAN
Defensive Back—Los Angeles Raiders
Born October 15, 1961, at Hartford, Conn.
Height, 6.01. Weight, 190.
High School—San Francisco, Calif., Lincoln.
Attended University of California at Berkeley.

Selected by Oakland in 1984 USFL territorial draft.
Signed by Oakland Invaders, January 20, 1984.
On developmental squad, May 25 through June 13, 1984; activated, June 14, 1984.
Selected by Green Bay in 3rd round (72nd player selected) of 1984 NFL supplemental draft.
Not protected in merger of Oakland Invaders and Michigan Panthers, selected by Oakland Invaders in USFL dispersal draft, December 6, 1984.
Released by Oakland Invaders, July 31, 1985; signed by Green Bay Packers, July 10, 1986.
Released by Green Bay Packers, October 17, 1986; awarded on waivers to San Diego Chargers, October 20, 1986.
Released by San Diego Chargers, August 29, 1987; signed as free agent replacement player by San Francisco 49ers, September 24, 1987.
Released by San Francisco 49ers, October 26, 1987; signed as free agent by Los Angeles Raiders, April 8, 1988.
On developmental squad for 3 games with Oakland Invaders in 1984.
Oakland USFL, 1984 and 1985; Green Bay (9) NFL, 1986; San Francisco NFL, 1987.
Games: 1984 (15), 1985 (18), 1986 (15), 1987 (1). Total USFL—33. Total NFL—16. Total Pro—49.
Pro statistics: Credited with one sack for five yards, 1984; intercepted four passes for four yards, credited with one sack for eight yards and fumbled once, 1985.
Played in USFL Championship Game following 1985 season.

DONALD O. SUMMERS
(Don)
Tight End—Green Bay Packers
Born February 22, 1961, at Grants Pass, Ore.
Height, 6.04. Weight, 235.
High Schools—Eagle Point, Ore.; and Medford, Ore.
Attended Oregon Tech and Boise State University.

Signed as free agent by Oakland Invaders, January 8, 1984.
Released by Oakland Invaders, January 30, 1984; signed as free agent by Denver Broncos, May 2, 1984.
Released by Denver Broncos, August 26, 1985; re-signed by Broncos, September 17, 1985.
Released by Denver Broncos, October 4, 1985; signed as free agent by Green Bay Packers, May 2, 1986.
Released by Green Bay Packers, August 25, 1986; re-signed as replacement player by Packers, October 2, 1987.
On injured reserve with knee injury, October 19 through remainder of 1987 season.

——PASS RECEIVING——

Year Club	G.	P.C.	Yds.	Avg.	TD.
1984—Denver NFL	16	3	32	10.7	0
1985—Denver NFL	2		None		
1987—Green Bay NFL	3	7	83	11.9	1
Pro Totals—3 Years	21	10	115	11.5	1

Additional pro statistics: Recovered one fumble, 1984.

WILLIAM SUTTON
(Mickey)
Cornerback—Los Angeles Rams
Born August 28, 1960, at Greenville, Miss.
Height, 5.08. Weight, 165.
High School—Union City, Calif., Logan.
Attended University of Montana.

Signed as free agent by Hamilton Tiger-Cats, April 15, 1983.
Released by Hamilton Tiger-Cats, July 25, 1983; signed by Pittsburgh Maulers, September 2, 1983.
Franchise disbanded, October 25, 1984.
Selected by Birmingham Stallions in USFL dispersal draft, December 6, 1984.
Granted free agency, August 1, 1985; signed by Los Angeles Rams, May 17, 1986.
Crossed picket line during players' strike, October 14, 1987.

— 399 —

Year Club	G.	INTERCEPTIONS				-PUNT RETURNS-				-KICKOFF RET.-				-TOTAL-		
		No.	Yds.	Avg.	TD.	No.	Yds.	Avg.	TD.	No.	Yds.	Avg.	TD.	TD.	Pts.	F.
1983—Hamilton CFL	1	None				None				None				0	0	0
1984—Pittsburgh USFL.........	17	1	16	16.0	0	None				9	232	25.8	0	1	6	0
1985—Birmingham USFL	17	2	30	15.0	0	1	0	0.0	0	15	244	16.3	0	0	0	2
1986—L.A. Rams NFL............	16	2	25	12.5	0	28	234	8.4	0	5	91	18.2	0	0	0	0
1987—L.A. Rams NFL............	12	1	4	4.0	0			None		2	37	18.5	0	0	0	0
CFL Totals—1 Year.......	1	0	0	0.0	0	0	0	0.0	0	0	0	0.0	0	0	0	0
USFL Totals—2 Years....	34	3	46	15.3	0	1	0	0.0	0	24	476	19.8	0	1	6	2
NFL Totals—2 Years.....	28	3	29	9.7	0	28	234	8.4	0	7	128	18.3	0	0	0	0
Pro Totals—5 Years.......	63	6	75	12.5	0	29	234	8.1	0	31	604	19.5	0	1	6	2

Additional CFL statistics: Recovered one fumble, 1983.
Additional USFL statistics: Recovered one fumble for 44 yards and a touchdown, 1984; recovered four fumbles, 1985.
Additional NFL statistics: Recovered one fumble, 1986; recovered two fumbles, 1987.

GEORGE SWARN
Running Back—Cleveland Browns
Born February 15, 1964, at Cincinnati, O.
Height, 5.10. Weight, 205.
High School—Mansfield, O., Malabar.
Attended Miami University (O.).

Selected by St. Louis in 5th round (118th player selected) of 1987 NFL draft.
Signed by St. Louis Cardinals, July 24, 1987.
Released by St. Louis Cardinals, September 7, 1987; signed as free agent replacement player by Cleveland Browns, October 15, 1987.
On injured reserve with ankle injury, December 25 through remainder of season.
Cleveland NFL, 1987.
Games: 1987 (1).

HARRY SWAYNE
Defensive End—Tampa Bay Buccaneers
Born February 2, 1965, at Philadelphia, Pa.
Height, 6.05. Weight, 268.
High School—Philadelphia, Pa., Cardinal Dougherty.
Attended Rutgers University.

Selected by Tampa Bay in 7th round (190th player selected) of 1987 NFL draft.
Signed by Tampa Bay Buccaneers, July 18, 1987.
On injured reserve with fractured hand, September 8 through October 30, 1987; activated, October 31, 1987.
Tampa Bay NFL, 1987.
Games: 1987 (8).

JAMES JOSEPH SWEENEY
(Jim)
Offensive Tackle-Guard—New York Jets
Born August 8, 1962, at Pittsburgh, Pa.
Height, 6.04. Weight, 275.
High School—Pittsburgh, Pa., Seton LaSalle.
Attended University of Pittsburgh.

Selected by Pittsburgh in 1984 USFL territorial draft.
Selected by New York Jets in 2nd round (37th player selected) of 1984 NFL draft.
Signed by New York Jets, July 12, 1984.
New York Jets NFL, 1984 through 1987.
Games: 1984 (10), 1985 (16), 1986 (16), 1987 (12). Total—54.

DENNIS NEAL SWILLEY
Center—Minnesota Vikings
Born June 28, 1955, at Bossier City, La.
Height, 6.03. Weight, 266.
High School—Pine Bluff, Ark.
Attended Texas A&M University and received degree in interior design/architectural design from North Texas State University.

Selected by Minnesota in 2nd round (55th player selected) of 1977 NFL draft.
On reserve/retired list entire 1984 season.
On injured reserve with broken leg, November 16 through remainder of 1987 season.
Minnesota NFL, 1977 through 1983 and 1985 through 1987.
Games: 1977 (14), 1978 (14), 1979 (16), 1980 (16), 1981 (16), 1982 (9), 1983 (16), 1985 (16), 1986 (16), 1987 (6). Total—139.
Pro statistics: Returned one kickoff for no yards and fumbled once, 1977; recovered one fumble, 1979, 1982 and 1985; fumbled once for minus 14 yards, 1986.
Played in NFC Championship Game following 1977 season.

PAT SWILLING
Linebacker—New Orleans Saints
Born October 25, 1964, at Toccoa, Ga.
Height, 6.03. Weight, 242.
High School—Toccoa, Ga., Stephens County.
Attended Georgia Tech.
Selected by Jacksonville in 1986 USFL territorial draft.
Selected by New Orleans in 3rd round (60th player selected) of 1986 NFL draft.
Signed by New Orleans Saints, July 21, 1986.
New Orleans NFL, 1986 and 1987.
Games: 1986 (16), 1987 (12). Total—28.
Pro statistics: Intercepted one pass for 10 yards and recovered three fumbles for one yard, 1987.

CRAIG AVERY SWOOPE
(Name pronounced Swope.)
Defensive Back—Indianapolis Colts
Born February 3, 1964, at Fort Pierce, Fla.
Height, 6.01. Weight, 200.
High School—Fort Pierce, Fla., Westwood.
Attended University of Illinois.
Selected by Orlando in 1986 USFL territorial draft.
Selected by Tampa Bay in 4th round (83rd player selected) of 1986 NFL draft.
Signed by Tampa Bay Buccaneers, June 27, 1986.
On injured reserve with hamstring injury, September 19 through November 2, 1987.
Released by Tampa Bay Buccaneers, November 3, 1987; awarded on waivers to Indianapolis Colts, November 4, 1987.
Tampa Bay NFL, 1986; Indianapolis NFL, 1987.
Games: 1986 (15), 1987 (3). Total—18.
Pro statistics: Intercepted one pass for 23 yards and recovered two fumbles, 1986.

PATRICK ROAMAN SWOOPES
Nose Tackle—New Orleans Saints
Born March 4, 1964, at Florence, Ala.
Height, 6.04. Weight, 280.
High School—Florence, Ala., Bradshaw.
Attended Mississippi State University.
Selected by New Jersey in 1986 USFL territorial draft.
Selected by New Orleans in 11th round (284th player selected) of 1986 NFL draft.
Signed by New Orleans Saints, July 14, 1986.
Released by New Orleans Saints, August 18, 1986; re-signed as replacement player by Saints, September 23, 1987.
New Orleans NFL, 1987.
Games: 1987 (9).

HARRY FLANROY SYDNEY III
Fullback—San Francisco 49ers
Born June 26, 1959, at Petersburg, Va.
Height, 6.00. Weight, 215.
High School—Fayetteville, N.C., 71st.
Received bachelor of general studies degree in criminal justice from University of Kansas in 1982.
Signed as free agent by Seattle Seahawks, April 30, 1981.
Released by Seattle Seahawks, August 25, 1981; signed as free agent by Cincinnati Bengals, February 2, 1982.
Released by Cincinnati Bengals, September 6, 1982; signed by Denver Gold, November 23, 1982.
Traded with 4th round pick in 1985 draft by Denver Gold to Memphis Showboats for right of first refusal to free agent defensive back Terry Love and 1st round pick in 1985 draft, January 3, 1985.
On developmental squad, April 14 through April 18, 1985; activated, April 19, 1985.
On developmental squad, May 18 through May 31, 1985; activated, June 1, 1985.
On developmental squad, June 7 through remainder of 1985 season.
Granted free agency when USFL suspended operations, August 7, 1986; signed as free agent by Montreal Alouettes, August 19, 1986.
Released by Montreal Alouettes, September 16, 1986; signed as free agent by San Francisco 49ers, April 8, 1987.
Crossed picket line during players' strike, October 7, 1987.
On developmental squad for 6 games with Memphis Showboats in 1985.

		—RUSHING—				PASS RECEIVING				—TOTAL—		
Year Club	G.	Att.	Yds.	Avg.	TD.	P.C.	Yds.	Avg.	TD.	TD.	Pts.	F.
1983—Denver USFL	18	176	801	4.6	9	31	306	9.9	2	11	66	9
1984—Denver USFL	18	230	961	4.2	10	44	354	8.1	2	12	72	5
1985—Memphis USFL	13	76	341	4.5	4	10	79	7.9	0	4	24	2
1986—Montreal CFL	4	38	115	3.0	2	18	162	9.0	0	2	†14	1
1987—San Francisco NFL	14	29	125	4.3	0	1	3	3.0	0	0	0	2
USFL Totals—3 Years	49	482	2103	4.4	23	85	739	8.7	4	27	162	16
CFL Totals—1 Year	4	38	115	3.0	2	18	162	9.0	0	2	14	1
NFL Totals—1 Year	14	29	125	4.3	0	1	3	3.0	0	0	0	2
Pro Totals—5 Years	67	549	2343	4.3	25	104	904	8.7	4	29	176	19

KICKOFF RETURNS

Year Club	G.	No.	Yds.	Avg.	TD.
1983—Denver USFL	18	1	13	13.0	0
1984—Denver USFL	18	3	24	8.0	0
1985—Memphis USFL	13	3	25	8.3	0
1986—Montreal CFL	4			None	
1987—San Francisco NFL	14	12	243	20.3	0
USFL Totals—3 Years	49	7	62	8.9	0
CFL Totals—1 Year	4	0	0	0.0	0
NFL Totals—1 Year	14	12	243	20.3	0
Pro Totals—5 Years	67	19	305	16.1	0

†Scored one 2-point conversion.
Additional pro statistics: Attempted three passes with one completion for 46 yards and one interception, 1983; recovered two fumbles, 1983 through 1985; attempted four passes with no completions and one interception, 1984; attempted one pass with one completion for 50 yards and a touchdown, 1987.

DARRYL VICTOR TALLEY
Linebacker—Buffalo Bills
Born July 10, 1960, at Cleveland, O.
Height, 6.04. Weight, 227.
High School—East Cleveland, O., Shaw.
Received degree in physical education from West Virginia University.

Named as linebacker on THE SPORTING NEWS College All-America Team, 1982.
Selected by New Jersey in 2nd round (24th player selected) of 1983 USFL draft.
Selected by Buffalo in 2nd round (39th player selected) of 1983 NFL draft.
Signed by Buffalo Bills, June 14, 1983.
Buffalo NFL, 1983 through 1987.
Games: 1983 (16), 1984 (16), 1985 (16), 1986 (16), 1987 (12). Total—76.
Pro statistics: Returned two kickoffs for nine yards and recovered two fumbles for six yards, 1983; recovered one fumble and intercepted one pass for no yards, 1984; recovered one fumble for 47 yards, 1986; recovered one fumble for one yard, 1987.

ROBERT STANLEY TALLEY
(Stan)
Punter—Los Angeles Raiders
Born September 5, 1958, at Dallas, Tex.
Height, 6.05. Weight, 220.
High School—Torrance, Calif., West Torrance.
Attended El Camino Junior College and received bachelor of business administration degree in marketing from Texas Christian University in 1982.

Named punter on THE SPORTING NEWS USFL All-Star Team, 1985.
Led USFL in punting yardage with 3,825 in 1983 and 4,569 in 1984.
Signed as free agent by Atlanta Falcons, May 5, 1981.
Released by Atlanta Falcons, August 23, 1981; signed as free agent by New Orleans Saints, May 6, 1982.
Released by New Orleans Saints, September 6, 1982; signed by Oakland Invaders, January 11, 1983.
Protected in merger of Oakland Invaders and Michigan Panthers, December 6, 1984.
Released by Oakland Invaders, August 25, 1985; signed as free agent by Cleveland Browns, April 21, 1986.
Released by Cleveland Browns, August 18, 1986; signed as free agent by Los Angeles Raiders, April 6, 1987.

		——PUNTING——		
Year Club	G.	No.	Avg.	Blk.
1983—Oakland USFL	18	87	*44.0	....
1984—Oakland USFL	18	*110	41.5	....
1985—Oakland USFL	18	66	*44.3	....
1987—L.A. Raiders NFL	12	56	40.7	1
USFL Totals—3 Years	54	263	43.0	....
NFL Totals—1 Year	12	56	40.7	1
Pro Totals—4 Years	66	319	42.6	....

Additional pro statistics: Fumbled twice and rushed once for no yards, 1983; recovered one fumble, 1984.
Played in USFL Championship Game following 1985 season.

BEN ALLEN TAMBURELLO JR.
(Name pronounced TAM-bur-RELL-o.)
Center-Guard—Philadelphia Eagles
Born September 9, 1964, at Birmingham, Ala.
Height, 6.03. Weight, 278.
High Schools—Birmingham, Ala., Shades Valley; and Sweetwater, Tenn.,
Tennessee Military Institute.
Attended Auburn University.

Named as center on THE SPORTING NEWS College All-America Team, 1986.
Selected by Philadelphia in 3rd round (65th player selected) of 1987 NFL draft.
Signed by Philadelphia Eagles, August 6, 1987.
On injured reserve with broken wrist, August 25 through December 16, 1987; activated, December 17, 1987.
Philadelphia NFL, 1987.
Games: 1987 (2).
Pro statistics: Recovered one fumble, 1987.

STEVE TASKER
Wide Receiver-Kick Returner—Buffalo Bills
Born April 10, 1962, at Leoti, Kan.
Height, 5.09. Weight, 185.
High School—Leoti, Kan., Wichita County.
Attended Dodge City Community College and Northwestern University.
Selected by Houston in 9th round (226th player selected) of 1985 NFL draft.
Signed by Houston Oilers, June 14, 1985.
On injured reserve with knee injury, October 23 through remainder of 1985 season.
On injured reserve with knee injury, September 15 through November 5, 1986.
Released by Houston Oilers, November 6, 1986; awarded on waivers to Buffalo Bills, November 7, 1986.

| | | KICKOFF RETURNS | | | |
Year Club	G.	No.	Yds.	Avg.	TD.
1985—Houston NFL..............	7	17	447	26.3	0
1986—Hou. (2)-Buff. (7) NFL.	9	12	213	17.8	0
1987—Buffalo NFL..............	12	11	197	17.9	0
Pro Totals—3 Years...........	28	40	857	21.4	0

Additional pro statistics: Rushed twice for 16 yards and caught two passes for 19 yards, 1985; credited with a safety and fumbled twice, 1987.
Played in Pro Bowl (NFL All-Star Game) following 1987 season.

MOSIULA TATUPU
(Mosi)
Running Back—New England Patriots
Born April 26, 1955, at Pago Pago, American Samoa.
Height, 6.00. Weight, 227.
High School—Honolulu, Haw., Punahou.
Attended University of Southern California.
Son of Mosi Tatupu, former Samoan boxing champ; and cousin of Terry Tautolo,
linebacker with Philadelphia Eagles, San Francisco 49ers, Detroit Lions and Miami Dolphins,
1976 through 1984; and John Tautolo, guard with Los Angeles Raiders.
Selected by New England in 8th round (215th player selected) of 1978 NFL draft.

Year Club		RUSHING				PASS RECEIVING				TOTAL		
	G.	Att.	Yds.	Avg.	TD.	P.C.	Yds.	Avg.	TD.	TD.	Pts.	F.
1978—New England NFL....................	16	3	6	2.0	0	None				0	0	0
1979—New England NFL....................	16	23	71	3.1	0	2	9	4.5	0	0	0	0
1980—New England NFL....................	16	33	97	2.9	3	4	27	6.8	0	3	18	0
1981—New England NFL....................	16	38	201	5.3	2	12	132	11.0	1	3	18	2
1982—New England NFL....................	9	30	168	5.6	0	None				0	0	0
1983—New England NFL....................	16	106	578	5.5	4	10	97	9.7	1	5	30	1
1984—New England NFL....................	16	133	553	4.2	4	16	159	9.9	0	4	24	4
1985—New England NFL....................	16	47	152	3.2	2	2	16	8.0	0	2	12	1
1986—New England NFL....................	16	71	172	2.4	1	15	145	9.7	0	2	12	1
1987—New England NFL....................	12	79	248	3.1	0	15	136	9.1	0	0	0	1
Pro Totals—10 Years....................	149	563	2246	4.0	16	76	721	9.5	2	19	114	10

Additional pro statistics: Returned one kickoff for 17 yards, 1978; returned three kickoffs for 15 yards, 1979; recovered three fumbles, 1981; recovered one fumble, 1983 through 1985; returned one kickoff for nine yards, 1984; returned blocked punt 17 yards for a touchdown, 1986; attempted one pass with one completion for 15 yards and a touchdown, 1987.
Played in AFC Championship Game following 1985 season.
Played in NFL Championship Game following 1985 season.
Played in Pro Bowl (NFL All-Star Game) following 1986 season.

TERRY WAYNE TAUSCH
Guard—Minnesota Vikings
Born February 5, 1959, at New Braunfels, Tex.
Height, 6.05. Weight, 276.
High School—New Braunfels, Tex.
Received bachelor of business administration degree in marketing from
University of Texas in 1981.
Named as offensive tackle on THE SPORTING NEWS College All-America Team, 1981.
Selected by Minnesota in 2nd round (39th player selected) of 1982 NFL draft.
On injured reserve with torn ankle tendon, November 14 through remainder of 1987 season.
Minnesota NFL, 1982 through 1987.
Games: 1982 (2), 1983 (10), 1984 (16), 1985 (16), 1986 (16), 1987 (5). Total—65.

TAIVALE TAUTALATASI JR.
(Name pronounced TIE-volley TAUGHT-a-la-TOSS-ee.)
(Junior)
Running Back—Philadelphia Eagles
Born March 24, 1962, at Oakland, Calif.
Height, 5.10. Weight, 210.
High School—Alameda, Calif., Encinal.
Attended Chabot College and Washington State University.

Selected by Philadelphia in 10th round (261st player selected) of 1986 NFL draft.
Selected by Baltimore in 8th round (60th player selected) of 1986 USFL draft.
Signed by Philadelphia Eagles, July 16, 1986.

Year Club	G.	RUSHING				PASS RECEIVING				—TOTAL—		
		Att.	Yds.	Avg.	TD.	P.C.	Yds.	Avg.	TD.	TD.	Pts.	F.
1986—Philadelphia NFL	16	51	163	3.2	0	41	325	7.9	2	2	12	6
1987—Philadelphia NFL	12	26	69	2.7	0	25	176	7.0	0	0	0	1
Pro Totals—2 Years	28	77	232	3.0	0	66	501	7.6	2	2	12	7

Year Club	G.	KICKOFF RETURNS			
		No.	Yds.	Avg.	TD.
1986—Philadelphia NFL	16	18	344	19.1	0
1987—Philadelphia NFL	12	3	53	17.7	0
Pro Totals—2 Years	28	21	397	18.9	0

Additional pro statistics: Recovered one fumble, 1986.

JOHN WILLIAM TAUTOLO
Name pronounced Ta-TOE-low.
Guard—Los Angeles Raiders
Born May 29, 1959, at Long Beach, Calif.
Height 6.03. Weight, 260.
High School—Long Beach, Calif., R.A. Millikan.
Attended University of California at Los Angeles.
Brother of Terry Tautolo, linebacker with Philadelphia Eagles, San Francisco 49ers, Detroit Lions and Miami Dolphins, 1976 through 1984; cousin of Manu Tuiasosopo, nose tackle with Seattle Seahawks and San Francisco 49ers, 1979 through 1986; Wilson Faumuina, defensive end with Atlanta Falcons, 1977 through 1981; Mosi Tatupu, running back with New England Patriots; Frank Manumaleuga, linebacker with Kansas City Chiefs, Oakland Invaders and Portland Breakers, 1979 through 1981 and 1983 through 1985; and Jack Thompson, quarterback with Cincinnati Bengals and Tampa Bay Buccaneers, 1979 through 1984.
Signed as free agent by New England Patriots, May 27, 1981.
On injured reserve with knee injury, August 18 through entire 1981 season.
Released by New England Patriots, September 6, 1982; signed as free agent by New York Giants, November 30, 1982.
Released by New York Giants, August 27, 1984; signed by New Jersey Generals, December 27, 1984.
Released by New Jersey Generals after failing physical, January 21, 1985; signed as free agent by Portland Breakers, January 25, 1985.
On developmental squad, May 17 through May 21, 1985.
Released by Portland Breakers, May 22, 1985; re-signed by Breakers, June 12, 1985.
Released by Portland Breakers, June 26, 1985; signed as free agent replacement player by Los Angeles Raiders, September 24, 1987.
Released by Los Angeles Raiders, October 21, 1987; re-signed by Raiders for 1988, December 2, 1987.
On developmental squad for 1 game with Portland Breakers in 1985.
New York Giants NFL, 1982 and 1983; Portland USFL, 1985; Los Angeles Raiders NFL, 1987.
Games: 1982 (1), 1983 (6), 1985 (11), 1987 (3). Total NFL—10. Total Pro—21.

EUGENE TAYLOR
(Gene)
Wide Receiver—Tampa Bay Buccaneers
Born November 12, 1962, at Oakland, Calif.
Height, 6.02. Weight, 189.
High School—Richmond, Calif., Salesian.
Attended Contra Costa College and Fresno State University.
Selected by New England in 6th round (163rd player selected) of 1987 NFL draft.
Signed by New England Patriots, July 26, 1987.
Released by New England Patriots, August 31, 1987; awarded on waivers to Tampa Bay Buccaneers, September 1, 1987.
Released by Tampa Bay Buccaneers, September 7, 1987; re-signed by Buccaneers, September 8, 1987.
Tampa Bay NFL, 1987.
Games: 1987 (7).
Pro statistics: Caught two passes for 21 yards, 1987.

JOHN GREGORY TAYLOR
Wide Receiver—San Francisco 49ers
Born March 31, 1962, at Pennsauken, N. J.
Height, 6.01. Weight, 185.
High School—Pennsauken, N. J.
Attended Delaware State College.
Selected by San Francisco in 3rd round (76th player selected) of 1986 NFL draft.
Selected by Baltimore in 2nd round (13th player selected) of 1986 USFL draft.
Signed by San Francisco 49ers, July 21, 1986.
On injured reserve with back injury, August 26 through entire 1986 season.

Year Club	G.	PASS RECEIVING			
		P.C.	Yds.	Avg.	TD.
1987—San Francisco NFL	12	9	151	16.8	0

Additional pro statistics: Recovered one fumble for 26 yards and a touchdown and returned one punt for nine yards, 1987.

JOHNNY HERBERT TAYLOR
Linebacker—San Diego Chargers
Born June 21, 1961, at Seattle, Wash.
Height, 6.04. Weight, 235.
High School—Garfield, Wash.
Attended Wenatchee Valley Junior College and University of Hawaii.

Signed as free agent by Atlanta Falcons, May 2, 1984.
Released by Atlanta Falcons, August 21, 1984; re-signed by Falcons after clearing procedural waivers, December 6, 1984.
Released by Atlanta Falcons, October 11, 1986; awarded on waivers to Miami Dolphins, October 13, 1986.
On injured reserve with ankle injury, October 23 through Novmeber 27, 1986.
Released by Miami Dolphins, November 28, 1986; signed as free agent replacement player by San Diego Chargers, September 24, 1987.
On injured reserve with hamstring injury, December 12 through remainder of 1987 season.
Atlanta NFL, 1984 and 1985; Atlanta (5)-Miami (1) NFL, 1986; San Diego NFL, 1987.
Games: 1984 (2), 1985 (15), 1986 (6), 1987 (7). Total—30.
Pro statistics: Recovered one fumble, 1985.

LAWRENCE TAYLOR
Linebacker—New York Giants
Born February 4, 1959, at Williamsburg, Va.
Height, 6.03. Weight, 243.
High School—Williamsburg, Va., Lafayette.
Attended University of North Carolina.

Named THE SPORTING NEWS NFL Player of the Year, 1986.
Named to THE SPORTING NEWS NFL All-Star Team, 1981 and 1983 through 1986.
Named as linebacker on THE SPORTING NEWS College All-America Team, 1980.
Selected by New York Giants in 1st round (2nd player selected) of 1981 NFL draft.
Crossed picket line during players' strike, October 14, 1987.

			—INTERCEPTIONS—			
Year Club	G.	No.	Yds.	Avg.	TD.
1981—N.Y. Giants NFL	16	1	1	1.0	0
1982—N.Y. Giants NFL	9	1	97	97.0	*1
1983—N.Y. Giants NFL	16	2	10	5.0	0
1984—N.Y. Giants NFL	16	1	−1	−1.0	0
1985—N.Y. Giants NFL	16		None		
1986—N.Y. Giants NFL	16		None		
1987—N.Y. Giants NFL	12	3	16	5.3	0
Pro Totals—7 Years	101	8	123	15.4	1

Additional pro statistics: Recovered one fumble for four yards, 1981; fumbled once, 1981 and 1983; recovered two fumbles for three yards, 1983; recovered two fumbles for 25 yards, 1985.
Played in NFC Championship Game following 1986 season.
Played in NFL Championship Game following 1986 season.
Played in Pro Bowl (NFL All-Star Game) following 1981 through 1987 seasons.

MALCOLM TAYLOR
Defensive Tackle—Los Angeles Raiders
Born June 20, 1960, at Crystal Springs, Miss.
Height, 6.06. Weight, 280.
High School—Crystal Springs, Miss.
Attended Tennessee State University.

Selected by Houston in 5th round (121st player selected) of 1982 NFL draft.
Signed by Chicago Blitz, January 4, 1984, for contract to take effect after being granted free agency, February 1, 1984.
USFL rights traded by Memphis Showboats to Chicago Blitz for past considerations, January 9, 1984.
On developmental squad, April 28 through May 17, 1984; activated, May 18, 1984.
On developmental squad, June 24 through remainder of 1984 season.
Franchise disbanded, November 20, 1984.
Selected by Houston Gamblers in USFL dispersal draft, December 6, 1984.
Traded by Houston Gamblers to Birmingham Stallions for offensive tackle Rob Taylor, February 12, 1985.
On developmental squad, March 16 through March 29, 1985; activated, March 30, 1985.
Granted free agency when USFL suspended operations, August 7, 1986; signed by Houston Oilers, August 24, 1986.
Granted roster exemption, August 24 through August 28, 1986; activated, August 29, 1986.
Released by Houston Oilers, October 2, 1986; signed as free agent by Los Angeles Raiders, April 17, 1987.
On developmental squad for 4 games with Chicago Blitz in 1984.
On developmental squad for 2 games with Birmingham Stallions in 1985.
Houston NFL, 1982, 1983 and 1986; Chicago USFL, 1984; Birmingham USFL, 1985; Los Angeles Raiders NFL, 1987.
Games: 1982 (9), 1983 (16), 1984 (14), 1985 (15), 1986 (3), 1987 (12). Total NFL—40. Total USFL—29. Total Pro—69.
NFL statistics: Recovered one fumble, 1982.
USFL statistics: Credited with six sacks for 47½ yards, 1984; credited with four sacks for 33 yards and recovered one fumble, 1985.

—DID YOU KNOW—
That when Tampa Bay defeated Atlanta in its 1987 season-opening game, it was the first time the Buccaneers had been above the .500 mark since their 5-4 finish in the strike-shortened 1982 season?

ROBERT EARL TAYLOR
(Rob)
Offensive Tackle—Tampa Bay Buccaneers
Born November 14, 1960, at St. Charles, Ill.
Height, 6.06. Weight, 290.
High School—Kettering, O., Fairmont East.
Received degree in electrical engineering from Northwestern University.
Selected by Philadelphia in 12th round (328th player selected) of 1982 NFL draft.
Released by Philadelphia Eagles, August 23, 1982; claimed on waivers by Baltimore Colts, August 25, 1982.
Released by Baltimore Colts, September 6, 1982; signed as free agent by Chicago Blitz, October 4, 1982.
Franchise transferred to Arizona, September 30, 1983.
Protected in merger of Arizona Wranglers and Oklahoma Outlaws, December 6, 1984.
Granted free agency, November 30, 1984; signed by Birmingham Stallions, January 23, 1985 (Arizona did not exercise right of first refusal).
Traded by Birmingham Stallions to Houston Gamblers for defensive end Malcolm Taylor, February 12, 1985.
On developmental squad, February 21 through March 2, 1985; activated, March 3, 1985.
Released by Houston Gamblers, July 31, 1985; awaded on waivers to Baltimore Stars, August 1, 1985.
Released by Baltimore Stars, August 2, 1985; signed as free agent by Tampa Bay Buccaneers, March 26, 1986.
On injured reserve with knee injury, November 11 through remainder of 1987 season.
On developmental squad for 1 game with Houston Gamblers in 1985.
Chicago USFL, 1983 and 1984; Houston USFL, 1985; Tampa Bay NFL, 1986 and 1987.
Games: 1983 (18), 1984 (18), 1985 (16), 1986 (16), 1987 (5). Total USFL—52. Total NFL—21. Total Pro—73.
Pro statistics: Recovered one fumble, 1983.
Played in USFL Championship Game following 1984 season.

TERRY TAYLOR
Cornerback—Seattle Seahawks
Born July 18, 1961, at Warren, O.
Height, 5.10. Weight, 188.
High School—Youngstown, O., Rayen.
Attended Southern Illinois University.
Cousin of Walter Poole, running back with Chicago Blitz
and Houston Gamblers, 1983 and 1984.
Selected by Chicago in 2nd round (25th player selected) of 1984 USFL draft.
Selected by Seattle in 1st round (22nd player selected) of 1984 NFL draft.
Signed by Seattle Seahawks, July 10, 1984.

| | | | —INTERCEPTIONS— | | |
Year Club	G.	No.	Yds.	Avg.	TD.
1984—Seattle NFL	16	3	63	21.0	0
1985—Seattle NFL	16	4	75	18.8	*1
1986—Seattle NFL	16	2	0	0.0	0
1987—Seattle NFL	12	1	11	11.0	0
Pro Totals—4 Years	60	10	149	14.9	1

Additional pro statistics: Returned blocked punt for 15 yards and a touchdown, 1985.

JIMMY DEWAYNE TEAL
Wide Receiver—Seattle Seahawks
Born August 18, 1962, at Lufkin, Tex.
Height, 5.11. Weight, 175.
High School—Diboll, Tex.
Attended Texas A&M University.
Selected by Houston in 1985 USFL territorial draft.
Selected by Buffalo in 5th round (130th player selected) of 1985 NFL draft.
Signed by Buffalo Bills, July 19, 1985.
On injured reserve with hamstring injury, September 3 through December 5, 1985; activated, December 6, 1985.
On injured reserve with shoulder injury, September 2 through November 20, 1986; activated, November 21, 1986.
Released by Buffalo Bills, August 10, 1987; awarded on waivers to New Orleans Saints, August 11, 1987.
On injured reserve, September 1 through September 6, 1987.
Released by New Orleans Saints, September 7, 1987; signed as free agent replacement player by Seattle Seahawks, Sepember 24, 1987.

| | | | —PASS RECEIVING— | | |
Year Club	G.	P.C.	Yds.	Avg.	TD.
1985—Buffalo NFL	3	1	24	24.0	0
1986—Buffalo NFL	5	6	60	10.0	1
1987—Seattle NFL	4	14	198	14.1	2
Pro Totals—3 Years	12	21	282	13.4	3

Additional pro statistics: Returned one kickoff for 20 yards, 1985; returned six punts for 38 yards, returned six kickoffs for 95 yards and fumbled once, 1987.

JOHN ROBERT TELTSCHIK
Punter—Philadelphia Eagles
Born March 8, 1964, at Floresville, Tex.
Height, 6.02. Weight, 209.
High School—Kerrville, Tex., Tivy.
Received degree in business administration from University of Texas in 1986.
Related to Fritz Connally, third baseman with Chicago Cubs and Baltimore Orioles, 1983 and 1985.

Led NFL in punting yards with 4,493 in 1986.
Selected by Chicago in 9th round (249th player selected) of 1986 NFL draft.
Selected by New Jersey in 8th round (55th player selected) of 1986 USFL draft.
Signed by Chicago Bears, July 15, 1986.
Released by Chicago Bears, August 26, 1986; signed as free agent by Philadelphia Eagles, August 28, 1986.

| | | ——PUNTING—— | | |
Year	Club	G.	No.	Avg.	Blk.
1986—Philadelphia NFL		16	*108	41.6	1
1987—Philadelphia NFL		12	*82	38.2	1
Pro Totals—2 Years......................		28	190	40.1	2

Additional pro statistics: Rushed once for no yards and recovered one fumble, 1986; rushed three times for 32 yards, 1987.

DEREK WAYNE TENNELL
(Name pronounced Te-NELL.)
Tight End—Cleveland Browns
Born February 12, 1964, at Los Angeles, Calif.
Height, 6.05. Weight, 245.
High School—West Covina, Calif.
Attended University of California at Los Angeles.

Selected by Seattle in 7th round (185th player selected) of 1987 NFL draft.
Signed by Seattle Seahawks, July 21, 1987.
Released by Seattle Seahawks, September 7, 1987; signed as free agent replacement player by Cleveland Browns, September 24, 1987.

| | | ——PASS RECEIVING—— | | | |
Year	Club	G.	P.C.	Yds.	Avg.	TD.
1987—Cleveland NFL..............		11	9	102	11.3	3

Played in AFC Championship Game following 1987 season.

VINCENT FRANK TESTAVERDE
(Vinny)
Quarterback—Tampa Bay Buccaneers
Born November 13, 1963, at Brooklyn, N. Y.
Height, 6.05. Weight, 220.
High School—Floral Park, N.Y., Sewanhaka;
and Fort Union, Vir., Fork Union Military.
Attended University of Miami (Fla.).

Heisman Trophy winner, 1986.
Named college football Player of the Year by THE SPORTING NEWS, 1986.
Named as quarterback on THE SPORTING NEWS College All-America Team, 1986.
Signed by Tampa Bay Buccaneers, April 3, 1987.
Selected officially by Tampa Bay in 1st round (1st player selected) of 1987 NFL draft.

| | | ————PASSING———— | | | | | | | ——RUSHING—— | | | —TOTAL— | | |
Year	Club	G.	Att.	Cmp.	Pct.	Gain	T.P.	P.I.	Avg.	Att.	Yds.	Avg.	TD.	TD.	Pts.	F.
1987—Tampa Bay NFL..............		6	165	71	43.0	1081	5	6	6.55	13	50	3.8	1	1	6	7

Quarterback Rating Points: 1987 (60.2).
Additional pro statistics: Recovered four fumbles and fumbled seven times for minus three yards, 1987.

THOMAS ALLEN THAYER
(Tom)
Guard—Chicago Bears
Born August 16, 1961, at Joliet, Ill.
Height, 6.04. Weight, 280.
High School—Joliet, Ill., Catholic.
Received bachelor of arts degree in communications and public relations
from University of Notre Dame.
Brother-in-law of John Scully, guard with Atlanta Falcons.

Selected by Chicago in 1983 USFL territorial draft.
Signed by Chicago Blitz, April 26, 1983.
Selected by Chicago in 4th round (91st player selected) of 1983 NFL draft.
Franchise transferred to Arizona, September 30, 1983.
Protected in merger of Arizona Wranglers and Oklahoma Outlaws, December 6, 1984.
On developmental squad, March 3 through March 10, 1985; activated, March 11, 1985.
Granted free agency, July 15, 1985; signed by Chicago Bears, July 19, 1985.
On developmental squad for 1 game with Arizona Outlaws in 1985.
Chicago USFL, 1983 and 1984; Arizona USFL, 1985; Chicago NFL, 1985 through 1987.
Games 1983 (10), 1984 (18), 1985 USFL (17), 1985 NFL (16), 1986 (16), 1987 (11). Total USFL—45. Total NFL—43.
Total Pro—88.
USFL statistics: Recovered two fumbles, 1985.
Played in USFL Championship Game following 1984 season.
Played in NFC Championship Game following 1985 season.
Played in NFL Championship Game following 1985 season.

RAY CHARLES THIELEMANN
Name pronounced TEEL-munn.
(R. C.)
Guard—Washington Redskins
Born August 12, 1955, at Houston, Tex.
Height, 6.04. Weight, 272.
High School—Houston, Tex., Spring Woods.
Attended University of Arkansas.
Selected by Atlanta in 2nd round (36th player selected) of 1977 NFL draft.
On injured reserve with shoulder separation, September 13 through October 12, 1979; activated, October 13, 1979.
On injured reserve with shoulder injury, December 13 through remainder of 1979 season.
On did not report list, August 16 through August 24, 1983.
Reported and granted exemption, August 25, 1983; activated, September 1, 1983.
Granted free agency, February 1, 1985; re-signed by Falcons and traded to Washington Redskins for wide receiver Charlie Brown, August 26, 1985.
Granted roster exemption, August 26 through August 29, 1985; activated, August 30, 1985.
On injured reserve with knee injury, October 2 through remainder of 1985 season.
Atlanta NFL, 1977 through 1984; Washington NFL, 1985 through 1987.
Games: 1977 (14), 1978 (16), 1979 (11), 1980 (16), 1981 (16), 1982 (9), 1983 (16), 1984 (16), 1985 (3), 1986 (14), 1987 (12). Total—143.
Pro statistics: Recovered one fumble, 1977, 1983 and 1984; recovered two fumbles, 1978 through 1981.
Played in NFC Championship Game following 1986 and 1987 seasons.
Played in NFL Championship Game following 1987 season.
Played in Pro Bowl (NFL All-Star Game) following 1981 through 1983 seasons.

BENJAMIN THOMAS JR.
(Ben)
Defensive End-Nose Tackle—Green Bay Packers
Born July 2, 1961, at Ashburn, Ga.
Height, 6.04. Weight, 275.
High School—Ashburn, Ga., Turner County.
Attended Auburn University.
Selected by Birmingham in 1985 USFL territorial draft.
Selected by New England in 2nd round (56th player selected) of 1985 NFL draft.
Signed by New England Patriots, July 24, 1985.
Released by New England Patriots, October 17, 1986; awarded on waivers to Green Bay Packers, October 20, 1986.
On injured reserve with knee injury, September 1 through entire 1987 season.
Crossed picket line during players' strike, October 14, 1987.
New England NFL, 1985; New England (4)-Green Bay (9) NFL, 1986.
Games: 1985 (15), 1986 (13). Total—28.
Played in AFC Championship Game following 1985 season.
Played in NFL Championship Game following 1985 season.

CALVIN LEWIS THOMAS
Fullback—Chicago Bears
Born January 7, 1960, at St. Louis, Mo.
Height, 5.11. Weight, 245.
High School—St. Louis, Mo., McKinley.
Attended University of Illinois.
Signed as free agent by Chicago Bears, May 21, 1982.
On inactive list, September 12, 1982.

		—RUSHING—				PASS RECEIVING				—TOTAL—		
Year	Club	G.	Att.	Yds.	Avg.	TD.	P.C.	Yds.	Avg.	TD.	TD.	Pts.	F.
1982—Chicago NFL		6	5	4	0.8	0	None				0	0	1
1983—Chicago NFL		13	8	25	3.1	0	2	13	6.5	0	0	0	0
1984—Chicago NFL		16	40	186	4.7	1	9	39	4.3	0	1	6	0
1985—Chicago NFL		14	31	125	4.0	4	5	45	9.0	0	4	24	0
1986—Chicago NFL		16	56	224	4.0	0	4	18	4.5	0	0	0	3
1987—Chicago NFL		12	25	88	3.5	0	None				0	0	0
Pro Totals—6 Years		77	165	652	4.0	5	20	115	5.8	0	5	30	5

Additional pro statistics: Recovered one fumble, 1984 and 1987; recovered two fumbles, 1986.
Played in NFC Championship Game following 1984 and 1985 seasons.
Played in NFL Championship Game following 1985 season.

CHUCK THOMAS
Center—San Francisco 49ers
Born December 24, 1960, at Houston, Tex.
Height, 6.03. Weight, 277.
High School—Houston, Tex., Stratford.
Attended University of Oklahoma.
Selected by San Antonio in 1985 USFL territorial draft.
Selected by Houston in 8th round (199th player selected) of 1985 NFL draft.
Signed by Houston Oilers, July 13, 1985.
Released by Houston Oilers, September 2, 1985; signed as free agent by Atlanta Falcons, November 22, 1985.
Released by Atlanta Falcons, August 12, 1986; signed as free agent by San Francisco 49ers, December 22, 1986.

On injured reserve with thigh injury, August 28 through September 6, 1987.
Released by San Francisco 49ers, September 7, 1987; re-signed as replacement player by 49ers, September 24, 1987.
Atlanta NFL, 1985; San Francisco NFL, 1987.
Games: 1985 (4), 1987 (7). Total—11.

CURTLAND PARRISH THOMAS
Wide Receiver—New York Jets
Born February 19, 1962, at St. Louis, Mo.
Height, 6.00. Weight, 185.
High School—St. Louis, Mo., Sumner.
Attended University of Missouri.
Selected by Philadelphia in 18th round (368th player selected) of 1984 USFL draft.
Selected by Washington in 12th round (335th player selected) of 1984 NFL draft.
Signed by Washington Redskins, July 12, 1984.
Released by Washington Redskins, August 13, 1984; signed by Orlando Renegades, December 20, 1984.
Released by Orlando Renegades, January 18, 1985; signed as free agent by St. Louis Cardinals, April 24, 1985.
Released by St. Louis Cardinals, August 27, 1985; signed as free agent by Toronto Argonauts, March 16, 1986.
Released by Toronto Argonauts, August 19, 1986; signed as free agent by New York Jets, March 27, 1987.
Released by New York Jets, August 31, 1987; signed as free agent replacement player by New Orleans Saints, September 24, 1987.
Released by New Orleans Saints, October 21, 1987; signed as free agent by New York Jets, May 3, 1988.
Toronto CFL, 1986; New Orleans NFL, 1987.
Games: 1986 (4), 1987 (2). Total—6.
Pro statistics: Caught one pass for 14 yards and returned one kickoff for 11 yards, 1987.

ERIC JASON THOMAS
Cornerback—Cincinnati Bengals
Born September 11, 1964, at Tucson, Ariz.
Height, 5.11. Weight, 175.
High School—Sacramento, Calif., Norte Del Rio.
Attended Pasadena City College and Tulane University.
Selected by Cincinnati in 2nd round (49th player selected) of 1987 NFL draft.
Signed by Cincinnati Bengals, July 27, 1987.
Cincinnati NFL, 1987.
Games: 1987 (12).
Pro statistics: Intercepted one pass for three yards, 1987.

HENRY LEE THOMAS JR.
Nose Tackle—Minnesota Vikings
Born January 12, 1965, at Houston, Tex.
Height, 6.02. Weight, 268.
High School—Houston, Tex., Dwight D. Eisenhower.
Attended Louisiana State University.
Selected by Minnesota in 3rd round (72nd player selected) of 1987 NFL draft.
Signed by Minnesota Vikings, July 14, 1987.
Minnesota NFL, 1987.
Games: 1987 (12).
Pro statistics: Intercepted one pass for no yards and recovered one fumble, 1987.
Played in NFC Championship Game following 1987 season.

BRODERICK THOMPSON
Guard-Offensive Tackle—San Diego Chargers
Born August 14, 1960, at Birmingham, Ala.
Height, 6.04. Weight, 290.
High School—Cerritos, Calif., Richard Gahr.
Attended Cerritos College and University of Kansas.
Signed as free agent by Dallas Cowboys, April 28, 1983.
Released by Dallas Cowboys, August 2, 1983; signed as free agent by San Antonio Gunslingers, November 12, 1983.
Traded with 1st round pick in 1984 draft by San Antonio Gunslingers to Chicago Blitz for rights to quarterback Bob Gagliano, January 3, 1984.
Released by Chicago Blitz, January 31, 1984; signed as free agent by Los Angeles Express, February 10, 1984.
Released by Los Angeles Express, February 13, 1984; signed as free agent by Los Angeles Rams, May 4, 1984.
Released by Los Angeles Rams, August 21, 1984; signed as free agent by Portland Breakers, January 23, 1985.
Released by Portland Breakers, July 31, 1985; awarded on waivers to Memphis Showboats, August 1, 1985.
Released by Memphis Showboats, August 2, 1985; signed as free agent by Dallas Cowboys, August 3, 1985.
Released by Dallas Cowboys, August 26, 1986; signed as free agent by San Diego Chargers, April 13, 1987.
Released by San Diego Chargers, September 7, 1987; re-signed by Chargers, September 8, 1987.
Portland USFL, 1985; Dallas NFL, 1985; San Diego NFL, 1987.
Games: 1985 USFL (18), 1985 NFL (11), 1987 (8). Total NFL—19. Total Pro—37.

GARY THOMPSON
Cornerback—Washington Redskins
Born February 23, 1959, at Castro Valley, Calif.
Height, 6.00. Weight, 180.
High School—Eureka, Calif.
Attended College of the Redwoods and San Jose State University.

Signed as free agent by San Francisco 49ers, May 4, 1982.
Released by San Francisco 49ers, August 21, 1982; signed as free agent by Winnipeg Blue Bombers, April, 1983.
Released by Winnipeg Blue Bombers, July 3, 1983; signed as free agent by Buffalo Bills, July 14, 1983.
Released by Buffalo Bills, October 24, 1984; signed as free agent by San Francisco 49ers, April 16, 1985.
Released by San Francisco 49ers, August 13, 1985; signed as free agent by Edmonton Eskimos, September, 1985.
Released by Edmonton Eskimos, September, 1986; signed as free agent by Toronto Argonauts for 1987, November, 1986.
Released by Toronto Argonauts, June 13, 1987; signed as free agent replacement player by Washington Redskins, October 13, 1987.
Released by Washington Redskins, October 20, 1987; re-signed by Redskins, April 15, 1988.

			—INTERCEPTIONS—		
Year	Club	G.	No.	Yds.	Avg.TD.
1983—Buffalo NFL		16		None	
1984—Buffalo NFL		8		None	
1985—Edmonton CFL		7	5	72	14.4	1
1986—Edmonton CFL		10	3	21	7.0	0
1987—Washington NFL		1		None	
NFL Totals—3 Years		25	0	0	0.0	0
CFL Totals—2 Years		17	8	93	11.6	1
Pro Totals—5 Years		42	8	93	11.6	1

Additional CFL statistics: Returned three punts for 20 yards and returned one kickoff for 21 yards, 1985; recovered one fumble for 22 yards, 1986.

LAWRENCE DONNELL THOMPSON
(Known by middle name.)
Defensive End—Indianapolis Colts
Born October 27, 1958, at Lumberton, N.C.
Height, 6.04. Weight, 272.
High School—Lumberton, N. C.
Received bachelor of arts and science degree from University of North Carolina.

Selected by Baltimore in 1st round (18th player selected) of 1981 NFL draft.
On physically unable to perform/active with shoulder injury, July 24 through August 22, 1982; activated, August 23, 1982.
Franchise transferred to Indianapolis, March 31, 1984.
Placed on suspended list, August 12 through September 11, 1984.
On non-football injury list with shoulder and back injuries, September 12 through October 11, 1984; activated, October 12, 1984.
Baltimore NFL, 1981 through 1983; Indianapolis NFL, 1984 through 1987.
Games: 1981 (13), 1982 (9), 1983 (14), 1984 (10), 1985 (15), 1986 (16), 1987 (12). Total—89.
Pro statistics: Recovered one fumble, 1981; credited with one safety, 1983; recovered one fumble for nine yards, 1985; recovered one fumble for 28 yards and a touchdown, 1987.

REYNA ONALD THOMPSON
First name pronounced Renee.
Cornerback—Miami Dolphins
Born August 28, 1963, at Dallas, Tex.
Height, 5.11. Weight, 194.
High School—Dallas, Tex., Thomas Jefferson.
Received bachelor of arts degree in communications from Baylor University in 1986.

Selected by Miami in 9th round (247th player selected) of 1986 NFL draft.
Signed by Miami Dolphins, July 17, 1986.
Released by Miami Dolphins, August 17, 1986; re-signed by Dolphins, August 18, 1986.
On injured reserve with shoulder injury, September 8 through October 23, 1987; activated, October 24, 1987.
Miami NFL, 1986 and 1987.
Games: 1986 (16), 1987 (9). Total—25.
Pro statistics: Returned one punt for no yards and fumbled once, 1986.

WILLIS HOPE THOMPSON
(Weegie)
Wide Receiver—Pittsburgh Steelers
Born March 21, 1961, at Pensacola, Fla.
Height, 6.06. Weight, 210.
High School—Midlothian, Va.
Received bachelor of science degree in management from Florida State University in 1984.

Selected by Tampa Bay in 1984 USFL territorial draft.
USFL rights traded with rights to quarterback Kelly Lowrey by Tampa Bay Bandits to Jacksonville Bulls for rights to wide receiver Mark Militello and running back Mike Grayson, January 4, 1984.
Selected by Pittsburgh in 4th round (108th player selected) of 1984 NFL draft.
Signed by Pittsburgh Steelers, July 22, 1984.

			—PASS RECEIVING—			
Year	Club	G.	P.C.	Yds.	Avg.	TD.
1984—Pittsburgh NFL		16	17	291	17.1	3
1985—Pittsburgh NFL		16	8	138	17.3	1
1986—Pittsburgh NFL		16	17	191	11.2	5
1987—Pittsburgh NFL		12	17	313	18.4	1
Pro Totals—4 Years		60	59	933	15.8	10

Additional pro statistics: Fumbled once, 1984; recovered one fumble, 1987.
Played in AFC Championship Game following 1984 season.

DONALD KEVIN THORP
(Don)
Defensive Lineman—Indianapolis Colts
Born July 10, 1962, at Chicago, Ill.
Height, 6.04. Weight, 260.
High School—Buffalo Grove, Ill.
Received bachelor of arts degree in finance from University of Illinois.

Named as defensive lineman on THE SPORTING NEWS College All-America Team, 1983.
Selected by Chicago in 1984 USFL territorial draft.
Selected by New Orleans in 6th round (156th player selected) of 1984 NFL draft.
Signed by New Orleans Saints, June 21, 1984.
On injured reserve with neck injury, October 9 through remainder of 1984 season.
Released by New Orleans Saints, August 26, 1985; signed as free agent by Chicago Bears, February 12, 1986.
Released by Chicago Bears, August 25, 1986; signed as free agent by New York Jets, March 16, 1987.
Released by New York Jets, September 6, 1987; signed as free agent replacement player by Indianapolis Colts, September 28, 1987.
New Orleans NFL, 1984; Indianapolis NFL, 1987.
Games: 1984 (5), 1987 (5). Total—10.

JOHN TICE
Tight End—New Orleans Saints
Born June 22, 1960, at Bayshore, N.Y.
Height, 6.05. Weight, 249.
High School—Central Islip, N.Y.
Attended University of Maryland.
Brother of Mike Tice, tight end with Seattle Seahawks.

Selected by Washington in 1983 USFL territorial draft.
Selected by New Orleans in 3rd round (65th player selected) of 1983 NFL draft.
Signed by New Orleans Saints, July 6, 1983.
On injured reserve with ankle injury, November 19 through remainder of 1984 season.

Year Club		G.	P.C.	Yds.	Avg.	TD.
			—PASS RECEIVING—			
1983—New Orleans NFL		16	7	33	4.7	1
1984—New Orleans NFL		10	6	55	9.2	1
1985—New Orleans NFL		16	24	266	11.1	2
1986—New Orleans NFL		16	37	330	8.9	3
1987—New Orleans NFL		12	16	181	11.3	6
Pro Totals—5 Years		70	90	865	9.6	13

Additional pro statistics: Recovered two fumbles, 1983; recovered one fumble, 1985 and 1986; fumbled once, 1986.

MICHAEL PETER TICE
(Mike)
Tight End—Seattle Seahawks
Born February 2, 1959, at Bayshore, N.Y.
Height, 6.07. Weight, 250.
High School—Central Islip, N.Y.
Attended University of Maryland.
Brother of John Tice, tight end with New Orleans Saints.

Signed as free agent by Seattle Seahawks, April 30, 1981.
On injured reserve with fractured ankle, October 15 through December 6, 1985; activated, December 7, 1985.

Year Club		G.	P.C.	Yds.	Avg.	TD.
			—PASS RECEIVING—			
1981—Seattle NFL		16	5	47	9.4	0
1982—Seattle NFL		9	9	46	5.1	0
1983—Seattle NFL		15		None		
1984—Seattle NFL		16	8	90	11.3	3
1985—Seattle NFL		9	2	13	6.5	0
1986—Seattle NFL		16	15	150	10.0	0
1987—Seattle NFL		12	14	106	7.6	2
Pro Totals—7 Years		93	53	452	8.5	5

Additional pro statistics: Recovered one fumble, 1982, 1983 and 1986; returned two kickoffs for 28 yards, 1983; returned one kickoff for 17 yards, 1985 and 1986.
Played in AFC Championship Game following 1983 season.

VAN TIFFIN
Placekicker—Tampa Bay Buccaneers
Born September 6, 1965, at Red Bay, Ala.
Height, 5.10. Weight, 163.
High School—Red Bay, Ala.
Attended University of Alabama.

Signed as free agent by Atlanta Falcons, May 6, 1987.

Released by Atlanta Falcons, August 11, 1987; signed as free agent replacement player by Tampa Bay Buccaneers, September 24, 1987.

Released by Tampa Bay Buccaneers, October 31, 1987; signed as free agent by Miami Dolphins, December 12, 1987.

Released by Miami Dolphins, December 15, 1987; signed as free agent by Tampa Bay Buccaneers, May 17, 1988.

		——PLACE KICKING——					
Year	Club	G.	XP.	XPM.	FG.	FGA.	Pts.
1987—TB (3)-Mia (1) NFL		4	11	0	5	7	26

SPENCER ALLEN TILLMAN
Running Back—Houston Oilers
Born April 21, 1964, at Tulsa, Okla.
Height, 5.11. Weight, 206.
High School—Tulsa, Okla., Thomas Edison.
Received bachelor of science degree in radio and television communications
from University of Oklahoma in 1987.

Selected by Houston in 5th round (133rd player selected) of 1987 NFL draft.
Signed by Houston Oilers, July 28, 1987.

			——RUSHING——				PASS RECEIVING				—TOTAL—		
Year	Club	G.	Att.	Yds.	Avg.	TD.	P.C.	Yds.	Avg.	TD.	TD.	Pts.	F.
1987—Houston NFL		5	12	29	2.4	1	None				1	6	1

Additional pro statistics: Returned one kickoff for no yards, 1987.

RONALD JOHN TILTON
(Ron)
Guard—New York Jets
Born August 9, 1963, at Homestead, Fla.
Height, 6.04. Weight, 250.
High School—Tampa, Fla., H. B. Plant.
Attended University of Florida and received bachelor's degree in
social science from Tulane University in 1986.

Signed as free agent by Washington Redskins, May 3, 1986.
Released by Washington Redskins, September 1, 1986; re-signed by Redskins, September 2, 1986.
Released by Washington Redskins, October 11, 1986; re-signed by Redskins, October 14, 1986.
Released by Washington Redskins, November 1, 1986; re-signed by Redskins, November 5, 1986.
Placed on did not report/retired list, June 1 through October 21, 1987.
Released by Washington Redskins, October 22, 1987; signed as free agent by New York Jets, May 24, 1988.
Washington NFL, 1986.
Games: 1986 (7).
Played in NFC Championship Game following 1986 season.

ANDRE BERNARD TIPPETT
Linebacker—New England Patriots
Born December 27, 1959, at Birmingham, Ala.
Height, 6.03. Weight, 241.
High School—Newark, N.J., Barringer.
Attended Ellsworth Community College and received bachelor of liberal arts degree from
University of Iowa in 1983.

Named to THE SPORTING NEWS NFL All-Star Team, 1985.
Selected by New England in 2nd round (41st player selected) of 1982 NFL draft.
Crossed picket line during players' strike, October 14, 1987.
New England NFL, 1982 through 1987.
Games: 1982 (9), 1983 (15), 1984 (16), 1985 (16), 1986 (11), 1987 (13). Total—80.
Pro statistics: Recovered one fumble, 1982, 1983 and 1986; recovered four fumbles for 25 yards and a touchdown, 1985; ran 32 yards with lateral from interception, 1986; recovered three fumbles for 29 yards and a touchdown, 1987.
Played in AFC Championship Game following 1985 season.
Played in NFL Championship Game following 1985 season.
Played in Pro Bowl (NFL All-Star Game) following 1984 through 1987 seasons.

GLEN WESTON TITENSOR
Name pronounced TIGHT-en-sir.
Guard—Dallas Cowboys
Born February 21, 1958, at Bellflower, Calif.
Height, 6.04. Weight, 275.
High School—Garden Grove, Calif., Bolsa Grande.
Attended University of California at Los Angeles and Brigham Young University.

Selected by Dallas in 3rd round (81st player selected) of 1981 NFL draft.
On injured reserve with knee injury, September 7 through entire 1987 season.
Dallas NFL, 1981 through 1986.
Games: 1981 (16), 1982 (4), 1983 (15), 1984 (15), 1985 (16), 1986 (16). Total—82.
Pro statistics: Recovered one fumble, 1981 and 1986.
Played in NFC Championship Game following 1981 season.
Member of Dallas Cowboys for NFC Championship Game following 1982 season; did not play.

ALVIN TOLES
Linebacker—New Orleans Saints
Born March 23, 1963, at Barnesville, Ga.
Height, 6.01. Weight, 227.
High School—Forsyth, Ga., Mary Persons.
Attended University of Tennessee.
Selected by Memphis in 1985 USFL territorial draft.
Selected by New Orleans in 1st round (24th player selected) of 1985 NFL draft.
Signed by New Orleans Saints, July 10, 1985.
New Orleans NFL, 1985 through 1987.
Games: 1985 (16), 1986 (16), 1987 (12). Total—44.
Pro statistics: Recovered one fumble, 1986; returned blocked punt 11 yards for a touchdown, 1987.

MIKE TOMCZAK
Name pronounced Tom-zak.
Quarterback—Chicago Bears
Born October 23, 1962, at Calumet City, Ill.
Height, 6.01. Weight, 195.
High School—Calumet City, Ill., Thornton Fractional North.
Attended Ohio State University.
Selected by New Jersey in 1985 USFL territorial draft.
Signed as free agent by Chicago Bears, May 9, 1985.

Year Club	G.	Att.	Cmp.	Pct.	Gain	T.P.	P.I.	Avg.	Att.	Yds.	Avg.	TD.	TD.	Pts.	F.
			—PASSING—						—RUSHING—				—TOTAL—		
1985—Chicago NFL	6	6	2	33.3	33	0	0	5.50	2	3	1.5	0	0	0	1
1986—Chicago NFL	13	151	74	49.0	1105	2	10	7.32	23	117	5.1	3	3	18	2
1987—Chicago NFL	12	178	97	54.5	1220	5	10	6.85	18	54	3.0	1	1	6	6
Pro Totals—3 Years	31	335	173	51.6	2358	7	20	7.04	43	174	4.0	4	4	24	9

Quarterback Rating Points: 1985 (52.8), 1986 (50.2), 1987 (62.0). Total—56.4.
Additional pro statistics: Recovered one fumble, 1985 and 1987; fumbled once for minus 13 yards, 1985.
Member of Chicago Bears for NFC Championship Game following 1985 season; did not play.
Played in NFL Championship Game following 1985 season.

ANTHONY TONEY
Fullback—Philadelphia Eagles
Born September 23, 1962, at Salinas, Calif.
Height, 6.00. Weight, 227.
High School—Salinas, Calif., North Salinas.
Attended Hartnell Community College and Texas A&M University.
Cousin of Del Rodgers, running back with Green Bay Packers
and San Francisco 49ers, 1982, 1984 and 1987.
Selected by Jacksonville in 1986 USFL territorial draft.
Selected by Philadelphia in 2nd round (37th player selected) of 1986 NFL draft.
Signed by Philadelphia Eagles, July 25, 1986.
On injured reserve with sprained ankle, September 2 through September 30, 1986; activated, October 1, 1986.

Year Club	G.	Att.	Yds.	Avg.	TD.	P.C.	Yds.	Avg.	TD.	TD.	Pts.	F.
		—RUSHING—				PASS RECEIVING				—TOTAL—		
1986—Philadelphia NFL	12	69	285	4.1	1	13	177	13.6	0	1	6	0
1987—Philadelphia NFL	11	127	473	3.7	5	39	341	8.7	1	6	36	5
Pro Totals—2 Years	23	196	758	3.9	6	52	518	10.0	1	7	42	5

Additional pro statistics: Attempted one pass with no completions and recovered three fumbles, 1987.

AL LEE TOON JR.
Wide Receiver—New York Jets
Born April 30, 1963, at Newport News, Va.
Height, 6.04. Weight, 205.
High School—Newport News, Va., Menchville.
Attended University of Wisconsin.
Selected by Jacksonville in 1985 USFL territorial draft.
Selected by New York Jets in 1st round (10th player selected) of 1985 NFL draft.
Signed by New York Jets, September 11, 1985.
Granted roster exemption, September 11 through September 13, 1985; activated, September 14, 1985.

Year Club	G.	P.C.	Yds.	Avg.	TD.
		—PASS RECEIVING—			
1985—N.Y. Jets NFL	15	46	662	14.4	3
1986—N.Y. Jets NFL	16	85	1176	13.8	8
1987—N.Y. Jets NFL	12	68	976	14.4	5
Pro Totals—3 Years	43	199	2814	14.1	16

Additional pro statistics: Rushed once for five yards, 1985; rushed twice for minus three yards, recovered one fumble and fumbled three times, 1986.
Played in Pro Bowl (NFL All-Star Game) following 1986 and 1987 seasons.

STACEY J. TORAN
Safety—Los Angeles Raiders
Born November 10, 1961, at Indianapolis, Ind.
Height, 6.02. Weight, 200.
High School—Indianapolis, Ind., Broad Ripple.
Received degree from University of Notre Dame in 1984.
Selected by Chicago in 1984 USFL territorial draft.
Selected by Los Angeles Raiders in 6th round (168th player selected) of 1984 NFL draft.
Signed by Los Angeles Raiders, June 2, 1984.

			—INTERCEPTIONS—			
Year	Club	G.	No.	Yds.	Avg.	TD.
1984—L. A. Raiders NFL........		16		None		
1985—L. A. Raiders NFL........		16	1	76	76.0	1
1986—L. A. Raiders NFL........		16	2	28	14.0	0
1987—L. A. Raiders NFL........		12	3	48	16.0	1
Pro Totals—4 Years............		60	6	152	25.3	2

Additional pro statistics: Recovered one fumble, 1986 and 1987.

THOMAS JEFFREY TOTH
(Tom)
Guard—Miami Dolphins
Born May 23, 1962, at Chicago, Ill.
Height, 6.05. Weight, 275.
High School—Orland Park, Ill., Carl Sandberg.
Attended Western Michigan University.
Selected by Oakland in 7th round (95th player selected) of 1985 USFL draft.
Selected by New England in 4th round (102nd player selected) of 1985 NFL draft.
Signed by New England Patriots, July 19, 1985.
On injured reserve with ankle injury, August 15 through entire 1985 season.
Released by New England Patriots, September 1, 1986; signed as free agent by Miami Dolphins, September 9, 1986.
Miami NFL, 1986 and 1987.
Games: 1986 (13), 1987 (12). Total—25.
Pro statistics: Returned one kickoff for no yards and fumbled once, 1986.

JOSEPH RAY TOWNSELL
(Jojo)
Wide Receiver-Kick Returner—New York Jets
Born November 4, 1960, at Reno, Nev.
Height, 5.09. Weight, 180.
High School—Reno, Nev., Hug.
Received degree in sociology from University of California at Los Angeles in 1982.
Selected by Los Angeles in 6th round (72nd player selected) of 1983 USFL draft.
Selected by New York Jets in 3rd round (78th player selected) of 1983 NFL draft.
Signed by Los Angeles Express, June 3, 1983.
Released by Los Angeles Express, August 1, 1985; signed by New York Jets, August 5, 1985.

			PASS RECEIVING				-PUNT RETURNS-				—KICKOFF RET.—				—TOTAL—		
Year	Club	G.	P.C.	Yds.	Avg.	TD.	No.	Yds.	Avg.	TD.	No.	Yds.	Avg.	TD.	TD.	Pts.	F.
1983—Los Angeles USFL......		5	21	326	15.5	3		None			1	8	8.0	0	3	18	0
1984—Los Angeles USFL......		18	58	889	15.3	7		None				None			7	42	2
1985—Los Angeles USFL......		16	47	777	16.5	6	8	33	4.1	0		None			6	36	2
1985—N.Y. Jets NFL		16	12	187	15.6	0	6	65	10.8	0	2	42	21.0	0	0	0	1
1986—N.Y. Jets NFL		14	1	11	11.0	0	4	52	13.0	0	13	322	24.8	★1	1	6	0
1987—N.Y. Jets NFL		12	4	37	9.3	0	32	381	11.9	1	11	272	24.7	0	1	6	3
USFL Totals—3 Years....		39	126	1992	15.8	16	8	33	4.1	0	1	8	8.0	0	16	96	5
NFL Totals—3 Years......		42	17	235	13.8	0	42	498	11.9	1	26	636	24.5	1	2	12	3
Pro Totals—6 Years.......		81	143	2227	15.6	16	50	531	10.6	1	27	644	23.9	1	18	108	8

Additional USFL statistics: Rushed eight times for 19 yards, 1984; rushed twice for nine yards and recovered one fumble, 1985.
Additional NFL statistics: Recovered one fumble, 1985; rushed once for two yards, 1986; rushed once for minus two yards and recovered two fumbles, 1987.

ANDRE TOWNSEND
Defensive End-Nose Tackle—Denver Broncos
Born October 8, 1962, at Chicago, Ill.
Height, 6.03. Weight, 265.
High School—Aberdeen, Miss.
Attended University of Mississippi.
Selected by Birmingham in 1984 USFL territorial draft.
Selected by Denver in 2nd round (46th player selected) of 1984 NFL draft.
Signed by Denver Broncos, June 18, 1984.
Denver NFL, 1984 through 1987.
Games: 1984 (16), 1985 (16), 1986 (16), 1987 (12). Total—60.
Pro statistics: Recovered one fumble, 1984 and 1985; recovered one fumble for seven yards and a touchdown, 1986.
Played in AFC Championship Game following 1986 and 1987 seasons.
Played in NFL Championship Game following 1986 and 1987 seasons.

GREG TOWNSEND
Defensive End—Los Angeles Raiders
Born November 3, 1961, at Los Angeles, Calif.
Height, 6.03. Weight, 250.
High School—Compton, Calif., Dominguez.
Attended Long Beach City College and Texas Christian University.
Selected by Oakland in 7th round (79th player selected) of 1983 USFL draft.
Selected by Los Angeles Raiders in 4th round (110th player selected) of 1983 NFL draft.
Signed by Los Angeles Raiders, July 7, 1983.
On suspended list, October 9, 1986; reinstated, October 10, 1986.
On suspended list, October 13 through October 19, 1986; activated, October 20, 1986.
Crossed picket line during players' strike, October 14, 1987.
Los Angeles Raiders NFL, 1983 through 1987.
Games: 1983 (16), 1984 (16), 1985 (16), 1986 (15), 1987 (13). Total—76.
Pro statistics: Recovered one fumble for 66 yards and a touchdown, 1983; recovered one fumble, 1985; credited with a safety, 1986.
Played in AFC Championship Game following 1983 season.
Played in NFL Championship Game following 1983 season.

STEPHEN PAUL TRAPILO
(Steve)
Guard—New Orleans Saints
Born September 20, 1964, at Boston, Mass.
Height, 6.05. Weight, 281.
High School—Boston, Mass., Boston College.
Received degree in sociology from Boston College in 1986.
Selected by New Orleans in 4th round (96th player selected) of 1987 NFL draft.
Signed by New Orleans Saints, July 27, 1987.
New Orleans NFL, 1987.
Games: 1987 (11).

MARK JOSEPH TRAYNOWICZ
Name pronounced TRAY-no-witz.
Guard—Buffalo Bills
Born November 20, 1962, at Omaha, Neb.
Height, 6.05. Weight, 280.
High School—Bellevue, Neb., West.
Received degree in civil engineering from University of Nebraska in 1985.
Selected by Houston in 1st round (9th player selected) of 1985 USFL draft.
Selected by Buffalo in 2nd round (29th player selected) of 1985 NFL draft.
Signed by Buffalo Bills, July 20, 1985.
Buffalo NFL, 1985 through 1987.
Games: 1985 (14), 1986 (16), 1987 (11). Total—41.
Pro statistics: Recovered one fumble, 1985 and 1986.

PAUL RANDALL TRIPOLI
Defensive Back—Tampa Bay Buccaneers
Born December 14, 1961, at Utica, N. Y.
Height, 6.00. Weight, 197.
High School—Liverpool, N. Y.
Attended University of Alabama.
Signed as free agent by Cleveland Browns, May 6, 1985.
Released by Cleveland Browns, August 20, 1985; signed as free agent by Toronto Argonauts, September, 1985.
Released by Toronto Argonauts, July 5, 1987; signed as free agent by Tampa Bay Buccaneers, July 10, 1987.
Released by Tampa Bay Buccaneers, August 31, 1987; re-signed as replacement player by Buccaneers, September 24, 1987.

| | | —INTERCEPTIONS— | | | |
Year Club	G.	No.	Yds.	Avg.	TD.
1986—Toronto CFL	9	3	15	5.0	0
1987—Toronto CFL	2	2	33	16.5	0
1987—Tampa Bay NFL	13	3	17	5.7	1
CFL Totals—2 Years	11	5	48	9.6	0
NFL Totals—1 Year	13	3	17	5.7	1
Pro Totals—3 Years	24	8	65	8.1	1

Additional CFL statistics: Returned four punts for 36 yards, 1987.
Additional NFL statistics: Recovered three fumbles, 1987.

JACK FRANCIS TRUDEAU
Quarterback—Indianapolis Colts
Born September 9, 1962, at Forest Lake, Minn.
Height, 6.03. Weight, 211.
High School—Livermore, Calif., Granada.
Received degree in political science from University of Illinois in 1986.
Brother of Kevin Trudeau, pitcher in Minnesota Twins' organization.

Selected by Orlando in 1986 USFL territorial draft.
Selected by Indianapolis in 2nd round (47th player selected) of 1986 NFL draft.
Signed by Indianapolis Colts, July 31, 1986.

					PASSING					RUSHING			TOTAL		
Year	Club	G.	Att.	Cmp.	Pct.	Gain	T.P.	P.I.	Avg.	Att.	Yds.	Avg.	TD.	TD.	Pts.	F.
1986—Indianapolis NFL		12	417	204	48.9	2225	8	18	5.34	13	21	1.6	1	1	6	*13
1987—Indianapolis NFL		10	229	128	55.9	1587	6	6	6.93	15	7	0.5	0	0	0	10
Pro Totals—2 Years		22	646	332	51.4	3812	14	24	5.90	28	28	1.0	1	1	6	23

Quarterback Rating Points: 1986 (53.5), 1987 (75.4). Total—61.4.
Additional pro statistics: Recovered six fumbles and fumbled 13 times for minus 15 yards, 1986; recovered two fumbles and fumbled 10 times for minus 28 yards, 1987.

ERIC TRUVILLION
Wide Receiver—Indianapolis Colts
Born June 18, 1959, at New York, N.Y.
Height, 6.04. Weight, 205.
High School—Queens, N.Y., Springfield Gardens.
Attended Florida A&M University.

Named as wide receiver on THE SPORTING NEWS USFL All-Star Team, 1983.
Signed as free agent by New York Jets, June 15, 1982.
Released by New York Jets after failing physical, July 27, 1982; re-signed by Jets after signing injury waiver, July 28, 1982.
Released by New York Jets, August 30, 1982; signed by Tampa Bay Bandits, November 2, 1982.
On developmental squad, June 6 through remainder of 1984 season.
On developmental squad, April 5 through May 17, 1985; activated, May 18, 1985.
On developmental squad, May 25 through June 6, 1985; activated, June 7, 1985.
On developmental squad, June 13 through remainder of 1985 season.
Traded with defensive back Warren Hanna by Tampa Bay Bandits to Arizona Outlaws for draft choice, August 2, 1985.
Granted free agency when USFL suspended operations, August 7, 1986; signed as free agent by Detroit Lions, March 4, 1987.
Released by Detroit Lions, September 7, 1987; re-signed as replacement player by Lions, September 29, 1987.
Released by Detroit Lions, November 3, 1987; signed as free agent by Indianapolis Colts, April 8, 1988.
On developmental squad for 3 games with Tampa Bay Bandits in 1984.
On developmental squad for 10 games with Tampa Bay Bandits in 1985.

			RUSHING				PASS RECEIVING				TOTAL		
Year	Club	G.	Att.	Yds.	Avg.	TD.	P.C.	Yds.	Avg.	TD.	TD.	Pts.	F.
1983—Tampa Bay USFL		18	4	11	2.8	0	66	1080	16.4	*15	15	†92	1
1984—Tampa Bay USFL		15	1	1	1.0	0	70	1044	14.9	9	9	†56	1
1985—Tampa Bay USFL		7			None		31	478	15.4	6	6	36	0
1987—Detroit NFL		3			None		12	207	17.3	1	1	6	1
USFL Totals—3 Years		40	5	12	2.4	0	167	2602	15.6	30	30	184	2
NFL Totals—1 Year		3	0	0	0.0	0	12	207	17.3	1	1	6	1
Pro Totals—4 Years		43	5	12	2.4	0	179	2809	15.7	31	31	190	3

†Includes one 2-point conversion.
Additional pro statistics: Attempted one pass with no completions, 1983; attempted one pass with one completion for 13 yards and a touchdown, 1984.

TRAVIS TYRONE TUCKER
Tight End—Cleveland Browns
Born September 19, 1963, at Brooklyn, N.Y.
Height, 6.03. Weight, 240.
High School—Brooklyn, N.Y., South Shore.
Attended Southern Connecticut State University.

Selected by Cleveland in 11th round (287th player selected) of 1985 NFL draft.
Signed by Cleveland Browns, July 11, 1985.
On injured reserve with knee injury, November 3 through remainder of 1987 season.

			PASS RECEIVING		
Year	Club	G.	P.C.	Yds.	Avg.	TD.
1985—Cleveland NFL		16	2	20	10.0	0
1986—Cleveland NFL		16	2	29	14.5	0
1987—Cleveland NFL		4			None	
Pro Totals—3 Years		36	4	49	12.3	0

Additional pro statistics: Recovered one fumble, 1986.
Played in AFC Championship Game following 1986 season.

JESSIE LLOYD TUGGLE
Linebacker—Atlanta Falcons
Born February 14, 1965, at Spalding County, Ga.
Height, 5.11. Weight, 225.
High School—Griffin, Ga.
Attended Valdosta State College.

Signed as free agent by Atlanta Falcons, May 2, 1987.
Atlanta NFL, 1987.
Games: 1987 (12).

MARK PULEMAU TUINEI
Name pronounced TWO-e-nay.
Offensive Tackle—Dallas Cowboys
Born March 31, 1960, at Nanakuli, Oahu, Haw.
Height, 6.05. Weight, 283.
High School—Honolulu, Haw., Punahou.
Attended University of California at Los Angeles and University of Hawaii.
Brother of Tom Tuinei, defensive tackle with Edmonton Eskimos.
Selected by Boston in 19th round (227th player selected) of 1983 USFL draft.
Signed as free agent by Dallas Cowboys, April 28, 1983.
On injured reserve with knee injury, December 2 through remainder of 1987 season.
Dallas NFL, 1983 through 1987.
Games: 1983 (10), 1984 (16), 1985 (16), 1986 (16), 1987 (8). Total—66.
Pro statistics: Returned one kickoff for no yards, recovered three fumbles and fumbled once, 1986; recovered one fumble, 1987.

WILLIE TULLIS
Cornerback—Indianapolis Colts
Born April 5, 1958, at Newville, Ala.
Height, 5.11. Weight, 195.
High School—Headland, Ala.
Attended University of Southern Mississippi and Troy State University.
Selected by Houston in 8th round (217th player selected) of 1981 NFL draft.
Released by Houston Oilers, September 3, 1985; signed as free agent by New Orleans Saints, September 17, 1985.
Released by New Orleans Saints, October 29, 1986; signed as free agent by Indianapolis Colts, May 11, 1987.

		INTERCEPTIONS			–PUNT RETURNS–			—KICKOFF RET.—			—TOTAL—		
Year	Club	G.	No.	Yds.	Avg.	TD.	No.	Yds.	Avg.	TD.	No.	Yds.	Avg.	TD.	TD.	Pts.	F.
1981—Houston NFL		16		None			2	29	14.5	0	32	779	24.3	⋆1	1	6	0
1982—Houston NFL		9		None				None			5	91	18.2	0	0	0	0
1983—Houston NFL		16	5	65	13.0	0		None			1	16	16.0	0	0	0	0
1984—Houston NFL		16	4	48	12.0	0		None				None			0	0	1
1985—New Orleans NFL		14	2	22	11.0	0	17	141	8.3	0	23	470	20.4	0	0	0	1
1986—New Orleans NFL		7		None			2	10	5.0	0	2	28	14.0	0	0	0	0
1987—Indianapolis NFL		12	3	0	0.0	0	4	27	6.8	0		None			0	0	0
Pro Totals—7 Years		90	14	135	9.6	0	25	207	8.3	0	63	1384	22.0	1	1	6	2

Additional pro statistics: Recovered one fumble, 1984.

JEFF TUPPER
Defensive Tackle—Kansas City Chiefs
Born December 26, 1962, at Joplin, Mo.
Height, 6.05. Weight, 269.
High School—Joplin, Mo., Parkwood.
Received degree in finance from University of Oklahoma in 1986.
Selected by St. Louis in 5th round (116th player selected) of 1986 NFL draft.
Signed by St. Louis Cardinals, July 14, 1986.
Released by St. Louis Cardinals, September 1, 1986; signed as free agent by Philadelphia Eagles, November 13, 1986.
Released by Philadelphia Eagles, September 11, 1987; signed as free agent replacement player by Denver Broncos, September 29, 1987.
Released by Denver Broncos, November 3, 1987; signed as free agent by Kansas City Chiefs, November 18, 1987.
Released by Kansas City Chiefs, November 25, 1987; re-signed by Chiefs, December 23, 1987.
Active for 1 game with Kansas City Chiefs in 1987; did not play.
Philadelphia NFL, 1986; Denver (4)-Kansas City (0) NFL, 1987.
Games: 1986 (3), 1987 (4). Total—7.

DANIEL ANTHONY TURK
(Dan)
Center—Tampa Bay Buccaneers
Born June 25, 1962, at Milwaukee, Wis.
Height, 6.04. Weight, 260.
High School—Milwaukee, Wis., James Madison.
Attended Drake University and University of Wisconsin.
Selected by Jacksonville in 1985 USFL territorial draft.
USFL rights traded with rights to running back Marck Harrison and tight end Ken Whisenhunt by Jacksonville Bulls to Tampa Bay Bandits for rights to running back Cedric Jones, kicker Bobby Raymond and defensive back Eric Riley, January 3, 1985.
Selected by Pittsburgh in 4th round (101st player selected) of 1985 NFL draft.
Signed by Pittsburgh Steelers, July 19, 1985.
On injured reserve with broken wrist, September 16 through remainder of 1985 season.
Traded by Pittsburgh Steelers to Tampa Bay Buccaneers for 6th round pick in 1987 draft, April 13, 1987.
Crossed picket line during players' strike, October 14, 1987.
Pittsburgh NFL, 1985 and 1986; Tampa Bay NFL, 1987.
Games: 1985 (1), 1986 (16), 1987 (13). Total—30.

DARYL TURNER
Wide Receiver—Seattle Seahawks
Born December 15, 1961, at Wadley, Ga.
Height, 6.03. Weight, 194.
High School—Flint, Mich., Southwestern.
Attended Michigan State University.
Selected by Michigan in 1984 USFL territorial draft.
Selected by Seattle in 2nd round (49th player selected) of 1984 NFL draft.
Signed by Seattle Seahawks, May 16, 1984.

		—PASS RECEIVING—			
Year Club	G.	P.C.	Yds.	Avg.	TD.
1984—Seattle NFL..................	16	35	715	20.4	10
1985—Seattle NFL..................	16	34	670	19.7	*13
1986—Seattle NFL..................	15	18	334	18.6	7
1987—Seattle NFL..................	12	14	153	10.9	6
Pro Totals—4 Years...........	59	101	1872	18.5	36

KEENA TURNER
Linebacker—San Francisco 49ers
Born October 22, 1958, at Chicago, Ill.
Height, 6.02. Weight, 219.
High School—Chicago, Ill., Vocational.
Attended Purdue University.
Selected by San Francisco in 2nd round (39th player selected) of 1980 NFL draft.
On injured reserve with knee injury, December 17 through remainder of 1987 season.

		—INTERCEPTIONS—			
Year Club	G.	No.	Yds.	Avg.	TD.
1980—San Francisco NFL	16	2	15	7.5	0
1981—San Francisco NFL	16	1	0	0.0	0
1982—San Francisco NFL	9		None		
1983—San Francisco NFL	15		None		
1984—San Francisco NFL	16	4	51	12.8	0
1985—San Francisco NFL	15		None		
1986—San Francisco NFL	16	1	9	9.0	0
1987—San Francisco NFL	10	1	15	15.0	0
Pro Totals—8 Years...........	113	9	90	10.0	0

Additional pro statistics: Recovered three fumbles, 1981; recovered one fumble, 1983; returned two fumbles for 65 yards and a touchdown, 1985.
Played in NFC Championship Game following 1981, 1983 and 1984 seasons.
Played in NFL Championship Game following 1981 and 1984 seasons.
Played in Pro Bowl (NFL All-Star Game) following 1984 season.

ODESSA TURNER
Wide Receiver—New York Giants
Born October 12, 1964, at Monroe, La.
Height, 6.03. Weight, 205.
High School—Monroe, La., Wossman.
Attended Northwestern State (La.) University.
Selected by New York Giants in 4th round (112th player selected) of 1987 NFL draft.
Signed by New York Giants, July 27, 1987.
On injured reserve with hamstring and shoulder injuries, September 7 through October 23, 1987; activated, October 24, 1987.

		—PASS RECEIVING—			
Year Club	G.	P.C.	Yds.	Avg.	TD.
1987—New York Giants NFL	7	10	195	19.5	1

THOMAS JAMES TURNER
(T. J.)
Defensive End—Miami Dolphins
Born May 16, 1963, at Lufkin, Tex.
Height, 6.04. Weight, 275.
High School—Lufkin, Tex.
Attended University of Houston.
Selected by Miami in 3rd round (81st player selected) of 1986 NFL draft.
Signed by Miami Dolphins, July 23, 1986.
Miami NFL, 1986 and 1987.
Games: 1986 (16), 1987 (12). Total—28.
Pro statistics: Recovered one fumble, 1987.

MILES JOHN TURPIN
Linebacker—Tampa Bay Buccaneers
Born May 15, 1964, at Minneapolis, Minn.
Height, 6.04. Weight, 230.
High School—Fremont, Calif., American.

Received degree in political science and social sciences from University of California at Berkeley in 1986.
Nephew of Jim Marshall, defensive end with Cleveland Browns and Minnesota Vikings, 1960 through 1979.
Signed by free agent by Green Bay Packers, May 2, 1986.
Released by Green Bay Packers, September 1, 1986; re-signed by Packers, September 2, 1986.
Released by Green Bay Packers, September 9, 1986; signed by free agent by Cleveland Browns, April 22, 1987.
Released by Cleveland Browns, September 1, 1987; signed as free agent replacement player by Tampa Bay Buccaneers, September 24, 1987.
Released by Tampa Bay Buccaneers, October 19, 1987; re-signed by Buccaneers for 1988, November 20, 1987.
Green Bay NFL, 1986; Tampa Bay NFL, 1987.
Games: 1986 (1), 1987 (3). Total—4.

TIMOTHY G. TYRRELL

Name pronounced Tuhr-RELL.

(Tim)

Fullback—Los Angeles Rams

Born February 19, 1961, at Chicago, Ill.
Height, 6.01. Weight, 201.
High School—Hoffman Estates, Ill., James B. Conant.
Attended William Rainey Harper College and Northern Illinois University.

Selected by Chicago in 1984 USFL territorial draft.
Signed as free agent by Atlanta Falcons, May 2, 1984.
Released by Atlanta Falcons, August 27, 1984; re-signed by Falcons, October 3, 1984.
Released by Atlanta Falcons, August 26, 1986; re-signed by Falcons, October 24, 1986.
Released by Atlanta Falcons, October 27, 1986; re-signed by Falcons, October 31, 1986.
Released by Atlanta Falcons, November 11, 1986; signed as free agent by Los Angeles Rams, November 13, 1986.
Crossed picket line during players' strike, October 14, 1987.

Year Club	G.	Att.	RUSHING Yds.	Avg.	TD.	PASS RECEIVING P.C. Yds.	Avg.	TD.	TOTAL TD.	Pts.	F.
1984—Atlanta NFL	11		None			None			0	0	0
1985—Atlanta NFL	16		None			None			0	0	1
1986—Atlanta (3)-L.A. Rams (6) NFL	9		None			1 9	9.0	0	0	0	1
1987—Los Angeles Rams NFL	11	11	44	4.0	0	6 59	9.8	0	0	0	0
Pro Totals—4 Years	47	11	44	4.0	0	7 68	9.7	0	0	0	2

Additional pro statistics: Returned one kickoff for no yards and recovered three fumbles, 1984; returned one kickoff for 13 yards, 1985; returned six kickoffs for 116 yards, 1987.

RICHARD KEITH UECKER

(Known by middle name.)

Guard-Offensive Tackle—Green Bay Packers

Born June 29, 1960, at Hollywood, Fla.
Height, 6.05. Weight, 284.
High School—Hollywood, Fla., Hollywood Hills.
Attended Auburn University.

Selected by Denver in 9th round (243rd player selected) of 1982 NFL draft.
On injured reserve with Achilles tendon injury, August 14 through October 21, 1984.
Awarded on procedural waivers to Green Bay Packers, October 23, 1984.
On injured reserve with knee injury, November 2 through remainder of 1985 season.
On injured reserve with knee injury, August 22 through entire 1986 season.
Crossed picket line during players' strike, October 14, 1987.
On injured reserve with knee injury, October 31 through December 4, 1987; activated, December 5, 1987.
Denver NFL, 1982 and 1983; Green Bay NFL, 1984, 1985 and 1987.
Games: 1982 (5), 1983 (16), 1984 (6), 1985 (7), 1987 (8). Total—42.
Pro statistics: Returned one kickoff for 12 yards and fumbled once, 1982; recovered one fumble, 1985.

TERRANCE LYNN UNREIN

(Terry)

Nose Tackle-Defensive End—San Diego Chargers

Born October 24, 1962, at Brighton, Colo.
Height, 6.05. Weight, 283.
High School—Fort Lupton, Colo.
Received bachelor of science degree in agricultural business
from Colorado State University in 1986.

Selected by San Diego in 3rd round (66th player selected) of 1986 NFL draft.
Signed by San Diego Chargers, July 15, 1986.
On injured reserve with knee injury, September 10 through October 10, 1986; activated, October 11, 1986.
Crossed picket line during players' strike, October 14, 1987.
San Diego NFL, 1986 and 1987.
Games: 1986 (12), 1987 (9). Total—21.

—DID YOU KNOW—

That a 78-yard touchdown by Minnesota's Leo Lewis on November 22 was the first punt return for a touchdown for the Vikings since Charlie West's 98-yard return on November 3, 1968?

BENJAMIN MICHAEL UTT
(Ben)
Guard—Indianapolis Colts
Born June 13, 1959, at Richmond, Calif.
Height, 6.06. Weight, 286.
High School—Vidalia, Ga.
Received bachelor of science degree in industrial management from Georgia Tech in 1982.
Signed as free agent by Dallas Cowboys, May, 1981.
Released by Dallas Cowboys, August 14, 1981; signed as free agent by Baltimore Colts, January 18, 1982.
Franchise transferred to Indianapolis, March 31, 1984.
On injured reserve with knee and back injuries, November 4 through remainder of 1986 season.
Baltimore NFL, 1982 and 1983; Indianapolis NFL, 1984 through 1987.
Games: 1982 (9), 1983 (16), 1984 (16), 1985 (16), 1986 (9), 1987 (12). Total—78.
Pro statistics: Recovered one fumble, 1984; caught one pass for minus four yards and recovered two fumbles, 1987.

IRA LYNN VALENTINE
Running Back—Houston Oilers
Born June 4, 1963, at Marshall, Tex.
Height, 6.00. Weight, 212.
High School—Marshall, Tex.
Attended Texas A&M University.
Selected by Houston in 12th round (314th player selected) of 1987 NFL draft.
Signed by Houston Oilers, July 22, 1987.
Released by Houston Oilers, November 7, 1987; re-signed by Oilers, November 12, 1987.

| | | —RUSHING— | | | | PASS RECEIVING | | | | —TOTAL— | | |
Year	Club	G.	Att.	Yds.	Avg.	TD.	P.C.	Yds.	Avg.	TD.	TD.	Pts.	F.
1987—Houston NFL		7	5	10	2.0	0	2	10	5.0	0	0	0	0

Additional pro statistics: Returned one kickoff for 13 yards, 1987.

KEITH VAN HORNE
Offensive Tackle—Chicago Bears
Born November 6, 1957, at Mt. Lebanon, Pa.
Height, 6.06. Weight, 285.
High School—Fullerton, Calif.
Received bachelor of arts degree in broadcast journalism from University of Southern California.
Brother of Pete Van Horne, first baseman in Chicago Cubs' organization, 1977;
and son-in-law of Walter Mondale, former Vice-President.
Named as offensive tackle on THE SPORTING NEWS College All-America Team, 1980.
Selected by Chicago in 1st round (11th player selected) of 1981 NFL draft.
Chicago NFL, 1981 through 1987.
Games: 1981 (14), 1982 (9), 1983 (14), 1984 (14), 1985 (16), 1986 (16), 1987 (12). Total—95.
Pro statistics: Recovered one fumble, 1981, 1982 and 1986.
Played in NFC Championship Game following 1984 and 1985 seasons.
Played in NFL Championship Game following 1985 season.

NORWOOD JACOB VANN JR.
Linebacker—Los Angeles Rams
Born February 18, 1962, at Philadelphia, Pa.
Height, 6.01. Weight, 237.
High School—Warsaw, N.C., James Kenan.
Attended East Carolina University.
Selected by Los Angeles Rams in 10th round (253rd player selected) of 1984 NFL draft.
On injured reserve with knee injury, October 21 through December 20, 1985; activated, December 21, 1985.
Los Angeles Rams NFL, 1984 through 1987.
Games: 1984 (16), 1985 (8), 1986 (16), 1987 (11). Total—51.
Pro statistics: Credited with one safety and recovered two fumbles, 1984; recovered one fumble, 1985 and 1987; recovered three fumbles, 1986.
Played in NFC Championship Game following 1985 season.

CLARENCE VAUGHN
Safety—Washington Redskins
Born July 17, 1964, at Chicago, Ill.
Height, 6.00. Weight, 202.
High School—Chicago, Ill., Gage Park.
Attended Northern Illinois University.
Selected by Washington in 8th round (219th player selected) of 1987 NFL draft.
Signed by Washington Redskins, July 24, 1987.
On injured reserve with ankle injury, December 5, 1987 through January 8, 1988; activated, January 9, 1988.
Washington NFL, 1987.
Games: 1987 (5).
Played in NFC Championship Game following 1987 season.
Played in NFL Championship Game following 1987 season.

ALAN STUART VEINGRAD
Offensive Tackle-Guard—Green Bay Packers
Born July 24, 1963, at Brooklyn, N.Y.
Height, 6.05. Weight, 277.
High School—Miami, Fla., Sunset.
Received bachelor of science degree in physical education and health
from East Texas State University in 1985.

Selected by San Antonio in 11th round (163rd player selected) of 1985 USFL draft.
Signed as free agent by Tampa Bay Buccaneers, June 26, 1985.
Released by Tampa Bay Buccaneers, July 30, 1985; awarded on waivers to Houston Oilers, August 1, 1985.
Released by Houston Oilers, August 20, 1985; signed as free agent by Green Bay Packers, March 28, 1986.
Green Bay NFL, 1986 and 1987.
Games: 1986 (16), 1987 (11). Total—27.
Pro statistics: Recovered one fumble, 1986.

CLARENCE VERDIN
Wide Receiver-Kick Returner—Indianapolis Colts
Born June 14, 1963, at New Orleans, La.
Height, 5.08. Weight, 160.
High School—Bourg, La., South Terrebonne.
Attended Southwestern Louisiana University.

Named as kick returner on THE SPORTING NEWS USFL All-Star Team, 1985.
Selected by Houston in 17th round (353rd player selected) of 1984 USFL draft.
Signed by Houston Gamblers, January 19, 1984.
On developmental squad, February 24 through March 22, 1984; activated, March 23, 1984.
Selected by Washington in 3rd round (83rd player selected) of 1984 NFL supplemental draft.
Traded with defensive backs Luther Bradley, Will Lewis, Mike Mitchell and Durwood Roquemore, defensive end Pete Catan, quarterbacks Jim Kelly and Todd Dillon, defensive tackles Tony Fitzpatrick, Van Hughes and Hosea Taylor, running back Sam Harrell, linebackers Andy Hawkins and Ladell Wills, wide receivers Richard Johnson, Scott McGhee, Gerald McNeil and Ricky Sanders, guard Rich Kehr, center Billy Kidd and offensive tackles Chris Riehm and Tommy Robison by Houston Gamblers to New Jersey Generals for past considerations, March 7, 1986.
Granted free agency when USFL suspended operations, August 7, 1986; signed by Washington Redskins, August 13, 1986.
Granted roster exemption, August 13 through August 24, 1986; activated, August 25, 1986.
On injured reserve with hamstring injury, September 1 through October 17, 1986; activated, October 18, 1986.
On injured reserve with ribs and shoulder injuries, December 9 through remainder of 1986 season.
On injured reserve with leg injury, September 7 through December 11, 1987; activated, December 12, 1987.
Traded by Washington Redskins to Indianapolis Colts for 6th round pick in 1988 draft, March 29, 1988.
On developmental squad for 4 games with Houston Gamblers in 1984.

		—————RUSHING—————				PASS RECEIVING				—TOTAL—		
Year Club	G.	Att.	Yds.	Avg.	TD.	P.C.	Yds.	Avg.	TD.	TD.	Pts.	F.
1984—Houston USFL	14	1	—2	—2.0	0	16	315	19.7	3	4	24	2
1985—Houston USFL	18	7	20	2.9	0	84	1004	12.0	9	12	72	0
1986—Washington NFL	8		None					None		0	0	0
1987—Washington NFL	3	1	14	14.0	0	2	62	31.0	0	0	0	0
USFL Totals—2 Years	32	8	18	2.3	0	100	1319	13.2	12	16	96	2
NFL Totals—2 Years	11	1	14	14.0	0	2	62	31.0	0	0	0	0
Pro Totals—4 Years	43	9	32	3.6	0	102	1381	13.5	12	16	96	2

		KICKOFF RETURNS			
Year Club	G.	No.	Yds.	Avg.	TD.
1984—Houston USFL	14	25	643	25.7	*1
1985—Houston USFL	18	28	746	*26.6	*3
1986—Washington NFL	8	12	240	20.0	0
1987—Washington NFL	3	12	244	20.3	0
USFL Totals—2 Years	32	53	1389	26.2	4
NFL Totals—2 Years	11	24	484	20.2	0
Pro Totals—4 Years	43	77	1873	24.3	4

Additional pro statistics: Recovered four fumbles, 1984.
Member of Washington Redskins for NFL Championship Game following 1987 season; inactive.

GARIN LEE VERIS
Name pronounced GARR-in VAIR-is.
Defensive End—New England Patriots
Born February 27, 1963, at Chillicothe, O.
Height, 6.04. Weight, 255.
High School—Chillicothe, O.
Attended Stanford University.

Selected by Oakland in 1985 USFL territorial draft.
Selected by New England in 2nd round (48th player selected) of 1985 NFL draft.
Signed by New England Patriots, July 25, 1985.
New England NFL, 1985 through 1987.
Games: 1985 (16), 1986 (16), 1987 (12). Total—44.
Pro statistics: Recovered two fumbles, 1985 and 1986.
Played in AFC Championship Game following 1985 season.
Played in NFL Championship Game following 1985 season.

ROGER VICK
Fullback—New York Jets
Born August 11, 1964, at Conroe, Tex.
Height, 6.03. Weight, 232.
High School—Tomball, Tex.
Attended Texas A&M University.

Selected by New York Jets in 1st round (21st player selected) of 1987 NFL draft.
Signed by New York Jets, July 21, 1987.

Year Club	G.	Att.	Yds.	Avg.	TD.	P.C.	Yds.	Avg.	TD.	TD.	Pts.	F.
		—RUSHING—				PASS RECEIVING				—TOTAL—		
1987—New York Jets NFL	12	77	257	3.3	1	13	108	8.3	0	1	6	3

DANNY VILLA
Offensive Tackle—New England Patriots
Born September 21, 1964, at Nogales, Ariz.
Height, 6.05. Weight, 305.
High School—Nogales, Ariz.
Attended Arizona State University.

Selected by New England in 5th round (113th player selected) of 1987 NFL draft.
Signed by New England Patriots, July 25, 1987.
New England NFL, 1987.
Games: 1987 (11).
Pro statistics: Fumbled once for minus 13 yards, 1987.

LIONEL VITAL
Running Back—Buffalo Bills
Born July 15, 1963, at Loreauville, La.
Height, 5.09. Weight 195.
High School—Loreauville, La.
Attended Nichols State University.

Selected by Arizona in 13th round (187th player selected) of 1985 USFL draft.
Selected by Washington in 7th round (185th player selected) of 1985 NFL draft.
Signed by Washington Redskins, July 18, 1985.
On injured reserve with hamstring injury, August 20 through entire 1985 season.
Released by Washington Redskins, August 19, 1986; awarded on waivers to New York Giants, August 20, 1986.
Released by New York Giants, August 26, 1986; signed as free agent by Calgary Stampeders, September 22, 1986.
Released by Calgary Stampeders, September 29, 1986; signed as free agent replacement player by Washington Redskins, September 23, 1987.
Released by Washington Redskins, November 3, 1987; signed as free agent by Buffalo Bills, December 8, 1987.

Year Club	G.	Att.	Yds.	Avg.	TD.	P.C.	Yds.	Avg.	TD.	TD.	Pts.	F.
		—RUSHING—				PASS RECEIVING				—TOTAL—		
1986—Calgary CFL	1	3	8	2.7	0		None			0	0	1
1987—Washington NFL	3	80	346	4.3	2	1	13	13.0	0	2	12	3
Pro Totals—2 Years	4	83	354	4.3	2	1	13	13.0	0	2	12	4

Additional CFL statistics: Returned two punts for one yard, 1986.
Additional NFL statistics: Returned two kickoffs for 31 yards, 1987.

RECORD AS BASEBALL PLAYER

Signed as free agent by Chicago White Sox' organization, October 16, 1986.
Released by Chicago White Sox, March, 1987.

MARK RICHARD VLASIC
Quarterback—San Diego Chargers
Born October 25, 1963, at Rochester, Pa.
Height, 6.03. Weight, 206.
High School—Monaca, Pa., Center.
Received degree in finance from University of Iowa in 1987.

Selected by San Diego in 4th round (88th player selected) of 1987 NFL draft.
Signed by San Diego Chargers, July 26, 1987.
San Diego NFL, 1987.
Games: 1987 (1).
Pro statistics: Attempted six passes with three completions for eight yards and one interception, recovered one fumble and fumbled once, 1987.

TIMOTHY GENE VOGLER
(Tim)
Guard—Buffalo Bills
Born October 2, 1956, at Troy, O.
Height, 6.03. Weight, 285.
High School—Covington, O.
Attended Ohio State University.

Signed as free agent by Buffalo Bills, May 5, 1979.
On injured reserve with broken hand, August 28 through October 5, 1979; activated, October 6, 1979.

On injured reserve with hamstring injury, November 29 through remainder of 1980 season.
On injured reserve with knee injury, August 19 through October 17, 1986; activated, October 18, 1986.
Buffalo NFL, 1979 through 1987.
Games: 1979 (10), 1980 (10), 1981 (14), 1982 (6), 1983 (16), 1984 (16), 1985 (14), 1986 (9), 1987 (12). Total—107.
Pro statistics: Returned one kickoff for no yards, 1980; recovered one fumble, 1985; recovered two fumbles, 1987.

BRYAN J. WAGNER
Punter—Chicago Bears
Born March 28, 1962, at Escondido, Calif.
Height, 6.02. Weight, 195.
High School—Chula Vista, Calif., Hilltop.
Attended California Lutheran College and California State University at Northridge.

Selected by Baltimore in 15th round (216th player selected) of 1985 USFL draft.
Signed as free agent by Dallas Cowboys, May 2, 1985.
Released by Dallas Cowboys, August 27, 1985; signed as free agent by New York Giants, May 10, 1986.
Released by New York Giants, August 11, 1986; signed as free agent by St. Louis Cardinals, August 19, 1986.
Released by St. Louis Cardinals, August 26, 1986; signed as free agent by Denver Broncos, May 1, 1987.
Traded with draft pick by Denver Broncos to Chicago Bears for guard Stefan Humphries, August 25, 1987.
On injured reserve with back injury, December 16, through remainder of 1987 season.

		—PUNTING—		
Year	Club	G.	No.	Avg.	Blk.
1987—Chicago NFL		10	36	40.6	1

MARK CHARLES WALCZAK
Tight End—San Diego Chargers
Born April 26, 1962, at Rochester, N. Y.
Height, 6.06. Weight, 246.
High School—Rochester, N. Y., Greece Athena.
Attended University of Arizona.

Signed as free agent by Kansas City Chiefs, May 6, 1986.
Released by Kansas City Chiefs, August 14, 1986; signed as free agent by Indianapolis Colts, May 14, 1987.
Released by Indianapolis Colts, August 31, 1987; signed as free agent replacement player by Buffalo Bills, September 24, 1987.
Released by Buffalo Bills, October 16, 1987; signed as free agent by Indianapolis Colts, October 27, 1987.
On injured reserve with knee injury, December 23 through remainder of 1987 season.
Released by Indianapolis Colts, April 18, 1988; signed as free agent by San Diego Chargers, May 23, 1988.
Buffalo (2)-Indianapolis (8) NFL, 1987.
Games: 1987 (10).
Pro statistics: Fumbled once, 1987.

MARK HARTLEY WALEN
Defensive Lineman—Dallas Cowboys
Born March 10, 1963, at San Francisco, Calif.
Height, 6.05. Weight, 262.
High School—Burlingame, Calif.
Received bachelor of science degree in history
from University of California at Los Angeles in 1986.

Selected by Arizona in 1986 USFL territorial draft.
Selected by Dallas in 3rd round (74th player selected) of 1986 NFL draft.
Signed by Dallas Cowboys, August 9, 1986.
On injured reserve with broken foot, August 26 through entire 1986 season.
Dallas NFL, 1987.
Games: 1987 (9).

HERSCHEL WALKER
Running Back—Dallas Cowboys
Born March 3, 1962, at Wrightsville, Ga.
Height, 6.01. Weight, 222.
High School—Wrightsville, Ga., Johnson County.
Received degree in criminal justice from University of Georgia in 1984.

Named THE SPORTING NEWS USFL Player of the Year, 1985.
Named as running back on THE SPORTING NEWS USFL All-Star Team, 1983 and 1985.
Heisman Trophy winner, 1982.
Named college football Player of the Year by THE SPORTING NEWS, 1982.
Named as running back on THE SPORTING NEWS College All-America Team, 1980 through 1982.
Signed by New Jersey Generals, February 22, 1983 (Generals forfeited 1st round pick in 1984 draft).
On developmental squad, April 8 through April 13, 1984; activated, April 14, 1984.
Selected by Dallas in 5th round (114th player selected) of 1985 NFL draft.
Granted free agency when USFL suspended operations, August 7, 1986; signed by Dallas Cowboys, August 13, 1986.
Granted roster exemption, August 13 through August 22, 1986; activated, August 23, 1986.
On developmental squad for 1 game with New Jersey Generals in 1984.

		—RUSHING—				PASS RECEIVING				—TOTAL—		
Year	Club	G.	Att.	Yds.	Avg.	TD.	P.C.	Yds.	Avg.	TD.	TD.	Pts.	F.
1983—New Jersey USFL		18	*412	*1812	4.4	*17	53	489	9.2	1	*18	†110	12
1984—New Jersey USFL		17	293	1339	4.6	16	40	528	13.2	5	*21	†128	6
1985—New Jersey USFL		18	*438	*2411	5.5	*21	37	467	12.6	1	*22	*132	9

		——RUSHING——				PASS RECEIVING				—TOTAL—		
Year	Club	G.	Att.	Yds.	Avg.	TD.	P.C.	Yds.	Avg.	TD.	TD.	Pts.	F.
1986—Dallas NFL		16	151	737	4.9	12	76	837	11.0	2	14	84	5
1987—Dallas NFL		12	209	891	4.3	7	60	715	11.9	1	8	48	4
USFL Totals—3 Years		53	1143	5562	4.9	54	130	1484	11.4	7	61	370	27
NFL Totals—2 Years		28	360	1628	4.5	19	136	1552	11.4	3	22	132	9
Pro Totals—5 Years		81	1503	7190	4.8	73	266	3036	11.4	10	83	502	36

†Includes one 2-point conversion.
Additional USFL statistics: Returned three kickoffs for 69 yards and recovered four fumbles, 1983; recovered two fumbles, 1984; recovered three fumbles, 1985.
Additional NFL statistics: Recovered two fumbles, 1986; recovered one fumble, 1987.
Played in Pro Bowl (NFL All-Star Game) following 1987 season.

JACKIE A. WALKER
Linebacker—Tampa Bay Buccaneers
Born November 3, 1962, at Monroe, La.
Height, 6.05. Weight, 245.
High School—Monroe, La., Carroll.
Attended Jackson State University.

Selected by Tampa Bay in 2nd round (28th player selected) of 1986 NFL draft.
Signed by Tampa Bay Buccaneers, July 22, 1986.
Tampa Bay NFL, 1986 and 1987.
Games: 1986 (15), 1987 (12). Total—27.

JEFFREY LYNN WALKER
(Jeff)
Offensive Tackle—Los Angeles Rams
Born January 22, 1963, at Jonesboro, Ark.
Height, 6.04. Wright, 295.
High School—Olive Branch, Miss.
Attended Memphis State University.

Selected by Memphis in 1986 USFL territorial draft.
Selected by San Diego in 3rd round (70th player selected) of 1986 NFL draft.
Signed by San Diego Chargers, July 23, 1986.
On injured reserve with knee injury, September 7, 1987.
Traded by San Diego Chargers to Los Angeles Rams for 11th round pick in 1988 draft, September 8, 1987.
On injured reserve with knee injury, September 8 through October 24 and October 27 through remainder of 1987 season.
San Diego NFL, 1986.
Games: 1986 (16).

KEVIN CORNELIUS WALKER
Defensive Back—Detroit Lions
Born October 20, 1963, at Greensboro, N.C.
Height, 5.11. Weight, 180.
High School—Greensboro, N.C., Ben L. Smith.
Attended East Carolina University.

Selected by Tampa Bay in 6th round (165th player selected) of 1986 NFL draft.
Selected by Tampa Bay in 9th round (64th player selected) of 1986 USFL draft.
Signed by Tampa Bay Buccaneers, July 16, 1986..
On injured reserve with shoulder injury, September 2 through November 20, 1986; activated, November 21, 1986.
Released by Tampa Bay Buccaneers, August 17, 1987; re-signed as replacement player by Buccaneers, September 24, 1987.
On injured reserve with ankle injury, October 19 through remainder of 1987 season.
Granted free agency with no qualifying offer, February 1, 1988; signed by Detroit Lions, May 5, 1988.

			–PUNT RETURNS-				—KICKOFF RET.—				—TOTAL—		
Year	Club	G.	No.	Yds.	Avg.	TD.	No.	Yds.	Avg.	TD.	TD.	Pts.	F.
1986—Tampa Bay NFL		4	9	27	3.0	0	8	146	18.3	0	0	0	1
1987—Tampa Bay NFL		3			None		1	0	0.0	0	1	6	0
Pro Totals—2 Years		7	9	27	3.0	0	9	146	16.2	0	1	6	1

Additional pro statistics: Recovered one fumble, 1986; intercepted two passes for 30 yards and a touchdown, 1987.

WESLEY DARCEL WALKER
Wide Receiver—New York Jets
Born May 26, 1955, at San Bernardino, Calif.
Height, 6.00. Weight, 179.
High School—Carson, Calif.
Attended University of California.

Selected by New York Jets in 2nd round (33rd player selected) of 1977 NFL draft.
On injured reserve with knee injury, October 31 through remainder of 1979 season.
On injured reserve with thigh injury, October 11 through November 14, 1980; activated, November 15, 1980.
Placed on did not report list, August 20 through August 26, 1984.
Reported and granted roster exemption, August 27 through August 31, 1984; activated, September 1, 1984.
On injured reserve with knee injury, September 3 through October 4, 1985; activated, October 5, 1985.
On injured reserve with separated shoulder, November 11 through remainder of 1987 season.

Year	Club	G.	P.C.	Yds.	Avg.	TD.
1977—New York Jets NFL....		14	35	740	*21.1	3
1978—New York Jets NFL....		16	48	*1169	*24.4	8
1979—New York Jets NFL....		9	23	569	24.7	5
1980—New York Jets NFL....		11	18	376	20.9	1
1981—New York Jets NFL....		13	47	770	16.4	9
1982—New York Jets NFL....		9	39	620	15.9	6
1983—New York Jets NFL....		16	61	868	14.2	7
1984—New York Jets NFL....		12	41	623	15.2	7
1985—New York Jets NFL....		12	34	725	21.3	5
1986—New York Jets NFL....		16	49	1016	20.7	12
1987—New York Jets NFL....		5	9	190	21.1	1
Pro Totals—11 Years......		133	404	7666	19.0	64

†Credited with one safety.

Additional pro statistics: Rushed three times for 25 yards, 1977; fumbled twice, 1977 and 1978; rushed once for minus three yards, 1978; recovered one fumble, 1978 and 1985; rushed once for one yard, 1984; fumbled once, 1985; fumbled three times, 1986.

Played in AFC Championship Game following 1982 season.
Played in Pro Bowl (NFL All-Star Game) following 1978 and 1982 seasons.

BARRON STEVEN WALLACE
(Steve)
Offensive Tackle—San Francisco 49ers

Born December 27, 1964, at Atlanta, Ga.
Height, 6.05. Weight, 276.
High School—Atlanta, Ga., Chamblee.
Attended Auburn University.

Selected by Birmingham in 1986 USFL territorial draft.
Selected by San Francisco in 4th round (101st player selected) of 1986 NFL draft.
Signed by San Francisco 49ers, July 18, 1986.
San Francisco NFL, 1986 and 1987.
Games: 1986 (16), 1987 (11). Total—27.

RAYMOND DURYEA WALLACE
(Ray)
Fullback—Houston Oilers

Born December 3, 1963, at Indianapolis, Ind.
Height, 6.00. Weight, 217.
High School—Indianapolis, Ind., North Central.
Attended Purdue University.

Selected by Houston in 6th round (145th player selected) of 1986 NFL draft.
Signed by Houston Oilers, July 21, 1986.
On injured reserve with neck injury, August 29 through October 16, 1986; activated, October 17, 1986.

			RUSHING				PASS RECEIVING				TOTAL		
Year	Club	G.	Att.	Yds.	Avg.	TD.	P.C.	Yds.	Avg.	TD.	TD.	Pts.	F.
1986—Houston NFL		8	52	218	4.2	3	17	177	10.4	2	5	30	1
1987—Houston NFL		12	19	102	5.4	0	7	34	4.9	0	0	0	1
Pro Totals—2 Years		20	71	320	4.5	3	24	211	8.8	2	5	30	2

Additional pro statistics: Recovered one fumble, 1987.

EVERSON COLLINS WALLS
Cornerback—Dallas Cowboys

Born December 28, 1959, at Dallas, Tex.
Height, 6.01. Weight, 194.
High School—Dallas, Tex., L.V. Berkner.
Received bachelor of arts degree in accounting from Grambling State University in 1981.
Cousin of Ralph Anderson, back with Pittsburgh Steelers and New England Patriots, 1971 through 1973; and Herkie Walls, wide receiver-kick returner with Houston Oilers and Tampa Bay Buccaneers, 1983 through 1985 and 1987.
Established NFL record for most seasons leading league in interceptions (3).
Signed as free agent by Dallas Cowboys, May, 1981.

			INTERCEPTIONS		
Year	Club	G.	No.	Yds.	Avg.TD.
1981—Dallas NFL		16	*11	133	12.1 0
1982—Dallas NFL		9	*7	61	8.7 0
1983—Dallas NFL		16	4	70	17.5 0
1984—Dallas NFL		16	3	12	4.0 0
1985—Dallas NFL		16	*9	31	3.4 0
1986—Dallas NFL		16	3	46	15.3 0
1987—Dallas NFL		12	5	38	7.6 0
Pro Totals—7 Years		101	42	391	9.3 0

Additional pro statistics: Recovered one fumble, 1981; fumbled once, 1982; recovered one fumble for four yards, 1985.

Played in NFC Championship Game following 1981 and 1982 seasons.
Played in Pro Bowl (NFL All-Star Game) following 1981 through 1983 and 1985 seasons.

JOSEPH FOLLMANN WALTER JR.
(Joe)
Offensive Tackle—Cincinnati Bengals
Born June 18, 1963, at Dallas, Tex.
Height, 6.06. Weight, 290.
High School—Garland, Tex., North.
Attended Texas Tech University.

Selected by Denver in 1985 USFL territorial draft.
Selected by Cincinnati in 7th round (181st player selected) of 1985 NFL draft.
Signed by Cincinnati Bengals, July 15, 1985.
Cincinnati NFL, 1985 through 1987.
Games: 1985 (14), 1986 (15), 1987 (12). Total—41.
Pro statistics: Recovered two fumbles, 1987.

MICHAEL DAVID WALTER
(Mike)
Linebacker—San Francisco 49ers
Born November 30, 1960, at Salem, Ore.
Height, 6.03. Weight, 238.
High School—Eugene, Ore., Sheldon.
Attended University of Oregon.

Selected by Los Angeles in 20th round (240th player selected) of 1983 USFL draft.
Selected by Dallas in 2nd round (50th player selected) of 1983 NFL draft.
Signed by Dallas Cowboys, July 7, 1983.
Released by Dallas Cowboys, August 27, 1984; awarded on waivers to San Francisco 49ers, August 28, 1984.
Dallas NFL, 1983; San Francisco NFL, 1984 through 1987.
Games: 1983 (15), 1984 (16), 1985 (14), 1986 (16), 1987 (12). Total—73.
Pro statistics: Intercepted one pass for no yards, 1985; recovered one fumble, 1986 and 1987; intercepted one pass for 16 yards, 1987.
Played in NFC Championship Game following 1984 season.
Played in NFL Championship Game following 1984 season.

ALVIN EARL WALTON
Safety—Washington Redskins
Born March 14, 1964, at Riverside, Calif.
Height, 6.00. Weight, 180.
High School—Banning, Calif.
Attended Mt. San Jacinto Junior College and University of Kansas.

Selected by Washington in 3rd round (75th player selected) of 1986 NFL draft.
Signed by Washington Redskins, July 18, 1986.

		—INTERCEPTIONS—			
Year Club	G.	No.	Yds.	Avg.TD.	
1986—Washington NFL	16	None			
1987—Washington NFL	12	3	28	9.3	0
Pro Totals—2 Years	28	3	28	9.3	0

Played in NFC Championship Game following 1986 and 1987 seasons.
Played in NFL Championship Game following 1987 season.

TIMMIE EUGENE WARE
Wide Receiver—San Diego Chargers
Born April 2, 1963, at Los Angeles, Calif.
Height, 5.10. Weight, 171.
High School—Compton, Calif., Centennial.
Attended University of Southern California.

Selected by Los Angeles in 1985 USFL territorial draft.
Signed as free agent by San Diego Chargers, June 20, 1985.
Released by San Diego Chargers, August 26, 1985; re-signed by Chargers, March 10, 1986.
On injured reserve with hamstring injury, September 1 through October 23, 1986; activated, October 24, 1986.
San Diego NFL, 1986 and 1987.
Games: 1986 (9), 1987 (12). Total—21.
Pro statistics: Caught one pass for 11 yards, 1986; caught two passes for 38 yards, 1987.

CURT WARNER
Running Back—Seattle Seahawks
Born March 18, 1961, at Wyoming, W. Va.
Height, 5.11. Weight, 205.
High School—Pineville, W. Va.
Attended Penn State University.

Selected by Philadelphia in 1983 USFL territorial draft.
Selected by Seattle in 1st round (3rd player selected) of 1983 NFL draft.
Signed by Seattle Seahawks, June 29, 1983.
On injured reserve with knee injury, September 5 through remainder of 1984 season.
Selected by Philadelphia Phillies' organization in 32nd round of free-agent draft, June 5, 1979.

Year Club	G.	Att.	RUSHING Yds.	Avg.	TD.	P.C.	PASS RECEIVING Yds.	Avg.	TD.	TOTAL TD.	Pts.	F.
1983—Seattle NFL	16	335	1449	4.3	13	42	325	7.7	1	14	84	6
1984—Seattle NFL	1	10	40	4.0	0	1	19	19.0	0	0	0	0
1985—Seattle NFL	16	291	1094	3.8	8	47	307	6.5	1	9	54	8
1986—Seattle NFL	16	319	1481	4.6	13	41	342	8.3	0	13	78	6
1987—Seattle NFL	12	234	985	4.2	8	17	167	9.8	2	10	60	4
Pro Totals—5 Years	61	1189	5049	4.2	42	148	1160	7.8	4	46	276	24

Additional pro statistics: Recovered two fumbles, 1983 and 1985; recovered five fumbles, 1986; recovered one fumble, 1987.
Played in AFC Championship Game following 1983 season.
Played in Pro Bowl (NFL All-Star Game) following 1983 season.
Named to play in Pro Bowl following 1986 season; replaced due to injury by Earnest Jackson.
Named to play in Pro Bowl following 1987 season; replaced due to injury by Marcus Allen.

DON WARREN
Tight End—Washington Redskins
Born May 5, 1956, at Bellingham, Wash.
Height, 6.04. Weight, 242.
High School—Covina, Calif., Royal Oak.
Attended Mt. San Antonio Junior College and San Diego State University.
Selected by Washington in 4th round (103rd player selected) of 1979 NFL draft.

Year Club	G.	P.C.	PASS RECEIVING Yds.	Avg.	TD.
1979—Washington NFL	16	26	303	11.7	0
1980—Washington NFL	13	31	323	10.4	0
1981—Washington NFL	16	29	335	11.6	1
1982—Washington NFL	9	27	310	11.5	0
1983—Washington NFL	13	20	225	11.3	2
1984—Washington NFL	16	18	192	10.7	0
1985—Washington NFL	16	15	163	10.9	1
1986—Washington NFL	16	20	164	8.2	1
1987—Washington NFL	12	7	43	6.1	0
Pro Totals—9 Years	127	193	2058	10.7	5

Additional pro statistics: Recovered one fumble, 1979, 1985 and 1986; fumbled once, 1980 and 1986; rushed once for five yards, 1985.
Played in NFC Championship Game following 1982, 1983, 1986 and 1987 seasons.
Played in NFL Championship Game following 1982, 1983 and 1987 seasons.

FRANK WILLIAM WARREN III
Defensive End—New Orleans Saints
Born September 14, 1959, at Birmingham, Ala.
Height, 6.04. Weight, 290.
High School—Birmingham, Ala., Phillips.
Attended Auburn University.
Selected by New Orleans in 3rd round (57th player selected) of 1981 NFL draft.
New Orleans NFL, 1981 through 1987.
Games: 1981 (16), 1982 (9), 1983 (16), 1984 (16), 1985 (16), 1986 (16), 1987 (12). Total—101.
Pro statistics: Recovered one fumble, 1981 and 1983; intercepted one pass for six yards, 1983; recovered one fumble for 50 yards and a touchdown and returned blocked field goal attempt 42 yards for a touchdown, 1985; recovered three fumbles, 1986.

JOHN M. WARREN JR.
Defensive Back—Detroit Lions
Born April 25, 1963, at Washington, D.C.
Height, 5.10. Weight, 190.
High School—Washington, D.C., Calvin Coolidge.
Attended Virginia Union University.
Selected by Los Angeles in 7th round (96th player selected) of 1985 USFL draft.
Signed by Los Angeles Express, January 21, 1985.
Released by Los Angeles Express, February 20, 1985; re-signed by Express, February 28, 1985.
On developmental squad, February 28 through March 9, 1985; activated, March 10, 1985.
Traded with defensive backs Dwight Drane and Troy West, running back Mel Gray, guard Wayne Jones, tight end Ken O'Neal and linebacker Howard Carson by Los Angeles Express to Arizona Outlaws for past considerations, August 1, 1985.
Granted free agency when USFL suspended operations, August 7, 1986; signed as free agent by Dallas Cowboys, April 30, 1987.
On injured reserve with knee injury, September 1 through November 11, 1987.
Crossed picket line during players' strike, October 1, 1987.
Released by Dallas Cowboys, November 12, 1987; signed as free agent by Detroit Lions, May 5, 1988.
On developmental squad for 1 game with Los Angeles Express in 1985.
Los Angeles USFL, 1985.
Games: 1985 (15).
Pro statistics: Recovered one fumble, 1985.

VINCENT LEO WARREN
(Vince)
Wide Receiver—Miami Dolphins
Born February 18, 1963, at Little Rock, Ark.
Height, 6.00. Weight, 180.
High School—Albuquerque, N.M., Eldorado.
Attended San Diego State University.

Selected by New York Giants in 5th round (130th player selected) of 1986 NFL draft.
Signed by New York Giants, July 19, 1986.
On injured reserve with hamstring injury, September 2 through October 17, 1986; activated, October 18, 1986.
Released by New York Giants, November 15, 1986; re-signed by Giants for 1987, November 17, 1986.
Released by New York Giants, August 19, 1987; signed as free agent by Miami Dolphins, January 6, 1988.
New York Giants NFL, 1986.
Games: 1986 (4).

CHRIS WASHINGTON
Linebacker—Tampa Bay Buccaneers
Born March 6, 1962, at Jackson, Miss.
Height, 6.04. Weight, 230.
High School—Chicago, Ill., Percy L. Julian.
Attended Iowa State University

Selected by Washington in 3rd round (49th player selected) of 1984 USFL draft.
Selected by Tampa Bay in 6th round (142nd player selected) of 1984 NFL draft.
Signed by Tampa Bay Buccaneers, June 5, 1984.
Tampa Bay NFL, 1984 through 1987.
Games: 1984 (16), 1985 (16), 1986 (16), 1987 (12). Total—60.
Pro statistics: Recovered one fumble, 1985; intercepted one pass for 12 yards and recovered two fumbles, 1986.

JOHN WASHINGTON
Defensive End—New York Giants
Born February 20, 1963, at Houston, Tex.
Height, 6.04. Weight, 275.
High School—Houston, Tex., Sterling.
Attended Oklahoma State University.

Selected by New Jersey in 1986 USFL territorial draft.
Selected by New York Giants in 3rd round (73rd player selected) of 1986 NFL draft.
Signed by New York Giants, July 17, 1986.
On injured reserve with back injury, January 3 through 1986 season playoffs.
New York Giants NFL, 1986 and 1987.
Games: 1986 (16), 1987 (12). Total—28.

LIONEL WASHINGTON
Cornerback—Los Angeles Raiders
Born October 21, 1960, at New Orleans, La.
Height, 6.00. Weight, 188.
High School—Lutcher, La.
Received degree in sports administration from Tulane University.

Selected by Tampa Bay in 20th round (229th player selected) of 1983 USFL draft.
Selected by St. Louis in 4th round (103rd player selected) of 1983 NFL draft.
Signed by St. Louis Cardinals, May 6, 1983.
On injured reserve with broken fibula, September 16 through November 21, 1985; activated, November 22, 1985.
Granted free agency, February 1, 1987; re-signed by Cardinals and traded to Los Angeles Raiders for 5th round pick in 1987 draft, March 18, 1987.

		—INTERCEPTIONS—			
Year Club	G.	No.	Yds.	Avg.	TD.
1983—St. Louis NFL..............	16	8	92	11.5	0
1984—St. Louis NFL..............	15	5	42	8.4	0
1985—St. Louis NFL..............	5	1	48	48.0	*1
1986—St. Louis NFL..............	16	2	19	9.5	0
1987—L.A. Raiders NFL.........	11		None		
Pro Totals—5 Years...........	63	16	201	12.6	1

Additional pro statistics: Recovered one fumble, 1983, 1984 and 1986.

RONNIE CARROLL WASHINGTON
Linebacker—Los Angeles Raiders
Born July 29, 1963, at Monroe, La.
Height, 6.01. Weight, 236.
High School—Monroe, La., Richwood.
Attended Northeast Louisiana University.

Selected by Arizona in 1st round (13th player selected) of 1985 USFL draft.
Selected by Atlanta in 8th round (215th player selected) of 1985 NFL draft.
Signed by Atlanta Falcons, July 18, 1985.
Traded with 6th round pick in 1987 draft by Atlanta Falcons to San Diego Chargers for rights to quarterback Ed Luther, August 13, 1986.

Released by San Diego Chargers, September 1, 1986; signed as free agent by Los Angeles Raiders, May 1, 1987.
Released by Los Angeles Raiders, September 7, 1987; re-signed as replacement player by Raiders, October 6, 1987.
Released by Los Angeles Raiders, December 5, 1987; re-signed by Raiders, April 22, 1988.
Atlanta NFL, 1985; Los Angeles Raiders NFL, 1987.
Games: 1985 (16), 1987 (2). Total—18.
Additional pro statistics: Returned one kickoff for no yards, 1985 and 1987; recovered one fumble and fumbled once, 1985.

ANDRE WATERS
Safety—Philadelphia Eagles
Born March 10, 1962, at Belle Glade, Fla.
Height, 5.11. Weight, 199.
High School—Pahokee, Fla.
Received degree in business administration from Cheyney State College.
Signed as free agent by Philadelphia Eagles, June 20, 1984.

		KICKOFF RETURNS			
Year	Club	G.	No.	Yds.	Avg.TD.
1984—Philadelphia NFL		16	13	319	24.5 ⋆1
1985—Philadelphia NFL		16	4	74	18.5 0
1986—Philadelphia NFL		16	6	39	6.5 0
1987—Philadelphia NFL		12	3	63	21.0 0
Pro Totals—4 Years		60	26	495	19.0 1

Additional pro statistics: Recovered one fumble and fumbled once, 1984 and 1985; returned one punt for 23 yards, 1985; recovered two fumbles for 81 yards, 1986; recovered two fumbles for 11 yards, 1987.

ROBERT MICHAEL WATERS
(Mike)
Tight End—New Orleans Saints
Born March 15, 1962, at San Diego, Calif.
Height, 6.02. Weight, 225.
High School—Ridgecrest, Calif., Ridgecrest Burroughs.
Attended Bakersfield College and San Diego State University.
Selected by New York Jets in 9th round (235th player selected) of 1985 NFL draft.
Signed by New York Jets, July 25, 1985.
Released by New York Jets, August 19, 1985; signed as free agent by Philadelphia Eagles, February 21, 1986.
Released by Philadelphia Eagles after failing physical, March 19, 1986; re-signed by Eagles, May 7, 1986.
Released by Philadelphia Eagles, October 8, 1986; signed as free agent by New Orleans Saints, February 23, 1987.
Released by New Orleans Saints, September 7, 1987; re-signed as replacement player by Saints, September 24, 1987.
On injured reserved with knee injury, November 3 through remainder of 1987 season.

			—RUSHING—				PASS RECEIVING				—TOTAL—		
Year	Club	G.	Att.	Yds.	Avg.	TD.	P.C.	Yds.	Avg.	TD.	TD.	Pts.	F.
1986—Philadelphia NFL		5	5	8	1.6	0	2	27	13.5	0	0	0	3
1987—New Orleans NFL		5		None			5	140	28.0	1	1	6	0
Pro Totals—2 Years		10	5	8	1.6	0	7	167	23.9	1	1	6	3

Additional pro statistics: Returned seven punts for 30 yards and recovered one fumble, 1986.

BOBBY LAWRENCE WATKINS
Cornerback—Detroit Lions
Born May 31, 1960, at Cottonwood, Ida.
Height, 5.10. Weight, 184.
High School—Dallas, Tex., Bishop Dunne.
Attended Southwest Texas State University.
Selected by Detroit in 2nd round (42nd player selected) of 1982 NFL draft.
On injured reserve with foot injury, October 16 through remainder of 1986 season.
On injured reserve with thigh injury, October 31 through November 24, 1987; activated, November 25, 1987.

			—INTERCEPTIONS—		
Year	Club	G.	No.	Yds.	Avg.TD.
1982—Detroit NFL		9	5	22	4.4 0
1983—Detroit NFL		16	4	48	12.0 0
1984—Detroit NFL		16	6	0	0.0 0
1985—Detroit NFL		16	5	15	3.0 0
1986—Detroit NFL		5		None	
1987—Detroit NFL		5		None	
Pro Totals—6 Years		67	20	85	4.3 0

Additional pro statistics: Recovered one fumble, 1982; recovered three fumbles for six yards and fumbled once, 1983; recovered two fumbles, 1985.

STEPHEN ROSS WATSON
(Steve)
Wide Receiver—Denver Broncos
Born May 28, 1957, at Baltimore, Md.
Height, 6.04. Weight, 195.
High School—Wilmington, Del., St. Mark's.
Received degree in parks administration from Temple University.

Signed as free agent by Denver Broncos, May 12, 1979.
Crossed picket line during players' strike, October 2, 1987.
On injured reserve with broken ribs, October 15 through December 17, 1987; activated, December 18, 1987.

Year Club	—PASS RECEIVING—				
	G.	P.C.	Yds.	Avg.	TD.
1979—Denver NFL	16	6	83	13.8	0
1980—Denver NFL	16	6	146	24.3	0
1981—Denver NFL	16	60	1244	20.7	*13
1982—Denver NFL	9	36	555	15.4	2
1983—Denver NFL	16	59	1133	19.2	5
1984—Denver NFL	16	69	1170	17.0	7
1985—Denver NFL	16	61	915	15.0	5
1986—Denver NFL	16	45	699	15.5	3
1987—Denver NFL	5	11	167	15.2	1
Pro Totals—9 Years	126	353	6112	17.3	36

Additional pro statistics: Returned one kickoff for five yards and recovered one fumble, 1980; rushed twice for six yards and recovered two fumbles, 1981; rushed once for minus four yards, 1982; fumbled once, 1982 and 1983; rushed three times for 17 yards, 1983.
Played in AFC Championship Game following 1986 and 1987 seasons.
Played in NFL Championship Game following 1986 and 1987 seasons.
Played in Pro Bowl (NFL All-Star Game) following 1981 season.

FRANK WATTELET
Name pronounced WATT-lit.
Safety—Los Angeles Rams
Born October 25, 1958, at Paola, Kan.
Height, 6.00. Weight, 190.
High School—Abilene, Kan.
Attended University of Kansas.

Signed as free agent by New Orleans Saints, May 27, 1981.
Released by New Orleans Saints after failing physical, July 15, 1981; re-signed by Saints, July 17, 1981.
Released by New Orleans Saints, November 3, 1987; signed as free agent by Los Angeles Rams, November 27, 1987.

Year Club	—INTERCEPTIONS—				
	G.	No.	Yds.	Avg.	TD.
1981—New Orleans NFL	16	3	16	5.3	0
1982—New Orleans NFL	9		None		
1983—New Orleans NFL	16	2	33	16.5	0
1984—New Orleans NFL	16	2	52	26.0	1
1985—New Orleans NFL	16	2	0	0.0	0
1986—New Orleans NFL	16	3	34	11.3	0
1987—N.O. (2)-Rams (5) NFL	7		None		
Pro Totals—7 Years	96	12	135	11.3	1

Additional pro statistics: Recovered one fumble, 1981, 1982, 1986 and 1987; returned one kickoff for four yards and recovered three fumbles for six yards, 1983; recovered two fumbles for 22 yards and a touchdown, 1984; recovered one fumble for four yards and rushed twice for 42 yards, 1985; attempted one pass with one completion for 13 yards, 1986.

ELBERT WATTS
Cornerback—Green Bay Packers
Born March 20, 1963, at Carson, Calif.
Height, 6.01. Weight, 205.
High School—Los Angeles, Calif., Venice.
Attended University of Oklahoma, East Los Angeles Junior College,
Santa Monica College and University of Southern California.

Selected by Los Angeles Rams in 9th round (243rd player selected) of 1986 NFL draft.
Signed by Los Angeles Rams, July 17, 1986.
On injured reserve with shoulder injury, August 19 through October 15, 1986.
Awarded on procedural waivers to Green Bay Packers, October 17, 1986.
On injured reserve with dislocated knee, August 10 through entire 1987 season.
Crossed picket line during players' strike, September 28, 1987.

Year Club	-INTERCEPTIONS-				—KICKOFF RET.—				—TOTAL—		
	G.	No.	Yds.	Avg.	TD.	No.	Yds.	Avg.	TD.	TD.	Pts.	F.
1986—Green Bay NFL	9	1	6	6.0	0	12	239	19.9	0	0	0	0

RANDY WATTS
Defensive End—Dallas Cowboys
Born June 22, 1963, at Sandersville, Ga.
Height, 6.06. Weight, 279.
High School—Sandersville, Ga., Washington County.
Attended East Carolina University and Catawba College.

Selected by Kansas City in 9th round (244th player selected) of 1987 NFL draft.
Signed by Kansas City Chiefs, July 19, 1987.
Released by Kansas City Chiefs, September 7, 1987; signed as free agent replacement player by Dallas Cowboys, September 23, 1987.
Left Dallas Cowboys camp and granted roster exemption, November 11 and November 12, 1987; activated, November 13, 1987.

Released by Dallas Cowboys, November 24, 1987; re-signed by Cowboys for 1988, November 27, 1987.
Dallas NFL, 1987.
Games: 1987 (5).
Pro statistics: Recovered one fumble, 1987.

DAVID BENJAMIN WAYMER JR.
(Dave)
Cornerback—New Orleans Saints
Born July 1, 1958, at Brooklyn, N.Y.
Height, 6.01. Weight, 188.
High School—Charlotte, N.C., West.
Received bachelor of arts degree in economics from University of Notre Dame in 1980.
Selected by New Orleans in 2nd round (41st player selected) of 1980 NFL draft.

| | | | —INTERCEPTIONS— | | |
Year Club	G.	No.	Yds.	Avg.	TD.
1980—New Orleans NFL........	16		None		
1981—New Orleans NFL........	16	4	54	13.5	0
1982—New Orleans NFL........	9		None		
1983—New Orleans NFL........	16		None		
1984—New Orleans NFL........	16	4	9	2.3	0
1985—New Orleans NFL........	16	6	49	8.2	0
1986—New Orleans NFL........	16	9	48	5.3	0
1987—New Orleans NFL........	12	5	78	15.6	0
Pro Totals—8 Years............	117	28	238	8.5	0

Additional pro statistics: Returned three punts for 29 yards, 1980; fumbled once, 1980 and 1985; recovered two fumbles, 1980, 1981 and 1982; recovered three fumbles, 1983; caught one pass for 13 yards and recovered one fumble, 1986; recovered three fumbles for two yards, 1987.
Played in Pro Bowl (NFL All-Star Game) following 1987 season.

CLARENCE WEATHERS
Wide Receiver—Cleveland Browns
Born January 10, 1962, at Green's Pond, S.C.
Height, 5.09. Weight, 170.
High School—Fort Pierce, Fla.
Attended Delaware State College.
Brother of Robert Weathers, running back with New England Patriots.
Signed as free agent by New England Patriots, July 20, 1983.
On injured reserve with broken foot, August 28 through October 19, 1984; activated, October 20, 1984.
Released by New England Patriots, September 2, 1985; awarded on waivers to Cleveland Browns, September 3, 1985.

| | | -PASS RECEIVING- | | | | -PUNT RETURNS- | | | | —TOTAL— | | |
Year Club	G.	P.C.	Yds.	Avg.	TD.	No.	Yds.	Avg.	TD.	TD.	Pts.	F.
1983—New England NFL.............	16	19	379	19.9	3	4	1	0.3	0	3	18	2
1984—New England NFL.............	9	8	115	14.4	2	1	7	7.0	0	2	12	0
1985—Cleveland NFL.............	13	16	449	28.1	3	28	218	7.8	0	3	18	3
1986—Cleveland NFL.............	16	9	100	11.1	0		None			0	0	0
1987—Cleveland NFL.............	12	11	153	13.9	2		None			2	12	0
Pro Totals—5 Years......................	66	63	1196	19.0	10	33	226	6.8	0	10	60	5

Additional pro statistics: Returned three kickoffs for 58 yards and rushed once for 28 yards, 1985; recovered one fumble, 1983 and 1985; returned one kickoff for 17 yards and rushed once for 18 yards, 1985.
Played in AFC Championship Game following 1986 and 1987 seasons.

ROBERT JAMES WEATHERS
Running Back—New England Patriots
Born September 13, 1960, at Westfield, N.Y.
Height, 6.02. Weight, 222.
High School—Fort Pierce, Fla.
Attended Arizona State University.
Brother of Clarence Weathers, wide receiver with Cleveland Browns.
Selected by New England in 2nd round (40th player selected) of 1982 NFL draft.
On injured reserve with knee injury, September 13 through December 7, 1984; activated, December 8, 1984.
On injured reserve with foot injury, November 13 through remainder of 1986 season.
On physically unable to perform/reserve with ankle injury, September 7 through entire 1987 season.

| | | ———RUSHING——— | | | | PASS RECEIVING | | | | —TOTAL— | | |
Year Club	G.	Att.	Yds.	Avg.	TD.	P.C.	Yds.	Avg.	TD.	TD.	Pts.	F.
1982—New England NFL.............	6	24	83	3.5	1	3	24	8.0	0	1	6	1
1983—New England NFL.............	15	73	418	5.7	1	23	212	9.2	0	1	6	4
1984—New England NFL.............	2		None				None			0	0	0
1985—New England NFL.............	16	41	174	4.2	1	2	18	9.0	0	1	6	0
1986—New England NFL.............	5	21	58	2.8	1	1	14	14.0	0	1	6	0
Pro Totals—5 Years......................	44	159	733	4.6	4	29	268	9.2	0	4	24	5

Additional pro statistics: Returned three kickoffs for 68 yards, 1983; returned one kickoff for 18 yards, 1985.
Played in AFC Championship Game following 1985 season.
Played in NFL Championship Game following 1985 season.

MICHAEL LEWIS WEBSTER
(Mike)
Center—Pittsburgh Steelers
Born March 18, 1952, at Tomahawk, Wis.
Height, 6.02. Weight, 254.
High School—Rhinelander, Wis.
Attended University of Wisconsin.

Named to THE SPORTING NEWS NFL All-Star Team, 1980, 1981 and 1983.
Named to THE SPORTING NEWS AFC All-Star Team, 1978 and 1979.
Selected by Pittsburgh in 5th round (125th player selected) of 1974 NFL draft.
On injured reserve with dislocated elbow, September 3 through October 2, 1986; activated, October 3, 1986.
Crossed picket line during players' strike, September 30, 1987.
Pittsburgh NFL, 1974 through 1987.
Games: 1974 (14), 1975 (14), 1976 (14), 1977 (14), 1977 (14), 1978 (16), 1980 (16), 1981 (16), 1982 (9), 1983 (16), 1984 (16), 1985 (16), 1986 (12), 1987 (15). Total—204.
Pro statistics: Fumbled twice, 1976; recovered two fumbles for two yards, 1979; recovered two fumbles, 1983; recovered one fumble, 1985.
Played in AFC Championship Game following 1974 through 1976, 1978, 1979 and 1984 seasons.
Played in NFL Championship Game following 1974, 1975, 1978 and 1979 seasons.
Played in Pro Bowl (NFL All-Star Game) following 1978 through 1985 and 1987 seasons.

MICHAEL WAYNE WEDDINGTON
Linebacker—Green Bay Packers
Born October 9, 1960, at Belton, Tex.
Height, 6.04. Weight, 245.
High School—Temple, Tex.
Attended University of Oklahoma.

Selected by New Jersey in 1983 USFL territorial draft.
Signed by New Jersey Generals, January 31, 1983.
On developmental squad, March 10 through May 4, 1984; activated, May 5, 1984.
On developmental squad, June 15 through June 22, 1984; activated, June 23, 1984.
Granted free agency when USFL suspended operations, August 7, 1986; signed as free agent by Green Bay Packers, August 13, 1986.
On injured reserve with shoulder injury, September 1 through December 5, 1986; activated, December 6, 1986.
On developmental squad for 9 games with New Jersey Generals in 1984.
New Jersey USFL, 1983 through 1985; Green Bay NFL, 1986 and 1987.
Games: 1983 (18), 1984 (9), 1985 (3), 1987 (12). Total USFL—45. Total NFL—15. Total Pro—60.
USFL statistics: Credited with six sacks for 46 yards, recovered one fumble and returned four kickoffs for 41 yards, 1983; credited with 3½ sacks for 39½ yards, 1984; credited with 2½ sacks for 23 yards and recovered two fumbles, 1985.
NFL statistics: Recovered one fumble, 1987.

CLAYTON CHARLES WEISHUHN
Name pronounced Why-SOON.
Linebacker—Green Bay Packers
Born October 7, 1959, at San Angelo, Tex.
Height, 6.01. Weight, 220.
High School—Wall, Tex.
Received bachelor of science degree in physical education from
Angelo State University in 1982.

Selected by New England in 3rd round (60th player selected) of 1982 NFL draft.
On injured reserve with knee injury, September 5 through remainder of 1984 season.
On injured reserve with knee injury, August 19 through entire 1985 season.
On injured reserve with groin injury, September 2 through October 23, 1986; activated, October 24, 1986.
On injured reserve with hamstring injury, November 19 through remainder of 1986 season.
Released by New England Patriots, September 7, 1987; awarded on waivers to Green Bay Packers, September 8, 1987.
New England NFL, 1982 through 1984 and 1986; Green Bay NFL, 1987.
Games: 1982 (9), 1983 (16), 1984 (1), 1986 (4), 1987 (9). Total—39.
Pro statistics: Recovered one fumble, 1982; ran 27 yards with lateral on interception for a touchdown and recovered three fumbles, 1983; returned one kickoff for one yard, 1987.

HERB DOYAN WELCH
Defensive Back—New York Giants
Born January 12, 1961, at Los Angeles, Calif.
Height, 5.11. Weight, 180.
High School—Downey, Calif., Warren.
Attended Cerritos College and University of California at Los Angeles.

Selected by Portland in 10th round (135th player selected) of 1985 USFL draft.
Selected by New York Giants in 12th round (326th player selected) of 1985 NFL draft.
Signed by New York Giants, July 9, 1985.

Year Club	G.	No.	Yds.	Avg.	TD.
		——INTERCEPTIONS——			
1985—N.Y. Giants NFL	16	2	8	4.0	0
1986—N.Y. Giants NFL	16	2	22	11.0	0
1987—N.Y. Giants NFL	12	2	7	3.5	0
Pro Totals—3 Years	44	6	37	6.2	0

Additional pro statistics: Recovered one fumble for seven yards, 1986.
Played in NFC Championship Game following 1986 season.
Played in NFL Championship Game following 1986 season.

RAIMUND WERSCHING
Name pronounced WERE-shing.
(Ray)
Placekicker—San Francisco 49ers
Born August 21, 1950, at Mondsee, Austria.
Height, 5.11. Weight, 215.
High School—Downey, Calif., Earl Warren.
Attended Cerritos College and received bachelor of science degree in
accounting from University of California at Berkeley.
Tied NFL records for most field goals, game, no misses (6) vs. New Orleans Saints, October 16, 1983; most extra
points, no misses, season (56), 1984.
Signed as free agent by Atlanta Falcons, 1971.
Released by Atlanta Falcons, 1971; signed as free agent by San Diego Chargers, 1973.
Released by San Diego Chargers, September 6, 1976; re-signed by Chargers, October 16, 1976.
Released by San Diego Chargers, August, 1977; signed as free agent by San Francisco 49ers, October 11, 1977.
On injured reserve with hip injury, September 12 through October 9, 1981; activated, October 10, 1981.

| | | ——PLACE KICKING—— | | | | | | | | ——PLACE KICKING—— | | | | |
Year	Club	G.	XP.	XPM.	FG.	FGA.	Pts.	Year	Club	G.	XP.	XPM.	FG.	FGA.	Pts.
1973—San Diego NFL		14	13	2	11	25	46	1981—San Fran. NFL		12	30	0	17	23	81
1974—San Diego NFL		14	0	0	5	11	15	1982—San Fran. NFL		9	23	2	12	17	59
1975—San Diego NFL		14	20	1	12	24	56	1983—San Fran. NFL		16	51	0	25	30	126
1976—San Diego NFL		9	14	2	4	8	26	1984—San Fran. NFL		16	56	0	25	35	*131
1977—San Fran. NFL		10	23	0	10	17	53	1985—San Fran. NFL		16	*52	1	13	21	91
1978—San Fran. NFL		16	24	1	15	23	69	1986—San Fran. NFL		16	41	1	25	35	116
1979—San Fran. NFL		16	32	3	20	24	92	1987—San Fran. NFL		12	*44	2	13	17	83
1980—San Fran. NFL		16	33	*6	15	19	78	Pro Totals—15 Years		206	456	21	222	329	1122

Additional pro statistics: Recovered one fumble, 1985.
Played in NFC Championship Game following 1981, 1983 and 1984 seasons.
Played in NFL Championship Game following 1981 and 1984 seasons.

EDWARD LEE WEST III
(Ed)
Tight End—Green Bay Packers
Born August 2, 1961, at Colbert County, Ala.
Height, 6.01. Weight, 242.
High School—Leighton, Ala., Colbert County.
Attended Auburn University.
Selected by Birmingham in 1984 USFL territorial draft.
Signed as free agent by Green Bay Packers, May 3, 1984.
Released by Green Bay Packers, August 27, 1984; re-signed by Packers, August 30, 1984.

| | | ——PASS RECEIVING—— | | | | |
Year	Club	G.	P.C.	Yds.	Avg.	TD.
1984—Green Bay NFL		16	6	54	9.0	4
1985—Green Bay NFL		16	8	95	11.9	1
1986—Green Bay NFL		16	15	199	13.3	1
1987—Green Bay NFL		12	19	261	13.7	1
Pro Totals—4 Years		60	48	609	12.7	7

Additional pro statistics: Rushed once for two yards and a touchdown, 1984; recovered one fumble, 1984 and 1986;
rushed once for no yards and fumbled once, 1985.

DWIGHT WHEELER
Center-Guard—Los Angeles Raiders
Born January 13, 1955, at Memphis, Tenn.
Height, 6.03. Weight, 285.
High School—Memphis, Tenn., Manassas.
Attended Tennessee State University.
Selected by New England in 4th round (102nd player selected) of 1978 NFL draft.
On injured reserve with broken leg, September 13 through remainder of 1978 season.
On injured reserve with ankle injury, December 12 through remainder of 1979 season.
Released by New England Patriots, August 27, 1984; signed as free agent by Los Angeles Raiders, November 8,
1984.
Released by Los Angeles Raiders, November 12, 1984; re-signed by Raiders, November 15, 1984.
Released by Los Angeles Raiders, September 2, 1985; re-signed by Raiders, March 20, 1986.
Released by Los Angeles Raiders, September 1, 1986; re-signed by Raiders, March 12, 1987.
Released by Los Angeles Raiders, September 7, 1987; signed as free agent by San Diego Chargers, September 18,
1987.
Released by San Diego Chargers, September 19, 1987; re-signed as replacement player by Chargers, September 30,
1987.
Released by San Diego Chargers, October 27, 1987; signed as free agent by Los Angeles Raiders, December 3, 1987.
New England NFL, 1978 through 1983; Los Angeles Raiders NFL, 1984; San Diego (3)-Los Angeles Raiders (4) NFL,
1987.

Games: 1978 (2), 1979 (13), 1980 (16), 1981 (16), 1982 (9), 1983 (16), 1984 (4), 1987 (7). Total—83.
Pro statistics: Returned one kickoff for no yards, 1978; fumbled once for minus 14 yards, 1979; fumbled once for minus 41 yards, 1980.

KENNETH MOORE WHISENHUNT
(Ken)
Tight End—Atlanta Falcons
Born February 28, 1962, at Atlanta, Ga.
Height, 6.03. Weight, 240.
High School—Augusta, Ga., Richmond.
Attended Georgia Tech.

Selected by Jacksonville in 1985 USFL territorial draft.
USFL rights traded with rights to running back Marck Harrison and center Dan Turk by Jacksonville Bulls to Tampa Bay Bandits for rights to kicker Bobby Raymond, running back Cedric Jones and defensive back Eric Riley, January 3, 1985.
Selected by Atlanta in 12th round (313th player selected) of 1985 NFL draft.
Signed by Atlanta Falcons, July 18, 1985.
On injured reserve with separated shoulder, December 2 through remainder of 1987 season.

		—PASS RECEIVING—			
Year Club	G.	P.C.	Yds.	Avg.	TD.
1985—Atlanta NFL	16	3	48	16.0	0
1986—Atlanta NFL	16	20	184	9.2	3
1987—Atlanta NFL	7	17	145	8.5	1
Pro Totals—3 Years	39	40	377	9.4	4

Additional pro statistics: Rushed once for three yards, returned four kickoffs for 33 yards, 1985; recovered one fumble, 1985 and 1987; rushed once for 20 yards, 1986; fumbled once, 1987.

ADRIAN DARNELL WHITE
Safety—New York Giants
Born April 6, 1964, at Orange Park, Fla.
Height, 6.00. Weight, 200.
High School—Orange Park, Fla.
Attended University of Southern Illinois at Carbondale and University of Florida.

Selected by New York Giants in 2nd round (55th player selected) of 1987 NFL draft.
Signed by New York Giants, July 27, 1987.
On injured reserve with knee injury, August 22 through October 13, 1987; activated, October 14, 1987.
Crossed picket line during players' strike, October 14, 1987.
New York Giants NFL, 1987.
Games: 1987 (6).

CHARLES RAYMOND WHITE
Running Back—Los Angeles Rams
Born January 22, 1958, at Los Angeles, Calif.
Height, 5.10. Weight, 190.
High School—San Fernando, Calif.
Attended University of Southern California.

Heisman Trophy winner, 1979.
Named to THE SPORTING NEWS NFL All-Star Team, 1987.
Named as running back on THE SPORTING NEWS College All-America Team, 1979.
Named THE SPORTING NEWS College Player of the Year, 1979.
Selected by Cleveland in 1st round (27th player selected) of 1980 NFL draft.
On injured reserve with broken ankle, August 16 through entire 1983 season.
On physically unable to perform/active with ankle injury, July 19 through August 11, 1984; activated, August 12, 1984.
On injured reserve with ankle and back injuries, November 30 through remainder of 1984 season.
Released by Cleveland Browns, June 4, 1985; signed as free agent by Los Angeles Rams, July 9, 1985.
Released by Los Angeles Rams, September 2, 1985; re-signed by Rams, September 3, 1985.
Crossed picket line during players' strike, October 1, 1987.

		—RUSHING—				PASS RECEIVING				—TOTAL—		
Year Club	G.	Att.	Yds.	Avg.	TD.	P.C.	Yds.	Avg.	TD.	TD.	Pts.	F.
1980—Cleveland NFL	14	86	279	3.2	5	17	153	9.0	1	6	36	1
1981—Cleveland NFL	16	97	342	3.5	1	27	219	8.1	0	1	6	8
1982—Cleveland NFL	9	69	259	3.8	3	34	283	8.3	0	3	18	2
1984—Cleveland NFL	10	24	62	2.6	0	5	29	5.8	0	0	0	0
1985—Los Angeles Rams NFL	16	70	310	4.4	3	1	12	12.0	0	3	18	3
1986—Los Angeles Rams NFL	16	22	126	5.7	0	1	7	7.0	0	0	0	2
1987—Los Angeles Rams NFL	15	*324	*1374	4.2	*11	23	121	5.3	0	11	66	8
Pro Totals—7 Years	96	692	2752	4.0	23	108	824	7.6	1	24	144	24

	KICKOFF RETURNS						KICKOFF RETURNS			
Year Club	G.	No.	Yds.	Avg.TD.		Year Club	G.	No.	Yds.	Avg.TD.
1980—Cleveland NFL	14	1	20	20.0	0	1985—L.A. Rams NFL	16	17	300	17.6	0
1981—Cleveland NFL	16	12	243	20.3	0	1986—L.A. Rams NFL	16	12	216	18.0	0
1982—Cleveland NFL	9			None		1987—L.A. Rams NFL	15	3	73	24.3	0
1984—Cleveland NFL	10	5	80	16.0	0	Pro Totals—7 Years	96	50	932	18.6	0

Additional pro statistics: Recovered one fumble, 1980 and 1987; recovered three fumbles, 1981; returned one punt for no yards, 1985.
Played in NFC Championship Game following 1985 season.
Played in Pro Bowl (NFL All-Star Game) following 1987 season.

RANDY LEE WHITE
Defensive Tackle—Dallas Cowboys
Born January 15, 1953, at Wilmington, Del.
Height, 6.04. Weight, 265.
High School—Wilmington, Del., Thomas McKean.
Attended University of Maryland.

Outland Trophy winner, 1974.
Named as defensive end on THE SPORTING NEWS College All-America Team, 1974.
Named to THE SPORTING NEWS NFC All-Star Team, 1978 and 1979.
Named to THE SPORTING NEWS NFL All-Star Team, 1980, 1981, 1983 and 1985.
Selected by Dallas in 1st round (2nd player selected) of 1975 NFL draft.
Placed on did not report list, August 21 through August 26, 1984.
Reported and granted roster exemption, August 27 through September 2, 1984; activated, September 3, 1984.
Crossed picket line during players' strike, September 23, 1987.
Dallas NFL, 1975 through 1987.
Games: 1975 (14), 1976 (14), 1977 (14), 1978 (16), 1979 (15), 1980 (16), 1981 (16), 1982 (9), 1983 (16), 1984 (16), 1985 (16), 1986 (16), 1987 (15). Total—193.
Pro statistics: Recovered two fumbles, 1975, 1977 and 1986; recovered one fumble, 1976, 1979, 1982 and 1983; returned one kickoff for 15 yards, 1978; intercepted one pass for no yards, 1987.
Played in NFC Championship Game following 1975, 1977, 1978 and 1980 through 1982 seasons.
Played in NFL Championship Game following 1975, 1977 and 1978 seasons.
Played in Pro Bowl (NFL All-Star Game) following 1977 and 1979 through 1985 seasons.
Named to play in Pro Bowl following 1978 season; replaced due to injury by Doug English.

REGINALD HOWARD WHITE
(Reggie)
Defensive End—Philadelphia Eagles
Born December 19, 1961, at Chattanooga, Tenn.
Height, 6.05. Weight, 285.
High School—Chattanooga, Tenn., Howard.
Attended University of Tennessee.

Named to THE SPORTING NEWS NFL All-Star Team, 1987.
Named as defensive end on THE SPORTING NEWS USFL All-Star Team, 1985.
Named as defensive end on THE SPORTING NEWS College All-America Team, 1983.
Selected by Memphis in 1984 USFL territorial draft.
Signed by Memphis Showboats, January 15, 1984.
On developmental squad, March 9 through March 23, 1984; activated, March 24, 1984.
Selected by Philadelphia in 1st round (4th player selected) of 1984 NFL supplemental draft.
Released by Memphis Showboats, September 19, 1985; signed by Philadelphia Eagles, September 21, 1985.
Granted roster exemption, September 21 through September 26, 1985; activated, September 27, 1985.
On developmental squad for 2 games with Memphis Showboats in 1984.
Memphis USFL, 1984 and 1985; Philadelphia NFL, 1985 through 1987.
Games: 1984 (16), 1985 USFL (18), 1985 NFL (13), 1986 (16), 1987 (12). Total USFL—34. Total NFL—41 Total Pro—75.
USFL statistics: Credited with 12 sacks for 84 yards and recovered one fumble, 1984; credited with 11½ sacks for 93½ yards, credited with one safety and recovered one fumble for 20 yards and a touchdown, 1985.
NFL statistics: Recovered two fumbles, 1985; recovered one fumble for 70 yards and a touchdown, 1987.
Played in Pro Bowl (NFL All-Star Game) following 1986 and 1987 seasons.

ROBERT A. WHITE
(Bob)
Offensive Lineman—Dallas Cowboys
Born April 9, 1963, at Fitchburg, Mass.
Height, 6.05. Weight, 267.
High School—Lunenburg, Mass.
Received bachelor of arts degree in journalism
from University of Rhode Island in 1986.

Seleted by New York Jets in 7th round (189th player selected) of 1986 NFL draft.
Signed by New York Jets, July 23, 1986.
Released by New York Jets, August 25, 1986; signed as free agent by Dallas Cowboys, March 17, 1987.
Released by Dallas Cowboys, September 7, 1987; re-signed as replacement player by Cowboys, September 23, 1987.
Dallas NFL, 1987.
Games: 1987 (4).
Pro statisitcs: Fumbled twice, 1987.

—DID YOU KNOW—
That Dallas defensive end Jim Jeffcoat has returned two interceptions for touchdowns in his five-year NFL career—both off passes tipped by teammate Ed Jones and thrown by Giants quarterback Phil Simms? The interceptions came in 1985 and 1987.

THOMAS LEON WHITE
(Known by middle name.)
Linebacker—Cincinnati Bengals
Born October 4, 1963, at San Diego, Calif.
Height, 6.02. Weight, 236.
High School—La Mesa, Calif., Helix.
Attended Brigham Young University.
Selected by Cincinnati in 5th round (123rd player selected) of 1986 NFL draft.
Signed by Cincinnati Bengals, July 20, 1986.
Cincinnati NFL, 1986 and 1987.
Games: 1986 (16), 1987 (12). Total—28.
Pro statistics: Credited with a safety, 1986.

WILFORD DANIEL WHITE
(Danny)
Quarterback—Dallas Cowboys
Born February 9, 1952, at Mesa, Ariz.
Height, 6.03. Weight, 198.
High School—Mesa, Ariz., Westwood.
Attended Arizona State University.
Son of Wilford White, halfback with Chicago Bears, 1951 and 1952.
Selected by Dallas in 3rd round (53rd player selected) of 1974 NFL draft.
Played in World Football League with Memphis Southmen, 1974 and 1975.
Signed by Dallas Cowboys after World Football League folded, April 15, 1976.
On injured reserve with broken wrist, November 14 through remainder of 1986 season.
Crossed picket line during players' strike, September 30, 1987.
Selected by Cleveland Indians' organization in 39th round of free-agent draft, June 5, 1973.
Selected by Houston Astros' organization in secondary phase of free-agent draft, January 9, 1974.
Selected by Cleveland Indians' organization in secondary phase of free-agent draft, June 5, 1974.
Selected by Cleveland Indians' organization in secondary phase of free-agent draft, January 9, 1975.

Year Club	G.	Att.	Cmp.	Pct.	Gain	T.P.	P.I.	Avg.	Att.	Yds.	Avg.	TD.	TD.	Pts.	F.
1974—Memphis WFL	....	155	79	51.0	1190	11	9	7.68	24	103	4.3	0	0	0	....
1975—Memphis WFL	....	195	104	53.3	1445	10	8	7.41	23	116	5.0	0	0	1	....
1976—Dallas NFL	14	20	13	65.0	213	2	2	10.65	6	17	2.8	0	0	0	0
1977—Dallas NFL	14	10	4	40.0	35	0	1	3.50	1	—2	—2.0	0	0	0	0
1978—Dallas NFL	16	34	20	58.8	215	0	1	6.32	5	7	1.4	0	0	0	2
1979—Dallas NFL	16	39	19	48.7	267	1	2	6.85	1	25	25.0	0	0	0	1
1980—Dallas NFL	16	436	260	59.6	3287	28	25	7.54	27	114	4.2	1	1	6	8
1981—Dallas NFL	16	391	223	57.0	3098	22	13	7.92	38	104	2.7	0	0	0	★14
1982—Dallas NFL	9	247	156	63.2	2079	16	12	8.42	17	91	5.4	0	0	0	★10
1983—Dallas NFL	16	533	334	62.7	3980	29	23	7.47	18	31	1.7	4	5	30	10
1984—Dallas NFL	14	233	126	54.1	1580	11	11	6.78	6	21	3.5	0	0	0	2
1985—Dallas NFL	14	450	267	59.3	3157	21	17	7.02	22	44	2.0	1	2	12	6
1986—Dallas NFL	7	153	95	62.1	1157	12	5	7.56	8	16	2.0	1	1	6	6
1987—Dallas NFL	11	362	215	59.4	2617	12	17	7.23	10	14	1.4	1	1	6	9
WFL Totals—2 Years	....	350	183	52.3	2635	21	17	7.53	47	219	4.7	0	0	0	....
NFL Totals—12 Years	163	2908	1732	59.6	21685	154	129	7.46	159	482	3.0	8	10	60	68
Pro Totals—14 Years	....	3258	1915	58.8	24320	175	146	7.46	206	701	3.4	8	10	60	....

NFL Quarterback Rating Points: 1976 (94.4), 1977 (10.4), 1978 (65.3), 1979 (58.6), 1980 (80.8), 1981 (87.5), 1982 (91.1), 1983 (85.6), 1984 (71.5), 1985 (80.6), 1986 (97.9), 1987 (73.2). Total—82.2.

		—————PUNTING—————		
Year Club	G.	No.	Avg.	Blk.
1974—Memphis WFL	....	80	40.9	0
1975—Memphis WFL	....	41	★45.1	0
1976—Dallas NFL	14	70	38.4	2
1977—Dallas NFL	14	80	39.6	1
1978—Dallas NFL	16	76	40.5	1
1979—Dallas NFL	16	76	41.7	0
1980—Dallas NFL	16	71	40.9	0
1981—Dallas NFL	16	79	40.8	0
1982—Dallas NFL	9	37	41.7	0
1983—Dallas NFL	16	38	40.6	1
1984—Dallas NFL	14	82	38.4	0
1985—Dallas NFL	14	1	43.0	0
1986—Dallas NFL	7	None		
1987—Dallas NFL	11	None		
WFL Totals—2 Years	....	121	42.3	0
NFL Totals—12 Years	163	610	40.3	5
Pro Totals—14 Years	....	731	40.6	5

Additional WFL statistics: Scored one action point, 1975.
Additional NFL statistics: Recovered one fumble, 1977; recovered two fumbles and fumbled twice for minus eight yards, 1978; recovered one fumble for 15 yards and caught one pass for minus nine yards, 1980; recovered eight fumbles and fumbled 14 times for minus 34 yards, 1981; recovered two fumbles, 1982; caught one pass for 15 yards and a touchdown and recovered four fumbles, 1983; recovered one fumble and fumbled twice for minus three yards, 1984; caught one pass for 12 yards and a touchdown, recovered two fumbles and fumbled six times for minus six yards, 1985;

recovered one fumble and fumbled six times for minus two yards, 1986; recovered three fumbles and fumbled nine times for minus seven yards, 1987.
Played in NFC Championship Game following 1977, 1978 and 1980 through 1982 seasons.
Played in NFL Championship Game following 1977 and 1978 seasons.
Played in Pro Bowl (NFL All-Star Game) following 1982 season.

BARRY T. WILBURN
Cornerback—Washington Redskins
Born December 9, 1963, at Memphis, Tenn.
Height, 6.03. Weight, 186.
High School—Memphis, Tenn., Melrose.
Attended University of Mississippi.

Selected by Washington in 8th round (219th player selected) of 1985 NFL draft.
Signed by Washington Redskins, July 18, 1985.

| | | | —INTERCEPTIONS— | | |
Year Club	G.	No.	Yds.	Avg.	TD.
1985—Washington NFL..........	16	1	10	10.0	0
1986—Washington NFL..........	16	2	14	7.0	0
1987—Washington NFL..........	12	*9	135	15.0	1
Pro Totals—3 Years............	44	12	159	3.3	1

Additional pro statistics: Recovered one fumble, 1985; recovered two fumbles, 1986.
Played in NFC Championship Game following 1986 and 1987 seasons.
Played in NFL Championship Game following 1987 season.

STEPHEN T. WILBURN
(Steve)
Defensive End—New England Patriots
Born February 25, 1961, at Chicago, Ill.
Height, 6.03. Weight, 255.
High School—Chicago, Ill., Mendel Catholic.
Attended Illinois State University.

Signed as free agent by Calgary Stampeders, June, 1983.
Released by Calgary Stampeders, August, 1985; signed as free agent by Saskatchewan Roughriders, September, 1985.
Released by Saskatchewan Roughriders, June, 1987; signed as free agent replacement player by New England Patriots, September 24, 1987.
Released by New England Patriots, October 26, 1987; re-signed by Patriots, January 27, 1988.
Calgary CFL, 1983 and 1984; Calgary (5)-Saskatchewan (4) CFL, 1985; Saskatchewan CFL, 1986; New England NFL, 1987.
Games: 1983 (11), 1984 (15), 1985 (9), 1986 (2), 1987 (3). Total CFL—37. Total Pro—40.
CFL statistics: Recovered one fumble, 1983 and 1984; intercepted one pass for no yards, 1984.

MIKE WILCHER
Linebacker—Los Angeles Rams
Born March 20, 1960, at Washington, D.C.
Height, 6.03. Weight, 235.
High School—Washington, D.C., Eastern.
Attended University of North Carolina.

Selected by Philadelphia in 1983 USFL territorial draft.
Selected by Los Angeles Rams in 2nd round (36th player selected) of 1983 NFL draft.
Signed by Los Angeles Rams NFL, June 16, 1983.
Los Angeles Rams NFL, 1983 through 1987.
Games: 1983 (15), 1984 (15), 1985 (16), 1986 (16), 1987 (12). Total—74.
Pro statistics: Intercepted one pass for no yards, 1985 and 1986; intercepted one pass for 11 yards and recovered one fumble for 35 yards and a touchdown, 1987.
Played in NFC Championship Game following 1985 season.

SOLOMON WILCOTS
Cornerback—Cincinnati Bengals
Born October 9, 1964, at Los Angeles, Calif.
Height, 5.11. Weight, 180.
High School—Riverside, Calif., Rubidoux.
Attended University of Colorado.

Selected by Cincinnati in 8th round (215th player selected) of 1987 NFL draft.
Signed by Cincinnati Bengals, July 22, 1987.
Cincinnati NFL, 1987.
Games: 1987 (12).
Pro statistics: Intercepted one pass for 37 yards, 1987.

JAMES CURTIS WILDER
Running Back—Tampa Bay Buccaneers
Born May 12, 1958, at Sikeston, Mo.
Height, 6.03. Weight, 225.
High School—Sikeston, Mo.
Attended Northeastern Oklahoma A&M and University of Missouri.

Established NFL records for most rushing attempts, season (407), 1984; most combined attempts, season (496), 1984.
Tied NFL record for most rushing attempts, game (43) vs. Green Bay Packers, September 30, 1984.
Selected by Tampa Bay in 2nd round (34th player selected) of 1981 NFL draft.
On injured reserve with broken ribs, November 15 through remainder of 1983 season.
On injured reserve with ankle injury, December 19 through remainder of 1986 season.

		—RUSHING—				PASS RECEIVING				—TOTAL—		
Year Club	G.	Att.	Yds.	Avg.	TD.	P.C.	Yds.	Avg.	TD.	TD.	Pts.	F.
1981—Tampa Bay NFL	16	107	370	3.5	4	48	507	10.6	1	5	30	3
1982—Tampa Bay NFL	9	83	324	3.9	3	53	466	8.8	1	4	24	5
1983—Tampa Bay NFL	10	161	640	4.0	4	57	380	6.7	2	6	36	1
1984—Tampa Bay NFL	16	*407	1544	3.8	13	85	685	8.1	0	13	78	10
1985—Tampa Bay NFL	16	365	1300	3.6	10	53	341	6.4	0	10	60	9
1986—Tampa Bay NFL	12	190	704	3.7	2	43	326	7.6	1	3	18	10
1987—Tampa Bay NFL	12	106	488	4.6	0	40	328	8.2	1	1	6	3
Pro Totals—7 Years	91	1419	5370	3.8	36	379	3033	8.0	6	42	252	41

Additional pro statistics: Returned one kickoff for 19 yards, 1981; recovered one fumble, 1981 and 1985; recovered one fumble for three yards, 1982; attempted one pass with one completion for 16 yards and a touchdown and recovered four fumbles, 1984; recovered three fumbles, 1986; recovered two fumbles, 1987.
Played in Pro Bowl (NFL All-Star Game) following 1984 season.

BRUCE ALAN WILKERSON
Guard-Offensive Tackle—Los Angeles Raiders
Born July 28, 1964, at Loudon, Tenn.
Height, 6.05. Weight, 280.
High School—Loudon, Tenn.
Attended University of Tennessee.
Selected by Los Angeles Raiders in 2nd round (52nd player selected) of 1987 NFL draft.
Signed by Los Angeles Raiders, July 10, 1987.
Crossed picket line during players' strike, October 2, 1987.
Los Angeles Raiders NFL, 1987.
Games: 1987 (11).

GARY CLIFTON WILKINS
Fullback—Atlanta Falcons
Born November 23, 1963, at West Palm Beach, Fla.
Height, 6.01. Weight, 235.
High School—West Palm Beach, Fla., Twin Lakes.
Attended Georgia Tech.
Selected by Jacksonville in 1985 USFL territorial draft.
Signed as free agent by Dallas Cowboys, May 3, 1985.
Released by Dallas Cowboys, August 16, 1985; signed as free agent by Buffalo Bills, July 19, 1986.
Released by Buffalo Bills, September 1, 1986; re-signed by Bills, September 2, 1986.
Released by Buffalo Bills, August 31, 1987; re-signed as replacement player by Bills, October 17, 1987.
Released by Buffalo Bills, November 3, 1987; signed as free agent by Atlanta Falcons for 1988, December 10, 1987.

		—RUSHING—				PASS RECEIVING				—TOTAL—		
Year Club	G.	Att.	Yds.	Avg.	TD.	P.C.	Yds.	Avg.	TD.	TD.	Pts.	F.
1986—Buffalo NFL	16	3	18	6.0	0	8	74	9.3	0	0	0	0
1987—Buffalo NFL	1			None				None		0	0	0
Pro Totals—2 Years	17	3	18	6.0	0	8	74	9.3	0	0	0	0

JIMMY RAY WILKS
(Jim)
Defensive End—New Orleans Saints
Born March 12, 1958, at Los Angeles, Calif.
Height, 6.05. Weight, 265.
High School—Pasadena, Calif.
Attended Pasadena Community College and San Diego State University.
Selected by New Orleans in 12th round (305th player selected) of 1981 NFL draft.
On inactive list, September 19, 1982.
New Orleans NFL, 1981 through 1987.
Games: 1981 (16), 1982 (8), 1983 (16), 1984 (16), 1985 (16), 1986 (16), 1987 (12). Total—100.
Pro statistics: Recovered two fumbles, 1981; recovered one fumble, 1983 and 1984; recovered one fumble for 10 yards, 1987.

GERALD WILLIAM WILLHITE
Running Back—Denver Broncos
Born May 30, 1959, at Sacramento, Calif.
Height, 5.10. Weight, 200.
High School—Rancho Cordova, Calif., Cordova.
Attended American River Junior College and San Jose State University.
Brother of Kevin Willhite, rookie running back with Green Bay Packers;
and Randy Willhite, defensive back at University of Oregon.
Selected by Denver in 1st round (21st player selected) of 1982 NFL draft.
On injured reserve with pulled hamstring, August 30 through October 27, 1983; activated, October 28, 1983.

— 438 —

On injured reserve with broken leg, October 28 through remainder of 1987 season.

Year Club	G.	Att.	RUSHING Yds.	Avg.	TD.	PASS RECEIVING P.C.	Yds.	Avg.	TD.	TOTAL TD.	Pts.	F.
1982—Denver NFL	9	70	347	5.0	2	26	227	8.7	0	2	12	5
1983—Denver NFL	8	43	188	4.4	3	14	153	10.9	1	4	24	0
1984—Denver NFL	16	77	371	4.8	2	27	298	11.0	0	2	12	3
1985—Denver NFL	15	66	237	3.6	3	35	297	8.5	1	4	24	2
1986—Denver NFL	16	85	365	4.3	5	64	529	8.3	3	9	54	5
1987—Denver NFL	3	26	141	5.4	0	9	25	2.8	0	0	0	1
Pro Totals—6 Years	67	367	1649	4.5	15	175	1529	8.7	5	21	126	16

Year Club	G.	PUNT RETURNS No.	Yds.	Avg.	TD.	KICKOFF RET. No.	Yds.	Avg.TD.	
1982—Denver NFL	9	6	63	10.5	0	17	337	19.8	0
1983—Denver NFL	8		None				None		
1984—Denver NFL	16	20	200	10.0	0	4	109	27.3	0
1985—Denver NFL	15	16	169	10.6	0	2	40	20.0	0
1986—Denver NFL	16	42	468	11.1	1	3	35	11.7	0
1987—Denver NFL	3	4	22	5.5	0		None		
Pro Totals—6 Years	67	88	922	10.5	1	26	521	20.0	0

Additional pro statistics: Attempted two passes with no completions and one interception, 1982; attempted one pass with no completions, 1983 and 1987; attempted two passes with one completion for 20 yards and recovered two fumbles, 1984; attempted three passes with no completions, 1985; attempted four passes with one completion for 11 yards and recovered three fumbles, 1986.

Played in AFC Championship Game following 1986 season.
Played in NFL Championship Game following 1986 season.

ALPHONSO WILLIAMS
(Al)
Wide Receiver—San Diego Chargers
Born February 4, 1962, at Vidalia, Ga.
Height, 5.10. Weight, 180.
High School—Long Beach, Calif., Poly.
Attended University of Nevada at Reno.

Selected by Denver in 18th round (361st player selected) of 1984 USFL draft.
USFL rights traded by Denver Gold to Oklahoma Outlaws for draft choice, March 7, 1984.
Signed by Oklahoma Outlaws, March 8, 1984.
Selected by Detroit in 1st round (20th player selected) of 1984 NFL supplemental draft.
Protected in merger of Oklahoma Outlaws and Arizona Wranglers, December 6, 1984.
Granted free agency, August 1, 1985; re-signed by Outlaws, August 21, 1985.
Granted free agency when USFL suspended operations, August 7, 1986; signed by Detroit Lions, September 16, 1986.
Granted roster exemption, September 16 through September 28, 1986; activated, September 29, 1986.
Released by Detroit Lions, October 3, 1986; signed as free agent by San Diego Chargers, April 13, 1987.
Released by San Diego Chargers, August 27, 1987; awarded on waivers to New Orleans Saints, August 28, 1987.
Released by New Orleans Saints, September 7, 1987; signed as free agent replacement player by San Diego Chargers, September 24, 1987.
On injured reserve with hamstring injury, November 21 through remainder of 1987 season.

Year Club	G.	PASS RECEIVING P.C.	Yds.	Avg.	TD.
1984—Oklahoma USFL	16	50	1087	*21.7	7
1985—Arizona USFL	18	55	1020	18.6	8
1987—San Diego NFL	3	12	247	20.6	1
USFL Totals—2 Years	34	105	2107	20.1	15
NFL Totals—1 Year	3	12	247	20.6	1
Pro Totals—3 Years	37	117	2354	20.1	16

Additional USFL statistics: Fumbled once, 1984 and 1985; rushed twice for two yards and recovered one fumble, 1985.
Additional NFL statistics: Returned 10 punts for 96 yards, rushed once for 11 yards and fumbled once, 1987.

BRENT DIONE WILLIAMS
Defensive End—New England Patriots
Born October 23, 1964, at Flint, Mich.
Height, 6.03. Weight, 278.
High School—Flint, Mich., Northern.
Received degree in marketing from University of Toledo in 1986.

Selected by New England in 7th round (192nd player selected) of 1986 NFL draft.
Signed by New England Patriots, July 16, 1986.
New England NFL, 1986 and 1987.
Games: 1986 (16), 1987 (12). Total—28.
Pro statistics: Recovered four fumbles for 54 yards and a touchdown, 1986.

—DID YOU KNOW—
That when the Bears and Vikings both won their respective games during Week 1 by the score of 34-19, it marked the first time that either franchise had won by that score?

DARRYL EUGENE WILLIAMS
(Dokie)
Wide Receiver—San Francisco 49ers

Born August 25, 1960, at Oceanside, Calif.
Height, 5.11. Weight, 180.
High School—Oceanside, Calif., El Camino.
Received degree in political science from University of California at Los Angeles.
Selected by Oakland in 8th round (90th player selected) of 1983 USFL draft.
Selected by Los Angeles Raiders in 5th round (138th player selected) of 1983 NFL draft.
Signed by Los Angeles Raiders, July 6, 1983.
On injured reserve with knee injury, December 17 through remainder of 1986 season.
Traded with 2nd and 4th round picks in 1988 draft by Los Angeles Raiders to San Francisco 49ers for 1st round pick in 1988 draft, April 24, 1988.

			PASS RECEIVING				—KICKOFF RET.—				—TOTAL—		
Year	Club	G.	P.C.	Yds.	Avg.	TD.	No.	Yds.	Avg.	TD.	TD.	Pts.	F.
1983—Los Angeles Raiders NFL		16	14	259	18.5	3	5	88	17.6	0	3	18	2
1984—Los Angeles Raiders NFL		16	22	509	23.1	4	24	621	25.9	0	4	24	0
1985—Los Angeles Raiders NFL		16	48	925	19.3	5	1	19	19.0	0	5	30	0
1986—Los Angeles Raiders NFL		15	43	843	19.6	8		None			8	48	2
1987—Los Angeles Raiders NFL		11	21	330	15.7	5	14	221	15.8	0	5	30	0
Pro Totals—5 Years		74	148	2866	19.4	25	44	949	21.6	0	25	150	4

Additional pro statistics: Rushed three times for 27 yards, 1986; recovered one fumble, 1986 and 1987.
Member of Los Angeles Raiders for AFC Championship Game following 1983 season; did not play.
Played in NFL Championship Game following 1983 season.

DERWIN DAWAYNE WILLIAMS
Wide Receiver—Tampa Bay Buccaneers

Born May 6, 1961, at Brownwood, Tex.
Height, 6.01. Weight, 185.
High School—Brownwood, Tex.
Attended University of New Mexico.
Selected by New England in 7th round (192nd player selected) of 1984 NFL draft.
On injured reserve with concussion, August 27 through entire 1984 season.
On injured reserve with knee injury, January 4, 1986 through remainder of 1985 season playoffs.
Granted free agency with no qualifying offer, February 1, 1988; signed by Tampa Bay Buccaneers, April 5, 1988.

			——PASS RECEIVING——			
Year	Club	G.	P.C.	Yds.	Avg.	TD.
1985—New England NFL		16	9	163	18.1	0
1986—New England NFL		16	2	35	17.5	0
1987—New England NFL		10	3	30	10.0	0
Pro Totals—3 Years		42	14	228	16.3	0

Additional pro statistics: Recovered one fumble, 1987.

DOUG WILLIAMS
Offensive Tackle-Guard—Houston Oilers

Born October 1, 1962, at Cincinnati, O.
Height, 6.05. Weight, 285.
High School—Cincinnati, O., Moeller.
Attended Texas A&M University.
Selected by Jacksonville in 1986 USFL territorial draft.
USFL rights traded with rights to center Leonard Burton by Jacksonville Bulls to Memphis Showboats for rights to wide receiver Tim McGee, May 6, 1986.
Selected by New York Jets in 2nd round (49th player selected) of 1986 NFL draft.
Signed by New York Jets, July 27, 1986.
Released by New York Jets, August 25, 1986; awarded on waivers to Houston Oilers, August 26, 1986.
Crossed picket line during players' strike, October 14, 1987.
Houston NFL, 1986 and 1987.
Games: 1986 (15), 1987 (8). Total—23.

DOUGLAS LEE WILLIAMS
(Doug)
Quarterback—Washington Redskins

Born August 9, 1955, at Zachary, La.
Height, 6.04. Weight, 220.
High School—Zachary, La., Chaneyville.
Received bachelor of science degree in education from Grambling State University in 1978.
Brother of Robert J. Williams, pitcher in Cleveland Indians' organization, 1964 and 1965.
Named as quarterback on THE SPORTING NEWS College All-America Team, 1977.
Selected by Tampa Bay in 1st round (17th player selected) of 1978 NFL draft.
Granted free agency, February 1, 1983; signed by Oklahoma Outlaws, August 8, 1983.
USFL rights traded by Boston Breakers to Oklahoma Outlaws for rights to running back Cliff Chatman and future draft pick, October 11, 1983.
On injured reserve with knee injury, June 4 through remainder of 1984 season.
Protected in merger of Oklahoma Outlaws and Arizona Wranglers, December 6, 1984.

Granted free agency when USFL suspended operations, August 7, 1986; re-signed by Tampa Bay Buccaneers and traded to Washington Redskins for 5th round pick in 1987 draft and conditional pick in 1988 draft, August 13, 1986.
Granted roster exemption, August 13 through August 22, 1986; activated, August 23, 1986.

				PASSING						RUSHING				—TOTAL—		
Year	Club	G.	Att.	Cmp.	Pct.	Gain	T.P.	P.I.	Avg.	Att.	Yds.	Avg.	TD.	TD.	Pts.	F.
1978—Tampa Bay NFL		10	194	73	37.6	1170	7	8	6.03	27	23	0.9	1	1	6	5
1979—Tampa Bay NFL		16	397	166	41.8	2448	18	24	6.17	35	119	3.4	2	2	12	2
1980—Tampa Bay NFL		16	521	254	48.8	3396	20	16	6.52	58	370	6.4	4	4	24	7
1981—Tampa Bay NFL		16	471	238	50.5	3563	19	14	7.56	48	209	4.4	4	4	24	9
1982—Tampa Bay NFL		9	307	164	53.4	2071	9	11	6.75	35	158	4.5	2	2	12	9
1984—Oklahoma USFL		15	528	261	49.4	3084	15	21	5.84	28	89	3.2	3	3	18	13
1985—Arizona USFL		17	509	271	53.2	3673	21	17	7.22	27	82	3.0	1	1	6	9
1986—Washington NFL		1	1	0	0.0	0	0	0	0.00		None			0	0	0
1987—Washington NFL		5	143	81	56.6	1156	11	5	8.08	7	9	1.3	1	1	6	3
NFL Totals—7 Years		73	2034	976	48.0	13804	84	78	6.79	210	888	4.2	14	14	84	35
USFL Totals—2 Years		32	1037	532	51.3	6757	36	38	6.52	55	171	3.1	4	4	24	22
Pro Totals—9 Years		105	3071	1508	49.1	20561	120	116	6.70	265	1059	4.0	18	18	108	57

NFL Quarterback Rating Points: 1978 (53.5), 1979 (52.6), 1980 (69.7), 1981 (76.5), 1982 (69.4), 1986 (39.6), 1987 (94.0). Total—68.2.
USFL Quarterback Rating Points: 1984 (60.5), 1985 (76.4). Total—68.3.
Additional NFL statistics: Recovered two fumbles, 1978 and 1980; fumbled five times for minus six yards, 1978; recovered one fumble and fumbled twice for minus five yards, 1979; recovered three fumbles and fumbled nine times for minus 13 yards, 1981; recovered four fumbles, 1982.
Additional USFL statistics: Recovered seven fumbles, 1984; recovered four fumbles, 1985.
Played in NFC Championship Game following 1979 and 1987 seasons.
Member of Washington Redskins for NFC Championship Game following 1986 season; did not play.
Played in NFL Championship Game following 1987 season.

COACHING RECORD
Assistant coach, Southern University, 1985.

EDMUND SCOTT WILLIAMS
(Known by middle name.)
Fullback—Detroit Lions
Born July 21, 1962, at Charlotte, N.C.
Height, 6.02. Weight, 234.
High School—Charlotte, N.C., North Mecklenburg.
Received bachelor of arts degree in speech communications from University of Georgia in 1985.
Selected by Jacksonville in 1985 USFL territorial draft.
Selected by St. Louis in 9th round (244th player selected) of 1985 NFL draft.
Signed by St. Louis Cardinals, July 21, 1985.
Released by St. Louis Cardinals, August 19, 1985; signed as free agent by Detroit Lions, March 6, 1986.
On injured reserve with shoulder injury, November 25 through remainder of 1987 season.

			RUSHING			PASS RECEIVING			—TOTAL—		
Year	Club	G.	Att.	Yds.	Avg.	TD.	P.C.	Yds.	Avg.	TD.	TD.	Pts.	F.
1986—Detroit NFL		16	13	22	1.7	2	2	9	4.5	0	2	12	0
1987—Detroit NFL		5	8	29	3.6	0	4	16	4.0	1	1	6	0
Pro Totals—2 Years		21	21	51	2.4	2	6	25	4.2	1	3	18	0

EDWARD EUGENE WILLIAMS
(Ed)
Linebacker—New England Patriots
Born August 9, 1961, at Odessa, Tex.
Height, 6.04. Weight, 244.
High School—Odessa, Tex., Ector.
Attended University of Texas.
Selected by San Antonio in 1984 USFL territorial draft.
Selected by New England in 2nd round (43rd player selected) of 1984 NFL draft.
Signed by New England Patriots, July 13, 1984.
On injured reserve with groin injury, November 14 through remainder of 1986 season.
New England NFL, 1984 through 1987.
Games: 1984 (14), 1985 (13), 1986 (8), 1987 (12). Total—47.
Pro statistics: Intercepted one pass for 51 yards and recovered two fumbles for eight yards, 1987.
Played in AFC Championship Game following 1985 season.
Played in NFL Championship Game following 1985 season.

ERIC MICHAEL WILLIAMS
Nose Tackle—Detroit Lions
Born February 24, 1962, at Stockton, Calif.
Height, 6.04. Weight, 280.
High School—Stockton, Calif., St. Mary's.
Attended Washington State University.
Son of Roy Williams, 2nd round selection of Detroit Lions in 1962 NFL draft.
Selected by New Jersey in 1st round (19th player selected) of 1984 USFL draft.
Selected by Detroit in 3rd round (62nd player selected) of 1984 NFL draft.

Signed by Detroit Lions, July 21, 1984.
On injured reserve with cracked cervical disc, December 4 through remainder of 1985 season.
Detroit NFL, 1984 through 1987.
Games: 1984 (12), 1985 (12), 1986 (16), 1987 (11). Total—51.
Pro statistics: Recovered one fumble, 1985 and 1986; intercepted one pass for two yards, 1986.

GERALD WILLIAMS
Defensive End-Defensive Tackle—Pittsburgh Steelers
Born September 3, 1963, at Waycross, Ga.
Height, 6.03. Weight, 270.
High School—Valley, Ala.
Attended Auburn University.

Selected by Birmingham in 1986 USFL territorial draft.
Selected by Pittsburgh in 2nd round (36th player selected) of 1986 NFL draft.
Signed by Pittsburgh Steelers, July 25, 1986.
Crossed picket line during players' strike, October 13, 1987.
Pittsburgh NFL, 1986 and 1987.
Games: 1986 (16), 1987 (9). Total—25.
Pro statistics: Recovered one fumble, 1987.

JAMES HENRY WILLIAMS
(Jimmy)
Linebacker—Detroit Lions
Born November 15, 1960, at Washington, D.C.
Height, 6.03. Weight, 230.
High School—Washington, D.C., Woodrow Wilson.
Attended University of Nebraska.
Brother of Toby Williams, nose tackle with New England Patriots.

Selected by Detroit in 1st round (15th player selected) of 1982 NFL draft.
On injured reserve with broken foot, December 20 through remainder of 1982 season.
Granted roster exemption, August 18 through August 21, 1986; activated, August 22, 1986.
On injured reserve with knee injury, November 11 through remainder of 1986 season.
Detroit NFL, 1982 through 1987.
Games: 1982 (6), 1983 (16), 1984 (16), 1985 (16), 1986 (10), 1987 (12). Total—76.
Pro statistics: Intercepted one pass for four yards, 1982; recovered one fumble, 1983 through 1986; intercepted two passes for 12 yards, 1986; intercepted two passes for 51 yards and recovered two fumbles, 1987.

JAMIE WILLIAMS
Tight End—Houston Oilers
Born February 25, 1960, at Vero Beach, Fla.
Height, 6.04. Weight, 245.
High School—Davenport, Ia., Central.
Attended University of Nebraska.

Selected by Boston in 1983 USFL territorial draft.
Selected by New York Giants in 3rd round (63rd player selected) of 1983 NFL draft.
Signed by New York Giants, June 30, 1983.
Released by New York Giants, August 29, 1983; signed as free agent by St. Louis Cardinals, September 13, 1983.
Released by St. Louis Cardinals, October 5, 1983; signed as free agent by Tampa Bay Buccaneers, January 25, 1984.
USFL rights traded by New Orleans Breakers to New Jersey Generals for past consideration, March 26, 1984.
Released by Tampa Bay Buccaneers, May 8, 1984; awarded on waivers to Houston Oilers, May 21, 1984.

| | | —PASS RECEIVING— | | | |
Year	Club	G.	P.C.	Yds.	Avg.	TD.
1983—St. Louis NFL		1		None		
1984—Houston NFL		16	41	545	13.3	3
1985—Houston NFL		16	39	444	11.4	1
1986—Houston NFL		16	22	227	10.3	1
1987—Houston NFL		12	13	158	12.2	3
Pro Totals—5 Years		61	115	1374	11.9	8

Additional pro statistics: Returned one kickoff for no yards and fumbled twice, 1984; recovered one fumble, 1984, 1986 and 1987; returned two kickoffs for 21 yards and fumbled once, 1985.

JOEL WILLIAMS
First name pronounced Jo-EL.
Linebacker—Atlanta Falcons
Born December 13, 1956, at Miami, Fla.
Height, 6.01. Weight, 225.
High School—Miami, Fla., North.
Attended Peru College and received bachelor of business administration degree
from University of Wisconsin at LaCrosse in 1979.

Signed as free agent by Miami Dolphins, July 12, 1979.
Released by Miami Dolphins, August 27, 1979; claimed on waivers by Atlanta Falcons, August 28, 1979.
On injured reserve with knee injury, December 19 through remainder of 1981 season.
USFL rights released by Birmingham Stallions, August 16, 1983; rights awarded on waivers to Pittsburgh Maulers, August 17, 1983.
Traded by Atlanta Falcons to Philadelphia Eagles for 2nd round pick in 1984 draft, August 21, 1983.

Granted free agency, February 1, 1985; re-signed by Eagles, October 23, 1985.
Granted roster exemption, October 23 through November 3, 1985; activated, November 4, 1985.
Traded by Philadelphia Eagles to Atlanta Falcons for 5th round pick in 1986 draft, April 29, 1986.
Atlanta NFL, 1979 through 1982, 1986 and 1987; Philadelphia NFL, 1983 through 1985.
Games: 1979 (16), 1980 (16), 1981 (10), 1982 (9), 1983 (16), 1984 (16), 1985 (7), 1986 (15), 1987 (8). Total—113.
Pro statistics: Intercepted two passes for 55 yards, recovered three fumbles for 42 yards and one touchdown and credited with one safety, 1980; intercepted one pass for 25 yards and recovered two fumbles for 57 yards and a touchdown, 1981; recovered one fumble, 1982 and 1983; recovered two fumbles, 1984; intercepted two passes for 18 yards and a touchdown, 1986.

JOEL DAVID WILLIAMS
Tight End—Atlanta Falcons
Born March 16, 1965, at Pittsburgh, Pa.
Height, 6.03. Weight, 242.
High School—Monroeville, Pa., Gateway.
Received bachelor of arts degree in communications from University of Notre Dame in 1987.
Selected by Miami in 8th round (210th player selected) of 1987 NFL draft.
Signed by Miami Dolphins, July 22, 1987.
Released by Miami Dolphins, November 3, 1987; signed as free agent by Atlanta Falcons, April 15, 1988.
Miami NFL, 1987.
Games: 1987 (3).

JOHN L. WILLIAMS
(John L.)
Fullback—Seattle Seahawks
Born November 23, 1964, at Palatka, Fla.
Height, 5.11. Weight, 226.
High School—Palatka, Fla.
Attended University of Florida.
Selected by Tampa Bay in 1986 USFL territorial draft.
Selected by Seattle in 1st round (15th player selected) of 1986 NFL draft.
Signed by Seattle Seahawks, July 23, 1986.

		—RUSHING—			PASS RECEIVING				—TOTAL—		
Year	Club	G.	Att.	Yds.	Avg.	TD.	P.C.	Yds.	Avg.	TD.	TD.	Pts.	F.
1986—Seattle NFL		16	129	538	4.2	0	33	219	6.6	0	0	0	1
1987—Seattle NFL		12	113	500	4.4	1	38	420	11.1	3	4	24	2
Pro Totals—2 Years		28	242	1038	4.3	1	71	639	9.0	3	4	24	3

Additional pro statistic: Recovered one fumble, 1987.

KEITH WILLIAMS
Running Back—Tampa Bay Buccaneers
Born September 30, 1964, at St. Louis, Mo.
Height, 5.10. Weight, 173.
High School—St. Louis, Mo., Sumner.
Attended Southwest Missouri State University.
Selected by Atlanta in 6th round (159th player selected) of 1986 NFL draft.
Signed by Atlanta Falcons, July 17, 1986.
On injured reserve with neck injury, October 31 through November 26, 1986; activated after clearing procedural waivers, November 28, 1986.
Traded by Atlanta Falcons to Tampa Bay Buccaneers for conditional 7th round pick in 1988 draft, August 13, 1987.
On injured reserve with knee injury, August 25 through entire 1987 season.
Crossed picket line during players' strike, October 14, 1987.

		—RUSHING—				PASS RECEIVING				—TOTAL—		
Year	Club	G.	Att.	Yds.	Avg.	TD.	P.C.	Yds.	Avg.	TD.	TD.	Pts.	F.
1986—Atlanta NFL		12	3	18	6.0	0	12	164	13.7	1	1	6	1

		KICKOFF RETURNS			
Year	Club	G.	No.	Yds.	Avg.TD.
1986—Atlanta NFL		12	14	255	18.2	0

KEVIN J. WILLIAMS
Defensive Back—San Diego Chargers
Born November 28, 1961, at San Diego, Calif.
Height, 5.09. Weight, 169.
High School—San Diego, Calif., Crawford.
Attended San Diego City College and Iowa State University.
Selected by Los Angeles in 1st round (38th player selected) of 1985 USFL draft.
Signed as free agent by Washington Redskins, May 13, 1985.
Released by Washington Redskins, August 27, 1985; re-signed by Redskins, October 2, 1985.
Released by Washington Redskins, August 26, 1986; signed as free agent by Buffalo Bills, December 20, 1986.
On injured reserve with shoulder injury, September 1 through November 16, 1987.
Released by Buffalo Bills, November 17, 1987; signed as free agent by San Diego Chargers, March 4, 1988.
Washington NFL, 1985; Buffalo NFL, 1986.
Games: 1985 (12), 1986 (1). Total—13.

LAWRENCE RICHARD WILLIAMS II
(Larry)
Guard—Cleveland Browns
Born July 3, 1963, at Orange, Calif.
Height, 6.05. Weight, 290.
High School—Santa Ana, Calif., Mater Dei.
Received bachelor of arts degree in American studies (journalism) and business
from University of Notre Dame in 1985.
Selected by Portland in 10th round (136th player selected) of 1985 USFL draft.
Selected by Cleveland in 10th round (259th player selected) of 1985 NFL draft.
Signed by Cleveland Browns, July 15, 1985.
On injured reserve with wrist injury, August 20 through entire 1985 season.
Cleveland NFL, 1986 and 1987.
Games: 1986 (16), 1987 (12). Total—28.
Played in AFC Championship Game following 1986 and 1987 seasons.

LEE ERIC WILLIAMS
Defensive End—San Diego Chargers
Born October 15, 1962, at Fort Lauderdale, Fla.
Height, 6.05. Weight, 263.
High School—Fort Lauderdale, Fla., Stranahan.
Received degree in business administration from Bethune-Cookman College.
Selected by Tampa Bay in 1984 USFL territorial draft.
USFL rights traded with rights to defensive tackle Dewey Forte by Tampa Bay Bandits to Los Angeles Express for
draft choice, March 2, 1984.
Signed by Los Angeles Express, March 6, 1984.
Granted roster exemption, March 6 through March 15, 1984; activated, March 16, 1984.
Selected by San Diego in 1st round (6th player selected) of 1984 NFL supplemental draft.
Released by Los Angeles Express, October 20, 1984; signed by San Diego Chargers, October 22, 1984.
Granted roster exemption, October 22 through October 28, 1984; activated, October 29, 1984.
Los Angeles USFL, 1984; San Diego NFL, 1984 through 1987.
Games: 1984 USFL (14), 1984 NFL (8), 1985 (16), 1986 (16), 1987 (12). Total NFL—52. Total Pro—66.
USFL statistics: Credited with 13 sacks for 92 yards, 1984.
NFL statistics: Intercepted one pass for 66 yards and a touchdown, 1984; intercepted one pass for 17 yards and
recovered one fumble for two yards, 1985; recovered one fumble for six yards, 1986; credited with a safety, 1987.

LESTER WILLIAMS
Nose Tackle—Seattle Seahawks
Born January 19, 1959, at Miami, Fla.
Height, 6.03. Weight, 272.
High School—Miami, Fla., Carol City.
Attended University of Miami (Fla.).
Named as defensive end on THE SPORTING NEWS College All-America Team, 1981.
Selected by New England in 1st round (27th player selected) of 1982 NFL draft.
On injured reserve with broken arm, October 17 through remainder of 1984 season.
On injured reserve with knee injury, September 3 through October 17, 1985; activated, October 18, 1985.
Released by New England Patriots, August 26, 1986; signed as free agent by San Diego Chargers, September 10,
1986.
Released by San Diego Chargers, October 11, 1986; signed as free agent by St. Louis Cardinals, July 14, 1987.
Placed on did not report list and released, July 18, 1987; signed as free agent replacement player by Seattle
Seahawks, October 9, 1987.
Released by Seattle Seahawks, October 19, 1987; re-signed by Seahawks for 1988, October 22, 1987.
New England NFL, 1982 through 1985; San Diego NFL, 1986; Seattle NFL, 1987.
Games: 1982 (9), 1983 (15), 1984 (7), 1985 (9), 1986 (4), 1987 (2). Total—46.
Pro statistics: Recovered one fumble, 1982 and 1984.
Played in AFC Championship Game following 1985 season.
Played in NFL Championship Game following 1985 season.

PERRY LAMAR WILLIAMS
Cornerback—New York Giants
Born May 12, 1961, at Hamlet, N.C.
Height, 6.02. Weight, 203.
High School—Hamlet, N.C., Richmond County.
Attended North Carolina State University.
Selected by Washington in 7th round (76th player selected) of 1983 USFL draft.
Selected by New York Giants in 7th round (178th player selected) of 1983 NFL draft.
Signed by New York Giants, June 13, 1983.
On injured reserve with foot injury, August 17 through entire 1983 season.
On injured reserve with pinched nerve, September 7 through October 23, 1987; activated, October 24, 1987.

Year Club	G.	No.	Yds.	Avg.	TD.
1984—N.Y. Giants NFL	16	3	7	2.3	0
1985—N.Y. Giants NFL	16	2	28	14.0	0
1986—N.Y. Giants NFL	16	4	31	7.8	0
1987—N.Y. Giants NFL	10	1	—5	—5.0	0
Pro Totals—4 Years	58	10	61	6.1	0

— 444 —

Additional pro statistics: Recovered one fumble, 1984 and 1985; recovered two fumbles for one yard, 1987.
Played in NFC Championship Game following 1986 season.
Played in NFL Championship Game following 1986 season.

REGINALD WILLIAMS
(Reggie)
Linebacker—Cincinnati Bengals
Born September 19, 1954, at Flint, Mich.
Height, 6.00. Weight, 228.
High School—Flint, Mich., Southwestern.
Received bachelor of arts degree in psychology from Dartmouth College.

Selected by Cincinnati in 3rd round (82nd player selected) of 1976 NFL draft.
Crossed picket line during players' strike, September 30, 1987.

| | | | —INTERCEPTIONS— | | |
Year Club	G.	No.	Yds.	Avg.	TD.
1976—Cincinnati NFL.............	14	1	17	17.0	0
1977—Cincinnati NFL.............	14	3	67	22.3	1
1978—Cincinnati NFL.............	16	1	11	11.0	0
1979—Cincinnati NFL.............	12	2	5	2.5	0
1980—Cincinnati NFL.............	14	2	8	4.0	0
1981—Cincinnati NFL.............	16	4	33	8.3	0
1982—Cincinnati NFL.............	9	1	20	20.0	0
1983—Cincinnati NFL.............	16		None		
1984—Cincinnati NFL.............	16	2	33	16.5	0
1985—Cincinnati NFL.............	16		None		
1986—Cincinnati NFL.............	16		None		
1987—Cincinnati NFL.............	15		None		
Pro Totals—12 Years.........	174	16	194	12.1	1

Additional pro statistics: Recovered blocked punt in end zone for a touchdown, recovered two fumbles, 1977, 1980 and 1987; returned one punt for no yards, 1977 and 1980; fumbled once, 1977 and 1980; recovered one fumble for 30 yards, 1978; recovered one fumble, 1979, 1980 and 1986; recovered three fumbles, 1981, recovered four fumbles and credited with one safety, 1982; recovered four fumbles for 59 yards and a touchdown, 1983; recovered four fumbles for four yards, 1985.
Played in AFC Championship Game following 1981 season.
Played in NFL Championship Game following 1981 season.

ROBERT COLE WILLIAMS
Cornerback—Dallas Cowboys
Born October 2, 1962, at Galveston, Tex.
Height, 5.10. Weight, 190.
High School—Galveston, Tex., Ball.
Attended Baylor University.

Signed as free agent by Washington Redskins, May 1, 1986.
Released by Washington Redskins, August 4, 1986; signed as free agent by Dallas Cowboys, April 10, 1987.
Released by Dallas Cowboys, September 7, 1987; re-signed as replacement player by Cowboys, September 23, 1987.
Dallas NFL, 1987.
Games: 1987 (11).
Pro statistics: Recovered one fumble, 1987.

TOBIAS WILLIAMS
(Toby)
Nose Tackle—New England Patriots
Born November 19, 1959, at Washington, D.C.
Height, 6.04. Weight, 270.
High School—Washington, D.C., Woodrow Wilson.
Received bachelor of arts degree in criminal justice from University of Nebraska in 1983.
Brother of Jimmy Williams, linebacker with Detroit Lions.

Selected by Boston in 1983 USFL territorial draft.
Selected by New England in 10th round (265th player selected) of 1983 NFL draft.
Signed by New England Patriots, May 25, 1983.
On injured reserve with knee injury, October 18 through remainder of 1985 season.
New England NFL, 1983 through 1987.
Games: 1983 (16), 1984 (16), 1985 (5), 1986 (16), 1987 (12). Total—65.
Pro statistics: Recovered one fumble, 1984.

CARLTON WILLIAMSON
Safety—San Francisco 49ers
Born June 12, 1958, at Atlanta, Ga.
Height, 6.00. Weight, 204.
High School—Atlanta, Ga., Brown.
Received degree in urban science from University of Pittsburgh in 1981.

Selected by San Francisco in 3rd round (65th player selected) of 1981 NFL draft.
On injured reserve with fractured fibula, August 30 through October 21, 1983; activated, October 22, 1983.
On injured reserve with knee injury, October 23 through November 20, 1987; activated, November 21, 1987.

Year Club	G.	No.	Yds.	Avg.	TD.
1981—San Francisco NFL	16	4	44	11.0	0
1982—San Francisco NFL	8		None		
1983—San Francisco NFL	9	4	51	12.8	0
1984—San Francisco NFL	15	2	42	21.0	0
1985—San Francisco NFL	16	3	137	45.7	*1
1986—San Francisco NFL	16	3	3	1.0	0
1987—San Francisco NFL	8	1	17	17.0	0
Pro Totals—7 Years...........	88	17	294	17.3	1

Additional pro statistics: Recovered two fumbles for three yards, 1981; recovered one fumble, 1986.
Played in NFC Championship Game following 1981, 1983 and 1984 seasons.
Played in NFL Championship Game following 1981 and 1984 seasons.
Played in Pro Bowl (NFL All-Star Game) following 1984 and 1985 seasons.

KEITH WILLIS
Defensive End—Pittsburgh Steelers
Born July 29, 1959, at Newark, N.J.
Height, 6.01. Weight, 260.
High School—Newark, N.J., Malcolm X. Shabazz.
Attended Northwestern University.

Signed as free agent by Pittsburgh Steelers, April 30, 1982.
Pittsburgh NFL, 1982 through 1987.
Games: 1982 (9), 1983 (14), 1984 (12), 1985 (16), 1986 (16), 1987 (11). Total—78.
Pro statistics: Recovered one fumble, 1983 and 1984.
Played in AFC Championship Game following 1984 season.

OTIS MITCHELL WILLIS
(Mitch)
Defensive Tackle—Los Angeles Raiders
Born March 16, 1962, at Dallas, Tex.
Height, 6.08. Weight, 280.
High School—Arlington, Tex., Lamar.
Received bachelor of business administration degree from Southern Methodist University in 1984.

Selected by San Antonio in 4th round (68th player selected) of 1984 USFL draft.
Selected by Los Angeles Raiders in 7th round (183rd player selected) of 1984 NFL draft.
Signed by Los Angeles Raiders, June 15, 1984.
On injured reserve with shoulder injury, August 27 through entire 1984 season.
On injured reserve with knee injury, September 7 through October 4, 1985; activated, October 5, 1985.
Los Angeles Raiders NFL, 1985 through 1987.
Games: 1985 (11), 1986 (16), 1987 (10). Total—37.

CHARLES WADE WILSON
(Known by middle name.)
Quarterback—Minnesota Vikings
Born February 1, 1959, at Greenville, Tex.
Height, 6.03. Weight, 206.
High School—Commerce, Tex.
Attended East Texas State University.

Selected by Minnesota in 8th round (210th player selected) of 1981 NFL draft.
On inactive list, September 12, 1982.
On commissioner's exempt list, November 20 through December 7, 1982; activated, December 8, 1982.
Active for 4 games with Minnesota Vikings in 1982; did not play.

Year Club	G.	Att.	Cmp.	Pct.	Gain	T.P.	P.I.	Avg.	Att.	Yds.	Avg.	TD.	TD.	Pts.	F.
1981—Minnesota NFL.............	3	13	6	46.2	48	0	2	3.69		None			0	0	2
1983—Minnesota NFL.............	1	28	16	57.1	124	1	2	4.43	3	−3	−1.0	0	0	0	1
1984—Minnesota NFL.............	8	195	102	52.3	1019	5	11	5.23	9	30	3.3	0	0	0	2
1985—Minnesota NFL.............	4	60	33	55.0	404	3	3	6.73		None			0	0	0
1986—Minnesota NFL.............	9	143	80	55.9	1165	7	5	8.15	13	9	0.7	1	1	6	3
1987—Minnesota NFL.............	12	264	140	53.0	2106	14	13	*7.98	41	263	6.4	5	5	30	3
Pro Totals—7 Years..........	37	703	377	53.6	4866	30	36	6.92	66	299	4.5	6	6	36	11

Quarterback Rating Points: 1981 (16.4), 1983 (50.3), 1984 (52.5), 1985 (71.8), 1986 (84.4), 1987 (76.7). Total—68.7.
Additional pro statistics: Recovered one fumble, 1981; punted twice for a 38.0 average with one blocked, recovered one fumble and fumbled three times for minus two yards, 1986; fumbled three times for minus three yards, 1987.
Played in NFC Championship Game following 1987 season.

DAVID CARLTON WILSON
(Dave)
Quarterback—New Orleans Saints
Born April 27, 1959, at Anaheim, Calif.
Height, 6.03. Weight, 206.
High School—Anaheim, Calif., Katella.
Attended Fullerton Junior College and University of Illinois.

Selected by New Orleans in NFL supplementary draft, July 7, 1981; Saints forfeited 1st round pick in 1982 draft.
On injured reserve with knee injury, August 15 through entire 1982 season.
On injured reserve with elbow injury, November 15 through remainder of 1985 season.

			PASSING						RUSHING				TOTAL		
Year Club	G.	Att.	Cmp.	Pct.	Gain	T.P.	P.I.	Avg.	Att.	Yds.	Avg.	TD.	TD.	Pts.	F.
1981—New Orleans NFL............	11	159	82	51.6	1058	1	11	6.65	5	1	0.2	0	0	0	4
1983—New Orleans NFL............	8	112	66	58.9	770	5	7	6.88	5	3	0.6	1	1	6	5
1984—New Orleans NFL............	5	93	51	54.8	647	7	4	6.96	3	—7	—2.3	0	0	0	2
1985—New Orleans NFL............	10	293	145	49.5	1843	11	15	6.29	18	7	0.4	0	0	0	6
1986—New Orleans NFL............	14	342	189	55.3	2353	10	17	6.88	14	19	1.4	1	1	6	8
1987—New Orleans NFL............	4	24	13	54.2	243	2	0	10.13			None		0	0	0
Pro Totals—6 Years...........	52	1023	546	53.4	6914	36	54	6.76	45	23	0.5	2	2	12	25

Quarterback Rating Points: 1981 (46.1), 1983 (68.7), 1984 (83.9), 1985 (60.7), 1986 (65.8), 1987 (117.2). Total—64.3.
Additional pro statistics: Recovered three fumbles and fumbled four times for minus eight yards, 1981; recovered one fumble and fumbled six times for minus 23 yards, 1985; recovered four fumbles and fumbled eight times for minus four yards, 1986.

KARL WENDELL WILSON
Defensive End—San Diego Chargers
Born September 10, 1964, at Amite, La.
Height, 6.04. Weight, 268.
High School—Baker, La.
Received degree in general studies from Louisiana State University in 1987.

Selected by San Diego in 3rd round (59th player selected) of 1987 NFL draft.
Signed by San Diego Chargers, July 29, 1987.
On injured reserve with hamstring injury, November 3 through December 4, 1987; activated, December 5, 1987.
San Diego NFL, 1987.
Games: 1987 (7).

MARC DOUGLAS WILSON
Quarterback
Born February 15, 1957, at Bremerton, Wash.
Height, 6.06. Weight, 205.
High School—Seattle, Wash., Shorecrest.
Received bachelor of arts degree in economics from Brigham Young University in 1980.

Selected by Oakland in 1st round (15th player selected) of 1980 NFL draft.
Franchise transferred to Los Angeles, May 7, 1982.
On injured reserve with dislocated shoulder, November 7 through December 30, 1983; activated, December 31, 1983.
Crossed picket line during players' strike, September 23, 1987.
Granted free agency, February 1, 1988; Los Angeles Raiders exercised option not to re-sign, June 1, 1988.

			PASSING						RUSHING				TOTAL		
Year Club	G.	Att.	Cmp.	Pct.	Gain	T.P.	P.I.	Avg.	Att.	Yds.	Avg.	TD.	TD.	Pts.	F.
1980—Oakland NFL....................	2	5	3	60.0	31	0	0	6.20	1	3	3.0	0	0	0	0
1981—Oakland NFL....................	13	366	173	47.3	2311	14	19	6.31	30	147	4.9	2	2	12	8
1982—L.A. Raiders NFL.............	8	2	1	50.0	4	0	0	2.00			None		0	0	0
1983—L.A. Raiders NFL.............	10	117	67	57.3	864	8	6	7.38	13	122	9.4	0	0	0	4
1984—L.A. Raiders NFL.............	16	282	153	54.3	2151	15	17	7.63	30	56	1.9	1	1	6	11
1985—L.A. Raiders NFL.............	16	388	193	49.7	2608	16	21	6.72	24	98	4.1	2	2	12	8
1986—L.A. Raiders NFL.............	16	240	129	53.8	1721	12	15	7.17	14	45	3.2	0	0	0	6
1987—L.A. Raiders NFL.............	15	266	152	57.1	2070	12	8	7.78	17	91	5.4	0	0	0	1
Pro Totals—7 Years..........	96	1666	871	52.3	11760	77	86	7.06	129	562	4.4	5	5	30	38

Quarterback Rating Points: 1980 (77.9), 1981 (58.8), 1982 (56.3), 1983 (82.0), 1984 (71.7), 1985 (62.7), 1986 (67.4), 1987 (84.6). Total—68.8.
Additional pro statistics: Recovered two fumbles and fumbled eight times for minus three yards, 1981; recovered one fumble, 1983; recovered three fumbles and fumbled 11 times for minus 11 yards, 1984; recovered two fumbles and fumbled eight times for minus four yards, 1985; recovered one fumble and fumbled six times for minus 10 yards, 1986.
Played in AFC Championship Game following 1983 season.
Member of Oakland Raiders for AFC Championship Game following 1980 season; did not play.
Played in NFL Championship Game following 1983 season.
Member of Oakland Raiders for NFL Championship Game following 1980 season; did not play.

MICHAEL RUBEN WILSON
(Mike)
Wide Receiver—San Francisco 49ers
Born December 19, 1958, at Los Angeles, Calif.
Height, 6.03. Weight, 215.
High School—Carson, Calif.
Attended Washington State University.

Selected by Dallas in 9th round (246th player selected) of 1981 NFL draft.
Released by Dallas Cowboys, August 24, 1981; signed as free agent by San Francisco 49ers, August 27, 1981.
On injured reserve with broken finger, September 9 through November 19, 1982; activated, November 20, 1982.
On injured reserve with neck injury, November 21 through remainder of 1986 season.

Year Club	G.	P.C.	Yds.	Avg.	TD.
1981—San Francisco NFL	16	9	125	13.9	1
1982—San Francisco NFL	6	6	80	13.3	1
1983—San Francisco NFL	15	30	433	14.4	0
1984—San Francisco NFL	13	17	245	14.4	1
1985—San Francisco NFL	16	10	165	16.5	2
1986—San Francisco NFL	11	9	104	11.6	1
1987—San Francisco NFL	11	29	450	15.5	5
Pro Totals—7 Years...........	88	110	1602	14.6	11

Additional pro statistics: Returned four kickoffs for 67 yards, 1981; recovered one fumble, 1981 and 1986; fumbled once, 1983; returned one kickoff for 14 yards, 1984; returned one kickoff for 10 yards and recovered two fumbles, 1986.
Played in NFC Championship Game following 1981, 1983 and 1984 seasons.
Played in NFL Championship Game following 1981 and 1984 seasons.

OTIS RAY WILSON
Linebacker—Chicago Bears
Born September 15, 1957, at New York, N.Y.
Height, 6.02. Weight, 227.
High School—Brooklyn, N.Y., Thomas Jefferson.
Attended Syracuse University and University of Louisville.

Named as linebacker on THE SPORTING NEWS College All-America Team, 1979.
Selected by Chicago in 1st round (19th player selected) of 1980 NFL draft.
On suspended list, December 2 through December 7, 1986; activated, December 8, 1986.
On injured reserve with knee injury, November 11 through December 13, 1987; activated, December 14, 1987.

Year Club	G.	No.	Yds.	Avg.	TD.
1980—Chicago NFL	16	2	4	2.0	0
1981—Chicago NFL	15		None		
1982—Chicago NFL	9	2	39	19.5	*1
1983—Chicago NFL	16	1	6	6.0	0
1984—Chicago NFL	15		None		
1985—Chicago NFL	16	3	35	11.7	*1
1986—Chicago NFL	15	2	31	15.5	0
1987—Chicago NFL	7		None		
Pro Totals—8 Years...........	109	10	115	11.5	2

Additional pro statistics: Fumbled once, 1980; recovered three fumbles for 31 yards, 1981; recovered two fumbles and credited with one safety, 1985; recovered three fumbles, 1986.
Played in NFC Championship Game following 1984 and 1985 seasons.
Played in NFL Championship Game following 1985 season.
Played in Pro Bowl (NFL All-Star Game) following 1985 season.

STANLEY T. WILSON
Running Back—Cincinnati Bengals
Born August 23, 1961, at Los Angeles, Calif.
Height, 5.10. Weight, 210.
High School—Banning, Calif.
Attended University of Oklahoma.

Selected by New Jersey in 1983 USFL territorial draft.
Selected by Cincinnati in 9th round (248th player selected) of 1983 NFL draft.
Signed by Cincinnati Bengals, May 19, 1983.
On non-football injury list with drug problem, August 23 through September 20, 1984; activated, September 21, 1984.
On injured reserve with dislocated shoulder, October 1 through October 31, 1984.
On NFL suspended list with drug problem, November 1 through remainder of 1984 season and 1985 season; reinstated, May 9, 1986.
On injured reserve with knee injury, August 25 through November 16, 1986; activated, November 17, 1986.
On NFL suspended list with drug problem, July 2, 1987 through April 19, 1988; reinstated, April 20, 1988.

Year Club	G.	Att.	Yds.	Avg.	TD.	P.C.	Yds.	Avg.	TD.	TD.	Pts.	F.
			RUSHING				PASS RECEIVING				TOTAL	
1983—Cincinnati NFL.............................	10	56	267	4.8	1	12	107	8.9	1	2	12	4
1984—Cincinnati NFL.............................	1	17	74	4.4	0	2	17	7.5	0	0	0	0
1986—Cincinnati NFL.............................	10	68	379	5.6	8	4	45	11.3	0	8	48	1
Pro Totals—3 Years.................................	21	141	720	5.1	9	18	167	9.3	1	10	60	5

Additional pro statistics: Returned seven kickoffs for 161 yards (23.0 avg.) and recovered two fumbles, 1983.

STEVEN ANTHONY WILSON
(Steve)
Cornerback—Denver Broncos
Born August 24, 1957, at Los Angeles, Calif.
Height, 5.10. Weight, 195.
High School—Durham, N.C., Northern.
Received bachelor of business administration degree in marketing from Howard University in 1979.
Son of (Touchdown) Tommy Wilson, halfback with Los Angeles Rams, Cleveland Browns
and Minnesota Vikings, 1956 through 1963.

Signed as free agent by Dallas Cowboys, May 6, 1979.

Released by Dallas Cowboys, August 14, 1979; re-signed by Cowboys, August 29, 1979.
Released by Dallas Cowboys, September 6, 1982; signed as free agent by Denver Broncos, September 14, 1982.

		INTERCEPTIONS			-PUNT RETURNS-			—KICKOFF RET.—			—TOTAL—		
Year Club	G.	No.	Yds.	Avg. TD.	No.	Yds.	Avg. TD.	No.	Yds.	Avg. TD.	TD.	Pts.	F.
1979—Dallas NFL	16		None		35	236	6.7	0	19	328	17.3	0	0	0	1
1980—Dallas NFL	16	4	82	20.5	0		None		7	139	19.9	0	0	0	0
1981—Dallas NFL	16	2	0	0.0	0		None		2	32	16.0	0	0	0	0
1982—Denver NFL	8	2	22	11.0	0		None		6	123	20.5	0	0	0	0
1983—Denver NFL	16	5	91	18.2	0		None		24	485	20.2	0	0	0	0
1984—Denver NFL	15	4	59	14.8	0	1	0	0.0	0		None		0	0	1
1985—Denver NFL	14	3	8	2.7	0		None			None		0	0	0
1986—Denver NFL	16	1	—5	—5.0	0		None			None		1	6	0
1987—Denver NFL	11		None			None			None		0	0	0
Pro Totals—9 Years	128	21	257	12.2	0	36	236	6.6	0	58	1107	19.1	0	1	6	2

Additional pro statistics: Recovered one fumble, 1979, 1981 and 1984; caught three passes for 76 yards, 1979; recovered one fumble for two yards, 1985; caught one pass for 43 yards and a touchdown, 1986.
Played in NFC Championship Game following 1980 and 1981 seasons.
Played in AFC Championship Game following 1986 and 1987 seasons.
Played in NFL Championship Game following 1986 and 1987 seasons.

WILLIAM MIKE WILSON
(Known by middle name.)
Offensive Tackle—Seattle Seahawks
Born May 28, 1955, at Norfolk, Va.
Height, 6.05. Weight, 280.
High School—Gainesville, Ga., Johnson.
Attended University of Georgia.

Selected by Cincinnati in 4th round (103rd player selected) of 1977 NFL draft.
Signed by Toronto Argonauts, May, 1977.
Released by Toronto Argonauts, July 6, 1978; signed by Cincinnati Bengals, July 6, 1978; activated, October 13, 1978.
Placed on physically unable to perform list with knee injury, July 6, 1978.
Traded by Cincinnati Bengals to Seattle Seahawks for 3rd round pick in 1987 draft, August 27, 1986.
Toronto CFL, 1977; Cincinnati NFL, 1978 through 1985; Seattle NFL, 1987.
Games: 1977 (16), 1978 (9), 1979 (16), 1980 (16), 1981 (16), 1982 (9), 1983 (16), 1984 (16), 1985 (16), 1986 (16), 1987 (12).
Total NFL—142. Total Pro—158.
Played in AFC Championship Game following 1981 season.
Played in NFL Championship Game following 1981 season.

SAMMY WINDER
Running Back—Denver Broncos
Born July 15, 1959, at Madison, Miss.
Height, 5.11. Weight, 203.
High School—Madison, Miss., Ridgeland.
Attended University of Southern Mississippi.

Selected by Denver in 5th round (131st player selected) of 1982 NFL draft.

		——RUSHING——				PASS RECEIVING				—TOTAL—		
Year Club	G.	Att.	Yds.	Avg.	TD.	P.C.	Yds.	Avg.	TD.	TD.	Pts.	F.
1982—Denver NFL	8	67	259	3.9	1	11	83	7.5	0	1	6	1
1983—Denver NFL	14	196	757	3.9	3	23	150	6.5	0	3	18	7
1984—Denver NFL	16	296	1153	3.9	4	44	288	6.5	2	6	36	5
1985—Denver NFL	14	199	714	3.6	8	31	197	6.4	0	8	48	4
1986—Denver NFL	16	240	789	3.3	9	26	171	6.6	5	14	84	2
1987—Denver NFL	12	196	741	3.8	6	14	74	5.3	1	7	42	5
Pro Totals—6 Years	80	1194	4413	3.7	31	149	963	6.5	8	39	234	24

Additional pro statistics: Recovered one fumble, 1982, 1985 and 1986; recovered two fumbles, 1984 and 1987; attempted one pass with no completions, 1985.
Played in AFC Championship Game following 1986 and 1987 seasons.
Played in NFL Championship Game following 1986 and 1987 seasons.
Played in Pro Bowl (NFL All-Star Game) following 1984 and 1986 seasons.

GEORGE ARTHUR WINSLOW
Punter—Buffalo Bills
Born July 28, 1963, at Philadelphia, Pa.
Height, 6.04. Weight, 205.
High School—Philadelphia, Pa., LaSalle.
Attended University of Wisconsin and received bachelor of arts degree in
communication arts from Villanova University in 1987.

Signed as free agent by Cleveland Browns, May 4, 1987.
On injured reserve with back injury, September 7 through November 6, 1987; activated, November 7, 1987.
Crossed picket line during players' strike, October 14, 1987.
On injured reserve with back injury, December 15 through remainder of 1987 season.
Released by Cleveland Browns, February 16, 1988; awarded on waivers to Buffalo Bills, February 29, 1988.

		——PUNTING——		
Year Club	G.	No.	Avg.	Blk.
1987—Cleveland NFL	5	18	34.2	0

KELLEN BOSWELL WINSLOW
Tight End—San Diego Chargers
Born November 5, 1957, at St. Louis, Mo.
Height, 6.05. Weight, 250.
High School—East St. Louis, Ill.
Attended University of Missouri.

Tied NFL record for most touchdowns, pass receptions, game (5), November 22, 1981, against Oakland Raiders.
Named as tight end on THE SPORTING NEWS College All-America Team, 1978.
Named to THE SPORTING NEWS NFL All-Star Team, 1980 and 1981.
Selected by San Diego in 1st round (13th player selected) of 1979 NFL draft.
On injured reserve with broken leg, October 19 through remainder of 1979 season.
Left San Diego Chargers voluntarily and granted roster exemption, September 3 through September 9, 1984; activated, September 10, 1984.
On injured reserve with knee injury, October 23 through remainder of 1984 season.
On physically unable to perform/active with knee injury, August 20 through October 17, 1985; activated, October 18, 1985.

		—PASS RECEIVING—				
Year	Club	G.	P.C.	Yds.	Avg.	TD.
1979—San Diego NFL		7	25	255	10.2	2
1980—San Diego NFL		16	*89	1290	14.5	9
1981—San Diego NFL		16	*88	1075	12.2	10
1982—San Diego NFL		9	54	721	13.4	6
1983—San Diego NFL		16	88	1172	13.3	8
1984—San Diego NFL		7	55	663	12.1	2
1985—San Diego NFL		10	25	318	12.7	0
1986—San Diego NFL		16	64	728	11.4	5
1987—San Diego NFL		12	53	519	9.8	3
Pro Totals—9 Years		109	541	6741	12.5	45

Additional pro statistics: Fumbled once, 1979, 1982, 1984 and 1987; fumbled twice, 1980 and 1981; attempted two passes with no completions, 1981; recovered two fumbles, 1981, 1983 and 1986; attempted one pass with no completions, 1982; fumbled three times, 1983; returned two kickoffs for 11 yards, 1986.
Played in AFC Championship Game following 1980 and 1981 seasons.
Played in Pro Bowl (NFL All-Star Game) following 1980 through 1983 and 1987 seasons.

BLAISE WINTER
Nose Tackle—Green Bay Packers
Born January 31, 1962, at Blauvelt, N.Y.
Height, 6.03. Weight, 274.
High School—Orangeburg, N.Y., Tappan Zee.
Attended Syracuse University.

Selected by New Jersey in 1984 USFL territorial draft.
Selected by Indianapolis in 2nd round (35th player selected) of 1984 NFL draft.
Signed by Indianapolis Colts, July 27, 1984.
On injured reserve with shoulder injury, August 27 through entire 1985 season.
On injured reserve with knee injury, August 18 through October 14, 1986.
Released by Indianapolis Colts, October 15, 1986; signed as free agent by San Diego Chargers, November 24, 1986.
Released by San Diego Chargers, August 29, 1987; re-signed as replacement player by Chargers, September 28, 1987.
On injured reserve with hand injury, October 27 through remainder of 1987 season.
Traded by San Diego Chargers to Green Bay Packers for past considerations, April 28, 1988.
Indianapolis NFL, 1984; San Diego NFL, 1986 and 1987.
Games: 1984 (16), 1986 (4), 1987 (3). Total—23.
Pro statistics: Recovered one fumble, 1984.

FRANK MITCHELL WINTERS
Center—Cleveland Browns
Born January 23, 1964, at Hoboken, N. J.
Height, 6.03. Weight, 290.
High School—Union City, N. J., Emerson.
Attended College of Eastern Utah and received degree in political science
administration from Western Illinois University in 1987.

Selected by Cleveland in 10th round (276th player selected) of 1987 NFL draft.
Signed by Cleveland Browns, July 25, 1987.
Cleveland NFL, 1987.
Games: 1987 (12).
Pro statistics: Fumbled once, 1987.
Played in AFC Championship Game following 1987 season.

MIKE WISE
Defensive End—Los Angeles Raiders
Born June 5, 1964, at Greenbrae, Calif.
Height, 6.07. Weight, 265.
High School—Novato, Calif.
Attended University of California at Davis.

Selected by Los Angeles Raiders in 4th round (85th player selected) of 1986 NFL draft.
Signed by Los Angeles Raiders, July 11, 1986.

On injured reserve with elbow injury, August 26 through October 31, 1986; activated, November 1, 1986.
On injured reserve with elbow injury, December 11 through remainder of 1986 season.
On non-football injury list with virus, September 7 through December 4, 1987; activated, December 5, 1987.
Active for 1 game with Los Angeles Raiders in 1987; did not play.
Los Angeles Raiders NFL, 1986 and 1987.
Games: 1986 (6).

JOHN JOSEPH WITKOWSKI
Quarterback—New York Jets
Born June 18, 1962, at Flushing, N.Y.
Height, 6.01. Weight, 205.
High School—Lindenhurst, N.Y.
Received bachelor of arts degree in economics from Columbia University in 1984.

Selected by Philadelphia in 7th round (138th player selected) of 1984 USFL draft.
Selected by Detroit in 6th round (160th player selected) of 1984 NFL draft.
Signed by Detroit Lions, June 10, 1984.
Released by Detroit Lions, September 2, 1985; re-signed by Lions, March 6, 1986.
Released by Detroit Lions, August 30, 1986; signed as free agent by Houston Oilers, November 5, 1986.
Released by Houston Oilers, September 6, 1987; re-signed as replacement player by Oilers, September 28, 1987.
Traded by Houston Oilers to Green Bay Packers for past considerations, October 20, 1987.
Released by Green Bay Packers, October 23, 1987; signed as free agent by New York Jets, April 14, 1988.
Active for 7 games with Houston Oilers in 1986; did not play.
Active for 3 games with Houston Oilers in 1987; did not play.

Year Club	G.	Att.	Cmp.	Pct.	Gain	T.P.	P.I.	Avg.	Att.	Yds.	Avg.	TD.	TD.	Pts.	F.
				PASSING						RUSHING				TOTAL	
1984—Detroit NFL	3	34	13	38.2	210	0	0	6.18	7	33	4.7	0	0	0	1

Quarterback Rating Points: 1984 (59.7).

JOHN STANLEY WOJCIECHOWSKI
Guard—Chicago Bears
Born July 30, 1963, at Detroit, Mich.
Height, 6.04. Weight, 262.
High School—Warren, Mich., Fitzgerald.
Received bachelor of science degree in education
from Michigan State University in 1986.

Selected by Birmingham in 1986 USFL territorial draft.
Signed as free agent by Buffalo Bills, May 6, 1986.
Released by Buffalo Bills, August 18, 1986; signed as free agent by Chicago Bears, March 10, 1987.
Released by Chicago Bears, September 7, 1987; re-signed as replacement player by Bears, September 28, 1987.
Chicago NFL, 1987.
Games: 1987 (4).
Pro statistics: Recovered one fumble, 1987.

CRAIG ALAN WOLFLEY
Guard—Pittsburgh Steelers
Born May 19, 1958, at Buffalo, N.Y.
Height, 6.01. Weight, 272.
High School—Orchard Park, N.Y.
Received bachelor of science degree in speech communication from Syracuse University in 1980.
Brother of Ronnie Wolfley, fullback with Phoenix Cardinals;
and Dale Wolfley, guard at West Virginia University.

Selected by Pittsburgh in 5th round (138th player selected) of 1980 NFL draft.
On injured reserve with pulled hamstring, October 5 through November 18, 1984; activated, November 19, 1984.
On injured reserve with knee injury, August 19 through October 24, 1986; activated, October 25, 1986.
Pittsburgh NFL, 1980 through 1987.
Games: 1980 (16), 1981 (16), 1982 (9), 1983 (14), 1984 (9), 1985 (13), 1986 (9), 1987 (12). Total—98.
Pro statistics: Recovered two fumbles, 1982; recovered one fumble, 1983 and 1985 through 1987.
Played in AFC Championship Game following 1984 season.

RONALD PAUL WOLFLEY
(Ron)
Fullback—Phoenix Cardinals
Born October 14, 1962, at Blasdel, N.Y.
Height, 6.00. Weight, 222.
High School—Hamburg, N.Y., Frontier Central.
Attended West Virginia University.
Brother of Craig Wolfley, guard with Pittsburgh Steelers;
and Dale Wolfley, guard at West Virginia University.

Selected by Birmingham in 1985 USFL territorial draft.
Selected by St. Louis in 4th round (104th player selected) of 1985 NFL draft.
Signed by St. Louis Cardinals, July 21, 1985.
Franchise transferred to Phoenix, March 15, 1988.

Year Club	G.	Att.	Yds.	Avg.	TD.	P.C.	Yds.	Avg.	TD.	TD.	Pts.	F.
			RUSHING			PASS RECEIVING				TOTAL		
1985—St. Louis NFL	16	24	64	2.7	0	2	18	9.0	0	0	0	1
1986—St. Louis NFL	16	8	19	2.4	0	2	32	16.0	0	0	0	0
1987—St. Louis NFL	12	26	87	3.3	1	8	68	8.5	0	1	6	0
Pro Totals—3 Years	44	58	170	2.9	1	12	118	9.8	0	1	6	1

Year Club		G.	No.	Yds.	Avg.	TD.
			KICKOFF RETURNS			
1985—St. Louis NFL		16	13	234	18.0	0
1986—St. Louis NFL		16	0	—6	....	0
1987—St. Louis NFL		12		None		
Pro Totals—3 Years		44	13	228	17.5	0

Played in Pro Bowl (NFL All-Star Game) following 1986 and 1987 seasons.

WILLIAM CHARLES WOLFORD
(Will)
Offensive Tackle—Buffalo Bills

Born May 18, 1964, at Louisville, Ky.
Height, 6.05. Weight, 276.
High School—Louisville, Ky., St. Xavier.
Attended Vanderbilt University.

Selected by Memphis in 1986 USFL territorial draft.
Selected by Buffalo in 1st round (20th player selected) of 1986 NFL draft.
Signed by Buffalo Bills, August 12, 1986.
Granted roster exemption, August 12 through August 21, 1986; activated, August 22, 1986.
Buffalo NFL, 1986 and 1987.
Games: 1986 (16), 1987 (9). Total—25.

GEORGE IVORY WONSLEY
Running Back—Indianapolis Colts

Born November 23, 1960, at Moss Point, Miss.
Height, 5.10. Weight, 220.
High School—Moss Point, Miss.
Attened Mississippi State University.

Brother of Otis Wonsley, running back with Washington Redskins, 1981 through 1985; and Nathan Wonsley, running back with Tampa Bay Buccaneers, 1986.

Selected by New Jersey in 1984 USFL territorial draft.
Selected by Indianapolis in 4th round (103rd player selected) of 1984 NFL draft.
Signed by Indianapolis Colts, May 24, 1984.

| | | | ——RUSHING—— | | | PASS RECEIVING | | | —TOTAL— | | |
Year Club		G.	Att.	Yds.	Avg. TD.	P.C.	Yds.	Avg. TD.	TD.	Pts.	F.
1984—Indianapolis NFL		14	37	111	3.0 0	9	47	5.2 0	0	0	0
1985—Indianapolis NFL		16	138	716	5.2 6	30	257	8.6 0	6	36	4
1986—Indianapolis NFL		16	60	214	3.6 1	16	175	10.9 0	1	6	1
1987—Indianapolis NFL		11	18	71	3.9 1	5	48	9.6 0	1	6	1
Pro Totals—4 Years		57	253	1112	4.4 8	60	527	8.8 0	8	48	6

Additional pro statistics: Returned four kickoffs for 52 yards, 1984; returned two kickoffs for 31 yards, 1986; returned one kickoff for 19 yards, 1987.

KENNETH EMIL WOODARD
(Ken)
Linebacker

Born January 22, 1960, at Detroit, Mich.
Height, 6.01. Weight, 227.
High School—Detroit, Mich., Martin Luther King.
Attended Tuskegee Institute.

Selected by Denver in 10th round (274th player selected) of 1982 NFL draft.
Traded by Denver Broncos to Pittsburgh Steelers for 10th round pick in 1988 draft, August 27, 1987.
On injured reserve with knee injury, September 18 through November 20, 1987; activated, November 21, 1987.
Traded by Pittsburgh Steelers to Indianapolis Colts for draft choice, May 5, 1988; trade voided after failing physical, May 23, 1988.
Released by Pittsburgh Steelers, June 6, 1988.
Denver NFL, 1982 through 1986; Pittsburgh NFL, 1987.
Games: 1982 (9), 1983 (16), 1984 (16), 1985 (16), 1986 (16), 1987 (7). Total—80.
Pro statistics: Recovered one fumble, 1983; intercepted one pass for 27 yards and a touchdown, 1984; intercepted one pass for 18 yards, 1985; recovered one fumble for 16 yards and a touchdown, 1986.
Played in AFC Championship Game following 1986 season.
Played in NFL Championship Game following 1986 season.

RAYMOND LEE WOODARD
(Ray)
Defensive End—Kansas City Chiefs

Born August 20, 1961, at Corrigan, Tex.
Height, 6.06. Weight, 290.
High School—Corrigan, Tex., Corrigan-Camden.
Attended University of Texas.

Selected by Houston in 1984 USFL territorial draft.
Selected by San Diego in 8th round (199th player selected) of 1984 NFL draft.
Signed by San Diego Chargers, June 27, 1984.

On injured reserve with dislocated shoulder, August 13 through entire 1984 season.
Released by San Diego Chargers, August 14, 1985; signed as free agent by Denver Broncos, March 18, 1986.
On injured reserve with knee injury, August 25 through entire 1986 season.
Released by Denver Broncos, September 7, 1987; re-signed as replacement player by Broncos, September 25, 1987.
Released by Denver Broncos, October 19, 1987; signed as free agent by Kansas City Chiefs, November 18, 1987.
Denver (3)-Kansas City (5) NFL, 1987.
Games: 1987 (8).

DENNIS EARL WOODBERRY
Cornerback—Washington Redskins
Born April 22, 1961, at Texarkana, Ark.
Height, 5.10. Weight, 180.
High School—Texarkana, Ark.
Attended Southern Arkansas University.
Cousin of Jessie Clark, fullback with Green Bay Packers.

Selected by Birmingham in 6th round (111th player selected) of 1984 USFL draft.
Signed by Birmingham Stallions, January 22, 1984.
Selected by Atlanta in 3rd round (63rd player selected) of 1984 NFL supplemental draft.
Granted free agency when USFL suspended operations, August 7, 1986; signed by Atlanta Falcons, August 13, 1986.
Granted roster exemption, August 13 through August 21, 1986; activated, August 22, 1986.
Released by Atlanta Falcons, September 1, 1986; re-signed by Birmingham Stallions for 1987, October 8, 1986.
Released from Birmingham Stallions contract and re-signed by Atlanta Falcons, October 27, 1986.
On developmental squad, June 23 through remainder of 1984 season.
Sold by Atlanta Falcons to Green Bay Packers, August 25, 1987.
Released by Green Bay Packers, September 7, 1987; signed as free agent replacement player by Washington Redskins, September 24, 1987.
On developmental squad for 1 game with Birmingham Stallions in 1984.

			—INTERCEPTIONS—		
Year	Club	G.	No.	Yds.	Avg.TD.
1984—Birmingham USFL		17	7	67	9.6 0
1985—Birmingham USFL		18	5	64	12.8 0
1986—Atlanta NFL		7	2	14	7.0 0
1987—Washington NFL		12		None	
USFL Totals—2 Years		35	12	131	10.9 0
NFL Totals—2 Years		19	2	14	7.0 0
Pro Totals—4 Years		54	14	145	10.4 0

Additional pro statistics: Recovered one fumble, 1987.
Played in NFC Championship Game following 1987 season.
Played in NFL Championship Game following 1987 season.

DWAYNE DONZELL WOODRUFF
Cornerback—Pittsburgh Steelers
Born February 18, 1957, at Bowling Green, Ky.
Height, 6.00. Weight, 198.
High School—New Richmond, O.
Received bachelor of science degree in commerce from University of Louisville in 1979;
and attending Duquesne Law School.

Selected by Pittsburgh in 6th round (161st player selected) of 1979 NFL draft.
USFL rights traded with rights to quarterback Jeff Hostetler by Pittsburgh Maulers to Arizona Wranglers for a draft pick, May 2, 1984.
On injured reserve with dislocated elbow, October 15 through November 14, 1985; activated, November 15, 1985.
On injured reserve with knee injury, August 26 through entire 1986 season.

			—INTERCEPTIONS—		
Year	Club	G.	No.	Yds.	Avg.TD.
1979—Pittsburgh NFL		16	1	31	31.0 0
1980—Pittsburgh NFL		16	1	0	0.0 0
1981—Pittsburgh NFL		16	1	17	17.0 0
1982—Pittsburgh NFL		9	5	53	10.6 0
1983—Pittsburgh NFL		15	3	85	28.3 0
1984—Pittsburgh NFL		16	5	56	11.2 1
1985—Pittsburgh NFL		12	5	80	16.0 0
1987—Pittsburgh NFL		12	5	91	18.2 1
Pro Totals—8 Years		112	26	413	15.9 2

Additional pro statistics: Recovered one fumble and fumbled once, 1981; recovered one fumble for 65 yards and a touchdown, 1984.
Played in AFC Championship Game following 1979 and 1984 seasons.
Played in NFL Championship Game following 1979 season.

CHRISTOPHER WYATT WOODS
(Chris)
Wide Reciever—Los Angeles Raiders
Born July 19, 1962, at Birmingham, Ala.
Height, 5.11. Weight, 190.
High School—Birmingham, Ala., A. H. Parker.
Attended Auburn University.

Selected by Birmingham in 1984 USFL territorial draft.
Signed as free agent by Edmonton Eskimos, March 5, 1984.
Selected by Los Angeles Raiders in 1st round (28th player selected) of 1984 NFL supplemental draft.
Traded by Edmonton Eskimos to Toronto Argonauts, June 10, 1986.
Granted free agency, March 1, 1987; signed by Los Angeles Raiders, April 17, 1987.
On injured reserve with knee injury, September 7 through October 30, 1987; activated, October 31, 1987.

			PASS RECEIVING			-PUNT RETURNS-			-KICKOFF RET.-			-TOTAL-	
Year Club	G.	P.C.	Yds.	Avg.	TD.	No.	Yds.	Avg.	TD.	No.	Yds.	Avg.	TD.	TD.	Pts.
1984—Edmonton CFL	15	38	837	22.0	6	31	303	9.8	1	18	442	24.6	0	7	42	3
1985—Edmonton CFL	13	41	779	19.0	6	36	366	10.1	0	10	239	23.9	0	6	36	1
1986—Toronto CFL	17	61	1163	19.1	6	64	595	9.3	0	8	152	19.0	0	6	36	1
1987—L.A. Raiders NFL	9	1	14	14.0	0	26	189	7.3	0	3	55	18.3	0	0	0	2
CFL Totals—3 Years	45	140	2779	19.9	18	131	1264	9.6	1	36	833	23.1	0	19	114	5
NFL Totals—1 Year	9	1	14	14.0	0	26	189	7.3	0	3	55	18.3	0	0	0	2
Pro Totals—4 Years	54	141	2793	19.8	18	157	1453	9.3	1	39	888	22.8	0	19	114	7

Additional CFL statistics: Rushed three times for 60 yards and recovered one fumble, 1984; rushed three times for nine yards, 1985; rushed two times for 10 yards, 1986.
Additional NFL statistics: Recovered one fumble, 1987.

STANLEY ANTHONY WOODS
(Tony)
Linebacker—Seattle Seahawks
Born September 11, 1965, at Newark, N. J.
Height, 6.04. Weight, 244.
High School—South Orange, N. J., Seton Hall Prep.
Attended University of Pittsburgh.

Named as defensive lineman on THE SPORTING NEWS College All-America Team, 1986.
Selected by Seattle in 1st round (18th player selected) of 1987 NFL draft.
Signed by Seattle Seahawks, July 20, 1987.
Seattle NFL, 1987.
Games: 1987 (12).
Pro statistics: Recovered one fumble, 1987.

RODERICK KEVIN WOODSON
(Rod)
Defensive Back-Kick Returner—Pittsburgh Steelers
Born March 10, 1965, at Fort Wayne, Ind.
Height, 6.00. Weight, 202.
High School—Fort Wayne, Ind., R. Nelson Snider.
Attended Purdue University.

Named as kick returner on THE SPORTING NEWS College All-America Team, 1986.
Selected by Pittsburgh in 1st round (10th player selected) of 1987 NFL draft.
Placed on reserve/unsigned list, August 31 through October 27, 1987.
Signed by Pittsburgh Steelers, October 28, 1987.
Granted roster exemption, October 28 through November 6, 1987; activated, November 7, 1987.

		INTERCEPTIONS			-PUNT RETURNS-			-KICKOFF RET.-			-TOTAL-	
Year Club	G.	No.	Yds.	Avg.	TD.	No.	Yds.	Avg.	TD.	No.	Yds.	Avg.	TD.	TD.	Pts.	F.
1987—Pittsburgh NFL	8	1	45	45.0	1	16	135	8.4	0	13	290	22.3	0	1	6	3

Additional pro statistics: Recovered two fumbles, 1987.

HAROLD WOOLFOLK
(Butch)
Running Back—Detroit Lions
Born March 1, 1960, at Milwaukee, Wis.
Height, 6.01. Weight, 212.
High School—Westfield, N.J.
Received bachelor of science degree in physical therapy
from University of Michigan in 1982.

Tied NFL record for more rushing attempts, game (43) vs. Philadelphia Eagles, November 20, 1983.
Selected by New York Giants in 1st round (18th player selected) of 1982 NFL draft.
Traded by New York Giants to Houston Oilers for 3rd round pick in 1985 draft, March 21, 1985.
On injured reserve with dislocated shoulder, November 12 through remainder of 1986 season.
Released by Houston Oilers, July 30, 1987; signed as free agent by Cleveland Browns, August 5, 1987.
Released by Cleveland Browns, September 7, 1987; awarded on waivers to Detroit Lions, September 8, 1987.

		——RUSHING——				PASS RECEIVING			-TOTAL-	
Year Club	G.	Att.	Yds.	Avg.	TD.	P.C.	Yds.	Avg.	TD.	TD.	Pts.	F.
1982—New York Giants NFL	9	112	439	3.9	2	23	224	9.7	2	4	24	5
1983—New York GiantsNFL	16	246	857	3.5	4	28	368	13.1	0	4	24	8
1984—New York Giants NFL	15	40	92	2.3	1	9	53	5.9	0	1	6	1
1985—Houston NFL	16	103	392	3.8	1	80	814	10.2	4	5	30	5
1986—Houston NFL	10	23	57	2.5	0	28	314	11.2	2	2	12	0
1987—Detroit NFL	12	12	82	6.8	0	19	166	8.7	0	0	0	1
Pro Totals—6 Years	78	536	1919	3.6	8	187	1939	10.4	8	16	96	20

Year Club	G.	No.	Yds.	Avg.	TD.
1982—N.Y. Giants NFL	9	20	428	21.4	0
1983—N.Y. Giants NFL	16	2	13	6.5	0
1984—N.Y. Giants NFL	15	14	232	16.6	0
1985—Houston NFL	16		None		
1986—Houston NFL	10	2	38	19.0	0
1987—Detroit NFL	12	11	219	19.9	0
Pro Totals—6 Years	78	49	930	19.0	0

Additional pro statistics: Recovered one fumble, 1982 through 1984; recovered two fumbles, 1985.

RONALD J. WOOTEN
(Ron)
Guard—New England Patriots

Born June 28, 1959, at Bourne, Mass.
Height, 6.04. Weight, 273.
High School—Kinston, N.C.
Received bachelor of science degree in chemistry
from University of North Carolina in 1982.

Selected by New England in 6th round (157th player selected) of 1981 NFL draft.
On injured reserve with back injury, August 31 through entire 1981 season.
Crossed picket line during players' strike, October 2, 1987.
New England NFL, 1982 through 1987.
Games: 1982 (9), 1983 (16), 1984 (16), 1985 (14), 1986 (16), 1987 (13). Total—84.
Pro statistics: Recovered one fumble, 1986.
Played in AFC Championship Game following 1985 season.
Played in NFL Championship Game following 1985 season.

BARRY QUENTIN WORD
Fullback—New Orleans Saints

Born July 17, 1964, at Long Island, Va.
Height, 6.02. Weight, 220.
High School—South Boston, Va., Halifax County.
Attended University of Virginia.

Selected by Jacksonville in 1986 USFL territorial draft.
Selected by New Orleans in 3rd round (62nd player selected) of 1986 NFL draft.
Missed 1986 season due to time spent in prison on drug charges, November, 1986 through March, 1987.
Signed by New Orleans Saints, April 14, 1987.

		—RUSHING—				PASS RECEIVING			—TOTAL—		
Year Club	G.	Att.	Yds.	Avg.	TD.	P.C.	Yds.	Avg.	TD.	TD. Pts.	F.
1987—New Orleans NFL	12	36	133	3.7	2	6	54	9.0	0	2 12	1

Additional pro statistics: Returned three kickoffs for 100 yards (33.3 avg.) and recovered one fumble, 1987.

ALVIN WRIGHT
Nose Tackle—Los Angeles Rams

Born February 5, 1961, at Wedowee, Ala.
Height, 6.02. Weight, 265.
High School—Wedowee, Ala., Randolph County.
Attended Jacksonville State University.

Selected by Birmingham in 14th round (199th player selected) of 1985 USFL draft.
Signed as free agent by Los Angeles Rams, June 22, 1985.
On injured reserve with neck injury, August 27 through September 3, 1985.
Released by Los Angeles Rams, September 4, 1985; re-signed by Rams, March 9, 1986.
On injured reserve with knee injury, September 2 through October 30, 1986; activated, October 31, 1986.
Crossed picket line during players' strike, September 30, 1987.
Los Angeles Rams NFL, 1986 and 1987.
Games: 1986 (4), 1987 (15). Total—19.

CHARLES JAMES WRIGHT
Defensive Back—Dallas Cowboys

Born April 3, 1964, at Carthage, Mo.
Height, 5.09. Weight, 170.
High School—Carthage, Mo.
Attended Highland Community College, Fort Scott Community College and
University of Tulsa.
Brother of Felix Wright, safety with Cleveland Browns.

Selected by St. Louis in 10th round (257th player selected) of 1987 NFL draft.
Signed by St. Louis Cardinals, July 19, 1987.
Released by St. Louis Cardinals, November 3, 1987; signed as free agent by Dallas Cowboys, February 2, 1988.
St. Louis NFL, 1987.
Games: 1987 (3).

DANA WRIGHT
Running Back—Cincinnati Bengals
Born June 2, 1963, at Ravenna, O.
Height, 6.01. Weight, 219.
High School—Kent, O., Theodore Roosevelt.
Attended Findlay College.
Selected by New York Giants in 9th round (251st player selected) of 1987 NFL draft.
Signed by New York Giants, June 20, 1987.
Released by New York Giants, August 31, 1987; signed as free agent replacement player by Cincinnati Bengals, September 25, 1987.
Released by Cincinnati Bengals, October 19, 1987; re-signed by Bengals, November 11, 1987.

		—RUSHING—			PASS RECEIVING			—TOTAL—		
Year Club	G.	Att.	Yds.	Avg. TD.	P.C.	Yds.	Avg. TD.	TD.	Pts.	F.
1987—Cincinnati NFL	5	24	74	3.1 0	4	28	7.0 0	0	0	1

		KICKOFF RETURNS		
Year Club	G.	No.	Yds.	Avg.TD.
1987—Cincinnati NFL	5	13	266	20.5 0

ERIC WRIGHT
Cornerback—San Francisco 49ers
Born April 18, 1959, at St. Louis, Mo.
Height, 6.01. Weight, 185.
High School—East St. Louis, Ill., Assumption.
Attended University of Missouri.
Named to THE SPORTING NEWS NFL All-Star Team, 1985.
Selected by San Francisco in 2nd round (40th player selected) of 1981 NFL draft.
On inactive list, September 19, 1982.
On injured reserve with pulled abdomen, December 24 through remainder of 1985 season playoffs.
On injured reserve with groin injury, September 3 through October 2, 1986; activated, October 3, 1986.
On injured reserve with groin injury, October 29 through remainder of 1986 season.
Crossed picket line during players' strike, October 7, 1987.
On injured reserve with groin injury, October 8 through remainder of 1987 season.

		—INTERCEPTIONS—		
Year Club	G.	No.	Yds.	Avg.TD.
1981—San Francisco NFL	16	3	26	8.7 0
1982—San Francisco NFL	7	1	31	31.0 0
1983—San Francisco NFL	16	7	*164	23.4 *2
1984—San Francisco NFL	15	2	0	0.0 0
1985—San Francisco NFL	16	1	0	0.0 0
1986—San Francisco NFL	2		None	
1987—San Francisco NFL	2		None	
Pro Totals—7 Years	74	14	221	15.8 2

Additional pro statistics: Recovered two fumbles, 1981; recovered one fumble, 1983.
Played in NFC Championship Game following 1981, 1983 and 1984 seasons.
Played in NFL Championship Game following 1981 and 1984 seasons.
Played in Pro Bowl (NFL All-Star Game) following 1984 season.
Named to play in Pro Bowl following 1985 season; replaced due to injury by Gary Green.

FELIX CARL WRIGHT
Safety—Cleveland Browns
Born June 22, 1959, at Carthage, Mo.
Height, 6.02. Weight, 190.
High School—Carthage, Mo.
Received bachelor of science degree in physical education and history from Drake University in 1981.
Brother of Charles Wright, defensive back with Dallas Cowboys.
Signed as free agent by Houston Oilers, May 17, 1982.
Released by Houston Oilers, August 23, 1982; signed as free agent by Hamilton Tiger-Cats, October 24, 1982.
Granted free agency, March 1, 1985; signed by Cleveland Browns, May 6, 1985.

		—INTERCEPTIONS—		
Year Club	G.	No.	Yds.	Avg.TD.
1982—Hamilton CFL	2	2	32	16.0 0
1983—Hamilton CFL	12	6	140	23.3 1
1984—Hamilton CFL	16	7	100	14.3 1
1985—Cleveland NFL	16	2	11	5.5 0
1986—Cleveland NFL	16	3	33	11.0 0
1987—Cleveland NFL	12	4	152	38.0 1
CFL Totals—3 Years	30	15	272	18.1 2
NFL Totals—3 Years	44	9	196	21.8 1
Pro Totals—6 Years	74	24	468	19.5 3

Additional CFL statistics: Returned one punt for three yards, 1982; returned seven punts for 36 yards, recovered three fumbles for 10 yards and fumbled twice, 1983; recovered two fumbles, 1984.
Additional NFL statistics: Recovered two fumbles, 1985; returned blocked punt 30 yards for a touchdown, 1986; recovered one fumble, 1986 and 1987.
Played in AFC Championship Game following 1986 and 1987 seasons.

RANDALL STEVEN WRIGHT
(Randy)
Quarterback—Green Bay Packers
Born January 12, 1961, at St. Charles, Ill.
Height, 6.02. Weight, 203.
High School—St. Charles, Ill.
Received degree in communications from University of Wisconsin.
Selected by Memphis in 9th round (188th player selected) of 1984 USFL draft.
USFL rights released by Memphis Showboats, February 7, 1984.
Selected by Green Bay in 6th round (153rd player selected) of 1984 NFL draft.
Signed by Green Bay Packers, June 30, 1984.
On injured reserve with knee injury, December 12 through remainder of 1984 season.

					—PASSING—				—RUSHING—			—TOTAL—		
Year	Club	G.	Att.	Cmp.	Pct.	Gain	T.P.	P.I.	Avg.	Att.	Yds.	Avg.	TD.	TD.	Pts.	F.
1984—Green Bay NFL		8	62	27	43.5	310	2	6	5.00	8	11	1.4	0	0	0	1
1985—Green Bay NFL		5	74	39	52.7	552	2	4	7.46	8	8	1.0	0	0	0	5
1986—Green Bay NFL		16	492	263	53.5	3247	17	23	6.60	18	41	2.3	1	1	6	8
1987—Green Bay NFL		9	247	132	53.4	1507	6	11	6.10	13	70	5.4	0	0	0	3
Pro Totals—4 Years		38	875	461	52.7	5616	27	44	6.42	47	120	2.8	1	1	6	17

Quarterback Rating Points: 1984 (30.4), 1985 (63.6), 1986 (66.2), 1987 (61.6). Total—62.3.
Additional pro statistics: Recovered one fumble, 1984; recovered two fumbles and fumbled five times for minus six yards, 1985; recovered three fumbles and fumbled eight times for minus four yards, 1986; recovered one fumble and fumbled three times for minus four yards, 1987.

STEPHEN HOUGH WRIGHT
(Steve)
Offensive Tackle—Los Angeles Raiders
Born April 8, 1959, at St. Louis, Mo.
Height, 6.06. Weight, 270.
High School—Wayzata, Minn.
Attended University of Northern Iowa.
Signed as free agent by Dallas Cowboys, May, 1981.
Traded by Dallas Cowboys to Baltimore Colts for 7th round pick in 1985 draft, August 27, 1983.
Franchise transferred to Indianapolis, March 31, 1984.
Signed by Oakland Invaders, December 1, 1984, for contract to take effect after being granted free agency, February 1, 1984.
Released by Oakland Invaders, May 28, 1986; re-signed by Indianapolis Colts, July 16, 1986.
Released by Indianapolis Colts, August 18, 1986; signed as free agent by Los Angeles Raiders, May 2, 1987.
Released by Los Angeles Raiders, September 7, 1987; re-signed as replacement player by Raiders, September 29, 1987.
On injured reserve with knee injury, December 26 through remainder of 1987 season.
Dallas NFL, 1981 and 1982; Baltimore NFL, 1983; Indianapolis NFL, 1984; Oakland USFL, 1985; Los Angeles Raiders NFL, 1987.
Games: 1981 (16), 1982 (9), 1983 (13), 1984 (12), 1985 (18), 1987 (9). Total NFL—59. Total Pro—77.
USFL statistics: Caught one pass for two yards and a touchdown, 1985.
Played in NFC Championship Game following 1981 and 1982 seasons.
Played in USFL Championship Game following 1985 season.

TERRY WRIGHT
Defensive Back—Indianapolis Colts
Born July 17, 1965, at Phoenix, Ariz.
Height, 6.00. Weight, 195.
High School—Phoenix, Ariz., South Mountain.
Attended Scottsdale Community College and Temple University.
Signed as free agent by Cleveland Browns, May 4, 1987.
Released by Cleveland Browns, August 2, 1987; signed as free agent replacement player by Indianapolis Colts, September 23, 1987.
Indianapolis NFL, 1987.
Games: 1987 (13).
Pro statistics: Recovered one fumble, 1987.

DAVID MATTHEW WYMAN
Linebacker—Seattle Seahawks
Born March 31, 1964, at San Diego, Calif.
Height, 6.02. Weight, 231.
High School—Reno, Nev., Earl Wooster.
Attended Stanford University.
Named as linebacker on THE SPORTING NEWS College All-America Team, 1986.
Selected by Seattle in 2nd round (45th player selected) of 1987 NFL draft.
Signed by Seattle Seahawks, July 21, 1987.
Traded with draft choice by Seattle Seahawks to San Francisco 49ers for draft choice, November 3, 1987; trade voided after failing physical, November 4, 1987.
On injured reserve with ankle injury, December 30 through remainder of 1987 season.
Seattle NFL, 1987.
Games: 1987 (4).

ERIC LAMONE YARBER
Wide Receiver-Kick Returner—Washington Redskins
Born September 22, 1963, at Chicago, Ill.
Height, 5.08. Weight 156.
High School—Los Angeles, Calif., Crenshaw.
Attended Los Angeles Valley College and University of Idaho.
Cousin of Chet Lemon, outfielder with Detroit Tigers.
Selected by Washington in 12th round (323rd player selected) of 1986 NFL draft.
Selected by Jacksonville in 9th round (61st player selected) of 1986 USFL draft.
Signed by Washington Redskins, July 18, 1986.
On injured reserve with hip injury, August 19 through December 7, 1986; activated after clearing procedural waivers, December 9, 1986.

		—PUNT RETURNS—			
Year	Club	G.	No.	Yds.	Avg.TD.
1986—Washington NFL.........		2	9	143	15.9 0
1987—Washington NFL.........		12	37	273	7.4 0
Pro Totals—2 Years............		14	46	416	9.0 0

Additional pro statistics: Caught one pass for five yards and fumbled once, 1987.
Played in NFC Championship Game following 1986 and 1987 seasons.
Played in NFL Championship Game following 1987 season.

FREDD YOUNG
Linebacker—Seattle Seahawks
Born November 14, 1961, at Dallas, Tex.
Height, 6.01. Weight, 233.
High School—Dallas, Tex., Woodrow Wilson.
Attended New Mexico State University.
Named to THE SPORTING NEWS NFL All-Star Team, 1987.
Selected by Arizona in 1984 USFL territorial draft.
Selected by Seattle in 3rd round (76th player selected) of 1984 NFL draft.
Signed by Seattle Seahawks, May 17, 1984.
Crossed picket line during players' strike, October 14, 1987.
Seattle NFL, 1984 through 1987.
Games: 1984 (16), 1985 (16), 1986 (15), 1987 (13). Total—60.
Pro statistics: Recovered one fumble for 13 yards, 1985; intercepted one pass for 50 yards and a touchdown and recovered four fumbles, 1987.
Played in Pro Bowl (NFL All-Star Game) following 1984 through 1987 seasons.

GLEN YOUNG
Wide Receiver-Kick Returner—Cleveland Browns
Born October 11, 1960, at Greenwood, Miss.
Height, 6.02. Weight, 205.
High School—Greenwood, Miss.
Attended Mississippi State University.
Selected by Oakland in 2nd round (18th player selected) of 1983 USFL draft.
Selected by Philadelphia in 3rd round (62nd player selected) of 1983 NFL draft.
Signed by Philadelphia Eagles, May 13, 1983.
Released by Philadelphia Eagles, August 27, 1984; awarded on waivers to St. Louis Cardinals, August 28, 1984.
Released by St. Louis Cardinals, September 5, 1984; signed as free agent by Cleveland Browns, November 14, 1984.
Released by Cleveland Browns, August 26, 1986; re-signed by Browns, February 20, 1987.
Active for 1 game with St. Louis Cardinals in 1984; did not play.

		PASS RECEIVING				-PUNT RETURNS-				—KICKOFF RET.—				—TOTAL—		
Year	Club	G.	P.C.	Yds.	Avg. TD.	No.	Yds.	Avg. TD.		No.	Yds.	Avg. TD.		TD.	Pts.	F.
1983—Philadelphia NFL.......		16	3	125	41.7 1	14	93	6.6 0		26	547	21.0 0		1	6	2
1984—St.L. (0)-Cle. (2) NFL...		2	1	47	47.0 0		None			5	134	26.8 0		0	0	0
1985—Cleveland NFL.............		15	5	111	22.2 1		None			35	898	25.7 0		1	6	1
1987—Cleveland NFL.............		10		None			None			18	412	22.9 0		0	0	0
Pro Totals—4 Years.......		43	9	283	31.4 2	14	93	6.6 0		84	1991	23.7 0		2	12	3

Additional pro statistics: Recovered one fumble, 1983.

LONNIE YOUNG
Safety—Phoenix Cardinals
Born July 18, 1963, at Flint, Mich.
Height, 6.01. Weight, 182.
High School—Flint, Mich., Beecher.
Received degree in communications from Michigan State University in 1985.
Selected by New Jersey in 8th round (112th player selected) of 1985 USFL draft.
Selected by St. Louis in 12th round (325th player selected) of 1985 NFL draft.
Signed by St. Louis Cardinals, July 15, 1985.
Franchise transferred to Phoenix, March 15, 1988.

		—INTERCEPTIONS—			
Year Club	G.	No.	Yds.	Avg.	TD.
1985—St. Louis NFL.................	16	3	0	0.0	0
1986—St. Louis NFL.................	13		None		
1987—St. Louis NFL.................	12	1	0	0.0	0
Pro Totals—3 Years...........	41	4	0	0.0	0

Additional pro statistics: Recovered one fumble, 1985; recovered three fumbles, 1987.

MICHAEL DAVID YOUNG
(Mike)
Wide Receiver—Los Angeles Rams
Born February 2, 1962, at Hanford, Calif.
Height, 6.01. Weight, 185.
High School—Visalia, Calif., Mount Whitney.
Attended University of California at Los Angeles.

Selected by Memphis in 1985 USFL territorial draft.
Selected by Los Angeles Rams in 6th round (161st player selected) of 1985 NFL draft.
Signed by Los Angeles Rams, July 23, 1985.
Crossed picket line during players' strike, October 14, 1987.

		—PASS RECEIVING—			
Year Club	G.	P.C.	Yds.	Avg.	TD.
1985—L.A. Rams NFL............	15	14	157	11.2	0
1986—L.A. Rams NFL............	16	15	181	12.1	3
1987—L.A. Rams NFL............	12	4	56	14.0	1
Pro Totals—3 Years...........	43	33	394	11.9	4

Additional pro statistics: Fumbled once, 1985; fumbled twice, 1986.
Played in NFC Championship Game following 1985 season.

ROYNELL YOUNG
Cornerback—Philadelphia Eagles
Born December 1, 1957, at New Orleans, La.
Height, 6.01. Weight, 185.
High School—New Orleans, La., Cohen.
Attended Alcorn State University.

Selected by Philadelphia in 1st round (23rd player selected) of 1980 NFL draft.
On injured reserve with strained abdominal muscles, October 12 through November 15, 1984; activated, November 16, 1984.
Granted free agency, February 1, 1987; re-signed by Eagles, September 16, 1987.
Granted roster exemption, September 16 and September 17, 1987; activated, September 18, 1987.

		—INTERCEPTIONS—			
Year Club	G.	No.	Yds.	Avg.	TD.
1980—Philadelphia NFL	16	4	27	6.8	0
1981—Philadelphia NFL	13	4	35	8.8	0
1982—Philadelphia NFL	9	4	0	0.0	0
1983—Philadelphia NFL	16	1	0	0.0	0
1984—Philadelphia NFL	7		None		
1985—Philadelphia NFL	14	1	0	0.0	0
1986—Philadelphia NFL	16	6	9	1.5	0
1987—Philadelphia NFL	11	1	30	30.0	0
Pro Totals—8 Years...........	102	21	101	4.8	0

Additional pro statistics: Returned one kickoff for 18 yards and recovered two fumbles, 1983; recovered two fumbles for 20 yards, 1987.
Played in NFC Championship Game following 1980 season.
Played in NFL Championship Game following 1980 season.
Played in Pro Bowl (NFL All-Star Game) following 1981 season.

STEVE YOUNG
Quarterback—San Francisco 49ers
Born October 11, 1961, at Salt Lake City, Utah.
Height, 6.02. Weight, 200.
High School—Greenwich, Conn.
Attended Brigham Young University.
Brother of Mike Young, quarterback at Brigham Young University.

Named as quarterback on THE SPORTING NEWS College All-America Team, 1983.
Selected by Los Angeles in 1st round (10th player selected) of 1984 USFL draft.
Signed by Los Angeles Express, March 5, 1984.
Granted roster exemption, March 5, 1984; activated, March 30, 1984.
Selected by Tampa Bay in 1st round (1st player selected) of 1984 NFL supplemental draft.
On developmental squad, March 31 through April 15, 1985; activated, April 16, 1985.
Released by Los Angeles Express, September 9, 1985; signed by Tampa Bay Buccaneers, September 10, 1985.
Granted roster exemption, September 10 through September 22, 1985; activated, September 23, 1985.
Traded by Tampa Bay Buccaneers to San Francisco 49ers for 2nd and 4th round pick in 1987 draft and cash, April 24, 1987.
On developmental squad for 3 games with Los Angeles Express in 1985.

		—————PASSING—————						—RUSHING—				—TOTAL—		
Year Club	G.	Att.	Cmp.	Pct.	Gain	T.P.	P.I.	Avg.	Att.	Yds.	Avg.	TD.	TD.	Pts.	F.
1984—Los Angeles USFL	12	310	179	57.7	2361	10	9	7.62	79	515	6.5	7	7	†48	7
1985—Los Angeles USFL	13	250	137	54.8	1741	6	13	6.96	56	368	6.6	2	2	12	7
1985—Tampa Bay NFL	5	138	72	52.2	935	3	8	6.78	40	233	5.8	1	1	6	4
1986—Tampa Bay NFL	14	363	195	53.7	2282	8	13	6.29	74	425	5.7	5	5	30	11
1987—San Francisco NFL	8	69	37	53.6	570	10	0	8.26	26	190	7.3	1	1	6	0
USFL Totals—2 Years	25	560	316	56.4	4102	16	22	7.33	135	883	6.5	9	9	60	14
NFL Totals—3 Years	27	570	304	53.3	3787	21	21	6.64	140	848	6.1	7	7	42	15
Pro Totals—5 Years	52	1130	620	54.9	7889	37	43	6.98	275	1731	6.3	16	16	102	29

†Includes three 2-point conversions.
USFL Quarterback Rating Points: 1984 (80.6), 1985 (63.1). Total—73.1.
NFL Quarterback Rating Points: 1985 (56.9), 1986 (65.5), 1987 (120.8). Total—71.1.
Additional USFL statistics: Recovered four fumbles, 1984; recovered one fumble and fumbled seven times for minus 11 yards, 1985.
Additional NFL statistics: Recovered one fumble and fumbled four times for minus one yard, 1985; recovered four fumbles and fumbled 11 times for minus 24 yards, 1986.

THEO THOMAS YOUNG
Tight End—Pittsburgh Steelers
Born April 25, 1965, at Newport, Ark.
Height, 6.02. Weight, 237.
High School—Newport, Ark., Remmel Park.
Attended University of Arkansas.

Selected by Pittsburgh in 12th round (317th player selected) of 1987 NFL draft.
Signed by Pittsburgh Steelers, July 26, 1987.
Pittsburgh NFL, 1987.
Games: 1987 (12).
Pro statistics: Caught two passes for 10 yards, 1987.

KENNY R. ZACHARY
(Ken)
Running Back—San Diego Chargers
Born November 19, 1963, at Salpulpa, Okla.
Height, 6.00. Weight, 225.
High School—Sapulpa, Okla.
Attended Oklahoma State University.

Signed as free agent by Hamilton Tiger-Cats, May 2, 1986.
Released by Hamilton Tiger-Cats, June 20, 1986; signed as free agent by Green Bay Packers, August 3, 1986.
Released by Green Bay Packers, August 18, 1986; signed as free agent by Hamilton Tiger-Cats, August, 1986.
Released by Hamilton Tiger-Cats, September 1, 1987; signed as free agent replacement player by San Diego Chargers, September 24, 1987.
Released by San Diego Chargers, October 20, 1987; re-signed by Chargers, February 22, 1988.

		—RUSHING—				PASS RECEIVING				—TOTAL—		
Year Club	G.	Att.	Yds.	Avg.	TD.	P.C.	Yds.	Avg.	TD.	TD.	Pts.	F.
1986—Hamilton CFL	4	59	275	4.7	2	12	116	9.7	0	2	12	2
1987—Hamilton CFL	6	71	356	5.0	6	14	111	7.9	1	7	42	5
1987—San Diego NFL	3	1	3	3.0	0			None		0	0	1
CFL Totals—2 Years	10	130	631	4.8	8	26	227	8.7	1	9	54	7
NFL Totals—1 Year	3	1	3	3.0	0	0	0	0.0	0	0	0	1
Pro Totals—3 Years	13	131	634	4.8	8	26	227	8.7	1	9	54	8

Additional CFL statistics: Returned two kickoffs for 38 yards, 1986; returned six kickoffs for 124 yards (20.7 avg.), 1987.
Additional NFL statistics: Returned one kickoff for two yards, 1987.

CARL AUGUST ZANDER JR.
Linebacker—Cincinnati Bengals
Born March 23, 1963, at Mendham, N.J.
Height, 6.02. Weight, 235.
High School—Mendham, N.J., West Morris.
Attended University of Tennessee.

Selected by Memphis in 1985 USFL territorial draft.
Selected by Cincinnati in 2nd round (43rd player selected) of 1985 NFL draft.
Signed by Cincinnati Bengals, July 21, 1985.
Cincinnati NFL, 1985 through 1987.
Games: 1985 (16), 1986 (16), 1987 (12).
Pro statistics: Returned one kickoff for 19 yards and recovered one fumble for 34 yards, 1985; intercepted one pass for 18 yards and recovered one fumble, 1986.

—DID YOU KNOW—
That Jim Mora now ranks as the second winningest coach in New Orleans Saints history with 19 victories after two seasons? Bum Phillips had 27 wins in his five-year tenure.

MAXIMMILLIAN JAVIER ZENDEJAS
(Max)
Placekicker—Green Bay Packers

Born September 2, 1963, at Curimeo Michucan, Mex.
Height, 5.11. Weight, 184.
High School—Chino, Calif., Don Antonio Lugo.
Attended University of Arizona.
Brother of Joaquin Zendejas, placekicker with New England Patriots, 1983; brother of Luis Zendejas, placekicker with Arizona Outlaws and Dallas Cowboys, 1985 and 1987; brother of Alan Zendejas, placekicker at Arizona State University; cousin of Tony Zendejas, placekicker with Houston Oilers.
Selected by Arizona in 1986 USFL territorial draft.
Selected by Dallas in 4th round (100th player selected) of 1986 NFL draft.
Signed by Dallas Cowboys, July 11, 1986.
Released by Dallas Cowboys, September 1, 1986; signed as free agent by Washington Redskins, October 13, 1986.
On injured reserve with leg injury, December 16 through remainder of 1986 season.
Released by Washington Redskins, August 20, 1987; signed as free agent replacement player by Green Bay Packers, September 25, 1987.

			—PLACE KICKING—				
Year	Club	G.	XP.	XPM.	FG.	FGA.	Pts.
1986—Washington NFL.....		9	23	*5	9	14	50
1987—Green Bay NFL.......		10	13	2	16	19	61
Pro Totals—2 Years.......		19	36	7	25	33	111

TONY ZENDEJAS
Placekicker—Houston Oilers

Born May 15, 1960, at Curimeo Michucan, Mexico.
Height, 5.08. Weight, 165.
High School—Chino, Calif.
Attended University of Nevada at Reno.
Cousin of Joaquin Zendejas, placekicker with New England Patriots, 1983; cousin of Max Zendejas, placekicker with Green Bay Packers; cousin of Luis Zendejas, placekicker with Arizona Outlaws and Dallas Cowboys, 1985 and 1987; and cousin of Alan Zendejas, placekicker at Arizona State University.
Tied NFL record for most field goals, 50 or more yards, game (2), against San Diego Chargers, November 24, 1985.
Named as kicker on THE SPORTING NEWS USFL All-Star Team, 1984 and 1985.
Selected by Los Angeles in 5th round (90th player selected) of 1984 USFL draft.
Signed by Los Angeles Express, February 21, 1984.
Selected by Washington in 1st round (27th player selected) of 1984 NFL supplemental draft.
Granted free agency, July 1, 1985; signed by Washington Redskins, July 3, 1985.
Traded by Washington Redskins to Houston Oilers for 5th round pick in 1987 draft, August 27, 1985.
Crossed picket line during players' strike, October 14, 1987.

			—PLACE KICKING—				
Year	Club	G.	XP.	XPM.	FG.	FGA.	Pts.
1984—Los Angeles USFL...		18	33	0	21	30	96
1985—Los Angeles USFL...		18	22	1	*26	*34	100
1985—Houston NFL...........		14	29	2	21	27	92
1986—Houston NFL...........		15	28	1	22	27	94
1987—Houston NFL...........		13	32	1	20	26	92
USFL Totals—2 Years...		36	55	1	47	64	196
NFL Totals—3 Years.....		42	89	4	63	80	278
Pro Totals—5 Years.......		78	144	5	110	144	474

Additional NFL statistics: Attempted one pass with one completion for minus seven yards and recovered one fumble, 1985; punted once for 36 yards, 1986.

GARY WAYNE ZIMMERMAN
Offensive Tackle—Minnesota Vikings

Born December 13, 1961, at Fullerton, Calif.
Height, 6.06. Weight, 284.
High School—Walnut, Calif.
Attended University of Oregon.
Named to THE SPORTING NEWS NFL All-Star Team, 1987.
Named as offensive tackle on THE SPORTING NEWS USFL All-Star Team, 1984 and 1985.
Selected by Los Angeles in 2nd round (36th player selected) of 1984 USFL draft.
Signed by Los Angeles Express, February 13, 1984.
Granted roster exemption, February 13 through February 23, 1984; activated, February 24, 1984.
Selected by New York Giants in 1st round (3rd player selected) of 1984 NFL supplemental draft.
NFL rights traded by New York Giants to Minnesota Vikings for two 2nd round picks in 1986 draft, April 29, 1986.
Released by Los Angeles Express, May 19, 1986; signed by Minnesota Vikings, May 21, 1986.
Los Angeles USFL, 1984 and 1985; Minnesota NFL, 1986 and 1987.
Games: 1984 (17), 1985 (17), 1986 (16), 1987 (12). Total USFL—34. Total NFL—28. Total Pro—62.
USFL statistics: Returned one kickoff for no yards, recovered two fumbles and fumbled once, 1984.
NFL statistics: Recovered two fumbles, 1986; recovered one fumble for four yards, 1987.
Played in NFC Championship Game following 1987 season.
Played in Pro Bowl (NFL All-Star Game) following 1987 season.

JEFFREY ALAN ZIMMERMAN
(Jeff)
Guard—Dallas Cowboys
Born January 10, 1965, at Enid, Okla.
Height 6.03. Weight, 316.
High School—Orlando, Fla., Evans.
Attended University of Florida.
Selected by Dallas in 3rd round (68th player selected) of 1987 NFL draft.
Signed by Dallas Cowboys, July 17, 1987.
Dallas NFL, 1987.
Games: 1987 (11).

MICHAEL EDWARD ZORDICH
(Mike)
Safety—New York Jets
Born October 12, 1963, at Youngstown, O.
Height, 5.11. Weight, 207.
High School—Youngstown, O., Chaney.
Received bachelor of science degree in hotel, restaurant and institutional management
from Penn State University in 1986.
Selected by Baltimore in 1986 USFL territorial draft.
Selected by San Diego in 9th round (235th player selected) of 1986 NFL draft.
Signed by San Diego Chargers, June 24, 1986.
Released by San Diego Chargers, August 22, 1986; signed as free agent by New York Jets, April 9, 1987.
Released by New York Jets, September 6, 1987; re-signed by Jets, September 14, 1987.
New York Jets NFL, 1987.
Games: 1987 (10).

ADDITIONAL PLAYER TRANSACTIONS

The following player transactions involve players in the Register occurring after June 1, 1988.

BELL, TODD—Signed as free agent by Philadelphia Eagles, June 14, 1988.

BOWMAN, KEVIN—Released by Tampa Bay Buccaneers, June 8, 1988.

BROPHY, JAY—Retired from Tampa Bay Buccaneers, June 2, 1988.

DAVIS, MIKE—Granted free agency, February 1, 1988; withdrew qualifying offer, June 3, 1988.

EDWARDS, DAVID—Released by Tampa Bay Buccaneers, June 8, 1988.

EVANS, DAVID—Released by Tampa Bay Buccaneers, June 8, 1988.

FRAIN, TODD—Released by New York Jets, June 7, 1988.

GILBERT, GALE—Granted free agency, February 1, 1988; withdrew qualifying offer, June 8, 1988.

HAYES, LESTER—Released by Los Angeles Raiders, June 6, 1988.

JOHNSON, LAWRENCE—Released by Buffalo Bills, June 6, 1988.

MARVE, EUGENE—Traded by Buffalo Bills to Tampa Bay Buccaneers for draft choice, June 13, 1988.

QUINN, MARCUS—Released by Tampa Bay Buccaneers, June 8, 1988.

NFL Head Coaches

RAYMOND EMMETT BERRY
New England Patriots

Born February 27, 1933, at Corpus Christi, Tex.
High School—Paris, Tex.
Attended Schreiner Institute and received bachelor of arts degree from
Southern Methodist University in 1955.

Played wide receiver.
Inducted into Pro Football Hall of Fame, 1973.
Named to THE SPORTING NEWS NFL Western Conference All-Star Team, 1957 through 1960.
Selected (as future choice) by Baltimore in 20th round of 1954 NFL draft.

Year—Club	G.	P.C.	Yds.	Avg.	TD.	Year—Club	G.	P.C.	Yds.	Avg.	TD.
		—PASS RECEIVING—						—PASS RECEIVING—			
1955—Baltimore NFL	12	13	205	15.8	0	1962—Baltimore NFL	14	51	687	13.5	3
1956—Baltimore NFL	12	37	601	16.2	2	1963—Baltimore NFL	9	44	703	16.0	3
1957—Baltimore NFL	12	47	*800	17.0	6	1964—Baltimore NFL	12	43	663	15.4	6
1958—Baltimore NFL	12	*56	794	14.2	*9	1965—Baltimore NFL	14	58	739	12.7	7
1959—Baltimore NFL	12	*66	*959	14.5	*14	1966—Baltimore NFL	14	56	786	14.0	7
1960—Baltimore NFL	12	*74	*1298	17.5	10	1967—Baltimore NFL	7	11	167	15.2	1
1961—Baltimore NFL	12	75	873	11.6	0	Pro Totals—13 Years	154	631	9275	14.7	68

Additional pro statistics: Returned two kickoffs for 27 yards, 1955; fumbled once, 1962.
Played in NFL Championship Game following 1958, 1959 and 1964 seasons.
Played in Pro Bowl (NFL All-Star Game) following 1958, 1959, 1961, 1963 and 1964 seasons.

COACHING RECORD

Assistant coach, Dallas Cowboys NFL, 1968.
Assistant coach at University of Arkansas, 1970 through 1972.
Assistant coach, Detroit Lions NFL, 1973 through 1975.
Assistant coach, Cleveland Browns NFL, 1976 and 1977.
Assistant coach, New England Patriots NFL, 1978 through 1981.
Training camp assistant coach, Minnesota Vikings NFL, 1984.

Year—Club	Pos.	W.	L.	T.
1984—New England NFL†	‡Second	4	4	0
1985—New England NFL	‡§Second	11	5	0
1986—New England NFL	‡First	11	5	0
1987—New England NFL	‡§Second	8	7	0
Pro Totals—4 Years		34	21	0

†Replaced Ron Meyer, October 25, 1984 with 5-3 record and in third place.
‡Eastern Division (American Conference).
§Tied for position.

PLAYOFF RECORD

Year—Club	W.	L.
1985—New England NFL	3	1
1986—New England NFL	0	1
Pro Totals—2 Years	3	2

1985—Won wild-card playoff game from New York Jets, 26-14; won conference playoff game from Los Angeles Raiders, 27-20; won conference championship game from Miami, 31-14; lost NFL championship game (Super Bowl XX) to Chicago, 46-10.
1986—Lost conference playoff game to Denver, 22-17.

JEROME MONAHAN BURNS
(Jerry)
Minnesota Vikings

Born January 24, 1927, at Detroit, Mich.
High School—Detroit, Mich., Catholic Central.
Received degree in physical education from University of Michigan.

COACHING RECORD

Assistant coach at University of Hawaii, 1951.
Assistant coach at Whittier College, 1952.
Head coach at St. Mary of Redford High School, Detroit, Mich., 1953.
Assistant coach at University of Iowa, 1954 through 1960.
Assistant coach, Green Bay Packers NFL, 1966 and 1967.
Assistant coach, Minnesota Vikings NFL, 1968 through 1985.

Year—Club	Pos.	W.	L.	T.
1961—Iowa	†‡Seventh	5	4	0
1962—Iowa	†‡Fifth	4	5	0
1963—Iowa	†Eighth	3	3	2
1964—Iowa	†‡Ninth	3	6	0
1965—Iowa	†Tenth	1	9	0
1986—Minnesota NFL	§Second	9	7	0
1987—Minnesota NFL	§Second	8	7	0
College Totals—5 Years		16	27	2
Pro Totals—2 Years		17	14	0

PLAYOFF RECORD

Year	Club	W.	L.
1987—Minnesota NFL		2	1

1987—Won wild-card playoff game from New Orleans, 44-10; won conference playoff game from San Francisco, 36-24; lost conference championship game to Washington, 17-10.

FRANCIS MARION CAMPBELL
(Known by middle name.)
Atlanta Falcons
Born May 25, 1929, at Chester, S. C.
High School—Chester, S. C.
Received bachelor of science degree in education from University of Georgia.

Played defensive lineman.
Named to THE SPORTING NEWS NFL East Division All-Star Team, 1960.
Selected by San Francisco in 4th round of 1952 NFL draft.
Military service, 1952 and 1953.
Traded by San Francisco 49ers to Philadelphia Eagles for 6th round draft choice, September 20, 1956.
San Francisco NFL, 1954 and 1955; Philadelphia NFL, 1956 through 1961.
Games: 1954 (12), 1955 (11), 1956 (12), 1957 (10), 1958 (11), 1959 (12), 1960 (12), 1961 (14). Total—94.
Pro statistics: Recovered two fumbles, 1954; recovered one fumble, 1955, 1958 and 1960; intercepted one pass for no yards, 1955 and 1959; intercepted one pass for one yard and fumbled once, 1956; recovered three fumbles, 1959.
Played in NFL Championship Game following 1960 season.
Played in Playoff Bowl Game following 1961 season.
Played in Pro Bowl (NFL All-Star Game) following 1960 and 1961 seasons.

COACHING RECORD

Assistant coach, Boston Patriots AFL, 1962 and 1963.
Assistant coach, Minnesota Vikings NFL, 1964 through 1966.
Assistant coach, Los Angeles Rams NFL, 1967 and 1968.
Assistant coach, Atlanta Falcons NFL, 1969 through part of 1974 and 1986.
Assistant coach, Philadelphia Eagles NFL, 1977 through 1982.

Year	Club	Pos.	W.	L.	T.
1974—Atlanta NFL†		‡Fourth	1	5	0
1975—Atlanta NFL		‡Third	4	10	0
1976—Atlanta NFL§		‡Fourth	1	4	0
1983—Philadelphia NFL		xFifth	5	11	0
1984—Philadelphia NFL		xFifth	6	9	1
1985—Philadelphia NFL y		xFourth	6	9	0
1987—Atlanta NFL		xFourth	3	12	0
Pro Totals—7 Years			26	60	1

†Replaced Norm Van Brocklin, November 5, 1974 with 2-6 record and tied for third place.
‡Western Division (National Conference).
§Replaced by General Manager Pat Peppler, October 11, 1976.
xEastern Division (National Conference).
yReplaced by interim coach Fred Bruney, December 16, 1986.

MICHAEL KELLER DITKA
(Mike)
Chicago Bears
Born October 18, 1939, at Carnegie, Pa.
High School—Aliquippa, Pa.
Attended University of Pittsburgh.

Played tight end.
Inducted into Pro Football Hall of Fame, 1988.
Named as end on THE SPORTING NEWS College All-America Team, 1960.
Named NFL Rookie of the Year by THE SPORTING NEWS, 1961.
Named to THE SPORTING NEWS NFL Western Conference All-Star Team, 1961 through 1965.
Selected by Chicago in 1st round of 1961 NFL draft.
Traded by Chicago Bears to Philadelphia Eagles for quarterback Jack Concannon and a 1968 draft choice, April 26, 1967.
Traded by Philadelphia Eagles to Dallas Cowboys for receiver Dave McDaniels, January 18, 1969.

Year	Club	G.	P.C.	Yds.	Avg.	TD.		Year	Club	G.	P.C.	Yds.	Avg.	TD.
		—PASS RECEIVING—								—PASS RECEIVING—				
1961—Chicago NFL		14	56	1076	19.2	12		1968—Philadelphia NFL		11	13	111	8.5	2
1962—Chicago NFL		14	58	904	15.6	5		1969—Dallas NFL		12	17	268	15.8	3
1963—Chicago NFL		14	59	794	13.5	8		1970—Dallas NFL		14	8	98	12.3	0
1964—Chicago NFL		14	75	897	12.0	5		1971—Dallas NFL		14	30	360	12.0	1
1965—Chicago NFL		14	36	454	12.6	2		1972—Dallas NFL		14	17	198	11.6	1
1966—Chicago NFL		14	32	378	11.8	2		Pro Totals—12 Years		158	427	5812	13.6	43
1967—Philadelphia NFL		9	26	274	10.5	2								

Additional pro statistics: Recovered one fumble for a touchdown, 1962 and 1964; fumbled once, 1969; rushed twice for two yards, returned three kickoffs for 30 yards and recovered one fumble, 1971.
Played in NFC Championship Game following 1970 through 1972 seasons.
Played in NFL Championship Game following 1963, 1970 and 1971 seasons.
Played in Pro Bowl (NFL All-Star Game) following 1961 through 1965 seasons.

COACHING RECORD

Named NFL Coach of the Year by THE SPORTING NEWS, 1985.
Assistant coach, Dallas Cowboys NFL, 1973 through 1981.

Year Club	Pos.	W.	L.	T.
1982—Chicago NFL	†‡Eleventh	3	6	0
1983—Chicago NFL	‡§Second	8	8	0
1984—Chicago NFL	§First	10	6	0
1985—Chicago NFL	§First	15	1	0
1986—Chicago NFL	§First	14	2	0
1987—Chicago NFL	§First	11	4	0
Pro Totals—6 Years.............................		61	27	0

†National Conference.
‡Tied for position.
§Central Division (National Conference).

PLAYOFF RECORD

Year Club	W.	L.
1984—Chicago NFL	1	1
1985—Chicago NFL	3	0
1986—Chicago NFL	0	1
1987—Chicago NFL	0	1
Pro Totals—4 Years.......................................	4	3

1984—Won conference playoff game from Washington, 23-19; lost conference championship game to San Francisco, 23-0.
1985—Won conference playoff game from New York Giants, 21-0; won conference championship game from Los Angeles Rams, 24-0; won NFL championship game (Super Bowl XX) from New England, 46-10.
1986—Lost conference playoff game to Washington, 27-13.
1987—Lost conference playoff game to Washington, 21-17.

FRANCIS VanRENSSELAER GANSZ
(Frank)
Kansas City Chiefs

Born November 22, 1938, at Altoona, Pa.
High School—Pittsburgh, Pa., Taylor Allerdice.
Received degree from U.S. Naval Academy in 1960.

COACHING RECORD

Served in U.S. Air Force as jet pilot, 1961 through 1966.
Assistant coach at U.S. Air Force Academy, 1964 through 1966.
Assistant coach at Colgate University, 1968.
Assistant coach at U.S. Naval Academy, 1969 through 1972.
Assistant coach at Oklahoma State University, 1973 and 1975.
Assistant coach at U.S. Military Academy, 1974.
Assistant coach at University of California at Los Angeles, 1976 and 1977.
Assistant coach, San Francisco 49ers NFL, 1978.
Assistant coach, Cincinnati Bengals NFL, 1979 and 1980.
Assistant coach, Kansas City Chiefs NFL, 1981, 1982 and 1986.
Assistant coach, Philadelphia Eagles NFL, 1983 through 1985.

Year Club	Pos.	W.	L.	T.
1987—Kansas City NFL	†Fifth	4	11	0

†Western Division (American Conference).

JOE JACKSON GIBBS
Washington Redskins

Born November 25, 1940, at Mocksville, N. C.
High School—Sante Fe, Calif., Spring.
Attended Cerritos Junior College, received bachelor of science degree in physical education from San Diego State University in 1964 and received master's degree from San Diego State in 1966.

COACHING RECORD

Named NFL Coach of the Year by THE SPORTING NEWS, 1982 and 1983.
Graduate assistant at San Diego State University, 1964 and 1965.
Assistant coach at San Diego State University, 1966.
Assistant coach at Florida State University, 1967 and 1968.
Assistant coach at University of Southern California, 1969 and 1970.
Assistant coach at University of Arkansas, 1971 and 1972.
Assistant coach, St. Louis Cardinals NFL, 1973 through 1977.
Assistant coach, Tampa Bay Buccaneers NFL, 1978.
Assistant coach, San Diego Chargers NFL, 1979 and 1980.

Year Club	Pos.	W.	L.	T.
1981— Washington NFL	†Fourth	8	8	0
1982— Washington NFL	‡First	8	1	0
1983— Washington NFL	†First	14	2	0
1984— Washington NFL	†First	11	5	0
1985— Washington NFL	†§ First	10	6	0
1986— Washington NFL	†Second	12	4	0
1987— Washington NFL	†First	11	4	0
Pro Totals—7 Years..................		74	30	0

†Eastern Division (National Conference).
‡National Conference.
§Tied for position.

PLAYOFF RECORD

Year Club	W.	L.
1982—Washington NFL.............................	4	0
1983—Washington NFL.............................	2	1
1984—Washington NFL.............................	0	1
1986—Washington NFL.............................	2	1
1987—Washington NFL.............................	3	0
Pro Totals—5 Years..................	11	3

1982—Won conference playoff game from Detroit, 31-7; won conference playoff game from Minnesota, 21-7; won conference championship game from Dallas, 31-17; won NFL championship game (Super Bowl XVII) from Miami, 27-17.

1983—Won conference playoff game from Los Angeles Rams, 51-7; won conference championship game from San Francisco, 24-21; lost NFL championship game (Super Bowl XVIII) to Los Angeles Raiders, 38-9.

1984—Lost conference playoff game to Chicago, 23-19.

1986—Won wild-card playoff game from Los Angeles Rams, 19-7; won conference playoff game from Chicago, 27-13; lost conference championship game to New York Giants, 17-0.

1987—Won conference playoff game from Chicago, 21-17; won conference championship game from Minnesota, 17-10; won NFL championship game (Super Bowl XXII) from Denver, 42-10.

JERRY MICHAEL GLANVILLE
Houston Oilers

Born October 14, 1941, at Detroit, Mich.
High School—Reading, O.
Attended Montana State University and received bachelor of science degree from Northern Michigan University in 1964 and master's degree in art western from Western Kentucky University in 1966.

COACHING RECORD

Assistant coach at Central Catholic High School, Lima, O., 1963 and 1964.
Assistant coach at Reading High School, Reading, O., 1965.
Assistant coach at Northern Michigan University, 1966.
Assistant coach at Western Kentucky University, 1967.
Assistant coach at Georgia Tech, 1968 through 1973.
Assistant coach, Detroit Lions NFL, 1974 through 1976.
Assistant coach, Atlanta Falcons NFL, 1977 through 1982.
Assistant coach, Buffalo Bills NFL, 1983.
Assistant coach, Houston Oilers NFL, 1984 and 1985.

Year Club	Pos.	W.	L.	T.
1985— Houston NFL†	‡Fourth	0	2	0
1986— Houston NFL	‡Fourth	5	11	0
1987— Houston NFL	‡Second	9	6	0
Pro Totals—3 Years..................		14	19	0

†Replaced Hugh Campbell, December 9, 1985, with 5-9 record and in fifth place.
‡Central Division (American Conference).

PLAYOFF RECORD

Year Club	W.	L.
1987—Houston NFL.............................	1	1

1987—Won wild-card playoff game in overtime from Seattle, 23-20; lost conference playoff game to Denver, 34-10.

JELINDO INFANTE
(Lindy)
Green Bay Packers

Born May 27, 1940, at Miami, Fla.
High School—Miami, Fla.
Received bachelor of science degree in education from University of Florida in 1964.

Selected by Cleveland in 12th round of 1963 NFL draft.
Selected by Buffalo in 11th round of 1963 AFL draft.
Signed by Buffalo Bills, 1963.
Released by Buffalo Bills, 1963; signed as free agent by Hamilton Tiger-Cats, 1963.
Released by Hamilton Tiger-Cats, 1963.
Hamilton CFL, 1963.
Games: 1963 (1).
CFL statistics: Rushed three times for 12 yards, 1963.

Assistant coach, Miami (Fla.) High School, 1964.
Head coach at Miami (Fla.) High School, 1965.
Assistant coach at University of Florida, 1966 through 1971.
Assistant coach at Memphis State University, 1972 through 1974.
Assistant coach, Charlotte WFL, 1975.
Assistant coach at Tulane University, 1976 and 1979.
Assistant coach, New York Giants NFL, 1977 and 1978.
Assistant coach, Cincinnati Bengals NFL, 1980 through 1982.
Assistant coach, Cleveland Browns NFL, 1986 and 1987.

Year	Club	Pos.	W.	L.	T.
1984—	Jacksonville USFL	†Fifth	6	12	0
1985—	Jacksonville USFL	‡Sixth	9	9	0
	Pro Totals—2 Years..................................		15	21	0

†Southern Division (Eastern Conference).
‡Eastern Conference.

CHARLES ROBERT KNOX SR.
(Chuck)
Seattle Seahawks

Born April 27, 1932, at Sewickley, Pa.
High School—Sewickley, Pa.
Received bachelor of arts degree in history from Juniata College in 1954.
Father of Chuck Knox Jr., running back at University of Arizona.

COACHING RECORD

Named NFL Coach of the Year by THE SPORTING NEWS, 1973, 1980 and 1984.
Assistant coach at Juniata College, 1954.
Assistant coach at Tyrone (Pa.) High School, 1955.
Head coach at Ellwood City (Pa.) High School, 1956 through 1958 (Won 10, Lost 16, Tied 2).
Assistant coach at Wake Forest University, 1959 and 1960.
Assistant coach at University of Kentucky, 1961 and 1962.
Assistant coach, New York Jets AFL, 1963 through 1966.
Assistant coach, Detroit Lions NFL, 1967 through 1972.

Year	Club	Pos.	W.	L.	T.	Year	Club	Pos.	W.	L.	T.
1973—	Los Angeles NFL	†First	12	2	0	1981—	Buffalo NFL	‡Third	10	6	0
1974—	Los Angeles NFL	†First	10	4	0	1982—	Buffalo NFL	x§Eighth	4	5	0
1975—	Los Angeles NFL	†First	12	2	0	1983—	Seattle NFL	ySecond	9	7	0
1976—	Los Angeles NFL	†First	10	3	1	1984—	Seattle NFL	ySecond	12	4	0
1977—	Los Angeles NFL	†First	10	4	0	1985—	Seattle NFL	y§Third	8	8	0
1978—	Buffalo NFL	‡§Fourth	5	11	0	1986—	Seattle NFL	y§Second	10	6	0
1979—	Buffalo NFL	‡Fourth	7	9	0	1987—	Seattle NFL	ySecond	9	6	0
1980—	Buffalo NFL	‡First	11	5	0		Pro Totals—15 Years		139	82	1

†Western Division (National Conference).
‡Eastern Division (American Conference).
§Tied for position.
xAmerican Conference.
yWestern Division (American Conference).

PLAYOFF RECORD

Year	Club	W.	L.
1973—Los Angeles NFL..............................		0	1
1974—Los Angeles NFL..............................		1	1
1975—Los Angeles NFL..............................		1	1
1976—Los Angeles NFL..............................		1	1
1977—Los Angeles NFL..............................		0	1
1980—Buffalo NFL..............................		0	1
1981—Buffalo NFL..............................		1	1
1983—Seattle NFL..............................		2	1
1984—Seattle NFL..............................		1	1
1987—Seattle NFL..............................		0	1
Pro Totals—10 Years..............................		7	10

1973—Lost conference playoff game to Dallas, 27-16.
1974—Won conference playoff game from Washington, 19-10; lost conference championship game to Minnesota, 14-10.
1975—Won conference playoff game from St. Louis, 35-23; lost conference championship game to Dallas, 37-7.
1976—Won conference playoff game from Dallas, 14-12; lost conference championship game to Minnesota, 24-13.
1977—Lost conference playoff game to Minnesota, 14-7.
1980—Lost conference playoff game to San Diego, 20-14.
1981—Won conference playoff game from New York Jets, 31-27; lost conference playoff game to Cincinnati, 28-21.
1983—Won wild-card playoff game from Denver, 31-7; won conference playoff game from Miami, 27-20; lost conference championship game to Los Angeles Raiders, 30-14.
1984—Won wild-card playoff game from Los Angeles Raiders, 13-7; lost conference playoff game to Miami, 31-10.
1987—Lost wild-card playoff game in overtime to Houston, 23-20.

THOMAS WADE LANDRY
(Tom)
Dallas Cowboys

Born September 11, 1924, at Mission, Tex.
High School—Mission, Tex.
Received bachelor of business administration degree from University of Texas in 1949
and bachelor of science degree in industrial engineering from University of Houston.
Played defensive back.
Selected in 4th round from New York AAFC by New York Giants NFL in AAFC-NFL merger, 1950.

Year Club	G.	No.	Yds.	Avg.	TD.	No.	Avg.	Blk.	TD.	Pts.	F.
		-INTERCEPTIONS-				—PUNTING—			—TOTAL—		
1949—New York AAFC	13	1	44	44.0	0	51	44.1	⋆2	0	0	..
1950—New York Giants NFL	12	2	0	0.0	0	58	36.8	1	1	6	0
1951—New York Giants NFL	10	8	121	15.1	⋆2	15	42.5	0	3	18	0
1952—New York NFL	12	8	99	12.4	1	82	41.0	1	2	12	5
1953—New York NFL	12	3	55	18.3	0	44	40.3	0	0	0	1
1954—New York NFL	12	8	71	8.9	0	64	42.5	0	0	0	1
1955—New York NFL	12	2	14	7.0	0	⋆75	40.3	1	0	0	0
AAFC Totals—1 Year	13	1	44	44.0	0	51	44.1	2	0	0	..
NFL Totals—6 Years	70	31	360	11.6	3	338	40.4	3	6	36	7
Pro Totals—7 Years	83	32	404	12.6	3	389	40.9	5	6	36	..

Year Club	G.	No.	Yds.	Avg.	TD.	No.	Yds.	Avg.	TD.
		—PUNT RETURNS—				—KICKOFF RET.—			
1949—New York AAFC	13	3	52	17.3	0	2	39	19.5	0
1950—New York Giants NFL	12	None				None			
1951—New York Giants NFL	10	1	0	0.0	0	1	0	0.0	0
1952—New York NFL	12	10	88	8.8	0	1	20	20.0	0
1953—New York NFL	12	1	5	5.0	0	2	38	19.0	0
1954—New York NFL	12	None				None			
1955—New York NFL	12	None				None			
AAFC Totals—1 Year	13	3	52	17.3	0	2	39	19.5	0
NFL Totals—6 Years	70	12	93	7.8	0	4	58	14.5	0
Pro Totals—7 Years	83	15	145	9.7	0	6	97	16.2	0

Additional AAFC statistics: Rushed 29 times for 91 yards and caught six passes for 109 yards, 1949.
Additional NFL statistics: Rushed seven times for 40 yards and a touchdown, 1952; attempted 47 passes with 11 completions for 172 yards, one touchdown and seven interceptions, 1952; recovered two fumbles for 41 yards and one touchdown, 1950; recovered one fumble for nine yards and a touchdown, 1951; recovered two fumbles, 1952; recovered one fumble, 1953 and 1955; recovered two fumbles for 14 yards, 1954.
Played in Pro Bowl (NFL All-Star Game) following 1954 season.

COACHING RECORD

Named NFL Coach of the Year by THE SPORTING NEWS, 1966.
Player-coach for New York Giants NFL, 1954 and 1955.
Assistant coach for New York Giants NFL, 1956 through 1959.

Year	Pos.	W.	L.	T.	Year	Pos.	W.	L.	T.
1960—Dallas NFL	†Seventh	0	11	1	1975—Dallas NFL	ySecond	10	4	0
1961—Dallas NFL	‡Sixth	4	9	1	1976—Dallas NFL	yFirst	11	3	0
1962—Dallas NFL	‡Fifth	5	8	1	1977—Dallas NFL	yFirst	12	2	0
1963—Dallas NFL	‡Fifth	4	10	0	1978—Dallas NFL	yFirst	12	4	0
1964—Dallas NFL	‡Fifth	5	8	1	1979—Dallas NFL	y§First	11	5	0
1965—Dallas NFL	§‡Second	7	7	0	1980—Dallas NFL	y§First	12	4	0
1966—Dallas NFL	‡First	10	3	1	1981—Dallas NFL	yFirst	12	4	0
1967—Dallas NFL	xFirst	9	5	0	1982—Dallas NFL	zSecond	6	3	0
1968—Dallas NFL	xFirst	12	2	0	1983—Dallas NFL	ySecond	12	4	0
1969—Dallas NFL	xFirst	11	2	1	1984—Dallas NFL	y§Second	9	7	0
1970—Dallas NFL	yFirst	10	4	0	1985—Dallas NFL	y§First	10	6	0
1971—Dallas NFL	yFirst	11	3	0	1986—Dallas NFL	yThird	7	9	0
1972—Dallas NFL	ySecond	10	4	0	1987—Dallas NFL	§ySecond	7	8	0
1973—Dallas NFL	§yFirst	10	4	0	Pro Totals—28 Years		247	149	6
1974—Dallas NFL	yThird	8	6	0					

†Western Conference.
‡Eastern Conference.
§Tied for position.
xCapitol Division (Eastern Conference).
yEastern Division (National Conference).
zNational Conference.

PLAYOFF RECORD

Year Club	W.	L.	Year Club	W.	L.
1965—Dallas NFL	0	1	1976—Dallas NFL	0	1
1966—Dallas NFL	0	1	1977—Dallas NFL	3	0
1967—Dallas NFL	1	1	1978—Dallas NFL	2	1
1968—Dallas NFL	1	1	1979—Dallas NFL	0	1
1969—Dallas NFL	0	2	1980—Dallas NFL	2	1
1970—Dallas NFL	2	1	1981—Dallas NFL	1	1
1971—Dallas NFL	3	0	1982—Dallas NFL	2	1
1972—Dallas NFL	1	1	1983—Dallas NFL	0	1
1973—Dallas NFL	1	1	1985—Dallas NFL	0	1
1975—Dallas NFL	2	1	Pro Totals—19 Years	21	18

1965—Lost Playoff Bowl to Baltimore, 35-3.
1966—Lost NFL championship game to Green Bay, 34-27.
1967—Won conference playoff game from Cleveland, 52-14; lost NFL championship game to Green Bay, 21-17.
1968—Lost conference playoff game to Cleveland, 31-20; won Playoff Bowl from Minnesota, 17-13.
1969—Lost conference playoff game to Cleveland, 38-14; lost Playoff Bowl to Los Angeles, 31-0.
1970—Won conference playoff game from Detroit, 5-0; won conference championship game from San Francisco, 17-10; lost NFL championship game (Super Bowl V) to Baltimore, 16-13.
1971—Won conference playoff game from Minnesota, 20-12; won conference championship game from San Francisco, 14-3; won NFL championship game (Super Bowl VI) from Miami, 24-3.
1972—Won conference playoff game from San Francisco, 30-28; lost conference championship game to Washington, 26-3.
1973—Won conference playoff game from Los Angeles, 27-16; lost conference championship game to Minnesota, 27-10.
1975—Won conference playoff game from Minnesota, 17-14; won conference championship game from Los Angeles, 37-7; lost NFL championship game (Super Bowl X) to Pittsburgh, 21-17.
1976—Lost conference playoff game to Los Angeles, 14-12.
1977—Won conference playoff game from Chicago, 37-7; won conference championship game from Minnesota, 23-6; won NFL championship game (Super Bowl XII) from Denver, 27-10.
1978—Won conference playoff game from Atlanta, 27-20; won conference championship game from Los Angeles, 28-0; lost NFL championship game (Super Bowl XIII) to Pittsburgh, 35-31.
1979—Lost conference playoff game to Los Angeles, 21-19.
1980—Won conference playoff game from Los Angeles, 34-13; won conference playoff game from Atlanta, 30-27; lost conference championship game to Philadelphia, 20-7.
1981—Won conference playoff game from Tampa Bay, 38-0; lost conference championship game to San Francisco, 28-27.
1982—Won conference playoff game from Tampa Bay, 30-17; won conference playoff game from Green Bay, 37-26; lost conference championship game to Washington, 31-17.
1983—Lost wild-card playoff game to Los Angeles Rams, 24-17.
1985—Lost conference playoff game to Los Angeles Rams, 20-0.

MARVIN DANIEL LEVY
(Marv)
Buffalo Bills

Born August 3, 1928, at Chicago, Ill.
High School—Chicago, Ill., South Shore.
Received degree from Coe College in 1950 and received master's degree
in history from Harvard University in 1951.

COACHING RECORD

Head coach at St. Louis (Mo.) Country Day School, 1951 and 1952 (won 13, lost 0, tied 1).
Assistant coach at Coe College, 1953 through 1955.
Assistant coach at University of New Mexico, 1956 and 1957.
Assistant coach, Philadelphia Eagles NFL, 1969.
Assistant coach, Los Angeles Rams NFL, 1970.
Assistant coach, Washington Redskins NFL, 1971 and 1972.

Year Club	Pos.	W.	L.	T.	Year Club	Pos.	W.	L.	T.
1958—New Mexico	†Second	7	3	0	1977—Montreal CFL	yFirst	11	5	0
1959—New Mexico	†Third	7	3	0	1978—Kansas City NFL	zFifth	4	12	0
1960—California	‡Fourth	2	7	1	1979—Kansas City NFL	zFifth	7	9	0
1961—California	‡§Fourth	1	8	1	1980—Kansas City NFL	z§Third	8	8	0
1962—California	‡Fifth	1	9	0	1981—Kansas City NFL	zThird	9	7	0
1963—California	‡Fourth	4	5	1	1982—Kansas City NFL	aEleventh	3	6	0
1964—William & Mary	x§Fourth	4	6	0	1984—Chicago USFL	bFifth	5	13	0
1965—William & Mary	xFirst	6	4	0	1986—Buffalo NFLc	dFourth	2	5	0
1966—William & Mary	x§First	5	4	1	1987—Buffalo NFL	dFourth	7	8	0
1967—William & Mary	xFourth	5	4	1	College Totals—11 Years		45	60	5
1968—William & Mary	x§Third	3	7	0	NFL Totals—7 Years		40	55	0
1973—Montreal CFL	yThird	7	6	1	CFL Totals—5 Years		43	31	4
1974—Montreal CFL	yFirst	9	5	2	USFL Totals—1 Year		5	13	0
1975—Montreal CFL	ySecond	9	7	0	Pro Totals—12 Years		88	99	4
1976—Montreal CFL	y§Third	7	8	1					

†Skyline Conference.
‡Athletic Association of Western Universities.
§Tied for position.
xSouthern Conference.
yEastern Conference.
zWestern Division (American Conference).
aAmerican Conference.
bCentral Division (Western Conference).
cReplaced Hank Bullough, November 3, 1986 with 2-7 record and in fourth place.
dEastern Division (American Conference).

PLAYOFF RECORD

Year Club	W.	L.
1973—Montreal CFL	1	1
1974—Montreal CFL	2	0
1975—Montreal CFL	2	1
1976—Montreal CFL	0	1
1977—Montreal CFL	2	0
CFL Totals—5 Years	7	3

1973—Won conference playoff game from Toronto, 32-10; lost conference championship game to Ottawa, 23-14.

— 469 —

1974—Won conference championship game from Ottawa, 14-4, won CFL championship game from Edmonton, 20-7.
1975—Won conference playoff game from Hamilton, 35-12; won conference championship game from Ottawa, 20-10; lost CFL championship game to Edmonton, 9-8.
1976—Lost conference playoff game to Hamilton, 23-0.
1977—Won conference championship game from Ottawa, 21-18; won CFL championship game from Edmonton, 41-6.

RONALD SHAW MEYER
(Ron)
Indianapolis Colts
Born February 17, 1941, at Columbus, O.
High School—Westerville, O.
Received bachelor of science degree in physical education from Purdue University in 1963 and master's degree in physical education from Purdue in 1965.

COACHING RECORD
Graduate assistant coach at Purdue University, 1963.
Head coach at Penn Hill High School, Mishawaka, Ind., 1964 (Won 5, Lost 4, Tied 1).
Assistant coach at Purdue University, 1965 through 1970.
Scout for Dallas Cowboys, 1971 and 1972.

Year	Club	Pos.	W.	L.	T.
1973—	Nevada-Las Vegas	....	8	3	0
1974—	Nevada-Las Vegas	....	12	1	0
1975—	Nevada-Las Vegas	....	7	4	0
1976—	Southern Methodist	†‡Seventh	3	8	0
1977—	Southern Methodist	†‡Sixth	4	7	0
1978—	Southern Methodist	†‡Sixth	4	6	1
1979—	Southern Methodist	‡Sixth	5	6	0
1980—	Southern Methodist	‡Second	8	4	0
1981—	Southern Methodist	‡First	10	1	0
1982—	New England NFL	§Seventh	5	4	0
1983—	New England NFL	†xSecond	8	8	0
1984—	New England NFLy	xThird	5	3	0
1986—	Indianapolis NFLz	xFifth	3	0	0
1987—	Indianapolis NFL	xFirst	9	6	0
	College Totals—9 Years.........................		61	40	1
	Pro Totals—5 Years................................		30	21	0

†Tied for position.
‡Southwest Conference.
§American Conference.
xEastern Division (American Conference).
yReplaced by Raymond Berry, October 25, 1984.
zReplaced Rod Dowhower, December 1, 1986 with 0-13 record and in fifth place.

PLAYOFF RECORD
Year	Club	W.	L.
1982—	New England NFL.............................	0	1
1987—	Indianapolis NFL	0	1
	Pro Totals—2 Years........................	0	2

1982—Lost conference playoff game to Miami, 28-13.
1987—Lost conference playoff game to Cleveland, 38-21.

NCAA DIVISION II PLAYOFF RECORD
Year	Club	W.	L.
1974—	Nevada-Las Vegas.....................................	1	1

1974—Nevada-Las Vegas 35, Alcorn State 22; Delaware 49, Nevada-Las Vegas 11.

COLLEGIATE BOWL GAME RECORD
Year	Club	W.	L.
1980—	Southern Methodist..................................	0	1

1980—Lost Holiday Bowl to Brigham Young, 46-45.

JAMES ERNEST MORA
(Jim)
New Orleans Saints
Born May 24, 1935, at Los Angeles, Calif.
High School—Los Angeles, Calif., University.
Received bachelor of arts degree in physical education from Occidental College in 1957; received master's degree in education from University of Southern California in 1967.
Played in U.S. Marines at Quantico in 1957 and at Camp Lejeune in 1958 and 1959.

COACHING RECORD
Named NFL Coach of the Year by THE SPORTING NEWS, 1987.
Named THE SPORTING NEWS USFL Coach of the Year, 1984.
Assistant coach at Occidental College, 1960 through 1963.

Assistant coach at Stanford University, 1967.
Assistant coach at University of Colorado, 1968 through 1973.
Assistant coach at University of California at Los Angeles, 1974.
Assistant coach at University of Washington, 1975 through 1977.
Assistant coach, Seattle Seahawks NFL, 1978 through 1981.
Assistant coach, New England Patriots NFL, 1982.

Year	Club	Pos.	W.	L.	T.
1964—	Occidental	†Third	5	4	0
1965—	Occidental	†First	8	1	0
1966—	Occidental	†Fourth	5	4	0
1983—	Philadelphia USFL	‡First	15	3	0
1984—	Philadelphia USFL	§First	16	2	0
1985—	Baltimore USFL	xFourth	10	7	1
1986—	New Orleans NFL	yFourth	7	9	0
1987—	New Orleans NFL	ySecond	12	3	0
	College Totals—3 Years		18	9	0
	USFL Totals—3 Years		41	12	1
	NFL Totals—2 Years		19	12	0
	Pro Totals—5 Years		60	24	1

†Southern California Intercollegiate Conference.
‡Atlantic Division.
§Atlantic Division (Eastern Conference).
xEastern Conference.
yWestern Division (National Conference).

PLAYOFF RECORD

Year	Club	W.	L.
1983—	Philadelphia USFL	1	1
1984—	Philadelphia USFL	3	0
1985—	Baltimore USFL	3	0
1987—	New Orleans NFL	0	1
	USFL Totals—3 Years	7	1
	NFL Totals—1 Year	0	1
	Pro Totals—4 Years	7	2

1983—Won divisional playoff game from Chicago, 44-38 (OT); lost USFL championship game to Michigan, 24-22.
1984—Won conference playoff game from New Jersey, 28-7; won conference championship game from Birmingham, 20-10; won USFL championship game from Arizona, 23-3.
1985—Won conference playoff game from New Jersey, 20-17; won conference championship game from Birmingham, 28-14; won USFL championship game from Oakland, 28-24.
1987—Lost wild-card playoff game to Minnesota, 44-10.

CHARLES HENRY NOLL
(Chuck)
Pittsburgh Steelers
Born January 5, 1932, at Cleveland, O.
High School—Cleveland, O., Benedictine.
Received bachelor of science degree in education from University of Dayton in 1953.
Played linebacker and offensive guard.
Selected by Cleveland in 21st round of 1953 NFL draft.

Year	Club	G.	INTERCEPTIONS No.	Yds.	Avg.	TD.	—KICKOFF RET.— No.	Yds.	Avg.	TD.	—TOTAL— TD.	Pts.	F.
1953—	Cleveland NFL	12		None			1	2	2.0	0	0	0	0
1954—	Cleveland NFL	12		None					None		0	0	0
1955—	Cleveland NFL	12	5	74	14.8	1			None		1	8	0
1956—	Cleveland NFL	12	1	13	13.0	0			None		1	6	0
1957—	Cleveland NFL	5		None					None		0	0	0
1958—	Cleveland NFL	12		None					None		0	0	0
1959—	Cleveland NFL	12	2	5	2.5	0	1	20	20.0	0	0	0	0
	Pro Totals—7 Years	77	8	92	11.5	1	2	22	11.0	0	2	14	0

Additional pro statistics: Recovered two fumbles for 10 yards, 1954; credited with one safety, 1955; recovered one fumble for 39 yards and a touchdown, 1956.
Played in NFL Championship Game following 1953 through 1955 seasons.

COACHING RECORD

Assistant coach, Los Angeles Chargers AFL, 1960.
Assistant coach, San Diego Chargers AFL, 1961 through 1965.
Assistant coach, Baltimore Colts NFL, 1966 through 1968.

Year	Club	Pos.	W.	L.	T.	Year	Club	Pos.	W.	L.	T.
1969—	Pittsburgh NFL	†Fourth	1	13	0	1979—	Pittsburgh NFL	‡First	12	4	0
1970—	Pittsburgh NFL	‡Third	5	9	0	1980—	Pittsburgh NFL	‡Third	9	7	0
1971—	Pittsburgh NFL	‡Second	6	8	0	1981—	Pittsburgh NFL	‡Second	8	8	0
1972—	Pittsburgh NFL	‡First	11	3	0	1982—	Pittsburgh NFL	x§Fourth	6	3	0
1973—	Pittsburgh NFL	†§First	10	4	0	1983—	Pittsburgh NFL	‡First	10	6	0
1974—	Pittsburgh NFL	‡First	10	3	1	1984—	Pittsburgh NFL	‡First	9	7	0
1975—	Pittsburgh NFL	‡First	12	2	0	1985—	Pittsburgh NFL	‡§Second	7	9	0
1976—	Pittsburgh NFL	‡§First	10	4	0	1986—	Pittsburgh NFL	‡Third	6	10	0
1977—	Pittsburgh NFL	‡First	9	5	0	1987—	Pittsburgh NFL	‡Third	8	7	0
1978—	Pittsburgh NFL	‡First	14	2	0		Pro Totals—19 Years		163	114	1

PLAYOFF RECORD

Year Club	W.	L.	Year Club	W.	L.
1972—Pittsburgh NFL	1	1	1978—Pittsburgh NFL	3	0
1973—Pittsburgh NFL	0	1	1979—Pittsburgh NFL	3	0
1974—Pittsburgh NFL	3	0	1982—Pittsburgh NFL	0	1
1975—Pittsburgh NFL	3	0	1983—Pittsburgh NFL	0	1
1976—Pittsburgh NFL	1	1	1984—Pittsburgh NFL	1	1
1977—Pittsburgh NFL	0	1	Pro Totals—11 Years	15	7

1972—Won conference playoff game from Oakland, 13-7; lost conference championship game to Miami, 21-17.
1973—Lost conference playoff game to Oakland, 33-14.
1974—Won conference playoff game from Buffalo, 32-14; won conference championship game from Oakland, 24-13; won NFL championship game (Super Bowl IX) from Minnesota, 16-6.
1975—Won conference playoff game from Baltimore, 28-10; won conference championship game from Oakland, 16-10; won NFL championship game (Super Bowl X) from Dallas, 21-17.
1976—Won conference playoff game from Baltimore, 40-14; lost conference championship game to Oakland, 24-7.
1977—Lost conference playoff game to Denver, 34-21.
1978—Won conference playoff game from Denver, 33-10; won conference championship game from Houston, 34-5; won NFL championship game (Super Bowl XIII) from Dallas, 35-31.
1979—Won conference playoff game from Miami, 34-14; won conference championship game from Houston, 27-13; won NFL championship game (Super Bowl XIV) from Los Angeles, 31-19.
1982—Lost conference playoff game to San Diego, 31-28.
1983—Lost conference playoff game to Los Angeles Raiders, 38-10.
1984—Won conference playoff game from Denver, 24-17; lost conference championship game to Miami, 45-28.

DUANE CHARLES PARCELLS
(Bill)
New York Giants
Born August 22, 1941, at Englewood, N.J.
High School—Oradell, N.J., River Dell.
Received bachelor of arts degree in education from Wichita State University in 1964.

COACHING RECORD

Named NFL Coach of the Year by THE SPORTING NEWS, 1986.
Assistant coach at Hastings College, 1964.
Assistant coach at Wichita State University, 1965.
Assistant coach at West Point, 1966 through 1969.
Assistant coach at Florida State University, 1970 through 1972.
Assistant coach at Vanderbilt University, 1973 and 1974.
Asstant coach at Texas Tech University, 1975 through 1977.
Assistant coach, New England Patriots NFL, 1980.
Assistant coach, New York Giants NFL, 1981 and 1982.

Year Club	Pos.	W.	L.	T.
1978—Air Force	....	3	8	0
1983—New York Giants NFL	†Fifth	3	12	1
1984—New York Giants NFL	†‡Second	9	7	0
1985—New York Giants NFL	†‡First	10	6	0
1986—New York Giants NFL	†First	14	2	0
1987—New York Giants NFL	†Fifth	6	9	0
College Totals—1 Year		3	8	0
Pro Totals—5 Years		42	36	1

†Eastern Division (National Conference).
‡Tied for position.

PLAYOFF RECORD

Year Club	W.	L.
1984—New York Giants NFL	1	1
1985—New York Giants NFL	1	1
1986—New York Giants NFL	3	0
Pro Totals—3 Years	5	2

1984—Won wild-card playoff game from Los Angeles Rams, 16-10; lost conference playoff game to San Francisco, 21-10.
1985—Won wild-card playoff game from San Francisco, 17-3; lost conference playoff game to Chicago, 21-0.
1986—Won conference playoff from San Francisco, 49-3; won conference championship from Washington, 17-0; won NFL championship game (Super Bowl XXI) from Denver, 39-20.

WALTER RAY PERKINS
(Known by middle name.)
Tampa Bay Buccaneers
Born December 6, 1941, at Mt. Olive, Miss.
High School—Petal, Miss.
Received bachelor of science degree in secondary education from University of Alabama in 1967.
Selected (as future choice) by Baltimore in 7th round of 1966 NFL draft.

Year	Club	G.	P.C.	Yds.	Avg.	TD.
1967—Baltimore NFL		8	16	302	18.9	2
1968—Baltimore NFL		14	15	227	15.1	1
1969—Baltimore NFL		11	28	391	14.0	3
1970—Baltimore NFL		11	10	194	19.4	1
1971—Baltimore NFL		14	24	424	17.7	4
Pro Totals—5 Years		58	93	1538	16.5	11

(—PASS RECEIVING—)

Additional pro statistics: Rushed three times for 36 yards, 1969; rushed twice for six yards, 1970; rushed five times for 35 yards, 1971.
Played in NFL Championship Game, 1968 and 1970.
Played in AFL-NFL Championship Game following 1968 season.

COACHING RECORD

Assistant coach at Mississippi State University, 1973.
Assistant coach, New England Patriots NFL, 1974 through 1977.
Assistant coach, San Diego Chargers NFL, 1978.

Year	Club	Pos.	W.	L.	T.
1979—New York Giants NFL		†Fourth	6	10	0
1980—New York Giants NFL		†Fifth	4	12	0
1981—New York Giants NFL		†Third	9	7	0
1982—New York Giants NFL		‡§Eighth	4	5	0
1983—Alabama		§xThird	8	4	0
1984—Alabama		§xSeventh	5	6	0
1985—Alabama		§xSecond	9	2	1
1986—Alabama		§xSecond	10	3	0
1987—Tampa Bay NFL		§yFourth	4	11	0
College Totals—4 Years			32	15	1
Pro Totals—5 Years			27	45	0

†Eastern Division (National Conference).
‡National Conference.
§Tied for position.
xSoutheastern Conference.
yCentral Division (National Conference).

PLAYOFF RECORD

Year	Club	W.	L.
1981—New York Giants NFL		1	1

1981—Won conference playoff game from Philadelphia, 27-21; lost conference playoff game to San Francisco, 38-24.

COLLEGIATE BOWL GAME RECORD

Year	Club	W.	L.
1983—Alabama		1	0
1985—Alabama		1	0
1986—Alabama		1	0
Totals—3 Years		3	0

1983—Won Sun Bowl from Southern Methodist, 28-7.
1985—Won Aloha Bowl from Southern California, 24-3.
1986—Won Sun Bowl from Washington, 28-6.

DANIEL EDWARD REEVES
(Dan)
Denver Broncos

Born January 19, 1944, at Rome, Ga.
High School—Americus, Ga.
Attended University of South Carolina.

Played running back.
Named to THE SPORTING NEWS NFL Eastern Conference All-Star Team, 1966.
Signed as free agent by Dallas NFL, 1965.

Year	Club	G.	Att.	Yds.	Avg.	TD.	P.C.	Yds.	Avg.	TD.	TD.	Pts.	F.
				RUSHING			PASS RECEIVING				TOTAL		
1965—Dallas NFL		13	33	102	3.1	2	9	210	23.3	1	3	18	0
1966—Dallas NFL		14	175	757	4.3	8	41	557	13.6	8	*16	96	6
1967—Dallas NFL		14	173	603	3.5	5	39	490	12.6	6	11	66	7
1968—Dallas NFL		4	40	178	4.5	4	7	84	12.0	1	5	30	0
1969—Dallas NFL		13	59	173	2.9	4	18	187	10.4	1	5	30	2
1970—Dallas NFL		14	35	84	2.4	2	12	140	11.7	0	2	12	4
1971—Dallas NFL		14	17	79	4.6	0	3	25	8.3	0	0	0	1
1972—Dallas NFL		14	3	14	4.7	0		None			0	0	0
Pro Totals—8 Years		100	535	1990	3.7	25	129	1693	13.1	17	42	252	20

Year	Club	G.	Att.	Cmp.	Pct.	Gain	T.P.	P.I.	Avg.	No.	Yds.	Avg.	TD.
					PASSING						KICKOFF RET.		
1965—Dallas NFL		13	2	1	50.0	11	0	0	5.50	2	45	22.5	0
1966—Dallas NFL		14	6	3	50.0	48	0	0	8.00	3	56	18.7	0
1967—Dallas NFL		14	7	4	57.1	195	2	1	27.86		None		
1968—Dallas NFL		4	4	2	50.0	43	0	0	10.75		None		

Year Club	G.	PASSING Att.	Cmp.	Pct.	Gain	T.P.	P.I.	Avg.	KICKOFF RET. No.	Yds.	Avg.	TD.
1969—Dallas NFL	13	3	1	33.3	35	0	1	11.67			None	
1970—Dallas NFL	14	3	1	33.3	14	0	1	4.67			None	
1971—Dallas NFL	14	5	2	40.0	24	0	1	4.80			None	
1972—Dallas NFL	14	2	0	00.0	0	0	0	0.00			None	
Pro Totals—8 Years	100	32	14	43.8	370	2	4	11.56	5	101	20.2	0

Additional pro statistics: Returned two punts for minus one yard, 1966.
Played in NFC Championship Game following 1970 and 1971 seasons.
Played in NFL Championship Game following 1966, 1967, 1970 and 1971 seasons.

COACHING RECORD

Player-coach, Dallas Cowboys NFL, 1970 and 1971.
Assistant coach, Dallas Cowboys NFL, 1972 and 1974 through 1980.

Year Club	Pos.	W.	L.	T.
1981—Denver NFL	†‡First	10	6	0
1982—Denver NFL	§12th	2	7	0
1983—Denver NFL	†‡Second	9	7	0
1984—Denver NFL	†First	13	3	0
1985—Denver NFL	†Second	11	5	0
1986—Denver NFL	†First	11	5	0
1987—Denver NFL	†First	10	4	1
Pro Totals—7 Years		66	37	1

†Western Division (American Conference).
‡Tied for position.
§American Conference.

PLAYOFF RECORD

Year Club	W.	L.
1983—Denver NFL	0	1
1984—Denver NFL	0	1
1986—Denver NFL	2	1
1987—Denver NFL	2	1
Pro Totals—4 Years	4	4

1983—Lost wild-card playoff game to Seattle, 31-7.
1984—Lost conference playoff game to Pittsburgh, 24-17.
1986—Won conference playoff game from New England, 22-17; won conference championship game in overtime from Cleveland, 23-20; lost NFL championship game (Super Bowl XXI) to New York Giants, 39-20.
1987—Won conference playoff game from Houston, 34-10; won conference championship game from Cleveland, 38-33; lost NFL championship game (Super Bowl XXII) to Washington, 42-10.

JOHN ALEXANDER ROBINSON

Los Angeles Rams

Born July 25, 1935, at Chicago, Ill.
High School—San Mateo, Calif.
Received bachelor of science degree in education from University of Oregon in 1958.

COACHING RECORD

Assistant coach at University of Oregon, 1960 through 1971.
Assistant coach at University of Southern California, 1972 through 1974.
Assistant coach, Oakland Raiders NFL, 1975.

Year Club	Pos.	W.	L.	T.
1976—Southern California	†First	11	1	0
1977—Southern California	†‡Second	8	4	0
1978—Southern California	§First	12	1	0
1979—Southern California	§First	11	0	1
1980—Southern California	§Third	8	2	1
1981—Southern California	‡§Second	9	3	0
1982—Southern California	§x.....	8	3	0
1983—Los Angeles Rams NFL	ySecond	9	7	0
1984—Los Angeles Rams NFL	ySecond	10	6	0
1985—Los Angeles Rams NFL	yFirst	11	5	0
1986—Los Angeles Rams NFL	ySecond	10	6	0
1987—Los Angeles Rams NFL	yThird	6	9	0
College Totals—7 Years		67	14	2
Pro Totals—5 Years		46	33	0

†Pacific-8 Conference.
‡Tied for position.
§Pacific-10 Conference.
xIneligible for conference title.
yWestern Division (National Conference).

PLAYOFF RECORD

Year Club	W.	L.
1983—Los Angeles Rams NFL	1	1
1984—Los Angeles Rams NFL	0	1
1985—Los Angeles Rams NFL	1	1
1986—Los Angeles Rams NFL	0	1
Pro Totals—4 Years	2	4

1983—Won wild-card playoff game from Dallas, 24-17; lost conference playoff game to Washington, 51-7.
1984—Lost wild-card game to New York Giants, 16-13.
1985—Won conference playoff game from Dallas, 20-0; lost conference championship game to Chicago, 24-0.
1986—Lost wild-card playoff game to Washington, 19-7.

COLLEGIATE BOWL GAME RECORD

Year Club	W.	L.
1976—Southern California	1	0
1977—Southern California	1	0
1978—Southern California	1	0
1979—Southern California	1	0
1981—Southern California	0	1
Totals—5 Years	4	1

1976—Won Rose Bowl from Michigan, 14-6.
1977—Won Bluebonnet Bowl from Texas A&M, 47-28.
1978—Won Rose Bowl from Michigan, 17-10.
1979—Won Rose Bowl from Ohio State, 17-16.
1981—Lost Fiesta Bowl to Penn State, 26-10.

DARRYL D. ROGERS
Detroit Lions

Born May 28, 1935, at Los Angeles, Calif.
High School—Long Beach, Calif., Jordan.
Attended Long Beach City College and received bachelor of arts degree
in 1957 and master's degree in physical education in
1964, both from Fresno State University.

Signed as free agent by Los Angeles Rams, April, 1959.
Released by Los Angeles Rams, August, 1959.
In U.S. Marine Corps, 1958 and 1959.

COACHING RECORD

Named College Coach of the Year by THE SPORTING NEWS, 1978.
Assistant coach at Fresno City College, 1961 through 1964.

Year Club	Pos.	W.	L.	T.	Year Club	Pos.	W.	L.	T.
1965—Hayward State	†§	3	7	0	1978—Michigan State	‡zFirst	8	3	0
1966—Fresno State	‡xSecond	7	3	0	1979—Michigan State	‡zSeventh	5	6	0
1967—Fresno State	‡xSecond	3	8	0	1980—Arizona State	aFourth	7	4	0
1968—Fresno State	xFirst	7	4	0	1981—Arizona State	‡aSecond	9	2	0
1969—Fresno State	‡yFifth	6	4	0	1982—Arizona State	‡aThird	10	2	0
1970—Fresno State	yThird	8	4	0	1983—Arizona State	‡aSixth	6	4	1
1971—Fresno State	yThird	6	5	0	1984—Arizona State	aSixth	5	6	0
1972—Fresno State	‡yThird	6	4	1	1985—Detroit NFL	bcThird	7	9	0
1973—San Jose State	ySecond	5	4	2	1986—Detroit NFL	bThird	5	11	0
1974—San Jose State	‡ySecond	8	3	1	1987—Detroit NFL	‡bFourth	4	11	0
1975—San Jose State	yFirst	9	2	0	College Totals—20 Years		129	84	7
1976—Michigan State	‡zSeventh	4	6	1	Pro Totals—3 Years		16	31	0
1977—Michigan State	zThird	7	3	1					

†Ineligible for conference title.
‡Tied for position.
§Far Western Conference.
xCalifornia Collegiate Athletic Association.
yPacific Coast Athletic Association.
zBig 10 Conference.
aPacific-10 Conference.
bCentral Division (National Conference).
cTied for position.

COLLEGIATE BOWL GAME RECORD

Year Club	W.	L.
1968—Fresno State	0	1
1971—Fresno State	0	1
1982—Arizona State	1	0
Totals—3 Years	1	2

1968—Lost Camelia Bowl to Humboldt State, 29-14.
1971—Lost Mercy Bowl to California State-Fullerton, 17-14.
1982—Won Fiesta Bowl from Oklahoma, 32-21.

JAMES DAVID RYAN
(Buddy)
Philadelphia Eagles

Born February 17, 1934, at Frederick, Okla.
High School—Frederick, Okla.

Received bachelor of arts degree in education from Oklahoma State University
in 1957; and received master's degree in education
from Middle Tennessee State University in 1966.

Served in Korea.
Played on Fourth Army Championship team in Japan for two years.
Discharged as master sergeant.

COACHING RECORD

Head Coach and Athletic Director at Gainesville High School, Gainesville, Tex., 1957 through 1959.
Assistant coach at Marshall High School, Marshall, Tex., 1960.
Assistant coach at University of Buffalo, 1961 through 1965.
Assistant coach at Vanderbilt University, 1966.
Assistant coach at University of The Pacific, 1967.
Assistant coach, New York Jets NFL, 1968 through 1975.
Assistant coach, Minnesota Vikings NFL, 1976 and 1977.
Assistant coach, Chicago Bears NFL, 1978 through 1985.

Year Club	Pos.	W.	L.	T.
1986— Philadelphia NFL	†Fourth	5	10	1
1987— Philadelphia NFL	†‡Second	7	8	0
Pro Totals—2 Years..................		12	18	1

†Eastern Division (National Conference).
‡Tied for position.

ALAN KEITH SAUNDERS
(Al)
San Diego Chargers
Born February 1, 1947, at London, England.
High School—San Francisco, Calif., St. Ignatius College Prep.
Received degree in physical education from San Jose State University in 1969; received master's degree in
education from Stanford University in 1970; and attending University of Southern California
in completing his doctorate in Athletic Administration Sports Management.

COACHING RECORD

Graduate assistant at University of Southern California, 1970 and 1971.
Assistant coach at University of Missouri, 1972.
Assistant coach at Utah State University, 1973 through 1975.
Assistant coach at University of California at Berkeley, 1976 through 1981.
Assistant coach at University of Tennessee, 1982.
Assistant coach, San Diego Chargers NFL, 1983 through part of 1986.

Year Club	Pos.	W.	L.	T.
1986— San Diego NFL†	‡Fifth	3	5	0
1987— San Diego NFL	‡Third	8	7	0
Pro Totals—2 Years..................		11	12	0

†Replaced Don Coryell, October 29, 1986, with 1-7 record and in fifth place.
‡Western Division (American Conference).

MARTIN EDWARD SCHOTTENHEIMER
(Marty)
Cleveland Browns
Born September 23, 1943, at Canonsburg, Pa.
High School—McDonald, Pa.
Received bachelor of arts degree in English from University of Pittsburgh in 1964.

Played linebacker.
Selected by Buffalo in 7th round of 1965 AFL draft.
Released by Buffalo Bills and signed with Boston Patriots, 1969.
Traded by New England Patriots to Pittsburgh Steelers for offensive tackle Mike Haggerty and a draft choice,
July 10, 1971.
Released by Pittsburgh Steelers, 1971.

Year Club	G.	No.	Yds.	Avg.TD.	Year Club	G.	No.	Yds.	Avg.TD.
		—INTERCEPTIONS—					—INTERCEPTIONS—		
1965—Buffalo AFL..................	14		None		1970—Boston NFL..................	12		None	
1966—Buffalo AFL..................	14	1	20	20.0 0	AFL Totals—5 Years.........	67	6	133	22.2 1
1967—Buffalo AFL..................	14	3	88	29.3 1	NFL Totals—1 Year..........	12	0	0	0.0 0
1968—Buffalo AFL..................	14	1	22	22.0 0					
1969—Boston AFL..................	11	1	3	3.0 0	Pro Totals—6 Years...........	79	6	133	22.2 1

Additional pro statistics: Returned one kickoff for 13 yards, 1969; returned one kickoff for eight yards, 1970.
Played in AFL Championship Game following 1965 and 1966 seasons.
Played in AFL All-Star Game following 1965 season.

Assistant coach, Portland WFL, 1974.
Assistant coach, New York Giants NFL, 1975 through 1977.
Assistant coach, Detroit Lions NFL, 1978 and 1979.
Assistant coach, Cleveland Browns NFL, 1980 through 1984.

Year	Club	Pos.	W.	L.	T.
1984—Cleveland NFL†		‡Third	4	4	0
1985—Cleveland NFL		‡First	8	8	0
1986—Cleveland NFL		‡First	12	4	0
1987—Cleveland NFL		‡First	10	5	0
Pro Totals—4 Years..................................			34	21	0

†Replaced Sam Rutigliano, October 22, 1984 with 1-7 record and in third place.
‡Central Division (American Conference).

PLAYOFF RECORD

Year	Club	W.	L.
1985—Cleveland NFL.............................		0	1
1986—Cleveland NFL.............................		1	1
1987—Cleveland NFL.............................		1	1
Pro Totals—3 Years...		2	3

1985—Lost conference playoff game to Miami, 24-21.
1986—Won conference playoff game in two overtimes from New York Jets, 23-20; lost conference championship game in overtime to Denver, 23-20.
1987—Won conference playoff game from Indianapolis, 38-21; lost conference championship game to Denver, 38-33.

MICHAEL EDWARD SHANAHAN
(Mike)
Los Angeles Raiders
Born August 24, 1952, at Oak Park, Ill.
High School—Franklin Park, Ill., East Leyden.
Received bachelor of science degree in physical education in 1974 and received master's degree in physical education in 1975, both from Eastern Illinois University.

COACHING RECORD

Graduate assistant at Eastern Illinois University, 1973 and 1974.
Assistant coach at University of Oklahoma, 1975 and 1976.
Assistant coach at Northern Arizona University, 1977.
Assistant coach at Eastern Illinois University, 1978.
Assistant coach at University of Minnesota, 1979.
Assistant coach at University of Florida, 1980 through 1983.
Assistant coach, Denver Broncos NFL, 1984 through 1987.

DONALD FRANCIS SHULA
(Don)
Miami Dolphins
Born January 4, 1930, at Painesville, O.
High School—Painesville, O., Harvey.
Received bachelor of arts degree in sociology from John Carroll University in 1951.
Father of David Shula, assistant coach with Miami Dolphins;
and Mike Shula, assistant coach with Tampa Bay Buccaneers.

Played defensive back.
Selected by Cleveland in 9th round of 1951 NFL draft.
Traded with quarterback Harry Agganis, defensive backs Bert Rechichar and Carl Taseff, end Gern Nagler, guards Elmer Willhoite, Ed Sharkey and Art Spinney and tackles Dick Batten and Stu Sheetz by Cleveland NFL to Baltimore NFL for linebacker Tom Catlin, guard Herschel Forester, halfback John Petitbon and tackles Don Colo and Mike McCormack, March 25, 1953.
Sold by Baltimore NFL to Washington NFL, 1957.

Year Club	G.	No.	Yds.	Avg.TD.	Year Club	G.	No.	Yds.	Avg.TD.
1951—Cleveland NFL..............	12	4	23	5.8 0	1955—Baltimore NFL.............	9	5	64	12.8 0
1952—Cleveland NFL..............	5		None		1956—Baltimore NFL.............	12	1	2	2.0 0
1953—Baltimore NFL.............	12	3	46	15.3 0	1957—Washington NFL..........	11	3	48	16.0 0
1954—Baltimore NFL.............	12	5	84	16.8 0	Pro Totals—7 Years............	73	21	267	12.7 0

Additional pro statistics: Returned one kickoff for six yards, 1951; caught one pass for six yards, 1953; rushed twice for three yards, 1954; recovered one fumble, 1953; recovered two fumbles for 26 yards, 1955; recovered one fumble for six yards and returned one kickoff for no yards, 1956.
Played in NFL Championship Game following 1951 and 1952 seasons.

COACHING RECORD

Named NFL Coach of the Year by The Sporting News, 1964, 1968, 1970 and 1972.
Assistant coach at University of Virginia, 1958.
Assistant coach at University of Kentucky, 1959.
Assistant coach, Detroit Lions NFL, 1960 through 1962.

Year Club	Pos.	W.	L.	T.	Year Club	Pos.	W.	L.	T.
1963—Baltimore NFL	†Third	8	6	0	1976—Miami NFL	§Third	6	8	0
1964—Baltimore NFL	†First	12	2	0	1977—Miami NFL	§xFirst	10	4	0
1965—Baltimore NFL	†Second	10	3	1	1978—Miami NFL	§xFirst	11	5	0
1966—Baltimore NFL	†Second	9	5	0	1979—Miami NFL	§First	10	6	0
1967—Baltimore NFL	†Second	11	1	2	1980—Miami NFL	§Third	8	8	0
1968—Baltimore NFL	‡First	13	1	0	1981—Miami NFL	§First	11	4	1
1969—Baltimore NFL	‡Second	8	5	1	1982—Miami NFL	yxSecond	7	2	0
1970—Miami NFL	§Second	10	4	0	1983—Miami NFL	§First	12	4	0
1971—Miami NFL	§First	10	3	1	1984—Miami NFL	§First	14	2	0
1972—Miami NFL	§First	14	0	0	1985—Miami NFL	§First	12	4	0
1973—Miami NFL	§First	12	2	0	1986—Miami NFL	§Third	8	8	0
1974—Miami NFL	§First	11	3	0	1987—Miami NFL	§xSecond	8	7	0
1975—Miami NFL	§xFirst	10	4	0	Pro Totals—25 Years		255	101	6

†Western Conference.
‡Coastal Division (Western Conference).
§Eastern Division (American Conference).
xTied for position.
yAmerican Conference.

PLAYOFF RECORD

Year Club	W.	L.	Year Club	W.	L.
1964—Baltimore NFL	0	1	1978—Miami NFL	0	1
1965—Baltimore NFL	1	1	1979—Miami NFL	0	1
1966—Baltimore NFL	1	0	1981—Miami NFL	0	1
1968—Baltimore NFL	2	1	1982—Miami NFL	3	1
1970—Miami NFL	0	1	1983—Miami NFL	0	1
1971—Miami NFL	2	1	1984—Miami NFL	2	1
1972—Miami NFL	3	0	1985—Miami NFL	1	1
1973—Miami NFL	3	0	Pro Totals—16 Years	18	13
1974—Miami NFL	0	1			

1964—Lost NFL championship game to Cleveland, 27-0.
1965—Lost conference playoff game to Green Bay, 13-10; won Playoff Bowl from Dallas, 35-3.
1966—Won Playoff Bowl from Philadelphia, 20-14.
1968—Won conference playoff game from Minnesota, 24-14; won NFL championship game from Cleveland, 34-0; lost AFL-NFL playoff game (Super Bowl III) to New York Jets, 16-7.
1970—Lost conference playoff game to Oakland, 21-14.
1971—Won conference playoff game from Kansas City, 27-24; won conference playoff game from Baltimore, 21-0; lost NFL championship game (Super Bowl VI) to Dallas, 24-3.
1972—Won conference playoff game from Cleveland, 20-14; won conference championship game from Pittsburgh, 21-17; won NFL championship game (Super Bowl VII) from Washington, 14-7.
1973—Won conference playoff game from Cincinnati, 34-16; won conference championship game from Oakland, 27-10; won NFL championship game (Super Bowl VIII) from Minnesota, 24-7.
1974—Lost conference playoff game to Oakland, 28-26.
1978—Lost conference playoff game to Houston, 17-9.
1979—Lost conference playoff game to Pittsburgh, 34-14.
1981—Lost conference playoff game in overtime to San Diego, 41-38.
1982—Won conference playoff game from New England, 28-13; won conference playoff game from San Diego, 34-13; won conference championship game from New York Jets, 14-0; lost NFL championship game (Super Bowl XVII) to Washington, 27-17.
1983—Lost conference playoff game to Seattle, 27-20.
1984—Won conference playoff game from Seattle, 31-10; won conference championship game from Pittsburgh, 45-28; lost NFL championship game (Super Bowl XIX) to San Francisco, 38-16.
1985—Won conference playoff game from Cleveland, 24-21; lost conference championship game to New England, 31-14.

EUGENE CLIFTON STALLINGS
(Gene)
St. Louis Cardinals

Born March 2, 1935, at Paris, Tex.
High School—Paris, Tex.
Received bachelor of science degree in physical education from Texas A&M University in 1957.

COACHING RECORD

Student assistant coach, freshman team at Texas A&M University, 1957.
Assistant coach at University of Alabama, 1958 through 1964.
Assistant coach, Dallas Cowboys NFL, 1972 through 1985.

Year Club	Pos.	W.	L.	T.	Year Club	Pos.	W.	L.	T.
1965—Texas A&M	†‡Seventh	3	7	0	1971—Texas A&M	†Fourth	5	6	0
1966—Texas A&M	†Fourth	4	5	1	1986—St. Louis NFL	§Fifth	4	11	1
1967—Texas A&M	†First	7	4	0	1987—St. Louis NFL	‡§Second	7	8	0
1968—Texas A&M	†‡Sixth	3	7	0	College Totals—7 Years		27	45	1
1969—Texas A&M	†‡Sixth	3	7	0	Pro Totals—2 Years		11	19	1
1970—Texas A&M	†Eighth	2	9	0					

COLLEGIATE BOWL GAME RECORD

Year	Club	W.	L.
1967—Texas A&M		1	0

1967—Won Cotton Bowl from Alabama, 20-16.

WILLIAM ERNEST WALSH
(Bill)
San Francisco 49ers

Born November 30, 1931, at Los Angeles, Calif.
High School—Los Angeles, Calif., Hayward.
Attended San Mateo Junior College and received bachelor of arts degree
and master's degree in education from San Jose State in 1959.

COACHING RECORD

Named NFL Coach of the Year by THE SPORTING NEWS, 1981.
Assistant coach at Monterey Peninsula College, 1955.
Assistant coach at San Jose State University, 1956.
Head coach at Washington Union High, Fremont, Calif., 1957 through 1959.
Assistant coach at University of California, 1960 through 1962.
Assistant coach at Stanford University, 1963 through 1965.
Assistant coach, Oakland Raiders AFL, 1966.
Assistant coach, Cincinnati Bengals AFL, 1968 and 1969.
Assistant coach, Cincinnati Bengals NFL, 1970 through 1975.
Assistant coach, San Diego Chargers NFL, 1976.

Year	Club	Pos.	W.	L.	T.	Year	Club	Pos.	W.	L.	T.
1967—San Jose CoFL		†Second	7	5	0	1984—San Francisco NFL		yFirst	15	1	0
1977—Stanford		‡§Second	9	3	0	1985—San Francisco NFL		ySecond	10	6	0
1978—Stanford		xFourth	8	4	0	1986—San Francisco NFL		yFirst	10	5	1
1979—San Francisco NFL		yFourth	2	14	0	1987—San Francisco NFL		yFirst	13	2	0
1980—San Francisco NFL		yThird	6	10	0	College Totals—2 Years			17	7	0
1981—San Francisco NFL		yFirst	13	3	0	Pro Totals—9 Years			82	53	1
1982—San Francisco NFL		z§11th	3	6	0						
1983—San Francisco NFL		yFirst	10	6	0						

†Continental League.
‡Pacific Eight Conference.
§Tied for position.
xPacific Ten Conference.
yWestern Division (National Conference).
zNational Conference.

PLAYOFF RECORD

Year	Club	W.	L.
1981—San Francisco NFL		3	0
1983—San Francisco NFL		1	1
1984—San Francisco NFL		3	0
1985—San Francisco NFL		0	1
1986—San Francisco NFL		0	1
1987—San Francisco NFL		0	1
Pro Totals—6 Years		7	4

1981—Won conference playoff game from New York Giants, 38-34; won conference championship game from Dallas,
28-27; won NFL championship game (Super Bowl XVI) from Cincinnati, 26-21.
1983—Won conference playoff game from Detroit, 24-23; lost conference championship game to Washington, 24-21.
1984—Won conference playoff game from New York Giants, 21-10; won conference championship game from Chicago,
23-0; won NFL championship game (Super Bowl XIX) from Miami, 38-16.
1985—Lost wild-card playoff game to New York Giants, 17-3.
1986—Lost conference playoff game to New York Giants, 49-3.
1987—Lost conference playoff game to Minnesota, 36-24.

COLLEGIATE BOWL GAME RECORD

Year	Club	W.	L.
1977—Stanford		1	0
1978—Stanford		1	0
Totals—2 Years		2	0

1977—Won Sun Bowl from Louisiana State, 24-14.
1978—Won Bluebonnet Bowl from Georgia, 25-22.

JOSEPH FRANK WALTON
(Joe)
New York Jets

Born December 15, 1935, at Beaver Falls, Pa.
High School—Beaver Falls, Pa.
Received bachelor of arts degree in history from University of Pittsburgh in 1957.
Son of Frank Walton, guard with Boston Redskins, 1934 and 1935;
and Washington Redskins, 1944 and 1945; assistant coach, Pittsburgh Steelers, 1946.

Played tight end.
Named end on THE SPORTING NEWS College All-America Team, 1956.
Selected by Washington in 2nd round of 1957 NFL draft.

		—PASS RECEIVING—						—PASS RECEIVING—			
Year Club	G.	P.C.	Yds.	Avg.	TD.	Year Club	G.	P.C.	Yds.	Avg.	TD.
1957—Washington NFL........	12	3	57	19.0	0	1961—N.Y. Giants NFL........	12	36	544	15.1	2
1958—Washington NFL........	12	32	532	16.6	5	1962—N.Y. Giants NFL........	14	33	406	12.3	9
1959—Washington NFL........	9	21	317	15.1	3	1963—N.Y. Giants NFL........	12	26	371	14.3	6
1960—Washington NFL........	12	27	401	14.9	3	Pro Totals—7 Years...........	83	178	2628	14.8	28

Additional pro statistics: Intercepted one pass for 55 yards, 1957; fumbled once, 1958, 1959, 1961 and 1962; recovered one fumble for four yards, 1960.

COACHING RECORD
Scout, New York Giants NFL, 1967 and 1968.
Assistant coach, New York Giants NFL, 1969 through 1973.
Assistant coach, Washington Redskins NFL, 1974 through 1980.
Assistant coach, New York Jets NFL, 1981 and 1982.

Year Club	Pos.	W.	L.	T.
1983—New York Jets NFL	†‡Fourth	7	9	0
1984—New York Jets NFL	†Third	7	9	0
1985—New York Jets NFL	†‡Second	11	5	0
1986—New York Jets NFL	†Second	10	6	0
1987—New York Jets NFL	†Fifth	6	9	0
Pro Totals—5 Years....................		41	38	0

†Eastern Division (American Conference).
‡Tied for position.

PLAYOFF RECORD

Year Club	W.	L.
1985—New York Jets NFL	0	1
1986—New York Jets NFL	1	1
Pro Totals—2 Years.................	1	2

1985—Lost wild-card playoff game to New England, 26-14.
1986—Won wild-card playoff game from Kansas City, 35-15; lost conference playoff game in two overtimes to Cleveland Browns, 23-20.

SAMUEL DAVID WYCHE
(Sam)
Cincinnati Bengals
Born January 5, 1945, at Atlanta, Ga.
High School—Atlanta, Ga., North Fulton.
Received bachelor of arts degree in business administration from Furman University
in 1966 and received master's degree from University of South Carolina.
Brother of Joseph (Bubba) Wyche, former quarterback with Saskatchewan Roughriders,
Detroit Wheels, Chicago Fire and Shreveport Steamer.
Played quarterback.
Played in Continental Football League with Wheeling Ironmen, 1966.
Signed as free agent by Cincinnati AFL, 1968.
Traded by Cincinnati Bengals to Washington Redskins for running back Henry Dyer, May 5, 1971.
Traded by Washington Redskins to Detroit Lions for quarterback Bill Cappelman, August 17, 1974.
Released by Detroit Lions, September 2, 1975; signed as free agent by St. Louis Cardinals, 1976.
Released by St. Louis Cardinals, September 23, 1976; signed as free agent by Buffalo Bills, October 26, 1976.
Member of Washington Redskins' taxi squad, 1973.
Active for 7 games with Buffalo Bills in 1976; did not play.

		—PASSING—							—RUSHING—				—TOTAL—		
Year Club	G.	Att.	Cmp.	Pct.	Gain	T.P.	P.I.	Avg.	Att.	Yds.	Avg.	TD.	TD.	Pts.	F.
1966—Wheeling CoFL................	....	18	9	50.0	101	0	1	5.61	5	—11	—2.2	0	0	0	0
1968—Cincinnati AFL	3	55	35	63.6	494	2	2	8.98	12	74	6.2	0	0	0	2
1969—Cincinnati AFL	7	108	54	50.0	838	7	4	7.76	12	107	8.9	1	1	6	1
1970—Cincinnati NFL................	13	57	26	45.6	411	3	2	7.21	19	118	6.2	2	2	12	3
1971—Washington NFL.............	1			None					1	4	4.0	0	0	0	0
1972—Washington NFL.............	7			None							None		0	0	0
1974—Detroit NFL....................	14	1	0	00.0	0	0	1	0.00	1	0	0.0	0	0	0	0
1976—St.L. (1)-Buf. (0).............	1	1	1	100.0	5	0	0	5.00			None		0	0	0
AFL Totals—2 Years........	10	163	89	54.9	1332	9	6	8.17	24	181	7.5	1	1	6	3
NFL Totals—5 Years........	36	59	27	45.8	416	3	3	7.05	21	122	5.8	2	2	12	3
Pro Totals—7 Years...........	46	222	116	52.3	1748	12	9	7.87	45	303	6.7	3	3	18	6

Additional CoFL statistics: Intercepted three passes for nine yards, 1966.
Additional AFL statistics: Caught one pass for five yards, 1968.
Additional NFL statistics: Recovered one fumble for minus one yard, 1970.
Played in NFL Championship Game following 1972 season.

COACHING RECORD
Graduate assistant at University of South Carolina, 1967.
Assistant coach, San Francisco 49ers NFL, 1979 through 1982.

Year	Club	Pos.	W.	L.	T.
1983—Indiana		††Eighth	3	8	0
1984—Cincinnati NFL		§Second	8	8	0
1985—Cincinnati NFL		§‡Second	7	9	0
1986—Cincinnati NFL		§Second	10	6	0
1987—Cincinnati NFL		§Fourth	4	11	0
College Totals—1 Year			3	8	0
Pro Totals—4 Years			29	34	0

†Big Ten Conference.
‡Tied for position.
§Central Division (American Conference).

Recently Retired Coach

THOMAS RAYMOND FLORES
(Tom)
Born March 21, 1937, at Fresno, Calif.
High School—Sanger, Calif.
Attended Fresno City College and received bachelor of arts degree in education
from University of the Pacific in 1958.

Played quarterback.
Threw six touchdown passes in a game, December 22, 1963.
Drafted by Calgary Stampeders, 1958.
Released by Calgary Stampeders, 1958; signed as free agent by Washington Redskins, 1959.
Released by Washington Redskins, 1959; signed as free agent by Oakland Raiders, 1960.
    Traded with offensive end Art Powell and 2nd round draft choice by Oakland AFL to Buffalo AFL for quarterback
Daryle Lamonica, offensive end Glenn Bass and 3rd and 5th round draft choices, 1967.
Released by Buffalo, signed by Kansas City, 1969.
On Kansas City Chiefs' taxi squad entire 1970 season.

Year	Club	G.	Att.	Cmp.	Pct.	Gain	T.P.	P.I.	Avg.	Att.	Yds.	Avg.	TD.	TD.	Pts.	F.
					PASSING						RUSHING			TOTAL		
1960—Oakland AFL		14	252	136	★54.0	1738	12	12	6.90	19	123	6.5	3	3	18	..
1961—Oakland AFL		14	366	190	51.9	2176	15	19	5.95	23	36	1.6	1	1	6	..
1962—Oakland AFL					Missed entire season because of illness.											
1963—Oakland AFL		14	247	113	45.7	2101	20	13	8.51	12	2	0.2	0	0	0	..
1964—Oakland AFL		14	200	98	49.0	1389	7	14	6.95	11	64	5.8	0	0	0	3
1965—Oakland AFL		14	269	122	45.3	1593	14	11	5.92	11	32	2.9	0	0	0	0
1966—Oakland AFL		14	306	151	49.4	2638	24	14	8.62	5	50	10.0	1	1	6	2
1967—Buffalo AFL		13	64	22	34.4	260	0	8	4.06	None				0	0	0
1968—Buffalo AFL		1	5	3	60.0	15	0	1	3.00	None				0	0	0
1969—Buf.-K.C. AFL		13	6	3	50.0	49	0	0	8.17	1	0	0.0	0	0	0	0
Pro Totals—10 Years		111	1715	838	48.9	11959	92	92	6.97	82	307	3.7	5	5	30	....

Played in AFL All-Star Game following 1966 season.

COACHING RECORD
Freshman coach at University of the Pacific, 1959.
Assistant coach, Buffalo Bills NFL, 1971.
Assistant coach, Oakland Raiders NFL, 1972 through 1978.

Year	Club	Pos.	W.	L.	T.	Year	Club	Pos.	W.	L.	T.
1979—Oakland NFL		†‡Third	9	7	0	1984—L.A. Raiders NFL		†Third	11	5	0
1980—Oakland NFL		†‡First	11	5	0	1985—L.A. Raiders NFL		‡First	12	4	0
1981—Oakland NFL		†First	7	9	0	1986—L.A. Raiders NFL		†Fourth	8	8	0
1982—L.A. Raiders NFL		§First	8	1	0	1987—L.A. Raiders NFL		†Fourth	5	10	0
1983—L.A. Raiders NFL		†First	12	4	0	Pro Totals—9 Years			83	53	0

†Western Division (American Conference).
‡Tied for position.
§American Conference.

PLAYOFF RECORD

Year	Club	W.	L.
1980—Oakland NFL		4	0
1982—Los Angeles Raiders NFL		1	1
1983—Los Angeles Raiders NFL		3	0
1984—Los Angeles Raiders NFL		0	1
1985—Los Angeles Raiders NFL		0	1
Pro Totals—5 Years		8	3

1980—Won conference playoff game from Houston, 27-7; won conference playoff game from Cleveland, 14-12; won
    conference championship game from San Diego, 34-27; won NFL championship game (Super Bowl XV) from
    Philadelphia, 27-10.
1982—Won conference playoff game from Cleveland, 27-10; lost conference playoff game to New York Jets, 17-14.
1983—Won conference playoff game from Pittsburgh, 38-10; won conference championship game from Seattle, 30-14;
    won NFL championship game (Super Bowl XVIII) from Washington, 38-9.
1984—Lost wild-card playoff game to Seattle, 13-7.
1985—Lost conference playoff game to New England, 27-20.

Recently Retired Players

BRADLEY WILLIAM BENSON
(Brad)
Born November 25, 1955, at Altoona, Pa.
Height, 6.03. Weight, 270.
High School—Altoona, Pa.
Attended Pennsylvania State University.
Brother of Troy Benson, linebacker with New York Jets.

Selected by New England in 8th round (219th player selected) of 1977 NFL draft.
Released by New England Patriots, September 1, 1977; signed as free agent by New York Giants, November 15, 1977.
On injured reserve with knee injury, August 28 through September 27, 1979; activated, September 28, 1979.
Active for 5 games with New York Giants in 1977; did not play.
New York Giants NFL, 1977 through 1987.
Games: 1978 (16), 1979 (10), 1980 (15), 1981 (11), 1982 (9), 1983 (16), 1984 (16), 1985 (16), 1986 (16), 1987 (12). Total—137.
Pro statistics: Recovered one fumble, 1979.
Played in NFC Championship Game following 1986 season.
Played in NFL Championship Game following 1986 season.
Played in Pro Bowl (NFL All-Star Game) following 1986 season.

RONALD JAMES BROWN
(Ron)
Born March 31, 1961, at Los Angeles, Calif.
Height, 5.11. Weight, 181.
High School—Baldwin Park, Calif.
Attended Arizona State University.
Won gold medal in 4x100 relay during 1984 Olympics.

Tied NFL record for most touchdowns scored by kickoff return, game (2), against Green Bay Packers, November 24, 1985.
Named as kick returner to THE SPORTING NEWS NFL All-Star Team, 1985.
Selected by Arizona in 1983 USFL territorial draft.
Selected by Cleveland in 2nd round (41st player selected) of 1983 NFL draft.
NFL rights traded by Cleveland Browns to Los Angeles Rams for 2nd round pick in 1984 draft, April 27, 1984.
Signed by Los Angeles Rams, August 16, 1984.
Crossed picket line during players' strike, October 14, 1987.

		PASS RECEIVING				—KICKOFF RET.—				—TOTAL—		
Year Club	G.	P.C.	Yds.	Avg.	TD.	No.	Yds.	Avg.	TD.	TD.	Pts.	F.
1984—Los Angeles Rams NFL	16	23	478	20.8	4	None				4	24	0
1985—Los Angeles Rams NFL	13	14	215	15.4	3	28	918	★32.8	★3	6	36	★2
1986—Los Angeles Rams NFL	14	25	396	15.8	3	36	794	22.1	0	3	18	1
1987—Los Angeles Rams NFL	12	26	521	20.0	2	27	581	21.5	1	3	18	2
Pro Totals—4 Years	55	88	1610	18.3	12	91	2293	25.2	4	16	96	5

Additional pro statistics: Rushed twice for 25 yards, 1984; rushed twice for 13 yards, 1985; rushed four times for five yards and recovered two fumbles, 1986; rushed twice for 22 yards and recovered one fumble, 1987.
Played in NFC Championship Game following 1985 season.
Played in Pro Bowl (NFL All-Star Game) following 1985 season.

DWIGHT EDWARD CLARK
Born January 8, 1957, at Kinston, N. C.
Height, 6.04. Weight, 215.
High School—Charlotte, N. C., Garinger.
Received bachelor of arts degree in history from Clemson University in 1980.

Selected by San Francisco in 10th round (249th player selected) of 1979 NFL draft.
On injured reserve with knee injury, December 21 through remainder of 1983 season.
Crossed picket line during players' strike, October 7, 1987.

		——PASS RECEIVING——			
Year Club	G.	P.C.	Yds.	Avg.	TD.
1979—San Francisco NFL	16	18	232	12.9	0
1980—San Francisco NFL	16	82	991	12.1	8
1981—San Francisco NFL	16	85	1105	13.0	4
1982—San Francisco NFL	9	★60	913	15.2	5
1983—San Francisco NFL	16	70	840	12.0	8
1984—San Francisco NFL	16	52	880	16.9	6
1985—San Francisco NFL	16	54	705	13.1	10
1986—San Francisco NFL	16	61	794	13.0	2
1987—San Francisco NFL	13	24	290	12.1	5
Pro Totals—9 Years	134	506	6750	13.3	48

Additional pro statistics: Recovered one fumble, 1979; fumbled twice, 1980; rushed three times for 32 yards, 1981; attempted one pass with no completions, 1981, 1983 and 1984; fumbled once, 1982 and 1987; rushed three times for 18 yards, 1983; recovered two fumbles, 1986.
Played in NFC Championship Game following 1981 and 1984 seasons.
Played in NFL Championship Game following 1981 and 1984 seasons.
Played in Pro Bowl (NFL All-Star Game) following 1981 and 1982 seasons.

ANTHONY COLLINS
(Tony)
Born May 27, 1959, at Sanford, Fla.
Height, 5.11. Weight, 212.
High School—Penn Yan, N.Y., Penn Yan Academy.
Attended East Carolina University.
Cousin of Kenny Jackson, wide receiver with Philadelphia Eagles, 1984 through 1987;
and uncle of Reggie Branch, running back with Washington Redskins.
Selected by New England in 2nd round (47th player selected) of 1981 NFL draft.
Crossed picket line during players' strike, October 1, 1987.

			—RUSHING—			PASS RECEIVING				—TOTAL—		
Year Club	G.	Att.	Yds.	Avg.	TD.	P.C.	Yds.	Avg.	TD.	TD.	Pts.	F.
1981—New England NFL	16	204	873	4.3	7	26	232	8.9	0	7	42	8
1982—New England NFL	9	164	632	3.9	1	19	187	9.8	2	3	18	5
1983—New England NFL	16	219	1049	4.8	10	27	257	9.5	0	10	60	10
1984—New England NFL	16	138	550	4.0	5	16	100	6.3	0	5	30	3
1985—New England NFL	16	163	657	4.0	3	52	549	10.6	2	5	30	6
1986—New England NFL	16	156	412	2.6	3	77	684	8.9	5	8	48	4
1987—New England NFL	13	147	474	3.2	3	44	347	7.9	3	6	36	6
Pro Totals—7 Years	102	1191	4647	3.9	32	261	2356	9.0	12	44	264	42

		KICKOFF RETURNS			
Year Club	G.	No.	Yds.	Avg.	TD.
1981—New England NFL	16	39	773	19.8	0
1982—New England NFL	9		None		
1983—New England NFL	16		None		
1984—New England NFL	16	25	544	21.8	0
1985—New England NFL	16		None		
1986—New England NFL	16		None		
1987—New England NFL	13	1	18	18.0	0
Pro Totals—7 Years	102	65	1335	20.5	0

Additional pro statistics: Returned three punts for 15 yards and attempted one pass with no completions, 1981; recovered two fumbles, 1981 through 1983, 1985 and 1987; recovered one fumble, 1986.
Played in AFC Championship Game following 1985 season.
Played in NFL Championship Game following 1985 season.
Played in Pro Bowl (NFL All-Star Game) following 1983 season.

JOHN OWEN DUTTON
Born February 6, 1951, at Rapid City, S. D.
Height, 6.07. Weight, 261.
High School—Rapid City, S. D.
Received degree in business administration from University of Nebraska.
Named to THE SPORTING NEWS AFC All-Star Team, 1975 and 1976.
Named as defensive tackle on THE SPORTING NEWS College All-America Team, 1973.
Selected by Baltimore in 1st round (5th player selected) of 1974 NFL draft.
Placed on retired reserve list by Baltimore Colts, August 21, 1979.
Traded by Baltimore Colts to Dallas Cowboys for 1st and 2nd round picks in 1980 draft, October 9, 1979; activated, October 22, 1979.
Released by Dallas Cowboys, November 13, 1987.
Baltimore NFL, 1974 through 1978; Dallas NFL, 1979 through 1987.
Games: 1974 (14), 1975 (14), 1976 (14), 1977 (12), 1978 (14), 1979 (8), 1980 (16), 1981 (16), 1982 (9), 1983 (16), 1984 (16), 1985 (16), 1986 (16), 1987 (4). Total—185.
Pro statistics: Recovered one fumble, 1974, 1975, 1977, 1983 and 1985; recovered three fumbles for 10 yards, 1978; intercepted one pass for 38 yards and a touchdown and recovered two fumbles, 1980; credited with one safety, 1981 and 1984.
Played in NFC Championship Game following 1980 and 1982 seasons.
Member of Dallas Cowboys for NFC Championship Game following 1981 season; did not play.
Played in Pro Bowl (NFL All-Star Game) following 1975 through 1977 seasons.

KEITH VICTOR FAHNHORST
Born February 6, 1952, at St. Cloud, Minn.
Height, 6.06. Weight, 273.
High School—St. Cloud, Minn., Technical.
Received degree in psychology from University of Minnesota.
Brother of Jim Fahnhorst, linebacker with San Francisco 49ers.
Selected by San Francisco in 2nd round (35th player selected) of 1974 NFL draft.
Granted free agency, February 1, 1986; re-signed by 49ers, August 17, 1986.
Granted roster exemption, August 17 through August 25, 1986; activated, August 26, 1986.
On injured reserve with neck injury, November 3 through remainder of 1987 season.
San Francisco NFL, 1974 through 1987.
Games: 1974 (14), 1975 (14), 1976 (13), 1977 (14), 1978 (15), 1979 (16), 1980 (16), 1981 (16), 1982 (9), 1983 (16), 1984 (15), 1985 (16), 1986 (16), 1987 (3). Total—193.
Pro statistics: Recovered two fumbles, 1974 and 1981; caught one pass for one yard and returned one kickoff for 13 yards, 1975; recovered one fumble, 1975, 1977, 1978 and 1983.
Played in NFC Championship Game following 1981, 1983 and 1984 seasons.
Played in NFL Championship Game following 1981 and 1984 seasons.
Played in Pro Bowl (NFL All-Star Game) following 1984 season.

JOHN GARY FENCIK

(Known by middle name.)
Born June 11, 1954, at Chicago, Ill.
Height, 6.01. Weight, 197.
High School—Barrington, Ill.
Received bachelor of arts degree in history from Yale University; attending
Northwestern University for master's degree in management.
Named to THE SPORTING NEWS NFC All-Star Team, 1979.
Named to THE SPORTING NEWS NFL All-Star Team, 1981.
Selected by Miami in 10th round (281st player selected) of 1976 NFL draft.
Released by Miami Dolphins, September 6, 1976; signed as free agent by Chicago Bears, September 15, 1976.
Granted free agency with no qualifying offer, February 1, 1988.

			—INTERCEPTIONS—			
Year	Club	G.	No.	Yds.	Avg.	TD.
1976—Chicago NFL		13	None			
1977—Chicago NFL		14	4	33	8.3	0
1978—Chicago NFL		16	4	77	19.3	0
1979—Chicago NFL		14	6	31	5.2	0
1980—Chicago NFL		15	1	8	8.0	0
1981—Chicago NFL		16	6	121	20.2	1
1982—Chicago NFL		9	2	2	1.0	0
1983—Chicago NFL		7	2	34	17.0	0
1984—Chicago NFL		16	5	102	20.4	0
1985—Chicago NFL		16	5	43	8.6	0
1986—Chicago NFL		16	3	37	12.3	0
1987—Chicago NFL		12	None			
Pro Totals—12 Years		164	38	488	12.8	1

Additional pro statistics: Recovered one fumble, 1976, 1981 and 1983 through 1986; recovered two fumbles for 13 yards, 1978; recovered two fumbles, 1979; recovered three fumbles for 52 yards, 1980; fumbled once, 1984.
Played in NFC Championship Game 1984 and 1985 seasons.
Played in NFL Championship Game following 1985 season.
Played in Pro Bowl (NFL All-Star Game) following 1980 and 1981 seasons.

JOSEPH CHARLES FIELDS JR.

(Joe)
Born November 14, 1953, at Woodbury, N. J.
Height, 6.02. Weight, 253.
High School—Gloucester City, N. J., Catholic.
Attended University of Rutgers at Camden and received bachelor of science degree
in accounting from Widener College.
Selected by New York Jets in 14th round (349th player selected) of 1975 NFL draft.
On injured reserve with knee injury, October 4 through November 23, 1986; activated, November 24, 1986.
Crossed picket line during players' strike, October 7, 1987.
On injured reserve with elbow injury, December 26 through remainder of 1987 season.
Released by New York Jets, March 8, 1988.
New York Jets NFL, 1975 through 1987.
Games: 1975 (14), 1976 (14), 1977 (14), 1978 (16), 1979 (15), 1980 (13), 1981 (16), 1982 (9), 1983 (12), 1984 (16), 1985 (15), 1986 (9), 1987 (10). Total—173.
Pro statistics: Fumbled once for minus 21 yards and recovered one fumble for four yards, 1975; fumbled once for minus 14 yards, 1976; recovered one fumble, 1977, 1980, 1984, 1985 and 1987; fumbled once for minus 15 yards, 1981.
Played in AFC Championship Game following 1982 season.
Played in Pro Bowl (NFL All-Star Game) following 1981 and 1982 seasons.

DANIEL FRANCIS FOUTS

(Dan)
Born June 10, 1951, at San Francisco, Calif.
Height, 6.03. Weight, 210.
High School—San Francisco, Calif., St. Ignatius Prep.
Received bachelor of science degree in political science from University
of Oregon in 1973 and attended University of California at San Diego.
Established NFL records for most 300-yard passing games, career (51); most 3,000-yard seasons (6).
Tied NFL record for most consecutive games, 400 yards passing (2), 1984; most 4,000-yard seasons (3).
Named THE SPORTING NEWS NFL Player of the Year, 1979.
Named THE SPORTING NEWS AFC Player of the Year, 1979.
Named to THE SPORTING NEWS AFC All-Star Team, 1979.
Selected by San Diego in 3rd round (64th player selected) of 1973 NFL draft.
On injured reserve with knee and groin injuries, December 8 through remainder of 1984 season.

			—————PASSING—————							——RUSHING——				—TOTAL—		
Year	Club	G.	Att.	Cmp.	Pct.	Gain	T.P.	P.I.	Avg.	Att.	Yds.	Avg.	TD.	TD.	Pts.	F.
1973—San Diego NFL		10	194	87	44.8	1126	6	13	5.80	7	32	4.6	0	0	0	2
1974—San Diego NFL		11	237	115	48.5	1732	8	13	7.31	19	63	3.3	1	1	6	4
1975—San Diego NFL		10	195	106	54.4	1396	2	10	7.16	23	170	7.4	2	2	12	3
1976—San Diego NFL		14	359	208	57.9	2535	14	15	7.06	18	65	3.6	0	0	0	4
1977—San Diego NFL		4	109	69	63.3	869	4	6	7.97	6	13	2.2	0	0	0	4
1978—San Diego NFL		15	381	224	58.8	2999	24	20	7.87	20	43	2.2	2	2	12	10
1979—San Diego NFL		16	530	332	*62.6	*4082	24	24	7.70	26	49	1.9	2	2	12	13
1980—San Diego NFL		16	*589	*348	59.1	*4715	30	24	8.01	23	15	0.7	2	2	12	11

Year Club	G.	PASSING							RUSHING				TOTAL		
		Att.	Cmp.	Pct.	Gain	T.P.	P.I.	Avg.	Att.	Yds.	Avg.	TD.	TD.	Pts.	F.
1981—San Diego NFL	16	*609	*360	59.1	*4802	*33	17	7.89	22	56	2.5	0	0	0	9
1982—San Diego NFL	9	330	204	61.8	*2883	*17	11	*8.74	9	8	0.9	1	1	6	2
1983—San Diego NFL	10	340	215	63.2	2975	20	15	8.75	12	—5	—0.4	1	1	6	5
1984—San Diego NFL	13	507	317	62.5	3740	19	17	7.38	12	—29	—2.4	0	0	0	8
1985—San Diego NFL	14	430	254	59.1	3638	27	20	*8.46	11	—1	—0.1	0	0	0	13
1986—San Diego NFL	12	430	252	58.6	3031	16	22	7.05	4	—3	—0.8	0	0	0	4
1987—San Diego NFL	11	364	206	56.6	2517	10	15	6.91	12	0	0.0	2	2	12	10
Pro Totals—15 Years	181	5604	3297	58.8	43040	254	242	7.68	224	476	2.1	13	13	78	106

Quarterback Rating Points: 1973 (46.0), 1974 (61.4), 1975 (59.3), 1976 (75.3), 1977 (77.5), 1978 (83.2), 1979 (82.6), 1980 (84.6), 1981 (90.6), 1982 (93.6), 1983 (92.5), 1984 (83.4), 1985 (88.1), 1986 (71.4), 1987 (70.0). Total—80.2.

Additional pro statistics: Recovered one fumble, 1973, 1975 and 1984; recovered four fumbles, 1976; recovered three fumbles, 1978, 1980 and 1982; fumbled 10 times for minus four yards, 1978; recovered six fumbles and fumbled 13 times for minus 20 yards, 1979; fumbled 11 times for minus five yards, 1980; recovered two fumbles and fumbled nine times for minus 22 yards, 1981; recovered two fumbles, 1983; caught one pass for no yards, 1984; recovered six fumbles and fumbled 13 times for minus 11 yards, 1985; recovered two fumbles and fumbled four times for minus 13 yards, 1986; recovered four fumbles and fumbled 10 times for minus 10 yards, 1987.

Played in AFC Championship Game following 1980 and 1981 seasons.
Played in Pro Bowl (NFL All-Star Game) following 1979 through 1983 and 1985 seasons.

ANTHONY DALE GALBREATH

Name pronounced GALL-breath.

(Tony)

Born January 29, 1954, at Fulton, Mo.
Height, 6.00. Weight, 228.
High School—Fulton, Mo.
Attended Centerville Community College and University of Missouri.

Established NFL record for pass receptions by running back, career (464).
Selected by New Orleans in 2nd round (32nd player selected) of 1976 NFL draft.
On injured reserve with knee injury, December 16 through remainder of 1979 season.
Traded by New Orleans Saints to Minnesota Vikings for 3rd round pick in 1982 draft, August 31, 1981.
On inactive list, September 19, 1982.
Traded by Minnesota Vikings to New York Giants for linebacker Brad Van Pelt, July 12, 1984.
Granted free agency with no qualifying offer, February 1, 1988.

Year Club	G.	RUSHING				PASS RECEIVING				TOTAL		
		Att.	Yds.	Avg.	TD.	P.C.	Yds.	Avg.	TD.	TD.	Pts.	F.
1976—New Orleans NFL	14	136	570	4.2	7	54	420	7.8	1	8	48	7
1977—New Orleans NFL	14	168	644	3.8	3	41	265	6.5	0	3	18	3
1978—New Orleans NFL	16	186	635	3.4	5	74	582	7.9	2	7	42	6
1979—New Orleans NFL	15	189	708	3.7	9	58	484	8.3	1	10	67	5
1980—New Orleans NFL	16	81	308	3.8	3	57	470	8.2	2	5	30	3
1981—Minnesota NFL	14	42	198	4.7	2	18	144	8.0	0	2	12	2
1982—Minnesota NFL	8	39	116	3.0	1	17	153	9.0	0	1	6	1
1983—Minnesota NFL	13	113	474	4.2	4	45	348	7.7	2	6	36	4
1984—New York Giants NFL	16	22	97	4.4	0	37	357	9.6	0	0	0	0
1985—New York Giants NFL	16	29	187	6.4	0	30	327	10.9	1	1	6	2
1986—New York Giants NFL	16	16	61	3.8	0	33	268	8.1	0	0	0	3
1987—New York Giants NFL	12	10	74	7.4	0	26	248	9.5	0	0	0	1
Pro Totals—12 Years	170	1031	4072	3.9	34	490	4066	8.3	9	43	265	37

Additional pro statistics: Recovered one fumble, 1976 and 1979; returned 20 kickoffs for 399 yards and returned two punts for eight yards, 1976; recovered two fumbles for one yard, 1978; made one two extra points and two of three field goals for seven points and attempted three passes with two completions for 70 yards and one interception, 1979; recovered two fumbles, 1980, 1983 and 1986; returned six kickoffs for 86 yards and attempted two passes with no completions, 1980; returned one kickoff for 16 yards, 1981; attempted one pass with one completion for 13 yards, 1984; returned seven kickoffs for 120 yards, 1985; returned three punts for one yard and attempted one pass with no completions, 1986.

Played in NFC Championship Game following 1986 season.
Played in NFL Championship Game following 1986 season.

DENNIS WAYNE HARRAH

Born March 9, 1953, at Charleston, W. Va.
Height, 6.05. Weight, 265.
High School—Charleston, W. Va., Stonewall Jackson.
Attended University of Miami (Fla.).

Named to THE SPORTING NEWS NFL All-Star Team, 1986.
Named as offensive tackle on THE SPORTING NEWS College All-America Team, 1974.
Selected by Los Angeles in 1st round (11th player selected) of 1975 NFL draft.
On injured reserve with knee injury, November 8 through remainder of 1977 season.
On did not report list, August 19 through September 7, 1980; activated, September 8, 1980.
On injured reserve with thigh injury, October 4 through October 31, 1985; activated, November 1, 1985.
Los Angeles Rams NFL, 1975 through 1987.
Games: 1975 (14), 1976 (14), 1977 (8), 1978 (15), 1979 (13), 1980 (15), 1981 (15), 1982 (9), 1983 (15), 1984 (16), 1985 (10), 1986 (16), 1987 (8). Total—168.
Pro statistics: Recovered one fumble, 1982.
Played in NFC Championship Game following 1975, 1976, 1978, 1979 and 1985 seasons.

— 485 —

Played in NFL Championship Game following 1979 season.
Played in Pro Bowl (NFL All-Star Game) following 1978 through 1980 and 1985 through 1987 seasons.

MICHAEL ALBERT HARTENSTINE
Name pronounced Heart-In-Stine.
(Mike)
Born July 27, 1953, at Bethlehem, Pa.
Height, 6.03. Weight, 258.
High School—Bethlehem, Pa., Liberty.
Attended Penn State University.

Selected by Chicago in 2nd round (31st player selected) of 1975 NFL draft.
Released by Chicago Bears, September 7, 1987; signed as free agent by Minnesota Vikings, October 30, 1987.
Released by Minnesota Vikings, December 15, 1987.
Chicago NFL, 1975 through 1986; Minnesota NFL, 1987.
Games: 1975 (14), 1976 (14), 1977 (14), 1978 (16), 1979 (16), 1980 (16), 1981 (16), 1982 (9), 1983 (16), 1984 (16), 1985 (16), 1986 (16), 1987 (5). Total—184.

Pro statistics: Scored a safety and recovered two fumbles for five yards, 1975; recovered three fumbles for three yards and scored one touchdown on a 12 yard lateral, 1976; recovered three fumbles, 1977; recovered three fumbles for 10 yards, 1978; recovered one fumble, 1979 and 1985; recovered one fumble for four yards, 1981; recovered one fumble for 10 yards and a touchdown, 1983; recovered two fumbles, 1984.
Played in NFC Championship Game following 1984 and 1985 seasons.
Played in NFL Championship Game following 1985 season.

MICHAEL CHRISTOPHER WILBERT LUCKHURST
(Mick)
Born March 31, 1958, at Redbourn, England.
Height, 6.02. Weight, 180.
High School—Redbourn, England, St. Columbus College.
Attended St. Cloud State University and University of California.
Husband of Terri Moody Luckhurst, former professional golfer.

Signed as free agent by Atlanta Falcons, May 5, 1981.
On injured reserve with back and groin injuries, November 12 through remainder of 1986 season.

| | | —PLACE KICKING— | | | | |
Year Club	G.	XP.	XPM.	FG.	FGA.	Pts.
1981—Atlanta NFL	16	51	0	21	33	114
1982—Atlanta NFL	9	21	1	10	14	51
1983—Atlanta NFL	16	43	2	17	22	94
1984—Atlanta NFL	16	31	0	20	27	91
1985—Atlanta NFL	16	29	0	24	31	101
1986—Atlanta NFL	10	21	0	14	24	63
1987—Atlanta NFL	12	17	0	9	13	44
Pro Totals—7 Years	95	213	3	115	164	558

Additional pro statistics: Punted once for 26 yards, 1985; punted once for 37 yards, 1987.

STEVEN LEE NELSON
(Steve)
Born April 26, 1951, at Farmington, Minn.
Height, 6.02. Weight, 230.
High School—Anoka, Minn.
Attended Augsburg College and received bachelor of science degree in education
from North Dakota State University in 1974.

Named to THE SPORTING NEWS NFL All-Star Team, 1980.
Selected by New England in 2nd round (34th player selected) of 1974 NFL draft.
On injured reserve with knee injury, November 16 through remainder of 1976 season.
On injured reserve with separated shoulder, October 2 through October 30, 1981; activated, October 31, 1981.
On injured reserve with broken thumb, September 28 through November 24, 1983; activated, November 25, 1983.
On injured reserve with knee injury, November 26 through remainder of 1986 season.

| | | —INTERCEPTIONS— | | | |
Year Club	G.	No.	Yds.	Avg.	TD.
1974—New England NFL	11		None		
1975—New England NFL	14	2	8	4.0	0
1976—New England NFL	10	2	32	16.0	0
1977—New England NFL	13		None		
1978—New England NFL	14	5	104	20.8	0
1979—New England NFL	15	1	18	18.0	0
1980—New England NFL	16	3	37	12.3	0
1981—New England NFL	12	1	9	9.0	0
1982—New England NFL	9		None		
1983—New England NFL	8	1	6	6.0	0
1984—New England NFL	16	1	0	0.0	0
1985—New England NFL	15		None		
1986—New England NFL	10	2	21	10.5	0
1987—New England NFL	11		None		
Pro Totals—14 Years	174	18	235	13.1	0

Additional pro statistics: Recovered one fumble, 1974, 1977, 1979, 1980, 1983 and 1987; recovered three fumbles, 1976 and 1985; recovered four fumbles, 1978.
Played in AFC Championship Game following 1985 season.
Played in NFL Championship Game following 1985 season.
Played in Pro Bowl (NFL All-Star Game) following 1980, 1984 and 1985 seasons.

WALTER JERRY PAYTON

Born July 25, 1954, at Columbia, Miss.
Height, 5.10. Weight, 202.
High School—Columbia, Miss.
Received bachelor of arts degree in communications and special education from Jackson State University.
Brother of Eddie Payton, kick returner with Cleveland Browns, Detroit Lions, Kansas City Chiefs, Toronto Argonauts and Minnesota Vikings, 1977 through 1982; and nephew of Rickey Young, running back with San Diego Chargers and Minnesota Vikings, 1975 through 1983.

Established NFL records for most yards gained, rushing, game (275), November 20, 1977, against Minnesota Vikings; most rushing yards, career (16,726); most rushing attempts, career (3,838); most combined yards, career (21,803); most combined attempts, career (4,368); most consecutive combined 2,000-yard seasons (3), 1983 through 1985; most games, 100 yards rushing, career (77); most seasons, 1,000 yards rushing (10); most rushing touchdowns, career (110).

Tied NFL record for most consecutive games, 100 yards rushing (9), 1985; most rushing touchdowns, career (106).
Named NFC Player of the Year by THE SPORTING NEWS, 1976 and 1977.
Named to THE SPORTING NEWS NFL All-Star Team, 1980, 1984 and 1985.
Named to THE SPORTING NEWS NFC All-Star Team, 1976 through 1979.
Selected by Chicago in 1st round (4th player selected) of 1975 NFL draft.
USFL rights traded by Birmingham Stallions to Chicago Blitz for rights to quarterback Phil Kessel and a draft pick, January 23, 1984.
Granted free agency with no qualifying offer, February 1, 1988.

		—RUSHING—				PASS RECEIVING				—TOTAL—		
Year Club	G.	Att.	Yds.	Avg.	TD.	P.C.	Yds.	Avg.	TD.	TD.	Pts.	F.
1975—Chicago NFL	13	196	679	3.5	7	33	213	6.5	0	7	42	9
1976—Chicago NFL	14	*311	1390	4.5	13	15	149	9.9	0	13	78	10
1977—Chicago NFL	14	*339	*1852	*5.5	*14	27	269	10.0	2	*16	96	11
1978—Chicago NFL	16	*333	1395	4.2	11	50	480	9.6	0	11	66	5
1979—Chicago NFL	16	*369	1610	4.4	14	31	313	10.1	2	16	96	7
1980—Chicago NFL	16	317	1460	4.6	6	46	367	8.0	1	7	42	5
1981—Chicago NFL	16	339	1222	3.6	6	41	379	9.2	2	8	48	9
1982—Chicago NFL	9	148	596	4.0	1	32	311	9.7	0	1	6	3
1983—Chicago NFL	16	314	1421	4.5	6	53	607	11.5	2	8	48	5
1984—Chicago NFL	16	381	1684	4.4	11	45	368	8.2	0	11	66	5
1985—Chicago NFL	16	324	1551	4.8	9	49	483	9.9	2	11	66	6
1986—Chicago NFL	16	321	1333	4.2	8	37	382	10.3	3	11	66	6
1987—Chicago NFL	12	146	533	3.7	4	33	217	6.6	1	5	30	5
Pro Totals—13 Years	190	3838	16726	4.4	110	492	4538	9.2	15	125	750	86

		—PASSING—							—KICKOFF RET.—			
Year Club	G.	Att.	Cmp.	Pct.	Gain	T.P.	P.I.	Avg.	No.	Yds.	Avg.	TD.
1975—Chicago NFL	13	1	0	0.0	0	0	1	0.00	14	444	*31.7	0
1976—Chicago NFL	14			None					1	0	0.0	0
1977—Chicago NFL	14			None					2	95	47.5	0
1978—Chicago NFL	16			None						None		
1979—Chicago NFL	16	1	1	100.0	54	1	0	54.00		None		
1980—Chicago NFL	16	3	0	0.0	0	0	0	0.00		None		
1981—Chicago NFL	16	2	0	0.0	0	0	0	0.00		None		
1982—Chicago NFL	9	3	1	33.3	39	1	0	13.00		None		
1983—Chicago NFL	16	6	3	50.0	95	3	2	15.83		None		
1984—Chicago NFL	16	8	3	37.5	47	2	1	5.88		None		
1985—Chicago NFL	16	5	3	60.0	96	1	0	19.20		None		
1986—Chicago NFL	16	4	0	0.0	0	0	1	0.00		None		
1987—Chicago NFL	12	1	0	0.0	0	0	1	0.00		None		
Pro Totals—13 Years	190	34	11	32.4	331	8	6	9.74	17	539	31.7	0

Additional pro statistics: Punted once for 39 yards, 1975; recovered one fumble, 1975, 1982, 1984 and 1985; recovered five fumbles, 1977; recovered two fumbles, 1978, 1979 and 1983; recovered three fumbles, 1980 and 1981.
Played in NFC Championship Game following 1984 and 1985 seasons.
Played in NFL Championship Game following 1985 season.
Played in Pro Bowl (NFL All-Star Game) following 1976 through 1980 and 1983 through 1986 seasons.

DONNIE SHELL

Born August 26, 1952, at Whitmire, S. C.
Height, 5.11. Weight, 197.
High School—Whitmire, S. C.
Received bachelor of science degree in health and physical education from South Carolina State in 1974; and received master's degree in guidance and counseling from South Carolina State.

Named to THE SPORTING NEWS AFC All-Star Team, 1979.
Named to THE SPORTING NEWS NFL All-Star Team, 1980.
Signed as free agent by Pittsburgh Steelers, 1974.
Crossed picket line during players' strike, October 14, 1987.
Granted free agency with no qualifying offer, February 1, 1988.

	—INTERCEPTIONS—						—INTERCEPTIONS—			
Year Club	G.	No.	Yds.	Avg. TD.	Year Club	G.	No.	Yds.	Avg. TD.	
1974—Pittsburgh NFL	14	1	0	0.0 0	1982—Pittsburgh NFL	9	5	27	5.4 0	
1975—Pittsburgh NFL	14	1	29	29.0 0	1983—Pittsburgh NFL	16	5	18	3.6 0	
1976—Pittsburgh NFL	14	1	4	4.0 0	1984—Pittsburgh NFL	16	7	61	8.7 1	
1977—Pittsburgh NFL	12	3	14	4.7 0	1985—Pittsburgh NFL	16	4	40	10.0 0	
1978—Pittsburgh NFL	16	3	21	7.0 0	1986—Pittsburgh NFL	15	3	29	9.7 0	
1979—Pittsburgh NFL	16	5	10	2.0 0	1987—Pittsburgh NFL	13	1	50	50.0 1	
1980—Pittsburgh NFL	16	7	135	19.3 0	Pro Totals—14 Years	201	51	490	9.6 2	
1981—Pittsburgh NFL	14	5	52	10.4 0						

Additional pro statistics: Recovered one fumble, 1974, 1975, 1976, 1982 and 1983; caught two passes for 39 yards, 1975; recovered five fumbles for 21 yards and one touchdown and returned one punt for six yards, 1978; recovered two fumbles, 1979, 1981 and 1985; recovered one fumble for seven yards, 1980; recovered one fumble for 19 yards and a touchdown, 1987.
Played in AFC Championship Game following 1974 through 1976, 1978, 1979 and 1984 seasons.
Played in NFL Championship Game following 1974, 1975, 1978 and 1979 seasons.
Played in Pro Bowl (NFL All-Star Game) following 1978 through 1982 seasons.

JOHNNY LEE STALLWORTH
(John)
Born July 15, 1952, at Tuscaloosa, Ala.
Height, 6.02. Weight, 202.
High School—Tuscaloosa, Ala.
Received bachelor of science degree in business from Alabama A&M University in 1974;
and received master's degree in business administration from Alabama A&M University.
Named to THE SPORTING NEWS AFC All-Star Team, 1979.
Selected by Pittsburgh in 4th round (82nd player selected) of 1974 NFL draft.
On injured reserve with cracked fibula, September 17 through October 31, 1980; activated, November 1, 1980.
On injured reserve with broken foot, November 13 through remainder of 1980 season.
On injured reserve with pulled hamstring, October 7 through November 3, 1983; activated, November 4, 1983.
On injured reserve with knee injury, October 3 through November 6, 1986; activated, November 7, 1986.
Crossed picket line during players' strike, October 14, 1987.
Granted free agency with no qualifying offer, February 1, 1988.

Year Club	G.	Att.	Yds.	Avg.	TD.	P.C.	Yds.	Avg.	TD.	TD.	Pts.	F.
			RUSHING				PASS RECEIVING				TOTAL	
1974—Pittsburgh NFL	13	1	—9	—9.0	0	16	269	16.8	1	1	6	0
1975—Pittsburgh NFL	11		None			20	423	21.2	4	4	24	0
1976—Pittsburgh NFL	8		None			9	111	12.3	2	3	18	0
1977—Pittsburgh NFL	14	6	47	7.8	0	44	784	17.8	7	7	42	1
1978—Pittsburgh NFL	16		None			41	798	19.5	9	9	54	2
1979—Pittsburgh NFL	16		None			70 *1183		16.9	8	8	48	4
1980—Pittsburgh NFL	3		None			9	197	21.9	1	1	6	0
1981—Pittsburgh NFL	16	1	17	17.0	0	63	1098	17.4	5	5	30	4
1982—Pittsburgh NFL	9	1	9	9.0	0	27	441	16.3	7	7	42	2
1983—Pittsburgh NFL	4		None			8	100	12.5	0	0	0	0
1984—Pittsburgh NFL	16		None			80	1395	17.4	11	11	66	1
1985—Pittsburgh NFL	16		None			75	937	12.5	5	5	30	0
1986—Pittsburgh NFL	11		None			34	466	13.7	1	1	6	0
1987—Pittsburgh NFL	12		None			41	521	12.7	2	2	12	1
Pro Totals—14 Years	165	9	64	7.1	0	537	8723	16.2	63	64	384	15

Additional pro statistics: Recovered one fumble, 1975 and 1978; advanced one lateral for 47 yards and a touchdown, 1976; recovered three fumbles, 1979.
Played in AFC Championship Game following 1974 through 1976, 1978, 1979 and 1984 seasons.
Played in NFL Championship Game following 1974, 1975, 1978 and 1979 seasons.
Played in Pro Bowl (NFL All-Star Game) following 1979, 1982 and 1984 seasons.